DISCRETE AND SWITCHING FUNCTIONS

Marc Davio Jean-Pierre Deschamps André Thayse

(MBLE RESEARCH LABORATORY, BRUSSELS)

DISCRETE AND SWITCHING FUNCTIONS

With a foreword by Raymond T. Yeh

GEORGI PUBLISHING COMPANY
St-Saphorin, Switzerland

McGraw-Hill International Book Company

New York · St Louis · San Francisco · Auckland · Beirut · Bogatá · Düsseldorf
Johannesburg · Lisbon · London · Lucerne · Madrid · Mexico · Montreal
New Dehli · Panama · Paris · São Paulo · San Juan · Singapore · Sydney
Tokyo · Toronto

British Library Cataloging in Publication Data

Davio, Marc

Discrete and switching functions.
1. Logic, Symbolic and mathematical
I. Title II. Deschamps, Jean Pierre
III. Thayse, André
511′.33 QA10 77-30718

ISBN 0-07-015509-7

Printed in Great Britain by Adlard & Son Ltd, Bartholomew Press, Dorking, and bound in Great Britain

Contents

List of Symbols

Conjunction: No symbol or $\wedge$

Disjunction: $\vee$ or $\bigvee$

Negation of a: $\bar{a}$ or $-a$

Ring sum or addition modulo an integer: $\oplus$ or $\textstyle\bigoplus\!\!\!\!\sum$

Ring product or multiplication modulo an integer: No symbol or Π

Sum in a finite field: + or Σ

Product in a finite field: No symbol or Π

Matrix product with additive law $\top$ and multiplicative law $\perp$: No symbol (only if the additive and multiplicative laws are unambiguously defined by the context) or $(\top, \perp)$

Kronecker matrix product with multiplicative law $\top$: $\otimes$ (only if the multiplicative law is unambiguously defined by the context) or $\overset{\top}{\otimes}$

Implication: $\Rightarrow$

Equivalence: $\Leftrightarrow$

Union of sets: $\cup$

Intersection of sets: $\cap$

Inclusion of a set in another set: $\subseteq$ or $\subset$ (strict inclusion)

$\in$ means *is an element of*

Number of elements: #

Inclusion relation: $\leqslant$ or $<$ (strict inclusion)

Subtraction of sets: \

Discrete constants are denoted by lower-case letters like $a, \ldots, e, \ldots, l$

Discrete variables are denoted by lower-case letters like x, y, z

Bold-face lower-case letters like $\boldsymbol{e}$ are used to denote a *vector of discrete constants*

Bold-face lower-case letters like $\boldsymbol{x}$ are used to denote a *vector of discrete variables*

Lattice exponentiation: For a fixed integer $r \geqslant 2$, a variable $x \in S = \{0, 1, \ldots, m-1\}$ and a subset C of S, the lattice exponentiation

$$x^{(C)}$$

is defined as follows:

$$x^{(C)} = r-1 \quad \text{iff } x \in C$$
$$= 0 \quad \text{otherwise.}$$

If C is formed by a set of consecutive integers in the ring, i.e.:

$$C = \{a, a \oplus 1, \ldots, a \oplus h = b\}, \quad h \geqslant 0$$

it will be convenient to write

$$x^{[a,b]} \quad \text{for} \quad x^{(C)}$$

The following notations are also used for sake of simplicity:

$x^{[a}$ holds for $x^{[a,m-1]}$

$x^{b]}$ holds for $x^{[0,b]}$.

Ring exponentiation:

$$\tilde{x}^{(C)} = 1 \text{ iff } x \in C$$
$$= 0 \text{ otherwise}$$

If $C = \{a, a \oplus 1, \ldots, a \oplus h = b\}$, then

$\tilde{x}^{[a,b]}$ holds for $\tilde{x}^{(C)}$
$\tilde{x}^{[a}$ holds for $\tilde{x}^{[a,m-1]}$
$\tilde{x}^{b]}$ holds for $\tilde{x}^{[0,b]}$

Field exponentiation:

$$x^k = \underbrace{xx \ldots x}_{k \text{ times}}$$

Preface

by Raymond T. Yeh

The invention of calculus and its concomitant reduction of physical processes to mathematics has caused a revolutionary change in our understanding and control of the environment. However, physics, or the study of energy change in a system, is inadequate to model many complex processes such as those existing in biological systems.

During the twentieth century, we are witnessing another revolutionary change in our relationship to environment caused by a new way of looking at things. For example, modern physiology is concerned with how information is transferred through the blood streams and nervous sytems by hormones. The problem of how parents pass their traits on to offspring in genetics can be solved by reducing the problem to that of encoding information in the genes. Indeed, the recognition of the fact that information can be transmitted in discrete forms, and that information change in a system can be measured discretely has stimulated the development of mathematical theories of discrete structures. The observation that many different kinds of processes are reducible to discrete mathematics is the root of many scientific and engineering breakthroughs in this century. And discrete functions are one of the most potent mathematical tools for studying discrete structures.

It is indeed a pleasure to discover that most relevant and recent works of discrete functions are collected and uniformly treated in this book! The choice of topics is balanced with an abundance of applications, and the presentation is extremely comprehensive with pointers to relevant literatures. The material presented in this volume is self-contained and can be followed by anyone with an interest in the subject and some background in algebra as provided in Chapter 1.

The main virtue of this book is in the completeness of its coverage, both in theory and application; in its uniform notation and treatment; and in its lucid presentation. Such a book could not have been written without the deep insights and broad knowledge on the part of the authors.

The book will no doubt be recognized as one of the outstanding achievements in systems engineering.

Austin, Texas, U.S.A. Raymond T. Yeh

Introduction

Discrete functions, i.e. functions having finite domain and codomain, play an increasing role in various fields of human activity.

Their most ancient use has probably been formal logics: the history of multivalued logics may indeed be traced back to Grecian times when early philosophers and logicians investigated excursions into the "excluded middle law". The need for non-binary logics indeed already appears in simple examples such as the bald-headed man paradox (see Moisil [1972]):

(i) a bald-headed man is one with little hair;
(ii) the union of the hair of two bald-headed men is the hair of a bald-headed man
(iii) the hair smaller than that of a bald-headed man is also the hair of a bald-headed man.

Similar dual statements are then introduced over the set of haired men: one then has to conclude that, with these premises, Aristotelian logics are not able to draw the border between bald-headed men and haired men. From these early times on, the interest in multivalued logics has not faded away and nowadays motivates numerous papers, journals and symposia.

Apart from rare exceptions, among which the realizations of Pascal [1640], Jacquart [1800] and Babbage [1800] perhaps are the most frequently quoted, technical applications of discrete functions had to await the early twentieth century: it is indeed then that the possibility of handling and transmitting information in discrete form was recognized. The works of Nyquist [1928] and Shannon [1938, 1948] have played a predominant role in this respect. Most often, handled and transmitted information was of binary nature and it could be argued that Boolean algebra was probably one of the only forms of discrete mathematics endowed with fitting technical applications. Since that time, the number of applications of discrete functions has considerably increased: four generations of general purpose computers have been developed and it would be quite impossible to enumerate the types of special purpose computers. Specifically, the domain of digital communications is expanding in a particularly explosive way. While in the examples mentioned above, the carried information mostly remains of binary nature, other forms of discrete mathematics also have found a useful place in everyday technical life: think of finite automata theory, that applies in the design of sequential switching circuits and in the description of microprogrammed systems, of the combinatorial algebra and of its impact on reliable communication and on econometrics, and also of the numerous applications of graph theory and pseudo-Boolean methods.

Various reasons motivate an ever-increasing use of multivalued logics and of multivalued circuitry. A first argument is that a discrete function may be represented in multivalued logics much more concisely than it could be in binary logics: in this sense, multivalued logics already may appear as an adequate tool for coping with problems of higher size or complexity and it is clear that the appearance of highly complex systems is a typical characteristic of today's technical trends. The practical counterpart of this first argument arises from the consideration of the recent technological advances and, in particular, of the mastery of electronic integration. The arguments encountered here are of an economical nature. The relative cost of the connections indeed becomes the most significant part of the overall system cost and multivalued logics appear as a means of increasing the information density over these connections and thus their efficiency. Similarly, technology imposes severe limitations on the number of connections of an integrated circuit with the external world. This argument again favours multivalued logics.

The present book attempts to give a unified presentation of the algebraic theory of discrete functions, and, as such, it hopefully can provide the logician, the system designer and the advanced student or scientist with tools as precise and efficient as possible.

Any claim to cover exhaustively the extremely large field of discrete function theory would clearly be conceited and difficult choices had to be made in delineating the subject matter of the book. Roughly speaking, the subject matter is divided into two main parts: **the general representation theory** (Chapters 2 to 9) and **the study of functional properties** (Chapters 11, 12, 13).

Chapter 1, which describes the mathematical prerequisites of the subsequent chapters, has been introduced in an attempt to make the book self-contained and to present the main concepts and notations. This chapter discusses the algebraic structures of lattice, closure system, Boolean algebra and module. It also describes the weighted numbering systems, the Gray code number representations and the Kronecker products of matrices which will prove to be essential tools from a technical representation point of view. Apart from the three latter topics, the subject matter of this chapter is classical and the results presented here also are available from textbooks such as Birkhoff [1967] and McLane and Birkhoff [1967]. It can be recommended to the reader to use this chapter as a reference more than for continuous reading.

Chapter 2 first defines discrete functions as mappings relating finite sets and without resorting to any underlying algebraic system: the tabular representation and that of the computation scheme may be viewed as the initial and final steps of a design process and are actually not referring to any algebraic system. This approach, however, motivates interest in the algebraic representation theory: indeed, tabular representations become inadequate when the number of variables and the cardinality of their domain increase. A classical method of circumventing such a difficulty is to introduce suitable algebraic structures that provide a way of writing well-formed expressions such as polynomial-type expressions. Two essential algebraic structures are studied at an elementary level in this chapter, namely that of lattice and that of module: the latter is particularized to a linear algebra in the case of Galois functions. Languages of well-formed expressions are introduced over these structures together with canonical expansions, such as the canonical disjunctive expansion over the lattice structure and the Lagrange expansion over the module structure. The former may be viewed as generalization of the well-known Shannon expansion of Boolean functions. The detailed study of the three algebraic structures introduced here is carried on in subsequent chapters but Chapter 2 is obviously essential for the understanding of the book.

The study of the lattice structure performed in *Chapter 3* allows for the detection of concise representations of discrete functions in terms of cubes, blocks and convex blocks: these terms represent various families of generating functions which may all be viewed as generalizations of the implicant concept in Boolean algebra, but which have distinct practical applications. We face here a new type of problem, namely that of detecting specificities of a given discrete function. This type of problem will receive a definite motivation in Chapter 11. Most of the classical algorithms for the research of prime implicants are generalized to discrete functions and the presentation has been rendered as homogeneous as possible by the use of a lattice-difference terminology. These concepts are applied to the research of maximal compatibility classes in a graph, to the representation of fuzzy functions, to the synthesis of logical circuits and to the study of their transient behaviour.

The module structure (*Chapter 4*) will probably sound more familiar to an analogous system designer: the concepts of vector space, of linear combination and of basis are indeed taught at college or undergraduate level. Similar concepts are developed here for discrete functions. If the Lagrange expansion, introduced in Chapter 2, may be viewed as the decomposition of a function as a sum of weighted unit impulses, the Nyquist expansion represents a function as a sum of weighted unit steps. Both families of summed functions are bases of the module of discrete functions. Similarly, Newton equidifferent products $x(x-1)\ldots(x-k)$ also form such a basis and, as in the classical calculus, the coefficients of the corresponding expansion are interpreted in terms of discrete differences. The applications developed in this chapter describe the synthesis of switching circuits, fault diagnosis in these circuits and the development of fault tolerant circuits.

In some cases, and particularly when the variables and the function take their values in some finite field, the module structure introduced in Chapter 4 specializes to that of vector space or, if one considers the product of functions, to that of linear algebra. This structure is studied in *Chapter 5* and it turns out that the parallelism with the classical calculus may be carried further on: in particular, it becomes possible to introduce discrete derivatives and Taylor expansions of discrete functions. As in classical calculus too, discrete derivatives and differences are related by Stirling numbers and that observation yields a method of computation of the Stirling numbers based on the techniques of residual arithmetics.

Chapter 6 states a first class of optimization problems: essentially, it consists in choosing a suitable base of the module of discrete functions in such a way that the representation of a given function as a linear combination of base elements contains a minimum number of these elements. If the optimization problem is stated in these general terms, it may be considered as widely unsolved, since no efficient methods for cutting down the enumeration process are available: even in the simple case of switching functions, the problem has only been solved for five variable functions. Partial problems may, however, reasonably be solved: it is indeed sufficient to restrict the set of bases among which the choice is made to an appropriate subset. Various subsets of bases such as coherent bases, Newton and Taylor bases are studied in this chapter.

It has been observed in the preceding chapters that the systematic introduction of differential-like operators was quite an efficient unifying tool. Apart from that unifying property, the discrete differential or difference calculus has various advantages: first, its relationship with classical calculus throws an additional light on the deep meaning of the introduced concepts. Next and more important is the fact that this formalism permits presentation of functional properties as such, i.e. in a representation independent way. That approach is systematically developed in *Chapter 7* which presents a difference calculus and a differential calculus for discrete functions. The central property of these calculi lies in their use in the case of functions of functions: it has thus an essential role to play in the synthesis of combinational switching circuits since a computation scheme is indeed a function of function. It also immediately applies to the study of the transient behaviour of switching circuits and in particular of asynchronous sequential circuits.

A second family of optimization problems is discussed in *Chapter 8* which presents various algorithms for obtaining optimal covers and optimal closed covers. These problems are presented independently of the other chapters of the book because of their numerous applications. The former problem is, however, strongly connected with Chapter 3 since it allows for obtaining optimal representations of discrete functions in terms of their prime implicants. The application of the closed cover algorithm to the state number minimization of finite automata is also presented.

The problem of functional completeness may be stated as follows: what are the conditions to be satisfied by a family of discrete functions so that any discrete function can be expressed by composition of members of this set only. Once again, no precise answer to this general problem is available and *Chapter 9* exposes the solutions of two partial problems, viz. those of functional completeness for binary and r-valued logics. These results are essentially those of Post and of Rosenberg, respectively.

The purpose of the complexity theory is to compare various representations of functions or the associated circuits. This theory introduces two quality measures: the cost of a realization (i.e. the number of members of a functionally complete set appearing in a particular representation) and the computation time (equivalent to the depth of composition in the particular representation). The essential result is of qualitative nature: one indeed exhibits asymptotically coincident upper and lower bounds for the complexity of an arbitrary set of m functions of n variables in the

r-valued logics. These results, presented in *Chapter 10*, provide a motivation for various optimization problems such as those studied in Chapters 6 and 8: indeed, the only way to evade the above universal bounds for particular functions is to take advantage of their specificity. That reflection also provides a link with the second part of the book devoted to the study of functional properties.

The latter study has been limited to three topics: functional decomposition, unateness and symmetry. Functional decomposition is handled in *Chapter 11.* This chapter is divided in two parts: the first part is devoted to general theorems about the decomposition of discrete functions. The second part presents more precise results about binary functions: in particular, Ashenhurst's decomposition theory is restated in the language of the discrete differential calculus. It has already been pointed out that decomposition theory is by nature practically oriented since the output of a decomposition procedure is a computation scheme, i.e. a synthesis. This clearly shows why the above results, as fragmentary as they are, are of fundamental concern to circuit designers.

Chapter 12 presents the classical concept of unateness and refines it to local unateness which is probably more interesting for practical purposes; in particular, one establishes the relationship between unateness and the absence of hazards in switching circuits. Detection of unateness receives a particular attention and the detection algorithms are applied to the discovery of malfunctions of switching circuits. This chapter also presents the important concepts of unate envelopes and applies them to the synthesis of hazard-free circuits.

The concept of symmetry is also of importance in a technical context: indeed, many important functions, e.g. those encountered when implementing arithmetic operations, present some form of symmetry. On the other hand, it turns out to be possible to take advantage of that symmetry by the use of specific representation methods. *Chapter 13* presents a new definition of partial symmetry that generalizes the corresponding definition for switching functions in a natural way. That definition allows for an extension to discrete functions of classical results concerning switching or r-valued functions such as the ρ-symmetry theory and the imbedding in a totally symmetric function.

While forming the project of writing this book, the authors had to solve two preliminary technical problems: they had indeed to delineate in a precise way the subject matter of the book and to decide of a systematic presentation method. An agreement was rapidly obtained on the latter problem and it was decided to adopt a presentation style similar to that of standard mathematical textbooks: in particular, in each chapter the general theorems are presented first and are then specialized progressively to more restricted situations. The theoretical contents was also rapidly agreed upon together with its prerequisite structure described by Figure 1. The crucial decision regarded the choice of, and the volume to give to applications. These have for the most been restricted to switching circuit applications, with some exceptions to problems requiring a restricted background. This choice is questionable since it may give a false or at least incomplete idea of the actual realm of

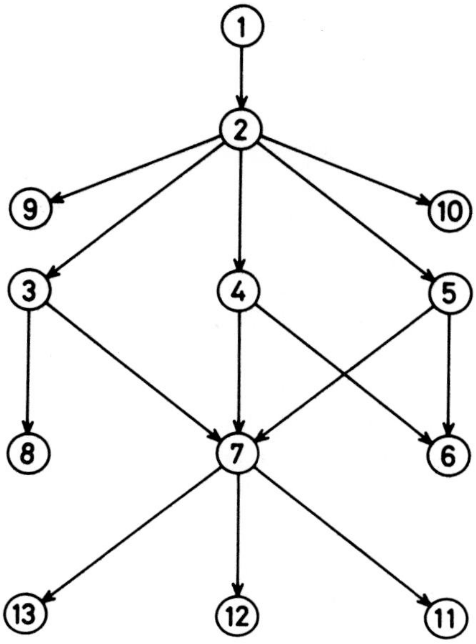

Figure 1. Prerequisite structure of the chapters

applications. It was, however, made necessary to keep the text within reasonable limits of length.

While writing this book, the authors have contracted important debts of gratitude. They wish to thank first Professor Vitold Belevitch, Director of the M.B.L.E. Research Laboratory, both for his constant interest and encouragement and for giving them the possibility of materializing this work within the framework of the M.B.L.E. Research Laboratory activities. Special thanks are also due to Professor Sergiu Rudeanu (University of Bucharest), who first suggested the writing of this book, and provided the authors with the invaluable help of his detailed knowledge of the literature.

The authors are also indebted to many of their colleagues of the Research Laboratory but particularly to Dr Philippe Delsarte who carefully read the manuscript and suggested numerous improvements and corrections and to MM. Géry Bioul and Jean-Jacques Quisquater for helpful discussions. Professor Raymond T. Yeh (University of Texas, Austin) kindly accepted to preface this book.

Mrs Edith Moës typed the manuscript with amability and competence. Mr Claude Semaille executed the numerous drawings with his usual care and Mr Heinz Georgi provided us with his kind editorial assistance.

Brussels, July 1977

Marc Davio
Jean-Pierre Deschamps
André Thayse

Chapter 1
Algebraic Structures

This chapter presents the algebraic background required for a thorough understanding of the theory of discrete functions. Most of its material is classical. The first section (1.1) introduces the concept of binary relation between sets; in particular the important notion of function is defined. The concept of binary relation on a set is also introduced, and some emphasis is put on the equivalence relations and on the order relations. Section 1.2 gives a short introduction to universal algebras; the definitions of homomorphism and congruence are given in that general context. Section 1.3 is devoted to ordered sets: semilattices, Boolean algebras and closure systems; some important results, directly applicable to the theory of discrete functions, are obtained such as a method for finding the prime implicants and the prime implicates of an element of a lattice (algorithm 1.2). Section 1.4 is devoted to rings, fields and modules. The important algebraic structures of rings of integers, Galois fields and extension fields are described; furthermore, an entire subsection (1.4.4) is devoted to matrices and matrix operations that play a key role in the module theory. The material contained in section 1.5 is perhaps less classical: numeration systems and lexicographical order, Gray codes, and Kronecker product of matrices. It is shown how the Kronecker product of matrices allows to obtain bases for a module of n-variable functions from the knowledge of bases of a module of one-variable functions; furthermore, the transformation matrices relating bases of that type are also obtained by Kronecker products.

1.1. Binary relations

1.1.1. Binary relations between two sets

Definitions 1.1. Given n sets $A_1, \ldots, A_n$, the *Cartesian product* $A_1 \times \ldots \times A_n$ is the set consisting of the ordered n-tuples $(a_1, \ldots, a_n)$ for every $a_1 \in A_1, \ldots, a_n \in A_n$: $A_1 \times \ldots \times A_n = \{(a_1, \ldots, a_n) | a_1 \in A_1, \ldots, a_n \in A_n\}$.

A *binary relation* from a set A to a set B is a triple $\langle A, B, R \rangle$ where:

A is the *domain* of R,

B is the *codomain* of R,

R is a subset of $A \times B$ called *graph* of the relation.

In the case where A and B are finite sets ($\# A = m$ and $\# B = n$) one uses a graphical representation for describing the relation $\langle A, B, R\rangle$: the elements of A and B are represented by points and with each pair (a_i, b_j) of R is associated an edge that connects the point representing a_i to the point representing b_j.

Another way to describe the relation $\langle A, B, R\rangle$ when both A and B are finite is the *adjacency matrix* $M(R)$; it is an $m \times n$ matrix the element of indices i and j of which is denoted m_{ij} and is defined as follows:

$$m_{ij} = 1 \quad \text{if } (a_i, b_j) \in R$$
$$m_{ij} = 0 \quad \text{if } (a_i, b_j) \notin R.$$

The *converse relation* $\langle B, A, R_c\rangle$ of a binary relation $\langle A, B, R\rangle$ is the binary relation from B to A the graph of which is defined by:

$$R_c = \{(b_j, a_i) \mid (a_i, b_j) \in R\}.$$

Designate by $\langle A, B, R\rangle$, $\langle B, C, S\rangle$ and $\langle C, D, T\rangle$ three binary relations. The *composition* of $\langle A, B, R\rangle$ and $\langle B, C, S\rangle$ is the binary relation $\langle A, C, R.S\rangle$ the graph of which is defined as follows:

$$R.S = \{(a_i, c_k) \mid \exists\, b_j : (a_i, b_j) \in R \text{ and } (b_j, c_k) \in S\}.$$

Theorem 1.1. The composition of binary relations is associative, i.e.

$$\langle A, D, (R.S).T\rangle = \langle A, D, R.(S.T)\rangle.$$

The proof of this theorem is omitted; it can be found in any classical textbook on algebra, e.g. Birkhoff and Bartee [1970]. In fact, all along sections 1.1 and 1.2 the proofs are omitted.

Definitions 1.2. In the sequel, $\langle A, B, R_i\rangle$ and $\langle B, C, S_j\rangle$, where i and j belong to some index set, designate binary relations. The *union* and the *intersection* of $\langle A, B, R_1\rangle$ and $\langle A, B, R_2\rangle$ are the relations $\langle A, B, R_1 \cup R_2\rangle$ and $\langle A, B, R_1 \cap R_2\rangle$, respectively. The relation $\langle A, B, R_1\rangle$ is *smaller than or equal to (included in)* the relation $\langle A, B, R_2\rangle$ iff $R_1 \subseteq R_2$.

Theorem 1.2. (a) *The composition of relations is distributive with respect to the union of relations:*

$$\langle A, C, (R_1 \cup R_2).S_1\rangle = \langle A, C, (R_1.S_1) \cup (R_2.S_1)\rangle,$$
$$\langle A, C, R_1.(S_1 \cup S_2)\rangle = \langle A, C, (R_1.S_1) \cup (R_1.S_2)\rangle.$$

(b) *The union and the intersection of relations are regular with respect to the inclusion of relations:*

$$R_1 \subseteq R_2 \text{ and } R_3 \subseteq R_4 \Rightarrow R_1 \cup R_3 \subseteq R_2 \cup R_4 \text{ and } R_1 \cap R_3 \subseteq R_2 \cap R_4.$$

(c) *The composition of relations is regular with respect to the inclusion of relations:*

$R_1 \subseteq R_2$ and $S_1 \subseteq S_2 \Rightarrow R_1 . S_1 \subseteq R_2 . S_2$.

Definition 1.3. Consider the subsets A' of A and B' of B. The *restriction* of $\langle A, B, R \rangle$ to A' and B' is the relation $\langle A', B', R|_{A'B'} \rangle$ where

$$R|_{A'B'} = \{(a, b) \in R \mid a \in A' \text{ and } b \in B'\}.$$

Definitions 1.4. Consider the binary relation $\langle A, B, R \rangle$. The *image* of $a \in A$ by R is the subset aR (or $R(a)$) of B defined as follows:

$$aR = \{b_i \in B \mid (a, b_i) \in R\}.$$

The *image of the subset* A' of A by R is the subset $A'R$ (or $R(A')$) of B defined by

$$A'R = \bigcup_{a \in A'} aR.$$

Finally, the image AR of A by R is called the *image* of R.

The *coimage* of $b \in B$ by R is the subset bR_c of A. The *coimage* of $B' \subseteq B$ by R is the subset $B'R_c$ of A. The *coimage* of R is the subset BR_c of A.

Definitions 1.5. Describe now some properties that a binary relation $\langle A, B, R \rangle$ can enjoy:

(a) it is *completely specified* if $aR \neq \emptyset$, for every $a \in A$ (i.e. $BR_c = A$);
(b) it is *onto* if $AR = B$;
(c) it is *functional* if $\#aR \leqslant 1$, for every $a \in A$;
(d) it is *one-to-one* if $\#bR_c \leqslant 1$, for every $b \in B$.

A *mapping* or *function* is a functional and completely specified binary relation. A *surjection* is an onto mapping. An *injection* is a one-to-one mapping. A *bijection* is a one-to-one and onto mapping.

Theorem 1.3. Given a mapping f, the converse relation f_c is also a mapping iff f is a bijection. In that case, f and f_c are called reciprocal bijections.

Remark. When no confusion can arise, the binary relation $\langle A, B, R \rangle$ is simply represented by its graph R.

Definitions 1.6. Consider a set A and its nth Cartesian power

$$A^n = \{(a_{i_1}, \ldots, a_{i_n}) \mid a_{i_k} \in A,\ k = 1, \ldots, n\}.$$

An *n-ary operation* on A is a mapping ω from A^n to A. The integer n is the *arity* of ω. An *O-ary operation* is a particular member of A.

The *restriction* of an n-ary operation ω on A to a subset A' of A is the restriction of the relation $\langle A^n, A, \omega \rangle$ to $((A')^n, A')$. The restriction of ω to A' is generally not an operation on A' since the image of an element of $(A')^n$ by ω is not necessarily an element of A'. In the case where the restriction of ω to A' is an operation on A', then A' is called a *stable part* of A with respect to ω.

There are two notations for the image a of $(a_{i_1}, \ldots, a_{i_n})$ by ω:

(a) the *prefixed or Polish notation*

$$a = (a_{i_1}, \ldots, a_{i_n})\,\omega;$$

(b) the classical *postfixed notation*

$$a = \omega(a_{i_1}, \ldots, a_{i_n}).$$

1.1.2. Binary relations on a set

Definitions 1.7. When the domain and the codomain of a binary relation are the same set A, it is called a *binary relation* on A and simply denoted $\langle A, R\rangle$. As it has been said above, in most cases it is not necessary to mention explicitly the set A.

A mapping (bijection) from A to A is also called a *transformation (permutation)* of A.

The relation $\langle A, \Delta_A\rangle$ where

$$\Delta_A = \{(a, a) \mid a \in A\}$$

is the *identity relation* on A or *diagonal relation* on A.

Theorem 1.4. If $\langle A, B, R\rangle$ is a binary relation from A to B, then

$$\langle A, B, \Delta_A . R\rangle = \langle A, B, R . \Delta_B\rangle = \langle A, B, R\rangle.$$

Definitions 1.8. The binary relations on A can have some particular features. The relation $\langle A, R\rangle$ is *reflexive* if

$$\Delta_A \subseteq R, \quad \text{i.e. } (a, a) \in R \text{ for every } a \text{ in } A.$$

It is *symmetric* if

$$R = R_c, \quad \text{i.e. } (a, b) \in R \Rightarrow (b, a) \in R.$$

It is *antisymmetric* if

$$R \cap R_c \subseteq \Delta_A, \quad \text{i.e. } (a, b) \in R \text{ and } (b, a) \in R \Rightarrow a = b.$$

It is *transitive* if

$$R . R \subseteq R, \quad \text{i.e. } (a, b) \in R \text{ and } (b, c) \in R \Rightarrow (a, c) \in R.$$

A relation that is reflexive and transitive is a *preorder relation.* An antisymmetric preorder relation is an *order relation* (section 1.1.4). A relation that is reflexive and symmetric is a *compatibility relation.* A transitive compatibility relation is an *equivalence relation.*

1.1.3. *Equivalence relations*

Definitions 1.9. Given an equivalence relation $\langle A, \mathcal{E}\rangle$ on A, the subset A' of A is an *equivalence class* of $\mathcal{E}$ if

(a) $(a, b) \in \mathcal{E}$ for every a and b in A';
(b) A' is maximal with respect to the property (a) i.e.

$$(a, b) \in \mathcal{E} \text{ with } a \in A' \Rightarrow b \in A'.$$

An indexed family $\{A_i | i \in I\}$ of nonempty subsets of A is a *partition* of A if

(a) $\bigcup_{i \in I} A_i = A$;

(b) $i \neq j \Rightarrow A_i \cap A_j = \emptyset$.

Theorem 1.5. (a) *If $\langle A, \mathcal{E}\rangle$ is an equivalence relation on A, the set of equivalence classes of $\mathcal{E}$ is a partition of A.*

(b) *Conversely, given a partition $\{A_i | i \in I\}$ of A, the relation $\langle A, \mathcal{E}\rangle$, where*

$$\mathcal{E} = \{(a, b) | \exists\, i \in I : a \in A_i \text{ and } b \in A_i\},$$

is an equivalence relation on A.

(c) *The two preceding properties establish a bijection between the set of equivalence relations on A and the set of partitions of A.*

Definition 1.10. Consider an equivalence relation $\langle A, \mathcal{E}\rangle$ on A. The set of equivalence classes of $\mathcal{E}$ is called the *quotient set* of A by $\mathcal{E}$, and is denoted by $A/\mathcal{E}$. The equivalence class containing a is represented by the symbol $[a]$. Finally, denoting by $\pi = \{A_i | i \in I\}$ the partition associated with $\mathcal{E}$ by theorem 2.5, one writes $a \equiv b(\pi)$ or even $a \equiv b$, modulo π, instead of $(a, b) \in \mathcal{E}$. The subsets A_i of A are called the *blocks of the partition.* A *binary partition* is a partition in two blocks.

Definition 1.11. Given a relation $\langle A, B, R\rangle$ from A to B, the *kernel* of that relation is the relation $\langle A, \ker R\rangle$ on A where

$$\ker R = R \,.\, R_c.$$

Theorem 1.6. (a) *$\ker R$ is a symmetric relation.*
(b) *If $\langle A, B, R\rangle$ is completely specified, $\ker R$ is reflexive.*
(c) *If $\langle A, B, R\rangle$ is onto, $\ker R_c$ is reflexive.*
(d) *If $\langle A, B, R\rangle$ is functional, $\ker R_c \subseteq \Delta_B$.*
(e) *If $\langle A, B, R\rangle$ is one-to-one, $\ker R \subseteq \Delta_A$.*
(f) *The kernel of a mapping is an equivalence relation.*

1.1.4. Order relations; duality

Definitions 1.12. Consider a set A on which is defined an order relation $\leqslant$. The general notation $(a_1, a_2) \in \leqslant$ is replaced by the classical notation $a_1 \leqslant a_2$ (a_1 smaller than or equal to a_2). Furthermore, in the case where $a_1 \leqslant a_2$ and $a_1 \neq a_2$, one simply writes $a_1 < a_2$. The set A is *ordered* by $\leqslant$. It is *totally ordered* by $\leqslant$ if for every pair (a_1, a_2) of elements of A one has either $a_1 \leqslant a_2$ or $a_2 \leqslant a_1$. In the opposite case, it is *partially ordered.* A totally ordered set is sometimes called a *chain.*

A finite chain is thus a finite totally ordered set like $\{a_0, a_1, \ldots, a_n\}$, with $a_0 < a_1 < \ldots < a_n$; its *length* is n and its *ends* are a_0 and a_n.

An *ordered set* is *of finite length* if all the chains it contains are finite; in that case, its *length* is the length of one of the greatest chains it contains.

The element a_2 of A *covers* the element a_1 of A if

(a) $a_1 < a_2$;
(b) there is no a_3 in A such that $a_1 < a_3 < a_2$.

A chain $a_0 < a_1 < \ldots < a_n$, such that a_i covers a_{i-1} for every $i = 1, \ldots, n$, is called a *maximal chain.*

It is obvious that if A is an ordered set of finite length, then given two elements a and b of A, such that $a < b$, there exists at least one maximal chain in A with a and b as ends. The set $[a, b]$ of elements of A that lie between a and b, i.e.

$$[a, b] = \{x \in A \mid a \leqslant x \leqslant b\}$$

is called an *interval* of A.

Every ordered set can be represented by a *Hasse diagram.* With each element of the ordered set A is associated a vertex of the diagram. If $a_1 \leqslant a_2$, the vertex representing a_2 is drawn higher than the vertex representing a_1. Furthermore, if a_2 covers a_1 there is an edge connecting a_1 and a_2.

Example 1.1. The set $\mathscr{P}(A)$ of all subsets of A is partially ordered under set inclusion. The corresponding Hasse diagram is given in Figure 1.1 in the case where $A = \{a, b, c, d\}$.

Theorem 1.7. (Duality principle.) The converse relation of an order relation is also an order relation.

Consequence. If some property P holds true in any ordered set, then the dual property obtained by replacing in P each occurrence of $\leqslant$ by $\geqslant$ also holds true in any ordered set.

Definitions 1.13. Consider an ordered set $\langle A, \leqslant \rangle$ and a subset B of A. An element a of A is an *upper bound* of B if $b \leqslant a$, for every b in B.

An element a of B is the *greatest element* of B (or the *maximum* element of B) if $b \leqslant a$, for every b in B.

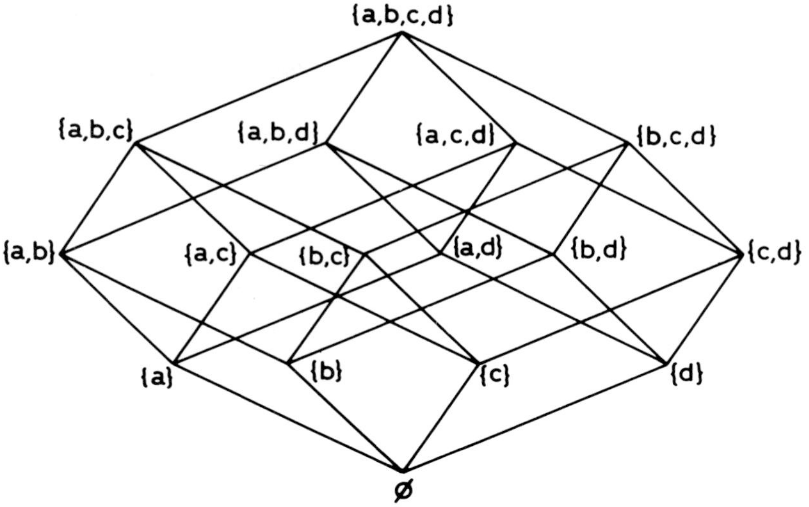

Figure 1.1. The set $\mathscr{P}$ ({a, b, c, d}) ordered by set inclusion

An element a of B is a *maximal element* of B if there is no b in B such that $a < b$.

It is obvious that a maximum element, when it exists, is unique. On the other hand, it can arise that a set has several maximal elements, but if there exists a maximum element it is at the same time the unique maximal element.

The concepts of *lower bound, least element (minimum element),* and *minimal element* are dually defined and enjoy dual properties.

Denote by $M(B)$ the set of upper bounds of B. If $M(B)$ has a minimum element, it is called the *least upper bound* of B (l.u.b.) or the *supremum* of B; it is denoted by sup B.

Denote similarly by $m(B)$ the set of lower bounds of B. If $m(B)$ has a maximum element, it is called the *greatest lower bound* of B (g.l.b.) or the *infimum* of B; it is denoted by inf B.

When the set A itself has a maximum element, this element is called the *universal element* of A and is denoted **1**. If A has a minimum element, it is called the *null element* of A and denoted **0**.

Definition 1.14. Given two ordered sets $\langle A, \leqslant_A \rangle$ and $\langle B, \leqslant_B \rangle$, an *order homomorphism* from A to B is a mapping ϕ from A to B that has the following property:

$$a_1 \leqslant_A a_2 \Rightarrow \phi(a_1) \leqslant_B \phi(a_2).$$

1.2. Universal algebras

Let $\Omega = \{n_1, \ldots, n_p\}$ be a finite set of non-negative integers, and A any set. With every n_i, $i = 1, \ldots, p$, associate an n_i-ary operation ω_i on A. This defines the algebraic structure

$$\langle A, \omega_1, \ldots, \omega_p \rangle$$

that is called *universal algebra* on A with the *operator domain* Ω.

If B is a stable part of A with respect to the p operations ω_i, then $\langle B, \omega_1, \ldots, \omega_p \rangle$ is a *subalgebra* of $\langle A, \omega_1, \ldots, \omega_p \rangle$.

Definition 1.15. Let $\langle A, \omega_1, \ldots, \omega_p \rangle$ be a universal algebra with the operator domain Ω, and $\mathcal{E}$ an equivalence relation on A. The equivalence relation $\mathcal{E}$ is a *congruence* on A if

$$(a_k, b_k) \in \mathcal{E}, \quad \forall\, k = 1, \ldots, n_i$$

$\Rightarrow$

$$((a_1, \ldots, a_{n_i})\, \omega_i, (b_1, \ldots, b_{n_i})\, \omega_i) \in \mathcal{E},$$

for every $i = 1, \ldots, p$.

If $\mathcal{E}$ is a congruence, one can easily define a universal algebra $\langle A/\mathcal{E}, \boldsymbol{\omega}_1, \ldots, \boldsymbol{\omega}_p \rangle$ on the quotient set $A/\mathcal{E}$, with Ω as operator domain, by putting

$$([a_1], \ldots, [a_{n_i}])\, \boldsymbol{\omega}_i = [(a_1, \ldots, a_{n_i})\, \omega_i],$$

for every $i = 1, \ldots, p$. By definition of a congruence, the class $[(a_1, \ldots, a_{n_i})\, \omega_i]$ is uniquely defined whatever may be the particular element a_j chosen in $[a_j]$, $\forall\, j = 1, \ldots, n_i$. The algebra $\langle A/\mathcal{E}, \boldsymbol{\omega}_1, \ldots, \boldsymbol{\omega}_p \rangle$ is the *quotient algebra* of $\langle A, \omega_1, \ldots, \omega_p \rangle$ by $\mathcal{E}$. The partition π associated with $\mathcal{E}$ is called a *partition with the substitution property* or *substitutive partition.*

Example 1.2. Consider a finite monoid $\langle A, o, e \rangle$ of order n, that is a set A of n elements on which is defined a binary associative operation o, and containing a particular element e such that:

$$e\, o\, a = a\, o\, e = a, \quad \forall a \in A,$$

i.e. a neutral element for o. Note that one writes $a\, o\, b$ for $o(a, b)$.

There are several ways for representing that monoid as a universal algebra. The most natural consists in choosing

$$\Omega = \{2, 0\}$$

where 2 is the arity of o and 0 the arity of e. However, two other representations deserve some attention. Associate indeed with every element a of A a unary operation r_a on A called the *right translation* by a and defined as follows:

$$(b)\, r_a = b\, o\, a, \quad \forall a \text{ and } b \in A.$$

The set r of n right translations on A completely characterizes the monoid $\langle A, o, e \rangle$ since it allows to reconstitute the "multiplication" table of o. The structure $\langle A, r \rangle$ can then be considered as a universal algebra with

$$\Omega = \{\underbrace{1, \ldots, 1}_{n \text{ times}}\}$$

as operator domain. The congruences on this algebra are the right congruences on the monoid.

Similarly, the *left translation* l_a is defined as follows:

$$l_a(b) = a \circ b, \quad \forall a \text{ and } b \in A.$$

The left congruences on the monoid are defined accordingly. Furthermore, the relations that are at the same time right and left congruences are the congruences on the monoid; they are indeed the congruences on A with $\Omega = \{2, 0\}$ as operator domain.

Definition 1.16. Given two universal algebras $\langle A, \omega_1^a, \ldots, \omega_p^a\rangle$ and $\langle B, \omega_1^b, \ldots, \omega_p^b\rangle$, with the same set Ω as operator domain, a mapping ϕ from A to B is a *homomorphism* if

$$((a_1, \ldots, a_{n_i})\, \omega_i^a)\, \phi = ((a_1\phi), \ldots, (a_{n_i}\phi))\, \omega_i^b,$$
$$\forall i = 1, \ldots, p,\ \forall (a_1, \ldots, a_{n_i}) \in A^{n_i}.$$

A one-to-one homomorphism is a *monomorphism.* An onto homomorphism is an *epimorphism.* A bijection that is a homomorphism is an *isomorphism.* A homomorphism from an algebra to itself is an *endomorphism* and an isomorphism from an algebra to itself is an *automorphism.*

Theorem 1.8. If ϕ is a homomorphism from $\langle A, \omega_1^a, \ldots, \omega_p^a\rangle$ to $\langle B, \omega_1^b, \ldots, \omega_p^b\rangle$, and ψ a homomorphism from $\langle B, \omega_1^b, \ldots, \omega_p^b\rangle$ to $\langle C, \omega_1^c, \ldots, \omega_p^c\rangle$, then $\phi.\psi$ is a homomorphism from $\langle A, \omega_1^a, \ldots, \omega_p^a\rangle$ to $\langle C, \omega_1^c, \ldots, \omega_p^c\rangle$.

Theorem 1.9. If ϕ is an epimorphism from $\langle A, \omega_1^a, \ldots, \omega_p^a\rangle$ to $\langle B, \omega_1^b, \ldots, \omega_p^b\rangle$, then

(a) *$\ker \phi$ is a congruence on A;*
(b) *$\langle A/\ker \phi, \boldsymbol{\omega}_1^a, \ldots, \boldsymbol{\omega}_p^a\rangle$ is isomorphic to $\langle B, \omega_1^b, \ldots, \omega_p^b\rangle$*

Definition 1.17. Given a universal algebra $\langle A, \omega_1, \ldots, \omega_p\rangle$ and a set of variables $\{x_1, x_2, \ldots\}$, a *well-formed algebraic expression* on this algebra is defined inductively as follows:

(a) the elements of A are well-formed algebraic expressions (in short: w.f.a.e.); they are sometimes called the constants.
(b) The variables are w.f.a.e.
(c) If $\alpha_1, \ldots, \alpha_{n_i}$ ($n_i \geq 1$) are w.f.a.e., then $(\alpha_1, \ldots, \alpha_{n_i})\, \omega_i$ is a w.f.a.e.
(d) There are no other w.f.a.e. than those generated by using a finite number of times rules (a), (b) and (c).

Consider a particular w.f.a.e. on the algebra $\langle A, \omega_1, \ldots, \omega_p \rangle$, with $\{x_1, \ldots, x_m\}$ as set of variables.

It is obvious that this w.f.a.e. defines a function from A^m to A; for evaluating that function at point $(a_1, \ldots, a_m)$ of A^m, it suffices to replace in the w.f.a.e. x_1 by $a_1, \ldots$, x_m by a_m, and to compute the obtained value in a step by step way (by rule (d) the number of steps is finite).

1.3. Lattice theory

1.3.1. Semilattices

Definition 1.18. A *sup-semilattice* is an ordered set $\langle S, \leqslant \rangle$ in which every pair of elements admits a supremum. Dually, an *inf-semilattice* is an ordered set $\langle S, \leqslant \rangle$ in which every pair of elements has an infimum.

A binary operation $\vee$ on a set S is a *lattice operation* if it has the three following properties:

(a) idempotence: $s \vee s = s, \ \forall s \in S$;
(b) associativity: $s \vee (t \vee v) = (s \vee t) \vee v, \ \forall s, t, v \in S$;
(c) commutativity: $s \vee t = t \vee s, \ \forall s, t \in S$.

Theorem 1.10. A set S is a sup-semilattice iff one can define a lattice operation $\vee$ *on S.*

Proof. (a) *Necessity.* Let $\langle S, \leqslant \rangle$ be a sup-semilattice. Define the binary operation $\vee$ on S by

$$s \vee t = \sup \{s, t\}, \ \forall s, t \in S,$$

and show that it is a lattice operation.

Idempotence. $s \vee s = \sup \{s, s\} = s$.

Associativity. It suffices to note that, given s, t and v in S, one has the following relations:

$$\sup \{s, \sup \{t, v\}\} = \sup \{s, t, v\} = \sup \{\sup \{s, t\}, v\}.$$

The supremum of s and $\sup \{t, v\}$ is obviously an upper bound of $\{s, t, v\}$ and thus

$$\sup \{s, \sup \{t, v\}\} \geqslant \sup \{s, t, v\}.$$

Conversely the supremum of $\{s, t, v\}$ in an upper bound of $\{s\}$ and $\{t, v\}$ and thus also of $\{s, \sup \{t, v\}\}$. Therefore

$$\sup \{s, t, v\} = \sup \{s, \sup \{t, v\}\}.$$

One proves similarly that

$$\sup \{s, t, v\} = \sup \{\sup \{s, t\}, v\}.$$

Commutativity. Obvious.

Note that if $\langle S, \leqslant \rangle$ is a sup-semilattice one has

$$s \leqslant t \quad \text{iff } \sup\{s, t\} = t$$

and thus also, by definition of the lattice operation $\vee$

$$s \leqslant t \quad \text{iff } s \vee t = t.$$

(b) *Sufficiency.* Let $\langle S, \vee \rangle$ be an algebraic structure where $\vee$ is a lattice operation. Define a binary relation R on S:

$$R = \{(s, t) \in S^2 \mid s \vee t = t\}. \tag{1.1}$$

The relation R is an order relation.

Reflexivity. The idempotence property of $\vee$ shows that $s \vee s = s$ and thus $(s, s) \in R$, $\forall s \in S$.

Antisymmetry. Suppose that $(s, t) \in R$ and $(t, s) \in R$; one has

$$s \vee t = t \quad \text{and} \quad t \vee s = s$$

and by the commutativity property of $\vee$ one deduces that $s = t$.

Transitivity. Suppose that $(s, t) \in R$ and $(t, u) \in R$, i.e.

$$s \vee t = t \quad \text{and} \quad t \vee u = u;$$

therefore

$$s \vee u = s \vee (t \vee u) = (s \vee t) \vee u = t \vee u = u,$$

and $(s, u) \in R$.

One can replace R by the classical notation $\leqslant$.

Note that $s \vee t = \sup\{s, t\}$, with respect to the order relation associated with $\vee$, for any s and t in S. First observe that:

$$s \vee (s \vee t) = (s \vee s) \vee t = s \vee t, \quad \text{i.e. } s \leqslant s \vee t$$

and

$$t \vee (t \vee s) = (t \vee t) \vee s = t \vee s, \quad \text{i.e. } t \leqslant t \vee s = s \vee t,$$

and thus $s \vee t$ is an upper bound of $\{s, t\}$. If furthermore u is another upper bound of $\{s, t\}$ one has:

$$(s \vee t) \vee u = s \vee (t \vee u) = s \vee u = u, \quad \text{i.e. } s \vee t \leqslant u.$$

Therefore $s \vee t$ is the supremum (or least upper bound) of $\{s, t\}$. ■

Remarks. (1) One can state a similar theorem in the case where $\langle S, \leqslant \rangle$ is an inf-semilattice. In that case one has

$$s \leqslant t \text{ iff } \inf\{s, t\} = s;$$

the associated lattice operation is then defined by

$$s \wedge t = \inf \{s, t\}.$$

Conversely, if $\wedge$ is a lattice operation on S, one defines the following order relation R' on S:

$$R' = \{(s, t) \in S^2 \mid s \wedge t = s\},$$

with respect to which

$$s \wedge t = \inf \{s, t\}$$

(2) Consider two sup-semilattices $\langle S, \leqslant_S \rangle$ and $\langle T, \leqslant_T \rangle$, and the associated lattice operations $\vee_S$ and $\vee_T$. Suppose that ϕ is a homomorphism from $\langle S, \vee_S \rangle$ to $\langle T, \vee_T \rangle$; then

$$s_1 \leqslant_S s_2 \Rightarrow s_1 \vee_S s_2 = s_2 \Rightarrow (s_1)\phi \vee_T (s_2)\phi = (s_2)\phi \Rightarrow (s_1)\phi \leqslant_T (s_2)\phi.$$

This proves that ϕ is also an order homomorphism from $\langle S, \leqslant_S \rangle$ to $\langle T, \leqslant_T \rangle$. The converse is generally not true, except when ϕ is a bijection, i.e. in the case of *order isomorphisms.*

Definition 1.19. Let $\langle S, \vee \rangle$ be a sup-semilattice. A subset G of S is a *$\vee$-generating system* iff every element s of S can be written in at least one way under the form

$$s = g_1 \vee \ldots \vee g_k$$

where the g_i's are well chosen elements of G. An element s of S is *$\vee$-irreducible* if any equality like

$$s = s_1 \vee \ldots \vee s_l, s_i \in S, \quad \forall i = 1, \ldots, l,$$

implies

$$s = s_i \text{ for some } i \in \{1, \ldots, l\}.$$

It is obvious that a $\vee$-generating system contains all the $\vee$-irreducible elements. Furthermore, if S is a finite set, this last condition is sufficient.

One defines dually the notions of *$\wedge$-generating system* and *$\wedge$-irreducible element* in the case of an inf-semilattice $\langle S, \wedge \rangle$.

Problem 1.1. Consider a finite sup-semilattice $\langle S, \vee \rangle$ a $\vee$-generating system G of which is known. Suppose furthermore that there exists a rule that allows one to perform the lattice operation $\vee$. One asks to reconstitute S from G and from the rule.

Algorithm 1.1.

Step 1. The elements of G constitute the list A_1.

Step *i.* Compute $s_k \vee s_j$ for all unordered pairs (s_k, s_j) of members of A_{i-1}. Delete in the obtained list elements of S that are already in one of the lists $A_1, \ldots, A_{i-1}$. One so gets the list A_i.

The algorithm stops after step i if A_i is empty or is a singleton, i.e. after at most $\#G$ steps.

The set S is the union of the lists $A_1, A_2, \ldots$.

One can briefly justify the method by proving that after step i one has obtained all the members of S of the type

$$s = g_1 \vee \ldots \vee g_i, g_j \in G, \quad \forall j = 1, \ldots, i.$$

This holds true for $i = 1$; the proof is completed by induction.

Consider the element $s = g_1 \vee \ldots \vee g_i$ of S. Then, by the induction hypothesis one has:

$$s_1 = g_2 \vee \ldots \vee g_i \in A_1 \cup \ldots \cup A_{i-1},$$
$$\vdots$$
$$s_i = g_1 \vee \ldots \vee g_{i-1} \in A_1 \cup \ldots \cup A_{i-1};$$

there are i elements of the type s_j and $(i-1)$ lists of the type A_j. It is thus possible to find two elements, say s_k and s_l, in the same list, say A_h. Therefore one has either

$$s = s_k \vee s_l \in A_{h+1}, \text{ with } h \leqslant i-1 \text{ and thus } h+1 \leqslant i,$$

or

$$s = s_k \vee s_l \in A_1 \cup \ldots \cup A_h.$$

Finally, note that a dual algorithm can be described in the case where $\langle S, \wedge \rangle$ is an inf-semilattice and G' a $\wedge$-generating system.

1.3.2. Lattices

Definition 1.20. A *lattice* is an ordered set $\langle L, \leqslant \rangle$ in which every pair of elements has a supremum and an infimum. It can easily be proven that any finite subset of L has also a supremum and an infimum. A *complete lattice* is an ordered set in which each subset has a supremum and an infimum. Thus every finite lattice is complete. Note that in a complete lattice one has:

$$\inf L = \sup \emptyset = \mathbf{0} \quad \text{and} \quad \sup L = \inf \emptyset = \mathbf{1}.$$

Theorem 1.11. A set L is a lattice iff one can define two lattice operations $\vee$ *and* $\wedge$ *on S for which the absorption law holds, i.e.*

$$l \vee (l \wedge m) = l \wedge (l \vee m) = l, \quad \forall l \text{ and } m \in L.$$

Proof. (a) *Necessity.* The two binary operations

$$l \vee m = \sup \{l, m\} \quad \text{and} \quad l \wedge m = \inf \{l, m\},$$

are lattice operations (see theorem 1.10). It suffices thus to prove that the absorption law holds:

$$l \vee (l \wedge m) = \sup \{l, \inf \{l, m\}\} = l$$

since

$$\inf \{l, m\} \leqslant l.$$

One proves similarly the second equality.

(b) *Sufficiency.* Let $\langle L, \vee, \wedge \rangle$ be an algebraic structure with two lattice operations that satisfy the absorption law. As it has been seen above (theorem 1.10) one can associate with each lattice operation $\vee$ and $\wedge$ an order relation on L:

$$l \leqslant_{\vee} m \quad \text{iff } l \vee m = m,$$

$$l \leqslant_{\wedge} m \quad \text{iff } l \wedge m = l.$$

Thanks to the absorption law one proves now that these two order relations are identical:

$$l \leqslant_{\vee} m \Rightarrow l \vee m = m \Rightarrow l = l \wedge (l \vee m) = l \wedge m \Rightarrow l \leqslant_{\wedge} m$$

and

$$l \leqslant_{\wedge} m \Rightarrow l \wedge m = l \Rightarrow m = m \vee (l \wedge m) = m \vee l \Rightarrow l \leqslant_{\vee} m. \qquad \blacksquare$$

The lattice operations $\vee$ and $\wedge$ are called *disjunction* and *conjunction*, respectively.

Theorem 1.12. In any lattice, the disjunction and the conjunction are isotone, i.e.

$$l \leqslant m \Rightarrow l \vee x \leqslant m \vee x \textit{ and } l \wedge x \leqslant m \wedge x, \quad \forall x \in L.$$

Proof. It suffices to write the following series of implications:

$$\begin{aligned} l \leqslant m \Rightarrow l \vee m = m \Rightarrow (l \vee m) \vee x = m \vee x \Rightarrow (l \vee m) \vee (x \vee x) \\ = m \vee x \Rightarrow (l \vee x) \vee (m \vee x) = m \vee x \Rightarrow l \vee x \leqslant m \vee x. \end{aligned}$$

The second proposition is dual of the first one. ■

Corollary. In any lattice the order relation is compatible with the disjunction and the conjunction, i.e.

$$a \leqslant b \quad \text{and} \quad c \leqslant d \Rightarrow a \vee c \leqslant b \vee d \quad \text{and} \quad a \wedge c \leqslant b \wedge d.$$

Proof. From the preceding theorem one deduces that

$$a \leqslant b \Rightarrow a \vee c \leqslant b \vee c,$$

and

$$c \leqslant d \Rightarrow b \vee c \leqslant b \vee d;$$

therefore, by transitivity one obtains: $a \vee c \leqslant b \vee d$.

The second proposition holds by duality. ■

Theorem 1.13. (Semidistributivity). In any lattice $\langle L, \vee, \wedge \rangle$ *the two following dual inequalities hold true:*

(a) $l \wedge (m \vee n) \geqslant (l \wedge m) \vee (l \wedge n)$,
(b) $l \vee (m \wedge n) \leqslant (l \vee m) \wedge (l \vee n)$,

$\forall l, m, n \in L$.

Proof. From the two relations

$$l \wedge m \leqslant l \quad \text{and} \quad l \wedge m \leqslant m \leqslant m \vee n,$$

and from the preceding corollary one deduces

$$l \wedge m \leqslant l \wedge (m \vee n);$$

one proves similarly that

$$l \wedge n \leqslant l \wedge (m \vee n)$$

and thus, again by the preceding corollary, one obtains

$$(l \wedge m) \vee (l \wedge n) \leqslant l \wedge (m \vee n).$$

The second relation holds by duality. ■

Definition 1.21. Given a lattice $\langle L, \vee, \wedge \rangle$, a subset L' of L is a *sublattice* iff it is a stable part of L with respect to the disjunction and to the conjunction. As an example it is obvious that every interval in a lattice L is also a sublattice of L.

Given two ordered sets $\langle L_1, \leqslant_1 \rangle$ and $\langle L_2, \leqslant_2 \rangle$, the *direct product* $\langle L_1 \times L_2, \leqslant \rangle$ of these sets is also an ordered set in which the order relation is defined componentwise, i.e.

$$(l_1, l_2) \leqslant (m_1, m_2) \quad \text{iff } l_1 \leqslant_1 m_1 \text{ and } l_2 \leqslant_2 m_2.$$

This definition can obviously be generalized to the product of a finite number of ordered sets.

Theorem 1.14. The direct product of two lattices is a lattice.

Proof. It suffices to define the lattice operations componentwise. ■

Definition 1.22. Given a lattice $\langle L, \vee, \wedge \rangle$ and a $\vee$-generating system G of L, any element g of G that is smaller than or equal to some element l of L is called an *implicant* of l. Furthermore, if g is maximal, i.e. if there is no g' in G that is greater than g and is also an implicant of l, then g is called a *prime implicant* of l.

Similarly, if H is a $\wedge$-generating system of L, any element h of H that is greater than or equal to some element l of L is called an *implicate* of l. A minimal implicate of l is a *prime implicate* of l.

Note that the notions of implicant and implicate are only defined with respect to some sets G and H. Once these sets have been chosen, one can state the two following theorems.

Theorem 1.15. Given a finite lattice $\langle L, \vee, \wedge\rangle$, *a* $\vee$*-generating system G of L, and a* $\wedge$*-generating system H of L, any element of L can be written as the disjunction of all its prime implicants or as the conjunction of all its prime implicates.*

Proof. Let

$$G = \{g_i \mid i \in I\}$$

where I is some finite index set. The set of prime implicants of $l \in L$ is of the type

$$\{g_i \mid i \in K\}$$

where K is some subset of I. By definition of an implicant one has

$$g_i \leqslant l, \quad \forall i \in K$$

and thus, using a generalized version of the corollary of theorem 1.12, one obtains

$$\bigvee_{i \in K} g_i \leqslant l.$$

Conversely since G is a $\vee$-generating set, there exists a subset J of I such that

$$l = \bigvee_{i \in J} g_i.$$

Furthermore, each g_i, with $i \in J$, is included in at least one prime implicant g_i' of l. Therefore,

$$l \leqslant \bigvee_{i \in J} g_i' \leqslant \bigvee_{i \in K} g_i$$

and thus

$$l = \bigvee_{i \in K} g_i. \qquad \blacksquare$$

Theorem 1.16. Given a finite lattice $\langle L, \vee, \wedge\rangle$ *and k elements* $l_1, \ldots, l_k$ *of L, represented by the set of their prime implicants* $\{g_i \mid i \in K_1\}, \ldots, \{g_i \mid i \in K_k\}$, *if g is a prime implicant of* $l = l_1 \wedge \ldots \wedge l_k$, *it is a prime implicant of* $g_{i_1} \wedge \ldots \wedge g_{i_k}$ *for some k-tuple* $(i_1, \ldots, i_k)$ *in* $K_1 \times \ldots \times K_k$.

(b) *Dual statement.*

Proof. If g is a prime implicant of $l_1 \wedge \ldots \wedge l_k$, g is an implicant of each l_i, $i = 1, \ldots, k$. Therefore g is included in some prime implicant g_{i_1} of $l_1, \ldots,$ in some prime implicant g_{i_k} of l_k. Hence

$$g \leqslant g_{i_1} \wedge \ldots \wedge g_{i_k} \leqslant l_1 \wedge \ldots \wedge l_k = l;$$

by maximality of g as implicant of l, it must also be maximal as implicant of $g_{i_1} \wedge \ldots \wedge g_{i_k}$. $\blacksquare$

State now two auxiliary problems.

Auxiliary problem 1. Compute the prime implicants of an element h of H and the prime implicates of an element g of G.

Auxiliary problem 2. Compute the prime implicants of the conjunction $g_1 \wedge g_2$ of two elements of G, and the prime implicates of the disjunction $h_1 \vee h_2$ of two elements of H.

Whenever a solution of both auxiliary problems is known, one has a solution of the following main problem.

Problem 1.2. Compute the prime implicants of an element l of L given as conjunction of elements of H, and compute the prime implicates of an element l of L given as disjunction of elements of G.

Suppose for instance that the element l of L is given as conjunction of elements of H:

$$l = h_1 \wedge \ldots \wedge h_k.$$

The following algorithm yields the prime implicants of l.

Algorithm 1.2.

Step 1. Compute the prime implicants of h_1 using the solution of the auxiliary problem 1.

Step i. At the end of step $(i-1)$ one has obtained the prime implicants $g_1, \ldots, g_q$ of $h_1 \wedge \ldots \wedge h_{i-1}$. Compute the prime implicants $g'_1, \ldots, g'_r$ of h_i using the solution of the auxiliary problem 1. Compute then the prime implicants of all the conjunctions $g_s \wedge g'_t$, $s = 1, \ldots, q$ and $t = 1, \ldots, r$, using the solution of the auxiliary problem 2. All the prime implicants of $(h_1 \wedge \ldots \wedge h_{i-1}) \wedge h_i$ are of that type (theorem 1.16); it thus suffices to delete in the obtained list the elements that are smaller than other elements in order to obtain all the prime implicants of $h_1 \wedge \ldots \wedge h_i$.

The algorithm stops after k steps.

It is obvious that a dual algorithm yields the solution of the second part of problem 1.2.

Note that the solution of the problem 1.2 yields also a solution of the two following ones: compute the prime implicants and the prime implicates of an element l of L given as disjunction of elements of G; compute the prime implicants and the prime implicates of an element l of L given as conjunction of elements of H. Suppose for instance that $l \in L$ is given under the form

$$l = g_1 \vee \ldots \vee g_q$$

i.e. as disjunction of elements of G. The solution of the second part of problem 1.2 gives a representation of l as conjunction of all its prime implicates, i.e. under the form

$$l = h_1 \wedge \ldots \wedge h_k.$$

The solution of the first part of problem 1.2, applied to that new expression of l, gives the set of prime implicants of l. This method is due to Davio and Bioul [1970]. In the sequel it will often be called the *"implicant–implicate method"*.

Definition 1.23. Given a lattice $\langle L, \vee, \wedge\rangle$, a subset G of L is $\wedge$*-closed* iff $g_i \wedge g_j \in G$, $\forall g_i$ and $g_j \in G$.

In other words, G is a stable part of L with respect to $\wedge$.

If G is a $\wedge$-closed $\vee$-generating system of L, the elements of G are called *classes.* Similarly, a subset H of L is $\vee$*-closed* iff it is a stable part of L with respect to $\vee$. If H is a $\vee$-closed $\wedge$-generating system, its elements are called *anticlasses.*

Suppose now that the notions of implicant and implicate are defined with respect to the $\wedge$-closed $\vee$-generating system G and to the $\vee$-closed $\wedge$-generating system H. In that case the solution of the auxiliary problem 2 is trivial: given for instance two classes g_i and g_j, their conjunction $g_i \wedge g_j$ is some class g_k that is the unique prime implicant of $g_i \wedge g_j$. The implicant–implicate method is then called the *class–anticlass method.*

1.3.3. Distributive, complemented and metric lattices

Definition 1.2.4. A lattice $\langle L, \vee, \wedge\rangle$ is *distributive* iff one of the two following dual equalities is satisfied:

$$a \wedge (b \vee c) = (a \wedge b) \vee (a \wedge c)$$

$$a \vee (b \wedge c) = (a \vee b) \wedge (a \vee c), \qquad \forall a, b, c \in L.$$

In fact, it can easily be proven that any one of these two equalities implies the other one.

Theorem 1.17. The lattice $\langle L, \vee, \wedge\rangle$ *is distributive iff the equalities*

$$x \wedge z = y \wedge z \text{ and } x \vee z = y \vee z \tag{1.2}$$

imply that $x = y$.

Proof. One only proves that the condition is necessary. The proof of the sufficiency can be found in any classical textbook, e.g. Rutherford [1965].

Suppose that $\langle L, \vee, \wedge\rangle$ is a distributive lattice and that the two equalities (1.2) hold true. Then by using the absorption law one has successively:

$$x = x \wedge (x \vee z) = x \wedge (y \vee z) = (x \wedge y) \vee (x \wedge z) = (x \wedge y) \vee (y \wedge z)$$
$$= (x \wedge z) \vee y = (y \wedge z) \vee y = y. \qquad \blacksquare$$

Definition 1.25. Consider a lattice $\langle L, \vee, \wedge\rangle$ and a finite indexed family $\{l_i \mid i \in I\}$ of $\vee$-irreducible elements of L. If for any proper subset K of I ($\emptyset \subset K \subset I$) one has the inequality

$$\bigvee_{i \in K} l_i < \bigvee_{i \in I} l_i,$$

then the family $\{l_i \mid i \in I\}$ is *irredundant.* The disjunction $\bigvee_{i \in I} l_i$ is called an *irredundant disjunction.*

Lemma 1.1. Given a distributive lattice $\langle L, \vee, \wedge \rangle$, a finite indexed family $\{l_i \mid i \in I\}$ of elements of L, and a $\vee$-irreducible element l of L, then the relation

$$l \leqslant \bigvee_{i \in I} l_i$$

implies that there exists i in I such that $l \leqslant l_i$.

Proof. Taking into account the distributive law, one has:

$$l \leqslant \bigvee_{i \in I} l_i \Rightarrow l \wedge \left(\bigvee_{i \in I} l_i \right) = l \Rightarrow \bigvee_{i \in I} (l \wedge l_i) = l$$

and thus, since l is $\vee$-irreducible, there exists i in I such that $l = l \wedge l_i$, i.e. $l \leqslant l_i$. ∎

Theorem 1.18. Every element l of a finite distributive lattice $\langle L, \vee, \wedge \rangle$ admits a unique representation as irredundant disjunction of $\vee$-irreducible elements.

Proof. First note that the set of $\vee$-irreducible elements is a $\vee$-generating system. Indeed, given some l in L, either l is $\vee$-irreducible or l can be written in the form

$$l = l_1 \vee \ldots \vee l_k, \; l_i < l, i = 1, \ldots, k.$$

Iterating the construction for each l_i and taking into account the fact that L is finite one obtains the result.

Suppose now that l admits two distinct representations as irredundant disjunction of $\vee$-irreducible elements:

$$l = \bigvee_{i \in I} l_i = \bigvee_{j \in J} m_j.$$

Then

$$l_i \leqslant \bigvee_{j \in J} m_j, \quad \forall i \in I$$

and thus (lemma 1.1)

$$l_i \leqslant m_j \quad \text{for some } j \in J.$$

One proves similarly

$$m_j \leqslant l_k \quad \text{for some } k \in I;$$

therefore, since $\bigvee_{i \in I} l_i$ is an irredundant disjunction, one has $i = k$ and $l_i = m_j$. ∎

Definition 1.26. Consider a lattice $\langle L, \vee, \wedge \rangle$ with a null element $\mathbf{0}$ and a universal element $\mathbf{1}$. The element l of L is a *complement* of the element m of L iff

$$l \vee m = \mathbf{1} \quad \text{and} \quad l \wedge m = \mathbf{0}.$$

A lattice in which every element has at least one complement is a *complemented lattice.*

Theorem 1.19. In a distributive lattice, every element has at most one complement.

Proof. Consider a distributive lattice $\langle L, \vee, \wedge \rangle$ and an element l of L that has two complements m_1 and m_2:

$$l \vee m_1 = l \vee m_2 = \mathbf{1},$$

$$l \wedge m_1 = l \wedge m_2 = \mathbf{0};$$

therefore (theorem 1.17)

$$m_1 = m_2. \qquad \blacksquare$$

In a distributive lattice, the unique complement of an element l is denoted by $\bar{l}$.

Definitions 1.27. Given a lattice $\langle L, \vee, \wedge \rangle$, a function ν from L to the set $\mathbb{R}$ of real numbers is a *valuation* of L iff

$$\nu(x) + \nu(y) = \nu(x \vee y) + \nu(x \wedge y),$$

for any x and y in L. It is a *positive valuation* if furthermore

$$x > y \Rightarrow \nu(x) > \nu(y).$$

A *metric lattice* is one with a positive valuation.

If L is a metric lattice, one can define a *distance* on L; the distance $d(l_1, l_2)$, between the points l_1 and l_2 of L, is defined as follows:

$$d(l_1, l_2) = \nu(l_1 \vee l_2) - \nu(l_1 \wedge l_2),$$

where ν is the positive valuation of L. The distance $d(l_1, l_2)$ is thus a non-negative real number; it satisfies the three following properties:

(a) $d(x, x) = 0$,

(b) $d(x, y) = d(y, x)$,

(c) $d(x, z) \leqslant d(x, y) + d(y, z)$,

$\forall x, y, z \in L$.

We now show how one can define a distance on every distributive lattice of finite length. For that we need the following statement.

Theorem 1.20. Given two elements l and m of a distributive lattice L, the intervals $[l \wedge m, l]$ and $[m, l \vee m]$ are isomorphic sublattices of L.

Proof. Define a mapping ϕ from $[l \wedge m, l]$ to $[m, l \vee m]$ and a mapping ψ from $[m, l \vee m]$ to $[l \wedge m, l]$ as follows:

$$\phi(x) = x \vee m, \quad \psi(y) = y \wedge l,$$

$\forall x \in [l \wedge m, l]$ and $y \in [m, l \vee m]$.

It suffices then to verify that ϕ is an order homomorphism, and that ψ is the converse relation of ϕ, i.e. $\phi(\psi(y)) = y$ and $\psi(\phi(x)) = x$, $\forall x \in [l \wedge m, l]$ and $y \in [m, l \vee m]$. ∎

Corollary. Let l and m be two different elements of a distributive lattice L. If the element k of L covers both l and m, then both l and m cover $l \wedge m$.

Proof. Since l and m are different, it is obvious that $l \vee m = k$. Consider now the two isomorphic intervals $[m, l \vee m]$ and $[l \wedge m, l]$; since $k = l \vee m$ covers m, one deduces that l covers $l \wedge m$. One proves similarly that m covers $l \wedge m$. ∎

The next theorem is the first part of the classical Jordan–Hölder–Dedekind theorem for modular lattices (see for instance McLane and Birkhoff [1967]).

Theorem 1.21. Let L be a distributive lattice of finite length. Then any two maximal chains in L which have the same ends have the same length.

Proof. Consider two elements c and d of L, and a maximal chain

$$c = x_0 < x_1 < \ldots < x_m = d$$

that joins c to d. The proof is achieved by induction on m. If $m = 1$, then d covers c and there is no other chain joining c to d.

Suppose now that there exists another chain

$$c = y_0 < y_1 < \ldots < y_n = d.$$

If $x_{m-1} = y_{n-1}$, then by the induction assumption one deduces $m - 1 = n - 1$ and thus $m = n$. In the contrary case $x_{m-1} \neq y_{n-1}$; then both x_{m-1} and y_{n-1} cover $x_{m-1} \wedge y_{n-1} = z$ (see the previous corollary). By the induction hypothesis any maximal chain

$$c = z_0 < z_1 < \ldots < z_p = z < x_{m-1}$$

from c to x_{m-1} has length $m - 1$. Therefore the maximal chain

$$c = z_0 < z_1 < \ldots < z_p = z < y_{n-1}$$

has length $m - 1$, and one deduces, again by the induction hypothesis, that the chain

$$c = y_0 < y_1 < \ldots < y_{n-1}$$

has length $m - 1$.

Thus $m - 1 = n - 1$, i.e. $m = n$. ∎

Definition 1.28. Given a distributive lattice L of finite length and two elements c and d of L, with $c \leqslant d$, the *length of the interval* $[c, d]$ is the length of any maximal chain with c and d as ends.

It is obvious that a lattice of finite length must contain a null element $\mathbf{0}$. The *length* $l(x)$ *of an element* x of L is the length of the interval $[\mathbf{0}, x]$.

Theorem 1.22. Given a distributive lattice L of finite length, the function l(x) is a positive valuation of L.

Proof. Given x and y in L one has:

$$l(x \vee y) = l(x) + \text{length } [x, x \vee y]$$

and

$$l(x \wedge y) = l(y) - \text{length } [x \wedge y, y];$$

since furthermore the intervals $[x, x \vee y]$ and $[x \wedge y, y]$ are isomorphic, they have the same length and thus

$$l(x) + l(y) = l(x \vee y) + l(x \wedge y).$$

The function $l(x)$ is thus a valuation, and it is obviously positive. ∎

As a conclusion we may state the following theorem.

Theorem 1.23. Every distributive lattice of finite length is a metric lattice.

1.3.4. Boolean algebras

Definition 1.29. A *Boolean algebra* is a distributive and complemented lattice. In a Boolean algebra one will sometimes use the terms "Boolean sum" and "Boolean product" instead of "disjunction" and "conjunction". Furthermore, in some cases the symbol $\wedge$ will be replaced by the usual multiplicative notation.

Theorem 1.24. In any Boolean algebra

(a) $\overline{(\bar{x})} = x$ *(involution);*

(b) $x \leqslant y$ *iff* $x \wedge \bar{y} = \mathbf{0}$ *(or dually iff* $\bar{x} \vee y = \mathbf{1}$*);*

(c) $\overline{\left(\bigvee_{i \in I} x_i\right)} = \bigwedge_{i \in I} \bar{x}_i, \overline{\left(\bigwedge_{i \in I} x_i\right)} = \bigvee_{i \in I} \bar{x}_i$ *(de Morgan's laws) where I is some finite indexing set;*

(d) $x \vee (\bar{x} \wedge y) = x \vee y, x \wedge (\bar{x} \vee y) = x \wedge y$ *(Boolean absorption).*

Proof. (a) This property results from the uniqueness of the complement.

(b) $x \leqslant y \Rightarrow x \wedge y = x \Rightarrow \mathbf{0} = x \wedge y \wedge \bar{y} = x \wedge \bar{y}; x \wedge \bar{y} = \mathbf{0} \Rightarrow (x \wedge \bar{y}) \vee (x \wedge y) = x \wedge y \Rightarrow x \wedge (y \vee \bar{y}) = x \wedge y \Rightarrow x = x \wedge y \Rightarrow x \leqslant y$.

(c) $\left(\bigvee_{i \in I} x_i\right) \vee \left(\bigwedge_{j \in I} \bar{x}_j\right) = \bigwedge_{j \in I}\left(\left(\bigvee_{i \in I} x_i\right) \vee \bar{x}_j\right) = \mathbf{1},$

and

$$\left(\bigvee_{i \in I} x_i\right) \wedge \left(\bigwedge_{j \in I} \bar{x}_j\right) = \bigvee_{i \in I}\left(x_i \wedge \left(\bigwedge_{j \in I} \bar{x}_j\right)\right) = \mathbf{0};$$

therefore

$$\overline{\left(\bigvee_{i\in I} x_i\right)} = \bigwedge_{j\in I} \bar{x}_j;$$

the second relation is obtained by duality.

(d) $x \vee (\bar{x} \wedge y) = (x \vee \bar{x}) \wedge (x \vee y) = \mathbf{1} \wedge (x \vee y) = x \vee y$. The second relation is again obtained by duality. ■

Definition 1.30. An *atom* of a Boolean algebra $\langle B, \vee, \wedge, \mathbf{0}, \mathbf{1}\rangle$ is an element of B that covers $\mathbf{0}$.

Lemma 1.2. Given a Boolean algebra $\langle B, \vee, \wedge, \mathbf{0}, \mathbf{1}\rangle$, an element x of B is an atom iff it is $\vee$-irreducible.

Proof. If x is an atom, it is clearly $\vee$-irreducible. Suppose now that x is not an atom. Then there exists p, such that $\mathbf{0} < p < x$. Consider the element $q = \bar{p} \wedge x$. It is not equal to $\mathbf{0}$:

$$q = \mathbf{0} \Rightarrow \bar{p} \wedge x = \mathbf{0} \Rightarrow x \leqslant p;$$

it is not equal to x:

$$q = x \Rightarrow \bar{p} \wedge x = x \Rightarrow x \leqslant \bar{p} \Rightarrow x \wedge p = \mathbf{0} \Rightarrow p = \mathbf{0} \quad \text{since } p < x.$$

Therefore

$$\mathbf{0} < q \leqslant x.$$

Furthermore

$$p \vee q = p \vee (\bar{p} \wedge x) = p \vee x = x,$$

and thus x is not $\vee$-irreducible. ■

Theorem 1.25. A finite Boolean algebra $\langle B, \vee, \wedge, \mathbf{0}, \mathbf{1}\rangle$ the set of atoms of which is $A = \{a_1, \ldots, a_p\}$ is isomorphic to the algebra $\langle \mathscr{P}(A), \cup, \cap, \emptyset, A\rangle$, where $\mathscr{P}(A)$ denotes the set of parts of A.

Proof. One proves first that any subset $\{a_{i_1}, \ldots, a_{i_k}\}$ of A is irredundant. Suppose for instance

$$a_{i_1} \vee \ldots \vee a_{i_{k-1}} = a_{i_1} \vee \ldots \vee a_{i_{k-1}} \vee a_{i_k}.$$

Thus

$$a_{i_k} \leqslant a_{i_1} \vee \ldots \vee a_{i_{k-1}}$$

and

$$a_{i_k} = (a_{i_k} \wedge a_{i_1}) \vee \ldots \vee (a_{i_k} \wedge a_{i_{k-1}});$$

since furthermore

$$i \neq j \Rightarrow a_i \wedge a_j = \mathbf{0}; \quad i, j \in \{1, \ldots, p\}$$

one has

$$a_{i_k} = \mathbf{0};$$

that contradicts the fact that a_{i_k} is an atom.

The proof is completed by noting that any disjunction of atoms gives an element of B, and that every element of B admits a unique representation as disjunction of atoms (theorem 1.18, lemma 1.2, and first part of the proof). ■

Corollary. Any Boolean algebra with p atoms contains 2^p elements.

Example 1.3. (a) The simplest Boolean algebra contains two elements. It is isomorphic to the algebra $\langle \mathscr{P}(\{a\}), \cup, \cap, \emptyset, \{a\} \rangle$. If one associates with $\emptyset$ and {a} the symbols 0 and 1, the operations of disjunction, conjunction and complementation are those described in Figure 1.2. This Boolean algebra is denoted B_2.

$\vee$	0	1
0	0	1
1	1	1

$\wedge$	0	1
0	0	0
1	0	1

x	$\bar{x}$
0	1
1	0

Figure 1.2. Operations in B_2

(b) Consider the algebra $\langle \mathscr{P}(A), \cup, \cap, \emptyset, A \rangle$ where $A = \{a_1, \ldots, a_n\}$. Every subset A' of A, i.e. every element of $\mathscr{P}(A)$, can be represented by its *characteristic vector* $\nu(A') = (\nu_1, \ldots, \nu_n)$:

$$\nu_i = 1 \quad \text{iff } a_i \in A'$$

$$\nu_i = 0 \quad \text{otherwise.}$$

One deduces from that last representation method that the algebra $\langle \mathscr{P}(A), \cup, \cap, \emptyset, A \rangle$ is isomorphic to the nth Cartesian power B_2^n of B_2. The operations in B_2^n are simply the componentwise extensions of the operations in B_2.

The *weight* $w(\nu)$ of an element ν of B_2^n is the number of 1's in ν. The *Hamming distance* between two elements ν and ν' of B_2^n is the number of coordinates in which they differ, i.e. the weight of $\nu \oplus \nu'$, where $\oplus$ stands for the componentwise sum modulo 2. In fact the weight is the valuation that is naturally associated with the distributive lattice B_2 (definition 1.28), and the Hamming distance is then the distance defined from this positive valuation.

Definition 1.31. Given a Boolean algebra $\langle B, \vee, \wedge, \mathbf{0}, \mathbf{1} \rangle$, an *n-variable Boolean function on B*, denoted $f(x_{n-1}, \ldots, x_0)$, is a mapping from B^n to B that can be described by a well-formed algebraic expression on the algebra $\langle B, \vee, \wedge, - \rangle$.

Lemma 1.3. Any n-variable Boolean function $f(x_{n-1}, \ldots, x_0)$ can be written in the form

$$f = (a_0 \wedge \bar{x}_{n-1} \wedge \ldots \wedge \bar{x}_0) \vee (a_1 \wedge \bar{x}_{n-1} \wedge \ldots \wedge \bar{x}_1 \wedge x_0) \vee \ldots \vee (a_{2^n-1} \wedge x_{n-1} \wedge \ldots \wedge x_0),$$

where $a_i \in B, \forall\, i = 0, \ldots, 2^n - 1$.

Proof. By induction on the number N of Boolean operators, i.e. $\vee$, $\wedge$ or $-$, in a w.f.a.e. describing f.

If $N = 0$, then $f = b \in B$ or $f = x_i, i \in \{0, \ldots, n-1\}$.

In the first case

$$f = b \wedge (\bar{x}_{n-1} \vee x_{n-1}) \wedge \ldots \wedge (\bar{x}_0 \vee x_0);$$

in the second case

$$f = 1 \wedge (\bar{x}_{n-1} \vee x_{n-1}) \wedge \ldots \wedge x_i \wedge \ldots \wedge (\bar{x}_0 \vee x_0).$$

Using the distributivity law yields the result.

Suppose now that g and h are n-variable Boolean functions written in the form

$$g = (b_0 \wedge \bar{x}_{n-1} \wedge \ldots \wedge \bar{x}_0) \vee \ldots \vee (b_{2^n-1} \wedge x_{n-1} \wedge \ldots \wedge x_0)$$

$$h = (c_0 \wedge \bar{x}_{n-1} \wedge \ldots \wedge \bar{x}_0) \vee \ldots \vee (c_{2^n-1} \wedge x_{n-1} \wedge \ldots \wedge x_0).$$

Using the de Morgan's laws and the distributivity law yields

$$\bar{g} = (\bar{b}_0 \wedge \bar{x}_{n-1} \wedge \ldots \wedge \bar{x}_0) \vee \ldots \vee (\bar{b}_{2^n-1} \wedge x_{n-1} \wedge \ldots \wedge x_0); \tag{1.3}$$

using again the distributivity law one obtains:

$$g \vee h = ((b_0 \vee c_0) \wedge \bar{x}_{n-1} \wedge \ldots \wedge \bar{x}_0) \vee \ldots \vee ((b_{2^n-1} \vee c_{2^n-1}) \wedge x_{n-1} \wedge \ldots \wedge x_0); \tag{1.4}$$

finally one may write:

$$\begin{aligned} g \wedge h = \overline{\bar{g} \vee \bar{h}} &= \overline{((\bar{b}_0 \vee \bar{c}_0)} \wedge \bar{x}_{n-1} \wedge \ldots \wedge \bar{x}_0) \vee \ldots \vee \overline{((\bar{b}_{2^n-1} \vee \bar{c}_{2^n-1})} \wedge x_{n-1} \wedge \ldots \wedge x_0) \\ &= ((b_0 \wedge c_0) \wedge \bar{x}_{n-1} \wedge \ldots \wedge \bar{x}_0) \vee \ldots \vee ((b_{2^n-1} \wedge c_{2^n-1}) \wedge x_{n-1} \wedge \ldots \wedge x_0) \end{aligned} \tag{1.5}$$ ■

Note that if $f(x_{n-1}, \ldots, x_0)$ admits the expression

$$f = (a_0 \wedge \bar{x}_{n-1} \wedge \ldots \wedge \bar{x}_0) \vee \ldots \vee (a_{2^n-1} \wedge x_{n-1} \wedge \ldots \wedge x_0), \tag{1.6}$$

then

$$f(0, \ldots, 0) = a_0, \ldots, f(1, \ldots, 1) = a_{2^n-1}. \tag{1.7}$$

This remark proves that the expression (1.6) is unique. It is called the *canonical disjunctive form* of f. Therefore with each Boolean function f can be associated one and only one vector $(a_0, \ldots, a_{2^n-1})$, the 2^n components of which are in B, and such that f admits the canonical disjunctive representation (1.6). Furthermore, as proven by the relations (1.3), (1.4) and (1.5), to the complementation, disjunction and conjunction of Boolean functions correspond the componentwise complementation, disjunction and conjunction of their associated vectors. We can thus state the following theorem.

Theorem 1.26. The set of n-variable Boolean functions on B is a Boolean algebra isomorphic to $B^{(2^n)}$.

Remarks. (1) If B is a finite Boolean algebra, the set of mappings from B^n to B is also a Boolean algebra isomorphic to $B^{((\# B)^n)}$. Therefore, except the case where $B = 2$, i.e. when $B = B_2$, the set of n-variable Boolean functions on B is a proper subalgebra of the Boolean algebra of the mappings from B^n to B. In fact, an n-variable Boolean function is completely defined once the values it takes at the 2^n points $(\mathbf{0}, \ldots, \mathbf{0}), \ldots, (\mathbf{1}, \ldots, \mathbf{1})$ are known. On the other hand, every function from $(B_2)^n$ to B_2, i.e. every *n-variable switching function*, is a Boolean function and can be represented as a w.f.a.e. on $\langle B_2, \vee, \wedge, - \rangle$.

(2) Given a Boolean algebra B, the Boolean functions of the type

$$b \wedge x_{n-1}^{(e_{n-1})} \wedge \ldots \wedge x_0^{(e_0)}, \quad b \in B, e_i \in \{0, 1\}, \tag{1.8}$$

where

$$x_i^{(1)} = x_i \text{ and } x_i^{(0)} = \bar{x}_i, \quad \forall i = 0, \ldots, n-1,$$

are atoms of the Boolean algebra of n-variable Boolean functions on B iff b is an atom of B, and in fact there are no other atoms. In other words, the expression (1.6) is generally not a representation of f as disjunction of the atoms included in f. Therefore one must be careful in what concerns the terminology since some authors reserve the appellation "canonical disjunctive representation" to disjunction of atoms. The two definitions coincide for switching functions. In that case the atoms, i.e. the functions of type (1.8) with $b = 1$, are called *minterms.*

(3) There exists a dual theory in which are defined *antiatoms, canonical conjunctive forms and maxterms.*

1.3.5. Closure systems and closure operators

Definitions 1.32. Given an ordered set $\langle A, \leqslant \rangle$, a mapping f from A to A is a *closure operator* on $\langle A, \leqslant \rangle$ if the three following conditions are satisfied:

(a) $a_1 \leqslant a_2 \Rightarrow f(a_1) \leqslant f(a_2)$,

(b) $a \leqslant f(a), \quad \forall a \in A$,

(c) $f(f(a)) = f(a), \quad \forall a \in A$.

On the other hand, if B is a subset of A such that, for any element a of A, the set $\{b \in B \mid a \leqslant b\}$ has a minimum element $g_B(a)$, then B is a *closure system* on $\langle A, \leqslant\rangle$.

Theorem 1.27. (a) *If f is a closure operator on the ordered set $\langle A, \leqslant\rangle$, then the set $B = \{a \in A \mid a = f(a)\}$ is a closure system for which $g_B = f$.* (b) *If B is a closure system on the ordered set $\langle A, \leqslant\rangle$, then the mapping g_B is a closure operator. Furthermore, $B = \{a \in A \mid a = g_B(a)\}$.*

Proof. (a) Given an element a of A, the set $\{b \in B \mid a \leqslant b\}$ is not empty since it contains $f(a)$; indeed:

$$f(f(a)) = f(a) \quad \text{and thus } f(a) \in B$$

and

$$a \leqslant f(a).$$

Furthermore, $f(a)$ is minimum in $\{b \in B \mid a \leqslant b\}$; indeed if

$$a \leqslant b, \quad \text{with } b \in B,$$

then

$$f(a) \leqslant f(b) = b.$$

Therefore the set B is a closure system for which $g_B = f$.

(b) Suppose

$$a_1 \leqslant a_2;$$

then the set

$$\{b \in B \mid a_2 \leqslant b\}$$

is included in the set

$$\{b \in B \mid a_1 \leqslant b\}$$

and thus

$$g_B(a_1) \leqslant g_B(a_2).$$

Furthermore since g_B is in the set $\{b \in B \mid a \leqslant b\}$, it is obvious that

$$a \leqslant g_B(a), \quad \forall a \in A.$$

Finally, note that $g_B(a)$ is the minimum element of the set $\{b \in B \mid g_B(a) \leqslant b\}$ since $g_B(a)$ is in B. Therefore

$$g_B(g_B(a)) = g_B(a), \quad \forall a \in A.$$

It remains to prove that $B = \{a \in A \mid a = g_B(a)\}$.

If b_1 is in B, it is the minimum element of the set $\{b \in B \mid b_1 \leqslant b\}$, and thus

$$g_B(b_1) = b_1, \quad \forall b_1 \in B.$$

This proves that

$$B \subseteq \{a \in A \mid a = g_B(a)\}.$$

Conversely, if $a = g_B(a)$, this proves in particular that a is an element of B and thus

$$\{a \in A \mid a = g_B(a)\} \subseteq B. \quad ■$$

This last theorem thus establishes a bijection between the set of closure operators on $\langle A, \leqslant\rangle$ and the set of closure systems on $\langle A, \leqslant\rangle$.

Theorem 1.28. If f is a closure operator on the complete lattice $\langle L, \leqslant\rangle$, and if M is the corresponding closure system, then the infimum of every subset M' of M is an element of M. Conversely, if M is a subset of L such that the infimum of every subset M' of M lies in M, then M is a closure system.

Proof. Suppose first that f is a closure operator on $\langle L, \leqslant\rangle$. One has then the following inclusion:

$$M' \subseteq \{m \in M \mid \inf M' \leqslant m\}, \quad \forall M' \subseteq M.$$

Taking the infimum of both members of the last inclusion one obtains:

$$\inf M' \geqslant f(\inf M')$$

and thus since f is a closure operator

$$\inf M' = f(\inf M'), \quad \text{i.e. } \inf M' \in M.$$

The second part of the statement is proven by putting:

$$g_M(l) = \inf\{m \in M \mid l \leqslant m\}, \quad \forall l \in L. \quad ■$$

Remark. In the case where L is a finite lattice, the theorem 1.28 can be stated as follows:

A subset M of L is a closure system iff

(a) $1 \in M$ (i.e. $\inf \emptyset \in M$);
(b) $m_1 \wedge m_2 \in M, \quad \forall m_1, m_2 \in M.$

Theorem 1.29. If f is a closure operator on the complete lattice $\langle L, \vee, \wedge\rangle$, then the corresponding closure system M is a complete lattice $\langle M, ⓥ, \wedge\rangle$, in which the disjunction is defined as follows:

$$m_1 ⓥ m_2 = f(m_1 \vee m_2), \quad \forall m_1, m_2 \in M.$$

Proof. Introduce the following notations:

$\inf_L$ and $\sup_L$ are the infimum and the supremum in the ordered set $\langle L, \leqslant\rangle$; $\inf_M$ and $\sup_M$ are the infimum and the supremum (if they exist) in the ordered set $\langle M, \leqslant\rangle$.

By theorem 1.28 one has

$$\inf_L(M') \in M, \quad \forall M' \subseteq M;$$

therefore

$$\inf_M(M') = \inf_L(M'), \quad \forall M' \subseteq M.$$

On the other hand, given a subset M' of M, the set

$$E = \{m \in M \mid m \text{ is an upper bound of } M'\}$$

admits an $\inf_L$ that is in M (theorem 1.28) and is also an upper bound of M' since every element of M' is a lower bound of E; it is thus the least upper bound of M' in M:

$$\begin{aligned}\sup_M M' &= \inf_L \{m \in M \mid m \text{ is an upper bound of } M'\}\\ &= \inf_L \{m \in M \mid \sup_L M' \leqslant m\}\\ &= f(\sup_L M').\end{aligned}$$

In particular

$$m_1 \circledV m_2 = f(m_1 \vee m_2).$$ ∎

Lemma 1.4. If f is a closure operator on the lattice $\langle L, \vee, \wedge \rangle$, *then* $f(l_1 \vee l_2) = f(f(l_1) \vee l_2)$, *for any* l_1 *and* l_2 *in L.*

Proof. (a)

$$l_1 \leqslant f(l_1) \Rightarrow l_1 \vee l_2 \leqslant f(l_1) \vee l_2 \Rightarrow f(l_1 \vee l_2) \leqslant f(f(l_1) \vee l_2). \tag{1.9}$$

(b)

$$\begin{aligned}l_1 \leqslant l_1 \vee l_2 &\Rightarrow f(l_1) \leqslant f(l_1 \vee l_2) \Rightarrow f(l_1) \vee l_2 \leqslant f(l_1 \vee l_2) \vee l_2 = f(l_1 \vee l_2)\\ &\Rightarrow f(f(l_1) \vee l_2) \leqslant f(l_1 \vee l_2).\end{aligned} \tag{1.10}$$

(1.9) and (1.10) $\Rightarrow f(l_1 \vee l_2) = f(f(l_1) \vee l_2)$. ∎

Lemma 1.5. If f is a closure operator on the complete lattice $\langle L, \vee, \wedge \rangle$, *then*

$$f(l_1 \vee \ldots \vee l_k) = f(l_1) \circledV \ldots \circledV f(l_k),$$

$\forall l_1, l_2, \ldots, l_k \in L.$

Proof. By a recursive use of lemma 1.4 one obtains:

$$f(l_1 \vee \ldots \vee l_k) = f(f(l_1) \vee \ldots \vee f(l_k)).$$

The proof is then completed by using theorem 1.29. ∎

Corollary. Given a closure operator f on the complete lattice $\langle L, \vee, \wedge \rangle$ *and the corresponding closure system M, if* $L' \subseteq L$ *is a* $\vee$*-generating system of L, then the set*

$$M' = \{m \in M \mid m = f(l') \text{ for some } l' \in L'\}$$

is a Ⓥ*-generating system of* $\langle M, Ⓥ, \wedge \rangle$.

Proof. Any element m of M admits a representation of the type

$$m = l'_1 \vee \ldots \vee l'_k, l'_i \in L', \quad \forall\, i = 1, \ldots, k,$$

and thus

$$m = f(m) = f(l'_1) Ⓥ \ldots Ⓥ f(l'_k).$$

■

This corollary suggests a solution of the following problem.

Problem 1.3. Given a finite lattice $\langle L, \vee, \wedge \rangle$, a $\vee$-generating set $L' \subseteq L$ and a closure operator f on $\langle L, \leqslant \rangle$, generate the lattice $\langle M, Ⓥ, \wedge \rangle$ corresponding to f. It suffices to consider the Ⓥ-generating system M' defined in the last corollary, and to use the solution of the problem 1.1.

Example 1.4. Consider the set of binary relations on a set E. It is a Boolean algebra isomorphic to $\langle \mathscr{P}(E^2), \cup, \cap, \emptyset, E^2 \rangle$ where $\mathscr{P}(E^2)$ is the set of subsets of $E^2 = E \times E$.

The set of equivalence relations on E is a closure system on $\langle \mathscr{P}(E^2), \subseteq \rangle$. Indeed, denote by M the set of equivalences on E; it suffices to verify that for any non-empty subset M' of M the relation

$$\inf M' = \{(e_i, e_j) \in E^2 \mid (e_i, e_j) \in m', \quad \forall\, m' \in M'\}$$

is an equivalence relation, and to note that the universal binary relation E^2 is also an equivalence relation. The complete lattice of equivalence relations on E is denoted $\langle M, \sqcup, \cap \rangle$. Given two equivalences m_1 and m_2, the disjunction $m_1 \sqcup m_2$ is the *transitive closure* of $m_1 \cup m_2$.

Suppose now that E is the set of states of a finite semiautomaton, deterministic and complete, i.e. the carrier of an algebra $\langle E, \sigma_1, \ldots, \sigma_p \rangle$ where each σ_i is a unary operation on E, $i = 1, \ldots, p$. The set N of congruences on that algebra is a closure system of $\langle M, \subseteq \rangle$. Consider indeed two congruences n_1 and n_2:

$$\begin{aligned}(e_i, e_j) \in n_1 \cap n_2 &\Rightarrow (e_i, e_j) \in n_1 \text{ and } (e_i, e_j) \in n_2\\ &\Rightarrow (\sigma_k(e_i), \sigma_k(e_j)) \in n_1 \text{ and } (\sigma_k(e_i), \sigma_k(e_j)) \in n_2,\\ &\Rightarrow (\sigma_k(e_i), \sigma_k(e_j)) \in n_1 \cap n_2, \forall k = 1, \ldots, p.\end{aligned}$$

Therefore $n_1 \cap n_2$ is also a congruence. Since furthermore the universal relation E^2 is also a congruence, one has proven that N is a closure system. It has a particular property:

Given two congruences n_1 and n_2, the disjunction $n_1 \cup n_2$ is also a congruence; in order to verify this fact it suffices to take into account the fact that $n_1 \sqcup n_2$ is the transitive closure of $n_1 \cup n_2$. Therefore, if the pair $(a, b) \in E^2$ is in $n_1 \sqcup n_2$, there exists a series of points in E

$$e_0 = a, e_1, \ldots, e_{r-1}, e_r = b$$

such that

$$(e_i, e_{i+1}) \in n_1 \cup n_2, \qquad \forall i = 0, \ldots, r-1,$$

and thus

$$(\sigma_k(e_i), \sigma_k(e_{i+1})) \in n_1 \cup n_2, \qquad \forall\, i = 0, \ldots, r-1 \text{ and } \forall\, k = 1, \ldots, p.$$

This proves that

$$(\sigma_k(a), \sigma_k(b)) \in n_1 \sqcup n_2, \qquad \forall\, k = 1, \ldots, p.$$

In other words the set of congruences is a sublattice of the lattice of equivalence relations. Such closure systems are sometimes called *topological closure systems.*

Apply now the solution of problem 1.3 to the research of all the congruences on $\langle E, \sigma_1, \ldots, \sigma_p \rangle$. One has a $\cup$-generating system of $\langle M, \cup, \cap \rangle$:

Let $E = \{e_1, \ldots, e_n\}$ and consider the $\binom{n}{2}$ equivalence relations m_{ij}, $1 \leqslant i < j \leqslant n$, defined as follows:

$$m_{ij} = \{(e_1, e_1), \ldots, (e_n, e_n), (e_i, e_j), (e_j, e_i)\}.$$

It corresponds to the partition

$$\pi_{ij} = \{(e_1), \ldots, (e_i, e_j), \ldots, (e_n)\}.$$

For every equivalence relation m_{ij} one looks for the smallest congruence containing m_{ij}; this gives a $\sqcup$-generating system of $\langle N, \sqcup, \cap \rangle$. It suffices then to use the solution of problem 1.1 for obtaining all the congruences.

1.4. Module theory

1.4.1. Groups

Definition 1.33. Given a set E on which is defined a binary operation T, the element e of E is an *identity element* with respect to T iff for any x in E one has

$$e\,T x = x\,T e = x.$$

Theorem 1.30. If there is an identity element e with respect to a binary operation T on a set E, it is unique.

Proof. Suppose that e' is another identity element; then

$$e' = e\,T e' = e.$$ ■

Definitions 1.34. A *monoid* is a set E on which is defined an associative binary operation T and that contains an identity element with respect to T. Recall that T is an associative binary operation if

$$(x\,T y)\,T z = x\,T(y\,T z), \qquad \forall\, x, y, z \in E.$$

Given a set E and a binary operation T on E with respect to which E contains an identity element e, the element x' of E is the *inverse* of the element x of E if

$$x\,T x' = x'\,T x = e.$$

Theorem 1.31. In a monoid $\langle E, T, e\rangle$, *the inverse of an element, if it exists, is unique.*

Proof. Suppose that x has two inverses x' and x'':

$$x' = x'\,T e = x'\,T(x\,T x'') = (x'\,T x)\,T x'' = e\,T x'' = x''. \qquad \blacksquare$$

Definition 1.35. A *group* is a monoid in which every element has an inverse. Very often one uses the additive or the multiplicative notation and terminology instead of T for representing the binary operation of a group.

(a) *Additive notation:* $x\,T y$ is replaced by $x + y$, x' is replaced by $-x$ and e by 0.
(b) *Multiplicative notation:* $x\,T y$ is replaced by xy, x' by x^{-1} and e by 1.

Note that if a and b are two elements of a group G, for which the multiplicative notation is used, one can find the two elements x and y of G for which the two following equalities hold:

$$ax = b \text{ and } ya = b.$$

Indeed the solutions are

$$x = a^{-1}b \text{ and } y = ba^{-1}.$$

Definitions 1.36. Consider a group $\langle G, ., 1\rangle$ for which one uses the multiplicative notation, and a non-empty subset H of G such that

(a) H is a stable part of G with respect to the multiplication in G;
(b) if h is in H, then h^{-1} is also in H.

A direct consequence of conditions (a) and (b) is that H contains 1. One can thus confer to H the algebraic structure of a group. It is a *subgroup* of $\langle G, ., 1\rangle$.

Define now a binary relation $R(H)$ on G:

$$(g_i, g_j) \in R(H) \text{ iff there exists } h \in H \text{ such that } g_i h = g_j.$$

Lemma 1.6. The relation $R(H)$ is an equivalence relation.

Proof. (a) It is reflexive since $1 \in H$: $g\,.\,1 = g, \forall g \in G$.

(b) It is symmetric:

$$g_i h = g_j \Rightarrow g_j h^{-1} = g_i, \quad \text{with } h^{-1} \in H.$$

(c) It is transitive:

$$g_i h_1 = g_j \quad \text{and} \quad g_j h_2 = g_k \Rightarrow g_i h_1 h_2 = g_k, \quad \text{with } h_1 h_2 \in H. \qquad \blacksquare$$

The equivalence classes of $R(H)$ are called the *right cosets* of G with respect to H.

Lemma 1.7. One can define a bijection between H and any right coset of G with respect to H.

Proof. Let K be a right coset and k some element of K. Define a function f from H to K:

$$f(h) = kh, \quad \forall\, h \in H.$$

It is obvious by definition of the equivalence $R(H)$ that kh is in K. The function f is *onto*: suppose that k' lies in K. There exists h' in H such that $k' = kh'$, i.e. $f(h') = k'$.

The function f is *one-to-one*: suppose that

$$f(h_1) = kh_1 = kh_2 = f(h_2)$$

then

$$h_1 = k^{-1}kh_1 = k^{-1}kh_2 = h_2.$$

■

Theorem 1.32. Consider a finite group $\langle G, ., 1\rangle$, with $\#G = N$, and a subgroup $\langle H, ., 1\rangle$, with $\#H = M$. Then M divides N.

Proof. It is a direct consequence of lemma 1.7: if there are Q right cosets of G with respect to H then

$$N = Q \times M.$$

■

Definition 1.37. Consider a finite group $\langle G, ., 1\rangle$ and an element g of G. Compute the successive powers of g: $g, g^2, g^3, \ldots,$ where g^i holds for

$$\overbrace{g.g\ldots g}^{i \text{ times}},$$

for any integer $i \geq 1$. By finiteness of G, it must arise that for some integers i and j, $1 \leq i < j$, one has $g^i = g^j$ and thus $g^{j-i} = 1$.

The smallest integer $m \geq 1$ such that $g^m = 1$ is called the *order of g*.

Lemma 1.8. If g is of order m then the set

$$\{g^0 = 1, g^1 = g, g^2, \ldots, g^{m-1}\}$$

is a subgroup of G.

Proof. Note first that the set $\{g^0, g^1, \ldots, g^{m-1}\}$ is well defined: suppose that $g^i = g^j$, $0 \leq i \leq j \leq m-1$. Then $g^{j-i} = 1$ and thus $j - i = 0$ since m is the smallest positive integer such that $g^m = 1$. Therefore all the g^i's, $i = 0, \ldots, m-1$, are different.

The proof is completed by noting that $g^i g^j = g^{i \oplus j}$, where $i \oplus j$ denotes the rest of the division of $i + j$ by m, $\forall i$ and $j \in \{0, \ldots, m-1\}$. ■

Theorem 1.33. Consider a finite group $\langle G, ., 1\rangle$, with $\#G = N$ and an element g of G of order m. Then m divides N.

Proof. This is a direct consequence of lemma 1.8 and theorem 1.32. ■

Definition 1.38. A group $\langle G, T, e\rangle$ for which T is a commutative binary operation is called a *commutative group.*

1.4.2. Rings

Definition 1.39. A *ring* is a set R on which are defined two binary operations, denoted + (addition) and . (multiplication), such that the following properties are satisfied:

(a) R is a commutative group $\langle R, +, 0\rangle$ with respect to the addition;
(b) R is a monoid $\langle R, ., 1\rangle$ with respect to the multiplication;
(c) the multiplication is distributive with respect to the addition:

$$(x+y)z = xz + yz \quad \text{and} \quad x(y+z) = xy + xz, \quad \forall x, y, z \in R.$$

The ring R is a *commutative ring* if the multiplication is commutative.

Theorem 1.34. Given two elements x and y of the ring R, the two following relations hold true:

(a) $x0 = 0x = 0;$
(b) $x(-y) = (-x)y = -xy, (-x)(-y) = xy.$

Proof. (a) $x0 = x(0+0) = x0 + x0 \Rightarrow x0 = 0;$
$0x = (0+0)x = 0x + 0x \Rightarrow 0x = 0.$
(b) $0 = x0 = x(y+(-y)) = xy + x(-y) \Rightarrow x(-y) = -xy;$
$0 = 0y = (x+(-x))y = xy + (-x)y \Rightarrow (-x)y = -xy;$

finally

$$(-x)(-y) = -(x(-y)) = -(-xy) = xy.$$ ■

Remark. The relations (b) of theorem 1.34 are often called the *sign rules.* They imply the following relations:

$$-x = (-1)x = x(-1), \quad \forall x \in R$$

and

$$(-1)(-1) = 1.$$

Introduce here a new notation; given an integer $n \geqslant 1$ and an element x of R, then nx stands for

$$\underbrace{x + x + \ldots + x}_{n \text{ times}}$$

Similarly x^n stands for

$$\underbrace{x \,.\, x \ldots x}_{n \text{ times}}$$

(this notation is already introduced in definition 1.37). We can now give another consequence of the sign rules:

$$(-x)^n = x^n \text{ if } n \text{ is even; } (-x)^n = -x^n \text{ if } n \text{ is odd.}$$

One can also state the following theorem (*binomial theorem*).

Theorem 1.35. Given two elements x and y of a commutative ring, then

$$(x+y)^n = \sum_{p=0}^{n} \binom{n}{p} x^p y^{n-p},$$

where $\binom{n}{p}$ *is the binomial coefficient giving the number* $\dfrac{n!}{p!(n-p)!}$ *of combinations of n objects taken p at a time.*

Proof. By using the distributivity law and the commutativity of the addition and of the multiplication, one deduces that $(x+y)^n$ can be written as a sum of terms of the type $x^p y^{n-p}$.

Furthermore, the number of terms of that type appearing in the sum is given by the number of ways one can choose p factors among n, i.e. $\binom{n}{p}$. ■

Example 1.5. The set Z of integers is a commutative ring with respect to the usual operations of addition and multiplication. It can be considered as a universal algebra $\langle Z, +, ., 0, 1 \rangle$.

Given an integer $m \geqslant 1$, define now a binary relation $\mathcal{E}$ on Z: the pair (a, b) of integers is in $\mathcal{E}$ iff the difference $a - b$ (i.e. $a + (-b)$) is a multiple of m, that is

$$a - b = mq, \quad \text{for some integer } q.$$

The relation $\mathcal{E}$ is clearly an equivalence:

$$a - a = m0; \quad a - b = mq \Rightarrow b - a = m(-q);$$

$$a - b = mq \quad \text{and} \quad b - c = mq' \Rightarrow a - c = m(q + q').$$

Furthermore it is a congruence. Suppose indeed that

$$a - b = mq \quad \text{and} \quad c - d = mq';$$

then

$$(a+c) - (b+d) = (a-b) + (c-d) = m(q+q')$$

and

$$ac - bd = (a-b)c + (c-d)b = m(qc + q'b).$$

In the sequel, instead of $(a, b) \in R$ one will write $a \equiv b$, modulo m. The equivalence class that contains an integer a is called the *class of a modulo m* and the quotient algebra $Z/\equiv$, denoted by Z_m, is also a ring that is called the *ring of integers modulo m*. If one represents each class, generated by the congruence, by the smallest non-negative integer it contains, it is obvious that $Z_m = \{0, 1, \ldots, m-1\}$. The addition, multiplication and negation (i.e. the inverse with respect to the addition) are called the *addition (or sum) modulo m*, the *multiplication (or product) modulo m* and the *negation modulo m*, respectively. The addition modulo m is often denoted by the symbol $\oplus$, whereas the same symbols are used for the multiplication and for the negation in Z and Z_m, respectively.

Definition 1.40. Given two rings $\langle R_1, \overset{1}{+}, \overset{1}{.}, 0_1, 1_1 \rangle$ and $\langle R_2, \overset{2}{+}, \overset{2}{.}, 0_2, 1_2 \rangle$, the *direct sum* $A_1 + A_2$ is an algebraic structure defined as follows:

$$R_1 + R_2 = \langle R_1 \times R_2, +, ., (0_1, 0_2), (1_1, 1_2) \rangle$$

where

$$(a_1, a_2) + (b_1, b_2) = (a_1 \overset{1}{+} b_1, a_2 \overset{2}{+} b_2),$$

and

$$(a_1, a_2) . (b_1, b_2) = (a_1 \overset{1}{.} b_1, a_2 \overset{2}{.} b_2),$$

$\forall a_1, b_1 \in R_1$ and $a_2, b_2 \in R_2$.

It can easily be proven that $R_1 + R_2$ is also a ring. Furthermore the definition can obviously be extended in order to define the *direct sum of k rings* $R_1, \ldots, R_k$.

Definition 1.41. Given the prime integer $p \geqslant 2$, the ring $\langle R, +, ., 0, 1 \rangle$ containing at least two elements (i.e. $0 \neq 1$) is a *p-ring* iff

$$x^p = x \text{ and } px = 0, \quad \forall x \in R.$$

We now state without proof two important theorems concerning the p-rings. The proofs can be found in McCoy [1948].

Theorem 1.36. Every p-ring is a commutative ring.

Theorem 1.37. If R is a p-ring, it contains p^k elements where k is some well-chosen positive integer. Furthermore R is isomorphic to the direct sum of k rings Z_p.

Remark. One can confer to the set $\{0, 1, \ldots, p-1\}$ the structure of distributive lattice by putting:

$$i \vee j = \max(i, j),$$

and

$$i \wedge j = \min(i, j),$$

$\forall i, j \in \{0, \ldots, p-1\}$; denote it by L_p. Therefore, if R is a p-ring isomorphic to the direct sum of k rings Z_p, R is also a distributive lattice isomorphic to the kth Cartesian power of the distributive lattice L_p. In the case where $p = 2$, this remark yields the more precise statement, known as the *Stone theorem.*

Definition 1.42. The ring $\langle B, \oplus, ., \mathbf{0}, \mathbf{1}\rangle$, that contains at least two elements, is a *Boolean ring* if the multiplication is idempotent, that is

$$x \,.\, x = x, \qquad \forall\, x \in B.$$

Theorem 1.38. (a) *Every Boolean ring is a 2-ring and, conversely, every 2-ring is a Boolean ring.*

(b) *In every Boolean ring one has:*

$$x \oplus y = \mathbf{0} \quad \text{iff } x = y.$$

(c) *Every Boolean ring is a commutative ring.*

Proof. (a) It suffices to prove that in the Boolean ring $\langle B, \oplus, ., \mathbf{0}, \mathbf{1}\rangle$ one has $x \oplus x = \mathbf{0}, \forall\, x \in B$. Indeed

$$(\mathbf{1} \oplus x)(\mathbf{1} \oplus x) = (\mathbf{1} \oplus x)$$
$$\Rightarrow (\mathbf{1} \oplus x) \oplus (x \oplus x) = (\mathbf{1} \oplus x)(\mathbf{1} \oplus x) = \mathbf{1} \oplus x$$
$$\Rightarrow x \oplus x = \mathbf{0}, \qquad \forall x \in B.$$

(b) It is a consequence of (a):

$$x \oplus y = \mathbf{0} \Rightarrow x \oplus y \oplus y = y \Rightarrow x = y;$$
$$x = y \Rightarrow x \oplus y = x \oplus x = \mathbf{0}.$$

(c) For any x and y in B one can write successively:

$$(x \oplus y)(x \oplus y) = x \oplus y$$
$$\Rightarrow x \oplus xy \oplus yx \oplus y = x \oplus y$$
$$\Rightarrow xy \oplus yx = \mathbf{0}$$
$$\Rightarrow xy = yx.$$

■

Theorem 1.39. (Stone [1935, 1936].) (a) *Every Boolean algebra* $\langle B, \vee, \wedge, \mathbf{0}, \mathbf{1}\rangle$ *is a Boolean ring if one defines as follows the addition and the multiplication:*

$$r \oplus s = (\bar{r} \wedge s) \vee (r \wedge \bar{s}),$$

and

$$r \,.\, s = r \wedge s,$$

$\forall\, r, s \in B.$

(b) *Conversely, any Boolean ring* $\langle B, \oplus, ., \mathbf{0}, \mathbf{1}\rangle$ *is a Boolean algebra if one defines as follows the disjunction and the conjunction:*

$$r \vee s = r \oplus s \oplus (r \,.\, s),$$

and

$$r \wedge s = r \,.\, s,$$

$\forall r, s \in B$. *Furthermore* $\bar{r} = 1 \oplus r$, $\forall r \in B$.

The routine proof of that theorem is left as an exercise.

Definition 1.43. Given a commutative ring R, a *one-variable polynomial function on the ring* R, denoted by $f(x)$, is a mapping from R to R that can be described by a well-formed algebraic expression on the algebra $\langle R, +, .\rangle$.

A *polynomial in one indeterminate with coefficients in* R is a well-formed algebraic expression of the type

$$r_0 + r_1 x + r_2 x^2 + \ldots + r_m x^m,$$

where the r_i's are elements or R. This polynomial can also be represented by the series

$$(r_0, r_1, \ldots, r_m, 0, 0, \ldots)$$

of elements of R. Recall that a *series* of elements of a set E is an indexed family $(e_i)_{i \in \mathbb{N}}$ of elements of E, where $\mathbb{N}$ denotes the set of natural numbers $0, 1, 2, \ldots$; in other words a series of elements of a set E is a mapping from $\mathbb{N}$ to E.

Conversely, a series $(r_i)_{i \in \mathbb{N}}$ of elements of R describes a polynomial if one of the two following properties is satisfied:

(a) there exists an index d, called *degree of the polynomial*, such that

$$r_d \neq 0 \text{ and } 0 = r_{d+1} = r_{d+2} = \ldots;$$

(b) $r_i = 0, \forall i \in \mathbb{N}$; in that case the polynomial is denoted 0, and its degree is conventionally chosen equal to 0.

One can define an addition and a multiplication on the set of polynomials in one indeterminate with coefficients in R; given two polynomials described by the series $(r_i)_{i \in \mathbb{N}}$ and $(r'_i)_{i \in \mathbb{N}}$ one defines their sum and their product as follows:

$$(r_i)_{i \in \mathbb{N}} + (r'_i)_{i \in \mathbb{N}} = (r_i + r'_i)_{i \in \mathbb{N}};$$

and

$$(r_i)_{i \in \mathbb{N}} \,.\, (r'_i)_{i \in \mathbb{N}} = (r_i r'_0 + r_{i-1} r'_1 + \ldots + r_0 r'_i)_{i \in \mathbb{N}}$$
$$= \left(\sum_{h+k=i} r_h r'_k \right)_{i \in \mathbb{N}}.$$

It can easily be proven that these operations confer the structure of commutative ring to the set of polynomials in one indeterminate with coefficients in R. The identity elements with respect to the addition and to the multiplication are $(0, 0, 0, \ldots)$ and $(1, 0, 0, \ldots)$, respectively.

If both polynomials are represented under the form

$$\sum_{i=0}^{m} r_i x^i \text{ and } \sum_{i=0}^{m} r_i' x^i,$$

with the classical convention that $x^0 = 1$, their sum and their product are obtained by considering x as an element of R, and by performing the operations in R, taking into account the properties of associativity and distributivity.

The following theorem justifies the naming "polynomial function".

Theorem 1.40. Every one-variable polynomial function on the commutative ring R admits a representation as polynomial in one indeterminate with coefficients in R.

Proof. The elements of R and the variable x can obviously be represented by polynomials. The proof can thus be achieved by induction on the number of operations (sum and product) that appear in a well-formed algebraic expression. It suffices then to take into account the definitions of sum and product of polynomials in order to complete the proof. ∎

Note that the representation of a polynomial function by a polynomial is generally not unique. Consider for instance the case of a finite commutative ring R. The set of functions from R to R is finite while the set of polynomials with coefficients in R is infinite.

One can extend definition 1.43 to the case of n-variable functions.

Definition 1.44. An n-variable polynomial function on the commutative ring R, denoted by $f(x_{n-1}, \ldots, x_0)$ is a mapping from R^n to R, that can be represented by a w.f.a.e. on $\langle R, +, . \rangle$.

A *polynomial in n indeterminates* with coefficients in R is a w.f.a.e. of the type:

$$\sum_{i_{n-1}=0}^{m_{n-1}} \left(\sum_{i_{n-2}=0}^{m_{n-2}} \left(\cdots \left(\sum_{i_0=0}^{m_0} r_{(i_{n-1}, \ldots, i_0)} x_{n-1}^{i_{n-1}} \ldots x_0^{i_0} \right) \cdots \right) \right);$$

the last expression will be denoted by

$$\sum_{i_{n-1}, \ldots, i_0} r_{(i_{n-1}, \ldots, i_0)} x_{n-1}^{i_{n-1}} \ldots x_0^{i_0}, (0, \ldots, 0) \leqslant (i_{n-1}, \ldots, i_0) \leqslant (m_{n-1}, \ldots, m_0),$$

with $r_{(i_{n-1}, \ldots, i_0)} \in R$.

One can also represent each polynomial by a family $(r_i)_{i \in \mathbb{N}^n}$ of elements of R indexed by the nth Cartesian power of $\mathbb{N}$.

The addition and the multiplication of two polynomials in n indeterminates with coefficients in R can be defined as above by considering the x_i's as elements of R and by performing the operations in R. This confers the structure of commutative ring to the set of polynomials in n indeterminates with coefficients in the commutative ring R.

1.4.3. Fields

Definition 1.45. A ring $\langle F, +, ., 0, 1\rangle$, that contains at least two elements (i.e. $0 \neq 1$), and in which the non-zero elements form a commutative group under the multiplication is a *field.*

Theorem 1.41. A finite commutative ring $\langle R, +, ., 0, 1\rangle$ is a field iff R does not contain divisors of zero, that is iff the equality

$$xy = 0, \quad x, y \in R$$

implies either $x = 0$ or $y = 0$.

Proof. (a) Suppose first that R is a field; then if $xy = 0$ with $x \neq 0$ and $y \neq 0$ one obtains

$$1 = x^{-1} x y y^{-1} = x^{-1} 0 y^{-1} = 0,$$

which leads to a contradiction.

(b) Suppose now that R is a finite commutative ring without divisors of zero. One must prove that the set

$$\{r_1, r_2, \ldots, r_{m-1}\}$$

of the non-zero elements of R is a commutative group under multiplication.

Note first that the set of non-zero elements of R is a stable part of R with respect to the multiplication since the equality $r_i r_j = 0$, with i and $j \in \{1, \ldots, m-1\}$ would imply that either $r_i = 0$ or $r_j = 0$.

It suffices then to prove that any element like r_i, $i \in \{1, \ldots, m-1\}$, admits a multiplicative inverse. Consider the $(m-1)$ products $r_i r_1, r_i r_2, \ldots, r_i r_{m-1}$, and suppose they are not all different, i.e. there exists indices j and k in $\{1, \ldots, m-1\}$ such that $r_i r_j = r_i r_k$; but then

$$r_i(r_j - r_k) = 0,$$

and thus

$$r_j - r_k = 0, \quad \text{i.e. } r_j = r_k$$

since $r_i \neq 0$.

Therefore the $(m-1)$ products are different and one of them is equal to 1. ■

Theorem 1.42. The ring Z_p of integers modulo p is a field iff p is a prime.

Proof. Suppose first that p is a prime. Given x and y in $\{1, \ldots, p-1\}$, if the product xy is equal to 0, modulo p, then the product of x by y in Z, that we denote $x \times y$ in order to avoid confusion, is a multiple of p: $x \times y = p \times q$, with $q \neq 0$. Since furthermore p is a prime, either x or y would admit p as prime factor, but this is impossible since both are smaller than p. Therefore Z_p does not contain divisors of zero; by theorem 1.41 it is a field.

Conversely, if $p = q \times r$, with q and r in $\{2, \ldots, p-1\}$, then $qr = 0$, modulo p, and thus Z_p is not a field. ■

If p is a prime, the field Z_p is called the *Galois field with p elements* and denoted by $GF(p)$.

Consider now the ring of polynomials in one indeterminate with coefficients in a field F.

Lemma 1.9. Given two polynomials $p_1(x)$ and $p_2(x)$ with coefficients in a field F, the degrees of which are d_1 and d_2, respectively, then (a) *the degree of $p_1(x)+p_2(x)$ is equal to max (d_1, d_2) if $d_1 \neq d_2$ and is smaller than or equal to d if $d_1 = d_2 = d$;* (b) *the degree of $p_1(x) \,.\, p_2(x)$ is equal to d_1+d_2.*

Proof. The first part of the statement obviously holds true. As to the second part, it suffices to note that the coefficient of index d_1+d_2 in $p_1(x) \,.\, p_2(x)$ is obtained by performing the product of the coefficient of index d_1 in $p_1(x)$ by the coefficient of index d_2 in $p_2(x)$; furthermore, since there are no divisors of zero in a field, the product is not equal to zero. ■

Theorem 1.43. Given two polynomials $D(x)$ and $d(x) \neq 0$, in one indeterminate with coefficients in a field F, then

(a) *there exist two polynomials $q(x)$ and $r(x)$ such that*

$$D(x) = d(x)\, q(x) + r(x)$$

with

$$\text{degree}\,(r(x)) < \text{degree}\,(d(x));$$

(b) *the polynomials $q(x)$ and $r(x)$ are unique.*

Proof. (a) It suffices to use the well-known Euclidean algorithm that allows a.o. to divide a polynomial in one indeterminate with rational coefficients by another polynomial of the same type.

(b) Suppose that

$$D(x) = d(x)q(x) + r(x) = d(x)q'(x) = r'(x),$$

with

$$\text{degree}\,(r(x)) < \text{degree}\,(d(x)) \text{ and degree}\,(r'(x)) < \text{degree}\,(d(x)).$$

Therefore

$$0 = d(x)\,(q(x) - q'(x)) + r(x) - r'(x).$$

If $q(x)-q'(x)$ is not equal to zero, one has an equality between 0 and a polynomial the degree of which is greater than or equal to the degree of $d(x) \neq 0$. This is impossible and thus

$$q(x)-q'(x)=0, \quad \text{i.e. } q(x)=q'(x),$$

and this implies

$$r(x)-r'(x)=0, \quad \text{i.e. } r(x)=r'(x). \qquad \blacksquare$$

The polynomial $r(x)$ is the *rest* of the division of $D(x)$ by $d(x)$; the polynomial $q(x)$ is the *quotient.*

Consider now a polynomial $f(x) \neq 0$, and define a binary relation $\mathcal{E}$ on the set of polynomials in one indeterminate with coefficients in a field F: the pair $(p(x), p'(x))$ of polynomials is in $\mathcal{E}$ iff the difference $p(x)-p'(x)$ is a multiple of $f(x)$, i.e.

$$p(x)-p'(x)=f(x)\,q(x).$$

This binary relation is obviously an equivalence relation, and one proves exactly as in section 1.4.2, in the case of the ring of integers modulo m, that the relation is a congruence. The fact that two polynomials $p(x)$ and $p'(x)$ are equivalent is denoted as follows:

$$p(x) \equiv p'(x), \text{ modulo } f(x).$$

The equivalence class containing $p(x)$ is called the *class of $p(x)$ modulo $f(x)$.* There is clearly a bijection between the set of equivalence classes and the set of polynomials the degree of which is smaller than the degree of $f(x)$; these polynomials are indeed all the possible rests with respect to the division by $f(x)$. Every class is represented by the unique polynomial it contains the degree of which is smaller than the degree of $f(x)$. The quotient ring is called the *ring of polynomials with coefficients in F modulo the polynomial $f(x)$.*

Note that this theory is quite similar to that developed in section 1.4.2. The question arises under what condition the ring of polynomials modulo $f(x)$ is a field; this condition must correspond for polynomials to the fact of being prime for an integer.

Definitions 1.46. A polynomial $D(x)$ with coefficients in F is *divisible* by a polynomial $d(x)$ with coefficients in F iff the rest of the division of $D(x)$ by $d(x)$ is 0. A polynomial $f(x)$ with coefficients in F the degree of which is $n \geqslant 1$, is *irreducible* iff it is divisible by no polynomial the degree of which is between 1 and $n-1$. Two polynomials $p_1(x) \neq 0$ and $p_2(x) \neq 0$, with coefficients in F are *relatively prime* iff there exists no polynomial $d(x)$, the degree of which is greater than or equal to 1, such that both $p_1(x)$ and $p_2(x)$ are divisible by $d(x)$.

Lemma 1.10. Given two polynomials $p_1(x) \neq 0$ and $p_2(x) \neq 0$, relatively prime, there exists two polynomials $a_1(x)$ and $a_2(x)$ such that

$$a_1(x)\, p_1(x) + a_2(x)\, p_2(x) = 1.$$

Proof. Suppose that the degree of $p_1(x)$ is d_1 and the degree of $p_2(x)$ is d_2, with $d_1 \leqslant d_2$. The proof is achieved by induction on d_1. In the case where $d_1 = 0$, $p_1(x)$ is a non-zero element of the field F, and it admits an inverse p_1^{-1}. One thus obtains the following relation

$$p_1^{-1}\, p_1(x) + 0\, p_2(x) = 1.$$

In the general case one may write

$$p_2(x) = p_1(x)\, q(x) + r(x) \tag{1.11}$$

with

$$\text{degree } (r(x)) < d_1.$$

If $r(x) = 0$, then $p_1(x)$ and $p_2(x)$ are divisible by $p_1(x)$, and this implies $d_1 = 0$ since $p_1(x)$ and $p_2(x)$ are relatively prime. If $r(x) \neq 0$, then $p_1(x)$ and $r(x)$ must be relatively prime since any polynomial that would divise $p_1(x)$ and $r(x)$ would also divise $p_2(x)$: this is a direct consequence of the equality (1.11) and of the distributive law. Thanks to the induction hypothesis one can find two polynomials $\alpha(x)$ and $\beta(x)$ such that

$$\alpha(x)\, p_1(x) + \beta(x)\, r(x) = 1; \tag{1.12}$$

from (1.11) and (1.12) one deduces

$$(\alpha(x) - \beta(x)\, q(x))\, p_1(x) + \beta(x)\, p_2(x) = 1.$$ ■

Lemma 1.11. The invertible elements of the ring of polynomials modulo $f(x)$ are the non-zero polynomials relatively prime with $f(x)$.

Proof. (a) If a polynomial $p(x) \neq 0$ is prime with $f(x)$, then there exists $a_1(x)$ and $a_2(x)$ such that (lemma 1.10)

$$a_1(x)\, p(x) + a_2(x)\, f(x) = 1$$

and thus

$$a_1(x)\, p(x) \equiv 1, \quad \text{modulo } f(x).$$

(b) Conversely, assume $p(x)$ is invertible modulo $f(x)$. Thus there exist $a(x)$ and $b(x)$ satisfying $p(x)\, a(x) + f(x)\, b(x) = 1$, which shows that $p(x)$ and $f(x)$ are relatively prime, since every polynomial that divides $p(x)$ and $f(x)$ also divides 1. ■

Theorem 1.44. The ring of polynomials, with coefficients in a field F, modulo a polynomial $f(x)$, is a field iff $f(x)$ is an irreducible polynomial.

Proof. This is a direct consequence of lemma 1.11 since $f(x)$ is relatively prime with *all* the non-zero polynomials, with degree smaller than the degree of $f(x)$, under the necessary and sufficient condition that it be irreducible. ■

The field of polynomials in one indeterminate, with coefficients in a field F, modulo an irreducible polynomial $f(x)$ is called an *extension field of F*. Note that if the degree of $f(x)$ is 1, the extension field is isomorphic to F.

Given now are two examples of extension fields.

Example 1.5. The ring of polynomials, with real coefficients, modulo the irreducible polynomial x^2+1 is an extension field of the real field, in which the operations of addition and multiplication are defined as follows:

$$(a_1+b_1x)+(a_2+b_2x)=(a_1+a_2)+(b_1+b_2)\,x,$$

$$(a_1+b_1x).(a_2+b_2x)=(a_1a_2-b_1b_2)+(a_1b_2+b_1a_2)\,x$$

since $x^2\equiv-1$, modulo x^2+1.

This extension field is thus isomorphic to the complex field.

Example 1.6. The most important example is that of the extension fields of $GF(p)$, for some prime p. One can prove the two following statements (see for instance Berlekamp [1968]):

(a) there exists at least one irreducible polynomial of degree n, with coefficients in $GF(p)$, for any $n \geqslant 1$ and for any prime p;

(b) any finite field is isomorphic to some extension field of $GF(p)$; furthermore all extension fields of $GF(p)$, with fixed p, deduced from irreducible polynomials of the same degree n are isomorphic.

These remarks justify the notation $GF(p^n)$, i.e. *Galois field of order p^n*, to designate an extension of $GF(p)$, modulo an irreducible polynomial of order n with coefficients in $GF(p)$. Such a field contains p^n elements, i.e. the number of polynomials the degree of which is smaller than n, with coefficients in $GF(p)$.

In the sequel one often uses the notation q instead of p^n, and thus $GF(q)$ instead of $GF(p^n)$.

Theorem 1.45. In any Galois field GF(q) the three following properties hold:

(a) $a^q=a, \quad \forall a\in GF(q);$

(b) if $q\geqslant 3$ then $\sum\limits_{x\in GF(q)} x=0;$

(c) $\sum\limits_{i=1}^{q-1} a^i=0, \quad \forall a\in GF(q), a\neq 1.$

Proof. (a) Consider the multiplicative group of the non-zero elements of $GF(q)$. The order of an element a of that group divides the number $(q-1)$ of elements of the group (theorem 1.33) and thus

$$a^{q-1}=1, \quad \forall a\in GF(q), a\neq 0.$$

Therefore

$$a^q = a, \quad \forall a \in GF(q).$$

(b) If one multiplies the elements of $GF(q)$ by some non-zero element a of $GF(q)$, one obtains the same elements in a different order since

$$ax = ax', \text{ with } a \neq 0$$

implies $x = x'$. Therefore

$$\sum_{x \in GF(q)} x = \sum_{x \in GF(q)} ax = a\left(\sum_{x \in GF(q)} x\right)$$

and thus

$$(a-1)\left(\sum_{x \in GF(q)} x\right) = 0, \quad \forall a \neq 0.$$

It then suffices to choose $a \neq 1$, and that is possible provided $q \geqslant 3$, in order to prove that

$$\sum_{x \in GF(q)} x = 0.$$

(c) From the identity

$$(a^q - 1) = (a-1)(1 + a + \ldots + a^{q-1}), \quad \forall a \in GF(q)$$

one deduces for $a \neq 1$ that

$$1 + a + \ldots + a^{q-1} = (a^q - 1)(a-1)^{-1} = 1$$

since by (a) $a^q = a, \quad \forall a \in GF(q)$.

Therefore

$$a + \ldots + a^{q-1} = 0, \quad \forall a \in GF(q).$$

■

Definition 1.47. The *Lagrange function* $\epsilon_a(x)$, with $a \in GF(q)$, is a function from $GF(q)$ to $GF(q)$ defined as follows:

$$\epsilon_a(x) = 0, \quad \forall x \in GF(q), x \neq a;$$

$$\epsilon_a(a) = 1.$$

Lemma 1.12. The Lagrange function $\epsilon_a(x)$ is a polynomial function that can be written under the form

$$\epsilon_a(x) = 1 - (x-a)^{q-1}.$$

Proof. This is a direct consequence of theorem 1.45(a), since

$$(x-a)^{q-1} = 1, \quad \forall x \neq a.$$

■

The next theorem proves that any function from $GF(q)$ to $GF(q)$ is a polynomial function.

Theorem 1.46. Any function $f(x)$ from $GF(q)$ to $GF(q)$ admits a unique expression under the form

$$f(x) = a_0 + a_1 x + \ldots + a_{q-1} x^{q-1},$$

i.e. as a polynomial of degree at most equal to $q-1$, with coefficients in $GF(q)$.

Proof. The fact that $f(x)$ can be represented by a polynomial is a consequence of lemma 1.12 and of the following canonical expansion:

$$f(x) = \sum_{a \in GF(q)} f(a)\, \epsilon_a(x).$$

The uniqueness comes from the fact that there are q^q functions from $GF(q)$ to $GF(q)$ and also q^q polynomials of degree at most equal to $q-1$ with coefficients in $GF(q)$. ∎

We now put emphasis on the multiplicative group of the non-zero elements. An important result is given by the following theorem, the proof of which is omitted, but can be found in any classical textbook on finite fields.

Theorem 1.47. In the multiplicative group of the non-zero elements of a Galois field of order $q = p^n$, there is at least one element α the order of which is $q-1$.

Such an element α is called a *primitive element* of $GF(q)$. A direct consequence of lemma 1.8 and of the fact that α has order $q-1$ is that the non-zero elements of $GF(q)$ are

$$\alpha^0 = 1, \alpha^1 = \alpha, \alpha^2, \ldots, \alpha^{q-2}.$$

This notation is often used for the non-zero elements of $GF(q)$; the multiplication in $GF(q)$ is then defined as follows:

$$0\alpha^i = 0, \quad \forall i = 0, \ldots, q-2$$

and

$$\alpha^i . \alpha^j = \alpha^{i \oplus j}, \quad \forall i \text{ and } j \in \{0, \ldots, q-2\}$$

where $\oplus$ is the sum modulo $q-1$.

If the irreducible polynomial $f(x)$, chosen in order to define $GF(q)$, is such that the class containing the polynomial x is a primitive element, then $f(x)$ is called a *primitive polynomial.*

Example 1.7. We can construct a field or order 4 from the field of two elements $GF(2)$ and the irreducible polynomial x^2+x+1. Let us name the field elements as $0, 1, \alpha, \beta$, and let us identify these elements with polynomials $0, 1, x$ and $x+1$, respectively. It is obvious that $x^2 \equiv x+1$, modulo (x^2+x+1), i.e. $\beta = \alpha^2$. Therefore x^2+x+1 is a primitive polynomial.

+	0	1	α	α^2
0	0	1	α	α^2
1	1	0	α^2	α
α	α	α^2	0	1
α^2	α^2	α	1	0

.	0	1	α	α^2
0	0	0	0	0
1	0	1	α	α^2
α	0	α	α^2	1
α^2	0	α^2	1	α

Figure 1.3. Addition and multiplication in $GF(4)$

Once we have identified the elements in $GF(4)$ with the polynomials over $GF(2)$, the addition and multiplication in the field can be conveniently performed through polynomial addition and multiplication; this yields the addition and multiplication tables of Figure 1.3.

1.4.4. Matrices

Definitions 1.48. Consider an algebraic structure $\langle S, +, . \rangle$ where S is some set, and + and . denote two binary operations on S called addition (sum) and multiplication (product), respectively. Furthermore, one supposes that the addition is *commutative*, that the addition and the multiplication are both *associative*, and that the multiplication is *distributive* with respect to the addition, i.e.

(a) $s_1 + s_2 = s_2 + s_1$,
(b) $s_1 + (s_2 + s_3) = (s_1 + s_2) + s_3$, $s_1(s_2 s_3) = (s_1 s_2) s_3$,
(c) $s_1(s_2 + s_3) = s_1 s_2 + s_1 s_3$, $(s_1 + s_2) s_3 = s_1 s_3 + s_2 s_3$, $\quad \forall s_1, s_2, s_3 \in S$.

Examples of such an algebraic structure are rings and distributive lattices.

Now, given two integers $r \geqslant 1$ and $s \geqslant 1$, a *matrix M of type $r \times s$ on S* is an array of elements of S consisting of r rows and s columns. In some cases the matrix M is denoted $[m_{ij}]$ where m_{ij} is the element of M appearing at the intersection of the ith row and of the jth column, with $1 \leqslant i \leqslant r$ and $1 \leqslant j \leqslant s$. Note that it will sometimes be convenient to number the rows from 0 to $r-1$ and the columns from 0 to $s-1$; see for instance section 1.5.3.

Given a matrix $A = [a_{ij}]$ of type $r \times s$ on S, the *transpose matrix* of A is the matrix $B = [b_{ij}]$ of type $s \times r$ defined by

$$b_{ij} = a_{ji}, \quad i = 1, \dots, s \quad \text{and} \quad j = 1, \dots, r.$$

One then writes

$$B = A^t.$$

The set of matrices of type $r \times s$ on S is denoted $\mathscr{M}_{rs}(S)$.

A matrix of type $r \times r$ on S is called a *square matrix of order r on S.* The set of those matrices is denoted $\mathscr{M}_r(S)$.

A matrix of type $1 \times s$ on S is called a *row vector with s components in S.* A row vector $\boldsymbol{e}$ is sometimes represented under the form $[e_j]$, where e_j is the jth component of $\boldsymbol{e}$, with $1 \leqslant j \leqslant s$. The set of those row vectors is denoted $\mathscr{V}_s(S)$.

A matrix of type $r \times 1$ on S is called a *column vector with r components in S.* A column vector is generally denoted $(\boldsymbol{e})^t$ or $[e_i]^t$, where e_i is the ith component of $(\boldsymbol{e})^t$, with $1 \leqslant i \leqslant r$. The set of column vectors with r components in S is denoted $\mathscr{V}_r^t(S)$.

Definitions 1.49. Various operations can be defined on the set of matrices on S.

(a) The *product aM of the matrix* $M = [m_{ij}]$ of type $r \times s$ *by the element a of S* is a matrix of type $r \times s$ defined as follows:

$$aM = [am_{ij}].$$

(b) The *sum* $M_1 + M_2$ of two matrices $M_1 = [m_{ij}^{(1)}]$ and $M_2 = [m_{ij}^{(2)}]$ of type $r \times s$ is a matrix of type $r \times s$ defined by

$$M_1 + M_2 = [m_{ij}^{(1)} + m_{ij}^{(2)}].$$

(c) The *product MN* of a matrix $M = [m_{ij}]$ of type $r \times s$ by a matrix $N = [n_{jk}]$ of type $s \times t$ is a matrix of type $r \times t$ defined as follows:

$$MN = \left[\sum_{j=1}^{s} m_{ij} n_{jk} \right].$$

The main properties of these various operations on matrices are gathered in the next theorem.

Theorem 1.48. (a) *Given two integers $r \geqslant 1$ and $s \geqslant 1$ the sum of matrices is a binary operation on $\mathscr{M}_{rs}(S)$ that is associative and commutative.*

(b) *Given four integers $r \geqslant 1$, $s \geqslant 1$, $t \geqslant 1$ and $u \geqslant 1$, then for any three matrices $M \in \mathscr{M}_{rs}(S)$, $N \in \mathscr{M}_{st}(S)$ and $P \in \mathscr{M}_{tu}(S)$ one has*

$$M(NP) = (MN)P.$$

(c) *Given four integers $r \geq 1$, $s \geq 1$, $t \geq 1$ and $u \geq 1$, then for any four matrices $M \in \mathcal{M}_{rs}(S)$, $N_1 \in \mathcal{M}_{st}(S)$, $N_2 \in \mathcal{M}_{st}(S)$ and $P \in \mathcal{M}_{tu}(S)$ one has*

$$M(N_1 + N_2) = MN_1 + MN_2 \text{ and } (N_1 + N_2)P = N_1P + N_2P.$$

Proof. (a) This is a direct consequence of the associativity and of the commutativity of the addition in S.

(b) Suppose that

$$M = [m_{ij}], N = [n_{jk}] \text{ and } P = [p_{kl}]$$

with

$$1 \leq i \leq r, 1 \leq j \leq s, 1 \leq k \leq t, 1 \leq l \leq u.$$

One has then

$$M(NP) = M\left(\left[\sum_{k=1}^{t} n_{jk}p_{kl}\right]\right)$$

$$= \left[\sum_{j=1}^{s} m_{ij}\left(\sum_{k=1}^{t} n_{jk}p_{kl}\right)\right].$$

By using the distributivity law in S one obtains

$$M(NP) = \left[\sum_{j=1}^{s}\left(\sum_{k=1}^{t} m_{ij}(n_{jk}p_{kl})\right)\right];$$

the associativity of the multiplication in S yields

$$M(NP) = \left[\sum_{j=1}^{s}\left(\sum_{k=1}^{t} (m_{ij}n_{jk})\,p_{kl}\right)\right],$$

and the commutativity of the addition in S allows one to write

$$M(NP) = \left[\sum_{k=1}^{t}\left(\sum_{j=1}^{s} (m_{ij}n_{jk})\,p_{kl}\right)\right];$$

finally by using the distributivity law in S one obtains:

$$M(NP) = \left[\sum_{k=1}^{t}\left(\sum_{j=1}^{s} (m_{ij}n_{jk})\right)p_{kl}\right],$$

i.e.

$$M(NP) = (MN)P.$$

(c) Suppose that

$$M = [m_{ij}], \quad N_1 = [n_{jk}^{(1)}] \quad \text{and} \quad N_2 = [n_{jk}^{(2)}]$$

with

$$1 \leqslant i \leqslant r, \quad 1 \leqslant j \leqslant s \quad \text{and} \quad 1 \leqslant k \leqslant t.$$

Then

$$M(N_1+N_2) = M([n_{jk}^{(1)} + n_{jk}^{(2)}])$$
$$= \left[\sum_{j=1}^{s} m_{ij}(n_{jk}^{(1)} + n_{jk}^{(2)})\right].$$

The distributivity law in S yields

$$M(N_1+N_2) = \left[\sum_{j=1}^{s} (m_{ij}n_{jk}^{(1)} + m_{ij}n_{jk}^{(2)}\right]$$

and the commutativity of the addition then allows one to write

$$M(N_1+N_2) = \left[\left(\sum_{j=1}^{s} m_{ij}n_{jk}^{(1)}\right) + \left(\sum_{j=1}^{s} m_{ij}n_{jk}^{(2)}\right)\right],$$

i.e.

$$M(N_1+N_2) = MN_1 + MN_2.$$ ■

Suppose now that S contains an identity element 0 with respect to the addition and an identity element 1 with respect to the multiplication, with the property that

$$0s = s0 = 0, \quad \forall s \in S.$$

Definitions 1.50. The *unit matrix of order r on S* is a square matrix $M = [m_{ij}]$ of order r on S defined as follows:

$$m_{ii} = 1, \quad \forall i = 1, \ldots, s;$$
$$i \neq j \Rightarrow m_{ij} = 0.$$

It is generally denoted $\mathbf{1}_r$.

The *zero matrix of order r on S* is a square matrix of order r on S all the elements of which are equal to 0. It is denoted $\mathbf{0}_r$.

Consider now the set $\mathscr{M}_r(S)$ of square matrices of order r on S. One can confer to it the algebraic structure $\langle \mathscr{M}_r(S), +, ., \mathbf{0}_r, \mathbf{1}_r \rangle$, where the addition and the multiplication are defined as in definition 1.49.

By theorem 1.48 one already knows that the addition is commutative and associative and that the multiplication is associative and distributive with respect to the addition. Furthermore, it can be easily shown that $\mathbf{0}_r$ is an identity with respect to the addition, that $\mathbf{1}_r$ is an identity with respect to the multiplication and that $\mathbf{0}_r M = M\mathbf{0}_r = \mathbf{0}_r$, for any square matrix M of order r on S. In other words the algebraic structure $\langle \mathscr{M}_r(S), +, ., \mathbf{0}_r, \mathbf{1}_r \rangle$ has the same properties as $\langle S, +, ., 0, 1 \rangle$.

One can thus define the *inverse of a matrix* $M \in \mathcal{M}_r(S)$: see definition 1.34. By theorem 1.31 the inverse of M, if it exists, is unique. One uses the notation M^{-1} for representing the inverse of M when it exists, and thus

$$MM^{-1} = M^{-1}M = \mathbf{1}_r.$$

We now give two important examples.

Example 1.8. Consider a ring $\langle R, +, ., 0, 1\rangle$ and the set $\mathcal{M}_r(R)$ of square matrices of order r on R. It can easily be verified that $\mathcal{M}_r(R)$ is a commutative group with respect to the addition and that consequently the algebraic structure $\langle \mathcal{M}_r(R), +, ., \mathbf{0}_r, \mathbf{1}_r\rangle$ is also a ring; it is the *ring of square matrices of order r on a ring R.*

In the case where the ring R is commutative one can define the determinant of a matrix M of $\mathcal{M}_r(R)$ just as in the case of a square matrix on the real field. It is possible to prove that a matrix M in $\mathcal{M}_r(R)$ admits an inverse iff its determinant that is an element of R admits an inverse in R. In the particular case where R is a field one obtains thus the well-known property that M has an inverse iff its determinant is not equal to 0.

Example 1.9. One can also define matrices on a distributive lattice and more particularly on a Boolean algebra. The theory of Boolean matrices has been extensively developed by Rudeanu [1974].

We conclude this section by an important remark that constitutes in fact a kind of generalization of the theory developed above. Consider two algebraic structures

$$\langle S, \overset{S}{+}, \overset{S}{.}, 0_S, 1_S\rangle \text{ and } \langle T, \overset{T}{+}, 0_T\rangle,$$

where $\overset{S}{+}$ and $\overset{S}{.}$ are binary operations on S, 0_S and 1_S are elements of S, $\overset{T}{+}$ is a commutative binary operation on T and 0_T is an element of T that is an identity with respect to $\overset{T}{+}$. One supposes furthermore that one has defined a mapping from $S \times T$ to T, denoted as a multiplication (i.e. it associates with $s \in S$ and $t \in T$ the element st of T), such that the five following properties are satisfied:

(a) $s(t_1 \overset{T}{+} t_2) = st_1 \overset{T}{+} st_2,$

(b) $(s_1 \overset{S}{+} s_2)\,t = s_1t \overset{T}{+} s_2t,$

(c) $(s_1 \overset{S}{.} s_2)\,t = s_1(s_2t),$

(d) $0_S t = 0_T,$

(e) $1_S t = t,$

for any s_1, s_2, s in S and for any t_1, t_2, t in T.

One can then define just as in definition 1.49:

(a) the *sum* $M_1 \overset{S}{+} M_2$ of two matrices $M_1 = [m_{ij}^{(1)}]$ and $M_2 = [m_{ij}^{(2)}]$ of type $r \times s$ on S:

$$M_1 \overset{S}{+} M_2 = [m_{ij}^{(1)} \overset{S}{+} m_{ij}^{(2)}];$$

(b) the *sum* $N_1 \overset{T}{+} N_2$ of two matrices $N_1 = [n_{ij}^{(1)}]$ and $N_2 = [n_{ij}^{(2)}]$ of type $r \times s$ on T:

$$N_1 \overset{T}{+} N = [n_{ij}^{(1)} \overset{T}{+} n_{ij}^{(2)}];$$

(c) the *product* $M \overset{S}{.} L$ of a matrix $M = [m_{ij}]$ of type $r \times s$ on S by a matrix $L = [l_{jk}]$ of type $s \times t$ on S:

$$M \overset{S}{.} L = \sum_{j=1}^{s}{}_{S}\ (m_{ij} l_{jk});$$

(d) the *product* MN of a matrix $M = [m_{ij}]$ of type $r \times s$ on S by a matrix $N = [n_{jk}]$ of type $s \times t$ on I:

$$MN = \left[\sum_{j=1}^{s}{}_{T}\ (m_{ij} n_{jk}) \right].$$

One can generalize the parts (b) and (c) of theorem 1.48, i.e. given four integers $r \geqslant 1, s \geqslant 1, t \geqslant 1$, and $u \geqslant 1$, then for any three matrices

$$M \in \mathscr{M}_{rs}(S), \quad L \in \mathscr{M}_{st}(S) \quad \text{and} \quad N \in \mathscr{M}_{tu}(T)$$

one has

$$(M \overset{S}{.} L) N = M(LN);$$

this property is called the *associativity property of the matrix product.*

For any four matrices

$$M_1 \in \mathscr{M}_{rs}(S),\ M_2 \in \mathscr{M}_{rs}(S),\ N_1 \in \mathscr{M}_{st}(S),\ N_2 \in \mathscr{M}_{st}(T),$$

one has

$$M_1(N_1 \overset{T}{+} N_2) = M_1 N_1 \overset{T}{+} M_1 N_2$$

and

$$(M_1 \overset{S}{+} M_2) N_1 = M_1 N_1 \overset{T}{+} M_2 N_1;$$

this last property is the *distributivity property of the matrix product with respect to the matrix sum.*

One can also define a zero matrix $\mathbf{0}_{S,\,r}$ of order r on S and a zero matrix $\mathbf{0}_{T,\,s}$ of order s on T and prove that

$$\mathbf{0}_{S,\,r} N = \mathbf{0}_{T,\,s}, \quad \forall N \in \mathscr{M}_{rs}(T).$$

Finally one defines a unit matrix $\mathbf{1}_{S,r}$ of order r on S and proves that

$$\mathbf{1}_{S,r}N = N, \quad \forall N \in \mathcal{M}_{rs}(T).$$

All these generalized concepts will be used in the next section.

1.4.5. Modules

Definition 1.51. Given a ring $\langle R, \overset{R}{+}, \overset{R}{.}, 0_R, 1_R\rangle$ and a commutative group $\langle M, \overset{M}{+}, 0_M\rangle$, one confers to M the structure of *module on R* or *R-module* by defining a mapping from $R \times M$ to M, denoted as a multiplication, such that the four following properties are satisfied:

(a) $r(m_1 \overset{M}{+} m_2) = rm_1 \overset{M}{+} rm_2,$

(b) $(r_1 \overset{R}{+} r_2)\, m = r_1 m \overset{M}{+} r_2 m,$

(c) $(r_1 \overset{R}{.} r_2)\, m = r_1(r_2 m),$

(d) $1_R m = m,$

$\forall r, r_1, r_2 \in R$ and $m, m_1, m_2 \in M.$

(This is in fact the definition of *left R-module.* A *right R-module* is defined by a mapping from $M \times R$ to M.)

Theorem 1.49. Given an R-module M, the three following relations are identically verified for any r in R and m in M:

(a) $0_R m = 0_M,$

(b) $r0_M = 0_M,$

(c) $(\overset{R}{-}r)m = \overset{M}{-}(rm) = r(\overset{M}{-}m).$

The proof of that property is quite similar to that of theorem 1.34, and is thus omitted.

In the sequel we will delete the indices R and M attached to the operations +, . , − and to the elements 0 and 1.

Example 1.10. Consider a ring R and an integer $s \geqslant 1$. One can confer to R^s the structure of ring (see definition 1.40) and thus in particular the structure of commutative group. Furthermore, one can define a mapping from $R \times R^s$ into R^s as follows:

$$r(r_1, \ldots, r_s) = (rr_1, \ldots, rr_s),$$

$\forall r \in R$ and $(r_1, \ldots, r_s) \in R^s.$

It can easily be verified that the four properties of definition 1.51 hold. Therefore R^s is an R-module.

Definition 1.52. Given an R-module M, a subset N of M is a *submodule* if

(a) N is a subgroup of M (see definition 1.36),
(b) $rn \in N$, $\forall r \in R$ and $n \in N$.

One easily concludes from these two last properties that N is also an R-module. One can also prove that the intersection of an indexed family $\{N_i\}_{i \in I}$ of submodules is still a submodule. Therefore, the property of a subset N of M to be a submodule is a closure property on the Boolean lattice $\mathscr{P}(M)$ of the parts of M. This remark gives a sense to the next definition.

Definitions 1.53. Given an R-module M and a subset X of M, the *submodule generated by* X is the smallest submodule of M that contains X. It is the set of elements of M that can be written as finite sums of elements of the type rx, with $r \in R$ and $x \in X$, i.e. as *linear combinations* of elements of X. The proof of that last assertion can be achieved by noting that

(a) every submodule that contains X must also contain all the linear combinations of elements of X (definition 1.52 (a) and (b));
(b) the set of linear combinations of elements of X has the two properties of the definition 1.45: this is a consequence of definition 1.51 and theorem 1.49.

If the submodule generated by X is M itself, then *M is generated by X* (or *X generates M*). The case where M is generated by a finite set $X = \{x_1, \ldots, x_s\}$ is particularly important. In that case every element m of M has at least one representation under the form

$$m = \sum_{i=1}^{s} r_i x_i,\ r_i \in R,\ x_i \in X,\ \forall\, i = 1, \ldots, s.$$

One then says that *M is finitely generated.*

Definition 1.54. Given two R-modules M and M', the mapping θ from M to M' is an *R-homomorphism* if

$$\theta(r_1 m_1 + r_2 m_2) = r_1 \theta(m_1) + r_2 \theta(m_2),$$

$\forall r_1, r_2 \in R$ and $m_1, m_2 \in M$.

This property implies a.o. that $\theta(0_M) = 0_{M'}$. If θ is a bijection it is called an *R-isomorphism*. An R-homomorphism from M into itself is an *R-endomorphism of M* and an R-isomorphism from M into itself is an *R-automorphism of M.*

Theorem 1.50. (a) *Given three R-modules M, M′ and M″, an R-homomorphism θ from M to M′, and an R-homomorphism ψ from M′ to M″, then the composition θ . ψ of θ and ψ is an R-homomorphism from M to M″.*

(b) *If θ is an R-isomorphism from M to M′, then the converse relation θ_c is an R-isomorphism from M′ to M.*

Proof. (a) Since θ and ψ are R-homomorphism, one has

$$\psi(\theta(r_1 m_1 + r_2 m_2)) = \psi(r_1 \theta(m_1) + r_2 \theta(m_2)) = r_1 \psi(\theta(m_1)) + r_2 \psi(\theta(m_2)),$$

$\forall r_1, r_2 \in R$ and $m_1, m_2 \in M$.

(b) If θ is an R-isomorphism, one can write

$$\begin{aligned} \theta(r_1\theta_c(m_1') + r_2\theta_c(m_2')) &= r_1\theta(\theta_c(m_1')) + r_2\theta(\theta_c(m_2')) \\ &= r_1 m_1' + r_2 m_2', \end{aligned}$$

and thus

$$r_1 \theta_c\,(m_1') + r_2 \theta_c\,(m_2') = \theta_c\,(r_1 m_1' + r_2 m_2'),$$

$\forall r_1, r_2 \in R$ and $m_1', m_2' \in M'$. ∎

We can now introduce the notion of free R-module.

Definitions 1.55. Given an R-module M generated by a subset $X \subseteq M$, one says that X *freely generates M* (or *M is freely generated by X*) iff every mapping φ from X to an R-module M' can be extended to an R-homomorphism ψ from M to M'. This means that with every mapping φ from X to M' can be associated an R-homomorphism ψ from M to M' with the property that

$$\psi(x) = \varphi(x), \ \forall x \in X.$$

This construction must be possible for any R-module M' and for any mapping φ from the generating set X to the chosen module M'.

An R-module freely generated by one of its subsets is a *free R-module.* Every subset that freely generates a module is a *basis* of that module. A free R-module that admits a finite basis is a *free R-module of finite type.* In the sequel one only considers modules of that type.

Definition 1.56. Given an R-module M, a finite subset $X = \{x_1, \ldots, x_s\}$ of M is *linearly independent* if the equality

$$\sum_{i=1}^{s} r_i x_i = 0, \quad r_i \in R, \quad \forall i = 1, \ldots, s,$$

implies

$$r_1 = \ldots = r_s = 0.$$

The following theorem yields a more concrete definition of free module of finite type.

Theorem 1.51. Given an R-module M and a finite subset $X = \{x_1, \ldots, x_s\}$ of M, the three following assertions are equivalent:

(a) *X freely generates M and is thus a basis of M;*
(b) *X is linearly independent and generates M;*
(c) *every element m of M admits a unique representation of the form*

$$m = \sum_{i=1}^{s} r_i x_i, \quad r_i \in R, \quad \forall i = 1, \ldots, s.$$

Proof. (a) ⇒ (b). It suffices to prove that if X freely generates M then it is linearly independent. Consider the mapping ϕ from X to the R-module R^s, that associates with x_i the vector ϵ_i all the components of which are equal to 0 except the ith that is equal to 1:

$$\phi(x_i) = (0, \ldots, 0, 1, 0, \ldots, 0).$$

This mapping can thus be extended to an R-homomorphism ψ from M to R^s. Suppose now that

$$\sum_{i=1}^{s} r_i x_i = 0;$$

then

$$\psi\left(\sum_{i=1}^{s} r_i x_i\right) = \sum_{i=1}^{s} r_i \psi(x_i) = \psi(0) = (0, \ldots, 0),$$

and since $\psi(x_i) = \phi(x_i) = \epsilon_i$, $\forall i = 1, \ldots, s$, one obtains

$$\sum_{i=1}^{s} r_i \epsilon_i = (r_1, \ldots, r_s) = (0, \ldots, 0)$$

i.e.

$$r_1 = \ldots = r_s = 0.$$

(b) ⇒ (c). Suppose that X is linearly independent and generates M. Every element m of M can thus be represented as a linear combination of elements of X. It suffices to prove the uniqueness of the representation. Suppose indeed that

$$m = \sum_{i=1}^{s} r_i x_i = \sum_{i=1}^{s} r_i' x_i;$$

then

$$0 = \sum_{i=1}^{s} (r_i - r_i')\, x_i$$

and thus

$$r_i - r_i' = 0, \quad \text{i.e. } r_i = r_i', \quad \forall i = 1, \ldots, s.$$

(c) ⇒ (d). Given an R-module M' and a mapping ϕ from X to M', one defines as follows the application ψ from M to M': an element m of M admits a unique representation under the form

$$m = \sum_{i=1}^{s} r_i x_i, \quad r_i \in R, x_i \in X, \quad \forall i = 1, \ldots, s.$$

Then, in order to define an R-homomorphism, one must choose

$$\psi(m) = \sum_{i=1}^{s} r_i \phi(x_i).$$

Prove now that ψ is effectively an R-homomorphism; suppose that

$$m_1 = \sum_{i=1}^{s} r_{i1} x_i \quad \text{and} \quad m_2 = \sum_{i=1}^{s} r_{i2} x_i;$$

then

$$r_1 m_1 + r_2 m_2 = \sum_{i=1}^{s} (r_1 r_{i1} + r_2 r_{i2}) x_i,$$

and thus

$$\psi(r_1 m_1 + r_2 m_2) = \sum_{i=1}^{s} (r_1 r_{i1} + r_2 r_{i2}) \phi(x_i)$$

$$= r_1 \sum_{i=1}^{s} r_{i1} \phi(x_i) + r_2 \sum_{i=1}^{s} r_{i2} \varphi(x_i) = r_1 \psi(m_1) + r_2 \psi(m_2).$$ ■

Note that in the last part of the preceding proof, the mapping ϕ can be extended in just one way to an R-homomorphism.

The coefficients r_i that appear in the unique representation of an element m of M as linear combination of the elements of a basis X of M are called the *coordinates of m in basis X.*

Example 1.11. The R-module R^s is free of finite type since it admits the basis $\{\epsilon_1, \ldots, \epsilon_s\}$.

Example 1.12. Denote by Z_m the ring of integers modulo $m \geqslant 2$ and Z the ring of integers. One can confer to Z_m the structure of Z-module by putting

$$ix = \underbrace{x \oplus \ldots \oplus x}_{i \text{ times}}, (-i)x = -(ix), \; 0x = 0,$$

$\forall i \in Z, i \geqslant 1$ and $\forall x \in Z_m$.

This module is not free since

$$mx = 0, \quad \forall x \in Z_m$$

and thus no non-empty subset of Z_m is linearly independent.

Example 1.13. If a module is free of finite type, that does not generally imply that every generating subset of the module contains a basis. Consider for instance the Z_6-module Z_6; it is free of finite type as seen in example 1.11. The subset $\{3, 4\}$ generates Z_6 since

$$i = i3 \oplus i4, \quad \forall i \in Z_6.$$

However, the singleton $\{3\}$ is not linearly independent since $2 . 3 = 0$, and the singleton $\{4\}$ is no linearly independent since $3 . 4 = 0$. Therefore the generating set $\{3, 4\}$ does not contain a basis.

Consider now two R-modules M and M', free of finite type. Suppose that $X = \{x_1, \ldots, x_p\}$ is a basis of M, $X' = \{x'_1, \ldots, x'_q\}$ is a basis of M', and θ is an R-homomorphism from M to M'. The R-homomorphism θ is entirely determined by the set of values

$$\theta(x_i), i = 1, \ldots, p.$$

Express now each $\theta(x_i)$ in the basis X':

$$\theta(x_i) = \theta_{i1}x'_1 + \ldots + \theta_{iq}x'_q, \quad \forall i = 1, \ldots, p.$$

i.e. in matrix notation:

$$[\theta(x_i)]^t = [\theta_{ij}]\,[x'_j]^t. \tag{1.13}$$

Consider an element m of M, the coordinates of which in basis X are $r_1, \ldots, r_p$, and compute the coordinates $r'_1, \ldots, r'_q$ of $\theta(m)$ in basis X'; one has by definition of the coordinates:

$$m = [r_i]\,[x_i]^t;$$

thus, thanks to the property of an R-homomorphism, one obtains

$$\theta(m) = [r_i]\,[\theta(x_i)]^t. \tag{1.14}$$

From (1.13) and (1.14) one deduces

$$\theta(m) = [r_i]\,([\theta_{ij}]\,[x'_j]^t),$$

and thanks to the associativity of the matrix product

$$\theta(m) = ([r_i]\,[\theta_{ij}])\,[x'_j]^t.$$

Therefore

$$[r'_j] = [r_i]\,[\theta_{ij}]. \tag{1.15}$$

Conversely, given two R-modules M and M', free of finite type, a basis $X = \{x_1, \ldots, x_p\}$ of M and a basis $X' = \{x'_1, \ldots, x'_q\}$ of M', then every matrix $[\theta_{ij}]$ of type $p \times q$ on R defines an R-homomorphism θ from M to M'; θ associates with an element m of M whose coordinates are $r_1, \ldots, r_p$ in basis X an element $\theta(m)$ of M' whose coordinates $r'_1, \ldots, r'_q$ in basis X' are given by the matrix relation (1.15).

Therefore, once one has chosen the bases X and X' of M and M', respectively, there is a bijection between the set of R-homomorphisms from M to M' and the set of matrices of type $p \times q$ on R.

Theorem 1.52. Given three R-modules M, M' and M", free of finite type, with bases $X = \{x_1, \ldots, x_p\}$, $X' = \{x'_1, \ldots, x'_q\}$ *and* $X'' = \{x''_1, \ldots, x''_s\}$, *given furthermore an R-homomorphism* θ *from M to M' and an R-homomorphism* ψ *from M' to M" with which are associated the matrices* $[\theta_{ij}]$ *of type* $p \times q$ *and* $[\psi_{jk}]$ *of type* $q \times s$, *then with the R-homomorphism* $\theta \,.\, \psi$ *from M to M" is associated the matrix* $[\gamma_{ik}] = [\theta_{ij}]\,[\psi_{jk}]$, *of type* $p \times s$.

Proof. Consider an element m of M and its coordinates $r_1, \ldots, r_p$ in basis X. Suppose that the coordinates of $\theta(m)$ in basis X' are $r'_1, \ldots, r'_q$ and that the coordinates of $\psi(\theta(m))$ in basis X'' are $r''_1, \ldots, r''_s$. Then one has

$$[r''_k] = [r'_j]\,[\psi_{jk}] = ([r_i]\,[\theta_{ij}])\,[\psi_{jk}] = [r_i]\,([\theta_{ij}]\,[\psi_{jk}]),$$

and thus

$$[\gamma_{ij}] = [\theta_{ij}]\,[\psi_{jk}].$$

■

A particularly interesting case is that of endomorphisms. Let M be a free R-module of finite type, and $X = \{x_1, \ldots, x_p\}$ one of its bases. Every R-endomorphism of M is described by a square matrix of order p on R.

Theorem 1.53. Given an R-module M, free of finite type and one of its bases $X = \{x_1, \ldots, x_p\}$, *then*

(a) *a square matrix* $[\theta_{ij}]$ *of order p on M defines an R-automorphism iff it admits an inverse;*

(b) *the subset* $Y = \{y_1, \ldots, y_p\}$ *of M is another basis iff the square matrix* $[\psi_{ji}]$ *of order p on R, the jth row of which gives the coordinates of* y_j *in X, admits an inverse.*

Proof. (a) The mapping θ from M to M that corresponds to the matrix $[\theta_{ij}]$ is a bijection iff there exists an application ψ from M to M such that

$$\theta \,.\, \psi = \psi \,.\, \theta = \Delta_M,$$

(see theorem 1.3(a)) where Δ_M is the diagonal relation on M. In terms of matrices, this condition is equivalent to the existence of an inverse for $[\theta_{ij}]$.

(b) If Y is a basis, each x_i, $i = 1, \ldots, p$, can be expressed in that basis:

$$[x_i]^t = [\theta_{ij}]\,[y_j]^t;$$

on the other hand

$$[y_j]^t = [\psi_{ji}]\,[x_i]^t;$$

thus

$$[x_i]^t = [\theta_{ij}]\,([\psi_{ji}]\,[x_i]^t) = ([\theta_{ij}]\,[\psi_{ji}])\,[x_i]^t,$$

and

$$[y_j]^t = [\psi_{ji}]\,([\theta_{ij}]\,[y_j]^t) = ([\psi_{ji}]\,[\theta_{ij}])\,[y_j]^t.$$

Therefore

$$[\theta_{ij}]\,[\psi_{ji}] = [\psi_{ji}]\,[\theta_{ij}] = 1_{R,p}.$$

Suppose conversely that $[\psi_{ji}]$ admits an inverse $[\theta_{ij}]$. One first proves that Y generates M. Indeed, given an element m of M with coordinates $r_1, \ldots, r_p$ in X, and taking into account the fact that

$$[y_j]^t = [\psi_{ji}]\,[x_i]^t$$

one obtains

$$m = [r_i]\,[x_i]^t = [r_i]\,([\theta_{ij}]\,[y_j]^t) = ([r_i]\,[\theta_{ij}])\,[y_j]^t.$$

Suppose that

$$[r_j]\,[y_j]^t = 0;$$

then

$$[r_j]\,([\psi_{ji}]\,[x_i]^t) = ([r_j]\,[\psi_{ji}])\,[x_i]^t = 0,$$

and thus

$$[r_j]\,[\psi_{ji}] = [0];$$

therefore

$$[r_j] = [0]\,[\theta_{ij}] = [0]$$

and Y is linearly independent. ∎

The matrix $[\psi_{ji}]$ is called the *transformation matrix* from basis Y to basis X, and its inverse $[\theta_{ij}]$ the transformation matrix from basis X to basis Y. Note indeed that if $m \in M$ has the coordinates $r_1, \ldots, r_p$ in X and the coordinates $\rho_1, \ldots, \rho_p$ in Y then

$$[\rho_j] = [r_i]\,[\theta_{ij}] \quad \text{and} \quad [r_i] = [\rho_j]\,[\psi_{ji}].$$

Recall that the jth row of $[\psi_{ji}]$ gives the coordinates of y_j in basis X and that the ith row of $[\theta_{ij}]$ gives the coordinates of x_i in basis Y.

Definition 1.57. A module M on a field F (i.e. an F-module) is called a *vector space on F.* One can prove that the vector spaces are always free modules and that any finitely generated vector space admits finite bases with a constant number of elements called the *dimension* of the vector space. The elements of the commutative group M are called *vectors*, and the elements of the field F are called *scalars.*

A *linear algebra* is a vector space for which is defined a binary operation on M, denoted as the multiplication, that is associative and for which the *bilinear* law holds, i.e.

$$m_1(f_1 m_2 + f_2 m_3) = f_1(m_1 m_2) + f_2(m_1 m_3)$$

and

$$(f_1 m_1 + f_2 m_2)\, m_3 = f_1(m_1 m_3) + f_2(m_2 m_2),$$

$\forall m_1, m_2, m_3 \in M$ and $f_1, f_2 \in F$.

Examples 1.14 Given a ring R, it is obvious that $\mathcal{M}_{pq}(R)$ is an $\mathcal{M}_p(R)$-module for any integers $p \geqslant 1$ and $q \geqslant 1$, since the set $\mathcal{M}_p(R)$ of the square matrices of order p on the ring R is itself a ring and that all the properties of a module are verified (see theorem 1.48).

One can also consider $\mathcal{M}_{pq}(R)$ as an R-module: with the element r of R and with the matrix A of $\mathcal{M}_{pq}(R)$ one associates the matrix rA.

If furthermore R is a field, then $\mathcal{M}_{pq}(R)$ is a vector space on R, and $\mathcal{M}_p(R)$, i.e. the set of square matrices of order p on a field R, is a linear algebra for which the associative composition law is the matrix product.

1.5. *Enumeration orders; Kronecker product*

1.5.1. *Lexicographical order; numeration systems*

Definitions 1.58. Let us use the notation S_i to represent the set of integers $\{0, 1, \ldots, m_i - 1\}$, with $m_i \geqslant 1$, and the notation S to represent the Cartesian product $S_{n-1} \times \ldots \times S_0$, with $n \geqslant 1$. One defines on S a total order called *lexicographical order*:

$$(a_{n-1}, \ldots, a_0) \leqslant (b_{n-1}, \ldots, b_0)$$

iff one of the two following assertions holds true

(a) $(a_{n-1}, \ldots, a_0) = (b_{n-1}, \ldots, b_0)$,
(b) there exists an index k in $\{0, \ldots, n-1\}$ such that

$$a_k < b_k \quad \text{and} \quad a_i = b_i, \forall\, i \geqslant k.$$

Define now a series of weights w_i:

$$w_0 = 1,$$

$$w_i = m_0 \times \ldots \times m_{i-1}, \quad \forall i = 1, \ldots, n-1, \text{ (}\times\text{ denotes the real product)}$$

and put

$$M = m_0 \times \ldots \times m_{n-1}.$$

Finally, define a function f from S to the set of integers

$$Z_M = \{0, 1, \ldots, M-1\}:$$

$$f(a_{n-1}, \ldots, a_0) = a_{n-1}w_{n-1} + \ldots + a_0 w_0,$$

$\forall (a_{n-1}, \ldots, a_0) \in S.$

Theorem 1.54. (a) *The function f is a bijection from S to Z_M.* (b) *If one considers the natural order in Z_M and the lexicographical order in S, then f is an order isomorphism.*

Proof. (a) The proof is by induction on n since the statement is verified when $n = 1$. The element x of Z_M admits a unique representation under the form

$$x = q_0 m_0 + a_0,$$

with $a_0 \in S_0$ and $q_0 \leqslant (m_1 \times \ldots \times m_{n-1}) - 1$ since $x \leqslant (m_0 \times \ldots \times m_{n-1}) - 1$. By the induction hypothesis, q_0 can be written in the form

$$q_0 = a_{n-1}(m_1 \times \ldots \times m_{n-2}) + \ldots + a_2 m_1 + a_1$$

and thus

$$\begin{aligned} x &= a_{n-1}(m_0 \times \ldots \times m_{n-2}) + \ldots + a_2(m_0 \times m_1) + a_1 m_0 + a_0 \\ &= a_{n-1}w_{n-1} + \ldots + a_2 w_2 + a_1 w_0 + a_0. \end{aligned}$$

Since furthermore S and Z_M both contain the same number $M = m_0 \times \ldots \times m_{n-1}$ of elements, f is a bijection.

(b) Suppose

$$(a_{n-1}, \ldots, a_0) < (b_{n-1}, \ldots, b_0).$$

Thus, there exists an index k such that

$$a_k < b_k \text{ and } a_i = b_i, \forall i > k.$$

Therefore

$$f(b_{n-1}, \ldots, b_0) - f(a_{n-1}, \ldots, a_0) = (b_k - a_k)\ \omega_k + \sum_{i=0}^{k-1} (b_i - a_i)\, w_i,$$

with

$$(b_k - a_k)\, w_k \geqslant w_k = m_0 \times \ldots \times m_{k-1},$$

and

$$\left|\sum_{i=0}^{k-1} (b_i - a_i)\, w_i\right| \leqslant \sum_{i=0}^{k-1} (m_i - 1)\, w_i < m_0 \times \ldots \times m_{k-1},$$

where $|z|$ denotes the absolute value of $z, \forall\, z \in Z$.

Thus

$$f(b_{n-1}, \ldots, b_0) - f(a_{n-1}, \ldots, a_0) > 0, \text{ i.e. } f(a_{n-1}, \ldots, a_0) < f(b_{n-1}, \ldots, b_0).$$

■

Definition 1.59. Since the function f defined above is a bijection, the converse relation f_c is a function from Z_M to S that is called *numeration system in basis* $(m_0, \ldots, m_{n-1})$. If $m_0 = \ldots = m_{n-1} = g$, then f_c is called *numeration system in basis g.* The numeration systems in bases 2, 3, 8, 10, 12 are called *binary, ternary, octal, decimal, duodecimal numeration systems.*

1.5.2. Gray code

Definition 1.60. Consider two elements $(a_{n-1}, \ldots, a_0)$ and $(b_{n-1}, \ldots, b_0)$ of S (see definition 1.58). They are *adjacent* or *at distance 1* iff there exists an index k in $\{0, \ldots, n-1\}$ such that

(a) $a_i = b_i, \quad \forall\, i \neq k,$
(b) $a_k - b_k \equiv 1, \quad$ modulo m_k or $b_k - a_k \equiv 1$, modulo m_k.

A *Gray code* is a list of all the elements of S, enumerated in such an order that two successive elements are at distance 1, and that the last element of the list is at distance 1 of the first one. More formally, it is a bijection g from Z_M to S such that:

$$g(x) \text{ and } g(x \oplus 1) \text{ are at distance } 1, \quad \forall\, x \in Z_M,$$

where $\oplus$ is the sum modulo M.

Theorem 1.55. For every n-tuple of integers $(m_{n-1}, \ldots, m_0)$, with $m_i \geqslant 1$, $i = 0, \ldots, n-1$, there exists at least one Gray code for enumerating the points of $S = S_{n-1} \times \ldots \times S_0$.

Proof. By induction on n, since the points of S_i are naturally enumerated according to a Gray code, $\forall\, i = 0, \ldots, n-1$. Suppose that the set $\{0, 1, \ldots, n-1\}$ is divided into two subsets $\{0, 1, \ldots, k-1\}$ and $\{k, \ldots, n-1\}$, with $k \geqslant 1$. Suppose furthermore that the points of $S_{n-1} \times \ldots \times S_k$ are enumerated by the following Gray code

$$a_0, a_1, \ldots, a_{K-1}, \quad \text{with } a_i \in S_{n-1} \times \ldots \times S_k, \quad \forall\, i \in \{0, \ldots, K-1\},$$

where $K = m_k \times \ldots \times m_{n-1}$, and suppose similarly that the points of $S_{k-1} \times \ldots \times S_0$

are enumerated by the Gray code

$$b_0, b_1, \ldots, b_{L-1}, \quad \text{with } b_i \in S_{k-1} \times \ldots \times S_0, \forall i \in \{0, \ldots, L-1\},$$

where $L = m_0 \times \ldots \times m_{k-1}$. One considers first two particular cases.

First case. $K = L$. The points of S are enumerated as follows by a Gray code:

$$(a_0, b_0), (a_1, b_0), \ldots, (a_{K-1}, b_0); (a_{K-1}, b_1), (a_0, b_1),$$
$$\ldots, (a_{K-2}, b_1); \ldots; (a_1, b_{K-1}), (a_2, b_{K-1}), \ldots, (a_0, b_{K-1}).$$

Second case. L is even. One constructs then the following Gray code:

$$(a_0, b_0), (a_1, b_0), \ldots, (a_{K-1}, b_0); (a_{K-1}, b_1), (a_{K-2}, b_1), \ldots, (a_0, b_1);$$
$$\ldots; (a_0, b_{L-2}), (a_1, b_{L-2}), \ldots, (a_{K-1}, b_{L-2}); (a_{K-1}, b_{L-1}), (a_{K-2}, b_{L-1});$$
$$\ldots; (a_0, b_{L-1}).$$

It remains to consider the case where $K \neq L$ and where K and L are odd. Suppose that $K \leqslant L$. The difference $D = L - K$ is even.

All points of the type (a_i, b_j) with $i \in \{0, \ldots, K-1\}$ and $j \in \{0, \ldots, K-1\}$ can be enumerated according to the scheme of the first case:

$$(a_0, b_0), (a_1, b_0), \ldots, (a_{K-1}, b_{K-1}), (a_0, b_{K-1}). \tag{1.16}$$

On the other hand, the points of the type (a_i, b_j), with $i \in \{0, \ldots, K-1\}$ and $j \in \{K, K+1, \ldots, K+(D-1) = L-1\}$ can be enumerated according to the scheme of the second case:

$$(a_0, b_K), (a_1, b_K), \ldots, (a_1, b_{K+D-1}), (a_0, b_{K+D-1}). \tag{1.17}$$

By concatening the lists (1.16) and (1.17) one obtains a Gray code that enumerates the points of S. ■

The proof of the preceding theorem is constructive, i.e. it gives a method for actually constructing a Gray code that enumerates the points of S. It is obvious that one could imagine other constructions. Give for instance a slightly generalized version of the first case: suppose that L be a multiple of K: $L = Q \,.\, K$. One has then the following Gray code:

$$(a_0, b_0), \ldots, (a_0, b_{K-1}); (a_0, b_K), \ldots, (a_0, b_{2K-1}); \ldots;$$
$$(a_0, b_{(Q-1)K}), \ldots, (a_0, b_{QK-1=L-1});$$

the list is divided into Q parts; that appearing in position $I (0 \leqslant I \leqslant Q-1)$ enumerates the points of type (a_i, b_j), with $i \in \{0, 1, \ldots, K-1\}$ and $j \in \{IK, IK+1, \ldots, IK+K-1 = (I+1)K-1\}$ according to the scheme of the first case. This method can obviously be used in a step by step way when $m_0 = \ldots = m_{n-1}$.

1.5.3. Kronecker product of matrices

Consider the algebraic structure $\langle S, +, .\rangle$ of definition 1.48. Given a matrix of type $r \times s$ on S, one chooses all along this section to number its rows from 0 to $r-1$, and its columns from 0 to $s-1$.

Definition 1.61. Given four integers $m_0 \geqslant 1, m'_0 \geqslant 1, m_1 \geqslant 1$ and $m'_1 \geqslant 1$, we define a mapping from $\mathcal{M}_{m_1 m'_1}(S) \times \mathcal{M}_{m_0 m'_0}(S)$ to $\mathcal{M}_{MM'}(S)$, where $M = m_0 \times m_1$ and $M' = m'_0 \times m'_1$, that is called the *Kronecker product of matrices.* Every element K of $\{0, 1, \ldots, M-1\}$ admits a unique representation

$$K = k_1 m_0 + k_0,$$

with

$$0 \leqslant k_1 \leqslant m_1 - 1 \quad \text{and} \quad 0 \leqslant k_0 \leqslant m_0 - 1,$$

in the numeration system of basis (m_0, m_1). Similarly, every element L of $\{0, 1, \ldots, M'-1\}$ admits a unique representation

$$L = l_1 m'_0 + l_0,$$

with

$$0 \leqslant l_1 \leqslant m'_1 - 1 \quad \text{and} \quad 0 \leqslant l_0 \leqslant m'_0 - 1,$$

in the numeration system of basis (m'_0, m'_1). Now, given a matrix $A = [a_{i_1 j_1}]$ in $\mathcal{M}_{m_1 m'_1}(S)$ and a matrix $B = [b_{i_0 j_0}]$ in $\mathcal{M}_{m_0 m'_0}(S)$, the Kronecker product $A \otimes B$ is defined as follows:

$$A \otimes B = [c_{KL}] \in \mathcal{M}_{MM'}(S)$$

where

$$c_{KL} = a_{k_1 l_1} b_{k_0 l_0}.$$

Theorem 1.56. (a) *For any three matrices $A \in \mathcal{M}_{m_2 m'_2}(S)$, $B \in \mathcal{M}_{m_1 m'_1}(S)$ and $C \in \mathcal{M}_{m_0 m'_0}(S)$ one has:*

$$A \otimes (B \otimes C) = (A \otimes B) \otimes C.$$

(Associativity of the Kronecker product.)

(b) *For any four matrices $A_1 \in \mathcal{M}_{m_1 m'_1}(S)$, $A_2 \in \mathcal{M}_{m_1 m'_1}(S)$, $B_1 \in \mathcal{M}_{m_0 m'_0}(S)$ and $B_2 \in \mathcal{M}_{m_0 m'_0}(S)$ one has:*

$$A_1 \otimes (B_1 + B_2) = (A_1 \otimes B_1) + (A_1 \otimes B_2)$$

and

$$(A_1 + A_2) \otimes B_1 = (A_1 \otimes B_1) + (A_2 \otimes B_1).$$

(Distributivity of the Kronecker product with respect to the addition of matrices.)

(c) *Consider p matrices* $A_i \in \mathcal{M}_{m_i m_i'}(S)$, $i = 0, \ldots, p-1$, *and p matrices* $B_i \in \mathcal{M}_{m_i' m_i''}(S)$, $i = 0, \ldots, p-1$, *then*

$$(A_{p-1} \otimes \ldots \otimes A_0)(B_{p-1} \otimes \ldots \otimes B_0) = (A_{p-1}B_{p-1}) \otimes \ldots \otimes (A_0 B_0).$$

Proof. (a) Compute the coefficient of indices (K, L) in $A \otimes (B \otimes C)$, where $A = [a_{i_2 j_2}]$, $B = [b_{i_1 j_1}]$ and $C = [c_{i_0 j_0}]$;

$$K = k_2(m_0 \times m_1) + k, \quad \text{in basis } (m_0 \times m_1, m_2),$$

$$L = l_2(m_0' \times m_1') + l, \quad \text{in basis } (m_0' \times m_1', m_2');$$

the coefficient of indices (K, L) of $A \otimes (B \otimes C)$ is thus equal to the product of $a_{k_2 l_2}$ by the coefficient of indices (k, l) of $(B \otimes C)$;

$$k = k_1 m_0 + k_0, \quad \text{in basis } (m_0, m_1),$$
$$l = l_1 m_0' + l_0, \quad \text{in basis } (m_0', m_1'),$$

and thus the coefficient of indices (K, L) of $A \otimes (B \otimes C)$ is

$$a_{k_2 l_2}(b_{k_1 l_1} c_{k_0 l_0})$$

where

$$K = k_2(m_0 \times m_1) + k_1 m_0 + k_0, \quad \text{in basis } (m_0, m_1, m_2)$$

and

$$L = l_2(m_0' \times m_1') + l_1 m_0' + l_0, \quad \text{in basis } (m_0', m_1', m_2').$$

One proves similarly that the coefficient of indices (K, L) in $(A \otimes B) \otimes C$ is equal to

$$(a_{k_2 l_2} \ b_{k_1 l_1})\, c_{k_0 l_0},$$

and thus by associativity of the multiplication in S one has

$$A \otimes (B \otimes C) = (A \otimes B) \otimes C.$$

(b) Compute the coefficient of indices (K, L) in $A_1 \otimes (B_1 + B_2)$, where $A_1 = [a_{i_1 j_1}^{(1)}]$, $B_1 = [b_{i_0 j_0}^{(1)}]$ and $B_2 = [b_{i_0 j_0}^{(2)}]$;

$$K = k_1 m_0 + k_0, \quad \text{in basis } (m_0, m_1),$$

$$L = l_1 m_0' + l_0, \quad \text{in basis } (m_0', m_1').$$

The coefficient of indices (K, L) of $A_1 \otimes (B_1 + B_2)$ is thus

$$a_{k_1 l_1}(b_{k_0 l_0}^{(1)} + b_{k_0 l_0}^{(2)}).$$

One proves similarly that the coefficient of indices (K, L) of $((A_1 \otimes B_1) + (A_1 \otimes B_2))$ is

$$a_{k_1 l_1} b_{k_0 l_0}^{(1)} + a_{k_1 l_1} b_{k_0 l_0}^{(2)}.$$

The property then results from the distributivity of the multiplication with respect to the addition in S.

The second relation, i.e. $(A_1+A_2) \otimes B_1 = (A_1 \otimes B_1)+(A_2 \otimes B_1)$, can be proven similarly.

(c) Consider first the case where $p = 2$ and prove that

$$(A_1 \otimes A_0)(B_1 \otimes B_0) = (A_1 B_1) \otimes (A_0 B_0),$$

where $A_1 = [a_{i_1 j_1}] \in \mathcal{M}_{m_1 m_1'}(S)$, $A_0 = [a_{i_0 j_0}] \in \mathcal{M}_{m_0 m_0'}(S)$, $B_1 = [b_{j_1 k_1}] \in \mathcal{M}_{m_1' m_1''}(S)$ and $B_0 = [b_{j_0 k_0}] \in \mathcal{M}_{m_0' m_0''}$.

Compute the coefficient of indices (K, L) of $(A_1 \otimes A_0)(B_1 \otimes B_0)$;

$K = k_1 m_0 + k_0$, in basis (m_0, m_1),

$H = h_1 m_0' + h_0$, in basis (m_0', m_1'),

$L = l_1 m_0'' + l_0$. in basis (m_0'', m_1'').

The coefficient of indices (K, L) is thus

$$\sum_{H=0}^{M'-1} (a_{k_1 h_1} a_{k_0 h_0})(b_{h_1 l_1} b_{h_0 l_0})$$

$$= \sum_{H=0}^{M'-1} (a_{k_1 h_1} b_{h_1 l_1})(a_{k_0 h_0} b_{h_0 l_0}) \text{ (associativity in } S)$$

$$= \left(\sum_{h_1=0}^{m_1'-1} a_{k_1 h_1} b_{h_1 l_1}\right)\left(\sum_{h_0=0}^{m_0'-1} a_{k_0 h_0} b_{h_0 l_0}\right) \text{ (distributivity in } S),$$

and it is equal to the product of the coefficient of indices (k_1, l_1) of $A_1 B_1$ by the coefficient of indices (k_0, l_0) of $A_0 B_0$, that is the coefficient of indices (K, L) of $(A_1 B_1) \otimes (A_0 B_0)$.

The proof can now be completed by induction on p:

$$\begin{aligned}(A_{p-1} \otimes (A_{p-2} \otimes \ldots \otimes A_0))&(B_{p-1} \otimes (B_{p-2} \otimes \ldots \otimes B_0)) \\ &= (A_{p-1} B_{p-1}) \otimes ((A_{p-2} \otimes \ldots \otimes A_0)(B_{p-2} \otimes \ldots \otimes B_0)) \\ &= (A_{p-1} B_{p-1}) \otimes (A_{p-2} B_{p-2}) \otimes \ldots \otimes (A_0 B_0).\end{aligned}$$

■

Consider now the case where S contains an identity element 0 with respect to the addition and an identity element 1 with respect to the multiplication, with the property that $0s = s0 = 0$, $\forall s \in S$. One can define a unit matrix $\mathbf{1}_r$ of order r on S.

The following statement is a direct consequence of theorem 1.52.

Corollary. Given p invertible square matrices $A_0, \ldots, A_{p-1}$ of order $r_0, \ldots, r_{p-1}$, respectively, then the matrix $A_{p-1} \otimes \ldots \otimes A_0$ admits $A_{p-1}^{-1} \otimes \ldots \otimes A_0^{-1}$ as inverse.

Proof.

$$\begin{aligned}(A_{p-1} \otimes \ldots \otimes A_0)(A_{p-1}^{-1} \otimes \ldots \otimes A_0^{-1}) &= (A_{p-1} A_{p-1}^{-1}) \otimes \ldots \otimes (A_0 A_0^{-1}) \\ &= (\mathbf{1}_{r_{p-1}} \otimes \ldots \otimes \mathbf{1}_{r_0}) = \mathbf{1}_R\end{aligned}$$

where $R = r_0 \times \ldots \times r_{p-1}$.

One proves similarly that

$$(A_{p-1}^{-1} \otimes \ldots \otimes A_0^{-1})(A_{p-1} \otimes \ldots \otimes A_0) = \mathbf{1}_R. \qquad \blacksquare$$

We give now an example of application of the Kronecker product. Consider a finite commutative ring R and the set $S = S_{n-1} \times \ldots \times S_0$ of definition 1.58. One can define functions $f(x_{n-1}, \ldots x_0)$ from S to R. The set of these functions is an R-module isomorphic to R^M where $M = m_0 \times \ldots \times m_{n-1}$; indeed, any function from $S_{n-1} \times \ldots \times S_0$ to R can be represented by a vector with M components, the ith component of which gives the value taken by f at the ith point of $S_{n-1} \times \ldots \times S_0$ in the lexicographical enumeration order (or in any other conventionally chosen order).

Some of these functions *degenerate* in all variables except one, for instance x_i; this means that their value at a point like $(e_{n-1}, \ldots, e_0)$ does not depend upon $e_{n-1}, \ldots, e_{i+1}, e_{i-1}, \ldots, e_0$, but only upon e_i. The set of these functions is a submodule isomorphic to R^{m_i}.

Use the notation $R^{m_{n-1}} \otimes \ldots \otimes R^{m_0}$ in order to represent the set of all products $f_{n-1}(x_{n-1}) \ldots f_0(x_0)$, where every $f_i(x_i)$ is a function from S to R that degenerates in all variables except x_i, $\forall i = 0, \ldots, n-1$.

Theorem 1.57. The module R^M is generated by $R^{m_{n-1}} \otimes \ldots \otimes R^{m_0}$.

Proof. Every function $f(x_{n-1}, \ldots, x_0)$ can be written in the form

$$f(x_{n-1}, \ldots, x_0) = \sum_{e_{n-1}, \ldots, e_0} f(e_{n-1}, \ldots, e_0)\, \epsilon_{e_{n-1}}(x_{n-1}) \ldots \epsilon_{e_0}(x_0),$$

where $(e_{n-1}, \ldots, e_0) \in S_{n-1} \times \ldots \times S_0$, and $\epsilon_{e_j}(x_j)$ is a Lagrange function defined just as in definition 1.47 in the case of finite fields, i.e.

$$\epsilon_{e_j}(e_j) = 1,$$
$$x_j \neq e_j \Rightarrow \epsilon_{e_j}(x_j) = 0. \qquad \blacksquare$$

Theorem 1.58. If $X_{n-1}, \ldots, X_0$ are bases of $R^{m_{n-1}}, \ldots, R^{m_0}$, then $X = X_{n-1} \otimes \ldots \otimes X_0$ is a basis of R^M.

Proof. If there are m elements in R, there are m^{m_i} elements in R^{m_i} and thus every basis of R^{m_i} must contain exactly m_i elements. Suppose thus that

$$X_i = \{x_0^{(i)}, \ldots, x_{m_i-1}^{(i)}\}, \quad \forall i = 0, \ldots, n-1.$$

The set

$$X = X_{n-1} \otimes \ldots \otimes X_0$$

(i.e. the set of all products of the type $x_{j_{n-1}}^{(n-1)} \ldots x_{j_0}^{(0)}$, with $j_{n-1} \in \{0, \ldots, m_{n-1}-1\}$, $\ldots, j_0 \in \{0, \ldots, m_0-1\}$) generates R^M. Indeed, every element $f_{n-1}(x_{n-1}) \ldots f_0(x_0)$

of $R^{m_{n-1}} \otimes \ldots \otimes R^{m_0}$ can be written as follows:

$$f_{n-1}(x_{n-1}) \ldots f_0(x_0) = ([r_{j_{n-1}}^{(n-1)}] [x_{j_{n-1}}^{(n-1)}]^t) \otimes \ldots \otimes ([r_{j_0}^{(0)}] [x_{j_0}^{(0)}]^t)$$
$$= ([r_{j_{n-1}}^{(n-1)}] \otimes \ldots \otimes [r_{j_0}^{(0)}])([x_{j_{n-1}}^{(n-1)}]^t \otimes \ldots \otimes [x_{j_0}^{(0)}]^t).$$

Every element of $R^{m_{n-1}} \otimes \ldots \otimes R^{m_0}$ is thus a linear combination of elements of $X = X_{n-1} \otimes \ldots \otimes X_0$, and so are also the elements of R^M since themselves are linear combinations of elements of $R^{m_{n-1}} \otimes \ldots \otimes R^{m_0}$.

The number of elements in X is $M = m_0 \times \ldots \times m_{n-1}$; this is the minimum number of elements for a generating set since R^M contains m^M elements. Therefore X is a basis of R^M. ■

Theorem 1.59. If $Y_{n-1}, \ldots, Y_0$ are other bases of $R^{m_{n-1}}, \ldots, R^{m_0}$, that are related to the bases $X_{n-1}, \ldots, X_0$ by the matrices $\Theta_{n-1}, \ldots, \Theta_0$, then $Y = Y_{n-1} \ldots \otimes Y_0$ is a basis of R^M related to the basis X by the matrix $= \Theta_{n-1} \otimes \ldots \otimes \Theta_0$.

Proof. One has thus

$$Y_i = \{y_0^{(i)}, \ldots, y_{m_i-1}^{(i)}\}, \quad \forall i = 0, \ldots, n-1,$$
$$[y_{j_i}^{(i)}]^t = \Theta_i [x_{j_i}^{(i)}]^t \quad \text{and} \quad [x_{j_i}^{(i)}]^t = \Theta_i^{-1} [y_{j_i}^{(i)}]^t.$$

Putting

$$[x_j] = [x_{j_{n-1}}^{(n-1)}] \otimes \ldots \otimes [x_{j_0}^{(0)}]$$

and

$$[y_j] = [y_{j_{n-1}}^{(n-1)}] \otimes \ldots \otimes [y_{j_0}^{(0)}],$$

one obtains

$$[y_j]^t = (\Theta_{n-1}[x_{j_{n-1}}^{(n-1)}]^t) \otimes \ldots \otimes (\Theta_0[x_{j_0}^{(0)}]^t)$$
$$= (\Theta_{n-1} \otimes \ldots \otimes \Theta_0)([x_{j_{n-1}}^{(n-1)}]^t \otimes \ldots \otimes [x_{j_0}^{(0)}]^t)$$

i.e.

$$[y_j]^t = \Theta[x_j]^t, \quad \text{where } \Theta = \Theta_{n-1} \otimes \ldots \otimes \Theta_0.$$

Similarly one obtains

$$[x_j]^t = \Theta^{-1} [y_j]^t, \quad \text{where } \Theta^{-1} = \Theta_{n-1}^{-1} \times \ldots \times \Theta_0^{-1}.$$

Therefore the set

$$Y = Y_{n-1} \otimes \ldots \otimes Y_0$$

of all products of the type $y_{j_{n-1}}^{(n-1)} \ldots y_{j_0}^{(0)}$ is also a basis of R^M related to the basis X by the matrix Θ. ■

The Kronecker product thus allows to obtain bases of R^M from the knowledge of bases of every R^{m_i}. Furthermore, the transformation matrices for the bases of R^M are deduced by Kronecker products from the transformation matrices for the basis of R^{m_i}.

Conclude this section by an important remark. Consider again the algebraic structure $\langle S, +, . \rangle$ of definition 1.48.

For every $i = 0, \ldots, n-1$ let

$$A_i = [a_{kl}^{(i)}]$$

be a square matrix of order m_i on S, and put

$$A = A_{n-1} \otimes \ldots \otimes A_0;$$

the matrix A is thus a square matrix of order $M = m_0 \times \ldots \times m_{n-1}$ on S.

Suppose now that one has to perform the product of a row vector

$$e = [e_L]$$

with M components in S by the matrix A.

As it has been in section 1.5.1, every integer J that lies in $\{0, \ldots, M-1\}$ may be represented under the form

$$J = j_{n-1} w_{n-1} + \ldots + j_0 w_0$$

in the numeration system of basis $(m_0, \ldots, m_{n-1})$. The function f and its converse f_c are defined as above in section 1.5.1, that is

$$f(j_{n-1}, \ldots, j_0) = j_{n-1} w_{n-1} + \ldots + j_0 w_0$$

and

$$f_c(J) = (j_{n-1}, \ldots, j_0).$$

A slightly generalized version of the proof of theorem 1.56(a) allows us to write:

$$eA = e' = [e'_L]$$

with

$$e'_L = \sum_{K=0}^{M-1} e_K a_{k_{n-1} l_{n-1}}^{(n-1)} \ldots a_{k_0 l_0}^{(0)}$$

where $(k_{n-1}, \ldots, k_0) = f_c(K)$ and $(l_{n-1}, \ldots, l_0) = f_c(L)$, for every $L = 0, \ldots, M-1$.

This last relation suggests a step by step method for computing eA. Define $e_L^{(i)}$ as follows, for every i in $\{1, \ldots, n\}$ and L in $\{0, \ldots, M-1\}$:

$$e_L^{(i)} = \sum_{k_{n-1}, \ldots, k_{n-i}} e_{f(k_{n-1}, \ldots, k_{n-i}, l_{n-i-1}, \ldots, l_0)} a_{k_{n-1} l_{n-1}}^{(n-1)} \ldots a_{k_{n-i} l_{n-i}}^{(n-i)}, \tag{1.18}$$

$0 \leqslant k_{n-1} \leqslant m_{n-1} - 1, \ldots, 0 \leqslant k_{n-i} \leqslant m_{n-i} - 1, (l_{n-1}, \ldots, l_0) = f_c(L)$.

Note in particular that $[e_L^{(n)}] = [e'_L]$.

The relation (1.18) may be written as follows:

$$e_L^{(i)} = \sum_{k_{n-i}} \left(\sum_{k_{n-1}, \dots, k_{n-i+1}} e_{f(k_{n-1}, \dots, k_{n-i}, l_{n-i-1}, \dots, l_0)} \times a^{(n-1)}_{k_{n-1}l_{n-1}} \dots a^{(n-i+1)}_{k_{n-i+1}l_{n-i+1}} \right) a^{(n-i)}_{k_{n-i}l_{n-i}},$$

and thus

$$e_L^{(i)} = \sum_{k_{n-i}=0}^{m_{n-i}-1} e^{(i-1)}_{f(l_{n-1}, \dots, l_{n-i+1}, k_{n-i}, l_{n-i-1}, \dots, l_0)} a^{(n-i)}_{k_{n-i}l_{n-i}}, \tag{1.19}$$

with $(l_{n-1}, \dots, l_0) = f_c(L)$, for every $i = 2, \dots, n$ and $L = 0, \dots, M-1$.

Furthermore, the same relation holds even for $i = 1$ if one put $e_L^{(0)} = e_L$, for every $L = 0, \dots, M-1$.

We are thus in place to compute eA step by step: at the end of step $(i-1)$ one has obtained a row vector $[e_L^{(i-1)}]$. The step i then consists in computing $e_L^{(i)}$, for every $L = 0, \dots, M-1$, according to the relation (1.19). The starting point is the vector $[e_L^{(0)}] = [e_L]$, and the algorithm yields $[e_L^{(n)}] = [e'_L]$ after n steps.

It is interesting to observe the saving in number of elementary operations and in number of storage locations that is obtained when using the step by step method rather than the direct matrix product.

The computation of $e_L^{(i)}$ according to relation (1.19) needs m_{n-i} products of two operands and $(m_{n-i}-1)$ sums of two operands. Since this computation must be performed for every $i = 0, \dots, M-1$, the step i requires $m_{n-i} \times M$ products of two operands and $(m_{n-i}-1) \times M$ sums of two operands.

The total number of products of two operands that must be computed in the step by step method is equal to $(m_0 + \dots + m_{n-1}) \times M$, and the total number of sums of two operands is equal to $(m_0 + \dots + m_{n-1} - n) \times M$.

The direct matrix product of e by A would require M^2 products of two operands and $(M-1) \times M$ sums of two operands. The saving in number of products when using the step by step method is thus equal to $M/(m_0 + \dots + m_{n-1})$ and the saving in number of sums is equal to $(M-1)/(m_0 + \dots + m_{n-1} - n)$.

The step by step method requires the memorizing of the n matrices A_i and of two M-component vectors: at each step indeed one computes a new M-component vector from the knowledge of one of the matrices A_i and of the M-component vector obtained at the end of the preceding step. One needs for that purpose $m_0^2 + \dots + m_{n-1}^2 + 2M$ memory locations.

The direct method requires the memorizing of A, e and eA; this corresponds to $(M^2 + 2M)$ memory locations. The saving in number of memory locations is equal to $(M^2 + 2M)/(m_0^2 + \dots + m_{n-1}^2 + 2M)$.

These facts have already been noted by Lechner in the case where $m_0 = \dots = m_{n-1} = 2$ (see Lechner [1963]).

An example of computation by the step by step method may be found in section 3.2.3.2.

Chapter 2

Elementary Theory of Discrete Functions

This chapter introduces the discrete functions, establishing the basic properties of logic functions, pseudo-logic functions and switching functions which are important particular cases of the concept of discrete function.

Representation modes of these functions are defined and studied. Particular attention is devoted to the study of:

the graphical representation methods,
the representation using the lattice operations of disjunction and of conjunction,
the representation using the ring operations of ring sum and of ring product,
the representation using polynomials over a finite field.

2.1. *Graphical representation methods*

2.1.1. *Definitions and elementary representations*

Definition 2.1. A function

$$f: S \to L$$

is a *discrete function* when the sets S and L are finite non-empty sets.

The function $f: S \to L$ will be denoted as $f(x)$ where the variable x takes its values in the set S and $f(x)$ takes its values in the set L.

Discrete functions can be described by tables.

Example 2.1. The function f from the set $S = \{0, 1, 2, 3, 4\}$ into the set $L = \{0, 1\}$ given by:

$$f(x) = \begin{cases} 0 & \text{if } x \text{ is even} \\ 1 & \text{if } x \text{ is odd} \end{cases}$$

is depicted by the value table shown in Figure 2.1.

x	0	1	2	3	4
$f(x)$	0	1	0	1	0

Figure 2.1. Value table of the example 2.1

As will be seen further on, in kinds of applications the domain S is the Cartesian product of n finite sets S_i:

$$S = S_{n-1} \times \ldots \times S_1 \times S_0 = \mathop{\times}_{i=n-1}^{0} S_i.$$

The function

$$f: \mathop{\times}_{i=n-1}^{0} S_i \rightarrow L$$

may then be denoted as $f(\boldsymbol{x})$, with $\boldsymbol{x} = (x_{n-1}, \ldots, x_1, x_0)$, the variable x_i taking its value in the set S_i. The particular type of domain S, that is a Cartesian product of finite sets, allows us however to introduce a slightly different kind of representation. Consider, for example, a partition of the finite sets S_i of the domain S:

$$S = (S_{n-1} \times \ldots \times S_q) \times (S_{q-1} \times \ldots \times S_0).$$

A useful representation of the domain S is a *logic chart* or *matrix*. Each q-tuple of $(S_{q-1} \times \ldots \times S_0)$ is assigned to a row of the matrix and, similarly, each $(n-q)$-tuple of $(S_{n-1} \times \ldots \times S_q)$ is assigned to a column of the matrix: the entries of the matrix are thus in bijection with the elements of the domain and will receive the corresponding function value. If the manner of dividing the sets S_i (and thus the corresponding variables x_i) into two groups does not follow directly from specific properties of the sets, one usually divides the variables so as to give both groups similar cardinalities.

Example 2.2. A *finite state machine M* is a system $[S, I, Z, \delta, \lambda]$, where S, I and Z are finite non-empty sets of states, input symbols and output symbols respectively; $\delta : S \times I \rightarrow S$ and $\lambda : S \times I \rightarrow Z$ are the next-state function and the output function respectively. Each of the two functions $\delta : S \times I \rightarrow S$ and $\lambda : S \times I \rightarrow Z$ may be viewed as a discrete function. The partition of the domain of the functions δ and λ naturally derives in this case from their definitions: the set of input symbols I determines the columns in the chart while the set of state symbols S determines the rows in the chart. It is of common use in the study of finite state machines to write in a unique tabular form both matrices corresponding to the functions δ and λ; such a table is known as a *flow-table.* $S = \{s_0, s_1, \ldots, s_{m-1}\}$ and $I = \{i_0, i_1, \ldots, i_{p-1}\}$, the general form of a flow-table, is shown in Figure 2.2.

Important special cases of discrete functions will now be given and some of their possible applications will be briefly outlined.

First of all, let us point out that it may be useful in some cases to consider discrete functions of the form

$$f: \mathop{\times}_{i=n-1}^{0} S_i \rightarrow L^m$$

that is where the codomain of f is the Cartesian mth power of a finite set L. These

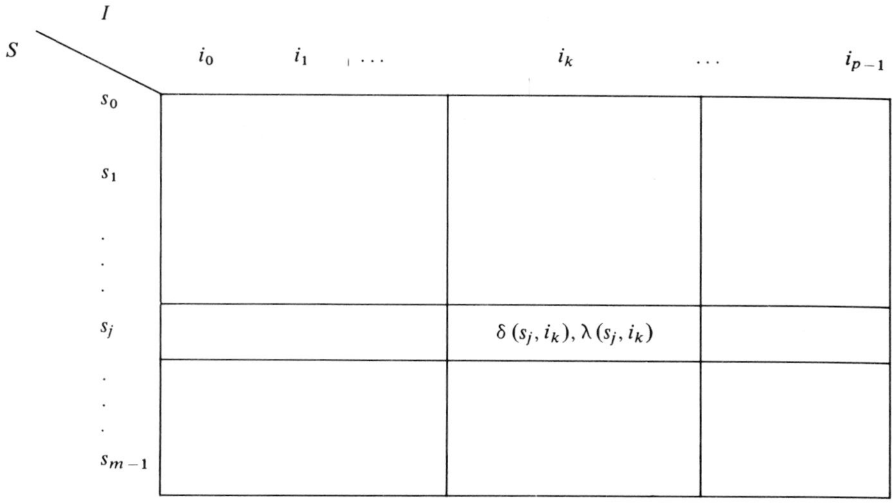

Figure 2.2. Matrix or logic chart for the functions δ and λ or, equivalently, general form of the flow-table describing a finite state machine.

functions will be referred to in the following as *general discrete functions.* A general discrete function is thus formed by a set of discrete functions:

$$f_j : \mathop{\times}_{i=n-1}^{0} S_i \to L, \quad 0 \leqslant j \leqslant m-1 .$$

Consequently, all the properties, theorems . . . which are derived in the sequel for discrete functions also hold for general discrete functions. It is however of common use in mathematics to consider functions instead of general functions. Therefore, the theory developed in this book will be in terms of discrete functions, while – when useful – applications, examples and remarks dealing with the concept of general discrete functions will appear within the text or as footnotes.

Definition 2.2. A discrete function

$$f\colon \mathop{\times}_{i=n-1}^{0} S_i \to L$$

is an *integer function* when each of the sets L and S_i are formed by non-negative integers.

An integer function is thus a mapping:

$$f\colon \mathop{\times}_{i=n-1}^{0} \{0, 1, \ldots, m_i - 1\} \to \{0, 1, \ldots, r-1\} ,$$

with r and m_i the cardinalities of the sets L and S_i respectively. It is important to note that any discrete function may be viewed as an integer function since it is always possible:

(a) to define a one-to-one mapping of S_i onto the set of integers $\{0, 1, \ldots, m_i - 1\}$, $i = 0, 1, \ldots, n-1$,
(b) to define a one-to-one mapping of L onto the set of integers $\{0, 1, \ldots, r-1\}$.

Definition 2.3. An integer function is a *logic function* when the sets L and S_i ($i = 0, 1, \ldots, n-1$) have the same cardinality.

A logic function is thus a mapping

$$f: \{0, 1, \ldots, r-1\}^n \to \{0, 1, \ldots, r-1\},$$

with r the cardinality of the sets L and S_i.

Definition 2.4. A logic function is a *switching function* when the cardinality of the sets L and S_i is 2.

A switching function is thus a mapping

$$f: \{0, 1\}^n \to \{0, 1\}.$$

Logic and switching functions are connected to formal (or mathematical) logic, the actual development of which dates back to the pioneering papers of Lukasiewicz [1920] and Post [1921], in which the first developed systematizations of multiple-valued logic (sometimes also referred to as multivalued logic or as many-valued logic) are presented.

Multiple-valued logic has been recognized for a long time to be of particular interest from the philosophical point of view. On the side of physical applications, a handful of writers have applied multiple-valued logic in the context of indeterminacy situations of quantum mechanics. It is however beyond the scope of this book to deal extensively with formal logic and with its numerous applications. A systematic historical survey of this theory may be found in the book by Rescher [1969] while a review of formal logic, including its most recent developments, is made in the book of Moisil [1972].

More importance will be attached in this book to the use of logic functions and of switching functions for the formal analysis and synthesis of some types of electronic networks.

Let us first consider networks, called *switching networks*, having n input terminals and one output terminal such that, when the input terminals are at the voltages V_0 or V_1, the output terminal is also at V_0 or V_1. Such networks therefore realize the mappings of an ordered n-tuple in $\{V_0, V_1\}^n$ to $\{V_0, V_1\}$. If we now denote conventionally by $\{0, 1\}$ the pair of logical voltages $\{V_0, V_1\}$, the mappings just mentioned coincide with the switching functions $f: \{0, 1\}^n \to \{0, 1\}$. Thus a switching network *realizes* a switching function. The analysis and the synthesis of a switching network which realizes a specific switching function, as well as the study of the problems pertaining to the satisfaction of some criteria of simplicity in this synthesis are the subject of a very important field, called *switching theory*. Several important algebraic problems arising in switching theory will be presented in the course of this book as applications of the concept of switching function. In switching theory, one deals also with *multiple-output switching networks*; such networks realize the mappings of an ordered n-tuple in $\{V_0, V_1\}^n$ to an ordered m-tuple in $\{V_0, V_1\}^m$. Therefore a multiple-output switching network realizes a general switching function. The pioneering work in switching theory is Shannon's paper [1938]; the present widespread interest in switching theory draws its motivation from the fact that switching networks are the basis of practically all today's digital computers.

Let us now consider networks called *logic networks* (or sometimes multiple-valued networks) having n input terminals and one output terminal, such that, when the input terminals are at the voltages $V_0, V_1, \ldots, V_{r-1}$, the output terminal is also at $V_0, V_1, \ldots, V_{r-1}$. Using similar arguments as for switching networks, one sees that logic networks realize mappings that coincide with logic functions f: $\{0, 1, \ldots, r-1\}^n \rightarrow \{0, 1, \ldots, r-1\}$, and that a logic network realizes a logic function. Similarly, multiple-output logic networks *realize* general logic functions.

Logic theory will be defined with respect to logic networks, as switching theory with respect to switching networks.

The main interest of logic networks comes from the fact that the amount of information carried by the wires of such networks may be increased at will by increasing the number r of different voltages. Practical feasibility of logic networks clearly depends upon two critical factors, namely the availability of reliable implementations of some basic logic networks (also called *logic gates* or *primitives*) and the adequacy of synthesis techniques. It now appears that device technology is maturing to produce some types of logic gates. For a survey of engineering aspects of logic systems, see e.g. the paper by Vranesic and Smith [1974]. Hence also the particular interest of logic functions which, as it will be seen further on in this book, will provide us with several analysis and synthesis techniques for logic networks.

Logic functions may finally also be of interest for studying some particular phenomena arising in switching networks. Switching functions are indeed a correct representation of switching networks only for steady-state conditions, i.e. when its input terminals do not change their value. Whenever the inputs are changing, some transient phenomena may occur at the network output. Some of these transients are classically referred to, in switching theory, as *hazards* (for a more rigorous definition of the hazard, see section 3.3.3). Yoeli and Rinon [1964] and Eichelberger [1965] use a three-valued logic function, that is a function f: $\{0, 1, 2\}^n \rightarrow \{0, 1, 2\}$, to perform hazard detection in switching networks (in the original papers by these authors, the function f is a mapping f: $\{0, 1/2, 1\}^n \rightarrow \{0, 1/2, 1\}$).

Definition 2.5. An integer function of the form

$$f: \mathop{\times}_{i=n-1}^{0} \{0, 1, \ldots, m_i - 1\} \rightarrow \{0, 1\},$$

is a *binary function.*

A binary function is thus a two-valued function of multiple-valued variables. The domains of applicability of these functions are numerous: let us enumerate some of them.

A partially *symmetric logic function* is a logic function which has the property of remaining unaltered when any two at least of its variables are interchanged (a more rigorous and complete definition of symmetry in discrete functions will take place in Chapter 13). It has been shown by Davio and Deschamps (Davio and Deschamps [1972], Deschamps [1973], Davio [1973]) that the study of a partially symmetric logic function may be performed in a very concise way by associating with this function a discrete function, called the *carrier function.*

Now it appears that, for the important particular case of partially symmetric switching functions, the carrier function is a binary function. Since the binary carrier function may always be represented in a much more concise form than the associated symmetric function, it is generally easier to study and to manipulate the carrier function instead of the function itself (see section 13.6).

It has been pointed out by Deschamps and Thayse (Deschamps and Thayse [1973b], Thayse [1974c]) that transient phenomena arising in switching networks when inputs of these networks are changing may be studied by associating a binary function to these networks (see section 12.5.2).

Several problems related to graph theory may be treated by using binary functions (see for example section 3.2.2 where one is faced with the problem of obtaining the maximal equivalence classes of an equivalence relation). Roughly speaking, a *graph* $\{V, E\}$ is a collection

$$E = \{e_0, e_1, \ldots, e_{m-1}\}$$

of edges e_k connecting a collection

$$V = \{v_0, v_1, \ldots, v_{n-1}\}$$

of vertices v_i. A graph $\{V, E\}$ may be described by its *adjacency matrix* which is an $(n \times n)$-matrix with binary entries a_{ij} defined by:

$$\begin{aligned} a_{ij} &= 1 \quad \text{iff there is an edge connecting vertices } v_j \text{ and } v_i, \\ &= 0 \quad \text{otherwise.} \end{aligned}$$

A graph $\{V, E\}$ may thus also be viewed as a binary function:

$$f: V^2 \to \{0, 1\}.$$

Definition 2.6. Let Z_r be the set of integers $\{0, 1, \ldots, r-1\}$; by a *pseudo-logic function* one means an integer function:

$$f: \{0, 1\}^n \to Z_r.$$

Let us first observe that a pseudo-logic function is a particular case of the concept of *pseudo-Boolean function* classically defined as a mapping:

$$f: \{0, 1\}^n \to R$$

where R is the field of the real numbers (see for example Hammer and Rudeanu [1968] and Rosenberg [1974]). From a practical point of view, however, distinction between the definition 2.6 and that of pseudo-Boolean function has no special importance. Indeed, the data found in applications are usually not real but rational numbers, and the latter can be transformed into integers by multiplying them by a suitable integer. One obtains then functions with integer values defined on $\{0, 1\}^n$ (note that these functions are called pseudo-logic functions by Klir [1972]).

Functions with integer values are finally transformed into functions with positive integer values by adding to them a suitable positive integer. It is principally for normalization purposes that only non-negative integers are considered in definition 2.6. for the codomain of a pseudo-logic function.

Applications of pseudo-logic functions have recently received considerable attention. A large class of problems in operations research, graph theory and combinatorics can be reduced to the following problem: find the set of all points in $\{0, 1\}^n$ where a given pseudo-logic function takes its minimum or its maximum value. Moreover pseudo-logic functions can be used in almost every problem associated with the design of switching and of logic networks.

An extensive survey of the class of problems which can be solved by using pseudo-logic functions and related methods can be found in the books by Hammer and Rudeanu [1968] and by Klir [1972].

As was seen in section 1.4.3, a field of finite order contains p^m elements where p is a prime and m is a positive integer. This field is referred to as a Galois field of order p^m; it is denoted by $GF(p^m)$.

Definition 2.7. A logic function

$$f: \mathop{\times}_{i=n-1}^{0} S_i \rightarrow L$$

is a *Galois function* when each of the sets L and S_i is the Galois field $GF(p^m)$.

A Galois function is thus a mapping:

$$f: \{GF(p^m)\}^n \rightarrow GF(p^m).$$

Many areas of coding theory (Peterson [1961]), linear sequential switching theory (Kautz [1965a]) and shift-register theory (Golomb *et al.* [1967], Green and Dimond [1970], Stern and Friedland [1961], Green and Kelsch [1973]) involve a widespread use of the Galois field theory. Apart from special-purpose devices, such as those used in shift-register theory, which can realize the Galois field operations, there is also a strong attraction for designing logic and switching networks directly in terms of operations between Galois field elements (see for example Bartee and Schneider [1963], Pradhan and Patel [1975], Pradhan [1976], Benjauthrit and Reed [1976], Davio and Quisquater [1972]). This question will be extensively developed in Chapter 5 of this book.

As a conclusion, the concept of discrete function generalizes and includes a wide class of functions already studied in the framework of applied mathematics and computer science. The rather wide and non-exhaustive range of applications quoted in this section provides us with a definite motivation for a deeper study of better computational means.

2.1.2. Graphical and tabular representation methods

An important simplification arises in tabular and matrix representations of discrete functions if one chooses an enumeration order of the points of the domain S.

Assume first that one defines a one-to-one mapping of S onto the set of integers $\{0, 1, \ldots, m-1\}$. With this convention we are able to define any discrete function by the corresponding set of values

$$[f(e)], \quad e = 0, 1, \ldots, m-1; \quad f(e) \in L \; \forall \, e.$$

The expression $[f(e)]$ will be referred to in the sequel as the *value vector* of $f(x)$; it will generally be written as $[f_e]$. The value vector may be considered as an economical tabular description of the function since the choice of an enumeration order allows us to drop the values of the argument x in the function representation. For example, the value vector of the function described by Figure 2.1 is:

$$[0 \quad 1 \quad 0 \quad 1 \quad 0].$$

Assume now that S is the Cartesian product $\bigtimes_i S_i$ of n finite sets. One shall first choose an enumeration order of the points of the sets S_i by defining a one-to-one mapping of S_i onto the set of integers $\{0, 1, \ldots, m_i-1\}$ with m_i the cardinality of S_i. It is then also useful for representation purposes to choose an enumeration order of the domain S

$$S = \bigtimes_{i=n-1}^{0} S_i.$$

The lexicographical order or the Gray code order, as defined in section 1.5, may then be chosen for this enumeration order. Again the value vector may then be used for representing a discrete function; it is denoted by:

$$[f(e)] \text{ or } [f_e], \quad e = (e_{n-1}, \ldots, e_1, e_0), \quad e_i \in S_i \, \forall \, i; \quad f(e) \in L \, \forall \, e.$$

Value vectors were obtained from the corresponding table by defining an enumeration order on S; *value charts* or *value matrices* will similarly be obtained by defining an enumeration order for the rows and columns of the logic charts or matrices.

Let us recall that a matrix is obtained by partitioning the domain

$$S = \bigtimes_{i=n-1}^{0} S_i$$

into two groups of sets, namely

$$(S_{n-1} \times \ldots \times S_q) \quad \text{and} \quad (S_{q-1} \times \ldots \times S_0).$$

If the set $(S_{n-1} \times \ldots \times S_q)$ determines the columns in the matrix while the set $(S_{q-1} \times \ldots \times S_0)$ determines the rows, we are able to define any discrete function by the corresponding rectangular matrix

$$[f(i,j)], \quad i = \text{row number}, \quad j = \text{column number}, \quad f(i,j) \in L \ \forall i,j$$

which could also equivalently be denoted as:

$$\begin{aligned} [f(e, \boldsymbol{\epsilon})], \quad & e = (e_{q-1}, \ldots, e_0), \ \boldsymbol{\epsilon} = (\epsilon_{n-1}, \ldots, \epsilon_q), \\ & e_i \in S_i, \quad 0 \leqslant i \leqslant q-1, \\ & \epsilon_j \in S_j, \quad q \leqslant j \leqslant n-1, \\ & f(e, \boldsymbol{\epsilon}) \in L. \end{aligned}$$

The *Veitch chart* corresponds to the lexicographical enumeration order in both groups of finite sets while the *Karnaugh chart* corresponds to a Gray code enumeration order. Both types of charts were originally described and used for switching functions. The Veitch chart was first suggested by Marquand [1881]; it was later rediscovered by Veitch [1952] and has been extensively used by Svoboda [1956, 1960]. Therefore it is sometimes called the Marquand chart or the Svoboda chart (see for example Klir [1972]). The Karnaugh chart, which is generally preferred in the contemporary literature concerning switching networks for a reason that will appear further on, was suggested by Karnaugh [1953] for switching functions.

Example 2.3. Let $S = \{0, 1, 2\}$

Enumeration of S^2:	0	1	2	3	4	5	6	7	8
Gray-code order:	0	0	0	1	1	1	2	2	2
	0	1	2	2	0	1	1	2	0
Lexicographical order:	0	0	0	1	1	1	2	2	2
	0	1	2	0	1	2	0	1	2

The function f from $S^2 \times S^2$ into the set $L = \{0, 1, \ldots, 8\}$ given by:

$$f(x_3, x_2, x_1, x_0) = x_3 + x_2 + x_1 + x_0$$

is depicted by the Figures 2.3 and 2.4.

The comparison of Veitch and Karnaugh matrices is generally performed in terms of adjacency. Indeed, the points of the domain $\times_i S_i$ may be considered as points of the n-dimensional Euclidean space R^n. Two points p_0 and p_1 are *adjacent* iff they only differ by a single of their coordinates. It turns out that, for some applications, it is important to detect these adjacencies and it is thus also important to use visual displays that exhibit a maximum amount of these adjacencies: clearly, two adjacent entries of a Karnaugh chart correspond to adjacent points of $\times_i S_i$. Such a property is

0	1	2	3	1	2	3	4	2
1	2	3	4	2	3	4	5	2
2	3	4	5	3	4	5	6	4
3	4	5	6	4	5	6	7	5
1	2	3	4	2	3	4	5	3
2	3	4	5	3	4	5	6	4
3	4	5	6	4	5	6	7	4
4	5	6	7	5	6	7	8	5
2	3	4	5	3	4	5	6	4

Figure 2.3. Karnaugh matrix of $f(x_3, x_2, x_1, x_0)$

0	1	2	1	2	3	2	3	4
1	2	3	2	3	4	3	4	5
2	3	4	3	4	5	4	5	6
1	2	3	2	3	4	3	4	5
2	3	4	3	4	5	4	5	6
3	4	5	4	5	6	5	6	7
2	3	4	3	4	5	4	5	6
3	4	5	4	5	6	5	6	7
4	5	6	5	6	7	6	7	8

Figure 2.4. Veitch matrix of $f(x_3, x_2, x_1, x_0)$

clearly not shared by the Veitch chart. This would favour the former with respect to the latter. However, even in the switching case, the number of displayed adjacencies is only a small part of the actually existing adjacencies and the situation is worse for discrete functions. It is finally difficult to put that discussion to a definite conclusion since, as Klir [1972] notes, the lexicographical order is a very convenient tool when used in computer simulation.

If the groups of sets $(S_{n-1} \times \ldots \times S_q)$ and $(S_{q-1} \times \ldots \times S_0)$ reduce each to a single set: S_1 and S_0 respectively (or, in other words, if $q = 1$ and $n = 2$), the Karnaugh and the Veitch matrices of the functions $f: S_1 \times S_0 \to L$ are evidently identical. Moreover, in this case there is a one-to-one correspondence between the adjacent points in the matrix and the adjacent points in $S_1 \times S_0$.

Finally, for $q = 0$, the value matrices reduce to value vectors.

Let us now give some more details about a type of representation for discrete functions briefly introduced above, namely when the points of the domain $\underset{i}{\times} S_i$ are considered as points of the n-dimensional Euclidean space R^n. This geometric representation of a discrete function has been extensively used by Lee [1954] for switching functions. It is then known as the *cubical representation* of a switching function and is obtained by mapping a switching function of n variables onto the n-dimensional unit cube (n-cube). Some of the concepts of this representation can be seen geometrically but, to circumvent the increase in geometric complexity encountered with an increase in the number of variables, one usually relies on an analytic description of this mapping. This analytic description provides us with another representation method known as the *cubical notation method.* An extensive development of cubical notations for switching functions may be found in the book by Miller [1965]. Cubical notations for logic functions have been presented by Su and Cheung [1972]; cubical notations are strongly connected to normal forms of discrete functions, which are introduced in section 2.2.2. They will be described in the same section.

The analytic description of the cubical representation for discrete functions is closely related to the converse of a discrete function (see section 1.1). For any discrete function $f(x)$ and any $l \in L$ we denote by $f_c(l)$, the set of points of the domain whose image by f is l. If the cardinality of L is r a discrete function is completely described when the converses of $r-1$ points of L are known. This kind of function description is particularly attractive for switching functions. Because for these functions the set L consists of two integers 0 and 1, a switching function is completely determined by either of its two converses

$$f_c(1) = \{x \in \{0, 1\}^n \mid f(x) = 1\}$$
$$f_c(0) = \{x \in \{0, 1\}^n \mid f(x) = 0\}$$

which are generally called the *on-set* and the *off-set* of the function $f(x)$.

Let us finally also point out that *Euler–Venn diagrams* (Euler [1772], Venn [1894]), initially defined to help us to visualize the fundamental notions concerning sets, may also be used for switching function description.

The different graphical representations of a discrete function are schematized in Figure 2.5.

The different tabular and graphical description methods described above evidently also hold when dealing with generalized discrete functions. Consider e.g. the value vector of a general discrete function; the entries of this vector are in this case a vector of constants: $\{f_0(e), f_1(e), \ldots, f_{m-1}(e)\}$ instead of a scalar $f(e)$. By use of the vectorial notation, general functions will sometimes be written $f(x) = \{f_0(x), f_1(x), \ldots, f_{m-1}(x)\}$; their value vector will then be denoted $[f(e)]$.

Further on in this book, the callings value vector and value matrix will always implicitly assume a lexicographical enumeration order on the domains. When dealing with switching functions and with binary functions, the value vector and matrix will generally be called *truth vector* and *truth matrix* respectively.

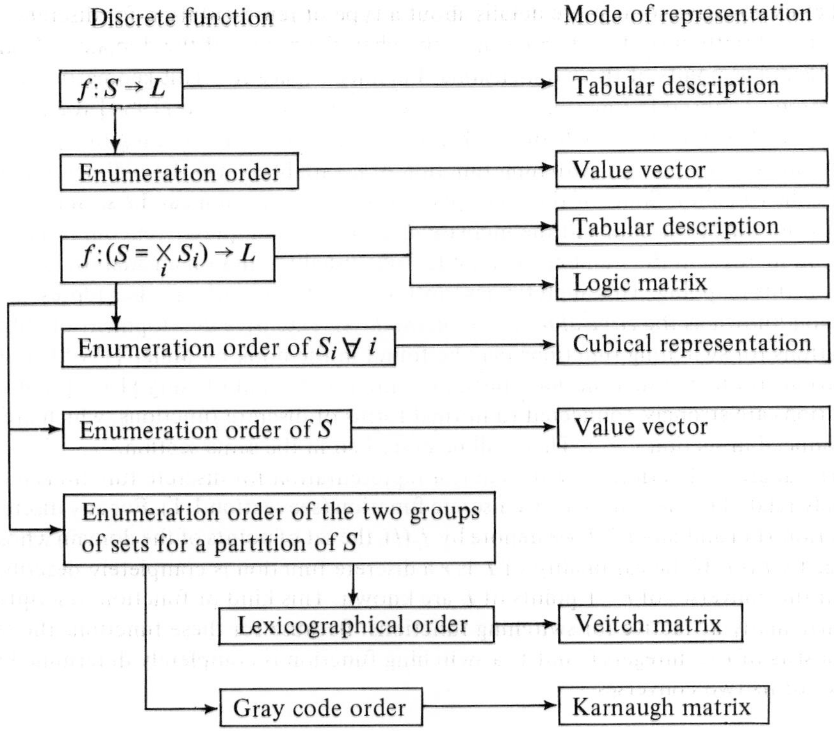

Figure 2.5. Graphical representations of discrete functions

An outstanding advantage of the graphical representation technique is that it enables the best use to be put to *don't care* conditions. In some problems it is not possible, or even desirable, to specify all the values of the domain S. These are generally referred to as *incompletely specified functions* although they are not really functions, from an algebraic point of view, but functional relations (see section 1.1).

Example 2.4. If we are designing a switching network to encode a four-bit binary coded decimal to Gray code, 6 out of the possible 16 four-bit combinations will not be used since only the decimal numbers 0 to 9 have to be represented (see Figure 2.6). Thus, since these combinations cannot occur, the outputs required for these input conditions are immaterial and can be assigned either 0 or 1 at will. These combinations are represented in Figure 2.6. by "–"; f_0, f_1, f_2 and f_3 are the four incompletely specified switching functions to be realized by means of four switching networks. (Let us also note that these four incompletely specified switching functions may be viewed as an incompletely specified general switching function.)

	x_3	x_2	x_1	x_0	f_3	f_2	f_1	f_0
0	0	0	0	0	0	0	0	0
1	0	0	0	1	0	0	0	1
2	0	0	1	0	0	0	1	1
3	0	0	1	1	0	0	1	0
4	0	1	0	0	0	1	1	0
5	0	1	0	1	0	1	1	1
6	0	1	1	0	0	1	0	1
7	0	1	1	1	0	1	0	0
8	1	0	0	0	1	1	0	0
9	1	0	0	1	1	0	0	0
	1	0	1	0	–	–	–	–
	1	0	1	1	–	–	–	–
	1	1	0	0	–	–	–	–
	1	1	0	1	–	–	–	–
	1	1	1	0	–	–	–	–
	1	1	1	1	–	–	–	–

Figure 2.6. Binary coded decimal to Gray code.

2.1.3. Computation schemes and discrete functions of functions

In what follows, we shall first be faced with logic functions, that is mappings $f: S^n \to S$. We assume that the cardinality of S is r ($r \geqslant 2$) and write

$$S = \{0, 1, \ldots, r-1\}.$$

We next consider a finite set Ω of p logic functions also called *primitives*:

$$\Omega = \{h_i | h_i: S^n \to S; \quad 0 \leqslant i \leqslant p-1\}.$$

An element of S^n is represented by an n-tuple:

$$e = (e_{n-1}, \ldots, e_1, e_0); \quad e_i \in S, \quad 0 \leqslant i \leqslant n-1.$$

We assume that the set Ω always contains a subset Γ that consists of

1. The constant functions ϕ_e

$$\phi_e: e \to e; \quad e \in S^n, \quad e \in S.$$

2. The projection functions x_i

$$x_i:(e_{n-1},\ldots,e_1,e_0)\to e_i,\quad 0\leqslant i\leqslant n-1$$

and define $\omega=\Omega\backslash\Gamma$. Note that the functions in ω may be independent of some of their arguments.

Definition 2.8. (Savage [1972]). *A computation scheme* σ over Ω is a finite sequence $\sigma=(f_0,f_1,\ldots,f_{N-1})$ of functions

$$f_j: S^n\to S$$

such that for each f_j one and only one of the two following conditions holds:

C1 : $f_j\in\Gamma$

C2: there exists a function $h_i\in\omega$ and n functions

$f_{j_0},f_{j_1},\ldots,f_{j_{n-1}}$ ($f_{j_k}\in\sigma; j_k<j$) such that: $f_j=h_i(f_{j_0},f_{j_1},\ldots,f_{j_{n-1}})$.

The computation scheme σ is said to *compute* any of the functions f_j. We shall furthermore assume, in what follows, that the set Ω is *complete*, i.e. that any function $f: S^n\to S$ can be computed by some computation scheme over Ω.

It is worthwhile pointing out the correspondence between the concepts of computation scheme and of well-formed expression (see section 1.2). To each well-formed expression may be associated at least one computation scheme the existence of which guarantees the fact that the initial expression is really a well-formed expression.

It is obviously possible to consider a computation scheme as the structural description of a logic network that computes (or realizes) the same function. In that case, the functions $h_i\in\omega$ are the *available operators* (which are generally elementary logic networks referred to as logic gates or primitives), the functions f_j satisfying condition C1 correspond to the *primary inputs* of the networks, while the functions f_j satisfying condition C2 provide the list of required operators together with a description of their interconnections.

The networks obtained by this correspondence are clearly the *well-behaved nets* in the sense of Burks and Wright [1953]. Thanks to this correspondence, we shall be able to speak either in terms of computation schemes, or in terms of the theory of logic networks.

Abstractly speaking, a switching network realizes a switching function. Thus, a switching network is viewed as a black-box computing a switching function; a more detailed definition of a switching network will now be given which allows us to describe some features of its internal structure.

Consider the elementary switching networks (gates or primitives) in Figure 2.7. The gates are defined as follows:

(1) AND: the output is 1 iff all the inputs are 1; it is 0 otherwise.
(2) OR: the output is 1 iff at least one of the inputs is 1; it is 0 otherwise.
(3) NOT: the output is 1 iff the input is 0, and vice versa.

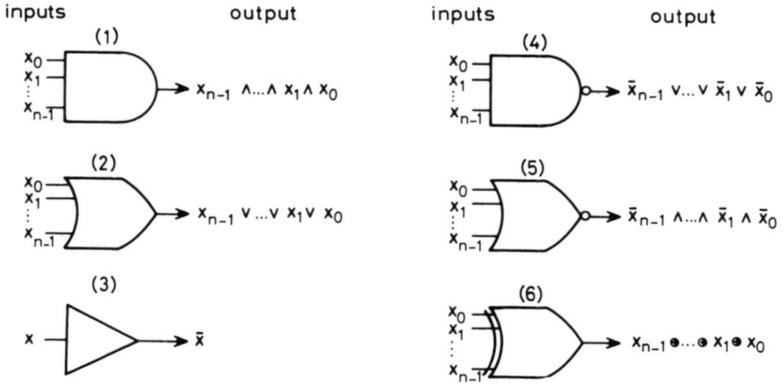

Figure 2.7. Switching gates or primitives

(4) NAND: the output is 1 iff at least one of the inputs is 0; it is 0 otherwise.
(5) NOR: the output is 1 iff all the inputs are 0, it is 0 otherwise.
(6) XOR: the output is 1 iff an odd number of inputs is 1; it is 0 otherwise.

A switching network is then defined as an interconnection of these gates so that:

(a) any gate input is connected to a gate output or to a primary input,
(b) no two outputs are connected together,
(c) no loops are present in the interconnection.

It must be noted that the switching networks thus defined correspond to the classical definition of *combinational switching networks.* Further on in this book, a switching network will thus always mean a combinational switching network. If the switching network has 1 output, it realizes 1 switching function; if it has m outputs, it realizes m switching functions or, equivalently, a general switching function.

Clearly the above definition of a switching network coincides with that given in section 2.1, since it realizes a mapping from $\{0, 1\}^n$ to $\{0, 1\}$.

Example 2.5. Consider the particular switching network of Figure 2.8 (Maley [1970]).

The primary inputs are: x, y, c;
the available operators are: h_1 = NAND-gate with two inputs,
h_2 = NAND-gate with three inputs.

The computation scheme is given by Figure 2.9. The interconnection scheme of Figure 2.8 is entirely described by the computation scheme of Figure 2.9.

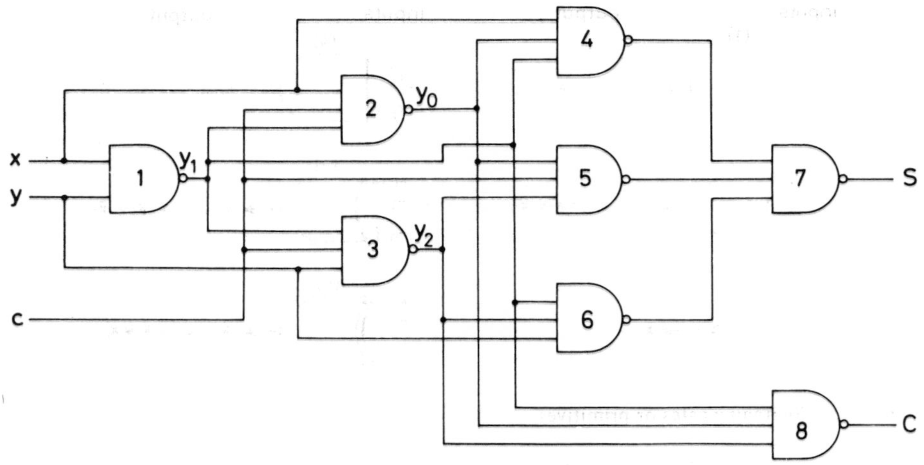

Figure 2.8. Switching network composed by an interconnection of NAND-gates

Function denomination	Operation it realizes
a	x
b	y
c	c
1	$h_1(a, b)$
2	$h_2(a, c, 1)$
3	$h_2(b, c, 1)$
4	$h_2(a, 1, 2)$
5	$h_2(c, 2, 3)$
6	$h_2(b, 1, 2)$
7	$h_2(4, 5, 6)$
8	$h_2(1, 2, 3)$

Figure 2.9. Computation scheme of the switching network of Figure 2.8

Computation schemes were defined for logic functions; they could similarly be defined for discrete functions. Since the notations are much more cumbersome for that case and since the most important applications of computation schemes are in in the frame of logic functions, no generalization of the above definitions and techniques applying to discrete functions will be given in this text.

Let us also point out that the development of an algebraic model for logic (and especially switching) networks which is isomorphic to the actual network structure down to the level of interconnected logic gates is of outstanding interest in switching theory. Numerous algebraic models and various techniques have already been developed in the treatment of this type of problem. Most of these models were presented in the framework of stuck-fault detection or diagnosis (see sections 4.4.2 and 7.3.2). The earliest model using this point of view was presented by Poage [1963]; other models were also developed, e.g. by Clegg [1972], Reese and McCluskey [1973], Armstrong [1966] and Thayse [1974e].

Closely related to the concept of computation scheme is that of discrete function of functions (Thayse [1974d]).

Definition 2.9. Consider a discrete function:

$$f:\left(\mathop{\times}_{i=n-1}^{0} S_i\right) \times \left(\mathop{\times}_{j=h-1}^{0} L_j\right) \rightarrow L.$$

This function is denoted $f(\boldsymbol{x}, \boldsymbol{y})$, with $\boldsymbol{x} = (x_{n-1}, \ldots, x_1, x_0)$ and $\boldsymbol{y} = (y_{h-1}, \ldots$ $\ldots, y_1, y_0)$, the variable x_i taking its value in the set $S_i = \{0, 1, \ldots, m_i - 1\}$ and the variable y_j taking its value in the set $L_j = \{0, 1, \ldots, r_j - 1\}$ $(0 \leqslant i \leqslant n-1, 0 \leqslant j \leqslant h-1)$; $f(\boldsymbol{x}, \boldsymbol{y})$ is a *discrete function of functions* if the variables y_j are mappings:

$$y_j : S \rightarrow L_j, \quad 0 \leqslant j \leqslant h-1.$$

Further on this kind of discrete function will be denoted by $f[\boldsymbol{x}, \boldsymbol{y}(\boldsymbol{x})]$ or $f(\boldsymbol{x}, \boldsymbol{y})$.

Cascaded types of functions of functions, as described by the system

$$\begin{aligned}
y_0 &= y_0(\boldsymbol{x}) \\
y_1 &= y_1(\boldsymbol{x}, y_0) \\
&\vdots \\
y_{q-1} &= y_{q-1}(\boldsymbol{x}, y_0, \ldots, y_{q-2}) \\
f &= f(\boldsymbol{x}, y_0, \ldots, y_{q-1})
\end{aligned} \tag{2.1}$$

will also be considered further on. The notation $\boldsymbol{y}_j$ means a finite set of mappings:

$$y_j = \{y_{j0}, y_{j1}, \ldots, y_{j(n_j-1)}\}$$

the domains of which being implicitly described by the set of relations (2.1).

Again, it is obviously possible to consider a discrete function of functions of the type (2.1) as the structural description of a combinational network that computes the function f. In this case, however, each of the functions y_k and f may be viewed as the description of a *black-box* computing that function. The set of equations (2.1) then only contains a description of these black-box interconnections (and no more longer the internal description of the black-box as the computation scheme did).

It will, however, be seen in the sequel that a judicious choice of the functions y_k allows us to solve a large number of problems arising in switching theory by using the concept of discrete function of functions, which may also be considered as a simplified computation scheme.

Example 2.5 (continued). Consider again the switching network of Figure 2.8. If the functions y_0, y_1, y_2 are a description of the outputs of the gates 2, 3 and 1 respectively, the following type of function of functions is a description of the structural interconnection of Figure 2.10:

$$\begin{aligned} y_1 &= y_1(x,y) \\ y_0 &= y_0(x,c,y) \\ y_2 &= y_2(y,c,y_1) \\ S &= S(x,y,c,y_0,y_1,y_2) \\ C &= C(y_0,y_1,y_2) \end{aligned} \tag{2.2}$$

Each of the functions (2.2) may for example be described by a table or by a matrix as shown in section 2.1.1. Functions (2.2) do not provide us with an internal description of the black-boxes realizing S, C, y_0, y_1 and y_2.

Let us consider some important particular types of discrete functions of functions. A *logic function of functions* is a discrete function of functions $f[\boldsymbol{x}, \boldsymbol{y}(\boldsymbol{x})]$ where f and each of the $y_j \in \boldsymbol{y}$ are logic functions (with the same codomain). A *switching function of functions* is a logic function of functions where f and the y_j's are switching functions.

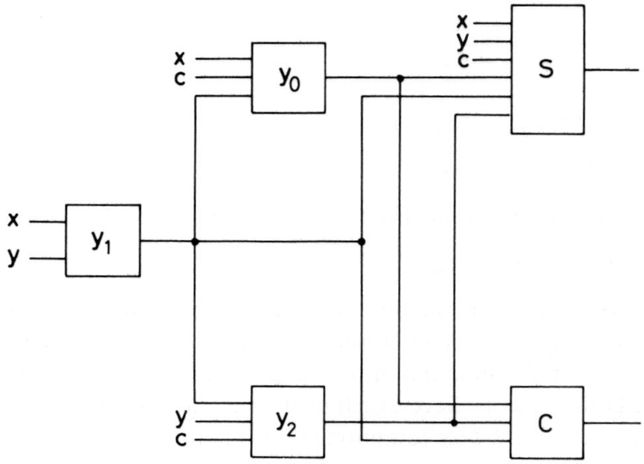

Figure 2.10. Interconnection scheme for the switching network of Figure 2.8

Definition 2.10. Consider a discrete function

$$f = \underset{i=n-1}{\overset{0}{\times}} S_i \to L,$$

usually denoted by $f(x)$; $f(x)$ will be called a *time-dependent discrete function* if the variables x_i are mappings:

$$x_i : L_t = \{0, 1, \ldots, m_t - 1\} \to S_i.$$

These functions will generally be denoted $f[x_{n-1}(t), \ldots, x_1(t), x_0(t)]$ or $f[x(t)]$, with t a discrete variable taking its values in L_t.

Since, in most applications, the variable t will be a discretized time index, these functions are called time-dependent discrete functions. One will also consider further on cascaded types of time-dependent discrete functions; they are described by adding the functions $x = x(t)$ on the top of system (2.1). Finally, *time-dependent logic functions* and *time-dependent switching functions* are defined according to the usual rules.

Time-dependent discrete functions are of practical interest in all the problems where a discretized time index may be used. Hence the possible use of these functions in simulation of logic networks (Breuer [1974], Thayse [1974c]). These functions are also of considerable theoretical interest since they lead to the concepts of increment and differential (see Chapter 7).

2.2. *The lattice structure of discrete functions*

2.2.1. *Definitions and lattice notations*

Further on in this text, it will always be assumed that the domain S is the Cartesian product

$$S = \underset{i=n-1}{\overset{0}{\times}} S_i;$$

this includes as particular case $n = 1$.

Let us choose an enumeration order of the points of the codomain L by defining a one-to-one mapping of L onto the set of integers $\{0, 1, \ldots, r-1\}$. Let $\{L, \vee, \wedge, 0, r-1\}$ be the lattice under disjunction $\vee$ and conjunction $\wedge$, having a least element 0 and a greatest element $(r-1)$. The disjunction $f \vee g$ and the conjunction $f \wedge g$ of two discrete functions given, e.g. (and without loss of generality) by their value vectors:

$$[f_e], [g_e], \quad e = (e_{n-1}, \ldots, e_1, e_0), \quad e_i \in S_i \ \forall i;$$
$$f_e, \quad g_e \in L \ \forall e,$$

are defined by the componentwise extensions of the disjunction and of the conjunction in L respectively, i.e.:

$$[(f \vee g)_e] = [f_e \vee g_e],$$
$$[(f \wedge g)_e] = [f_e \wedge g_e].$$

Let $l \in L$; the disjunction $l \vee f$ and the conjunction $l \wedge f$ of the function f with the lattice element l are defined by

$$[(l \vee f)_e] = [l \vee f_e],$$
$$[(l \wedge f)_e] = [l \wedge f_e].$$

The orderings on L and on S are denoted by the symbol $\geqslant$ with the usual terminology (see for example, Rutherford [1965] and Birkhoff [1967]). The following equivalences hold:

$$f \geqslant g \Leftrightarrow f(e) \geqslant g(e)\ \forall e \Leftrightarrow f \vee g = f \Leftrightarrow f \wedge g = g.$$

With these definitions, the set of discrete functions $S \to L$ is isomorphic to the product lattice L^N where $N = \Pi m_i$ is the cardinality of $S = \times_i S_i$ (m_i is the cardinality of $S_i\ \forall i$); it is thus a distributive lattice since L^N is a distributive lattice together with L.

When dealing with general functions, the lattice to be considered is $\{L^m, \vee, \wedge, \mathit{0}, \mathit{r-1}\}$ where $\mathit{0}$ and $(\mathit{r-1})$ mean m-tuples of 0 and of $(r-1)$ respectively. The lattice elements are then evidently m-tuples $(l_0, l_1, \ldots, l_{m-1})$, $l_j \in L = \{0, 1, \ldots, r-1\}\ \forall j$.

Let $\boldsymbol{x}$ denote the vector of variables $(x_{n-1}, \ldots, x_1, x_0)$; given a variable $x_i \in \boldsymbol{x}$ and a subset C_i of S_i, the function

$$x_i^{(C_i)}$$

is defined as follows.

Definition 2.11. Lattice exponentiation:

$$x_i^{(C_i)} = r-1 \quad \text{iff } x_i \in C_i,$$
$$= 0 \quad \text{otherwise.}$$

With this notation, $x_i^{(S_i)} = r-1$ and $x_i^{(\phi)} = 0$, where ϕ means the empty set.

Definitions 2.12. By a *lattice expression* we mean a well-formed expression (see section 1.2) made up of the following symbols:

(a) the lattice elements $0, 1, \ldots, r-1$,
(b) the variables $x_i^{(C_i)}$,
(c) the two binary lattice operations:

$\vee$ standing for the disjunction,
$\wedge$ standing for the conjunction.

As it will be seen in section 2.2.3, any discrete function may be described by a lattice expression. Conversely, every lattice expression is clearly a discrete function since its arguments x_i and values are in S and in L respectively. In order to determine the value of an expression for a given combination, it is sufficient to substitute the values for the variables in the expression.

Some particular types of lattice expressions (or equivalently of discrete functions) will now be considered.

Definition 2.13. A *cube function* (as introduced by Davio and Bioul [1970]) is a discrete function $c(\boldsymbol{x})$ of the form

$$c(\boldsymbol{x}) = l \wedge \bigwedge_{i=n-1}^{0} x_i^{(C_i)}, \quad l \in L;$$

l will be called the *weight* of the cube.

The cube $c(\boldsymbol{x})$ takes thus the value l iff $x_i \in C_i \; \forall \, i$ and takes the value 0 otherwise. A cube $c(\boldsymbol{x})$ such that the cardinality of each C_i is unity is a *join-irreducible element* of the lattice (see section 1.3). If moreover $l = 1$, $c(\boldsymbol{x})$ is an *atom* of L^N which is thus a discrete function of the form:

$$1 \wedge \bigwedge_{i=n-1}^{0} x_i^{(e_i)},$$

where e_i is an element of $S_i \; \forall \, i$. This function takes thus the value 1 iff $x_i = e_i \; \forall \, i$ and takes the value 0 otherwise.

Whenever at least one set C_i is empty, a cube $c(\boldsymbol{x})$ assumes the value 0 everywhere and is thus reduced to the smallest element of L^N, called *empty cube*. Let us also note that the conjunction of two cubes:

$$l_0 \wedge \bigwedge_{i=n-1}^{0} x_i^{(C_{i0})} \quad \text{and} \quad l_1 \wedge \bigwedge_{i=n-1}^{0} x_i^{(C_{i1})}, \quad l_0, l_1 \in L$$

is a cube the expression of which is:

$$l_0 \wedge l_1 \wedge \bigwedge_{i=n-1}^{0} x_i^{(C_{i0} \cap C_{i1})}. \tag{2.3}$$

The dual concepts are now introduced.

Definition 2.14. An *anticube function* is a discrete function $d(\boldsymbol{x})$ of the form:

$$d(\boldsymbol{x}) = l \vee \bigvee_{i=n-1}^{0} x_i^{(D_i)}$$

where $D_i \subseteq S_i \; \forall \, i$; l will be called the *weight* of the anticube. The anticube $d(\boldsymbol{x})$ takes thus the value $r-1$ iff $\exists i : x_i \in D_i$ and takes the value l otherwise. Denote by $\bar{D}_i$ the complement of D_i with respect to S_i, that is $\bar{D}_i = S_i \backslash D_i$; an anticube $d(\boldsymbol{x})$ such that the cardinality of each D_i is unity, is a *meet-irreducible element* of the lattice. If moreover $l = r-2$, $d(\boldsymbol{x})$ is an *antiatom* of L^N which is thus a discrete function of the form:

$$(r-2) \vee \bigvee_{i=n-1}^{0} x_i^{(\bar{e}_i)}.$$

This function takes thus the value $r-2$ iff $x_i = e_i \;\forall i$ and takes the value $r-1$ otherwise.

Whenever at least one $\bar{C}_i$ is empty the anticube assumes the value $r-1$ everywhere and is thus reduced to the greatest member of L^N -called hereafter *empty anticube*.

The disjunction of two anticubes

$$l_0 \vee \bigvee_{i=n-1}^{0} x_i^{(D_{i0})} \quad \text{and} \quad l_1 \vee \bigvee_{i=n-1}^{0} x_i^{(D_{i1})}$$

is an anticube the expression of which is:

$$l_0 \vee l_1 \vee \bigvee_{i=n-1}^{0} x_i^{(D_{i0} \cup D_{i1})}. \tag{2.4}$$

The terms cubes and anticubes are coined from an elementary geometric representation of lattice expressions widely used for switching functions (see for example, Kuntzmann [1965], Miller [1965], Su and Dietmeyer [1969], Dietmeyer [1971]). The terms irreducible element, atom and antiatom have their usual lattice theoretical meaning (see section 1.3 and for example, Crawley and Dilworth [1973]).

The relations between the dual concepts of cube and anticube and of atom and antiatom for example, may be illustrated by using the concept of *negation* of a discrete function (Su and Sarris [1972]).

Definition 2.15. The *negation* $\bar{f}$ of a discrete function is defined by

$$[\bar{f}_e] = [(r-1) - f_e]$$

where the minus sign represents arithmetic subtraction.

In view of the above definition it appears that the negation $\bar{f}(\boldsymbol{x})$ of a discrete function $f(\boldsymbol{x})$ is another discrete function.

The rules governing the negation operation are summarized by the following theorem.

Theorem 2.1 (*De Morgan theorem*). *For every discrete function one has*:

(a) $\bar{\bar{f}}(\boldsymbol{x}) = f(\boldsymbol{x})$

(b) $\left\{\overline{\bigvee_j f_j(x)}\right\} = \bigwedge_j \bar{f}_j(x)$

(c) $\left\{\overline{\bigwedge_j f_j(x)}\right\} = \bigvee_j \bar{f}_j(x).$

Proof

(a) Obvious in view of definition 2.13.
(b) Let $\boldsymbol{e}$ be a particular value of $\boldsymbol{x}$ and let, e.g. $f_i(\boldsymbol{e}) \geqslant f_j(\boldsymbol{e})$; then:

$$\left\{\overline{\bigvee_j f_j(\boldsymbol{e})}\right\} = \bar{f}_i(\boldsymbol{e}) = \bigwedge_j \bar{f}_j(\boldsymbol{e})$$

since $\bar{f}_j(\boldsymbol{e}) \geqslant \bar{f}_i(\boldsymbol{e})$.

Since this holds for any $\boldsymbol{e} \in S$, the relation (b) is true.
(c) Similar statement as (b). ∎

In view of theorem 2.1 it appears that the negation of a cube function (resp. anticube function) is an anticube function (resp. cube function); more precisely:

$$\overline{l \wedge \bigwedge_{i=n-1}^{0} x_i^{(C_i)}} = \bar{l} \vee \bigvee_{i=n-1}^{0} x_i^{(\bar{C}_i)} \tag{2.5}$$

$$\overline{l \vee \bigvee_{i=n-1}^{0} x_i^{(C_i)}} = \bar{l} \wedge \bigwedge_{i=n-1}^{0} x_i^{(\bar{C}_i)}. \tag{2.6}$$

The proofs of relations (2.5) and (2.6) are derived from theorem 2.1 and from the following identity:

$$\overline{x_i^{(C_i)}} = x_i^{(\bar{C}_i)}\,. \tag{2.7}$$

The following identities are immediate consequences of theorem 2.1:

$$\text{if } C_i = \bigcup_j C_{ij}, \quad \text{then } x_i^{(C_i)} = \bigvee_j x_i^{(C_{ij})} \tag{2.8}$$

$$\text{if } C_i = \bigcap_j C_{ij}, \quad \text{then } x_i^{(C_i)} = \bigwedge_j x_i^{(C_{ij})} \tag{2.9}$$

$$(r-1) \wedge x_i^{(C_i)} = x_i^{(C_i)}. \tag{2.10}$$

The following notation will also be used:

if $C_i = \{a_{i0}, a_{i1}, \ldots, a_{i(n_i-1)}\}$

then $x_i^{(C_i)}$ will be written $x_i^{(a_{i0}, a_{i1}, \ldots, a_{i(n_i-1)})}$.

Switching functions and switching variables

Let us define a switching variable as a binary variable taking its values in $B_2 = \{0, 1\}$; switching variables may evidently be present in any lattice expression when some of the cardinalities m_i are 2. For x a switching variable of a switching function, the following notations are of classical use for the lattice exponentiation:

$$x^{(1)} = x \quad \text{(direct form of } x\text{)}$$

$$x^{(0)} = 1 - x = \bar{x} \quad \text{(complemented form of } x\text{).} \tag{2.11}$$

One has evidently also

$$x^{(0,1)} = 1.$$

2.2.2. *Lattice expressions and their manipulation*

In view of definition (2.12), by a lattice expression we mean the combination of a finite number of literals $x_i^{(C_i)}$ and constants $\{0, 1, \ldots, r-1\}$ by means of the lattice operations: $\vee$, $\wedge$ and parentheses. Let $F(x_{n-1}, \ldots, x_1, x_0)$ be a lattice expression. Since each of the variables $x_{n-1}, \ldots, x_1, x_0$ can independently assume any one of the values in $S_{n-1}, \ldots, S_1, S_0$ respectively, there are Πm_i combinations of values to be considered in determining the value of F. In order to determine the value of an expression for a given combination, it is sufficient to substitute the values for the variables in the expression. The values assumed by an expression for all the combinations of the variables $x_{n-1}, \ldots, x_1, x_0$ define a discrete function. This correspondence is best specified by means of a value vector or of a value matrix. Note that each value vector or matrix defines only one discrete function although this function may be expressed in a number of ways by different lattice expressions.

Example 2.6. Consider a ternary function of two quaternary variables, that is:

$$f:\{0, 1, 2, 3\}^2 \to \{0, 1, 2\}.$$

It is described by the following lattice expression:

$$F = 2x_1^{(0,2)} x_0^{(2)} \vee 1x_1^{(2)} x_0^{(0)} \vee 1x_1^{(0,3)} x_0^{(1,3)} \vee 1x_1^{(0)} x_0^{(1,2,3)}. \tag{2.12}$$

(For sake of conciseness the symbol "$\wedge$" of the conjunction will be omitted in the examples.) For example, for the combination $x_1 = 0, x_0 = 2$, the value of F is 2 because $F(0, 2) = 2 \vee 0 \vee 0 \vee 1 = 2$.

In a similar manner the value of F may be computed for every combination and one obtains the tabular representation of a discrete function as shown in Figure 2.11.

The discrete function described by Figure 2.11 could also be described by another lattice expression, such as, e.g.:

$$G = (1 \vee x_1^{(0,2)} x_0^{(2)})(x_1^{(0,2)} \vee x_0^{(0)} \vee x_1^{(0,2,3)} x_0^{(0,1,3)})$$
$$(x_0^{(2)} \vee x_1^{(0,3)} x_0^{(1,2,3)} \vee x_1^{(2)} x_0^{(0,2)}). \tag{2.13}$$

$x_1 \backslash x_0$	0	1	2	3
0	0	1	2	1
1	0	0	0	0
2	1	0	2	0
3	0	1	0	1

Figure 2.11. Matrix representation of the lattice expression (2.12)

Since, as quoted above, every discrete function may be expressed in a number of ways by different lattice expressions, it comes naturally that some of these expressions will be preferred to some others according to, for example, a simplicity criterion; this will be extensively detailed in Chapters 3 and 8 devoted to the minimization of lattice expressions. Hence also the interest of the manipulation and simplification of lattice expressions.

The properties presented in section 1.3 provide the basic tools for the simplification of lattice expressions. In this section one will present an important type of lattice expression, namely the *normal form.*

Definition 2.16. If a discrete function is expressed as a disjunction of cube functions, it is called a *disjunctive normal form.* If a discrete function is expressed a conjunction of anticube functions, it is called a *conjunctive normal form.*

Every lattice expression may be expressed in a disjunctive normal form and in a conjunctive normal form by using the distributive laws in the lattice (see section 1.3); namely, if T_0, T_1 and T_2 are lattice expressions, then (distributivity) the following identities hold

$$T_0 \wedge (T_1 \vee T_2) = (T_0 \wedge T_1) \vee (T_0 \wedge T_2) \tag{2.14a}$$

$$T_0 \vee (T_1 \wedge T_2) = (T_0 \vee T_1) \wedge (T_0 \vee T_2). \tag{2.14b}$$

The expressions (2.14) permit a variety of manipulations on lattice expressions. In particular an iterative use of (2.14a) allows us to convert any lattice expression into a disjunctive normal form; dually, the use of (2.14b) leads to a conjunctive normal form of the lattice expression.

The distributive laws, together with the absorption law in the lattice (see section 1.3), enable us, for example (whenever possible) to convert a lattice expression into an equivalent one with fewer literals. This question will be extensively treated in Chapter 3.

Example 2.6 (continued). The lattice expression (2.12) is a disjunctive normal form of the discrete function represented by Figure 2.11. A discrete function may be expressed in a number of ways by disjunctive normal forms. For example, expression (2.15) constitutes another normal form of the same discrete function

$$F' = 2x_1^{(0,2)}\,x_0^{(2)} \vee 1x_1^{(2)}\,x_0^{(0)} \vee 1x_1^{(0,3)}\,x_0^{(1,3)}. \tag{2.15}$$

A conjunctive normal form of the discrete function is, for example, obtained from expression (2.15) by using distributivity of the disjunction with respect to the conjunction:

$$F'' = (1 \vee x_0^{(2)})\,(1 \vee x_1^{(0,2)})\,(x_1^{(2)} \vee x_0^{(1,2,3)})\,(x_1^{(0,3)} \vee x_0^{(0,2)})\,(x_1^{(0,2,3)} \vee x_0^{(0)})$$
$$(x_1^{(0,2)} \vee x_0^{(0,1,3)}). \tag{2.16}$$

General lattice expressions, and in particular the normal forms of a logic function, are of special importance for the design of logic networks.

As defined in section 2.1.1 a logic network may be viewed as a black-box computing a logic function; as was done in section 2.1.3 for switching networks, a more detailed definition of a logic network will now be given.

Consider the elementary logic networks (logic gates or primitives) of Figure 2.12. These are defined as follows:

(1) AND: the output is the minimum (or the conjunction) of all the inputs.
(2) OR: the output is the maximum (or the disjunction) of all the inputs.
(3) Exponentiation: the output is: $(\text{input})^{(C)}$.

Clearly the logic gates of Figure 2.12 correspond to the switching gates (1), (2) and (3) respectively of Figure 2.7.

A logic network is then defined as an interconnection of these gates in the same way as a switching network was defined as an interconnection of switching gates (see section 2.1.3).

Let us apply the above definition of a logic network to the realization of a logic expression (logic theory). First of all it should be noted that according to Vranesic

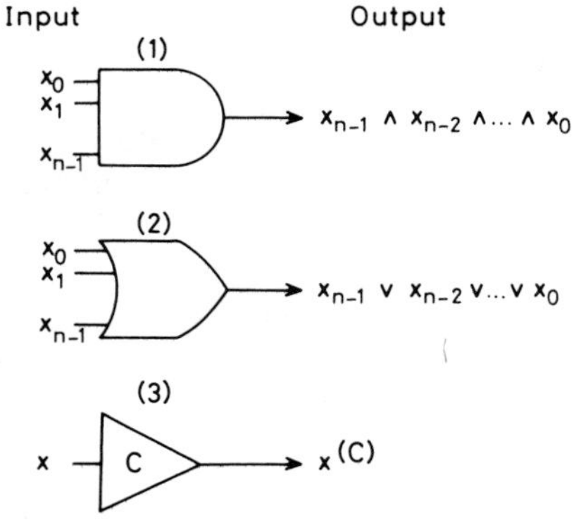

Figure 2.12. Logic gates or primitives

and Smith [1974] the number of useful and manageable logic gates is not large. Some of them, such as the AND- and the OR-gates, are very easily implemented; others require more complex electronic circuits, as in the case of the exponentiation gate (see for example, Allen and Givone [1968]).

Since a given logic function can be realized by a large number of logic networks, it is reasonable in selecting a network to use some criteria of simplicity. A traditional criterion of simplicity has been based on the cost of the electronics components (logic gates) used and on the interconnection complexity of these gates. Hence the importance of the logic design using standard forms.

Procedures for designing logic circuits corresponding to particularly attractive normal forms (from a simplicity criterion point of view) will be extensively discussed in Chapters 3 and 8. Let us however already now define a *normal logic network* associated to a normal logic expression. Consider for example a disjunctive normal form; corresponding to each cube function of a given normal form, let A_i be the output of an AND-gate. If all the AND-gate outputs feed the inputs of a single OR-gate, this type of network realizes the given lattice expression and is referred to as a *disjunctive normal logic network*, or simpler, as an *AND–OR network*. The general form of an AND–OR network is given in Figure 2.13.

The dual types of networks deriving from the conjunctive normal forms are called the *conjunctive normal logic networks*, or the *OR–AND networks*.

Note on cubical notations for normal forms

A cube is completely defined by its weight l and by the n subsets C_i; we use for a cube function

$$l \wedge \bigwedge_{i=n-1}^{0} x_i^{(C_i)}$$

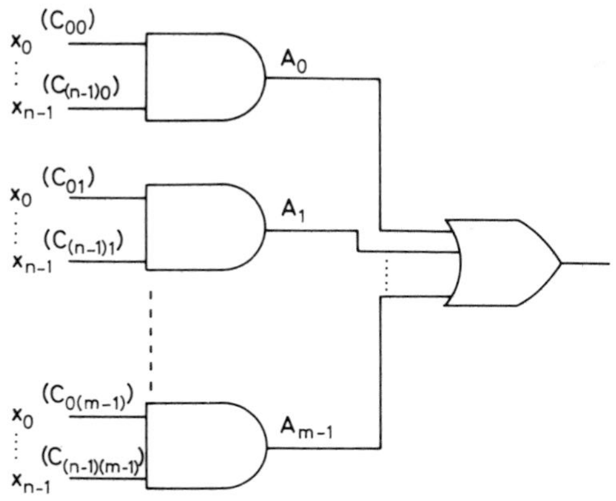

Figure 2.13. An AND–OR circuit realizing $\bigvee_{j=0}^{m-1} \left(\bigwedge_{i=n-1}^{0} x_i^{(C_{ij})} \right)$

the notation $\{l, C_{n-1}, \ldots, C_1, C_0\}$; a disjunctive normal form

$$\bigvee_{j=0}^{m-1} \left(l_j \wedge \bigwedge_{i=n-1}^{0} x_i^{(C_{ij})} \right)$$

may similarly be represented by an array:

$$\begin{bmatrix} l_0, & C_{(n-1)0}, \ldots, & C_{10}, & C_{00} \\ l_1, & C_{(n-1)1}, \ldots, & C_{11}, & C_{01} \\ \cdots & \cdots & \cdots & \cdots \\ l_{m-1}, & C_{(n-1)(m-1)}, \ldots, & C_{1(m-1)}, & C_{0(m-1)} \end{bmatrix}.$$

The above array is called the *cubical representation* of the corresponding normal form.

It must be recalled that cubical representations were introduced mainly because they are convenient for digital computer processing; for this reason it is generally also useful to represent the subsets C_{ij} of S_i by a vector of m_i bits or binary constants. The k_ith element of this vector is 1 if the element k_i of S_i is present in C_{ij}; it is 0 otherwise.

Example 2.6 (continued). The normal form (2.12) is the disjunction of four cubes; it is represented by the following cubical array:

$$\begin{bmatrix} 2 & (1\ 0\ 1\ 0) & (0\ 0\ 1\ 0) \\ 1 & (0\ 0\ 1\ 0) & (1\ 0\ 0\ 0) \\ 1 & (1\ 0\ 0\ 1) & (0\ 1\ 0\ 1) \\ 1 & (1\ 0\ 0\ 0) & (0\ 1\ 1\ 1) \end{bmatrix}.$$

Example 2.7. Consider the following normal form of a switching function:

$$x_5 x_4 \vee \bar{x}_4 x_0 \vee x_5 x_3 x_2 x_1.$$

It is represented by the following cubical array:

$$\begin{bmatrix} (0\ 1) & (0\ 1) & (1\ 1) & (1\ 1) & (1\ 1) & (1\ 1) \\ (1\ 1) & (1\ 0) & (1\ 1) & (1\ 1) & (1\ 1) & (0\ 1) \\ (0\ 1) & (1\ 1) & (0\ 1) & (0\ 1) & (0\ 1) & (1\ 1) \end{bmatrix}.$$

Clearly, since the weight of a cube is always 1 when dealing with switching functions, it may be dropped in the cube array representation. It is also of common use when dealing with switching functions (see for example Miller [1965] and Dietmeyer [1971]) to substitute the elements (0 1), (1 0) and (1 1) in the cubical arrays by 1,

0 and x respectively; the cubical array representation of the switching function of example 2.7 then becomes:

$$\begin{bmatrix} 1 & 1 & x & x & x & x \\ x & 0 & x & x & x & 1 \\ 1 & x & 1 & 1 & 1 & x \end{bmatrix}.$$

2.2.3. *Lattice canonical forms*

The discrete function f generated by a lattice expression F is the discrete function obtained from F by interpreting the letters $x_{n-1}, \ldots, x_1, x_0$ as variables in $S_{n-1}, \ldots, S_1, S_0$, the literals $x_{n-1}^{(C_{n-1})}, \ldots, x_1^{(C_1)}, x_0^{(C_0)}$ as the function defined by 2.9, and the operators $\vee$ and $\wedge$ as the lattice disjunction and conjunction respectively.

In the preceding sections we have emphasized the distinction between discrete functions and lattice expressions. The reason for doing so was that a lattice expression generates a single discrete function while a discrete function is generated by several lattice expressions. However, further on, we shall adopt the convention of using the same notations, that is, e.g. $f(\mathbf{x})$, for a lattice expression as well as for the discrete function.

We are now in position to carry out our promise and prove first that every discrete function is generated by at least one lattice expression.

Theorem 2.2. Every discrete function $f(\mathbf{x})$ can be written as the disjunction of the largest $\vee$-irreducible elements contained in $f(\mathbf{x})$:

$$f(\mathbf{x}) = \bigvee_{\mathbf{e}} \left[f(\mathbf{e}) \wedge \bigwedge_{i=n-1}^{0} x_i^{(e_i)} \right],$$

$$\mathbf{e} = (e_{n-1}, \ldots, e_1, e_0), \qquad 0 \leqslant e_i \leqslant m_i - 1. \tag{2.17}$$

Proof. As the variables $x_{n-1}, \ldots, x_1, x_0$ take on any of the Πm_i possible sets of values in $S = S_{n-1} \times \ldots \times S_1 \times S_0$, say for example $(x_{n-1}, \ldots, x_1, x_0) = (e_{n-1}, \ldots, e_1, e_0)$, only one term in the expression (2.17) is non-zero, namely the term

$$f(e_{n-1}, \ldots, e_1, e_0) \wedge x_{n-1}^{(e_{n-1})} \wedge \ldots \wedge x_1^{(e_1)} \wedge x_0^{(e_0)}$$

which at $x_{n-1} = e_{n-1}, \ldots, x_1 = e_1, x_0 = e_0$ is just $f(e_{n-1}, \ldots, e_1, e_0)$. ∎

It should be noted that theorem 2.2 derives from the general expansion theorem on distributive lattices which was proved in section 1.3.3.

Definition 2.17. The right-hand side of (2.17) is called the *canonical disjunctive form* of the function $f(\mathbf{x})$.

Each conjunction of the form $l \wedge x_{n-1}^{(e_{n-1})} \wedge \ldots \wedge x_1^{(e_1)} \wedge x_0^{(e_0)}$ is called a *minterm*.

The canonical disjunctive form was first obtained by Shannon [1949] for switching functions and by Davio and Bioul [1970] and Ying and Susskind [1971] for discrete functions.

Let $(\boldsymbol{x}_1, \boldsymbol{x}_0)$ be a partition of the set $\boldsymbol{x}$ of variables, with:

$$\boldsymbol{x}_1 = (x_{n-1}, \ldots, x_{q+1}, x_q),$$
$$\boldsymbol{x}_0 = (x_{q-1}, \ldots, x_1, x_0).$$

Every discrete function $f(\boldsymbol{x})$ can be written in the form:

$$f(\boldsymbol{x}) = \bigvee_{\boldsymbol{e}_0} \left\{ f(\boldsymbol{x}_1, \boldsymbol{e}_0) \wedge \bigwedge_{i=q-1}^{0} x_i^{(e_i)} \right\} \tag{2.18}$$

$$\boldsymbol{e}_0 = (e_{q-1}, \ldots, e_1, e_0), \quad 0 \leqslant e_i \leqslant m_i - 1.$$

Relation (2.18) is called the *partial canonical disjunctive form* of $f(\boldsymbol{x})$ with respect to $\boldsymbol{x}_0$. The proof of (2.18) is exactly the same as that of (2.17).

Theorem 2.3. Every discrete function $f(\boldsymbol{x})$ can be written as the conjunction of the smallest $\wedge$-irreducible elements containing $f(\boldsymbol{x})$:

$$f(\boldsymbol{x}) = \bigwedge_{\boldsymbol{e}} \left\{ f(\boldsymbol{e}) \vee \bigvee_{i=n-1}^{0} x_i^{(\bar{e}_i)} \right\}, \quad 0 \leqslant e_i \leqslant m_i - 1. \tag{2.19}$$

Proof. Similar to that of theorem 2.2.

Another proof is obtained by applying formula (2.17) to the function $\bar{f}$ and then taking the negation in both sides using theorem 2.1 and relations (2.5–2.10).

Definition 2.18. The right-hand side of relation (2.19) is called the *canonical conjunctive form* of the function $f(\boldsymbol{x})$.

Each disjunction of the form $l \vee x_{n-1}^{(\bar{e}_{n-1})} \vee \ldots \vee x_1^{(\bar{e}_1)} \vee x_0^{(\bar{e}_0)}$ is called a *maxterm*.

Every discrete function may also be written in the *partial canonical conjunctive form* with respect to $\boldsymbol{x}_0$, that is:

$$f(\boldsymbol{x}_1, \boldsymbol{x}_0) = \bigwedge_{\boldsymbol{e}} \left\{ f(\boldsymbol{x}_1, \boldsymbol{e}_0) \vee \bigvee_{i=q-1}^{0} x_i^{(\bar{e}_i)} \right\}, \quad 0 \leqslant e_i \leqslant m_i - 1. \tag{2.20}$$

One way of obtaining the canonical forms of any discrete function is by means of *Shannon's first expansion theorem* which states that any discrete function $f(x_{n-1}, \ldots, x_1, x_0)$ can be expressed as:

$$f(x_{n-1}, \ldots, x_1, x_0) = \bigvee_{e_{n-1}=m_{n-1}}^{0} \{(x_{n-1}^{(e_{n-1})} \wedge f(e_{n-1}, \ldots, x_1, x_0)\} \tag{2.21}$$

which is nothing but a particular case of (2.18). The expansion of (2.21) successively about the variables $x_{n-2}, \ldots, x_1$ and x_0 yields the canonical disjunctive form. In a similar manner, repeated applications of the dual expansion theorem:

$$f(x_{n-1},\ldots,x_1,x_0) = \bigwedge_{e_{n-1}=m_{n-1}}^{0} \{(x_{n-1}^{(\bar{e}_{n-1})} \vee f(e_{n-1},\ldots,x_1,x_0)\} \tag{2.22}$$

about the variables $x_{n-1},\ldots,x_1,x_0$ yield the canonical conjunctive form.

A probably faster procedure for obtaining the canonical disjunctive form of a discrete function is summarized as follows:

Algorithm 2.1. (a) Obtain a disjunctive normal form of the lattice expression by using the distributive laws.

(b) Examine each term; if it is a minterm, retain it and continue to the next term.

(c) In each cube which is not a minterm:

(1) Check the variables that do not occur; for each x_i that does not occur, multiply the cube by:

$(x_i^{(0)} \vee x_i^{(1)} \vee \ldots \vee x_i^{(m_i-1)})$.

(2) Check the literals $x_j^{(C_j)}$ with cardinality of $C_j > 1$; if:

$C_j = e_{j0} \cup e_{j1} \cup \ldots \cup e_{j(n_j-1)}$

with e_{ji} elements of C_j, replace $x_j^{(C_j)}$ by $\bigvee_i x_i^{(e_{ji})}$ (in view of (2.8)) in the cube.

(d) Multiply out all the cubes by using the distributive law of the disjunction with respect to the conjunction and retain only one occurrence of the terms that appear more than once and the terms that are not included in other ones.

An algorithm for obtaining the canonical conjunctive expansion of f is similarly obtained by applying the algorithm 2.1 to the function $\bar{f}$ and then taking the negation of the expression obtained, using theorem 2.1 and relations (2.5–2.10).

Example 2.6 (continued). Starting from the expression (2.12) one obtains successively:

$$\begin{aligned} f &= 2\,(x_1^{(0)} \vee x_1^{(2)})x_0^{(2)} \vee 1x_1^{(2)}x_0^{(0)} \vee 1(x_1^{(0)} \vee x_1^{(3)})\,(x_0^{(1)} \vee x_0^{(3)}) \vee 1x_1^{(0)}\,(x_0^{(1)} \vee \\ &\quad x_0^{(2)} \vee x_0^{(3)}) \\ &= 2x_1^{(0)}x_0^{(2)} \vee 2x_1^{(2)}x_0^{(2)} \vee 1x_1^{(2)}x_0^{(0)} \vee 1x_1^{(0)}x_0^{(1)} \vee 1x_1^{(0)}x_0^{(3)} \vee 1x_1^{(3)}x_0^{(1)} \vee \\ &\quad 1x_1^{(3)}x_0^{(3)} \end{aligned} \tag{2.23}$$

which is the canonical disjunctive form of the discrete function described by Figure 2.11.

Starting from the expression (2.16) one obtains successively:

$$\begin{aligned}\bar{f} &= 1x_0^{(0,1,3)} \vee 1x_1^{(1,3)} \vee 2x_1^{(0,1,3)}\, x_0^{(0)} \vee 2x_1^{(1,2)}\, x_0^{(1,3)} \vee 2x_1^{(1)}\, x_0^{(1,2,3)} \vee 2x_1^{(1,3)}\, x_0^{(2)}\\
&= 1(x_0^{(0)} \vee x_0^{(1)} \vee x_0^{(3)})\,(x_1^{(0)} \vee x_1^{(1)} \vee x_1^{(2)} \vee x_1^{(3)}) \vee 1(x_1^{(1)} \vee x_1^{(3)})\,(x_0^{(0)} \vee x_0^{(1)} \vee x_0^{(2)}\\
&\quad \vee x_0^{(3)}) \vee 2(x_1^{(0)} \vee x_1^{(1)} \vee x_1^{(3)})\,x_0^{(0)} \vee 2(x_1^{(1)} \vee x_1^{(2)})\,(x_0^{(1)} \vee x_0^{(3)}) \vee 2x_1^{(1)}(x_0^{(1)}\\
&\quad \vee x_0^{(2)} \vee x_0^{(3)}) \vee 2(x_1^{(1)} \vee x_1^{(3)})\,x_0^{(2)}\\
&= 2x_1^{(1)}\, x_0^{(2)} \vee 2x_1^{(3)}\, x_0^{(2)} \vee 2x_1^{(1)}\, x_0^{(1)} \vee 2x_1^{(1)}\, x_0^{(3)} \vee 2x_1^{(0)}\, x_0^{(0)} \vee 2x_1^{(1)}\, x_0^{(0)} \vee\\
&\quad 2x_1^{(3)}\, x_0^{(0)} \vee 2x_1^{(2)}\, x_0^{(1)} \vee 2x_1^{(2)}\, x_0^{(3)} \vee 1x_1^{(3)}\, x_0^{(1)} \vee 1x_1^{(3)}\, x_0^{(3)} \vee 1x_1^{(0)}\, x_0^{(1)} \vee\\
&\quad 1x_1^{(0)}\, x_0^{(3)} \vee 1x_1^{(2)}\, x_0^{(0)}\end{aligned}$$

$$\begin{aligned}f &= (x_1^{(0,2,3)} \vee x_0^{(0,1,3)})\,(x_1^{(0,1,2)} \vee x_0^{(0,1,3)})\\
&\quad (x_1^{(0,2,3)} \vee x_0^{(0,2,3)})\,(x_1^{(0,2,3)} \vee x_0^{(0,1,2)})\\
&\quad (x_1^{(1,2,3)} \vee x_0^{(1,2,3)})\,(x_1^{(0,2,3)} \vee x_0^{(1,2,3)})\\
&\quad (x_1^{(0,1,2)} \vee x_0^{(1,2,3)})\,(x_1^{(0,1,3)} \vee x_0^{(0,2,3)})\\
&\quad (x_1^{(0,1,3)} \vee x_0^{(0,1,2)})\,(1 \vee x_1^{(0,1,2)} \vee x_0^{(0,2,3)})\\
&\quad (1 \vee x_1^{(0,1,2)} \vee x_0^{(0,1,2)})\,(1 \vee x_1^{(1,2,3)} \vee x_0^{(0,2,3)})\\
&\quad (1 \vee x_1^{(1,2,3)} \vee x_0^{(0,1,2)})\,(1 \vee x_1^{(0,1,3)} \vee x_0^{(1,2,3)}).\end{aligned} \tag{2.24}$$

From the above theorems 2.2 and 2.3 we may conclude that the canonical disjunctive form and the canonical conjunctive form of a discrete function are unique (up to permutation of terms).

Two lattice expressions are said to be *equivalent* iff both expressions represent the same discrete function. Consequently, two lattice expressions are equivalent iff their canonical forms are identical. Thus in order to prove the equivalence of two lattice expressions, it is sufficient to expand both functions to their canonical forms and to compare the outcomes.

The value vector and the canonical forms are two unique representations of a discrete function. It is important to show that these representations are easily obtained from each other.

If a lattice expression which represents a discrete function is known, the value vector of this discrete function is obtained by giving to the variables $x_{n-1}, \ldots, x_1, x_0$ all the possible values successively in the lexicographical order. In particular, if the lattice expression is a canonical form, one has a systematic way to obtain the value vector (or any other graphical representation) from one of the two canonical forms.

Let us now assume that a function $f(x)$ be given by its value vector $[f(e)]$ considered here as a $(1 \times \Pi m_i)$ matrix. Define the $(1 \times m_i)$ matrix $[x_i^{(j)}]$ as follows:

$$[x_i^{(j)}] = [x_i^{(0)}, x_i^{(1)}, \ldots, x_i^{(m_i-1)}].$$

The notation $[\ \ ]^t$ means as usual the matrix transpose operation. Let the notation $\textcircled{\top\perp}$ denote a matrix multiplication with the additive law $\top$ and the multiplicative law $\perp$; let moreover $\overset{\perp}{\otimes}$ be a Kronecker matrix product with multiplication law $\perp$ (see section 1.5.3).

Theorem 2.4. The canonical disjunctive form of $f(\boldsymbol{x})$ is given by:

$$[f(e)] \textcircled{\vee\wedge} \left(\overset{\wedge}{\underset{i=n-1,0}{\otimes}} [x_i^{(j)}] \right)^t. \qquad (2.25)$$

Proof. The proof is achieved by perfect induction.
Initial step. For $n = 1$, a routine verification shows that:

$$[f(0), f(1), \ldots, f(m-1)] \textcircled{\vee\wedge} [x^{(0)}, x^{(1)}, \ldots, x^{(m-1)}]^t = \bigvee_{e=0}^{m-1} \{f(e) \wedge x^{(e)}\}.$$

Induction step. We assume as induction hypothesis that (2.25) holds true for any function $f(\boldsymbol{x})$ of n variables; now if $g_c(e_n, \boldsymbol{x})$, $0 \leqslant e_n \leqslant m_n - 1$, are the canonical disjunctive forms of the m_n functions $g(e_n, \boldsymbol{x})$ respectively, the canonical disjunctive form of the function $g(x_n, \boldsymbol{x})$, $x_n \in S_n = \{0, 1, \ldots, m_n - 1\}$ is:

$$[g_c(0, \boldsymbol{x}), g_c(1, \boldsymbol{x}), \ldots, g_c(m_n - 1, \boldsymbol{x})] \textcircled{\vee\wedge} [x_n^{(0)}, x_n^{(1)}, \ldots, x_n^{(m_n-1)}]^t.$$

This is a direct consequence of (2.25) and of the definition of the canonical disjunctive form. ■

Theorem 2.5. The canonical conjunctive form of $f(\boldsymbol{x})$ is given by:

$$[f(e)] \textcircled{\wedge\vee} \left(\overset{\vee}{\underset{i=n-1,0}{\otimes}} \overline{[x_i^{(j)}]} \right)^t \qquad (2.26)$$

with $\overline{[x_i^{(j)}]}$ *the negation of* $[x_i^{(j)}]$.

Proof. Dual type of proof to that of theorem 2.4.

Example 2.6 (continued). The value vector of the example 2.5 is:

[0 1 2 1 0 0 0 0 1 0 2 0 0 1 0 1]

One then easily verifies that

$$[0121 \ \ 0000 \ \ 1020 \ \ 0101] \textcircled{\vee\wedge} \left(\begin{bmatrix} x_1^{(0)} \\ x_1^{(1)} \\ x_1^{(2)} \\ x_1^{(3)} \end{bmatrix} \overset{\wedge}{\otimes} \begin{bmatrix} x_0^{(0)} \\ x_0^{(1)} \\ x_0^{(2)} \\ x_0^{(3)} \end{bmatrix} \right)$$

and

$$[0121 \quad 0000 \quad 1020 \quad 0101] \; \widehat{\wedge\vee} \left(\begin{bmatrix} x_1^{(\bar{0})} \\ x_1^{(\bar{1})} \\ x_1^{(\bar{2})} \\ x_1^{(\bar{3})} \end{bmatrix} \underset{\otimes}{\vee} \begin{bmatrix} x_0^{(\bar{0})} \\ x_0^{(\bar{1})} \\ x_0^{(\bar{2})} \\ x_0^{(\bar{3})} \end{bmatrix} \right)$$

yield expressions (2.23) and (2.24) respectively.

2.3. The module structure of discrete functions

2.3.1. Definitions and ring notations

Let $\{L, \oplus, ., 0, 1\}$ be the ring of integers $0, 1, \ldots, r-1$, under the modulo r sum ($\oplus$ or Σ) and the modulo r product (no symbol or Π) with the identity elements 0 and 1 for the sum and the product respectively. The modulo r sum (also called ring sum or sum) $f \oplus g$ and the modulo r product (also called ring product or product) fg of two discrete functions f and g

$$f: S \to L,$$

$$g: S \to L,$$

are defined to be the componentwise extensions of the modulo r sum and of the modulo r product in L respectively, i.e.:

$$[(f \oplus g)_e] = [f_e \oplus g_e]$$

$$[(fg)_e] = [f_e\, g_e].$$

Let $l \in L$; the modulo r sum $l \oplus f$ and the modulo r product lf of the discrete function f and of the ring element l are defined by

$$[(l \oplus f)_e] = [l \oplus f_e]$$

$$[(lf)_e] = [lf_e].$$

With these definitions, the set of discrete functions $S \to L$ is an L-module of functions (see section 1.4).

The additive inverse of f is denoted by $(-f)$. Generating sets and bases were already introduced in section 1.4. Consider the L-module of functions defined above.

A *generating set* of that module is a family $\{f_0, f_1, \ldots, f_{M-1}\}$ of functions such that any discrete function $f: S \to L$ may be expressed in the form:

$$f = \sum_{i=0}^{M-1} l_i f_i, \quad l_i \in L. \tag{2.27}$$

A generating set is a *basis* if it contains the minimum number of functions f_i; that number is given by the product $(m_{n-1} \times \ldots \times m_1 \times m_0) = N$. Indeed, since $f(e)$ takes its values in the set L (with cardinality r) and since e takes its values in the set S (with cardinality N) there are r^N discrete functions. Note also that since the number of functions in a basis is minimum, the expansion of a given function in a basis must be unique.

Definition 2.19 (*ring exponentiation*).

$$\tilde{x}_i^{(C_i)} = 1 \quad \text{iff} \quad x_i \in C_i,$$
$$= 0 \quad \text{otherwise.}$$

Since 1 is the identity element for the modulo r product, one has:

$$1\tilde{x}_i^{(C_i)} = \tilde{x}_i^{(C_i)}. \tag{2.28}$$

Let us compare the lattice exponentiation $x_i^{(C_i)}$ with the ring exponentiation $\tilde{x}_i^{(C_i)}$; the following relation holds:

$$l \wedge x_i^{(C_i)} = l\tilde{x}_i^{(C_i)}. \tag{2.29}$$

An equality such as (2.29) may evidently only be written if the element l always explicitly appears in both sides of the expression, even if it is the identity element $(r-1)$ for the conjunction or the identity element 1 for the modulo r product.

Definition 2.20. By a ***ring expression*** we mean a well-formed expression (see section 1.2) made up of the following symbols:

(a) the ring elements $0, 1, \ldots, r-1$,
(b) The variables $\tilde{x}_i^{(C_i)}$,
(c) the two binary ring operations
 $\oplus$ standing for the ring sum,
 . or absence of symbol standing for the ring product.

As it will be seen in section 2.3.2, any discrete function may be described by a ring expression. Conversely, every ring expression is clearly a discrete function since its arguments x_i and values are in S and in L respectively. Each of the variables $x_{n-1}, \ldots, x_1, x_0$ can independently assume any one of the values in $S_{n-1}, \ldots, S_1, S_0$ respectively. In order to determine the value of a ring expression for a given combination it is sufficient to substitute the value for the variables in the expression. A discrete function value vector or value matrix, for example, is obtained from any ring expression in the same way as it was obtained from a lattice expression (see section 2.2.2).

The relation (2.29) allows us to write any cube function in terms of ring operations, i.e.:

$$l \wedge \bigwedge_{i=n-1}^{0} x_i^{(C_i)} = l \prod_{i=n-1}^{0} \tilde{x}_i^{(C_i)}. \tag{2.30}$$

Further, the modulo r product of two cubes

$$l_0 \prod_{i=n-1}^{0} \tilde{x}_i^{(C_{i0})} \quad \text{and} \quad l_1 \prod_{i=n-1}^{0} \tilde{x}_i^{(C_{i1})}$$

is given by

$$l_0 l_1 \prod_{i=n-1}^{0} \tilde{x}_i^{(C_{i1} \cap C_{i0})}. \tag{2.31}$$

Definition 2.21. A cube function such that the cardinality of each C_i is unity and such that $l = 1$ is a *Lagrange function.*

Let us recall that in classical analysis a Lagrange function is defined as a function which takes the value 1 at one point of the domain to be considered, and the value 0 at any other point. If one takes $C_i = \{e_i\}\ \forall i$ with e_i an element of S_i, the Lagrange function taking the value 1 at $\boldsymbol{x} = \boldsymbol{e}$ is written:

$$\prod_{i=n-1}^{0} \tilde{x}_i^{(e_i)}. \tag{2.32}$$

The following notation will be adopted:

if $C_i = \{a_{i0}, a_{i1}, \ldots, a_{i(n_i-1)}\}$,

then $\tilde{x}_i^{(C_i)}$ will be written $\tilde{x}_i^{(a_{i0}, a_{i1}, \ldots, a_{i(n_i-1)})}$.

Example 2.8. Consider the ring expression

$$F = 3\tilde{x}_1^{(2,3,4)}\,\tilde{x}_0^{(2,3,4)} \oplus \tilde{x}_1^{(1,2,3)}\,\tilde{x}_0^{(1,2)} \oplus 4\tilde{x}_1^{(1)}. \tag{2.33}$$

If $S_1 = S_0 = L = \{0, 1, 2, 3, 4\}$, the above expression describes a logic function:

$$f: \{0, 1, 2, 3, 4\}^2 \to \{0, 1, 2, 3, 4\}.$$

This function is also described by the matrix of Figure 2.14 which is obtained from (2.33) in the way explained in this section.

$x_1 \backslash x_0$	0	1	2	3	4
0	0	0	0	0	0
1	4	0	0	4	4
2	0	1	4	3	3
3	0	1	4	3	3
4	0	0	3	3	3

Figure 2.14. Matrix representation of the ring expression (2.33)

It is also clear that every discrete function may be expressed in a number of ways by different ring expressions. The discrete function of Figure 2.14 may also be expressed by the ring expression (2.34):

$$\begin{aligned} F' = {} & \tilde{x}_1^{(2,3)}\,(4 \oplus \tilde{x}_0^{(1,2,3,4)}) \oplus \\ & \tilde{x}_1^{(2,3,4)}\,(2\tilde{x}_0^{(2,3,4)} \oplus 1\tilde{x}_0^{(2)}) \oplus \\ & 1\tilde{x}_1^{(1,3,4)}\,\tilde{x}_0^{(3,4)} \oplus 3\tilde{x}_1^{(1)}\,\tilde{x}_0^{(0,3,4)} \oplus \\ & 1\tilde{x}_1^{(1,2,3)}\,\tilde{x}_0^{(0)} \oplus 1\tilde{x}_1^{(2,3)}\,\tilde{x}_0^{(1,2)} \oplus 1\tilde{x}_1^{(2)}\,\tilde{x}_0^{(3,4)}. \end{aligned} \tag{2.34}$$

The ring expressions may be manipulated, e.g. by using the distributivity of the ring sum with respect to the ring product (see section 1.4.2).

Let us again note that when dealing with general functions the ring constants l become a vector of ring constants, and in the different relations and equations, the ring sum and the ring product have to be performed componentwise.

Let us briefly consider the particular case of switching and of binary functions. Since for these functions $(r-1) = 1$, the lattice exponentiation $x_i^{(C_i)}$ coincides with the ring exponentiation $\tilde{x}_i^{(C_i)}$ in the expressions describing them. Moreover, for the variables appearing in a switching expression (that is an expression describing a switching function), one has:

$$\begin{aligned} & \tilde{x}_i^{(1)} = x_i^{(1)} = x_i \quad \text{(direct form of } x_i\text{)} \\ & \tilde{x}_i^{(0)} = x_i^{(0)} = \bar{x}_i = 1 \oplus x_i \quad \text{(complemented form of } x_i\text{).} \end{aligned} \tag{2.35}$$

Let us make some comments on the logical design aspect of ring expressions. It will be proved in the next section that every discrete function may be represented by at least one ring expression. Thus, in the same way as elementary logic gates or primitives realizing basic lattice operations could be used for computing logic functions (see section 2.2.2), logic networks might be built up by interconnecting logic gates realizing the ring sum, the ring product and the ring exponentiation. Let us first observe that in view of relations (2.29–2.30) the same type of electronic devices may be used for realizing (a) the lattice and the ring exponentiations and (b) the conjunction and the ring product respectively. On the other hand electronic networks realizing the ring sum $\oplus$ are now available (see for example Brusentzov [1965], Druzeta, Vranesic and Sedra [1974]). Primitives realizing the ring sum are a generalization of the XOR-gate used in switching theory and defined in section 2.1.3; the same graphical symbol will thus be used in the sequel for describing both switching and logic gates.

2.3.2. *The Lagrange canonical form*

Let C_{i0} and $C_{i1} \subseteq S_i$ with $C_{i0} \cap C_{i1} = \phi$ (empty set); one has:

$$(l \wedge x_i^{(C_{i0})}) \vee (l \wedge x_i^{(C_{i1})}) = l x_i^{(C_{i0})} \oplus l x_i^{(C_{i1})} \tag{2.36}$$

since the sets C_{i0} and C_{i1} are disjoint.

Theorem 2.6 (Lagrange expansion theorem). The set of Lagrange functions is a basis for the discrete functions

$$f: S \to L.$$

Proof. The set of functions

$$\left\{ \prod_{i=n-1}^{0} \tilde{x}_i^{(e_i)}, \quad (e_{n-1}, \ldots, e_1, e_0) \in S_{n-1} \times \ldots \times S_1 \times S_0 \right\}$$

is a basis. Indeed, it contains $m_{n-1} \times \ldots \times m_1 \times m_0 = N$ functions and from theorem 2.2 one successively deduces that every discrete function $f(\boldsymbol{x})$ can be written in the forms:

$$f(\boldsymbol{x}) = \bigvee_{\boldsymbol{e}} [f(\boldsymbol{e}) \prod_{i=n-1}^{0} \tilde{x}_i^{(e_i)}] \quad \text{(in view of (2.30))}$$

$$= \sum_{\boldsymbol{e}} [f(\boldsymbol{e}) \prod_{i=n-1}^{0} \tilde{x}_i^{(e_i)}] \quad \text{(in view of (2.36))}$$

$$\boldsymbol{e} = (e_{n-1}, \ldots, e_1, e_0), \quad 0 \leqslant e_i \leqslant m_i - 1. \tag{2.37}$$

■

Definition 2.22. The right-hand side of relation (2.37) is said to be the *Lagrange (canonical) form* of the function $f(\boldsymbol{x})$.

It will sometimes be useful to describe *partial Lagrange forms*; they are defined according to the same rule as the partial disjunctive form. A similar type of proof as for theorem 2.6 shows that any discrete function $f(\boldsymbol{x})$ may be written in the partial Lagrange form:

$$f(\boldsymbol{x}_1, \boldsymbol{x}_0) = \sum_{\boldsymbol{e}_0} \left\{ f(\boldsymbol{x}_1, \boldsymbol{e}_0) \prod_{i=q-1}^{0} \tilde{x}_i^{(e_i)} \right\}, \quad \boldsymbol{e}_0 = (e_{q-1}, \ldots, e_1, e_0). \tag{2.38}$$

Two ring expressions are said to be equivalent iff both expressions represent the same discrete functions and thus, equivalently, if both expressions have the same Lagrange form.

Methods have been described in section 2.2.3 for obtaining canonical disjunctive forms of a discrete function from a lattice expression representing it. Expressions (2.30, 2.36) and theorem 2.6 allow us to transform any of these methods in order to obtain the Lagrange form of a discrete function from any of its ring expressions.

A first method derives from an iterated use of the following relation:

$$f(x_{n-1}, \ldots, x_1, x_0) = \sum_{e_{n-1}=m_{n-1}}^{0} \tilde{x}_{n-1}^{(e_{n-1})} f(e_{n-1}, x_{n-2}, \ldots, x_1, x_0) \tag{2.39}$$

which comes from (2.21).

Another procedure is:

Algorithm 2.2

(a) Obtain a (modulo r) sum of (modulo r) products form of the ring expression by using the distributive law.
(b) Examine each product term; if it is a Lagrange function (possibly multiplied by a ring element) retain it and continue to the next term.
(c) In each product term which is not a Lagrange function:

1. Check the variables that do not occur; for each x_i that does not occur, multiply the product by

$$(\tilde{x}_i^{(0)} \oplus \tilde{x}_i^{(1)} \oplus \ldots \oplus \tilde{x}_i^{(m_i-1)}).$$

2. Check the literals $\tilde{x}_j^{(C_j)}$ with cardinality of $C_j > 1$; if

$$C_j = e_{j0} \cup e_{j1} \cup \ldots \cup e_{j(n_j-1)}$$

with e_{ji} elements of C_j, replace $\tilde{x}_j^{(C_j)}$ by $\sum_j \tilde{x}_j^{(e_{ji})}$ in the product term.

(d) Multiply out all the products by using the distributive law and gather the terms by adding all the coefficients of the same Lagrange function.

Theorem 2.7. below allows us to obtain the Lagrange form of a discrete function from its value vector; it is a straightforward consequence of theorem 2.4.

Theorem 2.7. The Lagrange form of $f(x)$ is given by:

$$[f(e)] \; \textcircled{\oplus \cdot} \left\{ \dot{\bigotimes}_{i=n-1,0} (\tilde{x}_i^{(j_i)}) \right\}^t \tag{2.40}$$

with $[\tilde{x}_i^{(j_i)}]$ *the* $(1 \times m_i)$ *matrix*

$$[\tilde{x}_i^{(0)}, \tilde{x}_i^{(1)}, \ldots, \tilde{x}_i^{(m_i-1)}].$$

2.3.3. *Transformation of a lattice expression into a ring expression and vice versa*

It is always possible to transform a given lattice expression into a ring expression by transforming it first into, for example, its lattice disjunctive canonical form or its value vector form. The transformation from the canonical disjunctive form or from the value vector form into the Lagrange canonical form may then be performed by use of theorems 2.6 or 2.7 respectively. Conversely, the Lagrange form or the value vector form may be used as intermediate representation for obtaining a lattice expression equivalent to a ring expression. (A ring expression will be said to be equivalent to a lattice expression if they are both representations of the same discrete function.) While straightforward, these transformations using the value vector or any canonical form as intermediate step generally request lengthy computations, especially when the number of variables and when the cardinalities of their domains are large. Hence the interest of a method developed in this section for transforming directly ring and lattice expressions into each other without resorting to an intermediate form.

Let us first assume that a function $f(\boldsymbol{x})$ is given by means of a ring expression. We shall first transform this ring expression into a (modulo r) sum of (modulo r) products expression by using the distributivity law.

Lemma 2.1. Let f be given as a sum of k cubes:

$$f = \sum_{j=0}^{k-1} l_j \left(\prod_{i=n-1}^{0} \tilde{x}_i^{(C_{ij})} \right). \tag{2.41}$$

An equivalent disjunctive form of f is then:

$$f = \bigvee_{a} \left[\left(\sum_{j=0}^{k-1} l_j\, a_j \right) \prod_{j=0}^{k-1} \widetilde{\left(\prod_{i=n-1}^{0} \tilde{x}_i^{(C_{ij})} \right)}^{(a_j)} \right] \tag{2.42}$$

$$0 \leqslant a_j \leqslant 1, \quad 0 < a = (a_{k-1}, \ldots, a_1, a_0).$$

Proof. Consider a vertex $\boldsymbol{h} = (h_{n-1}, \ldots, h_1, h_0)$ of $\boldsymbol{x}$; at this point the following relations hold:

$$\widetilde{\left(\prod_{i=n-1}^{0} \tilde{x}_i^{(C_{ij})} \right)}_{\boldsymbol{x}=\boldsymbol{h}} = 1 \quad \forall\, j = 0, 1, \ldots, q-1,$$

$$\widetilde{\left(\prod_{i=n-1}^{0} \tilde{x}_i^{(C_{ij})} \right)}_{\boldsymbol{x}=\boldsymbol{h}} = 0 \quad \forall\, j = q, q+1, \ldots, k-1.$$

Both expressions (2.41) and (2.42) take then at this point the same value, namely $l_0 \oplus l_1 \oplus \ldots \oplus l_{q-1}$. Since the point $\boldsymbol{h}$ is arbitrarily chosen the lemma is proven. ∎

The expression (2.42) will now be transformed according to the following rules. First the exponentiation present in (2.42) will be performed as follows (in view of De Morgan's law):

$$\begin{aligned} \widetilde{\left(\prod_{i=n-1}^{0} \tilde{x}_i^{(C_{ij})} \right)}^{(a_j)} &= \prod_{i=n-1}^{0} \tilde{x}_i^{(C_{ij})} \quad \text{iff } a_j = 1 \\ &= \bigvee_{i=k-1}^{0} \tilde{x}_i^{(\bar{C}_{ij})} \quad \text{iff } a_j = 0. \end{aligned} \tag{2.43}$$

The distributive law allows us to transform the expression (2.42) (after substitution of the exponentiations by means of relations (2.43)) into a disjunctive form of the type

$$\bigvee_{j=0}^{k'-1} l'_j \left(\prod_{i=n-1}^{0} x_i^{(C'_{ij})} \right) \tag{2.44}$$

which can then, in view of relation (2.30), be transformed into the equivalent lattice expression:

$$\bigvee_{j=0}^{k'-1} l_j' \left(\bigwedge_{i=n-1}^{0} \tilde{x}_i^{(C_{ij}')} \right). \tag{2.45}$$

Starting from a sum of product ring expressions, the above algorithm allows us to obtain an equivalent disjunctive normal lattice expression.

Example 2.8 (continued). A ring expression of the type (2.41) is given by (2.33); this last relation will first be transformed into a disjunctive form (2.42), that is:

$$3\ [\widetilde{(\tilde{x}_1^{(2,3,4)}\ \tilde{x}_0^{(2,3,4)})^{(1)}}\ \widetilde{(\tilde{x}_1^{(1,2,3)}\ \tilde{x}_0^{(1,2)})^{(0)}}\ \widetilde{(\tilde{x}_1^{(1)})^{(0)}}]\ \vee$$

$$1\ [\widetilde{(\tilde{x}_1^{(1,2,3)}\ \tilde{x}_0^{(1,2)})^{(1)}}\ \widetilde{(\tilde{x}_1^{(2,3,4)}\ \tilde{x}_0^{(2,3,4)})^{(0)}}\ \widetilde{(\tilde{x}_1^{(1)})^{(0)}}]\ \vee$$

$$4\ [\widetilde{(\tilde{x}_1^{(1)})^{(1)}}\ \widetilde{(\tilde{x}_1^{(1,2,3)}\ \tilde{x}_0^{(1,2)})^{(0)}}\ \widetilde{(\tilde{x}_1^{(2,3,4)}\ \tilde{x}_0^{(2,3,4)})^{(0)}}]\ \vee$$

$$(3 \oplus 1)\ [\widetilde{(\tilde{x}_1^{(2,3,4)}\ \tilde{x}_0^{(2,3,4)})^{(1)}}\ \widetilde{(\tilde{x}_1^{(1,2,3)}\ \tilde{x}_0^{(1,2)})^{(1)}}\ \widetilde{(\tilde{x}_1^{(1)})^{(0)}}]\ \vee$$

$$(4 \oplus 3)\ [\widetilde{(\tilde{x}_1^{(2,3,4)}\ \tilde{x}_0^{(2,3,4)})^{(1)}}\ \widetilde{(\tilde{x}_1^{(1)})^{(1)}}\ \widetilde{(\tilde{x}_1^{(1,2,3)}\ \tilde{x}_0^{(1,2)})^{(0)}}]\ \vee$$

$$(4 \oplus 1)\ [\widetilde{(\tilde{x}_1^{(1,2,3)}\ \tilde{x}_0^{(1,2)})^{(1)}}\ \widetilde{(\tilde{x}_1^{(1)})^{(1)}}\ \widetilde{(\tilde{x}_1^{(2,3,4)}\ \tilde{x}_0^{(2,3,4)})^{(0)}}]\ \vee$$

$$(4 \oplus 3 \oplus 1)\ [\widetilde{(\tilde{x}_1^{(2,3,4)}\ \tilde{x}_0^{(2,3,4)})^{(1)}}\ \widetilde{(\tilde{x}_1^{(1,2,3)}\ \tilde{x}_0^{(1,2)})^{(1)}}\ \widetilde{(\tilde{x}_1^{(1)})^{(1)}}].$$

The formulae (2.43) applied to the above expression yield:

$$3\tilde{x}_1^{(2,3,4)}\ \tilde{x}_0^{(2,3,4)}\ (\tilde{x}_1^{(4,0)} \vee \tilde{x}_0^{(3,0)})\ \tilde{x}_1^{(2,3,4,0)} \vee$$

$$1\tilde{x}_1^{(1,2,3)}\ \tilde{x}_0^{(1,2)}\ (\tilde{x}_1^{(0,1)} \vee \tilde{x}_0^{(0,1)})\ \tilde{x}_1^{(2,3,4,0)} \vee$$

$$4\tilde{x}_1^{(1)}\ (\tilde{x}_1^{(4,0)} \vee \tilde{x}_0^{(3,4,0)})\ (\tilde{x}_1^{(1,2,3,4)} \vee \tilde{x}_0^{(0,1)}) \vee$$

$$(3 \oplus 1)\ \tilde{x}_1^{(2,3)}\ \tilde{x}_1^{(2,3,4,0)}\ \tilde{x}_0^{(2)} \vee$$

$$(4 \oplus 1)\ \tilde{x}_1^{(1)}\ \tilde{x}_0^{(1,2)}\ (\tilde{x}_1^{(0,1)} \vee \tilde{x}_0^{(0,1)}).$$

The distributive law and the simplification of the exponentiation expressions allow us to write:

$$4\tilde{x}_1^{(2,3)}\ \tilde{x}_0^{(2)} \vee 3\tilde{x}_1^{(2,3,4)}\ \tilde{x}_0^{(3,4)} \vee 3\tilde{x}_1^{(4)}\ \tilde{x}_0^{(2,3,4)} \vee 1\tilde{x}_1^{(2,3)}\ \tilde{x}_0^{(1)} \vee 4\tilde{x}_1^{(1)}\ \tilde{x}_0^{(3,4,0)},$$

which corresponds to the expression (2.42). The obtention of the lattice expression is then straightforward, i.e.:

$$4x_1^{(2,3)}\ x_0^{(2)} \vee 3x_1^{(2,3,4)}\ x_0^{(3,4)} \vee 3x_1^{(4)}\ x_0^{(2,3,4)} \vee 1x_1^{(2,3)}\ x_0^{(1)} \vee 4x_1^{(1)}\ x_0^{(3,4,0)}.$$

The intermediate steps in the above computation have been written explicitly for greater lucidity. Practically all of them may be avoided in the course of computation.

From a computational point of view the above algorithm is easily performed in a step-by-step way. If f is represented as a sum of cubes $c_0 \oplus c_1 \oplus \ldots \oplus c_{k-1}$, we will first compute the lattice expression of $c_0 \oplus c_1$ that is c_{01}, next, the lattice expression of $c_0 \oplus c_1 \oplus c_2 = c_2 \oplus c_{01}$, that is c_{012}, and so on.

It is worthwhile pointing out that for switching variables x_0 and x_1, lemma 2.1 allows us for example, to obtain the well-known identity

$$x_0 \oplus x_1 = x_0 \bar{x}_1 \vee x_1 \bar{x}_0. \tag{2.46}$$

One has indeed successively:

$$x_0 \oplus x_1 = (1 \oplus 1)\, x_1^{(1)} x_0^{(1)} \vee (0 \oplus 1)\, x_1^{(0)} x_0^{(1)} \vee (1 \oplus 0)\, x_1^{(1)} x_0^{(0)} \vee$$

$$(0 \oplus 0)\, x_1^{(0)} x_0^{(0)}$$

$$= x_1^{(0)} x_0^{(1)} \vee x_1^{(1)} x_0^{(0)} = \bar{x}_1 x_0 \vee x_1 \bar{x}_0.$$

Starting from a ring expression of f, an equivalent conjunctive form of f could, for example, be obtained by:

(a) applying lemma (2.1) to the negation $\bar{f}$ of f in order to obtain an equivalent disjunctive form of $\bar{f}$,
(b) taking the negation of the disjunctive form of $\bar{f}$ by using the De Morgan law.

An interesting application of lemma 2.1 may be found in the frame of maximization of pseudo-logic functions. It has been pointed out in section 2.1.1 that a large class of problems in operations research, graph theory and combinatorics can be reduced to the following one: find the set of all points in $\{0, 1\}^n$ where a given pseudo-logic function takes its maximum or its minimum value. It is quite evident that the set of all points in $\{0, 1\}^n$ where a given pseudo-logic function f takes its maximum value may easiest be found when the latter is given in a disjunctive normal form; dually, the set of all points in $\{0, 1\}^n$ where a given pseudo-logic function f takes its minimum value is trivially obtained when the latter is given as a conjunctive normal form. Now, the problems whose formulation results in the minimization or in the maximization of pseudo-logic functions generally provide us with a representation of that function as a real sum of cubes, that is:

$$f = \sum_{j=0}^{k-1} l_j \left(\prod_{i=n-1}^{0} \tilde{x}_i^{(\epsilon_{ij})} \right), \quad \epsilon_{ij} \in \{0, 1\} \forall i, j. \tag{2.47}$$

Lemma 2.1 allows us to write down a disjunctive equivalent expression of (2.47), that is:

$$f = \bigvee_a \left\{ \left(\sum_{j=0}^{k-1} l_j a_j \right) \overbrace{\prod_{j=0}^{k-1} \left(\prod_{i=n-1}^{0} \tilde{x}_i^{(\epsilon_{ij})} \right)^{(a_j)}} \right\} \tag{2.48}$$

which can then be transformed into a lattice equivalent expression according to the algorithm described in this section.

Example 2.9. Consider a pseudo-logic function given as a sum of cubes:

$$f = 3 + \tilde{x}_0^{(1)} + 2\tilde{x}_1^{(1)} + \tilde{x}_0^{(1)}\,\tilde{x}_2^{(1)} - \tilde{x}_1^{(1)}\,\tilde{x}_2^{(1)} - 2\tilde{x}_0^{(1)}\,\tilde{x}_1^{(1)}. \tag{2.49}$$

Application of formula (2.48) yields:

$$f = 3x_0^{(0)}\,x_1^{(0)} \vee 4x_0^{(1)}\,x_2^{(0)} \vee 4x_1^{(1)}\,x_2^{(1)} \vee 5x_0^{(0)}\,x_1^{(1)}\,x_2^{(0)} \vee 5x_0^{(1)}\,x_1^{(0)}\,x_2^{(1)}, \tag{2.50}$$

from which one deduces that f takes its maximal value 5 at the vertices:

$$x_2x_1x_0 = 0\ 1\ 0,$$
$$\ 1\ 0\ 1.$$

Let us observe that, for a pseudo-logic function described by a lattice expression, the lattice exponentiation $x_i^{(C_i)}$ can be strictly defined only once the maximum value of that pseudo-logic function is known, since, in view of definition 2.9, one has:

$$\begin{aligned} x_i^{(C_i)} &= \text{maximum value of the pseudo-logic function} \\ &\quad \text{iff} \quad x_i \in C_i \\ &= 0 \quad \text{otherwise.} \end{aligned}$$

However, for practical problems (e.g. as the one developed under example 2.9) the cubes appearing in the disjunctive normal form of a pseudo-logic function are always multiplied by a lattice constant so that the lattice exponentiations may practically be written down without knowing the maximal value of the function.

Let us note that the negation of a pseudo-logic function may only be written if the maximal value of this function is known, since by definition of the negation one has:

$$\bar{f} = (\text{maximal value}) - f.$$

This remark has its importance if one wants, for example, to use the inverse of a pseudo-logic function in order to determine its minimal values as it was suggested earlier in this section.

It is important to note that when dealing with pseudo-logic functions it is of common use and unambiguous (see for example, Hammer and Rudeanu [1968]) to substitute both

$$x^{(1)} \text{ and } \tilde{x}^{(1)} \text{ by } x$$

and both

$$x^{(0)} \text{ and } \tilde{x}^{(0)} \text{ by } \bar{x} = 1 - x.$$

Let us observe that this last definition of $\bar{x}$ is different from the definition of negation used before, i.e.:

$$\bar{x} = (r-1) - x.$$

Moreover, when using the above notation, the real product is always used in the cube terms instead of the conjunction. By use of the above conventions, equations (2.49) and (2.50) become respectively:

$$f = 3 + x_0 + 2x_1 + x_0x_2 - x_1x_2 - 2x_0x_1 \tag{2.51a}$$

$$f = 3\bar{x}_0\bar{x}_1 \vee 4x_0\bar{x}_2 \vee 4x_1x_2 \vee 5\bar{x}_0x_1\bar{x}_2 \vee 5x_0\bar{x}_1x_2. \tag{2.51b}$$

Let us also note that the De Morgan laws hold under the negation $\bar{x} = 1 - x$. Finally, it is not only because pseudo-logic functions were considered as a particular case of a more general theory that the notations of (2.47–2.50) were adopted above; these notations are indeed a more powerful tool for manipulating pseudo-logic expressions as it will be seen below.

Example 2.9 (*continued*). The negation of the logic function (2.49) is:

$$\bar{f} = 5 - f$$
$$= 2 - \tilde{x}_0^{(1)} - 2\tilde{x}_1^{(1)} - \tilde{x}_0^{(1)}\tilde{x}_2^{(1)} + \tilde{x}_1^{(1)}\tilde{x}_2^{(1)} + 2\tilde{x}_0^{(1)}\tilde{x}_1^{(1)}.$$

Application of formula (2.48) yields:

$$\bar{f} = 2x_1^{(0)}x_0^{(0)} \vee 1x_2^{(0)}x_0^{(1)} \vee 1x_2^{(1)}x_1^{(1)}.$$

Using the De Morgan theorem, one finally obtains:

$$f = (3 \vee x_1^{(1)} \vee x_0^{(1)})(4 \vee x_2^{(1)} \vee x_0^{(0)})(4 \vee x_2^{(0)} \vee x_1^{(0)}) \tag{2.52}$$

from which one deduces that f takes its minimal value, i.e. 3, at the vertices:

$x_2x_1x_0$: 0 0 0

1 0 0.

Let us now deal with the inverse problem, that is, a discrete function f being given by a lattice expression, find a ring expression which represents it.

Without loss of generality, let us assume that f is given as a disjunction of k cubes; the following lemma holds.

Lemma 2.2. Let f be given as a disjunction of cubes:

$$f = \bigvee_{j=0}^{k-1} \left(l_j \wedge \bigwedge_{i=n-1}^{0} x_i^{(C_{ij})} \right), \tag{2.53}$$

*a ring expression of f is then**

$$f \mathrel{\dot{=}} \sum_a (-1)^{[\mu(a)-1]} \left\{ \left(\bigwedge_{j=0}^{k-1} l_j\, a_j \right) \prod_{j=0}^{k-1} \left(\prod_{i=n-1}^{0} \tilde{x}_i^{(C_{ij})} \right)^{a_j} \right\} \tag{2.54}$$

$$0 \leqslant a_j \leqslant 1, \quad 0 < a.$$

* In expression (2.54), the exponentiation X^a has its usual meaning, i.e.:

$X^a = X$ iff $a = 1$
$= 1$ iff $a = 0$.

with $\mu(a)$ the weight of a (i.e. the number of its 1's).

Proof. Similar to that of lemma 2.1.

Example 2.8 (continued). Let the function of example 2.8 be given by the following lattice expression:

$$f = 4x_1^{(2,3)}\, x_0^{(2)} \vee 4x_1^{(1)}\, x_0^{(3,4,0)} \vee 3x_1^{(2,3,4)}\, x_0^{(2,3,4)} \vee 1x_1^{(2,3)}\, x_0^{(1,2,3,4)}.$$

Using lemma (2.2) and relation (2.29), one obtains

$$f = 4\tilde{x}_1^{(2,3)}\, \tilde{x}_0^{(2)} \oplus 4\tilde{x}_1^{(1)}\, \tilde{x}_0^{(3,4,0)} \oplus 3\tilde{x}_1^{(2,3,4)}\, \tilde{x}_0^{(2,3,4)} \oplus$$

$$1\tilde{x}_1^{(2,3)}\, \tilde{x}_0^{(1,2,3,4)} - 3\tilde{x}_1^{(2,3)}\, \tilde{x}_0^{(2)} - 1\tilde{x}_1^{(2,3)}\, \tilde{x}_0^{(2)} - 1\tilde{x}_1^{(2,3)}\, \tilde{x}_0^{(2,3,4)} \oplus$$

$$1\tilde{x}_1^{(2,3)}\, \tilde{x}_0^{(2)}$$

$$= 1\tilde{x}_1^{(2,3)}\, \tilde{x}_0^{(2)} \oplus 4\tilde{x}_1^{(1)}\, \tilde{x}_0^{(3,4,0)} \oplus 3\tilde{x}_1^{(2,3,4)}\, \tilde{x}_0^{(2,3,4)} \oplus$$

$$1\tilde{x}_1^{(2,3)}\, \tilde{x}_0^{(1,2,3,4)} - 1\tilde{x}_1^{(2,3)}\, \tilde{x}_0^{(2,3,4)}.$$

From a computational point of view the above algorithm may also be performed in a step-by-step way as suggested for the algorithm transforming a ring expression into a lattice expression.

It is also interesting to note that, for switching variables x_0 and x_1, lemma 2.2 reduces to the well-known identity:

$$x_0 \vee x_1 = x_0 \oplus x_1 \oplus x_0 x_1. \qquad (2.55)$$

2.4. *The linear algebra structure of Galois functions*

2.4.1. *Definitions and field notations*

By definition (see section 1.4.3) a *finite field* is a field having a finite number of elements. Such a field must have some (finite) prime characteristic p. Hence, as we have already observed, its order must be some power $q = p^m$ of the prime p; every finite field has prime-power order. Finite fields are also called *Galois fields*. For the rest of this section, we shall suppose that $GF(p^m)$ is a given field of prime-power order $q = p^m$.

The addition $f + g$ and the multiplication fg of two Galois functions f and g:

$$f: \{GF(q)\}^n \to GF(q)$$

$$g: \{GF(q)\}^n \to GF(q)$$

are defined to be the componentwise extensions of the addition and of the multiplication in $GF(q)$ respectively, i.e.:

$$[(f+g)_e] = [f(e)+g(e)],$$

$$[(fg)_e] = [f(e)\,g(e)].$$

Let $l \in GF(q)$; the addition $l+f$ and the multiplication lf of the Galois function f and of the field element l is defined by the above equalities when the function g reduces to a constant function l over $GF(q)$.

With these definitions, the set of Galois functions $\{GF(q)\}^n \to GF(q)$ is a linear algebra of functions.

A field expression is defined as follows (see also sections 1.2 and 1.4):

Definition 2.23. By a ***field expression*** we mean a well-formed expression made up of the following symbols:

(a) the field elements: $0, 1, \alpha, \alpha^2, \ldots, \alpha^{q-2}$,
(b) the variables x_i,
(c) the two binary field operations
  + standing for the addition,
  . or absence of symbol standing for the multiplication.

Field expressions play a similar role, with respect to the linear algebra structure of Galois functions, as lattice expressions and ring expressions with respect to the lattice structure and to the module structure of discrete functions respectively. In particular, as it will be seen in section 2.4.2, any Galois function may be described by a field expression. Conversely, every field expression represents a Galois function since its arguments x_i and values are both in $GF(q)$. Each of the variables $x_{n-1}, \ldots, x_1, x_0$ can independently assume any one of the values in $GF(q)$; in order to determine the value of an expression for a given combination, it is sufficient to substitute the values for the variables in the expression. The values assumed by an expression for all the combinations of the variables $x_{n-1}, \ldots, x_1, x_0$ define a Galois function.

Example 2.10. A field of order 2^2 has been constructed in section 1.4.3; addition and multiplication tables for this field are mapped in Figures 1.1 and 1.2 respectively.

Consider the following three-variable expression over $GF(4)$:

$$f = \beta x_1(\alpha + x_1^2)(1 + x_2^3 + x_1 x_0^2 + x_0) + \alpha x_1^2(1 + x_2^3 + x_1 x_0^2 + x_0) + \alpha x_1 x_0(\alpha x_1 x_0^2 + x_0^2 + \beta x_1^2 x_0^2). \tag{2.56}$$

This expression (2.56) describes a Galois function, the converse images of which are, in view of Figures 1.1 and 1.2:

$$f_c(\beta) = \{x_2 x_1 x_0 : 0\beta 0, 0\beta 1, 0\beta\beta\},$$

$$f_c(\alpha) = \{x_2 x_1 x_0 : 0\beta\alpha\},$$

$$f_c(1) = \{x_2 x_1 x_0 : 1\beta\alpha, \alpha\beta\alpha, \beta\beta\alpha\}.$$

Every Galois function may be expressed in a number of ways by means of different field expressions. Some of these expressions will be preferred to some others according to a simplicity criterion. It is, for example, of common use (see Birkhoff and Bartee [1970]) to specify as *standard polynomials* a small set of field expressions to which all others can be easily reduced (polynomials were already defined in section 1.4).

Definition 2.24. A *standard polynomial* in the variables $\boldsymbol{x}$ over $GF(q)$ is an expression of the form:

$$\sum_{e=0}^{q-1} a_e \left(\prod_{i=n-1}^{0} x_i^{e_i} \right), \quad a_e \in GF(q)\, \forall\, e \tag{2.57}$$

$$e = (e_{n-1}, \ldots, e_1, e_0), \quad q-1 = (q-1, \ldots, q-1).$$

The a_e are called the coefficients of the polynomial (2.57); any or all of them may be 0.

The standard polynomial is also specifiable by the vector of its coefficients, as:

$$[a_e] = [a_0, \ldots, a_{q-1}]$$

once an ordering on $\boldsymbol{e}$ has been defined; this ordering will generally be the lexicographical order and $[a_e]$ will then be called the *coefficient vector* of the standard polynomial.

Any field expression may evidently be transformed into a standard polynomial form by using the distributive law in the field, the multiplicative law

$$x^q = x$$

and by grouping the coefficients of the same powers of $\boldsymbol{x}$.

Usually two field expressions are said to be equivalent if they represent the same Galois function.

The following result is obvious.

Lemma 2.3. Two field expressions are equivalent iff they have the same standard polynomial (which is unique up to commutation of terms).

Example 2.10 (continued). The standard polynomial of the field expression (2.56) is:

$$x_1 + x_1x_0 + \beta x_1x_0^2 + \alpha x_1x_0^3 + \alpha x_1^2 + \alpha x_1^2x_0 + x_1^2x_0^2 + \beta x_1^2x_0^3 + \beta x_1^3 + \beta x_1^3x_0 + \alpha x_1^3x_0^2 + x_1^3x_0^3 + x_2^3x_1 + \alpha x_2^3x_1^2 + \beta x_2^3x_1^3. \tag{2.58}$$

2.4.2. *Polynomial expansions of Galois functions*

Theorems 2.8 and 2.9 below may both be viewed as another formulation of theorem 1.46.

Theorem 2.8. Any Galois function may be described by at least one field expression over GF(q).

Proof. The ring exponentiation operation $\tilde{x}^{(e)}$ may be written as the following field expression:

$$\tilde{x}^{(e)} = \prod_{j \neq e} \frac{x-j}{e-j}, \quad e, j \in GF(q). \tag{2.59}$$

Indeed, the right member of (2.59) takes the value 1 if $x = e$ and the value 0 on all the other points of $GF(q)$; moreover, $1/(e-j)$ is a field element. The Lagrange functions may thus be written as follows:

$$\prod_{i=n-1}^{0} \tilde{x}_i^{(e_i)} = \prod_{\substack{i=n-1,0 \\ j_i \neq e_i}} \frac{x_i - j_i}{e_i - j_i}, \quad e_i, j_i \in GF(q) \tag{2.60}$$

and a field expression for any Galois function directly derives from the expression (2.37) and from the above formula (2.60). ■

Theorem 2.9. The set of functions

$$\left\{ \prod_{i=n-1}^{0} x_i^{e_i}, \quad e_i \in \{0, 1, \ldots, q-1\} \right\}$$

is a basis for the Galois functions over GF(q); these functions may thus be written in the following polynomial form:

$$f(x) = \sum_{e} a_e \left(\prod_{i=n-1}^{0} x_i^{e_i} \right)$$

$$e = (e_{n-1}, \ldots, e_1, e_0); e_i \in \{0, 1, \ldots, q-1\} \tag{2.61}$$

$$a_e \in GF(q) \, \forall \, e.$$

Proof. The proof directly follows from theorem 2.8. and from the fact that any field expression over $GF(q)$ may be expanded according to its standard polynomial form.

Definition 2.25. The right-hand side of relation (2.61) is called the *standard polynomial form* of the Galois function $f(x)$. Partial standard polynomial forms of a Galois function may also be considered; they are defined according to the same rule as the partial disjunctive form (see section 2.2.3) or as the partial Lagrange form (see section 2.3.2).

Any given function over $GF(q)$ is uniquely specified by the set of the q^n coefficients a_e of the polynomial form. These coefficients select and weight the contributions of the general product terms involving the variables. It is important to have relationships between the coefficients a_e and the local values of the function: $f(e')$ which are also the entries of the polynomial vector and value vector respectively. To derive these relationships will be the purpose of the following theorems of this section.

Theorem 2.10. Any Galois function $f(\mathbf{x})$ can be expressed as:

$$f(\mathbf{x}) = \sum_{e} f(e) \prod_{i=n-1}^{0} [1-(x_i-e_i)^{q-1}], \quad e_i \in GF(q)\ \forall i. \tag{2.62}$$

Proof. Since for each element $u \neq 0$ of $GF(q)$

$u^{q-1} = 1$ (see section 1.4.3)

one has

$$\prod_{i=n-1}^{0} [1-(x_i-e_i)^{q-1}] = \begin{cases} 1 & \text{if } x_i = e_i\ \forall i \\ 0 & \text{otherwise} \end{cases}$$

which proves the theorem. ∎

Lemma 2.4

$$1-(x-e)^{q-1} = (1-e^{q-1}) - (x^{q-1} + ex^{q-2} + \ldots + e^{q-2}x), \quad \forall x, e \in GF(q). \tag{2.63}$$

Proof

$$\begin{aligned} 1-(x-e)^{q-1} &= 1 - \frac{(x-e)^q}{x-e} \\ &= 1 - \frac{x^q - e^q}{x-e} \\ &= 1 - \frac{(x-e)(x^{q-1} + ex^{q-2} + \ldots + e^{q-2}x + e^{q-1})}{x-e} \\ &= (1-e^{q-1}) - (x^{q-1} + ex^{q-2} + \ldots + e^{q-2}x). \end{aligned}$$ ∎

Theorem 2.11. Any Galois function $f(\mathbf{x})$ can be expressed as:

$$\begin{aligned} f(\mathbf{x}) = f(0) - &\sum_{\substack{i=n-1,0 \\ j_i=1,q-1}} x_i^{j_i} \left\{ \sum_{e_i \in GF(q)} f(0,\ldots,0,e_i,0,\ldots,0)\, e_i^{q-j_i-1} \right\} + \\ &\sum_{\substack{i,k=n-1,0 \\ j_i,j_k=1,q-1}} x_i^{j_i} x_k^{j_k} \left\{ \sum_{e_i, e_k \in GF(q)} f(0,\ldots,e_i,e_k,\ldots,0) e_i^{q-j_i-1} e_k^{q-j_k-1} \right\} - \\ &\vdots \\ &+(-1)^n \sum_{j_0,\ldots,j_{n-1}=1,q-1} x_{n-1}^{j_{n-1}} \ldots x_0^{j_0} \left\{ \sum_{e_0,\ldots,e_{n-1} \in GF(q)} f(e_{n-1},\ldots,e_0) \right. \\ &\left. e_{n-1}^{j_{n-1}} \ldots e_0^{j_0} \right\} \end{aligned} \tag{2.64}$$

Proof. The proof is obtained by substituting the expression (2.63) into the polynomial (2.62) of theorem 2.10 and by multiplying out the different factors in the expression thus obtained. ∎

The above theorem 2.11 allows us to obtain the polynomial coefficients a_e in terms of the values $f(e')$ of f $\forall e, e' \in \{GF(q)\}^n$ or, equivalently, the coefficient vector $[a_e]$ in terms of the value vector $[f_e]$.

It is obvious that arguments similar to those developed in theorems 2.10 and 2.11 allow us to derive partial polynomial expansions of $f(\boldsymbol{x})$ with respect to a subset $\boldsymbol{x}_0 = (x_{s-1}, \ldots, x_1, x_0)$ of $\boldsymbol{x}$. For example any Galois function $f(\boldsymbol{x}_1, \boldsymbol{x}_0)$ may be expanded as:

$$f(\boldsymbol{x}_1, \boldsymbol{x}_0) = \sum_{\boldsymbol{e}_0} f(\boldsymbol{x}_1, \boldsymbol{e}_0) \prod_{i=s-1}^{0} \{1-(x_i - e_i)^{q-1}\} \tag{2.65}$$

$$e_i \in GF(q), \quad \boldsymbol{e}_0 = (e_{s-1}, \ldots, e_1, e_0).$$

The substitution of expression (2.63) into (2.65) provides us, after multiplying out the different factors and simplifying the result, with a partial standard polynomial expansion with respect to $\boldsymbol{x}_0$ which is defined as the right-hand side of the following expression:

$$f(\boldsymbol{x}_1, \boldsymbol{x}_0) = \sum_{\boldsymbol{e}_0} a(\boldsymbol{x}_1, \boldsymbol{e}_0) \prod_{i=s-1}^{0} x_i^{e_i}. \tag{2.66}$$

These partial expansions may be used for obtaining the standard polynomial of a Galois function. In view of theorem 2.11, the following partial expansion with respect to the variable x_{n-1} holds:

$$f(x_{n-1}, \ldots, x_1, x_0) = f(0, x_{n-2}, \ldots, x_1, x_0) - \sum_{i=1}^{q-1} x_{n-1}^i \left\{ \sum_{e_{n-1} \in GF(q)} f(e_{n-1}, x_{n-2}, \ldots, x_0)\, e_{n-1}^{q-i-1} \right\}. \tag{2.67}$$

The expansion (2.67) performed successively with respect to the variables $x_{n-2}, \ldots, x_1$ and x_0 yields finally the polynomial form of theorem 2.11.

A slightly different formulation of the polynomial expansion (2.64) will now be given; it will appear to be of considerable theoretical interest further on in this book.

In view of the following relation which holds in $GF(q)$ (see theorem 1.38):

$$\sum_{\substack{u \in GF(q) \\ \neq 0}} u^j = -1 \quad \text{iff } j = 0$$
$$= 0 \quad \text{otherwise} \tag{2.68}$$

relation (2.67) may be written:

$$f(x_{n-1},\ldots,x_1,x_0) = f(0,x_{n-2},\ldots,x_1,x_0) + \sum_{i=1}^{q-1} x_{n-1}^{i} \left\{ \sum_{\substack{e_{n-1}\in GF(q)\\ \neq 0}} \frac{f(0,x_{n-2},\ldots,x_0) - f(e_{n-1},x_{n-2},\ldots,x_0}{e_{n-1}^{i}} \right\}. \tag{2.69}$$

For sake of conciseness, the following notation will be used in theorem 2.12 below:

$f(e_i, e_j, \ldots, e_k)$ means $f(0, \ldots, 0, e_i, 0, \ldots, e_j, 0, \ldots, e_k, 0, \ldots, 0)$

that is, that only the non-zero values of the arguments have been indicated in $f(e)$.

Theorem 2.12. Any Galois function $f(x)$ can be expressed as:

$$\begin{aligned} f(x) = f(0) &+ \sum_{\substack{i=n-1,0\\ j_i=1,q-1}} x_i^{j_i} \left\{ \sum_{\substack{e_i\in GF(q)\\ \neq 0}} \frac{f(0)-f(e_i)}{e_i^{j_i}} \right\} + \\ &\sum_{\substack{i,k=n-1,0\\ j_i j_k=1,q-1}} x_i^{j_i} x_k^{j_k} \left\{ \sum_{\substack{e_i,e_k\in GF(q)\\ \neq 0}} \frac{f(0)-f(e_i)-f(e_k)+f(e_i,e_k)}{e_i^{j_i} e_k^{j_k}} \right\} + \\ &\vdots \\ &\sum_{\substack{j_0,\ldots,j_{n-1}\\ =1,q-1}} x_{n-1}^{j_{n-1}}\ldots x_0^{j_0} \times \\ &\left\{ \sum_{\substack{e_0,\ldots,e_{n-1}\in GF(q)\\ \neq 0}} \frac{f(0)-\sum_i f(e_i)+\sum_{i,k} f(e_i,e_k)+\ldots+(-1)^n f(e)}{e_0^{j_0}\ldots e_{n-1}^{j_{n-1}}} \right\}. \end{aligned} \tag{2.70}$$

Proof. The proof is achieved by perfect induction.

Initial step. For $n = 1$, the proof results immediately from the examination of relation (2.69).

Induction step. Assume now that relation (2.70) is true and consider the expansion of a function $f(x_n, x)$ of $n+1$ variables.

By the induction hypothesis:

$$f(x_n, x) = f(x_n, 0) + \sum_{\substack{i=n-1,0\\ j_i=1,q-1}} x_i^{j_i} \left\{ \sum_{\substack{e_i\in GF(q)\\ \neq 0}} \frac{f(x_n,0)-f(x_n,e_i)}{e_i^{j_i}} \right\} + \ldots \tag{2.71}$$

But each of the functions $f(x_n, e_i, e_j \ldots)$ present in the above expression is a mapping $GF(q) \to GF(q)$, hence (2.69) can be used to develop these functions. The induction hypothesis results then from the substitution of the expansions of $f(x_n, e_i, e_j \ldots)$ into (2.71). ∎

Polynomial forms similar to those of theorems 2.11 and 2.12 have been derived by several authors; let us mention Bernstein [1928], Gazalé [1959], Menger [1969], Piret [1969], Tosik [1972], Thayse and Deschamps [1973b], Thayse [1974b], Pradhan [1974, 1976], Green and Taylor [1974], Benjauthrit and Reed [1976].

Let us now assume that the Galois function $f(\mathbf{x})$ be given by its value vector $[f_e]$ (or $\{f(\mathbf{e})\}$) considered here as *a* $(1 \times q^n)$ matrix. The coefficient vector $[a_e]$ (or $\{a(\mathbf{e})\}$) will also be considered as *a* $(1 \times q^n)$ matrix. Let us denote by $\{0, 1, \alpha, \ldots, \alpha^{q-2}\}$ the q elements of $GF(q)$ and by B^{-1} the $(q \times q)$ matrix (the reason for calling this matrix B^{-1} instead of B will appear in Chapter 5):

$$B^{-1} = [b'_{kj}] = \begin{bmatrix} 1 & 0 & 0 & \cdot & 0 & \cdot & 0 & 0 \\ 0 & -1 & -(\alpha)^{-1} & \cdot & -(\alpha^{j-1})^{-1} & \cdot & -(\alpha^{q-3})^{-1} & -(\alpha^{q-2})^{-1} \\ 0 & -1 & -(\alpha)^{-2} & \cdot & -(\alpha^{j-1})^{-2} & \cdot & -(\alpha^{q-3})^{-2} & -(\alpha^{q-2})^{-2} \\ \cdot & \cdot & \cdot & \cdot & \cdot & \cdot & \cdot & \cdot \\ 0 & -1 & -(\alpha)^{-k} & \cdot & -(\alpha^{j-1})^{-k} & \cdot & -(\alpha^{q-3})^{-k} & -(\alpha^{q-2})^{-k} \\ \cdot & \cdot & \cdot & \cdot & \cdot & \cdot & \cdot & \cdot \\ 0 & -1 & -(\alpha)^{-(q-2)} & \cdot & -(\alpha^{j-1})^{-(q-2)} & \cdot & -(\alpha^{q-3})^{-(q-2)} & -(\alpha^{q-2})^{-(q-2)} \\ -1 & -1 & -1 & \cdot & -1 & \cdot & -1 & -1 \end{bmatrix}$$

In the above matrix, a notation such as $(\alpha^j)^{-k}$ means $1/(\alpha^j)^k$ where α^j is a field element $\neq 0$.

Let us designate by $(B^{-1})^n$ the nth Kronecker power of the matrix B^{-1}, that is: $B^{-1} \dot{\otimes} B^{-1} \dot{\otimes} \ldots \dot{\otimes} B^{-1}$ (n times).

Theorem 2.13

$$[a_e]^t = (B^{-1})^n \; \textcircled{+ \cdot} \; [f_e]^t. \tag{2.72}$$

Proof. The proof is achieved by perfect induction.

Initial step. For $n = 1$ a routine verification shows that relation (2.67) allows us to write:

$$[a_e]^t = B^{-1} \; \textcircled{+ \cdot} \; [f_e]^t. \tag{2.73}$$

Induction step. We assume as induction hypothesis that (2.72) holds true for any Galois function $f(\mathbf{x})$ of n variables; now if $\{a_e(x_n)\}$ and $\{g_e(x_n)\}$, are the coefficient vectors and the value vectors of the q functions $\{g(e_n, \mathbf{x}) \colon e_n \in GF(q)\}$ respectively, one has in view of (2.71)

$$\{a_e(x_n)\}^t = (B^{-1})^n \; \textcircled{+ \cdot} \; \{g_e(x_n)\}^t. \tag{2.74}$$

Since the theorem holds true for $n = 1$, one has, in view of (2.73–2.74):

$$[a_{e_n e}]^t = (B^{-1})^{n+1} \, \textcircled{+ \cdot} \, [g_{e_n e}]^t. \qquad \blacksquare$$

The expression of the matrix B^{-1} is particularly attractive for Galois functions over $GF(p)$ since for these fields the elements are the integers modulo p. One has up to permutation:

$$B^{-1} = \begin{bmatrix} 1 & 0 & 0 & . & 0 & . & 0 & 0 \\ 0 & -1 & -2^{-1} & . & -j^{-1} & . & -(p-2)^{-1} & -(p-1)^{-1} \\ 0 & -1 & -2^{-2} & . & -j^{-2} & . & -(p-2)^{-2} & -(p-1)^{-2} \\ . & . & . & . & . & . & . & . \\ 0 & -1 & -2^{-k} & . & -j^{-k} & . & -(p-2)^{-k} & -(p-1)^{-k} \\ . & . & . & . & . & . & . & . \\ 0 & -1 & -2^{-(p-2)} & . & -j^{-(p-2)} & . & -(p-2)^{-(p-2)} & -(p-1)^{-(p-2)} \\ -1 & -1 & -1 & . & -1 & . & -1 & -1 \end{bmatrix}.$$

Finally, for switching functions the matrix B^{-1} reduces to

$$\begin{bmatrix} 1 & 0 \\ 1 & 1 \end{bmatrix}$$

and it could easily be verified that $(B^{-1})^n$ is the square matrix of dimension 2^n whose general element is:

$$b'_{kj} = \binom{k}{j}_2$$

where $\binom{k}{j}_2$ is the residue modulo 2 of the binomial coefficient $\binom{k}{j}$. The matrix $(B^{-1})^n$ coincides thus, for switching functions, with a Pascal triangle (of adequate dimension) reduced modulo 2; this has first been pointed out by Calingaert [1961]. Some generalizations of this result for logic functions will be developed further on in Chapter 4 of this book.

Example 2.8 (continued). The function described, for example, by the matrix of Figure 2.14 is a Galois function from $\{GF(5)\}^2$ to $GF(5)$; the matrix B^{-1} for this type of function is:

$$B^{-1} = \begin{bmatrix} 1 & 0 & 0 & 0 & 0 \\ 0 & 4 & 2 & 3 & 1 \\ 0 & 4 & 1 & 1 & 4 \\ 0 & 4 & 3 & 2 & 1 \\ 4 & 4 & 4 & 4 & 4 \end{bmatrix}.$$

The coefficients a_e will be obtained from B^{-1} and from the matrix of Figure 2.14 in two steps, using the properties of the Kronecker matrix product. One first obtains:

$$\begin{bmatrix} 1 & 0 & 0 & 0 & 0 \\ 0 & 4 & 2 & 3 & 1 \\ 0 & 4 & 1 & 1 & 4 \\ 0 & 4 & 3 & 2 & 1 \\ 4 & 4 & 4 & 4 & 4 \end{bmatrix} \textcircled{+ \cdot} \begin{bmatrix} \{f(x_1=0)\} = (0,0,0,0,0) \\ \{f(x_1=1)\} = (4,0,0,4,4) \\ \{f(x_1=2)\} = (0,1,4,3,3) \\ \{f(x_1=3)\} = (0,1,4,3,3) \\ \{f(x_1=4)\} = (0,0,3,3,3) \end{bmatrix} = \begin{bmatrix} \{a(x_1=0)\} = (0,0,0,0,0) \\ \{a(x_1=1)\} = (1,0,3,4,4) \\ \{a(x_1=2)\} = (1,2,0,4,4) \\ \{a(x_1=3)\} = (1,0,3,4,4) \\ \{a(x_1=4)\} = (1,3,4,2,2) \end{bmatrix}. \tag{2.75}$$

By applying the same transformation B^{-1} successively to the five vectors $\{a(x_1=i)\}$, $0 \leqslant i \leqslant 4$, considered as (5×1) matrices one finally obtains the coefficient vector $[a_e]$, i.e.:

$$[a_e] = [0\ 0\ 0\ 0\ 0 \quad 1\ 2\ 3\ 1\ 3 \quad 1\ 4\ 3\ 0\ 4 \quad 1\ 2\ 3\ 1\ 3 \quad 1\ 3\ 1\ 0\ 3]. \tag{2.76}$$

The standard polynomial expansion then immediately derives from the knowledge of $[a_e]$, that is:

$$\begin{aligned} p(x_1, x_0) = {} & x_1 + 2x_1 x_0 + 3x_1 x_0^2 + x_1 x_0^3 + 3x_1 x_0^4 + \\ & x_1^2 + 4x_1^2 x_0 + 3x_1^2 x_0^2 + 4x_1^2 x_0^4 + \\ & x_1^3 + 2x_1^3 x_0 + 3x_1^3 x_0^2 + x_1^3 x_0^3 + 3x_1^3 x_0^4 + \\ & x_1^4 + 3x_1^4 x_0 + x_1^4 x_0^2 + 3x_1^4 x_0^4. \end{aligned} \tag{2.77}$$

Let us also point out that the polynomial coefficients a_e are sometimes presented by means of a *coefficient matrix* instead of a coefficient vector. A coefficient matrix for the function of example 2.8 is given in Figure 2.15.

	x_0^0	x_0^1	x_0^2	x_0^3	x_0^4
x_1^0	0	0	0	0	0
x_1^1	1	2	3	1	3
x_1^2	1	4	3	0	4
x_1^3	1	2	3	1	3
x_1^4	1	3	1	0	3

Figure 2.15. Coefficient matrix of the function of example 2.8

Let us now consider the inverse transformation, that is the obtention of the value vector $[f_e]$ of a discrete function $f(\boldsymbol{x})$ from its coefficient vector $[a_e]$. The partial polynomial expansion of $f(x)$ with respect to the variable x_{n-1} is:

$$f(x_{n-1}, \ldots, x_1, x_0) = \sum_{i=0}^{q-1} a_i(x_{n-2}, \ldots, x_1, x_0)\, x_{n-1}^i \tag{2.78}$$

from which one deduces:

$$f(e_{n-1}, \ldots, x_1, x_0) = \sum_{i=0}^{q-1} a_i\, e_{n-1}^i, \quad e_{n-1} \in GF(q). \tag{2.79}$$

From relation (2.79) one concludes that, for a one variable function, the value vector $[f_e]$ is related to the coefficient vector $[a_e]$ by the matrix relation:

$$[f_e] = B \; (+\,\cdot) \; [a_e]$$

with $B = [b_{kj}]$:

$$[b_{kj}] = \begin{bmatrix} 1 & 0 & 0 & . & 0 & . & 0 & 0 \\ 1 & 1 & 1 & . & 1 & . & 1 & 1 \\ 1 & \alpha & \alpha^2 & . & \alpha^j & . & \alpha^{q-2} & 1 \\ . & . & . & . & . & . & . & . \\ 1 & \alpha^{k-2} & (\alpha^{k-2})^2 & . & (\alpha^{k-2})^j & . & (\alpha^{k-2})^{q-2} & 1 \\ . & . & . & . & . & . & . & . \\ 1 & \alpha^{q-3} & (\alpha^{q-3})^2 & . & (\alpha^{q-3})^j & . & (\alpha^{q-3})^{q-2} & 1 \\ 1 & \alpha^{q-2} & (\alpha^{q-2})^2 & . & (\alpha^{q-2})^j & . & (\alpha^{q-2})^{q-2} & 1 \end{bmatrix}.$$

The following theorem, the proof of which is quite similar to that of theorem 2.13, then holds:

Theorem 2.14

$$[f_e] = B^n \; (+\,\cdot) \; [a_e]. \tag{2.80}$$

Again, the expression of the matrix B is particularly attractive for Galois functions over $GF(p)$; for these functions one has up to permutation:

$$[b_{kj}] = \begin{bmatrix} 1 & 0 & 0 & . & 0 & . & 0 & 0 \\ 1 & 1 & 1 & . & 1 & . & 1 & 1 \\ 1 & 2 & 2^2 & . & 2^j & . & 2^{(p-2)} & 1 \\ . & . & . & . & . & . & . & . \\ 1 & k & k^2 & . & k^j & . & k^{(p-2)} & 1 \\ . & . & . & . & . & . & . & . \\ 1 & p-2 & (p-2)^2 & . & (p-2)^j & . & (p-2)^{(p-2)} & 1 \\ 1 & -1 & 1 & . & (-1)^j & . & (-1)^{p-2} & 1 \end{bmatrix}.$$

Finally, for switching functions the matrix B reduces to

$$\begin{bmatrix} 1 & 0 \\ 1 & 1 \end{bmatrix}.$$

It follows that for switching functions $(B^{-1})^n = B^n$; the transformation matrix B^n is thus its own inverse (see also Muller [1959], Calingaert [1961]).

Example 2.8 (continued). For a function over $GF(5)$ the matrix B is:

$$B = \begin{bmatrix} 1 & 0 & 0 & 0 & 0 \\ 1 & 1 & 1 & 1 & 1 \\ 1 & 2 & 4 & 3 & 1 \\ 1 & 3 & 4 & 2 & 1 \\ 1 & 4 & 1 & 4 & 1 \end{bmatrix}.$$

From the coefficient vector (2.76) one deduces:

$$\begin{bmatrix} 1 & 0 & 0 & 0 & 0 \\ 1 & 1 & 1 & 1 & 1 \\ 1 & 2 & 4 & 3 & 1 \\ 1 & 3 & 4 & 2 & 1 \\ 1 & 4 & 1 & 4 & 1 \end{bmatrix} (+\,\cdot) \begin{bmatrix} (0,0,0,0,0) \\ (1,2,3,1,3) \\ (1,4,3,0,4) \\ (1,2,3,1,3) \\ (1,3,1,0,3) \end{bmatrix} = \begin{bmatrix} (0,0,0,0,0) \\ (4,1,0,2,3) \\ (0,4,3,0,4) \\ (0,4,3,0,4) \\ (0,3,3,3,1) \end{bmatrix}. \tag{2.81}$$

By applying the same transformation B successively to the five vectors obtained at the right-hand side of (2.81) considered each as (5×1) matrices, one obtains the value vector:

$$[f_e] = [0\ 0\ 0\ 0\ 0 \quad 4\ 0\ 0\ 4\ 4 \quad 0\ 1\ 4\ 3\ 3 \quad 0\ 1\ 4\ 3\ 3 \quad 0\ 0\ 3\ 3\ 3]. \tag{2.82}$$

The Lagrange canonical form then derives from the knowledge of $[f_e]$:

$$\begin{aligned} f(x_1, x_0) = {} & 4\tilde{x}_1^{(1)}\tilde{x}_0^{(0)} \oplus 4\tilde{x}_1^{(1)}\tilde{x}_0^{(3)} \oplus 4\tilde{x}_1^{(1)}\tilde{x}_0^{(4)} \oplus 1\tilde{x}_1^{(2)}\tilde{x}_0^{(1)} \oplus 4\tilde{x}_1^{(2)}\tilde{x}_0^{(2)} \oplus \\ & 3\tilde{x}_1^{(2)}\tilde{x}_0^{(3)} \oplus 3\tilde{x}_1^{(2)}\tilde{x}_0^{(4)} \oplus 1\tilde{x}_1^{(3)}\tilde{x}_0^{(1)} \oplus 4\tilde{x}_1^{(3)}\tilde{x}_0^{(2)} \oplus 3\tilde{x}_1^{(3)}\tilde{x}_0^{(3)} \oplus \\ & 3\tilde{x}_1^{(3)}\tilde{x}_0^{(4)} \oplus 3\tilde{x}_1^{(4)}\tilde{x}_0^{(2)} \oplus 3\tilde{x}_1^{(4)}\tilde{x}_0^{(3)} \oplus 3\tilde{x}_1^{(4)}\tilde{x}_0^{(4)}. \end{aligned} \tag{2.83}$$

Theorem 2.15 below allows us to obtain the polynomial form of a Galois function from its value vector; it is a straightforward consequence of theorem 2.14.

Theorem 2.15. The polynomial form of $f(\mathbf{x})$ is given by:

$$[f(e)] (+\,\cdot) \{(B^{-1})^n\}^t \left(\dot{\bigotimes}_{i=n-1,0} [x_i^j] \right)^t \tag{2.84}$$

with $[x_i^j]$ the $(1 \times q)$ matrix

$$[x_i^0, x_i^1, \ldots, x_i^{q-1}].$$

Chapter 3

Lattice Expressions of Discrete Functions

One of the major areas in discrete function theory is concerned with obtaining suitable algorithms for the simplification of lattice expressions. By *simplification* of a lattice expression one means the obtention of an equivalent lattice expression which is better under some criterion. *Minimization* is the process of obtaining that expression of a lattice expression which is optimum under some criterion. Usually a *simplicity* criterion is established and the optimum expression is that which contains a minimum number of symbols and of literals.

The laws and theorems of lattice theory (such as, for example, the distributivity, the De Morgan's law . . .) can be used to minimize a lattice expression. But the use of these laws to minimize other than some simple kinds of lattice expressions has serious disadvantages. First, in what order should we apply the axioms and theorems? No answer can be given. With experience, insight, trial and error we may find a minimal expression, but an orderly procedure is certainly to be desired. Second, when do we stop attempting to apply the axioms and theorems to minimize further? With a few exceptions it is difficult to tell when a lattice expression has in fact been expressed in optimum fashion.

To simplify this chapter, we will consider only the minimization of normal forms (see definition 2.16). Several orderly procedures (algorithms) will be developed which, if followed, will give a minimal disjunctive normal form, or dually a minimal conjunctive normal form. All these procedures are essentially the same and can be divided into three parts:

1. (a) Select the type of normal form (disjunctive or conjunctive) to be minimized.
   (b) If the disjunctive normal form is chosen, the function is written as a disjunction of implicants; for discrete functions three kinds of implicants may be chosen (according to some criteria developed in section 3.1), namely, the cube, the block or the convex block functions (see definitions 2.13, 3.1 and 3.2). Select one of these types of implicants (for switching functions, the cube, block and convex block functions constitute a unique concept). If the conjunctive normal form is chosen, the function is written as a conjunction of implicates; three kinds of implicates are defined, namely the anticube, antiblock and convex antiblock functions (see definitions 2.14, 3.3 and 3.4). Select one of these types of implicates.

2. Find all the prime implicants or all the prime implicates (procedures are given in section 3.2).
3. A smallest subset of the set of all prime implicants is selected which expresses the discrete function as the disjunction of these selected prime implicants. Dually one searches for the smallest subset of all the prime implicates such that the function is expressed as the conjunction of the prime implicates belonging to that subset. The research of these smallest subsets will be considered in a separate chapter of this book (see Chapter 8) devoted to covering problems.

It could easily be shown that the above procedure verifies (for the restricted class of normal forms) the simplicity criterion quoted above. Indeed, prime implicants are particularly interesting since they correspond to cubes with a minimum number of literals; similarly prime implicates correspond to anticubes with also a minimum number of literals. Moreover, since prime implicants, for example, are the greatest cubes contained in a given discrete function, the number of these cubes required to describe the function is the smallest when using prime implicants. This minimizes the number of symbols to be used in an expression.

Applications of the minimization of lattice expressions are numerous in the frame of switching and automata theory.

The minimization of lattice expressions will be viewed as a common formalism which may be used, for example, in the research of the maximal compatibility classes of binary relations (see section 3.3.1), the covering problems (see Chapter 8), the research of prime implicants of fuzzy functions (see section 3.3.2) and the analysis and design of some switching and logic networks (see sections 3.3.3 and 3.3.4).

3.1. Definitions

Cube and anticube functions were defined in section 2.2.1 (see definitions 2.13 and 2.14). We shall consider in this section some particular types of cube and of anticube functions which will appear to be of special interest further on in this book.

Let $S = \times_i S_i$ and let C_i be a subset of S_i; if $C_i = \{a_i, a_i \oplus 1, \ldots, a_i \oplus k_i = b_i\}$, i.e. if C_i is formed by consecutive numbers in the ring of integers modulo m_i, the lattice exponentiation

$$x_i^{(C_i)} \quad (i = 0, 1, \ldots, n-1)$$

will be written

$$x_i^{[a_i, b_i]}.$$

If C_i reduces to the single element e_i of S_i, one will conventionally write

$$x_i^{(e_i)} = x_i^{[e_i, e_i]}.$$

Further on, it will also be convenient to denote the set $\{a_i, a_i \oplus 1, \ldots, a_i \oplus k_i = b_i\}$ of consecutive elements in S_i by $[a_i, b_i]$.

Definition 3.1. A *block function* is a cube function of the form

$$b(\mathbf{x}) = l \wedge \bigwedge_{i=n-1}^{0} x_i^{[a_i, b_i]}, \quad l \in L; a_i, b_i \in S_i \,\forall i. \tag{3.1}$$

A block function may thus be viewed as a cube function where the entries of weight l are adjacent in S (see Figure 3.2).

Definition 3.2. A block function (3.1) is a *convex block function* iff $a_i \leqslant b_i \;\forall i$.

In view of definition 3.1 it is obvious that the block functions will be of interest for the problems involving a cyclic or ring structure of the sets S_i (in this structure the elements 0 and (m_i-1) are consecutive numbers in S_i). The convex blocks will merely be used in the formulation of problems where the sets S_i have a chain structure; the condition $a_i \leqslant b_i$ involves indeed that no convex block may take the value l (which is also referred to as the *weight* of the block) on a proper subset C_i of S_i containing simultaneously the elements 0 and m_i-1.

It should already be pointed out now that, when dealing with switching functions, the concepts of cube function, block function and convex block function coincide with the unique concept of cube (sometimes also called *product term*) and which is written:

$$\bigwedge_{x_i \in \mathbf{x}_0} x_i^{(e_i)}, \quad e_i \in \{0, 1\}, \mathbf{x}_0 \subseteq \mathbf{x}.$$

A cube function may always be written as a disjunction of block functions. Indeed, any $C_i \subseteq S_i$ is the union of subsets formed by adjacent points in S_i (it is recalled that one assumes that 0 and (m_i-1) are adjacent in S_i):

$$C_i = \bigcup_{j_i} [a_{ij_i}, b_{ij_i}]. \tag{3.2}$$

One obtains successively, in view of relations (2.8), (3.2) and of the distributive law,

$$l \wedge \bigwedge_{i=n-1}^{0} x_i^{(C_i)} = l \wedge \bigwedge_{i=n-1}^{0} \left(\bigvee_{j_i} x_i^{[a_{ij_i}, b_{ij_i}]} \right)$$

$$= \bigvee_{j_0, j_1, \ldots, j_{n-1}} \left(l \wedge \bigwedge_{i=n-1}^{0} x_i^{[a_{ij_i}, b_{ij_i}]} \right). \tag{3.3}$$

Example 2.6 (continued). Consider the expression (2.12); each of the cube functions of (2.16) may be written as a disjunction of block functions according to (3.3).

One has, for example:

$$
\begin{aligned}
2x_1^{(0,2)}\,x_0^{(2)} &= 2(x_1^{(0)} \vee x_1^{(2)})\,x_0^{(2)} \\
&= 2x_1^{(0)}\,x_0^{(2)} \vee 2x_1^{(2)}\,x_0^{(2)} \\
1x_1^{(0,3)}\,x_0^{(1,3)} &= 1x_1^{[3,0]}\,(x_0^{(1)} \vee x_0^{(3)}) \\
&= 1x_1^{[3,0]}\,x_0^{(1)} \vee 1x_1^{[3,0]}\,x_0^{(3)}.
\end{aligned}
$$

A block function may similarly be written as a disjunction of k $(1 \leqslant k \leqslant 2^n)$ convex block functions; indeed, if $b_i \leqslant a_i$, then:

$$[a_i, b_i] = [a_i, m_i - 1] \cup [0, b_i] \tag{3.4}$$

so that any block function of the form (3.1) may be transformed as:

$$l \wedge \bigwedge_{i:b_i<a_i} (x_i^{[a_i, m_i-1]} \vee x_i^{[0,b_i]}) \wedge \bigwedge_{j:a_j \leqslant b_j} x_j^{[a_j,b_j]}. \tag{3.5}$$

Using again the distributive law, the above expression (3.5) is then obtained as a disjunction of at most 2^n convex blocks.

Example 2.6 (continued). In view of (3.5) the block

$$1x_1^{[3,0]}\,x_0^{(1)}$$

may be written successively:

$$
\begin{aligned}
1x_1^{[3,0]}\,x_0^{(1)} &= 1(x_1^{(3)} \vee x_1^{(0)})\,x_0^{(1)} \\
&= 1\,(x_1^{(3)}\,x_0^{(1)} \vee x_1^{(0)}\,x_0^{(1)}) \\
&= 1x_1^{[3,3]}\,x_0^{[1,1]} \vee 1x_1^{[0,0]}\,x_0^{[1,1]}.
\end{aligned}
$$

It is useful to define *partially convex blocks*; a block of the form (3.1) is said to be partially convex with respect to the set of variables $\boldsymbol{x}_0 \subseteq \boldsymbol{x} = (\boldsymbol{x}_1, \boldsymbol{x}_0)$ iff:

(a) $\forall\ x_i \in \boldsymbol{x}_0:\ \ a_i \leqslant b_i$.

(b) $\forall\ x_j \in \boldsymbol{x}_1:\ \ a_j > b_j$.

Lemma 3.1 The set of cubes, the set of blocks, the set of convex blocks are each $\vee$*-generating subsets of* L^N (see definition 1.19).

Proof. Since the minterms are at the same time cubes, blocks and convex blocks, the proof of lemma 3.1 immediately results from theorem 2.2. ■

Lemma 3.2. The set of cubes and the set of convex blocks are each ∧*-closure systems of* L^N (see definition 1.23).

Proof. That the set of cubes is a ∧-closure system of L^N results from (2.3). ∎

Consider the two convex blocks:

$$l_0 \wedge \bigwedge_{i=n-1}^{0} x_i^{[a_{i0}, b_{i0}]}, \quad a_{i0} \leqslant b_{i0} \; \forall i,$$

$$l_1 \wedge \bigwedge_{i=n-1}^{0} x_i^{[a_{i1}, b_{i1}]}, \quad a_{i1} \leqslant b_{i1} \; \forall i.$$

Since

$$[a_{i0}, b_{i0}] \cap [a_{i1}, b_{i1}] = [a_{i0} \vee a_{i1}, b_{i0} \wedge b_{i1}] \quad \text{iff } a_{i0} \vee a_{i1} \leqslant b_{i0} \wedge b_{i1} \; \forall i,$$
$$= 0 \text{ otherwise},$$

the conjunction of these two convex blocks is a convex block the expression of which is:

$$l_0 \wedge l_1 \wedge \bigwedge_{i=n-1}^{0} x_i^{[a_{i0} \vee a_{i1}, b_{i0} \wedge b_{i1}]} \quad \text{iff } a_{i0} \vee a_{i1} \leqslant b_{i0} \wedge b_{i1} \; \forall i,$$

and is 0 otherwise.

The two preceding lemmas allow us to state lemma 3.3.

Lemma 3.3. The set of cubes and the set of convex blocks are each systems of classes (see definition 1.23).

The conjunction of two blocks is not necessarily a block since (see also Figure 3.1):

$$lx^{[a_0, b_0]} \; x^{[a_1, b_1]} = lx^{[a_1, b_0]} \vee lx^{[a_0, b_1]} \tag{3.6}$$

if, for example, $a_0 < b_0, a_1 > b_1, a_1 < b_0$ and $a_0 < b_1$.

The set of blocks is thus not a system of classes.

The conjunction of two blocks may thus always be written as the disjunction of $k(1 \leqslant k \leqslant 2^n)$ blocks.

The concepts of cubes, blocks and convex blocks can best be illustrated by means of two-dimensional (or planar) discrete functions, that is functions:

$$f: S_1 \times S_0 \to L.$$

Consider, for example, Figure 3.2 which schematically describes some of these functions

Figures 3.2(a), (b), (c) and (d) represent respectively:

a cube function,
a block function,

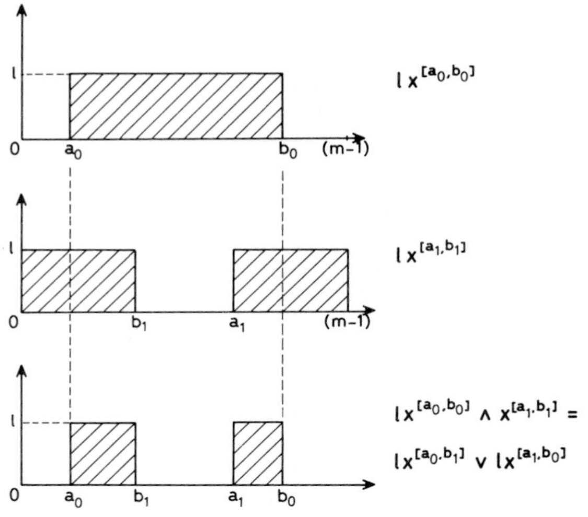

Figure 3.1. The conjunction of two blocks

a block function which is partially convex with respect to x_0,
a convex block function.

The shaded areas in Figure 3.2 represent the domain where the discrete function takes the value l; in the other areas, the function is zero.

In view of definition 1.22 and of lemma 3.1, the cubes, blocks and convex blocks smaller than a discrete function f are implicants of f; these implicants will be called cubes of f, blocks of f and convex blocks of f respectively. The *prime cubes* of f, *prime blocks* of f and *prime convex blocks* of f are defined accordingly.

The following theorem is a direct consequence of theorem 1.15.

Theorem 3.1. (a) *Any discrete function f is the disjunction of all its prime cubes.*
(b) *Any discrete function f is the disjunction of all its prime blocks.*
(c) *Any discrete function f is the disjunction of all its prime convex blocks.*

Several methods for obtaining the prime cubes, the prime blocks and the prime convex blocks of a discrete function f will be given in the next sections; examples and applications will be extensively detailed. It is however already useful to point out that the cubes, blocks and convex blocks are of outstanding interest in several domains related to logic design, compatibility relations, fuzzy logic and combinatorial theory.

Definition 3.3. An *antiblock function* is an anticube function of the form:

$$a(x) = l \vee \bigvee_{i=n-1}^{0} x_i^{[a_i,\, b_i]}, \quad l \in L; a_i, b_i \in S_i \ \forall i. \tag{3.7}$$

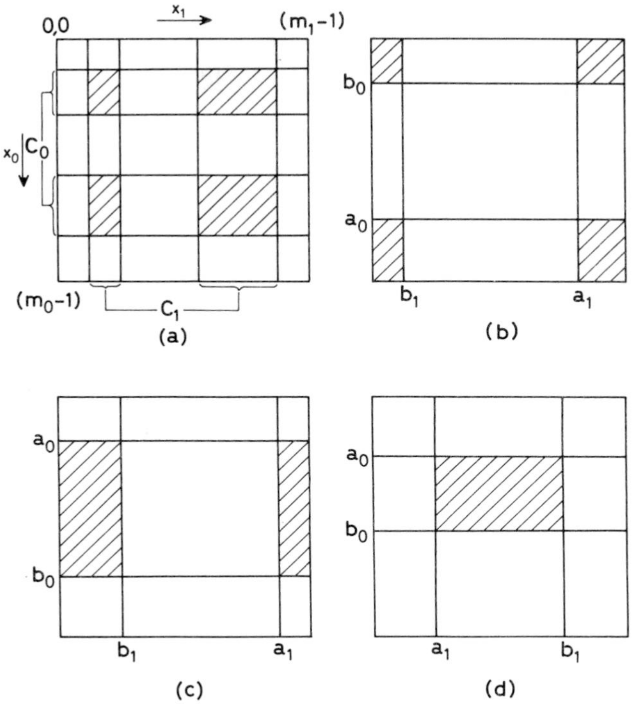

Figure 3.2. (a) Cube function $l \wedge x_1^{(C_1)} \wedge x_0^{(C_0)}$

(b) and (c) Block functions $l \wedge x_1^{[a_1, b_1]} \wedge x_0^{[a_0, b_0]}$

(d) Convex block function $l \wedge x_1^{[a_1, b_1]} \wedge x_0^{[a_0, b_0]}$

Definition 3.4. An antiblock function (3.7) is a *convex antiblock function* iff either $a_i > b_i$ or $a_i = 0$ or $a_i = m_i - 1$, $\forall i$.

An anticube function may always be written as a conjunction of antiblock functions. Indeed, any $C_i \subseteq S_i$ is the intersection of subsets formed by adjacent elements in S_i:

$$C_i = \bigcap_{j_i} \{a_{ij_i}, a_{ij_i} \oplus 1, \ldots, a_{ij_i} \oplus k_{ij_i} = b_{ij_i}\}. \qquad (3.8)$$

One way of obtaining C_i as an intersection of such subsets is, for example, to obtain first $S_i \backslash C_i$ as a union of subsets C_{ij}^* of the form (3.2) and to apply the De Morgan law:

$$S_i \backslash (\cup C_{ij}^*) = \cap (S_i \backslash C_{ij}^*) \qquad (3.9)$$

to the result. One obtains then successively:

$$l \vee \bigvee_{i=n-1}^{0} x_i^{(C_i)} = l \vee \bigvee_{i=n-1}^{0} \left(\bigwedge_{j_i} x_i^{[a_{ij_i}, b_{ij_i}]} \right),$$

$$= \bigwedge_{j_0, j_1, \ldots, j_{n-1}} \left(l \vee \bigvee_{i=n-1}^{0} x_i^{[a_{ij_i}, b_{ij_i}]} \right). \tag{3.10}$$

An antiblock function may similarly be written as a conjunction of k ($1 \leqslant k \leqslant 2^n$) convex antiblock functions by use of the following identity which holds if $a_i < b_i$

$$[a_i, b_i] = [0, b_i] \cap [a_i, m_i - 1]. \tag{3.11}$$

A dual form of (3.5) is then obtained.

Partially convex antiblocks are also defined accordingly.

Lemma 3.4. The set of anticubes, the set of antiblocks, the set of convex antiblocks are each $\bigwedge$*-generating subsets of* L^N (see definition 1.19).

Lemma 3.5. The set of anticubes, the set of convex antiblocks are each $\bigvee$*-closure subsets of* L^N (see definition 1.23).

Lemma 3.6. The set of anticubes and the set of convex antiblocks are each systems of anticlasses (see definition 1.23).

In view of definition 1.22, the anticubes, antiblocks and convex antiblocks greater than a discrete function f are implicates of f; these implicates will be called anticubes of f, antiblocks of f and convex antiblocks of f respectively. The *prime anticubes* of f, *prime antiblocks* of f and *prime convex antiblocks* of f are defined accordingly.

Theorem 3.2. (a) *Any discrete function is the conjunction of all its prime anticubes.*

(b) *Any discrete function is the conjunction of all its prime antiblocks.*

(c) *Any discrete function is the conjunction of all its prime convex antiblocks.*

The disjunction of two antiblocks is not necessarily an antiblock since:

$$(l \vee x^{[a_0, b_0]}) \vee (l \vee x^{[a_1, b_1]}) = (l \vee x^{[a_0, b_1]}) \wedge (l \vee x^{[a_1, b_0]}) \tag{3.12}$$

if $a_0 < b_0, a_1 > b_1, b_1 < a_0, b_0 < a_1$.

Relation (3.12) is illustrated by means of Figure 3.3.

The system of antiblocks is thus not a system of anticlasses. The disjunction of two antiblocks may generally be written as the conjunction of k ($1 \leqslant k \leqslant 2^n$) antiblocks.

The concepts of anticubes, antiblocks and convex antiblocks are illustrated for a two-dimensional discrete function

$$f: S_1 \times S_0 \to L$$

by means of Figure 3.4.

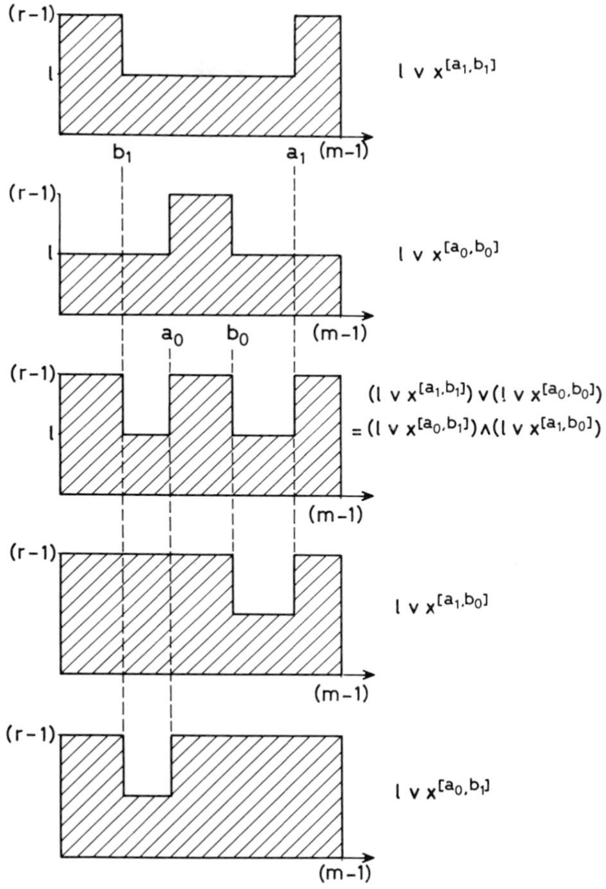

Figure 3.3. Disjunction of antiblock functions

Figures 3.4(a), (b), (c) and (d) represent respectively

an anticube function,
an antiblock function,
an antiblock function which is partially convex with respect to x_1,
a convex antiblock function.

The shaded areas in Figure 3.2 represent the domain where the discrete function takes the value $(r-1)$; on the other areas, the function is l.

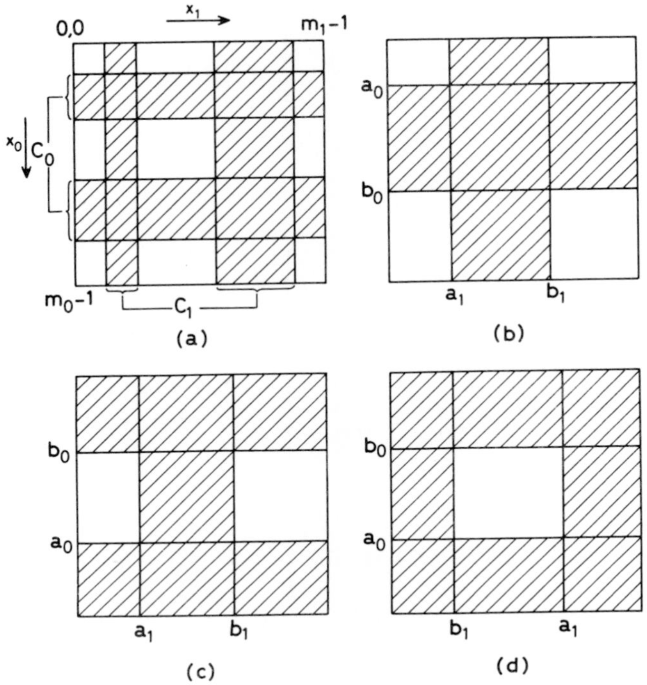

Figure 3.4. (a) Anticube function $l \vee x_1^{(C_1)} \vee x_0^{(C_0)}$

(b) and (c) Antiblock functions $l \vee x_1^{[a_1, b_1]} \vee x_0^{[a_0, b_0]}$

(d) Convex antiblock function $l \vee x_1^{[a_1, b_1]} \vee x_0^{[a_0, b_0]}$

The negation (see definition 2.5) of a block function is an antiblock function and conversely; one has indeed in view of the De Morgan law (theorem 2.1)

$$\overline{l \wedge \bigwedge_{i=n-1}^{0} x_i^{[a_i, b_i]}} = \bar{l} \vee \bigvee_{i=n-1}^{0} x_i^{[b_i \oplus 1, a_i - 1]}. \tag{3.13}$$

Since, moreover, $a_i \leqslant b_i$ implies either:

$$b_i \oplus 1 > a_i - 1$$

or

$$b_i \oplus 1 = 0 \quad (\text{if } b_i = m_i - 1)$$

or

$$a_i - 1 = m_i - 1 \quad (\text{if } a_i = 0)$$

the negation of a convex block function is a convex antiblock function and conversely.

Theorem 3.3. The prime implicants (resp. prime implicates) of a discrete function f are the negation of the prime implicates (resp. prime implicants) of $\overline{f}$.

Proof. It has been shown that the negation of a cube, of a block and of a convex block is an anticube, an antiblock and a convex antiblock respectively. Let m and m' be two implicants of f with $m \geqslant m'$; the proof results then from the following equivalence:

$$f \geqslant m \geqslant m' \Leftrightarrow \overline{m}' \geqslant \overline{m} \geqslant \overline{f}\,. \qquad \blacksquare$$

Since the representation of any discrete function f as the disjunction of all its prime implicants (resp. as the conjunction of all its prime implicates) is unique, this kind of representation will be called *canonical*.

An important feature of the sets of convex blocks and of convex antiblocks is that their intersection is not empty. The elements of that intersection are called the *unate generators* of L^N for a reason that will appear further on in this book.

The *unate generators* of L^N are:

(a) The functions assuming a constant value on all points of the domain S; these unate generators, actually reduced to the elements of L, are accordingly denoted by the corresponding symbol l.
(b) The functions defined by the lattice expressions $x_i^{[0,a_i]}$ or $x_i^{[a_i,m_i-1]}$.

In the intuitive cubical representation of discrete functions, the generators of the type (b) define, for example, a separation of the domain S by a hyperplane orthogonal to the ith coordinate axis and assume the value 0 on one side of that hyperplane and the value $r-1$ on the other side.

The unate generators constitute in fact the well-known Muehldorf system of multiple-valued logic (Muehldorf [1958]). Muehldorf [1959] himself applied his system to the synthesis of ternary logic networks. Yoeli and Rosenfeld [1965] developed the ternary case further on and arrived at a synthesis procedure with a minimization technique which is an extension of the Quine–McCluskey algorithm (see section 3.2). Although Muehldorf described the operators necessary for his system, he did not go any further. A complete development of his system for discrete functions may be found in the papers by Ying and Susskind [1971], Deschamps and Thayse [1973a] and in the course of this chapter.

Because of their importance and of their frequent use further on, the unate generators $x_i^{[0,a_i]}$ and $x_i^{[a_i,m_i-1]}$ will be written in a more concise form, i.e.

$$x_i^{a_i]} \quad \text{holds for} \quad x_i^{[0,a_i]},$$

and

$$x_i^{[a_i} \quad \text{holds for} \quad x_i^{[a_i,m_i-1]}.$$

Theorem 3.4. The unate generators together with the operations of disjunction and of conjunction can generate any discrete function.

Proof. For any $e_i \in S_i$ one has:

$$x_i^{(e_i)} = x_i^{[e_i} \wedge x_i^{e_i]} \tag{3.14}$$

so that expression (2.17) may be written:

$$f(x) = \bigvee_e \left[f(e) \wedge \bigwedge_{i=n-1}^{0} \left(x_i^{e_i]} \wedge x_i^{[e_i}\right)\right], \quad 0 \leqslant e_i \leqslant m_i - 1. \tag{3.15}$$

A dual expansion of (3.15) may be obtained from (2.19); since

$$x_i^{(\bar{e}_i)} = x_i^{[e_i+1} \vee x_i^{e_i-1]} \tag{3.16}$$

(it is conventionally assumed that $x_i^{-1]} = x_i^{[m_i} = 0$), the expansion (2.19) becomes:

$$f(x) = \bigwedge_e \left[f(e) \vee \bigvee_{i=n-1}^{0} \left(x_i^{[e_i+1} \vee x_i^{e_i-1]}\right)\right]. \quad \blacksquare \tag{3.17}$$

It is finally worthwhile pointing out that any convex block can be represented as a conjunction of unate generators, since for any $a_i, b_i \in S_i$ with $a_i \leqslant b_i$, one has:

$$x_i^{[a_i, b_i]} = x_i^{[a_i} \wedge x_i^{b_i]}. \tag{3.18}$$

Dually any convex antiblock can be represented as a disjunction of unate generators since for any $a_i, b_i \in S_i$, $a_i > b_i$, one has:

$$x_i^{[a_i, b_i]} = x_i^{[a_i} \vee x_i^{b_i]}. \tag{3.19}$$

Remark 1. Switching functions. For the important particular case of switching functions, the concepts of cube, block and convex block of a switching function f are identical and correspond to the classical concept of implicant of f. Similarly, the concepts of anticube, antiblock and convex antiblock of f correspond all to the concept of implicate of f.

Remark 2. General discrete functions. It should be noted that the concepts of blocks, cubes, . . . , etc., defined in this section and in the preceding chapter also hold for general discrete functions (see section 2.1.1). The only difference is that the weight l associated with each of these concepts and which is a scalar when dealing with discrete functions, becomes a vector of scalars $(l_{m-1}, \ldots, l_1, l_0)$ for general discrete functions.

3.2. *Prime implicant and prime implicate extraction methods*

In this section one will be faced with the problem of obtaining a discrete function as a disjunction of all its prime implicants or as a conjunction of all its prime implicates. These expressions of discrete functions are not only simpler than other types of lattice expressions (this has been discussed in the introduction to this chapter) but they constitute also canonical forms for discrete functions since they are unique for a given function.

Two basic types of algorithms will be proposed for detecting prime implicants and prime implicates of a discrete function.

Let us deal with the obtention of prime implicants; implicants are product terms of the form

$$\bigwedge_{i=n-1}^{0} x_i^{(C_i)}, \qquad C_i \subseteq S_i \; \forall i.$$

The set of product terms is a closure system of the lattice of discrete functions the lowest and highest elements of which are 0 and $(r-1)$ respectively. Given a discrete function f, its prime implicants may be detected as follows (*decreasing algorithm*):

1. Starting from the highest element $(r-1)$ of the lattice of product terms, test each product term for its inclusion in the discrete function.
2. The first product term encountered and which is included in the discrete function is a prime implicant of that function. The smaller product terms are evidently not prime implicants and are thus not to be tested.
3. All the prime implicants are detected once each of the paths in the lattice (starting from the element $(r-1)$) have been explored. The above algorithm is schematized by Figure 3.5.

The prime implicants are denoted by $A, B, C, D, \ldots, Y, Z$. The shaded area in this figure represents that part of the lattice which must not be tested.

An algorithm using this technique, and called *implicant–implicate algorithm*, is developed under section 3.2.2.

A second kind of computation scheme for detecting prime implicants may be built as follows (*increasing algorithm*):

1. Starting from the lowest element 0 of the lattice of product terms, test each product term for its inclusion in the discrete function.
2. Stop the testing when a product term is obtained which is not included in the function. The product term obtained just before this last term in the exploration scheme is a prime implicant of the function and the higher product terms are evidently not to be tested further on.
3. All the prime implicants are detected once each of the paths in the lattice (starting from the element 0) have been explored. A similar type of picture as that of Figure 3.5 could be used for illustrating that figure; it is obtained, for example, by interchanging in Figure 3.5 the elements 0 and $(r-1)$.

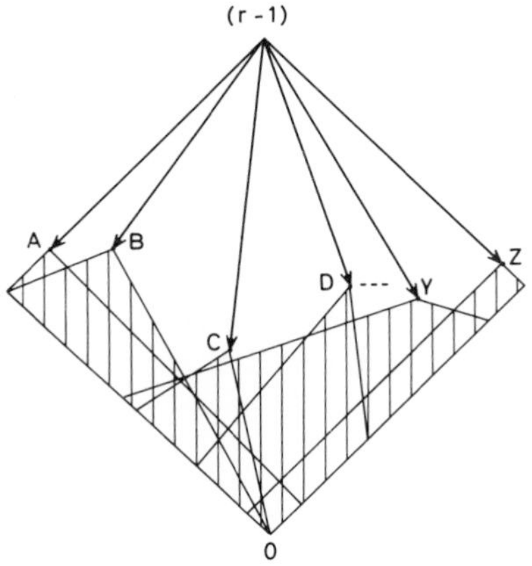

Figure 3.5. Detection of prime implicants of a discrete function in the lattice of product terms

Algorithms using this technique are developed in section 3.2.3; they are grounded on the concept of *lattice difference* of a discrete function which is defined in section 3.2.3.1. One shows that this concept allows us to develop several prime implicant extraction methods and among others, for example, a generalized Quine–McCluskey method and a generalized consensus method.

Dual statements evidently also hold for prime implicate extraction methods.

Before dealing with discrete functions in general, one shall consider in section 3.2.1 two-dimensional (or planar) discrete functions; the Karnaugh map allows us then to illustrate visually most of the concepts and methods described earlier in this chapter.

3.2.1. The Karnaugh map of two-dimensional discrete functions

The Karnaugh map is probably the simplest and the fastest tool for detecting prime implicants and prime implicates of a discrete function. The power of the Karnaugh map lies in its utilization of the ability of the human mind to perceive patterns (like those of Figures 3.2 and 3.4) in pictorial representations of data. The main drawback of the Karnaugh map representation, for detecting prime implicants and prime implicates, comes from the fact that it is practically limited to discrete functions of two variables and to switching functions of at most four variables. Indeed, a requirement for the Karnaugh map to be useful for prime implicant extraction is that its entries be so arranged that any pair of entries immediately adjacent to each other (horizontally or vertically) must correspond to a pair of input conditions that are logically adjacent, i.e. that differ by a single unit in a single of their coordinates (see section 2.1.2).

Let us first deal with the detection of prime implicants of a discrete function and consider, for example, Figure 3.2.

The pattern corresponding to a convex block is the easiest to perceive: a convex block of weight l is a square or a rectangle grouping entries larger than or equal to l. To the prime convex blocks correspond the squares or rectangles that cannot be included in others.

The pattern corresponding to a block of weight l is again a square or a rectangle grouping entries larger than or equal to l, but these rectangles have an additional property: when dealing with blocks it is assumed that the variables are arranged in ring patterns of symmetry so that these entries in a Karnaugh map would be adjacent if the map were drawn on a torus. Again the prime blocks correspond to the largest rectangles.

Patterns corresponding to cubes are probably the most difficult to identify. They are basically a set of rectangles generated by the intersection of horizontal rows with vertical columns; the prime cubes of weight l correspond to the largest patterns including only entries equal to or larger than l.

In order to detect prime implicants, the following two kinds of algorithms may be used.

Algorithm 3.1

(a) Start with the largest possible pattern, i.e. $S^* = S_1 \times S_0$ and with, for example, the largest weight, i.e. $l = (r-1)$.
(b) By deleting the smallest possible number of rows and/or columns in the pattern S^* try to obtain a pattern S^{**} such that each of its entries has a weight $\geq l$; (l, S^{**}) is then a prime implicant of the function and the patterns smaller than S^{**} are not to be tested for implicants of weight l.
(c) Perform the step (b) but by deleting in another manner the rows and/or columns of S^*; explore in this way all the possible patterns and determine all the prime implicants of weight l.
(d) Once the smallest patterns (which are eventually the entries of the matrix $S_1 \times S_0$) have been explored, perform the same operations (b) and (c) but for a new weight l = (old weight -1).
(e) The algorithm ends once the patterns of weight $l = 1$ have been explored.

Algorithm 3.1 corresponds evidently to a decreasing type of algorithm as described in the introduction of section 3.2. This kind of algorithm is called *decreasing* since the patterns are explored in decreasing order of their dimensions and since the weights of the patterns are also explored from the highest to the lowest.

Algorithm 3.2

(a) Start with the smallest possible pattern, i.e. S^* = (an entry of the Karnaugh map), and with the smallest non-zero weight, i.e. $l = 1$.
(b) By adding other entries of the Karnaugh map to the pattern, try to obtain another pattern S^{**} such that each of its entries has a weight l; once it is impossible to add an entry of weight l to the pattern S^{**}, (l, S^{**}) is a prime implicant

of the function and the patterns larger than S^{**} are not to be tested for implicants of weight l.

(c) Perform the step (b) but by adding in another way the entries to the initial pattern, or by choosing another initial entry S^*; explore in this way all the possible patterns and determine all the prime implicants of weight l.

(d) Once the largest patterns (which is eventually the function domain $S_1 \times S_0$ itself) have been explored, perform the same operations (b) and (c) but for a new weight $l =$ (old weight + 1).

(e) The algorithm ends once the patterns of weight $l = r - 1$ have been explored.

Algorithm 3.2 is an *increasing* type of algorithm (see the introduction to section 3.2).

It is however clear that, when dealing with two-dimensional discrete functions represented by means of their Karnaugh map, the visual aid of this map practically allows us to use simultaneously the two kinds of algorithms in order to achieve in the fastest and simplest way the prime implicant or prime implicate extraction.

Example 3.1. Consider the logic function

$$f:\{0, 1, 2, 3, 4\}^2 \to \{0, 1, 2, 3, 4\}$$

represented by the Karnaugh map of Figure 3.6(a). The circled entries which appear on the map are the prime convex blocks of that function. They are listed below with decreasing weights, which is the order for which they can generally the most easily be detected.

$$f = 4x_1^{(1)} x_0^{(0)} \vee 4x_1^{(1)} x_0^{[3,4]} \vee 4x_1^{[2,3]} x_0^{(2)} \vee 3x_1^{[2,4]} x_0^{[2,4]} \vee 3x_1^{[1,4]} x_0^{[3,4]} \vee$$
$$2x_1^{(4)} \vee 2x_1^{(0)} x_0^{[0,1]} \vee 2x_1^{[0,1]} x_0^{(0)} \vee 1x_1^{[2,4]} x_0^{[1,4]}. \tag{3.20}$$

The circled entries which appear on the map of Figure 3.6(b) are the prime blocks; one has:

$$f = 4x_1^{(1)} x_0^{[3,0]} \vee 4x_1^{[2,3]} x_0^{(2)} \vee 3x_1^{[2,4]} x_0^{[2,4]} \vee 3x_1^{[1,4]} x_0^{[3,4]} \vee 2x_1^{(4)} \vee$$
$$2x_1^{[4,0]} x_0^{[0,1]} \vee 2x_1^{[4,1]} x_0^{(0)} \vee 1x_1^{[2,4]} x_0^{[1,4]} \vee 1x_1^{[2,0]} x_0^{(1)}. \tag{3.21}$$

It could easily be verified that the prime blocks of Figure 3.6(b) are all at the same time prime cubes of the function. The only additional prime cube, schematically represented in Figure 3.6(c), is:

$$2x_1^{(1,4)} x_0^{(0,3,4)}.$$

Dual types of algorithms evidently hold for obtaining, from the Karnaugh map representation, the prime implicates of a discrete function. One has to detect in the map patterns similar to those of Figure 3.4, and then to select the smallest patterns of this kind. From a practical point of view, and since it is generally more difficult to visualize the patterns corresponding to implicates than those corresponding to implicants, it is preferable to obtain the prime implicants of the negation of the function considered and then to take the negation of the result by using the De Morgan laws (theorem 2.1).

Example 3.1 (*continued*). The negation of the function of Figure 3.6(a) is plotted in Figure 3.6(d); in view of this last map, the prime blocks of $\bar{f}$ are:

$$\begin{aligned}\bar{f} = {} & 4x_1^{(0)} x_0^{[2,4]} \vee 4x_1^{[0,1]} x_0^{(2)} \vee 4x_1^{(1)} x_0^{[1,2]} \vee 4x_1^{[2,3]} x_0^{(0)} \vee \\ & 3x_1^{[2,3]} x_0^{[0,1]} \vee 3x_1^{[1,3]} x_0^{(1)} \vee 2x_0^{(1)} \vee \\ & 2x_1^{[2,0]} x_0^{[0,1]} \vee 2x_1^{(0)} \vee 2x_1^{[0,1]} x_0^{[1,2]} \vee \\ & 1x_1^{[4,0]} \vee 1x_1^{[2,0]} x_0^{[3,1]} \end{aligned} \qquad (3.22)$$

from which one deduces the prime antiblocks of f:

$$\begin{aligned} f = {} & (x_1^{[1,4]} \vee x_0^{[0,1]})(x_1^{[2,4]} \vee x_0^{[3,1]})(x_1^{[2,0]} \vee x_0^{[3,0]})(x_1^{[4,1]} \vee x_0^{[1,4]}) \\ & (1 \vee x_1^{[4,1]} \vee x_0^{[2,4]})(1 \vee x_1^{[4,0]} \vee x_0^{[2,0]})(2 \vee x_0^{[2,0]}) \\ & (2 \vee x_1^{(1)} \vee x_0^{[2,4]})(2 \vee x_1^{[1,4]})(2 \vee x_1^{[2,4]} \vee x_0^{[3,0]}) \\ & (3 \vee x_1^{[1,3]})(3 \vee x_1^{(1)} \vee x_0^{(2)}). \end{aligned} \qquad (3.23)$$

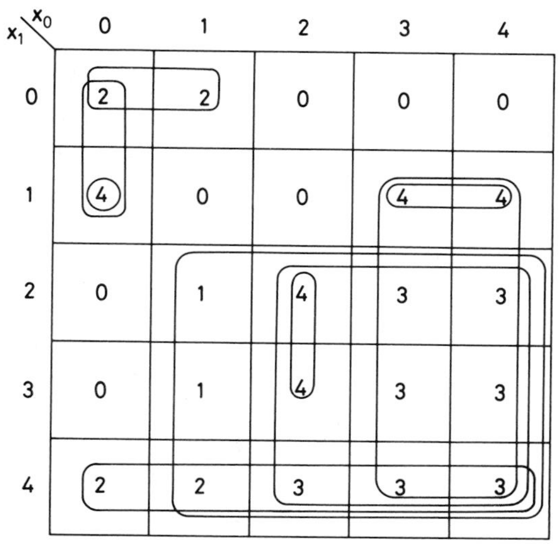

Figure 3.6 (a). Prime convex blocks

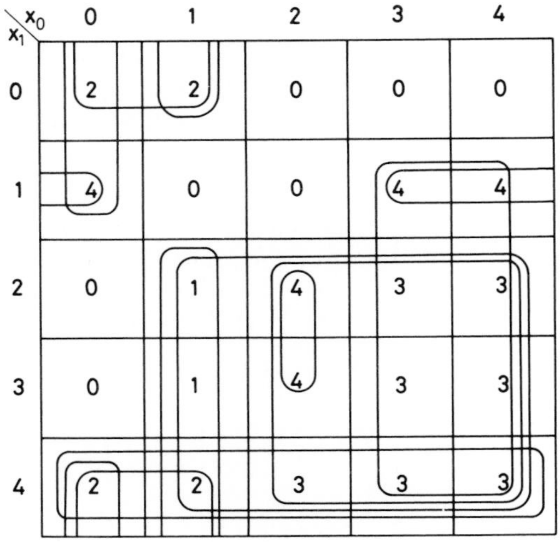

Figure 3.6 (b). Prime blocks

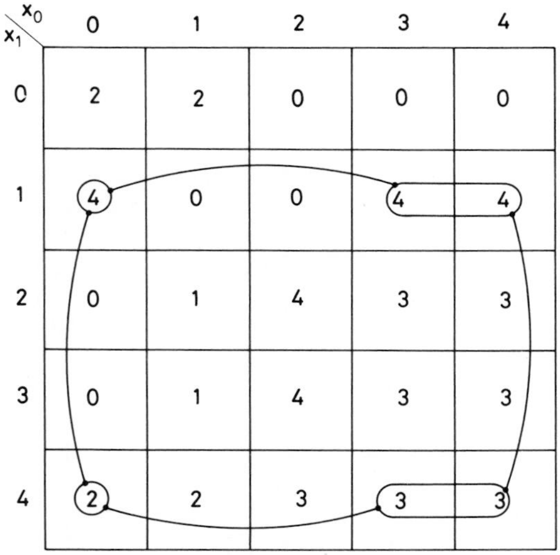

Figure 3.6 (c). Additional prime cube

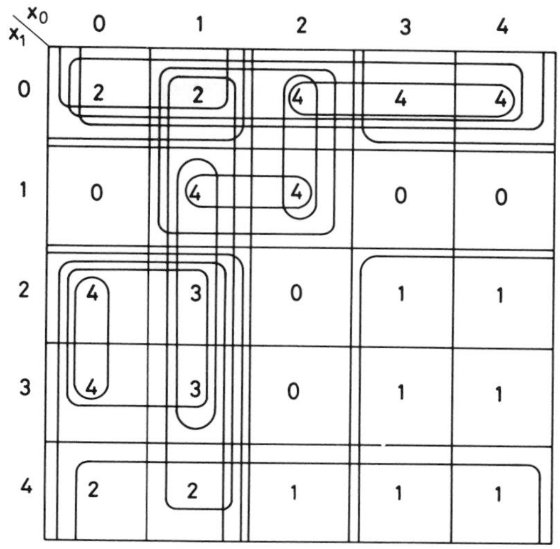

Figure 3.6 (d). Prime blocks of $\bar{f}$

Switching functions

For switching functions the concepts of prime cubes, prime blocks and prime convex blocks of f coincide; these entities are classically called prime implicants of the switching function f. Similarly, the prime anticubes, prime antiblocks and prime convex antiblocks of f are a unique concept and coincide with the prime implicates of the switching function.

Prime implicant and prime implicate extraction of switching functions may be performed through the Karnaugh map representation by means of algorithms identical to those proposed above for discrete functions. However, due to the adjacency properties of the Karnaugh map of switching functions, this method may be used for mappings having at most four variables (the introduction of conventional adjacencies allows us to deal also with switching functions of five and of six variables).

This method was developed in the original paper by Karnaugh [1953] and is generally extensively studied in all the books dealing with switching theory (see, for example, Marcus [1962], McCluskey [1965], Lewin [1968] and Hill and Peterson [1974]).

General discrete functions

It should be noted that since the notions of prime implicants and of prime implicates were defined for any kind of discrete functions, and thus also for general discrete functions (see section 2.1.1), the above methods grounded on the Karnaugh map representation (and the other methods developed in sections 3.2 and 3.3) may be used for obtaining the prime implicants and the prime implicates of any general discrete function.

As quoted above, the weight l of an implicant or of an implicate is a vector of constants when dealing with general discrete functions, i.e. $l = (l_{m-1}, \ldots, l_1, l_0)$.

It is also worthwhile pointing out that general switching functions are classically called *multiple-output switching functions* in the literature dealing with switching theory since, as it will be seen in the sequel, these functions correspond to multiple-output switching networks.

Example 3.2. A general switching function is described by the Karnaugh map of Figure 3.7.

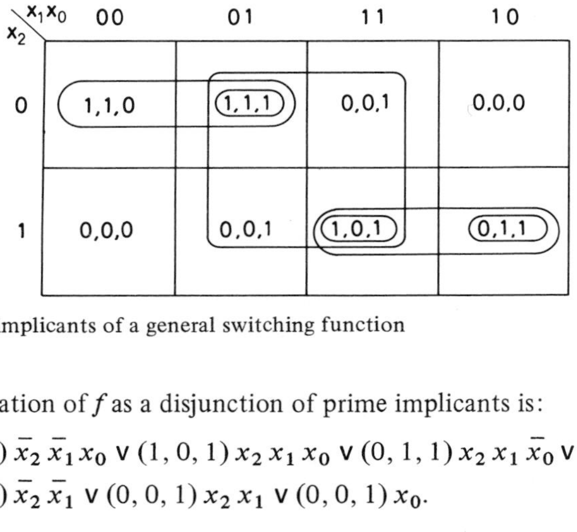

Figure 3.7. Prime implicants of a general switching function

The representation of f as a disjunction of prime implicants is:

$$f = (1, 1, 1)\, \bar{x}_2\, \bar{x}_1\, x_0 \vee (1, 0, 1)\, x_2\, x_1\, x_0 \vee (0, 1, 1)\, x_2\, x_1\, \bar{x}_0 \vee$$
$$(1, 1, 0)\, \bar{x}_2\, \bar{x}_1 \vee (0, 0, 1)\, x_2\, x_1 \vee (0, 0, 1)\, x_0. \tag{3.24}$$

3.2.2. *The implicant–implicate method*

The *implicant–implicate method* for obtaining the prime implicants and the prime implicates of a discrete function is grounded on the algorithm developed in section 1.3.2 (and which will be recalled hereafter for the cube and anticube functions) and on the solution of the two auxiliary problems quoted in the same section 1.3.2. It was first developed by Davio and Bioul [1970].

One will first describe the algorithm for obtaining the prime cubes and the prime anticubes of a discrete function; one then shows that the prime blocks, prime convex blocks, prime antiblocks and prime convex antiblocks are easily obtained from the prime cubes and prime anticubes.

Theorem 3.5 below brings the solution of the auxiliary problem 1 for cubes and anticubes.

Theorem 3.5. (a) *Let*

$$c(x) = l \wedge \bigwedge_{i=n-1}^{0} x_i^{(C_i)}$$

be a cube. The prime anticubes of $c(x)$ *are* l *and* $x_i^{(C_i)}$.

(b) *Let*

$$d(x) = l \vee \bigvee_{i=n-1}^{0} x_i^{(C_i)}$$

be an anticube. The prime cubes of $d(x)$ *are* l *and* $x_i^{(C_i)}$.

Proof. (a) 1. l and $x_i^{(C_i)}$ are anticubes of $c(x)$ since l and $x_i^{(C_i)}$ are greater than $c(x)$.

2. l is a prime anticube of $c(x)$. Indeed, the only anticubes smaller than l are the anticubes l' such that $l' < l$. These are obviously not anticubes of $c(x)$. Similarly, the anticubes smaller than $x_i^{(C_i)}$ are the anticubes $x_i^{(C_i')}$, with $C_i' \subset C_i$, which are not anticubes of $c(x)$.

3. Any prime anticube

$$d(x) = l' \vee \bigvee_{i=n-1}^{0} x_i^{(C_i')}$$

is either l or one of the $x_i^{(C_i)}$. Assume first $l \leqslant l'$. Then $d(x)$ has to be l since $l \leqslant d(x)$ and $d(x)$ is prime. Assume next $l \nleqslant l'$ (i.e. $l > l'$ or l and l' are not comparable). In this case, for one index at least, say k, $C_k \subseteq C_k'$ holds. In the opposite case, $d(x)$ would assume the value l' in at least one point where $c(x)$ assumes the value l: $d(x)$ would not be an implicate. Then $d(x) = x_k^{(C_k)}$ since $x_k^{(C_k)} \leqslant d(x)$ and $d(x)$ is prime.

(b) Dual statement. ■

The following algorithm may then be used for obtaining the prime cubes and the prime anticubes of any discrete function.

Algorithm 3.3. Obtention of prime cubes and/or prime anticubes.

(a) Assume that $f(x)$ is represented as a disjunction of cubes; in view of theorem 3.5(a), each of these cubes is represented as a conjunction of its prime anticubes.

(b) Compute the prime anticubes of f by performing disjunctions of anticubes, using theorem 1.16(b) (let us recall that the disjunction of two anticubes is an anticube).

(c) In view of theorem 3.5(b) each of these anticubes is represented as a disjunction of its prime cubes.

(d) Compute the prime cubes of $f(\boldsymbol{x})$ by performing conjunctions of cubes, using theorem 1.16(a) (let us recall that the conjunction of two cubes is a cube).

It is first interesting to note that the proposed algorithm provides at the same time the representation of f both by its prime cubes and by its prime anticubes. The algorithm is easily matched to partial problems, e.g. to the research of the prime anticubes from a disjunction of cubes or to other data presentation, i.e. to a representation of f as a conjunction of anticubes.

From the computational point of view, steps 2 and 4 of the algorithm are easily performed in a step-by-step way. If f is represented as the disjunction of cubes $C_0 \vee C_1 \vee C_2, \ldots$, we will first compute the prime anticubes of $C_{01} = C_0 \vee C_1$, next the prime anticubes of $C_{012} = C_0 \vee C_1 \vee C_2 = C_{01} \vee C_2$, and so on.

Example 3.3. Consider a ternary function of two quaternary variables:

$$f:\{0, 1, 2, 3\}^2 \to \{0, 1, 2\}$$

and assume it is given as a disjunction of cubes, i.e.

$$f = 1x_1^{(0)} x_0^{(1)} \vee 2x_1^{(0)} x_0^{(2)} \vee 1x_1^{(0)} x_0^{(3)} \vee 1x_1^{(2)} x_0^{(0)} \vee 2x_1^{(2)} x_0^{(2)} \vee 1x_1^{(3)} x_0^{(1)} \vee 1x_1^{(3)} x_0^{(3)}. \tag{3.25}$$

The disjunction of the two first terms is

$$x_1^{(0)} x_0^{(0,2)} (1 \vee x_0^{(2)}).$$

The result is next summed with the third term to give:

$$x_1^{(0)} x_0^{(1,2,3)} (1 \vee x_0^{(2)}).$$

The process is carried on until the last term and provides as resulting representation:

$$f = (1 \vee x_0^{(2)}) (1 \vee x_1^{(0,2)}) (1 \vee x_1^{(2)} \vee x_0^{(1,2,3)}) (x_1^{(2)} \vee x_0^{(1,2,3)}) (x_1^{(0,3)} \vee x_0^{(0,2)}) (x_1^{(0,2,3)} \vee x_0^{(0)}) (x_1^{(0,2)} \vee x_0^{(0,1,3)}) \tag{3.26}$$

(representation of f as a conjunction of prime anticubes).

Step (d) of algorithm 3.1 provides us finally with f as a disjunction of prime cubes, i.e.

$$f = 2x_1^{(0,2)} x_0^{(2)} \vee 1x_1^{(2)} x_0^{(0)} \vee 1x_1^{(0,3)} x_0^{(1,3)} \vee 1x_1^{(0)} x_0^{(1,2,3)}. \tag{3.27}$$

Example 3.4. Consider the general discrete function

$$f = \{0, 1\}^3 \to \{0, 1, 2\}^2$$

given as a disjunction of cubes, i.e.:

$$f = (2, 2)\,x_2^{(1)} x_1^{(0)} \vee (1, 1)\,x_3^{(1)} \vee (2, 1)\,x_3^{(1)} x_1^{(0)} \vee (1, 2)\,x_3^{(1)} x_2^{(0)} x_1^{(1)} \vee$$
$$(0, 1)\,x_1^{(0)} \vee (1, 0)\,x_2^{(0)} x_1^{(1)}. \tag{3.28}$$

The successive steps of the implicant–implicate algorithm are detailed in order to obtain (3.28) as a conjunction of prime anticubes.

(a) $(2, 2)\,x_2^{(1)} x_1^{(0)} \vee (1, 1)\,x_3^{(1)} = (x_3^{(1)} \vee x_1^{(0)})\,(x_3^{(1)} \vee x_2^{(1)})\,((1, 1) \vee x_1^{(0)})\,((1, 1) \vee x_2^{(1)})$.

(b) (Expression (a)) $\vee\, (2, 1)\,x_3^{(1)} x_1^{(0)} = (x_3^{(1)} \vee x_1^{(0)})\,(x_3^{(1)} \vee x_2^{(1)})\,((1, 1) \vee x_1^{(0)})\,((2, 1) \vee x_2^{(1)})\,((1, 1) \vee x_2^{(1)} \vee x_1^{(0)})\,((1, 1) \vee x_3^{(1)} \vee x_2^{(1)})$.

(c) (Expression (b)) $\vee\, (1, 2)\,x_3^{(1)} x_2^{(0)} x_1^{(1)} = (x_3^{(1)} \vee x_1^{(0)})\,(x_3^{(1)} \vee x_2^{(1)})\,((1, 2) \vee x_1^{(0)})\,((1, 1) \vee x_2^{(0)} \vee x_1^{(0)})\,((2, 2) \vee x_2^{(1)})\,((2, 1) \vee x_2^{(1)} \vee x_1^{(1)})$.

(d) (Expression (c)) $\vee\, (0, 1)\,x_1^{(0)} = (x_3^{(1)} \vee x_1^{(0)})\,((0, 1) \vee x_3^{(1)} \vee x_2^{(1)})\,((1, 2) \vee x_1^{(0)})\,((1, 1) \vee x_2^{(0)} \vee x_1^{(0)})\,((1, 1) \vee x_3^{(1)} \vee x_1^{(0)})\,((2, 2) \vee x_2^{(1)})\,((2, 1) \vee x_2^{(1)} \vee x_1^{(1)})$.

(e) (Expression (d)) $\vee\, (1, 0)\,x_2^{(0)} x_1^{(1)} = ((1, 0) \vee x_3^{(1)} \vee x_1^{(0)})\,(x_3 \vee x_2^{(0)} \vee x_1^{(0)})\,((1, 1) \vee x_3^{(1)} \vee x_2^{(1)})\,((0, 1) \vee x_3^{(1)} \vee x_2^{(1)} \vee x_1^{(1)})\,((1, 2) \vee x_1^{(0)})\,((1, 1) \vee x_2^{(0)} \vee x_1^{(1)})\,((2, 1) \vee x_2^{(1)} \vee x_1^{(1)})$. (3.29)

From (3.29) one then deduces by using a similar computation scheme that the representation of f as a disjunction of prime cubes is (3.28).

The results of algorithm 3.3 (i.e. the obtention of the prime cubes and of the prime anticubes of a discrete function) will now be used for obtaining the prime (convex) blocks and the prime (convex) antiblocks of a discrete function.

Let C_i be a subset of S_i; C_i can always be represented as the union of subsets formed by adjacent elements in S_i (see relation 3.2). These subsets will be called *maximal adjacent subsets of* C_i if they are not contained in any other subset formed by adjacent elements of C_i. Clearly, C_i can always be represented as the union of its maximal adjacent subsets. If, moreover, it is assumed that 0 and $m_i - 1$ are not adjacent elements in S_i, the adjacent subsets reduce to the classical notion of *interval*; the *maximal intervals* contained in C_i are defined accordingly, and C_i is also the union of its maximal intervals.

Lemma 3.7. (a) *The representation of a discrete function f as a disjunction of prime blocks (resp. prime convex blocks) can be deduced from its representation as a disjunction of prime cubes by representing each prime cube* $l \wedge \bigwedge_i x_i^{(C_i)}$ *in the form:*

$$l \wedge \bigwedge_i \left(\bigvee_j x_i^{[a_{ij}, b_{ij}]} \right)$$

where $[a_{ij}, b_{ij}]$ *is a maximal adjacent subset of* C_i *(resp. maximal interval of* C_i*), by obtaining that function as a disjunction of blocks (resp. convex blocks) using relation (3.3) and by deleting in the obtained list of blocks (resp. convex blocks) those which are included in other ones.*

(b) *The representation of a discrete function as a conjunction of prime antiblocks (resp. prime convex antiblocks) can be deduced from its representation as a conjunction of prime anticubes by representing each prime anticube* $l \vee \bigvee_i x_i^{(C_i)}$ *in the form:*

$$l \vee \bigvee_i \left(\bigwedge_j x_i^{[a_{ij}, b_{ij}]} \right),$$

where $S_i \backslash [a_i, b_i]$ *is a maximal adjacent subset (resp. maximal interval) of* $S_i \backslash C_i$, *by obtaining that function as a conjunction of antiblocks (resp. convex antiblocks) using relation (3.10) and by deleting in the obtained list of antiblocks (resp. convex antiblocks) those including other ones.*

The routine proof of theorem 3.7 is omitted.

Algorithm 3.4. 1. Obtention of the prime (convex) blocks of $f(\boldsymbol{x})$.

(a) Perform algorithm 3.3(a) and (b).
(b) Use lemma 3.7(a) for obtaining the prime blocks and/or the prime convex blocks of $f(\boldsymbol{x})$.

2. Obtention of the prime (convex) antiblocks of $f(\boldsymbol{x})$.

(a) Perform algorithm 3.3(c) and (d).
(b) Use lemma 3.7(b) for obtaining the prime antiblocks and/or the prime convex antiblocks of $f(\boldsymbol{x})$.

Example 3.3 (continued). From expression (3.27) and from lemma 3.7(a) one obtains successively the expression of $f(\boldsymbol{x})$ as a conjunction of prime blocks and of prime convex blocks:

$$f(\boldsymbol{x}) = 2x_1^{(0)} x_0^{(2)} \vee 2x_1^{(2)} x_0^{(2)} \vee 1x_1^{(2)} x_0^{(0)} \vee 1x_1^{[3,0]} x_0^{(1)} \vee 1x_1^{[3,0]} x_0^{(3)} \vee 1x_1^{(0)} x_0^{[1,3]}. \tag{3.30}$$

$$f(\boldsymbol{x}) = 2x_1^{(0)} x_0^{(2)} \vee 2x_1^{(2)} x_0^{(2)} \vee 1x_1^{(2)} x_0^{(0)} \vee 1x_1^{(3)} x_0^{(1)} \vee 1x_1^{(3)} x_0^{(3)} \vee 1x_1^{(0)} x_0^{[1,3]}. \tag{3.31}$$

Prime blocks and prime convex blocks are obtained, by the intermediate of the prime cubes and of lemma 3.7. An algorithm could also be constructed which gives us immediately the prime blocks and prime convex blocks of a function without resorting to a first representation in terms of prime cubes.

For the representation of f as a disjunction of prime convex blocks and as a conjunction of prime convex antiblocks one has to solve the auxiliary problem 1 (see section 1.3.2) and to apply the algorithm of section 1.3.2. The auxiliary problem 2 has again an immediate solution since the conjunction of two convex blocks is a convex block and since the disjunction of two convex antiblocks is a convex antiblock.

Prime blocks and prime antiblocks of a discrete function may also be obtained by solving the auxiliary problems 1 and 2 and by applying the algorithm of section 1.3.2.

3.2.3. The lattice difference algorithms

Contrarily to the implicant–implicate method (developed in section 3.2.2) the algorithms grounded on the lattice differences, and which will be studied in the present section, are only suited for detecting prime (convex) blocks and prime (convex) antiblocks of discrete functions. The detection of prime cubes and prime anticubes, while possible (see Deschamps and Thayse [1973a]), leads however to very tedious computations; therefore it will not be detailed here.

The concept of lattice difference is defined in section 3.2.3.1; it was introduced by Fadini [1961] (join difference) and Thayse [1973a] (meet difference) for switching functions. The relation of these differences with the classical concepts (in switching theory) of prime implicant and of prime implicate was pointed out by Thayse [1973a].

The lattice differences for discrete functions were introduced by Deschamps and Thayse [1973a] and Thayse [1976], and used among other applications to detection of prime (convex) blocks and prime (convex) antiblocks of a discrete function.

It will appear further on in this section that the lattice differences are a general theoretical concept which can lead to various computational schemes for detecting prime implicants and prime implicates. It allows, among other applications, to develop a generalized consensus theory (see section 3.2.3.4) and a generalized Quine–McCluskey method (see section 3.2.3.5).

3.2.3.1. The lattice differences of discrete functions

At this point we introduce the important concept of lattice difference of a discrete function since it is related to the block functions as it will be seen further on in this section.

Let T be any one of the lattice operations: $\vee$ (disjunction) and $\wedge$ (conjunction).

Definition 3.5. (a) *Simple differences*

Given a discrete function $f(\boldsymbol{x})$, the (partial) lattice difference of $f(\boldsymbol{x})$ with respect to a variable $x_i \in \boldsymbol{x}$ will be denoted Tf/Tx_i and is defined as follows:

$$\frac{Tf}{Tx_i} = f(x_i \oplus 1) \mathsf{T} f(\boldsymbol{x}) \tag{3.32}$$

where $\oplus$ is the sum modulo m_i.

(b) *Multiple differences.*

The multiple differences are defined according to a recurrence scheme:

$$\frac{T^{k_i}f}{Tx_i} = \frac{T}{Tx_i}\left(\frac{T^{k_i-1}f}{Tx_i}\right), \quad k_i \geq 1. \tag{3.33}$$

If $(\boldsymbol{x}_1, \boldsymbol{x}_0)$ is a partition of $\boldsymbol{x}$, the multiple lattice difference of f with respect to the q variables in $\boldsymbol{x}_0$ will be denoted $T^{\boldsymbol{k}_0}f/T\boldsymbol{x}_0$ and is defined as follows:

$$\frac{T^{\boldsymbol{k}_0}f}{T\boldsymbol{x}_0} = \frac{T^{k_0}}{Tx_0}\left[\frac{T^{k_1}}{Tx_1}\left(\cdots\frac{T^{k_{q-1}}f}{Tx_{q-1}}\right)\cdots\right] \tag{3.34}$$

with $\boldsymbol{k}_0 = (k_{q-1}, \ldots, k_1, k_0)$ and $\boldsymbol{x}_0 = (x_{q-1}, \ldots, x_1, x_0)$.

On the basis of the above definition, a set of important functional properties can be derived. They are gathered in theorem 3.6 below; since these functional properties are quite self-evident, this theorem needs no proof.

Theorem 3.6

(a)
$$\frac{T^{\boldsymbol{k}_0}f}{T\boldsymbol{x}_0} = \mathop{\mathsf{T}}_{\boldsymbol{e}_0} f(\boldsymbol{x}_1, \boldsymbol{x}_0 \oplus \boldsymbol{e}_0), \quad \boldsymbol{0} \leq \boldsymbol{e}_0 = (e_{q-1}, \ldots, e_1, e_0) \leq \boldsymbol{k}_0 \tag{3.35}$$

and for $\boldsymbol{k}_0 = (\boldsymbol{m}_0 - \boldsymbol{1}) = (m_{q-1}-1, \ldots, m_1-1, m_0-1)$, relation (3.35) becomes:

$$\frac{T^{(\boldsymbol{m}_0-\boldsymbol{1})}f}{T\boldsymbol{x}_0} = \mathop{\mathsf{T}}_{\boldsymbol{e}_0} f(\boldsymbol{x}_1, \boldsymbol{e}_0), \quad \boldsymbol{0} \leq \boldsymbol{e}_0 \leq (\boldsymbol{m}_0 - \boldsymbol{1}). \tag{3.36}$$

(b)
$$\frac{T^{\boldsymbol{k}_0}l}{T\boldsymbol{x}_0} = l, \quad l \in L. \tag{3.37}$$

(c)
$$\frac{T^{\boldsymbol{k}_0}}{T\boldsymbol{x}_0}[l_0 f(\boldsymbol{x}) \mathsf{T} l_1 g(\boldsymbol{x})] = l_0 \frac{T^{\boldsymbol{k}_0}f}{T\boldsymbol{x}_0} \mathsf{T} l_1 \frac{T^{\boldsymbol{k}_0}g}{T\boldsymbol{x}_0}, \quad l_0, l_1 \in L. \tag{3.38}$$

(d)
$$\frac{T^{k_i}}{Tx_i}\left(\frac{T^{k_j}f}{Tx_j}\right) = \frac{T^{k_j}}{Tx_j}\left(\frac{T^{k_i}f}{Tx_i}\right) = \frac{T^{k_ik_j}f}{Tx_ix_j}. \tag{3.39}$$

From (3.36) and (3.38) one deduces also

$$\frac{T^{k_0}f}{Tx_0} = \frac{T^{(m_0-1)}f}{Tx_0}, \quad k_0 \geqslant (m_0-1)$$

so that it will always be assumed in the following that $0 \leqslant k_i \leqslant m_i-1$, $\forall i = 0, 1, \ldots, n-1$. Further on $T^{k_0}f/Tx_0$ will also be denoted by Tf/Tx_0 for $k_0 = (1, \ldots, 1, 1)$, while $T^0 f/Tx_0$ will be assumed equal to $f(x)$ for $0 = (0, \ldots, 0, 0)$; in other words the following expressions are equivalent:

$$T^{(1,\ldots,1,1)} f/Tx_0 \text{ and } Tf/Tx_0,$$

$$T^{(0,k_0)} f/Tx_1 x_0 \quad \text{and} \quad T^{k_0}f/Tx_0.$$

Definition 3.6. (a) If T is the disjunction, the lattice differences Tf/Tx_i, $T^{k_i}f/Tx_i$ and $T^{k_0}f/Tx_0$ are called *join differences* and will be denoted qf/qx_i, $q^{k_i}f/qx_i$ and $q^{k_0}f/qx_0$ respectively.

(b) Dually, if T is the conjunction, the lattice differences Tf/Tx_i, $T^{k_i}f/Tx_i$ and $T^{k_0}f/Tx_0$ are called *meet differences* and will be denoted pf/px_i, $p^{k_i}f/px_i$ and p^{k_0}/px_0 respectively.

Definition 3.7. (a) A discrete function $f(x)$ is said to be *degenerate* in x_i iff $f(e_i) = f(l_i)$ for any $e_i, l_i \in S_i$.

(b) A discrete function $f(x)$ is said to be degenerate in x_0 iff it is degenerate in each of the variables $x_i \in x_0$, or, equivalently, iff $f(e_0) = f(l_0)$ for any $e_0, l_0 \in \underset{i=q-1,0}{\times} S_i$.

Let us designate by (prime) implicant, either a (prime) cube or a (prime) block or a (prime) convex block; dually let us designate by (prime) implicate either a (prime) anticube or a (prime) antiblock or a (prime) convex antiblock.

Theorem 3.7. (a) *The meet difference $p^{(m_0-1)}f/px_0$ is the largest function smaller than or equal to f and degenerate in x_0; it is the disjunction of all the prime implicants of f independent of x_0.*

(b) *The join difference $q^{(m_0-1)}f/qx_0$ is the smallest function larger than or equal to f and degenerate in x_0; it is the conjunction of all the prime implicates of f independent of x_0.*

Proof. (a) From relation (3.36) one deduces that $p^{(m_0-1)}f/px_0$ is smaller than f, degenerate in x_0 and equal to f for at least one value e_0 of x_0; it is thus the largest function smaller than or equal to f and degenerate in x_0. But the disjunction of the prime implicants of f degenerate in x_0 is also, by definition of the concept of prime implicant, the largest function smaller than or equal to f and degenerate in x_0.

(b) Dual statement. ■

Theorem 3.8. (a) *If* $(p^{k_0}f/p\boldsymbol{x}_0)_{\boldsymbol{x}=\boldsymbol{e}} = l$ *with* $l > 0$, *then*

$$l \wedge \bigwedge_{x_j \in \boldsymbol{x}_1} x_j^{(e_j)} \wedge \bigwedge_{x_i \in \boldsymbol{x}_0} x_i^{[e_i, e_i \oplus k_i]}, \quad \boldsymbol{x} = (\boldsymbol{x}_1, \boldsymbol{x}_0), \tag{3.40}$$

$$\boldsymbol{e} = (e_{n-1}, \ldots, e_1, e_0), \boldsymbol{k}_0 = (k_{q-1}, \ldots, k_1, k_0)$$

is a block of f.

(b) *If* $(q^{k_0}f/q\boldsymbol{x}_0)_{\boldsymbol{x}=\boldsymbol{e}} = l, (l < (r-1))$, *then*

$$l \vee \bigvee_{x_j \in \boldsymbol{x}_1} x_j^{[e_j \oplus 1, e_j - 1]} \vee \bigvee_{x_i \in \boldsymbol{x}_0} x_i^{[e_i \oplus k_i \oplus 1, e_i - 1]}, \quad \boldsymbol{x} = (\boldsymbol{x}_1, \boldsymbol{x}_0), \tag{3.41}$$

$$\boldsymbol{e} = (e_{n-1}, \ldots, e_1, e_0), \boldsymbol{k}_0 = (k_{q-1}, \ldots, k_1, k_0)$$

is an antiblock of f.

Proof. (a) Let us take $\boldsymbol{k}_1 = (k_{n-1}, \ldots, k_{q+1}, k_q) = (0, \ldots, 0, 0)$; from relation 3.35 one deduces $(p^{k_0}f/p\boldsymbol{x}_0)_{\boldsymbol{x}=\boldsymbol{e}} = l$ iff $f(\boldsymbol{x}) \geqslant l$ for

$$\boldsymbol{x} \in \mathop{\times}_{i=n-1}^{0} [e_i, e_i \oplus k_i]$$

and $f(\boldsymbol{x}) = l$ for at least one value of $\boldsymbol{x}$ in that domain; hence the function (3.40) is smaller than $f(\boldsymbol{x})$ and it is thus a block of $f(\boldsymbol{x})$.

(b) Dual statement. ■

The most important properties of the meet and join differences are given by theorems 3.7 and 3.8 hereabove; these theorems relate the concept of lattice difference to those of blocks and antiblocks of a discrete function.

From a computational point of view the evaluation of the lattice differences requests the knowledge of $f(x_i \oplus 1)$ and more generally of $f(\boldsymbol{x}_0 \oplus \boldsymbol{k}_0)$.

Let us first assume that $f(\boldsymbol{x})$ is given by its value vector or value matrix. The expression $f(x_i \oplus 1)$ is then obtained by shifting the function values of one unit along coordinate x_i. This can be performed either visually for planar functions, or by matrix multiplication of the value vector or value matrix with a permutation matrix. Explicit expressions for these matrices are given at the end of this section.

Assume now that f is given by a lattice expression and moreover that the presence of the variable x_i is denoted as follows in the expression:

$$f(\boldsymbol{x}) = f(x_i^{(a_{ij}, b_{ij}, \ldots, e_{ij})})$$

then

$$f(x_i \oplus k_i) = f(x_i^{(a_{ij} - k_i, b_{ij} - k_i, \ldots, e_{ij} - k_i)}). \tag{3.42}$$

Similarly, if all the exponentiations relative to x_i are in the block form, i.e.

$$f(\boldsymbol{x}) = f(x_i^{[a_{ij}, b_{ij}]})$$

then

$$f(x_i \oplus k_i) = f(x_i^{[a_{ij}-k_i,\, b_{ij}-k_i]}). \tag{3.43}$$

In (3.42) and (3.43) "–" stands for the subtraction in the ring.

Example 3.1 (continued). From the lattice expression (3.20) one deduces in view of (3.42)

$$\begin{aligned} f(x_1 \oplus 1) = {} & 4x_1^{(0)} x_0^{(0)} \vee 4x_1^{(0)} x_0^{[3,4]} \vee 4x_1^{[1,2]} x_0^{(2)} \vee 3x_1^{[1,3]} x_0^{[2,4]} \vee \\ & 3x_1^{[0,3]} x_0^{[3,4]} \vee 2x_1^{(3)} \vee 2x_1^{(4)} x_0^{[0,1]} \vee 2x_1^{[4,0]} x_0^{(0)} \vee \\ & 1x_1^{[1,3]} x_0^{[1,4]} \end{aligned} \tag{3.44}$$

$$\begin{aligned} pf/px_1 &= f \wedge f(x_1 \oplus 1) \\ &= 4x_1^{(2)} x_0^{(2)} \vee 3x_1^{(1)} x_0^{[3,4]} \vee 3x_1^{[2,3]} x_0^{[2,4]} \vee 2x_1^{(4)} x_0^{[0,1]} \vee \\ &\quad 2x_1^{[4,0]} x_0^{(0)} \vee 1x_1^{[2,3]} x_0^{[1,4]} \end{aligned} \tag{3.45}$$

$$\begin{aligned} (pf/px_1)_{x_1 = x_1 \oplus 1} = {} & 4x_1^{(1)} x_0^{(2)} \vee 3x_1^{(0)} x_0^{[3,4]} \vee 3x_1^{[1,2]} x_0^{[2,4]} \vee 2x_1^{(3)} x_0^{[0,1]} \vee \\ & 2x_1^{[3,4]} x_0^{(0)} \vee 1x_1^{[1,2]} x_0^{[1,4]} \end{aligned} \tag{3.46}$$

$$\begin{aligned} p^2f/px_1 &= f \wedge f(x_1 \oplus 1) \wedge f(x_1 \oplus 2) \\ &= p(pf/px_1)/px_1 \\ &= (pf/px_1)\,((pf/px_1)_{x_1 = x_1 \oplus 1}) \\ &= 3x_1^{(1)} x_0^{[3,4]} \vee 3x_1^{(2)} x_0^{[2,4]} \vee 1x_1^{(3)} x_0^{(1)} \vee 2x_1^{(4)} x_0^{(0)} \vee 1x_1^{(2)} x_0^{[1,4]} \end{aligned} \tag{3.47}$$

$$\begin{aligned} p^{21}f/px_1x_0 &= (p^2f/px_1)\,((p^2f/px_1)_{x_0 = x_0 \oplus 1}) \\ &= 3x_1^{(2)} x_0^{[2,3]} \vee 3x_1^{(1)} x_0^{(3)} \vee 1x_1^{(2)} x_0^{[1,3]} \end{aligned} \tag{3.48}$$

$$\begin{aligned} p^{22}f/px_1x_0 &= p(p^{21}f/px_1x_0)/px_0 \\ &= 3x_1^{(2)} x_0^{(2)} \vee 1x_1^{(2)} x_0^{[1,2]}. \end{aligned} \tag{3.49}$$

Since $(p^{22}f/px_1x_0)_{x_1, x_0 = 2,2} = 3$ one deduces that

$$3x_1^{[2,4]} x_0^{[2,4]}$$

is a block of f.

The functions $pf/px_1, p^2f/px_1, p^{21}f/px_1x_0$ and $p^{22}f/px_1x_0$ are also described by means of Figures 3.8(a), (b), (c) and (d) respectively. These Karnaugh maps for the lattice differences may be obtained directly from the function Karnaugh map of Figure 3.6(a).

$x_1 \backslash x_0$	0	1	2	3	4
0	2				
1				3	3
2		1	4	3	3
3		1	3	3	3
4	2	2			

(a)

			3	3
	1	3	3	3
	1			
2				

(b)

			3	
	1	3	3	

(c)

	1	3		

(d)

Figure 3.8. Meet differences
(a) pf/px_1
(b) $p^2 f/px_1$
(c) $p^{21} f/px_1 x_0$
(d) $p^{22} f/px_1 x_0$

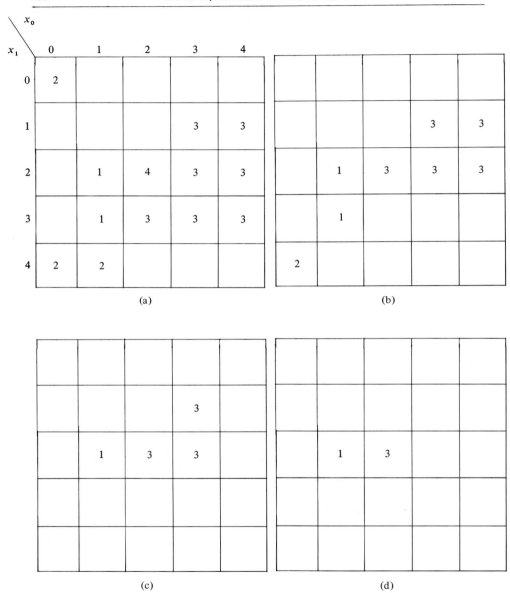

Expressions (3.42)–(3.43) allow us to compute the lattice differences of a discrete function f when the latter is given by means of a lattice expression. It is also important to have matrix relations allowing us to evaluate these differences when the function f is given by the intermediate of its value vector.

Consider first a single variable discrete function $f(x)$:

$$f(x) = \{0, 1, \ldots, m-1\} \rightarrow \{0, 1, \ldots, r-1\}.$$

Define the matrices $E_{m,k}$ as follows: $E_{m,0}$ is the $(m \times m)$ unit matrix (generally denoted I_m), i.e.

$$E_{m,0} = I_m = \begin{bmatrix} 1 & & & & & \\ & 1 & & & & \\ & & 1 & & & \\ & & & \cdot & & \\ & & & & \cdot & \\ & & & & & 1 \end{bmatrix}$$

Let P_m be the $(m \times m)$ primitive circulant, that is (only the 0's on the diagonal have been indicated):

$$P_m = \begin{bmatrix} 0 & & & & & & 1 \\ 1 & 0 & & & & & \\ & 1 & 0 & & & & \\ & & 1 & \cdot & & & \\ & & & & \cdot & & \\ & & & & & 0 & \\ & & & & & 1 & 0 \end{bmatrix}$$

$$E_{m,1} = I_m + P_m$$

$$E_{m,2} = I_m + P_m + P_m^2 \text{ where } P_m^2 = P_m . P_m$$

$$\vdots$$

$$E_{m,k} = I_m + \sum_{i=1}^{k} P_m^k .$$

$E_{m,k}$ is thus an $(m \times m)$ matrix of 0's and 1's; let us denote by $(r-1)E_{m,k}$ the matrix $E_{m,k}$ multiplied by the scalar $r-1$.

The following relations then immediately derive from the definitions 3.5.6:

$$\left[\frac{q^k f}{qx}(e)\right] = [f_e] \, \textcircled{\vee\wedge} \, (r-1)E_{m,k} \tag{3.50}$$

$$\left[\frac{p^k f}{px}(e)\right] = [f_e] \, \textcircled{\wedge\vee} \, \overline{(r-1)E_{m,k}} \tag{3.51}$$

The properties of the Kronecker matrix product (see section 1.5.3) allow us to state the following theorem:

Theorem 3.9

$$\text{(a)}\quad \left[\frac{q^k f}{qx}(e)\right] = [f_e] \; \bigcirc\!\!\!\!\!\!\!\vee\wedge \; (r-1)\left[\overset{\wedge}{\underset{i=n-1,0}{\otimes}} E_{m_i,k_i}\right] \tag{3.52}$$

$$\text{(b)}\quad \left[\frac{p^k f}{px}(e)\right] = [f_e] \; \bigcirc\!\!\!\!\!\!\!\wedge\vee \; \left[\overset{\vee}{\underset{i=n-1,0}{\otimes}} \overline{(r-1)\,E_{m_i,k_i}}\right] \tag{3.53}$$

$$k = (k_{n-1}, \ldots, k_1, k_0).$$

Switching functions

The meet and join differences of switching functions enjoy some special computational properties which allow an easy evaluation of these functions.

First of all, since for switching functions $(r-1) = 1$, the meet and join differences are of the form:

$$qf/q\boldsymbol{x}_0 \quad \text{and} \quad pf/p\boldsymbol{x}_0;$$

indeed, $q^{\boldsymbol{k}_0}f/q\boldsymbol{x}_0$ and $p^{\boldsymbol{k}_0}f/p\boldsymbol{x}_0$ are only meaningful for $k_i \leqslant 1$, $\vee\; k_i \in \boldsymbol{k}_0$.

The following theorems, which are a direct consequence of theorem 3.7, show the importance of the concepts of join and of meet differences as a theoretical tool by giving the relations of these differences with the classical concepts of prime implicant and prime implicate of a switching function.

Theorem 3.10. (a) *The function $pf/p\boldsymbol{x}_0$ is the disjunction of the prime implicants of $f(\boldsymbol{x})$ degenerate in $\boldsymbol{x}_0$.*

(b) *The function $qf/q\boldsymbol{x}_0$ is the conjunction of the prime implicates of $f(\boldsymbol{x})$ degenerate in $\boldsymbol{x}_0$.*

Theorem 3.10 is a particular case of theorem 3.7 and thus needs no proof.

Theorem 3.11. (a) *If $(\boldsymbol{x}_1, \boldsymbol{x}_0)$ is a partition of $\boldsymbol{x}$, the minterms of the function*

$$p_{\boldsymbol{x}_0}(f) = \frac{pf}{p\boldsymbol{x}_0} \wedge \bigwedge_{x_i \in \boldsymbol{x}_1} \overline{\frac{pf}{p\boldsymbol{x}_0 x_i}} \tag{3.54}$$

are the prime implicants of f degenerate in $\boldsymbol{x}_0$ and containing all the variables of $\boldsymbol{x}_1$.

(b) *The minterms of the function*

$$q_{\boldsymbol{x}_0}(f) = \overline{\frac{qf}{q\boldsymbol{x}_0}} \wedge \bigwedge_{x_i \in \boldsymbol{x}_1} \frac{qf}{q\boldsymbol{x}_0 x_i} \tag{3.55}$$

are the prime implicants of $\bar{f}$ degenerate in $\boldsymbol{x}_0$ and containing all the variables of $\boldsymbol{x}_1$.

Proof. (a) The function $pf/p\boldsymbol{x}_0$ is the disjunction of all the prime implicants of f degenerate in $\boldsymbol{x}_0$; if this last expression is multiplied by $pf/p\boldsymbol{x}_0 x_i$ one eliminates the prime implicants degenerate in $\boldsymbol{x}_0$ and in x_i. The expression (3.54) is the disjunction of the prime implicants containing all the variables of $\boldsymbol{x}_1$.

(b) Dual statement. ■

Theorems 3.10 and 3.11 will be used later in this chapter for deriving prime implicant and prime implicate extraction algorithms for switching functions.

It is important to have good computational formula for obtaining the lattice differences of a switching function f from any of its lattice expressions; from (3.35) one deduces:

$$pf/px_i = f \wedge f(\bar{x}_i) = f(x_i = 0) \wedge f(x_i = 1), \tag{3.56}$$

$$qf/qx_i = f \vee f(\bar{x}_i) = f(x_i = 0) \vee f(x_i = 1). \tag{3.57}$$

The higher order differences can either be evaluated by means of the recurrence formula and of (3.56)–(3.57), i.e.

$$pf/px_i x_j = p(pf/px_i)/px_j = (pf/px_i)_{x_j=0} \wedge (pf/px_i)_{x_j=1} \tag{3.58}$$

$$qf/qx_i x_j = q(qf/qx_i)/qx_j = (qf/qx_i)_{x_j=0} \vee (qf/qx_i)_{x_j=1} \tag{3.59}$$

or by means of the general formula:

$$pf/p\boldsymbol{x}_0 = \bigwedge_{\boldsymbol{e}_0} f(\boldsymbol{x}_1, \boldsymbol{e}_0), \quad 0 \leqslant e_i \leqslant 1, \quad e_i \in \boldsymbol{e}_0 \tag{3.60}$$

$$qf/q\boldsymbol{x}_0 = \bigvee_{\boldsymbol{e}_0} f(\boldsymbol{x}_1, \boldsymbol{e}_0), \quad 0 \leqslant e_i \leqslant 1, \quad e_i \in \boldsymbol{e}_0. \tag{3.61}$$

It is worth pointing out that the above formulae may also be used when the switching function is given by means of a well-formed expression made up of the lattice operations $\wedge$ and $\vee$, of the ring operation $\oplus$ and of the literals x_i and $\bar{x}_i$. Mixed lattice-ring expressions are indeed of frequent use for describing switching functions; the main reason why such expressions are not used for describing discrete functions is that the lattice exponentiation differs from the ring exponentiation, except for switching functions where the two concepts coincide.

Let us now assume $f(\boldsymbol{x})$ be given by its value vector $[f_e]$. The following theorem, which derives immediately from theorem 3.9, gives us the value vectors of the lattice differences.

Theorem 3.12

(a) $$\left[\frac{q^k f}{qx}(e)\right] = [f_e] \text{ (}\vee\ \wedge\text{) } \left(\overset{\wedge}{\underset{i=n-1,0}{\otimes}} E_{k_i}\right) \tag{3.62}$$

(b) $$\left[\frac{p^k f}{px}(e)\right] = [f_e] \text{ (}\wedge\ \vee\text{) } \left(\overset{\vee}{\underset{i=n-1,0}{\otimes}} \bar{E}_{k_i}\right) \tag{3.63}$$

with $k = (k_{n-1}, \ldots, k_1, k_0), \quad 0 \leqslant k_i \leqslant 1,$

$$E_{k_i} = \begin{bmatrix} 1 & k_i \\ k_i & 1 \end{bmatrix}$$

Example 3.5

$$f = x_0(x_1 \oplus x_2x_3) \oplus (\bar{x}_4 \vee x_5) \tag{3.64}$$

$$pf/px_0 = f(x_0 = 0) \wedge f(x_0 = 1) = (\bar{x}_4 \vee x_5)(\bar{x}_1 \oplus x_2x_3)$$

$$pf/px_0x_2 = (pf/px_0)_{x_2=0} \wedge (pf/px_0)_{x_2=1} = (\bar{x}_4 \vee \bar{x}_5)\bar{x}_3\bar{x}_1$$

$$pf/px_0x_2x_1 = 0, pf/px_0x_2x_3 = 0, pf/px_0x_2x_4 = \bar{x}_1\bar{x}_3x_5,$$

$$pf/px_0x_2x_5 = \bar{x}_1\bar{x}_3\bar{x}_4 .$$

Since:

$$\frac{pf}{px_0x_2} \wedge \overline{\frac{pf}{px_0x_2x_1}} \wedge \overline{\frac{pf}{px_0x_2x_3}} \wedge \overline{\frac{pf}{px_0x_2x_4}} \wedge \overline{\frac{pf}{px_0x_2x_5}} = 0$$

the function (3.64) has no prime implicant degenerate in x_0x_2 and containing the variables $x_1x_3x_4x_5$ (see theorem 3.11(a)).

$$pf/px_0x_4 = x_5(\bar{x}_1 \oplus x_2x_3)$$

$$pf/px_0x_4x_1 = 0, pf/px_0x_4x_2 = x_5\bar{x}_3\bar{x}_1, pf/px_0x_4x_3 = x_5\bar{x}_2\bar{x}_1,$$

$$pf/px_0x_4x_5 = 0$$

$$\frac{pf}{px_0x_4} \wedge \overline{\frac{pf}{px_0x_4x_1}} \wedge \overline{\frac{pf}{px_0x_4x_2}} \wedge \overline{\frac{pf}{px_0x_4x_3}} \wedge \overline{\frac{pf}{px_0x_4x_5}} = x_5x_3x_2x_1 .$$

This last expression $x_5x_3x_2x_1$ is a prime implicant of f in view of theorem 3.11(a).

3.2.3.2. The extended vector algorithm

The extended vector algorithm is the most general method making use of the lattice differences; it applies to any representation of discrete functions. The latter may thus be given either by any lattice expression or by its value vector. Other types of algorithms will be presented in next sections which apply, e.g. only when the lattice expression is given by a normal disjunctive form (see section 3.2.3.3) or when the discrete function is described by a value table (see the Quine–McCluskey method of section 3.2.3.5).

The extended vector algorithm will first be presented in its fundamental form; a simplified extended vector algorithm will then be derived, which permits several kinds of computational simplifications.

3.2.3.2.1. Fundamental form

The concept of *extended vector* was first defined by Bioul and Davio [1972] with respect to the operation of modulo-2 sum and for switching functions. This concept has been enlarged both to lattice operations (disjunction and conjunction) and to discrete functions by Thayse [1976]; it is applied in this section to the research of the prime (convex) blocks and prime (convex) antiblocks of these functions.

Let $[f(\boldsymbol{e})]$ be the value vector of $f(\boldsymbol{x})$, with $\boldsymbol{e} = (e_{n-1}, \ldots, e_1, e_0)$; $0 \leqslant e_j \leqslant m_j - 1 \;\forall j$. The *partial value vector* of f with respect to $x_i \in \boldsymbol{x}$, that is: $[f(x_i = 0), f(x_i = 1), \ldots, f(x_i = m_i - 1)]$ will be denoted by $[f(e_i)]$ and the partial value vector of f with respect to $\boldsymbol{x}_0 \subseteq \boldsymbol{x}$ will be denoted by $[f(\boldsymbol{e}_0)]$. Let T be either the disjunction "$\vee$" or the conjunction "$\wedge$" and $\perp$ the dual:

Definition 3.8. (a) The T-*partial extended vector* of a discrete function f with respect to a variable x_i will be denoted by $\phi_{x_i}^{(T)}(f)$ and is defined as follows:

$$\phi_{x_i}^{(T)}(f) = \left\{[f(e_i)], \left[\frac{Tf}{Tx_i}(e_i)\right], \ldots, \left[\frac{T^{m_i-2}f}{Tx_i}(e_i)\right], \frac{T^{m_i-1}f}{Tx_i}\right\}. \tag{3.65}$$

It is recalled that $T^{m_i-1}f/Tx_i$ is degenerate in x_i (see theorem 3.6). Clearly, in view of the above definitions, $\phi_{x_i}^{(T)}(f)$ associates to the function $f{:}S \to L$, $m_i(m_i - 1) + 1$ applications:

$$S_{n-1} \times \ldots \times S_{i+1} \times S_{i-1} \times \ldots \times S_0 \to L.$$

The T-partial extended vector of f with respect to the variables in $\boldsymbol{x}_0 = (x_{q-1}, \ldots, x_1, x_0) \subseteq \boldsymbol{x}$ is denoted $\phi_{\boldsymbol{x}_0}^{(T)}(f)$; it is defined according to the following iterative scheme:

Definition 3.8. (b) For any $x_i, x_j \in \boldsymbol{x}$, $\phi_{x_jx_i}^{(T)}(f)$ is defined as follows (in view of definition 3.8(a)):

$$\begin{aligned}
\phi_{x_jx_i}^{(T)}(f) &= \phi_{x_j}^{(T)}[\phi_{x_i}^{(T)}(f)] \\
&= \left(\phi_{x_j}^{(T)}\{[f(e_i)]\}, \phi_{x_j}^{(T)}\left\{\left[\frac{Tf}{Tx_i}(e_i)\right]\right\}, \ldots, \right. \\
&\quad \left. \phi_{x_j}^{(T)}\left\{\left[\frac{T^{m_i-2}f}{Tx_i}(e_i)\right]\right\}, \phi_{x_j}^{(T)}\left(\frac{T^{m_i-1}f}{Tx_i}\right)\right) \\
&= \left\{[f(e_i, e_j)], \left[\frac{Tf}{Tx_j}(e_i, e_j)\right], \ldots, \frac{T^{m_j-1}f}{Tx_j}(e_i), \right. \\
&\quad \left[\frac{Tf}{Tx_i}(e_i, e_j)\right], \left[\frac{Tf}{Tx_jx_i}(e_i, e_j)\right], \ldots, \frac{T^{(m_j-1)1}f}{Tx_jx_i}(e_i), \ldots, \\
&\quad \left. \frac{T^{(m_j-1)(m_i-1)}f}{Tx_jx_i}\right\}.
\end{aligned} \tag{3.66}$$

$\phi^{(\mathrm{T})}_{x_0}(f)$ derives immediately from the recurrence formula (3.66), i.e.

$$\phi^{(\mathrm{T})}_{x_0}(f) = \phi^{(\mathrm{T})}_{x_0}\{\phi^{(\mathrm{T})}_{x_1}[\ldots(\phi^{(\mathrm{T})}_{x_{q-1}}(f))\ldots]\}. \tag{3.67}$$

Definition 3.8. (c) The T-extended vector $\phi^{(\mathrm{T})}(f)$ finally derives from the above definitions when the complete set x of variables is considered, i.e.

$$\phi^{(\mathrm{T})}(f) = \phi^{(\mathrm{T})}_{x}(f). \tag{3.68}$$

Example 3.6. Consider a ternary function of a binary variable x_0 and of a ternary variable x_1, that is a function

$$f: \{0, 1, 2\} \times \{0, 1\} \rightarrow \{0, 1, 2\}$$

$$f = 2x_1^{(0)} x_0^{(1)} \vee 2x_1^{(0)} x_0^{(0)} \vee 2x_1^{(1)} x_0^{(0)} \vee 1x_1^{(2)} x_0^{(0)} \vee 1x_1^{(2)} x_0^{(1)}. \tag{3.69}$$

One has successively:

$$\begin{aligned}
\phi^{(\wedge)}_{x_1}(f) &= [f(x_1 = 0), f(x_1 = 1), f(x_1 = 2), (pf/px_1)_{x_1=0}, (pf/px_1)_{x_1=1},\\
&\quad (pf/px_1)_{x_1=2}, p^2 f/px_1]\\
&= (2x_0^{(1)} \vee 2x_0^{(0)}, 2x_0^{(0)}, 1x_0^{(0)} \vee 1x_0^{(1)}, 2x_0^{(0)}, 1x_0^{(0)}, 1x_0^{(0)} \vee 1x_0^{(1)}, 1x_0^{(0)})\\
\phi^{(\wedge)}_{x_1 x_0}(f) &= [f(x_1, x_0 = 0, 0), f(x_1, x_0 = 0, 1), (pf/px_0)_{x_1=0},\\
&\quad f(x_1, x_0 = 1, 0), \ldots, p^{21} f/px_1 x_0]\\
&= (2, 2, 2, 2, 0, 0, 1, 1, 1, 2, 0, 0, 1, 0, 0, 1, 1, 1, 1, 0, 0)
\end{aligned} \tag{3.70}$$

$$\begin{aligned}
\phi^{(\vee)}_{x_1}(f) &= [f(x_1 = 0), f(x_1 = 1), f(x_1 = 2), (qf/qx_1)_{x_1=0}, (qf/qx_1)_{x_1=1},\\
&\quad (qf/qx_1)_{x_1=2}, q^2 f/qx_1]\\
&= (2x_0^{(1)} \vee 2x_0^{(0)}, 2x_0^{(0)}, 1x_0^{(0)} \vee 1x_0^{(1)}, 2x_0^{(0)} \vee 2x_0^{(1)}, 2x_0^{(0)} \vee\\
&\quad 1x_0^{(1)}, 2x_0^{(0)} \vee 2x_0^{(1)}, 2x_0^{(0)} \vee 2x_0^{(1)})
\end{aligned} \tag{3.71}$$

$$\phi^{(\vee)}_{x_1 x_0}(f) = (2, 2, 2, 2, 0, 2, 1, 1, 1, 2, 2, 2, 2, 1, 2, 2, 2, 2, 2, 2, 2). \tag{3.72}$$

As mentioned above, the extended vectors may easily be computed when the discrete function f is given by its value vector; let us define the following matrices:

E_i is the $(m_i \times 1)$ matrix of 1's,

that is:

$$E_i = (1, 1, \ldots, 1)^t$$

(t indicates as usual the transpose operation).

$M_i^{(\vee)}$ is the $m_i \times (m_i(m_i-1)+1)$ matrix of 0's and of $(r-1)$'s defined as follows (see the definition of the matrix $E_{m,k}$ in the preceding section):

$$M_i^{(\vee)} = (r-1)\,(E_{m_i,0}, E_{m_i,1}, \ldots, E_{m_i,(m_i-2)}, E_i) \tag{3.73}$$

$$M_i^{(\wedge)} = [(r-1)] - M_i^{(\vee)} = \overline{M_i^{(\vee)}} \tag{3.74}$$

where $[(r-1)]$ denotes an $\{m_i \times [m_i(m_i-1)+1]\}$ matrix of $(r-1)$'s; otherwise, $M_i^{(\wedge)}$ is obtained from $M_i^{(\vee)}$ by interchanging the 0's and the $(r-1)$'s. Both types of matrices will be denoted by the single symbol $M_i^{(\top)}$.

In view of theorem 3.9 and of definitions 3.8, one has

$$\phi_{x_i}^{(\top)}(f) = [f(e_i)] \; \textcircled{\top\,\perp} \; [M_i^{(\top)}] \tag{3.75}$$

$$\phi^{(\top)}(f) = [f(e)] \; \textcircled{\top\,\perp} \left[\overset{\perp}{\underset{i=n-1,0}{\otimes}} M_i^{(\top)} \right]. \tag{3.76}$$

Example 3.6 (continued). The value vector of the function (3.69) is

$$[f(e_1, e_0)] = (2, 2, 2, 0, 1, 1).$$

The matrices $M_1^{(\wedge)}$ and $M_0^{(\wedge)}$ are respectively:

$$M_1^{(\wedge)} = \begin{bmatrix} 0 & 2 & 2 & 0 & 2 & 0 & 0 \\ 2 & 0 & 2 & 0 & 0 & 2 & 0 \\ 2 & 2 & 0 & 2 & 0 & 2 & 0 \end{bmatrix}$$

$$M_0^{(\wedge)} = \begin{bmatrix} 0 & 2 & 0 \\ 2 & 0 & 0 \end{bmatrix}$$

One verifies then easily

$$M^{(\wedge)} = M_1^{(\wedge)} \overset{\vee}{\otimes} M_0^{(\wedge)} = \left[\begin{array}{ccccccc|ccccccc|ccccccc} 0 & 2 & 0 & 2 & 2 & 2 & 2 & 2 & 2 & 0 & 2 & 0 & 2 & 2 & 2 & 0 & 2 & 0 & 0 & 2 & 0 \\ 2 & 0 & 0 & 2 & 2 & 2 & 2 & 2 & 2 & 2 & 0 & 0 & 2 & 2 & 2 & 2 & 0 & 0 & 2 & 0 & 0 \\ 2 & 2 & 2 & 0 & 2 & 0 & 2 & 2 & 2 & 0 & 2 & 0 & 0 & 2 & 0 & 2 & 2 & 2 & 0 & 2 & 0 \\ \hline 2 & 2 & 2 & 2 & 0 & 0 & 2 & 2 & 2 & 2 & 0 & 0 & 2 & 0 & 0 & 2 & 2 & 2 & 2 & 0 & 0 \\ 2 & 2 & 2 & 2 & 2 & 2 & 0 & 2 & 0 & 2 & 2 & 2 & 0 & 2 & 0 & 0 & 2 & 0 & 0 & 2 & 0 \\ 2 & 2 & 2 & 2 & 2 & 2 & 2 & 0 & 0 & 2 & 2 & 2 & 2 & 0 & 0 & 2 & 0 & 0 & 2 & 0 & 0 \end{array}\right].$$

The extended vector $\phi^{(\wedge)}(f)$ is then:

$$\phi^{(\wedge)}(f) = [f(e_1, e_0)] \; \textcircled{\wedge\,\vee} \; M^{(\wedge)} = (2, 2, 2, 2, 0, 0, 1, 1, 1, 2, 0, 0, 1, 0, 0, 1, 1, 1, 1, 0, 0).$$

The properties of the Kronecker matrix product however always allow us to avoid the cumbersome computation of the matrix $M^{(\wedge)}$. By considering first the value vector $[f(e_1, e_0)]$ as a (1×3) matrix, each element of which is formed by a pair of elements, that is:

$$[f(e_1, e_0)] = [(2,2), (2,0), (1,1)]$$

one obtains first:

$$[(2,2),(2,0),(1,1)] \textcircled{\wedge \vee} M_1^{(\wedge)} = [(2,2),(2,0),(1,1),(2,0),(1,0),(1,1),(1,0)].$$

By applying the transformation matrix $M_0^{(\wedge)}$ to each of the 2-tuples of the above vector, one obtains finally the extended vector (3.70).

Let us denote by $(x_i^{[j, j \oplus k]})$ the vector

$$(x_i^{[0,k]}, x_i^{[1,k \oplus 1]}, x_i^{[2,k \oplus 2]}, \ldots, x_i^{[m_i - 1, k \oplus m_i - 1]}).$$

The vectors $K_i^{(\top)}$ are then defined as follows

$$K_i^{(\wedge)} = [(x_i^{[j,j \oplus 0]}), (x_i^{[j,j \oplus 1]}), \ldots, (x_i^{[j,j \oplus (m_i - 2)]}), x_i^{[j,j \oplus (m_i - 1)]} = r - 1]^t \tag{3.77}$$

$$K_i^{(\vee)} = (r-1) - K_i^{(\wedge)} = \overline{K_i^{(\wedge)}} \tag{3.78}$$

$K^{(\top)}$ is the Kronecker product: $K^{(\top)} = \overset{\top}{\underset{i=n-1,\,0}{\otimes}} K_i^{(\top)}$.

Theorem 3,13. The blocks (antiblocks) of the function $f(x)$ are the terms of:

$$\phi^{(\top)}(f) \textcircled{\perp \top} K^{(\top)} \tag{3.79}$$

with $\top$ the conjunction (disjunction) and $\perp$ the dual operation.

Proof. For $n = 1, m = 3$, a routine verification shows that:

(a) $[f(0), f(1), f(2), f(0) \wedge f(1), f(1) \wedge f(2), f(2) \wedge f(0), f(0) \wedge f(1) \wedge f(2)] \textcircled{\vee \wedge}$ $[x^{[0,0]}, x^{[1,1]}, x^{[2,2]}, x^{[0,1]}, x^{[1,2]}, x^{[2,0]}, x^{[0,2]} = (r-1)]^t = f(0)\, x^{[0,0]} \vee$ $f(1)\, x^{[1,1]} \vee f(2)\, x^{[2,2]} \vee f(0) f(1)\, x^{[0,1]} \vee f(1) f(2)\, x^{[1,2]} \vee f(2) f(0)\, x^{[2,0]} \vee$ $f(0) f(1) f(2)$.

(b) $[f(0), f(1), f(2), f(0) \vee f(1), f(1) \vee f(2), f(2) \vee f(0), f(0) \vee f(1) \vee f(2)] \textcircled{\wedge \vee}$ $[x^{[1,2]}, x^{[2,0]}, x^{[0,1]}, x^{[2,2]}, x^{[0,0]}, x^{[1,1]}, 0]^t = [f(0) \vee x^{[1,2]}]$ $[f(1) \vee x^{[2,0]}]\ [f(2) \vee x^{[0,1]}]\ [f(0) \vee f(1) \vee x^{[2,2]}]\ [f(1) \vee f(2) \vee$ $x^{[0,0]}]\ [f(2) \vee f(0) \vee x^{[1,1]}]\ [f(0) \vee f(1) \vee f(2)]$.

The proof is easily achieved by perfect induction on m and on n. It will not be detailed here. ∎

The prime blocks and the prime antiblocks of f are then obtained from the above theorem 3.13 by deleting in the expression (3.79) the blocks smaller and the anti-blocks greater than other ones.

Let us now consider the detection of prime convex blocks and of prime convex antiblocks; in this respect we introduce first the concept of T-*convex extended vector.* The partial value vector of f with respect to x_i was denoted by $[f(e_i)]$, which implicitly means $[f(e_i)\colon 0 \leqslant e_i \leqslant m_i - 1]$; subvectors of $[f(e_i)]$ will be denoted as follows:

$$\{f(e_i)\colon e_i \in [a_i, b_i]\} = [f(a_i), f(a_i \oplus 1), \ldots, f(a_i \oplus h_i) = f(b_i)]$$

Definition 3.9. (a) The T-*partial convex extended vector* of a discrete function f with respect to a variable x_i will be denoted by $\psi_{x_i}^{(\mathrm{T})}(f)$ and is defined as follows:

$$\psi_{x_i}^{(\mathrm{T})}(f) = \left(\{f(e_i)\colon e_i \in [0, m_i - 1]\}, \left\{\frac{Tf}{Tx_i}(e_i)\colon e_i \in [0, m_i - 2]\right\}, \right.$$

$$\left\{\frac{T^2 f}{Tx_i}(e_i)\colon e_i \in [0, m_i - 3]\right\}, \ldots, \left\{\frac{T^{m_i - 2} f}{Tx_i}(e_i)\colon e_i \in [0, 1]\right\},$$

$$\left. \frac{T^{m_i - 1} f}{Tx_i}\right). \tag{3.80}$$

In view of the above definition $\psi_{x_i}^{(\mathrm{T})}(f)$ associates to $f\colon S \to L$, $m_i(m_i + 1)/2$ applications:

$$S_{n-1} \times \ldots \times S_{i+1} \times S_{i-1} \times \ldots \times S_0 \to L.$$

The T-partial convex extended vector $\psi_{x_0}^{(\mathrm{T})}(f)$ is defined by the same type of iteration formula as (3.66); it will thus not be detailed further on.

Definition 3.9. (b) The T-*convex extended vector* $\psi^{(\mathrm{T})}(f)$ derives from the above definitions when the complete set $\boldsymbol{x}$ of variables is considered, i.e.

$$\psi^{(\mathrm{T})}(f) = \psi_{\boldsymbol{x}}^{(\mathrm{T})}(f). \tag{3.81}$$

Let us briefly consider the matrix representation of the T-convex extended vectors. Consider an $(m_i \times m_i)$ matrix X; with the same kind of notation as above, $X[a_i, b_i]$ denotes the matrix obtained by deletion in X of the columns whose index $j \notin [a_i, b_i]$ and where a_i, b_i are column numbers of X (it is recalled that, in the matrices, rows and columns are numbered from 0 and not from 1).

The matrix $N_i^{(\vee)}$ is the $m_i \times [m_i(m_i+1)/2]$ matrix of 0's and of $(r-1)$'s derived from $M_i^{(\vee)}$ as follows:

$$N_i^{(\vee)} = (r-1)\,(E_{m_i,0}, E_{m_i,1}\,[0, m_i-2], E_{m_i,2}\,[0, m_i-3], \ldots, E_{m_i,(m_i-2)}\,[0, 1], E_i). \tag{3.82}$$

$N_i^{(\wedge)}$ is the negation of $N_i^{(\vee)}$.

In view of the above definitions one then obtains:

$$\psi_{x_i}^{(\mathsf{T})}(f) = [f(e_i)] \circledcirc_{\mathsf{T}\perp} N_i^{(\mathsf{T})} \tag{3.83}$$

$$\psi^{(\mathsf{T})}(f) = [f(e)] \circledcirc_{\mathsf{T}\perp} \left[\overset{\perp}{\underset{i=n-1,0}{\otimes}} N_i^{(\mathsf{T})}\right] \tag{3.84}$$

Example 3.6 (continued). From (3.69) amd (3.80) one deduces successively:

$$\psi_{x_1}^{(\wedge)}(f) = [f(x_1=0), f(x_1=1), f(x_1=2), (pf/px_1)_{x_1=0}, (pf/px_1)_{x_1=1}, p^2f/px_1]$$
$$= (2x_0^{(1)} \vee 2x_0^{(0)}, 2x_0^{(0)}, 1x_0^{(0)} \vee 1x_0^{(1)}, 2x_0^{(0)}, 1x_0^{(0)}, 1x_0^{(0)})$$

$$\psi_{x_1x_0}^{(\wedge)}(f) = (2, 2, 2, 2, 0, 0, 1, 1, 1, 2, 0, 0, 1, 0, 0, 1, 0, 0). \tag{3.85}$$

Using again the same notation as for the matrix (3.82), one deduces the vectors $J_i^{(\mathsf{T})}$ from the vectors $K_i^{(\mathsf{T})}$ as follows:

$$J_i^{(\wedge)} = \{(x_i^{[j,j\oplus 0]}), (x_i^{[j,j\oplus 1]})\,[0, m_i-2], \ldots, (x_i^{[j,j+m_i-1]})\,[0, 1], (r-1)\}^t \tag{3.86}$$

$$J_i^{(\vee)} = (r-1) - J_i^{(\wedge)} = \overline{J_i^{(\wedge)}} \tag{3.87}$$

$$J^{(\mathsf{T})} = \overset{\mathsf{T}}{\underset{i=n-1,0}{\otimes}} J_i^{(\mathsf{T})}.$$

Theorem 3.14. The convex blocks (convex antiblocks) of the function $f(\mathbf{x})$ are the terms of

$$\psi^{(\mathsf{T})}(f) \circledcirc_{\perp\mathsf{T}} J^{(\mathsf{T})} \tag{3.89}$$

with T the conjunction (disjunction) and $\perp$ the dual operation.

The same type of proof as for theorem 3.13 holds.

The prime convex blocks and the prime convex antiblocks are then obtained from the above theorem by deleting in (3.89) the convex blocks smaller than other convex blocks and the convex antiblocks greater than other convex antiblocks.

Example 3.6 (continued). For the function:

$$f: \{0, 1, 2\} \times \{0, 1\} \rightarrow \{0, 1, 2\}$$

the matrix $K^{(\wedge)}$ is:

$$K^{(\wedge)} = K_1^{(\wedge)} \overset{\wedge}{\otimes} K_0^{(\wedge)}$$
$$= [(x_1^{(0)}, x_1^{(1)}, x_1^{(2)}, x_1^{[0,1]}, x_1^{[1,2]}, x_1^{[2,0]}, 2) \overset{\wedge}{\otimes} (x_0^{(0)}, x_0^{(1)}, 2)]^t$$
$$= (x_1^{(0)} x_0^{(0)}, x_1^{(0)} x_0^{(1)}, x_1^{(0)}, x_1^{(1)} x_0^{(0)}, x_1^{(1)} x_0^{(1)}, x_1^{(1)}, x_1^{(2)} x_0^{(0)}, x_1^{(2)} x_0^{(1)}, x_1^{(2)},$$
$$x_1^{[0,1]} x_0^{(0)}, x_1^{[0,1]} x_0^{(1)}, x_1^{[0,1]}, x_1^{[1,2]} x_0^{(0)}, x_1^{[1,2]} x_0^{(1)}, x_1^{[1,2]}, x_1^{[2,0]} x_0^{(0)},$$
$$x_1^{[2,0]} x_0^{(1)}, x_1^{[2,0]}, x_0^{(0)}, x_0^{(1)}, 2)^t. \tag{3.90}$$

One obtains then in view of (3.70)–(3.90) and of theorem 3.13 the expression of f as a disjunction of blocks:

$$f = 2x_1^{(0)} x_0^{(0)} \vee 2x_1^{(0)} x_0^{(1)} \vee \underline{2x_1^{(0)}} \vee 2x_1^{(1)} x_0^{(0)} \vee 1x_1^{(2)} x_0^{(0)} \vee 1x_1^{(2)} x_0^{(1)} \vee 1x_1^{(2)} \vee$$
$$\underline{2x_1^{[0,1]} x_0^{(0)}} \vee 1x_1^{[1,2]} x_0^{(0)} \vee 1x_1^{[2,0]} x_0^{(0)} \vee 1x_1^{[2,0]} x_0^{(1)} \vee \underline{1x_1^{[2,0]}} \vee \underline{1x_0^{(0)}}$$

The prime blocks in the above expression have been underlined.

The prime convex blocks could be obtained in a similar way: the convex extended vector was obtained previously (see (3.85)); the matrix $J_1^{(\wedge)}$ is obtained from $K_1^{(\wedge)}$ by deletion in that matrix of the element $x_1^{[2,0]}$ while $J_0^{(\wedge)}$ equals $K_0^{(\wedge)}$. The computation will however not be detailed here since the properties of the Kronecker matrix product allow us again to avoid the computation of the matrix $J^{(\wedge)}$. This fact has already been explained several times previously; it will again be detailed below, but by using a visual method.

A visual or graphical scheme for the extended vector-algorithm will be presented now. This allows us first to show in a simple way how the Kronecker matrix product may be described visually; this will also be an introduction for the simplified form of the extended vector algorithm presented in section 3.2.3.2.2.

One will make use of a tree-like computation scheme as illustrated by Figure 3.9. Let us start from the discrete function f, the prime implicants (resp. prime implicates) of which are to be detected. In Figure 3.9 $[m_{n-1}(m_{n-1}-1)+1]$ arrows starting from f are labelled with the symbols:

$$m_{n-1}(m_{n-1}-1) \text{ arrow symbols} \quad \begin{cases} (n-1)^{(0)}, (n-1)^{(1)}, \ldots, (n-1)^{(m_{n-1}-1)}, \\ (n-1)^{[0,1]}, (n-1)^{[1,2]}, \ldots, (n-1)^{[m_{n-1}-1,\,0]}, \\ (n-1)^{[0,2]}, (n-1)^{[1,3]}, \ldots, (n-1)^{[m_{n-1}-1,1]}, \\ \ldots \\ (n-1)^{[0,m_{n-1}-2]}, (n-1)^{[1,m_{n-1}-1]}, \ldots, (n-1)^{[m_{n-1}-1,m_{n-1}-3]}, \end{cases}$$

plus a last arrow without symbol.

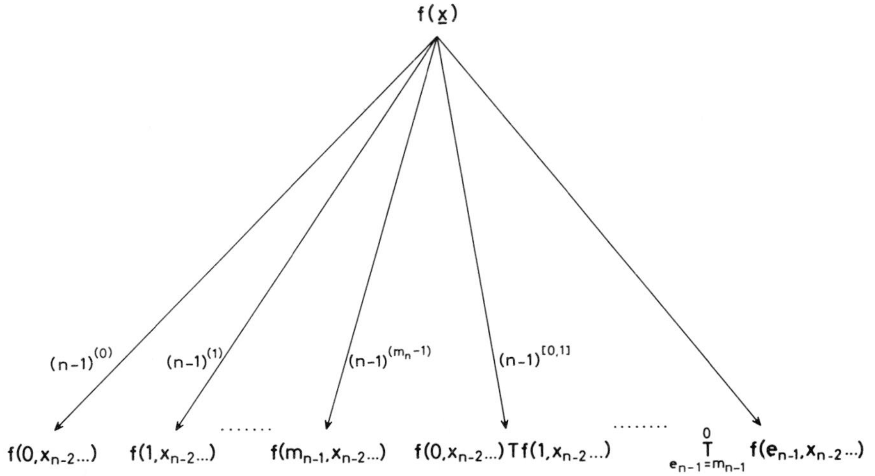

Figure 3.9. Extended vector computation scheme

These arrows correspond to the functions of $(x_{n-2}, \ldots, x_1, x_0)$ respectively:

$$f(e_{n-1}, x_{n-2}, \ldots, x_0),$$
$$f(e_{n-1}, x_{n-2}, \ldots, x_0) \mathsf{T} f(e_{n-1} \oplus 1, x_{n-2}, \ldots, x_0),$$
$$f(e_{n-1}, x_{n-2}, \ldots, x_0) \mathsf{T} f(e_{n-1} \oplus 1, x_{n-2}, \ldots, x_0) \mathsf{T} f(e_{n-1} \oplus 2, x_{n-2}, \ldots, x_0)$$
$$\ldots$$
$$(0 \leqslant e_{n-1} \leqslant m_{n-1}).$$

The arrow without symbol corresponds to the function:

$$\mathop{\mathsf{T}}_{e_{n-1}=0}^{m_n-1} f(e_{n-1}, x_{n-2}, \ldots, x_0).$$

The same scheme is then adopted for each of the above functions but with respect to the variable x_{n-2}; an iterative procedure is thus built with respect to the successive variables of x. Each arrow starting from a function g is labelled with the symbol $i^{[a_i, b_i]}$ if the operation to be performed at this level is

$$g(x_i = a_i) \mathsf{T} g(x_i = a_i \oplus 1) \mathsf{T} \ldots \mathsf{T} g(x_i \oplus h_i = b_i).$$

The arrow without symbol, at the same level, indicates the operation

$$\mathop{\mathsf{T}}_{e_i=0}^{m_i-1} g(x_i = e_i).$$

The T-extended vector is obtained after n steps of the above algorithm: it is formed by the constants which necessarily appear after all the variables from x_{n-1} to x_0 have been explored.

The blocks of the function f are of the form:

$$l \wedge x_i^{[a_i, b_i]} \wedge x_j^{[a_j, b_j]} \wedge \ldots \wedge x_k^{[a_k, b_k]}$$

if the set of consecutive arrows from $f(x)$ to a term l of the $\wedge$-extended vector are labelled:

$$i^{[a_i, b_i]}, j^{[a_j, b_j]}, \ldots, k^{[a_k, b_k]}.$$

The antiblocks of the function f are of the form

$$l \vee \overline{x_i^{[a_i, b_i]}} \vee \overline{x_j^{[a_j, b_j]}} \vee \ldots \vee \overline{x_k^{[a_k, b_k]}}$$

if the set of consecutive arrows from $f(x)$ to a term l of the $\vee$-extended vector are labelled in the way quoted above.

It could easily be verified (see also Figures 3.10 and 3.11 below) that the arrows at the ith level of the above treelike scheme correspond to the ith step of the iteration scheme (3.67) for obtaining the extended vector, or equivalently correspond to the

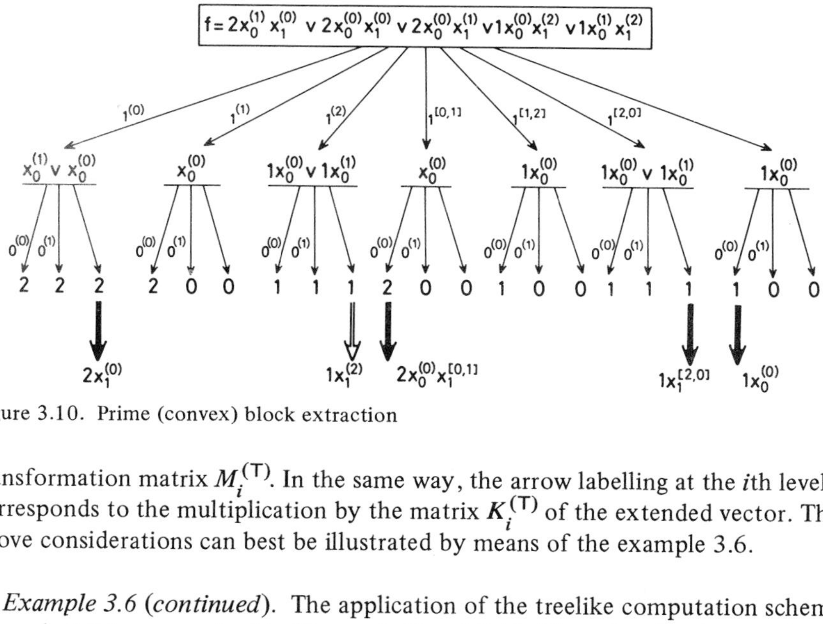

Figure 3.10. Prime (convex) block extraction

transformation matrix $M_i^{(T)}$. In the same way, the arrow labelling at the ith level corresponds to the multiplication by the matrix $K_i^{(T)}$ of the extended vector. The above considerations can best be illustrated by means of the example 3.6.

Example 3.6 (*continued*). The application of the treelike computation scheme to example 3.6 is summarized in Figures 3.10 and 3.11. The prime blocks and the prime convex blocks are obtained from Figure 3.10:

$$f = 2x_1^{[0,0]} \vee 2x_1^{[0,1]}\, x_0^{[0,0]} \vee 1x_1^{[2,0]} \vee 1x_0^{[0,0]} \text{ (prime blocks)} \tag{3.91}$$

$$f = 2x_1^{[0,0]} \vee 2x_1^{[0,1]}\, x_0^{[0,0]} \vee 1x_1^{[2,2]} \vee 1x_0^{[0,0]} \text{ (prime convex blocks)} \tag{3.92}$$

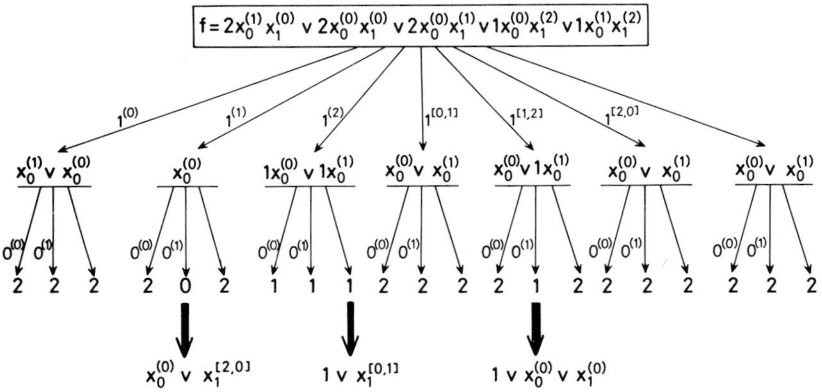

Figure 3.11. Prime (convex) antiblock extraction

Dual operations and notations are used in Figure 3.11 in order to obtain the prime antiblocks and the prime convex antiblocks:

$$f = (x_1^{[2,0]} \vee x_0^{[0,0]})\,(1 \vee x_1^{[0,1]})\,(1 \vee x_0^{[0,0]} \vee x_1^{[0,0]}) \text{ (prime antiblocks and prime convex antiblocks).} \tag{3.93}$$

It should be noted that the arrows which lead to non-convex blocks and non-convex antiblocks in Figures 3.10 and 3.11 are those labelled $1^{[2,0]}$ respectively.

Switching functions

From definition 3.8(a) one deduces that the T-partial extended vector of a switching function f with respect to a variable x_i is:

$$\phi_{x_i}^{(\mathrm{T})}(f) = \left[f(x_i = 0), f(x_i = 1), \frac{Tf}{Tx_i}\right]. \tag{3.94}$$

The iteration scheme (3.66) then becomes:

$$\begin{aligned}\phi_{x_j x_i}^{(\mathrm{T})}(f) &= \phi_{x_j}^{(\mathrm{T})}[\phi_{x_i}^{(\mathrm{T})}(f)]\\ &= \left\{\phi_{x_j}^{(\mathrm{T})}[f(x_i=0)],\ \phi_{x_j}^{(\mathrm{T})}[f(x_i=1)],\ \phi_{x_j}^{(\mathrm{T})}\left(\frac{Tf}{Tx_i}\right)\right\}\\ &= \left[f(x_j=0, x_i=0), f(x_j=1, x_i=0), \left(\frac{Tf}{Tx_j}\right)_{x_j=0},\right.\\ &\qquad f(x_j=0, x_i=1), f(x_j=1, x_i=1), \left(\frac{Tf}{Tx_j}\right)_{x_j=1},\\ &\qquad \left.\left(\frac{Tf}{Tx_i}\right)_{x_j=0}, \left(\frac{Tf}{Tx_i}\right)_{x_j=1}, \frac{Tf}{Tx_i x_j}\right].\end{aligned} \tag{3.95}$$

$\phi_{x_i}^{(T)}(f)$, associates to f: $\{0, 1\}^n \to \{0, 1\}$ three applications: $\{0, 1\}^{n-1} \to \{0, 1\}$; the matrices $M_i^{(T)}$ reduce to the following:

$$M_i^{(\vee)} = \begin{bmatrix} 1 & 0 & 1 \\ & & \\ 0 & 1 & 1 \end{bmatrix}, \quad M_i^{(\wedge)} = \begin{bmatrix} 0 & 1 & 0 \\ & & \\ 1 & 0 & 0 \end{bmatrix}.$$

The extended vector has 3^n components and from its definition it appears that it may be partitioned into three subvectors of equal length that are the extended vectors of the subfunctions $f(x_{n-1} = 0), f(x_{n-1} = 1)$ and of the T-difference Tf/Tx_{n-1}.

The matrices $K_i^{(T)}$ are:

$$K_i^{(\wedge)} = \begin{bmatrix} \bar{x}_i \\ x_i \\ 1 \end{bmatrix}, \quad K_i^{(\vee)} = \begin{bmatrix} x_i \\ \bar{x}_i \\ 0 \end{bmatrix}. \tag{3.96}$$

Finally, for switching functions, the algorithm schematized by Figure 3.9 reduces to a similar algorithm schematized by Figure 3.12. In this figure, the notations

$$i^{(0)} \quad \text{and} \quad i^{(1)}$$

are replaced by the simpler figures $\bar{i}$ and i respectively.

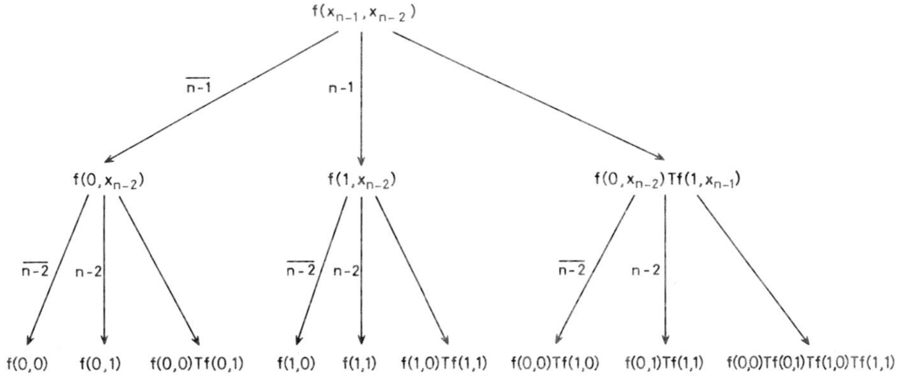

Figure 3.12. Extended vector computation scheme for switching functions

Examples of prime implicant extraction for switching functions are given under the section 3.2.3.2.2 below.

3.2.3.2.2. Modified form

The algorithm based on theorems 3.13–3.14 and developed along the rules summarized in Figures 3.9–3.11 can now significantly be simplified by use of the following remarks.

1. In the extended-vector algorithm, the computation of Figure 3.9 leads first to the obtention of the extended vector, which is a vector of discrete constants. If the computation is stopped before the obtention of the elements of the extended vector, the result is a vector of discrete functions. Now, during the research of the (convex) blocks, each branch of the algorithm (see Figures 3.9–3.11) may be ended once a (convex) block of the general form

$$x_i^{[a_i,b_i]} \wedge x_j^{[a_j,b_j]} \wedge \ldots \wedge x_k^{[a_k,b_k]}$$

has been obtained.

If the set of consecutive arrows from f until that (convex) block are labelled with symbols

$$p^{[a_p,b_p]}, q^{[a_q,b_q]}, \ldots, r^{[a_r,b_r]},$$

then the (convex) block:

$$x_i^{[a_i,b_i]} \wedge x_j^{[a_j,b_j]} \wedge \ldots \wedge x_k^{[a_k,b_k]} \wedge x_p^{[a_p,b_p]} \wedge x_q^{[a_q,b_q]} \wedge \ldots \wedge x_r^{[a_r,b_r]}$$

is a (convex) block of f. All the (convex) blocks which could be obtained by continuing the initial proposed algorithm once a (convex) block has been reached are smaller than or equal to the (convex) block of f noted above.

The main rule proposed here for simplifying the algorithm is to recognize as soon as possible the (convex) blocks during the obtention of the treelike scheme. This allows us to eliminate at this point all the subsequent computations.

2. If, at each step of the algorithm, the arrows with the largest domains $[a_i, b_i]$ are first explored, the prime (convex) blocks are detected in decreasing order of their dimension, so that those parts of the algorithm which would lead to smaller (convex) blocks could easily be detected and would thus be ended at once.

3. Assume that after a set of consecutive arrows labelled

$$i^{[a_i,b_i]}, j^{[a_j,b_j]}, \ldots, k^{[a_k,b_k]}$$

a function g is obtained, and assume moreover that this part of the algorithm issued from the continuation of the computation after the obtention of g, gives the p prime (convex) blocks of f:

$$\{x_i^{[a_i,b_i]} \wedge x_j^{[a_j,b_j]} \wedge \ldots \wedge x_k^{[a_k,b_k]} \wedge \alpha_0, \ldots,$$
$$x_i^{[a_i,b_i]} \wedge x_j^{[a_j,b_j]} \wedge \ldots \wedge x_k^{[a_k,b_k]} \wedge \alpha_{p-1}\},$$

with $\alpha_0, \alpha_1, \ldots, \alpha_{p-1}$, arbitrary (convex) blocks. Then, if the same function g is obtained in any other part of the algorithm and after a set of consecutive arrows labelled:

$$p^{[a_p,b_p]}, q^{[a_q,b_q]}, \ldots, r^{[a_r,b_r]},$$

the following (convex) blocks are the largest ones which could be obtained by developing further on that part of the algorithm which follows the obtention of g:

$$\{x_p^{[a_p, b_p]} \wedge x_q^{[a_q, b_q]} \wedge \ldots \wedge x_r^{[a_r, b_r]} \wedge \alpha_0, \ldots,$$
$$x_p^{[a_p, b_p]} \wedge x_q^{[a_q, b_q]} \wedge \ldots \wedge x_r^{[a_r, b_r]} \wedge \alpha_{p-1}\}.$$

This remark allows us again to achieve quicker the initial proposed extended-vector algorithm.

Example 3.6 (continued). The computation scheme of Figure 3.10 reduces to that of Figure 3.13, after application of the simplification rules 1 and 2 proposed above. Only the prime blocks have been indicated in Figure 3.13.

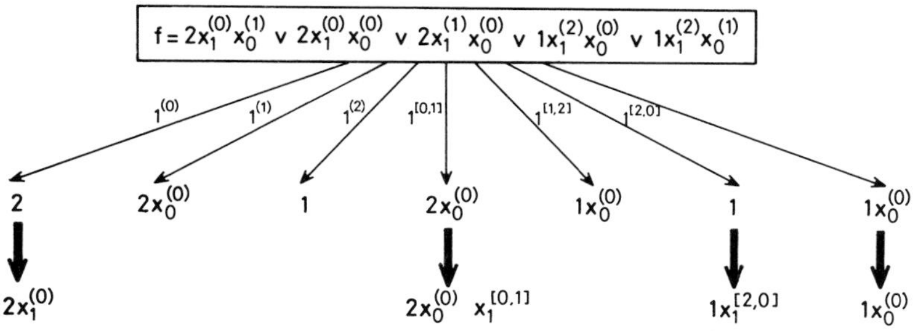

Figure 3.13. Simplified method for prime (convex) block extraction

Example 3.7. The simplifications (for detecting prime implicants) issued from the points 1–3 just quoted in this section are illustrated in Figure 3.14 by the research of the prime implicants of the switching function:

$$f = 1 \oplus x_1 x_0 \oplus x_4 \overline{x}_5 \oplus x_3 x_2 x_0. \qquad (3.97)$$

The prime implicants have been underlined in that figure. Moreover the identical functions that appear at different points of the algorithm (illustration of the simplification rule 3) are designated by asterisks, i.e. ( )* and ( )**.

One thus obtains f as the disjunction of its prime implicants, i.e.

$$f = \overline{x}_4 \overline{x}_0 \vee \overline{x}_4 \overline{x}_2 \overline{x}_1 \vee \overline{x}_4 x_3 x_2 x_1 \vee \overline{x}_4 \overline{x}_3 \overline{x}_1 \vee x_5 \overline{x}_0 \vee x_5 \overline{x}_2 \overline{x}_1 \vee x_5 x_3 x_2 x_1 \vee$$
$$x_5 \overline{x}_3 \overline{x}_1 \vee \overline{x}_5 x_4 \overline{x}_2 x_1 x_0 \vee \overline{x}_5 x_4 x_3 x_2 \overline{x}_1 x_0 \vee \overline{x}_5 x_4 \overline{x}_3 x_1 x_0. \qquad (3.98)$$

Example 3.2 (continued). The same algorithm applied to the research of the prime implicants of a general switching function is illustrated by means of Figure 3.15.

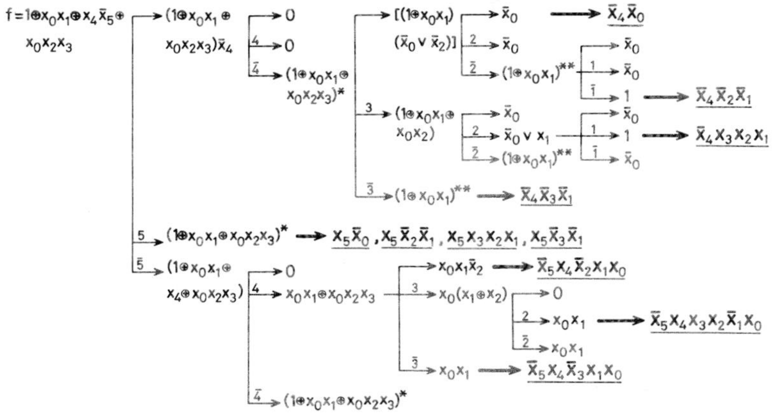

Figure 3.14. Prime implicants of a switching function

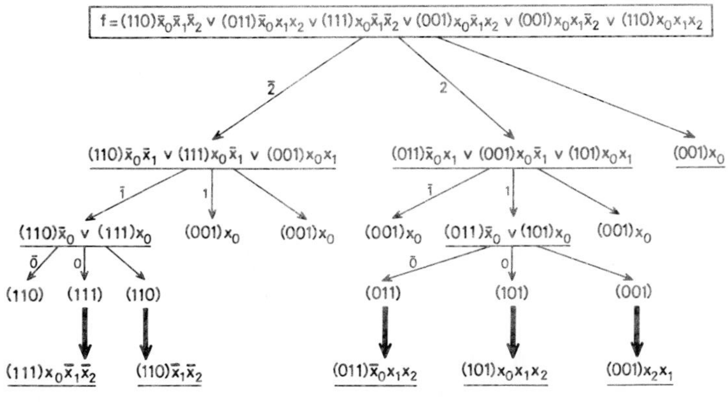

Figure 3.15. Prime implicants of a general switching function

3.2.3.3. The lattice-difference algorithms

Our main problem in this section will be the following: a discrete function f being represented as a disjunction of blocks, find all its prime blocks and/or all its prime convex blocks; or, dually, a discrete function f being represented as a conjunction of antiblocks, find all its prime antiblocks and/or all its prime convex antiblocks. This problem is thus less general than the one considered in the preceding section 3.2.3.1; indeed, one assumes that the initial form of the discrete function is, for example, a disjunction of blocks while no assumption was made previously concerning the initial form of the lattice expression.

The operators $I(p^k f/px)$ and $I(q^k f/qx)$ are defined as follows:
Let $p^k f/px$ be represented as a disjunction of blocks, that is:

$$\frac{p^k f}{px} = \bigvee_j \left(l_j \wedge \bigwedge_{i=n-1}^{0} x_i^{[a_{ij}, b_{ij}]} \right),$$

then

$$I\left(\frac{p^k f}{px}\right) = \bigvee_j \left(l_j \wedge \bigwedge_{i=n-1}^{0} x_i^{[a_{ij}, b_{ij} \oplus k_i]} \right) \qquad (3.99)$$

with $x = (x_{n-1}, \ldots, x_1, x_0)$ and $k = (k_{n-1}, \ldots, k_1, k_0)$, $0 \leqslant k_i \leqslant m_i - 1 \; \forall i$.
Let $q^k f/qx$ be represented as a conjunction of antiblocks, that is:

$$\frac{q^k f}{qx} = \bigwedge_j \left(l_j \vee \bigvee_{i=n-1}^{0} x_i^{[a_{ij}, b_{ij}]} \right),$$

then

$$I\left(\frac{q^k f}{qx}\right) = \bigwedge_j \left(l_j \vee \bigvee_{i=n-1}^{0} x_i^{[a_{ij} \oplus k_i, b_{ij}]} \right). \qquad (3.100)$$

Definition 3.10. (a) The *length of a block* with respect to its coordinate x_i is the number of non-zero elements of this block along x_i; the *dimension of a block* is the vector of its lengths.

(b) The *length of an antiblock* with respect to its coordinate x_i is the number of non-$(r-1)$ elements of this antiblock along x_i; the *dimension of an antiblock* is the vector of its lengths.

Theorem 3.15. (a) *The function $I(p^k f/px)$ is the disjunction of the prime blocks of f the dimensions of which are $\geqslant k + 1$.*

(b) *The function $I(q^k f/qx)$ is the conjunction of the prime antiblocks of f the dimensions of which are $\geqslant k + 1$.*

Proof. (a) From theorem 3.8(a) one deduces that $(p^k f/px)_{x=e} = l$ iff $f(x) \geqslant l$ for $x \in [e, k \oplus e]$ and $f(x) = l$ for at least one value of x in this domain. Hence the function $I(p^k f/px)$ is a function smaller than or equal to f, and, in view of relation (3.99) it is the disjunction of the prime blocks of f the dimensions of which are $\geqslant k + 1$.

(b) Dual statement of (a). ∎

In view of relations (3.99)–(3.100), one also sees that the dimension of each block present in the expression of $I(p^k f/px)$ (resp. of each antiblock present in the expression of $I(q^k f/qx)$) is at least equal to $k + 1$.

In view of theorem 3.15(a) the following algorithm may, for example, be used for detecting the prime blocks of a function f.

Algorithm 3.5.

(a) From the expression of f, compute

1. $p^{\boldsymbol{k}}f/p\boldsymbol{x}$, with $\{\boldsymbol{k}: \Sigma k_i = 1\}$, using (3.32), and obtain these functions as a disjunction of blocks, using the distributive law.
2. $I(p^{\boldsymbol{k}}f/p\boldsymbol{x})$, using (3.99).

(b) At the jth step, from the expression of

$$p^{\boldsymbol{k}}f/p\boldsymbol{x}, \text{ with } \{\boldsymbol{k}: \Sigma k_i = j-1\}, \text{ compute}$$

1. $p^{\boldsymbol{k}}f/p\boldsymbol{x}$, with $\{\boldsymbol{k}: \Sigma k_i = j\}$, using (3.33)–(3.34), and obtain these functions as a disjunction of blocks, using the distributive law.
2. $I(p^{\boldsymbol{k}}f/p\boldsymbol{x})$, using (3.99).

(c) $p^{\boldsymbol{m}-\boldsymbol{1}}f/p\boldsymbol{x}$ is obtained at the last step.
In view of theorem 3.15(a), the expressions $I(p^{\boldsymbol{k}}f/p\boldsymbol{x})$ contain all the blocks of f; the prime blocks are obtained by deleting in the obtained list of blocks those smaller than other ones.

The prime convex blocks and the prime convex antiblocks are deduced from the prime blocks and the prime antiblocks respectively by using lemma 3.8 below.

Lemma 3.8. The representation of a discrete function f as a disjunction of prime convex blocks (resp. as a conjunction of prime convex antiblocks) can be deduced from its representation as a disjunction of prime blocks (resp. as a conjunction of prime antiblocks) by representing each non-convex block as a disjunction of convex blocks using relation (3.5) (resp. each non-convex antiblock as a conjunction of convex antiblocks using relation (3.11)) and the distributive laws and by deleting in the obtained expression the convex blocks smaller (resp. the convex antiblocks larger) than other ones.

The routine proof of lemma 3.8 is omitted.

Let us point out that the division of algorithm 3.5 into successive steps is somewhat arbitrary; practically, one has to compute the meet differences $p^{\boldsymbol{k}}f/p\boldsymbol{x}$ from the lowest $\boldsymbol{k}$ until the highest. The above division of the algorithm into steps will however allow us a better comparison of the lattice-difference algorithm with the consensus theory (see section 3.2.3.4.).

Example 3.8. Consider first a ternary function of two quaternary variables given as a disjunction of blocks:

$$f = 1x_1^{[1,1]}\, x_0^{[3,0]} \vee 1x_1^{[1,1]}\, x_0^{[2} \vee 1x_1^{0]}\, x_0^{[1,1]} \vee 2x_1^{[1,2]}\, x_0^{[1,1]} \vee 2x_1^{[3}\, x_0^{1]} \vee$$
$$2x_1^{[2,2]}\, x_0^{[3,0]} \vee 2x_1^{[2}\, x_0^{[3}. \qquad (3.101)$$

Application of (3.99) yields the following expressions:

$$I(pf/px_0) = 1x_1^{[1,1]}\,x_0^{[2,0]} \vee 1x_1^{[1,1]}\,x_0^{[1,2]} \vee 1x_1^{[1,1]}\,x_0^{1]} \vee 2x_1^{[2,2]}\,x_0^{1]} \vee$$
$$2x_1^{[3}\,x_0^{1]} \vee 2x_1^{[3}\,x_0^{[3,0]} \vee 2x_1^{[2,2]}\,x_0^{[3,0]}$$
$$I(p^2f/px_0) = 1x_1^{[1,1]}\,x_0^{[2,0]} \vee 1x_1^{[1,1]}\,x_0^{[1} \vee 1x_1^{[1,1]}\,x_0^{2]} \vee 1x_1^{[1,1]}\,x_0^{[3,1]} \vee$$
$$2x_1^{[2,2]}\,x_0^{[3,1]} \vee 2x_1^{[3}\,x_0^{[3,1]}$$
$$I(p^3f/px_0) = \underline{1x_1^{[1,1]}}$$
$$I(pf/px_1) = 1x_1^{[3,0]}\,x_0^{[1,1]} \vee 1x_1^{1]}\,x_0^{[1,1]} \vee 2x_1^{[1,2]}\,x_0^{[1,1]} \vee 2x_1^{[2}\,x_0^{0]} \vee$$
$$1x_1^{[1,2]}\,x_0^{[3,0]} \vee 2x_1^{[2}\,x_0^{[3} \vee 2x_1^{[2}\,x_0^{[1,1]}$$
$$I(p^2f/px_1) = 1x_1^{[2,0]}\,x_0^{[1,1]} \vee 1x_1^{[3,1]}\,x_0^{[1,1]} \vee 1x_1^{2]}\,x_0^{[1,1]} \vee 1x_1^{[1}\,x_0^{0]} \vee$$
$$\underline{2x_1^{[1}\,x_0^{[1,1]}} \vee 1x_1^{[1}\,x_0^{[3}$$
$$I(p^3f/px_1) = \underline{1x_0^{[1,1]}}$$
$$I(pf/px_1x_0) = 1x_1^{[1,2]}\,x_0^{1]} \vee 1x_1^{[1,2]}\,x_0^{[3,0]} \vee 2x_1^{[2}\,x_0^{1]} \vee 2x_1^{[2}\,x_0^{[3,0]}$$
$$I(p^{21}f/px_1x_0) = 1x_1^{[1}\,x_0^{1]} \vee 1x_1^{[1}\,x_0^{[3,0]}$$
$$I(p^{22}f/px_1x_0) = \underline{1x_1^{[1}\,x_0^{[3,1]}}$$
$$I(p^{12}f/px_1x_0) = 1x_1^{[1,2]}\,x_0^{[3,1]} \vee \underline{2x_1^{[2}\,x_0^{[3,1]}}.$$

The prime blocks have been underlined in the above expressions, so that one obtains the following expression of f as a disjunction of prime blocks:

$$f = 1x_1^{[1,1]} \vee 1x_0^{[1,1]} \vee 1x_1^{[1}\,x_0^{[3,1]} \vee 2x_1^{[2}\,x_0^{[3,1]} \vee 2x_1^{[1}\,x_0^{[1,1]}. \qquad (3.102)$$

The only non-convex blocks are those where the term $x_0^{[3,1]}$ appears; in order to obtain the prime convex blocks of f one has to replace $x_0^{[3,1]}$ by $x_0^{[3} \vee x_0^{1]}$ in the above expression and to apply the distributive law. One obtains finally:

$$f = 1x_1^{[1,1]} \vee 1x_0^{[1,1]} \vee 1x_1^{[1}\,x_0^{[3} \vee 1x_1^{[1}\,x_0^{1]} \vee 2x_1^{[2}\,x_0^{[3} \vee 2x_1^{[2}\,x_0^{1]} \vee$$
$$2x_1^{[1}\,x_0^{[1,1]}. \qquad (3.103)$$

Consider now the same function given as a conjunction of antiblocks:

$$f = (1 \vee x_1^{[1} \vee x_0^{[2,0]})\,(1 \vee x_1^{[2,0]} \vee x_0^{[1})\,(1 \vee x_1^{[2} \vee x_0^{1]})\,(x_1^{[3,1]} \vee$$
$$x_0^{[3,1]})\,(x_1^{2]} \vee x_0^{[3,1]})\,(x_1^{[1} \vee x_0^{[1})\,(x_1^{[1} \vee x_0^{1]}). \qquad (3.104)$$

Application of (3.100) yields the following expressions:

$$I(qf/qx_0) = (1 \vee x_1^{[2} \vee x_0^{1]})\,(1 \vee x_1^{[1} \vee x_0^{[2]})\,(1 \vee x_1^{[2,0]} \vee x_0^{[1,2]})\,(x_1^{[1} \vee x_0^{[1,2]})\,(x_1^{[1} \vee x_0^{1]})$$

$$I(q^2f/qx_0) = (1 \vee x_1^{[1} \vee x_0^{[2,2]})\,(1 \vee x_1^{[1} \vee x_0^{[1,1]})\,(1 \vee x_1^{[1} \vee x_0^{[3]})\,(1 \vee x_1^{[1} \vee x_0^{0]})\,\underline{(x_1^{[1} \vee x_0^{[1,1]})}$$

$$I(q^3f/qx_0) = \underline{1 \vee x_1^{[1}}$$

$$I(qf/qx_1) = (1 \vee x_1^{[2} \vee x_0^{[1]})\,(1 \vee x_1^{[2} \vee x_0^{1]})\,(1 \vee x_1^{[3,0]} \vee x_0^{[3,1]})\,(x_1^{1]} \vee x_0^{[3,1]})\,(x_1^{[1,2]} \vee x_0^{[3,1]})$$

$$I(q^2f/qx_1) = (1 \vee x_1^{[3} \vee x_0^{[3,1]})\,(1 \vee x_1^{[2,2]} \vee x_0^{[3,1]})\,(1 \vee x_1^{0]} \vee x_0^{[3,1]})\,\underline{(x_1^{[1,1]} \vee x_0^{[3,1]})}$$

$$I(q^3f/qx_1) = \underline{1 \vee x_0^{[3,1]}}$$

$$I(qf/qx_1x_0) = (1 \vee x_1^{[2} \vee x_0^{1]})\,(1 \vee x_1^{[2} \vee x_0^{[1,2]})$$

$$I(q^{12}f/qx_1x_0) = \underline{1 \vee x_1^{[2} \vee x_0^{[1,1]}}.$$

The prime antiblocks have been underlined in the above expressions, so that one obtains the following expression of f as a conjunction of prime antiblocks:

$$f = (x_1^{[1} \vee x_0^{[1,1]})\,(x_1^{[1,1]} \vee x_0^{[3,1]})\,(1 \vee x_1^{[1})\,(1 \vee x_0^{[3,1]})\,(1 \vee x_1^{[2} \vee x_0^{[1,1]}). \tag{3.105}$$

In order to obtain the prime convex antiblocks of f, one has to replace $x_i^{[1,1]}$ by $x_i^{1]}\,x_i^{[1}$, $i = 0, 1$ in the above expression and to apply the distributive law and the absorption law. One finally obtains:

$$f = (x_1^{[1} \vee x_0^{1]})\,(x_1^{[1} \vee x_0^{[1})\,(x_1^{1]} \vee x_0^{[3,1]})\,(1 \vee x_1^{[1})\,(1 \vee x_0^{[3,1]})\,(1 \vee x_1^{[2} \vee x_0^{1]})\,(1 \vee x_1^{[2} \vee x_0^{[1}). \tag{3.106}$$

Example 3.9. Consider now a somewhat more elaborate example, a quaternary function of three ternary variables, i.e., a discrete function:

$$f\colon \{0, 1, 2\}^3 \to \{0, 1, 2, 3\};$$

f is given as a disjunction of blocks:

$$\begin{aligned} f = {} & 1x_2^{(2)} x_1^{(0)} x_0^{(2)} \vee 1x_2^{(2)} x_1^{(2)} x_0^{(2)} \vee 1x_2^{(0)} x_1^{(2)} x_0^{[0,1]} \vee 1x_2^{(2)} x_1^{[1,2]} x_0^{(0)} \vee \\ & 2x_2^{(1)} x_1^{[1,2]} x_0^{[0,1]} \vee 2x_2^{(1)} x_0^{(2)} \vee \underline{3x_2^{(1)} x_1^{(2)} x_0^{(2)}} \vee 3x_2^{(0)} x_1^{(0)} x_0^{[0,1]} \vee \\ & 3x_2^{(0)} x_1^{[0,1]} x_0^{(0)} \vee 3x_2^{[0,1]} x_1^{(1)} x_0^{(1)}. \end{aligned} \tag{3.107}$$

In view of (3.107) one obtains successively:

$$\begin{aligned} I(pf/px_0) = {} & 1x_2^{(0)} x_1^{(2)} x_0^{[0,1]} \vee 1x_2^{(2)} x_1^{(2)} x_0^{[2,0]} \vee 2x_2^{(1)} x_1^{[1,2]} x_0^{[0,1]} \vee \\ & 2x_2^{(1)} x_1^{[1,2]} x_0^{[2,0]} \vee 2x_2^{(1)} x_1^{[1,2]} x_0^{[1,2]} \vee 2x_2^{(1)} x_1^{(2)} x_0^{[1,2]} \vee \\ & 3x_2^{(0)} x_1^{(0)} x_0^{[0,1]} \vee 2x_2^{(1)} x_1^{(1)} x_0^{[0,1]} \vee 3x_2^{(0)} x_1^{(1)} x_0^{[0,1]} \\ I(p^2f/px_0) = {} & 2x_2^{(1)} x_1^{[1,2]} \\ I(pf/px_1) = {} & 1x_2^{(2)} x_1^{[2,0]} x_0^{(2)} \vee 1x_2^{(0)} x_1^{[1,2]} x_0^{(0)} \vee 1x_2^{(0)} x_1^{[1,2]} x_0^{(1)} \vee \\ & 1x_2^{(2)} x_1^{[1,2]} x_0^{(0)} \vee 2x_2^{(1)} x_1^{[1,2]} x_0^{[0,1]} \vee 2x_2^{(1)} x_0^{(2)} \vee \\ & 1x_2^{(0)} x_1^{[2,0]} x_0^{[0,1]} \vee 3x_2^{(0)} x_1^{[0,1]} x_0^{(0)} \vee 3x_2^{(0)} x_1^{[0,1]} x_0^{(1)} \\ I(p^2f/px_1) = {} & \underline{2x_2^{(1)} x_0^{(2)}} \vee 1x_2^{(0)} x_0^{(0)} \vee 1x_2^{(0)} x_0^{(1)} \\ I(pf/px_2) = {} & 1x_2^{[1,2]} x_1^{(0)} x_0^{(2)} \vee 1x_2^{[1,2]} x_1^{(2)} x_0^{(2)} \vee 1x_2^{[2,0]} x_1^{(2)} x_0^{(0)} \vee \\ & 1x_2^{[1,2]} x_1^{[1,2]} x_0^{(0)} \vee 1x_2^{[0,1]} x_1^{(2)} x_0^{[0,1]} \vee 2x_2^{[0,1]} x_1^{(1)} x_0^{(0)} \vee \\ & 1x_2^{[2,0]} x_1^{(1)} x_0^{(0)} \vee \underline{3x_2^{[0,1]} x_1^{(1)} x_0^{(1)}} \\ I(p^2f/px_2) = {} & 1x_1^{(2)} x_0^{(0)} \vee 1x_1^{(1)} x_0^{(0)} \\ I(pf/px_1x_0) = {} & 2x_2^{(1)} x_1^{[1,2]} x_0^{[2,0]} \vee 1x_2^{(0)} x_1^{[1,2]} x_0^{[0,1]} \vee 2x_2^{(1)} x_1^{[1,2]} x_0^{[0,1]} \vee \\ & 2x_2^{(1)} x_1^{[1,2]} x_0^{[1,2]} \vee 1x_2^{(0)} x_1^{[2,0]} x_2^{[0,1]} \vee \underline{3x_2^{(0)} x_1^{[0,1]} x_0^{[0,1]}} \\ I(p^{12}f/px_1x_0) = {} & \underline{2x_2^{(1)} x_1^{[1,2]}} \\ I(p^{21}f/px_1x_0) = {} & \underline{1x_2^{(0)} x_0^{[0,1]}} \\ I(pf/px_2x_1x_0) = {} & \underline{1x_2^{[0,1]} x_1^{[1,2]} x_0^{[0,1]}} \\ I(pf/px_2x_0) = {} & \underline{1x_2^{[1,2]} x_1^{(2)} x_0^{[2,0]}} \vee \underline{2x_2^{[0,1]} x_1^{(1)} x_0^{[0,1]}} \\ I(pf/px_2x_1) = {} & 1x_2^{[1,2]} x_1^{[1,2]} x_0^{(0)} \vee \underline{1x_2^{[1,2]} x_1^{[2,0]} x_0^{(2)}} \vee 1x_2^{[2,0]} x_1^{[1,2]} x_0^{(0)} \vee \\ & 1x_2^{[0,1]} x_1^{[1,2]} x_0^{(0)} \vee \underline{1x_2^{[2,0]} x_1^{[1,2]} x_0^{(1)}} \\ I(p^{21}f/px_2x_1) = {} & \underline{1x_1^{[1,2]} x_0^{(0)}} \end{aligned}$$

The prime blocks of f have been underlined in the above expressions, and the disjunction of these prime blocks is thus:

$$f = 1x_2^{[1,2]}\, x_1^{(2)}\, x_0^{[2,0]} \vee 3x_2^{(1)}\, x_1^{(2)}\, x_0^{(2)} \vee 2x_2^{(1)}\, x_0^{(2)} \vee 3x_2^{[0,1]}\, x_1^{(1)}\, x_0^{(1)} \vee$$
$$3x_2^{(0)}\, x_1^{[0,1]}\, x_0^{[0,1]} \vee 2x_2^{(1)}\, x_1^{[1,2]} \vee 1x_2^{(0)}\, x_0^{[0,1]} \vee 1x_2^{[0,1]}\, x_1^{[1,2]}\, x_0^{[0,1]} \vee$$
$$2x_2^{[0,1]}\, x_1^{(1)}\, x_0^{[0,1]} \vee 1x_2^{[1,2]}\, x_1^{[2,0]}\, x_0^{(2)} \vee 1x_1^{[1,2]}\, x_0^{(0)}. \qquad (3.108)$$

The prime blocks of weight 3, 2 and 1 are visualized in Figures 3.16(a), (b) and (c) respectively.

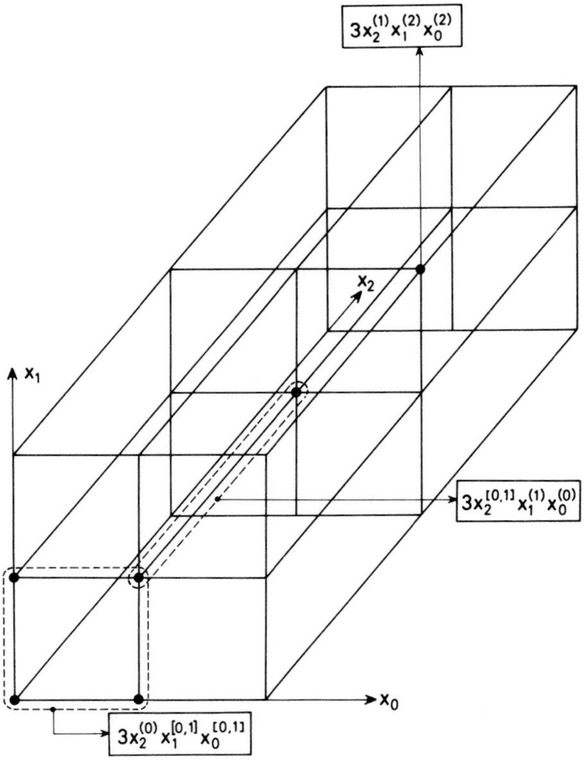

Figure 3.16(a). Prime blocks of weight 3; the vertices of weight 3 are denoted by •

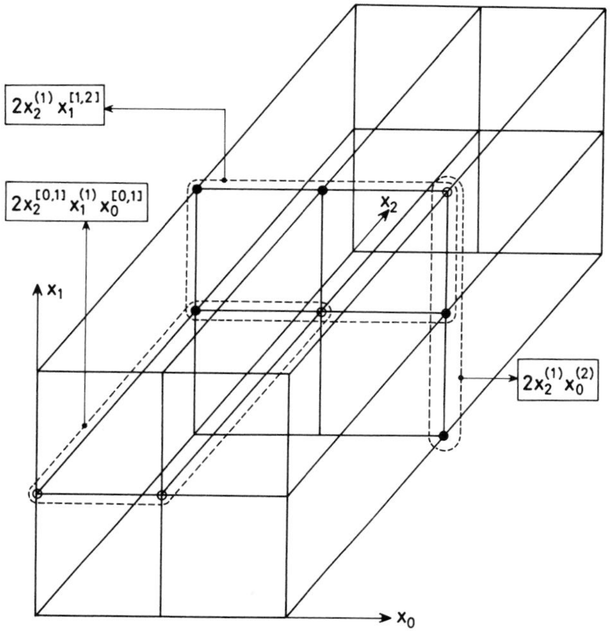

Figure 3.16(b). Prime blocks of weight 2; the vertices of weight 2 are denoted by •; the vertices of weight 3 included in some prime blocks of weight 2 are denoted by ○

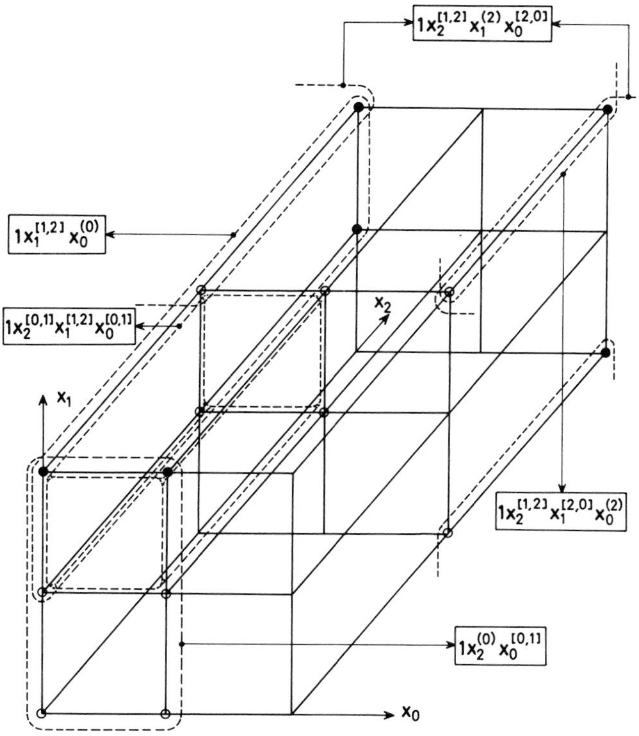

Figure 3.16(c). Prime blocks of weight 1; the vertices of weight 1 are denoted by •; the vertices of weights 2 or 3 included in some prime blocks of weight 1 are denoted by ○

Switching functions

The meet and join differences of switching functions enjoy some special computational properties which allow for an easy evaluation of these functions (see relations (3.56)–(3.61)). Moreover, in view of theorem 3.10(a), the algorithm 3.5 for detecting the implicants of a switching function reduces to the successive evaluation of the functions $p^k f/px$ (and no more $I(p^k f/px)$) from the lowest k until the highest.

Example 3.10

$$f = x_3\bar{x}_2x_1\bar{x}_0 \vee x_3\bar{x}_2\bar{x}_1\bar{x}_0 \vee x_3x_1x_0 \vee x_2\bar{x}_1x_0 \vee \bar{x}_3x_1\bar{x}_0 \vee \bar{x}_3x_1 \tag{3.109}$$

(a) $pf/px_0 = x_3\bar{x}_2x_1 \vee \bar{x}_3x_1$

$pf/px_1 = \underline{x_3\bar{x}_2\bar{x}_0} \vee \bar{x}_3x_2x_0 \vee x_3x_2x_0$

$pf/px_2 = x_3x_1x_0 \vee \bar{x}_3x_1$

$pf/px_3 = x_2\bar{x}_1x_0 \vee \bar{x}_2\bar{x}_0x_1 \vee x_1x_0$

(b) $pf/px_0x_1 = 0$

$pf/px_0x_2 = \underline{\bar{x}_3x_1}$

$pf/px_0x_3 = \underline{\bar{x}_2x_1}$

$pf/px_1x_3 = \underline{x_2x_0}$

$pf/px_2x_3 = \underline{x_1x_0}$

(c) $pf/px_ix_jx_k = 0 \quad \forall i, j, k.$

The prime implicants have been underlined in the above list of product terms.

All the algorithms for detecting the prime implicants (or the prime implicates) of a switching function may be divided into two successive parts:

The first part produces all the implicants of the function;
The second part selects the prime implicants by deleting in the obtained list the implicants smaller than other ones.

This second part may be avoided by use of theorem 3.11; the expressions (3.54) and (3.55) are indeed the prime implicants and the complement of the prime implicates of f respectively. From the result of this theorem, the following algorithm may be built.

Algorithm 3.6. (a) Compute all the meet differences from the lowest $pf/px_i, \forall i$, to the highest pf/px.

(b) Evaluate the expressions (3.54) from the highest, i.e. for $\boldsymbol{x}_0 = \boldsymbol{x}$, to the lowest, i.e. for $\boldsymbol{x}_0 = \phi$ (where ϕ means the empty set). The non-zero terms are the prime implicants of the function. It is conventionally assumed that $pf/p\phi = qf/q\phi = f$.

The above method is particularly attractive, since the algorithm provides us with the prime implicants only; the comparison of numerous implicants of $f(x)$ is thus avoided.

Example 3.7 (continued). Consider the switching function (3.97), i.e.

$$f = 1 \oplus x_1 x_0 \oplus x_4 \bar{x}_5 \oplus x_3 x_2 x_0.$$

The functions $p_{\boldsymbol{x}_0}(f)$ and $q_{\boldsymbol{x}_0}(f)$ are gathered in Figure 3.17. For sake of conciseness the entries $\boldsymbol{x}_0 = (x_i, \ldots, x_j)$ of the table of Figure 3.17 are denoted by $(i, \ldots, j)$. The prime implicants of $\bar{f}$ have been underlined in that figure.

$\boldsymbol{x}_0; p_{\boldsymbol{x}_0}(f), q_{\boldsymbol{x}_0}(f)$	$\boldsymbol{x}_0; p_{\boldsymbol{x}_0}(f), q_{\boldsymbol{x}_0}(f)$	$\boldsymbol{x}_0; p_{\boldsymbol{x}_0}(f), q_{\boldsymbol{x}_0}(f)$	$\boldsymbol{x}_0; p_{\boldsymbol{x}_0}(f), q_{\boldsymbol{x}_0}(f)$
(0 1 2 3) 0	(0 1 2) 0	(0 1) 0	0 $\underline{\bar{x}_5 x_4 x_3 x_2 x_1}$
(0 1 2 4) 0	(0 1 3) 0	(0 2) $\underline{\bar{x}_5 x_4 \bar{x}_3 \bar{x}_1}$	1 0
(0 1 2 5) 0	(0 1 4) 0	(0 3) $\underline{\bar{x}_5 x_4 \bar{x}_2 \bar{x}_1}$	2 $\bar{x}_5 x_4 \bar{x}_3 x_1 x_0$
(0 1 3 4) 0	(0 1 5) 0	(0 4) $x_5 x_3 x_2 x_1$	3 $\bar{x}_5 x_4 \bar{x}_2 x_1 x_0$
(0 1 4 5) 0	(0 2 3) 0	(0 5) $\bar{x}_4 x_3 x_2 x_1$	4 $\underline{x_5 x_3 x_2 \bar{x}_1 x_0}$
(0 2 3 4) 0	(0 2 4) $x_5 \bar{x}_3 \bar{x}_1$	(1 2) 0	5 $\underline{\bar{x}_4 x_3 x_2 \bar{x}_1 x_0}$
(0 2 3 5) 0	(0 2 5) $\bar{x}_4 \bar{x}_3 \bar{x}_1$	(1 3) 0	$\boldsymbol{x}_0; p_{\boldsymbol{x}_0}(f), q_{\boldsymbol{x}_0}(f)$
(0 2 4 5) 0	(0 3 4) $x_5 \bar{x}_2 \bar{x}_1$	(1 4) 0	$\phi; \bar{x}_5 x_4 x_3 x_2 \bar{x}_1 x_0$
(0 3 4 5) 0	(0 3 5) $\bar{x}_4 \bar{x}_2 \bar{x}_1$	(1 5) 0	
(1 2 3 4) $x_5 \bar{x}_0$	(0 4 5) 0	(2 3) 0	
(1 2 3 5) $\bar{x}_4 \bar{x}_0$	(1 2 3) $\underline{\bar{x}_5 x_4 \bar{x}_0}$	(2 4) $\underline{x_5 \bar{x}_3 x_1 x_0}$	
(1 2 4 5) 0	(1 2 4) 0	(2 5) $\underline{\bar{x}_4 \bar{x}_3 x_1 x_0}$	
(1 3 4 5) 0	(1 2 5) 0	(3 4) $\underline{x_5 \bar{x}_2 x_1 x_0}$	
(2 3 4 5) 0	(1 3 4) 0	(3 5) $\underline{\bar{x}_4 \bar{x}_2 x_1 x_0}$	
	(1 3 5) 0	(4 5) 0	
	(1 4 5) 0		
	(2 3 4) 0		
	(2 3 5) 0		
	(2 4 5) 0		

Figure 3.17. Prime implicants and negation of prime implicates of the switching function (3.97)

3.2.3.4. Lattice differences and consensus theory

A well-known procedure for finding prime implicants of a switching function is based on what Quine [1952, 1953, 1955] first called the *consensus* of implicants. The original method developed by Quine is generally referred to as the *iterative consensus*; it is fully detailed in most of the books dealing with switching theory (see, for example, Miller [1965], McCluskey [1965] and Dietmeyer [1971]).

This method has been improved, mainly by Tison [1964, 1965, 1967] who suggested a most efficient algorithm which is called the *generalized consensus*. Besides the original papers by Tison, a description of this algorithm may also be found in the books by Kuntzmann [1965], Kuntzmann and Naslin [1967], Perrin, Denouette and Daclin [1967a] and Dietmeyer [1971].

The main purpose of this section is to show that the concepts of meet and join differences are a convenient mathematical support for both the iterative and the generalized consensus. In this way, one shows that the consensus algorithms are implicitly contained in the lattice difference algorithms developed in the preceding sections.

The consensus theory, initially developed only for switching functions, has recently been extended by Tison [1971] to discrete functions. Again, the concepts of lattice differences for these functions generalize both the concept of consensus and the algorithms grounded on it.

It is not the purpose of this section to account fully for the consensus theory; only the basic definition will be recalled and a comparison between the results obtained by the consensus algorithms and the lattice difference algorithms will be made.

Consider first a switching function of, e.g. four variables, i.e. $f(x_3x_2x_1x_0)$. The function f and its meet differences $p^e f/p\boldsymbol{x}$ constitute a lattice which is schematized by Figure 3.18.

The extended-vector algorithm (see section 3.2.3.2.1) for this function may be schematized as follows:

Steps:

(a) From f one deduces pf/px_3.

(b) From f and pf/px_3 one deduces pf/px_2 and pf/px_3x_2 respectively.

(c) From f, pf/px_3, pf/px_2 and pf/px_3x_2 one deduces pf/px_1, pf/px_3x_1, pf/px_2x_1 and $pf/px_3x_2x_1$ respectively.

(d) From f, pf/px_3, pf/px_2, pf/px_3x_2, pf/px_1, pf/px_3x_1, pf/px_2x_1 and $pf/px_3x_2x_1$ one deduces pf/px_0, pf/px_3x_0, pf/px_2x_0, $pf/px_3x_2x_0$, pf/px_1x_0, $pf/px_3x_1x_0$, $pf/px_2x_1x_0$ and $pf/px_3x_2x_1x_0$ respectively.

All these functions are obtained in their value vector form from which one immediately deduces the implicants and thus the prime implicants. The steps (a), (b), (c) and (d) for the function $f(x_3x_2x_1x_0)$ are also schematically described by means of Figure 3.19.

Since, contrary to the consensus algorithms and to the lattice difference algorithm, the extended-vector algorithm holds whatever the initial form of the function may be, it constitutes the most general method for detecting prime implicants of a switching function.

Let us now turn to the important particular case where the switching function is given by a disjunctive normal form; both the consensus theory and the lattice difference algorithm apply for detecting prime implicants when the function is given in that form. We will first compare more thoroughly the definitions of consensus and of meet difference.

Definition 3.11. Let $c_0(\boldsymbol{x})$ and $c_1(\boldsymbol{x})$ be two cube functions; the *consensus operation* associates to the pair of cubes $\{c_0(\boldsymbol{x}), c_1(\boldsymbol{x})\}$ the cube denoted by $c_0(\boldsymbol{x}) * c_1(\boldsymbol{x})$ and which is defined as follows:

(a) If each of the variables which appear simultaneously in both $c_0(\boldsymbol{x})$ and $c_1(\boldsymbol{x})$

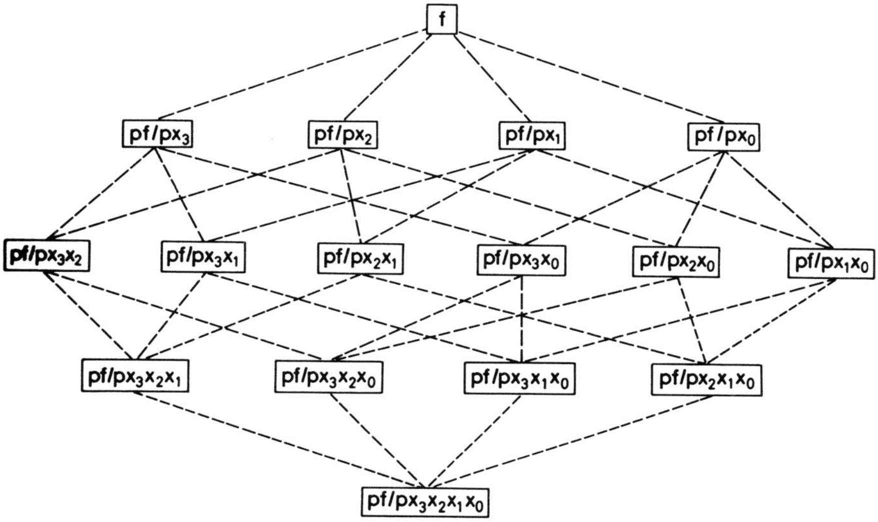

Figure 3.18. The lattice of the switching function $f(x_3 x_2 x_1 x_0)$ and of its meet differences

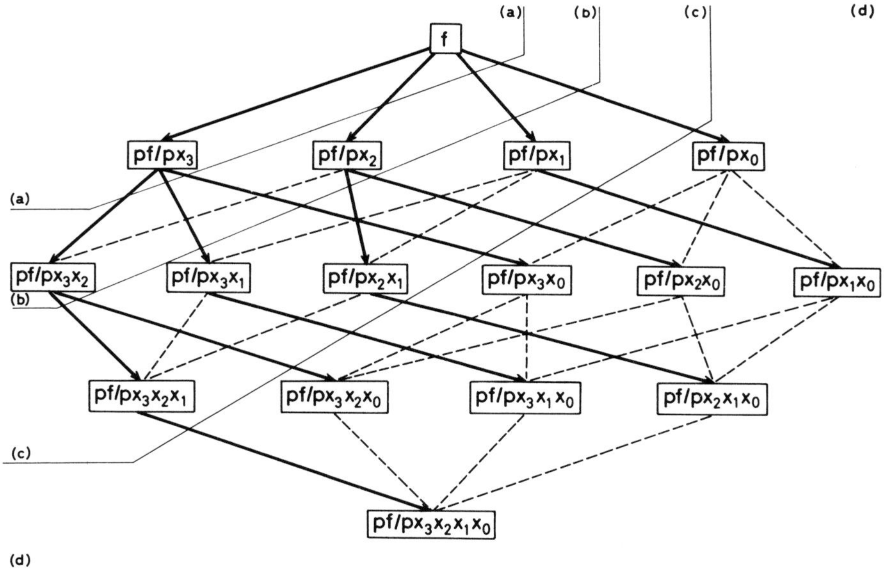

Figure 3.19. Scheme for the extended vector algorithm

have the same polarity (or equivalently are both in either direct or complemented form) then:

$$c_0(x) * c_1(x) = c_0(x) \wedge c_1(x)$$

(b) If only one variable has different polarities in $c_0(x)$ and $c_1(x)$, that is, for example, if: $c_0(x) = \bar{x}_0 \wedge c'_0(x)$ and $c_1(x) = x_0 \wedge c'_1(x)$, then:

$$c_0(x) * c_1(x) = c'_0(x) \wedge c'_1(x)$$

(c) If at least two variables have different polarities in $c_0(x)$ and $c_1(x)$, then

$$c_0(x) * c_1(x) = 0.$$

Consider now the meet differences of $c_0(x) \vee c_1(x)$; one has for the three possibilities mentioned in definition 3.10 respectively:

$$\begin{aligned} &\text{(a)} \quad \bigvee_{i=0,n-1} \frac{p[c_0(x) \vee c_1(x)]}{px_i} = 0. \\ &\text{(b)} \quad \bigvee_{i=0,n-1} \frac{p[c_0(x) \vee c_1(x)]}{px_i} = c'_0(x) \wedge c'_1(x). \\ &\text{(c)} \quad \bigvee_{i=0,n-1} \frac{p[c_0(x) \vee c_1(x)]}{px_i} = 0. \end{aligned} \tag{3.110}$$

One sees that the definition of consensus between two cubes coincides with the sum of the simple differences of the disjunction of these two cubes, except for the case (a). But it is well known that definition 3.11(a) of the consensus is completely arbitrary and the definition

$$c_0(x) * c_1(x) = 0$$

could also have been chosen without alteration of anything in the consensus algorithms. The consensus operation between two cubes may thus be related to the meet differences of the disjunction of these cubes as follows:

$$c_0(x) * c_1(x) = \bigvee_{i=0,n-1} \frac{p[c_0(x) \vee c_1(x)]}{px_i}. \tag{3.111}$$

It is however important to note that the consensus operation is only defined between two cubes while the meet differences apply to any form of switching functions. In particular, if the switching function is given as a disjunction of cubes, that is

$$f = \bigvee_j c_j(x)$$

the first step of the iterative consensus algorithm (see, for example, McCluskey [1965]) requires among others the computation of the consensus operation between each possible pair of cubes; one easily verifies that this operation corresponds to the evaluation of the function

$$\bigvee_{i=0,n-1} p\left[\bigvee_j c_j(x)\right] \Big/ px_i.$$

Let us now turn to the lattice-difference algorithm (see section 3.2.3.3) and consider again the four-variable switching function $f(x_3x_2x_1x_0)$: this algorithm may be schematized as follows: $f(x_3x_2x_1x_0)$ being given as a disjunction of cubes, perform the following steps successively.

Steps:

(a) From f one deduces $pf/px_3, pf/px_2, pf/px_1$ and pf/px_0 (if f is given as a disjunction of cubes these functions are also naturally obtained as a disjunction of cubes by use of the distributive law).
(b) From pf/px_3 one deduces, for example, $pf/px_3x_2, pf/px_3x_1$,
from pf/px_1 one deduces, for example, pf/px_2x_1,
from pf/px_0 one deduces, for example, $pf/px_3x_0, pf/px_2x_0, pf/px_1x_0$.
(c) From pf/px_3x_2 one deduces, for example, $pf/px_3x_2x_1, pf/px_3x_2x_0$,
from pf/px_1x_0 one deduces, for example, $pf/px_3x_1x_0, pf/px_2x_1x_0$.
(d) From, for example, $pf/px_3x_2x_0$ one deduces $pf/px_3x_2x_1x_0$.

These steps are schematically described by means of Figure 3.20. Now, if at each step of this algorithm one considers all the cubes already obtained (as a result of this step and of all the preceding steps) and if one deletes in the obtained list of cubes those which are contained in others, the remaining cubes are exactly those obtained at the corresponding step of the iterative consensus algorithm. Each step of the iterative consensus is thus fully described by the corresponding step of the lattice-difference algorithm.

Let us now turn to the description of the generalized consensus algorithm by means of the concept of meet difference.

First of all let us note that since $pf/px_i \leqslant f$ holds one has

$$f \vee pf/px_i = f. \tag{3.112}$$

Let us now assume that f be given as a disjunction of cubes; these cubes may be a completely random covering of the function. If pf/px_i is also given as a disjunction of cubes, one knows that the expression $f \vee pf/px_i$ is equal to f and contains certainly all the cubes of f degenerate in the variable x_i. Thus, while functionally equivalent, the expressions f and $f \vee pf/px_i$ are not identical since they may contain different sets of cubes; further on in this section one will assume that an expression such as $f \vee pf/px_i$ not only represents an expression functionally equivalent to f but has also the meaning, quoted above, of a disjunction of cubes.

The following relation holds

$$p(f \vee pf/px_i)/px_j = [f(x_j = 0) \vee pf(x_j = 0)/px_i] \wedge [f(x_j = 1) \vee pf(x_j = 1)/px_i]$$
$$= pf/px_j \vee pf/px_i x_j.$$

More generally, one has for a function $f(\boldsymbol{x}, y)$:

$$p(f \vee \bigvee_{e} pf/p\boldsymbol{x}^{e})/py = pf/py \vee \bigvee_{e} pf/p\boldsymbol{x}^{e}y. \tag{3.113}$$

On the basis of this observation the following algorithm may be stated for detecting all prime implicants of the function $f(x_3x_2x_1x_0)$.

Algorithm 3.7

Steps:

(a) From f one deduces pf/px_3.
(b) From $f \vee pf/px_3$ one deduces $p(f \vee pf/px_3)/px_2 = pf/px_2 \vee pf/px_3x_2$.
(c) From $f \vee pf/px_3 \vee pf/px_2 \vee pf/px_3x_2$ one deduces $p(f \vee pf/px_3 \vee pf/px_2 \vee pf/px_3x_2)/px_1 = pf/px_1 \vee pf/px_3x_1 \vee pf/px_2x_1 \vee pf/px_3x_2x_1$.
(d) From $f \vee pf/px_3 \vee pf/px_2 \vee pf/px_3x_2 \vee pf/px_1 \vee pf/px_3x_1 \vee pf/px_2x_1 \vee pf/px_3x_2x_1$ one deduces $p(f \vee pf/px_3 \vee pf/px_2 \vee pf/px_3x_2 \vee pf/px_1 \vee pf/px_3x_1 \vee pf/px_2x_1 \vee pf/px_3x_2x_1)/px_0 = pf/px_0 \vee pf/px_3x_0 \vee pf/px_2x_0 \vee pf/px_3x_2x_0 \vee pf/px_1x_0 \vee pf/px_3x_1x_0 \vee pf/px_2x_1x_0 \vee pf/px_3x_2x_1x_0$.

Now if at each step of this algorithm one deletes, in the expression $f \vee \bigvee_{e} pf/p\boldsymbol{x}^{e}$, the cubes contained in others, the remaining cubes are exactly those obtained at the corresponding step of the generalized consensus algorithm. These steps are schematically described by means of Figure 3.21. The generalization of algorithm 3.7 to a function $f(\boldsymbol{x})$ is quite clear and needs no further explanation.

It is clear that the iterative consensus algorithm and the generalized consensus algorithm were described in a very general form. More detailed explanations may be found in the papers and books quoted at the beginning of this section. In fact there exist many different types of iterative and generalized consensus algorithms which differ from each other by several kinds of improvements which are, for example, of interest for the improvement of the complexity of automatic computations. It is beyond the scope of this book to deal with these questions; our purpose was only to show here that, since the concept of lattice difference constitutes a more general concept than the consensus operation, the basic algorithms which are based on the consensus operation may easily be deduced from the meet differences.

Example 3.10 (continued)

Iterative consensus

$$f = x_3\bar{x}_2x_1\bar{x}_0 \vee x_3\bar{x}_2\bar{x}_1\bar{x}_0 \vee x_3x_1x_0 \vee x_2\bar{x}_1x_0 \vee \bar{x}_3x_1\bar{x}_0 \vee \bar{x}_3x_1.$$

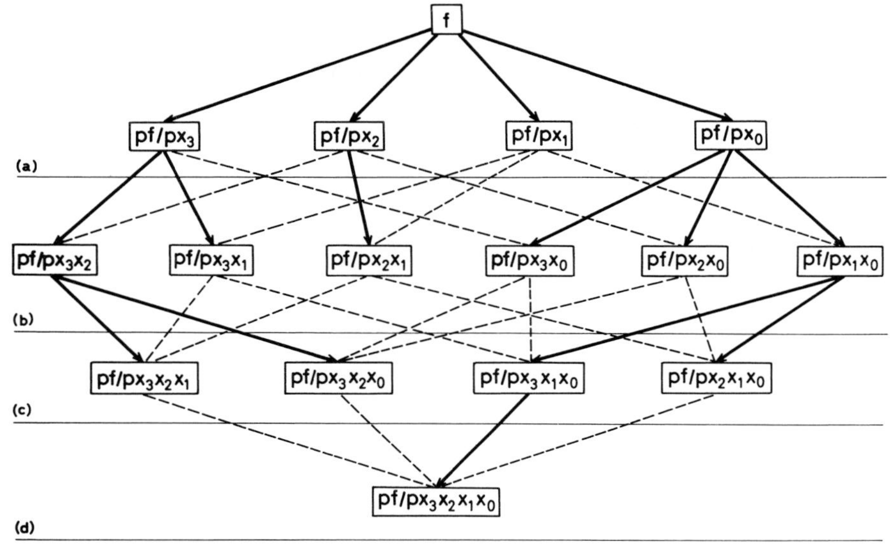

Figure 3.20. Scheme for the lattice-difference algorithm

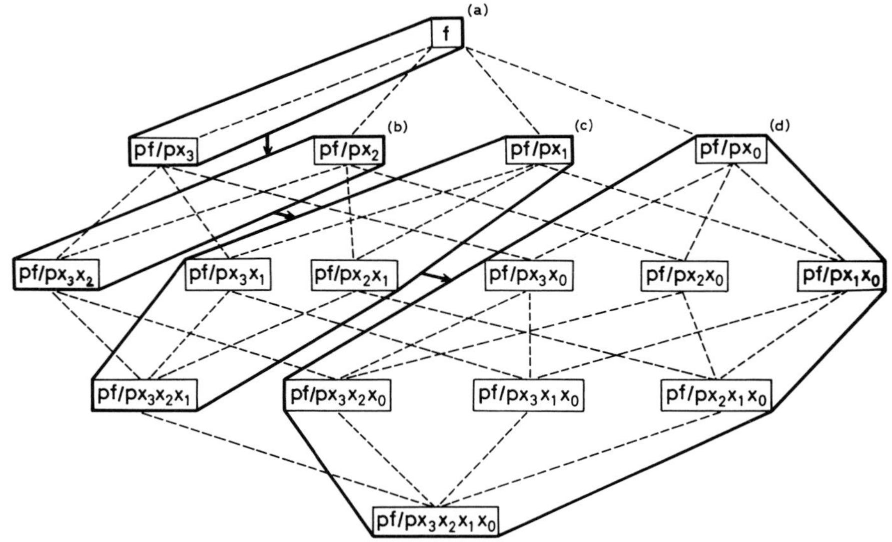

Figure 3.21. Scheme for the generalized consensus algorithm

Deleting the cubes contained in others, one obtains:

$$f = x_3\bar{x}_2x_1\bar{x}_0 \vee x_3\bar{x}_2\bar{x}_1\bar{x}_0 \vee x_3x_1x_0 \vee x_2\bar{x}_1x_0 \vee \bar{x}_3x_1$$

(a) $$\bigvee_{i=0,3} pf/px_i = x_1x_0 \vee \bar{x}_3x_1 \vee x_3\bar{x}_2x_1 \vee x_3\bar{x}_2\bar{x}_0 \vee \bar{x}_3x_2x_0 \vee x_3x_2x_0 \vee x_2\bar{x}_1x_0 \vee \bar{x}_2\bar{x}_0x_1$$

$$f \vee \bigvee pf/px_i = x_1x_0 \vee \bar{x}_3x_1 \vee x_3\bar{x}_2x_1 \vee x_3\bar{x}_2\bar{x}_0 \vee \bar{x}_3x_2x_0 \vee x_3x_2x_0 \vee x_2\bar{x}_1x_0 \vee \bar{x}_2\bar{x}_0x_1.$$

(b) $$\bigvee_{i,j} pf/px_ix_j = \bar{x}_3x_1 \vee \bar{x}_2x_1 \vee x_2x_0 \vee x_1x_0$$

$$f \vee \bigvee_i pf/px_i \vee \bigvee_{i,j} pf/px_ix_j = \bar{x}_3x_1 \vee \bar{x}_2x_1 \vee x_2x_0 \vee x_1x_0 \vee x_3\bar{x}_2\bar{x}_0$$

(c) $pf/px_ix_jx_k = 0 \;\forall\, i, j, k$ and (b) gives thus the prime implicants of f.

Generalized consensus

Let us start from an irredundant disjunction of product terms, that is a disjunction of cubes where no cube is contained in others:

$$f = x_3\bar{x}_2x_1\bar{x}_0 \vee x_3\bar{x}_2\bar{x}_1x_0 \vee x_3x_1x_0 \vee x_2\bar{x}_1x_0 \vee \bar{x}_3x_1$$

(a) $pf/px_3 = x_2\bar{x}_1x_0 \vee \bar{x}_2x_1\bar{x}_0 \vee x_1x_0$

$$f \vee pf/px_3 = x_2\bar{x}_1x_0 \vee \bar{x}_2x_1\bar{x}_0 \vee x_1x_0 \vee x_3\bar{x}_2\bar{x}_1\bar{x}_0 \vee \bar{x}_3x_1 = f_0.$$

(b) $pf_0/px_2 = x_1x_0 \vee \bar{x}_3x_1.$

$$f_0 \vee pf_0/px_2 = x_1x_0 \vee \bar{x}_3x_1 \vee x_2\bar{x}_1x_0 \vee \bar{x}_2x_1\bar{x}_0 \vee x_3\bar{x}_2\bar{x}_1\bar{x}_0 = f_0.$$

(c) $pf_0/px_1 = x_2x_0 \vee x_3\bar{x}_2\bar{x}_0$

$$f_0 \vee pf_0/px_1 = x_2x_0 \vee x_3\bar{x}_2\bar{x}_0 \vee \bar{x}_3x_1 \vee x_1x_0 \vee \bar{x}_2x_1\bar{x}_0 = f_1.$$

(d) $pf_1/px_0 = \bar{x}_3x_1 \vee \bar{x}_2x_1$

$$f_1 \vee pf_1/px_0 = x_2x_0 \vee \bar{x}_3x_1 \vee x_1x_0 \vee \bar{x}_2x_1 \vee x_3\bar{x}_2\bar{x}_0.$$

The consensus theory is actually well known and completely developed for switching functions; it has been extended by Tison [1971] for dealing also with discrete functions. This theory will not be developed in this book; only the definition of the consensus operation between two blocks in term of the meet difference will be given.

Definition 3.13. Let c_0 and c_1 be two (discrete) block functions; the *consensus operation* associates to the pair of blocks $\{c_0, c_1\}$ the function denoted by $c_0 * c_1$ and which is defined as follows:

$$c_0 * c_1 = \bigvee_{i=0,n-1} I\left[\frac{(c_0 \vee c_1)}{px_i}\right]. \tag{3.114}$$

3.2.3.5. *The Quine–McCluskey algorithm*

The *Quine–McCluskey method* for detection of prime implicants has been known for a long time in switching theory. It is basically a tabular method due to McCluskey [1956b] and based on an original technique due to Quine [1952]. In this section we present a generalized version of the Quine–McCluskey method that can be applied to the research of the prime convex blocks of a discrete function.

Definition 3.13. Consider a discrete function f and one of its (non-zero) convex blocks

$$g = l \wedge \bigwedge_{i=n-1}^{0} x_i^{[a_i, b_i]}, \quad l \in L, a_i, b_i \in S_i, \forall\, i.$$

In the sequel of this section, the notation h_i stands for the difference $b_i - a_i$ (i.e. $b_i = a_i + h_i$). One supposes that l has the maximum value in order that g is a block of f, i.e.

$$l = \left(\frac{p^h f}{px}\right)_{x=a},$$

where

$$h = (h_{n-1}, \ldots, h_0) \quad \text{and} \quad a = (a_{n-1}, \ldots, a_0).$$

The convex blocks *1-associated* with g are all the non-zero convex blocks of f of the form

$$g_j = l' \wedge x_{n-1}^{[a_{n-1}, b_{n-1}]} \wedge \ldots \wedge x_j^{[a_j+1, b_j+1]} \wedge \ldots \wedge x_0^{[a_0, b_0]},$$

for some j such that $b_j \leqslant m_j - 2$, and some value l' such that

$$l' = \left(\frac{p^h f}{px}\right)_{x=a+\epsilon_j},$$

with $\epsilon_j = (0, \ldots, 1 \ldots, 0)$. The number of convex blocks 1-associated with g is thus at most equal to n.

The *order* of a convex block is the sum of its lengths. The order of g is thus $n+h_{n-1}+\ldots+h_0$. It is obvious that a convex block and all its 1-associated convex blocks have necessarily the same order.

Let us now compute $g * g_j$ according to the definition 3.12:

$$g * g_j = \bigvee_{i=0}^{n-1} I\left[\frac{p(g \vee g_j)}{px_i}\right].$$

By definition of the meet difference one has

$$\frac{p(g \vee g_j)}{px_i} = [g(x_i) \vee g_j(x_i)] \wedge [g(x_i \oplus 1) \wedge g_j(x_i \oplus 1)]$$

$$= \frac{pg}{px_i} \vee \frac{pg_j}{px_i} \vee [g_j(x_i) \wedge g(x_i \oplus 1)] \vee [g(x_i) \wedge g_j(x_i \oplus 1)].$$

Consider then two cases.

1. $i \neq j$.

$$g_j(x_i) \wedge g(x_i \oplus 1) = 0 \quad \text{if} \quad a_i = b_i \quad \text{or if} \quad a_j = b_j,$$

$$= l \wedge l' \wedge \ldots \wedge x_j^{[a_j+1, b_j]} \wedge \ldots \wedge x_i^{[k_i, b_i'-1]} \wedge \ldots, \text{otherwise};$$

$$g(x_i) \wedge g_j(x_i \oplus 1) = g_j(x_i) \wedge g(x_i \oplus 1);$$

therefore

$$I\left[\frac{p(g \vee g_j)}{px_i}\right] = 0 \quad \text{if} \quad a_i = b_i,$$

$$= g \vee g_j \quad \text{otherwise}.$$

2. $i = j$.

$$g_j(x_j) \wedge g(x_j \oplus 1) = 0 \quad \text{if} \quad a_j = b_j \quad \text{or if} \quad a_j = b_j - 1,$$

$$= l \wedge l' \wedge \ldots \wedge x_j^{[a_j+1, b_j-1]} \wedge \ldots, \quad \text{otherwise};$$

$$g(x_j) \wedge g_j(x_j \oplus 1) = l \wedge l' \wedge \ldots \wedge x_j^{[a_j, b_j]} \wedge \ldots;$$

therefore

$$I\left[\frac{p(g \vee g_j)}{px_j}\right] = h \quad \text{if} \quad a_j = b_j,$$

$$= g \vee g_j \vee h, \quad \text{otherwise},$$

where

$$h = l \wedge l' \wedge x_{n-1}^{[a_{n-1}, b_{n-1}]} \wedge \ldots \wedge x_j^{[a_j, b_j+1]} \wedge \ldots \wedge x_0^{[a_0, b_0]};$$

it is a convex block of order $d+1$ if d denotes the order of g (and g_j). Finally one obtains

$$\begin{aligned} g * g_j &= h \quad \text{if} \quad a_i = b_i, \forall i = 0, \ldots, n-1, \\ &= g \vee g_j \vee h \quad \text{otherwise.} \end{aligned}$$

The convex block h is called the *consensus* between g and g_j since it is the only new block obtained by the consensus operation $*$. Note that

$$\begin{aligned} l \wedge l' &= \left(\frac{p^h f}{px}\right)_{x=a} \wedge \left(\frac{p^h f}{px}\right)_{x=a+\epsilon_j} \\ &= \left[\frac{p}{px_j}\left(\frac{p^h f}{px}\right)\right]_{x=a} = \left(\frac{p^{h+\epsilon_j} f}{px}\right)_{x=a}, \end{aligned}$$

and thus $l \wedge l'$ is maximum.

Lemma 3.9. If

$$g = \left(\frac{p^h f}{px}\right)_{x=a} \wedge \bigwedge_{i=n-1}^{0} x_i^{[a_i, b_i]}$$

is a convex block of f of order $d+1$, with $d \geqslant n$, it is obtained by consensus between two convex blocks of f of order d.

Proof. If g has order $d+1$, one of the intervals $[a_i, b_i]$ has a length greater than one. Suppose for instance $a_0 < b_0$. Then the two blocks

$$g' = \left(\frac{p^{h-\epsilon_0} f}{px}\right)_{x=a} \wedge \left(\bigwedge_{i=n-1}^{1} x_i^{[a_i, b_i]}\right) \wedge x_0^{[a_0, b_0-1]}$$

and

$$g'' = \left(\frac{p^{h-\epsilon_0} f}{px}\right)_{x=a+\epsilon_0} \wedge \left(\bigwedge_{i=n-1}^{1} x_i^{[a_i, b_i]}\right) \wedge x_0^{[a_0+1, b_0]}$$

are 1-associated; their order is d and their consensus is g. ■

Suppose now that it is possible to range all the (non-zero) convex blocks of f, of order $d \geqslant n$, with maximum weight, into classes $C_0^d, C_1^d, \ldots$, such that C_{k+1}^d contains all the convex blocks of f 1-associated with the convex blocks that lie in C_k^d, $k = 0, 1, \ldots$. By performing consensus between convex blocks appearing in adjacent classes, one obtains thus all the convex blocks of f of order $d+1$, with maximum weight (see lemma 3.9). They are arranged into classes $C_0^{d+1}, C_1^{d+1}, \ldots$, where C_k^{d+1} contains the convex blocks resulting from consensus between convex blocks of C_k^d and C_{k+1}^d. Furthermore, we prove now that the classes $C_0^{d+1}, C_1^{d+1}, \ldots$, have the same property as the classes $C_0^d, C_1^d, \ldots$, i.e. C_{k+1}^{d+1} contains all the convex blocks of f 1-associated with the convex blocks lying in C_k^{d+1}.

Lemma 3.10. If the convex block

$$g = \left(\frac{p^h f}{px}\right)_{x=a} \wedge \bigwedge_{i=n-1}^{0} x_i^{[a_i, b_i]}$$

is in C_k^{d+1}, if b_j is smaller than $m_j - 1$ and if

$$\left(\frac{p^h f}{px}\right)_{x=a+\epsilon_j}$$

is not equal to 0, then the convex block

$$g_j = \left(\frac{p^h f}{px}\right)_{x=a+\epsilon_j} \wedge x_j^{[a_j+1, b_j+1]} \wedge \bigwedge_{\substack{i=n-1 \\ i \neq j}}^{0} x_i^{[a_i, b_i]}$$

is in C_{k+1}^{d+1}.

Proof. The block g is obtained by consensus between a convex block g' of C_k^d and a convex block g'' of C_{k+1}^d:

$$g' = \left(\frac{p^{h-\epsilon_i} f}{px}\right)_{x=a} \wedge x_{n-1}^{[a_{n-1}, b_{n-1}]} \wedge \ldots \wedge x_i^{[a_i, b_i - 1]} \wedge \ldots \wedge x_0^{[a_0, b_0]},$$

$$g'' = \left(\frac{p^{h-\epsilon_i} f}{px}\right)_{x=a+\epsilon_i} \wedge x_{n-1}^{[a_{n-1}, b_{n-1}]} \wedge \ldots \wedge x_i^{[a_i+1, b_i]} \wedge \ldots \wedge x_0^{[a_0, b_0]}.$$

Consider again two cases.

1. $i \neq j$. Thus the non-zero convex block

$$g_j' = \left(\frac{p^{h-\epsilon_i} f}{px}\right)_{x=a+\epsilon_j} \wedge \ldots \wedge x_j^{[a_j+1, b_j+1]} \wedge \ldots \wedge x_i^{[a_i, b_i - 1]} \wedge \ldots$$

is 1-associated with g' and lies in C_{k+1}^d, while the non-zero convex block

$$g_j'' = \left(\frac{p^{h-\epsilon_i} f}{px}\right)_{x=a+\epsilon_i+\epsilon_j} \wedge \ldots \wedge x_j^{[a_j+1, b_j+1]} \wedge \ldots \wedge x_i^{[a_i+1, b_i]} \wedge \ldots$$

is 1-associated with g'' and lies in C_{k+2}^d. Therefore C_{k+1}^{d+1} contains the convex block g_j that is obtained by consensus between $g_j' \in C_{k+1}^d$ and $g_j'' \in C_{k+2}^d$.

2. $i = j$. Then the non-zero convex block

$$g''' = \left(\frac{p^{h-\epsilon_j} f}{px}\right)_{x=a+2\epsilon_j} \wedge x_{n-1}^{[a_{n-1}, b_{n-1}]} \wedge \ldots \wedge x_j^{[a_j+2, b_j+1]} \wedge \ldots \wedge x_0^{[a_0, b_0]}$$

is 1-associated with g'' and lies thus in C_{k+2}^d. The convex block g_j is then obtained by consensus between $g'' \in C_{k+1}^d$ and $g''' \in C_{k+2}^d$. ■

The next lemma gives the starting point of the Quine–McCluskey algorithm.

Lemma 3.11. The convex blocks of f of order n, with maximum weight, i.e. the minterms of f, can be ranged into classes $C_0^n, C_1^n, \ldots, C_{q-1}^n$, according to the scheme described above. Some class(es) may be empty. The number of classes is $q = m_0 + \ldots + m_{n-1} - n + 1$.

Proof. The class C_k^n contains all the minterms

$$f(a) \wedge \bigwedge_{i=n-1}^{0} x_i^{[a_i, a_i]},$$

with $f(a) \neq 0$ and such that

$$\sum_{i=n-1}^{0} a_i = k.$$

The index k takes thus all the values between 0 and

$$\sum_{i=n-1}^{0} (m_i - 1) = m_0 + \ldots + m_{n-1} - n. \qquad \blacksquare$$

The next algorithm gives then the prime convex blocks of a discrete function f.

Algorithm 3.8

Step 1. Range the minterms of f into classes $C_0^n, \ldots, C_q^n$, where C_k^n contains all the minterms

$$f(a) \wedge \bigwedge_{i=n-1}^{0} x_i^{[a_i, a_i]},$$

with $f(a) \neq 0$ and

$$\sum_{i=n-1}^{0} a_i = k.$$

Step i. Obtain the classes $C_0^{n+i-1}, \ldots, C_{q-i+1}^{n+i-1}$ of convex blocks: the class C_k^{n+i-1} contains the convex blocks resulting from the consensus between a convex block of C_k^{n+i-2} and a convex block of C_{k+1}^{n+i-2}, $k = 0, \ldots, q-i+1$.

After $q-1$ steps, all the convex blocks of f with maximum weight, among which lie all the prime convex blocks of f, have been found. In order to select the prime convex blocks, a marking technique can be used just as in the classical Quine–McCluskey algorithm for switching functions:

If a consensus is made between the convex block g_1 of weight l_1 and the convex block g_2 of weight l_2, then the block with the smallest weight is marked; if $l_1 = l_2$, then both are marked. The prime convex blocks of f are all the unmarked convex blocks: indeed, if one performs a consensus between two convex blocks, the new convex block is greater than the initial convex block with the smallest weight. Conversely, if a convex block g of weight l is not prime, then there must exist a convex block g' of weight $l' \geqslant l$ such that either g' is 1-associated with g or g is 1-associated with g'.

Example 3.8 (continued). The prime convex blocks of the ternary function of two quaternary variables

$$f = 1x_1^{[1,1]}\, x_0^{[3,0]} \vee 1x_1^{[1,1]}\, x_0^{[2} \vee 1x_1^{0]}\, x_0^{[1,1]} \vee 2x_1^{[1,2]}\, x_0^{[1,1]} \vee 2x_1^{[3}\, x_0^{1]} \vee$$
$$2x_1^{[2,2]}\, x_0^{[3,0]} \vee 2x_1^{[2}\, x_0^{[3}$$

are computed by the Quine–McCluskey method. The computations are summarized in Figure 3.22. There are thus seven prime convex blocks:

$$A = 2x_1^{[2}\, x_0^{[3};\ B = 2x_1^{[1}\, x_0^{[1,1]};\ C = 2x_1^{[2}\, x_0^{1]};\ D = 1x_1^{[1}\, x_0^{[3};\ E = 1x_0^{[1,1]};$$
$$F = 1x_1^{[1,1]};\ G = 1x_1^{[1}\, x_0^{1]}.$$

3.2.3.6. Iterative forms for switching functions

This section deals with a computation method for evaluating simultaneously the meet and join differences of a switching function. The iterative form of a switching function was defined by Lyngholm and Yoourgrau [1960] and used by Reischer and Simovici [1971] to discuss some special problems like the square rooting of a switching function. A more general definition of the iterative form was later given by Thayse [1973b] who used it to detect prime implicants and prime implicates of switching functions and to solve several design problems arising in hazard-free synthesis of switching networks (see Thayse [1975b]).

Let us recall that a notation such as $f(x_i = f)$ means that in the expression representing the function f, the variable x_i has to be replaced by the function f itself.

Definition 3.14. (a) *Simple iterative form*

Given a switching function $f(\boldsymbol{x})$, the iterative form of f with respect to a variable $x_i \in \boldsymbol{x}$ will be denoted by rf/rx_i and is defined as follows:

$$rf/rx_i = f(x_i = f) \tag{3.115}$$

(b) *Multiple iterative form*

The multiple iterative forms are defined according to a recurrence scheme:

$$\frac{rf}{r\boldsymbol{x}_0} = \frac{r}{rx_0}\left\{\frac{r}{rx_1}\left[\cdots\left(\frac{rf}{rx_{q-1}}\right)\cdots\right]\right\} \tag{3.116}$$

with $\boldsymbol{x}_0 = (x_{q-1}, \ldots, x_1, x_0)$.

Class	Term	Check	
C_0^2			
C_1^2	$1x_1^{0]}\,x_0^{[1,1]}$	v	
	$1x_1^{[1,1]}\,x_0^{0]}$	v	
C_2^2	$2x_1^{[1,1]}\,x_0^{[1,1]}$	v	
	$2x_1^{[2,2]}\,x_0^{0]}$	v	
C_3^2	$1x_1^{[1,1]}\,x_0^{[2,2]}$	v	
	$2x_1^{[2,2]}\,x_0^{[1,1]}$	v	
	$2x_1^{[3}\,x_0^{0]}$	v	
C_4^2	$1x_1^{[1,1]}\,x_0^{[3}$	v	
	$2x_1^{[3}\,x_0^{[1,1]}$	v	
C_5^2	$2x_1^{[2,2]}\,x_0^{[3}$	v	
C_6^2	$2x_1^{[3}\,x_0^{[3}$	v	

Class	Term	Check	
C_0^3			
C_1^3	$1x_1^{1]}\,x_0^{[1,1]}$	v	
	$1x_1^{[1,1]}\,x_0^{1]}$	v	
	$1x_1^{[1,2]}\,x_0^{0]}$	v	
C_2^3	$1x_1^{[1,1]}\,x_0^{[1,2]}$	v	
	$2x_1^{[1,2]}\,x_0^{[1,1]}$	v	
	$2x_1^{[2,2]}\,x_0^{1]}$	v	
	$2x_1^{[2}\,x_0^{0]}$	v	
C_3^3	$1x_1^{[1,1]}\,x_0^{[2}$	v	
	$2x_1^{[2}\,x_0^{[1,1]}$	v	
	$2x_1^{[3}\,x_0^{1]}$	v	
C_4^3	$1x_1^{[1,2]}\,x_0^{[3}$	v	
C_5^3	$2x_1^{[2}\,x_0^{[3}$		A

Class	Term	Check	
C_0^4			
C_1^4	$1x_1^{2]}\,x_0^{[1,1]}$	v	
	$1x_1^{[1,1]}\,x_0^{2]}$	v	
	$1x_1^{[1,2]}\,x_0^{1]}$	v	
	$1x_1^{[1}\,x_0^{0]}$	v	
C_2^4	$1x_1^{[1,1]}\,x_0^{[1}$	v	
	$2x_1^{[1}\,x_0^{[1,1]}$		B
	$2x_1^{[2}\,x_0^{1]}$		C
C_3^4			
C_4^4	$1x_1^{[1}\,x_0^{[3}$		D

Class	Term	
C_0^5		
C_1^5	$1x_0^{[1,1]}$	E
	$1x_1^{[1,1]}$	F
	$1x_1^{[1}\,x_0^{1]}$	G
C_2^5		
C_3^5		

Figure 3.22. The Quine–McCluskey method

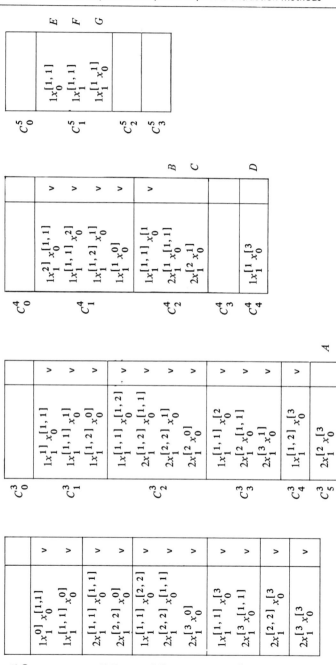

By developing (3.115) with respect to x_i, one obtains successively:

$$rf/rx_i = \bar{f}\ f(x_i = 0) \vee f\,f(x_i = 1)$$
$$= pf/px_i \vee x_i(qf/qx_i). \tag{3.117}$$

From (3.115)–(3.116) one then easily deduces that $rf/r\boldsymbol{x}_0$ can be expressed in the following symbolical form:

$$rf/r\boldsymbol{x}_0 = \bigvee_{x_i \in \boldsymbol{x}_0} [p/px_i \vee x_i(q/qx_i)]f. \tag{3.118}$$

It turns out that $rf/r\boldsymbol{x}_0$ contains in a parametrical form all the information relative to both the prime implicants and the prime implicates of f which are degenerate in $\boldsymbol{x}_0$. The following algorithm may then, for example, be used for detecting at the same time the prime implicants and the prime implicates.

Algorithm 3.9. (a) From the expression of f, compute successively

$$rf/r\boldsymbol{x}^k$$

from the lowest k to the highest one; since $\forall \boldsymbol{x}_0 \subseteq \boldsymbol{x}$ relation (3.118) allows us to write

$$pf/p\boldsymbol{x}_0 = (rf/r\boldsymbol{x}_0)_{\boldsymbol{x}_0=0}$$
$$qf/q\boldsymbol{x}_0 = (rf/r\boldsymbol{x}_0)_{\boldsymbol{x}_0=1}, \tag{3.119}$$

all the meet and join differences are obtained from $rf/r\boldsymbol{x}^k$.

(b) Evaluate the expressions (3.54)–(3.55) from the highest set, i.e. for $\boldsymbol{x}_0 = \boldsymbol{x}$, to the lowest set, i.e. for $\boldsymbol{x}_0 = \phi$; the non-0 terms of $p_{\boldsymbol{x}_0}(f)$ are the prime implicants while the non-1 terms of $\overline{q_{\boldsymbol{x}_0}(f)}$ are the prime implicates.

The above algorithm evidently holds, whatever the initial form of the switching function may be; one will however point out that the computations yielding the iterative forms are very easily performed when the switching function is given by a modulo-2 sum of cubes containing only letters in a direct form. Such an expression will be called the Reed–Muller expansion of the switching function for a reason that will appear further on in this book (see Chapter 5).

Example 3.11. Consider the switching function

$$f = x_0 \oplus x_1 \oplus x_2 \oplus x_0x_2 \oplus x_1x_3. \tag{3.120}$$

The iterative forms, meet and join differences are first obtained in increasing order of the dimension of $\boldsymbol{x}_0$; the functions $p_{\boldsymbol{x}_0}(f)$ and $\overline{q_{\boldsymbol{x}_0}(f)}$ are then obtained in decreasing order of the dimension of $\boldsymbol{x}_0$. All these results are gathered in the table of Figure 3.23. For sake of conciseness the entries $\boldsymbol{x}_0 = (x_i, \ldots, x_j)$ of the table of Figure 3.23 are denoted by $(i, \ldots, j)$.

x_0	rf/rx_0	pf/px_0
ϕ	$x_0 \oplus x_1 \oplus x_2 \oplus x_0x_2 \oplus x_1x_3$	$x_0 \oplus x_1 \oplus x_2 \oplus x_0x_2 \oplus x_1x_3$
0	$x_0 \oplus x_2 \oplus x_0x_2 \oplus x_1x_2 \oplus x_1x_2x_3$	$x_2 \oplus x_1x_2 \oplus x_1x_2x_3$
1	$x_1 \oplus x_1x_3 \oplus x_0x_3 \oplus x_2x_3 \oplus x_0x_2x_3$	$x_0x_3 \oplus x_2x_3 \oplus x_0x_2x_3$
2	$x_0 \oplus x_2 \oplus x_0x_1 \oplus x_0x_2 \oplus x_0x_1x_3$	$x_0 \oplus x_0x_1 \oplus x_0x_1x_3$
3	$x_0 \oplus x_2 \oplus x_0x_1 \oplus x_0x_2 \oplus x_1x_2 \oplus x_1x_3 \oplus x_0x_1x_3$	$x_0 \oplus x_2 \oplus x_0x_1 \oplus x_0x_2 \oplus x_1x_2 \oplus x_0x_1x_2$
01	$x_0 \oplus x_0x_2 \oplus x_1x_2 \oplus x_2x_3 \oplus x_1x_2x_3$	x_2x_3
02	$x_0 \oplus x_2 \oplus x_0x_2 \oplus x_1x_2 \oplus x_0x_1 \oplus x_0x_1x_3 \oplus x_1x_2x_3$	0
03	$x_0 \oplus x_2 \oplus x_0x_2 \oplus x_1x_2 \oplus x_1x_2x_3$	$x_2 \oplus x_1x_2$
12	$x_1 \oplus x_1x_3 \oplus x_0x_3 \oplus x_2x_3 \oplus x_0x_2x_3$	x_0x_3
13	$x_1x_3 \oplus x_0x_1 \oplus x_0x_3 \oplus x_1x_2 \oplus x_2x_3 \oplus x_0x_1x_2 \oplus x_0x_2x_3$	0
23	$x_0 \oplus x_2 \oplus x_0x_1 \oplus x_0x_2 \oplus x_0x_1x_3$	$x_0 \oplus x_0x_1$
012	$x_0x_2 \oplus x_0x_1 \oplus x_1x_2 \oplus x_0x_3 \oplus x_2x_3 \oplus x_0x_1x_3 \oplus x_0x_1x_2x_3$	0
013	$x_0 \oplus x_0x_2 \oplus x_2x_3 \oplus x_1x_2 \oplus x_1x_2x_3$	0
023	$x_0 \oplus x_2 \oplus x_0x_2 \oplus x_0x_1 \oplus x_0x_1x_3 \oplus x_1x_2 \oplus x_1x_2x_3$	0
123	$x_1x_3 \oplus x_0x_1 \oplus x_0x_3 \oplus x_0x_1x_2 \oplus x_1x_2 \oplus x_2x_3 \oplus x_0x_2x_3$	0
0123	$x_0x_3 \oplus x_0x_2 \oplus x_2x_3 \oplus x_0x_1 \oplus x_0x_1x_3 \oplus x_0x_1x_2 \oplus x_0x_1x_2x_3$	0

x_0	qf/qx_0	$p_{x_0}(f)$	$\overline{q_{x_0}(f)}$
ϕ	$x_0 \oplus x_1 \oplus x_2 \oplus x_0x_2 \oplus x_1x_3$	$\bar{x}_3\bar{x}_2x_1\bar{x}_0$	1
0	$1 \oplus x_1x_2 \oplus x_1x_2x_3$	0	$x_3 \vee \bar{x}_2 \vee \bar{x}_1$
1	$1 \oplus x_3 \oplus x_0x_3 \oplus x_2x_3 \oplus x_0x_2x_3$	0	$\bar{x}_3 \vee x_2 \vee x_0$
2	$1 \oplus x_0x_1 \oplus x_0x_1x_3$	0	$x_3 \vee \bar{x}_1 \vee \bar{x}_0$
3	$x_0 \oplus x_1 \oplus x_2 \oplus x_0x_1 \oplus x_0x_2 \oplus x_1x_2 \oplus x_0x_1x_2$	0	$x_2 \vee x_1 \vee x_0$
01	1	x_3x_2	1
02	1	0	1
03	1	$x_2\bar{x}_1$	1
12	1	x_3x_0	1
13	1	0	1
23	1	$\bar{x}_1x_0$	1
012	1	0	1
013	1	0	1
023	1	0	1
123	1	0	1
0123	1	0	1

Figure 3.23. Evaluation of the implicants and implicates from the iterative forms

3.3. Applications

The representation of a discrete function in terms of prime implicants and prime implicates applies to several kinds of problems arising in the fields of discrete mathematics and computing sciences.

Some applications are briefly considered in this section; other applications, in the frame of switching and logic theory, will be studied in other chapters of this book.

Section 3.3.1 will be devoted to the research of maximal compatibility classes of a compatibility relation while section 3.3.2 will deal with some representation modes of fuzzy functions. Finally section 3.3.3 will introduce some problems arising in synthesis and analysis of logic and of switching networks.

3.3.1. Research of the maximal compatibility classes of a compatibility relation

The implicant–implicate method, described in section 3.2.2, may be used for obtaining the prime implicants of functions which cannot be formulated by means of well-formed expressions; one will specially consider here the research of the maximal compatibility classes of binary relations.

A binary relation R on a set S is a subset of S^2; if a binary relation R is at the same time reflexive and symmetric, R is a compatibility relation on S (see section 1.1.2). If the cardinality of S is s, a compatibility relation is completely defined by specifying the inclusion in R of the $s(s-1)/2$ pairs of distinct elements of S. Otherwise stated, a compatibility relation R is a binary function

$$R: S \to \{0, 1\}$$

where the cardinality of S is $s(s-1)/2$.

A *compatibility class* is a compatibility relation C defined by a subset S_C of S: by definition $(s_1, s_2) \in S$ belongs to C iff $s_1 \in S_C$ and $s_2 \in S_C$. It is well known that the set of compatibility classes is a $\wedge$-closure and $\vee$-generating system of the compatibility relations, so that our main representation problem is meaningful. Recently, attention has been paid to this problem in view of its application in the Paull–Unger problems (Paull and Unger [1959], Das and Sheng [1969], Chaudhury, Basu and Desarkar [1969]).

The dual concept is that of anticlass*: an *anticlass* is a compatibility relation D defined by a subset S_D of S: by definition $(s_1, s_2) \in S$ belongs to D iff $s_1 \in S_D$ or $s_2 \in S_D$. It could be easily checked that the anticlass D introduced in this way defines an internally stable subset $S\backslash D$ of the graph R (Malgrange [1962]).

Let us now turn to the solution of the auxiliary problem 1 (see section 1.3.5).

Theorem 3.16. (a) *The prime implicates D_i of a compatibility class C characterized by the set S_C of cardinality r are the r anticlasses characterized by the r subsets S_{Di} obtained by deleting from S_C a single of its elements in all possible ways.*

*In this section the term "anticlass" means "compatibility anticlass".

(b) *The prime implicants C_i of an anticlass D characterized by the set S_D of cardinality r are the (s – r) classes characterized by the (s – r) sets S_{Ci} obtained from S_D by adding to it a single element of $S \in S_D$ in all possible ways.*

Proof. (a) Let $S_C = \{s_1, s_2, \ldots, s_r\}$ and, for example, $S_{D1} = \{s_2, \ldots, s_r\}$.

1. D_1 is an implicate of C: clearly, all couples of the form (s_i, s_j) $(i, j = 1, 2, \ldots, r)$ have at least one element in S_{D1}.

2. D_1 is a prime implicate of C: indeed, if we delete a single additional element of S_{D1}, say s_2, then the couple (s_1, s_2), member of C, is no longer a member of the new-formed anticlass.

The same argument proves that the set T_D characterizing any implicate of C should contain at least $(r - 1)$ of the elements of S_C. Hence, any prime implicate of C is one of the D_i's.

(b) Dual statement. ∎

Example 3.12. Let $S = \{1, 2, 3, 4, 5\}$ and let R be the compatibility relation described as the union of the classes:

$$\{1, 2\}, \{2, 3, 4\}, \{2, 4, 5\}, \{3, 5\}.$$

The prime implicates of these classes are (theorem 3.16(a)):

for $\{1, 2\}$: $\{1\}, \{2\}$,
for $\{2, 3, 4\}$: $\{2, 3\}, \{3, 4\}, \{2, 4\}$,
for $\{2, 4, 5\}$: $\{2, 4\}, \{2, 5\}, \{4, 5\}$,
for $\{3, 5\}$: $\{3\}, \{5\}$.

We compute then step by step the prime implicates of R (note that the disjunction of two anticlasses is described by the union of the corresponding subsets):

$$\{1, 2\} \cup \{2, 3, 4\} = \{2, 3\} \cap \{2, 4\} \cap \{1, 3, 4\},$$

$$\{1, 2\} \cup \{2, 3\ 4\} \cup \{2, 4, 5\} = \{2, 4\} \cap \{2, 3, 5\},$$

$$R = \{2, 3, 4\} \cap \{2, 4, 5\} \cap \{2, 3, 5\}.$$

The prime implicants of these anticlasses are (theorem 3.16(b)):

for $\{2, 3, 4\}$: $\{1, 2, 3, 4\}, \{2, 3, 4, 5\}$,

for $\{2, 4, 5\}$: $\{1, 2, 4, 5\}, \{2, 3, 4, 5\}$,

for $\{2, 3, 5\}$: $\{1, 2, 3, 5\}, \{2, 3, 4, 5\}$.

The prime implicants of R are next obtained step by step (note that the conjunction of two classes is described by the intersection of the corresponding subsets):

$$\{2, 3, 4\} \cap \{2, 4, 5\} = \{1, 2, 4\} \cup \{2, 3, 4, 5\}.$$

$$R = \{1, 2\} \cup \{2, 3, 4, 5\}.$$

An advantage of the present method is that it does apply to any description of the function by classes or anticlasses without resorting to an exhaustive enumeration of the component pairs by a graph or by a matrix.

Since the above problem is not formulated in terms of lattice expressions, the algebra of lattice expressions does not apply directly to its solution.

The theory of discrete functions, as it was defined in Chapters 2 and 3, does not apply directly to the solution of the research of the maximal compatibility classes of compatibility relations. However, with some precaution, this result may be achieved. Indeed, since a compatibility relation R is a binary function:

$$R: S^* \to \{0, 1\}$$

where S^* is the adjacency matrix of the graph representing R (see section 2.1.1) one could, for example, select the largest symmetrical submatrices (see Malgrange [1962]) of S^*. These submatrices are clearly the symmetrical prime cubes of R; in our case, by *symmetrical* one means a cube of the form

$$x_1^{(C)}\, x_0^{(C)}$$

and C is the compatibility class represented by this cube.

Example 3.12 (*continued*). The adjacency matrix of the compatibility relation R is given in Figure 3.24.

$x_1 \backslash x_0$	1	2	3	4	5
1	1	1	0	0	0
2	1	1	1	1	1
3	0	1	1	1	1
4	0	1	1	1	1
5	0	1	1	1	1

Figure 3.24. Adjacency matrix of the compatibility relation of example 3.12.

The matrix of Figure 3.24 may be viewed as a binary function, the prime cubes of which are (the cube–anticube method may, for example, be used for obtaining them):

$$f = x_1^{(1,2)}\, x_0^{(1,2)} \vee x_1^{(2,3,4,5)}\, x_0^{(2,3,4,5)} \vee x_1^{(2)} \vee x_0^{(2)}. \tag{3.121}$$

Since the two first prime cubes of the above function (3.121) are symmetrical, they correspond to the following compatibility classes respectively:

$$\{1, 2\} \quad \text{and} \quad \{2, 3, 4, 5\}.$$

It is worthwhile pointing out that the concept of compatibility relation has been extended by Yeh [1973] to the fuzzy domain (see also section 3.3.2). It is not the purpose of this section to define and develop extensively this theory; let us only point out that while a compatibility relation may, for example, be described by an adjacency matrix with entries 0 and 1, or equivalently by a binary function

$$f: S^* \to \{0, 1\}$$

a fuzzy compatibility relation is, for example, described by an adjacency matrix with entries $0, 1, \ldots, r-1$ or equivalently by a discrete function

$$f: S^* \to \{0, 1, \ldots, r-1\}.$$

This function may be written as

$$f = \bigvee_i l_i x_1^{(C_{1i})} x_0^{(C_{0i})} \tag{3.122}$$

and the maximal fuzzy classes correspond again to the prime symmetrical cubes of the above function (3.122).

3.3.2. Representation of fuzzy functions

The concepts of fuzzy sets, fuzzy languages, fuzzy automata, . . . , etc., have been introduced in a rather recent past (see, for example, Zadeh [1965], Wee and Fu [1967], Lee and Lee [1970], Marinos [1969]) in an attempt to provide mathematical models for classes of ill-defined events. The algebraic structure of *soft algebra* axiomatically introduced by Preparata and Yeh [1971, 1972] represents a first tool for approaching this goal. Motivated by the recognized inadequacy of conventional logic for the representation and manipulation of variables in areas related to artificial intelligence, the papers by Yeh and Preparata address themselves to the investigation of the formal systems obtained by extending well-known connectives to continuous arguments. The studied systems, called *soft algebras*, are generalizations of Boolean algebras in that they satisfy all the axioms of the latter except the laws of complementarity, i.e. $x \vee \bar{x} = 1$ and $x \wedge \bar{x} = 0$.

This section is devoted to the study of a specific soft algebra, namely the family of functions of n variables ranging in the closed interval $I = [0, 1]$. These functions, called *fuzzy functions*, have been studied in great detail by Preparata and Yeh, whose main results are briefly recalled in section 3.3.2.1. Section 3.3.2.2 studies the unique representation of a fuzzy function as the join-irredundant sum of join-irreducible elements. Section 3.3.2.3 introduces the concept of fuzzy function compatible with a switching function. This concept is a useful tool for deriving fuzzy properties from the corresponding switching properties; it has many applications in the frame of transient analysis of switching networks (see also section 3.3.3). Finally, section 3.3.2.4 presents two algorithms for computation of the prime implicants and the prime implicates of a fuzzy function. The first of these two algorithms is the application of the implicant–implicate method to fuzzy functions; the second of these algorithms is based on the use of the lattice differences. Both algorithms are due to Davio and Thayse [1973].

3.3.2.1. *Preliminaries*

One investigates well-formed expressions using the symbols x_i, $\vee$, $\wedge$ and $\overline{x}_i$. The variables x_i take their values in the closed interval $I = [0, 1]$ and the operators have their usual lattice theoretical meaning:

$$\begin{aligned} x_i \vee x_j &= \max(x_i, x_j) \\ x_i \wedge x_j &= \min(x_i, x_j) \\ \overline{x}_i &= 1 - x_i. \end{aligned} \qquad (3.123)$$

To those expressions are associated functions generally called fuzzy functions which will be denoted by $f(x_{n-1}, \ldots, x_1, x_0)$ or $f(\boldsymbol{x})$.

Definition 3.15. A *fuzzy function* is a mapping:

$$f: I^n \to I$$

which can be expressed by means of a well-formed expression using the symbols $x_i, \overline{x}_i$, $\vee$ and $\wedge$.

In view of the properties of the operators $\vee$ and $\wedge$, the set of fuzzy functions constitutes a bounded and distributive lattice. The following theorem, which appears to be of basic importance for the characterization of fuzzy functions, has been stated by Preparata and Yeh [1971, 1972].

Theorem 3.17. (a) *The value assumed by an expression $f(\boldsymbol{x})$ at the vertices of the n-cube can only be 0 or 1; at the centre of a k-cube ($k \leqslant n$), it can only be 0, 1/2 or 1.*

(b) *If the value assumed by an expression at the centre of a k-cube C is 1 or 0, the same value occurs at the centre of each (k − 1)-cube contained in C.*

(c) *The value of an expression at the centre of a k-cube whose vertices have mixed values is 1/2.*

(d) *The value of an expression $f(\boldsymbol{x})$ is completely determined by the values of f at the vertices of the n-cube and at the centres of each of its subcubes.*

The proof of this theorem 3.17 may be found in the papers by Preparata and Yeh; it will not be given extensively in this book.

The correctness of this theorem may however easily be appreciated by observing first that there are six fuzzy functions of one variable, namely:

$$0, 1, x, \overline{x}, x \wedge \overline{x} \text{ and } x \vee \overline{x}.$$

These functions are depicted in Figure 3.25(a)–(f) respectively.

In view of the functions plotted in Figure 3.25 the above theorem 3.12 evidently holds for a one-variable function. An intuitive proof of theorem 3.17 for a fuzzy function $f(\boldsymbol{x})$ may then be obtained by observing that any fuzzy function is a well-formed expression made up with the elementary functions of Figure 3.25.

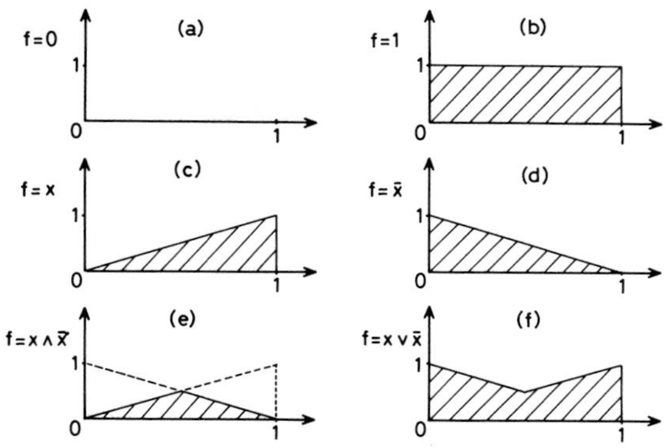

Figure 3.25. Fuzzy functions of one variable

The statement of theorem 3.17(d) is of particular importance; since the values of a fuzzy function $f(x)$ are completely determined by the values of f at a finite number of vertices, f may also be viewed as a discrete function, or more precisely, as a logic function of three-valued variables (0, 1/2 and 1).

For arbitrary x, y, z in $[0, 1]$, the following identities are easily verified

$$
\begin{aligned}
&x \vee y = y \vee x; x \wedge y = y \wedge x \\
&(x \vee y) \vee z = x \vee (y \vee z); (x \wedge y) \wedge z = x \wedge (y \wedge z) \\
&x \wedge (y \vee z) = (x \wedge y) \vee (x \wedge z); x \vee (y \wedge z) = (x \vee y) \wedge (x \vee z) \\
&x \vee x = x; x \wedge x = x \qquad (3.124) \\
&0 \vee x = x; 1 \wedge x = x; 0 \wedge x = 0; 1 \vee x = 1 \\
&\overline{(x \vee y)} = \bar{x} \wedge \bar{y}; \overline{x \wedge y} = \bar{x} \vee \bar{y} \\
&\bar{\bar{x}} = x.
\end{aligned}
$$

According to Preparata and Yeh it will be convenient to subdivide the product terms (that are fuzzy functions formed by product (or conjunction) of letters $x_i, \bar{x}_i$) into two categories, *P-terms* and *V-terms*, depending upon whether they contain or do not contain, respectively, *symmetric pairs* of the type $x_i \wedge \bar{x}_i$. A V-term β does not contain any symmetric pair, a P-term $\beta \wedge \gamma$ is the conjunction of a V-term β and a product term γ of symmetric pairs.

3.3.2.2. Unique representation of a fuzzy function

The two following theorems will be used further on.

Theorem 3.18 (Preparata and Yeh [1971, 1972]). *The set of fuzzy functions is a bounded and distributive lattice.*

Lemma 3.12 (Birkhoff [1967], p. 58). *If p is a join-irreducible element in a distributive lattice, then $p \leqslant \bigvee_i l_i$ implies $p \leqslant l_i$ for some i.*

Theorem 3.19 (Birkhoff [1967], p. 58). *In a distributive lattice of finite length, each element has a strictly unique representation as the join of a join-irredundant set of join-irreducible elements.*

Lemma 3.13. If p and q denote products of literals, then

(a) $p \leqslant q \Leftrightarrow p = q \wedge r$.

(b) $p < q \Leftrightarrow p = q \wedge r$ *where r is a non-void product of literals that do not belong to q.*

Proof. (a) If $p \leqslant q$, then $q \wedge p = p$ and the letters of q which do not belong to p play the role of r.

If $p = q \wedge r$, then by definition $p < q$.

(b) If $p < q$, then $p = q \wedge r$; moreover if r is empty, then $p = q$.

If $p = q \wedge r$ and if r is non-empty, then $p \leqslant q$. Moreover, if the value of the letters of q and r are such that $q = 1/2$ and $r = 0$, then $p = 0$ at this point.

Theorem 3.20 (Davio and Thayse [1973]). *In the lattice of fuzzy functions of n variables, the join-irreducible elements are:*

(a) *The products of literals containing no symmetric pair $x \wedge \bar{x}$;*

(b) *The products of literals containing each of the n variables at least with one polarity.*

Proof. (1) By definition, each join-irreducible element may be represented by a product term.

(2) Let p be a product-term which does not contain any symmetric pair of the type $x_i \wedge \bar{x}_i$. Let us give to the letters of p values such that $p = 1$ and to all remaining letters the value 1/2. In view of lemma 3.13, each product-term strictly smaller than p contains at least one letter having the value 1/2 or one letter having the value 0. Each product-term has thus the value 0 or 1/2 at the considered point and the maximum of such product-terms cannot reach the value 1.

(3) Let p be a product-term containing all the letters. Let us give to the letters belonging to symmetric pairs of the form $x_i \wedge \bar{x}_i$ the value 1/2 and to the remaining letters a value 0 or 1 such that their product is equal to 1. Each product term strictly smaller than p is obtained by substituting a letter x_k in p (x_k does not belong to a symmetric pair of p) by the symmetric pair $x_k \wedge \bar{x}_k$. The product-term thus obtained takes the value 0 at the considered point and the disjunction of such product-terms cannot have the value 1/2.

(4) The following equalities (due to Preparata and Yeh) are easily verified:

$$
\begin{aligned}
&(x \wedge \bar{x} \wedge y) \vee (x \wedge \bar{x} \wedge \bar{y}) = x \wedge \bar{x} \\
&(x \wedge y) \vee (\bar{x} \wedge y) \vee (x \wedge \bar{x}) = (x \wedge y) \vee (\bar{x} \wedge y) \qquad (3.125) \\
&x \vee (\bar{x} \wedge y \wedge \bar{y}) = x \vee (y \wedge \bar{y}).
\end{aligned}
$$

In view of these relations a product-term which contains at least one symmetric pair and does not contain all the letters is not join-irreducible. ■

In what follows, the join-irreducible elements containing no symmetric pair are called *V*-join irreducible elements. The other join-irreducible elements are called *P*-join irreducible elements. For illustrative purposes, the *Hasse diagram* of the join-irreducible elements for $n = 2$ is shown in Figure 3.26.

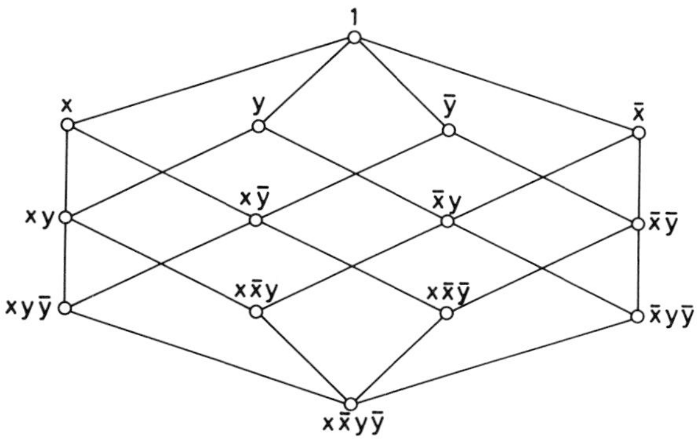

Figure 3.26. Hasse diagram of the join-irreducible elements for $n = 2$

An algorithm will now be given in order to obtain a canonical disjunctive form for the fuzzy functions as the union of their join-irreducible elements.

Algorithm 3.10 (Davio and Thayse [1973]). Obtaining the (unique) canonical disjunctive expression of a fuzzy function given by an arbitrary expression f.

(a) Reduce f to a normal disjunctive form using De Morgan's laws and the distributivity.
(b) Detect the non-join-irreducible elements and multiply them by a factor $x_i \vee \bar{x}_i$ for each of the missing literals. Reduce the new expression to the normal disjunctive form.
(c) Discard the products contained in other products by applying the absorption law.

Example 3.13

$$f = x_2 \{\overline{[\bar{x}_1(x_1 \vee \bar{x}_0)]} \vee \bar{x}_2 x_1 x_0 \bar{x}_0\} \vee \bar{x}_2 \bar{x}_1 (x_1 x_0 \bar{x}_0 \vee x_2). \tag{3.126}$$

(a) $f = x_1 x_2 \vee x_0 \bar{x}_1 x_2 \vee x_1 x_0 \bar{x}_0 x_2 \bar{x}_2 \vee \bar{x}_2 x_0 \bar{x}_0 x_1 \bar{x}_1 \vee \bar{x}_1 x_2 \bar{x}_2.$
(b) All the terms are join-irreducible except the last one which is replaced by $x_2 \bar{x}_2 \bar{x}_1 (x_0 \vee \bar{x}_0) = x_2 \bar{x}_2 \bar{x}_1 x_0 \vee x_2 \bar{x}_2 \bar{x}_1 \bar{x}_0.$

(c) Since $x_2\bar{x}_2x_1x_0\bar{x}_0 < x_2x_1$ and $x_2\bar{x}_2\bar{x}_1x_1 < x_2\bar{x}_1x_0$, the disjunctive normal form is:

$$f = x_1x_2 \vee x_0\bar{x}_1x_2 \vee x_0\bar{x}_0x_1\bar{x}_1\bar{x}_2 \vee \bar{x}_0\bar{x}_1\bar{x}_2x_2.$$

Other algorithms for obtaining canonical disjunctive forms for a fuzzy function may also be found in the papers by Preparata and Yeh [1971, 1972] and Davio and Thayse [1973].

3.3.2.3. *The lattice of fuzzy functions compatible with a given switching function*

Definition 3.16. A fuzzy function g is said to be *compatible* with a switching function f if f and g take the same values on the vertices of the n-cube.

Theorem 3.21. The set of fuzzy functions compatible with a given switching function f is a sublattice of the lattice of fuzzy functions.

Proof. In view of the lattice character of the operations min and max the disjunction and the conjunction of two fuzzy functions compatible with f are themselves fuzzy functions taking the same values as f on the vertices of the n-cube. ■

It must however be pointed out that the set of fuzzy functions compatible with a given switching function is not a Boolean algebra.

Let

$$f = \bigvee_e [f(e) \wedge \bigwedge_i x_i^{(e_i)}] = \bigwedge_e [f(e) \vee \bigvee_i x_i^{(e_i)}] \tag{3.127}$$

be the canonical disjunctive and conjunctive expansions of the switching function f respectively. Let further:

$$f = \bigvee_i p_i(x) = \bigwedge_j q_j(x) \tag{3.128}$$

be the representation of f as a disjunction of all its prime implicants and as the conjunction of all its prime implicates respectively. The following theorem then holds.

Theorem 3.22. (a) *The fuzzy functions.*

$$f_m = \bigvee_e [f(e) \wedge \bigwedge_i x_i^{(e_i)}] \tag{3.129}$$

and

$$f_M = \bigwedge_e [f(e) \vee \bigvee_i x_i^{(e_i)}] \tag{3.130}$$

are the minimum and the maximum elements respectively of the lattice of fuzzy functions compatible with f.

(b) *The fuzzy functions*

$$f_{Mm} = \bigvee_i p_i(x) = \bigwedge_j q_j(x) \tag{3.131}$$

are the functions compatible with f which take the largest value (that is 1) on the (1)-subcubes of f (i.e. the subcubes where the switching function f takes the value 1) and the smallest value (that is 0) on the (0)-subcubes of f (i.e. the subcubes where the switching function f takes the value 0).

Proof. Let us first consider the fundamental theorem 3.18 by Preparata and Yeh. In view of this theorem, one sees that the values of the fuzzy functions compatible with a given switching function are determined by the values of the latter function, except at the following vertices:

the centres of the (1)-cubes; at these points the compatible fuzzy function values may either be 1 or 1/2;
the centres of the (0)-cubes; at these points the compatible fuzzy function values may either be 0 or 1/2.

(a) Consider the fuzzy function f_m; this function takes the value 0 at the centres of the (0)-cubes of the compatible switching function. Indeed, a 1/2-value at this point may only be produced by a symmetric term $x_i \wedge \bar{x}_i$ which never appears in the switching function minterms. It moreover takes the value 1/2 at the centres of (1)-cubes since the minterms of f may only take values 0 or 1/2 at the k-cubes ($k \leqslant n$) centres; f_m is thus the smallest fuzzy function compatible with f.

In a similar way one states that f_M is the largest fuzzy function compatible with f.

(b) Consider the fuzzy function $\wedge\, q_j(x)$, that is a fuzzy function formed by the conjunction of all the prime implicants of the compatible switching function. This function is 0 on the (0)-subcubes of f since at least one prime implicate of f is 0 on these subcubes; it is 1 on the (1)-subcubes of f since all the prime implicates of f are 1 on these subcubes.

A similar type of proof holds for the fuzzy function $\vee p_i(x)$. ∎

In view of the above theorem 3.22, one has thus

$$f_m \leqslant f_{Mm} \leqslant f_M.$$

More precisely, one shows easily that the following relations hold:

$$f_m = f_{Mm} \wedge \bigwedge_{i=n-1}^{0} (x_i \vee \bar{x}_i) \tag{3.132}$$

$$f_M = f_{Mm} \vee \bigvee_{i=n-1}^{0} (x_i \wedge \bar{x}_i). \tag{3.133}$$

Example 3.14. Consider the switching function

$$f = x_2 x_0 \vee \bar{x}_2 x_1. \tag{3.134}$$

The value table of this function is given by Figure 3.27(a); the compatible fuzzy functions f_m, f_M and f_{Mm} are given by Figure 3.27(b), (c) and (d) respectively; the well-formed expressions representing these functions are also written below each of the corresponding figures.

$x_2 \backslash x_1 x_0$	0 0	0 1	1 1	1 0
0	0	0	1	1
1	0	1	1	0

$f = x_2 x_0 \vee \bar{x}_2 x_1$

(a)

$x_2 \backslash x_1 x_0$	0 0	0 1/2	0 1	1/2 1	1 1	1 1/2	1 0	1/2 0	1/2 1/2
0	$\underline{0}$	0	$\underline{0}$	1/2	$\underline{1}$	1/2	$\underline{1}$	1/2	1/2
1/2	0	1/2	1/2	1/2	1/2	1/2	1/2	1/2	1/2
1	$\underline{0}$	1/2	$\underline{1}$	1/2	$\underline{1}$	1/2	$\underline{0}$	0	1/2

$$\begin{aligned} f_m &= \underbrace{x_2 x_1 x_0 \vee x_2 \bar{x}_1 x_0} \vee \underbrace{\bar{x}_2 x_1 \bar{x}_0 \vee \bar{x}_2 x_1 x_0} \\ &= x_2 x_0 (x_1 \vee \bar{x}_1) \vee \bar{x}_2 x_1 (x_0 \vee \bar{x}_0) \\ &= (x_2 \vee x_1)(\bar{x}_2 \vee x_0)(x_1 \vee x_2)(x_2 \vee \bar{x}_2)(x_1 \vee \bar{x}_1)(x_0 \vee \bar{x}_0) \\ &= f_{Mm} \wedge [(x_2 \vee \bar{x}_2)(x_1 \vee \bar{x}_1)(x_0 \vee \bar{x}_0)] \end{aligned}$$

(b)

$x_2 \backslash x_1 x_0$	0 0	0 1/2	0 1	1/2 1	1 1	1 1/2	1 0	1/2 0	1/2 1/2
0	$\underline{0}$	1/2	$\underline{0}$	1/2	$\underline{1}$	1	$\underline{1}$	1/2	1/2
1/2	1/2	1/2	1/2	1/2	1	1/2	1/2	1/2	1/2
1	$\underline{0}$	1/2	$\underline{1}$	1	$\underline{1}$	1/2	$\underline{0}$	1/2	1/2

$$\begin{aligned} f_M &= \underbrace{(x_2 \vee x_1 \vee x_0)(x_2 \vee x_1 \vee \bar{x}_0)} \underbrace{(\bar{x}_2 \vee x_1 \vee x_0)(\bar{x}_2 \vee \bar{x}_1 \vee x_0)} \\ &= (x_2 \vee x_1 \vee x_0 \bar{x}_0)(\bar{x}_2 \vee x_0 \vee x_1 \bar{x}_1) \\ &= x_2 x_0 \vee x_1 x_0 \vee x_1 \bar{x}_2 \vee x_2 \bar{x}_2 \vee x_1 \bar{x}_1 \vee x_0 \bar{x}_0 \\ &= f_{Mm} \vee (x_2 \bar{x}_2 \vee x_1 \bar{x}_1 \vee x_0 \bar{x}_0) \end{aligned}$$

(c)

$x_2 \backslash x_1 x_0$	0 0	0 1/2	0 1	1/2 1	1 1	1 1/2	1 0	1/2 0	1/2 1/2
0	$\underline{0}$	0	$\underline{0}$	1/2	$\underline{1}$	1	$\underline{1}$	1/2	1/2
1/2	0	1/2	1/2	1/2	1	1/2	1/2	1/2	1/2
1	$\underline{0}$	1/2	$\underline{1}$	1	$\underline{1}$	1/2	$\underline{0}$	0	1/2

$$\begin{aligned} f_{Mm} &= (\bar{x}_2 \vee x_0)(x_2 \vee x_1)(x_1 \vee x_0) \\ &= \bar{x}_2 x_1 \vee x_2 x_0 \vee x_1 x_0 \end{aligned}$$

(d)

Figure 3.27

While implicitly assumed previously, it is worthwhile pointing out that any well-formed switching expression represents simultaneously a switching and a fuzzy function. These functions are most often unambiguously denoted by the same symbol such as f or $f(\boldsymbol{x})$.

An application of the lattice of fuzzy functions compatible with a given switching function will be presented in section 3.3.3. One shows that the fuzzy functions compatible with a switching function are models for describing the transient behaviours of switching networks realizing that switching function. The analysis of the transient behaviour of switching networks will be an important application of some of the results presented in this book; section 3.3.3 will only present some preliminary results.

3.3.2.4. Prime implicants and prime implicates of fuzzy functions

In what follows, we are dealing with two dual subsets of the lattice of fuzzy functions. The first one is the set of products of letters, the elements of which are classes; it is indeed closed under the conjunction and every fuzzy function may be expressed, at least in one way, as the disjunction of some classes. This last form may, for example, be obtained from any fuzzy expression by use of the distributive law.

The second subset is the set of sums of letters, the elements of which are called anticlasses. Indeed, it is closed under the disjunction and every fuzzy function may be expressed at least in one way as the product of some anticlasses.

With the usual callings (see section 1.3.2) a class smaller than or equal to a fuzzy function f is an implicant of f. A maximal implicant of f is also called a prime implicant of f. An anticlass larger than or equal to a fuzzy function f is an implicate of f. A minimal implicate of f is also called a prime implicate of f.

The research of the prime implicants and implicates of a fuzzy function will first be performed through the implicant–implicate algorithm (see section 3.2.2). The solution of the auxiliary problem 1 for fuzzy functions is given by the following theorem.

Theorem 3.23. (a) *The prime implicates of a join-irreducible class are all its literals. The prime implicates of a non-join-irreducible class are*

all its literals,
the disjunctions $x_j \vee \bar{x}_j$ corresponding to all of the missing literals in the given class.

(b) *The prime implicants of a meet-irreducible anticlass are all its literals. The prime implicants of a non-meet-irreducible anticlass are*

all its literals,
the conjunctions $x_j \wedge \bar{x}_j$ corresponding to all the missing literals in the given anticlass.

Proof. (a) The literals of a join-irreducible class are implicates of that class, by definition of the conjunction, and they are prime in view of lemma 3.12. Consider now an implicate of the given function. As an anticlass it is a disjunction of literals, and, again by lemma 3.12, if it contains a literal of the class, it can only be prime if it is reduced to that literal. If it contains no literal of the class, two cases are possible: either the class contains a symmetric pair and the candidate implicate then only contains the opposite polarity letters appearing in the class with a single polarity, but, in this case, there exists a point where the class and its candidate implicate have values 1/2 and 0 respectively; or the class contains no symmetric pair, and in this case a similar reasoning shows the existence of a point where the class and its candidate implicate have values 1 and 1/2 respectively.

A similar proof holds for the non-join-irreducible class

(b) Dual statement of (a). ■

Example 3.13 (*continued*).

$$f = x_2 x_1 \vee x_2 \bar{x}_1 x_0 \vee \bar{x}_2 \bar{x}_1 x_1 \bar{x}_0 x_0 \vee \bar{x}_2 x_2 \bar{x}_1 \bar{x}_0.$$

Prime implicates of f are obtained after steps (a) and (b) of algorithm 3.1:

$$(x_2 \vee \bar{x}_2)(x_2 \vee x_1)(x_2 \vee \bar{x}_1)(x_2 \vee x_0)(x_2 \vee \bar{x}_0)(\bar{x}_1 \vee x_1)(\bar{x}_2 \vee x_1 \vee x_0)$$

$$(x_1 \vee \bar{x}_0 \vee x_0).$$

Prime implicants of f are obtained after steps (c) and (d) of algorithm 3.1:

$$\bar{x}_2 x_2 \vee x_2 x_1 \vee \bar{x}_1 x_1 \bar{x}_0 x_0 \vee x_2 \bar{x}_1 x_0 \vee x_2 \bar{x}_0 x_0.$$

Another algorithm for obtention of prime implicants and prime implicates of a fuzzy function will now be developed; it is based on the use of lattice differences of the compatible switching function and was developed (as well as the preceding algorithm) in a paper by Davio and Thayse [1973].

Preparata and Yeh [1971, 1972] have subdivided the implicants into two categories, *P-implicants* and *V-implicants* depending upon whether they contain or do not contain, respectively, symmetric pairs of the type $x_i \wedge \bar{x}_i$.

A V-implicant β does not contain any symmetric pair $x_i \wedge \bar{x}_i$; a P-implicant $\beta \wedge \gamma$ is the product of a factor β which is a product of literals with a single polarity each and a factor γ built up with symmetric pairs $x_i \wedge \bar{x}_i$ only.

Lemma 3.14. The maximal V-join-irreducible elements of a function f appear in every disjunctive normal form of f.

Proof. Let $f = \bigvee m_i$ and let p be a maximal V-irreducible element of f. Assume that p is not contained in the set of m_i. This is impossible since one would have $p \leqslant \bigvee_i m_i$ and $p \leqslant m_j$ for at least one j. If $p \neq m_j$, p is not maximal. ■

Theorem 3.24 below then immediately follows from lemma 3.14.

Theorem 3.24. In order to obtain the V-prime implicants of a fuzzy function f it is necessary and sufficient to obtain a disjunctive expression of f by applying

De Morgan's laws and distributivity. The V-prime implicants are then the V-terms that remain in the expression after application of the absorption law.

The *P*-prime implicants are, generally, not obtained by simply applying an absorption rule and moreover the union of all the *P*-prime implicants does not usually constitute a minimum sum-of-product form for the fuzzy function.

The following notation, characterizing a *P*-term, will be used further on:

$$\gamma(\boldsymbol{x}_0) = \bigwedge_{x_i \in \boldsymbol{x}_0} (x_i \wedge \bar{x}_i). \tag{3.135}$$

Before going further, let us recall some notation conventions. One assumes first that the set $\boldsymbol{x}_0$ may be represented as $\boldsymbol{x}^{\boldsymbol{e}}$ provided an adequate choice of $\boldsymbol{e}$ is made. More precisely, if one assumes

$$\boldsymbol{x} = (\boldsymbol{x}_1, \boldsymbol{x}_0) \quad \text{and} \quad \boldsymbol{x}^{\boldsymbol{e}} = (\boldsymbol{x}_1^{\boldsymbol{e}_1}, \boldsymbol{x}_0^{\boldsymbol{e}_0})$$

one will have for $\boldsymbol{e}_1 = \boldsymbol{0}, \boldsymbol{e}_0 = \boldsymbol{1}$:

$$\boldsymbol{x}^{\boldsymbol{e}} = (\boldsymbol{x}_1^{\boldsymbol{0}}, \boldsymbol{x}_0^{\boldsymbol{1}}) = (\boldsymbol{1}, \boldsymbol{x}_0).$$

For the above choice of $\boldsymbol{e}$ one will also conventionally write

$$\gamma(\boldsymbol{x}^{\boldsymbol{e}}) = \gamma(\boldsymbol{x}_0).$$

It is also worthwhile pointing out that the same switching expression represents at the same time a switching and a fuzzy function. Further on in this section the expression $qf/q\boldsymbol{x}^{\boldsymbol{e}}$ will represent the fuzzy function which is the conjunction of the prime implicates degenerate in $\boldsymbol{x}^{\boldsymbol{e}}$ of the compatible switching function f. In view of theorem 3.22 the expression $qf/q\boldsymbol{x}^{\boldsymbol{e}}$ may equivalently be represented as the conjunction of all its prime implicates or as the disjunction of all its prime implicants.

Theorem 3.25. Let $qf/q\boldsymbol{x}^{\boldsymbol{e}}$ be the conjunction of the prime implicates of f degenerate in $\boldsymbol{x}^{\boldsymbol{e}}$; each product-term of the fuzzy function (written as a disjunction of product terms), i.e.

$$\bigvee_{\boldsymbol{e}} \left[\frac{qf}{q\boldsymbol{x}^{\boldsymbol{e}}} \wedge \gamma(\boldsymbol{x}^{\boldsymbol{e}})\right], \quad 0 \leqslant e_i \leqslant 1, 0 < \boldsymbol{e} = (e_{n-1}, \ldots, e_1, e_0) \tag{3.136}$$

is an implicant of any fuzzy function compatible with the switching function f.

Proof. The subcubes of the n-cube where the switching function f takes both 0 and 1 values are characterized by the relation

$$\frac{pf}{p\boldsymbol{x}_0} \oplus \frac{qf}{q\boldsymbol{x}_0} = 1. \tag{3.137}$$

Indeed, consider a partition $(\boldsymbol{x}_1, \boldsymbol{x}_0)$ of $\boldsymbol{x}$; for any fixed value $\boldsymbol{e}_1$ of $\boldsymbol{x}_1$ one has

$$\begin{aligned}(pf/p\boldsymbol{x}_0)_{\boldsymbol{x}_1 = \boldsymbol{e}_1} &= 1 \text{ if } f(\boldsymbol{x}_1 = \boldsymbol{e}_1) \text{ is a function equal to 1 everywhere,}\\ &= 0 \text{ otherwise}\end{aligned}$$

$$(qf/px_0)_{x_1=e_1} = 0 \text{ if } f(x_1 = e_1) \text{ is a function equal to 0 everywhere}$$
$$= 1 \text{ otherwise}$$

Since this holds for any value e_1 and for any partition of x (and thus for any subcube) relation (3.137) holds true.

Similarly the subcubes of the n-cube where f takes a constant value 1 are characterized by the relation.

$$\frac{pf}{px_0} = 1. \tag{3.138}$$

The subcubes on which f has either the constant value 1 or the mixed values 0 and 1 are thus such that

$$\left(\frac{pf}{px_0} \oplus \frac{qf}{qx_0}\right) \vee \frac{pf}{px_0} = 1$$

or, after simplification:

$$\frac{qf}{qx_0} = 1.$$

These subcubes have a value $\geqslant 1/2$ at their centre (see theorem 3.17) so that the terms of

$$\bigvee_e \left[\frac{qf}{qx^e} \wedge \gamma(x^e)\right]$$

are P-implicants of the fuzzy functions associated with f. ∎

Algorithm 3.11. Obtaining all the prime implicants of a fuzzy function.

(a) Obtain a disjunctive expression of the fuzzy function by applying dualization and distributivity.

(b) The V-prime implicants are the V-terms that remain in the expression after application of the absorption law.

(c) If $qf/qx^e = 1$, the P-term $\gamma(x^e)$ is an implicant of any fuzzy function compatible with the switching function f; the subsets $x^{\epsilon} \supseteq x^e$ are discarded.

If $qf/qx^e \neq 1$, then for the set of terms containing $\gamma(x^e)$ in the disjunctive expression of the fuzzy function, i.e. the terms

$$\beta_j \wedge \gamma(x^e), \quad j = 0, 1, \ldots, m-1,$$

obtain the following expression as a disjunction of its prime implicants

$$\left(\frac{qf}{qx^e} \vee \bigvee_j \beta_j\right) \wedge \gamma(x^e) \tag{3.139}$$

which will be denoted by:

$$\bigvee_k \, [\beta_k^* (x^e) \wedge \gamma(x^e)]. \qquad (3.140)$$

Note that, in view of relations (3.125), the prime implicants of $qf/qx^e \vee \bigvee_j \beta_j$, which are also denoted by $\beta_k^* (x^e)$, are obtained as if they were prime implicants of a switching function (otherwise the algorithm could evidently not be used).

(d) The *P*-prime implicants are the $\beta\gamma$-terms that remain in the expression

$$(V\text{-prime implicants}) \vee \bigvee_{e,k} \, [\beta_k^* (x^e) \wedge \gamma(x^e)]$$

after application of the absorption law (theorems 3.24, 3.25).

Example 3.15

$$f = (x_0 x_1 \vee x_2)(\bar{x}_0 \vee \bar{x}_1 \vee x_2 \vee \bar{x}_2)(x_0 \vee \bar{x}_0 \vee x_1 \vee \bar{x}_1 \vee \bar{x}_3) \vee$$
$$\bar{x}_1 \bar{x}_2 x_0 \bar{x}_0 \vee \bar{x}_0 \bar{x}_2 x_1 \bar{x}_1.$$

The *V*-prime implicants of f are obtained after steps (a) and (b) of algorithm 3.11:

$$\bar{x}_2 x_1 x_0 \vee x_2 x_0 \vee x_2 \bar{x}_0 \vee x_2 x_1 \vee x_2 \bar{x}_1.$$

Step (c): obtaining the expression (3.140):

$x_0 \bar{x}_0 \vee x_1 \bar{x}_1 \vee x_2 \bar{x}_2 \vee$ terms of the form $x_i \bar{x}_i x_j \bar{x}_j$ which disappear by absorption.

Step (d): obtaining the set of implicants:

$$f = \bar{x}_2 x_1 x_0 \vee x_2 x_0 \vee x_2 \bar{x}_0 \vee x_2 x_1 \vee x_2 \bar{x}_1 \vee x_0 \bar{x}_0 \vee x_1 \bar{x}_1 \vee x_2 \bar{x}_2.$$

It should be noted that, while a fuzzy function may be viewed as a ternary logic function (see the fundamental theorem 3.17 by Preparata and Yeh), the concept of implicant of a fuzzy function differs from that of implicant of a ternary function.

For example the fuzzy cube $x_1 x_0$ is written as the disjunction of two implicants of a ternary logic function, i.e.

$$x_1 x_0 = 1 x_0^{(1)} x_1^{(1)} \vee 1/2 \, x_1^{(1,1/2)} x_0^{(1,1/2)}.$$

This also clearly appears in Figure 3.28 representing the fuzzy implicant $x_1 x_0$:

x_1 \ x_0	0	1/2	1
0	0	0	0
1/2	0	1/2	1/2
1	0	1/2	1

Figure 3.28. Fuzzy cube $x_1 x_0$

It should finally be noted that other methods for simplification of a fuzzy function may be found in the paper by Kandel [1973].

3.3.3. Hazard detection in switching networks by fuzzy functions

This section constitutes a first introduction to a much larger subject, namely, the *transient analysis of logic networks.* This subject will extensively be treated in other chapters of this book; the aim of this section is to show that the concept of fuzzy function compatible with a given switching function provides us with a good approach to some aspects of transient analysis.

Switching networks constitute the most convenient model of representing information in electronic networks using two-level voltages. Actual methods for synthesis of switching networks almost exclusively rely on the use of switching functions. However a switching function is a correct representation of a logic network only for static conditions, i.e. when the signals in the circuit do not change. Whenever the input signals of a switching network are changed, i.e. for *transient conditions*, the use of the switching function, which is the mathematical model of the switching network, can lead to an incorrect prediction of the real behaviour of the network. The network is then said to contain a *hazard* for that input change. The specific reason for this incorrect prediction is that the switching function model inherently implies the assumption that the propagation time of signals in the logical gates and in the wires interconnecting these logical gates is strictly zero. However, no matter what types of switching gates we use to build a switching network, there will be an inherent time delay associated with the operation of each of the physical gates. Moreover, delays of signal propagation occur for signals to be transmitted along the wires interconnecting the switching gates of a network. These new degrees of freedom brought into the network make that the switching function model may no longer be used for the analysis of logical network under transient conditions. In section 3.3.3.2, we propose a fuzzy function model for a switching network and, in sections 3.3.3.3 and 3.3.3.4, we show how this fuzzy function model may be used for detecting some transient phenomena occurring at the switching network output. The concept of hazard will be defined more thoroughly in the next section.

3.3.3.1 Hazards

As shown before, due to the fact that gates and wires exhibit unplanned delays, generally called *stray delays*, transient output values of switching networks may differ from their final values. If it is possible (for at least one combination of the values of the stray delays) for the network output signal to behave in a different way than that predicted by the value table or the switching function, one says that the network possesses a hazard for the considered input transition.

Otherwise stated, transient errors in a network output due to the presence of stray delays are the result of a hazard; networks in which such transient errors may occur for some distribution of stray delays are said to have one or more hazards. Note that hazards are associated with network configurations, not with physical circuits. A particular physical circuit corresponding to a configuration with a hazard may or may not malfunction, depending upon the magnitudes and locations of its stray delays at a particular time. A *hazard-free* network is one that does not display the type of malfunction under discussion regardless of the distribution of the stray delays.

Hazards can be classified in different ways; according to the kind of the network output signal, there are two types of hazards: the *static hazard* and the *dynamic hazard.*

Definition 3.17. (a) The characteristic of the *static hazard* is that it causes a transition in an output, which is required to remain constant, during a given input variable change.

(b) The *dynamic hazard*, which can occur when the network output is meant to change, causes the output to change three or more times instead of only once.

While the concept of hazard was first used by Keister, Ritchie and Washburn [1951], it is Huffman [1957] who first defined the concepts of static and of dynamic hazards for (combinational) switching circuits.

Hazards are also classified according to whether they can or cannot be detected by means of tests on the switching function to be realized.

Definition 3.18 Function hazards can be detected by performing tests on the switching function (realized by the switching network) while *logic hazards* cannot.

This last classification has been introduced by Eichelberger [1964, 1965] but only for static hazards.

According to the four possibilities mentioned above one will speak of *function-static-hazard, function-dynamic-hazard, logic-static-hazard* and *logic-dynamic-hazard.* For sake of conciseness they will often be denoted f-s-hazard, f-d-hazard, *l*-s-hazard and *l*-d-hazard, respectively. Only static hazards, that is f-s- and *l*-s-hazards will be studied in this section; they will first be defined in a more mathematical way.

Let us define two vertices of $\boldsymbol{x} = (\boldsymbol{x}_1, \boldsymbol{x}_0)$ as follows:

$$\boldsymbol{a} = (a_{n-1}, \ldots, a_{q+1}, a_q; a_{q-1}, \ldots, a_1, a_0) = (\boldsymbol{a}_1; \boldsymbol{a}_0)$$
$$\boldsymbol{b} = (a_{n-1}, \ldots, a_{q+1}, a_q; \bar{a}_{q-1}, \ldots, \bar{a}_1, \bar{a}_0) = (\boldsymbol{a}_1; \bar{\boldsymbol{a}}_0).$$

Definition 3.19 A switching function $f(\boldsymbol{x})$ contains an f-s-hazard for the input change $\boldsymbol{a}$ to $\boldsymbol{b}$ iff

(a) $f(\boldsymbol{a}) = f(\boldsymbol{b})$;
(b) the function $f(\boldsymbol{a}_1, \boldsymbol{x}_0)$ is not degenerate in $\boldsymbol{x}_0$.

It is evident that if $f(\boldsymbol{a}_1, \boldsymbol{x}_0)$ is not degenerate in $\boldsymbol{x}_0$, then there must be some set of values for the changing input variables $(x_{q-1}, \ldots, x_1, x_0)$ for which $f(\boldsymbol{a}_1, \boldsymbol{x}_0)$ is not equal to $f(\boldsymbol{a})$ or $f(\boldsymbol{b})$; consequently it must be possible to detect this hazard by means of tests on the switching function and the definitions 3.18 and 3.19 are thus coherent.

It is also evident that, if one assumes that stray delays are present only in the network inputs, the delay values may always be chosen in such a way that these input changes reach the output in a sequence containing the vertex $(\boldsymbol{a}_1, \boldsymbol{e}_0)$ with

$f(\boldsymbol{a}_1, \boldsymbol{e}_0) = f(\boldsymbol{a})$. Since the same type of consideration holds for dynamic hazards, function hazards could also be defined as those the effects of which may always be made obvious by inserting stray delays only in the network inputs and not in the network internal wiring. Thus the following theorem is true (Eichelberger [1965]).

Theorem 3.26. If a switching function f contains a function hazard for the input change $\boldsymbol{a}$ *to* $\boldsymbol{b}$, *then it is impossible to construct a switching network realizing f such that the possibility of transient malfunction occurring for this transition is eliminated.*

Definition 3.20. A switching network realizing the switching function $f(\boldsymbol{x})$ contains an l-s-hazard for the variable input change $\boldsymbol{a}$ to $\boldsymbol{b}$ iff

(a) $f(\boldsymbol{a}) = f(\boldsymbol{b})$;
(b) the function $f(\boldsymbol{a}_1, \boldsymbol{x}_0)$ is degenerate in $\boldsymbol{x}_0$, i.e. $f(\boldsymbol{a}_1, \boldsymbol{x}_0) \equiv f(\boldsymbol{a})$;
(c) during the input change $\boldsymbol{a}$ to $\boldsymbol{b}$ a transient malfunction may occur on the output.

Condition (b) of definition 3.20 is equivalent to stating that the input change does not involve a function hazard.

In view of definitions 3.18 and 3.20 it is obvious that logic hazards cannot be detected only by means of some tests on the switching function $f(\boldsymbol{x})$. This type of hazard is thus closely related to internal propagation times on the signal paths, i.e. on the internal stray delays; logic hazards could thus also be defined as those the effects of which may only be made obvious by inserting stray delays in the network internal wiring.

Example 3.14 (continued). Consider the switching function (3.134), i.e.

$$f = x_0 x_2 \vee x_1 \bar{x}_2 .$$

When the input variables $\boldsymbol{x} = (x_2, x_1, x_0)$ switch from the initial input state $\boldsymbol{a} = (0, 1, 1)$ of $\boldsymbol{x}$ to the final input state $\boldsymbol{b} = (1, 0, 1)$ the function f remains constant at the value 1. Now, due to stray delays at the inputs of any network realizing f, the simultaneous change of the variables x_2, x_1 is practically impossible to realize. The effect of the stray delays at the network inputs means that the variable x_2 change will take place either before or after the variable x_1 change.

To the theoretical transition

$$(x_2, x_1, x_0; f)\colon (0, 1, 1; 1) \rightarrow (1, 0, 1; 1)$$

must thus be substituted the couple of possible transitions, i.e.

(a) $(x_2, x_1, x_0; f)\colon (0, 1, 1; 1) \rightarrow (1, 1, 1; 1) \rightarrow (1, 0, 1; 1)$,
(b) $(x_2, x_1, x_0; f)\colon (0, 1, 1; 1) \rightarrow (0, 0, 1; 0) \rightarrow (1, 0, 1; 1)$.

The real transition that the network will experience will, among others, depend on the relative values of the stray delays present at the inputs x_1 and x_2. If the transition is according to the scheme (a) the network output will remain correct at the value 1;

otherwise if the transition is according to the scheme (b) the network output will transiently be incorrect at the value 0. Now, whatever the real transition may be, the network will experience an f-s-hazard for that transition since for at least one kind of delay values a malfunction (sometimes also called *spurious hazard pulse*) occurs at the output. Let us now give an example of an l-s-hazard. Consider the network of Figure 3.29; it realizes the switching function (3.134). When the variables x_0 and x_1 are both fixed at the value 1 and when x_2 changes from 0 to 1 the network output presents a transient malfunction if the stray delay along the path ABD is larger than the stray delay along the path ACD. This clearly appears when considering the signals depicted in Figure 3.29. Since the considered transition is free of function hazard, the above quoted malfunction is produced by an l-s-hazard occurring for this transition.

The above example and Figure 3.29 allows us to make obvious the basic network scheme which produces logic hazards. In view of definition 3.20 one sees that logic hazards are due to internal stray delays present in the network; more precisely, the logic hazard occurs when there exist at least two signals issued from one fanout point (point A in Figure 3.29) that reconverges (at point D in Figure 3.29) in a network gate. The hazard is then produced by the different delays on the paths (ABD and ACD in Figure 3.29) between the fanout point and the reconvergent gate. Such scheme in a network is known as a *fanout-reconvergent structure*; logic hazards are produced by these structures.

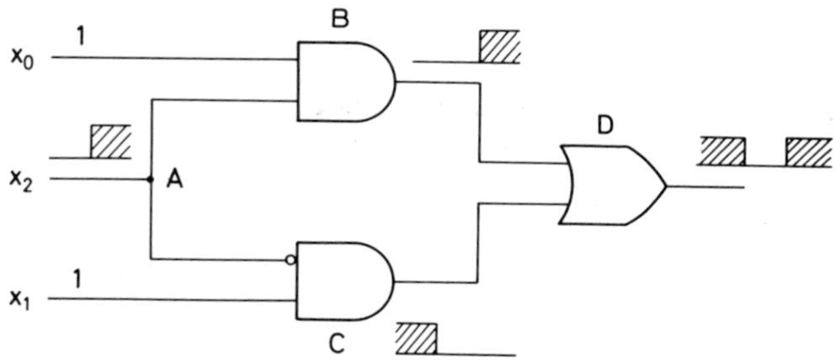

Figure 3.29. Switching network

3.3.3.2. *Static hazard detection by means of fuzzy simulation*

The static hazard detection method presented in this section and in the next one owns much of several ternary and fuzzy simulation methods developed by different authors (see, for example, Muller [1959], Yoeli and Rinon [1964], Eichelberger [1964, 1965], Kandel [1974]).

*Theorem 3.27. Let f(**x**) be a switching function; assume moreover that f(**x**) is represented by a lattice expression which may be either the disjunction of all the prime implicants of f, or the conjunction of all the prime implicates of f. Consider* *moreover this lattice expression as the fuzzy function f_{Mm}; $f(\mathbf{x})$ contains an f-s-hazard for the input change $\mathbf{a} = (\mathbf{a}_1, \mathbf{a}_0)$ to $\mathbf{b} = (\mathbf{a}_1, \bar{\mathbf{a}}_0)$ iff:*

(a) $f_{Mm}(\mathbf{a}) = f_{Mm}(\mathbf{b})$
(b) $f_{Mm}(\mathbf{a}_1, 1/2, \ldots, 1/2, 1/2) = 1/2$.

Proof. In view of theorem 3.2.2 (b), f_{Mm} takes the value 1 on the (1)-subcubes of f and the value 0 on the (0)-subcubes of f. If $f_{Mm}(\mathbf{a}_1, 1/2, \ldots, 1/2)$ takes the value 1/2, the function f takes thus necessarily mixed values 0 and 1 on the vertices of $f(\mathbf{a}_1, \mathbf{x}_0)$; if moreover $f(\mathbf{a}) = f(\mathbf{b})$; the transition $\mathbf{a} \to \mathbf{b}$ contains an f-s-hazard.

Example 3.14 (continued). Consider again the switching function (3.134); the representation of this function as a disjunction of its prime implicants is:

$$f(x_2 x_1 x_0) = x_0 x_2 \vee x_1 \bar{x}_2 \vee x_0 x_1. \tag{3.141}$$

Consider again the transition on (x_2, x_1, x_0): $(0, 1, 1) \to (1, 0, 1)$.
One has, in view of (3.141):

$$f(0, 1, 1) = 1$$
$$f(1/2, 1/2, 1) = 1/2$$
$$f(1, 0, 1) = 1$$

and the considered transition contains an f-s-hazard.

For the transition $(0, 1, 1) \to (1, 1, 1)$ one has:

$$f(0, 1, 1) = 1$$
$$f(1/2, 1, 1) = 1$$
$$f(1, 1, 1) = 1$$

and the considered transition is free of f-s-hazard.

Let us now turn to the detection of logic hazards; as mentioned above, these hazards are not connected to switching functions as the function hazards are, but to switching networks. One will also be faced only with the detection of l-s-hazards.

Let us designate by s a transition signal from 0 to 1 and by $\bar{s}$ a transition signal from 1 to 0 (see Figure 3.30). Assume moreover that these signals propagate through a switching network with stray delays and containing possibly substructures with fanout-reconvergent paths. The effect of the stray delays is to render arbitrary the time instant at which the variations from 0 to 1 and from 1 to 0 occur. The symbols s and $\bar{s}$ will thus designate binary signals with a fixed pattern but with arbitrary switching instant; these signals propagate through any switching network according to the patterns of Figure 3.30 and satisfy the relations (3.142).

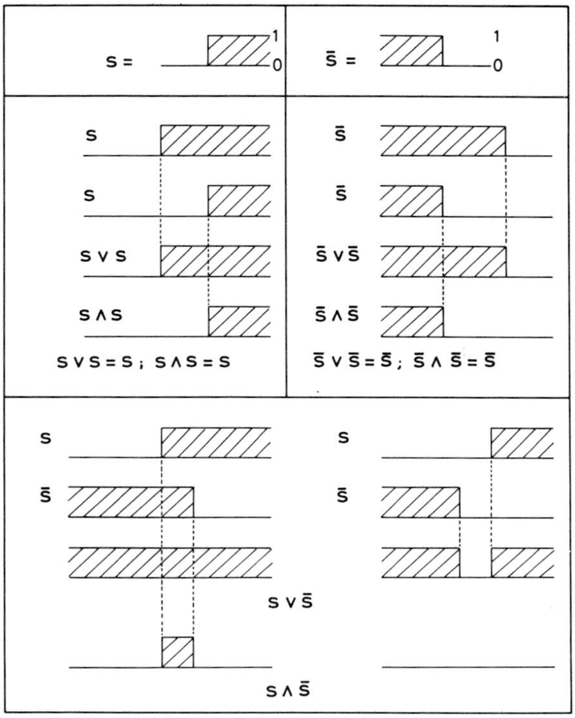

Figure 3.30. Binary patterns

$$
\begin{aligned}
&s \vee s = s \wedge s = 1 \wedge s = 0 \vee s = s = 1 - \bar{s} \\
&\bar{s} \vee \bar{s} = \bar{s} \wedge \bar{s} = 1 \wedge \bar{s} = 0 \vee \bar{s} = \bar{s} = 1 - s \\
&1 \vee s = 1 \vee \bar{s} = 1 \\
&0 \wedge s = 0 \wedge \bar{s} = 0 \\
&s \vee \bar{s} \text{ is not necessarily } 1 \\
&s \wedge \bar{s} \text{ is not necessarily } 0.
\end{aligned}
\tag{3.142}
$$

The symbol s may be viewed as a fuzzy variable compatible with a switching variable x which takes the values 0 and 1 before and after the transition represented by s respectively. Indeed, the relations (3.142) correspond to relations (3.124) which characterize fuzzy variables.

More precisely, one will define s as the fuzzy variable taking the same value as x, i.e. 0 and 1, before and after the transition respectively and the value 1/2 during the transition. It follows that:

$s \vee \bar{s}$ not necessarily 1

becomes

$s \vee \bar{s} = 1$ before and after the transition of the switching variable x,

$= 1/2$ during the transition of the switching variable x;

$s \wedge \bar{s}$ not necessarily 0,

becomes

$s \wedge \bar{s} = 0$ before and after the transition of the switching variable x;

$= 1/2$ during the transition of the switching variable x.

Further on, no distinction will be made between fuzzy and switching variables which will, as usual, be denoted by identical symbols, i.e. x. In view of Figure 3.30 and relations (3.142) one sees that the propagation of signals into a switching network containing stray delays may be simulated by a fuzzy variable; the use of this fuzzy variable allows us to detect static hazards.

Theorem 3.2.8. Consider a switching network built up by means of AND, OR and NOT gates (it is assumed that the possible XOR gates are replaced by a switching network realizing the modulo 2 sum by means of these last gates); assume that the AND, OR and NOT gates realize the operations of $\wedge$, $\vee$, *and* $\bar{x}$ *of fuzzy algebra respectively. The switching network may thus be viewed as a fuzzy network realizing a fuzzy function* $f(x)$. *The switching function or the switching network experiences a static hazard (function- or logic-) for the input change* a *to* b *iff:*

(a) $f(a) = f(b)$
(b) $f(a_1, 1/2, \ldots, 1/2) = 1/2$.

Proof. Since, in view of Figure 3.30 and relations (3.142),

(a) A switching network with stray delays is simulated by a fuzzy network,
(b) A hazard corresponds to an output sequence 0, 1/2, 0 or 1, 1/2, 1 consecutive to the sequence $(a_1, a_0), (a_1, 1/2, \ldots, 1/2), (a_1, \bar{a}_0)$ of the input variables,

the theorem is proven. ∎

Example 3.14 (*continued*). The fuzzy function corresponding to the network of Figure 3.29 considered as a fuzzy network is:

$$x_0 x_2 \vee x_1 \bar{x}_2.$$

If $x_0 = x_1 = 1$ the above fuzzy function becomes $x_2 \vee \bar{x}_2$, and a static hazard occurs thus when the variable x_2 changes.

The application of theorem 3.28 requests that a fuzzy function may easily be obtained from any network configuration. This fuzzy function is generally obtained in the easiest way by using the concept of function of functions (see section 2.1.3); to any network configuration may be associated a set of functions of functions (in our case a set of fuzzy functions of functions). The fuzzy function may then be obtained by substituting iteratively the different fuzzy expressions in terms of their input variables so that the remaining expression is finally a function of the primary input variables only. The distributive and absorption laws may be used for simplification of the remaining fuzzy expression which will be called the *fuzzy function compatible with the switching network.*

Example 3.16. Consider the network of Figure 3.31; it may be expressed by the following set of fuzzy functions:

$$\begin{aligned} f &= y_0 \vee y_1 \\ y_0 &= \bar{x}_0 y_2 \\ y_1 &= \bar{x}_1 y_2 \\ y_2 &= x_0 \vee x_1 \vee x_2. \end{aligned} \tag{3.143}$$

One obtains then successively

$$\begin{aligned} f &= \bar{x}_0(x_0 \vee x_1 \vee x_2) \vee \bar{x}_1(x_0 \vee x_1 \vee x_2) \\ &= \bar{x}_0 x_0 \vee \bar{x}_0 x_1 \vee \bar{x}_0 x_2 \vee \bar{x}_1 x_0 \vee \bar{x}_1 x_1 \vee \bar{x}_1 x_2 \end{aligned} \tag{3.144}$$

which is a disjunctive form of the fuzzy function representing the fuzzy network of Figure 3.31.

Theorem 3.27 allows us to detect the f-s-hazards while theorem 3.28 allows us to detect simultaneously the f-s- and the *l*-s-hazards; thus the use of these two theorems allows us, if requested, to separate the function-static from the logic-static hazard.

The following theorem, due to Eichelberger [1964, 1965], is a direct consequence of theorems 3.22(b) and 3.27.

Theorem 3.29. (a) *An AND-OR network has no l-s-hazards if its AND-gates are in one-to-one correspondence with the prime implicants of the function being realized.*

(b) *An OR-AND network has no l-s-hazards if its OR-gates are in one-to-one correspondence with the prime implicates of the function being realized.*

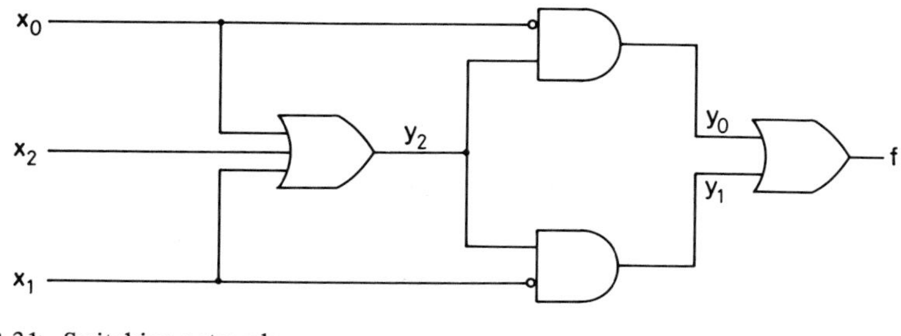

Figure 3.31. Switching network

The above theorem is fundamental since it provides us with a design method for building switching networks free of l-s-hazards. It states also the importance of the algorithms for obtaining the prime implicants and the prime implicates of a switching function.

The next section will be devoted to the detection of the only logic-static-hazards; the method that will be developed is based on the concepts of prime implicants and prime implicates of fuzzy functions obtained from switching networks configurations.

3.3.3.3. *Logic-static-hazard detection by means of fuzzy prime implicants and prime implicates*

The present section is devoted exclusively to l-s-hazard detection. These hazards are generally presented in the literature as the most important to be detected, since: (a) they are the cause of permanent fault in sequential systems (see, for example, Huffmann [1957], Unger [1969]), (b) they are easily eliminated by modification of the logical design of networks (see, for example, Eichelberger [1964, 1965] and theorem 3.29).

It is useful to partition l-s-hazards between 1-hazards and 0-hazards (McCluskey [1962]).

Definition 3.21. (a) A static hazard is a 1-hazard if the considered transition is between a pair of input states which both produce a 1-output, during which transition it is possible for a momentary 0-output to occur.

(b) A static hazard is a 0-hazard if the considered transition is between a pair of input states which both produce a 0-output, during which transition it is possible for a momentary 1-output to occur.

Consider the partition $(\boldsymbol{x}_1, \boldsymbol{x}_0)$ of $\boldsymbol{x}$ and a transition involving the change of each of the variables in $\boldsymbol{x}_0$; consider a switching network and the representation of its compatible fuzzy function as the conjunction of all its prime implicates. These prime implicates will be partitioned into two sets;

(a) The prime implicates containing a sum term of the form (see relation (3.135)):

$$\overline{\gamma(\boldsymbol{x}_0^e)} = \bigvee_{x_i \in \boldsymbol{x}_0^e} (x_i \vee \bar{x}_i).$$

These prime implicates are the disjunction of three kinds of sum terms, that is

(1) Sum terms containing variables $x_i \in \boldsymbol{x}_0^e \subseteq \boldsymbol{x}_0$ in both direct and complemented forms, i.e. $\overline{\gamma(\boldsymbol{x}_0^e)}$;
(2) Sum terms containing variables $x_i \in \boldsymbol{x}_0^{\bar{e}}$ $(\boldsymbol{x}_0^e \cup \boldsymbol{x}_0^{\bar{e}} = \boldsymbol{x}_0)$;
(3) Sum terms depending on $\boldsymbol{x}_1$, and which will be denoted by $h_j(\boldsymbol{x}_1)$.

Clearly the sum terms of the forms (2) and (3) may be absent in that kind of prime implicate while a sum term of the form (1) must always be present in order to characterize these prime implicates.

(b) The prime implicates free of terms of the form $\gamma(x_0^e)$; these prime implicates are the disjunction of two kinds of sum terms, i.e.

$$g_{0i}(x_0) \vee g_{1i}(x_1)$$

the first one being degenerate in x_1 and the second one in x_0. One of the two above sum terms may evidently be absent in these prime implicates.

Any fuzzy function $f(x) = f(x_1, x_0)$ may thus be written in the following form as a conjunction of prime implicates

$$f(x) = \bigwedge_j [\overline{\gamma(x_0^{e_j})} \vee h_j(x_1) \vee (\text{sum term in } x_0^{\bar{e}_j})] \wedge \bigwedge_i [g_{0i}(x_0) \vee g_{1i}(x_1)]. \tag{3.145}$$

Theorem 3.30. A switching network represented by the fuzzy function f(x) experiences a 1-hazard during an input change of the variables x_0 for the following conditions of the fixed variables x_1:

$$\left[\bigvee_j \bar{h}_j(x_1)\right] \wedge \bigwedge_i g_{1i}(x_1) = 1. \tag{3.146}$$

Proof. For each transition implying a change in the variables x_0, the presence of a transient malfunction of the form 1–0–1 is equivalent to the presence of a factor of the form $\overline{\gamma(x_0^{e_j})}$ in any conjunctive form of the fuzzy function. This in turn implies that at least one of the sum terms $h_j(x_1)$ be 0 or, equivalently,

$$\bigvee_j \bar{h}_j(x_1) = 1.$$

The fact that both initial and final values of f must be equal to 1 is equivalent to the presence of a sum term in x_1 which must remain equal to 1 in each of the remaining prime implicates of $f(x)$; hence the condition (3.146). ■

A dual kind of theorem could evidently be stated for detecting the 0-hazards; it is based on the presence (or absence) of product terms of the form $\gamma(x_0^e)$ in the representation of the fuzzy function as the disjunction of all its prime implicants.

Example 3.17. The switching networks of Figure 3.32(a) and (b) realize both the switching function:

$$f = x_1x_0 \vee x_3x_2 \vee x_3x_1.$$

To the switching network of Figure 3.32(a) corresponds the fuzzy function

$$f_0 = x_1x_0 \vee x_3x_2 \vee x_3\bar{x}_2x_1\bar{x}_0$$

the prime implicates of which are:

$$(x_3 \vee x_0)(x_2 \vee x_1)(x_3 \vee x_1)(x_2 \vee x_0 \vee \bar{x}_0)(x_2 \vee \bar{x}_2 \vee x_0).$$

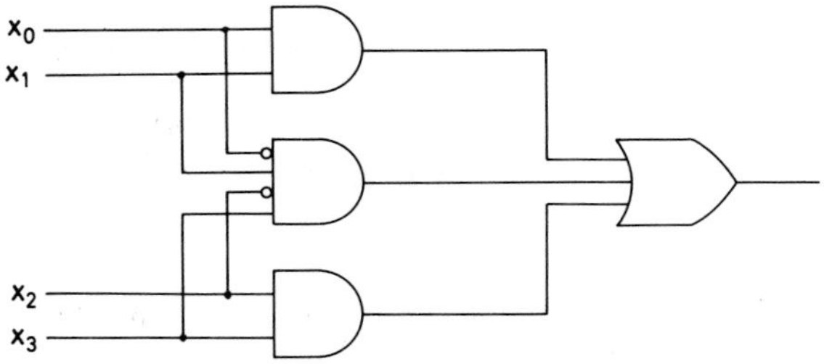

(a)

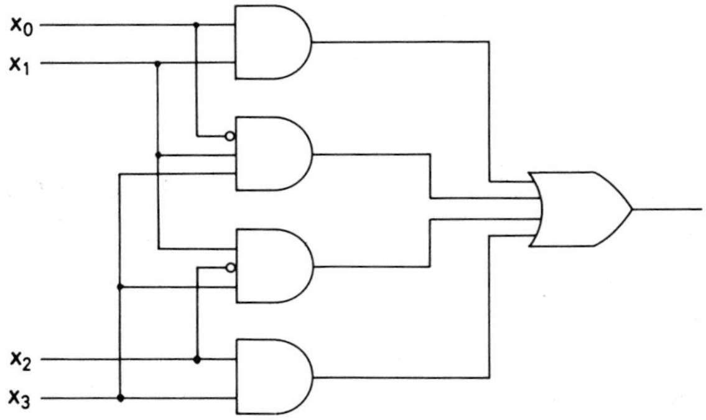

(b)

Figure 3.32. Switching networks

When the variable x_0 changes a 1-hazard occurs for the condition:

$$x_3\bar{x}_2x_1 = 1.$$

To the switching network of Figure 3.32(b) corresponds the fuzzy function

$$f_1 = x_1x_0 \vee x_3x_2 \vee x_3\bar{x}_2x_1 \vee x_3x_1\bar{x}_0$$

the prime implicates of which are

$$(x_0 \vee x_3)(x_1 \vee x_2)(x_1 \vee x_3)(x_0 \vee \bar{x}_0 \vee x_2 \vee \bar{x}_2).$$

When the variables x_2, x_0 change a 1-hazard occurs for the condition:

$$x_3x_1 = 1.$$

As a conclusion of *fuzzy analysis* of switching systems, it is important to note that, particularly when analysing large networks, it is useful to be able to determine whether timing problems exist for specific transitions. The fuzzy (or ternary) approach discussed here is particularly suitable for use in conjunction with computer simulations of digital systems.

3.3.4. Introduction to switching and to logic design

The subject of this section is only to give a short introduction to some problems related to different kinds of minimal designs with or without cost constraints; these questions will be more carefully studied in Chapter 8 devoted to the covering problems.

3.3.4.1. Two-level logic networks

First of all, the sum of products realization of a switching function, the products of which being in one-to-one correspondence with the prime implicants of the switching function appeared to be of particular importance in the preceding section. These networks are indeed free of l-s-hazards; so are also evidently the dual types of networks, i.e. the product of sums networks where the sums realize the prime implicates of the switching function.

These networks are also called two level AND-OR and OR-AND switching networks; similar kinds of networks evidently also exist when dealing with multiple-valued networks. One knows that in this case the concept of prime implicant may be replaced either by that of prime cube, or by that of prime block or by that of prime convex block of the multivalued network. The use of these concepts in logic design will briefly be introduced.

Consider first the problem of *multipositional switch design.* A multipositional switch is a network realizing or computing a binary function; it is formed by an interconnection (in the sense of section 2.1.3) of elementary gates, also called *elementary switches*, each of which realizes a binary function of one variable. For example, the elementary switch realizing the binary function:

$$f(x) \text{ is } 1 \quad \text{iff } x = 3, 4, 5 \text{ or } 7$$
$$\text{is } 0 \quad \text{if } x = 0, 1, 2 \text{ or } 6$$

is represented by Figure 3.33.

Any multipositional switch realizes a binary function; to normal forms of these binary functions correspond normal forms of the multipositional switches. More precisely, product terms are realized by serial connections of switches while sum terms are realized by parallel connections of switches. Otherwise stated, switches in serial

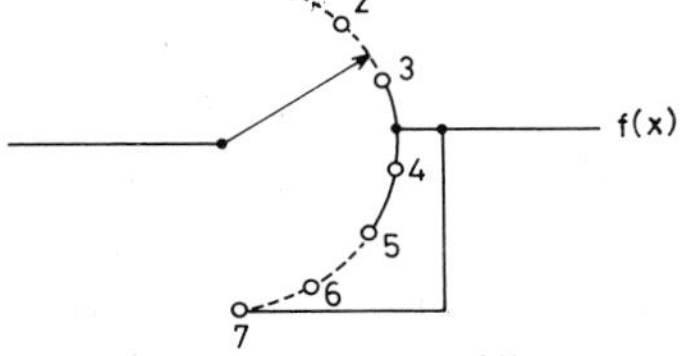

Figure 3.33. Elementary switch

configurations realize a cube function while switches in parallel configuration realize an anticube function.

Example 3.18. Consider the binary function described by the table of Figure 3.34.

$x_1 \backslash x_0$	0	1	2	3	4
0					
1			1	1	
2		1	1		
3					
4					

Figure 3.34. Binary function value table

It may also be described by the following representations:

conjunction of its prime anticubes:

$$x_1^{(1,2)}\, x_0^{(1,2,3)}\, (x_1^{(1)} \vee x_0^{(1,2)})\, (x_1^{(2)} \vee x_0^{(2,3)}) \tag{3.147}$$

disjunction of its prime cubes:

$$x_1^{(1)}\, x_0^{(2,3)} \vee x_1^{(2)}\, x_0^{(1,2)} \vee x_1^{(1,2)}\, x_0^{(2)}. \tag{3.148}$$

To the functions (3.147) and (3.148) correspond the realizations of Figures 3.35 and 3.36 respectively.

Let us now briefly consider the case of logic networks, that is, networks realizing a logic function. One knows (see, for example, Vranesic and Smith [1974], Su and Cheung [1972] or Su and Sarris [1972]) that in this case the available building blocks realize block and convex block functions or, dually, antiblock and convex antiblock functions. In the case of logic functions, the relevant expansions are thus those in terms of prime blocks, prime convex blocks, prime antiblocks and prime convex antiblocks.

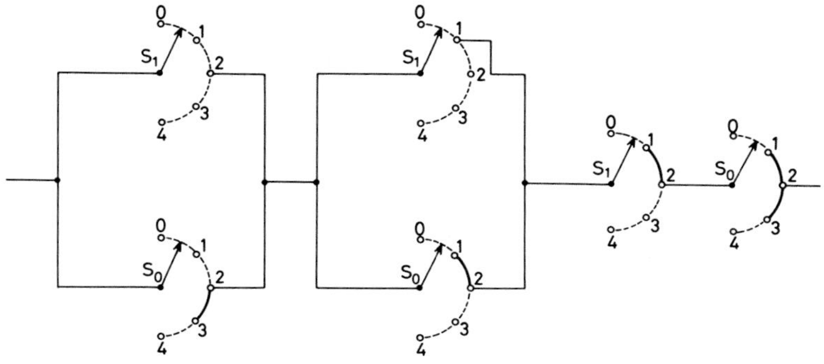

Figure 3.35. AND-OR realization of a multipositional switch

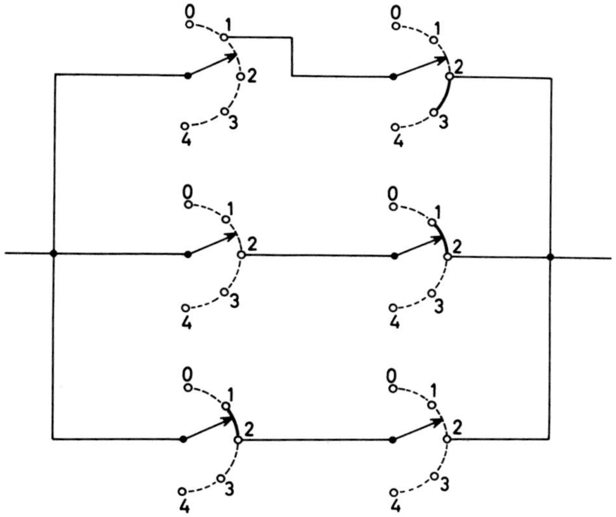

Figure 3.35. OR-AND realization of a multipositional switch

3.3.4.2. Cellular and hazard-free design of switching networks

The calling ***hazard-free*** will mean in this section free of logic static hazards. Our main purpose will be to present hazard-free ***cellular designs***, that is types of designs using a standardized type of cell and/or a standardized scheme of connection, for switching networks. These logical designs are a direct application of some prime implicants extraction methods developed in section 3.2.3.

Let us first consider the algorithms based on the extended vector and which were developed in section 3.2.3.2. From the extended vector method, as illustrated by Figure 3.12, it is obvious that the first step of this method may be designed by a ($\perp$)-cell as illustrated by Figure 3.37(a). In this cell, each AND and each OR gate is schematized by the operation it realizes within a circle; moreover the negated gate inputs are classically denoted by a small circle. The successive steps of the algorithm are then materialized by the interconnection of ⊥-cells as illustrated by Figure 3.37(a), (b).

Example 3.7 (continued). Consider the realization of the function

$$f = 1 \oplus x_0 x_1 \oplus x_4 \bar{x}_5 \oplus x_0 x_2 x_3.$$

The computations of Figure 3.14. lead to the interconnection of (⊥)-cells as described in Figure 3.38. Let us give some details about this realization. It is assumed in Figure 3.38 that the available inputs are products of direct and negated variables; if these products are not available, they can be constructed by adding an appropriate number of cells.

The network thus obtained is a multilevel hazard-free realization of f; this is a direct consequence of the following theorem by Unger [1969].

Theorem 3.31. Given any algebraic expression $\mathscr{E}$, if we transform it into a sum-of-products expression $\mathscr{S}$ through the use of the associative, distributive and De Morgan laws, then networks corresponding to $\mathscr{E}$ and $\mathscr{S}$ respectively have precisely the same static hazards.

The expressions $\mathscr{S}$ corresponding to Figures 3.37 and 3.38 and for ∧-cells are, by construction, the sum of all the prime implicants of $f(x)$, which is precisely free of any static hazard (see theorem 3.29). ■

Let us also point out that the recognition of identical functions g at different steps of the algorithm of section 3.2.3.2.2, gives rise to logical design simplifications. Indeed,

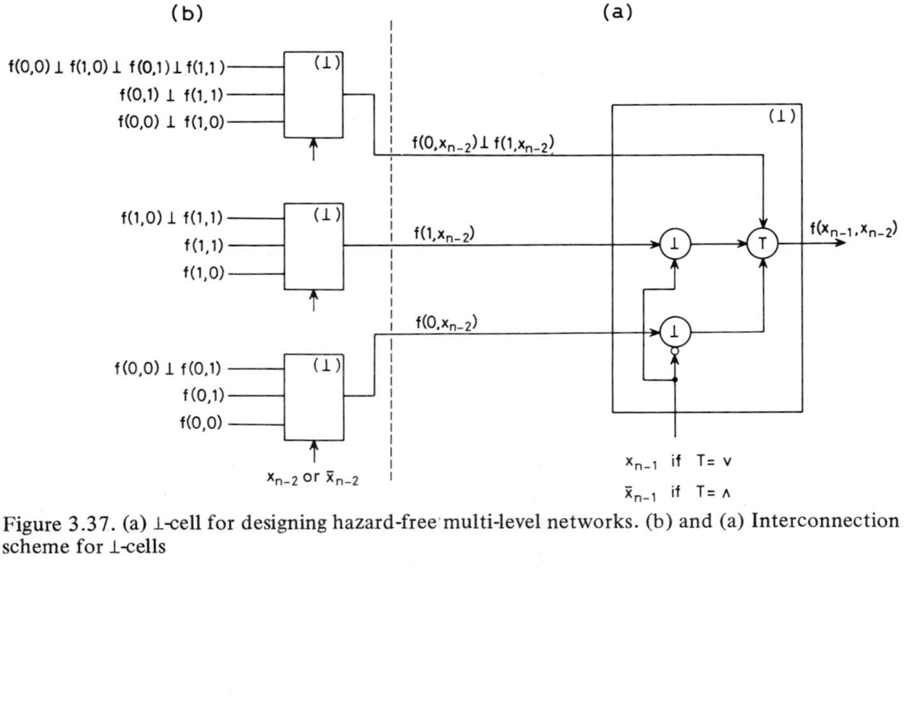

Figure 3.37. (a) ⊥-cell for designing hazard-free multi-level networks. (b) and (a) Interconnection scheme for ⊥-cells

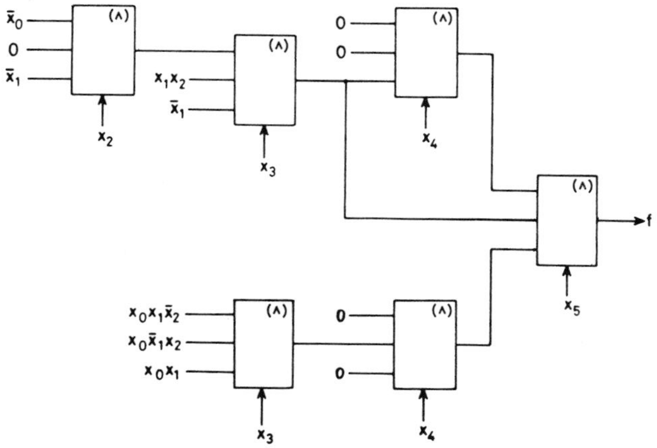

Figure 3.38. Hazard-free cellular realization of a switching function

these functions g may be fanned-out and reintroduced at several cell inputs, giving rise to a more economical realization; this is illustrated by the fanout-point of Figure 3.38.

Let us finally also point out that the extended vector algorithm, as schematized by Figure 3.12, gives rise to a method for building a *Universal Logic Module* (that is, a network able to compute any n-variables switching function) free of logic static hazards. It is clear that the interconnection of ⊥-cells along the scheme of Figure 3.37(a), (b) (which derives from the computation scheme of Figure 3.12) provides us with a hazard-free Universal Logic Module composed of $(3^{n-1}-1)/2$ cells. Theorem 3.31 by Unger allows us again to substitute the ⊥-cell of Figure 3.37(a) by that of Figure 3.39(a) which generates an Universal Logic Module free of logic static hazards and containing $2^{n-1}-1$ cells as schematized by Figure 3.39(a), (b).

Let us consider the problem of cellular realization of some types of switching functions. Assume that a realization of a function f is given as a black-box, that is, that nothing about its internal structure is known. First of all, expression (3.119) allows us to build in a cellular way, that is by interconnecting only identical cells realizing f, the prime implicants and the prime implicates of f degenerate in a set of variables. The importance of this logical design arises from the fact that prime implicants and implicates of a switching function play a key role in hazard-free logical design. Whatever the realization of f may be, the function $f \vee pf/px_0$ is hazard-free for the transitions involving a variation of the variables x_0 and for the 1-hazards. In the same way, the function $f \wedge qf/qx_0$ is hazard-free for the 0-hazards and the function $(f \vee pf/px_0) \wedge qf/qx_0$ is free of both types of hazards. Now, in view of section 3.2.3.6, it is clear that such realizations can always be obtained by a simple interconnection of a set of cells realizing f and two logical gates: an OR-gate which eliminates the l-hazards and an AND-gate which eliminates the 0-hazards.

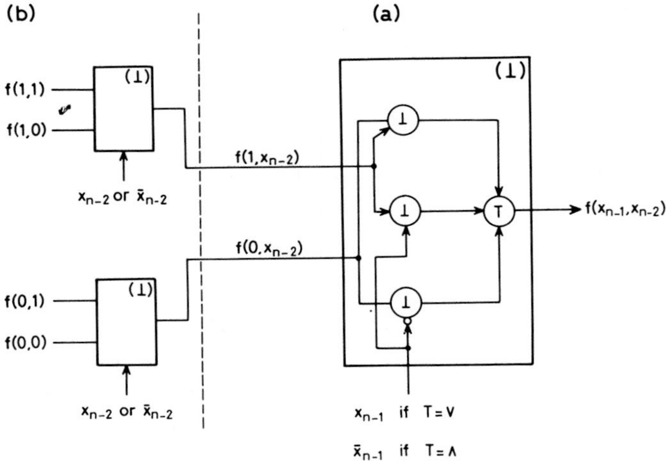

Figure 3.39. (a) ⊥-cell for designing a hazard-free ULM. (b) and (a) Interconnection scheme of ⊥-cells

Let us, for example, consider a realization of $f = x_0x_2 \oplus x_1\bar{x}_2$, the internal structure of which remains unknown. Assume that one has to be certain that the transition involving a change in the variable x_2 be hazard-free. The scheme of Figure 3.40 (with $n = 3$) satisfies this condition independently of the particular structure of the black-box realizing f.

The above kind of design may also be attractive from a cost point of view and for networks with a high number of non-essential prime implicants or implicates (see

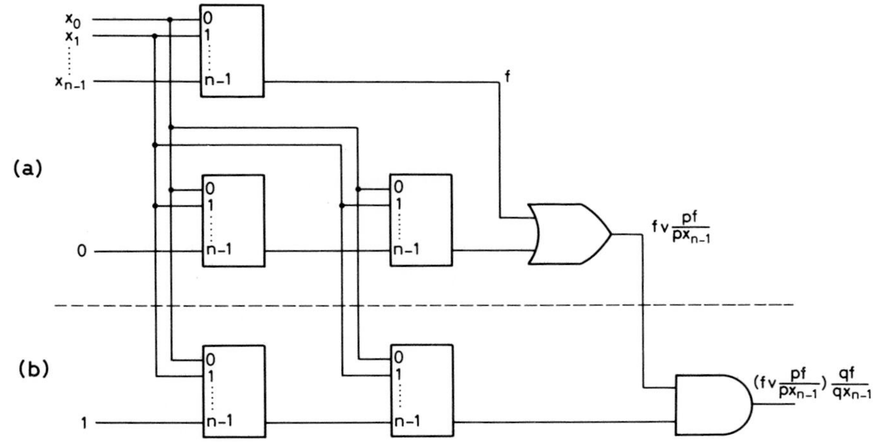

Figure 3.40. Example of hazard-free realization with hazard-containing components

Chapter 8). Consider, for example, a two-level AND-OR network where the AND-gates are in one-to-one correspondence with the prime implicants of f:

$$f = \bigvee_{i=1}^{p} x_{n-1} A_i \vee \bigvee_{j=1}^{q} \bar{x}_{n-1} B_j.$$

In order to be hazard-free for a transition involving a change of the variable x_{n-1}, the above network should also realize the pq prime implicants

$$\bigvee_{ij} A_i B_j.$$

Now these prime implicants may be built by interconnecting two modules realizing f as in Figure 3.40(a). The realization of f as a sum of prime implicants contains $p+q+pq+1$ gates while the hazard-free realization of f using recursive forms contains $3(p+q+1)+1$ gates. If p and q are high, the recursive realization becomes quickly much more economical than the two-level realization. The above example may easily be generalized for any type of transition.

Chapter 4

Ring Expressions of Discrete Functions

This chapter is mainly devoted to the study of *ring expansions* of discrete functions; a ring expansion is the representation of a discrete function as the ring sum of some elementary discrete functions sometimes referred to as primitives. If these elementary discrete functions are the elements of a basis, the ring expansions are *canonical ring forms* for the set of discrete functions. Let us recall that a canonical form (or a canonical expansion) for discrete functions is a form in which each function has a unique representation. Several types of bases are studied in section 4.2.3; to each of these bases operators (defined in section 4.1) are associated, which allow an easy interpretation of the coefficients of the basis elements in the ring expansions. Special attention is paid to the bases whose elements are Kronecker products of one-variable elementary functions (see section 4.2).

Ring expansions of switching functions are studied extensively and the present chapter includes most of the results available today on these functions. In particular, Reed–Muller, generalized Reed–Muller and pseudo-Kronecker expansions are carefully defined and their main properties are made obvious.

Section 4.4 is devoted to a short introduction to the domain of applicability of ring expansions.

In section 4.4.1 several design procedures for logic and for switching networks which derive from corresponding ring expansions are studied. The important problem of diagnosis of logic networks is introduced in sections 4.4.2 and 4.4.3. The analysis problem, that is, the detection of faults in logic networks, is studied in section 4.4.2; the synthesis problem, that is, the construction of networks the faults of which are easily detectable, is dealt with in section 4.4.3.

4.1. Bases, associated operators and expansions

As shown in Chapter 1, the set of discrete functions, i.e. the set of functions

$$f\colon S_{n-1} \times \ldots \times S_1 \times S_0 \to L,$$

viewed as an L-module, is isomorphic to L^N where $N = m_0 \times m_1 \times \ldots \times m_{n-1}$. Consider then a basis b of that module:

$$b = \{g_0(x), g_1(x), \ldots, g_{N-1}(x)\}.$$

All along this section it is convenient to use the following notation: given an integer i that lies between 0 and $N-1$, the vector $\boldsymbol{i} = (i_{n-1}, \ldots, i_1, i_0)$ gives the digits of i in the numeration system in basis $(m_{n-1}, \ldots, m_1, m_0)$, i.e.

$$i = i_{n-1}\, w_{n-1} + \ldots + i_1 w_1 + i_0 w_0,$$

the weights w_j being defined as in section 1.5.1.

The functions of b are related to the minterms (or equivalently to the Lagrange functions) by the identity:

$$[g_i(\boldsymbol{x})] = \left(\bigotimes_{i=n-1,0} [\tilde{x}_i^{(e_i)}]\right) G, \tag{4.1}$$

where the $(N \times N)$ matrix $G = [g_{ij}]$ is defined by

$$g_{ij} = g_j(\boldsymbol{i}), \qquad \forall\, i, j \in \{0, 1, \ldots, N-1\};$$

the $(1 \times m_i)$ matrix $[\tilde{x}_i^{(e_i)}]$ was defined in section 2.3.2 (see theorem 2.7); one will define the $(1 \times N)$ matrix:

$$[\tilde{\boldsymbol{x}}^{(e)}] = \bigotimes_{i=n-1,0} [\tilde{x}_i^{(e_i)}]. \tag{4.2}$$

The set of minterms is a basis; therefore, according to theorem 1.53, the matrix G admits an inverse. Let $G^{-1} = [g'_{ij}]$ be the inverse of G.

The functions $g'_0(\boldsymbol{x}), \ldots, g'_{N-1}(\boldsymbol{x})$, are defined by:

$$g'_j(\boldsymbol{i}) = g'_{ij}, \qquad \forall\, i, j \in \{0, 1, \ldots, N-1\}.$$

They are thus related to the minterms by the invertible matrix G^{-1}:

$$[g'_i(\boldsymbol{x})] = [\tilde{\boldsymbol{x}}^{(e)}]\, G^{-1}. \tag{4.3}$$

According again to theorem 1.53, the set

$$b' = \{g'_0(\boldsymbol{x}), g'_1(\boldsymbol{x}), \ldots, g'_{N-1}(\boldsymbol{x})\}$$

is a basis. It is called the *dual basis* of b.

Consider now the set of functions $\{g_0(\boldsymbol{x}-\boldsymbol{h}), g_1(\boldsymbol{x}-\boldsymbol{h}), \ldots, g_{N-1}(\boldsymbol{x}-\boldsymbol{h})\}$ where $\boldsymbol{h} = (h_{n-1}, \ldots, h_1, h_0) \in S_{n-1} \times \ldots \times S_1 \times S_0$; the ring subtractions are performed componentwise, i.e.

$$(\boldsymbol{x} - \boldsymbol{h}) = (x_{n-1} - h_{n-1}, \ldots, x_1 - h_1, x_0 - h_0)$$

where $x_i - h_i$ means clearly $x_i \oplus (m_i - 1)\, h_i$.

These functions are related to the minterms by a matrix $H = [h_{ij}]$:

$$[g_i(\boldsymbol{x} - \boldsymbol{h})] = [\tilde{\boldsymbol{x}}^{(e)}]\, H$$

with $h_{ij} = g_j(\boldsymbol{i} - \boldsymbol{h}) = g_{f(\boldsymbol{i}-\boldsymbol{h})j}$, where $f(\boldsymbol{i} - \boldsymbol{h})$ is defined as in (1.58), i.e.

$$f(\boldsymbol{i} - \boldsymbol{h}) = (i_0 - h_0)\, w_0 + (i_1 - h_1)\, w_1 + \ldots (i_{n-1} - h_{n-1})\, w_{n-1}.$$

The matrix H is thus deduced from G by a simple permutation of rows; therefore it will be denoted further on:

$$G^{f(i-h)}.$$

The inverse of this matrix, i.e. $(G^{f(i-h)})^{-1}$ has thus as (i,j)th element

$$g'_{i\,f(i-h)},$$

i.e. it is obtained by a corresponding permutation of the columns of G^{-1}. The set of functions

$$b_h = \{g_0(x-h), g_1(x-h), \ldots, g_{N-1}(x-h)\}$$

is thus a basis since it is related to the set of minterms by the invertible matrix $G^{f(i-h)}$; it is called a *translated basis* of b.

Definition 4.1. For every k in $\{0, 1, \ldots, N-1\}$, the *operator* $D^{(k)}$ associates with the function f the function $D^k f$ defined as follows:

$$D^k f = \sum_{e=0}^{N-1} g'_e(k) \quad f(x \oplus e). \tag{4.4}$$

Consider then the expression of f in the translated basis b_h:

$$f(x) = \sum_{i=0}^{N-1} l_i\, g_i(x-h), \quad l_i \in L \;\forall\, i.$$

Compute then the value of $D^k f$ at $x = h$:

$$\begin{aligned}(D^k f)_{x=h} &= \sum_{e=0}^{N-1} g'_e(k)\, f(h \oplus e)\\ &= \sum_{e=0}^{N-1} g'_e(k) \left[\sum_{i=0}^{N-1} l_i\, g_i(e)\right]\\ &= \sum_{i=0}^{N-1} l_i \sum_{e=0}^{N-1} g'_{ke}\, g_{ei}\\ &= l_k\end{aligned}$$

since

$$\sum_{e=0}^{N-1} g'_{ke} g_{ei} = 1 \text{ iff } k = i \text{ and is 0 otherwise.}$$

We may thus state the following theorem:

Theorem 4.1. Given a basis $b = \{g_0(x), g_1(x), \ldots, g_{N-1}(x)\}$ *of the module of discrete functions, and the dual basis* $b' = \{g'_0(x), g'_1(x), \ldots, g'_{N-1}(x)\}$*, every discrete function f admits the N expansions:*

$$f(x) = \sum_{e=0}^{N-1} (D^e f)_{x=h}\, g_e(x-h), \quad h = (h_{n-1}, \ldots, h_1, h_0) \in S_{n-1} \times \ldots \times S_1 \times S_0 \tag{4.5}$$

with

$$D^k f = \sum_{e=0}^{N-1} g'_e(k)\, f(x \oplus e), \quad k = 0, 1, \ldots, N-1. \tag{4.6}$$

The most important case is when the basis b is a Kronecker basis.

Definition 4.2. A *Kronecker basis b* for the n-variables discrete functions

$$f: S_{n-1} \times \ldots \times S_1 \times S_0 \to L$$

is a basis which can be expressed as the Kronecker product of n elementary bases:

$$b = b_{n-1} \otimes \ldots \otimes b_1 \otimes b_0$$

each of the elementary bases b_i being a basis for the 1-variable functions:

$$f_i: S_i \to L, \quad i = 0, 1, \ldots, n-1 \tag{4.7}$$

that is:

$$b_i = \{g_{0i}(x_i), g_{1i}(x_i), \ldots, g_{(m_i-1)i}(x_i)\}.$$

In that case one has thus (see theorems 1.58 and 1.59):

$$[g_i(x)] = \bigotimes_{j=n-1,0} [g_{i_j j}(x_j)]$$

$$G = \bigotimes_{j=n-1,0} G_j$$

$$G^{-1} = \bigotimes_{j=n-1,0} G_j^{-1}$$

$$[g'_i(x)] = \bigotimes_{j=n-1,0} [g'_{i_j j}(x_j)].$$

Definition 4.3(a). The *operators* D^{k_i}/Dx_i are defined as follows:

$$\frac{D^{k_i} f}{Dx_i} = \sum_{e_i=0}^{m_i-1} g'_{e_i i}(k_i)\, f(x_i \oplus e_i), \quad i = 0, 1, \ldots, n-1; \quad k_i = 0, 1, \ldots, m_i - 1. \tag{4.8}$$

Consider a partition $(\boldsymbol{x}_1, \boldsymbol{x}_0)$ of $\boldsymbol{x}$ with $\boldsymbol{x}_1 = (x_{n-1}, \ldots, x_{q+1}, x_q)$ and $\boldsymbol{x}_0 = (x_{q-1}, \ldots, x_1, x_0)$; let moreover $\boldsymbol{k}_0 = (k_{q-1}, \ldots, k_1, k_0)$.

Definition 4.3(b). The *operators* $D^{\boldsymbol{k}_0}/D\boldsymbol{x}_0$ are defined as follows:

$$\frac{D^{\boldsymbol{k}_0} f}{D\boldsymbol{x}_0} = \frac{D^{k_{q-1}}}{Dx_{q-1}} \left\{ \frac{D^{k_{q-2}}}{Dx_{q-2}} \left[\ldots \left(\frac{D^{k_0} f}{Dx_0} \right) \ldots \right] \right\}. \tag{4.9}$$

Lemma 4.1.

$$\frac{D^{\boldsymbol{k}_0} f}{D\boldsymbol{x}_0} = \sum_{\boldsymbol{e}_0} \left[\prod_{l=0}^{q-1} g'_{e_i i}(k_i) \right] f(\boldsymbol{x}_1, \boldsymbol{x}_0 \oplus \boldsymbol{e}_0)$$

$$\boldsymbol{e}_0 = (e_{q-1}, \ldots, e_1, e_0), \quad 0 \leqslant e_i \leqslant m_i - 1 \;\forall\; i = 0, 1, \ldots, q-1. \tag{4.10}$$

Proof. The property holds true for $q = 1$, the proof can then easily be achieved by induction on q ∎

Thanks to that lemma, we can now state the following theorem.

Theorem 4.2. In the case where b is the Kronecker basis $b_{n-1} \otimes \ldots \otimes b_1 \otimes b_0$, then:

$$D^k f = \frac{D^{\boldsymbol{k}} f}{D\boldsymbol{x}} \tag{4.11}$$

for every $k = 0, 1, \ldots, N-1$ and with $\boldsymbol{k} = (k_{n-1}, \ldots, k_1, k_0)$.

The operators D^{k_i}/Dx_i have some properties similar to those of the derivatives or differences in classical differential calculus.

1. They are *linear*

$$\frac{D^{k_i}}{Dx_i} (l_0 f_0(\boldsymbol{x}) \oplus l_1 f_1(\boldsymbol{x})) = l_0 \frac{D^{k_i} f_0}{Dx_i} \oplus l_1 \frac{D^{k_i} f_1}{Dx_i}. \tag{4.12}$$

2. $$\left(\frac{D^{k_i} f}{Dx_i} \right)_{\boldsymbol{x}=\boldsymbol{h}} = \left[\frac{D^{k_i}}{Dx_i} f(\boldsymbol{h}_1, \boldsymbol{x}_0) \right]_{\boldsymbol{x}_0 = \boldsymbol{h}_0} \tag{4.13}$$

$$\boldsymbol{h} = (\boldsymbol{h}_1; \boldsymbol{h}_0) = (h_{n-1}, \ldots, h_{q+1}, h_q; h_{q-1}, \ldots, h_1, h_0), \; 0 \leqslant i \leqslant q-1.$$

This last property immediately yields partial expansions for discrete functions.

Theorem 4.3. Given a Kronecker basis $b = b_{n-1} \otimes \ldots \otimes b_1 \otimes b_0$ of the module of discrete functions with

$$b_i = \{g_{0i}(x_i), g_{1i}(x_i), \ldots, g_{(m_i-1)i}(x_i)\}, \quad i = 0, \ldots, N-1,$$

and the dual basis $b' = b'_{n-1} \otimes \ldots \otimes b'_1 \otimes b'_0$ *with*

$$b'_i = \{g'_{0i}(x_i), g'_{1i}(x_i), \ldots, g'_{(m_i-1)i}(x_i)\}, \quad i = 0, 1, \ldots, N-1,$$

then, for every partition (x_1, x_0) *of* x *and for every* $h_0 \in S_{q-1} \times \ldots \times S_1 \times S_0$, *the discrete function* f *admits the following partial expansion:*

$$f(x_1, x_0) = \sum_{e_0} \left(\frac{D^{e_0} f}{Dx_0}\right)_{x_0 = h_0} \left[\prod_{i=0}^{q-1} g_{e_i i}(x_i - h_i)\right], \quad 0 \leqslant e_i \leqslant m_i - 1 \tag{4.14}$$

with:

$$\frac{D^{k_i} f}{Dx_i} = \sum_{e_i=0}^{m_i-1} g'_{e_i i}(k_i)\, f(x_i \oplus e_i), \quad i = 0, 1, \ldots, q-1.$$

Proof. According to theorems 4.1 and 4.2 one has for any point $(h_1, h_0) \in S_{n-1} \times \ldots \times S_1 \times S_0$:

$$\begin{aligned} f(h_1, x_0) &= \sum_{e_0} \left[\frac{D^{e_0}}{Dx_0} f(h_1, x_0)\right]_{x_0 = h_0} \left[\prod_{i=0}^{q-1} g_{e_i i}(x_i - h_i)\right] \\ &= \sum_{e_0} \left(\frac{D^{e_0} f}{Dx_0}\right)_{x = h} \left[\prod_{i=0}^{q-1} g_{e_i i}(x_i - h_i)\right] \end{aligned}$$

with $h = (h_1, h_0)$. The proof is completed by noting that this relation holds true for every choice of h_1. ■

Some other properties that hold for the derivatives in classical analysis generally do not hold for the operators associated with a given basis b. Among others, it is generally not true that

1. $\dfrac{D^{k_i} f}{Dx_i} = \dfrac{D}{Dx_i}\left(\dfrac{D^{k_i - 1} f}{Dx_i}\right), \quad 1 \leqslant k_i \leqslant m_i - 1.$

2. $\dfrac{D^0 f}{Dx_i} = f.$

3. $\dfrac{D^{k_i} l}{Dx_i} = 0, \quad l \in L.$

As will be seen later, another property that is interesting to detect, but is not always true, is that:

4. $\dfrac{D^{m_i - 1} f}{Dx_i}$ is a constant function.

The following theorem gives the conditions under which each of those properties is satisfied. It is stated, without loss of generality, for one-variable functions.

Theorem 4.4. Consider a basis $b = \{g_0(x), g_1(x), \ldots, g_{m-1}(x)\}$ *of the set of one-variable discrete functions* $f(x)$:

$$f: \{0, 1, \ldots, m-1\} \rightarrow \{0, 1, \ldots, r-1\}$$

and the dual basis $b' = \{g'_0(x), g'_1(x), \ldots, g'_{m-1}(x)\}$ *and define the operators* D^k/Dx, $k = 0, 1, \ldots, m-1$ *as above, i.e.*

$$\frac{D^k f}{Dx} = \sum_{e=0}^{m-1} g'_e(k) f(x \oplus e),$$

then:

(a) $\dfrac{D^k f}{Dx} = \dfrac{D}{Dx}\left(\dfrac{D^{k-1} f}{Dx}\right), \quad 1 \leqslant k \leqslant m-1$ *for every function f iff:*

iff

$$g'_e(k) = \sum_{e=0}^{m-1} g'_e(1)\, g'_{j-e}(k-1);$$

(b) $\dfrac{D^0 f}{Dx} = f$ *for every function f iff:*

$$g'_0(0) = 1, g'_1(0) = \ldots = g'_{m-1}(0) = 0;$$

(c) $\dfrac{D^k l}{Dx} = 0, \quad 1 \leqslant k \leqslant m-1, \quad l \in L,$ *iff:*

$$\sum_{e=0}^{m-1} g'_e(k) = 0;$$

(d) $\dfrac{D^{m-1} f}{Dx}$ *is a constant, for every function f, iff:*

$$g'_0(m-1) = g'_1(m-1) = \ldots = g'_{m-1}(m-1).$$

Proof. (a) Compute

$$\frac{D}{Dx}\left(\frac{D^{k-1} f}{Dx}\right);$$

one obtains

$$\frac{D}{Dx}\left(\frac{D^{k-1}f}{Dx}\right) = \sum_{e=0}^{m-1} g_e'(1) \left(\frac{D^{k-1}f}{Dx}\right)_{x=e}$$

$$= \sum_{e=0}^{m-1} g_e'(1) \left[\sum_{i=0}^{m-1} g_i'(k-1)\, f(x \oplus e \oplus i)\right]$$

$$= \sum_{i=0}^{m-1} \left[\sum_{e=0}^{m-1} g_e'(1)\, g_{i-e}'(k-1)\, f(x \oplus i)\right].$$

On the other hand

$$\frac{D^k f}{Dx} = \sum_{i=0}^{m-1} g_i'(k)\, f(x \oplus i).$$

In order that the two expressions above represent the same function for any choice of f, it is necessary and sufficient that:

$$g_i'(k) = \sum_{e=0}^{m-1} g_e'(1)\, g_{i-e}'(k-1).$$

(b) $$\frac{D^0 f}{Dx} = g_0'(0)\, f(x) \oplus \sum_{e=0}^{m-1} g_e'(0)\, f(x \oplus e).$$

The condition under which $D^0 f/Dx = f$, for every function f, is thus

$$g_0'(0) = 1, \quad g_1'(0) = \ldots g_{m-1}'(0) = 0.$$

(c) $$\frac{D^k l}{Dx} = l\left[\sum_{e=0}^{m-1} g_e'(k)\right],$$

and thus the condition under which $D^k l/dx = 0$, for every constant l, is

$$\sum_{e=0}^{m-1} g_e'(k) = 0.$$

(d) The condition is clearly sufficient. Furthermore, if it is not satisfied, it is possible to find a function f such that $D^{m-1} f/Dx$ is not a constant function. ■

The above theory on bases and associated operators was stated by Deschamps [1975]. It will be applied in next section 4.2 to several important kinds of canonical expansions.

4.2. *Kronecker bases and associated ring expansions*

4.2.1. *Coherent Kronecker bases*

Definition 4.4. A *coherent Kronecker basis b* is a Kronecker basis where the elements of the elementary bases b_i have either identical expressions for each of these bases b_i, or expressions that can be deduced from each other by means of a translation.

For example the basis of minterms is a Kronecker basis since (see theorem 2.2) it is the Kronecker product:

$$b = \bigotimes_{i=n-1,0} [\tilde{x}_i^{(e_i)}].$$

It is moreover a coherent basis since all the elementary bases contain elements having an identical expression for each basis b_i, namely

$$\tilde{x}_i^{(e_i)}, \quad i = 0, 1, \ldots, n-1.$$

The basis:

$$b = \bigotimes_{i=n-1,0} [\widetilde{(x_i - h_i)}^{(e_i)}]$$

is also a coherent Kronecker basis since the elements of its bases b_i may be deduced from each other by a simple translation.

The study of canonical ring expansions for discrete functions is important; this is partly due to the fact that a given canonical expansion is unique for a given discrete function and is generally easily obtained. Moreover, in many cases, the canonical expansions of a function will be the starting point for obtaining a minimal or a reduced expression for a function (see Chapter 6).

Three kinds of canonical ring expansions in a coherent basis will be considered in this section, namely the Newton expansions, the Nyquist expansions and the Kodandapani expansions.

4.2.1.1. *The binomial bases, the ring differences and the Newton expansions*

4.2.1.1.1. *General theory*

Let us denote by $\binom{k}{e}$ the *binomial coefficient* (see, for example, Jordan [1947] p. 62) evaluated in the ring of integers modulo-r (k and e are non-negative integers). The *binomial function* $\binom{x}{e}$ is a function of x which takes on the value $\binom{k}{e}$ when $x = k$. The binomial function is without doubt the most important function of the calculus of finite differences. It will be seen hereafter that the binomial function evaluated in the ring of integers modulo-r plays a similar role in the ring expansions studied in this section.

Consider first one-variable functions: $\{0, 1, \ldots, m-1\} \rightarrow \{0, 1, \ldots, r-1\}$.

Lemma 4.2

$$\binom{x}{k} = \sum_{e=0}^{m-1} \binom{e}{k} \tilde{x}^{(e)}. \tag{4.15}$$

Proof. The proof derives from the fact that $\tilde{x}^{(e)}$ is 1 iff $x = e$ and is 0 otherwise. ■

The set of binomial functions constitutes a basis for the discrete functions; indeed, define first the matrices:

$[\tilde{x}^{(e)}]$ is the $(1 \times m)$ matrix the eth entry of which is $\tilde{x}^{(e)}$ (see also theorem 2.7);

$\left[\binom{x}{e}\right]$ is the $(1 \times m)$ matrix the eth entry of which is $\binom{x}{e}$;

$A_m = [a_{ij}]$ is an $(m \times m)$ matrix with $a_{ij} = \binom{i}{j}$ (i = row number, j = column number, $0 \leqslant i, j \leqslant m-1$).

Lemma 4.2 may then be stated in the following matrix form which corresponds to relation (4.1):

$$\left[\binom{x}{e}\right] = [\tilde{x}^{(e)}]\, A_m. \tag{4.16}$$

Let $A_m^{-1} = [a'_{ij}]$ be the inverse of A_m; one knows (see, for example, Riordan [1968]) that $a'_{ij} = (-1)^{(i+j)} \binom{i}{j}$. One has thus:

$$[\tilde{x}^{(e)}] = \left[\binom{x}{e}\right] A_m^{-1} \tag{4.17}$$

or equivalently:

$$\tilde{x}^{(k)} = \sum_{e=0}^{m-1} (-1)^{(e+k)} \binom{e}{k} \binom{x}{e}. \tag{4.18}$$

To the basis of binomial functions:

$$\left\{\binom{x}{0}, \binom{x}{1}, \ldots, \binom{x}{m-1}\right\}$$

corresponds thus the dual basis

$$\left\{(-1)^x \binom{x}{0}, (-1)^{(x+1)} \binom{x}{1}, \ldots, (-1)^{(x+m-1)} \binom{x}{m-1}\right\}.$$

Consider now the translated basis:

$$b_h = \left\{\binom{x-h}{0}, \binom{x-h}{1}, \ldots, \binom{x-h}{m-1}\right\}.$$

These functions are related to the minterms by the matrix A^h_m which is the $(m \times m)$ matrix the (i, j)th entry of which is $a_{(i-h)j}$. The inverse of this matrix is the $(m \times m)$ matrix $(A^h_m)^{-1}$ the (i, j)th element of which is $a'_{i(j-h)}$. This clearly derives from the theory of section 4.1; the configurations of the matrices A^h_m and $(A^h_m)^{-1}$ derive also from lemma 4.3 below.

Lemma 4.3
If

$$f_k(x) = \sum_{e=0}^{m-1} d_{ek}\, \tilde{x}^{(e)} \tag{4.19}$$

and

$$\tilde{x}^{(k)} = \sum_{e=0}^{m-1} d'_{ek}\, f_e(x) \tag{4.20}$$

then

$$f_k(x-h) = \sum_{e=0}^{m-1} d_{(e-h)k}\, \tilde{x}^{(e)} \tag{4.21}$$

and

$$\tilde{x}^{(k)} = \sum_{e=0}^{m-1} d'_{e(k-h)}\, f_e(x-h) \tag{4.22}$$

where $x-h$ is computed modulo m.

Proof. From (4.19) one deduces first that

$$d_{ek} = f_k(e).$$

Substituting this last expression in (4.21) one obtains:

$$f_k(x-h) = \sum_{e=0}^{m-1} f_k(e-h)\, \tilde{x}^{(e)}.$$

From (4.20) one first deduces that:

$$\widetilde{(x-h)}^{(k)} = \tilde{x}^{(k \oplus h)} = \sum_{e=0}^{m-1} d'_{ek}\, f_k(x-h)$$

therefore

$$\tilde{x}^{(k)} = \sum_{e=0}^{m-1} d'_{e(k-h)} f_e(x-h). \qquad \blacksquare$$

Let us now consider the corresponding coherent bases for the n-variable discrete functions:

$$f = S_{n-1} \times \ldots \times S_1 \times S_0 \rightarrow L.$$

The $(1 \times \Pi m_i)$ matrices $[\tilde{x}^{(e)}]$ and $\left[\binom{x-h}{e}\right]$ are defined as follows:

$$[\tilde{x}^{(e)}] = \bigotimes_{i=n-1,\,0} [\tilde{x}_i^{(e_i)}] \tag{4.23}$$

$$\left[\binom{x-h}{e}\right] = \bigotimes_{i=n-1,\,0} \left[\binom{x_i-h_i}{e_i}\right] \tag{4.24}$$

$$h \in S_{n-1} \times \ldots \times S_1 \times S_0.$$

The $(\Pi m_i \times \Pi m_i)$ matrices A_m^h and $(A_m^h)^{-1}$ are simply defined by

$$A_m^h = \bigotimes_{i=n-1,\,0} A_{m_i}^{h_i}$$

$$(A_m^h)^{-1} = \bigotimes_{i=n-1,\,0} (A_{m_i}^{h_i})^{-1}. \tag{4.25}$$

The above definition and the properties of the Kronecker product allow us to state the following relations:

$$\left[\binom{x-h}{e}\right] = [\tilde{x}^{(e)}]\, A_m^h \tag{4.26}$$

$$[\tilde{x}^{(e)}] = \left[\binom{x-h}{e}\right] (A_m^h)^{-1}. \tag{4.27}$$

The set of binomial functions

$$\left\{ \prod_{i=0}^{n-1} \binom{x_i-h_i}{e_i}, \quad (e_{n-1}, \ldots, e_1, e_0) \in S_{n-1} \times \ldots \times S_1 \times S_0 \right\}$$

constitutes thus a basis for the discrete functions $f\colon S \rightarrow L$.

The following theorem 4.5 is a direct consequence of theorem 4.3 and of the above definition of the basis of binomial functions.

Theorem 4.5. (Partial Newton expansion evaluated at the point $\boldsymbol{h}_0$.) Given a canonical basis of binomial functions, for every partition $(\boldsymbol{x}_1, \boldsymbol{x}_0)$ of $\boldsymbol{x}$ and for every $\boldsymbol{h}_0 \in S_{q-1} \times \ldots \times S_1 \times S_0$, the discrete function f admits the following partial expansion:

$$f(\boldsymbol{x}_1, \boldsymbol{x}_0) = \sum_{\boldsymbol{e}_0} \left(\frac{\Delta^{\boldsymbol{e}_0} f}{\Delta \boldsymbol{x}_0}\right)_{\boldsymbol{x}_0 = \boldsymbol{h}_0} \left[\prod_{i=0}^{q-1} \binom{x_i - h_i}{e_i}\right] \tag{4.28}$$

$$\boldsymbol{e}_0 = (e_{q-1}, \ldots, e_1, e_0), \quad 0 \leqslant e_i \leqslant m_i - 1, \quad i = 0, 1, \ldots, q-1$$

with

$$\frac{\Delta^{\boldsymbol{k}_0} f}{\Delta \boldsymbol{x}_0} = \sum_{\boldsymbol{e}_0} (-1)^{\left[\sum_{j=0}^{q-1} (k_j + e_j)\right]} \left[\prod_{i=0}^{q-1} \binom{k_i}{e_i}\right] f(\boldsymbol{x}_0 \oplus \boldsymbol{e}_0). \tag{4.29}$$

The bases of binomial functions provide us thus with a type of expansion called *Newton expansion*, and with an operator that will be called hereafter *ring difference.* These expansions and operators were both derived from a general theory developed in section 4.1. Due to the importance of Newton expansions and of ring operators one will show that these concepts are also strongly connected to the Newton expansions and finite differences of numerical analysis (see e.g. Jordan [1947]); one will also prove that similar methods may be used in both finite difference calculus and ring difference calculus. For example, finite differences and Newton expansions, ring differences and Newton ring expansions are obtained by use of similar computation methods.

Let us define the ring differences of discrete functions by means of the same type of formula as the lattice differences (see definition 3.5); the simple ring difference is obtained by replacing in definition 3.5 the lattice operation T by the modulo-*r* subtraction.

Definition 4.5. (a) *Simple ring differences.*

Given a discrete function $f(\boldsymbol{x})$, the (partial) ring difference of $f(\boldsymbol{x})$ with respect to a variable $x_i \in \boldsymbol{x}$ is denoted by $\Delta f/\Delta x_i$, and is defined as follows:

$$\frac{\Delta f}{\Delta x_i} = f(x_i \oplus 1) - f(\boldsymbol{x}). \tag{4.30}$$

(b) *Multiple ring differences.*

The multiple ring differences $\Delta^{k_i} f/\Delta x_i$ and $\Delta^{\boldsymbol{k}_0} f/\Delta \boldsymbol{x}_0$ are defined according to the recurrence formulas (4.31) and (4.32), that is:

$$\frac{\Delta^{k_i} f}{\Delta x_i} = \frac{\Delta}{\Delta x_i}\left(\frac{\Delta^{k_i - 1} f}{\Delta x_i}\right), \quad 1 \leqslant k_i \leqslant m_i - 1 \tag{4.31}$$

$$\frac{\Delta^{\boldsymbol{k}_0} f}{\Delta \boldsymbol{x}_0} = \frac{\Delta^{k_0}}{\Delta x_0}\left\{\frac{\Delta^{k_1}}{\Delta x_1}\left[\cdots\left(\frac{\Delta^{k_{q-1}} f}{\Delta x_{q-1}}\right)\cdots\right]\right\} \tag{4.32}$$

with $\boldsymbol{k}_0 = (k_{q-1}, \ldots, k_1, k_0)$ and $\boldsymbol{x}_0 = (x_{q-1}, \ldots, x_1, x_0)$.

In view of the above definition, it is clear that the ring differences for discrete functions are strongly connected to the *finite differences* of numerical analysis (see, for example, Jordan [1947]): the ring difference is nothing but a finite difference evaluated modulo-r. It follows that the ring differences satisfy the properties (a), (b) and (c) of theorem 4.4.

Let E/Ex_i be the operation of displacement defined as follows for a function $f(\boldsymbol{x})$:

$$\frac{Ef}{Ex_i} = f(x_i \oplus 1).$$

In the same way:

$$\frac{E^{k_i} f}{Ex_i} = \frac{E}{Ex_i}\left(\frac{E^{k_i - 1} f}{Ex_i}\right) = f(x_i \oplus k_i).$$

In view of the formulas (4.30) and (4.31) one obtains successively:

$$\frac{\Delta f}{\Delta x_i} = \left(\frac{E}{Ex_i} - 1\right) f$$

$$\frac{\Delta^{k_i} f}{\Delta x_i} = \left(\frac{E}{Ex_i} - 1\right)^{k_i} f$$

$$= \sum_{e_i=0}^{k_i} (-1)^{k_i+e_i} \binom{k_i}{e_i} f(x_i \oplus e_i)$$

$$= \sum_{e_i=0}^{m_i-1} (-1)^{k_i+e_i} \binom{k_i}{e_i} f(x_i \oplus e_i), \quad 1 \leqslant k_i \leqslant m_i - 1. \tag{4.33}$$

The expression (4.29) for several variables is then obtained by induction on q, which shows in a direct way that the ring differences defined under 4.5 correspond to the operators associated with the basis of binomial functions and defined in theorem 4.5.

Lemma 4.4

$$f(\boldsymbol{x}_0 \oplus \boldsymbol{k}_0) = \sum_{\boldsymbol{e}_0} \left[\prod_{j=0}^{q-1} \binom{k_j}{e_j}\right] \frac{\Delta^{\boldsymbol{e}_0} f}{\Delta \boldsymbol{x}_0}, \quad 0 \leqslant e_i \leqslant m_i - 1. \tag{4.34}$$

Proof. The same type of proof as for relation (4.33) holds; it is based on the symbolical relation:

$$\frac{E^{k_i}}{Ex_i} = \left(1 \oplus \frac{\Delta}{\Delta x_i}\right)^{k_i}.$$

■

Lemma 4.4 provides us with a direct way for obtaining the partial Newton expansion (4.28); it is obtained from expression (4.34) by

(a) replacing in (4.34) $\boldsymbol{k}_0$ by $\boldsymbol{h}_0$,
(b) interchanging in the expression so obtained $\boldsymbol{x}_0$ and $\boldsymbol{h}_0$,
(c) replacing in the last expression $\boldsymbol{x}_0$ by $\boldsymbol{x}_0 - \boldsymbol{h}_0$.

The *Newton expansion* is derived in the same way, but by considering the complete set $\boldsymbol{x}$ of variables, that is:

Newton expansion evaluated at the point $\boldsymbol{h}$:

$$f(\boldsymbol{x}) = \sum_{e} \left(\frac{\Delta^e f}{\Delta \boldsymbol{x}}\right)_{\boldsymbol{x}=\boldsymbol{h}} \left[\prod_{i=0}^{n-1} \binom{x_i - h_i}{e_i}\right] \tag{4.35}$$

$$0 \leqslant \boldsymbol{e} = (e_{n-1}, \ldots, e_1, e_0) \leqslant \boldsymbol{m} - \boldsymbol{1}; \quad \boldsymbol{h} = (h_{n-1}, \ldots, h_1, h_0) \in \mathop{\times}_{i} S_i.$$

The expansion (4.35) is called Newton expansion since it corresponds in many respects to the Newton expansion of the finite difference calculus (see e.g. Jordan [1947]). The expansion (4.35) was obtained by Gazalé [1959] while the interpretation of its coefficients in terms of local values of ring differences is due to Thayse and Deschamps [1973b].

The following functional properties of the ring differences may either be deduced from the definition 4.5 or from the general theorem 4.4. For any $l_0, l_1, l \in L$ one has:

$$\frac{\Delta^{k_0}}{\Delta \boldsymbol{x}_0} [l_0 f(\boldsymbol{x}) \oplus l_1\, g(\boldsymbol{x})] = l_0 \frac{\Delta^{k_0} f}{\Delta \boldsymbol{x}_0} \oplus l_1 \frac{\Delta^{k_0} g}{\Delta \boldsymbol{x}_0}$$

$$\frac{\Delta^{k_i}}{\Delta x_i}\left(\frac{\Delta^{k_j} f}{\Delta x_j}\right) = \frac{\Delta^{k_j}}{\Delta x_j}\left(\frac{\Delta^{k_i} f}{\Delta x_i}\right) = \frac{\Delta^{k_i k_j} f}{\Delta x_i x_j}$$

$$\frac{\Delta l}{\Delta x_i} = 0 \tag{4.36}$$

$$\frac{\Delta \bar{f}}{\Delta x_i} = (r-1)\frac{\Delta f}{\Delta x_i}$$

$$\frac{\Delta (fg)}{\Delta x_i} = f \frac{\Delta g}{\Delta x_i} \oplus g \frac{\Delta f}{\Delta x_i} \oplus \frac{\Delta f}{\Delta x_i} \frac{\Delta g}{\Delta x_i}.$$

Example 4.1. For the discrete functions $f(x_1 x_0)$:

$f\colon \{0, 1, 2, 3\}^2 \to L$

the Newton expansion evaluated at $(h_1h_0) = (00)$ is, in view of (4.12):

$$f = f(00) \oplus \left(\frac{\Delta f}{\Delta x_0}\right)_{00} \binom{x_0}{1} \oplus \left(\frac{\Delta^2 f}{\Delta x_0}\right)_{00} \binom{x_0}{2} \oplus \left(\frac{\Delta^3 f}{\Delta x_0}\right)_{00} \binom{x_0}{3} \oplus \left(\frac{\Delta f}{\Delta x_1}\right)_{00} \binom{x_1}{1} \oplus$$

$$\left(\frac{\Delta^2 f}{\Delta x_1}\right)_{00} \binom{x_1}{1} \oplus \left(\frac{\Delta^3 f}{\Delta x_1}\right)_{00} \binom{x_1}{3} \oplus \left(\frac{\Delta f}{\Delta x_1 x_0}\right)_{00} \binom{x_1}{1} \binom{x_0}{1} \oplus$$

$$\left(\frac{\Delta^{12} f}{\Delta x_1 x_0}\right)_{00} \binom{x_1}{1} \binom{x_0}{2} \oplus \left(\frac{\Delta^{13} f}{\Delta x_1 x_0}\right)_{00} \binom{x_1}{1} \binom{x_0}{3} \oplus \left(\frac{\Delta^{21} f}{\Delta x_1 x_0}\right)_{00}$$

$$\binom{x_1}{2} \binom{x_0}{1} \oplus \left(\frac{\Delta^{31} f}{\Delta x_1 x_0}\right)_{00} \binom{x_1}{3} \binom{x_0}{1} \oplus \left(\frac{\Delta^{22} f}{\Delta x_1 x_0}\right)_{00} \binom{x_1}{2} \binom{x_0}{2} \oplus$$

$$\left(\frac{\Delta^{23} f}{\Delta x_1 x_0}\right)_{00} \binom{x_1}{2} \binom{x_0}{3} \oplus \left(\frac{\Delta^{32} f}{\Delta x_1 x_0}\right) \binom{x_1}{3} \binom{x_0}{2} \oplus \left(\frac{\Delta^{33} f}{\Delta x_1 x_0}\right)_{00}$$

$$\binom{x_1}{3} \binom{x_0}{3}.$$

Considering a discrete function $f(x_1x_0)$ given by its value matrix (Figure 4.1), let us compute the Newton expansion at $(h_1h_0) = (00)$.

$$\left(\frac{\Delta f}{\Delta x_0}\right)_{00} = 1, \quad \left(\frac{\Delta^2 f}{\Delta x_0}\right)_{00} = 1, \quad \left(\frac{\Delta^3 f}{\Delta x_0}\right)_{00} = 0$$

$$\left(\frac{\Delta f}{\Delta x_1}\right)_{00} = 1, \quad \left(\frac{\Delta^2 f}{\Delta x_1}\right)_{00} = 0, \quad \left(\frac{\Delta^3 f}{\Delta x_1}\right)_{00} = 2$$

$$\left(\frac{\Delta f}{\Delta x_1 x_0}\right)_{00} = 0, \quad \left(\frac{\Delta^{12} f}{\Delta x_1 x_0}\right)_{00} = 0, \quad \left(\frac{\Delta^{21} f}{\Delta x_1 x_0}\right)_{00} = 2$$

$$\left(\frac{\Delta^{22} f}{\Delta x_1 x_0}\right)_{00} = 0, \quad \left(\frac{\Delta^{13} f}{\Delta x_1 x_0}\right)_{00} = 0, \quad \left(\frac{\Delta^{31} f}{\Delta x_1 x_0}\right)_{00} = 2$$

$$\left(\frac{\Delta^{32} f}{\Delta x_1 x_0}\right)_{00} = 0, \quad \left(\frac{\Delta^{23} f}{\Delta x_1 x_0}\right)_{00} = 0, \quad \left(\frac{\Delta^{33} f}{\Delta x_1 x_0}\right)_{00} = 0.$$

In view of the local values of the differences, one obtains the following Newton expansion of f;

$$f = \binom{x_0}{1} \oplus \binom{x_0}{2} \oplus \binom{x_1}{1} \oplus 2\binom{x_1}{3} \oplus 2\binom{x_1}{2}\binom{x_0}{1} \oplus 2\binom{x_1}{3}\binom{x_0}{1}.$$

$x_1 \backslash x_0$	0	1	2	3
0	0	1	0	0
1	1	2	1	1
2	2	2	0	2
3	2	2	0	2

Figure 4.1. Value matrix

Computational formulae will now be derived for obtaining the Newton expansions and the ring differences of a discrete function when the latter is given by the intermediate of its value vector.

Let us first observe that formulae (4.16), (4.17), (4.26) and (4.27) provide us with transformation formulae allowing us to obtain the binary function bases at the point $\boldsymbol{h}$ from the basis of Lagrange functions and vice versa; in this respect the formulae (4.16) and (4.17) which allow us to derive the basis at the point $\boldsymbol{0}$ are only particular cases of the more general formulae (4.26) and (4.27).

Theorem 4.6. The Newton expansion at the point $\boldsymbol{h}$ *is given by:*

$$[f_e]\ [(A_m^h)^{-1}]^t \left[\binom{x-h}{e}\right]^t . \tag{4.37}$$

Proof. From relations (2.40) and (4.27) one deduces:

$$\begin{aligned} f(x) &= [f_e]\ [\tilde{x}^{(e)}]^t \\ &= [f_e]\ [(A_m^h)^{-1}]^t \left[\binom{x-h}{e}\right]^t . \end{aligned}$$

■

Corollary. The Newton expansion at the point $\boldsymbol{0}$ *is given by*

$$[f_e]\ (A_m^{-1})^t \left[\binom{x}{e}\right]. \tag{4.38}$$

Example 4.1 (continued). Consider a discrete function: $\{0, 1, 2, 3\}^2 \to \{0, 1, 2\}$ given by its value vector, i.e.

$$[0\ 1\ 0\ 0\ 1\ 2\ 1\ 1\ 2\ 2\ 0\ 2\ 2\ 2\ 0\ 2].$$

In order to obtain the Newton expansion at the point $\boldsymbol{0}$, one first multiplies the value vector by the matrix $(A_4^{-1} \otimes A_4^{-1})^t = (A_{44}^{-1})^t$. This operation is performed (without computing explicitly A_{44}^{-1}) by multiplying first the 4-tuples of $[f_e]$ (considered here as a (1 × 4) matrix with 4-tuples as elements) by $(A_4^{-1})^t$, that is:

$$[(0\ 1\ 0\ 0),\ (1\ 2\ 1\ 1),\ (2\ 2\ 0\ 2),\ (2\ 2\ 0\ 2)]\begin{bmatrix}1 & -1 & 1 & -1\\ 0 & 1 & -2 & 0\\ 0 & 0 & 1 & 0\\ 0 & 0 & 0 & 1\end{bmatrix}:$$

$$[(0\ 1\ 0\ 0),\ (1\ 1\ 1\ 1),\ (0\ 2\ 1\ 0),\ (2\ 1\ 0\ 2)].$$

By applying again the same transformation matrix $(A_4^{-1})^t$ successively to the four 4-tuples of the above matrix, one obtains finally:

$$[f_e]\ [A_4^{-1} \otimes A_4^{-1}] = [0\ 1\ 1\ 0\ \ 1\ 0\ 0\ 0\ \ 0\ 2\ 0\ 0\ \ 2\ 2\ 0\ 0].$$

The Newton expansion at the point 0 is then

$$[0\ 1\ 1\ 0\ \ 1\ 0\ 0\ 0\ \ 0\ 2\ 0\ 0\ \ 2\ 2\ 0\ 0]\left\{\left[\binom{x_1}{e_1}\right] \otimes \left[\binom{x_0}{e_0}\right]\right\}^t =$$

$$\binom{x_1}{1}\oplus 2\binom{x_1}{3}\oplus\binom{x_0}{1}\oplus 2\binom{x_1}{2}\binom{x_0}{1}\oplus 2\binom{x_1}{3}\binom{x_0}{1}\oplus\binom{x_0}{2}. \tag{4.39}$$

The above example allows us again to observe that the Kronecker-product structure of the various transformation matrices is equivalent to an order-lowering algorithm so that, for example, the matrix A_m^{-1} never must be explicitly evaluated: one has only to deal with the partial transformation matrices $A_{m_i}^{-1}$ (see also section 1.5.3).

One wants to compute the Newton expansion of the same function at the point $(h_1, h_0) = (2, 1)$. One multiplies first the 4-tuples of $[f_e]$ by $[(A_4^2)^{-1}]^t$, that is

$$[(0\ 1\ 0\ 0),\ (1\ 2\ 1\ 1),\ (2\ 2\ 0\ 2),\ (2\ 2\ 0\ 2)]\begin{bmatrix}0 & 0 & 1 & 0\\ 0 & 0 & 0 & 1\\ 1 & -1 & 1 & -1\\ 0 & 1 & -2 & 0\end{bmatrix} =$$

$$[(2\ 2\ 0\ 2),\ (0\ 0\ 0\ 0),\ (1\ 2\ 0\ 1),\ (2\ 0\ 1\ 2)].$$

By applying the transformation matrix

$$[(A_4^1)^{-1}]^t = \begin{bmatrix}0 & 0 & 0 & 1\\ 1 & -1 & 1 & -1\\ 0 & 1 & -2 & 0\\ 0 & 0 & 1 & 0\end{bmatrix}$$

successively to the four 4-tuples of this last matrix, one obtains:

$$[2\ 1\ 1\ 0\ 0\ 0\ 0\ 0\ 2\ 1\ 0\ 2\ 0\ 1\ 0\ 2].$$

The Newton expansion at the point $(h_1, h_0) = (2, 1)$ is then:

$$[2\ 1\ 1\ 0\quad 0\ 0\ 0\ 0\quad 2\ 1\ 0\ 2\quad 0\ 1\ 0\ 2]\left\{\left[\binom{x_1-2}{e_1}\right] \otimes \left[\binom{x_0-1}{e_0}\right]\right\}^t =$$

$$2 \oplus \binom{x_0-1}{1} \oplus \binom{x_0-1}{2} \oplus 2\binom{x_1-2}{2} \oplus \binom{x_1-2}{2}\binom{x_0-1}{1} \oplus 2\binom{x_1-2}{2}\binom{x_0-1}{3}$$

$$\oplus \binom{x_1-2}{3}\binom{x_0-1}{1} \oplus 2\binom{x_1-2}{3}\binom{x_0-1}{3}. \tag{4.40}$$

At this point we wish to compute the ring differences of a discrete function from its value vector; it will be seen that the matrices which allow the computation of these ring differences derive from the matrix A_m and from its inverse A_m^{-1} both defined above in this section.

Consider again first a function $f(x)$ of one variable with $x \in \{0, 1, \ldots, m-1\}$, and let us define the two following $(m \times 1)$ matrices:

$$\left[\frac{Ef}{Ex}\right] = \left[\frac{E^0 f}{Ex} = f, \frac{Ef}{Ex}, \frac{E^2 f}{Ex}, \ldots, \frac{E^{m-1} f}{Ex}\right]^t$$

$$\left[\frac{\Delta f}{\Delta x}\right] = \left[\frac{\Delta^0 f}{\Delta x} = f, \frac{\Delta f}{\Delta x}, \frac{\Delta^2 f}{\Delta x}, \ldots, \frac{\Delta^{m-1} f}{\Delta x}\right]^t.$$

Relations (4.29) and (4.28), for $x_0 = x$ may be stated in the following matrix form respectively:

$$[\mathbf{\Delta} f/\mathbf{\Delta} x] = A_m^{-1}\ [Ef/Ex] \tag{4.41}$$

$$[Ef/Ex] = A_m\ [\mathbf{\Delta} f/\mathbf{\Delta} x]. \tag{4.42}$$

Thanks to the fact that $[Ef/Ex]_{x=0} = [f_e]^t$, that is the transpose of the value vector of $f(x)$, the above relations (4.41) and (4.42) establish the connections between the coefficients appearing in the Newton expansions and the entries of the value vector. From (4.42) one deduces, for example,

$$[f_e]^t = A_m\ [\mathbf{\Delta} f/\mathbf{\Delta} x]_{x=0}. \tag{4.43}$$

The kth element from $[\mathbf{\Delta} f/\mathbf{\Delta} x]$ being $\Delta^k f/\Delta x$ (it is recalled that the elements are numbered from 0 to $m-1$), one deduces from relation (4.41):

$$\left(\frac{\Delta^k f}{\Delta x}\right)_{x=0} = \left[(-1)^k \binom{k}{0}, (-1)^{k+1}\binom{k}{1}, \ldots, (-1)^{(k+m-1)}\binom{k}{m-1}\right] [f_e]^t$$

$$= [a_k^{-1}]\ [f_e]^t,$$

where $[a_k^{-1}]$ is the kth row of the matrix A_m^{-1}.

$$\left(\frac{\Delta^k f}{\Delta x}\right)_{x=1} = \left[(-1)^{(k+m-1)}\binom{k}{m-1}, \ldots, (-1)^k \binom{k}{0}, \ldots, (-1)^{(k+m-2)}\binom{k}{m-2}\right] [f_e]^t$$

$$= [\nabla a_k^{-1}]\, [f_e]^t,$$

where $[\nabla a_k^{-1}]$ means a $(1 \times m)$ matrix obtained by shifting from one column to the right each element of $[a_k^{-1}]$. The $(1 \times m)$ matrix $[\nabla^j a_k^{-1}]$ is obtained by shifting from j columns to the right each element of $[a_k^{-1}]$, or otherwise:

$$[\nabla^j a_k^{-1}] = [\nabla(\nabla^{j-1} a_k^{-1})], \quad 1 \leqslant j \leqslant m-1.$$

The value vector $[\Delta^k f(e)/\Delta x]$ of the kth ring difference of f is then given by the following matrix relation:

$$\left[\frac{\Delta^k f}{\Delta x}(e)\right]^t = \begin{bmatrix} [a_k^{-1}] \\ [\nabla a_k^{-1}] \\ \cdots \\ [\nabla^{m-1} a_k^{-1}] \end{bmatrix} [f_e]^t \tag{4.44}$$

$$= [\nabla^k A_m^{-1}]\, [f_e]^t$$

where $[\nabla^k A_m^{-1}]$ is the $(m \times m)$ matrix obtained from the m $(1 \times m)$ vectors $[\nabla^j a_k^{-1}]$, $0 \leqslant j \leqslant m-1$, as defined by relation (4.44).

The extension of the above formulae to multivariable functions can now easily be performed by the use of the Kronecker product of matrices. The $(1 \times (\Pi m_i))$ matrices $[Ef/Ex]$ and $[\boldsymbol{\Delta} f/\boldsymbol{\Delta} \mathbf{x}]$ are defined as follows respectively:

$$[Ef/E\mathbf{x}] = \left[\bigotimes_{i=n-1,0} (E/Ex_i)\, f(\mathbf{x})\right] \tag{4.45}$$

$$[\boldsymbol{\Delta} f/\boldsymbol{\Delta} \mathbf{x}] = \left[\bigotimes_{i=n-1,0} (\Delta/\Delta x_i)\, f(\mathbf{x})\right]. \tag{4.46}$$

It is recalled that the following symbolical writing is of current use when dealing with operators:

$$(\Delta/\Delta x_i)\,(\Delta/\Delta x_j)\, f = (\Delta/\Delta x_i x_j)\, f = \Delta f/\Delta x_i x_j.$$

The same kind of notation is adopted for any type of operator so that the matrices (4.45) and (4.46) are unambiguously defined.

Theorem 4.5 (for $x_0 = x$) allows us to write:

$$[\Delta f/\Delta x] = A_m^{-1}\ [Ef/Ex] \tag{4.47}$$

$$[Ef/Ex] = A_m\ [\Delta f/\Delta x]. \tag{4.48}$$

Since $[Ef/Ex]_{x=0} = [f_e]^t$, and in view of relation (4.44), one finally obtains the following theorem which provides us with the value vector of the differences in terms of the value vector of the function.

Theorem 4.7

$$\left[\frac{\Delta^k f}{\Delta x}(e)\right]^t = \left[\frac{\Delta^{k_{n-1}\dots k_1 k_0} f}{\Delta x_{n-1}\dots x_1 x_0}(e)\right]^t$$

$$= \left(\bigotimes_{i=n-1,0} [\nabla^{k_i} A_{m_i}^{-1}]\right)\ [f_e]^t. \tag{4.49}$$

The remark made for theorem 4.6 evidently also holds for theorem 4.7: the Kronecker matrix structure of the transformation matrix present in (4.49) is equivalent to an order lowering algorithm.

Example 4.1 (continued). Assume one wants to compute $\Delta^{12} f/\Delta x_1 x_0$ for the discrete function f of example 4.1; the transpose of the value vector has thus to be multiplied by the matrix

$$\nabla A_4^{-1} \otimes \nabla^2 A_4^{-1}.$$

Using the same type of computation scheme as previously, one obtains successively in view of theorem 4.7:

$$\begin{bmatrix} -1 & 1 & 0 & 0 \\ 0 & -1 & 1 & 0 \\ 0 & 0 & -1 & 1 \\ 1 & 0 & 0 & -1 \end{bmatrix} [(0\ 1\ 0\ 0), (1\ 2\ 1\ 1), (2\ 2\ 0\ 2), (2\ 2\ 0\ 2)]^t =$$

$$[(1\ 1\ 1\ 1), (1\ 0\ 2\ 1), (0\ 0\ 0\ 0), (1\ 2\ 0\ 1)]^t.$$

By applying the transformation matrix

$$\begin{bmatrix} 1 & -2 & 1 & 0 \\ 0 & 1 & -2 & 1 \\ 1 & 0 & 1 & -2 \\ -2 & 1 & 0 & 1 \end{bmatrix}$$

to the four 4-tuples of this last vector, one obtains finally:

$$\left[\frac{\Delta^{12} f}{\Delta x_1 x_0}(e_1 e_0)\right]^t = ([\nabla A_4^{-1}] \otimes [\nabla^2 A_4^{-1}])\,[f_{e_1 e_0}]^t$$

$$= [0\ 0\ 0\ 0 \quad 0\ 0\ 1\ 2 \quad 0\ 0\ 0\ 0 \quad 0\ 0\ 2\ 1]^t.$$

4.2.1.1.2. *Switching functions*

When dealing with switching functions, the concept of ring difference reduces to a well-known concept, namely the *Boolean difference* or (equivalently) the *Boolean derivative* (it will be seen further on in this book that these two callings are equivalently meaningful). The concept of Boolean difference, introduced by Reed [1954], has been more thoroughly investigated in papers due to Akers [1959], Sellers, Hsiao and Bearnson [1968], Davio and Piret [1969] and Thayse and Davio [1973]. These Boolean differences constitute the algebraic support of ring expansions of switching functions generally referred to as the *Reed–Muller expansions* (they were indeed first introduced by Reed [1954] and by Muller [1954]) or as the *Taylor–Maclaurin* expansions. The reason for this last denomination will appear clearly in the next chapter; these expansions will be referred in the following as *Reed–Muller expansions.*

Besides the general properties (4.36) of the ring differences, the Boolean differences satisfy the following additional relations.

$$\frac{\Delta f}{\Delta x_i} = f(x_i) \oplus f(x)$$

$$= f(x_i = 0) \oplus f(x_i = 1). \tag{4.50}$$

$\Delta f/\Delta x_i$ is thus degenerate in x_i, and consequently

$$\frac{\Delta}{\Delta x_i}\left(\frac{\Delta f}{\Delta x_i}\right) = 0. \tag{4.51}$$

For switching functions the ring (or Boolean) differences are thus of the form

$$\Delta f/\Delta \boldsymbol{x}_0$$

since $\Delta^{\boldsymbol{k}_0} f/\Delta \boldsymbol{x}_0 = 0$ if there is at least one $k_i > 1$ in $\boldsymbol{k}_0$.

From (4.29) or from (4.50) one deduces:

$$\frac{\Delta f}{\Delta \boldsymbol{x}_0} = \sum_{\boldsymbol{e}_0} f(\boldsymbol{x}_1, \boldsymbol{x}_0^{(\boldsymbol{e}_0)}), \quad \boldsymbol{0} \leqslant \boldsymbol{e}_0 = (e_{q-1}, \ldots, e_1, e_0) \leqslant \boldsymbol{1}$$

$$= \sum_{\boldsymbol{e}_0} f(\boldsymbol{x}_1, \boldsymbol{x}_0 = \boldsymbol{e}_0) \tag{4.52}$$

$$\frac{\Delta \bar{f}}{\Delta x_i} = \frac{\Delta f}{\Delta x_i} \tag{4.53}$$

$$\frac{\Delta (f \vee g)}{\Delta x_i} = \bar{f}\,\frac{\Delta g}{\Delta x_i} \oplus \bar{g}\,\frac{\Delta f}{\Delta x_i} \oplus \frac{\Delta f}{\Delta x_i}\,\frac{\Delta g}{\Delta x_i}. \tag{4.54}$$

Let us now turn to the Reed–Muller expansions of switching functions; since in this case:

$$\binom{x_i \oplus h_i}{0} = 1 \quad \text{and} \quad \binom{x_i \oplus h_i}{1} = x_i \oplus h_i$$

one has:

$$\binom{x_i \oplus h_i}{e_i} = (x_i \oplus h_i)^{e_i}, \quad 0 \leqslant e_i \leqslant 1$$

so that expansion (4.35) becomes:

$$f(\boldsymbol{x}) = \sum_{\boldsymbol{e}} \left(\frac{\Delta^{\boldsymbol{e}} f}{\Delta \boldsymbol{x}}\right)_{\boldsymbol{x}=\boldsymbol{h}} \prod_{i=0}^{n-1} (x_i \oplus h_i)^{e_i} \tag{4.55}$$

which constitutes the Reed–Muller expansion of f at the point $\boldsymbol{h}$.

Let us point out that, for $\boldsymbol{h} = \boldsymbol{0}$, the expansion (4.55) becomes

$$f(\boldsymbol{x}) = \sum_{\boldsymbol{e}} \left(\frac{\Delta^{\boldsymbol{e}} f}{\Delta \boldsymbol{x}}\right)_{\boldsymbol{x}=\boldsymbol{0}} \prod_{i=0}^{n-1} x_i^{e_i}. \tag{4.56}$$

This expansion (sometimes called the *Maclaurin expansion* of the switching function) is also a polynomial in the variables $\boldsymbol{x}$ over GF(2) (see definition 2.24). The coefficients $(\Delta^{\boldsymbol{e}} f/\Delta \boldsymbol{x})_{\boldsymbol{x}=\boldsymbol{0}}$ are thus the elements of the coefficient vector of the polynomial; similarly, since for switching functions

$$x_i \oplus h_i = x_i^{(\bar{h}_i)},$$

the Reed–Muller expansions (4.55) are polynomials in the variables $\boldsymbol{x}^{(\bar{\boldsymbol{h}})}$. It is therefore useful to define more generally a *coefficient vector at the point* $\boldsymbol{h}$ which is the (1×2^n) matrix, the jth element of which is $(\Delta^{\boldsymbol{e}} f/\Delta \boldsymbol{x})_{\boldsymbol{x}=\boldsymbol{h}}, j = \Sigma e_i\, 2^i$.

The obtention of the Reed–Muller expansions for switching functions from any expression of these functions is evidently straightforward by use of the following identities:

$$\begin{aligned} x \vee y &= x \oplus y \oplus xy \\ \bar{x} &= 1 \oplus x \\ x \oplus x &= 0 \end{aligned} \tag{4.57}$$

together with the distributive law.

Example 4.2. The switching function

$$f = \bar{x}_2\bar{x}_1\bar{x}_0 \vee x_1x_0 \vee x_2x_1 \vee x_2x_0 \tag{4.58}$$

may be expressed as a Reed–Muller expansion at $(x_2x_1x_0) = (000)$ by replacing in (4.58) $\bar{x}_i$ by $(x_i \oplus 1)$, $i = 0, 1, 2$ and by using (4.57), i.e.

$$f = 1 \oplus x_0 \oplus x_1 \oplus x_2 \oplus x_0x_1x_2. \tag{4.59}$$

Similarly, the Reed–Muller expansion at $(x_2x_1x_0) = (111)$ is obtained by replacing in (4.58) or in (4.59) x_i by $(1 \oplus \bar{x}_i)$; one obtains:

$$f = 1 \oplus \bar{x}_2\bar{x}_1 \oplus \bar{x}_1\bar{x}_0 \oplus \bar{x}_2\bar{x}_0 \oplus \bar{x}_2\bar{x}_1\bar{x}_0. \tag{4.60}$$

In view of the relations (4.57), Reed–Muller expansions of switching functions are always easily derived from any expression of the switching function. Moreover, the transformation matrices, derived previously in this section for discrete functions, allow us to obtain in a straightforward way any Reed–Muller expansion from the switching function value vector.

Relations (4.16) and (4.17) become in the switching case:

$$[1, x] = [\bar{x}, x] \begin{bmatrix} 1 & 0 \\ 1 & 1 \end{bmatrix}$$

$$[\bar{x}, x] = [1, x] \begin{bmatrix} 1 & 0 \\ 1 & 1 \end{bmatrix}.$$

Thus:

$$A_2 = A_2^{-1} = \begin{bmatrix} 1 & 0 \\ 1 & 1 \end{bmatrix}.$$

In view of theorem 4.6, the Reed–Muller expansion of an n-variable function $f(\boldsymbol{x})$, evaluated at $\boldsymbol{h} = \boldsymbol{0}$, is thus:

$$[f_e] \begin{bmatrix} 1 & 1 \\ 0 & 1 \end{bmatrix}^n \left(\bigotimes_{i=n-1,0} \begin{bmatrix} 1 \\ x_i \end{bmatrix} \right). \tag{4.61}$$

In (4.55) the notation

$$\begin{bmatrix} 1 & 1 \\ 0 & 1 \end{bmatrix}^n$$

means the nth Kronecker power of the matrix $(A_2)^t$, that is:

$$\underbrace{(A_2)^t \otimes (A_2)^t \otimes \ldots . \otimes (A_2)^t}_{n \text{ times}}.$$

The Kronecker product structure of the transformation matrix $[(A_2)^t]^n$ allows us again to avoid the explicit computation of this matrix and to deal with the elementary matrices $(A_2)^t$ only. This is illustrated by the following example.

Example 4.2 (continued). The value vector of the switching function of example 4.2 is:

$$[1 \ 0 \ 0 \ 1 \ \ 0 \ 1 \ 1 \ 1].$$

The algorithm for obtaining from this vector the coefficient vector (evaluated at the point $\boldsymbol{0}$) is then illustrated by means of Figure 4.2 which visualizes the different steps corresponding to the matrix transformation $[(A_2)^t]^n$.

The Reed–Muller expansion at $\boldsymbol{h} = \boldsymbol{0}$ is then obtained by multiplication of the above vector of Figure 4.2 by the matrix

$$\left(\bigotimes_{i=2,0} \begin{bmatrix} 1 \\ x_i \end{bmatrix}\right).$$

One obtains

$$f = 1 \oplus x_0 \oplus x_1 \oplus x_2 \oplus x_2 x_1 x_0.$$

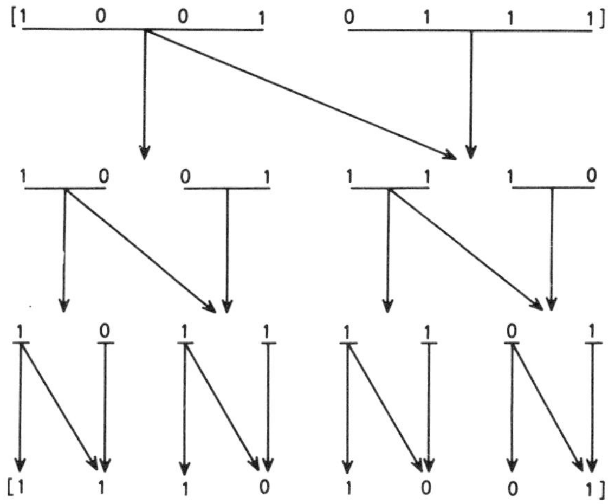

Figure 4.2. Obtention of the coefficient vector from the value vector

While it is generally unnecessary to compute explicitly the matrix $(A_2)^n$, it may be useful to point out that this matrix is the matrix of binomial coefficients evaluated modulo-2; this has been pointed out by Calingaert [1961]. The matrices A_2, $(A_2)^2$, $(A_2)^3$ are respectively:

$$\begin{bmatrix} 1 & 0 \\ 1 & 1 \end{bmatrix} \quad \left[\begin{array}{cc|cc} 1 & 0 & 0 & 0 \\ 1 & 1 & 0 & 0 \\ \hline 1 & 0 & 1 & 0 \\ 1 & 1 & 1 & 1 \end{array}\right] \quad \left[\begin{array}{cccc|cccc} 1 & 0 & 0 & 0 & 0 & 0 & 0 & 0 \\ 1 & 1 & 0 & 0 & 0 & 0 & 0 & 0 \\ 1 & 0 & 1 & 0 & 0 & 0 & 0 & 0 \\ 1 & 1 & 1 & 1 & 0 & 0 & 0 & 0 \\ \hline 1 & 0 & 0 & 0 & 1 & 0 & 0 & 0 \\ 1 & 1 & 0 & 0 & 1 & 1 & 0 & 0 \\ 1 & 0 & 1 & 0 & 1 & 0 & 1 & 0 \\ 1 & 1 & 1 & 1 & 1 & 1 & 1 & 1 \end{array}\right].$$

The matrices have been partitioned to emphasize their recurrent construction. One shows easily (see, for example, Davio [1968]) that the following recurrent form holds:

$$(A_2)^n = \left[\begin{array}{c|c} (A_2)^{n-1} & 0 \\ \hline (A_2)^{n-1} & (A_2)^{n-1} \end{array}\right].$$

Let us now turn to the computation of the Reed–Muller expansion at any point h. The relation (4.37) and the expression of A_2 allow us to state that

$$[f_e]\left(\bigotimes_{i=n-1,0} \begin{bmatrix} \bar{h}_i & 1 \\ h_i & 1 \end{bmatrix}\right)\left(\bigotimes_{i=n-1,0} \begin{bmatrix} 1 \\ x_i^{(\bar{h}_i)} \end{bmatrix}\right) \tag{4.62}$$

is the Reed–Muller expansion of $f(x)$ at $h = (h_{n-1}, \ldots, h_1, h_0)$.

Example 4.2 (continued). One wants to compute the Reed–Muller expansion of the switching function of example 4.2 at $h = (0, 1, 1)$; for $h_i = 0$ and 1, the partial transformation matrices are respectively:

$$\begin{bmatrix} 1 & 1 \\ 0 & 1 \end{bmatrix} \quad \text{and} \quad \begin{bmatrix} 0 & 1 \\ 1 & 1 \end{bmatrix}.$$

The algorithm for obtaining the coefficient vector evaluated at $h = (0, 1, 1)$ is illustrated in Figure 4.3.

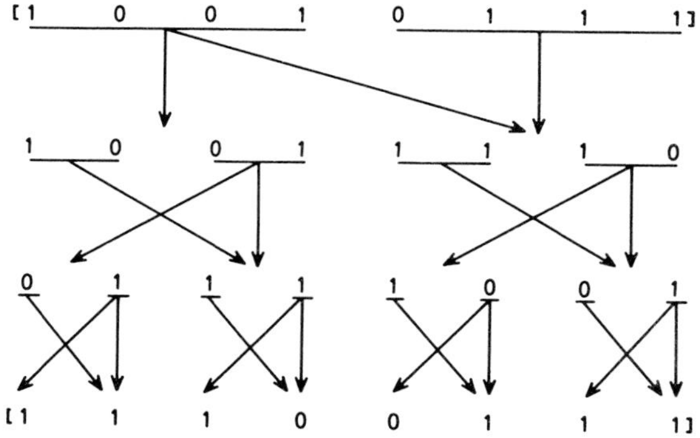

Figure 4.3. Obtention of the coefficient vector at $\boldsymbol{h}$ = (0, 1, 1) from the value vector

The Reed–Muller expansion at $\boldsymbol{h}$ = (0, 1, 1) is then obtained by multiplication of the above vector of Figure 4.3. by the matrix

$$\begin{bmatrix} 1 \\ \\ x_2 \end{bmatrix} \otimes \begin{bmatrix} 1 \\ \\ \bar{x}_1 \end{bmatrix} \otimes \begin{bmatrix} 1 \\ \\ \bar{x}_0 \end{bmatrix}$$

and one obtains accordingly:

$f = 1 \oplus \bar{x}_0 \oplus \bar{x}_1 \oplus x_2\bar{x}_0 \oplus x_2\bar{x}_1 \oplus x_2\bar{x}_1\bar{x}_0.$

The value vector of the differences is obtained from the value vector of f by application of theorem 4.7. Let us observe that the formalism of theorem 3.12 leads to the same result. Indeed, since for switching functions the join differences and the ring differences are respectively:

$$qf/qx_0 = \bigvee_{e_0} f(x_1, e_0)$$

$$\Delta f/\Delta x_0 = \bigoplus_{e_0} f(x_1, e_0)$$

one obtains the ring differences by replacing in the formal expression of the join differences the disjunction operation by the ring-sum operation; theorem 3.12 allows us to write:

$$\left[\frac{\Delta^k f}{\Delta x}(e)\right] = [f_e] \left(\bigotimes_{i=n-1,0} E_{k_i}\right) \tag{4.63}$$

with $k = (k_{n-1}, \ldots, k_1, k_0)$, $0 \leqslant k_i \leqslant 1$.

$$E_{k_i} = \begin{bmatrix} 1 & k_i \\ k_i & 1 \end{bmatrix}.$$

The above relations and computational formulae were deduced in a straightforward way from corresponding theorems which were derived in the frame of multiple-valued discrete functions. The theorems and algorithms derived below apply to switching functions only.

Recently, attention has been paid to the development of algorithms for determination of Reed–Muller expansions of switching functions from a disjunctive (or sum of products) representation of these functions. The main originality of the methods proposed in the following proceeds from the nature of the data, i.e. a disjunctive normal form.

Fisher [1974] derives a first algorithm allowing the determination of Reed–Muller expansions at a given point. Davio and Bioul [1974] present some theorems on ring-sum transformations duality which allow a simpler derivation of Fisher's method. Together with a suitable cube notation, an improvement of the method is given in order to avoid too prohibitive an increase of the computation.

Consider a switching function $f(\boldsymbol{x})$; the truth vector of that function is denoted by $[f_e]$; we also consider the $\boldsymbol{h}$-Reed–Muller expansion of $f(\boldsymbol{x})$, i.e. the Reed–Muller expansion of $f(\boldsymbol{x})$ at $\boldsymbol{x} = \boldsymbol{h}$. The coefficients of the $\boldsymbol{h}$-Reed–Muller expansion, expressed in the base (called $\boldsymbol{h}$-Reed–Muller or $\boldsymbol{h}$-R–M base) namely:

$$\bigotimes_{i=n-1,0} \begin{bmatrix} \bar{x}_i^{h_i} \\ x_i^{\bar{h}_i} \end{bmatrix}$$

form the vector [R–M $f_{\boldsymbol{h}}$] called $\boldsymbol{h}$-Reed–Muller vector (and also for sake of conciseness $\boldsymbol{h}$-R–M vector) of $f(\boldsymbol{x})$.

One has:

$$\begin{bmatrix} \bar{x}_i^{h_i} \\ x_i^{\bar{h}_i} \end{bmatrix} = \begin{bmatrix} 1 \\ x_i \end{bmatrix} \quad \text{iff } h_i = 0$$

$$= \begin{bmatrix} \bar{x}_i \\ 1 \end{bmatrix} \quad \text{iff } h_i = 1.$$

Let us note that another type of basis (see (4.62)), namely:

$$\begin{bmatrix} 1 \\ x_i^{(\bar{h}_i)} \end{bmatrix} = \begin{bmatrix} 1 \\ x_i \end{bmatrix} \quad \text{iff } h_i = 0$$

$$= \begin{bmatrix} 1 \\ \bar{x}_i \end{bmatrix} \quad \text{iff } h_i = 1.$$

was also used precedently in this section. It should be noted that both types of bases are meaningful for switching functions since they are both used to reduce the complexity of different minimization problems (see Chapter 6).

The *h-transform* of $f(\boldsymbol{x})$ is the switching function $f^h(\boldsymbol{x})$ defined by:

$$[f_e^h] = [\text{R–M}\ f_h]$$

or equivalently by

$$[\text{R–M}\ f_h^h] = [f_e].$$

The above relations simply express the fact that the functions $f(\boldsymbol{x})$ and $f^h(\boldsymbol{x})$ have interchanged truth and h-R–M vectors, and it turns out that the computation of the h-R–M vectors of $f(\boldsymbol{x})$ may be replaced by that of the truth vector of its h-R–M transform $f^h(\boldsymbol{x})$. This property has no computational impact whenever $f(\boldsymbol{x})$ is given by its truth vector; it becomes however a key point for other representations of $f(\boldsymbol{x})$ such as a disjunctive (normal) form.

The following theorem expresses two elementary properties of the h-transform.

Theorem 4.8. (a) *The* **h***-transform of the* **h***-transform of $f(\boldsymbol{x})$ is $f(\boldsymbol{x})$ itself (involution law).*

(b) $[(f^h \oplus g^h)_e] = [f_e^h] \oplus [g_e^h]$ *(morphism).*

Proof. These two properties are immediately understood in terms of the linear transformation that relates the minterm and the h-Reed–Muller bases. In these terms (a) expresses that the transformation matrix is its own inverse, while (b) results from the distributivity of the matrix product. ∎

It is rather easy to derive a ring-sum of products representation of $f(\boldsymbol{x})$. Theorem 4.8(b) then points out that the computation of the h-transform is immediate if a method of obtaining the h-transform of a cube is available. This is the purpose of theorem 4.9.

Lemma 4.5. The **h***-transform of the minterm*

$$m = \prod_{i \in I} x_i^{(\bar{h}_i)} \prod_{j \in J} x_j^{(h_j)}$$

is given by:

$$m^h = \prod_{i \in I} x_i^{(\bar{h}_i)}.$$

Proof. The enumeration order of the vectors in the h-Reed–Muller basis is derived from the usual minterm enumeration order by replacing by 1 the variables $x_j^{(\bar{h}_j)}$ that appear in the minterms with the unsuited polarity. Let now $\phi = \prod_{i \in I} x_i^{(\bar{h}_i)}$. It is clear from the above remark that $[m_e]$ and $[\phi_e^h]$ both have a single 1 and in the same position. Thus $\phi = m^h$. ■

Theorem 4.9. The h-transform of the cube

$$c = \prod_{i \in I} x_i^{(\bar{h}_i)} \prod_{j \in J} x_j^{(h_j)}$$

is given by

$$c^h = \prod_{i \in I} x_i^{(\bar{h}_i)} \prod_{k \in K} x_k^{(h_k)},$$

where K denotes the set of variables missing in c.

Proof. The expression of c is first expanded in a ring-sum of minterms, then transformed according to theorem 4.8(b) and lemma 4.5. That procedure immediately yields the announced result. ■

The above discussion immediately suggests an algorithm for obtaining the h-Reed–Muller expansion of $f(x)$ from an arbitrary initial representation R of $f(x)$ (e.g. a disjunctive form).

Algorithm 4.1

(a) Obtain from the given representation R of $f(x)$ a representation R' as a ring-sum of products.
(b) By theorems 4.8(b) and 4.9 obtain a representation S of $f^h(x)$ as a ring-sum of products.
(c) From S obtain the representation S' of $f^h(x)$ as a ring-sum of minterms.
(d) In S' replace by 1 the literals $x_j^{(h_j)}$. The obtained expression T is the h-Reed–Muller expansion of $f(x)$.

Remarks

1. In an actual computation, a ternary encoding of the cubes will be used; for instance, one might assume that x_i is represented by

X iff $i \in J$

1 iff $i \in I$

0 iff $i \in K$.

With such an encoding, steps (b) and (d) of algorithm 4.1 merely reduce to a change of the coding interpretation: they may thus be considered as computation-free. Attention has thus to be focused on steps (a) and (c) which are the significant ones from the computational point of view.

2. Algorithm 4.1 is essentially the algorithm presented by Fisher [1974] under a more complicated interpretation in terms of unateness properties. The concept of h-transform, introduced for unifying purposes, is even not essential to the understanding of algorithm 4.1. Some reflection shows indeed that the computations involved by algorithm 4.1 may be interpreted either in the minterm base of the h-transform or in the h-Reed–Muller base of the function f itself. Under the latter interpretation, Fisher's algorithm appears as a systematic procedure for performing the substitutions

$$x_i^{(h_i)} = 1 \oplus x_i^{(\bar{h}_i)}$$

implied by the Reed [1954] and Muller [1954] argument and for carrying out the necessary products and term cancellations.

3. To transform a disjunctive form into an equivalent ring-sum form, Fisher generates a set of pairwise disjoint cubes called *ON′-array* and equivalent to the cubical representations (see section 2.2.2).

It is possible to avoid the generation of the ON′-array by recursive use of the classical formula

$$a \vee b = a \oplus b \oplus ab$$

under the following computation scheme:

$$\left(\sum P_i\right) \vee [P \vee (\vee\, Q_j)] = \left(P \oplus \sum P_i \oplus P \sum P_i\right) \vee (\vee\, Q_j).$$

It may happen that this procedure, called hereafter generation of a P-form, yields less cubes in R' than any corresponding ON′-array.

Example 4.3. Compute the (1010101)-Reed–Muller expansion of the function $f(x_6, x_5, x_4, x_3, x_2, x_1, x_0)$ given by the following disjunctive form:

$$f(x) = x_2 x_1 x_0 \vee x_5 \bar{x}_4 x_3 \vee x_6 \bar{x}_3 \bar{x}_1 \vee \bar{x}_6 \bar{x}_5 x_0.$$

Step (a). The P-form corresponding to $f(x)$ is first produced according to the above remark (3).

$$f(x) = x_2 x_1 x_0 \oplus x_5 \bar{x}_4 x_3 \oplus x_5 \bar{x}_4 x_3 x_2 x_1 x_0 \oplus x_6 \bar{x}_3 \bar{x}_1 \oplus \bar{x}_6 \bar{x}_5 x_0 \oplus \bar{x}_6 \bar{x}_5 x_2 x_1 x_0.$$

Step (b). By theorems 4.8(b) and 4.9 one obtains

$$f^h(x) = x_6 \bar{x}_5 x_4 \bar{x}_3 x_1 \oplus x_6 x_5 \bar{x}_4 x_3 x_2 \bar{x}_1 x_0 \oplus x_6 x_5 \bar{x}_4 x_3 x_1 \oplus \bar{x}_5 x_4 x_2 x_0 \oplus \bar{x}_6 x_4 \bar{x}_3 x_2 \bar{x}_1 \oplus \bar{x}_6 x_4 \bar{x}_3 x_1.$$

Step (c). Minterm generation and cancellation.

$$
f^h(x) = \left\{ \begin{array}{lll}
x_6\bar{x}_5x_4\bar{x}_3\bar{x}_2x_1\bar{x}_0 & \cancel{\bar{x}_6\bar{x}_5x_4\bar{x}_3x_2\bar{x}_1x_0} & \bar{x}_6\bar{x}_5x_4\bar{x}_3\bar{x}_2x_1\bar{x}_0 \\
x_6\bar{x}_5x_4\bar{x}_3\bar{x}_2x_1x_0 & \cancel{\bar{x}_6\bar{x}_5x_4\bar{x}_3x_2x_1x_0} & \bar{x}_6\bar{x}_5x_4\bar{x}_3\bar{x}_2x_1x_0 \\
x_6\bar{x}_5x_4\bar{x}_3x_2x_1\bar{x}_0 & \bar{x}_6\bar{x}_5x_4x_3x_2\bar{x}_1x_0 & \bar{x}_6\bar{x}_5x_4\bar{x}_3x_2x_1\bar{x}_0 \\
\cancel{x_6\bar{x}_5x_4\bar{x}_3x_2x_1x_0} & \bar{x}_6\bar{x}_5x_4x_3x_2x_1x_0 & \cancel{\bar{x}_6\bar{x}_5x_4\bar{x}_3x_2x_1x_0} \\
 & x_6\bar{x}_5x_4\bar{x}_3x_2\bar{x}_1x_0 & \bar{x}_6x_5x_4\bar{x}_3\bar{x}_2x_1\bar{x}_0 \\
x_6x_5\bar{x}_4x_3x_2\bar{x}_1x_0 & \cancel{x_6\bar{x}_5x_4\bar{x}_3x_2x_1x_0} & \bar{x}_6x_5x_4\bar{x}_3\bar{x}_2x_1x_0 \\
 & x_6\bar{x}_5x_4x_3x_2\bar{x}_1x_0 & \bar{x}_6x_5x_4\bar{x}_3x_2x_1\bar{x}_0 \\
x_6x_5\bar{x}_4x_3\bar{x}_2x_1\bar{x}_0 & x_6\bar{x}_5x_4x_3x_2x_1x_0 & \bar{x}_6x_5x_4\bar{x}_3x_2x_1x_0 \\
x_6x_5\bar{x}_4x_3\bar{x}_2x_1x_0 & & \\
x_6x_5\bar{x}_4x_3x_2x_1\bar{x}_0 & \bar{x}_6\bar{x}_5x_4\bar{x}_3x_2\bar{x}_1\bar{x}_0 & \\
x_6x_5\bar{x}_4x_3x_2x_1x_0 & \cancel{\bar{x}_6\bar{x}_5x_4\bar{x}_3x_2\bar{x}_1x_0} & \\
 & \bar{x}_6x_5x_4\bar{x}_3x_2\bar{x}_1\bar{x}_0 & \\
 & \bar{x}_6x_5x_4\bar{x}_3x_2\bar{x}_1x_0 &
\end{array} \right\}
$$

Step (d). Deletion of the occurrences of $x_6, \bar{x}_5, x_4, \bar{x}_3, x_2, \bar{x}_1, x_0$

$$
\begin{aligned}
f(x) = {} & \bar{x}_2x_1\bar{x}_0 \oplus \bar{x}_2x_1 \oplus x_1\bar{x}_0 \oplus x_5\bar{x}_4x_3 \oplus x_5\bar{x}_4x_3\bar{x}_2x_1\bar{x}_0 \oplus x_5\bar{x}_4x_3\bar{x}_2x_1 \oplus \\
& x_5\bar{x}_4x_3x_1\bar{x}_0 \oplus x_5\bar{x}_4x_3x_1 \oplus \bar{x}_6x_3 \oplus \bar{x}_6x_5x_1 \oplus \bar{x}_6x_3x_1 \oplus 1 \oplus x_3 \oplus \\
& x_3x_1 \oplus \bar{x}_6\bar{x}_0 \oplus \bar{x}_6x_5\bar{x}_0 \oplus \bar{x}_6x_5 \oplus \bar{x}_6x_5x_1\bar{x}_0 \oplus \bar{x}_6\bar{x}_2x_1\bar{x}_0 \oplus \\
& \bar{x}_6\bar{x}_2x_1 \oplus \bar{x}_6x_1\bar{x}_0 \oplus \bar{x}_6x_5\bar{x}_2x_1\bar{x}_0 \oplus \bar{x}_6x_5\bar{x}_2x_1.
\end{aligned}
$$

This is the (1010101)-Reed–Muller expansion of $f(x)$. It contains 23 terms.

Remarks

4. Thanks to the coding described previously in remark (1) the expression provided in step (a) gives

$x_2x_1x_0$	0000X1X
$x_5\bar{x}_4x_3$	0111000
$x_5\bar{x}_4x_3x_2x_1x_0$	0111X1X
$x_6\bar{x}_3\bar{x}_1$	X00X0X0
$\bar{x}_6\bar{x}_5x_0$	1X0000X
$\bar{x}_6\bar{x}_5x_2x_1x_0$	1X00X1X

Inversion of the coding assumptions for 0 and X provides readily the coded expression given in step (b). Minterm generation is thus achieved by assignation in all ways of the values 0, 1 to the X's. After cancellation, minterms are decoded according to the initial code, i.e. 1 for **h**-polarity variables and 0 for missing variables.

5. The best ON′-array is the following

$$x_6\bar{x}_5x_2x_1x_0 \oplus x_5x_4x_2x_1x_0 \oplus x_5\bar{x}_4\bar{x}_3x_2x_1x_0 \oplus \bar{x}_6\bar{x}_5x_0 \oplus x_6\bar{x}_3\bar{x}_1 \oplus x_5\bar{x}_4x_3$$

obtained from the recursive application of the sharp operation (#-operation described in Miller [1965]). It contains 6 terms; however the following steps of the algorithm become harder because 45 minterms are now generated instead of 29. Other ON′-arrays have been produced which generated more than 100 minterms at the third step.

6. One has seen that the algorithm contains two main parts in the computation: the ring-sum form production and the minterm counting. The complexity of the first part is not negligible with regard to the second one. It is thus important to take it into account in any estimation of complexity.

Two methods have been described for ring-sum array construction: the ON′-array and the *P*-form generation. The #-operation needed by the first one involves more computation than the simple Boolean cube product implied by the second one. However the number of terms of an ON′-array never exceeds 2^n while 3^n terms can occur in a *P*-form.

The ON′-array is nevertheless not always the best as it appeared in the foregoing example. Moreover it must be noticed that the ring-sum array having the least number of terms is not always generating the least number of minterms in the third step of the algorithm. The choice of the method is thus not straightforward. One can expect however that for disjunctive form data involving a small number of terms with respect to 2^n, the *P*-form generation will often be more economical.

7. Let us compare now the algorithm 4.1 (A_1) with the Kronecker product method (A_3) described by relation (4.62).

Let the data be a disjunction of *P* cubes. Roughly, the complexity of truth table generation (A_3) has the same order of magnitude as the one of minterm generation in step (c) of A_1. This will not be the case if the number of cubes involved in the ring-sum form (step (a) of A_1) is much greater than P. It remains to compare the ring-sum form computation requirement (A_1) with $n.\ 2^{n-1}$: number of elementary modulo-2 requested by A_3. Obviously, whenever P is small the ring-sum form is easily provided for any n. However, if P is great the computation becomes quickly unmanageable; the number of pairwise comparisons has an order of magnitude greater than $\binom{P}{2}$; the number of elementary operations to be performed is thus greater than $K\binom{P}{2}$ where K takes into account an average number of operations to be performed after each comparison. The factor $K\binom{P}{2}$ dominates $n\,.\,2^{n-1}$ when P increases too much.

In conclusion the algorithm 4.1 is suitable for small P and large n, while A_3 appears as the best in most other cases.

The analysis of the foregoing example easily shows that step (c) of algorithm 4.1 is particularly computation consuming: this is due to the number of minterm generations needed.

A modification of algorithm 4.1 may be based on the following observation. If one disposes of a representation of $f^h(\boldsymbol{x})$ as a ring-sum of pairwise disjoint cubes, then all the minterms generated along step (c) will be distinct, i.e. no cancellation can happen. The terms of the h-Reed–Muller expansion of $f(\boldsymbol{x})$ may be written at once.

The following algorithm 4.2 generates from a ring-sum of cubes an equivalent ring-sum of disjoint cubes. The cubes of the given ring-sum are introduced one by one. Algorithm 4.2 thus only describes the introduction of a cube Q into a set $P_i \mid i \in I$ of pairwise disjoint cubes. The algorithm rests on the two following observations

1. $$\sum_{i \in I}\!\!\!\!\!\bigcirc\; P_i \oplus Q = \sum_{i \in I}\!\!\!\!\!\bigcirc\; P_i \bar{Q} \oplus Q \prod_{i \in I} \bar{P}_i.$$

The formula is obvious since the P_i are pairwise disjoint. Now, all the summed terms in the right-hand member of this formula are pairwise disjoint. Hence, the problem at hand will be solved if we obtain representations of $P_i\bar{Q}(\forall i)$ and of $Q\,\Pi\bar{P}_i$ as ring-sums of pairwise disjoint cubes.

2. It is easy to obtain a representation of the complement $\bar{c}$ of a cube

$$c = \prod_{i=1}^{p} c_i$$

as a ring-sum of pairwise disjoint cubes. Indeed:

$$\bar{c} = \bigvee_{i=1}^{p} \bar{c}_i = \bigvee_{i=1}^{p}\left(\bar{c}_i \prod_{j=1}^{i-1} c_j\right),$$

i.e.

$$\bar{c} = \sum_{i=1}^{p}\!\!\!\!\!\bigcirc\;\left(\bar{c}_i \prod_{j=1}^{i-1} c_j\right).$$

Algorithm 4.2. This algorithm generates, from a set $S = \{P_i, i \in I\}$ of pairwise disjoint cubes and from a cube Q, a set S' of pairwise disjoint cubes the ring-sum of which is equal to $\sum P_i \oplus Q$.

(a) Compute the products P_iQ. Let

$$I_1 = \{i \mid P_iQ = 0\}$$

and

$$I_2 = \{i \mid P_iQ \neq 0\}.$$

Put in S' the cubes P_i $(i \in I_1)$ and the cubes $P_i\bar{Q}(i \in I_2)$ computed according to the observation (2) hereabove.

(b) (Recursive computation of $Q \prod_i \bar{P}_i$). For sake of simplicity, we relabel the cubes P_i in such a way that

$$I_2 = \{1, 2, \dots, k\}.$$

Step (b) is then performed for $i = 1, 2, \dots, k$. One assumes available a representation of $Q\bar{P}_1\bar{P}_2 \dots \bar{P}_{i-1}$ as a set S_{i-1} of pairwise disjoint cubes. Let $S_{i-1} = \{Q_j \mid j \in J\}$. Compute the products Q_jP_i $(\forall j \in J)$ and put

$$J_1 = \{j \mid Q_jP_i = 0\}$$

and

$$J_2 = \{j \mid Q_jP_i \neq 0\}.$$

Put in S_i the cubes $Q_j(j \in J_1)$ and the cubes $Q_j\bar{P}_i(j \in J_2)$ computed according to observation (2) above.

Algorithm 4.3

(1) *Definition and notations.* Let the expression

$$\left\langle \prod_{j \in J} x_j^{(\bar{h}_j)} \right\rangle$$

be the ring-sum of the cubes containing

$$\prod_{j \in J} x_j^{(\bar{h}_j)};$$

one calls ***h*-*cube*** an expression such as

$$\prod_{i \in I} x_i^{(\bar{h}_i)} \left\langle \prod_{j \in J} x_j^{(\bar{h}_j)} \right\rangle$$

Obviously the hereabove ***h***-cube is the Boolean equivalent of the cube

$$c = \prod_{i \in I} x_i^{(\bar{h}_i)} \left\langle \prod_{j \in J} x_j^{(\bar{h}_j)} \right\rangle.$$

The usefulness of the notion of h-cube is twofold: the h-Reed–Muller expansion of any cube is readily obtained from complementing then bracketing the $\bar{h}$-polarity variables: h-cube provides a suitable condensed notation for a complex ring-sum. In what follows, two h-cubes will be called ***h*-*disjoint*** iff they do not contain any common cube in their ring-sum expansion.

(2) *First statement of the algorithm.*

(a) Obtain from the given representation R of $f(\boldsymbol{x})$ a representation R' as a ring-sum of products (cf. algorithm 4.1).

(b) Obtain from R' a ring-sum R'' of h-cubes.

(c) Obtain from R'' a pairwise h-disjoint h-cubes set. The remaining expression is the h-Reed–Muller expansion of $f(\boldsymbol{x})$ expressed as a ring-sum of h-cubes.

Remark

8. h-Transforms of h-cubes are easily derived thanks to the fact that h-cubes are actually cubes. Moreover, it is easy to point out the isomorphism existing between the cube development of any h-cube and the minterm development of its h-transform. It follows that pairwise h-disjoint h-cubes computation is isomorphic to pairwise disjoint h-transformed cubes generation.

(3) *Second statement of the algorithm.*

(a) Does not change.

(b) Obtain a representation S of $f^h(\boldsymbol{x})$ as a ring-sum of products (cf. algorithm 4.1).

(c) By algorithm 4.2 obtain from S a representation S' of $f^h(\boldsymbol{x})$ as a ring-sum of pairwise disjoint products.

(d) In any cube of S', replace by 1 the literals $x_j^{(h_j)}$ and by $\left\langle \prod_{k \in K} x_k^{(\bar{h}_k)} \right\rangle$ the missing variables x_k.

The remaining expression is the h-Reed–Muller expansion of $f(\boldsymbol{x})$ expressed as a ring-sum of h-cubes.

Example 4.3 (continued). Resume the example 4.3. After step (b) one gets:

$$x_6\bar{x}_5x_4\bar{x}_3x_1 \oplus x_6x_5\bar{x}_4x_3x_2\bar{x}_1x_0 \oplus x_6x_5\bar{x}_4x_3x_1 \oplus \bar{x}_5x_4x_2x_0 \oplus$$
$$\bar{x}_6x_4\bar{x}_3x_2\bar{x}_1 \oplus \bar{x}_6x_4\bar{x}_3x_1.$$

Step (c) pairwise disjoint cubes generation.

The first three terms are pairwise disjoint; the fourth has a non-void intersection with the first one. Then:

$$x_6\bar{x}_5x_4\bar{x}_3x_1 \to x_6\bar{x}_5x_4\bar{x}_3x_1\,(\overline{\bar{x}_5x_4x_2x_0}) = x_6\bar{x}_5x_4\bar{x}_3\bar{x}_2x_1 \oplus x_6\bar{x}_5x_4\bar{x}_3x_2x_1\bar{x}$$

$x_6x_5\bar{x}_4x_3x_2\bar{x}_1x_0$: disjoint

$x_6x_5\bar{x}_4x_3x_1$: disjoint

$$\bar{x}_5x_4x_2x_0 \to \bar{x}_5x_4x_2x_0\,(\overline{x_6\bar{x}_5x_4\bar{x}_3x_1}) = \bar{x}_6\bar{x}_5x_4x_2x_0 \oplus x_6\bar{x}_5x_4x_3x_2x_0 \oplus$$
$$x_6\bar{x}_5x_4\bar{x}_3x_2\bar{x}_1x_0.$$

One introduces now $\bar{x}_6 x_4 \bar{x}_3 x_2 \bar{x}_1$ in the above set, then:

$x_6 \bar{x}_5 x_4 \bar{x}_3 \bar{x}_2 x_1$: disjoint

$x_6 \bar{x}_5 x_4 \bar{x}_3 x_2 x_1 \bar{x}_0$: disjoint

$x_6 x_5 \bar{x}_4 x_3 x_2 \bar{x}_1 x_0$: disjoint

$x_6 x_5 \bar{x}_4 x_3 x_1$: disjoint

$\bar{x}_6 \bar{x}_5 x_4 x_2 x_0 \to \bar{x}_6 \bar{x}_5 x_4 x_2 x_0\ (\overline{\bar{x}_6 x_4 \bar{x}_3 x_2 \bar{x}_1}) = \bar{x}_6 \bar{x}_5 x_4 x_3 x_2 x_0 \oplus$
$\bar{x}_6 \bar{x}_5 x_4 \bar{x}_3 x_2 x_1 x_0$

$x_6 \bar{x}_5 x_4 x_3 x_2 x_0$: disjoint

$x_6 \bar{x}_5 x_4 \bar{x}_3 x_2 \bar{x}_1 x_0$: disjoint

$\bar{x}_6 x_4 \bar{x}_3 x_2 \bar{x}_1 \to \bar{x}_6 x_4 \bar{x}_3 x_2 \bar{x}_1\ (\overline{\bar{x}_6 \bar{x}_5 x_4 x_2 x_0}) = \bar{x}_6 x_5 x_4 \bar{x}_3 x_2 \bar{x}_1 \oplus$
$\bar{x}_6 \bar{x}_5 x_4 \bar{x}_3 x_2 \bar{x}_1 \bar{x}_0$.

Finally one introduces $\bar{x}_6 x_4 \bar{x}_3 x_1$,

$x_6 \bar{x}_5 x_4 \bar{x}_3 \bar{x}_2 x_1$: disjoint

$x_6 \bar{x}_5 x_4 \bar{x}_3 x_2 x_1 \bar{x}_0$: disjoint

$x_6 x_5 \bar{x}_4 x_3 x_2 \bar{x}_1 x_0$: disjoint

$x_6 x_5 \bar{x}_4 x_3 x_1$: disjoint

$\bar{x}_6 \bar{x}_5 x_4 x_3 x_2 x_0$: disjoint

$\bar{x}_6 \bar{x}_5 x_4 \bar{x}_3 x_2 x_1 x_0 \to \bar{x}_6 \bar{x}_5 x_4 \bar{x}_3 x_2 x_1 x_0 (\overline{\bar{x}_6 x_4 \bar{x}_3 x_1}) = \phi$

$x_6 \bar{x}_5 x_4 x_3 x_2 x_0$: disjoint

$x_6 \bar{x}_5 x_4 \bar{x}_3 x_2 \bar{x}_1 x_0$: disjoint

$\bar{x}_6 x_5 x_4 \bar{x}_3 x_2 \bar{x}_1$: disjoint

$\bar{x}_6 \bar{x}_5 x_4 \bar{x}_3 x_2 \bar{x}_1 \bar{x}_0$: disjoint

$\bar{x}_6 x_4 \bar{x}_3 x_1 \to \bar{x}_6 x_4 \bar{x}_3 x_1\ (\overline{\bar{x}_6 \bar{x}_5 x_4 \bar{x}_3 x_2 x_1 x_0}) = \bar{x}_6 x_5 \bar{x}_3 x_1 \oplus$

$\bar{x}_6 \bar{x}_5 x_4 \bar{x}_3 \bar{x}_2 x_1 \oplus \bar{x}_6 \bar{x}_5 x_4 \bar{x}_3 x_2 x_1 \bar{x}_0$.

In terms of h-cubes the solution is written as

$$\bar{x}_2 x_1 \langle \bar{x}_0 \rangle \oplus x_1 \bar{x}_0 \oplus x_5 \bar{x}_4 x_3 \oplus x_5 \bar{x}_4 x_3 x_1 \langle \bar{x}_2 \bar{x}_0 \rangle \oplus \bar{x}_6 x_3 \langle x_1 \rangle \oplus x_3 \langle x_1 \rangle \oplus 1 \oplus$$

$$\bar{x}_6 x_5 \langle \bar{x}_0 \rangle \oplus \bar{x}_6 \bar{x}_0 \oplus \bar{x}_6 x_5 x_1 \langle \bar{x}_2 \bar{x}_0 \rangle \oplus \bar{x}_6 \bar{x}_2 x_1 \langle \bar{x}_0 \rangle \oplus \bar{x}_6 x_1 \bar{x}_0.$$

Remark

9. According to the coding given by remark (1) the hereabove computation reduces to the following:

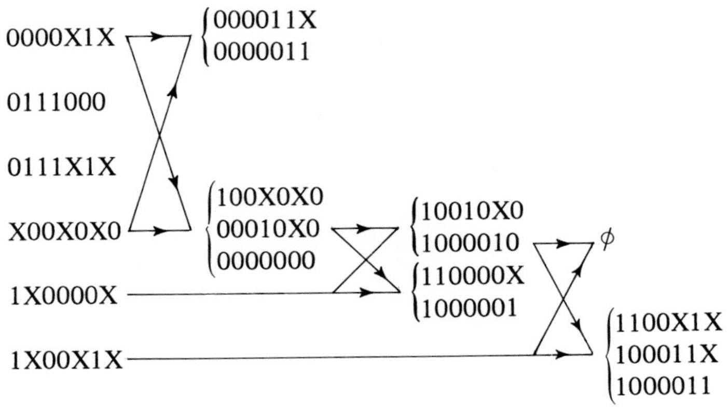

According to step (d) the decoding is now defined as

$$0 \to 1 \quad i \in K \text{ (missing variables)}$$

$$1 \to x_i^{(\bar{e}_i)} \quad i \in I$$

$$X \to \langle \ldots x_i^{(\bar{e}_i)} \ldots \rangle \quad i \in J.$$

Thanks to the coding, steps (b) and (d) remain computation free as in algorithm 4.1.

Concluding remark

The complexity of the foregoing algorithm depends more on the data than on the number of variables, the same remark holds for Fisher's method. Though those algorithms are not always the best, they can be very useful in some particular cases unmanageable by methods requesting truth table. One has shown that those suitable cases are characterized by a small number of cubes in the given disjunctive form and a large number of variables. The last algorithm presents some advantages compared to that of Fisher. First, one can save a lot of computation by avoiding minterm generation. For the same reason the memory span becomes smaller. Finally, the expression of the results (h-cubes ring-sum) is more condensed and therefore more useful for further processing.

4.2.1.2. The step functions base and the Nyquist expansions

Using similar notations as for the lattice exponentiation (see, for example, theorem 3.4) one will write:

$$\tilde{x}_i^{a_i]} \quad \text{instead of} \quad \tilde{x}_i^{[0,a_i]}$$

and

$$\tilde{x}_i^{[a_i} \text{ instead of } \tilde{x}_i^{[a_i, m_i - 1]}.$$

These functions will be called *step functions* since they define a separation of the domain S by a hyperplane orthogonal to the ith coordinate axis and assume the value 0 on one side of that hyperplane and the value 1 on the other side.

Consider first a one-variable function: $\{0, 1, \ldots, m-1\} \to \{0, 1, \ldots, r-1\}$; the following lemma is an immediate consequence of the definitions of the functions $\tilde{x}^{[i}$ and $\tilde{x}^{(i)}$.

Lemma 4.6

$$\text{(a) } \tilde{x}^{[k} = \sum_{e=0}^{m-1} \tilde{e}^{[k} \tilde{x}^{(e)} \tag{4.64}$$

$$0 \leqslant k \leqslant m-1$$

$$\text{(b) } \tilde{x}^{[k} = \tilde{x}^{[k} - \tilde{x}^{[k+1} \tag{4.65}$$

(It is conventionally assumed that $\tilde{x}^{[m} = 0$.)

The set of step functions $\tilde{x}^{[k}$ constitutes a basis for the discrete functions; define the matrices:

$[\tilde{x}^{[e}]$ is the $(1 \times m)$ matrix the eth entry of which is $\tilde{x}^{[e}$

$D_m = [d_{ij}]$ is the $(m \times m)$ matrix with $d_{ij} = \tilde{i}^{[j}$.

Lemma 4.6 may then be stated in the following matrix form which corresponds to relation 4.1:

$$[\tilde{x}^{[e}] = [\tilde{x}^{(e)}]\, D_m.$$

The inverse matrix $D_m^{-1} = [d'_{ij}]$ is deduced from (4.65):

$D_m^{-1} = [d'_{ij}]$ is an $(m \times m)$ matrix with

$d'_{00} = 1, d'_{01} = d'_{02} = \ldots = d'_{0(m-1)} = 0$

$d'_{i(i-1)} = -1, d'_{ii} = 1, d'_{ij} = 0$, for $i \geqslant 1, j \neq (i-1)$ and $j \neq i$.

The matrices D_m and D_m^{-1} are schematized below

$$D_m = \begin{bmatrix} 1 & & & & & & \\ 1 & 1 & & & & & \\ 1 & 1 & 1 & & & & \\ \cdot & & & \cdot & & & \\ \cdot & & & & \cdot & & \\ \cdot & & & & & \cdot & \\ 1 & 1 & 1 & \cdot & \cdot & \cdot & 1 \end{bmatrix}, \quad D_m^{-1} = \begin{bmatrix} 1 & & & & & \\ -1 & 1 & & & & \\ & -1 & 1 & & & \\ & & -1 & 1 & & \\ & & & \cdot & \cdot & \\ & & & & \cdot & \cdot \\ & & & & -1 & 1 \end{bmatrix}$$

One has thus also

$$[\tilde{x}^{(e)}] = [\tilde{x}^{[e}]\ D_m^{-1}.$$

To the basis of step functions:

$$b = \{\tilde{x}^{[0}, \tilde{x}^{[1}, \ldots, \tilde{x}^{[m-1}\}$$

corresponds thus the dual basis:

$$b' = \{\tilde{x}^{(0)} - \tilde{x}^{(1)}, \tilde{x}^{(1)} - x^{(2)}, \ldots, \tilde{x}^{(m-2)} - \tilde{x}^{(m-1)}, \tilde{x}^{(m-1)}\}.$$

Consider now the translated basis:

$$b_h = \{\widetilde{(x-h)}^{[0}, \widetilde{(x-h)}^{[1}, \ldots, \widetilde{(x-h)}^{[m-1}\}.$$

The functions of b_h are related to the minterms by the matrix D_m^h which is the $(m \times m)$ matrix the (i,j)th entry of which is $d_{(i-h)j}$ (see lemma 4.3). The inverse of this matrix is the $(m \times m)$ matrix $(D_m^h)^{-1}$, the (i,j)th element of which is $d'_{i(j-h)}$ (see lemma 4.3).

Let us now consider the corresponding bases for the n-variables discrete functions

$$f: S_{n-1} \times \ldots \times S_1 \times S_0 \to L.$$

The $(1 \times \Pi m_i)$ matrix $[\tilde{x}^{[e}]$ is defined as follows:

$$[\tilde{x}^{[e}] = \bigotimes_{i=n-1,0} [\tilde{x}^{[e_i}]. \tag{4.66}$$

The $(\Pi m_i \times \Pi m_i)$ matrices D_m^h and $(D_m^h)^{-1}$ are:

$$\begin{aligned} D_m^h &= \bigotimes_{i=n-1,0} D_{m_i}^{h_i} \\ (D_m^h)^{-1} &= \bigotimes_{i=n-1,0} (D_{m_i}^{h_i})^{-1}. \end{aligned} \tag{4.67}$$

One has thus:

$$[\widetilde{(x-h)}^{[e}] = [\tilde{x}^{(e)}]\ D_m^h \tag{4.68}$$

$$[\tilde{x}^{(e)}] = [\widetilde{(x-h)}^{[e}]\ (D_m^h)^{-1}. \tag{4.69}$$

The set of step functions

$$\left\{ \prod_{i=0}^{n-1} \widetilde{(x_i - h_i)}^{[e_i} \mid (e_{n-1}, \ldots, e_1, e_0) \in S_{n-1} \times \ldots \times S_1 \times S_0 \right\}$$

constitutes thus a basis for the discrete functions $f: S \to L$; the corresponding dual basis is

$$\left\{ \prod_{i=0}^{n-1} (\tilde{x}^{(e_i)} - \tilde{x}^{(e_i-1)}) \mid (e_{n-1}, \ldots, e_1, e_0) \in S_{n-1} \times \ldots \times S_1 \times S_0 \right\}.$$

The following theorem 4.10 is a direct consequence of theorem 4.3.

Theorem 4.10. (Partial Nyquist expansion evaluated at the point $\boldsymbol{h}_0$.) Given a canonical basis of step functions, for every partition $(\boldsymbol{x}_1, \boldsymbol{x}_0)$ of $\boldsymbol{x}$ and for every $\boldsymbol{h}_0 \in S_{q-1} \times \ldots \times S_1 \times S_0$, the discrete function f admits the following partial expansion:

$$f(\boldsymbol{x}_1, \boldsymbol{x}_0) = \sum_{\boldsymbol{e}_0} \left(\frac{D^{\boldsymbol{e}_0} f}{D\boldsymbol{x}_0}\right)_{\boldsymbol{x}_0 = \boldsymbol{h}_0} \left[\prod_{i=0}^{q-1} \widetilde{(x_i - h_i)}^{[e_i]}\right] \tag{4.70}$$

$$\boldsymbol{e}_0 = (e_{q-1}, \ldots, e_1, e_0), \quad 0 \leqslant e_i \leqslant m_i - 1, \quad i = 0, 1, \ldots, q-1$$

with

$$\frac{D^{\boldsymbol{k}_0} f}{D\boldsymbol{x}_0} = \sum_{\boldsymbol{e}_0} \left[\prod_{i=0}^{q-1} (\tilde{k}_i^{(e_i)} - \tilde{k}_i^{(e_i-1)})\right] f(\boldsymbol{x}_0 \oplus \boldsymbol{e}_0). \tag{4.71}$$

The operator $D^{\boldsymbol{k}_0} f / D\boldsymbol{x}_0$ associated with Nyquist expansions will no longer be used further on since it is easily expressed in terms of ring differences; one has indeed:

$$\frac{D^0 f}{D x_i} = f$$

$$\frac{D^{k_i} f}{D x_i} = f(x_i \oplus k_i) - f(x_i \oplus k_i - 1)$$

$$= \left(\frac{\Delta f}{\Delta x_i}\right)_{x_i = x_i \oplus k_i - 1}, \quad 1 \leqslant k_i \leqslant m_i - 1,$$

i.e.

$$\frac{D^{k_i} f}{D x_i} = \left(\frac{\Delta^{\tilde{k}_i^{[1}} f}{\Delta x_i}\right)_{x_i = x_i \oplus k_i - \tilde{k}_i^{[1}}.$$

One obtains finally by induction:

$$\frac{D^{\boldsymbol{k}_0} f}{D\boldsymbol{x}_0} = \left(\frac{\Delta^{\tilde{\boldsymbol{k}}_0^{[1}} f}{\Delta \boldsymbol{x}_0}\right)_{\boldsymbol{x}_0 = \boldsymbol{x}_0 \oplus \boldsymbol{k}_0 - \tilde{\boldsymbol{k}}_0^{[1}} \tag{4.72}$$

with

$$\tilde{k}_0^{[1} = (\tilde{k}_{q-1}^{[1}, \ldots, \tilde{k}_1^{[1}, \tilde{k}_0^{[1}).$$

In view of (4.70), the *Nyquist expansion* may be written as

$$f(\boldsymbol{x}) = \sum_{\boldsymbol{e}} \left(\frac{\Delta^{\tilde{\boldsymbol{e}}^{[1}} f}{\Delta \boldsymbol{x}}\right)_{\boldsymbol{x}=\boldsymbol{e} \oplus \boldsymbol{h} - \tilde{\boldsymbol{e}}^{[1}} \left[\prod_{i=0}^{n-1} \widetilde{(x_i - h_i)}^{[e_i}\right] \tag{4.73}$$

$$\boldsymbol{0} \leqslant \boldsymbol{e} \leqslant \boldsymbol{m} - \boldsymbol{1}.$$

Let us also point out that Nyquist expansions may easily be derived in a direct way, without resorting to the use of the general theorem 4.3. The function $f(\boldsymbol{x})$ may be expanded with respect to a variable x_i in the following way:

$$f = f(h_i) \oplus [f(h_i \oplus 1) - f(h_i)]\, \widetilde{(x_i - h_i)}^{[1} \oplus [f(h_i \oplus 2) - f(h_i \oplus 1)]\, \widetilde{(x_i - h_i)}^{[2} \oplus$$

$$\ldots$$

$$\oplus [f(h_i \oplus m_i - 1) - f(h_i \oplus m_i - 2)]\, [\widetilde{(x_i - h_i)}^{[m_i - 1}$$

$$= f(h_i) \oplus \sum_{e_i=1}^{m_i-1} \widetilde{(x_i - h_i)}^{[e_i} \left(\frac{\Delta f}{\Delta x_i}\right)_{x_i = e_i \oplus h_i - 1}. \tag{4.74}$$

The expansion (4.73) is then obtained from (4.74) by induction on the number of variables.

If $\boldsymbol{h} = \boldsymbol{0}$, the Nyquist expansion (4.73) may be expressed as follows:

$$f(\boldsymbol{x}) = \sum_{\boldsymbol{e}} \left(\frac{\Delta^{\tilde{\boldsymbol{e}}^{[1}} f}{\Delta \boldsymbol{x}}\right)_{\boldsymbol{x}=\boldsymbol{e}-\tilde{\boldsymbol{e}}^{[1}} \left[\prod_{i=0}^{n-1} \tilde{x}_i^{[e_i}\right] \tag{4.75}$$

$$= \sum_{\boldsymbol{e}} \left\{\left(\frac{\Delta^{\tilde{\boldsymbol{e}}^{[1}} f}{\Delta \boldsymbol{x}}\right)_{\boldsymbol{x}=\boldsymbol{e}-\tilde{\boldsymbol{e}}^{[1}} \wedge \left[\bigwedge_{i=0}^{n-1} x_i^{[e_i}\right]\right\}. \tag{4.76}$$

Expression (4.76) is a Nyquist expansion in terms of unate generators.

Ring-sum expansions using the lattice operation of conjunction as multiplicative law may be of interest since they constitute intermediate forms between the ring and the lattice expressions.

Example 4.1 (*continued*). Consider the discrete functions:

$$f\colon \{0, 1, 2, 3\}^2 \to L.$$

The Nyquist expansion evaluated at $(h_1, h_0) = (0, 0)$, is, in view of (4.73):

$$f = f(00) \oplus \left(\frac{\Delta f}{\Delta x_0}\right)_{00} \tilde{x}_0^{[1} \oplus \left(\frac{\Delta f}{\Delta x_0}\right)_{01} \tilde{x}_0^{[2} \oplus \left(\frac{\Delta f}{\Delta x_0}\right)_{02} \tilde{x}_0^{[3} \oplus$$

$$\left(\frac{\Delta f}{\Delta x_1}\right)_{00} \tilde{x}_1^{[1} \oplus \left(\frac{\Delta f}{\Delta x_1}\right)_{10} \tilde{x}_1^{[2} \oplus \left(\frac{\Delta f}{\Delta x_1}\right)_{20} \tilde{x}_1^{[3} \oplus$$

$$\left(\frac{\Delta f}{\Delta x_1 x_0}\right)_{00} \tilde{x}_1^{[1} x_0^{[1} \oplus \left(\frac{\Delta f}{\Delta x_1 x_0}\right)_{01} \tilde{x}_1^{[1} \tilde{x}_0^{[2} \oplus$$

$$\left(\frac{\Delta f}{\Delta x_1 x_0}\right)_{10} \tilde{x}_1^{[2} \tilde{x}_0^{[1} \oplus \left(\frac{\Delta f}{\Delta x_1 x_0}\right)_{02} \tilde{x}_1^{[1} \tilde{x}_0^{[3} \oplus$$

$$\left(\frac{\Delta f}{\Delta x_1 x_0}\right)_{20} \tilde{x}_1^{[3} \tilde{x}_0^{[1} \oplus \left(\frac{f}{\Delta x_1 x_0}\right)_{11} \tilde{x}_1^{[2} \tilde{x}_0^{[2} \oplus$$

$$\left(\frac{\Delta f}{\Delta x_1 x_0}\right)_{12} \tilde{x}_1^{[2} \tilde{x}_0^{[3} \oplus \left(\frac{\Delta f}{\Delta x_1 x_0}\right)_{21} \tilde{x}_1^{[3} \tilde{x}_0^{[2} \oplus$$

$$\left(\frac{\Delta f}{\Delta x_1 x_0}\right)_{22} \tilde{x}_1^{[3} \tilde{x}_0^{[3}.$$

Consider the particular discrete function mapped in Figure 4.1. In view of obtaining the Nyquist expansion at the vector $(h_1 h_0) = (00)$ one deduces from Figure 4.1:

$$\left(\frac{\Delta f}{\Delta x_1}\right)_{00} = 1, \quad \left(\frac{\Delta f}{\Delta x_1}\right)_{10} = 1, \quad \left(\frac{\Delta f}{\Delta x_1}\right)_{20} = 0$$

$$\left(\frac{\Delta f}{\Delta x_0}\right)_{00} = 1, \quad \left(\frac{\Delta f}{\Delta x_1 x_0}\right)_{00} = 0, \quad \left(\frac{\Delta f}{\Delta x_1 x_0}\right)_{10} = 2$$

$$\left(\frac{\Delta f}{\Delta x_1 x_0}\right)_{20} = 0, \quad \left(\frac{\Delta f}{\Delta x_0}\right)_{01} = 2, \quad \left(\frac{\Delta f}{\Delta x_1 x_0}\right)_{01} = 0$$

$$\left(\frac{\Delta f}{\Delta x_1 x_0}\right)_{11} = 2, \quad \left(\frac{\Delta f}{\Delta x_1 x_0}\right)_{21} = 0, \quad \left(\frac{\Delta f}{\Delta x_0}\right)_{02} = 0$$

$$\left(\frac{\Delta f}{\Delta x_1 x_0}\right)_{02} = 0, \quad \left(\frac{\Delta f}{\Delta x_1 x_0}\right)_{12} = 2, \quad \left(\frac{\Delta f}{\Delta x_1 x_0}\right)_{22} = 0$$

$$f = 1\tilde{x}_1^{[1} \oplus 1\tilde{x}_1^{[2} \oplus 1\tilde{x}_0^{[1} \oplus 2\tilde{x}_1^{[2} \tilde{x}_0^{[1} \oplus 2\tilde{x}_0^{[2} \oplus 2\tilde{x}_1^{[2} \tilde{x}_0^{[2} \oplus 2\tilde{x}_1^{[2} \tilde{x}_0^{[3}.$$

It is worthwhile pointing out that the transformation matrices D_m and D_m^{-1} were already used by Kautz [1968] and Kodandapani [1974] for performing switching network design. These matrices are also of current use in coding theory for the binary Golay code.

The formulas (4.68) and (4.69) provide us with transformation matrices allowing us to obtain the step functions basis at the point $\boldsymbol{h}$ from the basis of Lagrange functions and vice versa. The obtention of a Nyquist expansion from the discrete function value vector derives immediately from relations (2.40) and (4.69).

Theorem 4.11. The Nyquist expansion at the point $\boldsymbol{h}$ *is given by:*

$$[f_e]\ [(D_m^h)^{-1}]^t\ [\widetilde{(x-h)}^{[e}]^t. \tag{4.77}$$

Example 4.1 (*continued*). By applying the transformation matrix $(D_4^{-1})^t$ to the 4-tuples of the value matrix of example 4.1, one obtains:

$$[(0\ 1\ 0\ 0),\ (1\ 2\ 1\ 1),\ (2\ 2\ 0\ 2),\ (2\ 2\ 0\ 2)] \begin{bmatrix} 1 & -1 & 0 & 0 \\ 0 & 1 & -1 & 0 \\ 0 & 0 & 1 & -1 \\ 0 & 0 & 0 & 1 \end{bmatrix}$$

$$= [(0\ 1\ 0\ 0),\ (1\ 1\ 1\ 1),\ (1\ 0\ 2\ 1),\ (0\ 0\ 0\ 0)].$$

By applying again the same transformation matrix $(D_4^{-1})^t$ to the four 4-tuples of the above matrix, one obtains finally:

$$[f_e]\ [D_4^{-1} \otimes D_4^{-1}]^t = [0\ 1\ 2\ 0\ 1\ 0\ 0\ 0\ 1\ 2\ 2\ 2\ 0\ 0\ 0\ 0].$$

The Nyquist expansion at the point $\boldsymbol{0}$ is then:

$$1\tilde{x}_0^{[1} \oplus 2\tilde{x}_0^{[2} \oplus 1\tilde{x}_1^{[1} \oplus 1\tilde{x}_1^{[2} \oplus 2\tilde{x}_1^{[2}\ \tilde{x}_0^{[1} \oplus 2\tilde{x}_1^{[2}\ \tilde{x}_0^{[2} \oplus 2\tilde{x}_1^{[2}\ \tilde{x}_0^{[3}.$$

Let us finally point out that, as for Newton expansions, the Nyquist expansion of a switching function reduces to a Reed–Muller expansion.

One will now briefly consider the problem of obtaining the Nyquist expansion at $\boldsymbol{h} = \boldsymbol{0}$ for a discrete function $f(\boldsymbol{x})$ given as a disjunction of cubes. This problem has extensively been considered for switching functions in section 4.2.1.1.2.

Algorithm 4.4. Consider a discrete function given as a disjunction of cubes.

(a) Obtain the discrete function as a disjunction of convex blocks using lemma 3.7.

(b) Obtain the discrete function as a ring-sum of convex blocks using lemma 2.2 and grouping terms.

(c) Obtain the discrete function Nyquist expansion at $\boldsymbol{h} = \boldsymbol{0}$ by replacing the exponentiation

$$\tilde{x}_i^{[a_i, a_i + k_i]}$$

by

$$\tilde{x}_i^{[a_i} - \tilde{x}_i^{[a_i + k_i + 1}$$

(see lemma 4.6), using the distributive law and grouping terms.

A similar algorithm could be developed for obtaining the Nyquist expansion at any point $\boldsymbol{h}$ from a disjunctive representation of the discrete function. This would however request to define a more general kind of convex block, namely a block *convex with respect to a point* $\boldsymbol{h}$.

An example will now be treated which illustrates the algorithm 4.4.

Example 4.1 (continued). Consider the example of Figure 4.1 given as a disjunction of blocks:

$$f = 2x_1^{[2,3]}\, x_0^{[3,1]} \vee 2x_1^{[1,3]}\, x_0^{(1)} \vee 1x_1^{(1)} \vee 1x_0^{(1)}.$$

Step (a). The representation of f as a disjunction of convex blocks is obtained by use of the relation

$$x_0^{[3,1]} = x_0^{(3)} \vee x_0^{[0,1]}$$

and the distributivity law:

$$f = 2x_1^{[2,3]}\, x_0^{(3)} \vee 2x_1^{[2,3]}\, x_0^{[0,1]} \vee 2x_1^{[1,3]}\, x_0^{(1)} \vee 1x_1^{(1)} \vee 1x_0^{(1)}.$$

Step (b). Using lemma 2.2 and grouping terms one obtains:

$$f = 2\tilde{x}_1^{[2,3]}\, \tilde{x}_0^{(3)} \oplus 2\tilde{x}_1^{[2,3]}\, \tilde{x}_0^{[0,1]} \oplus 1\tilde{x}_1^{[1,3]}\, x_0^{(1)} \oplus 1\tilde{x}_1^{(1)} \oplus 1\tilde{x}_0^{(1)} \oplus$$
$$2\tilde{x}_1^{(1)}\, \tilde{x}_0^{(1)} \oplus 1\tilde{x}_1^{[2,3]}\, \tilde{x}_0^{(1)}.$$

Step (c). Substituting the exponentiations and using the distributive law one obtains:

$$f = 2\tilde{x}_1^{[2}\, \tilde{x}_0^{[3} \oplus 2\tilde{x}_1^{[2} \oplus 2\tilde{x}_1^{[2}\, \tilde{x}_0^{[2} \oplus 1\tilde{x}_1^{[1}\, \tilde{x}_0^{[1} \oplus 2\tilde{x}_1^{[1}\, \tilde{x}_0^{[2} \oplus 1\tilde{x}_1^{[1} \oplus 2\tilde{x}_1^{[2} \oplus$$
$$1\tilde{x}_0^{[1} \oplus 2\tilde{x}_0^{[2} \oplus 2\tilde{x}_1^{[1}\, \tilde{x}_0^{[1} \oplus 1\tilde{x}_1^{[1}\, \tilde{x}_0^{[2} \oplus 1\tilde{x}_1^{[2}\, \tilde{x}_0^{[2} \oplus 2\tilde{x}_1^{[2}\, \tilde{x}_0^{[1} \oplus 1\tilde{x}_1^{[2}\, \tilde{x}_0^{[1} \oplus$$
$$2\tilde{x}_1^{[2}\, \tilde{x}_0^{[2}.$$

One finally obtains by grouping terms:

$$f = 2\tilde{x}_1^{[2}\, \tilde{x}_0^{[3} \oplus 1\tilde{x}_1^{[2} \oplus 1\tilde{x}_1^{[1} \oplus 1\tilde{x}_0^{[1} \oplus 2\tilde{x}_0^{[2} \oplus 2\tilde{x}_1^{[2}\, \tilde{x}_0^{[2}.$$

4.2.1.3. The cube function bases and the Kodandapani expansions

The purpose of this section is to introduce briefly a ring expansion which was recently presented by Kodandapani and Setlur [1975] and Kodandapani [1974] as a generalization for discrete functions of the well-known Reed–Muller expansion for switching functions (Reed [1954], Muller [1954]). We have already seen that both Newton and Nyquist expansions reduce to Reed–Muller expansion in the switching case. The Kodandapani expansion will again be presented here as a particular case of the theory developed in section 4.1.

Consider again first a one-variable function; the sets of functions

$$b \;= \{1, \tilde{x}^{(1)}, \ldots, \tilde{x}^{(m-1)}\}$$

$$b' = \{\tilde{x}^{(0)} - \tilde{x}^{[1}, \tilde{x}^{(1)}, \ldots, \tilde{x}^{(m-1)}\}$$

are respectively a basis and its dual basis for the set of functions $\{0, 1, \ldots, m-1\} \rightarrow \{0, 1, \ldots, r-1\}$. One verifies indeed easily that the basis b is obtained from the basis of minterms by the intermediate of the transformation matrix D_m^* below; the inverse of this matrix is denoted $(D_m^*)^{-1}$:

$$D_m^* = \begin{bmatrix} 1 & & & & & \\ 1 & 1 & & & & \\ 1 & & 1 & & & \\ 1 & & & 1 & & \\ \vdots & & & & \ddots & \\ 1 & & & & & 1 \end{bmatrix} \qquad (D_m^*)^{-1} = \begin{bmatrix} 1 & & & & & \\ -1 & 1 & & & & \\ -1 & & 1 & & & \\ -1 & & & 1 & & \\ \vdots & & & & \ddots & \\ -1 & & & & & 1 \end{bmatrix}$$

To the basis b (called basis of cube functions) corresponds also the translated basis:

$$b_h \;= \{1, (\widetilde{x-h})^{(1)},\;\; (\widetilde{x-h})^{(2)}, \ldots, (\widetilde{x-h})^{(m-1)}\}$$

$$= \{1, \tilde{x}^{(h \oplus 1)},\;\; \tilde{x}^{(h \oplus 2)}, \ldots, \tilde{x}^{(h \oplus m-1)}\}.$$

Note that this basis may also be written as:

$$b_h = \{\tilde{x}^{k(0,h)},\;\; \tilde{x}^{k(1,h)}, \ldots, \tilde{x}^{k(m-1,h)}$$

with $k(e, h)$ defined as follows

$$k(e, h) = S \quad \text{iff} \quad e = 0$$

$$\qquad\quad = e \oplus h \quad \text{iff} \quad e \neq 0$$

and one has:

$$[\tilde{x}^{[k(e,h)]}] = [\tilde{x}^{(e)}]\,(D_m^*)^h. \tag{4.78}$$

Consider now n-variable discrete functions; define the matrices

$$[\tilde{x}^{[k(e,h)]}] = \bigotimes_{i=n-1,0} [\tilde{x}_i^{[k_i(e_i,h_i)]}]$$

$$(D_m^*)^h = \bigotimes_{i=n-1,0} (D_{m_i}^*)^{h_i}.$$

One has:

$$[\tilde{x}^{[k(e,h)]}] = [\tilde{x}^{(e)}]\,(D_m^*)^h \tag{4.79}$$

so that the set of functions

$$\left\{\prod_{i=0}^{n-1} \tilde{x}_i^{[k_i(e_i,h_i)]} \mid (e_{n-1},\ldots,e_1,e_0) \in S_{n-1} \times \ldots \times S_1 \times S_0\right\}$$

constitutes a basis for the functions: $S_{n-1} \times \ldots \times S_1 \times S_0 \to L$.

The following theorem then derives from theorem 4.3:

Theorem 4.12. (Partial Kodandapani expansion evaluated at the point $\boldsymbol{h}_0$.)

$$f(\boldsymbol{x}_1,\boldsymbol{x}_0) = \sum_{e_0} \left(\frac{K^{e_0}f}{K\boldsymbol{x}_0}\right)_{\boldsymbol{x}_0=\boldsymbol{h}_0} \left[\prod_{i=0}^{q-1} \tilde{x}_i^{[k_i(e_i,h_i)]}\right], \quad 0 \leqslant e_i \leqslant m_i - 1 \tag{4.80}$$

with $K^{e_0}f/K\boldsymbol{x}_0$ the operator associated with the basis of cube functions.

A formal expression of $K^{k_0}f/K\boldsymbol{x}_0$ is easily obtained from the expression of dual basis b'; from (4.8) one deduces:

$$\begin{aligned}
\frac{K^{k_i}f}{Kx_i} &= (\tilde{k}_i^{(0)} - \tilde{k}_i^{[1]})\, f(\boldsymbol{x}) \oplus \sum_{e_i=0}^{m_i-1} \tilde{k}_i^{(e_i)}\, f(x_i \oplus e_i)\\
&= (\tilde{k}_i^{(0)} - \tilde{k}_i^{[1]})\, f(\boldsymbol{x}) \oplus f(x_i \oplus k_i)\\
&= f(x_i \oplus k_i) - f(\boldsymbol{x}).
\end{aligned} \tag{4.81}$$

The operator $K^{k_i}f/Kx_i$ is easily expressed in terms of differences. One has indeed:

$$\begin{aligned}
\frac{K^{k_i}f}{Kx_i} &= \frac{E^{k_i}f}{Ex_i} - f\\
&= \left(\frac{E^{k_i}}{Ex_i} - 1\right) f\\
&= \left[\left(1 \oplus \frac{\Delta}{\Delta x_i}\right)^{k_i} - 1\right] f\\
&= \sum_{1 \leqslant e_i \leqslant k_i} \binom{k_i}{e_i} \frac{\Delta^{e_i}f}{\Delta x_i}.
\end{aligned} \tag{4.82}$$

An induction on the number of variables allows us to obtain the k_0th sensitivity of f with respect to $\boldsymbol{x}_0$, that is:

$$\frac{K^{k_0} f}{K\boldsymbol{x}_0} = \frac{K^{k_0}}{K\boldsymbol{x}_0}\left\{\frac{K^{k_1}}{K\boldsymbol{x}_1}\left[\ldots\left(\frac{K^{k_{q-1}} f}{K\boldsymbol{x}_{q-1}}\right)\ldots\right]\right\}$$

$$= \prod_{i=0}^{q-1}\left(\frac{E^{k_i}}{Ex_i} - 1\right) f$$

$$= \prod_{i=0}^{q-1}\left[\left(1 \oplus \frac{\Delta}{\Delta x_i}\right)^{k_i} - 1\right] f$$

$$= \sum_{1 \leqslant e_0 \leqslant k_0}\left[\prod_{i=0}^{q-1}\binom{k_i}{e_i}\right]\frac{\Delta^{e_0} f}{\Delta\boldsymbol{x}_0}. \tag{4.83}$$

From (4.33) one deduces:

$$\frac{\Delta^{k_i} f}{\Delta x_i} = \sum_{0 \leqslant e_i \leqslant m_i - 1}(-1)^{(k_i + e_i)}\binom{k_i}{e_i} f(x_i \oplus e_i)$$

$$= \sum_{1 \leqslant e_i \leqslant m_i - 1}(-1)^{(k_i + e_i)}\binom{k_i}{e_i}[f(x_i \oplus e_i) - f(\boldsymbol{x})]$$

$$= \sum_{1 \leqslant e_i \leqslant m_i - 1}(-1)^{(k_i + e_i)}\binom{k_i}{e_i}\frac{K^{k_i} f}{Kx_i}. \tag{4.84}$$

One obtains again by induction on the number of variables:

$$\frac{\Delta^{k_0} f}{\Delta\boldsymbol{x}_0} = \sum_{1 \leqslant e_0 \leqslant k_0}(-1)^{\left[\sum_{j=0}^{q-1}(k_j + e_j)\right]}\left[\prod_{j=0}^{q-1}\binom{k_j}{e_j}\right]\frac{K^{k_0} f}{K\boldsymbol{x}_0}. \tag{4.85}$$

Let us again note that Kodandapani expansions can easily be obtained directly without resorting to the use of theorem 4.3; let us expand f with respect to x_i as follows:

$$f(\boldsymbol{x}) = f(h_i) \oplus [f(h_i \oplus 1) - f(h_i)]\ \tilde{x}_i^{(h_i \oplus 1)} \oplus [f(h_i \oplus 2) - f(h_i)]\ \tilde{x}_i^{(h_i \oplus 2)} \oplus \ldots \oplus$$
$$[f(h_i \oplus m_i - 1) - f(h_i)]\ \tilde{x}_i^{(h_i \oplus m_i - 1)}$$

$$= f(h_i) \oplus \sum_{e_i = 1}^{m_i - 1}\tilde{x}_i^{(h_i \oplus e_i)}\left(\frac{K^{e_i} f}{Kx_i}\right)_{x_i = h_i}$$

$$= \sum_{e_i = 0}^{m_i - 1}\left(\frac{K^{e_i} f}{Kx_i}\right)_{x_i = h_i}\tilde{x}_i^{[k_i(e_i, h_i)]}.$$

The complete Kodandapani expansion:

$$f(x) = \sum_{1 \leq e \leq m-1} \left(\frac{K^e f}{Kx}\right)_{x=h} \left[\prod_{i=0}^{n-1} \tilde{x}_i^{[k_i(e_i,h_i)]}\right], \quad 0 \leq e_i \leq 1 \tag{4.86}$$

is obtained from this last expression by induction on the number of variables.

Example 4.1 (continued). Consider the discrete functions:

f: {0, 1, 2, 3} → L

the Kodandapani expansion evaluated at $(h_1, h_0) = (0, 0)$ is, in view of (4.86):

$$\begin{aligned} f = f(00) &\oplus \left(\frac{Kf}{Kx_0}\right)_{00} \tilde{x}_0^{(1)} \oplus \left(\frac{K^2 f}{Kx_0}\right)_{00} \tilde{x}_0^{(2)} \oplus \left(\frac{K^3 f}{Kx_0}\right)_{00} \tilde{x}_0^{(3)} \oplus \\ &\left(\frac{Kf}{Kx_1}\right)_{00} \tilde{x}_1^{(1)} \oplus \left(\frac{K^2 f}{Kx_1}\right)_{00} \tilde{x}_1^{(2)} \oplus \left(\frac{K^3 f}{Kx_1}\right)_{00} \tilde{x}_1^{(3)} \oplus \\ &\left(\frac{Kf}{Kx_1x_0}\right)_{00} \tilde{x}_1^{(1)} \tilde{x}_0^{(1)} \oplus \left(\frac{K^{12} f}{Kx_1x_0}\right)_{00} \tilde{x}_1^{(1)} \tilde{x}_0^{(2)} \oplus \\ &\left(\frac{K^{13} f}{Kx_1x_0}\right)_{00} \tilde{x}_1^{(1)} \tilde{x}_0^{(3)} \oplus \left(\frac{K^{21} f}{Kx_1x_0}\right)_{00} \tilde{x}_1^{(2)} \tilde{x}_0^{(1)} \oplus \\ &\left(\frac{K^{31} f}{Kx_1x_0}\right)_{00} \tilde{x}_1^{(3)} \tilde{x}_0^{(1)} \oplus \left(\frac{K^{22} f}{Kx_1x_0}\right)_{00} \tilde{x}_1^{(2)} \tilde{x}_0^{(2)} \oplus \\ &\left(\frac{K^{23} f}{Kx_1x_0}\right)_{00} \tilde{x}_1^{(2)} \tilde{x}_0^{(3)} \oplus \left(\frac{K^{32} f}{Kx_1x_0}\right)_{00} \tilde{x}_1^{(3)} \tilde{x}_0^{(2)} \oplus \\ &\left(\frac{K^{33} f}{Kx_1x_0}\right)_{00} \tilde{x}_1^{(3)} \tilde{x}_0^{(3)}. \end{aligned}$$

Consider now the particular function of Figure 4.1; one computes the operators at $(h_1, h_0) = (0, 0)$, that is:

$$\left(\frac{Kf}{Kx_0}\right)_{00} = 1, \quad \left(\frac{K^2 f}{Kx_0}\right)_{00} = 0, \quad \left(\frac{K^3 f}{Kx_0}\right)_{00} = 0$$

$$\left(\frac{Kf}{Kx_1}\right)_{00} = 1, \quad \left(\frac{K^2 f}{Kx_1}\right)_{00} = 2, \quad \left(\frac{K^3 f}{Kx_1}\right)_{00} = 2$$

$$\left(\frac{Kf}{Kx_1x_0}\right)_{00} = 0, \quad \left(\frac{K^{12}f}{Kx_1x_0}\right)_{00} = 0, \quad \left(\frac{K^{13}f}{Kx_1x_0}\right)_{00} = 0$$

$$\left(\frac{K^{21}f}{Kx_1x_0}\right)_{00} = 2, \quad \left(\frac{K^{31}f}{Kx_1x_0}\right)_{00} = 2, \quad \left(\frac{K^{22}f}{Kx_1x_0}\right)_{00} = 1$$

$$\left(\frac{K^{23}f}{Kx_1x_0}\right)_{00} = 0, \quad \left(\frac{K^{32}f}{Kx_1x_0}\right)_{00} = 1, \quad \left(\frac{K^{33}f}{Kx_1x_0}\right)_{00} = 0.$$

In view of the local values of these operators, one obtains the following Kodandapani expansion of f:

$$f = 1\tilde{x}_0^{(1)} \oplus 1\tilde{x}_1^{(1)} \oplus 2\tilde{x}_1^{(2)} \oplus 2\tilde{x}_1^{(3)} \oplus 2\tilde{x}_1^{(2)}\,\tilde{x}_0^{(1)} \oplus 2\tilde{x}_1^{(3)}\,\tilde{x}_0^{(1)} \oplus$$
$$1\tilde{x}_1^{(2)}\,\tilde{x}_0^{(2)} \oplus 1\tilde{x}_1^{(3)}\,\tilde{x}_0^{(2)}.$$

Clearly the Newton, Nyquist and Kodandapani expansions reduce to a unique form when dealing with switching functions.

The Kodandapani expansions may evidently be obtained from the function value vector by use of transformation matrices having the structure of a Kronecker product of matrices. One verifies, for example, that the Kodandapani expansions are obtained from the function value vector by means of the following formula:

$$f(x) = [f_e]\left\{\bigotimes_{i=n-1,0} [(D^*_{m_i})^{h_i}]^{-1}\right\}^t [\tilde{x}^{[k(e,h)]}]^t.$$

These transformation matrices have been extensively studied in the sections dealing with Newton and with Nyquist expansions, and the corresponding transformations with respect to Kodandapani expansions will not be given here. They may be found in the papers by Kodandapani and Setlur [1975] and Kodandapani [1974].

Remarks

1. We have considered four types of canonical expansions, namely the Lagrange expansion, the Newton expansion, the Nyquist expansion and the Kodandapani expansion. Lagrange and Newton expansions are of high theoretical interest because they are related to similar kinds of expansions arising in numerical analysis. Nyquist and Kodandapani expansions are also of use in logical design because their bases are formed by elements that can easily be realized by means of logic primitives. There are, however, a lot of other canonical expansions which are of interest for some particular types of problems; some of these expansions may, for example, be found in Pradhan and Patel [1975], Thayse and Deschamps [1973b] and Tosik [1972].

2. As for the Nyquist expansions, the Kodandapani expansions may readily be obtained from a disjunctive form of the discrete function. An algorithm for reaching this purpose may be summarized as follows:

(a) From any disjunctive form of a discrete function, obtain successively the canonical disjunctive form as a disjunction of minterms and the Lagrange canonical form as a ring sum of minterms.

(b) If one wants to obtain the Kodandapani expansion at the point $\boldsymbol{h}$, one replaces in the Lagrange canonical form the exponentiation

$$\tilde{x}_i^{(h_i)}$$

by

$$1 - \sum_{\substack{e_i=0\\ \neq h}}^{m_i-1} \tilde{x}_i^{(e_i)} = 1 \oplus (r-1)\left[\sum_{\substack{e_i=0\\ \neq h_i}}^{m_i-1} \tilde{x}_i^{(e_i)}\right]$$

and applies the distributivity law; the Kodandapani expansion is then obtained after grouping terms.

4.2.2. Change of Kronecker basis

Transformation matrices have been derived in the preceding sections to transform the value vector of a discrete function into, for example, its Newton or its Nyquist expansions and conversely. The different lemmas of sections 4.2.1.1 to 4.2.1.3 allow us also to transform, for example, the Newton and Nyquist expansions into the Lagrange expansion. It is however clear that the value vector form or the Lagrange expansion must not necessarily be used as an intermediate form if one wants, for example, to transform a Newton expansion into a Nyquist expansion or vice versa. Formulae and transformation matrices may easily be found for the transformation of, for example, the Newton, Nyquist and Kodandapani expansions into each other. It is not the purpose of this section to derive explicitly transformation formulae between each of these possible bases. For illustration purposes one will only briefly consider the transformation formulas and matrices for deriving, for example, a Nyquist basis from a Newton basis or vice versa. Some particularly important transformation matrices for switching functions are also studied.

Consider first a one-variable function.

Lemma 4.7

(a) $$\binom{x}{k} = \sum_{e=1}^{m-1} \binom{e-1}{k-1} \tilde{x}^{[e}, \quad 1 \leq e \leq m-1, k > 0 \tag{4.87}$$

$$\binom{x}{0} = 1 = \tilde{x}^{[0}$$

(b) $$\tilde{x}^{[k} = \sum_{e=1}^{m-1} (-1)^{(e+k)} \binom{e-1}{k-1} \binom{x}{e}. \tag{4.88}$$

Proof. (a) The proof follows from the combinatorial identity:

$$\binom{x}{j} = \binom{x-1}{j-1} + \binom{x-2}{j-1} + \ldots + \binom{1}{j-1} + \binom{0}{j-1}.$$

(b) The proof results from the fact that if a transformation matrix from one basis to another basis has $\binom{i-1}{j-1}$ as elements, then the inverse transformation matrix has $(-1)^{i+j}\binom{i-1}{j-1}$ as elements (see, for example, the matrices A_m and A_m^{-1} in section 4.2.1.1). ∎

The above lemma 4.7(a) allows us thus to replace the elements $\binom{x_i}{e_i}$ in any Newton expansion by the elements $\tilde{x}_i^{[e_i}$ and so obtain the Nyquist expansion at $h = 0$ from the Newton expansion at the same point. The inverse transformation is reached by use of lemma 4.7(b).

Lemma 4.7 may also easily be stated in a matrix form; define the following matrices:

$C_m = [c_{ij}]$ is an $(m \times m)$ matrix with $c_{ij} = \binom{i-1}{i-j}$

$i \neq 0, j \neq 0; c_{0j} = c_{i0} = c_{00} = 1$

$C_m^{-1} = [c'_{ij}]$ is an $(m \times m)$ matrix with $c'_{ij} = (-1)^{(i+j)}\binom{i-1}{i-j}$

$i \neq 0, j \neq 0; c'_{0j} = c'_{i0} = 0, c'_{00} = 1.$

Let us again note that, in all the above matrices, the rows and the columns are numbered from 0 and not from 1 as usual.

Lemma 4.7 and the above definitions allow us to write:

$$\left[\binom{x}{e}\right] = [\tilde{x}^{[e}]\, C_m \tag{4.89}$$

$$[\tilde{x}^{[e}] = \left[\binom{x}{e}\right] C_m^{-1}. \tag{4.90}$$

For dealing with n-variable bases, define the matrices

$$C_m = \bigotimes_{i=n-1,0} C_{m_i}$$

$$C_m^{-1} = \bigotimes_{i=n-1,0} C_{m_i}^{-1}.$$

The following lemma then holds.

Lemma 4.8

$$\left[\binom{x}{e}\right] = [\tilde{x}^{[e]}]\, C_m \tag{4.91}$$

$$[\tilde{x}^{[e]}] = \left[\binom{x}{e}\right] C_m^{-1}. \tag{4.92}$$

Transformation matrices and formulae may also easily be found for obtaining any Newton expansion at $\boldsymbol{h}'$ from any Nyquist expansion at $\boldsymbol{h}''$ and vice versa. The transformation formulae are given without proof; they are however easily derived from lemma 4.3.

For one-variable basis (or function) one has for any h_1 and $h_2 \in \{0, 1, \ldots, m-1\}$

$$\left[\binom{x-h_1}{e}\right] = [\widetilde{(x-h_2)}^{[e]}]\, (D_m^{h_2})^{-1}\, A_m^{h_1}$$

$$[\widetilde{(x-h_2)}^{[e]}] = \left[\binom{x-h_1}{e}\right] = (A_m^{h_1})^{-1}\, D_M^{h_2}.$$

Note that $(D_m^h)^{-1}\, A_m^h = (D_m)^{-1}\, A_m = C_m$ and that $(A_m^h)^{-1}\, D_m^h = (A_m)^{-1}\, D_m = C_m^{-1}$.

For an n-variables basis (or function) one has:

$$\left[\binom{\boldsymbol{x}-\boldsymbol{h}'}{e}\right] = [\widetilde{(\boldsymbol{x}-\boldsymbol{h}'')}^{[e]}]\, (D_m^{h''})^{-1}\, A_m^{h'} \tag{4.93}$$

$$[\widetilde{(\boldsymbol{x}-\boldsymbol{h}'')}^{[e]}] = \left[\binom{\boldsymbol{x}-\boldsymbol{h}'}{e}\right] (A_m^{h'})^{-1}\, D_m^{h''}. \tag{4.94}$$

Note furthermore that $(D_m^h)^{-1}\, A_m^h = C_m$ and $(A_m^h)^{-1}\, D_m^h = (C_m)^{-1}$.

Some of the matrices defined in this section and in the preceding ones are illustrated by the numerical example 4.4.

Example 4.4. Consider the two variable functions $f(x_1 x_0)$, with $m_1 = 3, m_0 = 2$, $h_1 = 2, h_0 = 1$ and $r = 3$.

$$\begin{aligned}[\tilde{x}^{(e)}] &= [\tilde{x}_1^{(0)}, \tilde{x}_1^{(1)}, \tilde{x}_1^{(2)}]^t \otimes [\tilde{x}_0^{(0)}, \tilde{x}_0^{(1)}]^t \\ &= [\tilde{x}_1^{(0)}\, \tilde{x}_0^{(0)}, \tilde{x}_1^{(0)}\, \tilde{x}_0^{(1)}, \tilde{x}_1^{(1)}\, \tilde{x}_0^{(0)}, \tilde{x}_1^{(1)}\, \tilde{x}_0^{(1)}, \tilde{x}_1^{(2)}\, \tilde{x}_0^{(0)}, \tilde{x}_1^{(2)}\, \tilde{x}_0^{(1)}]^t\end{aligned}$$

$$\begin{aligned}\left[\binom{\boldsymbol{x}-\boldsymbol{h}}{e}\right] &= \left[1, \binom{x_1-2}{1}, \binom{x_1-2}{2}\right]^t \otimes \left[1, \binom{x_0-1}{1}\right]^t \\ &= \left[1, \binom{x_0-1}{1}, \binom{x_1-2}{1}, \binom{x_1-2}{1}\binom{x_0-1}{1}, \binom{x_1-2}{2}, \binom{x_1-2}{2}\binom{x_0-1}{1}\right]^t;\end{aligned}$$

$$
\begin{aligned}
[\widetilde{(x-h)}^{[e]}] &= [1, \widetilde{(x_1-2)}^{[1}, \widetilde{(x_1-2)}^{[2}]^t \otimes [1, \widetilde{(x_0-1)}^{[1}]^t \\
&= [1, \widetilde{(x_0-1)}^{[1}, \widetilde{(x_1-2)}^{[1}, \widetilde{(x_1-2)}^{[1}\ \widetilde{(x_0-1)}^{[1}, \widetilde{(x_1-2)}^{[2}, \\
&\quad \widetilde{(x_1-2)}^{[2}\ \widetilde{(x_0-1)}^{[1}]^t
\end{aligned}
$$

$$
A_3^2 = \begin{bmatrix} 1 & 1 & 0 \\ 1 & 2 & 1 \\ 1 & 0 & 0 \end{bmatrix}; \quad A_2^1 = \begin{bmatrix} 1 & 1 \\ 1 & 0 \end{bmatrix};
$$

$$
A_{3,2}^{2,1} = \begin{bmatrix} 1 & 1 & 1 & 1 & 0 & 0 \\ 1 & 0 & 1 & 0 & 0 & 0 \\ 1 & 1 & 2 & 2 & 1 & 1 \\ 1 & 0 & 2 & 0 & 1 & 0 \\ 1 & 1 & 0 & 0 & 0 & 0 \\ 1 & 0 & 0 & 0 & 0 & 0 \end{bmatrix}
$$

$$
(A_{3,2}^{2,1})^{-1} = \begin{bmatrix} 0 & 0 & 0 & 0 & 0 & 1 \\ 0 & 0 & 0 & 0 & 1 & 2 \\ 0 & 1 & 0 & 0 & 0 & 2 \\ 1 & 2 & 0 & 0 & 2 & 1 \\ 0 & 1 & 0 & 1 & 0 & 1 \\ 1 & 2 & 1 & 2 & 1 & 2 \end{bmatrix}
$$

$$
(D_3^2)^{-1} = \begin{bmatrix} 0 & 0 & 1 \\ 1 & 0 & 2 \\ 2 & 1 & 0 \end{bmatrix}; \quad (D_2^1)^{-1} = \begin{bmatrix} 0 & 1 \\ 1 & 2 \end{bmatrix};
$$

$$
(D_{3,2}^{2,1})^{-1} = \begin{bmatrix} 0 & 0 & 0 & 0 & 0 & 1 \\ 0 & 0 & 0 & 0 & 1 & 2 \\ 0 & 1 & 0 & 0 & 0 & 2 \\ 1 & 2 & 0 & 0 & 2 & 1 \\ 0 & 2 & 0 & 1 & 0 & 0 \\ 2 & 1 & 1 & 2 & 0 & 0 \end{bmatrix}.
$$

$$(C_3)^{-1} = \begin{bmatrix} 1 & 0 & 0 \\ 0 & 1 & 0 \\ 0 & 2 & 1 \end{bmatrix}; \quad (C_2)^{-1} = \begin{bmatrix} 1 & 0 \\ 0 & 1 \end{bmatrix};$$

$$(C_{3,2})^{-1} = \begin{bmatrix} 1 & 0 & 0 & 0 & 0 & 0 \\ 0 & 1 & 0 & 0 & 0 & 0 \\ 0 & 0 & 1 & 0 & 0 & 0 \\ 0 & 0 & 0 & 1 & 0 & 0 \\ 0 & 0 & 2 & 0 & 1 & 0 \\ 0 & 0 & 0 & 2 & 0 & 1 \end{bmatrix}.$$

$$D_3^2 = \begin{bmatrix} 1 & 1 & 0 \\ 1 & 1 & 1 \\ 1 & 0 & 0 \end{bmatrix}; \quad D_2^1 = \begin{bmatrix} 1 & 1 \\ 1 & 0 \end{bmatrix};$$

$$D_{3,2}^{2,1} = \begin{bmatrix} 1 & 1 & 1 & 1 & 0 & 0 \\ 1 & 0 & 1 & 0 & 0 & 0 \\ 1 & 1 & 1 & 1 & 1 & 1 \\ 1 & 0 & 1 & 0 & 1 & 0 \\ 1 & 1 & 0 & 0 & 0 & 0 \\ 1 & 0 & 0 & 0 & 0 & 0 \end{bmatrix}.$$

$$C_3 = \begin{bmatrix} 1 & 0 & 0 \\ 0 & 1 & 0 \\ 0 & 1 & 1 \end{bmatrix}; \quad C_2 = \begin{bmatrix} 1 & 0 \\ 0 & 1 \end{bmatrix};$$

$$C_{3,2} = \begin{bmatrix} 1 & 0 & 0 & 0 & 0 & 0 \\ 0 & 1 & 0 & 0 & 0 & 0 \\ 0 & 0 & 1 & 0 & 0 & 0 \\ 0 & 0 & 0 & 1 & 0 & 0 \\ 0 & 0 & 1 & 0 & 1 & 0 \\ 0 & 0 & 0 & 1 & 0 & 1 \end{bmatrix}$$

$$(A_3^2)^{-1} = \begin{bmatrix} 0 & 0 & 1 \\ 1 & 0 & 2 \\ 1 & 1 & 1 \end{bmatrix}; \quad (A_2^1)^{-1} = \begin{bmatrix} 0 & 1 \\ 1 & 2 \end{bmatrix}.$$

Let us now consider a change of basis for switching functions which will appear to be of particular importance in Chapter 6; namely, one will be interested in the transformation matrix for computing the Reed–Muller expansion at the point $\boldsymbol{h}$ from the Reed–Muller expansion at the point $\boldsymbol{k}$.

The basis of the $\boldsymbol{h}$-Reed–Muller expansion is given by (see section 4.2.1.1.2):

$$\bigotimes_{i=n-1,0} \begin{bmatrix} \bar{x}_i^{h_i} \\ x_i^{\bar{h}_i} \end{bmatrix}.$$

Define moreover the matrix $A(h_i, k_i)$, $0 \leqslant k_i, h_i \leqslant 1$:

$$A(h_i, k_i) = \begin{bmatrix} k_i^{h_i \oplus k_i} & h_i \oplus k_i \\ h_i \oplus k_i & \bar{k}_i^{h_i \oplus k_i} \end{bmatrix}.$$

One has

$$\begin{bmatrix} k_i^{h_i \oplus k_i} & h_i \oplus k_i \\ h_i \oplus k_i & \bar{k}_i^{h_i \oplus k_i} \end{bmatrix} = \begin{bmatrix} 1 & 0 \\ 0 & 1 \end{bmatrix} \quad \text{iff} \quad h_i = k_i$$

$$\begin{bmatrix} k_i & 1 \\ 1 & \bar{k}_i \end{bmatrix} \quad \text{iff} \quad h_i = \bar{k}_i.$$

Theorem 4.13

$$[\text{R–M}\, f_h] = [\text{R–M}\, f_k] \left[\bigotimes_{i=n-1,0} A(h_i, k_i)\right]$$

$$\boldsymbol{h} = (h_{n-1}, \ldots, h_1, h_0), \quad \boldsymbol{k} = (k_{n-1}, \ldots, k_1, k_0), \; 0 \leqslant h_i, k_i \leqslant 1.$$

Proof. It is straightforward to check that:

$$\begin{bmatrix} k_i & 1 \\ 1 & \bar{k}_i \end{bmatrix} \begin{bmatrix} \bar{x}_i^{\bar{k}_i} \\ x_i^{k_i} \end{bmatrix} = \begin{bmatrix} \bar{x}_i^{k_i} \\ x_i^{\bar{k}_i} \end{bmatrix} \qquad \blacksquare$$

If the basis of the $\boldsymbol{h}$-Reed–Muller expansion is given by (see section 4.2.1.1.2):

$$\bigotimes_{i=n-1,0} \begin{bmatrix} 1 \\ x_i^{(\bar{h}_i)} \end{bmatrix},$$

theorem 4.13 remains true if the matrix $A(h_i, k_i)$ is replaced by $A'(h_i, k_i)$ defined by:

$$A'(h_i, k_i) = \begin{bmatrix} 1 & 0 \\ k_i^{(\bar{h}_i)} & 1 \end{bmatrix}.$$

Example 4.2 (continued). Consider the switching function given by the coefficient vector of Figure 4.2, that is:

$$[1 \quad 1 \quad 1 \quad 0 \quad 1 \quad 0 \quad 0 \quad 1].$$

The transformation matrix $A'(h_i, k_i)$ allows us to obtain the $\boldsymbol{h}$-coefficient vector from the $\boldsymbol{k}$-coefficient vector for any $\boldsymbol{k}, \boldsymbol{h}$. (Let us recall that the coefficient vector means in this terminology the $\boldsymbol{0}$-coefficient vector.) From theorem 4.13 one then deduces the following computation scheme for obtention of the (0, 1, 1)-coefficient vector from the (0, 0, 0)-coefficient vector.

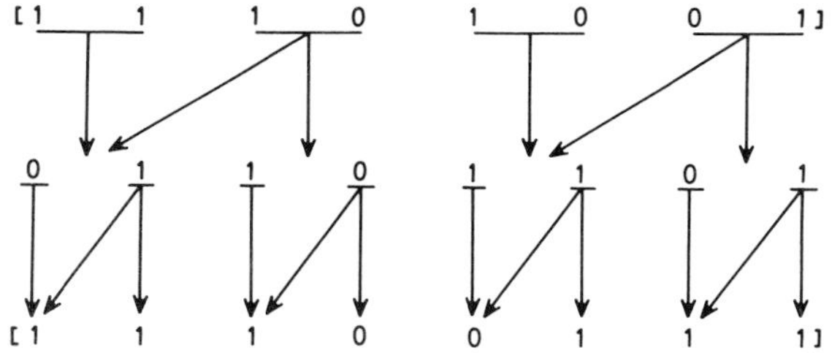

Figure 4.4. Obtention of the (0, 1, 1)-coefficient vector

4.2.3. *Non-coherent Kronecker bases*

In the canonical expansions considered in section 4.2.1, the bases were Kronecker products of matrices, each of these matrices being itself a basis for one-variable functions. These bases were said to be coherent since the elements of each of these bases were of the same type, that is, either all binomial functions (Newton expansions), or all step functions (Nyquist expansions) or all pulse or Lagrange functions (Lagrange expansions). Now, it turns out that the functions may partly be expanded (that is, with respect to a first subset of variables) along a first basis (e.g. a Newton basis) and partly (that is, with respect to the remaining variables) along a second basis (e.g. a Nyquist basis).

Example 4.1 (continued). Consider the function of Figure 4.1; let us develop this function with respect to the variable x_0 in the Newton basis at $h_0 = 0$, that is:

$$f(x_1, x_0) = f(x_1, 0) \oplus \left(\frac{\Delta f}{\Delta x_0}\right)_{x_0=0} \binom{x_0}{1} \oplus \left(\frac{\Delta^2 f}{\Delta x_0}\right)_{x_0=0} \binom{x_0}{2} \oplus \left(\frac{\Delta^3 f}{\Delta x_0}\right)_{x_0=0} \binom{x_0}{3}. \tag{4.95}$$

Now each of the functions of x_1 in the above expression may, for example, be expanded in the Nyquist basis at $h_1 = 0$; the value vectors of these functions are deduced from Figure 4.1, and from these vectors one in turn deduces the Nyquist expansions, that is:

$$\begin{aligned}
f(x_1, 0) &= [0\ 1\ 2\ 2] \\
&= 1\tilde{x}^{[1} \oplus 1\tilde{x}_1^{[2} \\
(\Delta f/\Delta x_0)_{x_0=0} &= f(x_1, 1) - f(x_1, 0) \\
&= [1\ 1\ 0\ 0] \\
&= 1 \oplus 2\tilde{x}_1^{[2} \\
(\Delta^2 f/\Delta x_0)_{x_0=0} &= f(x_1, 2) - 2f(x_1, 1) \oplus f(x_1, 0) \\
&= [1\ 1\ 1\ 1] \\
&= 1 \\
(\Delta^3 f/\Delta x_0)_{x_0=0} &= f(x_1, 3) - 3f(x_1, 2) \oplus 3f(x_1, 1) - f(x_1, 0) \\
&= [0\ 0\ 0\ 0] \\
&= 0.
\end{aligned}$$

By introducing these functions in (4.95) one obtains the following expansion of f:

$$f = 1\tilde{x}_1^{[1} \oplus 1\tilde{x}_1^{[2} \oplus (1 \oplus 2\tilde{x}_1^{[2})\binom{x_0}{1} \oplus \binom{x_0}{2}. \tag{4.96}$$

The Nyquist expansion at $(h_1, h_0) = (0, 0)$ may be obtained from this last expression by using the formula of lemma 4.6(a), that is:

$$\begin{aligned}
\binom{x_0}{1} &= 1\tilde{x}_0^{[1} \oplus 1\tilde{x}_0^{[2} \oplus 1\tilde{x}_0^{[3} \\
\binom{x_0}{2} &= 1\tilde{x}_0^{[2} \oplus 2\tilde{x}_0^{[3}
\end{aligned} \tag{4.97}$$

and by replacing in (4.96), $\binom{x_0}{1}$ and $\binom{x_0}{2}$ by their Nyquist expansion (4.97).

The expansions in non-coherent bases, as defined above, are clearly Kronecker expansions since they may be expressed as a Kronecker product of elementary bases. If one wants, for example, to expand a function $f(\boldsymbol{x}_1, \boldsymbol{x}_0)$ in the Newton basis at $\boldsymbol{h}_1 = \boldsymbol{0}$ for the variables $\boldsymbol{x}_1$ and in the Nyquist basis at $\boldsymbol{h}_0 = \boldsymbol{0}$ for the variables $\boldsymbol{x}_0$, one has to evaluate:

$$[f_e]\left(\bigotimes_{i=n-1,q} A_{m_i}^{-1} \otimes \bigotimes_{i=q-1,0} D_{m_i}^{-1}\right)^t \left\{\bigotimes_{i=n-1,q} \left[\binom{x_i}{e_i}\right] \otimes \bigotimes_{i=q-1,0} [\tilde{x}_i^{[e_i]}]\right\}^t$$

The Kronecker bases for discrete functions are numerous; for switching functions of n variables, there are 3^n possible Kronecker bases. These bases will be studied below.

A switching function $f(x_{n-1}, \ldots, x_1, x_0)$, or, in short, $f(\boldsymbol{x})$ is classically represented by its truth (or value) vector $[f_e]$, where $\boldsymbol{e} = (e_{n-1}, \ldots, e_1, e_0)$ is a binary vector having n components. A switching function $f(x)$ of a single binary variable x has the three ring expansions

$$f(x) = [f_0, f_0 \oplus f_1] \begin{bmatrix} 1 \\ x \end{bmatrix} \tag{4.98}$$

$$f(x) = [f_0 \oplus f_1, f_1] \begin{bmatrix} \bar{x} \\ 1 \end{bmatrix} \tag{4.99}$$

$$f(x) = [f_0, f_1] \begin{bmatrix} \bar{x} \\ x \end{bmatrix}. \tag{4.100}$$

The expansions (4.98) and (4.99) are the Reed–Muller expansions at $h = 0$ and at $h = 1$ respectively, while (4.100) is the Lagrange expansion. It is equivalent to say that the three pairs of functions:

$$\begin{bmatrix} 1 \\ x \end{bmatrix} \quad \begin{bmatrix} \bar{x} \\ 1 \end{bmatrix} \quad \begin{bmatrix} \bar{x} \\ x \end{bmatrix} \tag{4.101}$$

are as many bases of the linear algebra of functions of the variable x. Furthermore, these three bases are related by the linear transformations:

$$\begin{bmatrix} \bar{x} \\ x \end{bmatrix} = \begin{bmatrix} 1 & 1 \\ 0 & 1 \end{bmatrix} \begin{bmatrix} 1 \\ x \end{bmatrix}; \begin{bmatrix} \bar{x} \\ x \end{bmatrix} = \begin{bmatrix} 1 & 0 \\ 1 & 1 \end{bmatrix} \begin{bmatrix} \bar{x} \\ 1 \end{bmatrix}; \begin{bmatrix} \bar{x} \\ x \end{bmatrix} = \begin{bmatrix} 1 & 0 \\ 0 & 1 \end{bmatrix} \begin{bmatrix} \bar{x} \\ x \end{bmatrix}. \tag{4.102}$$

Denoting by the ternary exponentiation symbol $[x^{[h]}]$ $(h = 0, 1, 2)$ the three bases (4.101) respectively and by the symbol $A^{[h]}$ $(h = 0, 1, 2)$ the three transformation matrices appearing in (4.102) respectively, we may summarize the transformations (4.102) by:

$$\begin{bmatrix} \bar{x} \\ x \end{bmatrix} = A^{[h]} \; [x^{[h]}]. \tag{4.103}$$

The extension to functions of n variables is straightforward. The 3^n *Kronecker expansions* of $f(\boldsymbol{x})$ are its expansions in the bases:

$$\bigotimes_{i=n-1}^{0} \; [x_i^{[h_i]}] \tag{4.104}$$

where the symbol $\oplus$ stands for the Kronecker product of matrices.

Now, the Lagrange expansion of $f(\boldsymbol{x})$ may be written as:

$$f(\boldsymbol{x}) = [f_e] \left(\bigotimes_{i=n-1}^{0} \begin{bmatrix} \bar{x}_i \\ x_i \end{bmatrix} \right). \tag{4.105}$$

Hence:

Theorem 4.14. The transformation matrix from the Lagrange basis $\left(\bigotimes_{i=n-1}^{0} x_i^{[2]}] \right)$ *to the Kronecker basis (4.104) is the Kronecker product:*

$$\bigotimes_{i=n-1}^{0} A^{[h_i]}. \tag{4.106}$$

The proof of theorem 4.14 directly follows from the introduction of (4.103) in (4.105) and from the properties of the Kronecker product of matrices. ■

Clearly, a vector $\boldsymbol{h} = (h_{n-1}, \ldots, h_1, h_0)$ having n ternary components $h_i (h_i = 0, 1, 2)$ fully characterizes one of the 3^n expansions of a switching function $f(\boldsymbol{x})$. In what follows, we consider the vector $\boldsymbol{h}$ as the ternary representation of an integer (thus ranging from 0 to $3^n - 1$) and we agree to enumerate the 3^n expansions by increasing order of the attached integers.

Note further that the bracketed exponentiation symbol $[h_i]$ enjoys one more useful particularity. Indeed, if all the components h_i are restricted to take only the values 0 and 1, the corresponding expansion is one of the Reed–Muller expansions of the function, namely, the Reed–Muller expansion at $\boldsymbol{x} = \boldsymbol{h}$. In this case, the vector $\boldsymbol{h}$ may also be interpreted as the binary representation of an integer, and the Reed–Muller expansions are thus enumerated from 0 to $2^n - 1$. When we refer to this binary interpretation of $\boldsymbol{h}$, we use indices and exponents without brackets. Hence, the Reed–Muller expansions of $f(\boldsymbol{x})$ are represented by:

$$f(\boldsymbol{x}) = [f_e] \left(\bigotimes_{i=n-1}^{0} A^{h_i} \right) \left(\bigotimes_{i=n-1}^{0} [x_i^{h_i}] \right). \tag{4.107}$$

The Kronecker product structure of the transformation matrix (4.106) is known to be equivalent to an order lowering algorithm. Such an algorithm applies to any initial representation of the function.

Example 4.5. Consider the function of three variables $f(x_2, x_1, x_0)$ defined by the truth vector:

$$[f_e] = [1 \ 0 \ 0 \ 1 \ 0 \ 1 \ 1 \ 1],$$

and compute its expansion in the canonical basis:

$$\begin{bmatrix} \bar{x}_2 \\ 1 \end{bmatrix} \otimes \begin{bmatrix} \bar{x}_1 \\ x_1 \end{bmatrix} \otimes \begin{bmatrix} 1 \\ x_0 \end{bmatrix}.$$

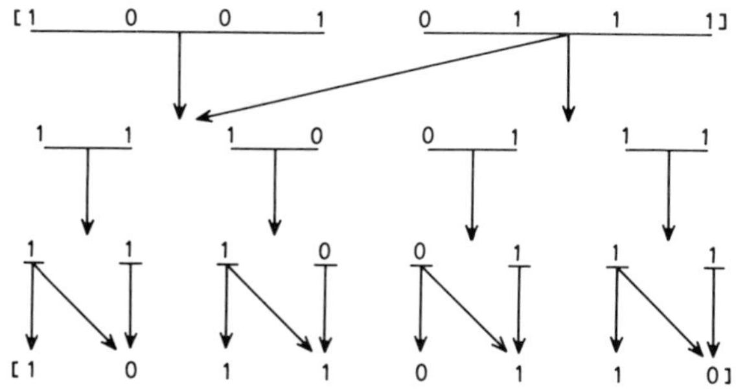

Figure 4.5. Computation of the coefficients of a canonical expansion

The coefficients of the expansion are computed in Figure 4.5 according to (4.106). The expansion itself is then given by:

$$f(x_2, x_1, x_0) = \bar{x}_2 \bar{x}_1 \oplus \bar{x}_2 x_1 \oplus \bar{x}_2 x_1 x_0 \oplus \bar{x}_1 x_0 \oplus x_1.$$

4.3. Other types of ring expansions for switching functions

One will first be faced with a type of ring expansion, first introduced by Cohn [1960, 1962], which will be referred to in the following as *generalized Reed–Muller expansions*, or in short G-R–M expansions.

Let us recall that Reed [1954] and Muller [1954] observed that an arbitrary switching function of n variables could be written in a canonical form as a modulo-2 sum of cubes, i.e.

$$f(x) = \bigoplus_{e} a_e \; [\Pi x_i^{e_i}].$$

Akers [1959] showed that the replacement, *consistently* throughout such a form, of any variable by its complement $\bar{x}_i$ should lead to an equally valid canonical form:

$$f(x) = \bigoplus_{e} a'_e \; [\Pi \dot{x}_i^{e_i}]$$

where $\dot{x}_i$ means consistently (that it has an identical meaning for each cube in the above expression) x_i or $\bar{x}_i$.

The two above forms are the Reed–Muller expansions at $h_i = 0 (\forall i)$ and at $\{h_i \mid \dot{x}_i \oplus h_i = x_i\}$ $(\forall i)$ respectively; they were written as follows (see equation (4.55)):

$$f(x) = \bigoplus_{e} a_{e,h} \; [\Pi (x_i \oplus h_i)^{e_i}].$$

Cohn [1960, 1962] showed that the restriction to *consistent* complementation is unnecessary; that is, in a given form a variable may occur complemented in some terms and uncomplemented in others, but nevertheless the form is canonical. It is recalled that a canonical form for discrete functions is a form in which each function has a unique representation.

The proof that all inconsistent forms are canonical is given in detail by Cohn [1960]; an outline is given below.

The proof begins with the observation that the set of n-variable switching functions under modulo-2 sum forms a 2^n-dimensional vector space over the field of integers modulo-2. Since all the forms under consideration are of the sum of products type, functions are expressed as linear combinations. Thus if a form is canonical it defines a basis for the vector space of n-variable switching functions; conversely, every basis defines a canonical form. But the set of terms which defines an inconsistent form can be shown to be related to the terms in the completely uncomplemented form (or Reed–Muller forms at $\boldsymbol{h} = 0$) by a non-singular linear transformation based on the following relation

$$\prod_i (x_i \oplus h_i) = \sum_j \left(\prod_i x_i^{\epsilon_{ij}}\right).$$

Since the uncomplemented form is known to be canonical, each inconsistent form is defined by a basis and is therefore canonical. This completes the proof.

A combinatorial argument can be used to prove that for n-variable functions there are 2^M G-R–M forms where $M = 2^{n2^{n-1}}$. Indeed, since the bases of these forms are of the type:

$$c, \dot{x}_i, \prod_{i,j} \dot{x}_i\dot{x}_j, \prod_{i,j,k} \dot{x}_i\dot{x}_j\dot{x}_k, \ldots, \prod_{i=0}^{n-1} \dot{x}_i$$

with c a binary constant, an elementary counting argument shows that, in each basis, there are:

1 constant term

n terms with 1 letter

$\binom{n}{2}$ terms with 2 letters

...

$\binom{n}{n-1}$ terms with $(n-1)$ letters

$\binom{n}{n}$ terms with n letters.

So the number of possible bases is:

$$2^n \, (2^2)^{\binom{n}{2}} \, (2^3)^{\binom{n}{3}} \ldots (2^{n-1})^{\binom{n}{n-1}} \, (2^n)^{\binom{n}{n}} = 2^M$$

with

$$M = n + 2\binom{n}{2} + 3\binom{n}{3} + \ldots + (n-1)\binom{n}{n-1} + n\binom{n}{n}.$$

Since $i\binom{n}{i} = n\binom{n-1}{i-1}$

$$M = n\left[1 + \binom{n-1}{1} + \binom{n-1}{2} + \ldots + \binom{n-1}{n-2} + \binom{n-1}{n-1}\right]$$

$$= n\,2^{n-1}.$$

These 2^M G-R–M expansions include evidently the 2^n Reed–Muller expansions so that there are 2^M-2^n inconsistent forms of n-variable switching functions.

The introduction of G-R–M expansions not only extends the class of Reed–Muller expansions (or consistent forms) but is a useful tool in the problem of minimization of ring-sum expansions.

Example 4.6. Consider the three-variable switching functions; the Reed–Muller basis at $(h_2, h_1, h_0) = (0, 0, 0)$ is:

$$(1, x_0, x_1, x_1x_0, x_2, x_2x_0, x_2x_1, x_2x_1x_0)$$

a G-R–M basis is then simply obtained from the above arbitrary complementation of any of its letters; consider, for example, the basis:

$$(1, \bar{x}_0, x_1, \bar{x}_1x_0, \bar{x}_2, x_2x_0, \bar{x}_2\bar{x}_1, x_2x_1x_0).$$

The switching function

$$x_2x_0 \vee \bar{x}_2x_1$$

is written in this basis as

$$x_2x_0 \oplus \bar{x}_2\bar{x}_1 \oplus \bar{x}_2.$$

The G-R–M bases are clearly not Kronecker bases; the *pseudo-Kronecker bases* studied below and first introduced by Davio [1971] are also not Kronecker bases.

Pseudo-Kronecker bases are grounded on the following observation; consider the explicit expansions of $f(\boldsymbol{x})$ with respect to x_{n-1} in the Lagrange basis and in the Reed–Muller bases at $h_{n-1} = 0$ and 1 respectively, i.e.

$$f = a_{00}\,\bar{x}_{n-1} \oplus a_{10}\,x_{n-1}$$

$$f = a_{01} \oplus a_{11}\,x_{n-1}$$

$$f = a_{02} \oplus a_{12}\,\bar{x}_{n-1}.$$

Each of these expansions is characterized by a pair of coefficients $(a_{0i}, a_{1i}), i = 0, 1, 2$; if one now assumes that in a second step the two coefficients a_{0i} and a_{1i} (for a given i) are in turn inconsistently developed with respect to the variable x_{n-2} along the three possibilities quoted above, one obtains 3×3^2 different kinds of ring expansions. If a switching function is expanded in that way with respect to each of its variables one obtains a *pseudo-Kronecker expansion* of the function, the corresponding bases are called *pseudo-Kronecker bases*. For the n-variable functions there are

$$3^{\left(\sum_{k=0}^{n} 2^k\right)} = 3^{2^{n+1}-1}$$

different pseudo-Kronecker bases including the 3^n Kronecker bases studied above.

Example 4.7. Consider the 3-variable functions $f(x_2, x_1, x_0)$; a pseudo-Kronecker expansion is generated by the scheme of Figure 4.6. It corresponds to the expansion

$$f = \bar{x}_0 f(0,1,0) \oplus x_0\, f(0,1,1) \oplus \bar{x}_1 \left(\frac{\Delta f}{\Delta x_1}\right)_{(x_2, x_0 = 0,0)} \oplus \bar{x}_1 x_0 \left(\frac{\Delta f}{\Delta x_1 x_0}\right)_{x_2 = 0} \oplus$$

$$x_2 \bar{x}_1 \left(\frac{\Delta f}{\Delta x_2}\right)_{(x_1, x_0 = 0,1)} \oplus x_2 \bar{x}_1 \bar{x}_0 \left(\frac{\Delta f}{\Delta x_2 x_0}\right)_{x_1 = 0} \oplus x_2 x_1 \bar{x}_0 \left(\frac{\Delta f}{\Delta x_2}\right)_{(x_1, x_0 = 1,0)} \oplus$$

$$x_2 x_1 x_0 \left(\frac{\Delta f}{\Delta x_2}\right)_{(x_1, x_0 = 1,1)}$$

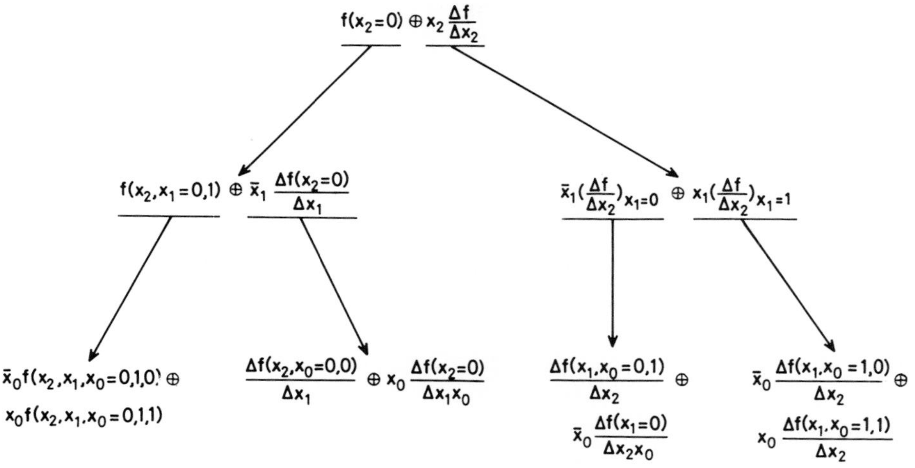

Figure 4.6. Pseudo-Kronecker basis

The switching function

$$x_2x_0 \vee \bar{x}_2x_1$$

is written in this basis as

$$\bar{x}_0 \oplus x_0 \oplus \bar{x}_1 \oplus x_2x_1\bar{x}_0 \oplus x_2\bar{x}_1 \oplus x_2\bar{x}_1\bar{x}_0.$$

The pseudo-Kronecker and the G-R–M bases do not contain all the possible bases for ring-sum expansion of switching functions. A summary of the principal bases studied above is schematized in Figure 4.7. An example of a basis for the 2-variable switching functions $f(x,y)$ is given for each of the entries of Figure 4.7. All these bases will be used further on in Chapter 6 devoted to the minimization of ring-sum expansions.

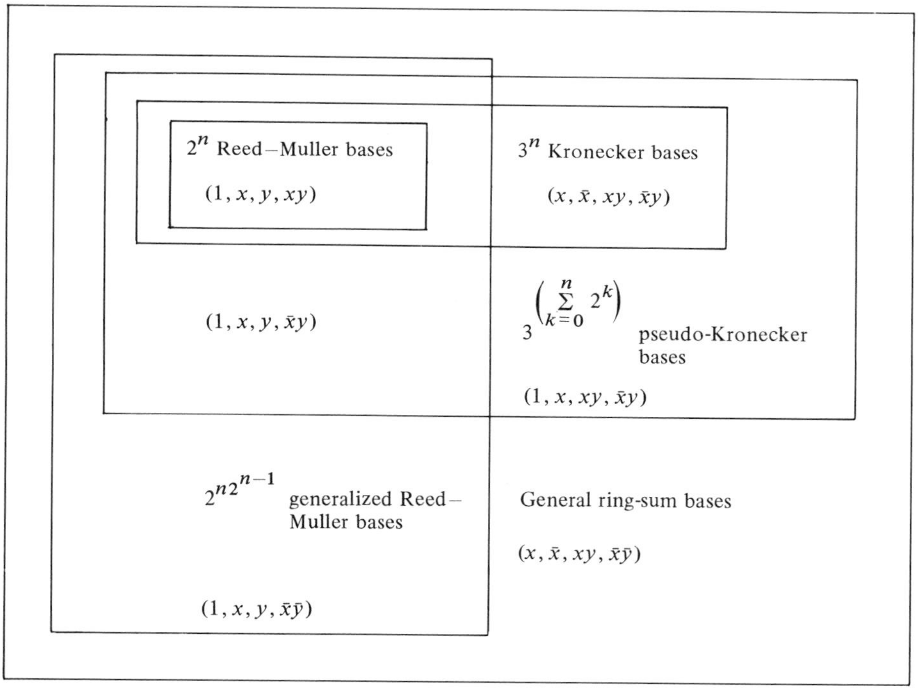

Figure 4.7. Ring-sum bases

4.4. Applications

4.4.1. Network synthesis

Ring expressions play a fundamental role in synthesis of logic networks. The most natural way for using these expressions is to consider them as a *structural description* of logic networks, that is, a topological meaning is added to the functional meaning of the expression. This interpretation of a logic expression has already been introduced in the section dealing with computation schemes and functions of functions (see section 2.1.3).

The ring-sum expansions studied in this chapter allow us to state that any logic function may be written as a linear combination:

$$f = \sum_{i=0}^{k-1} g_i \tag{4.108}$$

where the g_i's are terms of a basis. Let us designate by the symbol "T" within a square, the logical gates realizing the operation T (it is only for standardization purpose that these symbols are used instead of those already proposed by Figure 2.7).

The systems obtained by considering (4.108) as the structural description of a network have the general configuration of Figure 4.8(a). The associative character of the operator ⊕ however allows other possibilities; this property allows indeed the substitution of an operator ⊕ with k inputs by a cascade interconnection of $(k-1)$ operators ⊕ with two inputs as indicated by Figure 4.8(b). Two possibilities now remain for the synthesis of a logic network computing the function (4.108); both possibilities lead to networks having a regular geometrical structure.

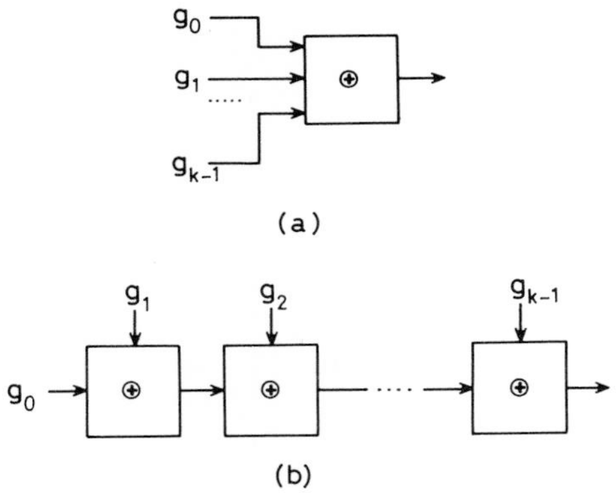

Figure 4.8. Associative character of the operation "⊕"

The simplest solution consists of materializing each of the functions g_i by means of a unique operator, namely a product operator (possibly preceded by exponentiation operators). Examples of a logic function and of a switching function realization are given below.

Example 4.8. Consider a logic function

$f\colon \{0, 1, 2\}^2 \to \{0, 1, 2\}$

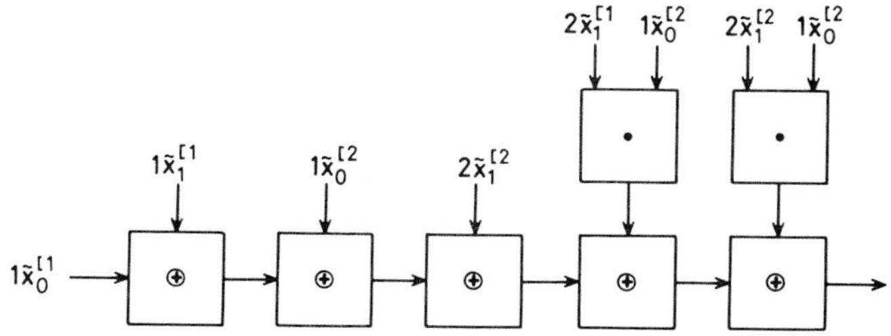

Figure 4.9. Realization of a logic function based on a Nyquist expansion

given by means of its Nyquist expansion at $(h_2, h_1, h_0) = (0, 0, 0)$, i.e.

$$f = 1\tilde{x}_0^{[1} \oplus 1\tilde{x}_1^{[1} \oplus 1\tilde{x}_0^{[2} \oplus 2\tilde{x}_1^{[2} \oplus 2\tilde{x}_1^{[1}\,\tilde{x}_0^{[2} \oplus 2\tilde{x}_1^{[2}\,\tilde{x}_0^{[2}.$$

A network realizing this function is given in Figure 4.9 (it is recalled that the actual technology allows the building of logic gates realizing ring sums, products and ring exponentiations).

Example 4.9. Consider a switching function $f(x_3, x_2, x_1, x_0)$ given by means of a ring-sum expansion, i.e.

$$f = \bar{x}_2 \oplus \bar{x}_2 x_1 x_0 \oplus x_3 \bar{x}_1 \oplus x_1.$$

The network realizing this function is given in Figure 4.10.

The second possibility for synthesizing a logic function consists in realizing (if possible) each of the functions g_i themselves by means of a cascade of operators: these cascades will be disposed perpendicularly to the cascade of "$\oplus$" operators also called *collecting cascade.* One so obtains two-dimensional arrays of operators called *cutpoint cellular arrays* (Mukhopadhyay [1971])

Only example 4.9 will be continued; the generalization of all that follows to logic functions is indeed straightforward.

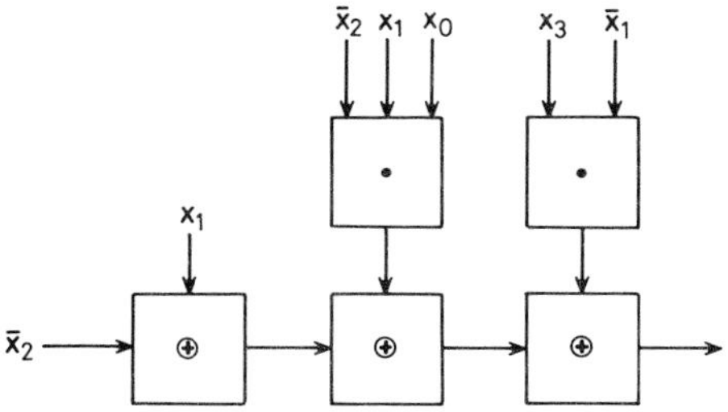

Figure 4.10. Realization of a switching function based on a ring-sum expansion

Example 4.9 (continued). The network of Figure 4.10 is transformed into a 2-dimensional rectangular array with adjacent cells in just two directions as shown in Figure 4.11. In this figure the symbols ↛, ⊙, and ⊕ mean complementation, product and modulo-2 sum gates respectively.

We briefly introduce the concept of *programmable cellular logic* (Mukhopadhyay [1971]) directly connected to the cutpoint cellular arrays. Let us consider the array of Figure 4.11. One sees that it is formed by means of four types of cells represented in Figure 4.12(a) where they are arbitrarily numbered from (0) to (3). The functional behaviours associated with these different cells are described by the following expressions respectively:

(0) $f_0 = y_0$; $\quad f_1 = y_0 \oplus y_1$

(1) $f_0 = y_0$; $\quad f_1 = y_1$

(2) $f_0 = y_0 y_1$; $\quad f_1 = y_1$

(3) $f_0 = y_0 \bar{y}_1$; $\quad f_1 = y_1$.

These functional behaviours may be realized by means of a unique *programmable cell* (Figure 4.12(b)) containing two additional binary inputs (c_0, c_1) the four possible

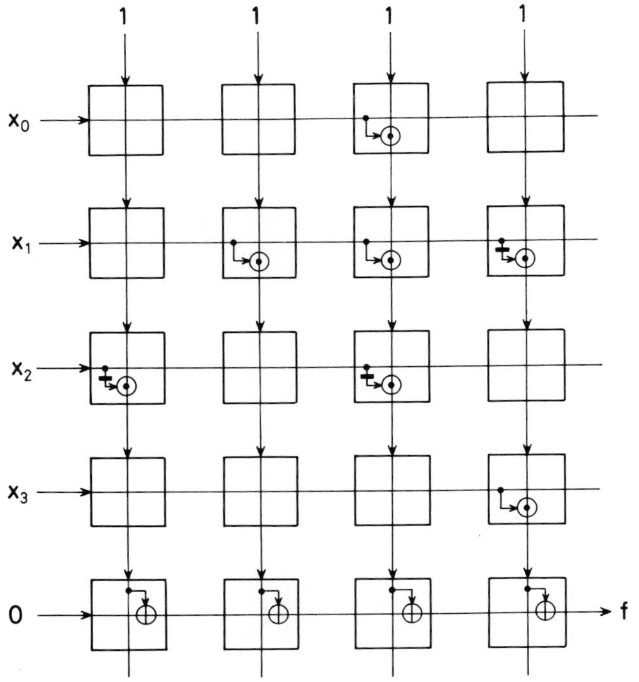

Figure 4.11. Cutpoint cellular array

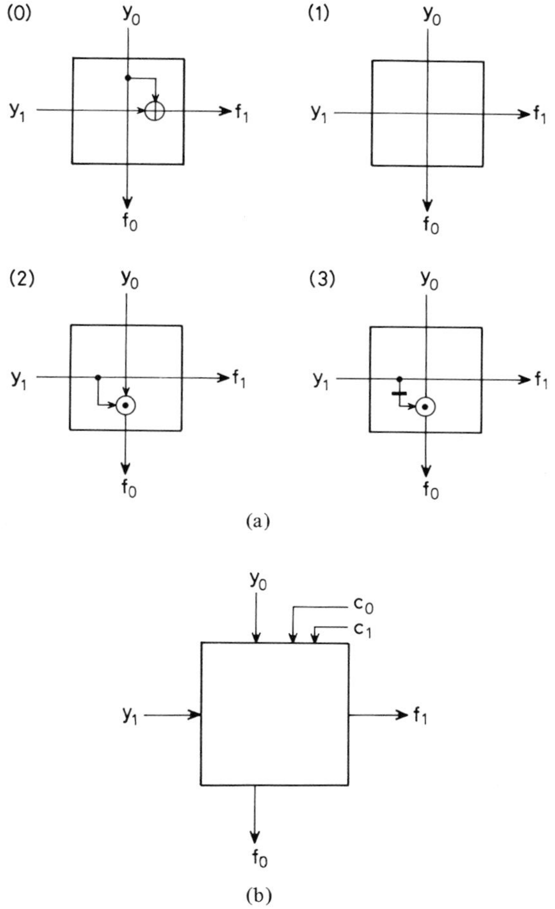

Figure 4.12. (a) Four basic cells. (b) Programmable cell

values of which are: (0, 0), (0, 1), (1, 0) and (1, 1), corresponding to the four functional behaviours requested respectively. If one chooses the following correspondence

$$(c_0, c_1)$$

$$(0) \leftrightarrow (0, 0)$$

$$(1) \leftrightarrow (0, 1)$$

$$(2) \leftrightarrow (1, 0)$$

$$(3) \leftrightarrow (1, 1)$$

one easily verifies that the programmable cell is described by the following equations:

$$f_0 = (\overline{c_0 \bar{y}_1})\, y_0 \oplus c_0 c_1 y_0$$

$$f_1 = y_1 \oplus \bar{c}_0 \bar{c}_1 y_0.$$

These equations are materialized by the scheme of Figure 4.13.

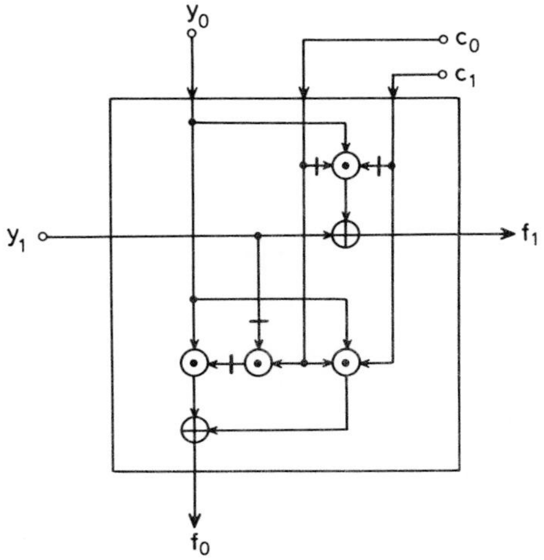

Figure 4.13. Scheme of a programmable cell

Let us finally note that a large survey of cellular logic may be found in the book by Mukhopadhyay [1971].

Both Reed–Muller expansions and cellular logic design may be used in the design of *universal logic modules* for switching functions: a universal logic module is a switching network capable of realizing every n-variable switching function, where function specialization is achieved by distributing the constants 0 and 1 freely among input terminals of the network.

Consider, for example, the network of Figure 4.15; it is built up as an interconnection of identical cells described by Figure 4.14.

This cell realizes the two switching functions

$$a \oplus bx \quad \text{and} \quad b.$$

It could then easily be verified that the network represented by Figure 4.1 as an interconnection of these cells realizes any 3-variable switching function $f(x_2, x_1, x_0)$ and all its ring differences. The network inputs are the elements of the function coefficient vector.

It is beyond the scope of this chapter to deal more extensively with cellular synthesis of switching and of discrete functions. More specialized material may be

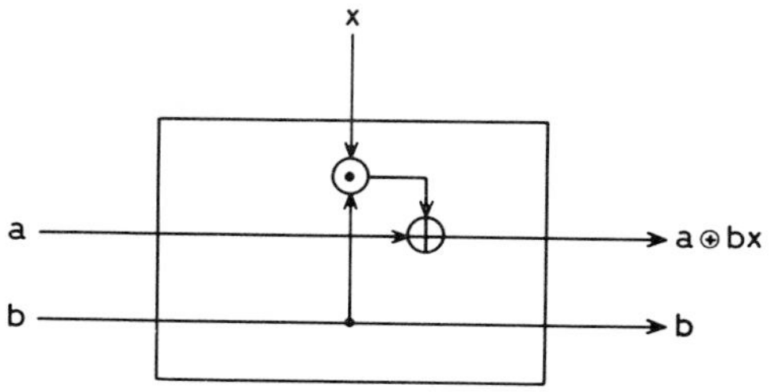

Figure 4.14. Basic cell for the network of Figure 4.15

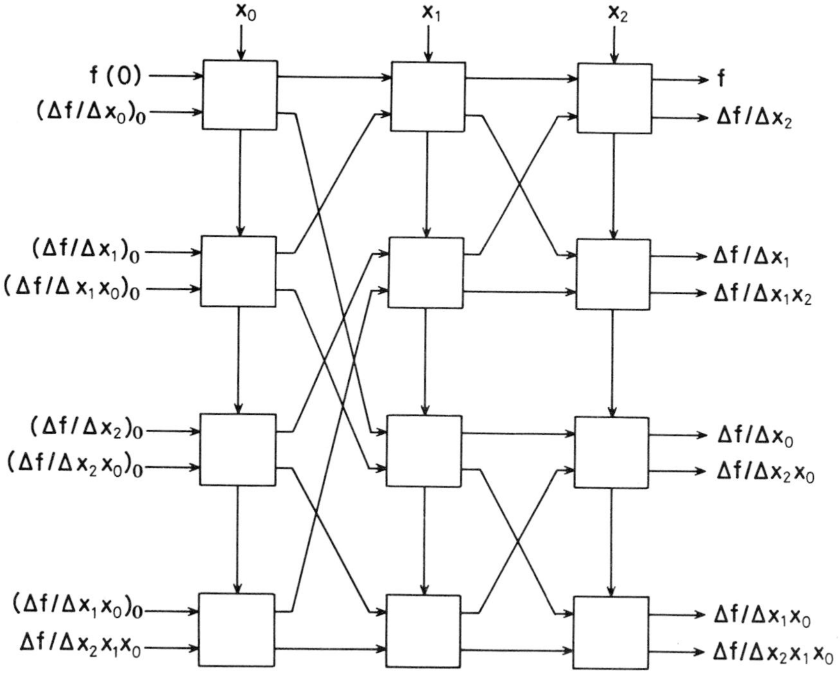

Figure 4.15. Universal module realizing any 3-variable switching function and all its ring differences

found in the papers by Yoeli [1970], Elspas [1971], Davio and Quisquater [1972] and Delsarte and Quisquater [1973].

4.4.2. Network diagnosis

In this section we briefly summarize the background material necessary for an understanding of the problems related to network diagnosis. Our treatment is however much too brief to allow for a relatively complete review of the theoretical aspects of diagnosis; the material presented here will be developed further in Chapter 7.

A *fault* or *failure* of an electrical circuit is a physical defect of one or more components, which can cause the circuit to malfunction. Faults can be roughly classified into several categories, according to the underlying physical causes. Many faults in electrical circuits create a *stuck-at-fault* in the corresponding logical network model: in this kind of fault-model, it is assumed that any electrical fault (such as, for example, short or open circuited diode, broken wire between gates, etc.) can be modelled by a number of connections in the corresponding logical network permanently fixed at a logical level ($0, 1, \ldots,$ or $m-1$ for a logic network and 0 or 1 for a switching network). The use of this fault model has many advantages which will appear further on in this section. The main purpose of network diagnosis is to *detect* and/or to *locate* faults in logic networks.

Consider a logic network realizing a logic function $f(\boldsymbol{x})$; assume further that the network, undergoing a specific fault, realizes the logic function $g(\boldsymbol{x})$ instead of $f(\boldsymbol{x})$.

Definition 4.6. Any n-tuple $\boldsymbol{a} \in S$ of particular values of the input variables $\boldsymbol{x}$ is called *test vector* for this specific fault iff

$$f(\boldsymbol{a}) \neq g(\boldsymbol{a}).$$

Consider next the function

$$t(\boldsymbol{x}) = f(\boldsymbol{x}) - g(\boldsymbol{x}).$$

This function assumes a value different from zero if a test vector $\boldsymbol{a}$ is substituted for $\boldsymbol{x}$. The function $t(\boldsymbol{x})$ will be called hereafter *test function* of the specific fault.

Definition 4.7. A particular fault having a test function $t(\boldsymbol{x}) = 0$ for all $\boldsymbol{x}$ will be said *undetectable*.

Another classical assumption of diagnosis theory that will be retained here is that all faults are detectable. In this case, it will be possible to detect any fault in the network by the simple observation of the actual output $g(\boldsymbol{x})$ for any of the m^n possible inputs and the comparison of these values with the prescribed values given by $f(\boldsymbol{x})$.

Definition 4.8. A set $\{\boldsymbol{a}\}$ of input vectors is called a *test* of a logic network if the observation of the corresponding outputs allows the detection of every possible fault in the network.

As the previous remark has shown, if all the faults are detectable, the set of m^n possible input vectors is a test of the network. However, if the network implementation (or scheme) is known, it will be possible to construct tests having less than m^n elements. One of the objectives of the diagnosis theory is the construction of minimal tests: a test is called a *minimal test* if it ceases to be a test at the suppression of any single of its components. Search for minimal tests is usually carried out in two well-distinct parts:

(a) For each of the possible faults, research of the corresponding test vectors, i.e. computation of the corresponding test function.

(b) Research of a *minimal cover* of the faults by a set of test vectors. The term *minimal cover* has been used here to point out the similarity of this research with the more classical problem of covering minterms by prime implicants (Chapter 8). In other terms, one searches the smallest possible number of test vectors which allows the detection of all the faults within the network.

Various practical methods will be developed in Chapter 8 to solve this covering problem and we shall not deal with it any more, focusing our attention on the computation of test functions.

Definition 4.9. Consider two faults having for respective test functions $t_0(\boldsymbol{x})$ and $t_1(\boldsymbol{x})$. These faults are said to be *indistinguishable* if

$$t_0(\boldsymbol{x}) = t_1(\boldsymbol{x});$$

they are distinguishable in the opposite case.

Indistinguishable faults are for instance the stuck-at-0 of either input of an AND-gate. Indistinguishability is an equivalence relation on the set of all possible faults: it is trivially reflexive, symmetric and transitive. The importance of indistinguishability comes from the following observation: the computation of the test functions has only to be performed for a single representative of each of its equivalence classes.

Let us now turn to the computation of the test functions. A first approach of the computation problem will be done in the case of a fault involving q input connections of the network. These q input connections correspond to the variables labelled $\boldsymbol{x}_0$ $[\boldsymbol{x} = (\boldsymbol{x}_1, \boldsymbol{x}_0)]$ and they will supposed to be stuck at $\boldsymbol{h}_0$; the other $n-q$ variables are denoted by $\boldsymbol{x}_1$ as usual. In this case, if the suitable output function is $f(\boldsymbol{x}_1, \boldsymbol{x}_0)$, the actual output function $g(\boldsymbol{x}_1, \boldsymbol{x}_0)$ is simply $f(\boldsymbol{x}_1, \boldsymbol{h}_0)$ and the test function $t(\boldsymbol{x})$ is given by:

$$t(\boldsymbol{x}) = f(\boldsymbol{x}_1, \boldsymbol{x}_0) - f(\boldsymbol{x}_1, \boldsymbol{h}_0).$$

Theorem 4.15. Consider the expansion of a logic function in a basis $b = \underset{i}{\oplus}\, b_i$ with

$$b_i = \{g_{e_i i}\,(x_i)\}$$

and assume moreover that the operators $D^{\boldsymbol{e}}/D\boldsymbol{x}$ associated with this basis are such that

$$D^{\boldsymbol{0}} f/D\boldsymbol{x} = f. \tag{4.109}$$

The test function for the input fault $f(\boldsymbol{x}_1, \boldsymbol{h}_0)$ is:

$$t(\boldsymbol{x}) = \sum_{\boldsymbol{e}_0} \left[\prod_{i=0}^{q-1} g_{e_i i}\,(x_i - h_i)\right] \left(\frac{D^{\boldsymbol{e}_0} f}{D\boldsymbol{x}_0}\right)_{\boldsymbol{x}_0 = \boldsymbol{h}_0} \tag{4.110}$$

$$0 \leqslant e_i \leqslant m_i - 1, \quad \boldsymbol{e}_0 \neq \boldsymbol{0}.$$

Proof. The assertion is a direct consequence of theorem 4.3. ■

Since it has been shown (see section 4.2.1) that the operators associated with the bases of the Newton expansions, of the Nyquist expansions and of the Kodandapani expansions satisfy the condition (4.109), any one of these expansions may be used for obtaining the expression (4.110) of the test function.

Definition 4.10. A fault is called a *simple fault* if a simple connection is affected. It is called a *multiple fault* or a *q-fault* if $q\ (q > 1)$ connections are affected.

For the simple fault x_i stuck at h_i, the test function (4.110) has a very simple expression:

$$t(\boldsymbol{x}) = \bigoplus_{e_i} g_{e_i i}\,(x_i - h_i) \left(\frac{D^{e_i} f}{D x_i}\right)_{x_i = h_i}, \quad 0 < e_i \leqslant m_i - 1. \tag{4.111}$$

The test function (4.110) is a function associated with a given fault at the inputs of a logic network. It must however be noted that $t(\boldsymbol{x})$ could also be defined as a function associated with any discrete function in order to study some of its functional properties. Further on we shall restrict ourselves to faults arising in switching networks; in this case the computational complexity for evaluating the test functions is greatly reduced. For switching functions, the expressions (4.110) and (4.111) become respectively:

$$\bigoplus_{e_0} \left[\prod_{i=0}^{q-1} (x_i \oplus h_i)\right] \left(\frac{\Delta^{e_0} f}{\Delta \boldsymbol{x}_0}\right)_{\boldsymbol{x}_0 = \boldsymbol{h}_0}, \quad 0 \leqslant e_i \leqslant 1, \boldsymbol{e}_0 \neq \boldsymbol{0} \tag{4.112}$$

$$(x_i \oplus h_i) \frac{\Delta f}{\Delta x_i}. \tag{4.113}$$

Let us now consider more carefully the expression (4.113); it is possible to illustrate in a simple way a fundamental principle of fault detection in terms of this expression.

In order to test any network for the presence of a fault, it is necessary and sufficient that two general conditions be satisfied. Namely, for each fault to be detected there must exist sets of input values to the network such that:

(a) The connection subject to the fault has a sufficient subset of input combinations applied to it to check it for the presence of this fault (the *local sensitivity condition*);

(b) For each such input combination applied to each connection, there is at least one path from the connection to the network output such that the faulty signal could propagate through this path (*propagation condition*).

Consider, for example, the simple fault $x_i = h_i$ and its corresponding test function (4.113); the local sensitivity condition becomes:

$$x_i \oplus h_i = 1, \quad \text{or equivalently } x_i = \bar{h}_i$$

while the propagation condition is:

$$\frac{\Delta f}{\Delta x_i} = 1.$$

Since $\Delta f/\Delta x_i$ is degenerate in x_i, the two above conditions can always be satisfied independently.

Let us give some more details about the propagation condition $\Delta f/\Delta x_i = 1$. Since $\Delta f/\Delta x_i = f(x_i = 0) \oplus f(x_i = 1)$, it is clear that the condition $\Delta f/\Delta x_i = 1$ implies that any change in the variable x_i propagates through the network realizing f, and results in a change of this network output. Thus, any fault in the input x_i is propagated up to the network output once the local sensitivity condition is satisfied.

Theorem 4.16. Let a switching function $f(\boldsymbol{x})$ be expanded according to its Reed–Muller expansion at $\boldsymbol{h}$; the test function for $\boldsymbol{x}_0$ fixed at $\boldsymbol{h}_0$ is the modulo-2 sum of the terms of the Reed–Muller expansion which are not degenerate in $\boldsymbol{x}_0$.

Proof. If one takes $x_i = h_i \; \forall x_i \in \boldsymbol{x}_0$ in the Reed–Muller expansion at $\boldsymbol{h}$, the remaining non-zero terms are those degenerate in $\boldsymbol{x}_0$; thus $f(\boldsymbol{x}) \oplus f(\boldsymbol{x}_1, \boldsymbol{x}_0 = \boldsymbol{h})$ is the modulo-2 sum of the terms not degenerate in $\boldsymbol{x}_0$. ■

Example 4.9 (continued). The Reed–Muller expansion at $\boldsymbol{h} = \boldsymbol{0}$ of the switching function of example 4.9. is:

$$1 \oplus x_2 \oplus x_1 \oplus x_3 \oplus x_3x_1 \oplus x_2x_1x_0.$$

The table of Figure 4.16 gives the corresponding test function for a set of faults at the network inputs and a possible test vector for each of the test functions.

Input stuck fault	Test function	Test vector
x_3 stuck at 0	$x_3 \oplus x_3x_1$	$x = (1, \times, 0, \times)$
x_2 stuck at 0	$x_2 \oplus x_2x_1x_0$	$x = (\times, 1, 0, \times)$
x_3 and x_2 stuck at 0	$x_3 \oplus x_2 \oplus x_3x_1 \oplus x_2x_1x_0$	$x = (1, 0, 0, \times)$

Figure 4.16. Test functions and test vectors

As usual the symbol "x" denotes an indeterminate value 0 or 1 in the switching variable.

Until now we have considered only stuck faults at the network inputs (*input faults*). We now turn to the more general case where any q connections in the network are involved in a fault (*internal faults*), and more precisely are stuck at $\boldsymbol{h}_0$. The situation is depicted in Figure 4.17(a): the q-involved connections normally carry the switching functions:

$$\boldsymbol{y}(\boldsymbol{x}) = [y_0(\boldsymbol{x}), y_1(\boldsymbol{x}), \ldots, y_{q-1}(\boldsymbol{x})]$$

and the output function is then $f(\boldsymbol{x})$. When the fault occurs, the connections carrying the function y_i are stuck at $h_i \; \forall i$. For the computation purposes, we introduce also the auxiliary network of Figure 4.17(b). This network is supposed to be fault-free and it is derived from the studied network by cutting the q-involved connections, considering them as additional inputs $\boldsymbol{y} = (y_0, y_1, \ldots, y_{q-1})$ to the network and putting

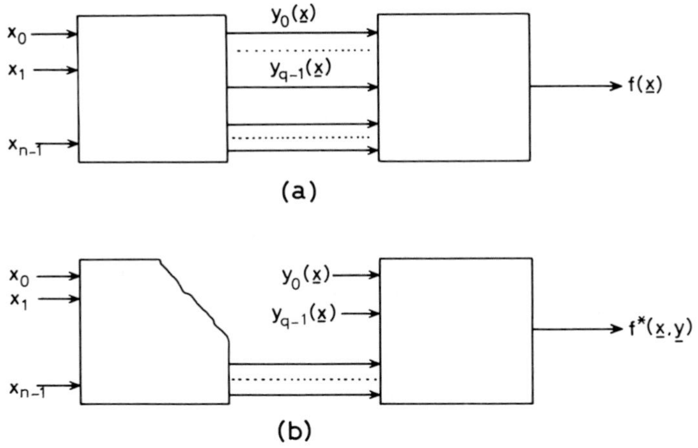

Figure 4.17. (a) Network under test. (b) Auxiliary network

away the unnecessary parts of the network. The output function of the auxiliary network is called $f^*(\boldsymbol{x}, \boldsymbol{y})$. It is clear that:

$$f(\boldsymbol{x}) = f^* [\boldsymbol{x}, \boldsymbol{y}(\boldsymbol{x})].$$

The test function for the q auxiliary inputs fixed at $\boldsymbol{h}_0$ is then given by:

$$t(\boldsymbol{x}) = f^*[\boldsymbol{x}, \boldsymbol{y}(\boldsymbol{x})] \oplus f^*(\boldsymbol{x}, \boldsymbol{h}_0).$$

The function $f^*(\boldsymbol{x}, \boldsymbol{y})$ may be expanded with respect to its variables $\boldsymbol{y}$ and according to a Reed–Muller scheme at $\boldsymbol{y} = \boldsymbol{h}$, that is:

$$f^*(\boldsymbol{x}, \boldsymbol{y}) = f^*(\boldsymbol{x}, \boldsymbol{h}_0) \oplus \sum_{\boldsymbol{e}_0} \left[\prod_{i=0}^{q-1}\right] (y_i \oplus h_i) \left(\frac{\Delta^{\boldsymbol{e}_0} f^*}{\Delta \boldsymbol{y}}\right)_{\boldsymbol{y} = \boldsymbol{h}_0}$$

$$0 \leqslant e_i \leqslant 1, \quad \boldsymbol{0} < \boldsymbol{e}_0.$$

The test function may thus be written in the form

$$t(\boldsymbol{x}) = \sum_{\boldsymbol{e}_0} \left\{\prod_{i=0}^{q-1} [y_i(\boldsymbol{x}) \oplus h_i]\right\} \left(\frac{\Delta^{\boldsymbol{e}_0} f^*}{\Delta \boldsymbol{y}}\right)_{\boldsymbol{y} = \boldsymbol{h}_0}. \tag{4.114}$$

This test function is again particularly attractive for the case of a simple fault in an internal connection y:

$$t(\boldsymbol{x}) = [y(\boldsymbol{x}) \oplus h] \frac{\Delta f^*}{\Delta y}. \tag{4.115}$$

According to theorem 4.16, the test function for the internal faults are easily obtained when f^* is expanded according to its Reed–Muller expansion at $\boldsymbol{y} = \boldsymbol{h}_0$.

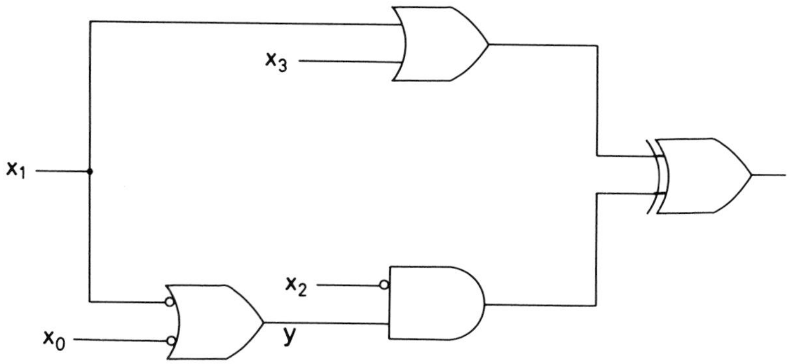

Figure 4.18. Realization of the switching function in example 4.9

Example 4.9 (*continued*). Consider the network of Figure 4.18; it realizes the switching function of example 4.9; assume that one wishes to test the internal connection y for a possible stuck at 1 fault.

The function f^* is:

$$f^*(x, y) = \bar{x}_2 y \oplus (x_3 \vee x_1)$$

with

$$y = \bar{x}_1 \vee \bar{x}_0.$$

According to (4.115) the test function for the considered fault is

$$t(x) = \bar{x}_2 \bar{y}$$
$$= \bar{x}_2 x_1 x_0.$$

A test vector is thus $(x_3, x_2, x_1, x_0) = (\times, 0, 1, 1)$.

4.4.3. *Synthesis of easily testable networks*

The problem of designing logic networks is normally solved under a set of specifications; let us quote, among others:

type of devices to be used in the network (e.g. AND, OR gates);
constraints on topology (e.g. cellular structure);
design criteria (e.g. minimum number of gates).

Several authors (see, for example, Betancourt [1971], Akers [1972], Reddy [1972], Saucier [1972]) proposed to include fault detection aspects into design specification. Otherwise stated, in this additional requirement we will have to consider the *testability* (or equivalently the ease of generating test vectors) of the network topology, since the test functions and test vectors for a network depend on its structure.

Desirable properties of easily testable networks are (see Reddy [1972]):

Small tests, i.e. tests with a small number of elements.
The test can be found without much extra work either during the design phase or after the network is designed. As an example it might be possible to design a network for a switching function which has a predetermined test set.
The structure of the test is such that it is easy to generate.

The purpose of this section is to show that network structures based on ring-sum expansions are *easily testable structures*; the material presented in this section owes much to a paper by Reddy [1972] devoted to the study of easily testable switching networks. Further on in this section one will be faced only with tests for detecting simple faults.

Consider, for example, the Nyquist expansions of an arbitrary logic function $f(x)$. For sake of simplicity (and without loss of generality) let us assume that the chosen vertex is $h = 0$ (Nyquist expansion at the origin of the variables). The function $f(x_{n-1}, \ldots, x_1, x_0)$ can then be realized by the network shown in Figure 4.19, which is built up by means of gates realizing the sum and the product modulo-m.

The inputs of the AND-gates are constants c_k and subsets of

$$\tilde{x}^{[i} = \{\tilde{x}_j^{[i} \mid 0 \leqslant j \leqslant n-1\}, \quad 1 \leqslant i \leqslant m-1.$$

Let us assume that the primary inputs are fault-free, but simple faults can occur at the inputs of the individual gates. The purpose of the test that will be performed is thus:

to test that no simple stuck-fault occurs at the inputs of the product and sum gates,
to test that the values $\{0, 1, \ldots, m-1\}$ may effectively be carried through each of these gates.

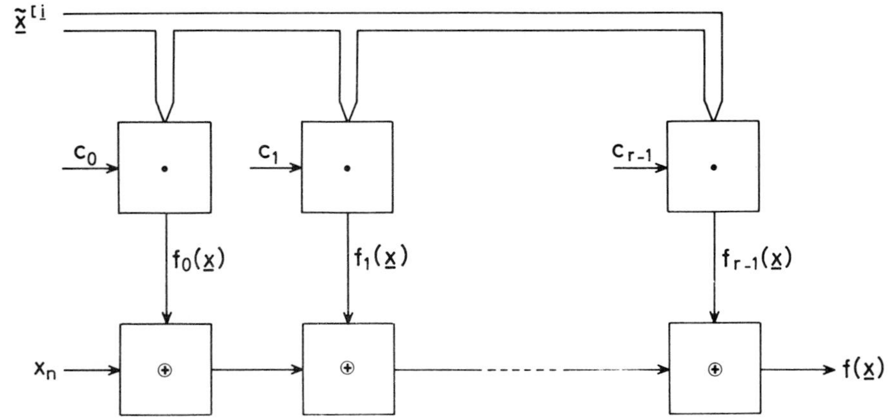

Figure 4.19. Easily diagnosable switching circuit structure

To detect a single faulty internal connection in a cascade of ring-sum gates, it is sufficient to apply the following set of test vectors t_i (see the lower part of Figure 4.19):

$$T_1^* \begin{cases} & x_n & x_{n-1} & x_{n-2} & \cdot & \cdot & \cdot & x_0 \\ t_1 = & 0 & 0 & 0 & \cdot & \cdot & \cdot & 0 \\ t_2 = & 1 & 0 & 0 & \cdot & \cdot & \cdot & 0 \\ t_3 = & 2 & 0 & 0 & \cdot & \cdot & \cdot & 0 \\ \cdot & \cdot\ \cdot & \cdot & \cdot & \cdot & \cdot & \cdot & \cdot \\ t_m = & m-1 & 0 & 0 & \cdot & \cdot & \cdot & 0 \end{cases}$$

The set T_1^* of test vectors clearly detects any simple fault occurring at the connection between the ring-sum gates. Furthermore, we see that any fault (except a stuck-at-0 fault) at any AND-gate output is detected by applying any one vector test of T_1^*; this is due to the fact that the ring-sum gates realize linear operations. The possible stuck-at-0 faults at the AND-gate outputs are detected by the test vector:

$$t_{m+1} = (1 \quad 1 \quad 1 \quad . \ . \ . \quad 1).$$

A first conclusion is thus that in order to detect a simple fault in a cascade of ring-sum gates, it is sufficient to apply the set of test vectors $T_1 = T_1^* \cup t_{m+1}$. A cascade of exclusive -OR gates (for a switching network) is thus completely tested by means of the three test vectors:

$$\begin{aligned} t_1 &= 0 \quad 0 \quad 0 \quad . \ . \ . \quad 0 \\ t_2 &= 1 \quad 0 \quad 0 \quad . \ . \ . \quad 0 \\ t_3 &= 1 \quad 1 \quad 1 \quad . \ . \ . \quad 1. \end{aligned}$$

The problem of testing the complete network thus reduces to detecting any fault (except a stuck-at-0 fault which is already detected by t_{m+1}) at the inputs of the AND-gates. It is quite evident that the single faults at the AND-gates inputs are detected by the following set of $n(m-1)$ test vectors in T_2.

$$T_2 = \begin{cases} x_n & x_{n-1} & x_{n-2} & \cdot & \cdot & \cdot & x_0 \\ \times & d & 1 & \cdot & \cdot & \cdot & 1 \\ \times & 1 & d & \cdot & \cdot & \cdot & 1 \\ \cdot & \cdot & \cdot & \cdot & \cdot & \cdot & \cdot \\ \times & 1 & 1 & \cdot & \cdot & \cdot & d \end{cases}$$

where $\times$ means any value between 0 and $m-1$ and where d must successively take the values $0, 2, \ldots, m-1$.

In conclusion, $m+1+n\ (m-1)$ tests are necessary to detect any simple fault into the network (it was assumed that the inputs x_i and c_i were fault-free); for switching networks the number of tests is thus $3+n$. It is important to note that the test $T_1 \cup T_2$ is independent of the function $f(x)$; e.g. for any switching function $f(x_3x_2x_1x_0)$, a test is:

	x_4	x_3	x_2	x_1	x_0
T_1	0	0	0	0	0
	1	0	0	0	0
	1	1	1	1	1
T_2	×	0	1	1	1
	×	1	0	1	1
	×	1	1	0	1
	×	1	1	1	0

More about the generation of test vectors for switching networks derived from Reed–Muller expansions may be found in the work by Reddy [1972] and Kodandapani [1974].

Chapter 5

Field Expressions of Galois Functions

The main purpose of this chapter is to introduce a new type of development for Galois functions, namely, the Taylor–Maclaurin expansion. The notion of derivative of a Galois function is introduced in section 5.1; these derivatives, as in classical differential calculus, are the coefficients of the Taylor–Maclaurin expansions. Explicit formulae are derived for the computation of the Taylor–Maclaurin expansions and the derivatives from the function value vector. One also shows that, in the same manner as in differential analysis, the derivatives of Galois functions are related to their differences through the intermediate of the Stirling numbers.

Section 5.2 is devoted to some possible applications of the theory developed in section 5.1. In section 5.2.1 we present an application which is closely connected to numerical analysis. We show that certain formulae derived from the relations between derivatives and differences allow us to obtain attractive closed expressions for computing the Stirling numbers in the field of integers modulo a prime number. The Chinese remainder theorem is then used to evaluate the real value of these Stirling numbers.

Section 5.2.2 is concerned with logic design; one shows that Taylor–Maclaurin expansions may be viewed as structure formulae for multiple-valued logic design.

The theory of section 5.1 is obtained from a general algebraic scheme for deriving operators associated with bases as developed under section 4.1. It could however also be derived in a more direct way by defining derivation operators over polynomials. This approach is developed in an appendix which constitutes thus another possible way of generating derivatives and field expansions for Galois functions; this approach owes much to a study of finite fields due to Berge [1968].

5.1. The Taylor expansions and the derivatives of Galois functions

Let us denote by x^e the field exponentiation, that is (see also sections 1.4.3 and 2.4.1):

$$x^e = \underbrace{x.x. \ldots .x}_{e \text{ times}} .$$

Consider first one-variable Galois functions from GF(q) to GF(q); one knows that the elements of a finite field may be denoted either as:

$$0, 1, \alpha, \alpha^2, \ldots, \alpha^{q-2}$$

or

$$0, 1, u_0, u_1, \ldots, u_{q-2}.$$

Lemma 5.1

$$x^k = \sum_{e \in \mathrm{GF}(q)} e^k \tilde{x}^{(e)}. \tag{5.1}$$

Proof. The proof derives from the fact that $\tilde{x}^{(e)}$ is 1 iff $x = e$ and is 0 otherwise. ■

One knows (see section 2.4.1) that the set of functions

$$b = \{x^0 = 1, x^1, x^2, \ldots, x^{q-1}\}$$

constitutes a basis for the Galois functions; this is also a straightforward consequence of lemma 5.1. Let us define the $(1 \times q)$ matrix $[x^e]$ as a matrix the eth entry of which is x^e; $B = [b_{ij}]$ is a $(q \times q)$ matrix with $b_{ij} = i^j$. Lemma 5.1 may then be stated in the following matrix form which corresponds to relations (4.1):

$$[x^e] = [\tilde{x}^{(e)}]\, B. \tag{5.2}$$

By using the three following identities

$$u^{q-1} = 1, \quad \forall u \in \mathrm{GF}(q), \quad u \neq 0$$

$$\sum_{u \in \mathrm{GF}(q)} u^i = 0, \quad \forall i = 1, 2, \ldots, q-2$$

$$\sum_{i=1}^{q-1} u^i = 0, \quad \forall u \in \mathrm{GF}(q), u \neq 1$$

one obtains the following inverse matrix for B:

$$B^{-1} = \begin{bmatrix} 1 & 0 & 0 & \cdot & 0 & \cdot & 0 & 0 \\ 0 & -1 & -u_0^{-1} & \cdot & -u_j^{-1} & \cdot & -u_{q-3}^{-1} & -u_{q-2}^{-1} \\ 0 & -1 & -u_0^{-2} & \cdot & -u_j^{-2} & \cdot & \cdot & \cdot \\ \cdot & \cdot & \cdot & \cdot & & \cdot & \cdot & \cdot \\ 0 & -1 & -u_0^{-k} & \cdot & -u_j^{-k} & \cdot & -u_{q-3}^{-k} & -u_{q-2}^{-k} \\ \cdot & \cdot & \cdot & \cdot & \cdot & \cdot & \cdot & \cdot \\ 0 & -1 & -u_0^{-(q-2)} & \cdot & -u_j^{-(q-2)} & \cdot & -u_{q-3}^{-(q-2)} & -u_{q-2}^{-(q-2)} \\ -1 & -1 & -1 & \cdot & -1 & \cdot & -1 & -1 \end{bmatrix}.$$

One has thus:

$$[\tilde{x}^{(e)}] = [x^e]\, B^{-1}. \tag{5.3}$$

Let us note that the above matrices B and B^{-1} were already derived in section 2.4.1.

Consider now the translated basis:

$$b_h = \{(x-h)^0, (x-h)^1, \ldots, (x-h)^{q-1}\}, \quad h \in \mathrm{GF}(q).$$

In view of the theory of section 4.1, the $(1 \times q)$ matrix b_h is related to the minterms basis by the matrix B^h, which is the $(q \times q)$ matrix the (i, j)th element of which is $b_{(i-h)j}$; the matrix $(B^{-1})^h$ is defined as usual (see section 4.1).

Definition 4.1 and the matrix B^{-1} allow us to state that the operators associated with the basis $[x^e]$ are:

$$\frac{D^0 f}{Dx} = f(x) \tag{5.4}$$

$$\frac{D^k f}{Dx} = -\sum_{\substack{e \in \mathrm{GF}(q)\\ e \neq 0}} \frac{f(x+e)}{e^k}, \quad 1 \leqslant k \leqslant q-2 \tag{5.5}$$

$$\frac{D^{q-1} f}{Dx} = -f(x) - \sum_{\substack{e \in \mathrm{GF}(q)\\ e \neq 0}} \frac{f(x+e)}{e^{q-1}}$$

$$= -\sum_{e \in \mathrm{GF}(q)} f(x+e). \tag{5.6}$$

Consider now a particular function x^i, $0 \leqslant i \leqslant q-1$. In view of relation (5.5), one has:

$$\frac{D^k x^i}{Dx} = -\sum_{\substack{e \in \mathrm{GF}(q)\\ e \neq 0}} \frac{(x+e)^i}{e^k}, \quad 1 \leqslant k \leqslant q-2.$$

Since furthermore

$$\frac{(x+e)^i}{e^k} = \sum_{j=0}^{i} \binom{i}{j} x^{i-j} e^{j-k}$$

one obtains

$$\frac{D^k x^i}{Dx} = -\sum_{j=0}^{i} \binom{i}{j} x^{i-j} \left(\sum_{\substack{e \in \mathrm{GF}(q)\\ e \neq 0}} e^{j-k} e \right).$$

From the fact that:

$$\sum_{\substack{e \in GF(q) \\ e \neq 0}} e^i = q-1 \quad \text{if} \quad i = 0 \text{ or } q-1$$

$$= 0 \quad \text{otherwise}$$

the expression of $D^k x^i / Dx$ is finally:

$$\frac{D^k x^i}{Dx} = \binom{i}{k} x^{i-k} \quad \text{if} \quad k \leqslant i$$

$$= 0 \quad \text{if} \quad k > i, \quad k = 1, 2, \ldots, q-2. \tag{5.7}$$

One proves similarly that:

$$\frac{D^{q-1} x^i}{Dx} = 1 \quad \text{if} \quad i = q-1$$

$$= 0 \quad \text{if} \quad i < q-1.$$

We may also define formal *derivatives* of discrete functions; the first derivative of x^i is defined by:

$$\frac{\partial x^i}{\partial x} = i x^{i-1}, \quad i = 0, 1, \ldots, q-1. \tag{5.8}$$

The multiple derivatives are then defined by induction, i.e.

$$\frac{\partial^k x^i}{\partial x} = \frac{\partial}{\partial x} \left(\frac{\partial^{k-1} x^i}{\partial x} \right) \tag{5.9}$$

and thus, in view of (5.8):

$$\frac{\partial^k x^i}{\partial x} = i(i-1) \ldots (i-k+1) x^{i-k} \quad \text{if} \quad k \leqslant i$$

$$= 0 \quad \text{if} \quad k > i. \tag{5.10}$$

Therefore, taking into account the formula

$$\binom{i}{k} = \frac{i(i-1) \ldots (i-k+1)}{k(k-1) \ldots 1}$$

one obtains the following relation between formal derivatives and operators associated with the basis $[x^e]$

$$\frac{\partial^k x^i}{\partial x} = k! \, \frac{D^k x^i}{Dx}, \quad k = 1, 2, \ldots, q-1.$$

Since every function f from GF(q) to GF(q) has a unique expression (see section 2.4.1):

$$f = \sum_{i=0}^{q-1} a_i x^i$$

the derivative of f can be defined as follows:

$$\frac{\partial f}{\partial x} = \sum_{i=0}^{q-1} a_i \frac{\partial x^i}{\partial x}. \tag{5.11}$$

The multiple derivatives are then defined by induction and one obtains:

$$\frac{\partial^k f}{\partial x} = \sum_{i=0}^{q-1} a_i \frac{\partial^k x^i}{\partial x}. \tag{5.12}$$

Taking into account the fact that the operators D^k/Dx are also linear operators (see relation (4.11)) one may write:

$$\begin{aligned}\frac{\partial^k f}{\partial x} &= \sum_{i=0}^{q-1} a_i \frac{\partial^k x^i}{\partial x}\\ &= k!\left(\sum_{i=0}^{q-1} a_i \frac{D^k x^i}{Dx}\right)\\ &= k!\,\frac{D^k f}{Dx}, \quad k = 0, 1, \ldots, q-1.\end{aligned} \tag{5.13}$$

At this point, consider the important particular case of functions from GF(p) to GF(p), where p is a prime. We know (see sections 1.4.3 and 2.4.1) that for this case the field elements are the integers $0, 1, \ldots, p-1$ and that the field addition "+" reduces to the addition modulo-p currently written "$\oplus$".

Let i be an integer that lies between 1 and $(p-1)$, and x be some element of GF(p); there is obviously no difference between $ix = x \oplus x \oplus \ldots \oplus x$, ($i$ times), and the product of i by x in GF(p). Consider now the factorial $k!$ with $k = 1, 2, \ldots, p-1$; it is the product of elements of $\{1, 2, \ldots, p-1\}$ that are all invertible in GF(p). Thus $k!$ is invertible in GF(p) and this allows us to write:

$$\frac{D^k f}{Dx} = \frac{1}{k!}\frac{\partial^k f}{\partial x}, \quad k = 0, 1, \ldots, p-1.$$

Theorem 5.1. (Taylor expansion) Every function f from GF(q) to GF(q) admits the following canonical expansion:

$$f(x) = f(h) + \sum_{\substack{e \in \mathrm{GF}(q)\\ e \neq 0}} \left(\frac{D^e f}{Dx}\right)_{x=h} (x-h)^e \tag{5.14}$$

where h is some chosen element of GF(q) and

$$\frac{D^k f}{Dx} = -\sum_{\substack{e \in \mathrm{GF}(q)\\ e \neq 0}} \frac{f(x+e)-f(x)}{e^k}, \quad k = 1, 2, \ldots, q-1. \tag{5.15}$$

Proof. The proof immediately follows from theorem 4.3 and from the following relation:

$$\sum_{\substack{e \in \mathrm{GF}(q)\\ e \neq 0}} \frac{f(x)}{e^k} = f(x) \cdot \left[\sum_{\substack{e \in \mathrm{GF}(q)\\ e \neq 0}} \left(\frac{1}{e}\right)^k \right]$$

$$= 0 \quad \text{if} \quad k = 1, 2, \ldots, q-2$$

$$= q-1 \quad \text{if} \quad e = q-1.$$

The following theorem 5.2 constitutes a particular case of theorem 5.1 for the Galois functions from GF(p) to GF(p).

Theorem 5.2. (Taylor expansion). Every function f from GF(p) to GF(p) admits the following canonical expansion:

$$f(x) = f(h) \oplus \sum_{e=1}^{p-1} \left(\frac{\partial^e f}{\partial x}\right)_{x=h} \frac{1}{e!}(x-h)^e \tag{5.16}$$

where h is some chosen element of GF(p) and

$$\frac{\partial^k f}{\partial x} = -k! \left[\sum_{e=1}^{p-1} \frac{f(x \oplus e) - f(x)}{e^k} \right]. \tag{5.17}$$

Theorems 5.1 and 5.2 are the Taylor expansions for Galois functions from GF(q) to GF(q) and from GF(p) to GF(p) respectively; the operators associated with these expansions are called *derivatives* or sometimes *partial derivatives* when dealing with Galois functions of several variables. The similarity between expansions (5.14) and (5.16) and the Taylor expansions of analytic functions in numerical analysis is quite self-evident. The correspondence between Taylor expansions and derivatives in finite fields and in classical analysis respectively will appear more explicitly further on in this section.

It is of current use to call the Taylor expansions at $h = 0$, i.e.

$$f(x) = f(0) + \sum_{\substack{e \in \mathrm{GF}(q)\\ e \neq 0}} \left(\frac{D^e f}{Dx}\right)_{x=0} x^e \tag{5.18}$$

and

$$f(x) = f(0) \oplus \sum_{e=1}^{p-1} \left(\frac{\partial^e f}{\partial x}\right)_{x=0} \frac{x^e}{e!} \tag{5.19}$$

the *Maclaurin expansions* of the Galois function $f(x)$.

It is only for sake of simplicity that we have considered until now one-variable Galois functions; the properties of the Kronecker matrix product and the theory of section 4.1 allow us to extend immediately the concepts of Taylor expansions and of derivatives to multiple-variable Galois functions.

Consider the Galois functions $[\mathrm{GF}(q)]^n \to \mathrm{GF}(q)$; define the matrices:

$$\begin{aligned} [(x-h)^e] &= \bigotimes_{i=n-1,0} [(x_i-h_i)^{e_i}] \\ B^h &= \bigotimes_{i=n-1,0} B^{h_i} \\ (B^h)^{-1} &= \bigotimes_{i=n-1,0} (B^{h_i})^{-1}. \end{aligned} \tag{5.20}$$

One has then:

$$\begin{aligned} [(x-h)^e] &= [\tilde{x}^{(e)}]\, B^h \\ [\tilde{x}^{(e)}] &= [(x-h)^e]\, (B^h)^{-1}. \end{aligned} \tag{5.21}$$

For $h = \mathbf{0}$, the above relations reduce to

$$\begin{aligned} [x^e] &= [\tilde{x}^{(e)}]\, (B)^n \\ [\tilde{x}^{(e)}] &= [x^e]\, (B^{-1})^n \end{aligned} \tag{5.22}$$

where $(B)^n$ means as usual the nth Kronecker power of the matrix B with the multiplication in the field as multiplicative law.

The set of functions:

$$\left\{\prod_{i=0}^{n-1} (x_i-h_i)^{e_i}, (e_{n-1}, \ldots, e_1, e_0) \in [\mathrm{GF}(q)]^n\right\}$$

constitutes thus a basis for the Galois functions $[\mathrm{GF}(q)]^n \to \mathrm{GF}(q)$.

The following theorem 5.3 is a direct consequence of theorems 4.3 and 5.1.

Theorem 5.3. (Taylor expansion) Every function $f(\boldsymbol{x})$ from $[GF(q)]^n$ to $GF(q)$ admits the following canonical expansion for every $\boldsymbol{h} \in [GF(q)]^n$:

$$f(x) = f(h) + \sum_{\substack{e \in \mathrm{GF}(q) \\ e \neq 0}} \left(\frac{D^e f}{Dx}\right)_{x=h} \left[\prod_{i=0}^{n-1} (x_i - h_i)^{e_i}\right] \tag{5.23}$$

with

$$\frac{D^k f}{Dx} = -\sum_{\substack{e \in GF(q) \\ \mathbf{0} \notin e}} \frac{f(x+e)-f(x)}{\Pi e_i^{k_i}}, \quad k = (k_{n-1}, \ldots, k_1, k_0). \tag{5.24}$$

Using similar definitions as for one-variable functions, we define formal derivatives as follows:

$$\frac{\partial}{\partial \boldsymbol{x}_0} \prod_{x_i \in \boldsymbol{x}_0} x_i^{i_j} = \prod_{x_i \in \boldsymbol{x}_0} i_j \, x_i^{i_j - 1}, \quad \boldsymbol{x}_0 \subseteq \boldsymbol{x}. \tag{5.25}$$

The multiple derivatives are defined by induction from (5.25) and (5.9); one obtains accordingly:

$$\frac{\partial^k}{\partial \boldsymbol{x}} (x_i^{i_j}) = \prod_i i_j(i_j-1) \ldots (i_j-k_j+1) \, x_i^{i_j - k_j}.$$

Since every function f from $[GF(q)]^n$ to GF(q) has a unique expansion (see section 2.4.1):

$$f = \sum_e a_e (\Pi \, x_i^{e_i})$$

the derivative of f with respect to $\boldsymbol{x}_0$ can be defined as follows:

$$\frac{\partial f}{\partial \boldsymbol{x}_0} = \sum_e a_e \frac{\partial}{\partial \boldsymbol{x}_0} (\Pi x_i^{e_i}).$$

The multiple derivatives are then defined by induction; using similar arguments as for one variable functions, one obtains:

$$\frac{\partial^k f}{\partial \boldsymbol{x}} = \prod_i k_i! \frac{D^k f}{Dx}, \quad k = (k_{n-1}, \ldots, k_1, k_0), \quad k_i \in \{0, 1, \ldots, q-1\}. \tag{5.26}$$

Since for Galois functions from $[GF(p)]^n \to GF(p)$, $k_i!$ is invertible one has also for these functions:

$$\frac{D^k f}{Dx} = \frac{1}{\prod_i k_i!} \frac{\partial^k f}{\partial \boldsymbol{x}}. \tag{5.27}$$

Theorem 5.4. (Taylor expansion) Every function f from $[GF(p)]^n$ to GF(p) admits the following canonical expansion:

$$f(\boldsymbol{x}) = f(\boldsymbol{h}) \oplus \sum_e \left(\frac{\partial^e f}{\partial \boldsymbol{x}}\right)_{\boldsymbol{x}=\boldsymbol{h}} \left[\prod_i \frac{(x_i - h_i)^{e_i}}{e_i!}\right] \tag{5.28}$$

$$e = (e_{n-1}, \ldots, e_1, e_0), \quad 0 \leqslant e_i \leqslant p-1, \mathbf{0} < e$$

$$\boldsymbol{h} \in [GF(p)]^n$$

with

$$\frac{\partial^k f}{\partial x} = -\prod_i k_i! \left[\sum_e \frac{f(x \oplus e) - f(x)}{\prod_i e_i^{k_i}} \right]. \tag{5.29}$$

The Maclaurin expansions are defined accordingly.

Let us now consider more attentively the switching functions. Switching functions are Galois functions from $[\mathrm{GF}(2)]^n$ to GF(2). The Taylor expansions for these functions are, in view of (5.28):

$$f(x) = f(h) \oplus \sum_e \left(\frac{\partial^e f}{\partial x}\right)_{x=h} \left[\prod_i (x_i \oplus h_i)^{e_i}\right] \tag{5.30}$$

with

$$\frac{\partial^k f}{\partial x} = \frac{\partial f}{\partial x^k}$$

$$= \sum_{e_0} f(x_1, x_0 \oplus e_0), \quad 0 \leqslant e_i \leqslant 1$$

with $x^k = x_0$.

It follows that for switching functions (and for switching functions only) the concepts of *difference* and of *derivative* coincide; consequently, *Taylor–Maclaurin expansions* and *Newton expansions* of switching functions coincide also and, as quoted in Chapter 4, are generally called *Reed–Muller expansions.* Our purpose is now to compare the Taylor–Maclaurin expansions defined above with the classical *Taylor–Maclaurin series expansions* used in numerical analysis.

Switching functions can be expressed as a disjunction of partial products of the variables; the variables may be complemented or uncomplemented independently from term to term. Such forms are known as *normal forms* (see Chapter 3). When the operation of disjunction is replaced by the ring-sum, the expressions thus obtained are known as (consistent or inconsistent) ring-sum expansions (see Chapter 4). By repeated use of the three identities (5.31) below, switching functions may be expressed as *real sums* of partial products of uncomplemented variables; the required identities are:

$$\begin{aligned} \bar{x} &= 1 - x \\ x \oplus y &= x + y - 2xy \\ x \vee y &= x + y - xy. \end{aligned} \tag{5.31}$$

(In the above relations, the operations + and – mean the real sum and the real subtraction respectively and no longer the corresponding operations in the finite field.) After the use of the distributivity law and after simplification of product terms one obtains a *real expansion* of the switching function as a real sum of consistent partial products.

Example 5.1

$$f = x_0 x_2 \vee x_1 \bar{x}_2$$
$$= x_0 x_2 + x_1(1-x_2) - x_0 x_1 x_2 (1-x_2)$$
$$= x_0 x_2 + x_1 - x_1 x_2. \tag{5.32}$$

Any real expression (i.e. an expression using the real connectives of sum + and of product) of a switching function $f(\boldsymbol{x})$ will from now on be denoted $f^r(\boldsymbol{x})$. The expression $f^r(\boldsymbol{x})$ represents a uniformly continuous function having derivatives at any point; this function may be expanded according to the classical Taylor–Maclaurin expansion, i.e.

$$f^r(\boldsymbol{x}) = f^r(\boldsymbol{h}) + \sum_e \left(\frac{\partial^r f^r}{\partial \boldsymbol{x}^e}\right)_{\boldsymbol{x}=\boldsymbol{h}} \left[\prod_i (x_i - h_i)^{e_i}\right], \quad 0 \leqslant e_i \leqslant 1 \tag{5.33}$$

where $\partial^r f^r / \partial \boldsymbol{x}^e$ means the real derivative (or the derivative in the sense of the classical differential calculus) of the function $f^r(\boldsymbol{x})$ with respect to $\boldsymbol{x}^e$. In view of (5.30) and (5.33) it is clear that the (finite field) Taylor expansion of f at $\boldsymbol{h}$ is obtained by substituting in the (real) Taylor expansion of f^r at $\boldsymbol{h}$ the real connectives + and – by the ring-sum $\oplus$.

Example 5.1 (continued). Expression (5.32) is the Taylor expansion of the function f^r at $\boldsymbol{h} = \boldsymbol{0}$, or equivalently the Maclaurin expansion; the Maclaurin expansion of f is thus:

$$x_0 x_2 \oplus x_1 \oplus x_1 x_2.$$

We will now compare more thoroughly the concepts of the (finite field) derivative $\partial / \partial \boldsymbol{x}_0$ and of the (real) derivative $\partial^r / \partial \boldsymbol{x}_0$. Any real expression f^r may be partially developed with respect to x_i, i.e.

$$f^r = a + b\, x_i \tag{5.34}$$

where a and b are functions of the $(n-1)$ remaining variables. One obtains then the following expression of the real derivatives $\partial^r f^r / x_i$:

$$\frac{\partial^r f^r}{\partial x_i} = b$$
$$= f(x_i{=}1) - f(x_i{=}0). \tag{5.35}$$

Since:

$$\frac{\partial f}{\partial x_i} = f(x_i = 1) \oplus f(x_i = 0)$$

$$= f(x_i = 1) + f(x_i = 0) - 2f(x_i = 1)\, f(x_i = 0)$$

$$= [f(x_i = 1) - f(x_i = 0)]^2$$

one has immediately:

$$\frac{\partial f}{\partial x_i} = \left(\frac{\partial^r f^r}{\partial x_i}\right)^2. \tag{5.36}$$

This last formula will be used in Chapter 6 for minimization purpose.

From (5.34) one deduces, by induction on the number of variables:

$$\frac{\partial^r f^r}{\partial x_{q-1} \ldots x_1 x_0} = \sum_{e_{q-1}, \ldots, e_1 e_0} (-1)^{(q + \Sigma e_i)} f(\boldsymbol{x}_1, e_{q-1}, \ldots, e_1, e_0) \tag{5.37}$$

$$0 \leqslant e_i \leqslant 1.$$

It follows that the (finite field or Boolean) derivatives could also be obtained from the (real) derivatives by replacing in (5.37) the real addition and subtraction by the modulo-2 addition operation.

Example 5.1 (continued)

$$f = x_0 x_2 \vee x_1 \bar{x}_2$$

$$f^r = x_0 x_2 + x_1 - x_1 x_2$$

$$\frac{\partial^r f^r}{\partial x_0} = x_2; \qquad \frac{\partial f}{\partial x_0} = x_2;$$

$$\frac{\partial^r f^r}{\partial x_1} = 1 - x_2; \qquad \frac{\partial f}{\partial x_1} = \bar{x}_2;$$

$$\frac{\partial^r f^r}{\partial x_2} = x_0 - x_1; \qquad \frac{\partial f}{\partial x_2} = x_0 \oplus x_1;$$

$$\frac{\partial^r f^r}{\partial x_0 x_2} = 1; \qquad \frac{\partial f}{\partial x_0 x_2} = 1;$$

$$\frac{\partial^r f^r}{\partial x_1 x_2} = -1; \qquad \frac{\partial f}{\partial x_1 x_2} = 1.$$

The above theory of derivatives and of Taylor–Maclaurin expansions for Galois functions was derived from a more general calculus of operators defined in section 4.1. From a historical point of view, the concepts of derivatives and of Taylor–Maclaurin expansions were first studied for switching functions by Reed [1954], Muller [1954] and Akers [1959]. The operators associated with the Taylor–Maclaurin (or Reed–Muller) expansions were either called Boolean differences (see, for example, Akers [1959], Sellers, Hsiao and Bearnson [1968] Ku and Masson [1975]) or Boolean derivatives (see, for example, Davio and Piret [1969], Thayse and Davio [1973]). It is clear in view of the material of this section that both callings are meaningful since the concepts of derivative and of difference coincide for switching functions. It seems that the concept of derivative of a Galois function was suggested in a note by Piret [1969]; this note gave rise to the actual definition of derivative presented in this text and originally published in papers by Thayse and Deschamps [1973b] and Thayse [1974b]. These authors defined the concepts of derivative and of Taylor–Maclaurin expansion by making use of normal and binomial families of polynomials (see the appendix to this chapter) without applying therefore the general theory of section 4.1. The derivatives and Taylor–Maclaurin expansions of Galois functions were also independently obtained by Benjauthrit and Reed [1976].

Some additional computation theorems relative to derivatives and to Taylor–Maclaurin expansions will now briefly be stated.

*Theorem 5.5. The Taylor–Maclaurin expansion at the point **h** for Galois functions from $[GF(q)]^n$ into $GF(q)$ is given by:*

$$f(\mathbf{x}) = [f_e]\ [(B^{\mathbf{h}})^{-1}]^t\ [(\mathbf{x}-\mathbf{h})^e]^t. \tag{5.38}$$

Proof. From relations (2.40), (5.20) and (5.21) one deduces:

$$\begin{aligned} f(\mathbf{x}) &= [f_e]\ [\tilde{\mathbf{x}}^{(e)}]^t \\ &= [f_e]\ [(B^{\mathbf{h}})^{-1}]^t\ [(\mathbf{x}-\mathbf{h})^e]^t. \end{aligned}$$ ∎

Corollary. The Maclaurin expansion is given by:

$$f(\mathbf{x}) = [f_e]\ [(B^{-1})^n]^t\ [\mathbf{x}^e]^t.$$

At this point we wish to compute the derivation operators $D^k f/D\mathbf{x}$ of a Galois function from its value vector; it will be seen that the matrices which allow the computation of these derivation operators derive from the matrix B and from its inverse B^{-1}.

Consider again first a Galois function $f(x)$ of one variable and let us define the $(q \times 1)$ matrix:

$$\left[\frac{Df}{Dx}\right] = \left[\frac{D^0 f}{Dx} = f, \frac{Df}{Dx}, \frac{D^2 f}{Dx}, \ldots, \frac{D^{q-1} f}{Dx}\right]^t.$$

Relations (5.24) and (5.23) for $\mathbf{x}_0 = \mathbf{x}$ may be stated in the following matrix form respectively:

$$[Df/Dx] = B^{-1}\,[Ef/Ex] \tag{5.39}$$

$$[Ef/Ex] = B\,[Df/Dx]. \tag{5.40}$$

Thanks to the fact that $[Ef/Ex]_{x=0} = [f_e]^t$ (see section 4.2.1.1.1) the above relations (5.39) and (5.40) establish relations between the coefficients appearing in the Taylor–Maclaurin expansions and the entries of the value vector. The kth element of $[Df/Dx]$ being $D^k f/Dx$, one deduces from (5.39)

$$\left(\frac{D^k f}{Dx}\right)_{x=0} = [b_k^{-1}]\,[f_e]^t$$

where b_k^{-1} is the kth row of the matrix B^{-1}. Using similar notations as in section 4.2.1.1.1, one will write:

$$\left(\frac{D^k f}{Dx}\right)_{x=j} = [\nabla^j\, b_k^{-1}]\,[f_e]^t$$

where $[\nabla^j b_k^{-1}]$ means a $(1 \times q)$ matrix obtained by shifting from j columns to the right each element of $[b_k^{-1}]$. The value vector $[D^k f(e)/Dx]$ of the kth derivation operator of f is then given by the following matrix relation:

$$\left[\frac{D^k f}{Dx}(e)\right]^t = \begin{bmatrix} [b_k^{-1}] \\ [\nabla b_k^{-1}] \\ \cdots \\ [\nabla^{q-1}\, b_k^{-1}] \end{bmatrix} [f_e]^t \tag{5.41}$$

$$= [\nabla^k\, B^{-1}]\,[f_e]^t$$

where $[\nabla^k\, B^{-1}]$ is the $(q \times q)$ matrix obtained from the q $(1 \times q)$ vectors $[\nabla^j\, b_k^{-1}]$, $0 \leqslant j \leqslant q-1$, as defined by relation (5.41).

The extension of (5.41) to multivariable functions is again straightforward through the use of the Kronecker product of matrices. Define first the $(1 \times q^n)$ matrix $[Df/D\mathbf{x}]$ as follows:

$$[Df/D\mathbf{x}] = \left[\bigotimes_{i=n-1,0} (D/Dx_i)\, f(\mathbf{x})\right]. \tag{5.42}$$

Relations (5.24) and (5.23) for $\mathbf{x}_0 = \mathbf{x}$ allow us again to write:

$$[Df/D\mathbf{x}] = (B^{-1})^n\,[Ef/E\mathbf{x}] \tag{5.43}$$

$$[Ef/E\mathbf{x}] = (B)^n\,[Df/D\mathbf{x}]. \tag{5.44}$$

Using similar types of arguments as for single-variable functions, one states the following theorem which provides us with the value vector of the derivation operators in terms of the value vector of the function:

Theorem 5.6

$$\left[\frac{D^k f}{Dx}(e)\right]^t = \left[\frac{D^{k_{n-1}\cdots k_1 k_0} f}{Dx_{n-1}\cdots x_1 x_0}(e)\right]^t$$

$$= \left(\bigotimes_{i=n-1,0} [\nabla^{k_i} B^{-1}]\right)[f_e]^t. \tag{5.45}$$

Corollary. The value vector $[\partial^k f(e)/\partial x]$ of $\partial^k f/\partial x$ is given by:

$$\left[\frac{\partial^k f}{\partial x}(e)\right]^t = \left(\bigotimes_{i=n-1,0} [k_i!\nabla^{k_i} B^{-1}]\right)[f_e]^t. \tag{5.46}$$

We conclude this section by giving the relations between the differences and the derivatives for Galois functions from $[GF(p)]^n$ to $GF(p)$.

Let $S_i^{(k)}$ and $\mathscr{S}_i^{(k)}$ be the Stirling numbers (evaluated modulo-p) of the first and of the second kind, respectively. The following theorem relates in closed form the differences and the derivatives.

Theorem 5.7

$$\text{(a)}\quad \frac{\Delta^k f}{\Delta x} = \sum_{e=k}^{p-1}\left[\prod_i \frac{\mathscr{S}_{e_i}^{(k_i)}\, k_i!}{e_i!}\right]\frac{\partial^e f}{\partial x},\quad 0 \leqslant k_i \leqslant p-1 \tag{5.47}$$

$$\text{(b)}\quad \frac{\partial^k f}{\partial x} = \sum_{e=k}^{p-1}\left[\prod_i \frac{S_{e_i}^{(k_i)}\, k_i!}{e_i!}\right]\frac{\Delta^e f}{\Delta x},\quad 0 \leqslant k_i \leqslant p-1. \tag{5.48}$$

Proof. According to theorem 4.5, one has:

$$\frac{\Delta^{k_i} f}{\Delta x_i} = \sum_{e_i=0}^{p-1} (-1)^{e_i+k_i}\binom{k_i}{e_i} f(x_i \oplus e_i).$$

The partial Maclaurin expansion of the function $f(x_i \oplus e_i)$ gives the following relation (in view of theorem 5.4):

$$f(x_i \oplus e_i) = \sum_{j_i=0}^{p-1}\left(\frac{\partial^{j_i} f}{\partial x_i}\right)_{x_i=e_i}\frac{x_i^{j_i}}{j_i!}.$$

An interchange of the roles played in this last relation by x_i and e_i allows us to write:

$$f(x_i \oplus e_i) = \sum_{j_i=0}^{p-1}\frac{\partial^{j_i} f}{\partial x_i}\frac{e_i^{j_i}}{j_i!}.$$

Therefore:

$$\frac{\Delta^{k_i} f}{\Delta x_i} = \sum_{j_i=0}^{p-1} \frac{1}{j_i!}\left[\sum_{e_i-0}^{p-1} (-1)^{e_i+k_i} \binom{k_i}{e_i} e_i^{j_i}\right] \frac{\partial^{j_i} f}{\partial x_i}.$$

From the definition of the Stirling numbers of the second kind (see, for example, Abramowitz and Stegun [1964], pp. 824–825)

$$\mathcal{S}_j^{(k)} = \frac{1}{k!} \sum_{e=0}^{k} (-1)^{e+k} \binom{k}{e} e^j$$

one then deduces:

$$\frac{\Delta^{k_i} f}{\Delta x_i} = \sum_{e_i=k_i}^{p-1} \frac{\mathcal{S}_{e_i}^{(k_i)} k_i!}{e_i!} \frac{\partial^{e_i} f}{\partial x_i}. \tag{5.49}$$

Relation (5.47) derives from (5.49) by induction on the number of variables and by the fact that differences and derivatives are linear operators.

The inverse transformation (5.48) then derives from (5.47) and from the following property of the Stirling numbers:

$$\sum_{i=k}^{j} \mathcal{S}_i^{(k)} S_j^{(i)} = \sum_{i=k}^{j} S_i^{(k)} \mathcal{S}_j^{(i)} = \delta_{jk} \text{ (Kronecker symbol).} \tag{5.50}$$ ∎

Since $S_{p-1}^{(p-1)} = \mathcal{S}_{p-1}^{(p-1)}$, one has:

$$\frac{\Delta^{p-1} f}{\Delta x_i} = \frac{\partial^{p-1} f}{\partial x_i} \tag{5.51}$$

and since the derivative $\partial^{p-1} f/\partial x_i$ is degenerate in x_i (in view of (5.12)), $\Delta^{p-1} f/\Delta x_i$ is also degenerate in x_i. It could easily be proven that $\Delta^{m_i-1} f/\Delta x_i$ is degenerate in x_i iff m_i is a prime.

The above theorem 5.7 may also easily be stated in a matrix form. Let S and S^{-1} be two $(p \times p)$ matrices defined as follows:

$$S = [s_{ij}] = [i\,!\mathcal{S}_j^i/j!] \tag{5.52}$$

$$S^{-1} = [s_{ij}^{-1}] = [i!\, S_j^i/j!]. \tag{5.53}$$

Theorem (5.7) allows us to state:

$$[\Delta f/\Delta \mathbf{x}] = (S)^n\, [\partial f/\partial \mathbf{x}] \tag{5.54}$$

$$[\partial f/\partial \mathbf{x}] = (S^{-1})^n\, [\Delta f/\Delta \mathbf{x}]. \tag{5.55}$$

Example 5.2. Consider the Galois function $f(x_1, x_0)$ from $[GF(3)]^2$ to GF(3) given by the value table of Figure 5.1.

x_1 \ x_0	0	1	2
0	0	1	2
1	1	2	2
2	0	1	0

Figure 5.1. Value table

Theorem 5.5 allows us, for example, to obtain the Taylor expansion at $(h_1, h_0) = (2, 2)$; for $p = 3$, the matrix B^{-1} is:

$$B^{-1} = \begin{bmatrix} 1 & 0 & 0 \\ 0 & 2 & 1 \\ 2 & 2 & 2 \end{bmatrix}$$

from which one deduces $(B^2)^{-1}$, that is:

$$(B^2)^{-1} = \begin{bmatrix} 0 & 0 & 1 \\ 2 & 1 & 0 \\ 2 & 2 & 2 \end{bmatrix}.$$

The coefficient vector at $(h_1, h_0) = (2, 2)$ is then obtained from $[(B^2)^{-1}]^t$ as shown in Figure 5.2, from which one immediately deduces the Taylor expansion (5.56):

$$f = (x_0 - 2) \oplus 2(x_0 - 2)^2 \oplus (x_1 - 2)(x_0 - 2)^2 \oplus 2(x_1 - 2)^2. \tag{5.56}$$

The Maclaurin expansion is then obtained from the above expression by developing the terms $(x_i - 2)^2$, using the distributivity and simplifying the obtained expression, that is:

$$f = x_0 \oplus 2x_1 \oplus 2x_1x_0 \oplus x_1x_0^2 \oplus 2x_1^2. \tag{5.57}$$

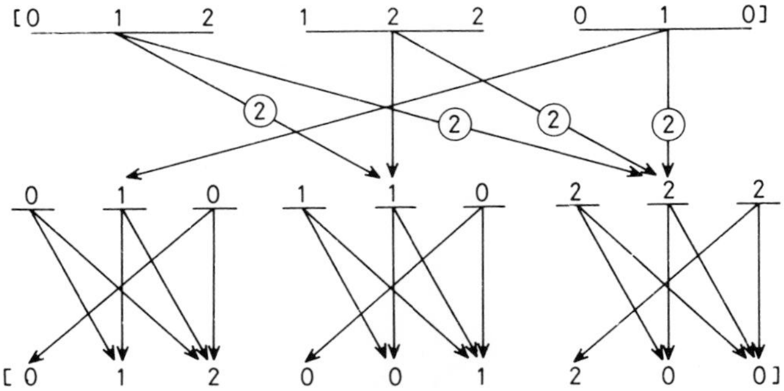

Figure 5.2. Obtention of the coefficient vector at $(h_1, h_0) = (2, 2)$ from the value vector

The derivatives may be obtained from (5.57) by using (5.13); one has, for example:

$$\frac{\partial f}{\partial x_0} = 1 \oplus 2x_1 \oplus 2x_1x_0$$

$$\frac{\partial f}{\partial x_1} = 2 \oplus 2x_0 \oplus x_0^2 \oplus x_1$$

$$\frac{\partial f}{\partial x_1 x_0} = 2 \oplus 2x_0.$$

5.2. *Applications*

5.2.1. *Derivatives and computation of Stirling numbers*

The Stirling numbers may be computed either by means of closed formulas such as, for example:

$$\mathcal{S}_i^{(k)} = \frac{1}{k!} \sum_{h=0}^{k} (-1)^{h+k} \binom{k}{h} h^i \tag{5.58}$$

$$S_i^{(k)} = \sum_{h=0}^{i-k} (-1)^h \binom{i-1+h}{i-k+h} \binom{2i-k}{i-k-h} \mathcal{S}_{i-k+h}^{(h)}, \tag{5.59}$$

or by means of recurrence formulae which are not given here but which may be found, for example, in Abramowitz and Stegun [1964] or in Jordan [1947]. If one wants to use the formulae (5.58) and (5.59) it is quite clear that the evaluation of the Stirling numbers of the first kind is much more tedious to perform than the evaluation of the Stirling numbers of the second kind. Our purpose is first to show that, for computation these numbers in the field of integers modulo-p, the two evaluations are of the same degree of complexity.

Theorem 5.8. The Stirling numbers of the first kind evaluated in the field of integers modulo-p are obtained from the closed formula:

$$S_i^{(k)} = -i! \mathop{\Sigma}_{h=i}^{p-1} \frac{\binom{h}{i}}{h^k}, \quad k \leqslant p-1. \tag{5.60}$$

Proof. According to theorem 5.4, one has for a one-variable function:

$$\frac{\partial^k f}{\partial x} = -k! \left[\mathop{\Sigma}_{h=1}^{p-1} \frac{f(x \oplus h) - f(x)}{h^k} \right].$$

According to theorem 2.4 one may write (Newton expansion of $f(x \oplus h)$):

$$f(x \oplus h) = f(h) \oplus \sum_{i=1}^{p-1} \binom{x}{i} \left(\frac{\Delta^i f}{\Delta x}\right)_{x=h} .$$

An interchange of the roles played by x and h in this last relation allows us to write:

$$f(x \oplus h) - f(x) = \sum_{i=1}^{p-1} \binom{h}{i} \frac{\Delta^i f}{\Delta x}$$

so that the expression of $\partial^k f/\partial x$ becomes:

$$\frac{\partial^k f}{\partial x} = \sum_{i=1}^{p-1} \left\{ -k! \left[\sum_{h=1}^{p-1} \frac{\binom{h}{i}}{h^k} \right] \frac{\Delta^i f}{\Delta x} \right\} . \tag{5.61}$$

On the other hand, theorem (5.7(b)) allows us to write

$$\frac{\partial^k f}{\partial x} = \sum_{i=0}^{p-1} S_i^{(k)} \frac{k!}{i!} \frac{\Delta^i f}{\Delta x} . \tag{5.62}$$

Relation (5.60) derives then from the comparison of (5.61) with (5.62). ∎

Expression (5.60) allows us to compute $S_i^{(k)}$ in the field of integers modulo-p, with p a prime $\geqslant k+1$. Advantage will now be taken of formula (5.60) in order to derive a computation algorithm for the evaluation of the real value of $S_i^{(k)}$.

First of all, one has:

$$\begin{aligned} &\operatorname{sign}(S_i^{(k)}) = (-1)^{i+k} \\ &|S_i^{(k)}| \sim \frac{(i-1)!}{(k-1)!} (\gamma + \ln i)^{k-1} \quad \text{for} \quad k = 0\ (\ln) \end{aligned} \tag{5.63}$$

where γ is known as Euler's constant and is approximately 0.577. The value of $S_i^{(k)}$ may then be deduced from its values in a set of fields of integers modulo-p by use of the *Chinese remainder theorem* (see, for example, Vinogradov [1961] or Dickson [1957]) which can be summarized as follows.

Consider a system of congruences:

$$\begin{aligned} &x = b_1 \text{ (modulo-}m_1) \\ &x = b_2 \text{ (modulo-}m_2) \\ &\dots \\ &x = b_k \text{ (modulo-}m_k) \end{aligned} \tag{5.64}$$

where m_i and m_j are mutually prime $\forall i, j$ (that is, have no common divisors). To solve the system (5.64), i.e. to find all the values of x for which it is satisfied, we shall use the Chinese remainder theorem.

Theorem 5.9. (Chinese remainder theorem). Let M_j and M_j' be given by

$$m_1 m_2 \ldots m_j \ldots m_k = M_j m_j, \quad M_j M_j' = 1 \text{ (modulo-}m_j\text{)}$$

and let

$$x_0 = M_1 M_1' b_1 + M_2 M_2' b_2 + \ldots + M_k M_k' b_k.$$

Then the set of values of x satisfying system (5.64) is defined by the congruence:

$$x = x_0 \text{ (mod } m_1 m_2 \ldots m_k\text{)}. \tag{5.65}$$

A proof of this theorem may, for example, be found in the books of Vinogradov [1961] and Dickson [1957].

Using the above formulae and theorem, the following algorithm may now be used for evaluating $S_i^{(k)}$.

Algorithm 5.1. (a) Evaluate an approximate value of $S_i^{(k)}$ using formulae (5.63) for instance.

(b) Select a set of primes $p_0, p_1, \ldots, p_l$ such that

$$p_0 p_1 \ldots p_l \geqslant S_i^{(k)}, \quad p_j \geqslant k+1 \ \forall j.$$

(c) Evaluate $S_i^{(k)}$ in the set of integers modulo $p_j \ \forall j$.

(d) Use the Chinese remainder theorem to compute $S_i^{(k)}$.

Example 5.3. (a) Computation of $S_5^{(2)}$.

Upper limit: $|S_5^{(2)}| < 7 \times 11 = 77$

Evaluation of $M_j M_j'$: $7 \times 8 = 56 = 1$ (modulo 11),

$11 \times 2 = 22 = 1$ (modulo 7).

$$(S_5^{(2)}) \text{ (modulo 7)} = -5!\left[\frac{\binom{5}{5}}{5^2} \oplus \frac{\binom{6}{5}}{6^2}\right] = 6$$

$$(S_5^{(2)}) \text{ (modulo 11)} = 5!\left[\frac{\binom{5}{5}}{5^2} \oplus \frac{\binom{6}{5}}{6^2} \oplus \frac{\binom{7}{5}}{7^2} \oplus \frac{\binom{8}{5}}{8^2} \oplus \frac{\binom{9}{5}}{9^2} \oplus \frac{\binom{10}{5}}{10^2}\right] = 5$$

$$x = 5 \times 56 + 6 \times 22 = 412$$

$$S_5^{(2)} = -(412) \text{ (modulo 77)} = -50.$$

(b) Computation of $S_6^{(2)}$

Upper limit: $|S_6^{(2)}| < 7 \times 11 \times 13 = 1001$

Evaluation of $M_j M_j'$: $(7 \times 11) \times 12 = 924 = 1$ (modulo 13),

$(7 \times 13) \times 4 = 364 = 1$ (modulo 11),

$(11 \times 13) \times 5 = 715 = 1$ (modulo 7).

$$(S_6^{(2)}) \text{ (modulo 7)} = -6! \left[\frac{\binom{6}{6}}{6^2} \right] = 1$$

$$(S_6^{(2)}) \text{ (modulo 11)} = -6! \left[\frac{\binom{6}{6}}{6^2} \oplus \frac{\binom{7}{6}}{7^2} \oplus \frac{\binom{8}{6}}{8^2} \oplus \frac{\binom{9}{6}}{9^2} \oplus \frac{\binom{10}{6}}{10^2} \right] = 10$$

$$(S_6^{(2)}) \text{ (modulo 13)} = -6! \left[\frac{\binom{6}{6}}{6^2} \oplus \frac{\binom{7}{6}}{7^2} \oplus \frac{\binom{8}{6}}{8^2} \oplus \frac{\binom{9}{6}}{9^2} \oplus \frac{\binom{10}{6}}{10^2} \oplus \frac{\binom{11}{6}}{11^2} \oplus \frac{\binom{12}{6}}{12^2} \right] = 1$$

$$x = 924 \times 1 + 364 \times 10 + 715 \times 1 = 5279$$

$$S_6^{(2)} = (5269) \text{ (modulo 1001)} = 274.$$

5.2.2. Logic design

Examples will now be presented to illustrate the use of Taylor–Maclaurin expansions of Galois functions for synthesizing logic networks. Such functions can be implemented in the same manner as logic functions by use of, for example, AND, OR and ring-sum gates. Indeed, in implementing a Taylor expansion we would need multipliers and adders over GF(q); since $q = p^r$ for some prime number p, every element in GF(q) can be expressed as an r-tuple over GF(p). Then the addition can be performed by use of r modulo-p adders (or ring-sum gates), and multiplication can be performed either by use of networks consisting of modulo-p adders and multipliers or by use of shift register networks as suggested by Peterson and Weldon [1972]. Another approach would be, instead of using only these simple gates, to employ complex modules realizing the field sum and product. Rigorous treatments of these gates may be found in the papers by Bartee and Schneider [1963], Ellison and Kolman [1970] and Benjauthrit [1974].

Most of the material and the examples presented below come from the papers by Pradhan [1974], Pradhan and Patel [1975] and Benjauthrit and Reed [1976].

Example 5.4. Consider the general Galois function over GF(3) represented by the table of Figure 5.3; from the function value vector (implicitly contained in Figure 5.3), one obtains the function coefficient vector (at $\mathbf{h} = \mathbf{0}$) by using formula (5.38), that is:

$$
\begin{array}{lllllllll}
[a_e] = [(00) & (02) & (20) & (10) & (00) & (00) & (00) & (00) & (00) \\
(12) & (02) & (00) & (00) & (00) & (21) & (00) & (11) & (10) \\
(00) & (00) & (10) & (00) & (00) & (00) & (10) & (00) & (20) \\
(01) & (12) & (00) & (20) & (00) & (02) & (00) & (12) & (00) \\
(00) & (00) & (00) & (00) & (00) & (00) & (00) & (00) & (00) \\
(00) & (12) & (00) & (22) & (00) & (10) & (00) & (02) & (00) \\
(00) & (00) & (10) & (00) & (00) & (00) & (10) & (00) & (20) \\
(00) & (02) & (00) & (21) & (20) & (01) & (00) & (00) & (20) \\
(00) & (00) & (20) & (00) & (10) & (10) & (20) & (10) & (20)].
\end{array}
$$

From the coefficient vector, one deduces the Maclaurin expansion (see theorem 5.5), that is:

$$
\begin{aligned}
f = {} & (02)\,u_0 \oplus (20)\,u_0^2 \oplus (10)\,u_1 \oplus (12)\,u_2 \oplus (02)\,u_2 u_0 \oplus (21)\,u_2 u_1 u_0^2 \oplus \\
& (11)\,u_2 u_1^2 u_0 \oplus (10)\,u_1^2 u_0^2 \oplus (10)\,u_2^2 u_1^2 \oplus (20)\,u_2^2 u_1^2 u_0^2 \oplus (01)\,u_3 \oplus (12)\,u_3 u_0 \oplus \\
& (20)\,u_3 u_1 \oplus (02)\,u_3 u_1 u_0^2 \oplus (12)\,u_3 u_1^2 u_0 \oplus (12)\,u_3 u_2^2 u_0 \oplus (22)\,u_3 u_2^2 u_1 \oplus \\
& (10)\,u_3 u_2^2 u_1 u_0^2 \oplus (02)\,u_3 u_2^2 u_1^2 u_0 \oplus (10)\,u_3^2 u_0^2 \oplus (10)\,u_3^2 u_1^2 \oplus (20)\,u_3^2 u_1^2 u_0^2 \oplus \\
& (02)\,u_3^2 u_2 u_0 \oplus (21)\,u_3^2 u_2 u_1 \oplus (20)\,u_3^2 u_2 u_1 u_0 \oplus (01)\,u_3^2 u_2 u_1 u_0^2 \oplus \\
& (20)\,u_3^2 u_2 u_1^2 u_0^2 \oplus (20)\,u_3^2 u_2^2 u_0^2 \oplus (10)\,u_3^2 u_2^2 u_1 u_0 \oplus (10)\,u_3^2 u_2^2 u_1 u_0^2 \oplus \\
& (20)\,u_3^2 u_2^2 u_1^2 \oplus (10)\,u_3^2 u_2^2 u_1^2 u_0 \oplus (20)\,u_3^2 u_2^2 u_1^2 u_0^2 \oplus (10)\,u_2 u_1^2 u_0^2.
\end{aligned}
$$

Clearly the above Maclaurin expansion of f constitutes a structural description of a logic network using ring-sum and ring-product elementary gates. It is worthwhile pointing out that if one uses the associative character of the ring-sum in order to obtain a network having cascaded ring-sum operators (as shown in Figures 4.8 and 4.9), this network has the same testing properties as those described in section 4.4.3.

u_3	u_2	u_1	u_0	v_1	v_0	u_3	u_2	u_1	u_0	v_1	v_0	u_3	u_2	u_1	u_0	v_1	v_0
0	0	0	0	0	0	1	0	0	0	0	1	2	0	0	0	0	2
0	0	0	1	2	2	1	0	0	1	1	2	2	0	0	1	2	2
0	0	0	2	1	1	1	0	0	2	1	0	2	0	0	2	0	2
0	0	1	0	1	0	1	0	1	0	1	1	2	0	1	0	0	2
0	0	1	1	0	2	1	0	1	1	2	2	2	0	1	1	0	2
0	0	1	2	2	1	1	0	1	2	0	2	2	0	1	2	0	0
0	0	2	0	2	0	1	0	2	0	1	1	2	0	2	0	2	2
0	0	2	1	1	2	1	0	2	1	2	0	2	0	2	1	2	1
0	0	2	2	0	1	1	0	2	2	0	0	2	0	2	2	2	2
0	1	0	0	1	2	1	1	0	0	1	0	2	1	0	0	1	1
0	1	0	1	1	0	1	1	0	1	0	1	2	1	0	1	2	0
0	1	0	2	0	1	1	1	0	2	1	2	2	1	0	2	2	2
0	1	1	0	0	2	1	1	1	0	0	0	2	1	1	0	1	0
0	1	1	1	2	2	1	1	1	1	0	0	2	1	1	1	0	0
0	1	1	2	2	1	1	1	1	2	1	0	2	1	1	2	1	2
0	1	2	0	1	2	1	1	2	0	1	0	2	1	2	0	0	2
0	1	2	1	2	0	1	1	2	1	0	0	2	1	2	1	0	0
0	1	2	2	2	2	1	1	2	2	1	0	2	1	2	2	1	2
0	2	0	0	2	1	1	2	0	0	2	2	2	2	0	0	2	0
0	2	0	1	2	1	1	2	0	1	1	1	2	2	0	1	0	0
0	2	0	2	1	1	1	2	0	2	2	0	2	2	0	2	0	0
0	2	1	0	1	1	1	2	1	0	0	0	2	2	1	0	1	0
0	2	1	1	0	2	1	2	1	1	2	1	2	2	1	1	2	1
0	2	1	2	1	1	1	2	1	2	2	0	2	2	1	2	2	2
0	2	2	0	2	1	1	2	2	0	0	1	2	2	2	0	2	0
0	2	2	1	2	1	1	2	2	1	1	1	2	2	2	1	1	1
0	2	2	2	0	0	1	2	2	2	1	0	2	2	2	2	1	2

Figure 5.3. General Galois function over GF(3)

Example 5.4 (*continued*). The general Galois function over GF(3) represented by the table of Figure 5.3 may be considered as a Galois function over GF(3^2) by defining the following correspondences:

$$x_1 = \{u_3, u_2\}, x_0 = \{u_1, u_0\}, f = \{v_1, v_0\}$$

A field of nine elements can be generated from the field GF(3) = {0, 1, 2} (see section 1.4.3) by using the primitive polynomial $x^2 + x + 2$ over GF(3). Let $0, 1, \alpha, \alpha^2, \alpha^3, \alpha^4, \alpha^5, \alpha^6, \alpha^7$ be the field elements. Using the rule for forming the α^i described in section 1.4.3. we find that:

$$1 = \alpha^0 = (1, 0); \alpha^1 = (0, 1); \alpha^2 = (1, 2); \alpha^3 = (2, 2); \alpha^4 = (2, 0); \alpha^5 = (0, 2);$$
$$\alpha^6 = (2, 1); \alpha^7 = (1, 1).$$

From the above correspondences, the field addition and multiplication tables (see Figure 5.4) together with the truth table (see Figure 5.5) are deduced.

The Galois function over GF(3^2) represented by its value table in Figure 5.5 can

(a)
Addition defined for field GF(3^2)

$+$	0	1	α	α^2	α^3	α^4	α^5	α^6	α^7
0	0	1	α	α^2	α^3	α^4	α^5	α^6	α^7
1	1	α^4	α^7	α^3	α^5	0	α^2	α	α^6
α	α	α^7	α^5	1	α^4	α^6	0	α^3	α^2
α^2	α^2	α^3	1	α^6	α	α^5	α^7	0	α^4
α^3	α^3	α^5	α^4	α	α^7	α^2	α^6	1	0
α^4	α^4	0	α^6	α^5	α^2	1	α^3	α^7	α
α^5	α^5	α^2	0	α^7	α^6	α^3	α	α^4	1
α^6	α^6	α	α^3	0	1	α^7	α^4	α^2	α^5
α^7	α^7	α^6	α^2	α^4	0	α	1	α^5	α^3

(b)
Multiplication defined for field GF(3^2)

$\cdot$	0	1	α	α^2	α^3	α^4	α^5	α^6	α^7
0	0	0	0	0	0	0	0	0	0
1	0	1	α	α^2	α^3	α^4	α^5	α^6	α^7
α	0	α	α^2	α^3	α^4	α^5	α^6	α^7	1
α^2	0	α^2	α^3	α^4	α^5	α^6	α^7	1	α
α^3	0	α^3	α^4	α^5	α^6	α^7	1	α	α^2
α^4	0	α^4	α^5	α^6	α^7	1	α	α^2	α^3
α^5	0	α^5	α^6	α^7	1	α	α^2	α^3	α^4
α^6	0	α^6	α^7	1	α	α^2	α^3	α^4	α^5
α^7	0	α^7	1	α	α^2	α^3	α^4	α^5	α^6

Figure 5.4. Operations over GF(3^2)

now be obtained in its Maclaurin expansion form by using again the formulation of theorem 5.5; one obtains finally:

$$f = \alpha x_1 + x_0^3 + x_0 x_1 + x_0^7 x_1^5 + x_0^8 x_1^8.$$

This expansion may again be considered as a structural description of a logic network using field addition and field multiplication elementary gates (or modules).

We now provide more carefully an application of theorems 5.3 and 5.5 in terms of switching (two-valued) elements.

Example 5.5. Consider the general Galois (or switching) function over GF(2) given by its truth table in Figure 5.6. Let $x_1 = (u_3, u_2)$, $x_0 = (u_1, u_0)$ and $f = (v_1, v_0)$; f can be realized as a Galois function over GF(2^2). A field of four elements can be generated from the field GF(2) by use of the primitive polynomial $x^2 + x + 1$ over GF(2); the 2-tuples of GF(2): (0, 0), (0, 1), (1, 0) and (1, 1) are represented by 0, 1, α and α^2 respectively. The multiplication and addition tables in GF(2^2) were given in Figure 1.3. From the table in Figure 5.6 one deduces the table in Figure 5.7 which represents the same function as a Galois function over GF(2^2). Our intention is now to represent

x_1	x_0	f	x_1	x_0	f	x_1	x_0	f
0	0	0	1	0	α	α^4	0	α^5
0	α	α^3	1	α	α^2	α^4	α	α^3
0	α^5	α^7	1	α^5	1	α^4	α^5	α^5
0	1	1	1	1	α^7	α^4	1	α^5
0	α^7	α^5	1	α^7	α^3	α^4	α^7	α^5
0	α^2	α^6	1	α^2	α^5	α^4	α^2	0
0	α^4	α^4	1	α^4	α^7	α^4	α^4	α^3
0	α^6	α^2	1	α^6	α^4	α^4	α^6	α^6
0	α^3	α	1	α^3	0	α^4	α^3	α^3
α	0	α^2	α^7	0	1	α^6	0	α^7
α	α	1	α^7	α	α	α^6	α	α^4
α	α^5	α	α^7	α^5	α^2	α^6	α^5	α^3
α	1	α^5	α^7	1	0	α^6	1	1
α	α^7	α^3	α^7	α^7	0	α^6	α^7	0
α	α^2	α^6	α^7	α^2	1	α^6	α^2	α^2
α	α^4	α^2	α^7	α^4	1	α^6	α^4	α^5
α	α^6	α^4	α^7	α^6	0	α^6	α^6	0
α	α^3	α^3	α^7	α^3	1	α^6	α^3	α^2
α^5	0	α^6	α^2	0	α^3	α^3	0	α^4
α^5	α	α^6	α^2	α	α^7	α^3	α	0
α^5	α^5	α^7	α^2	α^5	α^4	α^3	α^5	0
α^5	1	α^7	α^2	1	0	α^3	1	1
α^5	α^7	α^5	α^2	α^7	α^6	α^3	α^7	α^6
α^5	α^2	α^7	α^2	α^2	α^4	α^3	α^2	α^3
α^5	α^4	α^6	α^2	α^4	α	α^3	α^4	α^4
α^5	α^6	α^6	α^2	α^6	α^7	α^3	α^6	α^7
α^5	α^3	0	α^2	α^3	1	α^3	α^3	α^2

Figure 5.5. Galois function over GF(3^2)

this function in its Maclaurin expansion form; the transformation matrix B^{-1} is:

$$B^{-1} = \begin{bmatrix} 1 & 0 & 0 & 0 \\ 0 & -1 & -1/\alpha & -1/\alpha^2 \\ 0 & -1 & -1/\alpha^2 & -1/\alpha^4 \\ -1 & -1 & -1 & -1 \end{bmatrix}$$

$$= \begin{bmatrix} 1 & 0 & 0 & 0 \\ 0 & 1 & \alpha^2 & \alpha \\ 0 & 1 & \alpha & \alpha^2 \\ 1 & 1 & 1 & 1 \end{bmatrix}.$$

Theorem 5.5 allows us to compute the coefficient vector of f by using a Kronecker algorithm schematized by Figure 5.8.

u_3	u_2	u_1	u_0	v_1	v_0
0	0	0	0	0	0
0	0	0	1	0	1
0	0	1	0	1	1
0	0	1	1	1	0
0	1	0	0	0	0
0	1	0	1	0	0
0	1	1	0	0	1
0	1	1	1	0	1
1	0	0	0	0	1
1	0	0	1	1	1
1	0	1	0	1	1
1	0	1	1	0	1
1	1	0	0	0	1
1	1	0	1	1	0
1	1	1	0	0	1
1	1	1	1	1	0

Figure 5.6. General Galois function over GF (2)

x_1	x_0	f
0	0	0
0	1	1
0	α	α^2
0	α^2	α
1	0	0
1	1	0
1	α	1
1	α^2	1
α	0	1
α	1	α^2
α	α	α^2
α	α^2	1
α^2	0	1
α^2	1	α
α^2	α	1
α^2	α^2	α

Figure 5.7. Galois function over GF (2^2)

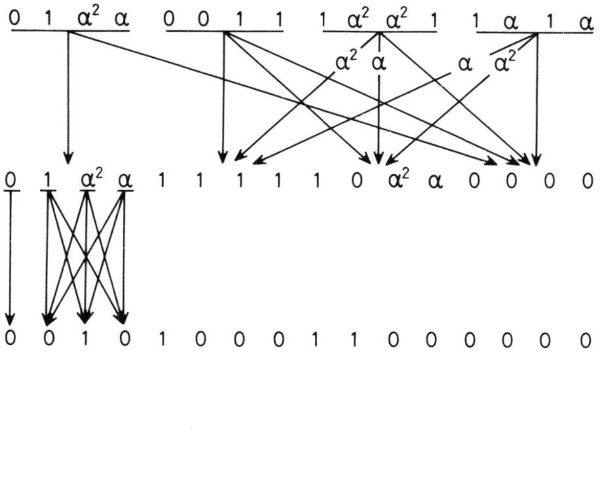

Figure 5.8

The Maclaurin expansion of the Galois function is then:

$$f = x_0^2 + x_1 + x_1^2 + x_1^2 x_0$$

This expansion can be realized by using the network shown in Figure 5.9; in this realization the network consists of GF(2^2) multipliers (schematized by the symbol ⊗) and adders (schematized by the symbol ⊕). As mentioned above, the multiplication in GF(2^2) is performed by polynomial multiplication modulo an irreducible polynomial. A network realizing this kind of multiplication is illustrated in Figure 5.10; this network is made up with switching gates. The addition in GF(2^2) can be performed by using two modulo-2 sum gates as shown in Figure 5.11.

The technique illustrated by the two above examples may be used for realization of any general Galois function over GF(p^r) where p is a prime number and r an integer. Consider, for example, a function having g input variables and h output variables; let the input variables be $\{u_{g-1}, \ldots, u_1, u_0\}$ and the output variables be $\{v_{h-1}, \ldots, v_1, v_0\}$. If the greatest common divisor of g and h is d, then the input and output variables can be partitioned into subsets of d (or a factor of d) variables. We may denote these new variables $\{x_{n-1}, \ldots, x_1, x_0\}$ and $\{f_{n-1}, \ldots, f_1, f_0\}$ where the x_i's and f_i's represent some subset of d (or of a factor of d) of the original input and output variables respectively. Now each f_i can be realized as a function of $x_{n-1}, \ldots,$ x_1, x_0 in an N^d (or a factor of d) valued logic. Though d is fixed for a given g and h, we can make it arbitrary by augmenting the input and the output variables; these augmented variables can be constants; in that case there will be large numbers of DON'T CARE conditions.

For logic functions, that is, for m-valued functions where m is not the power of a prime, we may apply the same realization technique by taking a p^r-valued algebra where $p^r > m$.

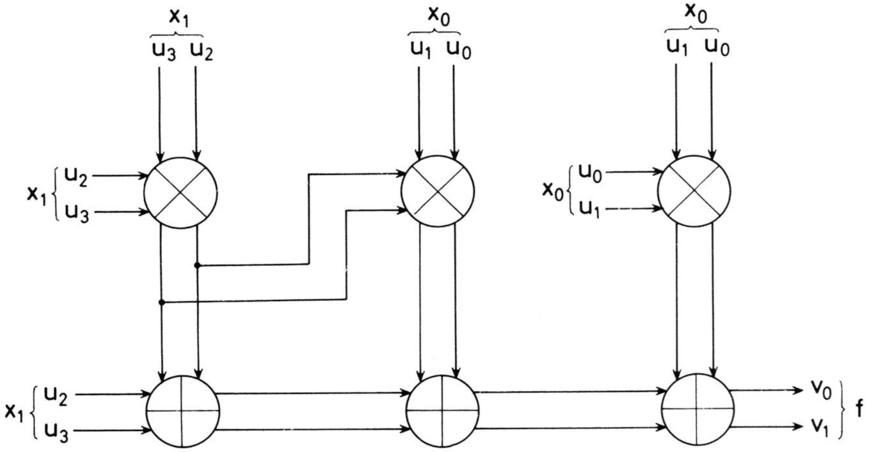

Figure 5.9. Realization of a general switching function

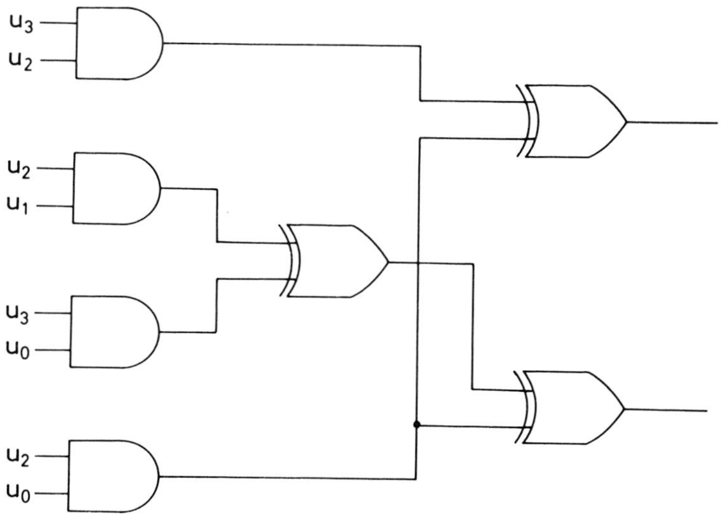

Figure 5.10. GF(2^2) multiplier

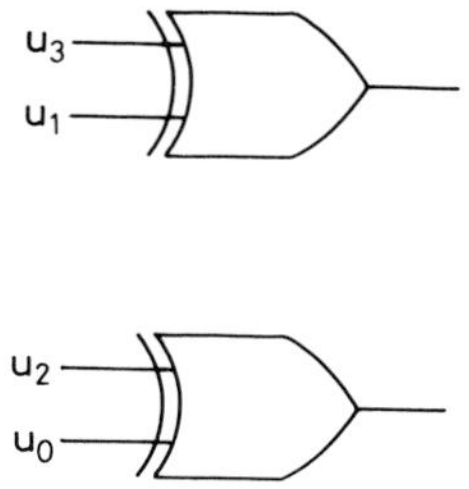

Figure 5.11. GF(2^2) adder

Appendix

Derivation operators over polynomials

Consider the finite field GF(q), with $q = p^N$, and the set $K[x]$ of polynomials $\phi(x)$ over that field, the degree of which is less than or equal to $(q-1)$ in each variable $x_j, j = 0, 1, \ldots, n-1$.

Definition A.1. The *degree* of the monomial $x_{n-1}^{i_{n-1}} \ldots x_1^{i_1} x_{i_0}$ is the vector $i = (i_{n-1}, \ldots, i_1, i_0)$; this allows us to define a total order relation on the set of monomials in $K[x]$.

The monomial m is greater than the monomial m' iff the degree of m is greater than the degree of m' in a q-ary numeration system.

The degree of a polynomial $\phi(x)$ is the degree of its maximum monomial.

Definition A.2. A subset $\mathscr{F} = \{p_i(x) \mid i \in \{0, 1, \ldots, q-1\}^n\}$ of $K[x]$ is a *quasinormal family of polynomials* iff

$$\deg P_i(x) = i, \qquad \forall\, i \in \{0, 1, \ldots, q-1\}^n.$$

In the sequel the set $\{0, 1, \ldots, q-1\}^n$ is denoted by L_q.

Theorem A. 1. Any polynomial $\phi(x) \in K[x]$ has a unique expansion

$$\phi(x) = \sum_{i \in L_q} \alpha_i P_i(x), \quad \alpha_i \in \mathrm{GF}(q), \tag{A.1}$$

in terms of the members of a quasinormal family of polynomials over GF(q).

Proof. Let d be the degree of ϕ; then $\alpha_i = 0$ for $i \succ d$, where $\succ$ denotes the lexicographic order.

Furthermore,

$$\phi(x) = \beta\, x_{n-1}^{d_{n-1}} \ldots x_1^{d_1} x_0^{d_0} + \phi'(x)$$

and

$$P_d(x) = \gamma\, x_{n-1}^{d_{n-1}} \ldots x_1^{d_1} x_0^{d_0} + P'_d(x),$$

with $\beta \neq 0, \gamma \neq 0$, $\deg \phi'(x) \prec d$ and $\deg P'_d(x) \prec d$; therefore

$$\phi(x) = \frac{\beta}{\gamma} P_d(x) + \left[\phi'(x) - \frac{\beta}{\gamma} P'_d(x)\right];$$

putting $\alpha_d = \beta/\gamma$ yields:

$$\phi(x) = \alpha_d P_d(x) + \phi''(x)$$

where

$$\deg \phi''(x) \prec d.$$

By iterating the procedure one shows that an expression exists. The uniqueness is a direct consequence of the fact that there are $q^{(q^n)}$ polynomials in $K[x]$ and also $q^{(q^n)}$ different expressions of the type (A. 1), for a given quasinormal family. ■

Definition A. 3. Derivation operators $D_{\mathscr{F}}^{(k)}$, $\forall k \in L_q$, over $K[x]$, associated with the quasinormal family $\mathscr{F}$, are mappings

$$D_{\mathscr{F}}^{(k)}: K[x] \to K[x],$$

such that

(1) $i \geqslant k$ (componentwise) $\Rightarrow D_{\mathscr{F}}^{(k)} P_i(x) = P_{i-k}(x) \prod_{j=0}^{n-1} \binom{i_j}{k_j}$;

(2) $i \ngeq k \Rightarrow D_{\mathscr{F}}^{(k)} P_i(x) = 0$;

(3) $D_{\mathscr{F}}^{(k)}(\lambda_1 \phi_1 + \lambda_2 \phi_2) = \lambda_1 D_{\mathscr{F}}^{(k)} \phi_1 + \lambda_2 D_{\mathscr{F}}^{(k)} \phi_2$, λ_1 and $\lambda_2 \in GF(q)$.

Note that $(i - k)$ is obtained by componentwise subtraction.

Theorem A.2. To any quasinormal family $\mathscr{F}$ of polynomials is associated a unique derivation operator $D_{\mathscr{F}}^{(k)}$, $\forall k \in L_q$.

Proof. From the unique expansion

$$\phi(x) = \sum_{i \in L_q} \alpha_i P_i(x),$$

we construct a mapping $D_{\mathscr{F}}^{(k)}$ of $K[x]$ into $K[x]$, by defining

$$D_{\mathscr{F}}^{(k)} \phi(x) = \sum_{\substack{i \in L_q \\ i \geq k}} \alpha_i \left[\prod_{j=0}^{n-1} \binom{i_j}{k_j} \right] P_{i-k}(x). \qquad \text{(A. 2)}$$

The properties (1), (2) and (3) of definition A.3 clearly hold true for that operator. The uniqueness results from theorem A.1 and from conditions (1), (2) and (3) of definition A. 3. ■

Note that

$$D_{\mathscr{F}}^{(0)} \phi(x) = \sum_{i \in L_q} \alpha_i P_i(x) = \phi(x).$$

Definition A. 4. A quasinormal family of polynomials $\mathscr{F} = \{P_i(x)\}$ *is normal* iff

(1) $P_0(x) = 1$,

(2) $P_i(\mathbf{0}) = 0$, $\forall i > 0$.

Theorem A.3. Any polynomial $\phi(x) \in K[x]$ has the unique expansion

$$\phi(x) = \sum_{i \in L_q} \left[D_{\mathscr{F}}^{(i)} \phi(x) \right]_{x=0} P_i(x),$$

(Maclaurin expansion) in terms of the members of a normal family of polynomials $\mathscr{F} = \{P_i(x)\}$.

Proof. From relation (A.2) and from conditions (1) and (2) of definition A.4 one deduces:

$$[D_{\mathscr{F}}^{(k)} \phi(x)]_{x=0} = \alpha_k. \qquad ■$$

Definition A.5. A normal family of polynomials $\mathcal{F} = \{P_i(x)\}$ is *binomial* iff

$$P_i(x+h) = \sum_{0 \leqslant k \leqslant i} \left[\prod_{j=0}^{n-1} \binom{i_j}{k_j}\right] P_k(x)\, P_{i-k}(h), \qquad \forall h \in [\mathrm{GF}(q)]^n.$$

Lemma A. 1. A normal family of polynomials $\mathcal{F}$ is binomial iff each of its associated derivation operators $D_{\mathcal{F}}^{(k)}$, $\forall k \in L_q$, verifies the condition:

$$[D_{\mathcal{F}}^{(k)}\, \phi(x+h)]_{x=0} = [D_{\mathcal{F}}^{(k)}\, \phi(x)]_{x=h}. \tag{A.3}$$

Proof. Assume first that $\mathcal{F}$ is binomial. Starting from the Maclaurin expansion

$$\phi(x) = \sum_{i \in L_q} [D_{\mathcal{F}}^{(i)}\, \phi(x)]_{x=0}\, P_i(x),$$

we deduce successively:

$$D_{\mathcal{F}}^{(k)}\, \phi(x) = \sum_{i \geqslant k} [D_{\mathcal{F}}^{(i)}\, \phi(x)]_{x=0} \left[\prod_{j=0}^{n-1} \binom{i_j}{k_j}\right] P_{i-k}(x),$$

and

$$[D_{\mathcal{F}}^{(k)}\, \phi(x)]_{x=h} = \sum_{i \geqslant k} [D_{\mathcal{F}}^{(i)}\, \phi(x)]_{x=0} \left[\prod_{j=0}^{n-1} \binom{i_j}{k_j}\right] P_{i-k}(h). \tag{A.4}$$

Next, we have, again from the Maclaurin expansion:

$$\phi(x+h) = \sum_{i \in L_q} [D_{\mathcal{F}}^{(i)}\, \phi(x)]_{x=0}\, P_i(x+h).$$

Taking into account the binomial character of $\mathcal{F}$, one obtains:

$$\phi(x+h) = \sum_{i \in L_q} [D_{\mathcal{F}}^{(i)}\, \phi(x)]_{x=0} \left\{ \sum_{0 \leqslant k \leqslant i} \left[\prod_{j=0}^{n-1} \binom{i_j}{k_j}\right] P_k(x)\, P_{i-k}(h) \right\}$$

$$= \sum_{k \in L_q} \left\{ \sum_{i \geqslant k} [D_{\mathcal{F}}^{(i)}\, \phi(x)]_{x=0} \left[\prod_{j=0}^{n-1} \binom{i_j}{k_j}\right] P_{i-k}(h) \right\} P_k(x);$$

thanks to the unicity of the Maclaurin expansion one has:

$$D_{\mathcal{F}}^{(k)}\, \phi(x+h)_{x=0} = \sum_{i \geqslant k} \Big[(D_{\mathcal{F}}^{(i)}\, \phi(x)\Big]_{x=0} \left[\prod_{j=0}^{n-1} \binom{i_j}{k_j}\right] P_{i-k}(h),$$

and thus, according to (A. 4): $[D_{\mathcal{F}}^{(k)}\, \phi(x+h)]_{x=0} = [D_{\mathcal{F}}^{(k)}\, \phi(x)]_{x=h}$.

Suppose conversely that condition (A. 3) holds. One has then:

$$P_i(x+h) = \sum_{0 \leqslant k \leqslant i} [D_{\mathscr{F}}^{(k)} P_i(x+h)]_{x=0} P_k(x)$$

$$= \sum_{0 \leqslant k \leqslant i} D_{\mathscr{F}}^{(k)} P_i(x)]_{x=r} P_k(x)$$

$$= \sum_{0 \leqslant k \leqslant i} \left[\prod_{j=0}^{n-1} \binom{i_j}{k_j}\right] P_{i-k}(h) P_k(x).$$ ∎

As a straightforward consequence of the foregoing lemma one obtains:

Theorem A.4. Any polynomial $\phi(x) \in K[x]$ has the unique expansion

$$\phi(x+h) = \sum_{i \in L_q} [D_{\mathscr{F}}^{(i)} \phi(x)]_{x=h} P_i(x),$$

(Taylor expansion) in terms of the members of a binomial family of polynomials $\mathscr{F} = \{P_i(x)\}$.

We give now an example of binomial family.

Theorem A.5. The set $\{x_{n-1}^{i_{n-1}} \ldots x_1^{i_1} x_0^{i_0} \mid i \in L_q\}$ of monomials is a binomial family of polynomials over GF(q).

Proof. The normal character is readily verified. The binomial character is a direct consequence of the fact that:

$$(x_j + h_j)^{i_j} = \sum_{k_j=0}^{i_j} \binom{i_j}{k_j} x_j^{i_j} h_j^{i_j - k_j}, \quad \forall\ j = 0, 1, \ldots, n-1.$$ ∎

Finally, we state some propositions that allow for computing $D_{\mathscr{F}}^{(k)} \phi(x)$ from the set of values $\phi(h)$, for each h in $[\mathrm{GF}(q)]^n$, in the case where $\mathscr{F}$ is the set of monomials in $K[x]$.

Lemma A.2. Given a partition (x_1, x_0) of x where

$$x_0 = (x_{q-1}, \ldots, x_1, x_0) \text{ and } x_1 = (x_{n-1}, \ldots, x_q),$$

$$D_{\mathscr{F}}^{(k_1,k_0)} \phi(x) = D_{\mathscr{F}}^{(k_1,0)} [D_{\mathscr{F}}^{(0,k_0)} \phi(x)],$$

for any $\phi(x) \in K[x]$ and for any quasinormal family $\mathscr{F}$.

Proof. According to (A.2) one has:

$$D_{\mathscr{F}}^{(0,k_0)} \phi(x) = \sum_{\substack{i_1 \geqslant 0 \\ i_0 \geqslant k_0}} \alpha_i \left[\prod_{j=0}^{l-1} \binom{i_j}{k_j}\right] P_{i_1, i_0 - k_0}(x);$$

according to the rules (1), (2) and (3) of definition A.3 one deduces:

$$D_{\mathscr{F}}^{(k_1,0)}\,[D_{\mathscr{F}}^{(0,k_0)}\phi(x)] = \sum_{\substack{i_1 \geqslant k_1 \\ i_0 - k_0 \geqslant 0}} \alpha_i \left[\prod_{j=0}^{l-1}\binom{i_j}{k_j}\right]\left[\prod_{j=l}^{n-1}\binom{i_j}{k_j}\right] P_{i_1-k_1,i_0-k_0}(x)$$

$$= D_{\mathscr{F}}^{(k_1,k_0)}\,\phi(x).$$ ■

We introduce the following notation:

$$D_{\mathscr{F}}^{(k_j)}\,\phi(x) = D_{\mathscr{F}}^{(0\ldots k_j\ldots 0)}\,(x).$$

A direct consequence of lemma A. 2 is given by the next theorem:

Theorem A.6

$$D_{\mathscr{F}}^{(k)}\,\phi(x) = D_{\mathscr{F}}^{(k_{n-1})}\,\{\ldots D_{\mathscr{F}}^{(k_1)}\,[D_{\mathscr{F}}^{(k_0)}\,\phi(x)]\,\ldots\}$$

for any $\phi(x) \in K[x]$ and for any quasinormal family.

Recall now the following classical proposition.

Lemma A.3

(a) $i \neq 0$ and $i \neq q-1 \Rightarrow \sum_{h \in \mathrm{GF}(q)} h^i = 0;$

(b) $h^0 = h^{q-1} = q-1, \quad \forall \quad h \in \mathrm{GF}(q), \quad h \neq 0.$

Theorem A.7. If $\mathscr{F}$ is the set of monomials in $K[x]$ then:

(a) $D_{\mathscr{F}}^{(k_j)}\,\phi(x) = \phi(x) \quad \text{if} \quad k_j = 0;$

(b) $$D_{\mathscr{F}}^{(k_j)}\,\phi(x) = -\sum_{\substack{h \in \mathrm{GF}(q) \\ h \neq 0}} \frac{\phi(x_{n-1}, \ldots, x_j + h, \ldots, x_0) - \phi(x)}{h^{k_j}},$$

$$\forall\, k_j = 1, 2, \ldots, q-1,$$

for any index $j = 0, 1, \ldots, n-1$.

Proof. (a) This has already been proved.

(b) According to the Taylor expansion one has, after permutation of $\boldsymbol{x}$ and $\boldsymbol{h}$:

$$\phi(x + h) = \sum_{i \in L_q} D_{\mathscr{F}}^{(i)}\,\phi(x)\, h_{n-1}^{i_{n-1}} \ldots h_1^{i_1}\, h_0^{i_0}.$$

In particular:

$$\phi(x_{n-1}, \ldots, x_j + h, \ldots, x_0) = \sum_{i_j=0}^{q-1} D_{\mathscr{F}}^{(i_j)}\,\phi(x)\, h_j^{i_j}$$

Therefore:

$$\sum_{\substack{h \in GF(q)\\ h \neq 0}} \frac{\phi(x_{n-1}, \ldots, x_j + h, \ldots, x_0)}{h^{k_j}} = \sum_{i_j=0}^{q-1} D_{\mathscr{F}}^{(i_j)} \phi(\boldsymbol{x}) \left(\sum_{\substack{h \in GF(q)\\ h \neq 0}} h^{i_j - k_j} \right)$$

$$= \phi(\boldsymbol{x}) \sum_{\substack{h \in GF(q)\\ h \neq 0}} \frac{1}{h^{k_j}} + \sum_{i_j=1}^{q-1} D_{\mathscr{F}}^{(i_j)} \phi(\boldsymbol{x}) \left(\sum_{\substack{h \in GF(q)\\ h \neq 0}} h^{i_j - k_j} \right);$$

for $1 \leqslant i_j \leqslant q-1$ and $1 \leqslant k_j \leqslant q-1$, one has (see lemma A. 3)

$$\sum_{\substack{h \in GF(q)\\ h \;\; h \neq 0}} h^{i_j - k_j} = q-1 \quad \text{iff} \quad i_j = k_j;$$

$$= 0 \quad \text{otherwise.}$$

Thus

$$\sum_{\substack{h \in GF(q)\\ h \neq 0}} \frac{\phi(x_{n-1}, \ldots, x_j + h, \ldots, x_0)}{h^{k_j}} = \phi(\boldsymbol{x}) \left[\sum_{\substack{h \in GF(q)\\ h \neq 0}} \frac{1}{h^{k_j}} + (q-1)\, D_{\mathscr{F}}^{(k_j)} \phi(\boldsymbol{x}) \right].$$

■

From the Taylor expansion and from the preceding theorem, one can deduce a formula due to Menger [1969].

Corollary A.1. Any polynomial $\phi(x) \in K[x]$ admits the expansion

$$\phi(x) = \phi(0) + \sum_{i=1}^{q-1} \left[\sum_{\substack{h \in GF(q)\\ h \neq 0}} \frac{\phi(0) - \phi(h)}{h^i} \right] x^i.$$

Let us now consider the derivation operators for functions from $[GF(p)]^n$ to $GF(p)$.

Any function from $[GF(p)]^n$ into $GF(p)$ can be described by a unique polynomial of degree at most $(p-1)$ in each variable and with coefficients in $GF(p)$. Denoting by $\phi_f(\boldsymbol{x})$ the polynomial associated with $f(\boldsymbol{x})$, one deduces:

$$D_{\mathscr{F}}^{(\boldsymbol{k})} f(\boldsymbol{x}) = D_{\mathscr{F}}^{(\boldsymbol{k})} \phi_f(\boldsymbol{x}), \quad \forall \boldsymbol{k} \in L_p,$$

$\mathscr{F}$ being the set of monomials in $K[\boldsymbol{x}]$.

Another family of derivation operators is now introduced. The reason why one introduces these new derivation operators is that one wishes to obtain derivatives with the classical property that the kth derivative is the first derivative of the $(k-1)$-th derivative. Furthermore, with these new operators one obtains a Taylor expansion similar to the classical Taylor expansion in analysis, where x_j^i is divided by $i!$. In the case of functions from $[\mathrm{GF}(q)]^n$ into $\mathrm{GF}(q)$ this was not possible, since $i! = 0$, $\forall i = p, p+1, \ldots, q-1$.

In the sequel, $\mathscr{F}$ denotes always the set of monomials.

Definition 3.6. The *partial derivative* of f with respect to x_j is defined as follows:

$$\frac{\partial f}{\partial x_j} = D_{\mathscr{F}}^{(1)} f;$$

the *multiple derivatives* are defined by induction:

$$\frac{\partial^{k_j} f}{\partial x_j} = \frac{\partial}{\partial x_j}\left(\frac{\partial^{k_j-1} f}{\partial x_j}\right), \quad k_j = 1, \ldots, p-1;$$

finally:

$$\frac{\partial^{k} f}{\partial \boldsymbol{x}} = \frac{\partial^{k_{n-1}}}{\partial x_{n-1}}\left[\cdots \frac{\partial^{k_1}}{\partial x_1}\left(\frac{\partial^{k_0} f}{\partial x_0}\right)\cdots\right]$$

with the convention that $\partial^0 f/\partial x_j = f$.

We relate now the operators $\partial^k/\partial \boldsymbol{x}$ with the operators $D_{\mathscr{F}}^{(k)}$.

Lemma A. 4. If

$$f(\boldsymbol{x}) = \sum_{i \in L_p} \alpha_i \, x_{n-1}^{i_{n-1}} \ldots x_0^{i_0},$$

then

$$\frac{\partial^{k_j} f}{\partial x_j} = \sum_{\substack{i \in L_p \\ i_j \geqslant k_j}} \alpha_i \, i_j(i_j-1) \ldots (i_j-k_j+1) \, x_n^{i_{n-1}} \ldots x_j^{i_j-k_j} \ldots x_0^{i_0}, \quad k_j = 1, 2, \ldots, p-1.$$

Proof. It suffices to note that

$$\frac{\partial f}{\partial x_j} = D_{\mathscr{F}}^{(1)} f = \sum_{\substack{i \in L_p \\ i_j \geqslant 1}} \alpha_i \binom{i_j}{1} x_{n-1}^{i_{n-1}} \ldots x_j^{i_j-1} \ldots x_0^{i_0}$$

$$= \sum_{\substack{i \in L_p \\ i_j \geqslant 1}} \alpha_i \, i_j \, x_{n-1}^{i_{n-1}} \ldots x_j^{i_j-1} \ldots x_0^{i_0}.$$

The proof can then be completed by induction. ■

Lemma A. 5

$$\frac{\partial^{k_j} f}{\partial x_j} = k_j!\, D_{\mathscr{F}}^{(k_j)} f, \quad k_j = 0, 1, \ldots, p-1.$$

Proof

$$D_{\mathscr{F}}^{(k_j)} f = \sum_{\substack{i \in L_p \\ i_j \geqslant k_j}} \alpha_i \binom{i_j}{k_j} x_{n-1}^{i_{n-1}} \ldots x_j^{i_j - k_j} \ldots x_0^{i_0}$$

where

$$\binom{i_j}{k_j} = \frac{i_j(i_j-1)\ldots(i_j-k_j+1)}{k_j!};$$

furthermore, $k_j! \not\equiv 0$ modulo-p, $\forall k_j \leqslant p-1$. Therefore:

$$k_j!\, D_{\mathscr{F}}^{(k_j)} f = \bigoplus_{\substack{i \in L_p \\ i_j \geqslant k_j}} \alpha_i\, i_j(i_j-1)\ldots(i_j-k_j \oplus 1)\, x_{n-1}^{i_{n-1}} \ldots x_j^{i_j-k_j} \ldots x_0^{i_0}$$

$$= \frac{\partial^{k_j} f}{\partial x_j}.$$

■

A direct consequence of lemma A. 5, definition A. 6 and theorem A. 5 is given by the next theorem.

Theorem A.8

$$\frac{\partial^k f}{\partial \boldsymbol{x}} = \prod_{j=0}^{n-1} k_j!\, D_{\mathscr{F}}^{(k)} f.$$

We can now state the following theorem.

*Theorem A.9. (Taylor expansion). Any function f(**x**) over GF(p) has the expansion*

$$f(\boldsymbol{x} \oplus \boldsymbol{h}) = \bigoplus_{i \in L_p} \left[\frac{\partial^i f(\boldsymbol{x})}{\partial \boldsymbol{x}}\right]_{\boldsymbol{x}=\boldsymbol{h}} \frac{x_{n-1}^{i_{n-1}} \ldots x_0^{i_0}}{i_{n-1}! \ldots i_0!}.$$

According to lemma A.5 and theorem A.6 one has:

Theorem A.10

$$\frac{\partial^{k_j} f(\boldsymbol{x})}{\partial x_j} = -k_j! \left[\bigoplus_{i=1}^{p-1} \frac{f(x_{n-1}, \ldots, x_j \oplus i, \ldots, x_0) - f(\boldsymbol{x})}{i^{k_j}}\right], \quad k_j = 1, 2, \ldots, p-1.$$

Remark. The definition of derivation operators and of derivatives introduced in this appendix correspond to those of section 5.1; so also are the notions of Taylor expansions. In order to obtain the Taylor expansions as quoted in section 5.1 one has only to replace in theorems A.4 and A.9 the variables $\boldsymbol{x}$ by $\boldsymbol{x}-\boldsymbol{h}$. Otherwise stated, the Taylor expansions of section 5.1 are formulated in terms of the Galois function $f(\boldsymbol{x})$ while the Taylor expansions of this appendix are formulated in terms of the Galois function $f(\boldsymbol{x} \oplus \boldsymbol{h})$.

Chapter 6
Minimization of Ring Expansions

Ring-sum expansions of switching functions are well known and their study goes back to Muller [1954]; ring-sum expansions of discrete functions were studied in Chapter 4 of this book. The main purpose of the present chapter is to describe algorithms for obtaining ring-sum expansions with a minimum number of terms. Besides providing a solution to an important algebraic problem, the logic designs corresponding to minimal ring-sum expansions correspond to a simplicity criterion (see also Chapters 3 and 8). Two types of problems will be considered.

Problem 1. Among all the ring-sum expansions of a discrete function, find the expansions having a minimum number of summed terms.

Problem 2. Among all the ring-sum expansions with a coherent Kronecker basis of a discrete function, find the expansions having a minimum number of summed terms.

In this chapter we shall propose a solution to the second problem (see section 6.1) while the more general problem 1 will receive a solution for some particular types of switching functions.

6.1. Minimization of canonical ring expansions with coherent bases

The present section is devoted to the description of algorithms for solving the following problem: among all the canonical ring expansions of a given discrete function in a given coherent basis (see section 4.2.1), find the expansions having a minimum number of summed terms.

Besides providing a solution to a classical minimization problem in discrete function theory, the algorithms described in this section are also motivated by several applications in switching theory. Hence the minimization of ring expansions for switching functions will receive particular attention.

The present section will be divided into two parts; in section 6.1.1 one deals with exhaustive methods for obtaining the minimal ring-sum expansions, so that *all* the ring expansions of a given class are exhaustively derived from which one then immediately selects the minimal expansion(s). Section 6.1.2 will be concerned with non-exhaustive methods, so that the minimal expansions are derived without resorting to the computation of *all* the ring expansions.

6.1.1. *Exhaustive minimization methods*

6.1.1.1. *Row-wise and column-wise construction of the polarity coefficient matrix*

Consider any ring-sum expansion evaluated at the point $\boldsymbol{h}$; we know that ring expansions at $\boldsymbol{h}$ are completely characterized by a $(1 \times \Pi m_i)$ matrix of coefficients of the form:

$$[f_e]\ [(X^h_m)^{-1}]^t. \tag{6.1}$$

In the above expression $[f_e]$ is the value vector considered here as a $(1 \times \Pi m_i)$ matrix while $(X^h_m)^{-1}$ is a $(\Pi m_i \times \Pi m_i)$ matrix depending on the type of ring expression chosen. For example:

$$\begin{aligned} X^h_m &= A^h_m \text{ for Newton expansions (see (4.37))} \\ &= D^h_m \text{ for Nyquist expansions (see (4.77))} \\ &= B^h \text{ for Taylor–Maclaurin expansions (see 5.38).} \end{aligned}$$

This last type of expansion (which is a field sum expansion) evidently holds for Galois functions only.

The $(\Pi m_i \times \Pi m_i)$ matrix

$$\{[f_e]\ [(X^h_m)^{-1}]^t\} \tag{6.2}$$

obtained from (6.1) by giving successively to $\boldsymbol{h}$ its Πm_i possible values in lexicographical order and by considering each matrix (6.1) as the $\boldsymbol{h}$th row of (6.2) will be called the *polarity coefficient matrix* for f. Each row of this matrix uniquely determines a ring-sum expansion of the discrete function f; the minimal expansions are evidently those corresponding to the rows containing the highest number of zero terms. The above formula (6.2) corresponds to a row-wise construction of the ring expansion matrix since each row corresponds to one expansion.

Let us now deal with a column-wise construction of the polarity coefficient matrix. Consider any difference operator $D^h f/Dx$ associated with a given basis and thus with a given ring (or field) sum expansion (see section 4.1). We know (see Chapter 4) that the value vector $[D^h f(e)/Dx]$ of any difference operator $D^h f/Dx$ is obtained from the value vector $[f(e)]$ of f through the following matrix form

$$[f_e]\ (Y^h_m)^t. \tag{6.3}$$

In the above expression, Y^h_m is a $(\Pi m_i \times \Pi m_i)$ matrix depending on the type of ring expression chosen; for example:

$$Y^h_m = \bigotimes_{i=n-1,0} [\nabla^{h_i} A^{-1}_{m_i}]$$

for Newton expansions (see (4.49))

$$= \bigotimes_{i=n-1,0} [\nabla^{h_i} B^{-1}]$$

for Taylor–Maclaurin expansions (see (5.46)).

The $(\Pi m_i \times \Pi m_i)$ matrix

$$\{[f_e]\,(Y_m^h)^t\} \tag{6.4}$$

obtained from (6.3) by giving successively to $\boldsymbol{h}$ its Πm_i possible values in lexicographical order and by considering each matrix (6.3) as the $\boldsymbol{h}$th row of (6.2) is clearly the transpose of the polarity coefficient matrix for f. Indeed, each column of this matrix uniquely determines a ring-sum expansion of the discrete function f. The minimal expansions are those containing the highest number of zero terms; the above matrix (6.4) corresponds thus to a column-wise construction of the polarity coefficient matrix.

An example will now be given; for sake of conciseness the Reed–Muller expansions of a switching function will be evaluated.

Example 6.1. The polarity coefficient matrix of the function

$$f = x_0 \vee \bar{x}_1 x_2$$

is:

$h_2h_1h_0$ \ h_2	0	0	0	0	1	1	1	1	
h_1	0	0	1	1	0	0	1	1	
h_0	0	1	0	1	0	1	0	1	Weight
0 0 0	0	1	0	0	1	1	1	1	5
0 0 1	1	1	0	0	0	1	0	1	4
0 1 0	0	1	0	0	0	0	1	1	3
0 1 1	1	1	0	0	0	0	0	1	3
1 0 0	1	0	1	1	1	1	1	1	7
1 0 1	1	0	0	1	0	1	0	1	4
1 1 0	0	1	1	1	0	0	1	1	5
1 1 1	1	1	0	1	0	0	0	1	4

Figure 6.1. Polarity coefficient matrix

The row $(h_2\ h_1\ h_0)$ of the matrix 6.1 contains the coefficients of the Reed–Muller expansion at the point $(h_2\ h_1\ h_0)$; the weight (number of non-zero coefficients) of each of these expansions is indicated at the right side of Figure 6.1. The minimal expansions are those corresponding to the vertices $(h_2\ h_1\ h_0) = (0\ 1\ 0)$ and $(0\ 1\ 1)$; they are respectively:

$$x_0 \oplus x_2\bar{x}_1 \oplus x_2\bar{x}_1 x_0$$

and

$$1 \oplus \bar{x}_0 \oplus x_2\bar{x}_1\bar{x}_0.$$

The column $(h_2\ h_1\ h_0)$ of the matrix 6.1 is the truth vector of the difference $\Delta f/\Delta x_2^{h_2} x_1^{h_1} x_0^{h_0}$.

6.1.1.2. *The Marinkovic–Tosic procedure and the Gray code approach*

Marinkovic and Tosic [1974] have suggested a method for obtaining minimal Reed–Muller expansions for switching functions. Their criterion of minimization is minimizing the total number of literals which does not always minimize the total number of terms. However, by a minor modification of their method, Reed–Muller expansions with the least number of terms can be obtained; this is the criterion which will be adopted here. Kodandapani [1974] extended the Marinkovic–Tosic procedure to the case of discrete function minimization; for sake of conciseness, only the switching function minimization will be considered here. The ensuing discussion follows very closely that of Marinkovic and Tosic.

Two vectors $\boldsymbol{h} = (h_{n-1}, \ldots, h_i, \ldots, h_0)$ and $\boldsymbol{h}^i = (h_{n-1}, \ldots, \bar{h}_i, \ldots, h_0)$ are called adjacent with respect to the element h_i. Let us denote by $\mathrm{RM}_{\boldsymbol{h}}(f)$ the Reed–Muller expansion of f at the point $\boldsymbol{h}$. The Reed–Muller expansion $\mathrm{RM}_{\boldsymbol{h}}(f)$ will be called *adjacent* to the Reed–Muller expansion $\mathrm{RM}_{\boldsymbol{h}^i}(f)$ with respect to the variable x_i; the set of n Reed–Muller expansions adjacent to $\mathrm{RM}_{\boldsymbol{h}}(f)$ will be denoted:

$$\{\mathrm{RM}_{\boldsymbol{h}}(f)\} = \{\mathrm{RM}_{\boldsymbol{h}^{n-1}}(f), \ldots, \mathrm{RM}_{\boldsymbol{h}^1}(f), \mathrm{RM}_{\boldsymbol{h}^0}(f)\}.$$

The total number of non-zero terms $W_{\boldsymbol{h}}(f)$ in $\mathrm{RM}_{\boldsymbol{h}}(f)$ will be called the *weight* of the given Reed–Muller expansion. The vector

$$\{W_{\boldsymbol{h}}(f)\} = (w_{n-1}, \ldots, w_1, w_0)$$

where

$$w_i = W_{\boldsymbol{h}}(f) - W_{\boldsymbol{h}^i}(f)$$

will be called the *influence vector* of the expansion $\mathrm{RM}_{\boldsymbol{h}}(f)$.

Let two adjacent Reed–Muller expansions $\mathrm{RM}_{\boldsymbol{h}^i}(f)$ and $\mathrm{RM}_{\boldsymbol{h}}(f)$ be given where $\mathrm{RM}_{\boldsymbol{h}}(f)$ will be called the starting expansion. Let us consider the characteristics of transition from one expansion to another.

Theorem 6.1. At the transition from the Reed–Muller expansion $RM_{\boldsymbol{h}}(f)$ to the adjacent expansion $RM_{\boldsymbol{h}^i}(f)$ all the terms of the form $p\dot{x}_i$ (p = term degenerate in x_i, $\dot{x}_i$ = either x_i or $\bar{x}_i$) from $RM_{\boldsymbol{h}}(f)$ appear in $RM_{\boldsymbol{h}^i}(f)$ as well under the form $p\bar{\dot{x}}_i$.

Proof. The proof follows from the fact that the ring difference

$$\Delta f/\Delta p x_i$$

is degenerate in x_i. ∎

Let $p\dot{x}_i$ be a term present in $\mathrm{RM}_{\boldsymbol{h}}(f)$; it may be represented as:

$$p\dot{x}_i = p\bar{\dot{x}}_i \oplus p. \tag{6.5}$$

The first term of the right-hand side of (6.5) is the term which will, on the basis of theorem 6.1, also exist in $\mathrm{RM}_{\boldsymbol{h}^i}(f)$ so that it does not affect the value of the element w_i of the influence vector; the cube p, which does not include the variable x_i, affects the value of the element w_i. If in $\mathrm{RM}_h(f)$, besides $p\dot{x}_i$, there exists a term p, the latter will, at transition to $\mathrm{RM}_{h^i}(f)$, be eliminated since $p \oplus p = 0$. Thus it increases the value of w_i for the value 1; on the contrary if p does not appear in $\mathrm{RM}_h(f)$, the appearance of p at the transition to $\mathrm{RM}_{h^i}(f)$ decreases the value of w_i for the value 1. As a conclusion, in order to compute w_i one has to consider the terms $p_j\dot{x}_i$ $(0 \leqslant j \leqslant k)$ appearing in $\mathrm{RM}_h(f)$; one has:

$$w_i = [\text{number of terms } p_j \text{ present in } \mathrm{RM}_{h^i}(f)] - [\text{number of terms } p_j \text{ which are not present in } \mathrm{RM}_{h^i}(f)].$$

Starting from a Reed–Muller expansion $\mathrm{RM}_h(f)$, the following algorithm may be used for obtaining a better expansion, that is an expansion with a smaller number of terms.

Algorithm 6.1

(a) Form the Reed–Muller expansion $\mathrm{RM}_h(f)$ for the starting expansion vertex $\boldsymbol{h}$.
(b) Form the influence vector $\{W_h(f)\}$.
(c) Determine the element w_i in $\{W_h(f)\}$ from the condition

$$w_i = \operatorname*{Max}_k\,(w_k), \quad k = n-1, \ldots, 1, 0.$$

If $w_i > 0$, modify the polarity of the element h_i of $\boldsymbol{h}$ and form the Reed–Muller expansion at $(h_{n-1}, \ldots, \bar{h}_i, \ldots, h_0)$; this new vertex will be denoted by $\boldsymbol{h}$. Go to step (b) of the algorithm.

If $w_i \leqslant 0$ declare that $\mathrm{RM}_h(f)$ is a *locally-minimal expansion* and stop the algorithm.

It is clear that algorithm 6.1 provides us only with a locally minimal expansion since all the vertices $\boldsymbol{h}$ are not necessarily examined. A minimal expansion could however easily be obtained by applying algorithm 6.1 for an adequate choice of different starting points $\boldsymbol{h}$.

Example 6.2

$$-\mathrm{RM}_{(000)}(f) = 1 \oplus x_0 \oplus x_1 \oplus x_0x_2 \oplus x_2x_1x_0$$

$$\{W_{(000)}(f)\} = (-1, 2, 0)$$

$$-\mathrm{RM}_{(010)}(f) = x_0 \oplus \bar{x}_1 \oplus x_2\bar{x}_1x_0$$

$$\{W_{(010)}(f)\} = (-2, -2, -1).$$

$\mathrm{RM}_{(010)}(f)$ is thus locally minimal with respect to the initial vertex (000).

A slight improvement from a complexity point of view (see section 6.1.3) over the Marinkovic–Tosic procedure is obtained by the following algorithm.

Algorithm 6.2. (Gray code algorithm).

(a) From the truth vector of $f(\boldsymbol{x})$ generate any ring-sum expansion, say at the point $\boldsymbol{h}$, and compute its weight.
(b) Starting from the ring-sum expansion at the point $\boldsymbol{h}$ and enumerating the n-tuples by means of a Gray code, generate from the given $\boldsymbol{h}$-Reed–Muller expansion the 2^n-1 remaining $\boldsymbol{h}$-Reed–Muller expansions, and compute their weight.

The computation of the step (b) of algorithm 6.2 can best be performed by making use of theorem 4.13.

6.1.2. Non-exhaustive minimization methods for Galois functions

6.1.2.1. Methods grounded on the extended vector

The minimization of ring-sum expansions reduces to the problem of determining the point (or points) where a maximum number of difference operators vanish. Since for discrete functions $f\colon (\bigtimes_i S_i) \to L$, there are $\prod_i m_i$ difference operators which must be evaluated at $\prod_i m_i$ vertices, the exhaustive computation of all the ring-sum expansions leads to the evaluation of $(\prod_i m_i)^2$ coefficients. The purpose of this section is to show that this exhaustive computation may be avoided for the class of Galois functions:

$$f\colon [\mathrm{GF}(p)]^n \to \mathrm{GF}(p)$$

by using a technique based on the extended vector (see section 3.2.3.2.1). This technique, initially developed by Bioul and Davio [1972] for switching functions, was extended by Thayse [1974b] to the Galois functions quoted above. It is based on the observation that, for some type of ring-sum expansions, the associated operators are such that $D^{p-1}f/Dx_i$ is degenerate in x_i. For example the difference $\Delta^p f/\Delta x_i$ and the derivative $\partial^p f/\partial x_i$ are each identically zero. It is a consequence of theorem 4.4; let us also give, for illustration purposes, a direct proof of the fact that $\Delta^p f/\Delta x_i$ is zero.

In view of relation (4.29) one has:

$$\frac{\Delta^p f}{\Delta x_i} = \sum_{e_i=0}^{p} (-1)^{(p+e_i)} \binom{p}{e_i} f(x_i \oplus e_i). \tag{6.6}$$

Since:

$$\binom{p}{e} = \frac{p!}{(p-e)!\,e!}$$

one has $\binom{p}{e} = 0$ (modulo-p) $\forall e\colon 1 < e < p$. Indeed, the expression (6.7) contains p in the numerator and since p is prime this factor cannot disappear by simplification with one of the factors of the denominator. Expression (6.6) thus becomes

$$\frac{\Delta^p f}{\Delta x_i} = f(x_i \oplus p) - f(x) = 0 \tag{6.7}$$

since $f(x_i \oplus p) = f(x_i)$. Since the pth difference of f with respect to x_i is zero the $(p-1)$-th difference is degenerate with respect to x_i. It could easily be shown that the degenerescence of the $(p-1)$-th difference only occurs for p a prime.

Let us turn to the computation of Newton expansions for Galois functions. The difference

$$\frac{\Delta^{k_1(p-1)}f}{\Delta x_1 x_0}$$

with $k_1 = (k_{n-1}, \ldots, k_{q+1}, k_q)$, $(p-1) = (p-1, \ldots, p-1)$ (q times), and with $k_i < p-1 \;\forall\, i$, depends only on the $n-q$ variables in x_1. There are

$$\binom{n}{q} p^{(n-q)}$$

differences of this kind, each of which must be evaluated at $(p-1)^{(n-q)}$ different points. Hence, there are

$$\sum_{q=0}^{n} \binom{n}{q} p^{(n-q)} (p-1)^{(n-q)} = [p(p-1) + 1]^n$$

local values of differences to be evaluated instead of the p^{2n} initially counted (for $m_i = p \;\forall i$, one has indeed $(\Pi m_i)^2 = p^{2n}$).

One will now show that the extended vector allows us to compute in a direct way these $(p^2-p+1)^n$ local values and, from that point on, computing the weights of the Newton expansions with a corresponding $(1-1/p+1/p^2)^n$ saving in complexity; the same type of argument evidently also holds when dealing with Taylor–Maclaurin expansions.

6.1.2.1.1. Extended vectors for Newton and for Taylor–Maclaurin expansions

T-extended vectors have been defined in section 3.2.3.2.1; they were defined (see definition 3.8) with respect to an operator T or, equivalently with respect to a difference operator Tf/Tx. The case where T was either the disjunction, or the conjunction, the corresponding differences being then the join and meet differences respectively, was examined in Chapter 3 dealing with lattice expressions. In this section one will be interested in T-extended vectors with respect to the ring-sum operation and the corresponding difference-operators $\Delta f/\Delta x$ and $\partial f/\partial x$ respectively.

From definition 3.8(a) one deduces that the partial extended vectors of a Galois function $f(\boldsymbol{x})$, with respect to a variable x_i, and with respect to the difference-operator and the derivation operator are respectively:

$$\phi_{x_i}^{(\Delta)}(f) = \left[f(e_i), \frac{\Delta f}{\Delta x_i}(e_i), \ldots, \frac{\Delta^{p-2} f}{\Delta x_i}(e_i), \frac{\Delta^{p-1} f}{\Delta x_i}\right] \tag{6.8}$$

$$\phi_{x_i}^{(\partial)}(f) = \left[f(e_i), \frac{\partial f}{\partial x_i}(e_i), \ldots, \frac{\partial^{p-2} f(e_i)}{\partial x_i}, \frac{\partial^{p-1} f}{\partial x_i}\right]. \tag{6.9}$$

The partial extended vectors $\phi_{\boldsymbol{x}_0}^{(\Delta)}(f)$ and $\phi_{\boldsymbol{x}_0}^{(\partial)}(f)$ are defined according to the computing scheme (3.66) and (3.67); the Δ- and ∂-extended vectors are finally defined according to the usual rule (see definition 3.8(c)), that is:

$$\phi^{(\Delta)}(f) = \phi_{\boldsymbol{x}}^{(\Delta)}(f)$$

$$\phi^{(\partial)}(f) = \phi_{\boldsymbol{x}}^{(\partial)}(f)$$

Computational formulae will now be given for obtaining the extended vectors of f when the latter is given by its value vector. Consider theorem 4.7; since $m_i = p$ for Galois functions, let us first simply denote by $\nabla^k A^{-1}$ the matrix $\nabla^{k_i} A_{m_i}^{-1}$ (see (4.44)). From relation (6.8) and from theorem 4.7. one then deduces that the expressions of the partial extended vector $\phi_{x_i}^{(\Delta)}(f)$ and of the extended vector $\phi^{(\Delta)}(f)$ are given by the following theorem (the symbol $(\oplus\,\cdot)$ is again used in this section for matrix multiplication in the ring, since matrix multiplication with other operations is also used).

Theorem 6.2

$$\phi_{x_i}^{(\Delta)}(f) = [f(e_i)] \,(\oplus\,\cdot)\, M^{(\Delta)} \tag{6.10}$$

$$\phi^{(\Delta)}(f) = [f(e)] \,(\oplus\,\cdot)\, (M^{(\Delta)})^n \tag{6.11}$$

with $M^{(\Delta)}$ the $[p \times (p(p-1)+1)]$ matrix:

$$[(A^{-1})^t, (\nabla A^{-1})^t, \ldots, (\nabla^{(p-2)} A^{-1})^t, E_p] \tag{6.12}$$

and where $(M^{(\Delta)})^n$ is the nth Kronecker power of the matrix $M^{(\Delta)}$.

It is recalled that in section 3.2.3.2.1 the matrix E_p was defined as the $(p \times 1)$ unit matrix; the extended vector has thus $[p(p-1)+1]^n$ components.

Theorem 5.6 and relation (6.9) finally allow us to state the following theorem 6.3.

Theorem 6.3

$$\phi_{x_i}^{(\partial)}(f) = [f(e_i)] \,(\oplus\,\cdot)\, M^{(\partial)} \tag{6.13}$$

$$\phi^{(\partial)}(f) = [f(e_i)] \,(\oplus\,\cdot)\, (M^{(\partial)})^n \tag{6.14}$$

with $M^{(\partial)}$ the $[p \times (p(p-1)+1)]$ matrix:

$$\{(B^{-1})^t, (1!\,\nabla B^{-1})^t, (2!\,\nabla^2 B^{-1})^t, \ldots, [(p-2)!\nabla^{(p-2)} B^{-1}]^t, (p-1)!E_p\}. \tag{6.15}$$

6.1.2.1.2. Minimal Newton expansions

The main purpose of this section will be to obtain the weights of all the Newton expansions of a given Galois function $f(x)$ through the intermediate of its extended vector $\phi^{(\Delta)}(f)$; the Newton expansions may then be computed at the vertices whose weight is minimal. This provides us clearly with a non-exhaustive method for obtaining the best Newton expansions.

Before dealing with this non-exhaustive method, one shows that the extended vector may be used for obtaining *all* the Newton expansions of a given Galois function, providing us thus with a new formulation of an exhaustive method; the non-exhaustive method based on the weight computation derives then immediately from this last one.

Let $f(x)$ be a Galois function of a single variable x; the symbol $N_h f$ denotes the Newton expansion of f at the vertex h. The notation $[N_h]$ will denote the $(1 \times p)$ matrix of operators:

$$[N_h] = [N_0, N_1, \ldots, N_{p-1}].$$

Next, for a function $f(x)$ of n variables, the $(1 \times p^n)$ matrix $[N_h]$ is defined as the formal Kronecker product

$$\bigotimes_{i=n-1,0} [N_{h_i}]$$

where the product of operators is achieved by concatenating the indices h_i. Consider the $\{[p(p-1)+1] \times p\}$ matrix $K_i^{(\Delta)}$ defined as follows:

$$\left[\begin{array}{cccc}
\binom{x_i-0}{0} & & & 0 \\
& \binom{x_i-1}{0} & & \\
& & \ddots & \\
0 & & & \binom{x_i-p+1}{0} \\
\hline
\binom{x_i-0}{1} & & & 0 \\
& \binom{x_i-1}{1} & & \\
& & \ddots & \\
0 & & & \binom{x_i-p+1}{1} \\
\hline
\vdots & & & \\
\hline
\binom{x_i-0}{p-2} & & & 0 \\
& \binom{x_i-1}{p-2} & & \\
& & \ddots & \\
0 & & & \binom{x_i-p+1}{p-2} \\
\hline
\binom{x_i-0}{p-1} & \binom{x_i-1}{p-1} & \cdots & \binom{x_i-1}{p-1}
\end{array}\right]$$

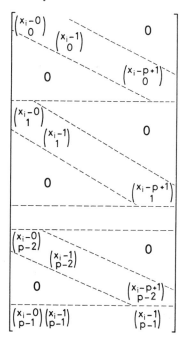

Theorem 6.4 below relates the p^n Newton expansions of f to the extended vector.

Theorem 6.4. The p^n Newton expansions of the Galois function $f(x)$ are given by:

$$[N_h\, f(x)] = \phi^{(\Delta)}(f) \,(\oplus\,\cdot)\, \left(\bigotimes_{i=n-1,0} K_i^{(\Delta)} \right). \tag{6.16}$$

Proof. The proof is achieved by perfect induction.

For $n = 1$, a routine verification shows that the theorem holds true. We assume as induction hypothesis that (6.16) is satisfied for every function $f(x)$ of n variables and show that

$$[N_{h_n h}\, g(x_n x)] = \{\phi^{(\Delta)}[g(0x)], \phi^{(\Delta)}[g(1x)], \ldots, \phi^{(\Delta)}[g(p-1, x)]\} \,(\oplus\,\cdot)\, \left[\left(\bigotimes_{i=n-1,0} K_i^{(\Delta)} \right) \otimes K_n^{(\Delta)} \right] \tag{6.17}$$

where $\phi^{(\Delta)}[g(ix)]$ is the extended vector of $g(i, x)$. Now, each column of (6.17) is a straightforward consequence of (6.16) and of the definition of the extended vector. ■

The number of summed terms in a ring expansion is the *weight* of the ring expansion; as quoted in the introduction of this section our purpose is to find a ring expansion having a *minimum weight* or equivalently a minimum number of summed terms. Theorem 6.4 computes all the Newton expansions; from this result one may evidently select the expansions having the minimum weight. It is an *exhaustive method* for obtaining the minimum expansions since it requests computation of all expansions. Theorem 6.5 below provides us with a non-exhaustive method for obtaining the best expansions since the method grounded on this theorem does not require an explicit computation of all expansions.

Let us define the matrices $WK_i^{(\Delta)}$ and $W\phi^{(\Delta)}(f)$ which are nothing but the matrices $K_i^{(\Delta)}$ *and* $\phi^{(\Delta)}(f)$ respectively, where the non-zero entries have been replaced by 1. The vector of the weights of Newton expansions, that we denote $[WN_h f(x)]$, may be evaluated by means of the following theorem.

Theorem 6.5. The weights of the p^n Newton expansions of the functions $f(x)$ are given by

$$\{WN_h\,[f(x)]\} = W\phi^{(\Delta)}(f) \,(+\,\times)\, \left(\bigotimes_{i=n-1,0} WK_i^{(\Delta)} \right) \tag{6.18}$$

where $\times$ means a real product and + a real sum.

Proof. One easily observes that each column of $\bigotimes_{i=n-1,0} K_i^{(\Delta)}$ contains as non-zero entries the functions forming the appropriate basis for the corresponding Newton expansion. Furthermore, these basis functions are enumerated in lexicographical order. Hence the only information needed about $\bigotimes_{i=n-1,0} K_i^{(\Delta)}$ is the actual position of its non-zero entries. The announced result is then achieved by performing in (6.18) a real matrix product. ■

Since all the matrices $WK_i^{(\Delta)}$ coincide for any index i, they will generally be denoted $WK^{(\Delta)}$.

The vector $[WN_h f(x)]$ will be called the *Newton weight vector.*

Example 6.3. Consider the Galois function:

$$f: \{0, 1, 2\}^2 \to \{0, 1, 2\}$$

given by its value vector:

$$[f_{e_1 e_0}] = [0\ 1\ 2 \quad 1\ 2\ 2 \quad 0\ 1\ 0].$$

The partial extended vector of f with respect to x_1, that is $\phi_{x_1}^{(\Delta)}(f)$, is obtained by multiplying the value vector $[f_{e_1 e_0}]$, considered here as a (1×3) matrix whose elements are 3-tuples, by the (3×7) matrix $M^{(\Delta)}$, that is

$$[(0\ 1\ 2)(1\ 2\ 2)(0\ 1\ 0)] \, (\oplus \cdot) \begin{bmatrix} 1 & 0 & 0 & 2 & 0 & 1 & 1 \\ 0 & 1 & 0 & 1 & 2 & 0 & 1 \\ 0 & 0 & 1 & 0 & 1 & 2 & 1 \end{bmatrix} =$$

$$[(0\ 1\ 2)(1\ 2\ 2)(0\ 1\ 0)(1\ 1\ 0)(2\ 2\ 1)(0\ 0\ 2)(1\ 1\ 1)].$$

The extended vector $\phi^{(\Delta)}(f)$ is then obtained by multiplying each of the 3-tuples of $\phi_{x_1}^{(\Delta)}(f)$ by the same matrix $M^{(\Delta)}$, and one obtains accordingly the (1×49) matrices:

$$\begin{aligned} \phi^{(\Delta)}(f) = [&(0\ 1\ 2\ 1\ 1\ 1\ 0)(1\ 2\ 2\ 1\ 0\ 2\ 2)(0\ 1\ 0\ 1\ 2\ 0\ 1) \\ &(1\ 1\ 0\ 0\ 2\ 1\ 2)(2\ 2\ 1\ 0\ 2\ 1\ 2)(0\ 0\ 2\ 0\ 2\ 1\ 2) \\ &(1\ 1\ 1\ 0\ 0\ 0\ 0)] \end{aligned}$$

$$\begin{aligned} W\phi^{(\Delta)}(f) = [&(0\ 1\ 1\ 1\ 1\ 1\ 0)(1\ 1\ 1\ 1\ 0\ 1\ 1)(0\ 1\ 0\ 1\ 1\ 0\ 1) \\ &(1\ 1\ 0\ 0\ 1\ 1\ 1)(1\ 1\ 1\ 0\ 1\ 1\ 1)(0\ 0\ 1\ 0\ 1\ 1\ 1) \\ &(1\ 1\ 1\ 0\ 0\ 0\ 0)]. \end{aligned}$$

In order to compute the weights of the Newton expansions one first multiplies the vector $W\phi^{(\Delta)}(f)$, considered here as a (1×7) matrix, whose elements are 7-tuples, by the (7×3) matrix $WK^{(\Delta)}$:

$$\begin{bmatrix} 1 & 0 & 0 \\ 0 & 1 & 0 \\ 0 & 0 & 1 \\ 1 & 0 & 0 \\ 0 & 1 & 0 \\ 0 & 0 & 1 \\ 1 & 1 & 1 \end{bmatrix}.$$

One obtains:

$$[(2\ 3\ 2\ 1\ 2\ 2\ 1)(3\ 3\ 3\ 1\ 1\ 2\ 2)(1\ 2\ 2\ 1\ 2\ 1\ 2)].$$

The value vector of the weights of the Newton expansions is then obtained by multiplying each of the 7-tuples of the above (1×3) matrix by the matrix $WK^{(\Delta)}$, that is, finally:

$$[4\ 6\ 5 \quad 6\ 6\ 7 \quad 4\ 6\ 5].$$

The minimal Newton expansions of f occur thus at $(x_1, x_0) = (0, 0)$ and $(2, 0)$; they are respectively:

$$\binom{x_1}{1} \oplus \binom{x_0}{1} \oplus 2\binom{x_1}{1}\binom{x_0}{2} \oplus \binom{x_1}{2}$$

$$\binom{x_0}{1} \oplus \binom{x_0}{2} \oplus 2\binom{x_1-2}{1}\binom{x_0}{2} \oplus \binom{x_1-2}{2}.$$

Assume now that one wants to compute explicitly all Newton expansions of the function f; the extended vector $\phi^{(\Delta)}(f)$ (considered again as a (1×7) matrix of 7-tuples) has first to be multiplied by the matrix $K_0^{(\Delta)}$, that is:

$$\begin{bmatrix} 1 & 0 & 0 \\ 0 & 1 & 0 \\ 0 & 0 & 1 \\ \binom{x_0}{1} & 0 & 0 \\ 0 & \binom{x_0-1}{1} & 0 \\ 0 & 0 & \binom{x_0-2}{1} \\ \binom{x_0}{2} & \binom{x_0-1}{2} & \binom{x_0-2}{2} \end{bmatrix}.$$

One obtains:

$$\left\{\left[\binom{x_0}{1}, 1 \oplus \binom{x_0}{1} \oplus 2\binom{x_0}{2}, \binom{x_0}{1} \oplus \binom{x_0}{2}, 1 \oplus 2\binom{x_0}{2}, 2 \oplus 2\binom{x_0}{2}, 2\binom{x_0}{2}, 1\right]\right.$$

$$\left[1 \oplus \binom{x_0-1}{1}, 2 \oplus 2\binom{x_0-1}{2}, 1 \oplus 2\binom{x_0-1}{1} \oplus \binom{x_0-1}{2}, 1 \oplus 2\binom{x_0-1}{2} \oplus 2\binom{x_0-1}{2}\right.$$

$$\left. 2 \oplus 2\binom{x_0-1}{1} \oplus 2\binom{x_0-1}{2}, 2\binom{x_0-1}{1} \oplus 2\binom{x_0-1}{2}, 1\right]$$

$$\left[2 \oplus \binom{x_0-2}{1}, 2 \oplus 2\binom{x_0-2}{1} \oplus 2\binom{x_0-2}{2}, \binom{x_0-2}{2}, \binom{x_0-2}{1} \oplus 2\binom{x_0-2}{2},\right.$$

$$\left.\left. 1 \oplus \binom{x_0-2}{1} \oplus 2\binom{x_0-2}{2}, 2 \oplus \binom{x_0-2}{1} \oplus 2\binom{x_0-2}{2}, 1\right]\right\}.$$

Each of the 7-tuples of the above (1×3) matrix are then to be multiplied by $K_1^{(\Delta)}$; one obtains finally the nine Newton expansions of (x_1, x_0), that is:

Vertex (0, 0):

$$\binom{x_1}{1} \oplus \binom{x_0}{1} \oplus 2\binom{x_1}{1}\binom{x_0}{2} \oplus \binom{x_1}{2}$$

Vertex (0, 1):

$$1 \oplus \binom{x_0-1}{1} \oplus \binom{x_1}{1} \oplus 2\binom{x_1}{1}\binom{x_0-1}{1} \oplus 2\binom{x_1}{1}\binom{x_0-1}{2} \oplus \binom{x_1}{2}$$

Vertex (0, 2):

$$2 \oplus \binom{x_0-2}{1} \oplus \binom{x_1}{1}\binom{x_0-2}{1} \oplus 2\binom{x_1}{1}\binom{x_0-2}{2} \oplus \binom{x_1}{2}$$

Vertex (1, 0):

$$1 \oplus \binom{x_0}{1} \oplus 2\binom{x_0}{2} \oplus 2\binom{x_1-1}{1} \oplus 2\binom{x_1-1}{1}\binom{x_0}{2} \oplus \binom{x_1-1}{2}$$

Vertex (1, 1):

$$2 \oplus 2\binom{x_0-1}{2} \oplus 2\binom{x_1-1}{1} \oplus 2\binom{x_1-1}{1}\binom{x_0-1}{1} \oplus 2\binom{x_1-1}{1}\binom{x_0-1}{2} \oplus \binom{x_1-1}{2}$$

Vertex (1, 2):

$$2 \oplus 2\binom{x_0-2}{1} \oplus 2\binom{x_0-2}{2} \oplus \binom{x_1-1}{1} \oplus \binom{x_1-1}{1}\binom{x_0-2}{1} \oplus 2\binom{x_1-1}{1}\binom{x_0-2}{2} \oplus$$
$$\binom{x_1-1}{2}$$

Vertex (2, 0):

$$\binom{x_0}{1} \oplus \binom{x_0}{2} \oplus 2\binom{x_1-2}{1}\binom{x_0}{2} \oplus \binom{x_1-2}{2}$$

Vertex (2, 1):

$$1 \oplus 2\binom{x_0-1}{1} \oplus \binom{x_0-1}{2} \oplus 2\binom{x_1-2}{1}\binom{x_0-1}{1} \oplus 2\binom{x_1-2}{1}\binom{x_0-1}{2} \oplus \binom{x_1-2}{2}$$

Vertex (2, 2):

$$\binom{x_0-2}{2} \oplus 2\binom{x_1-2}{1} \oplus \binom{x_1-2}{1}\binom{x_0-2}{1} \oplus 2\binom{x_1-2}{1}\binom{x_0-2}{2} \oplus \binom{x_1-2}{1}.$$

Switching functions

For switching functions, one deduces from functions (6.8) and (6.9) that the partial extended vector with respect to a variable x_i is given by:

$$\phi_{x_i}^{(\Delta)}(f) = \left[f(x_i = 0), f(x_i = 1), \frac{\Delta f}{\Delta x_i}\right]. \tag{6.19}$$

The matrix $M^{(\Delta)}$ is the (2×3) matrix

$$M^{(\Delta)} = \begin{bmatrix} 1 & 0 & 1 \\ 0 & 1 & 1 \end{bmatrix}$$

identical to the matrix $M_i^{(\vee)}$ (see section 3.2.3.2.1).

The extended vector $\phi^{(\Delta)}(f)$ has 3^n components and, from its definition, it clearly appears that it may be partitioned into three subvectors of equal length that are the extended vectors of the subfunctions $f(x_{n-1} = 0), f(x_{n-1} = 1)$ and of the difference $\Delta f/\Delta x_{n-1}$, respectively.

The matrix $K_i^{(\Delta)}$ becomes for switching functions:

$$K_i^{(\Delta)} = \begin{bmatrix} 1 & 0 \\ 0 & 1 \\ x_i & \bar{x}_i \end{bmatrix}$$

and the matrix $WK^{(\Delta)}$ is nothing but the transpose of $M^{(\Delta)}$.

Example 6.4. Let us compute the optimal Reed–Muller expansions of the function

$$[1\ 0\ 1\ 0\ 0\ 0\ 1\ 1].$$

The extended vector is first constructed:

$$[1\ 0\ 1\ 1\ 0\ 1\ 0\ 0\ 0 \quad 0\ 0\ 0\ 1\ 1\ 0\ 1\ 1\ 0 \quad 1\ 0\ 1\ 0\ 1\ 1\ 1\ 1\ 0].$$

The weights of the 8 Newton expansions are next computed from (6.18) taking into account the Kronecker product structure of $(M^{(\Delta)})^n$. The computation is sketched in Figure 6.2.

There are two optimal Reed–Muller expansions having three terms, namely $N_{001}f$ and $N_{101}f$. According to theorem 6.5, the latter expansion is given by:

$$[\phi^{(\Delta)}(f)] \textcircled{\oplus \cdot} \left(\begin{bmatrix} 0 \\ 1 \\ \bar{x}_2 \end{bmatrix} \otimes \begin{bmatrix} 1 \\ 0 \\ x_1 \end{bmatrix} \otimes \begin{bmatrix} 0 \\ 1 \\ \bar{x}_0 \end{bmatrix} \right) = x_1 \oplus \bar{x}_2\bar{x}_0 \oplus \bar{x}_2 x_1.$$

It is important to note at this point that the Newton weight vector constitutes a complete representation of the function. Indeed, theorem 4.13 allows us to compute

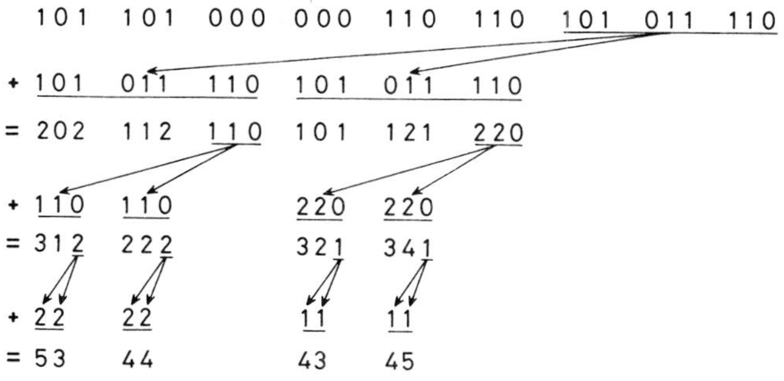

Figure 6.2. Weights of the Reed–Muller expansions

the Newton weight vector $[WN_e f]$ from the truth vector. Conversely, it is particularly simple to compute the truth vector from the Newton weight vector.

Theorem 6.6

$$[WN_e f]_{(\mathrm{mod}\,(2))} = [f_{\bar{e}}] \tag{6.20}$$

Proof. The coefficients of the Reed–Muller expansion at $\boldsymbol{x} = \boldsymbol{e}$ are computed from the truth vector $[f_h]$ by the transformation matrix $(\underset{i}{\oplus} A^{e_i})$ (see (4.107)). Any row of that matrix contains an even number of 1, except the row $\bar{e}$. Hence, the mod-2 sum of the coefficients of the Reed–Muller expansion at $\boldsymbol{x} = \boldsymbol{e}$ contains any $f(\boldsymbol{h})$ an even number of times, except $f(\bar{e})$, which appears only once. ■

In the case of example 6.4, the Newton weight vector is

$$[5\ \ 3\ \ 4\ \ 4\ \ 4\ \ 3\ \ 4\ \ 5].$$

Reducing this vector modulo-2 and reading it from right to left to account for the complementation of variables, one obtains

$$[1\ \ 0\ \ 1\ \ 0\ \ 0\ \ 0\ \ 1\ \ 1]$$

which is the function truth vector.

6.1.2.1.3. Minimal Taylor–Maclaurin expansions

It is clear that all that was said in the preceding section 6.2.1.1.2 concerning the Newton expansions of $f(\boldsymbol{x})$ could be transposed with some minor modifications to the Taylor–Maclaurin expansions. Some results are briefly quoted in this section; the statements would be the same as those of section 6.2.1.1.2.

The symbol $T_h f(\boldsymbol{x})$ denotes the Taylor expansion at the vertex $\boldsymbol{h}$ of f; the $(1 \times p^n)$ matrix $[T_h]$ is defined as the formal Kronecker product

$$\underset{i=n-1,0}{\otimes} [T_{h_i}]$$

where the product of operators is obtained by concatenating the indices h_i. The $\{[p(p-1)+1] \times p\}$ matrix $K_i^{(\partial)}$ is defined as follows:

$$\left[\begin{array}{cccc}
\frac{(x_i-0)^0}{0!} & & & \\
 & \frac{(x_i-1)^0}{0!} & & \\
 & & \ddots & \\
 & & & \frac{(x_i-p+1)^0}{0!} \\
\hline
\frac{(x_i-0)^1}{1!} & & & \\
 & \frac{(x_i-1)^1}{1!} & & \\
 & & \ddots & \\
 & & & \frac{(x_i-p+1)^1}{1!} \\
\hline
\vdots & & & \\
\hline
\frac{(x_i-0)^{(p-2)}}{(p-2)!} & & & \\
 & \frac{(x_i-1)^{(p-2)}}{(p-2)!} & & \\
 & & \ddots & \\
 & & & \frac{(x_i-p+1)^{(p-2)}}{(p-2)!} \\
\hline
\frac{(x_i-0)^{(p-1)}}{(p-1)!} & \frac{(x_i-1)^{(p-1)}}{(p-1)!} & \cdots & \frac{(x_i-p+1)^{(p-1)}}{(p-1)!}
\end{array}\right]$$

Theorem 6.7. The p^n Taylor expansions of the Galois function $f(\mathbf{x})$ are given by:

$$[T_h f(\mathbf{x})] = \phi^{(\partial)}(f) \boxed{\oplus\ \cdot} \left(\bigotimes_{i=n-1,0} K_i^{(\partial)} \right).$$

Let $[WT_h f(\mathbf{x})]$ be the vector of the weights of the Taylor expansions; define moreover $W\phi^{(\partial)}(f)$ and $WK_i^{(\partial)}$ in the same manner as $W\phi^{(\Delta)}(f)$ and $WK_i^{(\Delta)}$ respectively.

Theorem 6.8. The weights of the p^n Taylor expansions of the function $f(\mathbf{x})$ are given by:

$$[WT_h f(\mathbf{x})] = W\phi^{(\partial)}(f) \boxed{+\ \times} \left(\bigotimes_{i=n-1,0} WK_i^{(\partial)} \right). \tag{6.21}$$

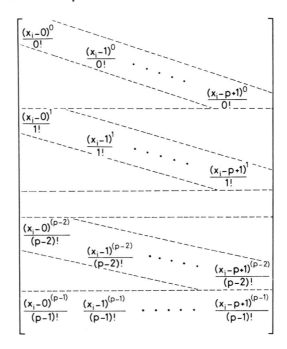

Example 6.3 (continued). Consider the function of example 6.3; the partial extended vector of f with respect to x_1, that is $\phi_{x_i}^{(\partial)}(f)$, is obtained by multiplying the value vector $[f_{e_1 e_0}]$, considered here as a (1×3) matrix, whose elements are 3-tuples,

by the (3×7) matrix $M^{(\partial)}$, that is:

$$[(0\ 1\ 2)\,(1\ 2\ 2)\,(0\ 1\ 0)] \ (\oplus\ \cdot)\ \begin{bmatrix} 1 & 0 & 0 & 0 & 1 & 2 & 2 \\ 0 & 1 & 0 & 2 & 0 & 1 & 2 \\ 0 & 0 & 1 & 1 & 2 & 0 & 2 \end{bmatrix} =$$

$$[(0\ 1\ 2)\,(1\ 2\ 2)\,(0\ 1\ 0)\,(2\ 2\ 1)\,(0\ 0\ 2)\,(1\ 1\ 0)\,(2\ 2\ 2)].$$

The extended vector $\phi^{(\partial)}(f)$ is then obtained by multiplying each of the 3-tuples of $\phi^{(\partial)}_{x_1}(f)$ by the same matrix $M^{(\partial)}$, and one obtains accordingly the (1×49) matrices:

$$\begin{aligned} \phi^{(\partial)}(f) = [&(0\ 1\ 2\ 1\ 1\ 1\ 0)\,(1\ 2\ 2\ 0\ 2\ 1\ 1)\,(0\ 1\ 0\ 2\ 0\ 1\ 2) \\ &(2\ 2\ 1\ 2\ 1\ 0\ 1)\,(0\ 0\ 2\ 2\ 1\ 0\ 1)\,(1\ 1\ 0\ 2\ 1\ 0\ 1) \\ &(2\ 2\ 2\ 0\ 0\ 0\ 0)] \\ W\phi^{(\partial)}(f) = [&(0\ 1\ 1\ 1\ 1\ 1\ 0)\,(1\ 1\ 1\ 0\ 1\ 1\ 1)\,(0\ 1\ 0\ 1\ 0\ 1\ 1) \\ &(1\ 1\ 1\ 1\ 1\ 0\ 1)\,(0\ 0\ 1\ 1\ 1\ 0\ 1)\,(1\ 1\ 0\ 1\ 1\ 0\ 1) \\ &(1\ 1\ 1\ 0\ 0\ 0\ 0)]. \end{aligned}$$

In order to compute the weights of the Taylor expansions one first multiplies the vector $W\phi^{(\partial)}(f)$, considered here as a (1×7) matrix, whose elements are 7-tuples by the (7×3) matrix $WK^{(\partial)}$; one obtains:

$$[(2\ 3\ 3\ 2\ 2\ 1\ 1)\,(2\ 2\ 3\ 1\ 2\ 1\ 2)\,(2\ 3\ 1\ 2\ 1\ 1\ 2)].$$

The value vector of the weights of the Taylor expansions is then obtained by multiplying each of the 7-tuples of the above (1×3) matrix by the matrix $WK^{(\partial)}$, that is finally:

$$[5\ 6\ 5 \quad 5\ 6\ 6 \quad 6\ 6\ 4].$$

The minimal Taylor expansion of f occurs at $(x_1, x_0) = (2, 2)$; it is:

$$(x_0-2) \oplus 2\,(x_0-2)^2 \oplus (x_1-2)\,(x_0-2)^2 \oplus 2\,(x_1-2)^2.$$

6.1.2.2. Methods for switching functions based on the use of real connectives

The purpose of this section is to present a minimization method for Reed–Muller expansions of switching functions and which is based on the use of *real expansions* for switching functions (see relation (5.33)). The method is based on a comparison between Taylor–Maclaurin expansions using real connectives and Taylor–Maclaurin expansions using ring connectives; therefore, one will adopt in this section the notations and callings of Boolean differential calculus, i.e. Boolean derivatives and Taylor expansions, instead of those of the Boolean difference calculus, i.e. ring differences and Newton expansions.

To each switching function one will associate a pseudo-logic function whose value at any vertex is the weight (number of summed terms) of the switching function Taylor expansion at the same vertex. Some well-known theorems of differential analysis will allow us then to obtain easily a formal expression of this pseudo-logic function. Any pseudo-logic minimizing method may then be used to derive the optimal Taylor expansions (Thayse [1974a]).

Given a switching function f of n variables $(x_{n-1}, \ldots, x_1, x_0) = \boldsymbol{x}$, the Taylor expansion of $f(\boldsymbol{x})$ evaluated at the vector $\boldsymbol{h}$ is

$$T_{\boldsymbol{h}} f(\boldsymbol{x}) = \bigoplus_{\boldsymbol{e}} \left(\frac{\partial f}{\partial \boldsymbol{x}^{\boldsymbol{e}}}\right)_{\boldsymbol{x}=\boldsymbol{h}} \left[\prod_{i=0}^{n-1} (x_i \oplus h_i)^{e_i}\right], \quad 0 \leqslant e_i \leqslant 1. \tag{6.22}$$

Consequently, the weight of the Taylor expansion of f at the point $\boldsymbol{h}$ is given by (+ and Σ stand in this section for the real sums):

$$WT_{\boldsymbol{h}} f(\boldsymbol{x}) = \sum_{\boldsymbol{e}} \left(\frac{\partial f}{\partial \boldsymbol{x}^{\boldsymbol{e}}}\right)_{\boldsymbol{x}=\boldsymbol{h}}, \quad 0 \leqslant e_i \leqslant 1. \tag{6.23}$$

In relations (6.22) and (6.23) it is conventionally assumed that the **0**-derivative $\partial f/\partial \boldsymbol{x}^{\boldsymbol{0}}$ is $f(\boldsymbol{x})$. The following algorithm may then be used for building a pseudo-logic function $W(f)$ that gives us the weights of the Taylor expansions at any vertex and, from that on, the weight of the optimal Taylor expansions.

Algorithm 6.3. (a) From any formal representation of $f(\boldsymbol{x})$, compute the (finite field) derivatives $\partial f/\partial \boldsymbol{x}^{\boldsymbol{e}}$, $0 \leqslant e_i \leqslant 1$.

(b) Obtain the real expansion $(\partial f/\partial \boldsymbol{x}^{\boldsymbol{e}})^r$ of these derivatives by using the identities (5.31).

(c) Compute the pseudo-logic function

$$W(f) = \sum_{\boldsymbol{e}} (\partial f/\partial \boldsymbol{x}^{\boldsymbol{e}})^r.$$

(d) The vertices where $W(f)$ takes its minimal value may then be obtained by using any pseudo-Boolean method (see e.g. Hammer and Rudeanu [1968]).

Let us illustrate this algorithm by means of a short example.

Example 6.4

Switching functions	Corresponding real expansions
$f = x_0 x_2 \vee x_1 \bar{x}_2$	$f^r = x_0 x_2 + x_1 - x_1 x_2$
$\partial f/\partial x_0 = x_2$	$(\partial f/\partial x_0)^r = x_2$
$\partial f/\partial x_1 = \bar{x}_2$	$(\partial f/\partial x_1)^r = 1 - x_2$
$\partial f/\partial x_2 = x_0 \oplus x_1$	$(\partial f/\partial x_2)^r = x_0 + x_1 - 2x_0 x_1$
$\partial f/\partial x_0 x_2 = \partial f/\partial x_1 x_2 = 1$	$(\partial f/\partial x_0 x_2)^r = (\partial f/\partial x_1 x_2)^r = 1$

$$W(f) = 3 + x_0 + 2x_1 + x_0 x_2 - x_1 x_2 - 2x_0 x_1.$$

The vertices where $W(f)$ takes its minimal values are:

$$h_2 h_1 h_0 = \times\ 0\ 0 \quad (\times = \text{indeterminate value, 0 or 1}).$$

The minimal value is 3 and the corresponding Taylor expansions are

$$x_0 x_2 \oplus x_1 \oplus x_1 x_2 \quad \text{for} \quad h_2 h_1 h_0 = 0\ 0\ 0$$

$$x_0 \oplus x_0 \bar{x}_2 \oplus x_1 \bar{x}_2 \quad \text{for} \quad h_2 h_1 h_0 = 1\ 0\ 0.$$

The above algorithm may be improved by using several simplifications. First, let us observe that the real expansions $(\partial f/\partial \mathbf{x}^{\mathbf{e}})^r$, $\mathbf{e} > \mathbf{0}$, may be computed by starting from the real expansion f^r without resorting to a first evaluation of the derivatives $\partial f/\partial \mathbf{x}^{\mathbf{e}}$. In view of relation (5.36), the real expansions of the field derivatives may be obtained by a formal derivation of f^r, i.e. (see (5.36)):

$$\left(\frac{\partial f}{\partial x_i}\right)^r = \left(\frac{\partial^r f^r}{\partial x_i}\right)^2. \tag{6.24}$$

It is recalled that the expression

$$\frac{\partial^r f^r}{\partial x_i}$$

means the (real) derivative of f with respect to x_i in the sense of the classical differential calculus. The higher order (field) derivatives are then obtained by a recurrence formula of the form:

$$\left[\frac{\partial}{\partial x_j}\left(\frac{\partial f}{\partial x_i}\right)\right]^r = \left[\frac{\partial^r}{\partial x_j}\left(\frac{\partial^r f^r}{\partial x_i}\right)^2\right]^2.$$

The real expansions of f and of all its (finite field) derivatives may then be computed in the following way by introducing partial real expansions of f with respect to a subset of its variables.

Algorithm 6.4

1. From $f(\mathbf{x})$ compute the partial real expansion with respect, for example, to x_0, that is:

$$f(x_0 = 0) + x_0 \frac{\partial^r f^r}{\partial x_0}$$

with $\dfrac{\partial^r f^r}{\partial x_0} = f(x_0 = 1) - f(x_0 = 0).$

From $\dfrac{\partial^r f^r}{\partial x_0}$ deduce $\dfrac{\partial f}{\partial x_0} = \left(\dfrac{\partial^r f^r}{\partial x_0}\right)^2.$

2. From $f(x_0 = 0) + x_0 \dfrac{\partial^r f^r}{\partial x_0}$ compute the partial real expansion with respect to x_0 and x_1, that is:

$$\left[f(x_0 = 0) + x_0 \frac{\partial^r f^r}{\partial x_0}\right]_{x_1=0} + x_1 \frac{\partial^r f^r}{\partial x_1}$$

with $\dfrac{\partial^r f^r}{\partial x_1} = \left[f(x_0 = 0) + x_0 \dfrac{\partial^r f^r}{\partial x_0}\right]_{x_1=1} - \left[f(x_0 = 0) + x_0 \dfrac{\partial^r f^r}{\partial x_0}\right]_{x_1=0}$.

From $\dfrac{\partial^r f^r}{\partial x_1}$ deduce $\dfrac{\partial f}{\partial x_1} = \left(\dfrac{\partial^r f^r}{\partial x_1}\right)^2$.

From $\left(\dfrac{\partial^r f^r}{\partial x_0}\right)^2$ compute the partial expansion with respect to x_1, that is:

$$\left(\frac{\partial^r f^r}{\partial x_0}\right)^2_{x_1=0} + x_1 \frac{\partial^r}{\partial x_1}\left(\frac{\partial^r f^r}{\partial x_0}\right)^2$$

with $\dfrac{\partial^r}{\partial x_1}\left(\dfrac{\partial^r f^r}{\partial x_0}\right)^2 = \left(\dfrac{\partial^r f^r}{\partial x_0}\right)^2_{x_1=1} - \left(\dfrac{\partial^r f^r}{\partial x_0}\right)^2_{x_1=0}$.

From $\dfrac{\partial^r}{\partial x_1}\left(\dfrac{\partial^r f^r}{\partial x_0}\right)^2$ deduce $\dfrac{\partial f}{\partial x_1 x_0} = \left[\dfrac{\partial^r}{\partial x_1}\left(\dfrac{\partial^r f^r}{\partial x_0}\right)^2\right]^2$.

(*n*) At the *n*th step of this algorithm (schematized by Figure 6.3) one obtains the real expansions of f and of all its (finite field) derivatives; $W(f)$ is then obtained by adding the functions obtained at this *n*th step.

It must be noted that at the *j*th step of this algorithm one uses a partial expansion of f with respect to its j first variables; for sake of conciseness, and without ambiguity, this expansion is denoted by f^r at each step. The importance of algorithm 6.4 comes from the fact that partial real expansions are performed with respect to one variable at a time and that the partial expansion with respect to $x_0 x_i$ derives easily from the partial expansion with respect to x_0. Algorithm 6.4 is illustrated by means of the following example.

Example 6.5

$$f = x_0 \bar{x}_2 x_3 \vee \bar{x}_0 x_2 x_3 \vee [(\bar{x}_0 \vee x_1) \oplus x_2] x_3.$$

From the last row of Figure 6.4 one deduces:

$$W(f) = 4 + 2x_0 - x_2 + 2x_3 - x_0 x_1 + x_1 - x_0 x_2 - x_0 x_3 - x_1 x_3 + x_0 x_1 x_3 + 2x_0 x_2 x_3 + 2x_0 x_1 x_2 x_3.$$

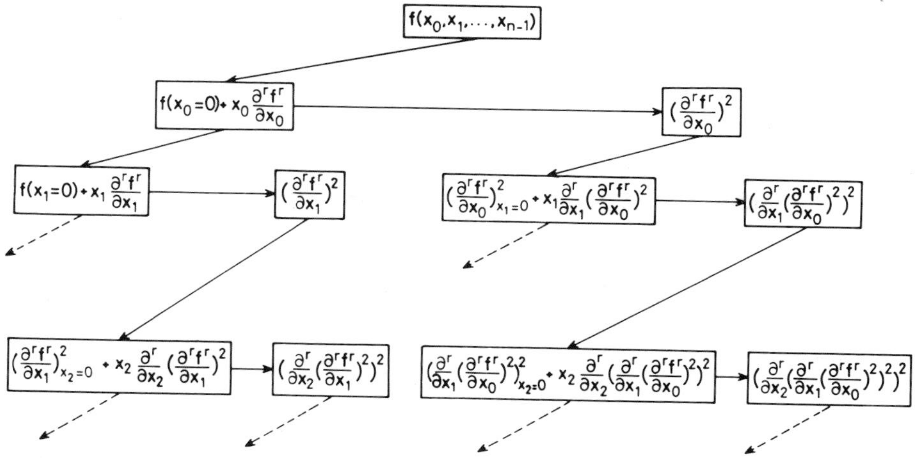

Figure 6.3. Illustration of algorithm 6.4

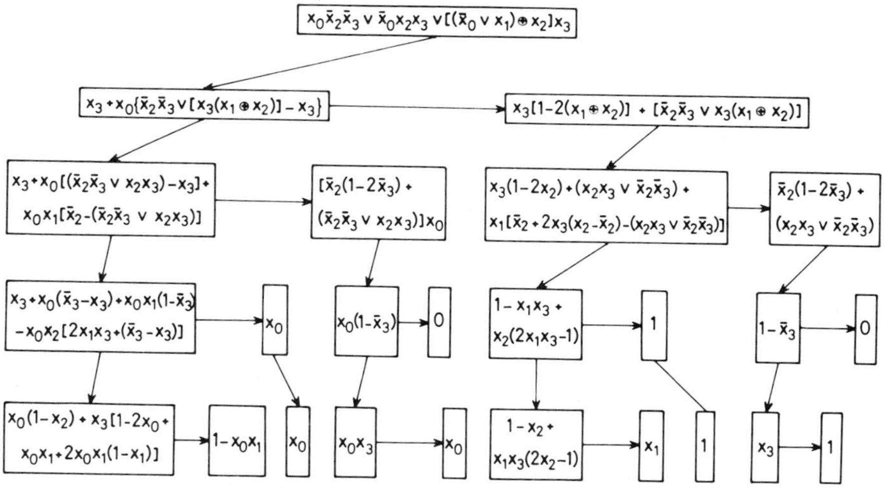

Figure 6.4. Computation scheme for example 6.5

At the vertex $x_3x_2x_1x_0 = 0\ 1\ 0\ 0$ $W(f) = 3$.

The Taylor expansion at this vertex is:

$$x_0\bar{x}_2 \oplus x_3 \oplus x_0x_1x_3.$$

The use of real expansions for obtaining minimal Taylor expansions is probably the most attractive, from a computational point of view, when the switching function $f(x)$ is given as a modulo-2 sum of cubes. Indeed, the above methods suggested in algorithms 6.3 and 6.4 both request the computation of all derivatives $\partial f/\partial \boldsymbol{x}^e$. Since the number of derivatives of $f(\boldsymbol{x})$ is 2^n, the amount of computation increases rapidly with the number of variables, except for those functions for which many multiple derivatives vanish. The evaluation of the derivatives may, however, be avoided, by use of some well-known expansions of numerical analysis. First, the classical Taylor formula allows us to write:

$$f^r(x_{n-1}+1,\ldots,x_1+1,x_0+1)=\sum_e \frac{\partial^r f^r}{\partial \boldsymbol{x}^e},\quad 0\leqslant e_i\leqslant 1. \tag{6.25}$$

It follows that $W(f)=f^r(x_{n-1}+1,\ldots,x_1+1,x_0+1)$ for the class of functions f such that

$$\frac{\partial^r f^r}{\partial \boldsymbol{x}^e}=\frac{\partial f}{\partial \boldsymbol{x}^e}\quad \forall e.$$

In view of relations (5.35) and (5.36), this class of functions reduces to the monotone increasing functions whose derivatives are also monotone increasing functions in the variables' domain {0, 1}. These functions are the cubes $\prod_i x_i$, and then, trivially:

$$W\left(\prod_i x_i\right) = \prod_i (x_i+1). \tag{6.26}$$

Let us observe that the cubes $\prod_i x_i^{(e_i)}$, $e_i \in \{0, 1\}$ are monotone increasing functions in the variables $x_i^{(e_i)}$, and we have:

$$W\left(\prod_i x_i^{(e_i)}\right) = \prod_i \left(x_i^{(e_i)}+1\right). \tag{6.27}$$

Consider now a switching function f given as a modulo-2 sum of m-cubes:

$$f(\boldsymbol{x}) = \bigoplus_{j=0,\,m-1}\left(\prod_{x_i\in \boldsymbol{x}_j} x_i^{(e_{ij})}\right),\quad \boldsymbol{x}_j\subseteq \boldsymbol{x}\ \forall j,\quad e_{ij}\in\{0,1\}\ \forall i,j. \tag{6.28}$$

For each subset of q cubes of $f(2\leqslant q\leqslant m)$, let us define the subsets of $\boldsymbol{x}$: $\boldsymbol{x}_\alpha, \boldsymbol{x}_\beta, \boldsymbol{x}_\gamma$ as follows:

$\boldsymbol{x}_\gamma$ is a subset of $\boldsymbol{x}$ composed of the literals appearing with both polarities in the q considered cubes.

If each of the q cubes includes *all* the literals of $\boldsymbol{x}_\gamma$, then $\boldsymbol{x}_\alpha$ and $\boldsymbol{x}_\beta$ are defined as follows:

$\boldsymbol{x}_\alpha$ is a subset of $\boldsymbol{x}$ composed of literals appearing with the same polarity in all the q cubes and $\boldsymbol{x}_\beta$ is a subset of $\boldsymbol{x}$ composed of literals appearing with the same polarity in a proper subset of the q cubes.

If some of the q cubes include only a subset of the literals of $\boldsymbol{x}_\gamma$, then $\boldsymbol{x}_\alpha$ and $\boldsymbol{x}_\beta$ are not defined.

The following algorithm may be used for obtaining the weights of the Taylor expansions of a function given as a modulo-2 sum of cubes:

Algorithm 6.5. (a) for each cube, evaluate

$$\prod_i (x_i^{(e_{ij})}+1).$$

(b) For each subset of q cubes ($2 \leqslant q \leqslant m$), evaluate

$$(-2)^{(q-1)} \prod_{x_k \in \boldsymbol{x}_\alpha} (x_k^{(e_{kj})} + 1) \prod_{x_l \in \boldsymbol{x}_\beta} x_l^{(e_{lj})}. \tag{6.29}$$

It is recalled that, by definition of $\boldsymbol{x}_\alpha$ and $\boldsymbol{x}_\beta$, the e_{kj} and e_{lj} do not depend on j.

(c) The function $W(f)$ is the (real) sum of the functions evaluated under (a) and (b).

Let us indicate a method of proof for this algorithm. For a function $f(\boldsymbol{x})$ given as a modulo-2 sum of two cubes:

$$f(\boldsymbol{x}) = \prod_{x_i \in \boldsymbol{x}_0} x_i^{(e_{i0})} \oplus \prod_{x_j \in \boldsymbol{x}_1} x_j^{(e_{j1})}$$

one has

$$W(f) \leqslant \prod_{x_i \in \boldsymbol{x}_0} (x_i^{(e_{i0})} + 1) + \prod_{x_j \in \boldsymbol{x}_1} (x_j^{(e_{j1})} + 1).$$

Indeed, the Taylor expansions of the two above cubes contain generally identical terms that disappear by modulo-2 addition. It is then easily verified that the contribution of these terms is taken into account by the quantity

$$-2 \prod_{x_k \in \boldsymbol{x}_\alpha} (x_k^{(e_{k0})} + 1) \prod_{x_l \in \boldsymbol{x}_\beta} x_l^{(e_{l0})}.$$

The general formula (6.29) for q cubes is then derived by induction on the number of cubes.

Let us finally note that

$$x^{(e)} + 1 = 1 + x \quad \text{iff} \quad e = 1$$

$$x^{(e)} + 1 = 2 - x \quad \text{iff} \quad e = 0.$$

Example 6.4 (continued)

$$f = x_0 x_2 \vee x_1 \bar{x}_2$$

$$= x_0 x_2 \oplus x_1 \bar{x}_2$$

$$W(f) = (x_0 + 1)(x_2 + 1) + (x_1 + 1)(2 - x_2) - 2x_0 x_1.$$

Consider now a somewhat more elaborate example.

Example 6.6

$$f = x_0 x_3 x_4 \oplus \bar{x}_1 \bar{x}_2 \bar{x}_3 x_4 \oplus \bar{x}_0 x_1 x_2 x_4$$

$$W(f) = [(1 + x_0)(1 + x_3) + (2 - x_1)(2 - x_2)(2 - x_3) + (2 - x_0)(1 + x_1)(1 + x_2)(1 + x_3)$$
$$-2(1 - x_0) - 2x_0(1 - x_1)(1 - x_2) - 2x_1 x_2 (1 + x_3)](1 + x_4).$$

The function $W(f)$ takes its minimal value 6 at the vertex

$$h_4 h_3 h_2 h_1 h_0 = 0\ 0\ 1\ 1\ 1;$$

the minimal expansion is:

$$x_3 x_4 \oplus \bar{x}_1 \bar{x}_2 x_4 \oplus \bar{x}_1 \bar{x}_2 x_3 x_4 \oplus \bar{x}_0 \bar{x}_1 x_3 x_4 \oplus \bar{x}_0 \bar{x}_2 x_3 x_4 \oplus \bar{x}_0 \bar{x}_1 \bar{x}_2 x_3 x_4.$$

The method developed by algorithm 6.5 is particularly attractive for the functions whose expression contains a small number of cubes. Let us also note that if $f(\boldsymbol{x})$ is given by the intermediate of one of its Taylor expansions, the subset $\boldsymbol{x}_\gamma$ is always empty.

6.1.3. Complexity of Reed–Muller minimization algorithms

This section reviews some of the algorithms presented in the preceding sections for computing an optimal Reed–Muller expansion of switching function. These algorithms are compared from the complexity point of view under the assumption that the function is initially represented by its truth vector. It is only in this case that simple complexity measures can be derived. In other cases, e.g. when the function is given as a disjunction of cubes, the number of operations to be performed becomes representation dependent and no satisfactory complexity bound has been obtained.

The result of that complexity study is that the algorithms fall into two main classes:

(a) The exhaustive class (see section 6.1.1) with a complexity given by $0(2^{2n})$ and a memory-span $0(3^n)$.

(b) The weight computation-type class (see section 6.1.2.1) with a complexity $0(3^n)$ and a memory span $0(3^n)$.

Marinkovic–Tosic procedure (see section 6.1.1.2)

The method is basically the following:

Step 1. Compute the Reed–Muller expansion at some points $\boldsymbol{e}_i$ such that the set of points adjacent to the $\boldsymbol{e}_i$'s covers the set of the 2^n n-tuples; compute their weight.

Step 2. For each $\boldsymbol{e}_i$, compute the variation of weight from the Reed–Muller expansion at $\boldsymbol{e}_i$ to the Reed–Muller expansion at $\boldsymbol{h}$, for any $\boldsymbol{h}$ adjacent to $\boldsymbol{e}_i$.

The smallest number of e_i's to be chosen for step 1 is obviously $2^n/(n+1)$, then, if the truth vector is given, step 1 requires $n\,2^{2n-1}/(n+1)$ 2-adic operations $\overset{2}{\oplus}$ (the symbol $\overset{2}{\oplus}$ means the diadic modulo-2 sum, that is the bit by bit modulo-2 sum) for the computation of $[\text{RM}f_{e_i}]$ (see section 4.2.1.1.2) and $2^n/(n+1)\overset{2n}{+}$ -operations (the symbol $\overset{k}{+}$ means similarly the k-adic real sum) for the weight computation.

For each e_i, step 2 implies, for weight comparison at the n adjacent points $\boldsymbol{h}$, $n\,2^{n-1}$ operations each of which has a complexity equivalent to diadic modulo-2 sum.

Then $n\,2^{2n-1}/(n+1)\ \overset{2}{\oplus}$ -operations are requested by step 2. Moreover $n\,2^n/(n+1)\ \overset{2n-1}{+}$ -operations are performed for weight variations determination.

In total one gets $n\,2^{2n}/(n+1)\ \overset{2}{\oplus}$ -operations and $2^n(2^n-1+n\,2^{n-1}-n)\ \overset{2}{+}$ -operations.

Gray code enumeration procedure (see section 6.1.1.2)

The method is the following:

Step 1. Generate any Reed–Muller expansion, say at the point $\boldsymbol{e}$, and compute its weight.

Step 2. Enumerating the n-tuples by means of a Gray code, generate from the given Reed–Muller expansion at $\boldsymbol{e}$ the 2^n-1 remaining Reed–Muller expansions at $\boldsymbol{h}$ and compute their weight.

When starting from the truth vector, step 1 requires $n\,2^{n-1}\ \overset{2}{\oplus}$ -operations for obtaining $[\mathrm{RM}f_e]$ and one $\overset{2n}{+}$-operation for the weight computation.

It follows from theorem 4.13 that the number of diadic modulo-2 sums $\overset{2}{\oplus}$ to be performed from any Taylor expansion to another is exactly $p\,2^{n-1}$, where p is the number of inverted polarities, i.e. the weight of $\boldsymbol{e} \oplus \boldsymbol{h}$. Thanks to a suitable enumeration order of polarities (Gray code order), all vectors $[\mathrm{RM}f_e]$ can be produced without requesting for p a value greater than 1. Step 2 requires thus $(2^n-1)\,2^{n-1}\ \overset{2}{\oplus}$ -operations for $[\mathrm{RM}\ f_h]$ computation and $(2^n+1)\ \overset{2n}{+}$-operations for the weight computation.

In total one gets $(2^n+n-1)\,2^{n-1}\ \overset{2}{\oplus}$ -operations and $2^n(2^n-1)\ \overset{2}{+}$ -operations.

Kronecker weight computation algorithm (see section 6.1.2.1.2)

This method starts from the truth vector $[f_e]$ of the given function.

Step 1. Compute the extended vector $\phi^{(\Delta)}(f)$ by

$$\phi^{(\Delta)}(f) = [f_e]\ \textcircled{\oplus\ \cdot}\ (M^{(\Delta)})^n$$

where $(M^{(\Delta)})^n$ is the nth Kronecker power of the matrix

$$M^{(\Delta)} = \begin{bmatrix} 1 & 0 & 1 \\ \\ 0 & 1 & 1 \end{bmatrix}.$$

Step 2. Compute the list of weights of the 2^n Reed–Muller expansions by

$$[W\ \mathrm{RM}_h\ f(x)] = \phi^{(\Delta)}(f)\ \textcircled{+\ \times}\ [(M^{(\Delta)})^n]^t$$

($[\quad]^t$ means as usual the transpose operation).

Step 3. Compute the e-Reed–Muller expansion at the point $\boldsymbol{e}$ giving the smallest weight.

Step 1 requires $(3^n-2^n)\ \overset{2}{\oplus}$ -operations, step 2 requires $2.(3^n-2^n)\ \overset{2}{+}$ -operations while $n\,2^{n-1}\ \overset{2}{\oplus}$ -operations are requested by step 3.

Comparison of complexities

The characteristics of complexity of the three foregoing algorithms are resumed at the following table.

	Gray code	Marinkovic–Tosic	Weight computation
$\overset{2}{\oplus}$	$0\,(2^{2n})$	$0\,(2^{2n})$	$0\,(3^n)$
$\overset{2}{+}$	$0\,(2^{2n})$	$0\,(2^{2n})$	$0\,(3^n)$
memory span	$0\,(2^n)$	$0\,(2^n)$	$0\,(3^n)$

Figure 6.5. Comparison of complexities

One sees that the asymptotic characteristics of the two first methods are given by the same factor 2^{2n}. However the Gray code algorithm implies roughly a factor 2 saving in computation with respect to Marinkovic–Tosic algorithm. The memory span is the same for these two methods; the only quantities to be recorded are in both cases:

1. The list of points already scanned (2^n bits).
2. The label A of the best expansion found at a given time (n bits) and its cost B ($n + 1$ bits for number of terms minimization, $n - 1 + \log_2 n$ bits for number of literals minimization).
3. The components of a particular $[RM_h f]$ vector that serve as data for a particular computation step (2^n bits).

The weight computation algorithm has an asymptotic computational complexity of 3^n thus a $(3/4)^n$ saving with respect to the others. It can be shown however that the memory span has an order of magnitude of 3^n, thus a loss of $(3/2)^n$ with respect to the others. In conclusion the weight computation method seems to be suitable as far as the memory capacity is not exceeded; in other cases the Gray code method appears as the best.

6.2. *The general minimization problem for switching functions*

The purpose of the present section will be to consider the minimization problem for a larger class of ring-sum expansions in the particular case of switching functions. This section may be considered as a further development of sections 4.2.3 and 4.3. More precisely, one will successively be concerned with the problems of minimizing Kronecker expansions, generalized Reed–Muller expansions, pseudo-Kronecker expansions and general ring-sum expansions.

6.2.1. *Minimization of Kronecker expansions*

Kronecker expansions for switching functions were defined in section 4.2.3; the present section is devoted to a minimization method for these expansions. There are 3^n different Kronecker expansions for a switching function of n variables; let us recall that the *weight* of a ring expansion is the number of *cubes* (or equivalently of *product terms*) it contains. The *extended weight vector* $\phi_w(f)$ of a switching function is a vector, the 3^n integer valued components of which are the weights of the 3^n Kronecker expansions of the function, enumerated by increasing value of $\boldsymbol{h}$; it is recalled (see section 4.2.3) that $\boldsymbol{h} = (h_{n-1}, \ldots, h_1, h_0)$ is a vector having n ternary components $h_i \in \{0, 1, 2\}$, which fully characterizes one of the 3^n Kronecker expansions of $f(\boldsymbol{x})$. Theorem 6.9 provides us with a simple computation scheme for the extended weight vector $\phi_w(f)$ from the Δ-extended vector $\phi^{(\Delta)}(f)$.

Theorem 6.9. The extended weight vector $\phi_w(f)$ is given by:

$$\phi_w(f) = \phi^{(\Delta)}(f) \; \textcircled{+ \times} \; K^n \tag{6.30}$$

where K^n is the nth Kronecker power of the matrix:

$$K = \begin{bmatrix} 1 & 0 & 1 \\ 0 & 1 & 1 \\ 1 & 1 & 0 \end{bmatrix}.$$

Proof. The induction proof of theorem 6.9 is straightforward. We only mention the initial step of that induction. For $n = 1$, one has:

$$\phi^{(\Delta)}(f) = [f_0, f_1, f_0 \oplus f_1]. \tag{6.31}$$

The expressions (4.98) to (4.100) of the canonical expansions of $f(x)$ show that:

$$\phi_w(f) = [f_0 + (f_0 \oplus f_1), f_1 + (f_0 \oplus f_1), f_0 + f_1]. \tag{6.32}$$

The comparison of (6.31) and (6.32) clearly yields:

$$\phi_w(f) = \phi^{(\Delta)}(f) \; \textcircled{+ \times} \; K.$$ ■

Example 6.7. Consider the function of three variables $f(x_2 x_1 x_0)$ defined by the truth vector:

$$f_e = [0\ 0\ 0\ 1\ 1\ 0\ 1\ 1].$$

The computation of the extended weight vector from the extended truth vector, again based on the Kronecker product structure of the transformation matrix, is displayed in Figure 6.6. Observation of the results shows that there is a single canonical expansion of weight 2; it corresponds to $(h_2\ h_1\ h_0) = (0\ 0\ 2)$, i.e. to the expansion with respect to the basis:

$$[x_2]^{[0]}\ [x_1]^{[0]}\ [x_0]^{[2]},$$

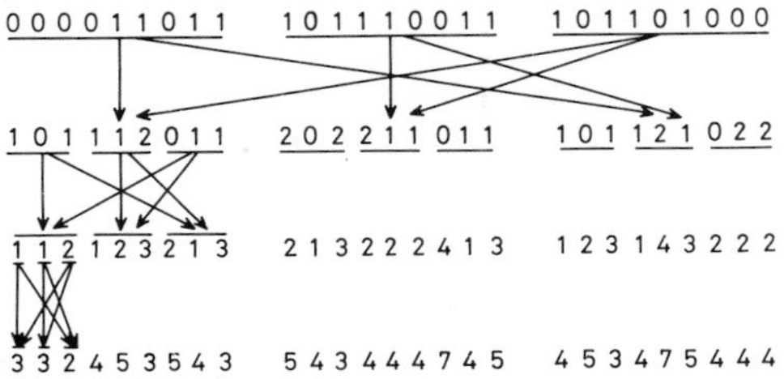

Figure 6.6. Computation of the extended weight vector

namely:

$$f(x_2 x_1 x_0) = x_1 x_0 \oplus x_2 \bar{x}_0.$$

Once again, we may restrict the components h_i of $\boldsymbol{h}$ to take only the values 0 and 1. The corresponding components of $\phi_w(f)$ form the vector $[WN_h f]$ having 2^n integer valued components (see (6.18)).

6.2.2. Minimization of generalized Reed–Muller expansions

The contents of this section comes principally from a paper by Csanky [1973]. Generalized Reed–Muller expansions of switching functions were defined in section 4.3. The main results quoted in this section are the following: given any switching function $f(\boldsymbol{x})$ of n variables, there are products of literals (i.e. cube functions), corresponding to *prime terms* (see definition 6.1 below), which must appear in any generalized Reed–Muller expansion of f and there are products of literals which cannot exist in any generalized Reed–Muller expansion of $f(\boldsymbol{x})$. There are switching functions $f(\boldsymbol{x})$ whose minimal generalized Reed–Muller expansion contains at least $\binom{n}{n/2}$ terms if n is even and $\binom{n}{(n-1)/2}$ terms if n is odd. Every switching function of n variables can be realized by at most $3(2^n-1)/4$ terms for $n \geqslant 3$.

Definition 6.1

$$\prod_{x_i \in \boldsymbol{x}_0} \dot{x}_i, \quad (\dot{x}_i = x_i \text{ or } \bar{x}_i)$$

is a *prime term* of the switching function $f(\boldsymbol{x})$ iff

$$\frac{\Delta f}{\Delta \boldsymbol{x}_0} \equiv 1.$$

Theorem 6.10 and its corollaries then result from the fact that the classical rules of formal derivation of polynomials hold true for generalized Reed–Muller expansions.

Theorem 6.10. For any subset $\boldsymbol{x}_0$ *of* $\boldsymbol{x}$, *the condition*

$$\frac{\Delta f}{\Delta \boldsymbol{x}_0} \equiv 1$$

implies the presence of a product term

$$\prod_{x_i \in \boldsymbol{x}_0} \dot{x}_i$$

in any generalized Reed–Muller form of $f(\boldsymbol{x})$.

A term of the form

$$\prod_{x_i \in \boldsymbol{x}_0^e} \dot{x}_i, \quad 0 \leqslant e \leqslant 1$$

will be called a subcombination of the term

$$\prod_{x_i \in \boldsymbol{x}_0} \dot{x}_i.$$

All existing terms in any generalized Reed–Muller expansion of a switching function are subcombinations of prime terms; indeed these terms correspond necessarily to differences

$$\frac{\Delta f}{\Delta \boldsymbol{x}_0^e} \not\equiv 1.$$

Theorem 6.11. There are switching functions $f(\boldsymbol{x})$ *whose minimal generalized Reed–Muller expansion will contain as many as*

$$\binom{n}{n/2}$$

terms if n *is even*

$$\binom{n}{(n-1)/2}$$

terms if n *is odd.*

Proof. For n even consider the function whose generalized Reed–Muller expansion contains all terms with $n/2$ variables and no other terms. Since none of those terms is a subcombination of any of the other terms all these terms are prime terms.

For n odd consider either the function whose generalized Reed–Muller expansion contains all terms with $(n-1)/2$ variables and no other terms or the function whose generalized Reed–Muller expansion contain all terms with $(n+1)/2$ variables and no other terms. It is easy to see that in both cases all terms are prime terms. ■

Let us finally note that there are terms that never can appear in any generalized Reed–Muller expansion of $f(\boldsymbol{x})$; indeed, if

$$\frac{\Delta f}{\Delta \boldsymbol{x}_0} \equiv 0$$

terms of the form

$$\prod_{x_i \in \boldsymbol{x}_0} \dot{x}_i$$

cannot appear in any of these expansions of $f(\boldsymbol{x})$.

Example 6.8. Some functions are listed below with the prime terms underlined and terms that cannot appear listed.

Functions	Terms that cannot appear
$1 \oplus \dot{x}_0 \oplus \dot{x}_1 \oplus \underline{\dot{x}_0 \dot{x}_1 \dot{x}_2}$	
$1 \oplus \dot{x}_0 \oplus \underline{\dot{x}_0 \dot{x}_1} \oplus \underline{\dot{x}_0 \dot{x}_2} \oplus \underline{\dot{x}_1 \dot{x}_2}$	$\dot{x}_0 \dot{x}_1 \dot{x}_2$
$1 \oplus \underline{\dot{x}_0} \oplus \dot{x}_1 \oplus \underline{\dot{x}_1 \dot{x}_2}$	$\dot{x}_0 \dot{x}_1, \dot{x}_0 \dot{x}_2, \dot{x}_0 \dot{x}_1 \dot{x}_2$

Some minimal generalized Reed–Muller expansions for switching functions of 3 variables are listed in the table of Figure 6.7. The functions of this table are not arbitrarily chosen; they are each representative of 3 variable equivalence classes. Two functions $f(x_2 x_1 x_0)$ and $g(x_2 x_1 x_0)$ are in the same equivalence class iff they differ by a negation and/or a permutation of the variables; equivalence classes of functions will more thoroughly be studied in section 6.2.4.

The table of Figure 6.7 contains thus the information needed for obtaining a minimal generalized Reed–Muller expansion of any switching function of 3 variables.

6.2.3. *Minimization of pseudo-Kronecker expansions*

Pseudo-Kronecker expansions for switching functions were defined in section 4.3. A ring expansion of a switching function stops being of the Kronecker type if, for some variable x_i, the three possible types of terms, i.e. terms containing x_i, $\bar{x}_i$ and no occurrence of x_i, are present.

Consider the expressions:

$$f = a_0\, \bar{x}_{n-1} \oplus a_1\, x_{n-1}$$

$$f = a_0 \oplus (a_0 \oplus a_1)\, x_{n-1}$$

$$f = a_1 \oplus (a_0 \oplus a_1)\, \bar{x}_{n-1}.$$

Function number	Minimal generalized Reed–Muller expansion
1	0
1C	1
2	$x_0x_1x_2$
2C	$1 \oplus x_0x_1x_2$
3	x_0x_1
3C	$1 \oplus x_0x_1$
4	$x_0\bar{x}_2 \oplus x_0x_1$
4C	$1 \oplus x_0\bar{x}_2 \oplus x_0x_1$
5	$x_0x_1 \oplus \bar{x}_0\bar{x}_2 \oplus x_1\bar{x}_2$
5C	$x_0\bar{x}_1 \oplus \bar{x}_0x_2 \oplus x_1\bar{x}_2$
6	$x_0 \oplus x_0\bar{x}_1\bar{x}_2$
6C	$\bar{x}_0 \oplus x_0\bar{x}_1\bar{x}_2$
7	$x_0x_1 \oplus \bar{x}_0\bar{x}_1x_2$
7C	$1 \oplus x_0x_1 \oplus \bar{x}_0\bar{x}_1x_2$
8	$x_0x_1 \oplus x_1x_2 \oplus x_0\bar{x}_1x_2$
8C	$\bar{x}_0 \oplus x_1x_2 \oplus x_0\bar{x}_1\bar{x}_2$
9	x_0
10	$x_0 \oplus x_1$
11	$x_0 \oplus x_1 \oplus x_2$
12	$x_0x_1 \oplus x_0x_2 \oplus x_1x_2$
13	$x_0\bar{x}_2 \oplus x_1x_2$
14	$x_0 \oplus \bar{x}_1\bar{x}_2$

Figure 6.7. Minimal expansions.

Any choice between these three expansions results in a choice of a couple of functions of $(n-1)$ variables among the triple

$$a_0, a_1, a_0 \oplus a_1.$$

The number of variables upon which the three functions depend has been lowered by one unit and the process may thus be iterated: namely the first part of the construction will amount to build extended vector $\phi^{(\Delta)}(f)$; in this vector:

(a) Each triple of components represents a function of the single variable x_0; after selection of an appropriate couple of binary components such a function will require 0 or 1 term.

(b) Each 9-tuple represents a function of two variables; for its synthesis one selects two triples requiring together a minimum number of terms.

(c) The process is carried on for the functions of 3, 4, 5, . . . , n variables selecting at each step the couple of subfunctions leading to the minimum number of terms.

Example 6.9. Consider a switching function f given by its truth vector:

$$[1\ 0\ 1\ 0\ 0\ 0\ 1\ 1].$$

The extended vector $\phi^{(\Delta)}(f)$ is:

$$[1\ 0\ 1, 1\ 0\ 1, 0\ 0\ 0; 0\ 0\ 0, 1\ 1\ 0, 1\ 1\ 0; 1\ 0\ 1, 0\ 1\ 1, 1\ 1\ 0].$$

The selection process is now carried on; the eliminated subvectors are replaced by dashes:

(a) At the triples level, one selects, e.g.:

$$[-0\ 1, -0\ 1, 0\ 0\ 0; 0\ 0\ 0, 1-0, 1-0; -0\ 1, 0-1, 1-0].$$

(b) At the 9-tuples level one selects

$$[-0\ 1, ---, 0\ 0\ 0; 0\ 0\ 0, ---, 1-0; -0\ 1, ---, 1-0].$$

(c) Finally at the function level

$$[-0\ 1, ---, 0\ 0\ 0; 0\ 0\ 0, ---, 1-0; ---, ---, ---].$$

One obtains an expansion having only two terms:

$$f = \bar{x}_2\bar{x}_0 \oplus x_2x_1.$$

It should finally be pointed out that pseudo-Kronecker ring expansions are not always optimal. The simplest example of this fact is the function

$$[1\ 0\ 0\ 1\ 0\ 1\ 1\ 1].$$

The best Reed–Muller expansions of this function have 5 terms. There are 5 such expansions, among which:

$$\bar{x}_0 \oplus x_1 \oplus x_2 \oplus x_1x_2 \oplus \bar{x}_0x_1x_2.$$

The best pseudo-Kronecker expansions have 4 terms; an example of such an expansion is

$$\bar{x}_0 \oplus x_1 \oplus x_2 \oplus x_0x_1x_2.$$

Finally the function has 3 ring expansions with 3 terms, e.g.:

$$x_0 \oplus \bar{x}_1\bar{x}_2 \oplus \bar{x}_0x_1x_2.$$

The most general case of ring-sum expansion minimization will be studied in the next section.

6.2.4. Minimization of general ring-sum expansions

It is well known that any switching function may be represented as a modulo-2 sum of products and the problem of minimizing the number of products in such a representation, first stated by Muller [1954], has long been, and still is, an open one. This problem has received various formulations in terms of coding theory and of graph theory (Kautz [1965a], Mukhopadhyay and Schmitz [1970]) but the underlying computations seem unmanageable when the number n of variables is greater than or equal to 4. The computational complexity of the problem has led various authors to present heuristic minimization algorithms (Even, Kohavi and Paz [1967], Rao and Nordstrom [1971], Ungern [1972]).

The present section, based on a paper by Bioul, Davio and Deschamps [1973], provides a complete solution of the minimization problem for $n = 4$. That solution is ultimately based on the concepts of Kronecker expansions of switching functions (see sections 4.2.3 and 6.2.1) and of D-equivalence (see section 6.2.4). These concepts also provide an improved approach to the solution for $n \geqslant 5$.

6.2.4.1. *Reed–Muller weight-vector and N-equivalence*

The concept of N-equivalence is due to Ninomiya [1961]; the concepts of N-equivalence as well as invariance will roughly be defined in this section. The reader will find a more complete and a more rigorous development of these concepts in Chapter 5 of the book by Harrison [1965] which constitutes a prerequisite before reading this section.

There are so many switching functions, that enumerative techniques for solving problems such as obtaining minimal ring-sum expansions are not particularly useful. The technique to be used is to impose an equivalence relation on the family of functions; this will reduce the set of functions which must be checked to a set of representatives of each equivalence class. The equivalence relation must be picked in a sensible way so that functions in the same class have similar properties. Most of the times, the equivalences are generated by permutation groups acting on the domain or on the range of the functions: such groups are, for example, the symmetric group S_n, the complementing group C_2^n and their semi-direct product G_n (see Harrison [1965] pp. 141 and 145). In the sequel we say that two functions of n variables $f(\boldsymbol{x})$ and $g(\boldsymbol{x})$ are *N-equivalent* if they are equivalent under G_n. In other words, two functions are N-equivalent if they may be derived from each other by a finite number of permutation and negation of their variables. We write in this case $f(\boldsymbol{x}) \overset{N}{\sim} g(\boldsymbol{x})$.

Invariants are numbers associated with switching functions such that when two functions have the same invariants, they are equivalent under the group; invariants for N-equivalence classes were first computed by Golomb [1959]. They may also be found in the book by Harrison [1965].

It is known that the action of an element of G_n on the function $f(\boldsymbol{x})$ reduces to a permutation of its truth vector. Clearly too, that same action also reduces to a permutation of the Reed–Muller weight vector $[WN_h f]$. Hence, by theorem 6.6, the set of Reed–Muller weights, rearranged by a suitable element of G_n to give the least sequence in lexicographical order, is an invariant characterizing the N-class of $f(\boldsymbol{x})$.

In what follows, we shall make an extensive use of the available tables of N-classes for $n = 3, 4$ (Harrison [1965]). Such an N-class will be denoted by its number in the Ninomiya–Harrison classification preceded by the symbol N and possibly followed by the symbol C to denote the complementation of the class. (That is, if f is in the class k, the class of $\bar{f}$ will be denoted kC.)

6.2.4.2. *The D-equivalence*

6.2.4.2.1. *Definition. Invariants of the D-classes*

Any ring expansion of a switching function $f(\mathbf{x})$ may be written in the form

$$f(\mathbf{x}) = g_0 \bar{x} \oplus g_1 x \oplus g_2 \tag{6.33}$$

by grouping terms containing $\bar{x}$, terms containing x, and terms in which x does not appear under any polarity.

Consider the symmetric group of permutations S_3 on the set of symbols $\{\bar{x}, x, 1\}$; denote by σ an element of this group and by $a\sigma$ ($a \in \{\bar{x}, x, 1\}$) the image of a by σ. We define the action of σ on the expression (6.33) of f by:

$$f\sigma = g_0(\bar{x}\sigma) \oplus g_1(x\sigma) \oplus g_2(1\sigma). \tag{6.34}$$

That action is well defined: indeed, the function $f\sigma$ represented by the expression (6.34) is independent of the initial representation (6.33) chosen for f. An elementary proof of this property is based on the following fact: any ring polynomial

$$f(\mathbf{x}) = h_0 \bar{x} \oplus h_1 x \oplus h_2$$

representing the function $f(\mathbf{x})$ is related to the representation (6.33) of $f(\mathbf{x})$ by the equations:

$$h_0 \oplus h_2 = g_0 \oplus g_2; h_1 \oplus h_2 = g_1 \oplus g_2; h_0 \oplus h_1 = g_0 \oplus g_1.$$

The transformations we have just defined have an interesting interpretation in terms of the ring difference $\Delta f/\Delta x = f_0 \oplus f_1$ of $f(\mathbf{x})$ with respect to x. Let us illustrate this point by an example. Consider the permutation $\sigma = (1\ x\ \bar{x})$ having one cycle of length 3. The transform of f by σ has the representation:

$$g(\mathbf{x}) = f(1\ x\ \bar{x}) = g_0 \oplus g_1 \bar{x} \oplus g_2 x.$$

Its subfunctions (residues) are thus:

$$g(0) = g_0 \oplus g_1 = f(0) \oplus f(1) = \Delta f/\Delta x$$

$$g(1) = g_0 \oplus g_2 = f(0).$$

More generally, the images of $f(\mathbf{x})$ by the six permutations σ are the functions the residues in x of which are the six couples of functions present in the set

$$\{f(0), f(1), \Delta f/\Delta x\}.$$

Let now $\sigma^{(j)}$ denote a permutation on the set $\{\bar{x}_j, x_j, 1\}$. The group of transformations generated by the permutations $\sigma^{(j)}$ is clearly a group of order 6^n isomorphic to the nth Cartesian power S_3^n. As earlier, we denote by S_n the symmetric group of permutations of the variables. The group of transformations generated by the elements of S_3^n and by those of S_n is easily seen to be isomorphic to the semi-direct product $H_n = S_3^n \times S_n$ of S_3^n by S^n. Finally, two functions $f(\mathbf{x})$ and $g(\mathbf{x})$ are *D-equivalent* iff there exists a transformation $R \in H_n$ such that $fR = g$. We write in this case $f(\mathbf{x}) \overset{D}{\sim} g(\mathbf{x})$. The equivalence classes are called *D-classes.*

The importance of the concept of D-equivalence to our problem is easy to perceive. Indeed, the cost $C(f)$ of $f(x)$ is, by definition, the weight of its optimal ring-sum expansion. Clearly,

Theorem 6.12. Two D-equivalent functions have the same cost.

Theorem 6.12 clearly results from the fact that the number of terms in a ring polynomial remains unchanged under any transformation $R \in H_n$. Furthermore:

Theorem 6.13. The D-equivalence is stronger than the N-equivalence, i.e.:

$$f \overset{N}{\sim} g \Rightarrow f \overset{D}{\sim} g.$$

Theorem 6.13 follows from the fact that C_2^n is a subgroup of S_3^n. As a consequence, the D-classes are in general the set union of some N-classes. Practically, the number of "essentially different" functions to be considered in the problem at hand is reduced to the number of D-classes.

Remarks

1. The concept of D-equivalence is related to that of B-transformation introduced and used for heuristic purposes by Ungern [1972].

2. Thanks to a heuristic programme, Rao and Nordstrom [1971] conjecture that the N-classes $N58$-C and $N71$-C have both cost 6. Actually, these classes are D-equivalent. It will be shown hereafter that their cost is actually 6.

It is easy to characterize the D-classes by invariants. Indeed, the expansion resulting from the action of $R \in H_n$ on a Kronecker expansion is itself a Kronecker expansion. This amounts to saying that R acts as a permutation on the extended weight vector. Hence, the set of weights of the Kronecker expansions, rearranged by a suitable element of H_n so as to obtain the least sequence in lexicographic order, is an invariant of the D-class. Note furthermore that the set of 2^n Reed–Muller weights extracted from that least sequence is in turn characteristic of the D-class.

6.2.4.2.2. D-equivalent N-classes

The existence of invariants characterizing the D-classes provide a theoretical means for obtaining an exhaustive list of these D-classes. This section describes another method method for obtaining such a list by regrouping N-classes. The availability of tables of N-classes for $n = 3$ and 4 renders the latter approach more effective in these cases.

Consider a function $f(x)$ of n variables. There are at most $6^n.n!$ functions D-equivalent to $f(x)$. However, these functions belong to at most 3^n distinct N-classes. This fact arises from the following three observations:

(a) The elements of the symmetric group S_n do not generate new N-classes.
(b) The permutations $(\bar{x}_j\, x_j)$ (1), that belong to the complementing group C_2^n, do not generate new N-classes.

(c) The pairs of permutations $\{(1\ x_i)(\bar{x}_i); (1\bar{x}_i\ x_i)\}$ and $\{(1\ \bar{x}_i)(x_i); (1\ x_i\ \bar{x}_i)\}$ generate pairs of N-equivalent functions, since, for example, $[(1\ x_i)(\bar{x}_i)] . [(\bar{x}_i\ x_i)(1)] = (1\ \bar{x}_i\ x_i)$.

Hence, in order to generate new N-classes from a typical representative of a given class, we have only to consider, with respect to each of the n variables, the three transformations $(1)(x_i)(\bar{x}_i)$, $(1\ x_i)(\bar{x}_i)$ and $(1\ \bar{x}_i)(x_i)$.

These computations have been performed on the functions of 3 and 4 variables. For $n = 3$ the 22 N-classes are regrouped in 6 D-classes, while for $n = 4$, the 402 N-classes fall into 30 D-classes. The results of these computations are summarized under the form of cross-tables (Figures 6.8 to 6.11). Computational evidence shows that, for $n = 3$, the set of distinct canonical weights completely characterizes the D-class. The same statement holds true for $n = 4$, but for two ambiguities. In these two cases, however, the number of occurrences of the involved weights are different. Hence, for $n = 4$, the set of distinct canonical weights along with their numbers of occurrences completely characterizes the D-class. These shortened lists of invariants are given in Figure 6.9. for $n = 3$ and in Figure 6.12 for $n = 4$. Together with the computational methods described in section 6.21, they provide a rapid method of D-class identification. In the case of example 6.7 the set of distinct canonical weights is (see Figure 6.6) 2, 3, 4, 5, 7: from Figure 6.9, the corresponding class is immediately identified as $D4$.

The above remarks also provide a rather crude lower bound on the number U_n of D-classes. Indeed, if T_n denotes the number of N-classes, one has clearly $U_n \geqslant T_n/3^n$. This simple reasoning shows that $U_5 \geqslant 5.054$. The latter figure gives a more precise idea of the problem complexity for $n = 5$.

6.2.4.3. *Cost of the D-classes*

This section presents an algorithm that generates the set of D-classes having cost w from the set of D-classes having a cost at most equal to $(w-1)$. This algorithm is based on the following theorem:

Theorem 6.14. If $C(f) = w$, then, there exists a function g such that:

(a) $g \overset{D}{\sim} f$

(b) $C(\bar{g}) = w - 1$.

Proof. Consider an expansion of f having w terms, and assume that one of these terms is the product of literals $x_1^{(e_1)} x_2^{(e_2)} \ldots x_k^{(e_k)}$. Applying to that expansion the transformations $(x_i^{(e_i)}\ 1)(x_i^{(\bar{e}_i)})$, one obtains an expansion of a D-equivalent function g a term of which is 1. Clearly, the cost of g is w while the cost of $\bar{g}$ is $(w-1)$.

Algorithm 6.6. (a) Consider the set of D-classes having a cost equal to $(w-1)$.

(b) List the N-classes contained in these D-classes.

(c) List the complementary N-classes.

N-class No.	D-class No.
1	1
2	2
3	2
4	3
5	4
6	3
7	4
8	5
9	2
10	3
11	5
12	5
13	4
14	4
1C	2
2C	4
3C	3
4C	5
5C	6
6C	4
7C	5
8C	6

Figure 6.8. Functions of three variables N-classes to D-classes

D-class No.	N-classes No.	Weights of the canonical expansions
1	1	0
2	2 3 9 1C	1 2 4 8
3	4 6 10 3C	2 3 4 6
4	5 7 13 14 6C 2C	2 3 4 5 7
5	8 11 12 7C 4C	3 4 5 6
6	5C 8C	5 6

Figure 6.9. Functions of three variables: D-classes to N-classes and invariants

(d) List the D-classes to which belong these complementary N-classes.

(e) Eliminate in the latter list the D-classes having a cost at most equal to $(w-1)$. The remaining D-classes have a cost w.

For $n = 3$ and 4, the costs of the D-classes are given in Figures 6.13 and 6.14 respectively, along with a typical representative of the class and an optimal expansion of that representative.

Number of the *N*-class: Tens ↓ / Units →	0	1	2	3	4	5	6	7	8	9
0		1	2	2	3	4	7	3	4	5
1	7	8	9	2	3	5	4	10	11	5
2	4	4	9	12	8	9	8	7	13	14
3	8	15	4	5	6	7	8	9	15	16
4	9	11	17	18	19	12	9	8	14	13
5	9	16	14	8	14	20	14	16	21	3
6	5	6	4	5	9	10	11	19	11	18
7	17	22	9	13	14	7	9	16	8	14
8	9	20	14	14	15	16	16	16	13	8
9	23	11	24	14	15	13	24	14	23	25
10	20	23	18	26	27	26	14	8	7	4
11	8	15	26	9	8	16	15	8	14	16
12	14	20	12	9	19	18	28	13	20	11
13	18	15	14	17	27	23	25	18	23	23
14	24	11	23	23	26	25	8	14	16	20
15	24	23	27	14	16	16	15	20	18	21
16	23	27	25	25	29	2	3	5	12	20
17	14	8	7	21	16	26	22	14	16	8
18	14	16	5	4	19	11	4	9	18	9
19	20	24	15	13	9	8	14	11	17	9
20	24	23	23	18	13	25	23	18	25	21
21	23	18	25	27	29	24	25	23	27	23
22	18	23	20							

Figure 6.10 (a). Functions of four variables: uncomplemented *N*-classes to *D*-classes

Number of the N-class (Tens ↓) \ Units →	0	1	2	3	4	5	6	7	8	9
0		2	7	4	9	20	29	8	14	16
1	20	25	27	3	5	12	6	19	28	15
2	13	9	25	21	23	18	17	14	18	27
3	16	21	8	14	16	9	15	16	26	21
4	16	26	21	22	22	26	23	24	25	23
5	17	21	18	11	18	27	19	28	30	4
6	9	20	5	6	12	11	19	28	18	28
7	27	30	11	24	23	8	15	26	14	23
8	20	25	16	23	25	27	27	26	20	14
9	27	18	18	16	18	15	25	16	27	21
10	18	26	21	22	22	22	16	14	8	7
11	9	16	21	14	13	18	23	9	15	25
12	20	29	16	14	26	26	22	14	16	23
13	27	16	20	18	21	25	27	27	25	25
14	23	17	18	18	21	27	10	11	19	17
15	23	18	28	24	18	18	23	23	27	22
16	25	21	26	27	25					
17										
18										
19								15	16	
20	20	16			9	18	17		19	28
21		19	18		23	11		17	26	
22			15							

Figure 6.10 (b). Functions of four variables: complemented N-classes to D-classes

D-class No.	*N*-classes No.														
1	1														
2	2	3	13	165	1C										
3	4	7	14	59	166	13C									
4	5	8	16	20	21	32	62	109	183	186		3C	59C		
5	9	15	19	33	60	63	167	182	14C	62C					
6	34	61	16C	63C											
7	6	10	27	35	75	108	172	2C	109C						
8	11	24	26	30	36	47	53	78	89	107	110	114	117	146	171
	179	195	7C	32C	75C	108C									
9	12	22	25	37	40	46	50	64	72	76	80	113	123	187	189
	194	199	4C	21C	35C	60C	110C	117C	204C						
10	17	65	146C												
11	18	41	66	68	91	129	141	185	197	53C	65C	72C	147C	215C	
12	23	45	122	168	15C	64C									
13	28	49	73	88	95	127	193	204	20C	114C					
14	29	48	52	54	56	74	79	82	83	93	97	106	118	120	132
	147	153	170	177	180	196	8C	27C	33C	78C	89C	107C	113C	123C	127C
15	31	38	84	94	111	116	131	156	192	19C	36C	76C	95C	118C	197C
	222C														
16	39	51	57	77	85	86	87	115	119	148	154	155	174	178	181
	9C	30C	34C	37C	40C	82C	93C	97C	106C	111C	122C	128C	131C	198C	201C
17	42	70	133	198	26C	50C	141C	149C	206C	217C					
18	43	69	102	125	130	137	158	188	203	207	211	220	25C	28C	52C
	54C	68C	91C	92C	94C	100C	115C	133C	142C	143C	151C	154C	155C	205C	212C
19	44	67	124	184	17C	56C	66C	148C	208C	211C					
20	55	81	100	121	128	149	157	169	190	222	5C	10C	61C	80C	88C
	120C	132C	200C												
21	58	159	173	209	23C	31C	39C	42C	51C	99C	102C	112C	134C	144C	161C
22	71	176	43C	44C	103C	104C	105C	126C	159C						
23	90	98	101	135	138	139	142	143	151	160	201	202	206	210	217
	219	221	24C	46C	49C	74C	79C	83C	116C	129C	140C	150C	156C	157C	214C
24	92	96	140	150	191	200	215	47C	73C	153C					
25	99	136	145	162	163	205	208	212	216	11C	22C	48C	81C	84C	96C
	119C	135C	138C	139C	160C	164C									
26	103	105	112	144	175	38C	41C	45C	77C	87C	101C	124C	125C	162C	218C
27	104	134	152	161	213	218	12C	29C	55C	70C	85C	86C	90C	98C	130C
	136C	137C	145C	158C	163C										
28	126	18C	57C	67C	69C	152C	209C								
29	164	214	6C	121C											
30	58C	71C													

D-class No.	Weights of the canonical expansions									
1	0									
2	1	2	4	8	16					
3	2	3	4	6	8	12				
4	2	3	4	5	6	7	8	10	14		
5	3	4	5	6	8	10	12				
6	5	6	10	12							
7	2	3	4	5	6	8	9	15			
8	3	4	5	6	7	8	10	11	13		
9	3	4	5	6	7	8	9	10	11	12	14
10	4	6	9								
11	4	5	6	7	8	9	10	11			
12	4	5	7	8	10	12					
13	4	5	6	7	8	9	12				
14	4	5	6	7	8	9	10	11	12	13	
15	4	5	6	7	8	9	10	11	12		
16	5	6	7	8	9	10	11	12	13		
17	5	6	7	8	9	11	12				
18	5(2)	6(3)	7(12)	8(21)	9(22)	10(9)	11(8)	12(4)			
19	5(4)	6(4)	7(8)	8(24)	9(16)	10(8)	11(16)	12(1)			
20	5	6	7	8	9	10	13	14			
21	5	7	8	9	10	11	12				
22	6	8	9	10	11						
23	6	7	8	9	10	11	12				
24	6(16)	7(24)	8(17)	9(8)	10(8)	11(8)					
25	6	7	8	9	10	11	12	13			
26	6(5)	7(5)	8(10)	9(30)	10(20)	11(11)					
27	6	7	8	9	10	11	12	13			
28	7	8	9	10	11	12					
29	7	8	9	14							
30	10	11									

Figure 6.12. Functions of four variables; invariants

D-Class No.	Cost	Representative	Optimal expansion
1	0	$\emptyset$	0
2	1	7	$x_0 x_1 x_2$
3	2	4, 7	$\bar{x}_1 x_2 \oplus x_0 x_2$
4	2	0, 7	$\bar{x}_0 \bar{x}_1 \bar{x}_2 \oplus x_0 x_1 x_2$
5	3	3, 5, 6	$x_0 \oplus x_1 x_2 \oplus x_0 \bar{x}_1 \bar{x}_2$
6	3	1, 2, 3, 4, 5, 6	$1 \oplus \bar{x}_0 \bar{x}_1 \bar{x}_2 \oplus x_0 x_1 x_2$

Figure 6.13. Functions of three variables. Costs and typical expansions

D-class No.	Cost	Representative	Optimal expansion
1	0	ϕ	0
2	1	15	$x_0x_1x_2x_3$
3	2	13, 14	$x_0x_2x_3 \oplus x_1x_2x_3$
4	2	10, 13	$x_0\bar{x}_1x_2x_3 \oplus \bar{x}_0x_1\bar{x}_2x_3$
5	3	9, 10, 15	$x_0x_1x_3 \oplus x_0\bar{x}_2x_3 \oplus \bar{x}_0x_1\bar{x}_2x_3$
6	3	8, 11, 12, 13, 14	$\bar{x}_1x_3 \oplus x_0\bar{x}_2x_3 \oplus \bar{x}_0x_1x_2x_3$
7	2	0, 15	$\bar{x}_0\bar{x}_1x_2\bar{x}_3 \oplus x_0x_1x_2x_3$
8	3	3, 12, 15	$x_0x_1x_2 \oplus x_0x_1\bar{x}_3 \oplus \bar{x}_0\bar{x}_1x_2x_3$
9	3	3, 13, 14	$x_0x_2x_3 \oplus x_1x_2x_3 \oplus x_0x_1\bar{x}_2\bar{x}_3$
10	4	0, 3, 12, 15	$x_0x_2 \oplus x_0\bar{x}_3 \oplus \bar{x}_1x_2 \oplus \bar{x}_1\bar{x}_3$
11	4	0, 3, 13, 14	$x_0x_2x_3 \oplus x_1x_2x_3 \oplus x_0\bar{x}_2\bar{x}_3 \oplus \bar{x}_1\bar{x}_2\bar{x}_3$
12	4	7, 11, 13, 14	$x_0x_1x_2 \oplus x_0x_1x_3 \oplus x_0x_2x_3 \oplus x_1x_2x_3$
13	3	4, 9, 14, 15	$x_2x_3 \oplus x_0\bar{x}_1x_3 \oplus \bar{x}_0\bar{x}_1x_2$
14	3	7, 8, 13, 14	$x_2x_3 \oplus x_0x_1x_2 \oplus \bar{x}_0\bar{x}_1x_3$
15	4	0, 11, 13, 14	$x_0x_1x_3 \oplus x_1x_2x_3 \oplus x_0\bar{x}_1x_2x_3 \oplus \bar{x}_0\bar{x}_1\bar{x}_2\bar{x}_3$
16	4	7, 8, 11, 13, 14	$x_2x_3 \oplus x_0x_1x_2 \oplus \bar{x}_0\bar{x}_1x_3 \oplus x_0x_1\bar{x}_2x_3$
17	4	0, 3, 13, 14, 15	$x_2x_3 \oplus x_0\bar{x}_2\bar{x}_3 \oplus \bar{x}_1\bar{x}_2\bar{x}_3 \oplus \bar{x}_0\bar{x}_1x_2x_3$
18	4	3, 5, 8, 14, 15	$x_2x_3 \oplus x_0\bar{x}_1x_2 \oplus \bar{x}_0\bar{x}_1x_3 \oplus x_0x_1\bar{x}_2\bar{x}_3$
19	4	5, 6, 9, 10, 15	$x_1x_2 \oplus x_0x_2\bar{x}_3 \oplus \bar{x}_0\bar{x}_1x_3 \oplus x_0\bar{x}_1\bar{x}_2x_3$
20	3	3, 8, 13, 14, 15	$x_2x_3 \oplus \bar{x}_0\bar{x}_1x_3 \oplus x_0x_1\bar{x}_2\bar{x}_3$
21	5	0, 1, 11, 13, 14	$x_0x_1x_2 \oplus x_0x_2x_3 \oplus \bar{x}_0x_1x_3 \oplus x_1\bar{x}_2x_3 \oplus \bar{x}_0\bar{x}_1\bar{x}_2\bar{x}_3$
22	5	3, 5, 6, 9, 10, 12	$x_1\bar{x}_3 \oplus \bar{x}_0x_1\bar{x}_2 \oplus x_0x_2\bar{x}_3 \oplus x_0\bar{x}_1x_3 \oplus \bar{x}_1x_2x_3$
23	4	0, 6, 11, 13, 14, 15	$x_0x_1x_3 \oplus \bar{x}_0x_1x_2 \oplus x_0\bar{x}_1x_2x_3 \oplus \bar{x}_0\bar{x}_1\bar{x}_2\bar{x}_3$
24	4	3, 4, 10, 13, 14, 15	$x_2x_3 \oplus x_0x_1\bar{x}_2 \oplus x_1\bar{x}_2x_3 \oplus \bar{x}_0\bar{x}_1x_2$
25	4	3, 4, 8, 14, 15	$x_2x_3 \oplus \bar{x}_0\bar{x}_1 \oplus x_0\bar{x}_2\bar{x}_3 \oplus \bar{x}_1\bar{x}_2\bar{x}_3$
26	5	0, 7, 9, 10, 12, 15	$x_1x_2 \oplus \bar{x}_0x_1 \oplus x_0\bar{x}_1x_3 \oplus \bar{x}_1x_2x_3 \oplus \bar{x}_0\bar{x}_2\bar{x}_3$
27	4	2, 3, 4, 8, 13, 15	$x_0x_2x_3 \oplus x_1\bar{x}_2\bar{x}_3 \oplus \bar{x}_0\bar{x}_1x_2 \oplus \bar{x}_0\bar{x}_1x_3$
28	5	4, 7, 8, 11, 13, 14, 15	$x_2x_3 \oplus x_0x_1\bar{x}_3 \oplus x_0x_1\bar{x}_2 \oplus \bar{x}_0\bar{x}_1x_2 \oplus \bar{x}_0\bar{x}_1\bar{x}_2x_3$
29	3	0, 3, 7, 11, 12, 13, 14	$x_0x_1 \oplus x_2x_3 \oplus \bar{x}_0\bar{x}_1\bar{x}_2\bar{x}_3$
30	6	0, 1, 2, 4, 7, 9, 10, 11, 12, 13, 14	$\bar{x}_1 \oplus x_0x_2\bar{x}_3 \oplus x_1x_2x_3 \oplus x_0x_1x_3 \oplus \bar{x}_0\bar{x}_2x_3 \oplus \bar{x}_0x_1\bar{x}_2\bar{x}_3$

Figure 6.14. Functions of four variables; costs and typical expansions

Chapter 7

Difference and Differential Calculus for Discrete Functions

The concept of *Boolean difference*, introduced by Reed [1954], has been more thoroughly investigated in a paper by Akers [1959] who obtained the algebraic properties of the Boolean difference. With the Boolean difference, Akers was able to determine the conditions under which changes in the variables of a switching function would cause change in the function. This led to the discovery of a number of relationships and theorems for switching functions that correspond to those of finite differences and of differential calculus of real functions. For example, Akers gives a series expansion for switching functions that closely resembles the Taylor–Maclaurin series. Amar and Condulmari [1967] and Sellers, Hsiao and Bearnson [1968] applied the Boolean difference to the problem of fault diagnosis; this gave rise to a considerable number of papers using the Boolean difference for fault detection. Thayse [1971] and Thayse and Davio [1973] describe a *Boolean differential calculus* which encompasses and generalizes the algebraic concepts introduced by the authors quoted above; it is considered as a general method of representation of an arbitrary switching function and as such could be applied to any classical switching problem. Moreover, Davio and Thayse have shown that the Boolean difference is applicable to a number of areas other than fault diagnosis, e.g. hazard detection, function decomposition (see Chapter 11) and analysis and synthesis of sequential switching networks. The essentials of the theory of Boolean differential calculus have been extended by several authors to discrete functions (see Thayse and Deschamps [1973a, b], Thayse [1974b], Kodandapani [1974] and Benjauthrit and Reed [1976]). Independently of the above results, Fadini [1961] suggests a theory of Boolean differences making use of disjunction instead of ring-sum. This theory has been extended by Thayse [1973a] and Deschamps and Thayse [1973a] to discrete functions. The differences are called in this case *lattice differences*.

The present chapter is devoted to a unified theory of the concepts and theories quoted above; section 7.1 deals with discrete functions while section 7.2 is devoted to a study of switching functions. Possible applications are discussed in section 7.3.

7.1. Difference and differential operators for discrete functions

This section will be devoted merely to general definitions and theorems relative to difference calculus and differential calculus for discrete functions. The case of binary and of switching functions consists as usual in a particular case of the theory of discrete functions. Due to its practical importance and to its attractive computational properties, the differential calculus for switching functions will also be studied more extensively in section 7.2.

7.1.1. *Total differences and increments of discrete functions*

Let us recall the concept of discrete function of functions (see also definition 2.9); the function $f[\boldsymbol{x}, \boldsymbol{y}(\boldsymbol{x})]$:

$$f:\left(\mathop{\times}_{i=n-1}^{0} S_i\right) \times \left(\mathop{\times}_{j=h-1}^{0} L_j\right) \rightarrow L$$

with $\boldsymbol{x} = (x_{n-1}, \ldots, x_1, x_0), x_i \in S_i = \{0, 1, \ldots, m_i-1\}\ \forall i$, and $\boldsymbol{y} = (y_{h-1}, \ldots, y_1, y_0), y_j \in L_j = \{0, 1, \ldots, r_j-1\}\ \forall j$, is a discrete function of functions if the variables y_j are mappings:

$$y_j: S \rightarrow L_j, \quad 0 \leqslant j \leqslant h-1.$$

The *total differences* of functions $f[\boldsymbol{x}, \boldsymbol{y}(\boldsymbol{x})]$ are defined as follows:

Definition 7.1. (a) Simple total difference

$$\frac{\Delta_t f}{\Delta_t x_i} = f[x_i \oplus 1, \boldsymbol{y}(x_i \oplus 1)] - f[\boldsymbol{x}, \boldsymbol{y}(\boldsymbol{x})] \tag{7.1}$$

(b) Multiple total differences

$$\frac{\Delta_t^{k_i} f}{\Delta_t x_i} = \frac{\Delta_t}{\Delta_t x_i}\left(\frac{\Delta_t^{k_i-1} f}{\Delta_t x_i}\right), \quad 1 \leqslant k_i \leqslant m_i \tag{7.2}$$

$$\frac{\Delta_t^{\boldsymbol{k}_0} f}{\Delta_t \boldsymbol{x}_0} = \frac{\Delta_t^{k_0}}{\Delta_t x_0}\left\{\frac{\Delta_t^{k_1}}{\Delta_t x_1}\left[\ldots\left(\frac{\Delta_t^{k_{q-1}} f}{\Delta_t x_{q-1}}\right)\ldots\right]\right\} \tag{7.3}$$

with $\boldsymbol{x}_0 = (x_{q-1}, \ldots, x_1, x_0)$ and $\boldsymbol{k}_0 = (k_{q-1}, \ldots, k_1, k_0), k_j \in S_j\ \forall j$.

The following theorem provides us with a formula giving the simple total difference as a function of the (partial) differences of f with respect to $x_i \in \boldsymbol{x}$ and to $y_k \in \boldsymbol{y}$.

Theorem 7.1

$$\frac{\Delta_t f}{\Delta_t x_i} = \frac{\Delta f}{\Delta x_i} \oplus \sum_e \left(\frac{\Delta^e f}{\Delta \boldsymbol{y}} \oplus \frac{\Delta^{1e} f}{\Delta x_i \boldsymbol{y}}\right) \prod_{j=0}^{h-1} \binom{\Delta y_j / \Delta x_i}{e_j} \tag{7.4}$$

$$0 \leqslant e_j \leqslant r_j-1, \quad 0 < e = (e_{h-1}, \ldots, e_1, e_0)$$

Proof. From relation (7.1) one deduces:

$$\frac{\Delta_t f}{\Delta_t x_i} = f[x_i \oplus 1, y_0(x_i \oplus 1), \ldots, y_{h-1}(x_i \oplus 1)] - f[x, y(x)]$$
$$= f\left[x_i \oplus 1, y_0 \oplus \frac{\Delta y_0}{\Delta x_i}, \ldots, y_{h-1} \oplus \frac{\Delta y_{h-1}}{\Delta x_i}\right] - f[x, y(x)]. \qquad (7.5)$$

From relation (4.34) written in the following form:

$$f(x_1, x_0 \oplus k_0) - f(x) = \sum_{e_0} \prod_{j=0}^{q-1} \binom{k_j}{e_j} \frac{\Delta^{e_0} f}{\Delta x_0}, \qquad 0 \leqslant e_i \leqslant m_i - 1, 0 < e \qquad (7.6)$$

one deduces by replacing k_0 by $(1, \Delta y_{h-1}/\Delta x_i, \ldots, \Delta y_0/\Delta x_i)$ in (7.6) that $\Delta_t f/\Delta_t x_i$ may be written successively as follows:

$$\frac{\Delta_t f}{\Delta_t x_i} = \sum_{\epsilon e} \frac{\Delta^{\epsilon e} f}{\Delta x_i y} \binom{1}{\epsilon} \left[\prod_{j=0}^{h-1} \binom{\Delta y_j/\Delta x_i}{e_j}\right]$$

$$0 \leqslant \epsilon \leqslant m_i - 1, \quad 0 \leqslant e_j \leqslant r_j - 1, \quad 0 < (\epsilon, e) = (\epsilon, e_{h-1}, \ldots, e_1, e_0)$$

$$= \frac{\Delta f}{\Delta x_i} \oplus \sum_{e} \left(\frac{\Delta^e f}{\Delta y} \oplus \frac{\Delta^{1e} f}{\Delta x_i y}\right) \left[\prod_{j=0}^{h-1} \binom{\Delta y_j/\Delta x_i}{e_j}\right]$$

$$0 \leqslant e_j \leqslant r_j - 1, \quad 0 < e. \qquad \blacksquare$$

Let us now briefly extend the above definition and theorem to cascaded types of functions of functions as described by the system (2.1), that is:

$$y_0 = y_0(x)$$
$$y_1 = y_1(x, y_0)$$
$$\vdots$$
$$y_{q-1} = y_{q-1}(x, y_0, \ldots, y_{q-2})$$
$$f = f(x, y_0, \ldots, y_{q-2}).$$

Let us denote moreover the vector $(y_{q-1}, y_{q-2}, \ldots, y_0)$ by y which is assumed to be, as above, a vector with h elements. The total difference of f with respect to x_i is defined as follows:

$$\frac{\Delta_t f}{\Delta_t x_i} = f\{x_i \oplus 1, y_0(x_i \oplus 1), y_1[x_i \oplus 1, y_0(x_i \oplus 1)], \ldots\} - f. \qquad (7.7)$$

The multiple total differences are defined with the recurrence relations (7.2) and (7.3).

Theorem 7.2

$$\frac{\Delta_t f}{\Delta_t x_i} = \frac{\Delta f}{\Delta x_i} \oplus \sum_e \left(\frac{\Delta^e f}{\Delta y} \oplus \frac{\Delta^{1e} f}{\Delta x_i y}\right)\left[\prod_{j=0}^{h-1} \binom{\Delta_t y_j/\Delta_t x_i}{e_j}\right] \tag{7.8}$$

Proof. Let y be partitioned into y_1 and y_0, that is:

$$y_0 = y_0(x)$$
$$y_1 = y_1[x, y_0(x)]$$
$$f = f(x, y_0, y_1).$$

One has:

$$\frac{\Delta_t f}{\Delta_t x_i} = f\{x_i \oplus 1, y_0(x_i \oplus 1), y_1\,[x_i \oplus 1, y_0(x_i \oplus 1)]\} - f$$

$$= f(x_i \oplus 1, y_0 \oplus \Delta y_0/\Delta x_i, y_1 \oplus \Delta_t y_1/\Delta_t x_i) - f$$

where $\Delta y_j/\Delta x_i$ means $(\Delta y_{l-1}/\Delta x_i, \ldots, \Delta y_1/\Delta x_i, \Delta y_0/\Delta x_i)$ for $y_j = (y_{l-1}, \ldots, y_1, y_0), j = 0$ or 1.

The proof then immediately follows from theorem 7.1. When y is partitioned into q subfunctions, the proof is achieved by induction on the number of subfunctions. ■

Expansions similar to those of theorems 7.1 and 7.2, but for multiple total differences and for other difference operators, may be found in the paper by Thayse [1974d]. As a conclusion, the above theorem 7.1 embodies a generalized chaining rule for the evaluation of the total difference operators for the functions of functions of the type (2.1): one has only to substitute, in the expansion of this theorem, the partial differences $\Delta y_j/\Delta x_i$ by the total differences $\Delta_t y_j/\Delta_t x_i$.

One will now be faced with a particular type of functions of functions which was previously called *time-dependent discrete functions* (see definition 2.10). The simplest time-dependent discrete functions are characterized by an expression of the form:

$$f = f[x_{n-1}(t), \ldots, x_1(t), x_0(t)] \tag{7.9}$$

where t is a discrete variable: $t \in \{0, 1, \ldots, m_t - 1\}$. Since in most applications, the variable t will be a discretized time index, the function represented by (7.9) will be called a time-dependent discrete function. In this case, the cardinality m_t of the domain of t is generally assumed to be an arbitrarily large positive integer. One will also consider in what follows more elaborate forms of time-dependent discrete functions; these are characterized by systems of the form:

$$x = x(t)$$
$$y_0 = y_0(x)$$
$$\vdots$$
$$y_{q-1} = y_{q-1}(x, y_0, \ldots, y_{q-2})$$
$$f = f(x, y_0, \ldots, y_{q-1}).$$

From theorems 7.1 and 7.2 one deduces the following theorem which gives us total differences of time dependent discrete functions.

Theorem 7.3

$$\frac{\Delta_t f}{\Delta_t t} = \sum_{\epsilon e} \frac{\Delta^{\epsilon e} f}{\Delta x y} \left[\prod_{\substack{j=0,h-1 \\ i=0,n-1}} \binom{\Delta x_i/\Delta t}{\epsilon_i} \binom{\Delta_t y_j/\Delta_t t}{e_j} \right]. \tag{7.10}$$

When dealing with discrete functions of the above type, that is functions which depend of only one variable (namely the variable t in our case), it is convenient to replace the notations $\Delta_t f/\Delta_t t$, $\Delta x_i/\Delta t$ and $\Delta_t y_j/\Delta_t t$ by Δf, Δx_i and Δy_j respectively. These notations will then be called the *increments* of f, x_i and y_j respectively. The expression giving the increment of f is then obtained from (7.10), that is:

$$\Delta f = \sum_{\epsilon e} \frac{\Delta^{\epsilon e} f}{\Delta x y} \left[\prod_{j,i} \binom{\Delta x_i}{\epsilon_i} \binom{\Delta y_j}{e_j} \right] \tag{7.11}$$

It is clear that the replacement of $\Delta_t f/\Delta_t t$ by Δf is unnecessary, but this substitution is classical in finite-difference calculus and in differential calculus. The expression (7.11) allows us to compute the increment of f as a function of the increments of its variables; for a function $f = f[x(t)]$, the expression (7.11) becomes:

$$\Delta f = \sum_{e} \frac{\Delta^{e} f}{\Delta x} \left[\prod_{i=0}^{n-1} \binom{\Delta x_i}{e_i} \right]. \tag{7.12}$$

$$0 \leqslant e_i \leqslant m_i - 1, \quad 0 < e = (e_{n-1}, \ldots, e_1, e_0).$$

The increment Δx_i of the variable x_i is the difference between its future and its present value:

$$\Delta x_i = x_i(t+1) - x_i(t).$$

The increment Δf of a function $f[x(t)]$ is the increment of this function due to the increments $(\Delta x_{n-1}, \ldots, \Delta x_1, \Delta x_0) = \Delta x$ of x.

One has thus:

$$\Delta f = f(y_{n-1} \oplus \Delta y_{n-1}, \ldots, y_1 \oplus \Delta y_1, y_0 \oplus \Delta y_0) - f(x_{n-1}, \ldots, x_1, x_0) \tag{7.13}$$
$$= f(x \oplus \Delta x) - f(x).$$

Let us now assume that $f(x)$ is a simple discrete function and no more a time-dependent discrete function. The expression (7.13) is then taken as the definition of the increment of f; in this case it is clear that the increments Δx_i are no more considered as a difference between future and present values of x_i. The increments Δx_i are now considered as new independent variables taking their values in S_i $\forall i$. Similarly, the increment of discrete functions $f(x, y)$ is defined by (7.11) which is the Newton expansion:

$$\Delta f = f(x \oplus \Delta x, y \oplus \Delta y) - f(x, y). \tag{7.14}$$

The Δx_i are again new independent variables, while the y_j are functions of x and Δx, that is, in view of (7.13):

$$\Delta y_j = y_j(x \oplus \Delta x) - y_j(x). \tag{7.15}$$

Consider two discrete functions $f(x)$ and $g\,[x, y(x)]$ such that $f = g$; one has:

$$\begin{aligned}\Delta g &= g(x \oplus \Delta x, y \oplus \Delta y) - g \\ &= g\,[x \oplus \Delta x, y(x \oplus \Delta x)] - g \\ &= f(x \oplus \Delta x) - f = \Delta f.\end{aligned} \tag{7.16}$$

The expression (7.13) is thus general and holds when the variables x_i are independent variables or functions.

We have first defined total differences for functions of functions; the total differences of time-dependent functions (which constitute a particular case of functions of functions) lead to the concept of increment for these functions. From the definition of the increment for time-dependent functions we finally obtained the concept of increment for any kind of discrete function. One could evidently also define the increment of any type of discrete function by relation (7.13) and (7.14) and deduce from this the concept of total difference.

Multiple increments may evidently be defined along the usual rule, that is:

$$\Delta^k f = \Delta(\Delta^{k-1} f). \tag{7.17}$$

One easily shows that $\Delta^k f$ may be expanded in terms of differences and of increments $\Delta^j x_i$ as follows:

$$\Delta^k f = \sum_{el} \frac{\Delta^e f}{\Delta x} (-1)^{(k+l)} \binom{k}{l} \left\{ \prod_{i=0}^{n-1} \binom{\sum_{j=1}^{l} \binom{l}{j} \Delta^j x_i}{e_i} \right\}. \tag{7.18}$$

These multiple increments will no further be studied here; their most important properties may be found in Thayse [1974d].

Remark. To simplify the writing of some functions, it is often useful to define a new operator, namely the *sensitivity*; the k_0-th sensitivity of $f(x)$ with respect to the q variables in x_0 will be denoted by $S^{k_0}f/Sx_0$ and defined as follows:

$$\frac{S^{k_0} f}{S x_0} = f(x_0 \oplus k_0) - f(x).$$

The following relations hold between sensitivities and differences:

$$\frac{S^{k_0} f}{S x_0} = \sum_{e_0} \prod_{j=0}^{q-1} \binom{k_j}{e_j} \frac{\Delta^{e_0} f}{\Delta x_0}$$

$$0 < e_0 \leqslant m_0 - 1$$

$$\frac{\Delta^{k_0} f}{\Delta x_0} = \sum_{e_0} (-1)^{\sum_{j=0}^{q-1} (k_j + e_j)} \prod_{j=0}^{q-1} \binom{k_j}{e_j} \frac{S^{e_0} f}{S x_0}.$$

7.1.2. *Total derivatives and differentials of Galois functions*

The concepts of *total derivatives* and of *differentials* for Galois functions from $[GF(p)]^n$ to $GF(p)$ will now briefly be introduced. It is not our purpose to investigate this subject in great detail since the developments of differential operators for Galois functions generally lead to tedious formulae. Moreover the most important case occurs for Galois functions from $[GF(2)]^n$ to $GF(2)$; one knows that for these functions the concepts of difference and of derivative coincide. Similarly, the concepts of total difference and of total derivative and the concepts of increment and of differential also coincide respectively. More about the differentials of Galois functions may be found in the paper by Thayse [1974b].

Definition 7.2. (a) Simple total derivatives of functions $f[\boldsymbol{x}, \boldsymbol{y}(\boldsymbol{x})]$:

$$\frac{df}{dx_i} = -\left\{\sum_{e=1}^{p-1} \frac{f[x_i \oplus e, y(x_i \oplus e)] - f[x, y(x)]}{e}\right\}. \tag{7.19}$$

(b) Multiple derivatives

$$\frac{d^{k_i}f}{dx_i} = \frac{d}{dx_i}\left(\frac{d^{k_i-1}f}{dx_i}\right) \tag{7.20}$$

$$\frac{d^{k_0}f}{dx_0} = \frac{d^{k_0}}{dx_0}\left\{\frac{d^{k_1}}{dx_1}\left[\cdots\left(\frac{d^{k_{q-1}}f}{dx_{q-1}}\cdots\right)\right]\right\}. \tag{7.21}$$

In view of (5.17) and (7.19), it is clear that the definition of the total derivative has been taken in such a way that, for two functions $f(\boldsymbol{x})$ and $g[\boldsymbol{x}, \boldsymbol{y}(\boldsymbol{x})]$, one has $dg/dx_i = \partial f/\partial x_i$ if $g = f$; the same relation then evidently holds between higher order derivatives. Since moreover $\Delta_t^k g/\Delta_t \boldsymbol{x} = \Delta^k f/\Delta \boldsymbol{x}$, the following relation holds between total derivatives and total differences:

$$\frac{d^k f}{dx_i} = \sum_{e=k}^{p-1} \frac{\mathscr{S}_e^{(k)}\, k!}{e!} \frac{\Delta_t^k f}{\Delta_t x_i}. \tag{7.22}$$

Relation (7.22) is a direct consequence of theorem 3.7.

The formal expansions of (7.19) and (7.22) in terms of partial derivatives with respect to any $x_i \in \boldsymbol{x}$ and $y_j \in \boldsymbol{y}$ are generally cumbersome and working them out is tedious, so that they will not be detailed here. The formula (7.22), however, constitutes a powerful tool for deriving useful formulas for some given p and f. Let us give an example; let f and g be two Galois functions, and $F = fg$ another Galois function defined as the product of f by g. From formula (7.22) one will derive the expression of the derivative of a product in terms of the derivatives of the components.

(a) $p = 2$; since for switching functions the derivatives and the differences coincide, one deduces from the last formula of (4.36):

$$\frac{d(fg)}{dx_i} = g\frac{\partial f}{\partial x_i} \oplus f\frac{\partial g}{\partial x_i} \oplus \frac{\partial f}{\partial x_i}\frac{\partial g}{\partial x_i}. \tag{7.23}$$

(b) $p = 3$; from (7.22) one deduces:

$$\frac{d(fg)}{dx_i} = \frac{\Delta_t(fg)}{\Delta_t x_i} \oplus \frac{\Delta_t^2(fg)}{\Delta_t x_i}. \tag{7.24}$$

In view of (4.36) one has successively:

$$\frac{\Delta_t(fg)}{\Delta_t x_i} = f\frac{\Delta g}{\Delta x_i} \oplus g\frac{\Delta f}{\Delta x_i} \oplus \frac{\Delta f}{\Delta x_i}\frac{\Delta g}{\Delta x_i}$$

$$\frac{\Delta_t^2(fg)}{\Delta_t x_i} = f\frac{\Delta^2 g}{\Delta x_i} \oplus g\frac{\Delta^2 f}{\Delta x_i} \oplus 2\frac{\Delta f}{\Delta x_i}\frac{\Delta g}{\Delta x_i} \oplus 2\frac{\Delta f}{\Delta x_i}\frac{\Delta^2 g}{\Delta x_i} \oplus 2\frac{\Delta g}{\Delta x_i}\frac{\Delta^2 f}{\Delta x_i} \oplus \frac{\Delta^2 g}{\Delta x_i}\frac{\Delta^2 f}{\Delta x_i}.$$

By introducing the two above expressions in (7.24) and by taking into account the following relations

$$\frac{\partial f}{\partial x_i} = \frac{\Delta f}{\Delta x_i} \oplus \frac{\Delta^2 f}{\Delta x_i}, \quad \frac{\partial g}{\partial x_i} = \frac{\Delta g}{\Delta x_i} \oplus \frac{\Delta^2 g}{\Delta x_i}, \quad \frac{\partial^2 f}{\partial x_i} = \frac{\Delta^2 f}{\Delta x_i}, \quad \frac{\partial^2 g}{\partial x_i} = \frac{\Delta^2 g}{\Delta x_i}$$

one finally obtains the following formula:

$$\frac{d(fg)}{dx_i} = \frac{\partial f}{\partial x_i}\left(g \oplus 2\frac{\partial^2 g}{\partial x_i}\right) \oplus \frac{\partial g}{\partial x_i}\left(f \oplus 2\frac{\partial^2 f}{\partial x_i}\right). \tag{7.25}$$

Thus the usual rule of derivation which holds in the real field:

$$\frac{d(fg)}{dx_i} = f\frac{\partial g}{\partial x_i} + g\frac{\partial f}{\partial x_i} \tag{7.26}$$

does not apply in a finite field. The correcting terms may however easily be computed.

Differentials for Galois functions from $[GF(p)]^n$ to $GF(p)$ may now be defined according to a scheme similar to the one used for the increments of discrete functions. This scheme holds for Galois functions $f(\boldsymbol{x})$ or for Galois functions of functions $f[\boldsymbol{x}, \boldsymbol{y}(\boldsymbol{x})]$; it may be summarized as follows:

(a) Consider the function $f(\boldsymbol{x})$ as a time-dependent function $f[\boldsymbol{x}(t)]$ (in this case t takes its values in $GF(p)$); obtain the total derivative of f: $d^k f/dt$ in terms of the total differences $\Delta_t^k f/\Delta_t t$, applying formula (7.22).

(b) The total differences $\Delta_t^k f/\Delta_t t$ are expressed in terms of the partial differences using formula (7.4) and more elaborate formulas for $k > 1$ (see Thayse [1974b]); all the partial differences are in turn expressed in terms of partial derivatives by using relation (5.47); replace in the expression of $d^k f/dt$ the total differences successively by partial differences and partial derivatives using the formulae quoted above.

(c) Replace $d^k f/dt$ by $d^k f$ and $\partial^j x_i/\partial t$ by $d^j x_i$ in the expression obtained; this last expansion is then by definition the expression of the kth differential of f in terms of the differentials $d^j x_i$ of the independent variables x_i.

One obtains finally the following expression for $d^k f$ (see also Thayse [1974b])

$$d^k f = k! \sum_{i,j} \frac{S_i^{(k)}}{i!} (-1)^{(i+j)} \binom{i}{j} f\left[x = \sum_{r,l} \binom{j}{l} \frac{\mathcal{S}_r^{(l)}\, l!}{r!} d^r x\right] \tag{7.27}$$

with $d^r x = (d^r x_{n-1}, \ldots, d^r x_1, d^r x_0)$. (An expression such as $f(x = \sum_j \alpha_j d^j x)$ means that each x_i in f must be replaced by $\sum_j \alpha_j d^j x_i$.)

The above formula (7.27) yields for $p = 2$ and 3 respectively (the corresponding expressions of the increments are also given):

$p = 2$:

$$\begin{aligned} df = \Delta f &= f(x \oplus \Delta x) \oplus f(x) \\ &= f(x \oplus dx) \oplus f(x) \end{aligned}$$

$p = 3$:

$$\begin{aligned} \Delta f &= f(x \oplus \Delta x) \oplus 2f(x) \\ &= f(x \oplus dx \oplus 2d^2 x) \oplus 2f(x) \\ df &= f(x \oplus 2\Delta x \oplus \Delta^2 x) \oplus 2f(x \oplus \Delta x) \\ &= f(x \oplus 2dx \oplus 2d^2 x) \oplus 2f(x \oplus dx \oplus 2d^2 x) \\ d^2 f = \Delta^2 f &= f(x \oplus 2\Delta x \oplus \Delta^2 x) \oplus f(x \oplus \Delta x) \oplus f(x) \\ &= f(x \oplus 2dx \oplus 2d^2 x) \oplus f(x \oplus dx \oplus 2d^2 x) \oplus f(x). \end{aligned}$$

Theorem 7.4

(a) $$\Delta^k f = \sum_{i=k}^{p-1} \frac{\mathcal{S}_i^{(k)}\, k!}{i!} d^i f, \quad k \leqslant p-1 \tag{7.28}$$

(b) $$d^k f = \sum_{i=k}^{p-1} \frac{S_i^{(k)}\, k!}{i!} \Delta^i f, \quad k \leqslant p-1. \tag{7.29}$$

Proof. The proof follows from theorem 5.7 and from the definitions of total differences, total derivatives, increments and differentials. ∎

Since $\mathscr{S}_i^{(1)} = 1$ and $S_i^{(1)} = (-1)^{(i+1)}\,(i-1)!$, the following relations, which constitute an important particular case of theorem 7.4 apply:

$$\Delta f = \sum_{i=1}^{p-1} \frac{1}{i!}\, d^i f \tag{7.30}$$

$$df = \sum_{i=1}^{p-1} \frac{(-1)^{(i+1)}}{i!}\, \Delta^i f. \tag{7.31}$$

In finite fields, relation (7.28) corresponds to the following classical formula in numerical analysis (if convergent):

$$\Delta^k f = k! \sum_{i=k}^{\infty} \frac{\mathscr{S}_i^{(k)}}{i!}\, d^i f. \tag{7.32}$$

In particular, for $k = 1$ the above relation yields

$$\Delta f = \sum_{i=1}^{\infty} \frac{d^i f}{i!} \tag{7.33}$$

which may also be written in the form

$$\Delta f = \sum_{i=1}^{n-1} \frac{d^i f}{i!} + R_n \tag{7.34}$$

where R_n is the remainder of the Taylor expansion. This last expression (7.34) constitutes the most general form of the Taylor expansion in classical analysis (see, for example, de la Vallée-Poussin [1959], pp. 85 and 134–137). Similarly, for finite fields, relation (7.29) constitutes the extension of the following formula which applies in numerical analysis (if convergent):

$$d^k f = k! \sum_{i=k}^{\infty} \frac{S_i^{(k)}}{i!}\, \Delta^i f. \tag{7.35}$$

As a conclusion theorem 7.4 generalizes to the fields of integers modulo-p some well-known relations of classical numerical analysis and so the definitions of differentials and of increments adopted in this book appear to be the adequate generalizations of the corresponding concepts defined in classical analysis for the real field. These concepts were introduced in the papers by Thayse [1974b, d].

7.1.3. Lattice differences and variations of discrete functions of functions

Lattice differences for discrete functions were defined in Chapter 3; the first purpose of this section will be to define lattice differences for functions of functions.

From these concepts one deduces a new operator namely the *variation* which will appear to be useful in the applications relative to logical design.

We shall first again consider discrete functions of the type:

$$f[x_{n-1}, \ldots, x_1, x_0, y_{h-1}(x_{n-1}, \ldots, x_1, x_0), \ldots, y_1(x_{n-1}, \ldots, x_1, x_0), y_0(x_{n-1}, \ldots, x_1, x_0)]$$
$$= f[x, y(x)]$$

Definition 7.3. (a) *Simple total join differences:*

$$\frac{q_t f}{q_t x_i} = \bigvee_{e_i} f[x_i \oplus e_{ih}, y_{h-1}(x_i \oplus e_{i(h-1)}), \ldots, y_0(x_i \oplus e_{i0})] \tag{7.36}$$

(b) *Simple total meet differences:*

$$\frac{p_t f}{p_t x_i} = \bigwedge_{e_i} f[x_i \oplus e_{ih}, y_{h-1}(x_i \oplus e_{i(h-1)}), \ldots, y_0(x_i \oplus e_{i0})] \tag{7.37}$$

$$e_i = (e_{ih}, e_{i(h-1)}, \ldots, e_{i1}, e_{i0}); \quad 0 \leqslant e_{ij} \leqslant 1.$$

The multiple total join and meet differences are defined according to the usual recurrence rule (see, for example (7.2) and (7.3)); they are denoted $q_t^{k_i} f/q_t x_i$, $q_t^{k_0} f/q_t x_0$, $p_t^{k_i} f/p_t x_i$ and $p_t^{k_0} f/p_t x_0$ respectively. These definitions immediately lead to the following relations (which could evidently also be taken as definition for these operators):

$$\frac{q_t^{k_i} f}{q_t x_i} = \bigvee_{e_i} f[x_i \oplus e_{ih}, y_{h-1}(x_i \oplus e_{i(h-1)}), \ldots, y_0(x_i \oplus e_{i0})] \tag{7.38}$$

$$0 \leqslant e_{ij} \leqslant k_i$$

$$\frac{q_t^{k_0} f}{q_t x_0} = \bigvee_{e} f[x_0 \oplus e_h, y_{h-1}(x_0 \oplus e_{h-1}), \ldots, y_0(x_0 \oplus e_0)] \tag{7.39}$$

$$e_j = (e_{(q-1)j}, \ldots, e_{1j}, e_{0j}); 0 \leqslant j \leqslant h, \quad 0 \leqslant e_{ij} \leqslant k_i$$

$$e = (e_h, \ldots, e_1, e_0).$$

Clearly dual expressions hold for the total meet differences.

The most important property of the total lattice differences is that the occurrences of the same variable, which appear both in the expression of f and in the expressions of the functions y_j, become in a certain way independent variables. Otherwise stated, in the k_ith lattice difference, the occurrences of x_i which appear in the funcion f itself and in each of the functions y_j may take independently any value between the limits x_i and $x_i \oplus k_i$; let us define an auxiliary function F as follows:

$$F = f[x_{ih}, y_{h-1}(x_{i(h-1)}), \ldots, y_1(x_{i1}), y_0(x_{i0})]$$

one has then:

$$\frac{q_t^{k_i} f}{q_t x_i} = \left(\frac{q^{k_i \ldots k_i k_i} F}{q x_{ih} \ldots x_{i1} x_{i0}} \right)_{x_{ij} = x_i}$$

$$\frac{p_t^{k_i} f}{p_t x_i} = \left(\frac{p^{k_i \ldots k_i k_i} F}{p x_{ih} \ldots x_{i1} x_{i0}} \right)_{x_{ij} = x_i} . \tag{7.40}$$

It may be useful to point out already now that these definitions are strictly oriented to the possible applications of the lattice differences in logical design. Some of these applications are discussed at the end of this chapter.

The above property of the total lattice differences (i.e. independence between identical limits of the different occurrences of the same variable) will be taken as a definition when dealing with more elaborate functions of functions of the type (2.1). If one has, for example, to compute a total lattice difference with respect to a variable x_i, the occurrences of this variable are denoted $x_{ih}, \ldots, x_{i1}, x_{i0}$ as in the following function:

$$\begin{aligned} F &= F(x_{ih}, y_{h-1}, \ldots, y_1, y_0) \\ y_0 &= y_0(x_{i0}) \\ y_1 &= y_1[x_{i1}, y_0(x_{i2})] \\ y_2 &= y_2\{x_{i3}, y_1[x_{i4}, y_0(x_{i5})], y_0(x_{i6})\} \\ &\vdots \end{aligned} \tag{7.41}$$

For the k_ith total lattice difference, the variables x_{ij} take their values between x_i and $x_i \oplus k_i$ as described by (7.40). The generalization of the above definition to $\boldsymbol{k}_0$th total differences and to sets of functions $\boldsymbol{y}_0, \boldsymbol{y}_1, \ldots, \boldsymbol{y}_{k-1}$ is straightforward.

A direct consequence of the above definitions is that the expression of the total lattice difference does not only depend on the logic value of the discrete function of functions but also on the presence of the functions y_j. Consider two discrete functions $f(\boldsymbol{x})$ and $g[\boldsymbol{x}, \boldsymbol{y}(\boldsymbol{x})]$ such that $g = f$; one has:

$$\begin{aligned} &p_t^{\boldsymbol{k}_0} g / p_t \boldsymbol{x}_0 \leqslant p^{\boldsymbol{k}_0} f / p \boldsymbol{x}_0 \\ &q_t^{\boldsymbol{k}_0} g / q_t \boldsymbol{x}_0 \geqslant q^{\boldsymbol{k}_0} f / q \boldsymbol{x}_0 . \end{aligned} \tag{7.42}$$

Let us recall that for total differences and derivatives we had:

$$\begin{aligned} \Delta_t^{\boldsymbol{k}_0} g / \Delta_t \boldsymbol{x}_0 &= \Delta^{\boldsymbol{k}_0} f / \Delta \boldsymbol{x}_0 \\ d^{\boldsymbol{k}_0} g / d \boldsymbol{x}_0 &= \partial^{\boldsymbol{k}_0} f / \partial \boldsymbol{x}_0 . \end{aligned} \tag{7.43}$$

Let us finally remember (see Chapter 3) that the lattice differences may be interpreted in terms of maximal and of minimal values of the function f on some of its subdomains.

One will now introduce a new operator, namely the *variation*; this operator will appear of outstanding interest in view of its applications in logical design.

Definition 7.4. (a) *k_0th variation* of a discrete function f:

$$\frac{\delta^{k_0} f}{\delta x_0} = \frac{q^{k_0} f}{q x_0} - \frac{p^{k_0} f}{p x_0} \tag{7.44}$$

(b) *k_0th total variation* of a discrete function of functions g:

$$\frac{\delta_t^{k_0} g}{\delta_t x_0} = \frac{q_t^{k_0} g}{q_t x_0} - \frac{p_t^{k_0} g}{p_t x_0} \tag{7.45}$$

In view of (7.42), (7.44) and (7.45) one has for functions $f = g$:

$$\delta_t^{k_0} g/\delta_t x_0 \geqslant \delta^{k_0} f/\delta x_0. \tag{7.46}$$

The k_0th variation and k_0th total variation were introduced by Thayse [1974d]; these operators generalize a switching operator introduced by Akers [1959] for switching functions and sometimes referred to as the Δ-*operator.* The importance of the variations comes from their utilization in several domains of switching theory such as hazard detection (see section 7.3.1 and Thayse [1971], Thayse and Davio [1973], Deschamps and Thayse [1973b]), function decomposition (see Chapter 11 and Akers [1959], Shen, McKellar and Weiner [1971], Thayse [1972c]) and in several problems arising in sequential logic (see section 7.3.3 and Thayse [1970, 1974c]).

General theorems relating the total lattice differences and the variations to partial difference operators may be found in Thayse [1974c]; in this section, detailed computational formulas for variations and total lattice differences will only be given in the frame of binary functions. These formulas will be used in Chapters 11, 12 and 13.

Theorems 7.5. (Relations between lattice differences and variations.) Let f be a binary function; one has:

(a) $$\frac{\delta^{k_0} f}{\delta x_0} = \overline{\left(\frac{p^{k_0} f}{p x_0}\right)} \wedge \frac{q^{k_0} f}{q x_0} \tag{7.47}$$

(b) $$\frac{q^{k_0} f}{q x_0} = f \vee \frac{\delta^{k_0} f}{\delta x_0} \tag{7.48}$$

(c) $$\frac{p^{k_0} f}{p x_0} = f \wedge \overline{\left(\frac{\delta^{k_0} f}{\delta x_0}\right)}. \tag{7.49}$$

Proof. In view of the definition of meet and join differences (see section 3.2.3.1) one has:

$$p^{k_0} f/px_0 \leqslant f \leqslant q^{k_0} f/qx_0. \tag{7.50}$$

For binary functions relation (7.43) becomes successively:

$$\begin{aligned}
\delta^{k_0} f/\delta x_0 &= q^{k_0} f/qx_0 \oplus p^{k_0} f/px_0 \quad (\oplus \text{ stands for the modulo-2 sum})\\
&= [\overline{(p^{k_0} f/px_0)} \wedge (q^{k_0} f/qx_0)] \vee [(p^{k_0} f/px_0) \wedge \overline{(q^{k_0} f/qx_0)}]\\
&= \overline{(p^{k_0} f/px_0)} \wedge (q^{k_0} f/qx_0) \quad \text{(in view of (7.50))}\\
f \vee \delta^{k_0} f/\delta x_0 &= f \vee [\overline{(p^{k_0} f/px_0)} \wedge q^{k_0} f/qx_0]\\
&= q^{k_0} f/qx_0 \quad \text{(in view of (7.50))}\\
f\overline{(\delta^{k_0} f/\delta x_0)} &= f \wedge (p^{k_0} f/px_0 \vee \overline{q^{k_0} f/qx_0})\\
&= p^{k_0} f/px_0 \quad \text{(in view of (7.50)).}
\end{aligned}$$

■

Corollary. If f is a binary function of functions, relations (7.47) and (7.49) hold between total lattice differences and total variations.

Proof. The proof immediately follows from the definitions of total operators (7.38), (7.39) and (7.46), from relation (7.50) which also holds for total lattice differences and from the above theorem 7.5. ■

The main properties of the variation operator for binary functions are gathered in theorem 7.6 below.

Theorem 7.6. (Properties of the variations.)

(a) $\delta^{m_0 - 1} f/\delta x_0$ *is degenerate in* x_0.

(b) $\delta^{m-1} f/\delta x$ *is 0 or 1 and is 0 iff f is itself 0 or 1 (degenerate function).*

(c) $(\delta^{m_0-1} f/\delta x_0)_{x_1=a_1}$ *is 0 or 1 and is 0 iff* $f(a_1, x_0)$ *is degenerate in* x_0.

Proof. (a) Since p^{m_0-1}/px_0 and $q^{m_0-1} f/qx_0$ are both degenerate in x_0, so is also $\delta^{m_0-1} f/\delta x_0$.

(b) $\delta^{m-1} f/\delta x$ is degenerate in x (see (a)); it is 0 iff $p^{m-1} f/px = q^{m-1} f/qx$, i.e. if f is degenerate.

(c) This point immediately results from (a) and (b) applied to the function $f(x_1 = a_1, x_0)$. ■

Corollary. $(\delta^{k_0} f/\delta x_0)_{x_1=a_1, x_0=a_0}$ is 0 iff $f(x_1 = a_1, x_0)$ is degenerate for $a_0 \leqslant x_0 \leqslant a_0 \oplus k_0$; it is 1 otherwise.

Theorem 7.7. (Relation between ring differences and variations.)

$$\frac{\delta^{k_0} f}{\delta x_0} = \bigvee_{e_0} \frac{\Delta^{e_0} f}{\Delta x_0}, \quad 0 \leqslant e_i \leqslant k_i, \quad 0 < e_0 \tag{7.51}$$

$$k_0 = (k_{q-1}, \ldots, k_1, k_0), \quad e_0 = (e_{q-1}, \ldots, e_1, e_0), \quad x_0 = (x_{q-1}, \ldots, x_1, x_0).$$

Proof. The proof may, for example, be achieved by verifying that the function $\bigvee_{e_0} \Delta^{e_0} f/\Delta x_0$ satisfies the properties of theorem 7.6 and of its corollary. ■

Let us now consider time-dependent binary functions of the form:

$$f[x_{n-1}(t), \ldots, x_1(t), x_0(t)]$$

where each of the x_i's are binary functions of one variable t.

The join and meet total differences for these functions are respectively:

$$\frac{q_t^k f}{q_t t} = \bigvee_{e} f[x_{n-1}(t \oplus e_{n-1}), \ldots, x_1(t \oplus e_1), x_0(t \oplus e_0)], \tag{7.52}$$

$$\frac{p_t^k f}{p_t t} = \bigwedge_{e} f[x_{n-1}(t \oplus e_{n-1}), \ldots, x_1(t \oplus e_1), x_0(t \oplus e_0)], \tag{7.53}$$

$$0 \leqslant e_i \leqslant k.$$

One will be interested (see section 7.3) in obtaining the expression of $\delta_t^k f/\delta_t t$ in terms of the differences $\Delta^e f/\Delta x$ and of the variations $\delta^k x_j/\delta t$.

Theorem 7.8

$$\frac{\delta_t^k f}{\delta_t t} = \bigvee_{e} \frac{\Delta f}{\Delta x^e} \left[\prod_{i=0}^{n-1} \left(\frac{\delta^k x_i}{\delta t} \right)^{e_i} \right], \quad 0 \leqslant e_i \leqslant 1, \quad 0 < e. \tag{7.54}$$

Proof. In view of the definition of simple difference (see section 4.2.1.1) one has:

$$x_i(t \oplus e_i) = x_i(t) \oplus e_i \frac{\Delta x_i}{\Delta t}, \quad e_i = 0, 1$$

so that relation (7.52) for $k = 1$ may be written in the following form:

$$\frac{q_t f}{q_t t} = \bigvee_{e} f\left(x_{n-1} \oplus e_{n-1} \frac{\Delta x_{n-1}}{\Delta t}, \ldots, x_1 \oplus e_1 \frac{\Delta x_1}{\Delta t}, x_0 \oplus e_0 \frac{\Delta x_0}{\Delta t}\right)$$

$$= f \vee \bigvee_{e} \left[f \oplus f\left(x_{n-1} \oplus e_{n-1} \frac{\Delta x_{n-1}}{\Delta t}, \ldots, x_1 \oplus e_1 \frac{\Delta x_1}{\Delta t}, x_0 \oplus e_0 \frac{\Delta x_0}{\Delta t}\right)\right].$$

Let us expand each of the terms of the above disjunctive expression according to the Newton expansion (see section 4.2.1.1); one obtains:

$$\frac{q_t f}{q_t t} = f \vee \bigvee_{i=0,n-1} \frac{\Delta f}{\Delta x_i}\frac{\Delta x_i}{\Delta t} \vee$$

$$\bigvee_{i,j=0,n-1} \left(\frac{\Delta f}{\Delta x_i}\frac{\Delta x_i}{\Delta t} \oplus \frac{\Delta f}{\Delta x_j}\frac{\Delta x_j}{\Delta t} \oplus \frac{\Delta f}{\Delta x_i x_j}\frac{\Delta x_i}{\Delta t}\frac{\Delta x_j}{\Delta t}\right) \vee \ldots \vee$$

$$\left\{ \sum_e \frac{\Delta f}{\Delta x^e}\left[\prod_{i,0,n-1}\left(\frac{\Delta x_i}{\Delta t}\right)^{e_k}\right]\right\}.$$

By repeated application of the classical rule

$$a \vee (a \oplus b) = a \vee b$$

the above expression reduces to the following:

$$\frac{q_t f}{q_t t} = f \vee \bigvee_e \frac{\Delta f}{\Delta x^e}\left[\prod_{i=0,n-1}\left(\frac{\Delta x_i}{\Delta t}\right)^{e_i}\right].$$

Expression (7.48) and the inequality $qf/q\boldsymbol{x}^{\boldsymbol{e}} \leqslant qf/q\boldsymbol{x}^{\boldsymbol{\epsilon}}$ if $\boldsymbol{e} \subseteq \boldsymbol{\epsilon}$ allow us to write successively

$$\frac{q_t f}{q_t t} = \bigvee_e \frac{qf}{q\boldsymbol{x}^{\boldsymbol{e}}}\left[\prod_{i=0,n-1}\left(\frac{\Delta x_i}{\Delta t}\right)^{e_i}\right]$$

$$= \bigvee_e \frac{qf}{q\boldsymbol{x}^{\boldsymbol{e}}}\left[\prod_{i=0,n-1}\left(\frac{\Delta x_i}{\Delta t}\right)^{(e_i)}\right]. \tag{7.55}$$

Similar arguments allow us to write

$$\frac{p_t f}{p_t t} = \bigvee_e \frac{pf}{p\boldsymbol{x}^{\boldsymbol{e}}}\left[\prod_{i=0,n-1}\left(\frac{\Delta x_i}{\Delta t}\right)^{(e_i)}\right]. \tag{7.56}$$

From (7.55), (7.56) and from the relation $pf/p\boldsymbol{x}^{\boldsymbol{e}} \oplus qf/q\boldsymbol{x}^{\boldsymbol{e}} = \delta f/\delta \boldsymbol{x}^{\boldsymbol{e}}$ one then deduces:

$$\frac{\delta_t f}{\delta_t t} = \frac{p_t f}{p_t t} \oplus \frac{q_t f}{q_t t}$$

$$= \bigvee_e \frac{\delta f}{\delta \boldsymbol{x}^{\boldsymbol{e}}}\left[\prod_{i=0,n-1}\left(\frac{\Delta x_i}{\Delta t}\right)^{(e_i)}\right]. \tag{7.57}$$

Finally, since $\delta f/\delta \boldsymbol{x}^{\boldsymbol{e}} \leqslant \delta f/\delta \boldsymbol{x}^{\boldsymbol{\epsilon}}$ if $\boldsymbol{e} \subseteq \boldsymbol{\epsilon}$ and since

$$\frac{\delta f}{\delta \boldsymbol{x}^{\boldsymbol{e}}} = \bigvee_{\boldsymbol{\epsilon} \subseteq \boldsymbol{e}} \frac{\Delta f}{\Delta \boldsymbol{x}^{\boldsymbol{\epsilon}}}$$

relation (7.57) may be transformed into the following:

$$\frac{\delta_t f}{\delta_t t} = \bigvee_e \frac{\Delta f}{\Delta x^e} \left[\prod_{i=,n-1} \left(\frac{\Delta x_i}{\Delta t}\right)^{e_i} \right]$$

which is nothing but (7.54) for $k = 1$; the proof for any k is obtained by exactly the same scheme. ■

A more detailed proof of the above theorem 7.8 may be found in Thayse [1974c].

When dealing with time-dependent binary functions, it is again convenient to replace the notations $\delta_t^k f/\delta_t t$ and $\delta^k x_i/\delta t$ by $\delta^k f$ and $\delta^k x_i$ respectively. This allows us to introduce a new parametrical operator, namely the *variational* (see Thayse [1971]).

Definition 7.5. Let $f(x)$ be a binary function; the kth variational of f is the function:

$$\delta^k f = \bigvee \frac{\Delta f}{\Delta x^e} \left[\prod_{i=0}^{n-1} (\delta^k x_i)^{e_i} \right], \quad 0 \leqslant e_i \leqslant 1, \quad 0 < e$$

where the $\delta^k x_i$ are new variables called the kth variationals of the variables x_i.

Definition 7.6. Let $f[x, y(x)]$ and $(y_{h-1}, \ldots, y_1, y_0) = y$ be binary functions. The kth variational of f is the function:

$$\delta^k f = \frac{\Delta f}{\Delta x^e y^\epsilon} \left[\prod_{i,j} (\delta^k x_i)^{e_i} (\delta^k y_j)^{\epsilon_j} \right]$$

$$0 \leqslant e_i, \epsilon_j \leqslant 1, \quad 0 < (e\ \epsilon).$$

Let us point out now that the variationals will be used in the frame of transient analysis of sequential switching networks (see section 7.3.3).

The following theorem, which is an immediate consequence of the definition of sensitivity, holds.

Theorem 7.9. *(Relation between ring differences and sensitivities.)*

$$\frac{S^{k_0} f}{S x_0} = \sum_{e_0} \frac{\Delta^{e_0} f}{\Delta x_0}, \quad 0 \leqslant e_i \leqslant k_i, \quad 0 < e_0$$

$$\frac{\Delta^{k_0} f}{\Delta x_0} = \sum_{e_0} \frac{S^{e_0} f}{S x_0}, \quad 0 \leqslant e_i \leqslant k_i, \quad 0 < e_0. \tag{7.58}$$

7.2. *Difference and differential operators for switching functions*

Section 7.1 was merely devoted to some general theorems and definitions relative to total operators for discrete functions. The main purpose of the present section will be to derive computational formulae for obtaining these operators in the particular case of switching functions. These computational formulae will then be used in section 7.3, which deals with possible applications of difference and of differential calculus in logical design.

Consider the case where the functions f and y_j are switching functions; since for these functions $r_j = r = 2$, the expression (7.4) giving the total difference of f becomes:

$$\frac{\Delta_t f}{\Delta_t x_i} = \frac{\Delta f}{\Delta x_i} \oplus \sum_e \left(\frac{\Delta f}{\Delta y^e} \oplus \frac{\Delta f}{\Delta x_i y^e}\right) \prod_{j=0}^{h-1} \left(\frac{\Delta y_j}{\Delta x_i}\right)^{e_j} \tag{7.59}$$

$$0 \leqslant e_j \leqslant 1, \quad 0 < e = (e_{n-1}, \ldots, e_1, e_0).$$

(It is recalled that if $0 \leqslant e_i \leqslant 1$, the notations $\Delta^e f/\Delta x$ and $\Delta f/\Delta x^e$ are equivalent.)

Since moreover $\Delta^2 f/\Delta x_i = 0$ for any switching function f, one has also $\Delta_t^2 f/\Delta_t x_i = 0$ for any switching function of functions. Therefore only multiple differences of the form $\Delta_t f/\Delta_t x_0$ are meaningful for these functions. The following expression of the total difference derives from (7.59):

$$\frac{\Delta_t f}{\Delta_t x_0} = \frac{\Delta f}{\Delta x_0} \oplus \sum_{l_0 e} \left(\frac{\Delta f}{\Delta y^e} \oplus \sum_{\epsilon} \frac{\Delta f}{\Delta x_0^{\epsilon} y^e}\right) \left\{\prod_{j=0}^{h-1} [y_j(x_0 \oplus l_0) \oplus y_j]^{e_j}\right\}$$

$$0 \leqslant e_j, \epsilon_i, l_k \leqslant 1 \tag{7.60}$$

$$0 < e = (e_{h-1}, \ldots, e_1, e_0), \quad 0 < \epsilon = (\epsilon_{q-1}, \ldots, \epsilon_1, \epsilon_0)$$

$$0 < l = (l_{q-1}, \ldots, l_1, l_0).$$

From (7.12) one deduces that the increment Δf of a switching function f is:

$$\Delta f = \sum_e \frac{\Delta f}{\Delta x^e} \left[\prod_{i=0}^{n-1} (\Delta x_i)^{e_i}\right]. \tag{7.61}$$

Since $\Delta_t^2 f/\Delta_t t = 0$, the increments $\Delta^k f$ are also zero for $k > 1$.

For switching functions the concepts of increment and of differential coincide; expression (7.61) may thus also be written in the form:

$$df = \sum_e \frac{\partial f}{\partial x^e} \left[\prod_{i=0,n-1} (dx_i)^{e_i}\right]. \tag{7.62}$$

Similarly, the expression of the total derivative coincides with that of the total difference, i.e. in view of (7.59):

$$\frac{df}{dx_i} = \frac{\partial f}{\partial x_i} \oplus \sum_e \left(\frac{\partial f}{\partial y^e} \oplus \frac{\partial f}{\partial x_i y^e}\right) \left[\prod_{j=0}^{h-1} \left(\frac{\partial y_j}{\partial x_i}\right)^{e_j}\right]. \tag{7.63}$$

The differentials and increments are called parametrical operators since they depend on parameters, namely the differentials and the increments of the independent variables respectively. Parametrical operators for switching functions will later appear of outstanding interest in view of their applications in switching theory. From (7.61) one deduces, for example:

$$(\Delta f)_{(\Delta x_1=0,\, \Delta x_0=1)} = \sum_{e_0} \frac{\Delta f}{\Delta x_0^{e_0}}$$

$$= f(x_1, x_0) \oplus f(x_1, \bar{x}_0). \qquad (7.64)$$

This last function (7.64) is called *sensitivity of f with respect to* x_0 (see for example, Sellers *et al.* [1968], Davio and Piret [1969] and the remark at the end of section 7.1.1; it is denoted Sf/Sx_0. The increment Δf is thus a parametrical form of the sensitivity functions, the parameters being the increments of the independent variables.

From definition 7.5 one deduces that the *variational* δf of the switching function $f(x)$ is the function:

$$\delta f = \bigvee_{e} \frac{\Delta f}{\Delta x^{e}} \left[\prod_{i=0,n-1} (\delta x_i)^{e_i} \right], \quad 0 \leqslant e_i \leqslant 1, \quad 0 < e \qquad (7.65)$$

where the δx_i are new switching variables, called the variationals of the variables x_i.

Further on, for x_i an independent variable, one will always take $\delta x_i = \Delta x_i = dx_i$. In view of (7.65), one has:

$$(\delta f)_{(\Delta x_1=0,\, \Delta x_0=1)} = \bigvee_{e_0} \frac{\Delta f}{\Delta x_0^{e_0}}, \quad 0 \leqslant e_i \leqslant 1, \quad 0 < e_0$$

$$= \frac{\delta f}{\delta x_0}. \qquad (7.66)$$

The variational δf is thus a parametrical form of the variations $\delta f/\delta x_0$, the parameters being the differentials of the independent variables x_i.

Let us recall that the increment was functionally defined as:

$$\Delta f = f(x \oplus \Delta x) \oplus f(x).$$

A similar expression holds for the variational; it is given by theorem 7.10 below:

Theorem 7.10. For any switching f(x) one has:

$$\delta f = \bigvee_{e} [f(x \oplus e\Delta x) \oplus f(x)], \quad 0 \leqslant e_i \leqslant 1 \qquad (7.67)$$

with

$$e\Delta x = (e_{n-1}\Delta x_{n-1}, \ldots, e_1 \Delta x_1, e_0 \Delta x_0).$$

Proof. By expanding the right-hand side of (7.67) according to Newton expansions for a given $\boldsymbol{e}$, one obtains:

$$\delta f = \bigvee_{i=0}^{n-1} \frac{\Delta f}{\Delta x_i} \Delta x_i \vee \bigvee_{i,j=0}^{n-1} \left(\frac{\Delta f}{\Delta x_i} \Delta x_i \oplus \frac{\Delta f}{\Delta x_j} \Delta x_j \oplus \frac{\Delta f}{\Delta x_i x_j} \Delta x_i \Delta x_j \right) \vee \ldots \vee$$

$$\left\{ \sum_{\boldsymbol{e}} \frac{\Delta f}{\Delta \boldsymbol{x}^{\boldsymbol{e}}} \left[\Pi (\Delta x_i)^{e_i} \right] \right\}. \tag{7.68}$$

By iterative application of the relation

$$a \vee (a \oplus b) = a \vee b$$

the above relation (7.68) becomes finally:

$$\delta f = \bigvee_{\boldsymbol{e}} \frac{\Delta f}{\Delta \boldsymbol{x}^{\boldsymbol{e}}} \left[\Pi (\Delta x_i)^{e_i} \right].$$

■

From the definition 7.6 one deduces that the variational δf of the switching function $f[\boldsymbol{x}, \boldsymbol{y}(\boldsymbol{x})]$ is the function

$$\delta f = \bigvee_{\boldsymbol{e}, \boldsymbol{\epsilon}} \frac{\Delta f}{\Delta \boldsymbol{x}^{\boldsymbol{e}} \boldsymbol{y}^{\boldsymbol{\epsilon}}} \left[\prod_{\substack{i=0,n-1 \\ j=0,h-1}} (\delta x_i)^{e_i} (\delta y_j)^{\epsilon_j} \right] \tag{7.69}$$

$$0 \leqslant e_i,\ \epsilon_j \leqslant 1, \quad 0 < \boldsymbol{e}\,\boldsymbol{\epsilon}.$$

Theorem 7.11. For any switching function $f[\boldsymbol{x}, \boldsymbol{y}(\boldsymbol{x})]$ one has:

$$(\delta f)_{(\Delta x_1 = 0,\, \Delta x_0 = 1)} = \frac{\delta_t f}{\delta_t x_0} \tag{7.70}$$

Proof: From definition 7.6 one successively deduces:

$$(\delta f)_{(\Delta x_1 = 0,\, \Delta x_0 = 1)} = \bigvee_{\boldsymbol{\epsilon}} \frac{\Delta f}{\Delta x_0 \boldsymbol{y}^{\boldsymbol{\epsilon}}} \left[\prod_j (\delta y_j)^{\epsilon_j}_{(\Delta x_1 = 0,\, \Delta x_0 = 1)} \right]$$

$$= \bigvee_{\boldsymbol{\epsilon}} \frac{\Delta f}{\Delta x_0 \boldsymbol{y}^{\boldsymbol{\epsilon}}} \left[\prod_j \left(\frac{\delta y_j}{\delta x_0} \right)^{\epsilon_j} \right], \quad 0 \leqslant \epsilon \leqslant 1. \tag{7.71}$$

The proof then derives from theorem 7.10. ■

As a conclusion the definition of the variational

$$\delta f = \bigvee_{\boldsymbol{e}} \frac{\Delta f}{\Delta \boldsymbol{x}^{\boldsymbol{e}}} \left(\prod_i \delta x_i^{e_i} \right) \tag{7.72}$$

holds, the variables x_i being independent variables or switching functions while the expression

$$\delta f = \bigvee_{e} \left(\frac{\Delta f}{\Delta x^e}\right) \prod_{i} \Delta x_i^{e_i} \tag{7.73}$$

holds only for x_i independent variables.

The notions of variational and of variation of functions of functions were first used by Thayse [1970, 1971] in the frame of hazard detection for switching networks.

We will terminate this section by giving some computational formulae for deriving the variations and total variations of functions given as a sum of product terms or as a product of sum terms.

Let us consider the representation of a switching function f by means of an arbitrary set of implicants p_i or by means of an arbitrary set of implicates q_j, i.e.

$$f(x) = \bigvee_{i} p_i(x) = \bigwedge_{j} q_j(x). \tag{7.74}$$

If $(\boldsymbol{x}_1, \boldsymbol{x}_0)$ is a partition of $\boldsymbol{x}$, let us define $p_{\boldsymbol{x}_0}(f)$ and $q_{\boldsymbol{x}_0}(f)$ as follows:

$$p_{\boldsymbol{x}_0}(f) = \bigvee_{i} p_i, \quad \{p_i \text{ does not contain } x_k \in \boldsymbol{x}_0\}$$

$$q_{\boldsymbol{x}_0}(f) = \bigwedge q_j, \quad \{q_j \text{ does not contain } x_k \in \boldsymbol{x}_0\}.$$

The p_i which contain a subset of $\boldsymbol{x}_0$ are each the product of two monomials $A_i(\boldsymbol{x}_1)$ and $B_i(\boldsymbol{x}_0)$, $A_i(\boldsymbol{x}_1)$ being the product of variables $x_j \in \boldsymbol{x}_1$ and $B_i(\boldsymbol{x}_0)$ being the product of variables $x_j \in \boldsymbol{x}_0$. Similarly, the q_i which contain a subset of $\boldsymbol{x}_0$ are each the sum of two terms, $C_i(\boldsymbol{x}_1)$ and $D_i(\boldsymbol{x}_0)$, $C_i(\boldsymbol{x}_1)$ being the sum of variables $x_j \in \boldsymbol{x}_1$ and $D_i(\boldsymbol{x}_0)$ being the sum of variables $x_j \in \boldsymbol{x}_0$. The following theorem then holds:

Theorem 7.12

(a) $$\frac{\delta f}{\delta \boldsymbol{x}_0} = \overline{\left(\frac{pf}{p\boldsymbol{x}_0}\right)} \wedge \left[\bigvee_{i} A_i(\boldsymbol{x}_1)\right]. \tag{7.75}$$

(b) $$\frac{\delta f}{\delta \boldsymbol{x}_0} = \frac{qf}{q\boldsymbol{x}_0} \wedge \left[\bigvee_{i} \overline{C_i(\boldsymbol{x}_1)}\right]. \tag{7.76}$$

(c) $$\frac{\delta f}{\delta \boldsymbol{x}_0} = \left[\bigvee_{i} A_i(\boldsymbol{x}_1)\right] \wedge \left[\bigvee_{j} \overline{C_j(\boldsymbol{x}_1)}\right]. \tag{7.77}$$

Proof. One has:

$$f = p_{\boldsymbol{x}_0}(f) \vee \bigvee_{i} A_i(\boldsymbol{x}_1)\, B_i(\boldsymbol{x}_0).$$

Since

$$\frac{qf}{qx_0} = p_{x_0}(f) \vee \bigvee_i A_i(x_1)$$

and

$$\frac{pf}{px_0} \geqslant p_{x_0}(f)$$

the following relation holds:

$$\frac{\delta f}{\delta x_0} = \left(\overline{\frac{pf}{px_0}}\right) \wedge \left[p_{x_0}(f) \vee \bigvee_i A_i(x_1)\right]$$

$$= \left(\overline{\frac{pf}{px_0}}\right) \wedge \left[\bigvee_i A_i(x_1)\right]$$

which proves part (a) of the theorem.

A dual type of statement holds for the second part.

By multiplying (7.75) with (7.76) one obtains:

$$\frac{\delta f}{\delta x_0} = \frac{\delta f}{\delta x_0} \wedge \left[\bigvee_i A_i(x_1)\right] \wedge \left[\bigvee_j \overline{C_j(x_1)}\right]$$

so that

$$\frac{\delta f}{\delta x_0} \leqslant \left[\bigvee_i A_i(x_1)\right] \wedge \left[\bigvee_j \overline{C_j(x_1)}\right]. \tag{7.78}$$

On the other hand one has:

$$\frac{pf}{px_0} = q_{x_0}(f) \wedge \bigwedge_j C_j(x_1)$$

so that:

$$\frac{\delta f}{\delta x_0} = \left[\overline{q_{x_0}}(f) \vee \bigvee_j \overline{C_j(x_1)}\right] \wedge \left[p_{x_0}(f) \vee \bigvee_i A_i(x_1)\right]$$

$$\geqslant \left[\bigvee_i A_i(x_1)\right] \wedge \left[\bigvee_j \overline{C_j(x_1)}\right]. \tag{7.79}$$

The proof of part (c) of the theorem results then from (7.78) and (7.79). ■

A similar theorem will now be proven for computing the total variations of switching functions of functions given as a product of sums or as a sum of products of auxiliary functions.

Consider again the representation (7.74) of a switching function f by means of an arbitrary set of implicants p_i or by means of an arbitrary set of implicates q_j respectively. Consider moreover two switching functions of functions $f_0[y(x)]$ and

$f_1[y^*(x)]$ such that $y_i = p_i\ \forall i$ and $y_j^* = q_j\ \forall j$:

$$f_0 = \bigvee_i y_i(x) \tag{7.80}$$

$$f_1 = \bigwedge_j y_i^*(x). \tag{7.81}$$

With the same symbols and notations as in theorem 7.12, the following theorem then holds:

Theorem 7.13.

$$\text{(a)}\ \frac{\delta_t f_0}{\delta_t x_0} = \overline{p_{x_0}(f)} \wedge \left[\bigvee_i A_i(x_1)\right]. \tag{7.82}$$

$$\text{(b)}\ \frac{\delta_t f_1}{\delta_t x_0} = q_{x_0}(f) \wedge \left[\bigvee_j \overline{C_j(x_1)}\right]. \tag{7.83}$$

Proof. By definition of the total meet and join differences one deduces from (7.80) and (7.81):

$$\frac{q_t f_0}{q_t x_0} = p_{x_0}(f) \vee \bigvee_i A_i(x_1), \quad \frac{q_t f_1}{q_t x_0} = q_{x_0}(f);$$

$$\frac{p_t f_0}{p_t x_0} = p_{x_0}(f), \quad \frac{p_t f_1}{p_t x_0} = q_{x_0}(f) \wedge \bigwedge_j C_j(x_1).$$

Relations (7.82) and (7.83) then result from the above equalities and form the definition of the total variation. ∎

We terminate this section by giving an algorithm for computing all the variations $\delta f/\delta \boldsymbol{x}^e$ of a switching function f; this algorithm will be used further on in this book (see Chapter 11) to obtain decomposition methods for switching functions.

We know (see (7.47)) that the following formula holds

$$\frac{\delta f}{\delta x_0} = \left(\overline{\frac{pf}{px_0}}\right) \frac{qf}{qx_0}. \tag{7.84}$$

The formal expression of (7.84) will now slightly be modified in order to allow the building of an iterative computation scheme for the set of variations of a switching function. Let us define $\hat{p}_{x_0}(f)$ and $\hat{q}_{x_0}(f)$ as follows:

$\hat{p}_{x_0}(f)$ is the disjunction of all the prime implicants of f degenerate in $\boldsymbol{x}_0$ and which contain *all* the variables of $\boldsymbol{x}_1$ (with $\boldsymbol{x}_1$ and $\boldsymbol{x}_0$ a partition of $\boldsymbol{x}$);

$\hat{q}_{x_0}(f)$ is the conjunction of all the prime implicates of f degenerate in $\boldsymbol{x}_0$ and which contain *all* the variables of $\boldsymbol{x}_1$.

The following equality then directly derives from (7.84):

$$\frac{\delta f}{\delta \boldsymbol{x}_0} = \bigwedge_{x_i \in \boldsymbol{x}_1} \frac{\delta f}{\delta \boldsymbol{x}_0 x_i} \overline{[\hat{p}_{\boldsymbol{x}_0}(f)\ \hat{q}_{\boldsymbol{x}_0}(f)]}. \tag{7.85}$$

Expression (7.85) allows us to compute immediately the variations $\delta f/\delta \boldsymbol{x}_0$ when the variations $\delta f/\delta \boldsymbol{x}_0 x_i$ and the prime implicates and implicants of f are known. Since, for a non-degenerate switching function, $\delta f/\delta \boldsymbol{x} = 1$ holds, all the variations may trivially be computed when starting with the variation $\delta f/\delta \boldsymbol{x}_0$ with the highest cardinality of the set $\boldsymbol{x}_0$. Let us note that the computation scheme based on (7.85) requires to take into account each of the prime implicants and prime implicates once and only once.

Example 7.1. Consider the switching function of example 3.7. Obtain first this function as a disjunction of all its prime implicants and as a conjunction of all its prime implicates, i.e.

$$f = \bar{x}_4\bar{x}_0 \vee \bar{x}_4\bar{x}_2\bar{x}_1 \vee \bar{x}_4x_3x_2x_1 \vee \bar{x}_4\bar{x}_3\bar{x}_1 \vee x_5\bar{x}_0 \vee x_5\bar{x}_2\bar{x}_1 \vee x_5x_3x_2x_1 \vee$$
$$x_5\bar{x}_3\bar{x}_1 \vee \bar{x}_5x_4\bar{x}_2x_1x_0 \vee \bar{x}_5x_4x_3x_2\bar{x}_1x_0 \vee \bar{x}_5x_4\bar{x}_3x_1x_0 \tag{7.86}$$
$$= (x_4 \vee \bar{x}_3 \vee \bar{x}_2 \vee x_1 \vee \bar{x}_0)(\bar{x}_5 \vee \bar{x}_3 \vee \bar{x}_2 \vee x_1 \vee \bar{x}_0)(x_5 \vee \bar{x}_4 \vee \bar{x}_3 \vee \bar{x}_2 \vee \bar{x}_1)$$
$$(x_4 \vee x_2 \vee \bar{x}_1 \vee \bar{x}_0)(\bar{x}_5 \vee x_2 \vee \bar{x}_1 \vee \bar{x}_0)(x_4 \vee x_3 \vee \bar{x}_1 \vee \bar{x}_0)(\bar{x}_5 \vee x_3 \vee \bar{x}_1 \vee$$
$$\bar{x}_0)(x_5 \vee \bar{x}_4 \vee x_2 \vee x_1)(x_5 \vee \bar{x}_4 \vee x_3 \vee x_1)(x_5 \vee \bar{x}_4 \vee x_0). \tag{7.87}$$

The variations are gathered in the table of Figure 7.1.

$\{i\ldots j\}\delta f/\delta x_i \ldots x_j$		$\{i\ldots j\}\delta f/\delta x_i \ldots x_j$		$\{i\ldots j\}\delta f/\delta x_i \ldots x_j$		$\{i\ldots j\}\delta f/\delta x_i \ldots x_j$	
0123	1	012	1	01	1	0	$x_1 \oplus x_2x_3$
0124	1	013	1	02	$x_1 \vee x_3$	1	x_0
0125	1	014	1	03	$x_1 \vee x_2$	2	x_0x_3
0134	1	015	1	04	$\bar{x}_5 \vee (x_1 \oplus x_2x_3)$	3	x_0x_2
0135	1	023	1	05	$x_4 \vee (x_1 \oplus x_2x_3)$	4	$\bar{x}_5$
0145	1	024	$x_1 \vee x_3 \vee \bar{x}_5$	12	x_0	5	x_4
0234	1	025	$x_1 \vee x_3 \vee x_4$	13	x_0		
0235	1	034	$x_1 \vee x_2 \vee \bar{x}_5$	14	$x_0 \vee \bar{x}_5$		
0245	1	035	$x_1 \vee x_2 \vee x_4$	15	$x_0 \vee x_4$		
0345	1	045	1	23	x_0		
1234	$x_0 \vee \bar{x}_5$	123	x_0	24	$\bar{x}_5 \vee x_0x_3$		
1235	$x_0 \vee x_4$	124	$x_0 \vee \bar{x}_5$	25	$x_4 \vee x_0x_3$		
1245	1	125	$x_0 \vee x_4$	34	$\bar{x}_5 \vee x_0x_2$		
1345	1	134	$x_0 \vee \bar{x}_5$	35	$x_4 \vee x_0x_2$		
2345	1	135	$x_0 \vee x_4$	45	1		
		145	1				
		234	$x_0 \vee \bar{x}_5$				
		235	$x_0 \vee x_4$				
		245	1				
		345	1				

Figure 7.1. The set of variations of f

Remarks

1. *Other kinds of operators for switching functions*

Several other kinds of difference operators for switching functions were derived by numerous authors; some of the most important operators (in view of their possible applications) will briefly be reviewed here.

The differential df of f is an *unoriented operator* since it does not distinguish a $0 \to 1$ change from $1 \to 0$ change of a switching function. *Oriented differential operators* may be defined as follows:

The *decreasing differential* d_1f of f is a switching function equal to 1 iff f changes from 1 to 0 and equal to 0 otherwise (i.e. if f does not change or changes from 0 to 1).

The *increasing differential* d_0f of f is a switching function equal to 1 iff f changes from 0 to 1 and equal to 0 otherwise (i.e. if f does not change or changes from 1 to 0).

The following relations hold between the operators d_0 and d_1 and the differential operator d:

$$d_1f = f\,df$$

$$d_0f = \bar{f}\,df$$

$$df = d_1f \oplus d_0f.$$

These operators were introduced by Hsiao, Sellers and Chia [1970] and Smith and Roth [1969] and studied by Tucker [1974].

A *reduced variational* is a variational operator, expressed in terms of differences, where all the terms containing multiple differences are dropped. The reduced variational of f will be denoted $\delta^R f$; let us first observe that the independent variables x_i are such that

$$dx_i = \delta x_i = \delta^R x_i.$$

For the function $f(\mathbf{x})$ one has:

$$\delta^R f = \bigvee_i \frac{\Delta f}{\Delta x_i}\, \delta^R x_i$$

For a function of functions $f[\mathbf{x}, \mathbf{y}(\mathbf{x})]$, one has:

$$\delta^R f = \bigvee_i \frac{\Delta f}{\Delta x_i}\, \delta^R x_i \vee \bigvee_j \frac{\Delta f}{\Delta y_j}\, \delta^R y_j$$

$$\delta^R y_j = \bigvee_i \frac{\Delta y_j}{\Delta x_i}\, \delta^R x_i$$

so that the following relation holds true:

$$\delta^R f = \bigvee_i \left(\frac{\Delta f}{\Delta x_i} \vee \bigvee_j \frac{\Delta f}{\Delta y_j} \frac{\Delta y_j}{\Delta x_i} \right) \delta^R x_i.$$

The importance of the reduced variational arises from the following theorem.

Theorem 7.14. The variational δf of a switching function f is identically zero iff the reduced variational $\delta^R f$ is identically 0.

Proof. Since $\delta f \geqslant \delta^R f$, $\delta f \equiv 0$ implies $\delta^R f \equiv 0$. If $\delta^R f \equiv 0$, then $\Delta f/\Delta x_i = 0\ \forall x_i$ and $\Delta f/\Delta x_i \boldsymbol{x}_0 \equiv 0\ \forall \boldsymbol{x}_0$. ■

The reduced variational was extensively used by Thayse [1970] for performing hazard detection in switching networks.

Finally Tucker [1974] introduced operators called *partial derivatives with respect to $x_i^{(e_i)}$* and defined as follows:

$$\frac{\partial f}{\partial x_i^{(1)}} = f(x_i = 1)\bar{f}(x_i = 0)$$

$$\frac{\partial f}{\partial x_i^{(0)}} = f(x_i = 0)\bar{f}(x_i = 1).$$

One has evidently

$$\frac{\partial f}{\partial x_i} = \frac{\partial f}{\partial x_i^{(1)}} \oplus \frac{\partial f}{\partial x_i^{(0)}}$$

and these operators are thus connected to the increasing and decreasing differentials. The differential defined by Tucker has the following expression.

$$df = \sum_{i=1}^{n-1} \left(\frac{\partial f}{\partial x_i^{(1)}}\, d_1 x_i \oplus \frac{\partial f}{\partial x_i^{(0)}}\, d_0 x_i \right).$$

2. *Symbolic computation of Fourier transforms of switching functions*

The Fourier transform or coordinate representation of a switching function has initially been used for classification purposes. Nowadays, however, it is more appropriately considered as a representation of a switching function, i.e. as a possible alternative to other, more classical representations such as ring and lattice expressions. The authoritative work of Lechner [1963, 1971] deserves a special mention. We study the relationships of the Fourier transform with the differential operators studied in this section 7.2. More precisely, explicit formulae are derived for direct computation of the differential operators from the Fourier transform (see also Davio, Thayse and Bioul [1972]).

The *partial Fourier transform* of the vector of switching functions $(f, \ldots, g)$ with respect to a variable x_i will be denoted $t_{x_i}(f, \ldots, g)$ and defined as follows:

$$t_{x_i}(f, \ldots, g) = [f(x_i = 0) + f(x_i = 1), f(x_i = 0) - f(x_i = 1), \ldots, g(x_i = 0) + g(x_i = 1), g(x_i = 0) - g(x_i = 1)]. \tag{7.88}$$

The partial Fourier transform of the vector of switching functions $(f, \ldots g)$ with respect to the variables in $\boldsymbol{x}_0$ will be denoted $t_{\boldsymbol{x}_0}(f, \ldots, g)$ and defined as follows:

$$t_{\boldsymbol{x}_0}(f, \ldots, g) = t_{x_0} [\![t_{x_1} \{ \ldots [t_{x_{q-1}}(f, \ldots, g)] \ldots \}]\!] \tag{7.89}$$

with $\boldsymbol{x}_0 = (x_{q-1}, \ldots, x_1, x_0)$.

The above definitions evidently hold whatever the representation of the switching functions $f, \ldots, g$ may be. In particular it is important to note that they may be given as ring or lattice expressions or by means of their truth vector.

Let us denote by H the Hadamard matrix:

$$\begin{bmatrix} 1 & 1 \\ 1 & -1 \end{bmatrix}.$$

One has, in view of the definitions of partial truth vector (see section 3.2.3.2.1) and of partial Fourier transform:

$$t_{x_i}(f) = [f(e_i)] \; \textcircled{+ \times} \; H \tag{7.90}$$

$$t_{\boldsymbol{x}_0}(f) = [f(\boldsymbol{e}_0)] \; \textcircled{+ \times} \; H^q \tag{7.91}$$

where q is the cardinality of $\boldsymbol{x}_0$ and H^q is the qth Kronecker power of the Hadamard matrix H. The orthogonality of the Hadamard matrix H^q allows us to write, in view of (7.91):

$$[f(\boldsymbol{e}_0)] = 2^{-q} \, t_{\boldsymbol{x}_0}(f) \; \textcircled{+ \times} \; H^q. \tag{7.92}$$

Let us now assume that f is given by its truth vector $[f(\boldsymbol{e})]$. The following expression then holds:

$$t_{x_i}(f) = [f(\boldsymbol{e})] \; \textcircled{+ \times} \; T_i. \tag{7.93}$$

Matrix T_i has a simple expression as a Kronecker product:

$$T_i = \begin{bmatrix} 1 & 0 \\ 0 & 1 \end{bmatrix}^{n-i-1} \otimes \begin{bmatrix} 1 & 1 \\ 1 & -1 \end{bmatrix} \otimes \begin{bmatrix} 1 & 0 \\ 0 & 1 \end{bmatrix}^{i}. \tag{7.94}$$

Let us define E^{d_i} as follows:

$$E^{d_i} = \begin{bmatrix} 1 & d_i \\ d_i & (-1)^{d_i} \end{bmatrix}, \quad d_i \in \{0, 1\}.$$

One has:

$$t_x d(f) = [f(e)] \textcircled{+\times} \left(\bigotimes_{i=n-1,0} E^{d_i} \right), \quad d = (d_{n-1}, \ldots, d_0). \tag{7.95}$$

The proof of (7.95) directly follows from relations (7.88), (7.94) and of the following well-known property of the Kronecker product:

$$(M_0 \otimes M_1 \otimes \ldots \otimes M_{n-1}) \textcircled{+\times} (N_0 \otimes N_1 \otimes \ldots \otimes N_{n-1}) =$$
$$(M_0 \textcircled{+\times} N_0) \otimes (M_1 \textcircled{+\times} N_1) \otimes \ldots \otimes (M_{n-1} \textcircled{+\times} N_{n-1}).$$

The *Fourier transform* $t(f)$ was defined by Lechner [1971] as follows:

$$t(f) = [f(e)] \textcircled{+\times} H^n. \tag{7.96}$$

One has thus immediately:

$$t_x(f) = t_{x_0} \{t_{x_1} [\ldots t_{x_{n-1}}(f)] \ldots\} = t(f). \tag{7.97}$$

The above relation (7.97) is fundamental; it relates the concept of Fourier transform to the concept of partial Fourier transform. Moreover, it provides us with a very simple recurrent scheme for the computation of the Fourier transform of a switching function. Let us recall that the computation of the Fourier transform according to the classical methods requires the switching function f to be completely expanded in its minterms. As mentioned above, this is not required for the computation of the partial Fourier transform. The recurrent scheme associated with the expression (7.97) allows us to use at each step of the computation a partial expansion of f with respect to only one of its variables.

From relation (7.88) one deduces successively:

$$t_{x_i}(f)_{(\text{modulo-2})} = [f(x_i = 0) \oplus f(x_i = 1), f(x_i = 0) \oplus f(x_i = 1)]$$

$$= \left[\frac{\Delta f}{\Delta x_i} (e_i)\right]$$

$$t_{x_0}(f)_{(\text{modulo-2})} = \left[\frac{\Delta f}{\Delta x_0} (e_0)\right] \tag{7.98}$$

$$t(f)_{(\text{modulo-2})} = \left[\frac{\Delta f}{\Delta x} (e)\right].$$

Relations (7.98) allow us to state that all the properties of the partial derivatives (or equivalently differences) of switching functions can be obtained by reducing modulo-2 the corresponding properties of the partial Fourier transforms (see Davio, Thayse and Bioul [1972]).

Since, in view of relation (7.92):

$$[f(e)] = 2^{-n} t(f) \mathbin{\textcircled{$+\times$}} H^n$$

one obtains successively by using relation (4.63):

$$\frac{\Delta f}{\Delta x^d}(e) = \left[t(f) \mathbin{\textcircled{$+\times$}} \frac{H^n}{2^n}\right] \mathbin{\textcircled{$\oplus\cdot$}} \left(\underset{i=n-1,0}{\otimes} E_{d_i}\right)$$

$$\left[t(f) \mathbin{\textcircled{$+\times$}} \frac{H^n}{2^n} \mathbin{\textcircled{$+\times$}} \left(\underset{i=n-1,0}{\otimes} E_{d_i}\right)\right]_{(\text{modulo-2})}$$

$$= 2^{q-n} t(f) \mathbin{\textcircled{$\oplus\cdot$}} \left(\underset{i=n-1,0}{\otimes} H_i^{d_i}\right) \qquad (7.99)$$

with q the weight of d and

$$H_i^{d_i} = \begin{bmatrix} 1 & 1 \\ 1-d_i & -1+d_i \end{bmatrix}.$$

The above formula provides us with a way for obtaining directly the truth vector of any difference of f from the Fourier representation of this function without, recurring, for example, to a first evaluation of the function value vector. Other formulae of this form, allowing us, for example, to obtain the sensitivities and the variations of switching functions, may be found in the paper by Davio, Thayse and Bioul [1972].

7.3. Applications

7.3.1. Transient analysis of switching networks

7.3.1.1. Function hazard detection

Hazards were defined in section 3.3.3 where hazard detection methods based on fuzzy functions were developed. The present section will be devoted to hazard detection methods based on difference and differential calculus (Thayse [1970, 1971]).

Theorem 7.15 (Thayse [1970]). *A transition involving a change in the variables $\mathbf{x}_0 \subseteq \mathbf{x}$ gives rise to a function static hazard for the function $f(\mathbf{x})$ iff*

$$\left(\frac{Sf}{S\mathbf{x}_0} \oplus \frac{\delta f}{\delta \mathbf{x}_0}\right)_{\mathbf{x}=\mathbf{a}} = 1, \qquad (7.100)$$

where $\mathbf{a}$ is either the initial or the final state of the transition.

Proof. In view of definition 3.19, a switching function $f(\boldsymbol{x})$ experiences a function static hazard for an input change $\boldsymbol{a} = (\boldsymbol{a}_1, \boldsymbol{a}_0)$ to $\boldsymbol{b} = (\boldsymbol{a}_1, \bar{\boldsymbol{a}}_0)$ iff:

(a) $f(\boldsymbol{a}) = f(\boldsymbol{b})$, which is equivalent to $\left(\dfrac{Sf}{S\boldsymbol{x}_0}\right)_{\boldsymbol{x}=\boldsymbol{a}} = 0.$

(b) the function $f(\boldsymbol{a}_1, \boldsymbol{x}_0)$, is not degenerate in $\boldsymbol{x}$ which is equivalent to $(\delta f/\delta \boldsymbol{x}_0)_{\boldsymbol{x}=\boldsymbol{a}} = 1.$ ∎

Let us observe that once the functions $Sf/S\boldsymbol{x}_0$ and $\delta f/\delta \boldsymbol{x}_0$ have been evaluated, their modulo-2 sum provides us with the information necessary to detect any function static hazard arising during a transition involving the change of the variables $\boldsymbol{x}_0$: one only has to evaluate the same function for different vertices. It follows that the function $(Sf/S\boldsymbol{x}_0 \oplus \delta f/\delta \boldsymbol{x}_0)$ contains in a relatively condensed form the information necessary to detect hazards for a large number of transitions.

A transition may always be characterized by:

(a) its initial or final state;
(b) the variables which are modified.

The latter variables will be characterized by their increment equal to 1 during the transition while the remaining variables have their increment equal to 0. Theorem 7.16 is an immediate consequence of theorem 7.15 and from the fact that the increments and the variationals are parametric forms of the functions $Sf/S\boldsymbol{x}^e$ and $\delta f/\delta \boldsymbol{x}^e$ respectively.

Theorem 7.16. A switching function $f(\boldsymbol{x})$ experiences a function static hazard for the transitions satisfying the relation:

$$\Delta f \oplus \delta f = 1. \tag{7.101}$$

Example 7.2. Consider the switching function $f = x_0 x_2 \vee x_1 \bar{x}_2$; one has:

$$\Delta f = x_2\, \Delta x_0 \oplus \bar{x}_2\, \Delta x_1 \oplus (x_0 \oplus x_1)\, \Delta x_2 \oplus \Delta x_0\, \Delta x_2 \oplus \Delta x_1\, \Delta x_2 \tag{7.102}$$

$$\delta f = x_2\, \Delta x_0 \vee \bar{x}_2\, \Delta x_1 \vee (x_0 \oplus x_1)\, \Delta x_2 \vee \Delta x_0\, \Delta x_2 \vee \Delta x_1\, \Delta x_2 \tag{7.103}$$

$$\delta f \oplus \Delta f = (x_0 \oplus x_1 \oplus x_2)\, \Delta x_0\, \Delta x_2 \oplus (x_0 \oplus x_1 \oplus \bar{x}_2)\, \Delta x_1\, \Delta x_2 \oplus (\bar{x}_0 \oplus x_1)\, \Delta x_0\, \Delta x_1\, \Delta x_2. \tag{7.104}$$

The function f experiences thus a function static hazard for the following transitions (a_i = fixed value 0 or 1 of x_i).

1. $\Delta x_0 = \Delta x_2 = 1, \Delta x_1 = 0, a_0 \oplus a_1 \oplus a_2 = 1,$
2. $\Delta x_1 = \Delta x_2 = 1, \Delta x_0 = 0, a_0 \oplus a_1 \oplus a_2 = 0,$
3. $\Delta x_0 = \Delta x_1 = \Delta x_2 = 1, a_0 \oplus a_1 = 1.$

When dealing with more elaborate examples the explicit computation of all transitions containing a function static hazard generally leads to an overwhelming size of results. It is then much easier to compute in a formal way the function $(Sf/S\boldsymbol{x}_0 \oplus \delta f/\delta \boldsymbol{x}_0)$ or $(df \oplus \delta f)$ and to test for each of the considered transitions the presence of a function static hazard.

$\{i\ldots j\}\dfrac{Sf}{Sx_i\ldots x_j} \oplus \dfrac{\delta f}{\delta x_i\ldots x_j}$		$\{i\ldots j\}\dfrac{Sf}{Sx_i\ldots x_j} \oplus \dfrac{\delta f}{\delta x_i\ldots x_j}$	
012	$x_0 \oplus x_1 \oplus x_3(\bar{x}_0 \oplus x_2)$	01	$x_0 \oplus x_1 \oplus x_2x_3$
013	$x_0 \oplus x_1 \oplus x_2(\bar{x}_0 \oplus x_3)$	02	$x_3(x_0 \oplus x_1 \oplus x_2)$
014	$x_0 \oplus x_1 \oplus \bar{x}_5 \oplus x_2x_3$	03	$x_2(x_0 \oplus x_1 \oplus x_3)$
015	$x_0 \oplus x_1 \oplus x_4 \oplus x_2x_3$	04	$\bar{x}_5(x_1 \oplus x_2x_3)$
023	$\bar{x}_1 \oplus x_0x_2x_3 \oplus \bar{x}_0\bar{x}_2\bar{x}_3$	05	$x_4(x_1 \oplus x_2x_3)$
024	$x_3(x_0 \oplus x_1 \oplus x_2) \oplus \bar{x}_5(x_1 \vee x_3)$	12	x_0x_3
025	$x_3(x_0 \oplus x_2 \oplus x_1) \oplus x_4(x_3 \vee x_1)$	13	x_0x_2
034	$x_2(x_0 \oplus x_1 \oplus x_3) \oplus \bar{x}_5(x_1 \vee x_2)$	14	$x_0\bar{x}_5$
035	$x_2(x_0 \oplus x_2 \oplus x_3) \oplus x_4(x_1 \vee x_2)$	15	x_0x_4
045	$\bar{x}_1 \oplus x_4 \oplus x_5 \oplus x_2x_3$	23	$x_0(x_2 \oplus x_3)$
123	$x_0(\bar{x}_2 \oplus x_3)$	24	$x_0x_3\bar{x}_5$
124	$x_0(x_3 \oplus \bar{x}_5)$	25	$x_0x_3x_4$
125	$x_0(x_3 \oplus x_4)$	34	$x_0x_2\bar{x}_5$
134	$x_0(x_2 \oplus \bar{x}_5)$	35	$x_0x_2x_4$
135	$x_0(x_2 \oplus x_4)$		
145	$\bar{x}_0 \oplus x_4 \oplus x_5$		
234	$x_0(\bar{x}_2 \oplus x_3 \oplus x_5)$		
235	$x_0(x_2 \oplus x_3 \oplus x_4)$		
245	$x_0x_3 \oplus x_4 \oplus \bar{x}_5$		
345	$x_0x_2 \oplus x_4 \oplus \bar{x}_5$		

Figure 7.2. The functions $Sf/S\boldsymbol{x}_0 \oplus \delta f/\delta \boldsymbol{x}_0$

Example 7.1 (continued). The functions $(Sf/S\boldsymbol{x}_0 \oplus \delta f/\delta \boldsymbol{x}_0)$, for $\boldsymbol{x}_0$ a set of 2 or 3 variables of $\boldsymbol{x}$, are gathered in the table of Figure 7.2. This table contains in a relatively condensed form the material needed for the analysis of the 480 transitions involving the change of two variables and of the 640 transitions involving a change of three variables. We may also compute the function $\Delta f \oplus \delta f$ which gives us under a parametrical form the material for the analysis of the 1824 transitions involving a change of at least two variables:

$$\begin{aligned}\Delta f \oplus \delta f = {} & [(x_1 \oplus x_2x_3)\,\Delta x_0 \oplus x_0\Delta x_1 \oplus x_0x_3\Delta x_2 \oplus x_0x_2\Delta x_3 \oplus \bar{x}_5\Delta x_4 \oplus \\ & x_4\Delta x_5 \oplus \Delta x_0\Delta x_1 \oplus x_3\Delta x_0\Delta x_2 \oplus x_2\Delta x_0\Delta x_3 \oplus x_0\Delta x_2\Delta x_3 \oplus \\ & \Delta x_4\Delta x_5 \oplus \Delta x_0\Delta x_2\Delta x_3] \oplus [(x_1 \oplus x_2x_3)\,\Delta x_0 \vee x_0\Delta x_1 \vee \\ & x_0x_3\Delta x_2 \vee x_0x_2\Delta x_3 \vee \bar{x}_5\Delta x_4 \vee x_4\Delta x_5 \vee \Delta x_0\Delta x_1 \vee x_3\Delta x_0\Delta x_2 \vee \\ & x_2\Delta x_0\Delta x_3 \vee x_0\Delta x_2\Delta x_3 \vee \Delta x_4\Delta x_5 \vee \Delta x_0\Delta x_2\Delta x_3]. \qquad (7.105)\end{aligned}$$

Let us now briefly consider the problem of function dynamic hazard detection.

Theorem 7.17. A transition involving a change in the variables $\boldsymbol{x}_0 \subseteq \boldsymbol{x}$ gives rise to a function dynamic hazard for the function $f(\boldsymbol{x})$ iff:

$$\left\{\frac{Sf}{S\boldsymbol{x}_0}\left[\bigvee_{e_0}\left(\frac{Sf}{S\boldsymbol{x}_0^{e_0}} \oplus \frac{\delta f}{\delta \boldsymbol{x}_0^{e_0}}\right)\right]\right\}_{\boldsymbol{x}=\boldsymbol{a}} = 1, \quad 0 < e_0 < 1. \tag{7.106}$$

Proof. A function dynamic hazard occurs for the considered transition iff:

(a) $f(\boldsymbol{a}) \neq f(\boldsymbol{b})$ or, equivalently, $(Sf/S\boldsymbol{x}_0)_{\boldsymbol{x}=\boldsymbol{a}} = 1$.

(b) The function f may change at least three times during the transition, or, equivalently, a function static hazard occurs for a transition involving a change in the variables $\boldsymbol{x}_0^{e_0} \subseteq \boldsymbol{x}_0$, i.e.

$$\bigvee_{e_0}\left(\frac{Sf}{S\boldsymbol{x}_0^{e_0}} \oplus \frac{\delta f}{\delta \boldsymbol{x}_0^{e_0}}\right) = 1$$

for $\boldsymbol{x} = \boldsymbol{a}$ or $\boldsymbol{b}$. ■

7.3.1.2. *Logic hazard detection*

It has been seen in section 3.3.3 that the logic hazards are associated with *switching network structures* and not with *switching functions* as the function hazards did. More precisely, logic hazards are produced by a type of network structure generally referred to as the *fanout-reconvergent-structure* (see section 3.3.1 and Figure 3.27). In order to detect logic hazards, we shall describe the network structure by a switching function of functions; this function of functions will be obtained from the network model in the following way:

Remove a set of internal connections from the network in such a way that the new network structure obtained in this way is no longer a fanout-reconvergent-structure. To each of the removed connections associate a switching function y_j the algebraic expression of which represents the output function carried by the removed connection. By doing this, we associate to the switching network realizing f a function whose the simplest expression will be:

$$F = F(\boldsymbol{x}, \boldsymbol{y})$$

$$\boldsymbol{y} = \boldsymbol{y}(\boldsymbol{x}).$$

More generally one will obtain a cascaded function of functions of the type 2.1; the following theorem then holds.

Theorem 7.18. A transition involving a change in the variables $\boldsymbol{x}_0 \subseteq \boldsymbol{x}$ gives rise to a logic static hazard for the network described by the functions F, $\boldsymbol{y}$ and realizing the function f iff

$$\left(\frac{\delta f}{\delta \boldsymbol{x}_0} \oplus \frac{\delta_t F}{\delta_t \boldsymbol{x}_0}\right)_{\boldsymbol{x}=\boldsymbol{a}} = 1 \tag{7.107}$$

where $\boldsymbol{a}$ is either the initial or the final state of the transition.

Proof. In view of definition 3.20 a switching network experiences a logic static hazard for an input change $\boldsymbol{a} = (\boldsymbol{a}_1, \boldsymbol{a}_0)$ to $\boldsymbol{b} = (\boldsymbol{a}_1, \bar{\boldsymbol{a}}_0)$ iff:

(a) The function $f(\boldsymbol{a}_1, \boldsymbol{x}_0)$ is degenerate in $\boldsymbol{x}_0$, i.e. $(\delta f/\delta \boldsymbol{x}_0)_{\boldsymbol{x}=\boldsymbol{a}} = 0$.
(b) During the input change $\boldsymbol{a}$ to $\boldsymbol{b}$ the network output does not remain constant, i.e. equivalently $(\delta_t F/\delta_t \boldsymbol{x}_0)_{\boldsymbol{x}=\boldsymbol{a}} = 1$. This equivalence results from the way the function of functions F was built and from the definition of the total variation. ■

Let us again observe that once the functions $\delta f/\delta \boldsymbol{x}_0$ and $\delta_t F/\delta_t \boldsymbol{x}_0$ have been evaluated, their sum modulo-2 provides us with the information necessary to detect any logic static hazard arising during a transition involving the change of the variables $\boldsymbol{x}_0$.

The following theorem 7.19 constitutes a parametrical form of theorem 7.18.

Theorem 7.19. A switching network F realizing a switching function f experiences a logic static hazard for the transitions satisfying the relation

$$\delta f \oplus \delta F = 1. \tag{7.108}$$

Example 7.2 (continued). Consider the switching function $f = x_0 x_2 \vee x_1 \bar{x}_2$ realized by means of the switching network of Figure 3.27; the functions F, y associated with this network are:

$$\begin{aligned} F &= x_0 x_2 \vee y \\ y &= x_1 \bar{x}_2. \end{aligned} \tag{7.109}$$

From (7.109) one deduces:

$$\delta F = x_2 \Delta x_0 \vee \bar{x}_2 \Delta x_1 \vee (x_0 \vee x_1)\, \Delta x_2 \vee \Delta x_0 \Delta x_2 \vee \Delta x_1 \Delta x_2. \tag{7.110}$$

Relations (7.103) and (7.110) allow us to write:

$$\delta f \oplus \delta F = x_0 x_1 \Delta x_2.$$

The only transition containing a logic static hazard is thus characterized by $x_0 = x_1 = \Delta x_2 = 1$.

Let us note that the above theorem 7.19 allowed us to analyse in a very concise way the $\binom{2^3}{2} = 28$ possible transitions for the function f and to detect the only transition containing a logic static hazard.

Let us now consider a more elaborate example.

Example 7.3. The network of Figure 2.8 produces the functions

$S = x \oplus y \oplus c$ (sum function)

$C = cx \vee cy \vee xy$ (carry function).

We wish to detect the logic static hazards consecutive to the change of only one input variable. Let us first consider the sum function S; since S is a linear function it is free of any logic hazard. Consider the carry function C; removal of the connections y_0, y_1, y_2 (see Figure 2.8) renders the switching network free of fanout-reconvergent-structure with respect to the output C. The functions describing the network obtained in this way are:

$$\begin{aligned} F &= \bar{y}_0 \vee \bar{y}_1 \vee \bar{y}_2 \\ y_0 &= \bar{x} \vee \bar{c} \vee \bar{y}_1 \\ y_2 &= \bar{y} \vee \bar{c} \vee \bar{y}_1 \\ y_1 &= \bar{x} \vee \bar{y}. \end{aligned} \tag{7.111}$$

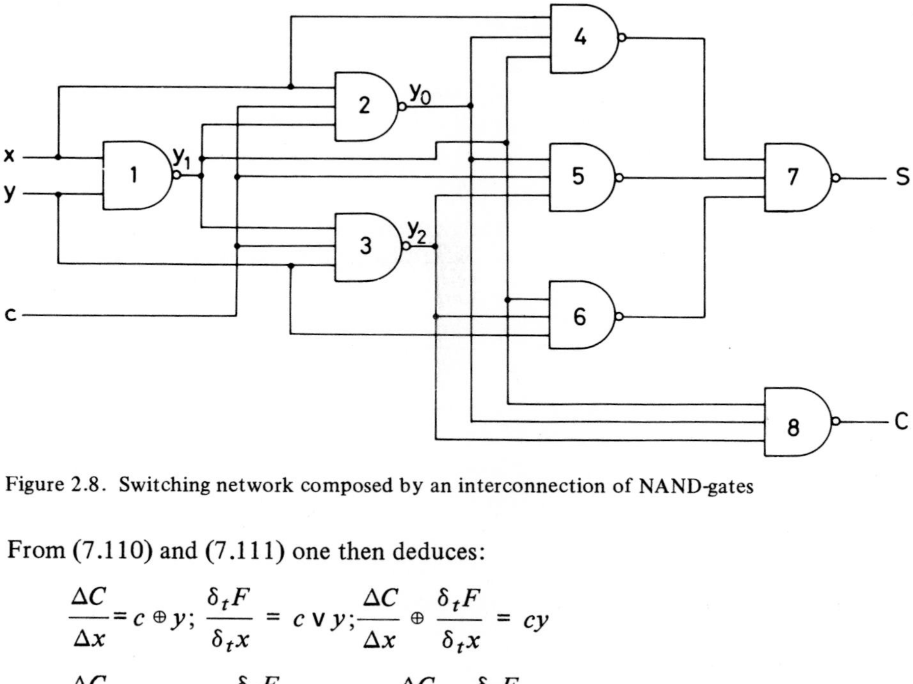

Figure 2.8. Switching network composed by an interconnection of NAND-gates

From (7.110) and (7.111) one then deduces:

$$\begin{aligned} &\frac{\Delta C}{\Delta x} = c \oplus y; \ \frac{\delta_t F}{\delta_t x} = c \vee y; \frac{\Delta C}{\Delta x} \oplus \frac{\delta_t F}{\delta_t x} = cy \\ &\frac{\Delta C}{\Delta y} = c \oplus x; \frac{\delta_t F}{\delta_t y} = c \vee x; \ \frac{\Delta C}{\Delta y} \oplus \frac{\delta_t F}{\delta_t y} = cx \\ &\frac{\Delta C}{\Delta c} = x \oplus y; \ \frac{\delta_t F}{\delta_t c} = x \oplus y; \frac{\Delta C}{\Delta c} \oplus \frac{\delta_t F}{\Delta_t c} = 0 \end{aligned} \tag{7.112}$$

so that logic static hazards occur for:

$$cy\Delta x = 1$$
$$cx\Delta y = 1.$$

The detection of logic dynamic hazards could be performed by using a theorem similar to the one used in the detection of function dynamic hazard (see theorem 7.17).

7.3.2. *Fault detection*

Let us consider the problem of detecting single stuck faults in switching networks described by functions of functions. First of all let us point out that functions of functions are a powerful tool for describing the internal structure of a switching network (see also section 2.1.3); it may also be easier to describe the functional properties of a switching function by the intermediate of a set of small relations rather than by a unique cumbersome relation.

The test functions for detecting stuck faults at the input x_i are (see section 4.4.2):

$$x_i \frac{\Delta f}{\Delta x_i} \quad \text{and} \quad \bar{x}_i \frac{\Delta f}{\Delta x_i}.$$

It turns out that the test functions for detecting the same faults when the network is described by a set of functions of functions are of the type:

$$x_i \frac{\Delta_t f}{\Delta_t x_i} \quad \text{and} \quad \bar{x}_i \frac{\Delta_t f}{\Delta_t x_i}. \tag{7.113}$$

The computational formulae derived in this chapter for computing the total differences allow us to evaluate these test functions directly from the set of functions of functions without rearranging them in order to obtain a single switching expression.

Example 7.4. Consider the set of functions

$$\begin{aligned} f &= y_0\bar{y}_1 \vee \bar{y}_0 y_1 y_3 \vee \bar{y}_1\bar{y}_3 \\ y_0 &= x_1 y_2 \vee \bar{x}_1\bar{y}_2 \\ y_1 &= x_1 y_2 \vee \bar{x}_1\bar{y}_2 \\ y_2 &= x_2 x_3 \\ y_3 &= x_0 x_6 \vee \bar{x}_0 x_3. \end{aligned} \tag{7.114}$$

From (7.59) one first derives the total differences:

$$\frac{\Delta_t f}{\Delta_t x_0} = \frac{\Delta f}{\Delta y_3}\frac{\Delta y_3}{\Delta x_0} = \bar{y}_0(x_3 \oplus x_6)$$

$$\frac{\Delta_t f}{\Delta_t x_1} = \frac{\Delta f}{\Delta y_0}\frac{\Delta y_0}{\Delta x_1} = y_3$$

$$\frac{\Delta_t f}{\Delta_t x_2} = \frac{\Delta f}{\Delta y_0}\frac{\Delta y_0}{\Delta y_2}\frac{\Delta y_2}{\Delta x_2} \oplus \frac{\Delta f}{\Delta y_1}\frac{\Delta y_1}{\Delta x_2} \oplus \frac{\Delta f}{\Delta y_0 y_1}\frac{\Delta y_0}{\Delta y_2}\frac{\Delta y_2}{\Delta x_2}\frac{\Delta y_1}{\Delta x_2}$$

$$= y_3 x_3 \oplus \bar{x}_4 \bar{x}_5$$

$$\frac{\Delta_t f}{\Delta_t x_3} = \frac{\Delta f}{\Delta y_0}\frac{\Delta y_0}{\Delta y_2}\frac{\Delta y_2}{\Delta x_3} \oplus \frac{\Delta f}{\Delta y_3}\frac{\Delta y_3}{\Delta x_3} \oplus \frac{\Delta f}{\Delta y_0 y_3}\frac{\Delta y_0}{\Delta y_2}\frac{\Delta y_2}{\Delta x_3}\frac{\Delta y_3}{\Delta x_3}$$

$$= y_3 x_2 \oplus \bar{y}_0 \bar{x}_0 \oplus \bar{x}_0 x_2$$

$$\frac{\Delta_t f}{\Delta_t x_4} = \frac{\Delta f}{\Delta y_1}\frac{\Delta y_1}{\Delta x_4} = \bar{x}_5(x_2 \oplus x_6)$$

$$\frac{\Delta_t f}{\Delta_t x_5} = \frac{\Delta f}{\Delta y_1}\frac{\Delta y_1}{\Delta x_5} = x_2 \bar{x}_4 \vee x_4 x_6$$

$$\frac{\Delta_t f}{\Delta_t x_6} = \frac{\Delta f}{\Delta y_1}\frac{\Delta y_1}{\Delta x_6} \oplus \frac{\Delta f}{\Delta y_3}\frac{\Delta y_3}{\Delta x_6} \oplus \frac{\Delta f}{\Delta y_1 y_3}\frac{\Delta y_1}{\Delta x_6}\frac{\Delta y_3}{\Delta x_6}.$$

The test functions derive immediately from the above expressions and from formula (7.113).

Let us now consider the problem of testing some internal stuck-faults (see section 4.4.2). We know that the set of functions (7.114) may be considered as a structure formula describing a switching network. This network is partially described in Figure 7.3 which gives explicitly the structure associated with the first relation of (7.114).

To detect any internal stuck-fault, each fanout connection from each fanout point must be tested. Consider, for example, the fanout point labelled y_0 in Figure 7.3; two fanout connections, namely y_{01} and y_{02}, are from this point. In order to detect the

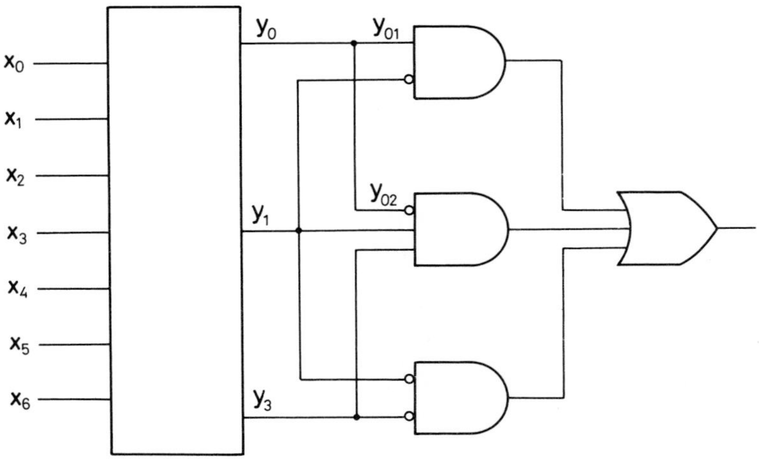

Figure 7.3. Switching network

single internal faults at y_{01} and y_{02}, the expression of f must be replaced by the following:

$$f = y_{01}\bar{y}_1 \vee \bar{y}_{02}y_1y_3 \vee \bar{y}_1\bar{y}_3$$

from which one deduces the differences:

$$\frac{\Delta f}{\Delta y_{01}} = \bar{y}_1y_3$$

$$\frac{\Delta f}{\Delta y_{02}} = y_1y_3$$

and the test functions:

$$y_0\bar{y}_1y_3, \bar{y}_0\bar{y}_1y_3, y_0y_1y_3, \bar{y}_0y_1y_3.$$

As a conclusion, the set of switching functions of functions (which may constitute the structure description of a switching network) together with the total difference operators for functions of functions studied in section 7.2 allow us to obtain computational formulae for deriving test functions for detecting input and internal stuck-faults.

Let us now briefly consider the multiple-fault-detection problem. From relation (4.112) one deduces that the test function for the stuck-fault $x_0 = h_0$ is:

$$\sum_{e_0} \frac{\Delta_t f}{\Delta_t x_0^{e_0}} \left[\prod_{i=0}^{q-1} (x_i \oplus h_i)^{e_i}\right]$$

where f is a switching function of functions (see formula (7.60)).

Differential tests for detecting a large class of multiple faults will now briefly be considered (Thayse [1971]). Consider first the input variable x_i; in the pair of test functions:

$$x_i \frac{\Delta f}{\Delta x_i}, \bar{x}_i \frac{\Delta f}{\Delta x_i} \tag{7.115}$$

for the stuck-at-0 and the stuck-at-1 faults on x_i, it is assumed that the do-not-care terms in any pair of test patterns which could be generated by these test functions may take arbitrary values. On the contrary, when the same pair of test functions is written in the following form (differential test function):

$$\frac{\Delta f}{\Delta x_i} \Delta x_i \tag{7.116}$$

it is assumed that the do-not-care terms take the same value in any pair of test patterns which could be generated by these functions. Let us observe that the pair of test patterns generated by (7.116) have their corresponding variables at the same polarity except x_i which takes both values 1 and 0. A multiple fault will be said to *contain* a fault on the variable x_i if that multiple fault involves a stuck-fault on x_i. The following theorem then holds.

Theorem 7.20. A pair of test patterns generated by the differential test function $(\Delta f/\Delta x_i)\Delta x_i$, where x_i is an input variable, detects any multiple stuck-fault containing a stuck-fault on the variable x_i.

Proof. If x_i is an input variable, the pair of test patterns satisfies the equation

$$\Delta f = (\Delta f/\Delta x_i)\Delta x_i = 1.$$

A stuck-fault on the variable x_i implies $\Delta x_i = 0$ and thus $\Delta f = 0$, independently of the other faults which could occur. ■

Example 7.5. Consider the switching function:

$$f = x_0 x_1 x_2 \vee x_3 x_4.$$

The test functions for x_1 stuck at 0 and at 1 are respectively:

$$x_1 \frac{\Delta f}{\Delta x_1} = x_1 x_0 x_2 (\bar{x}_3 \vee \bar{x}_4)$$

$$\bar{x}_1 \frac{\Delta f}{\Delta x_1} = \bar{x}_1 x_0 x_2 (\bar{x}_3 \vee \bar{x}_4)$$

A pair of test patterns for detecting these faults are, for example:

$$x_4 x_3 x_2 x_1 x_0 = (0\ 1\ 1\ 1\ 1)$$
$$(1\ 0\ 1\ 0\ 1).$$

The multiple fault x_1 stuck-at-0, x_4 stuck-at-1 is not detected by these test patterns. The variational test function

$$\frac{\Delta f}{\Delta x_1} \Delta x_1 = x_0 x_2 (\bar{x}_3 \vee \bar{x}_4) \Delta x_1$$

generates the pair of test patterns

$$x_4 x_3 x_2 x_1 x_0 = (0\ 1\ 1\ 1\ 1)$$
$$(0\ 1\ 1\ 0\ 1).$$

It can be verified that this pair of test patterns detects the multiple fault (x_4, x_1) stuck at $(1, 0)$.

Theorem 7.21. If $f(\boldsymbol{x})$ is a switching function realized by a network whose graph is a tree, a set of test patterns generated by the test functions

$$\frac{\Delta f}{\Delta x_i} \Delta x_i, \quad x_i \in \boldsymbol{x}$$

detects all simple and multiple stuck-faults of the network.

Proof. Any pair of test patterns generated by the test functions $(\Delta f/\Delta x_i)\Delta x_i$ implies that a signal must be able to be propagated through the connections following the connection x_i. A stuck-fault which destroys at least one of these connections destroys the only possible propagation path between the arc x_i and the network output. ■

7.3.3. *Sequential switching network description and analysis*

7.3.3.1. *Introduction to sequential logic*

It is traditional to divide switching networks into two categories; those for which the output is dependent only on the inputs present at the same instant of time: the combinational networks (which are until now the only ones considered in this book) and those for which the output not only depends on present inputs but also on the past history of inputs: the *sequential networks* (which will be considered in this section). The outputs of these networks at any given time are functions of the external inputs, as well as of the stored information at that time.

Finite state machines were briefly introduced in Chapter 2 (see example 2.2). The physical device that realizes a finite state machine is a sequential network; indeed, the concept of state corresponds to what we have called the past history of the inputs. The relation between a finite state and a sequential network that realizes it is conceptually analogous to that between a switching function and a switching network that implements it.

Sequential networks are in turn divided into two categories: *synchronous sequential networks* and *asynchronous sequential networks.*

In general, a synchronous sequential network is represented schematically by the circuit of Figure 7.4(a). This circuit has a finite number n of input terminals. The signals entering the circuit via these terminals constitute the n-tuple $(x_{n-1}, \ldots, x_1, x_0) = \boldsymbol{x}$ of input variables; an ordered n-tuple of 0's and 1's is an *input state* and the set of 2^n distinct input states is called the *input alphabet.* The box labelled *combinational network* contains only logic primitives connected in the way described on page 86. The network has a finite number m of output terminals, which define the m-tuple $(z_{m-1}, \ldots, z_1, z_0) = \boldsymbol{z}$ of output variables; an ordered m-tuple of 0's and 1's is an *output state* and the set of 2^m ordered m-tuples is the *output alphabet.*

Every finite-state machine contains a finite number of memory devices, which store the information regarding the past input history. The signal value at the output of each memory element is referred to as the *state variable* and the p-tuple $(y_{p-1}, \ldots, y_1, y_0) = \boldsymbol{y}$ constitutes the set of state variables; an ordered p-tuple of 0's and 1's is called the *internal state* or the *state* of the network. An ordered $(n + p)$-tuple of 0's and 1's (which represents a possible configuration of $(\boldsymbol{xy})$) is a *total state* of the network.

The inputs $\boldsymbol{x}$ and the values of the state variables $\boldsymbol{y}$ are supplied to the combinational network which in turn produces the outputs z and the values $(Y_{p-1}, \ldots, Y_1, Y_0) = \boldsymbol{Y}$. The values of the Y_j's, which appear at the outputs of the combinational network at time t, are identical with the values of the state variables y_j at $t+1$, and therefore they define the *next state* of the machine, i.e. the state that the machine will assume next; the Y_j's are called *next-state variables.* The switching functions which describe the effect of the circuit inputs $\boldsymbol{x}$ and the state variables $\boldsymbol{y}$ on the memory elements are called *next-state functions*; these functions are:

$$Y_j = Y_j(\boldsymbol{x}, \boldsymbol{y}), \quad j = 0, 1, \ldots, p-1. \tag{7.117}$$

The *output functions* are of the same type, i.e.

$$z_j = z_j(\boldsymbol{x}, \boldsymbol{y}), \quad j = 0, 1, \ldots, m-1. \tag{7.118}$$

The principal characteristic of *synchronous networks* is the input constraint, illustrated by the circuit of Figure 7.4(a), which restricts input changes to intervals defined by externally generated clock signals. These signals define the periods during which input changes are permitted. In practice, it may be accomplished by applying the clock pulses to the various AND gates which the inputs enter. This allows the gates to transmit signals only at instants which coincide with the arrival of the clock pulses. For a synchronous circuit to operate correctly, it is necessary to restrict the inherent delays within the combinational logic and to ensure that no input changes will occur when the clock pulse is present.

The theory of synchronous sequential networks was stated in the original papers by Moore [1956], Mealy [1955], Cadden [1959] and Brzozowski [1962]; the presentation given above comes in a large part from the book by Kohavi [1970].

In many practical situations the synchronizing clock pulses are not available and the sequential network is then called an *asynchronous sequential network*; the sequential network takes then the form of Figure 7.4(b). Externally, the network is characterized by the fact that its inputs can change at any time; internally it is characterized by the use of delay elements as memory devices. Input, output, state and next-state variables, internal and total states, next-state and output functions are defined in the same way as for synchronous networks.

For a given input state, the network is said to be in a *stable state* iff $y_i = Y_i \; \forall i = 0, 1, \ldots, p-1$. In response to a change in the input state, the combinational logic produces a new set of values for the next-state variables, and as a result the circuit enters what is called an *unstable state.* When the state variables assume their new values, i.e. when the y_j's become equal to the corresponding Y_j's, the circuit enters its next-stable state. Thus a transition from one stable state to another occurs only in response to a change in the input state. We shall assume that, after a change in one input has occurred, no other change in any input occurs until the circuit enters a stable state. Such a mode of operation is often referred to as a *fundamental mode*; a different mode of operation, called *pulse mode,* is obtained when the above requirement on input changes does not hold true. Only the fundamental mode of operation will be considered in this book.

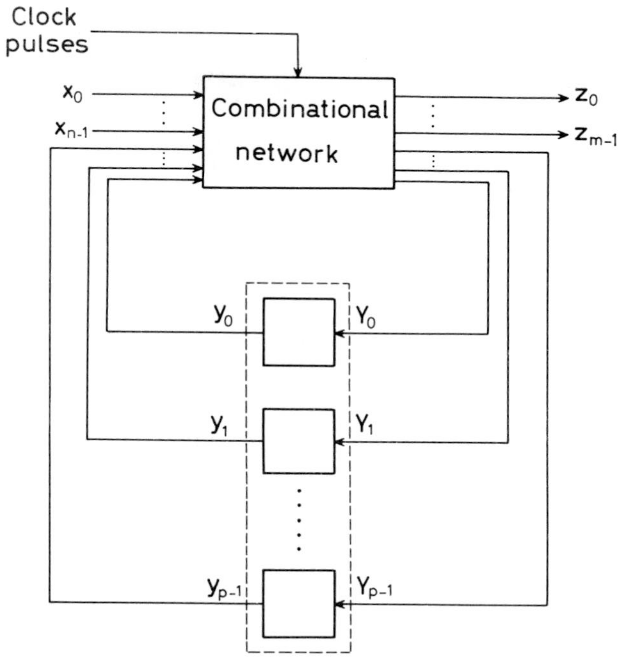

Figure 7.4 (a). Circuit representation of a synchronous sequential network

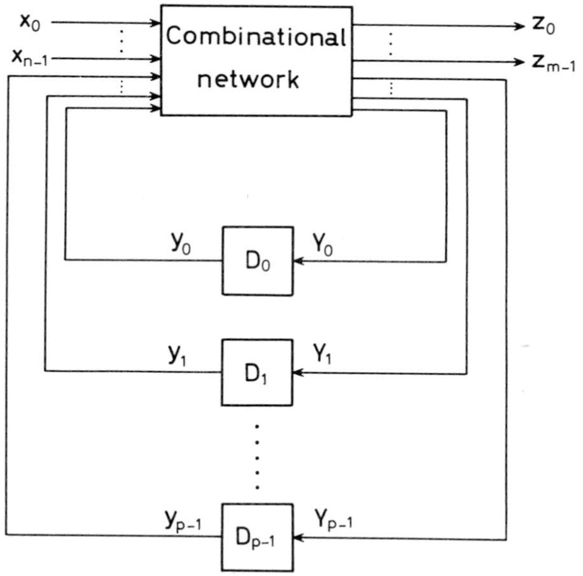

Figure 7.4 (b). Circuit representation of an asynchronous sequential network

When the restrictions that only one input variable at a time may change, that any transition leads to a next stable-state by the intermediary of no more than one unstable state and when operation is in fundamental mode, the term *normal fundamental mode* will be used.

Let us finally note that the theory of asynchronous sequential networks is mainly due to Huffman [1954].

7.3.3.2. Representations of asynchronous networks working in the fundamental mode

The output functions and the next-state functions (7.117) and (7.118) completely specify the behaviour of an asynchronous sequential network working in the fundamental mode. Another common representation of the sequential network is the *next-state table* which is a matrix having the next-state variables Y_j as entries (sometimes the output variables z_j are also added); the 2^n possible values of the input variables $\boldsymbol{x}$ specify the columns while the 2^p possible values of the state variables specify the rows. To describe the behaviour of a network it is sufficient to have a technique for determining the succession of the internal states; this can easily be achieved by using the next-state table as it will be seen further on. Consider the table of Figure 7.5(a). Initially the inputs are $\boldsymbol{x}=\boldsymbol{a}$ and the network is in the stable state $(\boldsymbol{x}=\boldsymbol{a}, \boldsymbol{y}=\boldsymbol{Y}=\boldsymbol{c})$; if now $\boldsymbol{x}$ changes from $\boldsymbol{a}$ to $\boldsymbol{b}$ as illustrated in Figure 7.5(a) the circuit enters a different total state $(\boldsymbol{x}=\boldsymbol{b}, \boldsymbol{y}=\boldsymbol{c})$ which is unstable since $\boldsymbol{Y}=\boldsymbol{d}\neq\boldsymbol{c}$. The circuit should then enter another stable state $(\boldsymbol{x}=\boldsymbol{b}, \boldsymbol{y}=\boldsymbol{Y}=\boldsymbol{d})$; thus a change in the value of the network inputs causes a horizontal move in the next-state table to the column whose heading corresponds to the new input value. A change in the internal state of the circuit is reflected by a vertical move, as shown by the arrows of Figure 7.5(a).

Assume an asynchronous sequential network working in the fundamental mode and any transition of which leads to a next-stable state by the intermediary of no more than one unstable state; by taking the first increment of both sides of (7.117) one obtains:

$$\Delta Y_j = \underbrace{\sum_{e} \frac{\Delta Y_j}{\Delta \boldsymbol{x}^e} \prod_i (\Delta x_i)^{e_i}}_{\text{I}} \oplus \underbrace{\sum_{e\epsilon} \frac{\Delta Y_j}{\Delta \boldsymbol{x}^e \boldsymbol{y}^\epsilon} \prod_i (\Delta x_i)^{e_i} \prod_j (\Delta y_j)^{\epsilon_j}}_{\text{II}} \tag{7.119}$$

$$0 \leqslant e_i,\ \epsilon_j \leqslant 1, \quad 0 < \epsilon.$$

The above difference relation has been partitioned into two parts; part I of relation (7.119) uniquely defines the increment of the next-state variable Y_j if it is assumed that any transition leads to a stable state by the intermediary of no more than one unstable state. Indeed, if one assumes that the initial state is stable $(\Delta y_j = 0\ \forall j)$,

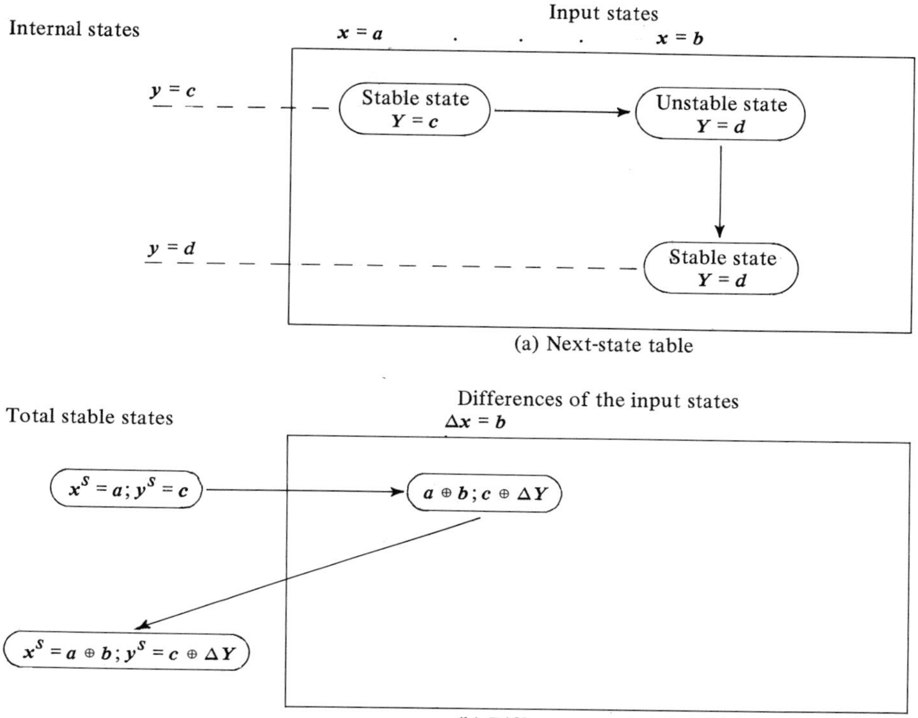

(a) Next-state table

(b) Difference next-state table

Figure 7.5. Next-state table

part II of (7.119) is then identically zero. Let $x^s y^s$ be a stable state of a network having the just quoted property

$$x^s y^s = (x^s_{n-1}, \ldots, x^s_1, x^s_0; y^s_{p-1}, \ldots, y^s_0).$$

The next-state functions may be rewritten in the following form:

$$Y_j = y_j^s \oplus (\Delta y_j)_{xy=x^s y^s}$$

$$= y_j^s \oplus \sum_e (\Delta y_j/\Delta x^e)_{xy=x^s y^s} \prod_i (\Delta x_i)^{e_i}. \qquad (7.120)$$

Indeed, if the input variable do not change, Y_j remains at its stable value y_j^s while, if the input variables are changing, Y_j changes or not according to whether $\Delta y_j = 0$ or 1. If the set of total stable states $x^s y^s$ and the increments Δx_i are considered as independent variables instead of x, y, then the relations (7.120) provide us with a representation of the asynchronous network, called *difference next-state functions*

(Thayse [1972b]); the corresponding tabular representation is the *difference next-state table* (see Figure 7.5(b)), which is a matrix having $(\boldsymbol{x}^s \oplus \Delta \boldsymbol{x}, \boldsymbol{y}^s \oplus \Delta \boldsymbol{Y})$ as entries ($\Delta \boldsymbol{x}$ means $(\Delta x_{n-1}, \ldots, \Delta x_1, \Delta x_0)$ while $\Delta \boldsymbol{Y}$ means $(\Delta Y_{p-1}, \ldots, \Delta Y_1, \Delta Y_0)$); the 2^n-1 possible values of the increments $\Delta \boldsymbol{x}$ (clearly $\Delta \boldsymbol{x} = \boldsymbol{0}$ is not considered as a possible value) specify the columns while the total stable states specify the rows. Consider the table of Figure 7.5(b); the initial total stable state is $(\boldsymbol{x}^s = \boldsymbol{a}, \boldsymbol{y}^s = \boldsymbol{c})$. If the input change corresponds to $\Delta \boldsymbol{x} = \boldsymbol{b}$, and if the entry of the table at the coordinate $\Delta \boldsymbol{x} = \boldsymbol{b}, \boldsymbol{x}^s\boldsymbol{y}^s = \boldsymbol{ac}$ is $(\boldsymbol{a} \oplus \boldsymbol{b}, \boldsymbol{c} \oplus \Delta \boldsymbol{Y})$ the network reaches the new total stable state $(\boldsymbol{x}^s = \boldsymbol{a} \oplus \boldsymbol{b}, \boldsymbol{y}^s = \boldsymbol{c} \oplus \Delta \boldsymbol{Y})$.

Let us finally note that difference next-state functions of the type (7.120) may be used for describing asynchronous sequential networks working in the fundamental mode but where any transition leads to a next-stable state by the intermediary of no more than q unstable states. The first increments in equation (7.120) are then to be replaced by qth increments; the algebraic aspect of this problem may be found in Thayse [1974c].

The description of asynchronous sequential networks by means of next-state functions or by means of next-state tables (sometimes also called *excitation tables*) is classical and is due to Huffman [1954]). Good presentations of asynchronous networks are available in Caldwell [1958], McCluskey [1962] and Miller [1965].

The difference next-state functions were introduced by Thayse [1972b,c] who showed the importance of this description mode in several problems in sequential logic, such as, for example, fault detection and hazard detection. The difference next-state tables were developed independently by Ashkinazy [1970] Smith and Roth [1971] and Thayse [1972b, 1974c].

Example 7.6. Consider the asynchronous sequential network of Figure 7.6; this network is classically known as an rs flip-flop. The next-state function of this flip-flop is:

$$Y = \bar{x}_0 \vee x_1 y \tag{7.121}$$

from which one deduces the next-state table (Figure 7.7)

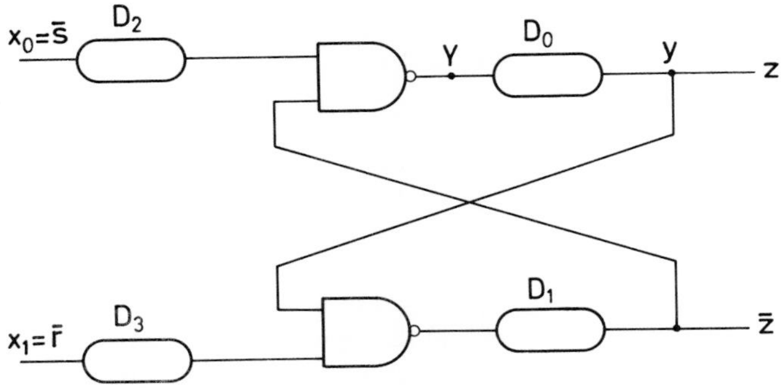

Figure 7.6. Realization of an rs flip-flop

$y \backslash x_1 x_0$	0 0	0 1	1 0	1 1
0	1	$\underline{0}$	1	$\underline{0}$
1	$\underline{1}$	0	$\underline{1}$	$\underline{1}$

Figure 7.7. Next-state table for an rs flip-flop

The stable states have been underlined in the above table. When a network is being operated in fundamental mode, the use of the transition table is as follows: the network is assumed to be started in some stable state with a particular value of the input variables (input state). Assume that in Figure 7.7 the starting state is 0 and the 0 1 input combination is present. The network will remain indefinitely in this condition if the input is not changed, since the internal state is stable. Now suppose that one of the inputs, say x_1, is changed. At first the input state will change to 1 0 and the internal state will remain the same. Consider now another transition, let the initial state be the same, i.e. $x_1 x_0 y = 0\ 1\ 0$. Suppose now that x_0 changes; the input state will become 0 0 and the initial state will first remain the same. Since the entry in this position of the table is 1, the internal state will change until it becomes equal to 1; the state $x_1 x_0 y = 0\ 0\ 1$ being stable, the network will remain in this state.

From the table of Figure 7.7 one deduces that the stable states $\boldsymbol{x}^s, \boldsymbol{y}^s$ are:

$$(x_1^s\, x_0^s\, y^s) = (0\ 0\ 1; 0\ 1\ 0; 1\ 0\ 1; 1\ 1\ 0; 1\ 1\ 1). \tag{7.122}$$

The increment ΔY is (it is recalled that Δy is assumed to be 0 for a network working in the fundamental mode)

$$\Delta Y = (\bar{x}_1 \vee y)\, \Delta x_0 \oplus y_0 x_0\, \Delta x_1 \oplus y_0\, \Delta x_1\, \Delta x_0. \tag{7.123}$$

From (7.122) and (7.123) one then deduces the table of Figure 7.8, which is the difference next-state table of the asynchronous network (7.6). The entries of this table are:

$$x_1^s \oplus \Delta x_1, x_0^s \oplus \Delta x_0, y^s \oplus \Delta Y.$$

$x_1^s x_0^s; y^s \backslash \Delta x_1 \Delta x_0$	0 1	1 0	1 1
0 0;1	0 1;0	1 0;1	1 1;0
0 1;0	0 0;1	1 1;0	1 0;1
1 0;1	1 1;0	0 0;1	0 1;0
1 1;0	1 0;1	0 1;0	0 0;1
1 1;1	1 0;1	0 1;0	0 0;1

Figure 7.8. Difference next-state table for an rs flip-flop

This table must be used as follows for determining the next stable states of a network; assume that the network corresponding to the table in Figure 7.8 is in state (0 0; 1). If the input x_1 changes, Δx_1 takes the value 1 during the transition while Δx_0 remains 0; the network goes to the final stable state 1 0; 1 (see Figure 7.8).

7.3.3.3. Hazard detection in asynchronous networks

Let us first deal with some features relative to asynchronous network description. We suppose first that the network to be analysed is specified by a structural description, that is, a circuit diagram depicting the gates and showing how they are interconnected. A classical way to reduce the analysis of a sequential network to a combinational problem is to remove connections of the network in order to obtain a loop-free structure (or a structure without feedback). A next-state variable and a state variable are then associated with each of the signals of the removed connections. This provides us with a set of functions, namely the next-state functions, which are a mathematical description of the network behaviour. It must be noted that the process of obtaining a set of next-state functions from a sequential network by removing some connections does not generally lead to a unique set of functions independent of the set of connections removed in the network. Consequently, some results of the network analysis, and in particular hazard detection (hazards in sequential networks will be defined further on), are also dependent on the chosen set of connections. One has however shown (see Thayse [1970]) that some sets of functions are equivalent in view of detecting hazards in sequential networks. More precisely, one has to determine in the network scheme an arbitrary set of connections which, if removed, leaves the resultant diagram without any loops and fanout reconvergent structure. The next-state functions are then obtained from the network by the above process where a state and a next-state are associated to each of the removed connections. Let us now turn to the hazard-detection problem.

Let us first recall that hazards were defined in section 3.3.3 as possibilities of transient errors in a combinational network due to the presence of delays in the gates and wires of this network. When dealing with hazard detection in sequential networks, we assume that stray delays may be present in both the combinational part of the network and in the feedback connections. Moreover, it turns out that, because of the memory function of the sequential networks, transient phenomena due to hazards may be memorized and thus produce a permanent error at the sequential network output.

Definition 7.6. A sequential network is free of *sequential hazard* for a given transition if a unique stable state is always reached, whatever the values of the network stray delays may be.

The *critical race* defined by Huffman [1954] and the *essential hazard* discovered by Unger [1959] are both sequential hazards. Eichelberger [1965] observed that the possibility of reaching two or more stable states after a transition involving a permanent hazard might be characterized mathematically by an oscillation of the state variables between these stable states; hence the following procedure, first proposed by Eichelberger [1965] for detecting hazards in sequential networks.

Algorithm 7.1. (a) Determine all the state variables (or equivalently the next-state variables) which may change as a result of a given input state; this part of the algorithm is generally referred to as the *variation phase.*

(b) Determine whether or not these state variables will stabilize in some stable state; the transition is said to experience a sequential hazard iff some state variables do not stabilize. This part of the algorithm is generally referred to as the *stabilization phase.*

The detection of state variables which do not stabilize (or equivalently which oscillate) was performed by Eichelberger [1965] by using a ternary algebra. We shall perform the steps (a) and (b) of algorithm 7.1 by using the concept of variation defined in section 7.1.3.

From the network scheme, one deduces by the way explained in the beginning of this section a set of p next-state functions:

$$Y_j = Y_j(\boldsymbol{x}, \boldsymbol{y}), \quad j = 0, 1, \ldots, p-1$$

with

$$\boldsymbol{x} = (x_{n-1}, \ldots, x_1, x_0) \quad \text{(input variables)},$$

$$\boldsymbol{y} = (y_{p-1}, \ldots, y_1, y_0) \quad \text{(internal variables)}.$$

Since the sequential network will be studied during a certain time duration (to be defined further on), these variables will be considered as time-dependent functions, and the next-state functions will be written accordingly ($t = 0$; initial time instant):

$$y_j(1) = Y_j[\boldsymbol{x}(0), \boldsymbol{y}(0)].$$

Further on, the time index $t = 0$ will generally be dropped in the equations. The stable states of the network are deduced by solving the following equation

$$\bigvee_{j=0,p-1} [y_j \oplus Y_j(\boldsymbol{x}, \boldsymbol{y})] = 0 \tag{7.124}$$

in the p unknowns $y_0, y_1, \ldots, y_{p-1}$.

Let us consider an asynchronous sequential network where the inputs are constrained so as to change only when the system is in a stable state. The term *fundamental mode* was used for this mode of operation. In view of performing the analysis of the variation phase one will be first interested in the possibility of changing for the next-state variables during a transition. Each transition is characterized by its initial conditions, which are:

The initial input state $\boldsymbol{x}$ and the initial internal state $\boldsymbol{y}$ which is necessarily a solution of equation (7.124).

The input change which can be characterized, for example, by the vector $\Delta \boldsymbol{x}$, that is:

$$\Delta \boldsymbol{x} = (\Delta x_{n-1}, \ldots, \Delta x_1, \Delta x_0).$$

The condition of working in fundamental mode implies moreover that:

$$\Delta y_j(t) = 0, \quad j = 0, 1, \ldots, p-1; \Delta x_i(t-1) = 0, \quad i = 0, 1, \ldots, n-1; \quad t \leqslant 0$$

$$\Delta^k x_i = \Delta x_i, \quad i = 0, 1, \ldots, n-1; \quad k \geqslant 1.$$

The first one of the two above kinds of conditions may also be written:

$$\Delta^k y_j(1-k) = 0, \Delta^k x_i(-k) = 0; \quad k \geqslant 1.$$

The variations will satisfy the same initial conditions, that is:

$$\delta^k y_j(1-k) = 0, \delta^k x_i(-k) = 0; \quad k \geqslant 1.$$

Let us point out that the above conditions on the variations imply the same conditions on the differences.

The following theorem entirely solves the variation phase.

Theorem 7.22. If p is the number of next-state variables, the next-state variables which may change as a result of a given input change are characterized by the condition:

$$(\delta^p Y_j)_{\text{initial conditions}} = 1, \quad j = 0, 1, \ldots, p-1. \tag{7.125}$$

Proof. Theorem 7.6 allows us to state that the next-state variables which may change as a result of a given input change are characterized by the relation

$$(\delta Y_j)_{\text{initial conditions}} = 1. \tag{7.126}$$

Similarly, the next-state variables which may change as a result of:

(a) the input variables which change,
(b) the state variables which change, that is those which satisfy the condition (7.126),

are characterized by the relation:

$$(\delta^2 Y_j)_{\text{initial conditions}} = 1.$$

The condition (7.125) then results from the fact that there are exactly p state and next-state variables. ∎

The computation of the expression $\delta^p Y_j$ evaluated for the initial conditions can best be done by using expression (7.54), that is:

$$\delta^k Y_j = \bigvee_e \frac{\Delta Y_j}{\Delta x^e} \left[\prod_i (\delta^k x_i)^{e_i}\right] \vee$$
$$\bigvee_\epsilon \frac{\Delta Y_j}{\Delta y^\epsilon} \left[\prod_l (\delta^k y_l)^{\epsilon_l}\right] \vee$$
$$\bigvee_{e\epsilon} \frac{\Delta Y_j}{\Delta x^e y^\epsilon} \left[\prod_{i,l} (\delta^k x_i)^{e_i} (\delta^k y_l)^{\epsilon_l}\right]. \tag{7.127}$$

By use of the initial conditions, the above expression is transformed into the following one:

$$\delta^k Y_j = \bigvee_e \frac{\Delta Y_j}{\Delta x^e} \left[\prod_i (\Delta x_i)^{e_i}\right] \vee$$
$$\bigvee_\epsilon \frac{\Delta Y_j}{\Delta y^\epsilon} \left[\prod_l (\delta^{k-1} Y_l)^{\epsilon_l}\right] \vee$$
$$\bigvee_{e\epsilon} \frac{\Delta Y_j}{\Delta x^e y^\epsilon} \left[\prod_{i,l} (\Delta x_i)^{e_i} (\delta^{k-1} Y_l)^{\epsilon_l}\right] \tag{7.128}$$

which allows us to compute $\delta^k Y_j$ when the $\delta^{k-1} Y_l$'s are known. Since the initial conditions allow us to write

$$\delta Y_j = \bigvee_e \frac{\Delta Y_j}{\Delta x^e} \left[\prod_i (\Delta x_i)^{e_i}\right] \tag{7.129}$$

the computation of $\delta^p Y_j$ can be performed by evaluating successively δY_l, $\delta^2 Y_l, \ldots, \delta^{p-1} Y_l$.

The evaluation of the variation phase according to the preceding computation scheme is illustrated by example 7.6.

Example 7.6 (continued). From (7.121) one deduces that the stable states of the network are solutions of the equation:

$$y \oplus (\bar{x}_0 \vee x_1 y) = 0.$$

The stable states y^s are thus:

$$y^s = \bar{x}_0 \vee \bar{\lambda} x_1 \ \forall\, x_1, x_0, \lambda \in \{0, 1\}. \tag{7.130}$$

The first variation of (7.121) is:

$$\delta Y = (\bar{x}_1 \vee \bar{y})\, \Delta x_0 \vee x_0 y\, \Delta x_1 \vee x_1 x_0\, \delta y \vee y_0\, \Delta x_0\, \Delta x_1 \vee x_1\, \Delta x_0\, \delta y \vee$$
$$x_0\, \Delta x_1\, \delta y \vee \Delta x_0\, \Delta x_1\, \delta y_0. \tag{7.131}$$

The result of the variation phase is then obtained by putting the initial conditions: $y = y^s$, $\Delta y = 0$ in (7.131), i.e.

$$\delta Y = (\bar{x}_1 \vee x_0\bar{\lambda})\,\Delta x_0 \vee x_0 x_1 \lambda \Delta x_1 \vee \Delta x_0\,\Delta x_1. \tag{7.132}$$

Let us now turn to the analysis of the stabilization phase. Assume that, as for the variation phase, the initial conditions take place at the time $t = 0$. The initial conditions of the stabilization phase are the final conditions of the variation phase. More precisely:

The initial input state $\boldsymbol{x}$ is:

$$\boldsymbol{x} \oplus \Delta\boldsymbol{x}(\nu)$$

where $\Delta\boldsymbol{x}(\nu)$ is the vector $\Delta\boldsymbol{x}$ of the first differences of $\boldsymbol{x}$ evaluated at the final step of the variation phase.

The initial conditions on the variations of the state variables are the final conditions on the variations of the next-state variables at the end of the variation phase, that is:

$$\delta y_j = \delta^p Y_j(\nu).$$

The following theorem solves the stabilization phase.

Theorem 7.23. The next-state variables which may oscillate as a result of a given input change are characterized by the relation

$$(\delta^p Y_j)_{(\text{final conditions of the variation phase})} = 1.$$

Proof. The proof is the same as that of theorem 7.22. ■

The computation of the expression $\delta^p Y_j/\delta t$ evaluated for the initial conditions can be done by using the same expression (7.54) as for the variation phase. By use of the initial conditions of the stabilization phase this expression is transformed into the following one:

$$\delta^k Y_j = \bigvee_{\epsilon} \left(\frac{\Delta Y_j}{\Delta y^{\epsilon}}\right)_{(x \oplus \Delta x)} \left\{\prod_i \,[\delta^{k-1}(\delta^p Y_j)]^{\epsilon_j}\right\}. \tag{7.133}$$

The evaluation of $\delta^p Y_j$ can now be performed according to the same iterative scheme as for the variation phase. This will be illustrated by continuing example 7.6.

Example 7.6 (continued). In view of (7.131) and (7.132) one successively has:

$$\delta Y = \left(\frac{\Delta Y}{\Delta y}\,\delta y\right)_{\text{initial conditions}}$$

$$= (x_1 \oplus \Delta x_1)(x_0 \oplus \Delta x_0)\,[(\bar{x}_1 \vee x_0\bar{\lambda})\,\Delta x_0 \vee x_0 x_1 \lambda\,\Delta x_1 \vee \Delta x_0\,\Delta x_1]$$

$$= \bar{x}_0\bar{x}_1\,\Delta x_0\,\Delta x_1. \tag{7.134}$$

The state and next-state variables will experience an oscillation if and only if the transition starts with the input state $(x_1, x_0) = (0, 0)$ and if both variables change. This transition is thus the only one producing a sequential hazard.

Several remarks may now be made about the above network analysis. First of all, because of the physical properties of the delays, the sequential hazard does not generally produce an oscillation between the stable states that may be reached. Instead of this, the network really reaches a stable state but this state is a function of the relative values of the delays; the delays are then called ***inertial delays*** (for a more rigorous definition of inertial delays see, for example, Miller [1965], Thayse [1970, 1974c], Mange [1973]). The effects of inertial delays in hazard-containing transitions may be made obvious in the difference model of the network. Consider, for example, the difference next-state table of Figure 7.8 which represents the rs flip-flop considered above. If one substitutes in the hazard-containing transitions the binary entries of the state variables which do not stabilize by a binary parameter depending on the stray delay values, a new kind of information about the real behaviour of the network is introduced. Let us illustrate this fact by means of example 7.6.

Example 7.6 (continued). Consider the transition table 7.8; we know that the only transition containing a hazard is: (x_1, x_0): $(0, 0) \rightarrow (1, 1)$. The transition table in Figure 7.6 must be replaced by the following.

$x_1^s\, x_0^s, y^s$ \ $\Delta x_1, \Delta x_0$	01	10	11
00, 1	01, 0	10, 1	11, α
01, 0	00, 1	11, 0	10, 1
10, 1	11, 0	00, 1	01, 0
11, 0	10, 1	01, 0	00, 1
11, 1	10, 1	01, 0	00, 1

Figure 7.9. Difference next-state table containing information about sequential hazards

By giving to the binary parameter α of the table in Figure 7.9 the values 0 and 1 successively, one sees that the stable states that may be reached are 11, 0 and 11, 1.

For a network containing several hazardous transitions, the table has several parameters α_i; the possible stable states are then obtained by giving in all the possible ways the values 0 and 1 to the parameters α_i. Clearly, the value to be given to these parameters depends on the relative delay values of the network. How to relate the delay values to the parameter values will be the subject of next section.

Remark. Comparison between binary and ternary simulations.

The analysis and simulation of fundamental mode sequential switching networks can be based either on some switching methods, as in this section, or alternatively on a three-valued representation as proposed by Eichelberger [1965]. Three-valued logic simulation systems have become quite prevalent in the last few years mostly because of the computational efficiency of the ternary approach. Let us point out the similarities of ternary simulation and of switching differential methods. The expression of $\delta^p Y_j$ obtained at the end of the stabilization phase may either be computed by means of the differential operators defined in section 7.1, or by a ternary simulation of the network. If the network has s stable states and n input variables, one has to perform $2s(2^n-1)$ ternary simulations. Let us now build a truth table by considering each of the $s(2^n-1)$ fundamental mode variations of the network: a 1 entry in this table will denote an oscillation produced by the corresponding input change while a 0 entry will denote a change free of oscillation. The expression of $\delta^p Y_j$ is then nothing but the switching expression of the corresponding truth table.

Moreover, since the results of the analysis based on the use of the differential operators allow us to obtain, in a very concise form, the complete information relative to a large number of ternary simulations, an efficient use of these operators will lead in most cases to considerably shorter computations than any other computational means.

For example, consider the rs flip-flop of example 7.6. In order to obtain the result of the stabilization phase one has only to evaluate 2 variations while the Eichelberger method requests the computation of $2 \times 5 \times 3 = 30$ ternary simulations.

As a conclusion, when one is interested in hazard detection for a small subset of transitions relative to a given network, it seems that ternary simulations generally lead to more rapid results. However, if one wants a complete information about any transition, the technique using differential operators is certainly the most concise now available.

7.3.3.4. Delay conditions and sequential hazards

In the preceding section 7.3.3.2 one has obtained a new type of next-state equations (7.120) which immediately leads to a difference next-state table (see, for example, the table in Figure 7.8 of example 7.6). This table, together with the conditions of theorem 7.23, allows us to determine all the possible ultimate stable states which may be reached by a network after a given input change (see table in Figure 7.9). The several possible stable states are obtained by giving all the allowed values to the binary parameters α_i of the parametrical form of the transition table. Now, each allowed stable state is reached in the real network for a given value of some internal delays. Neither the next-state functions (7.120) nor the resulting transition table give us any information about the relations between ultimate stable states and relative delay values. The main purpose of this section will be to build a systematic procedure allowing us to compute the delay conditions leading to the different possible ultimate stable states of a hazard-containing transition. This procedure will reduce practically to replace each occurrence of an α_i in the difference table by a switching relation in some delay values. Since the complexity of these switching relations increases quickly with the number of possible delays in a network, a computer program has been built which gives as result the transition table with the several delay conditions (Decroly, Fosséprez and Thayse [1969], Thayse [1969], Davio and Thayse [1969]).

The network studied is built up by means of an undetermined number of gates and of inertial delays the value of which generally remains unknown. For each delay of characteristic value D_j, one introduces two switching variables Y_j and y_j, namely the next-state variable and the state variable respectively. In view of the definition of the inertial delay element, if Y_j switches at a time t, then y_j takes the new value of Y_j after a time $t + D_j$ iff Y_j's new value remains constant during at least a time interval D_j; otherwise y_j is not affected by the considered variation of Y_j. It is thus clear that a distinction must be made between the state of excitation of an inertial delay and the state of its response as reflected by the variables Y_j and y_j respectively. Obviously, if each Y_j and y_j have the same value 0 or 1, the delay and the corresponding variable are in a stable state; otherwise they are in an unstable state. The stability or instability of any delay is thus reflected by the value of its first increment:

$$\Delta Y_i = y_i(1) \oplus y_i(0) = Y_i(0) \oplus y_i(0).$$

Let us for example consider a transition starting in a given total state $\boldsymbol{x}, \boldsymbol{y}$, and assume that the variables $\boldsymbol{x}_0 \subseteq \boldsymbol{x}$ are changing. Let us compute the set of first increment ΔY_i evaluated for that input change and let, for example, the variable $Y_0 = (Y_{00}, Y_{01}, \ldots, Y_{0k}) \subseteq Y$ be the variables the first differences of which are equal to 1. If one assumes that the delay values are such that $D_{00} < D_{01}, D_{02}, \ldots, D_{0k}$, the internal variable y_{00} will change first and the other excited variables will temporarily remain unchanged. The network will thus go into a new state where only the variable y_0 has taken a new value. At this state the first increments are again evaluated, and let, for example, the variables $Y_1 = (Y_{10}, Y_{12}, \ldots, Y_{1k}) \subseteq Y$ be the variables whose first increments are equal to 1. If one assumes that the delay values are such that:

$$\begin{aligned} D_{10} &< D_{1i} \ \forall\, Y_{1i} \in Y_1 \text{ and } \notin Y_0 \\ &< D_{1j} - D_{00} \ \forall\, Y_{1j} \in Y_1 \cap Y_0 \end{aligned}$$

it is the internal variable y_{10} which will change and lead to an internal state which differs from its predecessor only in that variable y_{10}. Let us observe that the second type of delay condition hereabove comes from the fact that the inertial delay D_{1j} has already been excited during a time interval D_{00} when the variable y_{00} was changing. The procedure briefly described above is then continued until an ultimate stable state has been reached. The delay conditions leading to this particular stable state are those derived at the successive steps of the procedure.

When an ultimate stable state has been reached for a given set of delay values, the procedure is repeated for another set of delay values. The final aim of the procedure is to explore all the possible conditions between the delay values of the unstable variables. This has been performed systematically by a computer program which has been developed on the basis of the method described above. It must however be noted that in this program, instead of imposing some delay conditions in order to detect the variables which are changing, when a race condition appears one selects a variable to win the race which imposes conditions between the delay values.

The program described in Decroly, Fosséprez and Thayse [1969] gives as result all the possible evolutions of a logical network starting from every stable state if the input change occurs in the fundamental mode. These evolutions are functions of the input change, of the network configuration and of the distribution and values of the delays. Together with the delay conditions associated with the hazard-containing transitions, the program gives also as result for each transition:

1. The sequence of the total states.
2. The time interval between intermediate total states.
3. The conditions between delay values.
4. The sequence of the input states.
5. The transition time between stable states.

Example 7.6 (continued). The example 7.6 can easily be treated by hand. Consider Figure 7.6 and assume first that the delays D_2 and D_3 are strictly zero. Consider also the table in Figure 7.9; one sees, by performing the procedure described above, that after the input has performed a change: $(x_0, x_1):(0,0) \rightarrow (1,1)$, the system reaches the stable state $(y_0, y_1) = (0, 1)$ if $D_0 < D_1$ and the stable state $(y_0, y_1) = (1, 0)$ if $D_1 < D_0$. The parameter α in the table in Figure 7.9 obeys thus the following switching relation:

$$\begin{aligned} \alpha &= 0 \quad \text{if} \quad D_0 < D_1 \\ &= 1 \quad \text{if} \quad D_1 < D_0 \end{aligned}$$

which can be written symbolically:

$$\alpha = D_0 > D_1.$$

Consider now the model with four delays (see Figure 7.6); one obtains accordingly:

$$\begin{aligned} \alpha = {} & 0 \text{ if } D_0 + D_2 < D_3 \\ & \text{or if } D_2 < D_3 < D_0 + D_2 < D_1 + D_3 \\ & \text{or if } D_0 + D_3 < D_2 \\ & \text{or if } D_3 < D_2 < D_0 + D_3 < D_1 + D_2 \\ = {} & 1 \text{ if } D_2 < D_3 < D_0 + D_2 \quad \text{and} \quad D_1 + D_3 < D_0 + D_2 \\ & \text{or if } D_3 < D_2 < D_0 + D_3 \quad \text{and} \quad D_1 + D_2 < D_0 + D_3 \end{aligned}$$

which can be written:

$$\alpha = (D_2 < D_3 < D_0 + D_2)\,(D_1 + D_3 < D_0 + D_2) \vee$$
$$(D_3 < D_2 < D_0 + D_3)\,(D_1 + D_2 < D_0 + D_3)$$

Example 7.7 (Master-slave synchronized rs flip-flop.)

Consider the network shown in Figure 7.10; it can easily be recognized that this network is built up through the intermediate of two rs flip flops (see Figure 7.6).

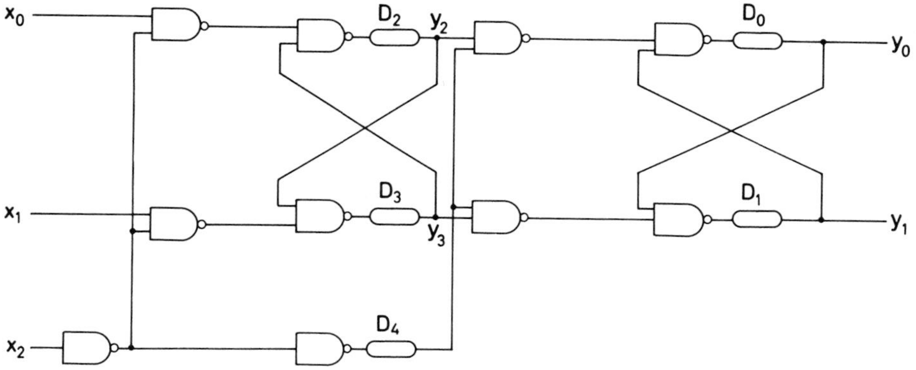

Figure 7.10. Master-slave synchronized rs flip-flop

Consider first the outputs $y_2 y_3$ of the first rs flip-flop. The behaviour of these outputs is described by the following functions:

Next-state functions:

$$Y_2 = x_0 \bar{x}_2 \vee \bar{y}_3$$
$$Y_3 = x_1 \bar{x}_2 \vee \bar{y}_2.$$

Parametric form of the stable states:

$$y_2^s = x_0 \bar{x}_2 \vee \bar{\lambda}_0(\bar{x}_1 \vee x_2)$$
$$y_3^s = x_1 \bar{x}_2 \vee \lambda_0(\bar{x}_0 \vee x_2).$$

Variations:

$$\delta^k Y_2 = \bar{x}_2 y_3\, \Delta x_0 \vee x_0 y_3\, \Delta x_2 \vee (\bar{x}_0 \vee x_2)\, \delta^k y_3 \vee y_3\, \Delta x_0\, \Delta x_2 \vee$$
$$\bar{x}_2\, \Delta x_0\, \delta^k y_3 \vee x_0\, \Delta x_2\, \delta^k y_3 \vee \Delta x_0\, \Delta x_2\, \delta^k y_3$$
$$\delta^k Y_3 = \bar{x}_2 y_2\, \Delta x_1 \vee x_1 y_2\, \Delta x_2 \vee (\bar{x}_1 \vee x_2)\, \delta^k y_2 \vee y_2\, \Delta x_1\, \Delta x_2 \vee$$
$$\bar{x}_2\, \Delta x_1\, \delta^k y_2 \vee x_1\, \Delta x_2\, \delta^k y_2 \vee \Delta x_1\, \Delta x_2\, \delta^k y_2.$$

Result of the stabilization phase:

$$\delta^2 Y_2 = \delta^2 Y_3 = x_0 x_1 \bar{x}_2 \, \Delta x_2 \vee x_0 x_1 \bar{x}_2 \, \Delta x_0 \, \Delta x_1 \vee$$
$$[x_1 \bar{x}_2 \vee \bar{x}_0 \bar{x}_2 \lambda_0 \vee x_0 \bar{x}_1 x_2 \lambda_0 \, \overline{\Delta x_1}] \, \Delta x_0 \, \Delta x_2 \vee$$
$$[x_0 \bar{x}_2 \vee \bar{x}_1 \bar{x}_2 \bar{\lambda}_0 \vee \bar{x}_0 x_1 x_2 \, \bar{\lambda}_0 \, \overline{\Delta x_0}] \, \Delta x_1 \, \Delta x_2 \vee$$
$$(\bar{x}_2 \vee x_0 x_1) \, \Delta x_0 \, \Delta x_1 \, \Delta x_2.$$

Consider the outputs $y_0 y_1$ of the second rs flip-flop. The behaviour of these outputs is described by the following functions:

Next-state functions:

$$Y_0 = x_2 y_2 \vee \bar{y}_1$$
$$Y_1 = x_2 y_3 \vee \bar{y}_0$$

Parametric form of the stable states:

$$y_0 = x_2 \bar{\lambda}_0 \vee \bar{x}_2 \bar{\lambda}_1$$
$$y_1 = x_2 \lambda_0 \vee \bar{x}_2 \lambda_1.$$

Variations:

$$\delta^k Y_0 = y_1 y_2 \, \Delta x_2 \vee (\bar{x}_2 \vee \bar{y}_2) \, \delta^k y_1 \vee x_2 y_1 \, \delta^k y_2 \vee y_2 \, \Delta x_2 \, \delta^k y_1 \vee$$
$$y_1 \, \Delta x_2 \, \delta^k y_2 \vee x_2 \, \delta^k y_1 \, \delta^k y_2 \vee \Delta x_2 \, \delta^k y_1 \, \delta^k y_2$$
$$\delta^k Y_1 = y_0 y_3 \, \Delta x_2 \vee (\bar{x}_2 \vee \bar{y}_3) \, \delta^k y_0 \vee x_2 y_0 \, \delta^k y_3 \vee y_3 \, \Delta x_2 \, \delta^k y_0 \vee$$
$$y_0 \, \Delta x_2 \, \delta^k y_3 \vee x_2 \, \delta^k y_0 \, \delta^k y_3 \vee \Delta x_2 \, \delta^k y_0 \, \delta^k y_3.$$

Result of the stabilization phase

$$\delta^2 Y_0 = \delta^2 Y_1$$
$$= (x_0 x_1 \vee x_1 x_2 \bar{\lambda}_0 \vee x_0 x_2 \, \lambda_0) \, \Delta x_2 \vee (x_1 \vee \bar{x}_0 \lambda_0 \vee x_2 \lambda_0) \, \Delta x_0 \, \Delta x_2 \vee$$
$$(x_0 \vee \bar{x}_1 \bar{\lambda}_0 \vee x_2 \bar{\lambda}_0) \, \Delta x_1 \, \Delta x_2 \vee \Delta x_0 \, \Delta x_1 \, \Delta x_2.$$

The above equations are then used to build the difference next-state table in Figure 7.11 for the rs synchronized flip-flop. Figure 7.11 reproduces only that part of the difference table representing any single input change and the multiple input change in the variables x_0 and x_1. The parameters of Figure 7.11 which appear in the hazard-containing transitions satisfy the following relations:

$$\alpha = (D_4 < D_3) \vee (D_3 < D_4) \, (D_4 < D_1 + D_3) \, (D_4 < D_2 + D_3) \vee$$
$$(D_2 < D_1) \, (D_2 + D_3 < D_4) \, (D_4 < D_1 + D_3) \vee (D_2 < D_1) \, (D_1 + D_3 < D_4)$$
$$(D_4 < D_0 + D_3) \vee$$
$$(D_1 < D_2) \, (D_1 + D_3 < D_4) \, (D_4 < D_2 + D_3) \, (D_2 + D_3 < D_1 + D_4)$$
$$(D_1 < D_0) \vee$$
$$(D_1 < D_2) \, (D_1 + D_3 < D_4) \, (D_4 < D_3 + D_2) \, (D_1 < D_0)$$
$$(D_1 + D_4 < D_2 + D_3) \vee$$
$$(D_1 < D_2) \, (D_2 + D_3 < D_4) \, (D_1 + D_4 < D_0 + D_2 + D_3)$$

	$\Delta x_0\,\Delta x_1\,\Delta x_2$			
	001	010	100	110
$x_0^s x_1^s x_2^s . y_0^s y_1^s y_2^s y_3^s$				
000.0110	001.1010	010.0101	100.0110	110.0111
000.0101	001.0101	010.0101	100.0110	110.0111
000.1010	001.1010	010.1001	100.1010	110.1011
000.1001	001.0101	010.1001	100.1010	100.1011
001.0101	000.0101	011.0101	101.0101	111.0101
001.1010	000.1010	011.1010	101.1010	111.1010
011.0101	010.0101	001.0101	111.0101	101.0101
011.1010	$010.\alpha\bar{\alpha}01$	001.1010	111.1001	101.1010
010.0101	011.0101	000.0101	110.0111	100.0110
010.1001	011.0101	000.1001	110.1011	100.1010
110.0111	$111.\beta\bar{\beta}\beta\bar{\beta}$	100.0110	010.0101	$000.01\beta\bar{\beta}$
110.1011	$111.\beta\bar{\beta}\beta\bar{\beta}$	100.1010	010.1001	$000.10\beta\bar{\beta}$
111.0101	$110.\gamma\bar{\gamma}11$	101.0101	011.0101	001.0101
111.1010	$110.\delta\bar{\delta}11$	101.1010	011.1010	001.1010
101.0101	$100.\epsilon\bar{\epsilon}10$	111.0101	001.0101	011.0101
101.1010	100.1010	111.1010	001.1010	011.1010
100.0110	101.0110	110.0111	000.0110	010.0101
100.1010	101.1010	110.1011	000.1010	010.1001

Figure 7.11. Difference next-state table for the network of Figure 7.10

$$\beta = D_3 < D_2$$
$$\gamma = (D_0 + D_2 < D_4)\,(D_1 < D_0)$$
$$\delta = (D_4 < D_3) \vee (D_3 < D_4)\,(D_4 < D_1 + D_2) \vee (D_1 + D_3 < D_4)\,(D_1 < D_0)$$
$$\begin{aligned}\epsilon = {} & (D_3 < D_0)\,(D_0 + D_2 < D_4)\,[(D_0 + D_1 + D_2 < D_4) \vee (D_4 < D_0 + D_1 + D_2) \\ & (D_1 + D_2 < D_4)] \vee (D_0 < D_3)\,(D_0 + D_2 < D_4)\,(D_4 < D_2 + D_3) \\ & [(D_1 < D_0)\,(D_1 + D_4 < D_3 + D_2) \vee (D_3 + D_2 < D_0)\,(D_3 + D_2 < D_1) \\ & (D_1 < D_0)] \vee (D_0 < D_3)\,(D_3 + D_2 < D_4)\,[(D_1 + D_2 + D_3 < D_4) \vee \\ & (D_4 < D_1 + D_2 + D_3)\,(D_1 + D_2 + D_3 < D_0 + D_4)].\end{aligned}$$

7.3.3.5. Fault detection in asynchronous switching circuits

The purpose of this section is to develop a fault detection procedure for asynchronous sequential networks which is based on the difference next-state table representation of the network. It will be assumed in this section that the reader is familiar with the vocabulary relative to state-identification and fault-detection experiments of finite-state machines (see, for example, Kohavi [1970] pp. 407–435).

Fault-detection experiments are generally performed through the use of homing and distinguishing input sequences whose definition is recalled below.

Definition 7.8. (a) An input sequence H is said to be a *homing sequence* if the final stable state of the sequential network can be determined uniquely from the network's response (or output state) to H, regardless of the initial stable state.

(b) An input sequence D is said to be a *distinguishing sequence* if the network's response to D is different for each initial stable state.

Assume the sequential network is available to the experimenter as a *black box*, which means that he has access to its input and output terminals (which are thus the observable signals fo the network) but cannot inspect the internal devices and their interconnections. The experiments thus consist of a set of input sequences and their corresponding output sequences. In addition, it will be assumed that the number of stable states does not increase under fault conditions.

According to Kohavi [1970] each fault-detection experiment can be summarized as follows:

Algorithm 7.2. (a) A fault-detection experiment starts with a homing sequence, followed by the appropriate transfer sequence, so as to manoeuvre the network to an initial pre-specified state.

(b) The network is next supplied with an input sequence which causes it to visit each state and to display its response to the distinguishing sequence.

(c) Finally, the network is made to go through every possible transition between two states, and in each case the transition is verified by displaying its response to the distinguishing sequence.

The following remarks must be done about this algorithm:

The algorithm 7.2 was formulated by Kohavi for synchronous networks. This is mainly due to the fact that the natural way to describe a synchronous network is the difference next-state table. Now the homing and distinguishing sequences, upon which the algorithm is based, can be built in a relatively easy way when starting from the difference next-state table; the level next-state table is less appropriate for deriving these sequences.

Since the network is viewed as a black box, the class of faults that can be detected by applying algorithm 7.2 is larger than the class of stuck-at-faults defined for combinational networks.

The algorithm 7.2 will be illustrated by means of the following example 7.8.

Example 7.8. Consider the asynchronous sequential network described by its next-state function:

$$Y = y\bar{x}_1 \vee x_1 x_0.$$

From the equation

$$y^s \oplus (y^s \bar{x}_1 \vee x_1 x_0) = 0$$

one deduces that the stable states y^s are obtained by giving the values 0 and 1 to x_0, x_1 and λ in the relation

$$y^s = x_1 x_0 \vee \lambda \bar{x}_1.$$

The difference next-state function is then:

$$Y = (x_1 x_0 \vee \lambda \bar{x}_1) \oplus x_1 \; \Delta x_0 \oplus \bar{x}_1 (x_0 \oplus \lambda) \; \Delta x_1 \oplus \Delta x_0 \; \Delta x_1.$$

The next-state table and difference next-state table are presented in Figures 7.12(a) and (b) respectively.

y \ $x_1 x_0$	00	01	11	10
0	$\underline{0}$	$\underline{0}$	1	$\underline{0}$
1	$\underline{1}$	$\underline{1}$	$\underline{1}$	0

(a) Next-state table

$x_1^s x_0^s, y^s$ \ $\Delta x_1 \Delta x_0$	01	11	10
00, 0	01, 0	11, 1	10, 0
01, 0	00, 0	10, 0	11, 1
11, 1	10, 0	00, 1	01, 1
01, 1	00, 1	10, 0	11, 1
00, 1	01, 1	11, 1	10, 0
10, 0	11, 1	01, 1	00, 0

(b) Difference next-state table

Figure 7.12

In order to simplify the notations, we shall designate the binary observable responses (which are the total states $x_1 x_0 y$ in our example) by decimal numbers, i.e. 000 will be designated by 1; 010 by 2; 111 by 3; 011 by 4; 001 by 5 and 100 by 6. Suppose that the fault-free detection experiment is designed so that state 1 is the initial state to which it is necessary to transfer the network. To this end we apply the homing sequence $d_1 = (\Delta x_1 = 1, \Delta x_0 = 0)$ and observe the response

1. If the response is 100, the network is in state 6. Apply the transfer sequence $T(6 \to 1) = d_0$ to transfer the network to state 1 ($d_0 = (\Delta x_1 = 0, \Delta x_0 = 1)$).
2. If it is 000, the network is in state 1.
3. If it is 111, the network is in state 3; apply the transfer sequence $T(3 \to 1) = d_0, d_1$. (Part (a))
4. If it is 011, the network is in state 4; apply the transfer sequence $T(4 \to 1) = d_1, d_0, d_1$.

This terminates part (a) of the fault-detection experiment. The sequence d_0 is a distinguishing experiment for the network. Part (b) of the fault-detection experiment can be achieved as follows:

Input:		d_0	d_0	d_1	d_0	d_0	d_0	d_1	d_0	d_0	d_0
State:	1	$\underline{2}$	$\underline{1}$	6	$\underline{3}$	$\underline{6}$	3	4	$\underline{5}$	$\underline{4}$	5

(Part (b))

The above sequence thus verifies the existence of at least six states by means of the six different underlined observable output sequences as response to the same input sequence d_0. The last input sequence d_0 guarantees that the network terminates in state 5. To complete the experiment, it is now necessary to verify each state transition. Up to this point, the remaining transitions to be verified are: $(2 \to 3)$; $(5 \to 6)$; $(6 \to 1)$; $(4 \to 3)$. Each transition will be checked by applying the suitable transfer sequence followed each by the distinguishing sequence.

The experiment is then achieved as follows:

Input:		d_1	d_0	d_0	d_1	d_0	d_1	d_0	d_0	d_1	d_1	d_0
State:	5	6	3	6	1	2	3	6	3	4	3	6
Transition checking:		$(5 \to 6)$			$(6 \to 1)$		$(2 \to 3)$				$(4 \to 3)$.	

(Part (c))

The fault-detection method outlined above may be found in the papers by Ashkinazy [1970] and Thayse [1972b]; it applies to any asynchronous network having at least one distinguishing sequence. Fault-detection experiments for networks, which do not have any distinguishing sequence, exist (see, for example, Hennie [1964]); it is however beyond the scope of this book to deal with these too specialized questions.

We have assumed until now that the asynchronous network was available to the experimenter as a black box. The testing experiment described precedently distinguishes the given m-state network from all possible p-state networks ($p \leqslant m$). Kohavi [1970] shows that the class of networks into which the given network can be transformed, as a result of stuck-fault type, form a subset of the set of all $p \leqslant m$-state networks. An expected result of this is that the testing of a network whose internal structure is known will result in a shorter experiment than the testing of a network whose model is a black box.

Let us assume that the sequential asynchronous network is given by means of its logical scheme. One has first to determine the minimum number of state variables of the network in order to be able to write its next-state functions. Let us consider example 7.8, a realization of which is given in Figure 7.13; the minimum number of state variables is 1 and each of the arcs 7 or 8 may be associated with the state variable. The determination of the state variables allows us to obtain the next-state functions and, consequently, the difference next-state table can be built. Let us now perform parts (a) and (b) of the testing experiment of algorithm 7.2. It is apparent that stuck-faults in the arcs likely to be associated with state variables cause the number of states of the network to decrease. Consequently, this type of faults will be detected in part (b) of the experiment in which one identifies the m distinct states of the network. For example, that part of the experiment would detect any stuck-fault in the arcs 1 and 2 of the example of Figure 7.13. Thus the only faults that are still to be checked are the stuck-faults in the remaining arcs of the combinational part of the sequential network.

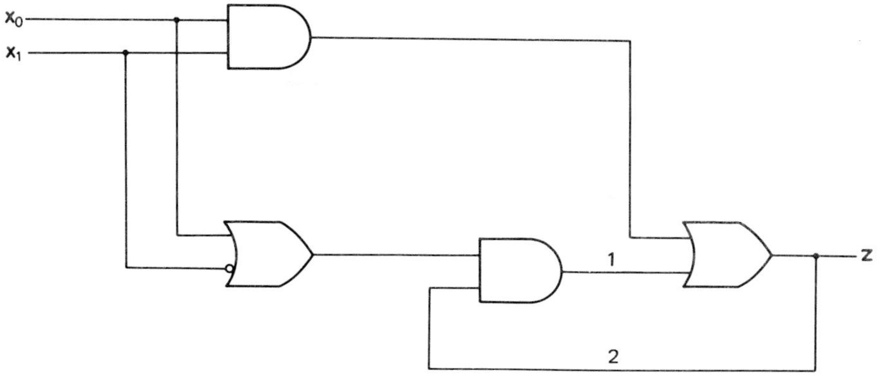

Figure 7.13. Asynchronous sequential network

Let us illustrate this by continuing example 7.8 realized by means of the logical scheme 7.13. Parts (a) and (b) of the test procedure remain valid, while part (c) may be performed by means of the following difference test functions:

$$x_2 \, \Delta x_0 \;\; = 1$$

$$\bar{y} x_0 \, \Delta x_1 = 1$$

which are equivalent to the following sequence

Input:		d_1	d_0	d_0	d_1	d_0	d_1	(Part (c′))
State:	5	6	3	6	1	2	3	

Evidently the sequence of part (c′) is shorter than that of part (c).

The following remark must be made concerning the test procedure described above; these test procedures cannot always directly be applied to the combinational part of the sequential network in the way suggested. Indeed, part of the state $\boldsymbol{y}$ (considered also as an input vector for fault detection) and part of the next-state vector $\boldsymbol{Y}$ (considered also as an output vector for fault-detection) are generally not available to the experimenter. Thus, in general, the procedure of applying a set of input variations and observing the output response is not always applicable. Kohavi [1969] suggests the following procedure to overcome this drawback: although it is impossible to apply directly an input combination to the combinational part of the network and observe the output response, it is possible to perform the test indirectly. In other words, since we cannot use inputs $\boldsymbol{y}$ and outputs $\boldsymbol{Y}$ in real time, we will force through the inputs $\boldsymbol{x}$ a desired input combination $\boldsymbol{y}$ and instead of observing the output response $\boldsymbol{Y}$, we will identify it by observing its response to a distinguishing sequence.

Chapter 8

The Optimal Covering Problem

We introduce this chapter by stating two problems; the first is chosen in switching theory and the second in automata theory.

Consider a switching function f and the set of its prime implicants: $m_1, m_2, \ldots, m_q$. The function f can be written as the disjunction of all its prime implicants (theorem 1.15). However, in many cases f can be written as the disjunction of only a subset of its prime implicants; it can indeed happen that some prime implicant, say m_k, be included in the disjunction of some other prime implicants. Suppose for instance that

$$m_k \leqslant m_1 \vee \ldots \vee m_{k-1};$$

then any representation of f as a disjunction of some of its prime implicants among which lie $m_1, \ldots, m_{k-1}$ and m_k is redundant, i.e. the implicant m_k may be deleted.

One of the main problems studied in switching theory is to find representations of f as the disjunction of a minimum number of its prime implicants; the problem may be stated as follows:

Find a subset M' of $M = \{m_1, \ldots, m_q\}$ such that

(a) for every point where f takes the value 1, there exists at least one prime implicant in M' that also takes the value 1;
(b) the number of elements in M' is as small as possible.

One could also associate with every prime implicant of f some cost, for instance the number of complemented and uncomplemented variables it contains. Then, point (b) can be replaced by:

(b′) the cost of M' is as small as possible,

where the cost of M' is defined as being the sum of the costs of its elements.

This is an example of covering problem: one has to "cover" the 1's of f by means of the prime implicants of f, while minimizing some cost function.

As a second example, consider a finite automaton $\langle \Sigma, \Theta, S, \delta, \lambda \rangle$, where S is the set of states, Σ the input alphabet, Θ the output alphabet, δ the transition function that maps a subset of $S \times \Sigma$ into S, and λ the output function that maps a subset of $S \times \Sigma$ into Θ.

Two states s_i and s_j of S are compatible iff they are not distinguishable by any finite length input word, i.e. there exists no finite length input word w such that the automaton produces two different output letters when applying to it the word w either in starting state s_i or in starting state s_j.

A compatibility class is a set of states that are pairwise compatible.

Consider now a compatibility class C; with C and with the input letter σ one associates a new class $\Delta(C, \sigma)$ defined as follows:

$$\Delta(C, \sigma) = \{s' \in S \mid \exists\, s \in C\colon \delta(s, \sigma) = s'\}.$$

A set $\{C_1, \ldots, C_r\}$ of compatibility classes is closed iff for every i in $\{1, \ldots, r\}$, and for every σ in Σ, there exists j in $\{1, \ldots, r\}$ such that

$$\Delta(C_i, \sigma) \subseteq C_j.$$

The solution of the following problem plays a key role in automata theory:

Find a set D of compatibility classes such that

(a) every element of S appears in at least one compatibility class of D;
(b) D is closed;
(c) the number of elements in D is as small as possible.

This is an example of covering-closure problem: one must "cover" the states of the automaton by means of a "closed" set of compatibility classes, while minimizing some cost function.

This chapter is devoted to the study of these two types of problems: the covering problem (8.1) and the covering-closure problem (8.2).

The first subsection (8.1.1) gives the general statement of the covering problem and its translation in Boolean, pseudo-Boolean and tabular form. The subsection 8.1.2 describes some methods for solving the covering problem. The subsection 8.1.3 is devoted to the covering of a switching function by means of its prime implicants.

The subsection 8.2.1 gives the general statement of the covering-closure problem and its translation in Boolean, pseudo-Boolean and tabular form. The subsection 8.2.2 gives some general methods of solution, while the subsection 8.2.3 is devoted to the covering of the states of an automaton by means of compatibility classes.

8.1. The covering problem

8.1.1. General statement

Consider the finite sets

$$A = \{a_0, \ldots, a_{n-1}\}$$

and

$$B = \{b_0, \ldots, b_{m-1}\},$$

and a binary relation $R \subseteq A \times B$. Associate with every element a of A a positive real number $c(a)$ that is the *cost* of a. The *optimal covering problem* can be stated as follows:

Find a subset A' of A such that

(a) A' *covers* B, i.e. $R(A') = B$;
(b) A' has a minimum cost $c(A') = \sum_{a \in A'} c(a)$.

We may associate with every element a_i of A a binary variable x_i:

$$x_i \in \{0, 1\}, \quad \forall\, i = 0, \ldots, n-1.$$

Every subset A' of A can thus be characterized by an n-tuple $(x_0, \ldots, x_{n-1})$ defined as follows:

$$\begin{aligned} x_i &= 1 \quad \text{if} \quad a_i \in A', \\ &= 0 \quad \text{otherwise.} \end{aligned}$$

On the other hand, define an $n \times m$ matrix $[r_{ij}]$ by

$$\begin{aligned} r_{ij} &= 1 \quad \text{if} \quad (a_i, b_j) \in R, \\ &= 0 \quad \text{otherwise,} \end{aligned}$$

$\forall\, i = 0, \ldots, n-1$ and $j = 0, \ldots, m-1$.

The subsets A' for which the condition (a) holds are those that are characterized by an n-tuple $(x_0, \ldots, x_{n-1})$ such that

$$\sum_{i=0}^{n-1} r_{ij} x_i \geqslant 1, \quad \forall\, j = 0, \ldots, m-1.$$

Indeed, this last condition means that for every b_j in B there exists at least one a_i in A such that $r_{ij} = 1$, i.e. such that $(a_i, b_j) \in R$.

The cost of A' is equal to

$$\sum_{i=0}^{n-1} c(a_i) x_i.$$

In the sequel, one uses the notation c_i instead of $c(a_i)$. The covering problem can now be stated in pseudo-Boolean form:

Minimize the cost function

$$c = \sum_{i=0}^{n-1} c_i x_i \tag{8.1}$$

under the m constraints

$$\sum_{i=0}^{x-1} r_{ij} x_i \geqslant 1, \quad \forall\, j = 0, \ldots, m-1. \tag{8.2}$$

The constraints may also be formulated in Boolean form:

$$\bigvee_{i=0}^{n-1} (r_{ij} \wedge x_i) = 1, \quad \forall\, j = 0, \ldots, m-1. \tag{8.2 bis}$$

It is also classical to represent the constraints in tabular form. For that purpose, one draws a rectangular table with n rows and m columns; the column j that corresponds to the element b_j of B has a *cross* in every row i corresponding to an element a_i of A such that $(a_i, b_j) \in R$. In other words, the table is directly deduced from the matrix $[r_{ij}]$ by indexing the rows and columns by means of the elements of A and B, respectively, by replacing the 1's by crosses and by deleting the 0's.

If a column j has a cross in row i, one then says that the row i covers the column j. The problem is thus to find a family of rows such that every column is covered by at least one of these rows.

8.1.2. General methods of solution

Suppose thus that one has to minimize the cost function (8.1) under the m constraints (8.2) or (8.2 bis).

The first natural question is clearly whether the constraints can be satisfied or not. The answer is given by the next theorem.

Theorem 8.1. The constraints (8.2) can be satisfied iff

$$\sum_{i=0}^{n-1} r_{ij} \geqslant 1$$

for every $j = 0, \ldots, m-1$.

In terms of constraint table this last condition is that every column must have at least one cross and is thus covered by at least one row. We now give some rules that allow deletion of some rows or columns in the constraint table.

Definitions 8.1. If for some $k \in \{0, \ldots, m-1\}$ one has

$$r_{lk} = 1 \quad \text{and} \quad r_{ik} = 0, \quad \forall i \neq l,$$

then the row l is an *essential row*. That means that there exists a column k in which appears only one cross in position l.

The column k *dominates* the column k' iff

$$r_{ik} \geqslant r_{ik'}, \quad \forall i = 0, \ldots, n-1.$$

That means that with each cross in column k' is associated a corresponding cross in column k.

The row l *dominates* the row l' iff

$$r_{lj} \geqslant r_{l'j}, \quad \forall j = 0, \ldots, m-1$$

and

$$c_l < c_{l'}.$$

The row l *weakly dominates* the row l' iff

$$r_{lj} \geqslant r_{l'j}, \quad \forall j = 0, \ldots, m-1$$

and

$$c_l \leqslant c_{l'}.$$

The various simplification rules are summarized by the next theorem.

Theorem 8.2. (a) *If the row l is essential, then in every solution of (8.2) x_l is equal to 1. Furthermore every column that has a cross in position l may be deleted from the constraint table.*

(b) *If the column k dominates the column k', then the column k may be deleted.*

(c) *If the row l dominates the row l', then the row l' may be deleted. In every minimum cost solution, $x_{l'} = 0$.*

(d) *If the row l weakly dominates the row l', and if one searches for only one minimum cover (and not for all minimum covers), then the row l' may be deleted. There exists a minimum cost solution with $x_{l'} = 0$.*

Proof. (a) If the row l is essential, there exists k such that

$$r_{lk} = 1 \quad \text{and} \quad r_{ik} = 0, \quad \forall i \neq l;$$

the constraint corresponding to the column k then becomes

$$x_l \geqslant 1$$

and thus, in every solution, x_l is equal to 1. Furthermore, suppose that for some k' one has $r_{lk'} = 1$; the constraint corresponding to column k' is then always satisfied once one has chosen the value 1 for x_l.

(b) It is obvious that every row that covers the column k' also covers the column k. Since in every solution there must exist a row that covers the column k', the constraint corresponding to column k is no longer necessary.

(c) Consider a solution to the constraints in which $x_{l'} = 1$. By putting $x_{l'} = 0$ and $x_l = 1$ one has also a solution to the constraints since every column covered by the row l' is also covered by the row l. Furthermore, the solution with $x_{l'} = 1$ cannot have a minimum cost since $c_{l'} > c_l$.

(d) The proof is similar to that of (c). ∎

It is interesting to note that if the initial problem is consistent, i.e. if the condition of theorem 8.1 is satisfied, then the rules indicated in theorem 8.2 yield simpler consistent problems. A repeated use of these simplification rules can thus be the first step of any optimal covering algorithm. At the end of this first step one obtains a constraint table in which none of the simplification rules may be applied. Such a table is called *cyclic*.

We now describe a Boolean method that allows to minimize (8.1) under the constraints (8.2 bis). First, we need the following definition.

Definition 8.2. A subset A' of A that covers B, and such that none of its proper subsets covers B, is an *irredundant cover* of B.

The Boolean method is based on the two following propositions.

Lemma 8.1. Every cover of minimum cost is an irredundant cover. ■

Lemma 8.2. A subset A' is an irredundant cover of B iff the conjunction

$$\bigwedge_{i:a_i\in A'} x_i$$

is a prime implicant of the switching function r defined by

$$r(x_0, \ldots, x_{n-1}) = \bigwedge_{j=0}^{m-1} \left[\bigvee_{i=0}^{n-1} (r_{ij} \wedge x_i)\right].$$

Proof. A subset A' covers B iff the corresponding n-tuple $(x_0, \ldots, x_{n-1})$ is a solution of each of the m Boolean equations (8.2 bis), i.e. if it is a solution of the equation

$$r(x_0, \ldots, x_{n-1}) = 1,$$

i.e. iff the conjunction

$$\bigwedge_{i:\, a_i \in A'} x_i$$

is an implicant of r. Furthermore, it is obvious that to an irredundant cover corresponds a prime implicant, and conversely. ■

Taking into account theorem 1.16 and the fact that r is given as a conjunction of variables, one concludes that the prime implicants of r may be simply computed as follows: transform the conjunction of disjunctions in a disjunction of conjunctions (by using the distributivity law), and delete the implicants that are contained in other implicants.

It is interesting to note that the rules (a) and (b) of theorem 8.2 have an obvious Boolean interpretation: in case (a), the function r admits x_l as factor, and thus x_l appears in every prime implicant of r. The case (b) is based on the following remark: if

$$r_{ik} \geqslant r_{ik'}, \quad \forall i = 0, \ldots, n-1,$$

then

$$\bigvee_{i=0}^{n-1} (r_{ik} \wedge x_i) \geqslant \bigvee_{i=0}^{n-1} (r_{ik'} \wedge x_i),$$

and thus

$$\left[\bigvee_{i=0}^{n-1} (r_{ik} \wedge x_i)\right] \wedge \left[\bigvee_{i=0}^{n-1} (r_{ik'} \wedge x_i)\right] = \bigvee_{i=0}^{n-1} (r_{ik'} \wedge x_i).$$

The Boolean method thus runs as follows.

Algorithm 8.1. Step 1. Compute the prime implicants of r. As noted above it suffices for that to use the distributivity law and delete the implicants that are not maximal.

Step 2. For every prime implicant $x_{i_1} \wedge \ldots \wedge x_{i_h}$ of r, compute the cost

$$c_{i_1} + \ldots + c_{i_h};$$

that is in fact the cost of the subset $\{a_{i_1}, \ldots, a_{i_h}\}$ of A.

Step 3. Delete the prime implicants the cost of which is not minimum.

To every prime implicant obtained at the end of step 3 corresponds a cover of B with minimum cost.

Example 8.1. Let us illustrate the various simplification rules on the constraint table of Figure 8.1.

	0	1	2	3	4	5	6	7
0	×	×		×	×			
1		×	×	×				
2			×			×	×	
3				×	×			×
4		×	×					
5			×	×				
6			×			×		
7			×				×	
8						×	×	
9				×				×
10	×						×	
11						×		

Figure 8.1. Initial constraint table

The various costs are:

$$c(a_0) = 2, c(a_1) = 3, c(a_2) = 2, c(a_3) = 2, c(a_4) = 2, c(a_5) = 3, c(a_6) = 3,$$
$$c(a_7) = 1, c(a_8) = 1, c(a_9) = 3, c(a_{10}) = 3, c(a_{11}) = 3.$$

Column 3 dominates column 4; one may thus delete column 3 and this gives the table of Figure 8.2.

	0	1	2	4	5	6	7
0	X	X		X			
1		X	X				
2			X		X	X	
3				X			X
4		X	X				
5			X				
6			X		X		
7			X			X	
8					X	X	
9							X
10	X					X	
11					X		

Figure 8.2. Simplified constraint table (1)

Taking into account the value of the costs associated with the rows of the table of Figure 8.2, one may verify that:

row 4 dominates row 1,

row 3 dominates row 5,

row 2 dominates row 6,

row 2 dominates row 11,

row 3 dominates row 9.

This allows to delete rows 1, 5, 6, 9 and 11; one so obtains the table of Figure 8.3.

	0	1	2	4	5	6	7
0	X	X		X			
2			X		X	X	
3				X			X
4		X	X				
7			X			X	
8					X	X	
10	X					X	

Figure 8.3. Simplified constraint table (2)

In the table of Figure 8.3, row 3 is essential being the only row that covers column 7. Therefore a_3 belongs to every minimum solution; one may delete row 3, column 4 and column 7. The new constraint table is given in Figure 8.4.

	0	1	2	5	6
0	×	×			
2			×	×	×
4		×	×		
7			×		×
8				×	×
10	×				×

Figure 8.4. Simplified constraint table (3)

In the table of Figure 8.4, column 6 that dominates column 5 may be deleted and that yields the table of Figure 8.5 in which row 0 dominates row 10. By deleting this last row, one obtains the table of Figure 8.6 in which row 0 is essential. Therefore, a_0 belongs to every minimum solution; one may delete row 0, column 0 and column 1, and so obtain the table of Figure 8.7.

	0	1	2	5
0	×	×		
2			×	×
4		×	×	
7			×	
8				×
10	×			

Figure 8.5

	0	1	2	5
0	×	×		
2			×	×
4		×	×	
7			×	
8				×

Figure 8.6

	2	5
2	×	×
4	×	
7	×	
8		×

Figure 8.7

Simplified constraint tables (4), (5) and (6)

In the table of Figure 8.7, row 7 dominates row 4 and may thus be deleted; one so obtains the cyclic table of Figure 8.8.

	2	5
2	×	×
7	×	
8		×

Figure 8.8 Cyclic table

This very simple constraint table can be solved by the Boolean method; one must find the prime implicants of the switching function

$$r(x_2, x_7, x_8) = (x_2 \vee x_7)(x_2 \vee x_8).$$

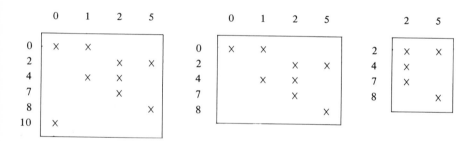

There are two prime implicants

$$x_2 \quad \text{and} \quad x_7x_8$$

and both have a cost equal to 2.

The two minimum cost solutions of the covering problem are thus:

$$\{a_0, a_2, a_3\} \quad \text{and} \quad \{a_0, a_3, a_7, a_8\}.$$

Their cost is equal to 6.

Many other methods exist for the determination of minimum covers. Among others, it is interesting to note that the problem of minimizing (8.1) under the m constraints (8.2) is an integer linear program that can be solved by classical methods of operation research; as proven by the next proposition, it is not necessary in that case to add constraints like

$$x_i \leqslant 1, \quad \forall i = 0, \ldots, n-1.$$

Lemma 8.3. Every positive integer solution of (8.2) that minimize (8.1) is composed of 0's and 1's.

Proof. Suppose that $(e_0, \ldots, e_{n-1})$ is a positive integer solution of (8.2), and that for some l in $\{0, \ldots, n-1\}$ one has: $e_l \neq 0$ and $e_l \neq 1$. Since by hypothesis e_l is a positive integer, it is greater than or equal to 2. Now, taking into account the fact that the second member of each inequation in (8.2) is equal to 1 and that r_{ij} is either 0 or 1, it is clear that putting $x_l = 1$ and $x_i = e_i$, $\forall i \neq l$, also yields a solution; furthermore the cost of that new solution is smaller than the cost of the previous solution. ∎

Methods based on linear programming have been proposed by Cobham *et al.* [1961], Balinski [1965] and Goethals [1965]. Among the authors of methods based on restricted enumeration, let us quote Balas [1965], Breuer [1972] and Kohler and Steiglitz [1974].

In the case of large covering problems, it could become impractical to use a method giving a minimum cost solution due to the computational time and to the memory space required for that purpose. That is the reason why several authors have designed methods that give solutions with a quasi-minimum cost, in a reasonable computational time. Let us quote Roth [1969], Lin [1970], Batni *et al.* [1974], Das [1971], Bubenik [1972], Bowman and McVey [1970] and Servit [1975].

We now describe a little known method, due to Fosséprez and Noé [1966] that is based on a restricted enumeration. Consider the sets A and B, and the binary relation R defined above. Introduce first the following definitions.

Definitions 8.3. Let A^* be a subset of A. The subset A' of A^* is *admissible* in A^* iff

$$R(A') \cup R(A \backslash A^*) = B.$$

The subset A' of A *dominates* the subset A'' of A iff

$$R(A') \supseteq R(A'')$$

and

$$c(A') < c(A'').$$

The subset A' of A *weakly dominates* the subset A'' of A iff

$$R(A') \supseteq R(A'')$$

and

$$c(A') \leqslant c(A'').$$

There is an obvious relation between these definitions and the definitions 8.1: row l is essential iff the empty set is not admissible in $\{a_l\}$; row l (weakly) dominates row l' iff the subset $\{a_l\}$ (weakly) dominates the subset $\{a_{l'}\}$.

A subset A' of A^* is *optimal* in A^* iff there is no other subset of A^* that dominates A'. A subset of A^* that is both admissible in A^* and optimal in A^* is called *optimal admissible* in A^*.

The method is based upon the following theorem.

Theorem 8.3. (a) *The subset A' of A is a solution of the optimal covering problem iff it is optimal admissible in A.*

(b) *The optimal covering problem admits a solution iff the empty set is admissible in the empty set.*

(c) *If A' is optimal admissible in A^*, and if A^{**} is a subset of A^*, then $A' \cap A^{**}$ is optimal admissible in A^{**}.*

Proof. (a) If A' is optimal admissible in A that means that

$$R(A') \cup R(A \backslash A) = R(A') = B$$

and that no other subset of A has the same property while having a smaller cost.

(b) If ϕ is admissible in ϕ then

$$R(\phi) \cup R(A \backslash \phi) = R(A) = B.$$

(c) Denote

$$A_1' = A' \cap A^{**} \quad \text{and} \quad A_0' = A' \cap (A^* \backslash A^{**}).$$

One has thus:

$$A' = A_1' \cup A_0' \quad \text{and} \quad A_1' \cap A_0' = \phi.$$

We first prove that A_1' is admissible in A^{**}:

$$\begin{aligned} R(A_1') \cup R(A \backslash A^{**}) &= R(A_1') \cup R(A \backslash A^*) \cup R(A^* \backslash A^{**}) \\ &\supseteq R(A_1') \cup R(A \backslash A^*) \cup R(A_0') \\ &= R(A') \cup R(A \backslash A^*) = B. \end{aligned}$$

Suppose now that A_1' is dominated by $A_2' \subseteq A^{**}$, i.e.

$$R(A_1') \subseteq R(A_2')$$

and

$$c(A_1') > c(A_2').$$

But then one has

$$R(A_2' \cup A_0') \supseteq R(A_1' \cup A_0') = R(A')$$

and

$$c(A_2' \cup A_0') = c(A_2') + c(A_0') < c(A_1') + c(A_0') = c(A');$$

therefore A' is dominated by $A_2' \cup A_0'$ in A^* and that contradicts the fact that A' is optimal admissible in A^*. ■

In the particular case where $A^* = A^{**} \cup \{a_l\}$ for some l in $\{0, \ldots, n-1\}$, there are two cases:

1. if A' is optimal admissible in A^* and if $a_l \in A'$, then $A' \backslash \{a_l\}$ is optimal admissible in A^{**};
2. if A' is optimal admissible in A^* and if $a_l \notin A'$, then A' is also optimal admissible in A^{**}.

Therefore, in this particular case, one can easily compute the list $L(A^*)$ of all the subsets of A^* that are optimal admissible in A^* from the knowledge of the list $L(A^{**})$ of all the subsets of A^{**} that are optimal admissible in A^{**}: suppose that

$$L(A^{**}) = (X_1, X_2, \ldots, X_s)$$

and put

$$Y_k = X_k \cup \{a_l\}, \qquad \forall k = 1, \ldots, s.$$

Form now the following list of subsets of A^*:

$$(X_1, \ldots, X_s, Y_1, \ldots, Y_s).$$

It then suffices to delete in that list the subsets that are not admissible in A^* and those that are dominated by other subsets in order to obtain the list $L(A^*)$.

This is in fact the base of the Fosséprez–Noé algorithm.

Algorithm 8.2. One successively computes the lists

$$L(A_0), L(A_1), \ldots, L(A_{n-1})$$

where

$$A_0 = \phi \quad \text{and thus} \quad L(A_0) = (\phi);$$

$$A_i = A_{i-1} \cup \{a_{l(i)}\} \quad \text{where} \quad a_{l(i)} \quad \text{is some element chosen in} \quad A \backslash A_{i-1};$$

$$A_{n-1} = A.$$

The computation is performed in n steps; at the end of step i one has obtained $L(A_{i-1})$; step i then runs as follows:

Step i. Choose an element $a_{l(i)}$ of A that does not lie in A_{i-1}; put $A_i = A_{i-1} \cup \{a_{l(i)}\}$ and compute the list $L(A_i)$ by the method indicated above.

At the end of step n one obtains the list $L(A)$ of all the subsets of A that are optimal admissible in A, i.e. all the solutions of the optimal covering problem.

Some remarks are now justified.

Remarks. 1. The choice of the new element $a_{l(i)}$ at step i can influence the efficiency of the algorithm. The authors have proposed two empirical rules for that choice. Let us quote one of them: choose an element $a_{l(i)}$ such that its entering maximizes the number of elements of B covered by no element of $A \backslash A_i$; then, in case of multiple solution, by only one element of $A \backslash A_i$; then by two, three ... elements of $A \backslash A_i$. It is expected that this rule will produce many non-admissible subsets in A_i among those formed at step i.

2. The authors have proposed some short-cuts in the performing of step i again in order to increase the efficiency of the algorithm.

3. In the case where one looks for only one minimum cost solution, one may use the concept of weak dominance instead of that of dominance.

Example 8.1 (continued). Consider the same covering problem as above, and solve it by the algorithm 8.2.

$A_0 = \phi$; ϕ is admissible in ϕ; $L(A_0) = (\phi)$.

Step 1. $A_1 = \{a_0\}$;

$L(A_1) = (\phi, \{a_0\})$.

Step 2. $A_2 = A_1 \cup \{a_3\} = \{a_0, a_3\}$;

ϕ is not admissible in A_2;

$L(A_2) = (\{a_0\}, \{a_3\}, \{a_0, a_3\})$.

Step 3. $A_3 = A_2 \cup \{a_9\} = \{a_0, a_3, a_9\}$;

$\{a_0\}$ is not admissible in A_3;

$\{a_0, a_9\}$ is dominated by $\{a_0, a_3\}$;

$\{a_3, a_9\}$ is dominated by $\{a_3\}$;

$\{a_0, a_3, a_9\}$ is dominated by $\{a_0, a_3\}$;

$L(A_3) = (\{a_3\}, \{a_0, a_3\})$.

Step 4. $A_4 = A_3 \cup \{a_{10}\} = \{a_0, a_3, a_9, a_{10}\}$;

$\{a_3\}$ is not admissible in A_4;

$L(A_4) = (\{a_0, a_3\}, \{a_3, a_{10}\}, \{a_0, a_3, a_{10}\})$.

Step 5. $A_5 = A_4 \cup \{a_1\} = \{a_0, a_1, a_3, a_9, a_{10}\}$;
$\{a_0, a_1, a_3, a_{10}\}$ is dominated by $\{a_1, a_3, a_{10}\}$;
$L(A_5) = (\{a_0, a_3\}, \{a_3, a_{10}\}, \{a_0, a_3, a_{10}\}, \{a_0, a_1, a_3\}, \{a_1, a_3, a_{10}\})$.

Step 6. $A_6 = A_5 \cup \{a_4\} = \{a_0, a_1, a_3, a_4, a_9, a_{10}\}$;
$\{a_3, a_{10}\}$ is not admissible in A_6;
$\{a_0, a_1, a_3\}$ is dominated by $\{a_0, a_3, a_4\}$;
$\{a_1, a_3, a_{10}\}, \{a_0, a_3, a_4, a_{10}\}, \{a_0, a_1, a_3, a_4\}$ and $\{a_1, a_3, a_4, a_{10}\}$ are dominated by $\{a_3, a_4, a_{10}\}$;
$L(A_6) = (\{a_0, a_3\}, \{a_0, a_3, a_{10}\}, \{a_0, a_3, a_4\}, \{a_3, a_4, a_{10}\})$.

Step 7. $A_7 = A_6 \cup \{a_5\} = \{a_0, a_1, a_3, a_4, a_5, a_9, a_{10}\}$;
$\{a_0, a_3, a_5\}$ and $\{a_0, a_3, a_4, a_5\}$ are dominated by $\{a_0, a_3, a_4\}$;
$\{a_0, a_3, a_5, a_{10}\}$ and $\{a_3, a_4, a_5, a_{10}\}$ are dominated by $\{a_3, a_4, a_{10}\}$;
$L(A_7) = (\{a_0, a_3\}, \{a_0, a_3, a_{10}\}, \{a_0, a_3, a_4\}, \{a_3, a_4, a_{10}\})$.

Step 8. $A_8 = A_7 \cup \{a_2\} = \{a_0, a_1, a_2, a_3, a_4, a_5, a_9, a_{10}\}$;
$\{a_0, a_3, a_{10}\}, \{a_3, a_4, a_{10}\}, \{a_0, a_2, a_3, a_{10}\}, \{a_0, a_2, a_3, a_4\}$ and $\{a_2, a_3, a_4, a_{10}\}$ are dominated by $\{a_0, a_2, a_3\}$;
$L(A_8) = (\{a_0, a_3\}, \{a_0, a_3, a_4\}, \{a_0, a_2, a_3\})$.

Step 9. $A_9 = A_8 \cup \{a_7\} = \{a_0, a_1, a_2, a_3, a_4, a_5, a_7, a_9, a_{10}\}$;
$\{a_0, a_3, a_4, a_7\}$ and $\{a_0, a_2, a_3, a_7\}$ are dominated by $\{a_0, a_2, a_3\}$;
$L(A_9) = (\{a_0, a_3\}, \{a_0, a_3, a_4\}, \{a_0, a_2, a_3\}, \{a_0, a_3, a_7\})$.

Step 10. $A_{10} = A_9 \cup \{a_6\} = \{a_0, a_1, a_2, a_3, a_4, a_5, a_6, a_7, a_9, a_{10}\}$;
$\{a_0, a_3\}$ is not admissible in A_{10};
$\{a_0, a_3, a_6\}, \{a_0, a_3, a_4, a_6\}, \{a_0, a_2, a_3, a_6\}$ and $\{a_0, a_3, a_6, a_7\}$ are dominated by $\{a_0, a_2, a_3\}$;
$L(A_{10}) = (\{a_0, a_3, a_4\}, \{a_0, a_2, a_3\}, \{a_0, a_3, a_7\})$.

Step 11. $A_{11} = A_{10} \cup \{a_8\} = \{a_0, a_1, a_2, a_3, a_4, a_5, a_6, a_7, a_8, a_9, a_{10}\}$;
$\{a_0, a_3, a_4\}$ is not admissible in A_{11};
$\{a_0, a_3, a_4, a_8\}$ and $\{a_0, a_2, a_3, a_8\}$ are dominated by $\{a_0, a_2, a_3\}$;
$L(A_{11}) = (\{a_0, a_2, a_3\}, \{a_0, a_3, a_7\}, \{a_0, a_3, a_7, a_8\})$.

Step 12. $A_{12} = A_{11} \cup \{a_{11}\} = A$;

$\{a_0, a_3, a_7\}$ is not admissible in A;

$\{a_0, a_2, a_3, a_{11}\}$, $\{a_0, a_3, a_7, a_{11}\}$ and $\{a_0, a_3, a_7, a_8, a_{11}\}$ are dominated by $\{a_0, a_2, a_3\}$;

$L(A) = (\{a_0, a_2, a_3\}, \{a_0, a_3, a_7, a_8\})$.

8.1.3. Minimization of discrete functions

Consider an n-variable discrete function f. It can be represented as a disjunction of implicants, i.e. under the form

$$f = \bigvee_{j=0}^{k-1} z_j$$

where

$$z_j = l^{(j)} \wedge x_{n-1}^{(C_{n-1}^{(j)})} \wedge \ldots \wedge x_0^{(C_0^{(j)})}$$

is a cube, a block or a convex block of f. With this disjunctive expression of f can be associated the logic circuit of Figure 8.9 to which can be confered some cost. Let us define two different costs:

(a) the number of gates;
(b) the number of gate inputs.

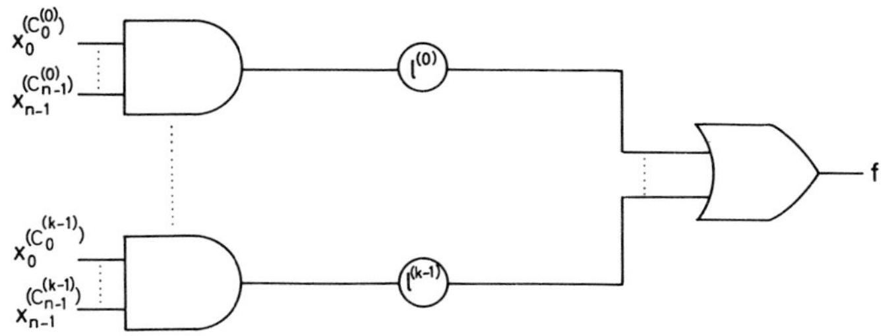

Figure 8.9. Logic circuit realizing a discrete function

Note that if in the circuit of Figure 8.9 one has $C_i^{(j)} = S_i$ for some i and j, then the corresponding AND-gate input wire may be deleted. If furthermore this can be done for all the input wires but one, the corresponding AND-gate itself may be deleted.

For every implicant z_j, denote $t(z_j)$ the number of indices i such $C_i \neq S_i$. Define then the two following cost functions:

(a) $c_1(z_j) = 1$ if $t(z_j) \geqslant 2$,
$\quad = 0$ if $t(z_j) = 0$ or 1.

(b) $c_2(z_j) = t(z_j) + 1$ if $t(z_j) \geqslant 2$,
$= 1$ if $t(z_j) = 0$ or 1.

The number of gates in the circuit of Figure 8.9 is thus

$$\sum_{j=0}^{k-1} c_1(z_j);$$

and the number of gate inputs is

$$\sum_{j=0}^{k-1} c_2(z_j)$$

(except in the trivial case where f itself is a cube and where the OR-gate may be deleted).

Denote now by $M(f)$ the set of the minterms of f, i.e. the set of conjunctions of the type

$$f(e) \wedge x_{n-1}^{(e_{n-1})} \wedge \ldots \wedge x_0^{(e_0)}$$

with $f(e) \neq 0$ and $e = (e_{n-1}, \ldots, e_0) \in S_{n-1} \times \ldots \times S_0$.

Denote also by $Z(f)$ the set of implicants of f; by implicant one means either cube or block or convex block. Define then in a very natural way a binary relation $R(f) \subseteq Z(f) \times M(f)$:

$$(z_i, m_j) \in R(f) \quad \text{iff} \quad z_i \geqslant m_j,$$

where $z_i \in Z(f)$ and $m_j \in M(f)$.

The problem of finding a minimum cost logic realization of f is thus an optimal covering problem; one must find a subset Z' of $Z(f)$ such that

(a) Z' covers $M(f)$;
(b) Z' has a minimum cost $c_1(Z')$ or $c_2(Z')$ according to the chosen cost.

At this point it is interesting to note that if for two implicants z_i and z_j of f one has

$$z_i < z_j$$

then

$$c_1(z_i) \geqslant c_1(z_j), c_2(z_i) \geqslant c_2(z_j)$$

while

$$z_i R(f) \subseteq z_j R(f).$$

In other words, the row corresponding to z_i is weakly dominated by the row corresponding to z_j. For the purpose of obtaining a minimum cost circuit realization of f, one will delete the implicants contained in others and thus only consider the prime implicants of f. For that reason, in the sequel $Z(f)$ will denote the set of prime implicants of f. That simplification would be forbidden for other cost functions violating the above condition, e.g. for the number of complemented literals in the case of switching functions.

Note that if f is a switching function, then $t(z_i)$ is the number of complemented and uncomplemented variables that appear in z_i; furthermore, if $z_i < z_j$, then $c_2(z_i) > c_2(z_j)$ and thus the row corresponding to z_i is dominated by the row corresponding to z_j.

Example 8.2. Consider the function f of example 3.8. It is a ternary function of two quaternary variables the minterms of which are:

$$m_0 = 1 \wedge x_1^{(0)} \wedge x_0^{(1)}, m_1 = 1 \wedge x_1^{(1)} \wedge x_0^{(0)}, m_2 = 2 \wedge x_1^{(1)} \wedge x_0^{(1)}, m_3 = 2 \wedge x_1^{(2)} \wedge x_0^{(0)}, m_4 = 1 \wedge x_1^{(1)} \wedge x_0^{(2)}, m_5 = 2 \wedge x_1^{(2)} \wedge x_0^{(1)}, m_6 = 2 \wedge x_1^{(3)} \wedge x_0^{(0)}, m_7 = 1 \wedge x_1^{(1)} \wedge x_0^{(3)}, m_8 = 2 \wedge x_1^{(3)} \wedge x_0^{(1)}, m_9 = 2 \wedge x_1^{(2)} \wedge x_0^{(3)}, m_{10} = 2 \wedge x_1^{(3)} \wedge x_0^{(3)}.$$

Its prime convex blocks have been computed by the Quine–McCluskey method in section 3.2.3.5:

$$z_0 = 2 \wedge x_1^{[2} \wedge x_0^{[3}, z_1 = 2 \wedge x_1^{[1} \wedge x_0^{[1,1]}, z_2 = 2 \wedge x_1^{[2} \wedge x_0^{1]}, z_3 = 1 \wedge x_1^{[1} \wedge x_0^{[3}, z_4 = 1 \wedge x_0^{[1,1]}, z_5 = 1 \wedge x_1^{[1,1]}, z_6 = 1 \wedge x_1^{[1} \wedge x_0^{1]}.$$

One obtains the constraint table of Figure 8.10.

This constraint table can be directly solved since rows 0, 1, 2, 4 and 5 are essential. They yield the unique solution of the optimal covering problem whatever may be the chosen costs.

The minimum cost representation of f in terms of prime convex blocks is thus

$$f = (2 \wedge x_1^{[2} \wedge x_0^{[3}) \vee (2 \wedge x_1^{[1} \wedge x_0^{[1,1]}) \vee (2 \wedge x_1^{[2} \wedge x_0^{1]}) \vee (1 \wedge x_0^{[1,1]}) \vee (1 \wedge x_1^{[1,1]}).$$

	0	1	2	3	4	5	6	7	8	9	10
0										×	×
1			×			×			×		
2				×		×	×		×		
3								×			
4	×										
5		×			×			×			
6		×									

Figure 8.10. Covering of f by means of its prime convex blocks

We now treat the problem of optimal representation for incompletely specified discrete functions.

Definition 8.4. A function f from a proper non-empty subset S' of $S_{n-1} \times \ldots \times S_0$ to L is an *incompletely specified discrete function* (or *partial discrete function*). A discrete function is *compatible* with the partial discrete function f if both take the same value at every point of S'.

Given a partial discrete function f, there are two discrete functions, compatible with f, that play a key role; the *greatest discrete function f_M compatible* with f and the *smallest discrete function f_m compatible* with f. They are defined as follows:

$$f_M(x) = f_m(x) = f(x), \quad \forall x \in S';$$

$$f_M(x) = r-1 \quad \text{and} \quad f_m(x) = 0, \quad \forall x \notin S',$$

where $r-1$ is the greatest member of L.

A *disjunctive representation* of a partial discrete function f is a disjunctive representation of any discrete function compatible with f. One can associate a cost c_1 or c_2 with every implicant and define an *optimal disjunctive representation* as one with a minimum cost.

As noted above, we may write the following implication:

$$z_i < z_j \Rightarrow c_1(z_i) \geqslant c_1(z_j) \quad \text{and} \quad c_2(z_i) \geqslant c_2(z_j). \tag{8.3}$$

Theorem 8.4. An optimal disjunctive representation of an incompletely specified discrete function f can be obtained by optimally covering $M(f_m)$ by means of $Z(f_M)$.

Proof. Consider a set $\{z_1, \ldots, z_k\}$ of implicants. Their disjunction is a representation of f iff the function

$$g = z_1 \vee \ldots \vee z_k$$

is compatible with f, i.e. iff

$$f_m \leqslant z_1 \vee \ldots \vee z_k \leqslant f_M.$$

This last relation is clearly equivalent to the conjunction of the two following properties:

(a) each z_i is an implicant of f_M;
(b) $M(f_m)$ is covered by $\{z_1, \ldots, z_k\}$.

The proof is then completed by taking into account the implication (8.3). ■

One can also be interested in optimally representing *general discrete functions,* i.e. functions from $S_{n-1} \times \ldots \times S_0$ to L^m. As noted in section 3.1 (remark 2), the concepts of cubes, blocks ... also hold for generalized discrete functions. In this case, the cubes are discrete functions of the type

$$l \wedge x_{n-1}^{(C_{n-1})} \wedge \ldots \wedge x_0^{(C_0)}$$

where l is an m-tuple of L^m.

One may associate a cost with every cube, block ... and look for optimal disjunctive representations of a given general discrete function f. There is however an important difference with the case of simple discrete functions. Consider the circuit of Figure 8.11: it gives the logic realization of the general discrete function

$$f = \bigvee_{j=0}^{k-1} (l^{(j)} \wedge x_{n-1}^{(C_{n-1}^{(j)})} \wedge \ldots \wedge x_0^{(C_0^{(j)})}),$$

where $f = (f_{m-1}, \ldots, f_0)$ and $l^{(j)} = (l_{m-1}^{(j)}, \ldots, l_0^{(j)})$.

Note that with the input wires of the OR-gates, weights $l_s^{(j)}$ are associated; in the case where $l_s^{(j)} = 0$, the corresponding wire may be deleted. Similarly, if $C_i^{(j)} = S_i$, the corresponding AND-gate input wire may be deleted.

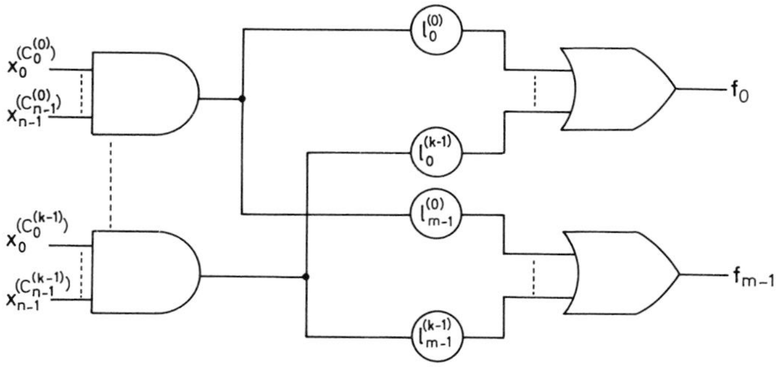

Figure 8.11. Logic circuit realizing a generalized discrete function

Given a cube

$$z = l \wedge x_{n-1}^{(C_{n-1})} \wedge \ldots \wedge x_0^{(C_0)},$$

denote $t(z)$ the number of indices i such that $C_i \neq S_i$, and $\nu(z)$ the number of nonzero components in l.

If one looks for a circuit with a minimum number of gate inputs, one must associate with z a cost $c_2(z)$ defined as follows:

$$\begin{aligned} c_2(z) &= t(z) + \nu(z) \quad \text{if} \quad t(z) \geqslant 2, \\ &= \nu(z) \quad \text{if} \quad t(z) = 0 \text{ or } 1. \end{aligned}$$

On the other hand, if one wants to minimize the number of gates, one must associate with z a cost $c_1(z)$ defined by

$$\begin{aligned} c_1(z) &= 1 \quad \text{if} \quad t(z) \geqslant 2, \\ &= 0 \quad \text{if} \quad t(z) = 0 \text{ or } 1. \end{aligned}$$

Note that this last definition is based on the assumption that none of the m OR-gates may be deleted.

Consider now two cubes z_i and z_j such that

$$z_i < z_j.$$

It is obvious that

$$c_1(z_i) \geqslant c_1(z_j),$$

but this does not necessarily hold for c_2. Consider for instance the two one-variable cubes

$$z = (0, 1) \wedge x^{(0)} \quad \text{and} \quad z' = (1, 1) \wedge x^{(0)};$$

one has

$$z < z'$$

while

$$c_2(z) = 1 \quad \text{and} \quad c_2(z') = 2.$$

In the case where one chooses c_1 as cost function, one may use the same method as for simple discrete functions: first find the prime implicants of the general discrete function, and then search for an optimal covering of the minterms of the general discrete function by means of its prime implicants.

In the case where one uses c_2 as cost function, the problem may be solved by introducing a new ordering on the set of cubes:

$$z_i \preccurlyeq z_j$$

iff

$$z_i \leqslant z_j \quad \text{and} \quad \nu(z_i) \geqslant \nu(z_j).$$

Lemma 8.4. If $z_i \preccurlyeq z_j$, then $c_2(z_i) \geqslant c_2(z_j)$.

Proof. If $z_i \preccurlyeq z_j$ then $z_i \leqslant z_j$ and thus $t(z_i) \geqslant t(z_j)$; on the other hand, $\nu(z_i) \geqslant \nu(z_j)$. Therefore

$$t(z_j) \geqslant 2 \Rightarrow t(z_i) \geqslant 2 \quad \text{and thus} \quad c_2(z_i) \geqslant c_2(z_j);$$

$$t(z_j) = 0 \text{ or } 1 \Rightarrow c_2(z_j) = \nu(z_j) \quad \text{and thus} \quad c_2(z_i) \geqslant \nu(z_i) \geqslant \nu(z_j) = c_2(z_j). \qquad \blacksquare$$

The maximal elements for that new ordering relation are given by the following lemma.

Lemma 8.5. If the implicant $z = l \wedge x_{n-1}^{(C_{n-1})} \wedge \ldots \wedge x_0^{(C_0)}$ of f is maximal with respect to $\preccurlyeq$ then there exists a prime implicant $z' = l' \wedge x_{n-1}^{(C_{n-1})} \wedge \ldots \wedge x_0^{(C_0)}$ of f such that either $l_s = l_s'$ or $l_s = 0$.

Proof. If z is an implicant of f, it is included in a prime implicant

$$z' = l' \wedge x_{n-1}^{(C_{n-1}')} \wedge \ldots \wedge x_0^{(C_0')}$$

of f, with $l \leqslant l'$, $C_{n-1} \subseteq C'_{n-1}, \ldots, C_0 \subseteq C'_0$; therefore

$$z \preccurlyeq z'' = l \wedge x_{n-1}^{(C'_{n-1})} \wedge \ldots \wedge x_0^{(C'_0)} \leqslant z'$$

since

$$z \leqslant z'' \quad \text{and} \quad \nu(z) = \nu(z'').$$

By maximality of z, one deduces that

$$C_{n-1} = C'_{n-1}, \ldots, C_0 = C'_0.$$

On the other hand, if $z \neq z'$, then $\nu(z) < \nu(z')$. There thus exists at least one index s such that $l_s = 0$ and $l'_s \neq 0$. For all the indices s for which $l_s \neq 0$, one has

$$0 \neq l_s \leqslant l'_s,$$

and by maximality of z one deduces that $l_s = l'_s$. ∎

The method for finding the maximal implicants of f with respect to the new ordering runs as follows:

(a) find the prime implicants of f;
(b) for every prime implicant like $l \wedge x_{n-1}^{(C_{n-1})} \wedge \ldots \wedge x_0^{(C_0)}$ replace in all ways some of the non-zero components of l by 0; add these new implicants to the list of prime implicants;
(c) delete the implicants smaller than ($\preccurlyeq$) other implicants of the list.

The definition of minterm must also be modified; it is obvious indeed that a minterm z, for which for instance $\nu(z) = 2$ could be covered by the disjunction of two maximal cubes z_i and z_j such that $\nu(z_i) = \nu(z_j) = 1$. The minterms are all the functions of the type

$$(0, \ldots, f_s(e), \ldots, 0) \wedge x_{n-1}^{(e_{n-1})} \wedge \ldots \wedge x_0^{(e_0)}.$$

With these new definitions of maximal implicant and of minterm, the classical method can again be used.

Example 8.3. Define a ternary general function of two ternary variables:

$$f(x_1, x_0) = [(1, 1) \wedge x_1^{(0)} \wedge x_0^{(1)}] \vee [(2, 1) \wedge x_1^{(0)} \wedge x_0^{(2)}].$$

It has two prime cubes:

$$z_0 = (1, 1) \wedge x_1^{(0)} \wedge x_0^{(1,2)}$$

and

$$z_1 = (2, 1) \wedge x_1^{(0)} \wedge x_0^{(2)}$$

that are both essential. The corresponding realization is given in Figure 8.12.

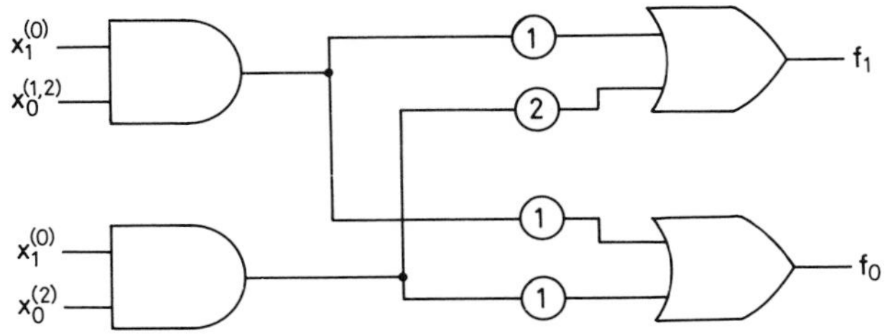

Figure 8.12. First realization of f

Use now the new definitions of minterms and maximal implicants. There are four minterms:

$$m_0 = (1, 0) \wedge x_1^{(0)} \wedge x_0^{(1)},$$

$$m_1 = (0, 1) \wedge x_1^{(0)} \wedge x_0^{(1)},$$

$$m_2 = (2, 0) \wedge x_1^{(0)} \wedge x_0^{(2)},$$

$$m_3 = (0, 1) \wedge x_1^{(0)} \wedge x_0^{(2)};$$

there are five maximal implicants:

$$z_0 = (1, 1) \wedge x_1^{(0)} \wedge x_0^{(1,2)},$$

$$z_1 = (2, 1) \wedge x_1^{(0)} \wedge x_0^{(2)},$$

$$z_2 = (1, 0) \wedge x_1^{(0)} \wedge x_0^{(1,2)},$$

$$z_3 = (0, 1) \wedge x_1^{(0)} \wedge x_0^{(1,2)},$$

$$z_4 = (2, 0) \wedge x_1^{(0)} \wedge x_0^{(2)};$$

note indeed that the second implicant deduced from z_1, i.e. $(0, 1) \wedge x_1^{(0)} \wedge x_0^{(2)}$ is smaller than ($\preccurlyeq$) z_3. The costs of these implicants are:

$$c(z_0) = 4, c(z_1) = 4, c(z_2) = c(z_3) = c(z_4) = 3.$$

The constraint table is given in Figure 8.13. The unique optimal cover is given by rows 0 and 4 to which corresponds the realization of Figure 8.14. Furthermore one could delete the OR-gate fed by only one wire and obtain a circuit with one gate less.

The methods developed above are based on the knowledge of the minterms of the considered functions. They are thus very convenient in the case where the functions are defined by truth tables. However, it could arise that the functions be given under another form, for instance as disjunction of cubes that are not necessarily minterms. In that case it would be inconvenient to have to compute the minterms before solving the optimal covering problem.

	0	1	2	3
0	X	X		X
1			X	X
2	X			
3		X		X
4			X	

Figure 8.13. Constraint table for the covering of f

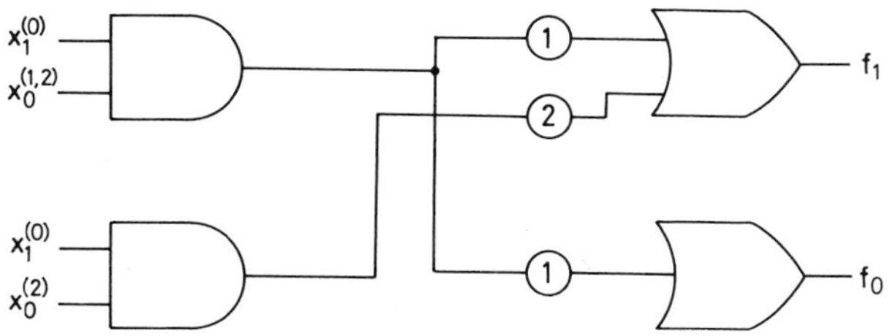

Figure 8.14. Realization of f with the minimum number of gate inputs

Miller [1965] has proposed a simplification method for switching functions in which the covering problem is solved with the list of prime implicants as starting point, without computing the minterms if they are not known. This method could certainly be generalized to the case of discrete functions.

Another very ingenious method has been found by Mott [1960], also in the case of switching functions; the method has been thoroughly studied by Kuntzmann [1965]. We conclude this section by summarizing the principles of this method.

Consider a switching function f and the list of its prime implicants: $m_1, m_2, \ldots, m_q$. If some implicant, say m_1, does not appear in a cover of f, then all the minterms covered by m_1 must be covered by the disjunction of some implicants that do appear in the cover, say $m_2, \ldots, m_k$. In that case one has an implication relation of the type

$$m_1 \leqslant m_2 \vee \ldots \vee m_k. \tag{8.4}$$

Suppose now that one has found *all* the implications of that type; for instance, using two indices, these relations could be

$$\begin{aligned} &m_1 \leqslant m_{11} \vee \ldots \vee m_{1k_1}, \\ &\vdots \\ &m_1 \leqslant m_{r1} \vee \ldots \vee m_{rk_r}; \end{aligned} \tag{8.5}$$

where

$$m_{ij} \in \{m_2, \ldots, m_q\}, \quad \forall i = 1, \ldots, r \quad \text{and} \quad j = 1, \ldots, k_i.$$

Consider a set C of prime implicants that covers f; then at least one of the following assertions is true:

1. m_1 is in C;
2. m_{11} and ... and m_{1k_1} are in C;

⋮

$(r+1)$ m_{r1} and ... and m_{rk_r} are in C.

This condition may be translated in Boolean form by associating a Boolean variable with every prime implicant:

$$x_1 \vee (x_{11} \wedge \ldots \wedge x_{1k_1}) \vee \ldots \vee (x_{r1} \wedge \ldots \wedge x_{rk_r}) = 1. \tag{8.6}$$

Such a Boolean condition may be written for every prime implicant; one thus obtains q Boolean conditions of the type (8.6) that must all be fulfilled. One has to perform the conjunction of these conditions and to compute the prime implicants of the so-obtained switching function in order to obtain all the irredundant covers of f.

It thus remains to compute for every prime implicant the implications of the type (8.5).

Suppose that

$$m_1 \leqslant m_2 \vee \ldots \vee m_k \leqslant f.$$

Then, m_1 being by hypothesis a prime implicant of f, it is also a prime implicant of

$$f' = m_2 \vee \ldots \vee m_k.$$

For that reason, m_1 is obtained by a series of consensus on the set $\{m_2, \ldots, m_k\}$. Therefore, if one performs consensus on the set of all the prime implicants, and if, by a suitable marking system, one keeps track of the way some prime implicant is obtained by consensus between some other prime implicants, one gets at the same time a list of all the implications between prime implicants. This is the basic principle of the Mott's method. For further details, see Kuntzmann [1965].

8.2. *The covering-closure problem*

8.2.1. *General statement*

Consider as above two finite sets

$$A = \{a_0, \ldots, a_{n-1}\}$$

and

$$B = \{b_0, \ldots, b_{m-1}\},$$

and a binary relation $R \subseteq A \times B$. Consider furthermore another binary relation $S \subseteq A \times \mathscr{P}(A)$, where $\mathscr{P}(A)$ denotes the set of all the subsets of A.

Definition 8.5. A subset A' of A is *closed* iff the fact that

$$a \in A' \quad \text{and} \quad (a, A'') \in S$$

implies that

$$A' \cap A'' \neq \phi.$$

As above one associates a cost with every element of A. The *optimal covering-closure problem* can be stated as follows:

Find a subset A' of A such that

(a) A' covers B, i.e. $R(A') = B$;
(b) A' is closed;
(c) A' has a minimum cost.

Introduce now a new notation: the subset of A that is characterized by the n-tuple $(x_0, \ldots, x_{n-1})$ will be denoted A_x where

$$x = x_0 + 2x_1 + \ldots + 2^{n-1} x_{n-1}.$$

The elements of $\mathscr{P}(A)$ may thus be written:

$$A_0 = \phi, A_1, \ldots, A_{2^n-1} = A.$$

The relation S is described by a matrix $[s_{ik}]$ of type $n \times 2^n$:

$$s_{ik} = 1 \quad \text{iff} \quad (a_i, A_k) \in S,$$
$$= 0 \quad \text{otherwise.}$$

Define also a matrix $[t_{ik}]$ of type $n \times 2^n$:

$$t_{ik} = k_i,$$

i.e. the digit of order i of the basis two representation of k.

Let us express now that the subset A_x of A is closed:

the condition $a_l \in A_x$ may be written $x_l = 1$;

the condition $(a_l, A_k) \in S$ may be written $s_{lk} = 1$;

by conjunction of these last two conditions one obtains:

$$s_{lk} x_l = 1;$$

on the other hand, the condition $A_x \cap A_k \neq \phi$ may be written

$$(k_0 x_0, \ldots, k_{n-1} x_{n-1}) \neq (0, \ldots, 0),$$

i.e.

$$\sum_{i=0}^{n-1} t_{ik} x_i \geqslant 1.$$

Thus, the closure condition may be written

$$\sum_{i=0}^{n-1} t_{ik}\, x_i \geqslant s_{lk}\, x_l, \quad \forall l = 0, \ldots, \quad n-1 \quad \text{and} \quad k = 0, \ldots, 2^n-1.$$

The covering-closure problem can now be stated in pseudo-Boolean form:

minimize the cost function

$$c = \sum_{i=0}^{n-1} c_i x_i \tag{8.7}$$

under the m covering constraints

$$\sum_{i=0}^{n-1} r_{ij} x_i \geqslant 1, \quad \forall j = 0, \ldots, m-1, \tag{8.8}$$

and under the closure constraints

$$\sum_{i=0}^{n-1} t_{ik}\, x_i \geqslant s_{lk} x_l, \quad \forall l = 0, \ldots, n-1 \quad \textit{and} \quad k = 0, \ldots, 2^n-1. \tag{8.9}$$

The constraints may also be formulated in Boolean form:

$$\bigvee_{i=0}^{n-1} (r_{ij} \wedge x_i) = 1, \quad \forall j = 0, \ldots, m-1 \tag{8.8 bis}$$

and

$$\bigvee_{i=0}^{n-1} (t_{ik} \wedge x_i) \geqslant (s_{lk} \wedge x_l), \quad \forall l = 0, \ldots, n-1 \quad \text{and} \quad k = 0, \ldots, 2^n-1. \tag{8.9 bis}$$

Note that the only constraints (8.9) that must be taken into account are those for which $s_{lk} = 1$ and $t_{lk} = 0$. They are the only non-trivial covering constraints.

There exists a tabular representation for the constraints: the CC-table (Grasselli and Luccio [1965]). It consists in a rectangular table with n rows and a number of columns equal to the number of constraints: the m covering constraints and the non-trivial closure constraints. Column j that corresponds to the covering constraint

$$\sum_{i=0}^{n-1} r_{ij} x_i \geqslant 1$$

has a cross in every row i such that $r_{ij} = 1$. The column that corresponds to the closure constraint

$$\sum_{\substack{i=0 \\ i \neq l}}^{n-1} t_{ik}\, x_i \geqslant x_l,$$

for some l and k such that $t_{lk} = 0$ and $s_{lk} = 1$, has a dot (.) in row l and a cross in every row i such that $t_{ik} = 1$.

There are thus two groups of columns corresponding to the covering and closure constraints, respectively. If a column has a cross in row i, one says that this column is covered by row i. The covering-closure problem may be stated as follows: select a family of rows such that

(a) every column of the first group is covered by at least one of them;
(b) if there is a dot at the intersection of one of the selected rows with a column of the second group, this last column must be covered by at least one of the selected rows.

8.2.2. *General methods of solution*

First note that if some element a_l of A is such that

$$(a_l, \phi) \in S,$$

then a_l cannot belong to a closed subset of A and A itself is not closed. In the constraints (8.9) this corresponds to the fact that $s_{l0} = 1$. Thus in every solution of (8.9) one must have $x_l = 0$.

This last remark suggests a first simplification rule of the CC-table.

Definition 8.6. If a column has a dot in row l and has no crosses, i.e. if $s_{l0} = 1$. then row l is *non-selectionable.*

Theorem 8.5. If row l is non-selectionable, then in every solution of (8.9) $x_l = 0$. Row l may be deleted along with the columns having a dot in row l.

The simplification rule of theorem 8.5 can be used iteratively until the point where one obtains a CC-table without any non-selectionable row; the set of remaining rows then corresponds to a closed subset of A. The consistency of the problem may be checked as follows:

(a) use iteratively the simplification rule of theorem 8.5 in order to obtain a table without any non-selectionable row;
(b) check whether the remaining rows can cover the columns corresponding to the covering constraints (theorem 8.1).

We now give some other simplification rules.

Definitions 8.7. If there is a column of the first group in which only one cross appears in position l, then row l is *essential*. That means that for some j in$\{0, \dots, m-1\}$ one has

$$r_{lj} = 1 \quad \text{and} \quad r_{ij} = 0, \quad \forall i \neq l.$$

Column K *dominates* column K' iff K has all the crosses and the dot (if any) of K'. Suppose first that K' belongs to the first group and corresponds to the constraint

$$\sum_{i=0}^{n-1} r_{ik'} x_i \geqslant 1$$

for some k' in $\{0, \ldots, m-1\}$. If K also belongs to the first group and corresponds to the constraint

$$\sum_{i=0}^{n-1} r_{ik} x_i \geqslant 1$$

for some k in $\{0, \ldots, m-1\}$, then one must verify that

$$r_{ik} \geqslant r_{ik'}, \quad \forall i = 0, \ldots, n-1;$$

if K is in the second group and corresponds to the constraint

$$\sum_{i=0}^{n-1} t_{ik} x_i \geqslant x_l \tag{8.10}$$

for some k in $\{0, \ldots, 2^n-1\}$ and l in $\{0, \ldots, n-1\}$, then one must verify that

$$t_{ik} \geqslant r_{ik'}, \quad \forall i = 0, \ldots, n-1.$$

On the other hand, if K' is in the second group and corresponds to the constraint

$$\sum_{i=0}^{n-1} t_{ik'} x_i \geqslant x_{l'} \tag{8.11}$$

for some k' in $\{0, \ldots, 2^n-1\}$ and l' in $\{0, \ldots, n-1\}$, then K must be in the second group; furthermore, if K corresponds to the constraint (8.10), then

$$l = l' \quad \text{and} \quad t_{ik} \geqslant t_{ik'}, \quad \forall i = 0, \ldots, n-1.$$

The row l *dominates* the row l' iff the three following conditions are verified

(a) the row l has no dot, i.e. $s_{lk} = 0, \forall k \in \{0, \ldots, 2^n-1\}$;
(b) the row l has all the crosses of the row l', i.e.

$$r_{lj} \geqslant r_{l'j}, \quad \forall j = 0, \ldots, m-1$$
$$t_{lk} \geqslant t_{l'k}, \quad \forall k = 0, \ldots, 2^n-1;$$

(c) $c_l < c_{l'}$.

The row l *weakly dominates* the row l' iff the conditions (a) and (b) above are verified, and if

(c′) $c_l \leqslant c_{l'}$.

A row that contains no crosses is a *non-covering* row.
The various simplification rules are given by the next theorem.

Theorem 8.6. (a) *If row l is essential, then in every solution of (8.8) x_l is equal to 1. Every column that has a cross in position l may be deleted from the CC-table while every column that has a dot in position l becomes a column of the first group.*

(b) *If column K dominates column K', then column K may be deleted.*

(c) *If row l dominates row l', then row l' may be deleted along with the columns having a dot in row l'. In every minimum cost solution $x_{l'} = 0$.*

(d) *If row l weakly dominates row l', and if one does not look for all the minimum cost solutions, then row l' may be deleted along with the columns having a dot in that row. There exists a minimum cost solution with $x_{l'} = 0$.*

(e) *Every non-covering row along with the columns having a dot in that row may be deleted.*

Proof. (a) The proof is similar to that of the part (a) of theorem 8.2. Note furthermore that if x_l is equal to 1, then a closure constraint like (8.10) becomes the covering constraint

$$\sum_{i=0}^{n-1} t_{ik} x_i \geqslant 1.$$

(b) Every row that covers K' also covers column K. If K' belongs to the first group, then in every solution a row must exist that covers K' and thus also covers K. If both K and K' belong to the second group then either both must be covered or none of them must be covered. Thus if K must be covered, then K' must also be covered and every row that covers K' will also cover K. The constraint corresponding to column K is thus not necessary since it is automatically satisfied once the constraint corresponding to column K' is satisfied.

(c) The proof is similar to that of the part (c) of theorem 8.2; one must take into account the fact that the row l does not introduce new closure constraints since it does not contain any dot. Furthermore, if $x_{l'}$ is equal to 0, every closure constraint like (8.11) becomes

$$\sum_{i=0}^{n-1} t_{ik'} x_i \geqslant 0,$$

and is thus always verified.

(d) The proof is similar to that of (c).

(e) A non-covering row is dominated by a virtual empty row the cost of which is zero and the entries of which are all blanks. ∎

A repeated use of the simplification rules of theorems 8.5 and 8.6 can be the first step of any algorithm for solving the optimal covering-closure problem. At the end of this first step one obtains thus a CC-table in which none of the simplification rules can still be applied; it is a *cyclic* table.

As for the covering problem, one may use a Boolean method.

Definition 8.8. A subset A' of A that is closed and covers B is an *irredundant closed cover* of B iff none of its proper subsets has the same two properties.

Lemma 8.6. Every solution of the optimal covering-closure problem is an irredundant closed cover. ■

Definitions 8.9. The switching function r is defined as above in lemma 8.2:

$$r(x_0, \ldots, x_{n-1}) = \bigwedge_{j=0}^{m-1} \left[\bigvee_{i=0}^{n-1} (r_{ij} \wedge x_i) \right].$$

The switching function s is defined as follows:

$$s(x_0, \ldots, x_{n-1}) = \bigwedge_{l=0}^{n-1} \bigwedge_{k=0}^{2^n-1} \left[\bar{s}_{kl} \vee \bar{x}_l \vee \bigwedge_{i=0}^{n-1} (t_{ik} \wedge x_i) \right]$$

$$= \bigwedge_{\substack{l,k \\ s_{lk}=1 \\ t_{lk}=0}} [(t_{0k} \wedge x_0) \vee \ldots \vee \bar{x}_l \vee \ldots \vee (t_{n-1k} \wedge x_{n-1})].$$

Lemma 8.7. A subset A' of A is an irredundant closed cover of B iff the switching function $r \wedge s$ admits a prime implicant of the type

$$p \wedge \bigwedge_{i: a_i \in A'} x_i,$$

where p is a conjunction of complemented variables.

Proof. The proof is similar to that of lemma 8.2, with the difference that $r \wedge s$ is no longer a positive unate switching function and can thus have prime implicants with complemented variables. ■

The functions r and s, and thus also the function $r \wedge s$, are given as a conjunction of disjunctions of variables. The prime implicants of $r \wedge s$ can be simply computed by transforming the conjunction of disjunctions into a disjunction of conjunctions (distributivity law), and by deleting the conjunctions that are included in other ones (a.o. those that are equal to zero).

The Boolean method thus runs as follows.

Algorithm 8.3

Step 1. Compute the prime implicants of $r \wedge s$. As noted above it suffices for that to use the distributivity law.

Step 2. For every prime implicant

$$x_{i_1} \wedge \ldots \wedge x_{i_h} \wedge \bar{x}_{j_1} \wedge \ldots \wedge \bar{x}_{j_k}$$

of $r \wedge s$, compute the cost

$$c_{i_1} + \ldots + c_{i_h}.$$

Step 3. Delete the prime implicants the cost of which is not minimum.
To every prime implicant obtained at the end of step 3 corresponds a closed cover of B with minimum cost.

Example 8.4. Consider the CC-table of Figure 8.15, the covering part of which is the constraint table of Figure 8.1.

	0	1	2	3	4	5	6	7	8	9	10	11	12	13	14	15	16	17	18	19
0	X	X		X	X						X	X					X			
1		X	X	X							X		•				•			
2			X			X	X		X				X				X			
3				X	X			X			X	X	X		X	X				
4		X	X						X	X			X							
5			X	X						•	X				X		X	X		X
6			X			X								•		•				
7			X				X			X	•	•						•		
8						X	X			X									X	•
9				X				X			X				•	X				
10	X						X		X					X					•	
11						X			•					X		X				

Figure 8.15. Initial CC-table

The various costs are:

$$c(a_0) = 2, c(a_1) = 3, c(a_2) = 2, c(a_3) = 2, c(a_4) = 2, c(a_5) = 1, c(a_6) = 3,$$
$$c(a_7) = 1, c(a_8) = 1, c(a_9) = 3, c(a_{10}) = 3, c(a_{11}) = 3.$$

Column 10 dominates columns 3, 4, 7, 11 and 17; column 3 dominates column 4; column 11 dominates column 4 and column 15 dominates column 7. One may delete columns 3, 10, 11, 15 and so obtain the table of Figure 8.16.

Taking into account the value of the costs associated with the rows of Figure 8.16, one deduces that:

row 4 dominates row 1;
row 2 dominates row 6;
row 3 dominates row 9.

One may thus delete rows 1, 6, 9 and columns 12, 13, 14 and 16. This gives the table of Figure 8.17 in which row 3 is essential. Therefore a_3 belongs to every solution. One may delete row 3 and columns 4 and 7. The new CC-table is given in Figure 8.18.

In Figure 8.18, row 2 dominates row 11; one thus deletes row 11 and column 8. This yields the table of Figure 8.19 in which column 6 dominates column 5. One may delete column 6 and obtain the table of Figure 8.20.

	0	1	2	4	5	6	7	8	9	12	13	14	16	17	18	19
0	X	X		X									X			
1		X	X							•			•			
2			X		X	X		X		X			X			
3				X			X			X		X				
4		X	X					X	X	X						
5			X						•			X	X	X		X
6			X		X						•					
7			X			X			X					•		
8					X	X			X						X	•
9							X					•				
10	X					X		X			X				•	
11					X			•			X					

Figure 8.16. Simplified CC-table (1)

	0	1	2	4	5	6	7	8	9	17	18	19
0	X	X		X								
2			X		X	X		X				
3				X			X					
4		X	X					X	X			
5			X						•	X		X
7			X			X			X	•		
8					X	X			X		X	•
10	X					X		X			•	
11					X			•				

Figure 8.17. Simplified CC-table (2)

	0	1	2	5	6	8	9	17	18	19
0	X	X								
2			X	X	X	X				
4		X	X			X	X			
5			X				•	X		X
7			X		X		X	•		
8				X	X		X		X	•
10	X				X	X			•	
11				X		•				

Figure 8.18. Simplified CC-table (3)

	0	1	2	5	6	9	17	18	19
0	X	X							
2			X	X	X				
4		X	X			X			
5			X			•	X		X
7			X		X	X	•		
8				X	X	X		X	•
10	X				X			•	

Figure 8.19

	0	1	2	5	9	17	18	19
0	X	X						
2			X	X				
4		X	X		X			
5			X		•	X		X
7			X		X	•		
8				X	X		X	•
10	X						•	

Figure 8.20
Simplified CC-tables (4) and (5)

In Figure 8.20 row 0 dominates row 10; this allows deletion of row 10 and column 18 and to obtain the table of Figure 8.21 in which row 0 is essential. Thus a_0 belongs to every solution. After deleting row 0, and columns 0 and 1, one obtains the cyclic table of Figure 8.22.

The table of Figure 8.22 may be solved by the Boolean method; one must find the prime implicants of

$$(x_2 \vee x_4 \vee x_5 \vee x_7)\ (x_2 \vee x_8)\ (x_4 \vee \bar{x}_5 \vee x_7 \vee x_8)\ (x_5 \vee \bar{x}_7)\ (x_5 \vee \bar{x}_8);$$

	0	1	2	5	9	17	19
0	X	X					
2			X	X			
4		X	X		X		
5			X		•	X	X
7			X		X	•	
8				X	X		•

Figure 8.21
Simplified CC-tables (6) and (7)

	2	5	9	17	19
2	X	X			
4	X		X		
5	X		•	X	X
7	X		X	•	
8		X	X		..

Figure 8.22

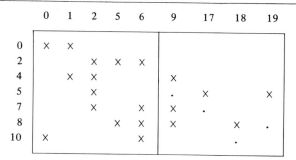

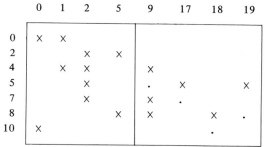

there are five prime implicants:

$$x_2x_4x_5, x_2x_5x_7, x_5x_8, x_2x_4\bar{x}_7\bar{x}_8 \quad \text{and} \quad x_2\bar{x}_5\bar{x}_7\bar{x}_8.$$

There are two minimum cost prime implicants:

$$x_5x_8 \quad \text{and} \quad x_2\bar{x}_5\bar{x}_7\bar{x}_8.$$

The two optimal solutions of the covering-closure problem are thus:

$$\{a_0, a_3, a_5, a_8\} \quad \text{and} \quad \{a_0, a_2, a_3\}.$$

Their cost is equal to 6.

Of course, many other methods exist for the determination of minimum covers. Among others, there exist methods based on linear programming (lemma 8.3 can be generalized to the case of covering-closure problems) and on restricted enumeration. To this last category belongs a method due to Noé [1968] and that we describe now.

Consider thus the sets A and B, and the binary relations $R \subseteq A \times B$ and $S \subseteq A \times \mathscr{P}(A)$ defined above.

Definitions 8.10. Let A^* be a subset of A. The subset A' of A^* is *admissible* in A^* iff the two following conditions are verified:

(a) $R(A') \cup R(A \backslash A^*) = B;$ (8.12)

(b) if $a \in A'$ and $(a, A_k) \in S$,

then either $A' \cap A_k \neq \phi$,

or $(A \backslash A^*) \cap A_k \neq \phi$. (8.13)

The subset A' of A^* *dominates* the subset A'' of A^*, in A^*, iff the four following conditions are verified:

(a) $R(A') \supseteq R(A'');$ (8.14)

(b) $c(A') < c(A'');$ (8.15)

(c) if $a \in A' \backslash A''$ and if $(a, A_k) \in S$, (8.16)
then $A' \cap A_k \neq \phi;$

(d) if $a \in [(A' \cap A'') \cup (A \backslash A^*)]$, if $(a, A_k) \in S$ and if $A'' \cap A_k \neq \phi$,
then $A' \cap A_k \neq \phi$. (8.17)

The subset A' of A^* *weakly dominates* the subset A'' of A^*, in A^*, iff the conditions (8.14), (8.16) and (8.17) are verified, and if

$(b')\ c(A') \leqslant c(A'').$

Note the relation between these definitions and the definitions 8.6 and 8.7. If a row l is non-selectionable, then every subset A' of A^*, that contains a_l, is not admissible in A^*. Row l is essential iff the empty set is not admissible in $\{a_l\}$. Row l (weakly) dominates row l' iff the subset $\{a_l\}$ (weakly) dominates the subset $\{a_{l'}\}$, in $\{a_l, a_{l'}\}$.

A subset A' of A^* is *optimal* in A^* iff there is no other subset of A^* that dominates A', in A^*. A subset of A^* that is both admissible in A^* and optimal in A^* is called *optimal admissible* in A^*.

The method is based upon the following theorem.

Theorem 8.7. (a) *The subset A' of A is a solution of the optimal covering-closure problem iff it is optimal admissible in A.*

(b) *If A' is optimal admissible in A^* and if A^{**} is a subset of A^*, then $A' \cap A^{**}$ is optimal admissible in A^{**}.*

Proof. (a) If A' is admissible in A that means that

$$R(A') \cup R(A \backslash A) = R(A') = B$$

and

$$a \in A', (a, A_k) \in S \Rightarrow A' \cap A_k \neq \phi$$

(since $(A \backslash A) \cap A_k = \phi$); therefore A' is admissible in A iff A' is a closed cover of B.

Suppose now that A' is admissible in A, and that it is dominated by A''. Then

(1) $R(A'') \supseteq R(A') = B$;
(2) $c(A'') < c(A')$;
(3) $a \in A'' \backslash A'$ and $(a, A_k) \in S \Rightarrow A'' \cap A_k \neq \phi$;
(4) $a \in A'' \cap A'$ and $(a, A_k) \in S \Rightarrow A' \cap A_k \neq \phi$ since A' is closed, and thus $A'' \cap A_k \neq \phi$ since A'' dominates A' in A;

from (3) and (4) one deduces that A'' is closed. Thus the subset A'' is also a closed cover of A', but with a lower cost, and A' is not a solution of the optimal covering-closure problem.

Conversely, if A' is a closed cover of B that is not of minimum cost, it can easily be shown that every minimum cost closed cover of B dominates A' in A.

(b) Denote

$$A_1' = A' \cap A^{**} \quad \text{and} \quad A_0' = A' \cap (A^* \backslash A^{**}).$$

One has thus:

$$A' = A_1' \cup A_0' \quad \text{and} \quad A_1' \cap A_0' = \phi.$$

We first prove that A_1' is admissible in A^{**}:

(1)
$$\begin{aligned} R(A_1') \cup R(A \backslash A^{**}) &= R(A_1') \cup R(A \backslash A^*) \cup R(A^* \backslash A^{**}) \\ &\supseteq R(A_1') \cup R(A \backslash A^*) \cup R(A_0') \\ &= R(A') \cup R(A \backslash A^*) = B. \end{aligned}$$

(2) If $a \in A_1'$ and $(a, A_k) \in S$, then, taking into account the fact that $A_1' \subseteq A'$ with A' admissible in A^*, one deduces that:

either

$$A' \cap A_k \neq \phi$$

or

$$(A \backslash A^*) \cap A_k \neq \phi;$$

in other words

$$[A' \cup (A \backslash A^*)] \cap A_k \neq \phi.$$

Furthermore

$$A' \cup (A \backslash A^*) = A_1' \cup A_0' \cup (A \backslash A^*) \subseteq A_1' \cup (A^* \backslash A^{**}) \cup (A \backslash A^*)$$
$$= A_1' \cup (A \backslash A^{**}),$$

and thus

$$[A_1' \cup (A \backslash A^{**})] \cap A_k \neq \phi.$$

It remains to prove that A_1' is optimal in A^{**}. Suppose that A_1' is dominated by $A_2' \subseteq A^{**}$, in A^{**}. We prove that A' is dominated by $(A_2' \cup A_0')$ in A^*.

(1) $R(A_2' \cup A_0') = R(A_2') \cup R(A_0') \supseteq R(A_1') \cup R(A_0') = R(A')$;
(2) $c(A_2' \cup A_0') = c(A_2') + c(A_0') < c(A_1') + c(A_0') = c(A')$;
(3) if $a \in (A_2' \cup A_0') \backslash (A_1' \cup A_0')$, then $a \in A_2' \backslash A_1'$; if furthermore $(a, A_k) \in S$, then $A_2' \cap A_k \neq \phi$ since A_2' dominates A_1' in A^{**}, and thus

$$(A_2' \cup A_0') \cap A_k' \neq \phi;$$

(4) if $a \in [(A_2' \cup A_0') \cap (A_1' \cup A_0')] \cup (A \backslash A^*)$, i.e. $a \in A_0' \cup (A_1' \cap A_2') \cup (A \backslash A^*)$, then $a \in (A_1' \cap A_2') \cup (A \backslash A^{**})$;

if furthermore $(a, A_k) \in S$ and $(A_1' \cup A_0') \cap A_k \neq \phi$, then either

$$A_1' \cap A_k \neq \phi$$

and thus

$$A_2' \cap A_k \neq \phi$$

since A_2' dominates A_1' in A^{**}, or

$$A_0' \cap A_k \neq \phi.$$

In both cases one has

$$(A_2' \cup A_0') \cap A_k \neq \phi.$$

From points (1) to (4) one deduces that $(A_2' \cup A_0')$ dominates A' in A^*, but this contradicts the hypothesis that A' is optimal admissible in A^*. Therefore A_2' cannot dominate A_1' in A^{**}, and A_1' is optimal admissible in A^{**}. ∎

The algorithm is exactly the same as the algorithm 8.2, the definitions 8.3 being replaced by the definitions 8.10. Note however that in this case, even if ϕ is admissible in ϕ, it could arise that the problem does not admit of any solution; at some step of the algorithm, one will obtain a list of subsets, none of which is admissible.

Before treating an example, we give the pseudo-Boolean counterpart of the definitions 8.10. Suppose that

$$A^* = \{a_0, \ldots, a_{d-1}\};$$

the subsets A' and A'' of A^* are described by the n-tuples

$$(e_0', \ldots, e_{d-1}', 0, \ldots, 0) \text{ and } (e_0'', \ldots e_{d-1}'', 0, \ldots, 0),$$

respectively. With these notations, the condition (8.12) becomes:

$$\sum_{i=0}^{d-1} r_{ij}\, e_i' + \sum_{i=d}^{n-1} r_{ij} \geqslant 1, \quad \forall j = 0, \ldots, m-1; \tag{8.12 bis}$$

the condition (8.13) becomes

$$\sum_{i=0}^{d-1} t_{ik}\, e_i' + \sum_{i=d}^{n-1} t_{ik} \geqslant s_{lk}\, e_l, \quad \forall l = 0, \ldots, d-1 \quad \text{and} \quad \forall k = 0, \ldots, 2^n-1. \tag{8.13 bis}$$

The conditions (8.14) to (8.16) become:

$$\bigvee_{i=0}^{d-1} (r_{ij} \wedge e_i') \geqslant \bigvee_{i=0}^{d-1} (r_{ij} \wedge e_i''), \quad \forall j = 0, \ldots, m-1; \tag{8.14 bis}$$

$$\sum_{i=0}^{d-1} c_i\, e_i' < \sum_{i=0}^{d-1} c_i\, e_i''; \tag{8.15 bis}$$

$$\bar{e}_l' \vee \bigvee_{i=0}^{d-1} (t_{ik} \wedge e_i') \geqslant s_{lk} \wedge \bar{e}_l'', \quad \forall l = 0, \ldots, d-1 \quad \text{and} \quad \forall k = 0, \ldots, 2^n-1; \tag{8.16 bis}$$

the condition (8.17) gives the two following conditions:

$$\bigvee_{i=0}^{d-1} (t_{ik} \wedge e_i') \geqslant s_{lk} \wedge \bigvee_{i=0}^{d-1} (t_{ik} \wedge e_i''), \quad \forall l = d, \ldots, n-1 \quad \text{and} \quad \forall k = 0, \ldots, 2^n-1; \tag{8.17 bis}$$

$$\bar{e}_l' \vee \bigvee_{i=0}^{d-1} (t_{ik} \wedge e_i') \geqslant s_{lk} \wedge e_l'' \wedge \bigvee_{i=0}^{d-1} (t_{ik} \wedge e_i''), \quad \forall l = 0, \ldots, d-1 \quad \text{and} \quad \forall k = 0, \ldots, 2^n-1. \tag{8.17 ter}$$

Note that by combining (8.16 bis) and (8.17 ter) one obtains the unique condition

$$e'_l \vee \bigvee_{i=0}^{d-1} (t_{ik} \wedge e'_i) \geqslant s_{lk} \wedge \left[\bar{e}''_l \vee \bigvee_{i=0}^{d-1} (t_{ik} \wedge e''_i)\right], \quad \forall l = 0, \ldots, \quad d-1 \quad \text{and}$$
$$k = 0, \ldots, 2^n-1. \tag{8.18}$$

Example 8.4 (continued). Let us solve the same covering-closure problem by the method of Noé.

$A_0 = \phi; L(A_0) = (\phi)$.

Step 1. $A_1 = \{a_7\}$;
$L(A_1) = (\phi, \{a_7\})$.

Step 2. $A_2 = A_1 \cup \{a_5\} = \{a_5, a_7\}$;
$\{a_7\}$ is not admissible in A_2;
$L(A_2) = (\phi, \{a_5\}, \{a_5, a_7\})$.

Step 3. $A_3 = A_2 \cup \{a_8\} = \{a_5, a_7, a_8\}$;
$\{a_8\}$ is not admissible in A_3;
$\{a_5, a_7, a_8\}$ is dominated by $\{a_5, a_8\}$ in A_3;
$L(A_3) = (\phi, \{a_5\}, \{a_5, a_7\}, \{a_5, a_8\})$.

Step 4. $A_4 = A_3 \cup \{a_{10}\} = \{a_5, a_7, a_8, a_{10}\}$;
$\{a_{10}\}, \{a_5, a_{10}\}$ and $\{a_5, a_7, a_{10}\}$ are not admissible in A_4;
$L(A_4) = (\phi, \{a_5\}, \{a_5, a_7\}, \{a_5, a_8\}, \{a_5, a_8, a_{10}\})$.

Step 5. $A_5 = A_4 \cup \{a_0\} = \{a_0, a_5, a_7, a_8, a_{10}\}$;
$\phi, \{a_5\}, \{a_5, a_7\}$ and $\{a_5, a_8\}$ are not admissible in A_5;
$L(A_5) = (\{a_5, a_8, a_{10}\}, \{a_0\}, \{a_0, a_5\}, \{a_0, a_5, a_7\}, \{a_0, a_5, a_8\}, \{a_0, a_5, a_8, a_{10}\})$.

Step 6. $A_6 = A_5 \cup \{a_3\} = \{a_0, a_3, a_5, a_7, a_8, a_{10}\}$;
$\{a_5, a_8, a_{10}\}$ is not admissible in A_6.

At this point we may use a simple short-cut: the subset $\{a_0, a_3, a_5, a_8\}$ is closed and covers B; its cost is equal to 6; we may thus delete the subsets $\{a_0, a_5, a_8, a_{10}\}$, $\{a_3, a_5, a_8, a_{10}\}$, and $\{a_0, a_3, a_5, a_8, a_{10}\}$, the costs of which are greater than 6, since they certainly do not yield optimal solutions. We may also delete the subset $\{a_0, a_3, a_5, a_7\}$, the cost of which is equal to 6, but that do not cover b_5.

$L(A_6) = (\{a_0\}, \{a_0, a_5\}, \{a_0, a_5, a_7\}, \{a_0, a_5, a_8\}, \{a_0, a_3\}, \{a_0, a_3, a_5\}, \{a_0, a_3, a_5, a_8$

Step 7. $A_7 = A_6 \cup \{a_9\} = \{a_0, a_3, a_5, a_7, a_8, a_9, a_{10}\}$;

$\{a_0\}$, $\{a_0, a_5\}$, $\{a_0, a_5, a_7\}$, $\{a_0, a_5, a_8\}$ and $\{a_0, a_9\}$ are not admissible in A_7;

$\{a_0, a_5, a_9\}$ is dominated by $\{a_0, a_3, a_5\}$ in A_7;

the cost of the subsets $\{a_0, a_5, a_7, a_9\}$, $\{a_0, a_5, a_8, a_9\}$, $\{a_0, a_3, a_9\}$, $\{a_0, a_3, a_5, a_9\}$ and $\{a_0, a_3, a_5, a_8, a_9\}$ is greater than 6; they may be deleted;

$L(A_7) = (\{a_0, a_3\}, \{a_0, a_3, a_5\}, \{a_0, a_3, a_5, a_8\})$.

Step 8. $A_8 = A_7 \cup \{a_2\}$;

$\{a_0, a_3\}$ and $\{a_0, a_3, a_5\}$ are not admissible in A_8;

$\{a_0, a_2, a_3, a_5\}$ and $\{a_0, a_2, a_3, a_5, a_8\}$ are dominated by $\{a_0, a_2, a_3\}$ in A_8;

$L(A_8) = (\{a_0, a_2, a_3\}, \{a_0, a_3, a_5, a_8\})$.

Since both $\{a_0, a_2, a_3\}$ and $\{a_0, a_3, a_5, a_8\}$ are closed and cover B, they are the solutions of the optimal covering-closure problem. Their cost is equal to 6.

8.2.3. *Minimization of finite automata*

This last subsection is devoted to the problem of covering the states of a finite automaton by means of a closed set of compatibility classes. Let us use the notations of Ginzburg [1968].

Definitions 8.11. A *finite deterministic Mealy automaton A* is a 5-tuple

$$A = \langle \Sigma, \Theta, S, M, N \rangle$$

where

Σ and Θ are the finite input and output alphabets, respectively,

S is the finite set of internal states,

$M = \{M_\sigma \mid \sigma \in \Sigma\}$ is a set of functional binary relations on S, i.e. $M_\sigma \subseteq S^2$ and $\# [M_\sigma(s)] \leqslant 1$, for every σ in Σ and s in S,

$N = \{N_\sigma \mid \sigma \in \Sigma\}$ is a set of functional binary relations from S to Θ.

Given a finite non-empty word

$$x = \sigma_1 \sigma_2 \ldots \sigma_p$$

over Σ, the functional binary relations $M_x \subseteq S^2$ and $N_x \subseteq S \times \Theta$ are defined as follows:

$$M_x = M_{\sigma_1} . M_{\sigma_2} . \ldots . M_{\sigma_p}$$

and

$$N_x = M_{\sigma_1} . M_{\sigma_2} . \dots . M_{\sigma_{p-1}} . N_{\sigma_p}.$$

Two elements s_1 and s_2 of S are *compatible* iff the fact that

$$(s_1, \theta_1) \in N_x \quad \text{and} \quad (s_2, \theta_2) \in N_x$$

implies that $\theta_1 = \theta_2$. A *compatibility class* is a set of states that are pairwise compatible.

Consider a set

$$\pi = \{C_1, \dots, C_r\}$$

of compatibility classes. The set π is a cover of S iff

$$C_1 \cup \dots \cup C_r = S;$$

it is a closed cover of S iff for every i in $\{1, \dots, r\}$, and for every σ in Σ, there exists j in $\{1, \dots, r\}$ such that

$$M_\sigma(C_i) \subseteq C_j.$$

The problem of finding a closed cover of S is obviously a covering-closure problem. Denote indeed by $\mathscr{C}$ the set of all the compatibility classes; the binary relation R from $\mathscr{C}$ to S contains all the pairs

$$(C, s) \quad \text{with} \quad s \in C;$$

the binary relation $\mathscr{S}$ from $\mathscr{C}$ to $\mathscr{P}(\mathscr{C})$ contains all the pairs

$$(C, \mathscr{C}')$$

where

$$\mathscr{C}' = \{C' \in \mathscr{C} \mid M_\sigma(C) \subseteq C'\},$$

for some σ in Σ.

Theorem 8.8. A set π of compatibility classes is a closed cover of S iff the two following properties are satisfied:

(a) $R(\pi) = S$;
(b) *if* $(C, \mathscr{C}') \in \mathscr{S}$ *with* $C \in \pi$, *then* $\pi \cap C' \neq \phi$.

Proof. It is obvious that

$$R(\pi) = \bigcup_{C \in \pi} C,$$

and that π is a cover of S iff $R(\pi) = S$.

On the other hand, the condition $(C, \mathscr{C}') \in \mathscr{S}$ means that $\mathscr{C}'$ is the set of compatibility classes that contain $M_\sigma(C)$ for some $\sigma \in \Sigma$, and thus the condition $\pi \cap \mathscr{C}' \neq \phi$ holds iff there exists in π a class that contains $M_\sigma(C)$. ∎

Definitions 8.12. Consider two finite deterministic Mealy automata

$$A = \langle \Sigma, \Theta, S, M, N \rangle$$

and

$$A' = \langle \Sigma, \Theta, S', M', N' \rangle$$

over the same input and output alphabets. The state s' of S' *covers* the state s of S iff the following implication is verified for every finite non-empty word x over Σ:

$$(s, \theta) \in N_x \Rightarrow (s', \theta) \in N'_x.$$

More intuitively, that means that A' starting in state s' does "at least as much" as does A starting in state s.

The automaton A' *covers* the automaton A iff every state of S is covered by at least one state of S'.

Consider now a closed cover π of S. One may then define at least one *quotient automaton*

$$A/\pi = \langle \Sigma, \Theta, \pi, M^\pi, N^\pi \rangle$$

in which the relations M^π_σ and N^π_σ are constructed according to the following rules:

(a) For every $C \in \pi$ and $\sigma \in \Sigma$ such that $M_\sigma(C) \neq \phi$, choose C' in π such that $M_\sigma(C) \subseteq C'$, and add the pair (C, C') to M^π_σ. This construction is always possible once π is closed. In some cases, there are several classes C' that contain $M_\sigma(C)$ and thus several ways to define the quotient automaton. Furthermore, if $M_\sigma(C) = \phi$, one could add a pair (C, C') to M^π_σ, where C' is arbitrarily chosen.

(b) If for some $C \in \pi$ and $\sigma \in \Sigma$ one has $N_\sigma(C) \neq \phi$, then $N_\sigma(C) = \{\theta\}$ for some $\theta \in \Theta$, since C is a compatibility relation. In that case, add the pair (C, θ) to N^π_σ. Note again that if $N_\sigma(C) = \phi$, one could add a pair (C, θ) to N^π_σ, where θ is arbitrarily chosen.

The importance of that new concept is given by the next theorem, the proof of which can be found in any classical textbook on automata theory, such as Ginzburg [1968].

Theorem 8.9. The quotient automaton A/π covers A. ■

One of the main goals in automata minimization is to obtain an automaton that covers a given automaton A and has a minimum number of internal states. It can be proven that if A has no *output empty state*, i.e. a state s such that $N_x(s) = \phi$ for every finite non-empty word x over Σ, then every automaton that covers A and has a minimum number of states is isomorphic to one of the quotient automata of A (see Zahnd [1969]). In the case where A contains some output empty state(s), a simple transformation yields an equivalent automaton without any output empty state (Davio and De Lit [1970]).

The problem can thus be solved in two phases. In a first phase, one looks for the set $\mathscr{C}$ of all the compatibility classes of A. In the second phase one searches for a subset π of $\mathscr{C}$ that is a closed cover of S and contains a minimum number of classes. It suffices then to construct the quotient automaton A/π.

The main contribution to the first phase is due to Paull and Unger [1959]. Their method yields the set of maximal compatibility classes. It then suffices to write the list of all the subsets of S that are included in some maximal compatibility class. Furthermore, as noted by Grasselli and Luccio [1965], it is not necessary to consider all the compatibility classes but only the so-called prime compatibility classes.

Some other methods for finding the maximal or the prime compatibility classes have been proposed. Let us quote a.o. Marcus [1964], Davio [1969], Davio and Bioul [1970] and Sinha Roy and Sheng [1972].

The second phase is a covering-closure problem: one looks for a subset π of $\mathscr{C}$ that has a minimum number of elements and satisfies the two conditions of theorem 8.8. It suffices to give to every class in $\mathscr{C}$ the same cost, for instance a cost equal to 1.

We conclude this section by giving a method due to Meisel [1967] that is quite suitable for solving that particular type of covering-closure problem. Introduce first some new definitions.

Definitions 8.12. Consider the automaton A and two compatibility classes C and C' of A. The class C' is *induced* by the class C iff the three following conditions are satisfied:

(a) $C' = M_\sigma(C)$ for some $\sigma \in \Sigma$;
(b) C' is not included in C;
(c) C' contains at least two elements.

Consider now a set α of compatibility classes. The class C' is *induced* by α iff the two following conditions are satisfied:

(a) C' is induced by some class $C \in \alpha$;
(b) C' is included in none of the classes of α.

The set β of compatibility classes is a *closure* of the set α of compatibility classes iff the two following conditions hold:

(a) $\alpha \subseteq \beta$;
(b) every class induced by α is included in at least one class of β.

Furthermore, β is a *minimal closure* of α iff none of its proper subsets is a closure of α.

Define now an enumeration order of the elements of S:

$$S = \{s_1, s_2, \ldots, s_p\}.$$

The set β of compatibility classes is a *successor* of the set α of compatibility classes iff it verifies one of the two following conditions:

(a) if α induces some class, then β is a minimal closure of α;

(b) If α does not induce any class, then $\beta = \alpha \cup \{C\}$ where C is a compatibility class containing the state s_j that has the smallest index among the states that do not lie in any class of α.

The method of Meisel consists then in drawing a tree in a step by step way. Every node of the tree represents a set α of compatibility classes and is connected to all its successors; the starting point of the tree (i.e. its root) is the empty set. It is obvious that if a node, corresponding to a set α, has no successor, then α is a closed cover of S. Conversely, one can easily prove that every *irredundant closed cover* of S is obtained in that way (a closed cover π of S is irredundant iff none of its proper subsets is still a closed cover): in fact, at each node of the tree, one considers all the possibilities of completing a set α of classes in order that either it becomes closed or that it covers some new state, but without introducing unnecessary classes.

It is important to note that once one has found a node that has no successor and corresponds thus to a closed cover π, it is no longer necessary to consider nodes corresponding to sets α containing more classes than does π.

Note that a generalized version of that method could be used for solving any covering-closure problem.

Examples 8.5 (Zahnd and Mange [1975]). Consider the automaton of Figure 8.23 for which

$$\Sigma = \{00, 01, 11, 10\},$$

$$\Theta = \{0, 1\},$$

$$S = \{a, b, c, d, e\}.$$

M/N	00	01	11	10
a	$b/-$	$e/0$	$e/0$	$b/-$
b	$c/0$	$d/-$	$-/-$	$-/-$
c	$-/-$	$e/-$	$a/0$	$b/0$
d	$a/-$	$b/1$	$-/-$	$-/-$
e	$b/1$	$-/-$	$-/-$	$d/1$

Figure 8.23. Automaton A

It has four maximal compatibility classes: $\{a, e\}, \{b, d\}, \{d, e\}$ and $\{a, b, c\}$. The table of Figure 8.24 gives the twelve compatibility classes along with the corresponding induced classes. One associates a score with every element of S, namely the number of compatibility classes containing the considered element of S, and range them by increasing score: d, e, c, a, b.

	Compatibility classes	Induced classes
C_1	$\{a\}$	–
C_2	$\{b\}$	–
C_3	$\{c\}$	–
C_4	$\{d\}$	–
C_5	$\{e\}$	–
C_6	$\{a, b\}$	$\{b, c\}, \{d, e\}$
C_7	$\{a, c\}$	$\{a, e\}$
C_8	$\{a, e\}$	$\{b, d\}$
C_9	$\{b, c\}$	$\{d, e\}$
C_{10}	$\{b, d\}$	$\{a, c\}$
C_{11}	$\{d, e\}$	$\{a, b\}$
C_{12}	$\{a, b, c\}$	$\{d, e\}, \{a, e\}$

Figure 8.24. Compatibility classes and induced classes

The tree that yields the optimal closed cover of S is given in Figure 8.25; every edge is indexed by the rule (a) or (b) giving the corresponding successor. There are two minimum closed covers:

$$\pi_1 = \{C_7, C_8, C_{10}\}$$

and

$$\pi_2 = \{C_6, C_9, C_{11}\}.$$

The two corresponding quotient automata are described in Figures 8.26 and 8.27.

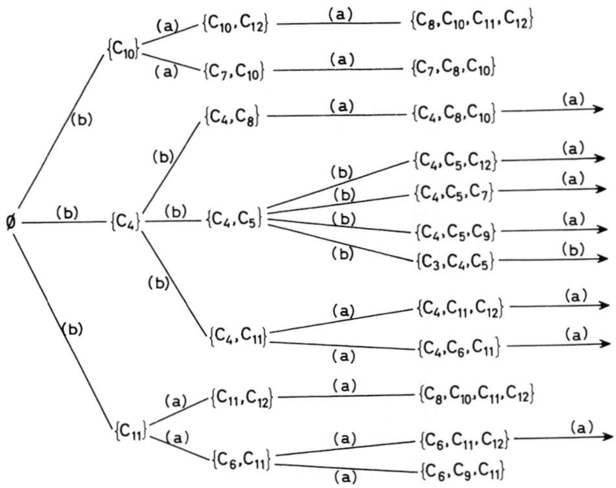

Figure 8.25. Covering-closure tree

M^{π_1}/N^{π_1}	00	01	11	10
C_7	$C_{10}/-$	$C_8/0$	$C_8/0$	$C_{10}/0$
C_8	$C_{10}/1$	$C_8/0$	$C_8/0$	$C_{10}/1$
C_{10}	$C_7/0$	$C_{10}/1$	$-/-$	$-/-$

Figure 8.26. Quotient automaton A/π_1

M^{π_2}/N^{π_2}	00	01	11	10
C_6	$C_9/0$	$C_{11}/0$	$C_{11}/0$	C_6 or $C_9/-$
C_9	$C_9/0$	$C_{11}/-$	$C_6/0$	C_6 or $C_9/-$
C_{11}	$C_6/1$	C_6 or $C_9/1$	$-/-$	$C_{11}/1$

Figure 8.27. Quotient automaton A/π_2

8.3. Comments

We conclude this chapter by two comments. The first one concerns the usefulness of the theory developed above. Beyond the problems of discrete function minimization and finite automata minimization, there are several other problems that can be stated in terms of covering and covering-closure problems. Let us quote some of them that arise in switching theory:

design of minimum cost TANT networks (Gimpel [1967]);
synthesis of three-level logic networks (Grasselli and Gimpel [1966]);
finding of a minimum test set (Kautz [1968], Thayse [1972a]);
minimizing the bit dimension of the control memory in a microprogrammed system (Montangero [1974], Das *et al.* [1973]).

The second comment concerns the algorithms that have been proposed above. In fact we have described methods or principles of solution rather than precise algorithms, and efficient algorithms could use successively and iteratively several of the stated principles. For instance, one could imagine the following scheme for solving a CC-table:

use the simplification rules of theorems 8.5 and 8.6 as much as possible;
branching step: obtain two new CC-tables by fixing the value of some variable x_i in (8.7), (8.8) and (8.9) to 0 and 1 successively;
use the simplification rules for the two tables, and so on.

Some branching can be avoided because they yield CC-tables that are not consistent. Furthermore, at some step of the algorithm one could decide to use the Boolean method or the linear programming method for solving the remaining CC-tables.

Chapter 9
Functional Completeness

This chapter is devoted to the functional completeness in r-ary logic. The problem is to find conditions that a family of logic functions must satisfy in order that all logic functions can be expressed as a finite composition of those functions. The solution of that problem plays an important role in the study of logic circuits; indeed, it is sometimes necessary to decide whether a family of logic gates allows synthesization of all the logic functions or not.

The first section (9.1) relates the study of the functional completeness to the existence of closed classes of logic functions. The main result (theorem 9.1) is that having a description of the maximal classes yields good criteria for functional completeness.

The second section (9.2) is devoted to the functional completeness in binary logic. The main result is a theorem due to Post (theorem 9.8) that gives a necessary and sufficient condition under which a set of switching functions is functionally complete.

The functional completeness in r-ary logic, with r greater than 2, is studied in the third section (9.3). The most important result is a theorem due to Rosenberg (theorem 9.9) that is stated here without proof. The case of the ternary logic ($r = 3$) is studied more thoroughly.

In the next section (9.4) the well-known Slupecki theorem is stated and proven, while the last section (9.5) is devoted to some examples.

9.1. *Closed classes*

Definition 9.1. Denote by $0_S^{(n)}$ the set of functions from S^n to S, and by 0_S the set of functions $0_S^{(1)} \cup 0_S^{(2)} \cup \ldots$, i.e. the set of logic functions.

Consider now a subset F of 0_S:

$$F = \{f_i \mid i \in I\},\ f_i \in 0_S^{(n_i)} \quad \forall i \in I,$$

where I is an index set. Given a set of variables $\{x_1, x_2, \ldots\}$, a *well-formed functional expression* on F is defined inductively as follows:

(a) the variables are well-formed functional expressions (in short: w.f.f.e.);

(b) if $\alpha_1, \ldots, \alpha_{m_i}$ are w.f.f.e., then $f_i(\alpha_1, \ldots, \alpha_{n_i})$ is a w.f.f.e.;
(c) there are no other w.f.f.e. than those generated by using a finite number of times rules (a) and (b).

It is obvious that every w.f.f.e. on F, with $\{x_1, \ldots, x_n\}$ as set of variables, defines a function of $0_S^{(n)}$. One can thus associate with every subset F of 0_S the set $J(F)$ of all functions in 0_S that can be defined by a w.f.f.e. on F with a suitable set of variables. Note that $J(F)$ does not necessarily contain the constant functions.

The operator J satisfies the three following rules:

(a) $F \subseteq J(F), \quad \forall F \subseteq 0_S;$
(b) $F \subseteq F' \Rightarrow J(F) \subseteq J(F');$
(c) $J[J(F)] = J(F), \quad \forall F \subseteq 0_S.$

It is thus a closure operator. The closed subsets of 0_S are called *closed classes.*

We now give the main definition: a subset F of 0_S is *functionally complete* iff $J(F) = 0_S$. It is thus a set of logic functions that allows one to express all other logic functions by finite composition.

The set of closed classes is a lattice in which the two binary operations $\vee$ and $\wedge$ are defined as follows (see section 1.3.5):

$$F \wedge F' = J(F \cap F') \quad \text{and} \quad F \vee F' = J(F \cup F').$$

The closed classes covered by 0_S are called the *maximal classes* of logic functions; they are thus the greatest classes properly included in 0_S.

The analysis of that lattice and, in particular, the description of its maximal classes plays a key role in the research of functional completeness criteria. This fact is attested by the next theorem.

Theorem 9.1. A subset F of 0_S is functionally complete iff for every maximal class C_i there is at least one function f_i in F such that $f_i \notin C_i$.

Proof. The condition is necessary: suppose indeed that every function f of F lies in some maximal class C. One has then

$$J(F) \subseteq C \subset 0_S.$$

Suppose conversely that the condition is verified. Then $J(F)$ being included in none of the maximal classes must be equal to 0_S. ■

As will be seen later, some closed classes, among which are the maximal classes, can be described as the set of functions that preserve some given relation. Recall that an h-ary relation on S is a subset of L^h, for every integer $h \geqslant 1$.

Definition 9.2. The logic function $f(x_{n-1}, \ldots, x_0)$ *preserves the h-ary relation R iff the fact that*

$$(s_{n-1}^1, \ldots, s_{n-1}^h) \in R \text{ and } \ldots \text{ and } (s_0^1, \ldots, s_0^h) \in R$$

implies that

$$[f(s^1_{n-1}, \ldots, s^1_0), \ldots, f(s^h_{n-1}, \ldots, s^h_0)] \in R.$$

Lemma 9.1. Given an h-ary relation R on L, the set of logic functions that preserve R is a closed class.

Proof. Let F be the set of logic functions that preserve R. One must prove that every function that is in $J(F)$ preserves R and is thus also in F. It is obvious that the variables define functions preserving R. The proof is completed by induction on the number of occurrences of elements of F in a w.f.f.e.

Let $g(x_{n-1}, \ldots, x_0)$ be in $J(F)$ and suppose that it is defined by a w.f.f.e. in which appear $m + 1$ occurrences of elements of F. It can thus be written under the form

$$g(x) = f_i[g_{n_i-1}(x), \ldots, g_0(x)]$$

where each $g_j(x)$ can be defined by a w.f.f.e. in which appear at most m occurrences of elements of F. Therefore, each function g_j preserves R. Note that some functions g_j could be independent of some of their arguments.

Suppose now that

$$(s^1_{n-1}, \ldots, s^h_{n-1}) \in R \text{ and } \ldots \text{ and } (s^1_0, \ldots, s^h_0) \in R.$$

Therefore

$$[g_j(s^1_{n-1}, \ldots, s^1_0), \ldots, g_j(s^h_{n-1}, \ldots, s^h_0)] \in R,$$

for any $j = 0, \ldots, n_i-1$, and since f_i is in F and preserves also R one obtains:

$$\{f_i[\ldots, g_j(s^1_{n-1}, \ldots, s^1_0), \ldots], \ldots, f_i[\ldots, g_j(s^h_{n-1}, \ldots, s^h_0), \ldots]\} \in R,$$

i.e.

$$[g(s^1_{n-1}, \ldots, s^1_0), \ldots, g(s^h_{n-1}, \ldots, s^h_0)] \in R.$$

This proves that g preserves R. ∎

9.2. The functional completeness in binary logic

In the case of binary logic, i.e. for $S = B_2 = \{0, 1\}$, the lattice of closed classes has been thoroughly studied by Post [1941]. It contains five maximal classes. Let us describe them:

(1) The set of functions that preserve the order relation in B_2, i.e. the *monotone increasing* functions.

(2) The set of functions that preserve the binary relation

$$R = \{(b, b \oplus 1) \mid b \in B_2\} = \{(0, 1), (1, 0)\},$$

i.e. the functions f such that

$$f(x_{n-1}, \ldots, x_0) \oplus 1 = f(x_{n-1} \oplus 1, \ldots, x_0 \oplus 1).$$

These functions are the *self-dual* functions.

(3) The set of functions that preserve the quaternary relation

$$R' = \{(b_1, b_2, b_3, b_4) \in B_2^4 \mid b_1 \oplus b_2 = b_3 \oplus b_4\}.$$

It is obvious that every linear function preserves R'. Suppose conversely that $f(x_{n-1}, \ldots, x_0)$ preserves R'; then

$$\frac{\Delta f}{\Delta x_i} = f(x_{n-1}, \ldots, x_i \oplus 1, \ldots, x_0) \oplus f(x_{n-1}, \ldots, x_i, \ldots, x_0)$$

$$= f(0, \ldots, 1, \ldots, 0) \oplus f(0, \ldots, 0, \ldots, 0).$$

Therefore all the first differences have a constant value and f is a linear function. This third class is thus the class of all the *linear* functions.

(4) The set of functions that preserve the unary relation $R'' = \{0\}$, i.e. the functions f such that $f(0, \ldots, 0) = 0$. They are called the *0-preserving* functions.

(5) The set of functions that preserve the unary relation $R''' = \{1\}$, i.e. the functions f for which $f(1, \ldots, 1) = 1$. They are called the *1-preserving* functions.

By lemma 9.1 one already knows that these five sets of functions are closed classes. Furthermore it can easily be proven that they are maximal classes. In order to prove that a closed class C is a maximal class it suffices to verify that by adding to C any function that is not in C one obtains a functionally complete set.

Theorem 9.2. The set of monotone increasing functions is a maximal class.

Proof. Consider a function $f(x_{n-1}, \ldots, x_0)$ that is not monotone increasing. There thus exists an element i in $\{0, 1, \ldots, n-1\}$ and $n-1$ elements $e_0, \ldots, e_{i-1}, e_{i+1}, \ldots, e_{n-1}$ in B_2 such that

$$f(e_{n-1}, \ldots, e_{i+1}, x_i, e_{i-1}, \ldots, e_0) = \bar{x}_i.$$

In the contrary case f would be monotone increasing.

The set of monotone increasing functions contains the constant functions; thus, by adding f to that set, one can express the complement. Since furthermore the conjunction and the disjunction are also monotone increasing functions, one obtains a functionally complete set in which every function can be expressed for instance by the disjunction of its minterms. ■

Theorem 9.3. The set of self-dual functions is a maximal class.

Proof. Consider a function $f(x_{n-1}, \ldots, x_0)$ that is not self-dual. Thus, there exists an element $(e_{n-1}, \ldots, e_0)$ in B_2^n such that

$$f(e_{n-1}, \ldots, e_0) = f(e_{n-1} \oplus 1, \ldots, e_0 \oplus 1).$$

Suppose that $e_{n-1} = \ldots = e_q = 0$ and $e_{q-1} = \ldots = e_0 = 1$. Thus

$$f(0, \ldots, 0, 1, \ldots, 1) = f(1, \ldots, 1, 0, \ldots, 0) = b$$

and

$$f(x, \ldots, x, \bar{x}, \ldots, \bar{x}) \equiv b,$$

where b is either 0 or 1.

The complement is a self-dual function; thus by adding f to the set of self-dual functions, one can define the constant function b and also the constant function $\bar{b}$.

On the other hand, the majority function $M(x_2, x_1, x_0) = x_2x_1 \vee x_2x_0 \vee x_1x_0$ is a self-dual function. Taking into account the fact that

$$x_1 \vee x_0 = M(1, x_1, x_0) \quad \text{and} \quad x_1x_0 = M(0, x_1, x_0),$$

one concludes that by adding f to the set of self-dual functions one obtains a functionally complete set. ∎

Theorem 9.4. The set of linear functions is a maximal class.

Proof. Consider a function f that is not linear. Its Mclaurin expansion contains at least one term in which appear two or more variables; choose one term of that kind in which a minimum number of variables appears. Its general form is x_ix_jp where either $p = 1$ or p is a product of variables. Give the value 1 to the variables appearing in p, and the value 0 to the other variables except x_i and x_j. One obtains a function of the type $a \oplus bx_i \oplus cx_j \oplus x_ix_j = a \oplus bc \oplus (x_i \oplus c)(x_j \oplus b)$.

The constant functions and the complement are linear functions. By adding f to the set of linear functions, one can thus define the conjunction; by De Morgan's laws, one can also define the disjunction. One has thus obtained a functionally complete set. ∎

Theorem 9.5. The set of 0-preserving functions is a maximal class.

Proof. Consider a function f that is not 0-preserving. Therefore $f(0, \ldots, 0) = 1$. Taking into account the fact that the constant function 0, the sum modulo-2 and the product are 0-preserving functions, one concludes that by adding f to the set of 0-preserving functions one obtains a functionally complete set: every function can indeed be represented by its Mclaurin expansion. ∎

Theorem 9.6. The set of 1-preserving functions is a maximal class.

Proof. Dual statement of the preceding theorem. ∎

One proves now that there are no other maximal classes.

Theorem 9.7. Every closed class, different from the set of all functions, is included in at least one of the five maximal classes defined above.

Proof. Suppose that a closed class F is contained in none of the five maximal classes defined above. It contains a function g that is not 0-preserving, i.e.

$$g(x, \ldots, x) = 1 \quad \text{or} \quad g(x, \ldots, x) = \bar{x}.$$

It contains also a function h that is not 1-preserving, i.e.

$$h(x, \ldots, x) = 0 \quad \text{or} \quad h(x, \ldots, x) = \bar{x}.$$

Therefore F contains either the two constant functions or the complement. In that last case, taking into account the fact that F contains a function that is not self-dual, the same reasoning as in the proof of theorem 9.3 shows that F contains the two constant functions.

Now, since F contains the two constant functions and a function that is not monotone increasing, the same reasoning as in the proof of theorem 9.2 shows that F contains the complement.

Finally, since F contains the constant functions, the complement, and a non-linear function, the same reasoning as in the proof of theorem 9.4 shows that F is functionally complete. But then F is the set of all functions since it is a closed class. ■

We can now state the main theorem of this section.

Theorem 9.8. A set of switching functions is functionally complete iff it contains

(a) *at least one function that is not monotone increasing;*
(b) *at least one function that is not self-dual;*
(c) *at least one function that is not linear;*
(d) *at least one function that is not 0-preserving;*
(e) *at least one function that is not 1-preserving.* ■

Introduce now a new definition.

Definition 9.3. A set F of switching function is *weakly functionally complete* or in short, *weakly complete* if by adding the constant functions 0 and 1 to F one obtains a functionally complete set.

From the logician's point of view, this notion has little meaning, one of the goals being precisely to generate the constant functions from other functions and to conclude in such a way that some propositions are always true or always false. However, from the logic circuit designer's point of view, the weak functional completeness is the main notion: the constant functions are indeed always available, being, for example, two voltage levels provided by the power supply.

Corollary 9.1. A set of switching functions is weakly complete iff it contains

(a) *at least one function that is not monotone increasing;*
(b) *at least one function that is not linear.*

Proof. It suffices to note that the constant functions are not self-dual, that the constant 0 is not a 1-preserving function, and that the constant 1 is not a 0-preserving function. ■

The next definition introduces another important notion, that of universal function (sometimes called Sheffer function).

Definition 9.4. A switching function f is a *universal function* iff the singleton $\{f\}$ is a functionally complete set. The function f thus allows to define all the other switching functions. Well-known examples of universal functions are the NOR and the NAND functions.

Corollary 9.2. A switching function $f(x_{n-1}, \ldots, x_0)$ is universal iff

(a) *it is not a self-dual function;*
(b) *it is not a 0-preserving function;*
(c) *it is not a 1-preserving function.*

Proof. It suffices to prove that if f satisfies the three conditions, then it is neither monotone increasing nor linear.

It is not monotone increasing since

$$f(0, \ldots, 0) = 1 \quad \text{and} \quad f(1, \ldots, 1) = 0.$$

Suppose that f is a linear function, i.e.

$$f = a \oplus \sum_{i=0}^{n-1} b_i x_i,$$

and thus

$$f(x_{n-1} \oplus 1, \ldots, x_0 \oplus 1) = f(x_{n-1}, \ldots, x_0) \oplus b,$$

where

$$b = \sum_{i=0}^{n-1} b_i.$$

If $b = 1$, then f is self-dual, and this contradicts the hypothesis. If $b = 0$, then $f(0, \ldots, 0) = f(1, \ldots, 1)$ and this contradicts also the hypothesis. ■

9.3. *The functional completeness in r-ary logic*

In the case of the r-ary logic, i.e. for $S = \{0, 1, \ldots, r-1\}$ with $r \geqslant 3$, the maximal classes of the lattice of closed classes have been found by Rosenberg [1965]. They are again sets of functions preserving some relations. The main result is that these relations belong to only six different types of relations. They are described below.

(1) The *order relations* with minimum element and maximum element.
(2) The binary relations of the type

$$R = \{(s_1, s_2) \in S^2 \mid s_2 = \pi(s_1)\},$$

where π is a non-trivial permutation, acting on S, that is composed of cycles having the same prime length.

(3) In the case where $r = p^m$, with p a prime, the quaternary relations of the type

$$R' = \{(s_1, s_2, s_3, s_4) \in S^4 \mid s_1 + s_2 = s_3 + s_4\},$$

where the addition confers to S the structure of commutative group of order p (i.e. a commutative group in which all elements have order p).

(4) The non-trivial *equivalence relations.*

(5) The *central h-ary relations.* An h-ary relation R'' is central iff it is *totally reflexive, totally symmetric* and if its *centre* is neither empty nor S itself.

An h-ary relation R'' is *totally reflexive* if the fact that in an h-tuple $(s_1, \ldots, s_h)$ all the components are not different (i.e. $s_i = s_j$ for some i and j) implies that $(s_1, \ldots, s_h)$ is in the relation.

An h-ary relation R'' is *totally symmetric* iff the fact that $(s_1, \ldots, s_h)$ is in R'' implies that $(s_{\pi(1)}, \ldots, s_{\pi(h)})$ is also in R'', for every permutation π acting on $\{1, \ldots, h\}$.

The *centre* of an h-ary relation R'' is the following subset of S:

$$\{s \in S \mid (s_1, \ldots, s_{h-1}, s) \in R'', \quad \forall (s_1, \ldots, s_{h-1}) \in S^{h-1}\}.$$

Note that the central unary relations can be confounded with their centre; they are thus all the proper non-empty subsets of S.

(6) The h-ary relations deduced as follows from an onto mapping ψ from S to $\{0, 1, \ldots, h^m - 1\}$, with

$$3 \leqslant h \leqslant r \quad \text{and} \quad 1 \leqslant m:$$

the h-tuple $(s_1, \ldots, s_h)$ is in the relation iff for every $l = 0, \ldots, m-1$, there are at most $h-1$ different values among $[\psi(s_1)]_l, \ldots, [\psi(s_h)]_l$, where $[\psi(s_i)]_l$ stands for the digit of order l in the expression of $\psi(s_i)$ in basis h, i.e.

$$\psi(s_i) = [\psi(s_i)]_0 + [\psi(s_i)]_1 h + \ldots + [\psi(s_i)]_{m-1} h^{m-1}.$$

In other words, $(s_1, \ldots, s_h)$ is in the relation iff for every $l = 0, \ldots, m-1$, two at least of the numbers $\psi(s_1), \ldots, \psi(s_h)$ have the same digit of order l when they are expressed in basis h.

We can now state the main result of this section.

Theorem 9.9 (Rosenberg [1965]). *A set F of logic functions is functionally complete iff for each relation belonging to one of the six types quoted above there is at least one function in F that does not preserve that relation.* ■

The proof of that remarkable property is very long. It has been published by Rosenberg in 1970.

It is obvious that two relations belonging to the same type could be equivalent, i.e. they could be preserved by exactly the same logic functions. Consider for instance an order relation with minimum and maximum element, and the converse relation.

Therefore the number of maximal classes is smaller than the number of relations belonging to one of the six types. The number of maximal classes, for each value of r, has been computed by Rosenberg [1973]. The results, for $r = 3$ to 7, are summarized in Figure 9.1 in which k_i gives the number of relations of type (i) that must be considered.

r	k_1	k_2	k_3	k_4	k_5	k_6	Total
3	3	1	1	3	9	1	18
4	18	3	1	13	40	7	82
5	190	6	6	50	355	36	643
6	3 285	35	0	201	11 490	171	15 182
7	88 851	120	120	875	7 758 205	813	7 848 984

Figure 9.1. Number of maximal classes

The concepts introduced in definitions 9.3 and 9.4 for switching functions can obviously be generalized.

Definitions 9.5. A set F of logic functions is *weakly complete* if by adding the r constant functions $0, 1, \ldots, r-1$ to F one obtains a functionally complete set.
A logic function f is *universal* iff the singleton $\{f\}$ is a functionally complete set.

Corollary 9.3. A set F of logic functions is weakly complete iff for each relation belonging to one of the types (1), (3), (4), and (6), quoted above, and for each central h-ary relation, with $h \geqslant 2$, there is at least one function in F that does not preserve that relation.

Proof. For every non-trivial permutation π, there is at least one constant function that does not preserve the relation $\{(s_1, s_2) \in S^2 \mid s_2 = \pi(s_1)\}$: there is at least one element s in S such that $\pi(s) \neq s$. Then the constant function s does not preserve the relation.

For every central unary relation there is also at least one constant function that does not preserve the relation: it suffices to choose an element s that does not lie in the centre of the relation. Then the constant function s does not preserve the relation. ■

The conditions that a logic function $f(x_{n-1}, \ldots, x_0)$ must fulfil in order to be universal have been studied by Rousseau [1967].

Theorem 9.10 (Rousseau [1967]). *A logic function f is universal iff it preserves none of the relations belonging to one of the three following types:*

(a) *the central unary relations;*

(b) *the binary relations of the type*

$$\{(s_1, s_2) \in S^2 \mid s_2 = \pi(s_1)\},$$

where π is a non-trivial permutation acting on S;

(c) *the non-trivial equivalence relations.*

Note that Rousseau has stated the theorem in terms of universal algebra; one may indeed consider $\langle S, f\rangle$ has a universal algebra in which f is an n-ary operator.

(a) If f preserves the central relation $S' \subseteq S$, that means that S' is a stable part of S with respect to f, and thus $\langle S', f'\rangle$ is a *subalgebra* of $\langle S, f\rangle$, where f' stands for the restriction of f to S'.

(b) If f preserves the binary relation

$$\{(s_1, s_2) \in S^2 \mid s_2 = \pi(s_1)\},$$

then π is an *automorphism* of $\langle S, f\rangle$.

(c) If f preserves an equivalence relation ρ on S, then ρ is a *congruence* on $\langle S, f\rangle$.

The theorem can thus be stated as follows: *a logic function f is universal iff the three following conditions are satisfied:*

(a) *there is no proper subalgebra of $\langle S, f\rangle$;*

(b) *there is non-trivial automorphism of $\langle S, f\rangle$;*

(c) *there is no non-trivial congruence on $\langle S, f\rangle$.*

The point (b) of the last theorem can be slightly modified, as noted by Schofield [1969], thanks to the following proposition.

Lemma 9.2. If π is an automorphism of the algebra $\langle S, f\rangle$, then one of the two following assertions holds true:

(a) *there is an automorphism ψ of $\langle S, f\rangle$, such that the permutation ψ is composed of cycles having the same prime length.*

(b) *There is a proper subalgebra of $\langle S, f\rangle$.*

Proof. Note that if π is an automorphism, then its successive powers

$$\pi^2 = \pi.\pi, \pi^3 = \pi.\pi^2, \ldots$$

are also automorphisms, since the composition of two automorphisms is an automorphism.

Suppose that the cycles of π have not all the same length, and let i be the length of a cycle of minimum length. Consider then the automorphism $\phi = \pi^i$ and the subset S' of S of all points belonging to a cycle of length i in π. It is obvious that

$\phi(s') = s', \forall s' \in S'$, and thus, since ϕ is an automorphism, one obtains:

$$f(s'_{n-1}, \ldots, s'_0) = f[\phi(s'_{n-1}), \ldots, \phi(s'_0)] = \phi\,[f(s'_{n-1}, \ldots, s'_0)],$$

for any $(s'_{n-1}, \ldots, s'_0) \in S'$; since ϕ maps $f(s'_{n-1}, \ldots, s'_0)$ on itself, that means that $f(s'_{n-1}, \ldots, s'_0)$ is also in S'. Therefore S' is a stable part of S with respect to f and $\langle S, f\rangle$ admits a proper subalgebra.

Suppose now that the cycles of π have all the same length $p \times q$. It is obvious that the automorphism $\psi = \pi^q$ has cycles of length p. ■

From theorem 9.10 and from the last lemma one then deduces the next proposition.

Corollary 9.4. The logic function f is universal iff it preserves none of the relations belonging to one of the types (2) and (4) quoted above, and none of the central unary relations.

We conclude this section by describing the eighteen maximal classes in the case of the ternary logic. Consider for this purpose the six types of relations.

(1) One can define six order relations, with minimum and maximum elements, on the set $\{0, 1, 2\}$. However, it is clear that an order relation and the converse relation yield the same classes of functions. One has thus to consider only three order relations:

$$0 < 1 < 2, \quad 0 < 2 < 1 \quad \text{and} \quad 1 < 0 < 2.$$

(2) There are two non-trivial permutations composed of cycles of the same prime length:

$$\sigma_1(x) = x \oplus 1 \quad \text{and} \quad \sigma_2(x) = x \oplus 2:$$

since furthermore $\sigma_1 = \sigma_2^2$ and $\sigma_2 = \sigma_1^2$, both yield the same maximal class. It thus suffices to choose one of these permutations, say σ_1, in order to define the maximal class: it contains all the functions $f(x_{n-1}, \ldots, x_0)$ for which the following relation is verified

$$f(x_{n-1}, \ldots, x_0) \oplus 1 = f(x_{n-1} \oplus 1, \ldots, x_0 \oplus 1).$$

By analogy with the binary case, these functions are called *self-dual.*

(3) Consider a commutative group of order 3, defined on $\{0, 1, 2\}$, the composition law of which is denoted +. Let s be an element of $\{0, 1, 2\}$ that is not the zero element of the group; the three elements of $\{0, 1, 2\}$ can thus be denoted $0.s = s + s + s$, i.e. the zero element, $1.s = s$ and $2.s = s + .s$. With that notation it is obvious that

$$i.s + j.s = (i \oplus j).s, \quad \forall i, j \in \{0, 1, 2\}.$$

This establishes an isomorphism between the chosen commutative group of order 3 and the additive group of Z_3 that we denote G. Let ϕ be that isomorphism. On the other hand, the permutation ψ, acting on $\{0, 1, 2\}$, that transposes 1 with 2 and leaves 0 fixed, is an automorphism of G. Therefore, $\phi.\psi$ is also an isomorphism between the chosen group and G. Whatever may be the permutation ϕ, either ϕ or $\phi.\psi$ is a permutation of the type $\pi(x) = x \oplus s$ for some $s \in \{0, 1, 2\}$. Therefore, since π is an isomorphism, one has

$$s_1 + s_2 = s_3 + s_4 \Leftrightarrow \pi(s_1 + s_2) = \pi(s_3 + s_4) \Leftrightarrow \pi(s_1) \oplus \pi(s_2) = \pi(s_3) \oplus \pi(s_4) \Leftrightarrow$$
$$(s_1 \oplus s) \oplus (s_2 \oplus s) = (s_3 \oplus s) \oplus (s_4 \oplus s) \Leftrightarrow s_1 \oplus s_2 = s_3 \oplus s_4.$$

There is thus only one maximal class; it contains all the functions that preserve the quaternary relation

$$\{(s_1, s_2, s_3, s_4) \in \{0, 1, 2\}^4 \mid s_1 \oplus s_2 = s_3 \oplus s_4\}.$$

Consider now a function $f(x_{n-1}, \ldots, x_0)$ that preserves that relation; then we may write

$$f(x_{n-1}, \ldots, x_i, \ldots, x_0) \oplus f(0, \ldots, 1, \ldots, 0) = f(x_{n-1}, \ldots, x_i \oplus 1, \ldots, x_0) \oplus f(0, \ldots, 0, \ldots, 0),$$

and thus

$$\frac{\Delta f}{\Delta x_i} = f(0, \ldots, 1, \ldots, 0) - f(0, \ldots, 0, \ldots, 0).$$

The first order differences are constant functions and the differences of higher order are then identically equal to 0. By the Newton expansion one obtains

$$f(x_{n-1}, \ldots, x_0) = f(0, \ldots, 0) \oplus s_0 x_0 \oplus \ldots \oplus s_{n-1} x_{n-1},$$

where $s_i = \Delta f / \Delta x_i$, $\forall i = 0, \ldots, n-1$. The function is thus a linear function.

It is obvious that conversely every linear function preserves the relation. This maximal class is thus the class of all the *linear functions.*

(4) There are three non-trivial equivalence relations on $\{0, 1, 2\}$; they correspond to the three following partitions:

$$(0, 1; 2), (0, 2; 1) \quad \text{and} \quad (0; 1, 2).$$

(5) There are six central unary relations corresponding to the six non-empty proper subsets of $\{0, 1, 2\}$:

$$\{0\}, \{1\}, \{2\}, \{0, 1\}, \{0, 2\}, \{1, 2\}.$$

There are three central binary relations with a singleton as centre:

$$\text{centre } \{0\} \Rightarrow \{(0, 0), (1, 1), (2, 2), (0, 1), (1, 0), (0, 2), (2, 0)\},$$
$$\text{centre } \{1\} \Rightarrow \{(0, 0), (1, 1), (2, 2), (1, 0), (0, 1), (1, 2), (2, 1)\},$$
$$\text{centre } \{2\} \Rightarrow \{(0, 0), (1, 1), (2, 2), (2, 0), (0, 2), (2, 1), (1, 2)\}.$$

There is no central binary relation with a two element centre: it would contain all the pairs of elements, but then the centre would be $\{0, 1, 2\}$.

(6) When $r = 3$, the only possible choice for h and m is $h = 3$ and $m = 1$. In that case, the onto mapping ψ is a bijection. Therefore, the ternary relation

$$\{(s_1, s_2, s_3) \in \{0, 1, 2\}^3 \mid \psi(s_1) = \psi(s_2) \text{ or } \psi(s_1) = \psi(s_3) \text{ or } \psi(s_2) = \psi(s_3)\}$$

is the same as the relation

$$\{(s_1, s_2, s_3) \in \{0, 1, 2\}^3 \mid s_1 = s_2 \quad \text{or} \quad s_1 = s_3 \quad \text{or} \quad s_2 = s_3\},$$

whatever may be the bijection ψ. There is thus only one relation to consider.

Note that the three central binary relations are in fact three compatibility relations that can be described by the three following decompositions:

$$(0, 1; 0, 2), (0, 1; 1, 2), (0, 2; 1, 2).$$

These three relations and the three non-trivial equivalence relations are the only non-trivial compatibility relations on $\{0, 1, 2\}$.

On the other hand introduce the next definition.

Definition 9.6. Given a subset S' of S, a function that preserves the unary relation S', i.e. a function $f(x_{n-1}, \ldots, x_0)$ such that

$$f(s'_{n-1}, \ldots, s'_0) \in S', \quad \forall\, (s'_{n-1}, \ldots, s'_0) \in (S')^{n-1},$$

is called a *S'-preserving function.*

We are now in place to state the main theorem in what concerns the ternary logic.

Theorem 9.11. A set of functions of the ternary logic is functionally complete iff it contains

(a) *for each of the three order relations $0 < 1 < 2$, $0 < 2 < 1$ and $1 < 0 < 2$, at least one function that is not monotone increasing with respect to that order;*
(b) *at least one function that is not self-dual;*
(c) *at least one function that is not linear;*
(d) *for each of the six non-trivial compatibility relations on $\{0, 1, 2\}$, at least one function that does not preserve that relation;*
(e) *for each of the six non-empty proper subsets S' of $\{0, 1, 2\}$, at least one function that is not S'-preserving;*
(f) *at least one function that does not preserve the ternary relation $\{(s_1, s_2, s_3) \in \{0, 1, 2\}^3 \mid s_1 = s_2 \text{ or } s_1 = s_3 \text{ or } s_2 = s_3\}$.*

Note that the number of classes of functions that must be considered is eighteen as indicated in Figure 9.1.

Corollary 9.5. A set of functions of the ternary logic is weakly complete iff it contains

(a) *for each of the three order relations $0 < 1 < 2$, $0 < 2 < 1$ and $1 < 0 < 2$, at least one function that is not monotone increasing with respect to that order;*

(b) *at least one function that is not linear;*
(c) *for each of the six non-trivial compatibility relations on* $\{0, 1, 2\}$, *at least one function that does not preserve that relation;*
(d) *at least one function that does not preserve the ternary relation*

$$\{(s_1, s_2, s_3) \in \{0, 1, 2\}^3 \mid s_1 = s_2 \text{ or } s_1 = s_3 \text{ or } s_2 = s_3\}.$$

Corollary 9.6. A function f of the ternary logic is universal iff

(a) *it is not* S'*-preserving, for every non-empty proper subset* S' *of* $\{0, 1, 2\}$;
(b) *it is not self-dual;*
(c) *it preserves none of the three non-trivial equivalence relations on* $\{0, 1, 2\}$.

9.4. The Slupecki theorem

We give in this section a proof of a well-known theorem on functional completeness that is due to Slupecki [1939]. It is stated in the frame of the r-ary logic, with $r \geqslant 3$.

Definition 9.7. A logic function $f(x_{n-1}, \ldots, x_0)$ is an *essential function* (or *Slupecki function*) iff it effectively depends on at least two variables and takes on all values from S.

The theorem can then be stated as follows: *a set F of logic functions, that allows to define all the one-variable functions, is functionally complete iff it contains at least one essential function.*

The proof of that theorem is decomposed in a series of intermediary steps.

Let $f(x_{n-1}, \ldots, x_0)$ be an essential function that lies in F, and suppose that f effectively depends upon x_1 and x_0.

Lemma 9.3. s_1, s'_1, s_0, s'_0 *exist in S, and e and* e' *in* S^{n-2}, *such that either:*

$$f(e, s_1, s_0) \neq f(e, s_1, s'_0) \neq f(e', s'_1, s'_0) \neq f(e, s_1, s_0),$$

or

$$f(e, s_1, s_0) \neq f(e', s_1, s'_0) \neq f(e', s'_1, s'_0) \neq f(e, s_1, s_0).$$

Proof. Since f is not degenerate with respect to x_0, e exists in S^{n-2} and s_1 in S such that $f(e, s_1, x_0)$ is not a constant function. Consider then two cases.

Case 1. $f(e, s_1, x_0)$ does not take on all values from S. There is thus an element s in S such that

$$f(e, s_1, x_0) \neq s, \tag{9.1}$$

for every x_0 in S.

On the other hand, since f is essential, there is a point (e', s'_1, s'_0) in S^n such that $f(e', s'_1, s'_0) = s$. Thus

$$f(e, s_1, s'_0) \neq f(e, s'_1, s'_0) = s.$$

Furthermore, since $f(e, s_1, x_0)$ is not a constant function, there is s_0 in S such that

$$f(e, s_1, s_0) \neq f(e, s_1, s'_0),$$

and by (9.1)

$$f(e, s_1, s_0) \neq f(e', s'_1, s'_0) = s.$$

Therefore

$$f(e, s_1, s_0) \neq f(e, s_1, s'_0) \neq f(e', s'_1, s'_0) \neq f(e, s_1, s_0).$$

Case 2. $f(e, s_1, x_0)$ takes on all values. Since f is not degenerate with respect to x_1, e' exists in S^{n-2} and s'_0 in S such that $f(e', x_1, s'_0)$ is not a constant function. Thus one can find s'_1 in S such that

$$f(e', s'_1, s'_0) \neq f(e', s_1, s'_0);$$

since furthermore $f(e, s_1, x_0)$ takes on all values and since $r \geqslant 3$, there is s_0 in S such that

$$f(e, s_1, s_0) \neq f(e', s'_1, s'_0)$$

and

$$f(e, s_1, s_0) \neq f(e', s_1, s'_0).$$

Therefore

$$f(e, s_1, s_0) \neq f(e', s_1, s'_0) \neq f(e', s'_1, s'_0) \neq f(e, s_1, s_0).$$ ■

Lemma 9.4. For every integer p, $2 \leqslant p \leqslant r-1$, one can find n subsets $S_p^{(0)}, \ldots, S_p^{(n-1)}$ of S, each of them containing p elements, and such that f takes on at least $p+1$ different values on $S_p^{(n-1)} \times \ldots \times S_p^{(0)}$, i.e. $\# f(S_p^{(n-1)} \times \ldots \times S_p^{(0)}) \geqslant p+1$.

Proof. For $p = 2$, this is a direct consequence of lemma 6.3. The proof is then achieved by induction. Let $S_{p-1}^{(0)}, \ldots, S_{p-1}^{(n-1)}$ be subsets of S such that

$$\# S_{p-1}^{(i)} = p-1, \quad \forall i = 0, \ldots, n-1, \quad \text{and} \quad \# f(S_{p-1}^{(n-1)} \times \ldots \times S_{p-1}^{(0)}) = q \geqslant p.$$

If $q \geqslant p+1$, then it suffices to add to each $S_{p-1}^{(i)}$ an element of S arbitrarily chosen in order to obtain $S_p^{(i)}, \forall i = 0, \ldots, n-1$.

If $q = p$, there exists at least one value s in S that is not taken on by f on $S_{p-1}^{(n-1)} \times \ldots \times S_{p-1}^{(0)}$. But, since f is essential, the value s is taken on by f at least in one point of S^n. It is thus possible to add an element of S to each $S_{p-1}^{(i)}$ in order to obtain subsets $S_p^{(i)}$ such that f takes on at least $p+1$ different values on $S_p^{(n-1)} \times \ldots \times S_p^{(0)}$.

■

Lemma 9.5. Every function $g(x, y) \in 0_S^2$, that takes on $p + 1$ different values on S^2 with $2 \leqslant p \leqslant r-1$, admits a decomposition of the type

$$g(x,y) = \phi\{f[\alpha_{n-1}(x,y), \dots, \alpha_0(x,y)]\},$$

where every $\alpha_i(x, y)$ is a member of 0_S^2 that takes on at most p different values on S^2, $i = 0, \dots, n-1$, and where ϕ is in 0_S^1.

Proof. By lemma 9.4 we know that there are n subsets $S_p^{(0)}, \dots, S_p^{(n-1)}$ of S, each of them containing p elements, and such that

$$\# S' \geqslant p + 1 \quad \text{where} \quad S' = f(S_p^{(n-1)} \times \dots \times S_p^{(0)}).$$

By hypothesis one has

$$\# S'' = p + 1 \quad \text{where} \quad S'' = g(S \times S).$$

It is thus possible to define an onto mapping ϕ from S' to S'' (ϕ is arbitrarily chosen). One can then define an onto mapping h from $S_p^{(n-1)} \times \dots \times S_p^{(0)}$ to S'':

$$h(s_{n-1}, \dots, s_0) = \phi\,[f(s_{n-1}, \dots, s_0)].$$

Since h is an onto mapping, there exists at least one mapping k from S'' to $S_p^{(n-1)} \times \dots \times S_p^{(0)}$ such that $k.h = \Delta_{S''}$, i.e.

$$h\,[k(s'')] = s'', \quad \forall s'' \in S''.$$

Use the notation

$$[k_{n-1}(s''), \dots, k_0(s'')] \quad \text{for} \quad k(s'') \in L_p^{(n-1)} \times \dots \times L_p^{(0)},$$

and put

$$\alpha_i(x,y) = k_i\,[g(x,y)], \quad \forall i = 0, \dots, n-1.$$

The functions α_i take on their values in $L_p^{(i)}$, $\forall i = 0, \dots, n-1$; thus they take on at most p different values. Furthermore $\phi\{f[\alpha_{n-1}(x,y), \dots, \alpha_0(x,y)]\} = h\,[\alpha_{n-1}(x,y), \dots, \alpha_0(x,y)] = h\{k\,[g(x,y)]\} = g(x,y)$. ■

Lemma 9.6. Every function $g(x, y) \in 0_S^2$, taking on only two distinct values, can be defined by means of the one-variable functions and f.

Proof. Suppose that g takes on the values s and s'. It can be written under the form

$$g(x,y) = \psi\,[h(x,y)]$$

where h takes on the values 0 and $r-1$, and where ψ is a one-variable function that maps 0 on s and $r-1$ on s'. It thus suffices to define h by means of f and one-variable functions.

Consider the points e, e', s_1, s_1', s_0 and s_0' defined in lemma 6.3, and suppose that the first series of inequalities holds, i.e.

$$f(e, s_1, s_0) \neq f(e, s_1, s_0') \neq f(e', s_1', s_0') \neq f(e, s_1, s_0).$$

Put

$$f(e,s_1,s_0)=a, f(e,s_1,s_0')=b, f(e',s_1',s_0')=c, f(e',s_1',s_0)=d.$$

Since $a \neq b \neq c \neq a$, one has either $d \neq a$ or $d \neq c$. Suppose that $d \neq a$. Therefore one has:

$$a \neq b, a \neq c, \quad \text{and} \quad a \neq d.$$

Suppose now that k_1 and k_0 are two functions of 0_S that only take the values 0 and $r-1$. Choose n one-variable functions $\alpha_0, \ldots, \alpha_{n-1}$ such that

$$[\alpha_{n-1}(0), \ldots, \alpha_2(0)] = e, \alpha_1(0) = s_1, \alpha_0(0) = s_0,$$
$$[\alpha_{n-1}(r-1), \ldots, \alpha_2(r-1)] = e'; \alpha_1(r-1) = s_1', \alpha_0(r-1) = s_0'.$$

Finally choose a one-variable function ϕ such that

$$\phi(a) = 0, \phi(b) = \phi(c) = \phi(d) = r-1.$$

One can then easily verify that

$$\phi\{f[\alpha_{n-1}(k_1), \ldots, \alpha_2(k_1), \alpha_1(k_1), \alpha_0(k_0)]\} = k_0 \vee k_1.$$

The conjunction can also be realized thanks to De Morgan's law:

$$k_0 \wedge k_1 = \overline{(\bar{k}_0 \vee \bar{k}_1)}$$

where

$$\bar{k} = (r-1) - k, \quad \forall k \in 0_S.$$

In the case where $a = d$, and thus $c \neq a, c \neq b$ and $c \neq d$, it suffices to exchange e with e', s_1 with s_1' and s_0 with s_0' in the definition of the functions α_i, and to choose ϕ such that $\phi(c) = 0$, $\phi(a) = \phi(b) = \phi(d) = r-1$.

The case where the second series of inequalities holds in lemma 6.3 obviously corresponds to a permutation of the roles played by x_0 and x_1.

Taking into account the associativity of the disjunction, and the canonical expansion

$$h(x,y) = \bigvee (x^{(s_1)} \wedge y^{(s_2)}),$$

in which the disjunction is extended to all pairs $(s_1, s_2) \in S^2$ such that $h(s_1, s_2) = r-1$, one concludes that h is definable by means of f and one-variable functions. ∎

We are now in a position to prove the theorem of Slupecki.

1. *The condition is sufficient.* It suffices to prove that any two-variable function can be defined since every logic function admits canonical expansions in which appear binary associative operations and unary operations.

Consider now a two-variable function $g(x,y)$. A repeated use of lemma 9.5 shows that g is definable by means of f, of one-variable functions and of functions taking on only two values. Furthermore, these last functions are also definable by means of f and of one-variable functions (lemma 9.6). This concludes the proof.

2. *The condition is necessary.* It is obvious that the functions that depend upon only one variable and the functions that do not take on the r possible different values all preserve the r-ary relation

$$R = \{(s_1, \ldots, s_r) \in S^r \mid \text{there exist } i \text{ and } j \text{ such that } s_i = s_j\}.$$

Therefore, if a set of functions F does not contain any essential function, then the set $J(F)$ of functions definable by F is included in the closed class formed by the functions preserving R. Thus, F is not functionally complete.

Remark. Several authors have improved that theorem by replacing the set 0_S^1 of all one-variable functions by a proper subset of 0_S^1 called *basic set.*

Consider for instance the set

$$\{f \in 0_S^1 \mid f(s) \subset S\},$$

i.e. the one-variable functions that are not onto. A reasoning quite similar to that used in the proof of lemma 9.5 proves that combining that set of functions with an essential function allows to define all other one-variable functions. This result is due to Iablonskii [1958]. Other basic sets have been found by Salomaa [1962, 1963] and by Mal'cev [1967].

9.5. *Examples*

We conclude this chapter by some examples of universal functions and of functionally complete sets.

Theorem 9.12. The Webb function defined by

$$W(x, x) = x \oplus 1,$$

$$x \neq y \Rightarrow W(x, y) = 0$$

is universal.

Proof. In the case where $r = 2$ (binary logic), the Webb function is the NOR function $\overline{x \vee y}$; it is well known to be universal. In the general case, let us use the theorem 9.10.

(1) The algebra $\langle S, W\rangle$ has no proper subalgebra since $w(x, x) = x \oplus 1$.

(2) Suppose that $\langle S, W\rangle$ has a non-trivial automorphism π; choose then s_1 and s_2 in S, with $s_1 \neq s_2$ and thus also $\pi(s_1) \neq \pi(s_2)$:

$$0 = W[\pi(s_1), \pi(s_2)] = \pi[W(s_1, s_2)] = \pi(0).$$

Furthermore

$$\pi(s) \oplus 1 = W[\pi(s), \pi(s)] = \pi[W(s, s)] = \pi(s \oplus 1), \quad \forall s \in S.$$

Starting from the relation $\pi(0) = 0$, one proves in a step by step way that $\pi(1) = 1$, $\pi(2) = 2, \ldots, \pi(r-1) = r-1$, and π is the trivial automorphism.

(3) Suppose that $\langle S, W \rangle$ admits a non-trivial congruence $\equiv$. Let s_1 and s_2 be two elements of S such that

$$s_1 \neq s_2 \quad \text{and} \quad s_1 \equiv s_2.$$

Thus

$$W(s_1, s_2) \equiv W(s_1, s_1) \equiv W(s_2, s_2),$$

i.e.

$$0 \equiv s_1 \oplus 1 \equiv s_2 \oplus 1.$$

One proves in a step by step way that

$$0 \equiv s_1 \oplus i \equiv s_2 \oplus i, \qquad \forall i = 0, \ldots, r-1.$$

All the elements of S are thus equivalent to 0 and $\equiv$ is a trivial congruence. ■

Theorem 9.13. The function $(x \vee y) \oplus 1$ is universal.

Proof. In the case where $r = 2$, it is the NOR function. In the general case, use again the theorem 9.10.

(1) The algebra $\langle S, (x \vee y) \oplus 1 \rangle$ has no subalgebra since $(x \vee x) \oplus 1 = x \oplus 1$.

(2) Let π be an automorphism of $\langle S, (x \vee y) \oplus 1 \rangle$. Then

$$\{\pi(r-1) \vee \pi[\pi^{-1}(r-1)]\} \oplus 1 = \pi\{[(r-1) \vee \pi^{-1}(r-1)] \oplus 1\},$$

i.e.

$$(r-1) \oplus 1 = \pi[(r-1) \oplus 1]$$

and thus

$$0 = \pi(0).$$

On the other hand

$$[\pi(s) \vee \pi(s)] \oplus 1 = \pi[(s \vee s) \oplus 1], \qquad \forall s \in S,$$

i.e.

$$\pi(s) \oplus 1 = \pi(s \oplus 1).$$

Starting from the equality $\pi(0) = 0$, one inductively proves that $\pi(1) = 1, \ldots$, $\pi(r-1) = r-1$, and π is the trivial automorphism.

(3) Let $\equiv$ be a non-trivial congruence. Choose two elements s_1 and s_2 such that

$$s_1 < s_2 \quad \text{and} \quad s_1 \equiv s_2.$$

Then

$$s_2 \oplus 1 = (s_1 \vee s_2) \oplus 1 \equiv (s_1 \vee s_1) \oplus 1 = s_1 \oplus 1.$$

One proves in a step by step way that

$$s_1 \oplus i \equiv s_2 \oplus i, \quad \forall i = 0, \dots, (r-1). \tag{9.2}$$

Putting $i_0 = (r-1) - s_2$, one obtains

$$s_1 \oplus i_0 \equiv r-1 \tag{9.3}$$

and thus

$$[(s_1 \oplus i_0) \vee (s_1 \oplus i_0 \oplus 1)] \oplus 1 \equiv [(r-1) \vee (s_1 \oplus i_0 \oplus 1)] \oplus 1,$$

i.e.

$$s_1 \oplus i_0 \oplus 2 \equiv 0.$$

Since furthermore by (9.2) and (9.3)

$$s_1 \oplus i_0 \oplus 1 \equiv (r-1) \oplus 1 = 0,$$

one deduces that

$$s_1 \oplus i_0 \oplus 1 \equiv s_1 \oplus i_0 \oplus 2.$$

But once two consecutive elements of S are equivalent, then by (9.2) they are all equivalent, and $\equiv$ is a trivial congruence. ∎

Corollary 9.7. The two functions $x \vee y$ and $x \oplus 1$ form a functionally complete set

Proof. This is obvious since these functions allow one to define the universal function $(x \vee y) \oplus 1$. ∎

Theorem 9.14. The two functions $\bar{x}$ and $x \rightarrow y$, where

$$\bar{x} = (r-1) - x$$

and

$$x \rightarrow y = r-1 \quad \text{if} \quad x \leqslant y,$$
$$= \overline{x-y} \quad \text{if} \quad x \geqslant y,$$

form a weakly complete set.

Proof. We give a direct proof of that theorem. One has to prove that every function is definable by means of $\bar{x}, x \rightarrow y$ and the constant functions.

(1) One can define the conjunction and the disjunction:

$$x \vee y = (x \rightarrow y) \rightarrow y;$$
$$x \wedge y = \overline{\bar{x} \vee \bar{y}}.$$

(2) One can define the r functions of type $1x^{(i)}$:

$$1x^{(0)} = \overline{1 \to x};$$
$$1x^{(i)} = \overline{[x \to (i-1)]} \wedge \overline{[(i+1) \to x]}, \qquad \forall i = 1, \ldots, r-2;$$
$$1x^{(r-1)} = \overline{x \to (r-2)}.$$

(3) One can define every function of the type $jx^{(i)}$: if

$$x + y \leqslant r-1,$$

then

$$x + y = \bar{x} \to y.$$

Therefore

$$jx^{(i)} = 1x^{(i)} + \ldots + 1x^{(i)} = \overline{1x^{(i)}} \to [\ \ldots \to (1x^{(i)}) \ldots].$$

From the points (1) and (3), it is obvious that every function is definable. ■

Note that the functions $\bar{x}$ and $x \to y$ are $\{0, r-1\}$-preserving functions. Thus, except in the binary case, they do not form a functionally complete set, but only a weakly complete set.

As a last example, recall that the unate generators, together with the operations of disjunction and conjunction can generate any logic function, and thus form a complete set (theorem 3.4).

Chapter 10

Complexity of Logic Functions

It has been seen in Chapter 2 that every logic function can be evaluated by means of a computation scheme and that this computation scheme describes a logic circuit, which in a certain sense, realizes the logic function. The problem then arises of appreciation of the complexity of the logic circuit associated with a logic function. This is the aim of the complexity theory.

In order to develop a theory of the complexity, it is necessary to have objective measures of the complexity of a logic circuit. Two such measures are defined in section 10.1: the computation cost and the computation time. The most significant result of this section is that, for a constant multiplying factor, the behaviour of both the computation cost and the computation time does not depend upon the set of chosen primitives (theorems 10.1 and 10.2).

Section 10.2 is devoted to the computation complexity; the main result is the generalization of a theorem stated by Muller in the frame of binary logic. A slightly different approach due to Lupanov is also presented.

The next section (10.3) contains theorems due to both Winograd and Spira about the time complexity.

Finally section 10.4 establishes the relationship between the theory of complexity and the theory of universal logic modules.

10.1. Complexity measures

In this section we introduce two complexity measures for logic functions. They essentially correspond to the amount of work required to perform a computation, and to the time needed to obtain the result. The presentation of this section is widely inspired from Davio and Quisquater [1975] and Savage [1972].

The main tool used for that purpose is the *computation scheme.* It has been defined in section 2.1.3.

Definition 10.1. Consider a set Ω of primitives. A set $\{f_0, \ldots, f_{m-1}\}$ of logic functions is *Ω-realizable* iff there exists at least one computation scheme σ over Ω

that computes every function f_i, $\forall i = 0, \ldots, m-1$, i.e.

$$\sigma = (g_0, \ldots, g_{N-1})$$

and

$$\{f_0, \ldots, f_{m-1}\} \subseteq \{g_0, \ldots, g_{N-1}\}.$$

The logic circuit associated with σ (see section 2.1.3) is said an *Ω-realization* of $f_0, \ldots, f_{m-1}$.

For every logic circuit, one can define the two following parameters:

(a) the number of logic gates it contains;
(b) its *depth*, i.e. the maximum number of logic gates encountered when passing from an arbitrary input to an arbitrary output.

The two complexity measures defined below are closely related to these two parameters.

Definition 10.2. The *computation cost* $C_\Omega(f_0, \ldots, f_{m-1})$ of the set of logic functions $\{f_0, \ldots, f_{m-1}\}$ with respect to Ω is the minimum number of logic gates in any Ω-realization of these functions. The *computation time* $D_\Omega(f_0, \ldots, f_{m-1})$ of the set of functions $\{f_0, \ldots, f_{m-1}\}$ with respect to Ω is the minimum depth of any Ω-realization of these functions.

In order that C_Ω and D_Ω were well defined, one must assume that Ω is functionally complete.

The *computation complexity* $\mathscr{C}_\Omega(n, m)$ and the *time complexity* $\mathscr{D}_\Omega(n, m)$ are defined by

$$\mathscr{C}_\Omega = \max \{C_\Omega(f_0, \ldots, f_{m-1})\},$$

and

$$\mathscr{D}_\Omega = \max \{D_\Omega(f_0, \ldots, f_{m-1})\},$$

where each f_i is a function from S^n to S and where the maximum is over the set of all possible m-tuples of functions f_i. Thus, for example, the computation complexity represents the maximum number of logic gates required to realize an arbitrarily chosen m-tuple of logic functions.

The quantities C_Ω, D_Ω and the complexities $\mathscr{C}_\Omega, \mathscr{D}_\Omega$ are functions both of the parameters n and m, and of the family ω of available operators. A noteworthy consequence of the following theorem 10.1 is that the family Ω is an irrelevant parameter in the evaluation of that dependence. This theorem extends to the time complexity a result first obtained by Muller [1956] for additive cost functions.

Consider two functionally complete sets of primitives

$$\Omega = \{h_0, \ldots, h_{p-1}\} \quad \text{and} \quad \Omega' = \{h'_0, \ldots, h'_{q-1}\},$$

and denote by $T_\Omega(f_0, \ldots, f_{m-1})$ any one of the quantities $C_\Omega(f_0, \ldots, f_{m-1})$ and $D_\Omega(f_0, \ldots, f_{m-1})$.

Theorem 10.1. For any set of logic functions $\{f_0, \ldots, f_{m-1}\}$,

$$K_{T1} T_\Omega(f_0, \ldots, f_{m-1}) \leqslant T_{\Omega'}(f_0, \ldots, f_{m-1}) \leqslant K_{T2} T_\Omega(f_0, \ldots, f_{m-1})$$

where K_{T1} *and* K_{T2} *are positive rational numbers that depend on* Ω *and* Ω' *but not on the functions* $f_0, \ldots, f_{m-1}$.

Proof. Since the set Ω is complete, every operation h_i' may be realized by a computation scheme over Ω with a cost equal to $T_\Omega(h_i')$. Consider now a computation scheme over Ω' that computes $f_0, \ldots, f_{m-1}$, with a cost equal to $T_{\Omega'}(f_0, \ldots, f_{m-1})$. Replace in that scheme each of the operations h_i' by the corresponding scheme over Ω. One obtains in this way a computation scheme σ over Ω that computes $f_0, \ldots, f_{m-1}$. Since, by definition, $T_\Omega(f_0, \ldots, f_{m-1})$ is minimum over the set of schemes that compute $f_0, \ldots, f_{m-1}$ from operations in Ω, we only have to show that an upper bound on the appropriate parameter of σ is given by

$$(1/K_{T1})\, T_{\Omega'}(f_0, \ldots, f_{m-1}).$$

Clearly, that result is obtained if one chooses

$$1/K_{T1} = \max \{T_\Omega\,(h_i')\}.$$

This completes the proof of the left-hand inequality in the theorem. The right-hand inequality is obtained in a parallel way. ■

A further argument, also due to Muller [1956], shows that similar inequalities hold true for the complexities. Denote by $\mathscr{T}_\Omega(n, m)$ any one of the complexities $\mathscr{C}_\Omega(n, m)$ and $\mathscr{D}_\Omega(n, m)$.

Theorem 10.2. For any value of the parameters n and m,

$$K_{T1}\, \mathscr{T}_\Omega(n, m) \leqslant \mathscr{T}_{\Omega'}(n, m) \leqslant K_{T2}\, \mathscr{T}_\Omega(n, m),$$

where K_{T1} *and* K_{T2} *are positive rational numbers that depend on* Ω *and* Ω', *but not on n and m.*

Proof. There exists at least one m-tuple of logic functions $f_0, \ldots, f_{m-1}$ such that:

$$\mathscr{T}_{\Omega'}(n, m) = T_{\Omega'}(f_0, \ldots, f_{m-1}).$$

For that particular set of functions, one has thus:

$$T_\Omega(f_0, \ldots, f_{m-1}) \leqslant \mathscr{T}_\Omega(n, m),$$

and, by theorem 10.1:

$$\mathscr{T}_{\Omega'}(n, m) = T_{\Omega'}(f_0, \ldots, f_{m-1}) \leqslant K_{T2}\, T_\Omega(f_0, \ldots, f_{m-1}) \leqslant K_{T2} \mathscr{T}_\Omega(n, m).$$

The second inequality in the theorem is obtained in a similar way.

10.2. The computation complexity

Our aim in this section is to derive for the computation complexity lower and upper bounds, depending on n and m, and having the same asymptotic behaviour. The lower bound is obtained by a counting argument, while the upper bound is obtained constructively. The last construction consists in producing a "universal module", i.e. a logic circuit that, thanks to a family of available operators is able to produce any m-tuple of functions from S^n to S.

The essential contribution in the study of the computation complexity in binary gate circuits is due to Muller [1956]. The present section generalizes Muller's arguments to r-valued circuits. These arguments are actually closely related to those used by Shannon [1949] and Lupanov [1958] in their study of the complexity of relay circuits. An account of the results of Shannon and Lupanov may be found in Harrison [1965] and Mukhopadhyay [1971].

Since our main concern is to trace the asymptotic dependence of $\mathscr{C}_\Omega(n,m)$, theorem 10.2 allows us to choose at will the set Ω. In this section we make use of a single type of operator called *U-operator.* It realizes the function U from S^{r+1} to S defined as follows:

$$U(x, x_{r-1}, \ldots, x_0) = x_{r-1} x^{(r-1)} \vee \ldots \vee x_0 x^{(0)}.$$

The results are condensed in the following theorem (10.3). The proof of theorem 10.3 is rather lengthy and most of the numerical arguments it contains may be skipped at first reading. However, the construction used in the proof of the upper bound is important for the understanding of the subsequent sections. It is based on the following lemma.

Lemma 10.1. The set of all n-variable logic functions can be realized by means of $r^{(r^n)}$ U-operators.

Proof. Every one-variable function can be realized by means of one U-operator:

$$f(x) = U[x, f(r-1), \ldots, f(0)].$$

One thus needs r^r U-operators in order to realize the r^r one-variable functions. The proof is then achieved by induction on n. Suppose that one has a logic circuit, that contains $r^{(r^{n-1})}$ U-operators, and realizes the $r^{(r^{n-1})}$ functions of $(n-1)$ variables. It remains to synthesize the $(r^{(r^n)} - r^{(r^{n-1})})$ functions depending effectively on n variables. Each of them can be written under the form

$$f(x_{n-1}, \ldots, x_0) = U[x_{n-1}, f(r-1, x_{n-2}, \ldots, x_0), \ldots, f(0, x_{n-2}, \ldots, x_0)].$$

One needs one additional U-operator per function. The total number of U-operators is thus equal to $r^{(r^n)}$. ■

Theorem 10.3. The computation complexity $\mathscr{C}_\Omega(n, m)$ is bounded by:

$$K_1 \frac{r^s}{s} \leqslant \mathscr{C}_\Omega(n,m) \leqslant K_2 \frac{r^s}{s}$$

where

$$s = n + \log_r m,$$

and where K_1 and K_2 only depend upon the complete set Ω.

Proof. (a) *Lower bound.* With a set of N U-operators, it is possible to produce at most

$$\gamma(N) = (N + n + r)^{[N(r+1)+m]}$$

distinct input–output behaviours. Indeed, in order to define an input–output behaviour, each of the m circuit outputs and each of the $N(r+1)$ operator inputs has to be connected to some source chosen among the r elements of S, the n input variables, and the N gate outputs. Clearly, $\gamma[\mathscr{C}_\Omega(n,m)]$ should exceed the number

$$r^{(m\, r^n)}$$

of distinct m-tuples of n-variable functions. Clearly too, any number N such that

$$\gamma(N) \leqslant r^{(m\, r^n)}$$

is a lower bound on $\mathscr{C}_\Omega(n,m)$.

Note also that any N such that

$$N + n + r < m$$

is also a lower bound $\mathscr{C}_\Omega(n,m)$ since in that case there exist more circuit outputs than distinct available signals.

To achieve the proof, it suffices thus to show that there exists a value of K_1 such that either

$$\gamma\left(K_1 \frac{r^s}{s}\right) \leqslant r^{(m\, r^n)} \tag{10.1}$$

or

$$K_1 \frac{r^s}{s} + n + r < m, \tag{10.2}$$

for any n and m.

Taking the logarithms in base r of both members of (10.1) one obtains:

$$\log_r \left[\gamma\left(K_1 \frac{r^s}{s}\right)\right] = \left[K_1 (r+1) \frac{r^s}{s} + m\right] \log_r \left(K_1 \frac{r^s}{s} + n + r\right) \leqslant m\, r^n = r^s.$$

In the cases where (10.2) does not hold one has:

$$m \leqslant K_1 \frac{r^s}{s} + n + r,$$

and thus

$$\log_r \left[\gamma\left(K_1 \frac{r^s}{s}\right)\right] \leqslant \left[K_1 (r+2) \frac{r^s}{s} + n + r\right] \log_r \left(K_1 \frac{r^s}{s} + n + r\right).$$

Furthermore, if s is large enough:

$$n + r \leqslant K_1 \frac{r^s}{s}$$

and thus

$$\log_r \left[\gamma\left(K_1 \frac{r^s}{s}\right)\right] \leqslant \left[K_1 (r+3) \frac{r^s}{s}\right] \log_r \left(2K_1 \frac{r^s}{s}\right).$$

For $K_1 = 1/(r+3)$, the last inequality becomes

$$\log_r \left[\gamma\left(K_1 \frac{r^s}{s}\right)\right] \leqslant r^s \frac{s - \log_r s + \log\,[2/(r+3)]}{s} \leqslant r^s,$$

and the inequality (10.1) holds true.

There only exists a finite number of cases under which s is smaller than a given amount, i.e. does not satisfy the above assumptions. Since this number is finite, it will always be possible to handle these cases by an appropriate choice of K_1.

(b) *Upper bound.* Any m-tuple of functions of n variables may be synthesized by the following two steps:

Step 1. Compute all the functions of k variables $(1 \leqslant k \leqslant n)$. This requires

$$r^{(rk)}$$

U-operators (lemma 10.1).

Step 2. Compute each of the m output functions from the k-variable functions obtained in step 1. Consider a function f depending on n variables; it can be written under the form:

$$f(x) = U\,[x_{n-1}, f(r-1, x_{n-2}, \ldots, x_0), \ldots, f(0, x_{n-2}, \ldots, x_0)].$$

Every $(n-1)$-variable function $f(e_{n-1}, x_{n-2}, \ldots, x_0)$, with $e_{n-1} \in S$, can also be decomposed according to the same rule, and so on. Finally, one obtains a realization of f by a tree of U-operators, the depth of which is $(n-k)$ and the inputs of which are k-variable functions. The number of U-operators in that tree is

$$1 + r + r^2 + \ldots + r^{(n-k-1)} = \frac{r^{(n-k)} - 1}{r-1}.$$

The total number of operators required for the realization of m functions is thus

$$N = r^{(rk)} + m\,\frac{r^{(n-k)}-1}{r-1}. \qquad (10.3)$$

Furthermore, since the choice of k has not been fixed, we may adjust k in order to minimize N. However, a formal minimization procedure yields a transcendental equation, and one merely tries to obtain an approximate minimum which satisfies the wanted upper bound. The discussion considers two cases.

Case 1. $\log_r (s - \log_s r) \leqslant n$.

In this case, we choose for k the unique integer defined by:

$$k'' = \log_r (s - \log_r s) - 1 \leqslant k < \log_r (s - \log_r s) = k'.$$

Since the second derivative of N with respect to k is always positive, the value $N(k)$ of N at point k cannot be simultaneously greater than $N(k')$ and $N(k'')$. The larger of $N(k')$ and $N(k'')$ is thus an upper bound of $N(k)$ and thus of $\mathscr{C}_\Omega(n, m)$. The substitution of k' and k'' in (10.3) yields:

$$N(k'') = \frac{r^s}{s} + \frac{1}{r-1}\,\frac{r^s}{s - \log_r s} - \frac{m}{r-1},$$

$$N(k') = \left(\frac{r^s}{s}\right)^{1/r} + \frac{1}{r-1}\,\frac{r^{s+1}}{s - \log_r s} - \frac{m}{r-1}.$$

In order to compare the values $N(k')$ and $N(k'')$ with $K_2\,(r^s/s)$, we first study the inequality:

$$\frac{1}{r-1}\,\frac{r^s}{s - \log_r s} \leqslant Q\,\frac{r^s}{s}.$$

It is equivalent to

$$\frac{s}{\log_r s} \geqslant \frac{Q(r-1)}{Q(r-1) - 1},$$

and the latter inequality can always be fulfilled by some value of Q. Note however that the ratio $s/\log_r s$ is minimum for $s = e$, and that its minimum value is $e.\ln r$. We thus choose Q in order to satisfy

$$e \ln r \geqslant \frac{Q(r-1)}{Q(r-1) - 1},$$

i.e.

$$Q \geqslant \frac{1}{r-1}\,\frac{e \ln r}{(e \ln r) - 1}.$$

A numerical computation shows that the last inequality is satisfied by $Q = 3$ if $r = 2$, and by $Q = 1$ if $r \geqslant 3$. Thus:

$$\text{for } r = 2, N(k'') \leqslant 4.\frac{2^s}{s}, \qquad N(k') \leqslant 7.\frac{2^s}{s},$$

$$\text{for } r \geqslant 3, N(k'') \leqslant 2.\frac{r^s}{s}, \qquad N(k') \leqslant (r+1)\frac{r^s}{s}.$$

Case 2. $\log_r(s - \log_r s) > n$.

In this case, we choose $k = n$, i.e. we only construct all the functions of n variables by step 1 of the synthesis procedure. The number of operators is then

$$r^{(r^n)} \leqslant r^{(r^{\log_r (s - \log_r s)})} = r^{(s - \log_r s)} = \frac{r^s}{s}.$$

Lupanov [1958] has proposed an original method that allows to synthesize any m-tuple of n-variable switching functions. His method may easily be generalized to the case of logic functions; it yields in some cases a better upperbound for $\mathscr{C}_\Omega(n, m)$.

Definition 10.3. An n-variable logic function f *strongly depends on* x_i iff there are $n-1$ points $e_0, \ldots, e_{i-1}, e_{i+1}, \ldots, e_{n-1}$ in S such that

$$f(e_{n-1}, \ldots, e_{i+1}, x_i, e_{i-1}, \ldots, e_0) = \pi(x_i),$$

where π denotes a permutation of S.

Let us consider a logic function F that depends on N variables, with N greater than or equal to some power r^p of r: $N \geqslant r^p$. Furthermore, suppose that F strongly depends on the r^p variables $x_0, \ldots, x_{r^p-1}$. Therefore, for every i in $\{0, \ldots, r^p - 1\}$ one may find N points $e_0(i), \ldots, e_{i-1}(i), e_{i+1}(i), \ldots, e_{N-1}(i)$ in S such that

$$F[e_{N-1}(i), \ldots, e_{i+1}(i), x_i, e_{i-1}(i), \ldots, e_0(i)] = \pi_i(x_i).$$

In the sequel of this section, the same symbol $\boldsymbol{x}_0$ will be used for representing either the point $(x_{p-1}, \ldots, x_0)$ of S^p or the integer $x_{p-1}\, r^{p-1} + \ldots + x_0\, r^0$.

We define r^p logic functions $\psi_{\boldsymbol{k}_0}$ depending on $(p+1)$ variables:

$$\begin{aligned} \psi_{\boldsymbol{k}_0}(z, \boldsymbol{x}_0) &= \overset{-1}{\pi}_{\boldsymbol{k}_0}(z) \quad \text{if} \quad \boldsymbol{x}_0 = \boldsymbol{k}_0, \\ &= e_{\boldsymbol{k}_0}(\boldsymbol{x}_0) \quad \text{otherwise,} \end{aligned}$$

for every $\boldsymbol{k}_0 = 0, \ldots, r^p - 1$.

In the case where N is greater than r^p, one also defines $(N - r^p)$ logic functions χ_j, depending on p variables:

$$\chi_j(\boldsymbol{x}_0) = e_j(\boldsymbol{x}_0),$$

for every $j = r^p, \ldots, N-1$.

Lemma 10.2. Every n-variable discrete function f, with $n \geqslant p$, admits the following canonical decomposition:

$$f(x_1, x_0) = F\{\ldots, \chi_j(x_0), \ldots, \psi_{k_0}[f(x_1, k_0), x_0], \ldots\}.$$

Proof. The second member of this last relation is equal to

$$F\{\ldots, e_j(x_0), \ldots, e_{x_0+1}(x_0), \overset{-1}{\pi}_{x_0}[f(x_1, x_0)], e_{x_0-1}(x_0), \ldots\}$$

$$= \pi_{x_0}\{\overset{-1}{\pi}_{x_0} f(x_1, x_0)]\} = f(x_1, x_0).$$ ■

Let ϕ be a logic function that strongly depends on all its $(\nu + 1)$ variables, with $\nu \geqslant 1$; one may then define a logic function F, that strongly depends on its $N = (v\nu + 1)$ variables by a repeated use of v times the function ϕ:

$$F(x_{v\nu}, \ldots, x_0) = \phi[\![\{\ldots \phi[\phi(x_{v\nu}, \ldots, x_{(v-1)\nu}), x_{(v-1)\nu-1}, \ldots, x_{(v-2)\nu}], \ldots, x_{2\nu-1}, \ldots, x_\nu\}, x_{\nu-1}, \ldots, x_0]\!]. \tag{10.4}$$

This function F may be used for the canonical decomposition of lemma 10.2. It is the main tool in the Lupanov synthesis method.

Lupanov synthesis method. Let us construct a logical circuit that realizes m logic functions f_l, $l = 1, \ldots, m$, depending on n variables. The variables are divided in three groups:

$$x_2 = (x_{n-1}, \ldots, x_{p+q}), x_1 = (x_{p+q-1}, \ldots, x_p), x_0 = (x_{p-1}, \ldots, x_0).$$

The r^q points of S^q are partitioned in t subsets

$$\Lambda_1, \ldots, \Lambda_t;$$

each of which contains h points, except possibly Λ_t which may contain less points. Hence,

$$\text{either } r^q = th \quad \text{or} \quad r^q = (t-1)h + h', \quad \text{with } h' < h;$$

in other words

$$t = \left\lceil \frac{r^q}{h} \right\rceil,$$

where $\lceil a \rceil$ stands for the smaller integer greater than or equal to a.

Every function f_l, $l = 1, \ldots, m$, may be written as follows:

$$f_l = \bigvee_{j=1}^{t} f_{lj}, \tag{10.5}$$

where

$$f_{lj}(x_2, x_1, x_0) = f_l(x_2, x_1, x_0) \quad \text{if } x_1 \in \Lambda_j,$$
$$= 0 \quad \text{otherwise,}$$

for every $j = 1, \ldots, t$.

Every function f_{lj} may be canonically expanded with respect to x_2:

$$f_{lj}(x_2, x_1, x_0) = \bigvee_{e_2 \in S^{n-p-q}} [x_2^{(e_2)} \wedge f_{lj}(e_2, x_1, x_0)]. \tag{10.6}$$

According to lemma 10.2 we may write:

$$f_{lj}(e_2, x_1, x_0) = F\{\ldots, \chi_j(x_0), \ldots, \psi_{k_0}[f_{lj}(e_2, x_1, k_0), x_0], \ldots\}. \tag{10.7}$$

It is important to notice that

$$f_{lj}(e_2, x_1, k_0) = \bigvee_{e_1 \in \Lambda_j} [x_1^{(e_1)} \wedge f_{lj}(e_2, e_1, k_0)];$$

therefore, for fixed j, the number of different subfunctions $f_{lj}(e_2, x_1, k_0)$ cannot exceed r^h. By taking into account the fact that j takes on t different values, one deduces that the total number of different subfunctions $f_{lj}(e_2, x_1, k_0)$ is at most equal to (tr^h).

Let c_1 denote the cost of an ∪-operator, c_2 the cost of an operator performing the disjunction of two operands, and c_3 the cost of an operator realizing ϕ.

The number $N = (v\nu + 1)$ must be greater than or equal to r^p; let us choose for v the smallest integer such that $(v\nu + 1) \geqslant r^p$ that is

$$v = \left\lceil \frac{r^p - 1}{\nu} \right\rceil.$$

The synthesis process is decomposed in several steps.

Step 1. Compute all the subfunctions $f_{lj}(e_2, x_1, k_0)$. Each of them is a q-variable function that may be synthesized by means of

$$1 + r + \ldots + r^{q-1} = \frac{r^q - 1}{r - 1} < r^q$$

∪-operators.

Since the number of different subfunctions is not greater than tr^h, and since $t = \lceil r^q/h \rceil$, the cost of the circuit associated with step 1 is bounded by

$$\left(\frac{r^q}{h} + 1\right) r^{h+q} c_1.$$

Step 2. Compute $\chi_j(x_0)$ for $j = r^p, \ldots, v\nu$. Each of them requires

$$\frac{r^p - 1}{r - 1} < r^p$$

∪-operators. Their number is

$$v\nu + 1 - r^p < \left(\frac{r^p - 1}{\nu} + 1\right) \nu + 1 - r^p = \nu.$$

The cost of the associated circuit is bounded by

$$\nu r^p \, c_1.$$

Step 3. Compute $\psi_k[f_{lj}(e_2, x_1, k_0), x_0]$ for all $k = 0, \ldots, r^p - 1$ and all different subfunctions $f_{lj}(e_2, x_1, k_0)$. Each of them may be synthesized by means of

$$\frac{r^{p+1} - 1}{r - 1} < r^{p+1}$$

$\cup$-operators, while their number does not exceed $r^p t r^h$.

The associated cost is bounded by

$$\left(\frac{r^q}{h} + 1\right) r^{2p+h+1} \, c_1.$$

Step 4. Compute $f_{lj}(e_2, x_1, x_0)$ for all $l \in \{1, \ldots, m\}, j \in \{1, \ldots, t\}, e_2 \in S^{n-p-q}$. According to (10.4) and (10.7), each of them requires υ operators realizing ϕ.

For this step the cost is bounded by

$$m \left(\frac{r^q}{h} + 1\right) r^{n-p-q} \left(\frac{r^p}{\nu} + 1\right) c_3.$$

Step 5. Compute f_{lj} for all $l \in \{1, \ldots, m\}$ and $j \in \{1, \ldots, t\}$. According to (10.6), each of them may be synthesized by means of

$$\frac{r^{n-p-q} - 1}{r - 1} < r^{n-p-q}$$

$\cup$-operators.

The cost associated with this step is bounded by

$$m \left(\frac{r^q}{h} + 1\right) r^{n-p-q} \, c_1.$$

Step 6. Compute f_l for all $l \in \{1, \ldots, m\}$. According to (10.5), the cost associated with this last step is bounded by

$$m \, \frac{r^q}{h} \, c_2.$$

The total cost of the circuit is thus not greater than

$$\left[\left(\frac{r^q}{h} + 1\right) r^{h+q} + \nu r^p + \left(\frac{r^q}{h} + 1\right) r^{2p+h+1} + m \left(\frac{r^q}{h} + 1\right) r^{n-p-q}\right] c_1$$

$$+ m \, \frac{r^q}{h} \, c_2 + m \left(\frac{r^n}{h\nu} + \frac{r^{n-q}}{\nu} + \frac{r^{n-p}}{h} + r^{n-p-q}\right) c_3.$$

Suppose that

$$3 \log_r s \leqslant n \quad \text{and} \quad 5 \log_r s \leqslant s-1,$$

where s stands for $(n + \log_r m)$. We may choose the following values for p, q and h:

$$p = \lfloor \log_r s \rfloor, q = \lfloor 2 \log_r s \rfloor, h = \lfloor s-5 \log_r s \rfloor,$$

where $\lfloor a \rfloor$ stands for the greatest integer smaller than or equal to a.

One obtains the following upper bound:

$$b(s) = \left[\beta(s) \frac{r^s}{s^5} s^2 + \nu s + \beta(s) s^2 \frac{r^{s+1}}{s^5} + \beta(s) \frac{r^{s+2}}{s^3}\right] c_1 + \frac{r^s}{s(s-5 \log_r s-1)} c_2 + \left[\frac{r^s}{(s-5 \log_r s-1) \nu} + \frac{r^{s+1}}{s^2 \nu} + \frac{r^{s+1}}{s(s-5 \log_r s-1)} + \frac{r^{s+2}}{s^3}\right] c_3$$

where

$$\beta(s) = \frac{s^2}{s-5 \log_r s-1} + 1.$$

In order to verify that $b(s)$ is an upper bound, it is important to note that

$$q \leqslant 2 \log_r s = 3 \log_r s - \log_r s \leqslant n - \log_r s,$$

and thus

$$mr^q \leqslant m \frac{r^n}{s} = \frac{r^s}{s}.$$

It is obvious that

$$b(s) = \frac{r^s}{s} \frac{c_3}{\nu} [1 + \alpha(s)],$$

where

$$\lim_{s \to \infty} \alpha(s) = 0.$$

Let us notice that the ∪-operator strongly depends on all its $(r + 1)$ variables:

$$\cup (e, x_{r-1}, \ldots, x_0) = x_e,$$
$$\cup (x_r, r-1, \ldots, 0) = x_r.$$

It can thus be chosen as function ϕ. In that particular case, $\nu = r$ and

$$b(s) = \frac{r^{s-1}}{s} [1 + \alpha(s)]$$

if one considers that the cost of an ∪-operator is equal to one.

Let us conclude this section by quoting another paper of Lupanov [1965] the appendix of which contains more precise values of both the lower and the upper bound, in function of the values taken by the parameters n and m.

10.3. *The time complexity*

We start this section with the observation that $\mathscr{D}_\Omega(n, m) = \mathscr{D}_\Omega(n, 1)$: this is clearly a consequence of the fact that m functions $f_0, \ldots, f_{m-1}$ may always be computed in parallel.

Accordingly, we shall denote $\mathscr{D}_\Omega(n, m)$ as $\mathscr{D}_\Omega(n)$, and confine our investigations to computation times of isolated functions $D_\Omega(f)$.

As a second remark, we note that if f has computation time $D_\Omega(f)$, there always exists a tree circuit that realizes f with computation time $D_\Omega(f)$; such a circuit is obtained by using recursively the following rule: if a gate output feeds k gate inputs, replace that gate by k copies of itself, each of them feeding one gate input. These operations leave unchanged the depth of the circuit.

We finally note that an upper bound on $\mathscr{D}_\Omega(n)$ is given by

$$\mathscr{D}_\Omega(n) \leqslant n.$$

This is an immediate consequence of the construction used in theorem 10.3. The theorems in this section essentially show that $\mathscr{D}_\Omega(n)$ is a linear function of n. However, the numerical results obtained by using the U-operator in the above way are rather poor: it will turn out that the main reason for this is a lack of parallelism. This is the reason why we use, in the study of the time complexity, the set ω of all q-input operators. In what follows, $\lceil a \rceil$ denotes the smallest integer greater than or equal to a.

Theorem 10.4. The computation time $D_\Omega(f)$ of any function f that actually depends on its n arguments has the lower bound:

$$D_\Omega(f) \geqslant \lceil \log_q n \rceil. \tag{10.8}$$

Proof. Consider a tree realizing f with depth D. The number T of primary inputs of that tree is such that

$$T \leqslant q^D,$$

since it cannot exceed the number of inputs of a complete tree of depth D. Furthermore, one should have $S \geqslant n$, since each of the input variables should appear at least once. Hence the proof. ■

By definition, the lower bound (10.8) also applies to the time complexity $\mathscr{D}_\Omega(n)$. However, the following theorem, due to Winograd [1967] provides us with a stronger lower bound.

Theorem 10.5. There always exists a positive number ϵ *such that*

$$D_\Omega(n) \geqslant \lceil \{n - \log_r [\log_r n(1+\epsilon)]\} \log_q r \rceil . \tag{10.9}$$

Proof. A complete tree made up of q-input operators and having depth D has q^D inputs and contains

$$(q^D - 1)/(q-1)$$

operators. The number of distinct trees of depth $\mathscr{D}_\Omega(n)$ should exceed the number of n-variable functions. One has thus

$$n^{(q^{\mathscr{D}_\Omega(n)})} \; r^{(r^q)\,[(q^{\mathscr{D}_\Omega(n)}-1)/(q-1)]} \geqslant r^{(r^n)} \tag{10.10}$$

since any of the

$$q^{\mathscr{D}_\Omega(n)}$$

inputs can receive the n variables, and since each of the operators may be one of the

$$r^{(r^q)}$$

q-variable functions. By taking the logarithm of both sides of (10.10) one obtains:

$$\Delta[\mathscr{D}_\Omega(n)] = q^{\mathscr{D}_\Omega(n)} \log_r n + r^q \, \frac{q^{\mathscr{D}_\Omega(n)} - 1}{q-1} \geqslant r^n .$$

Now, any number D that satisfies the inequality

$$\Delta(D) < r^n$$

is a lower bound of $\mathscr{D}_\Omega(n)$. This last inequality is clearly satisfied by any number D that fulfils the stronger inequality:

$$q^D (\log_r n + r^q) < r^n .$$

The quantity

$$\lceil n \log_q r - \log_q(\log_r n + r^q) \rceil$$

is thus a lower bound of $\mathscr{D}_\Omega(n)$. It is equal to

$$\lceil [n - \log_r(\log_r n + r^q)] \log_q r \rceil$$

since

$$\log_q x = \log_r x . \log_q r .$$

Clearly, there always exists a positive number ϵ such that:

$$\log_r n + r^q = \log_r n\,(1+\epsilon).$$

Furthermore

$$\lim_{n\to\infty} \log_r n\,(1+\epsilon) = \log_r n . \qquad \blacksquare$$

The essential contribution of the lower bound (10.9) is clearly $\lceil n \log_q r \rceil$. Winograd [1967] was probably the first to obtain an upper bound:

$$\mathscr{D}_\Omega(n) \leqslant \lceil n \log_q r \rceil + \lceil \log_q n \rceil + 1, \tag{10.11}$$

in which the essential contribution is also of the form $\lceil n \log_q r \rceil$.

The bound (10.11) is easily derived from the canonical disjunctive expansion of a function. In what follows, we describe an improvement on the bound (10.11). obtained by Spira [1971b, 1973].

Spira introduces a family $\{A_i\}$ of integers, and a function B from $\mathbb{N}$ to $\mathbb{N}$. The numbers A_i are defined recursively by:

$$A_0 = a$$

$$A_{i+1} = A_i + (q-1)\, q^{\mathscr{D}_\Omega(A_i)},$$

while

$$B(n) = \min \{i \mid A_i \geqslant n\}.$$

The construction is based on an inductive process indexed by $B(n)$. In that construction, the numbers A_i represent the border values of n at the different steps of the induction.

Theorem 10.6

(a) $\mathscr{D}_\Omega(n) \leqslant \lceil n \log_q r \rceil + 2B(n)$;
(b) *if* $r = q^s$, *then* $\mathscr{D}_\Omega(n) \leqslant sn + B(n)$.

Proof. The propositions (a) and (b) are clearly true if $B(n) = 0$, since in this case, $n \leqslant q$ and $\mathscr{D}_\Omega(n) = 1$. We thus assume as induction hypothesis that the theorem holds true for any n such that $B(n) \leqslant i$. We consider now the functions such that $B(n) = i + 1$, i.e. that $A_i < n \leqslant A_{i+1}$. The partial canonical disjunctive expansion of such a function with respect to $n - A_i$ variables contains a maximum of

$$r^{(n-A_i)}$$

terms, each of which is the product of a function of A_i variables by a minterm involving $(n - A_i)$ variables. Since $n \leqslant A_{i+1}$, one has

$$n - A_i \leqslant A_{i+1} - A_i = (q-1)\, q^{\mathscr{D}_\Omega(A_i)}; \tag{10.12}$$

the product of a minterm involving $(n - A_i)$ variables by a function of A_i variables can be considered as the product of $(q-1)$ minterms involving at most $\lceil (n - A_i)/(q-1) \rceil$ variables by a function of A_i variables. Each minterm involving $\lceil (n - A_i)/(q-1) \rceil$ variables may be computed in time $\mathscr{D}_\Omega(A_i)$ since by (10.12):

$$\frac{n - A_i}{q-1} \leqslant a^{\mathscr{D}_\Omega(A_i)};$$

on the other hand, any function of A_i variables can also be computed in time $\mathscr{D}_\Omega(A_i)$.

Therefore, the product of a minterm involving $(n-A_i)$ variables by a function of A_i variables may be computed in time $\mathscr{D}_\Omega(A_i) + 1$.

It remains then to compute the disjunction of the $r^{(n-A_i)}$ terms: this can be done in time

$$\lceil (n-A_i)\log_q r\rceil .$$

Hence:

$$\mathscr{D}_\Omega(n) \leqslant \mathscr{D}_\Omega(A_i) + 1 + \lceil (n-A_i)\log_q r\rceil .$$

Since $B(A_i) = \min\{j \mid A_j \geqslant A_i\} = i$, the induction hypothesis applies to $\mathscr{D}_\Omega(A_i)$.

Thus, in case (a), since

$$\mathscr{D}_\Omega(A_i) \leqslant \lceil A_i \log_q r\rceil + 2i,$$

one obtains

$$\begin{aligned}\mathscr{D}_\Omega(n) &\leqslant \lceil A_i \log_q r\rceil + 2i + 1 + \lceil (n-A_i)\log_q r\rceil \\ &\leqslant \lceil n \log_q r\rceil + 2i + 2 = \lceil n\log_q r\rceil + 2B(n);\end{aligned}$$

similarly, in case (b), since

$$\mathscr{D}_\Omega(A_i) \leqslant s\,A_i + i,$$

one obtains

$$\mathscr{D}_\Omega(n) \leqslant s\,A_i + i + 1 + (n-A_i)\,s = sn + i + 1 = sn + B(n).$$

Remarks. (1) Theorems 10.3 and 10.6 suggest a logarithmic dependence of the time complexity with respect to the computation complexity. Such a result has been obtained by Spira [1971a] for the restricted class of tree circuits.

(2) The numerical results obtained by theorem 10.6 may be improved. Various improvements have been described by Preparata and Muller [1970] when $r = q = 2$. Other examples of improvements may be observed when $r = 2$ and $q = 3$. In this case, for $n = 14$, theorem 10.6 would imply the partial expansion with respect to 5 variables and realization would require a depth 11. However, a partial expansion with respect to 11 variables immediately yields an equivalent computation scheme of depth 10.

10.4. Universal logic modules

In this section, we propose a rather general definition of *universal logic module* (ULM), and show how this concept is related to the foregoing study of complexity. A universal logic module is schematically described by Figure 10.1. It consists of:

(a) the source set Γ, i.e. the n variables and the r elements of S;

(b) a well-behaved net $\mathcal{N}$ made up of available operators from the set $\omega = \{h_i \mid i \in I\}$ where I is some index set and h_i is an q_i-ary operation of S:

$$h_i : S^{q_i} \to S.$$

The numbers of inputs, of outputs, of operators h_i and the total number of operators in $\mathcal{N}$ are denoted by P, M, G_i and G, respectively.

(c) m output terminals

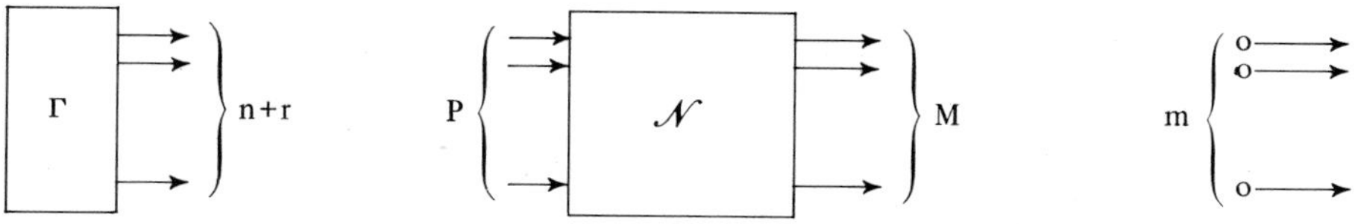

Figure 10.1. The general scheme of a ULM

The circuit displayed in Figure 10.1 is a universal logic module if it is able to produce any m-tuple of logic functions of n variables under one of the following allowed operations:

(a) if $q_i = q_j$, replacement of an h_i operator by an h_j operator;
(b) connection of the P inputs of $\mathcal{N}$ and of the m circuit outputs to an element of Γ or to one of the M outputs of $\mathcal{N}$. The latter operation is constrained to produce a well-behaved net.

The above definition is general enough to cover the classical concept of ULM discussed by Preparata and Muller [1970] and universal modules using auxiliary functions, such as those studied by Yau and Tang [1970]. For a recent account of the state of the art in the field, we refer to the work of Stone [1971].

We shall furthermore consider two extreme cases of ULM's. In a *free ULM*, the network $\mathcal{N}$ consists of totally disconnected gates, all the terminals of which are accessible. Thus, in a free ULM:

$$P = \sum_{i \in I} G_i q_i; M = G.$$

In a *wired ULM*, the network $\mathcal{N}$ has exactly m outputs which are preassigned to be the m module outputs. The only freedom degrees in a wired ULM are thus the allowed replacements of modules and the connections of the P inputs to the $(n + r)$ source nodes. Finally, a *canonical ULM* is a wired ULM each input of which may only be connected to a subset γ of the source nodes with the condition that $\#\gamma$ is independent of n.

The *input complexity* $\mathcal{P}_\Omega(n, m)$ and the *gate complexity* $\mathcal{G}_\Omega(n, m)$ are defined by

$$\mathcal{P}_\Omega(n, m) = \min_{\mathcal{N}} P; \ \mathcal{G}_\Omega(n, m) = \min_{\mathcal{N}} G,$$

respectively, where the minimum is over the set of all ULM's realizing the m-tuples of n-variable functions. The classical goal of ULM's theory is the study of $\mathscr{P}_\Omega(n,m)$. However, if $q = \max_{i \in I} q_i$, one has for any ULM:

$$Gq \geqslant P,$$

since the number of inputs to $\mathscr{N}$ cannot exceed the number of operator inputs which admits in turn the upper bound Gq. An argument similar to that of theorem 10.2 then allows to be written:

$$r\,\mathscr{G}_\Omega(n,m) \geqslant \mathscr{P}_\Omega(n,m). \tag{10.13}$$

Similarly, by definition of $\mathscr{C}_\Omega(n,m)$, one also has:

$$\mathscr{G}_\Omega(n,m) \geqslant \mathscr{C}_\Omega(n,m). \tag{10.14}$$

The knowledge of upper bounds on $\mathscr{G}_\Omega(n,m)$ thus provides upper bounds both on $\mathscr{P}_\Omega(n,m)$ and on $\mathscr{C}_\Omega(n,m)$, and appears as a particularly desirable goal. Actually, the relation (10.14) was implicitly used in the construction of theorem 10.3.

The relation (10.14) requires an additional comment; it reduces indeed to an equality when $\omega = \Omega \backslash \Gamma$ contains a single operator: it suffices for that to consider the free ULM that consists of $\mathscr{C}_\Omega(n,m)$ operators of the given type. In this particular case, by (10.13), any lower bound on $\mathscr{P}_\Omega(n,m)$ thus appears as the second desirable goal of ULM's theory. This is the purpose of the following theorem. Since we only expect to draw conclusion on the asymptotic behaviour of $\mathscr{C}_\Omega(n,m)$, we confine ourselves to the case where $\#\omega = 1$.

Theorem 10.7 (Quisquater [1973]). *When $\#\omega = 1$, the input complexity has the following lower bounds:*

(a) *for free ULM's, $\mathscr{P}_\Omega(n,m) \geqslant K_1\, r^s/s$ $(s = n + \log_r m)$;*
(b) *for wired ULM's, $\mathscr{P}_\Omega(n,m) \geqslant m\, r^n/\log_r(n+r)$;*
(c) *for canonical ULM's, $\mathscr{P}_\Omega(n,m) \geqslant m\, r^n/\log_r a$, where $a = \#\gamma$.*

Proof. The three bounds essentially result of the same counting argument: if A denotes the number of possible source signals and if B denotes the number of terminals to be connected, one should have

$$A^B \geqslant r^{(m\, r^n)}.$$

Hence

(a) For free ULM's

$$A = G + n + r, \quad B = P + m \text{ with } P = Gq,$$

and the discussion reduces to that given in theorem 10.3.

(b) For wired ULM's

$$A = n + r, \quad B = P.$$

One should have

$$(n + r)^P \geqslant r^{(m\, r^n)}.$$

The latter equality provides the proposition.

(c) For canonical ULM's A is a constant a independent of n and $B = P$.

Hence

$$a^P \geqslant r^{(m\, r^n)}.$$

■

It is interesting to compare the lower bounds on $\mathscr{P}_\Omega(n, m)$ obtained in theorem 10.7 with constructive upper bounds obtained in the literature. For free ULM's, it has been shown in theorem 10.3 that $\mathscr{G}_\Omega(n, m)$ has the adequate upper bound r^s/s. The results on canonical ULM's are numerous: the construction of theorem 10.3 used with $k = 1$ already yields $\mathscr{G}_\Omega(n, m) \leqslant m(r^{n-1}-1)/(r-1)$. It is noteworthy that rather strong constraints may be imposed on the wiring without altering the exponential behaviour. In particular, one may impose the cascade structure (Davio and Quisquater [1972], Delsarte and Quisquater [1973]), or, if $m = 1$, the iterative structure (Canaday [1964], Davio and Quisquater [1973a], Minnick *et al.* [1966], Quisquater [1973]). The weakest part of the theory thus concerns non-classical wired ULM's. The main result is an upper bound on $\mathscr{P}_\Omega(n, m)$ which has the asymptotic behaviour (b) (Preparata and Muller [1970]).

10.5. Conclusion

If we look at the asymptotic behaviour of the various complexity measures that have been discussed in this chapter, the situation appears to be satisfactory. In most cases, indeed, the lower and upper bounds are asymptotically identical for large values of n. This is however not completely the case when practical values n are of concern, and this raises the first type of open problems in complexity theory. This problem reappears even more stronger when one considers the numerical gap which separates the two bounds: the situation here is rather troublesome, since methods which are asymptotically poor may turn out to be quite effective for small values of n.

The essential conclusion to be drawn from the above study is however that the only way to escape the general bounds in a specific problem is to take advantage of the peculiarities of this problem. The preceding theory however provides us with two essential tools for dealing with specific problems: the detection of appropriate decompositions in terms of auxiliary functions (theorem 10.3) is the key method for obtaining cost reduction, while parallelism (theorem 10.6) plays the prominent role in the diminution of the computation time.

Chapter 11
Decomposition

The fact that a function undergoes some type of decomposition is certainly an important functional property as illustrated by the following classical example: consider a switching function f that undergoes the simple disjunctive decomposition

$$f(x_{n-1}, \ldots, x_0) = F[x_{n-1}, \ldots, x_p, y(x_{p-1}, \ldots, x_0)]$$

where F and y are also switching functions. In this case, f is entirely defined by the truth table of F that contains 2^{n-p+1} rows, by the truth table of y that contains 2^p rows and by the knowledge that f undergoes the given decomposition; thanks to that knowledge, the number of bits to memorize in order to define f completely is $(2^{n-p+1} + 2^p)$ in place of 2^n. Now, if one realizes f by means of read only memory (r.o.m.) circuits, the saving in the number of bits necessary for defining f corresponds to an actual hardware saving in the realization of f.

The chapter is divided in two parts. The first one (section 11.1) presents some general results about the decomposition of discrete functions while the second one (section 11.2) is mainly devoted to switching functions. In this section, we have voluntarily put emphasis on the results obtained by Ashenhurst for it seems to us they form a very unified, attractive theory; all along this section we have employed techniques issued from the differential calculus.

11.1. Decomposition of discrete functions

11.1.1. Generalities and main definitions

The functional decomposition of discrete functions may be presented as a mathematical tool for designing logic circuits. Indeed, it is often possible to express a discrete function f, depending on n variables, as a composite function of functions as in the following equation:

$$f(\boldsymbol{x}) = F[(\boldsymbol{x}_1, y(\boldsymbol{x}_0)] \qquad (11.1)$$

where

$$\boldsymbol{x}_1 = (x_{n-1}, \ldots, x_p),$$
$$\boldsymbol{x}_0 = (x_{p-1}, \ldots, x_0),$$
$$y: S_{p-1} \times \ldots \times S_0 \to E,$$
$$F: S_{n-1} \times \ldots \times S_p \times E \to L.$$

Sometimes, such a composite expression can be found in which F and y are essentially simpler functions than f. Thus, if we wish to design a logic circuit for realizing a discrete function like f, we may accomplish this by designing circuits realizing the several simpler functions of the composite representation.

We now give a more formal and precise definition.

Definition 11.1. A *decomposition* of the n-variable discrete function f is a series of discrete functions

$$y_0, y_1, \ldots, y_{M-1}$$

such that the value taken by f at point $\boldsymbol{x}$ may be computed according to the following M-step computation algorithm ($M \geqslant 2$):

$$\xi_0 = y_0(\boldsymbol{x}_0),$$
$$\xi_j = y_j(\boldsymbol{x}_j, \boldsymbol{\xi}_{j-1}), \quad \forall j = 1, \ldots, M-2,$$
$$f(\boldsymbol{x}) = y_{M-1}(\boldsymbol{x}_{M-1}, \boldsymbol{\xi}_{M-2}),$$

where

$$\boldsymbol{x}_j \subseteq \{x_0, \ldots, x_{n-1}\}, \quad \forall j = 0, \ldots, M-1,$$

and

$$\boldsymbol{\xi}_j \subseteq \{\xi_0, \ldots, \xi_j\}, \quad \forall j = 0, \ldots, M-2;$$

the function y_j takes its values in the r_j-element set

$$L_j = \{0, \ldots, r_j - 1\};$$

the domain of y_j is thus $S_{i_1} \times \ldots \times S_{i_k} \times L_{j_1} \times \ldots \times L_{j_t}$ if $\boldsymbol{x}_j = (x_{i_1}, \ldots, x_{i_k})$ and $\boldsymbol{\xi}_{j-1} = (\xi_{j_1}, \ldots, \xi_{j_t})$.

The similarity with the notion of computation scheme (see section 2.1.3) is quite obvious; in fact, if f is a logic function and if the y_j's are also logic functions, then the finite sequence of logic functions

$$(f_0, f_1, \ldots, f_{M-1})$$

with

$$f_j(\boldsymbol{x}) = \xi_j, \quad \forall j = 0, \ldots, M-1,$$

and

$$f_{M-1} = f,$$

is a computation scheme over a set of primitives that contains each y_j.

The decompositions may be classified in different ways. According to the value of M, there are two types of decompositions: the *simple decompositions* and the *complex decompositions*. A decomposition is simple iff $M = 2$; its general form is thus

$$f(x) = y_1 [x_1, y_0(x_0)].$$

If M is greater than two, the decomposition is said to be complex.

The following definitions are also classical (see for instance Curtis [1962]);

A *multiple decomposition* is characterized by an expression of the form ($M \geqslant 3$):

$$f(x) = y_{M-1} [x_{M-1}, y_{M-2} (x_{M-2}), \ldots, y_0 (x_0)],$$

that is $\xi_j = \phi$ for every $j = 0, \ldots, M-3$; an *iterative decomposition* is characterized by an expression of the form ($M \geqslant 3$):

$$f(x) = y_{M-1}(x_{M-1}, y_{M-2} [\![x_{M-2}, y_{M-3}\{\ldots [x_1, y_0(x_0)] \ldots\}]\!]),$$

that is $\xi_j = \{\xi_j\}$ for every $j = 0, \ldots, M-2$. Multiple and iterative decompositions are evidently of the complex decomposition class.

The decompositions may also be classified according to the fact that the subsets x_j of variables are disjoint or not. If for every pair of distinct indices i and j in $\{0, \ldots, M-1\}$ one has $x_i \cap x_j = \phi$, then the decomposition is said to be *disjunctive*; if not it is *non-disjunctive*. The proper subset x_{ip} of x_i is the set of variables of x_i that lie in none of the other subsets x_j:

$$x_{ip} = x_i \cap \bigcup_{j \neq i} \bar{x}_j$$

where the upper bar denotes the set complementation with respect to x. The decompositions may finally be classified according to the fact that some of the proper subsets x_{ip} are empty or not. A decomposition is said to be *proper* if each of its proper subsets x_{ip} is non-empty. If not it is *improper*. The simplest non-trivial improper decompositions of f are characterized by expressions of the form

$$f(x) = y_2 [x_1, y_1(x_0), y_0(x_0)],$$

and

$$f(x) = y_2\{x_0, y_1 [x_1, y_0(x_0)]\},$$

where (x_1, x_0) is a partition of x.

Rather few papers have been published on decomposition in the general frame of discrete function theory. One of the most important is certainly a paper due to Karp [1963] in which can be found some of the definitions introduced above as well as the material of the next subsection (with many other things). We must also quote the classical paper of Ashenhurst [1957] devoted to switching functions but, the author says, many results of which still hold for logic functions.

References concerning the decomposition of switching functions will be given in section 11.2 that is entirely devoted to binary functions.

We may also quote two references concerning the ternary logic: Muzio and Miller [1973], Thelliez [1973]; note that this last book contains a commented bibliography.

11.1.2. Disjunctive tree-like decompositions

Consider the decomposition of definition 11.1. One can associate with it the following oriented graph:

it has $(n + M)$ nodes labelled $a_0, \ldots, a_{n-1}, b_0, \ldots, b_{M-1}$;
there is an arc from a_i to b_j iff $x_i \in \boldsymbol{x}_j$ and there is an arc from b_k to b_l iff $\xi_k \in \boldsymbol{\xi}_l$.

The graph thus describes the skeleton of the circuit naturally associated with the decomposition.

In this section we consider the particular case where the graph is a tree; this occurs if the decomposition is disjunctive and if furthermore the $\boldsymbol{\xi}_j$'s are also disjoint, i.e.

$$\boldsymbol{x}_i \cap \boldsymbol{x}_j = \phi \quad \text{and} \quad \boldsymbol{\xi}_i \cap \boldsymbol{\xi}_j = \phi$$

for every pair of distinct indices i and j in $\{0, \ldots, M-1\}$. These decompositions are called *disjunctive tree-like decompositions.*

Consider for instance the following decomposition:

$$\xi_0 = y_0(x_1, x_0),$$
$$\xi_1 = y_1(x_4, x_3, x_2),$$
$$\xi_2 = y_2(x_6, x_5),$$
$$\xi_3 = y_3(x_7, \xi_0),$$
$$\xi_4 = y_4(x_8, \xi_2, \xi_1),$$
$$f(x_8, \ldots, x_0) = y_5(\xi_4, \xi_3).$$

It is a disjunctive tree-like decomposition of f the graph of which is given in Figure 11.1.

Definition 11.2. Consider a subset $\boldsymbol{x}_0$ of $\boldsymbol{x}$ and, in order to simplify the notations, suppose that $\boldsymbol{x}_0 = (x_{q-1}, \ldots, x_0)$. For every discrete function f define then an equivalence relation $R(\boldsymbol{x}_0, f)$ on $S_{q-1} \times \ldots \times S_0$ as follows:

$$(\boldsymbol{e}_0, \boldsymbol{e}_0') \in R(\boldsymbol{x}_0, f) \quad \text{iff} \quad f(\boldsymbol{x}_1, \boldsymbol{e}_0) = f(\boldsymbol{x}_1, \boldsymbol{e}_0')$$

for every $\boldsymbol{x}_1$ in $S_{n-1} \times \ldots \times S_q$.

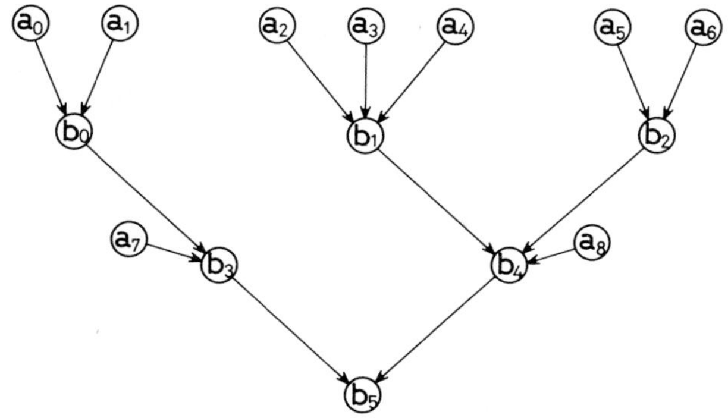

Figure 11.1. Graph associated with a disjunctive tree-like decomposition

The number of equivalence classes generated by $R(\boldsymbol{x}_0, f)$ is denoted $k(\boldsymbol{x}_0, f)$. In other words, it is the number of different functions among the set $\{f(\boldsymbol{x}_1, \boldsymbol{e}_0) \mid \boldsymbol{e}_0 \in S_{q-1} \times \ldots \times S_0\}$.

The number $k(\boldsymbol{x}_0, f)$ plays a key role in decomposition theory as proven by the fundamental theorem 11.1 stated below. It answers the following question: given a discrete function f and a tree that could correspond to some disjunctive tree-like decomposition of f, is there a way to define the functions y_j's such that f actually does admit a disjunctive tree-like decomposition to which corresponds the given graph. In other words, given a logic circuit composed of building blocks the behaviour of which is left undefined, is it possible to choose the input–output behaviour of every building block in such a way that the whole circuit realizes some given discrete function. The answer to that question is that one can always find suitable functions y_j's under the condition that their codomains L_j contain a sufficient number of points.

For every node b_j of the graph, $j = 0, \ldots, M-1$, let us define

$$X_j = \{x_i \in \boldsymbol{x} \mid \text{for every } i \text{ such that there exists a path from } a_i \text{ to } b_j\}.$$

Consider for instance the graph of Figure 11.1:

$$X_0 = (x_1, x_0),$$
$$X_1 = (x_4, x_3, x_2),$$
$$X_2 = (x_6, x_5),$$
$$X_3 = (x_7, x_1, x_0),$$
$$X_4 = (x_8, x_6, x_5, x_4, x_3, x_2),$$
$$X_5 = (x_8, x_7, x_6, x_5, x_4, x_3, x_2, x_1, x_0).$$

Theorem 11.1. The discrete function f has a disjunctive tree-like decomposition with a given associated graph iff the number r_j of points in the codomain L_j of y_j is greater than or equal to $k(X_j, f)$, for every $j = 0, \ldots, M-1$.

Proof. The condition is necessary. Suppose indeed that the y_j's are defined in such a way that the circuit realizes f. Consider then the output of the building block corresponding to the node b_j: it realizes a function f_j depending on the variables in X_j. Taking into account the disjunctive tree-like character of the circuit, one deduces that f admits an expression of the type

$$f(X_j, \bar{X}_j) = F[\bar{X}_j, f_j(X_j)]$$

where $\bar{X}_j$ is the set of variables that do not lie in X_j.

Therefore, given two points E_j and E_j' in the domain of f_j, if

$$f_j(E_j) = f_j(E_j')$$

then

$$f(E_j, \bar{X}_j) = f(E_j', \bar{X}_j), \quad \forall \bar{X}_j$$

and thus

$$(E_j, E_j') \in R(X_j, f).$$

As a consequence, the number of equivalence classes of $R(X_j, f)$ may not exceed the number of different values taken by f_j.

Let us now prove that the condition is sufficient. Let

$$\{a_{i_1}, \ldots, a_{i_t}, b_{j_1}, \ldots, b_{j_\nu}\}$$

be the set of all the nodes from which is originated an arc towards b_{M-1}. We first prove that f admits an expression of the type

$$f(x) = F[x_{M-1}, f_1(X_{j_1}), \ldots, f_\nu(X_{j_\nu})] \tag{11.2}$$

where

$$x_{M-1} = (x_{i_1}, \ldots, x_{i_t}),$$

and f_s takes on $k_s = k(X_{j_s}, f)$ different values, for every $s = 1, \ldots, \nu$.

Number for that purpose the equivalence classes of $R(X_{j_s}, f)$ from 0 to (k_s-1); the function f_s associates then with every X_{j_s} the number of the equivalence class in which it lies. It remains to define F: for every $\alpha_1 \in \{0, \ldots, k_1-1\}, \ldots,$ $\alpha_\nu \in \{0, \ldots, k_\nu-1\}$, put

$$F(x_{M-1}, \alpha_1, \ldots, \alpha_\nu) = f(x_{M-1}, E_{j_1}, \ldots, E_{j_\nu})$$

where, for every s, E_{j_s} is some element of the class numbered α_s. By definition of the equivalence $R(X_{j_s}, f)$, the value taken by f at this point does not depend on the choice of E_{j_s} in its class.

We now prove that this kind of construction may be iterated. Consider for that purpose one of the functions f_s and a partition $(X_{j_s 1}, X_{j_s 0})$ of X_{j_s}. We intend to prove that

$$k(X_{j_s0}, f_s) = k(X_{j_s0}, f);$$

from this equality one will deduce that the hypothesis of the theorem still holds for every f_s and that the construction may be continued further on.

Let us first suppose that

$$(E_{j_s0}, E'_{j_s0}) \in R(X_{j_s0}, f), \tag{11.3}$$

and that

$$(E_{j_s0}, E'_{j_s0}) \notin R(X_{j_s0}, f_s); \tag{11.4}$$

this yields a contradiction. From (11.4) one deduces that for some E_{j_s1} one has

$$f_s(E_{j_s1}, E_{j_s0}) \neq f_s(E_{j_s1}, E'_{j_s0})$$

and thus, by definition of f_s,

$$[(E_{j_s1}, E_{j_s0}), (E_{j_s1}, E'_{j_s0})] \notin R(X_{j_s}, f),$$

but this contradicts (11.3).

Conversely, if (E_{j_s0}, E'_{j_s0}) is in $R(X_{j_s0}, f_s)$, then

$$f_s(X_{j_s1}, E_{j_s0}) = f_s(X_{j_s1}, E'_{j_s0})$$

for every X_{j_s1} and by (11.2) the pair (E_{j_s0}, E'_{j_s0}) is also in $R(X_{j_s0}, f)$. ■

Note that the construction described in the second part of the proof yields a circuit in which every function f_j, i.e. the function corresponding to the node b_j, takes on exactly $k(X_j, f)$ different values.

We conclude this subsection by considering two particular types of disjunctive tree-like decompositions, namely the *multiple disjunctive decompositions* and the *iterative disjunctive decompositions.* We may easily particularize theorem 11.1 to these types of decompositions and so obtain the two following propositions.

Corollary 11.1. Given a discrete function f and the disjoint subsets of variables $\mathbf{x}_0, \ldots, \mathbf{x}_{M-1}$, *it is possible to define M functions* $y_0, \ldots, y_{M-1}$ *such that*

$$f(\mathbf{x}) = y_{M-1}\ [\mathbf{x}_{M-1}, y_{M-2}(\mathbf{x}_{M-2}), \ldots, y_0(\mathbf{x}_0)]$$

iff the number of points in the codomain L_j *of* y_j *is greater than or equal to* $k(\mathbf{x}_j, f)$, *for every* $j = 0, \ldots, M-2$, *and the number of points in the codomain* L_{M-1} *or* y_{M-1} *is greater than or equal to* $k(\mathbf{x}, f)$.

Corollary 11.2. Given a discrete function f and the disjoint subsets of variables $\mathbf{x}_0, \ldots, \mathbf{x}_{M-1}$, *it is possible to define M functions* $y_0, \ldots, y_{M-1}$ *such that*

$$f(\mathbf{x}) = y_{M-1}(\mathbf{x}_{M-1}, y_{M-2}\ [\![\mathbf{x}_{M-2}, y_{M-3}\{\ldots [\mathbf{x}_1, y_0(\mathbf{x}_0)]\ldots\}]\!])$$

iff the number of points in the codomain L_j *of* y_j *is greater than or equal to* $k[(\mathbf{x}_j, \ldots, \mathbf{x}_0), f]$, *for every* $j = 0, \ldots, M-1$.

11.1.3. Some other types of decompositions

We open this subsection by a remark concerning the incompletely specified discrete functions (see definition 8.4). Consider again a subset $\boldsymbol{x}_0 = (x_{q-1}, \ldots, x_0)$ of variables; for every incompletely specified discrete function f one defines a compatibility relation $R(\boldsymbol{x}_0, f)$ on $S_{p-1} \times \ldots \times S_0$:

$$(\boldsymbol{e}_0, \boldsymbol{e}_0') \in R(\boldsymbol{x}_0, f) \quad \text{iff} \quad f(\boldsymbol{x}_1, \boldsymbol{e}_0) = f(\boldsymbol{x}_1, \boldsymbol{e}_0')$$

for every $\boldsymbol{x}_1$ in $S_{n-1} \times \ldots \times S_q$ such that $f(\boldsymbol{x}_1, \boldsymbol{e}_0)$ and $f(\boldsymbol{x}_1, \boldsymbol{e}_0')$ are both specified. Furthermore, denote by $k(\boldsymbol{x}_0, f)$ the minimum number of classes in a cover of $S_{q-1} \times \ldots \times S_0$ by means of maximum compatibility classes.

We may then state the following theorem.

Theorem 11.2. Given an incompletely specified discrete function f it is possible to define a function y_0 from $S_{q-1} \times \ldots \times S_0$ to L_0, and a function y_1 from $S_{n-1} \times \ldots \times S_q \times L_0$ to L, such that

$$f(\boldsymbol{x}) = y_1 [\boldsymbol{x}_1, y_0(\boldsymbol{x}_0)]$$

*at every point **x** where f is specified iff the number of points in L_0 is greater than or equal to $k(\boldsymbol{x}_0, f)$.*

Proof. The condition is necessary since the equality of $y_0(\boldsymbol{e}_0)$ and $y_0(\boldsymbol{e}_0')$ clearly implies that $(\boldsymbol{e}_0, \boldsymbol{e}_0') \in R(\boldsymbol{x}_0, f)$. In order to prove that the condition is sufficient, consider a set of $k = k(\boldsymbol{x}_0, f)$ maximal compatibility classes that cover $S_{q-1} \times \ldots \times S_0$ and number them from 0 to $k-1$. The function y_0 associates then with every $\boldsymbol{x}_0$ the number of one of the compatibility classes in which it lies. It remains to define y_1: for every α in $\{0, \ldots, k-1\}$ put

$$y_1(\boldsymbol{x}_1, \alpha) = f(\boldsymbol{x}_1, \boldsymbol{e}_0)$$

where $\boldsymbol{e}_0$ is some element of the class numbered α and such that $f(\boldsymbol{x}_1, \boldsymbol{e}_0)$ is specified (if any). By definition of the compatibility relation $R(\boldsymbol{x}_0, f)$ there is no ambiguity. ■

The fact that simple disjunctive decompositions may be found for incompletely specified discrete functions allows us to treat the case of *simple non-disjunctive decompositions.*

Consider a discrete function f and suppose that one looks for a decomposition of the type

$$f(\boldsymbol{x}) = y_1 [\boldsymbol{x}_2, \boldsymbol{x}_1, y_0(\boldsymbol{x}_1, \boldsymbol{x}_0)]$$

where the subsets of variables $\boldsymbol{x}_0, \boldsymbol{x}_1$ and $\boldsymbol{x}_2$ are disjoint. Define then an incompletely specified discrete function g:

$$g(\boldsymbol{x}_2, \boldsymbol{x}_1, \boldsymbol{x}_{1'} \boldsymbol{x}_0) = f(\boldsymbol{x}_2, \boldsymbol{x}_1, \boldsymbol{x}_0);$$

if $\boldsymbol{x}_1' \neq \boldsymbol{x}_1$ then $g(\boldsymbol{x}_2, \boldsymbol{x}_1', \boldsymbol{x}_1, \boldsymbol{x}_0)$ is not specified.

It is obvious that

$$g(x_2, x'_1, x_1, x_0) = y_1\,[x_2, x'_1, y_0(x_1, x_0)]$$

at every point where g is specified.

The condition under which a discrete function f admits some type of simple non-disjunctive decomposition is thus that an associated incompletely specified discrete function g admits a simple disjunctive decomposition.

Another type of non-disjunctive decomposition that can easily be detected is given by the next theorem; it may be seen as a corollary of theorem 11.1.

Theorem 11.3. Given a discrete function f and the disjoint subsets of variables x_0 and x_1, it is possible to define M functions $y_0, \ldots, y_{M-1}$ such that

$$f(x) = y_{M-1}\,[x_1, y_{M-2}(x_0), \ldots, y_0(x_0)]$$

iff

$$r_0 \times \ldots \times r_{M-2} \geqslant k(x_0, f)$$

and

$$r_{M-1} \geqslant k(x, f),$$

where r_j is the number of points in the codomain L_j of y_j, for every $j = 0, \ldots, M-1$.

Remark. More rigorously speaking the condition $r_{M-1} \geqslant k(x, f)$ should be replaced by the following one: the codomain L_{M-1} of y_{M-1} contains $f(S_{n-1} \times \ldots \times S_0)$; a similar remark may be stated concerning the theorem 11.1 and its corollaries. Note however that the difference between these two conditions is only a matter of encoding of the points in L_{M-1}.

Still other types of decompositions may be discovered by using the concept of *partition pair* introduced by Hartmanis and Stearns [1966]. Consider a discrete function f and a partition (x_1, x_0) of the variables with $x_1 = (x_{n-1}, \ldots, x_q)$ and $x_0 = (x_{q-1}, \ldots, x_0)$. Define then an equivalence relation R_0 on $S_{q-1} \times \ldots \times S_0$ and an equivalence relation R on L, to which correspond the partitions π_0 and π, respectively. One says that the partitions π_0 and π form a partition pair iff the following implication is verified for every x_1 in $S_{n-1} \times \ldots \times S_q$:

$$(e_0, e'_0) \in R_0 \Rightarrow [(f(x_1, e_0), f(x_1, e'_0)] \in R.$$

Note that this definition generalizes in some way the notions introduced in definition 11.2: $R(x_0, f)$ is the greatest equivalence relation such that its associated partition forms a pair with the trivial partition of L in r blocks.

If one knows to which block of π_0 the point e_0 belongs, it is obvious that for every x_1 one can compute to which block of π the value $f(x_1, e_0)$ belongs. Suppose now that one has obtained k partition pairs

$$(\pi_0^1, \pi^1), \ldots, (\pi_0^k, \pi^k),$$

such that

$$\pi^1 \wedge \ldots \wedge \pi^k = 0 \tag{11.5}$$

where the operation $\wedge$ is the conjunction of partitions that corresponds to the set intersection of the equivalence relations they represent, and 0 stands for the trivial partition in r singletons. If one knows to which blocks of $\pi_0^1, \ldots, \pi_0^k$ the point $\boldsymbol{e}_0$ belongs, for every $\boldsymbol{x}_1$ one can compute to which blocks of $\pi^1, \ldots, \pi^k$ the value $f(\boldsymbol{x}_1, \boldsymbol{e}_0)$ belongs and thus, according to (11.5), actually compute $f(\boldsymbol{x}_1, \boldsymbol{e}_0)$.

Therefore, the function f admits the following decomposition:

$$f(\boldsymbol{x}) = F\{F_1[\boldsymbol{x}_1, y_1(\boldsymbol{x}_0)], \ldots, F_k[\boldsymbol{x}_1, y_k(\boldsymbol{x}_0)]\} \tag{11.6}$$

where

y_i is a function from $S_{q-1} \times \ldots \times S_0$ to $L_0^{(i)} = \{0, \ldots, m_0^{(i)}-1\}$,
$m_0^{(i)}$ is the number of blocks in π_0^i, $\forall i = 1, \ldots, k$;
F_i is a function from $S_{n-1} \times \ldots \times S_q \times L_0^{(i)}$ to $L^{(i)} = \{0, \ldots, m^{(i)}-1\}$,
$m^{(i)}$ is the number of blocks in π^i, $\forall i = 1, \ldots, k$;
F is a function from $L^{(1)} \times \ldots \times L^{(k)}$ to L.

The definition of these various functions is rather simple. Suppose that one has numbered the blocks of π_0^i from 0 to $(m_0^{(i)}-1)$, and the blocks of π^i from 0 to $(m^{(i)}-1)$, for every $i = 1, \ldots, k$. The function y_i associates with every $\boldsymbol{x}_0$ the number of the block of $\pi_0^{(i)}$ that contains $\boldsymbol{x}_0$. The function F_i is defined as follows:

Suppose that $\boldsymbol{x}_0$ lies in the block number α_0 of π_0^i and that $f(\boldsymbol{x}_1, \boldsymbol{x}_0)$ lies in the block number α of π^i; put then

$$F_i(\boldsymbol{x}_1, \alpha_0) = \alpha.$$

There is no ambiguity in that last definition since (π_0^i, π^i) is a partition pair. It remains to define F: for every $\alpha^{(1)} \in L^{(1)}, \ldots, \alpha^{(k)} \in L^{(k)}$, the value $F(\alpha^{(1)}, \ldots, \alpha^{(k)})$ is obtained by looking for the only element of L (if any) that lies in the block number $\alpha^{(1)}$ of $\pi^1, \ldots$, in the block number $\alpha^{(k)}$ of π^k.

Suppose conversely that f admits a decomposition characterized by equations (11.6). If F is a one-to-one function, one may define k equivalence relations $R^{(1)}, \ldots, R^{(k)}$ on L: two elements l and l' of L are equivalent in $R^{(i)}$ iff

(a) l and l' both lie in $f(S_{n-1} \times \ldots \times S_0)$;

(b) $F^{-1}(l)$ and $F^{-1}(l')$ have the same ith component in $L^{(1)} \times \ldots \times L^{(k)}$, where $L^{(j)}$ is the codomain of y_j, $\forall j = 1, \ldots, k$.

One may also define k equivalence relations $R_0^{(1)}, \ldots, R_0^{(k)}$ on $S_{p-1} \times \ldots \times S_0$:

$$(\boldsymbol{e}_0, \boldsymbol{e}_0') \in R_0^{(i)} \quad \text{iff} \quad y_i(\boldsymbol{e}_0) = y_i(\boldsymbol{e}_0').$$

It is obvious that the associated partitions form partition pairs

$$(\pi_0^1, \pi^1), \ldots, (\pi_0^k, \pi^k)$$

and that

$$\pi^1 \wedge \ldots \wedge \pi^k = 0.$$

In the case where F is not one-to-one, the converse relation F^{-1} no longer induces k equivalence relations but k compatibility relations.

The next theorem summarizes the results obtained above.

Theorem 11.4. A sufficient condition under which a discrete function f admits a decomposition of the type

$$f(x) = F\{F_1[x_1, y_1(x_0)], \ldots, F_k[x_1, y_k(x_0)]\}$$

is that there exist k partition pairs $(\pi_0^1, \pi^1), \ldots, (\pi_0^k, \pi^k)$ *such that*

(a) $\pi^1 \wedge \ldots \wedge \pi^k = 0$,

(b) *for every* $i = 1, \ldots, k$ *the number of blocks in* π_0^i *does not exceed the number of points in the codomain of* y_i, *and the number of blocks in* π^i *does not exceed the number of points in the codomain of* F_i.

If F is one-to-one, the condition is necessary.

Methods for finding the partition pairs induced by a given discrete function may be found in Hartmanis and Stearns [1966], Kohavi [1970], Deschamps [1974].

The concept of partition pair may be slightly generalized; consider indeed a discrete function f that has an iterative disjunctive decomposition

$$f(x) = y_{M-1}[\![x_{M-1}, y_{M-2}\{\ldots [x_1, y_0(x_0)] \ldots\}]\!].$$

For every $j = 0, \ldots, M-1$, let R_j be an equivalence relation on the domain of y_j, to which corresponds the partition π_j. These M partitions form a *partition M-tuple* $(\pi_0, \ldots, \pi_{M-1})$ iff for every $j = 1, \ldots, M-1$ the partitions π_{j-1} and π_j form a partition pair with respect to the function y_j.

Suppose now that one has obtained k partition M-tuples $(\pi_0^1, \ldots, \pi_{M-1}^1), \ldots, (\pi_0^k, \ldots, \pi_{M-1}^k)$, such that

$$\pi_{M-1}^1 \wedge \ldots \wedge \pi_{M-1}^k = 0;$$

the function f then admits a decomposition of the type:

$$f(x) = F[F_1(x), \ldots, F_k(x)]$$

where

$$F_i(x) = y_{M-1}^{(i)}[\![x_{M-1}, y_{M-2}^{(i)}\{\ldots [x_1, y_0^{(i)}(x_0)] \ldots\}]\!],$$

for every $i = 1, \ldots, k$.

The number of values taken by $y_j^{(i)}$ is given by the number of blocks in π_j^i. The corresponding logic circuit is given in Figure 11.2. More details about partition M-tuples along with some other types of decompositions related to partition computations may be found in Deschamps [1974].

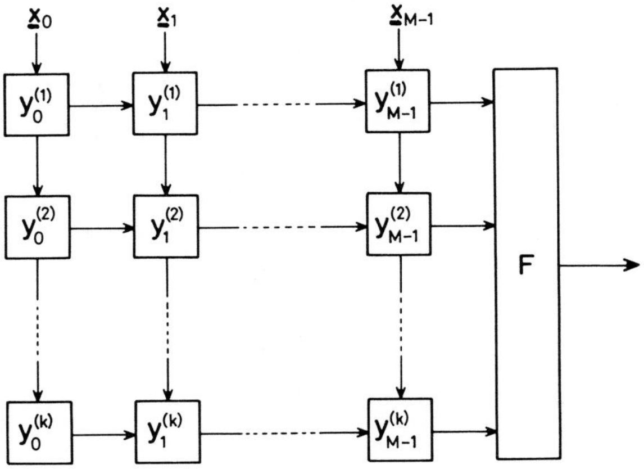

Figure 11.2. Decomposition based upon partition M-tuples

We conclude this section by defining an important particular type of non-disjunctive iterative decomposition: the *cascade decomposition.* For that purpose, use again the notations of definition 11.1. As it has already been seen, an iterative decomposition is characterized by the fact that every $\xi_j, j = 0, \ldots, M-2$, is a singleton; if furthermore every $x_j, j = 0, \ldots, M-1$, is also a singleton, the decomposition is called a cascade decomposition.

A very important result concerning cascade decompositions has been obtained by Delsarte and Quisquater [1973] in the case of logic functions, that is when $m_0 = \ldots = m_{n-1} = m$ (but with r not necessarily equal to m): they proved that every logic function admits a cascade decomposition for which

$$M = 2\,m^{n-1} - 1 \quad \text{if} \quad r \not\equiv 2, \quad \text{modulo-4},$$

and

$$M = 4\,m^{n-1} - 2 \quad \text{if} \quad r \equiv 2, \quad \text{modulo-4}.$$

In fact many papers have been published about this particular type of decompositions. Let us quote some of them: Elspas and Stone [1967], Shinahr and Yoeli [1969], Harao, Noguchi and Oizumi [1971], Kolp [1972] and also Davio and Quisquater [1972], this last paper being devoted to the case of r-ary functions of binary variables. It is interesting to note that the permutation cascades described by these two last authors are in some way "canonical": the variables appear in an *a priori* fixed order while all the functions y_j's realize a so-called affine transformation; this remark suffices to establish that there are common points in the study of topics like decomposition, complexity and universal logic modules.

11.2. Decomposition of switching functions

This section is mainly devoted to the disjunctive decomposition of switching functions. This type of decomposition has been thoroughly investigated by Ashenhurst [1957] in an almost historical paper; furthermore, his theory seems to us very attractive from a theoretical point of view while being likely very valuable as starting point for circuit synthesis purposes.

Nevertheless, some indications concerning as well the case of binary functions of non-binary variables as the non-disjunctive decompositions will be given.

11.2.1. Partition matrices and decomposition charts

Given a switching function f, we already know that a simple disjunctive decomposition of f is characterized by an equation of the type

$$f(\boldsymbol{x}) = y_1\,[\boldsymbol{x}_1, y_0(\boldsymbol{x}_0)] \tag{11.7}$$

where $\boldsymbol{x}_0 = (x_{q-1}, \ldots, x_0)$.

Furthermore, we impose the further condition that y_0 and y_1 be also switching functions.

Every subset $\boldsymbol{x}_0$ of variables such that f has a decomposition of the type (11.7) is called a *bound set* for f. The variables $\boldsymbol{x}_1$ form the *free set.* Note that the empty set ϕ, the whole set $\boldsymbol{x}$ and the singletons $\{x_i\}$ are bound sets for any switching functions f.

For every switching function f define a *partition matrix* with 2^{n-q} rows and 2^q columns. The rows correspond to the points of B_2^{n-q} and the columns to the points of B_2^q, both sets of points being enumerated in lexicographical order. Every entry of the matrix corresponds to a point of B_2^n and receives the value taken by f at that point.

The number of distinct rows in a partition matrix is called its *row multiplicity*, and similarly the number of distinct columns is its *column multiplicity.*

It is clear that the column multiplicity is equal to $k(\boldsymbol{x}_0, f)$. The next theorem is thus a direct consequence of theorem 11.1.

Theorem 11.5. (a) *A switching function f has a simple disjunctive decomposition with bound set* $\boldsymbol{x}_0$ *iff the column multiplicity of the corresponding partition is smaller than or equal to two.*

There is another condition in which one compares between them the rows rather than the columns.

Theorem 11.5. (b) *A switching function f has a simple disjunctive decomposition with bound set* $\boldsymbol{x}_0$ *iff the corresponding partition matrix has at most four distinct kinds of columns that can be classified into the following categories:*

(a) *all* 0's;
(b) *all* 1's;
(c) *a fixed pattern of* 0's *and* 1's;
(d) *the componentwise complement of* (c).

Proof. Suppose first that f admits the following decomposition:

$$f(\boldsymbol{x}) = y_1\,[\boldsymbol{x}_1, y_0(\boldsymbol{x}_0)];$$

then for every $\boldsymbol{e}_1$ in B_2^{n-q} the one-variable function $y_1(\boldsymbol{e}_1, y_0)$ is equal to 0, 1, y_0 or $\bar{y}_0$ and the corresponding row of the partition matrix lies in category (a), (b), (c) or (d).

Conversely, if the partition matrix has the property, one may associate with each row of category (c) a function y_0. It remains then to put: $y_1(\boldsymbol{e}_1, y_0) = 0, 1, y_0$ or $\bar{y}_0$ according to the category ((a), (b), (c) or (d)) to which belongs the row corresponding to $\boldsymbol{e}_1$. ■

For every partition $(\boldsymbol{x}_1, \boldsymbol{x}_0)$ of the set of variables one may draw a *decomposition chart*; it is constructed as a partition matrix in which the entry corresponding to the point $\boldsymbol{e}$ of B_2^n is the number $(e_0 + 2e_1 + \ldots + 2^{n-1}e_{n-1})$ that is the representation of $\boldsymbol{e}$ in the decimal numeration system.

Given a switching function f, one circles then the entries of the decomposition chart corresponding to the points where f takes the value 1; in this way one may check for the conditions of theorems 11.5 or 11.6 by simple visual inspection.

It is obvious that the decomposition chart corresponding to the bound set $\boldsymbol{x}_0$ and the free set $\boldsymbol{x}_1$ may also be used in the case where $\boldsymbol{x}_0$ is the free set and $\boldsymbol{x}_1$ the bound set: it suffices indeed to permute the roles of the rows and columns. Hence, for a given number n of variables, only $(2^{n-1}-1)$ charts are needed to represent all partition matrices.

Example 11.1. The seven decomposition charts obtained in the case of four-variable functions are shown in Figure 11.3. The circles correspond to the switching function f defined by the following Boolean expression (in which the conjunction symbols have been omitted):

$$f(x_3, x_2, x_1, x_0) = \bar{x}_3\bar{x}_2\bar{x}_1\bar{x}_0 \vee \bar{x}_3x_2x_1x_0 \vee x_3\bar{x}_2\bar{x}_1x_0 \vee x_3x_2x_1\bar{x}_0.$$

	$x_2x_1x_0$							
x_3	(0)	1	2	3	4	5	6	(7)
	8	(9)	10	11	12	13	(14)	15

	$x_3x_1x_0$							
x_2	(0)	1	2	3	8	(9)	10	11
	4	5	6	(7)	12	13	(14)	15

	$x_3x_2x_0$							
x_1	(0)	1	4	5	8	(9)	12	13
	2	3	6	(7)	10	11	(14)	15

	$x_3x_2x_1$							
x_0	(0)	2	4	6	8	10	12	(14)
	1	3	5	(7)	(9)	11	13	15

	x_1x_0			
x_3x_2	(0)	1	2	3
	4	5	6	(7)
	8	(9)	10	11
	12	13	(14)	15

	x_2x_0			
x_3x_1	(0)	1	4	5
	2	3	6	(7)
	8	(9)	12	13
	10	11	(14)	15

	x_2x_1			
x_3x_0	(0)	2	4	6
	1	3	5	(7)
	8	9	12	(14)
	(9)	11	13	15

Figure 11.3. Four-variable decomposition charts

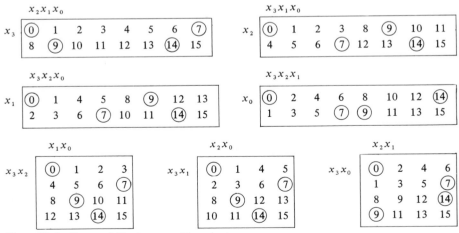

		x_3x_0 00	01	10	11
x_2x_1	00	1	0	0	1
	01	0	0	0	0
	10	0	0	0	0
	11	0	1	1	0

Figure 11.4. Partition matrix

One observes that (x_3, x_0) is a bound set for f: this can be viewed in the decomposition chart corresponding to the partition $[(x_3, x_0), (x_2, x_1)]$ in which appear two types of rows. The partition matrix is given in Figure 11.4; its column multiplicity is equal to two and its rows may be classified into three categories: all 0's, a fixed pattern (1, 0, 0, 1) and the complement pattern (0, 1, 1, 0).

The function f then admits the following simple disjunctive decomposition:

$$f(x_3, x_2, x_1, x_0) = y_1\,[x_2, x_1, y_0\,(x_3, x_0)]$$

where

$$y_0\,(x_3, x_0) = \bar{x}_3\bar{x}_0 \vee x_3x_0$$

and

$$y_1(x_2, x_1, y_0) = \bar{x}_2\bar{x}_1y_0 \vee x_2x_1\bar{y}_0.$$

The decomposition charts for functions of five and six variables may be found in Curtis [1962]. For functions of more than six variables, the decomposition charts become rather cumbersome for manual use. One has then to mechanize the method with the aid of a special or general purpose computer.

We now describe another tabular method for detecting the bound sets of a given switching function f. Consider for that purpose the Maclaurin expansion of f (see section 4.2.1.1.2):

$$f(x) = \sum_{e \in B_2^n} g(e)\, x^e$$

where

$$g(e) = \left(\frac{\Delta f}{\Delta x^e}\right)_{x=0}, \quad \forall e \in B_2^n.$$

For every partition (x_1, x_0) of the set of variables, one may define the *partition matrix associated with the Maclaurin expansion of f*: the entry corresponding to the point e of B_2^n is $g(e)$. In other words, it is the partition matrix associated with the function g.

Theorem 11.6 (Shen and McKellar [1970]). *A switching function f has a simple disjunctive decomposition with bound set* $\boldsymbol{x}_0$ *iff the corresponding partition matrix associated with its Maclaurin expansion only contains two types of rows after that one has deleted the first column, namely:*

(a) *all* 0's;
(b) *a fixed pattern of* 0's *and* 1's.

Proof. Note first that a partition matrix associated with a function g has the property iff one may find two functions a and b such that

$$g(\boldsymbol{e}_1, \boldsymbol{e}_0) = b(\boldsymbol{e}_1)\, a(\boldsymbol{e}_0)$$

for every $\boldsymbol{e}_1$ in B_2^{n-q} and for every non-zero $\boldsymbol{e}_0$ in B_2^q:

$b(\boldsymbol{e}_1) = 1$ iff the row $\boldsymbol{e}_1$ is not an all 0's row, and

$a(\boldsymbol{e}_0)$ describes the fixed pattern of 0's and 1's.

Prove now that the condition is necessary. If f has the decomposition

$$f(\boldsymbol{x}_1, \boldsymbol{x}_0) = y_1[\boldsymbol{x}_1, y_0(\boldsymbol{x}_0)],$$

then for every non-zero $\boldsymbol{e}_0$ in B_2^q one has:

$$\frac{\Delta f}{\Delta \boldsymbol{x}_0^{\boldsymbol{e}_0}} = \frac{\Delta y_1}{\Delta y_0} \cdot \frac{\Delta y_0}{\Delta \boldsymbol{x}_0^{\boldsymbol{e}_0}},$$

and thus

$$g(\boldsymbol{e}_1, \boldsymbol{e}_0) = \left(\frac{\Delta f}{\Delta \boldsymbol{x}_1^{\boldsymbol{e}_1}\, \boldsymbol{x}_0^{\boldsymbol{e}_0}}\right)_0 = b(\boldsymbol{e}_1)\, a(\boldsymbol{e}_0) \tag{11.8}$$

where

$$b(\boldsymbol{e}_1) = \left(\frac{\Delta y_1}{\Delta y_0\, \boldsymbol{x}_1^{\boldsymbol{e}_1}}\right)_0,$$

and

$$a(\boldsymbol{e}_0) = \left(\frac{\Delta y_0}{\Delta \boldsymbol{x}_0^{\boldsymbol{e}_0}}\right)_0.$$

Suppose conversely that (11.8) holds for every $\boldsymbol{e}_1$ in B_2^{n-q} and for every non-zero $\boldsymbol{e}_0$ in B_2^q. Then, according to the Maclaurin expansion of f one obtains:

$$f(\boldsymbol{x}) = y_1[\boldsymbol{x}_1, y_0(\boldsymbol{x}_0)]$$

where

$$y_0(\boldsymbol{x}_0) = \sum_{\substack{\boldsymbol{e}_0 \in B_2^q \\ \boldsymbol{e}_0 \neq \boldsymbol{0}}} a(\boldsymbol{e}_0)\, \boldsymbol{x}_0^{\boldsymbol{e}_0},$$

and

$$y_1(\boldsymbol{x}_1, y_0) = f(\boldsymbol{x}_1, \boldsymbol{0}) \oplus y_0 \left[\sum_{\boldsymbol{e}_1 \in B_2^{n-q}} b(\boldsymbol{e}_1)\, \boldsymbol{x}_1^{\boldsymbol{e}_1} \right]. \qquad \blacksquare$$

Example 11.2. Consider the same function f as in example 11.1. It has the following Maclaurin expansion:

$$f(x_3, x_2, x_1, x_0) = 1 \oplus x_0 \oplus x_1 \oplus x_1 x_0 \oplus x_2 \oplus x_2 x_0 \oplus x_2 x_1 \oplus x_3 \oplus x_3 x_1 \oplus x_3 x_2;$$

the partition matrix associated with its Maclaurin expansion and corresponding to the bound set (x_3, x_0) is given in Figure 11.5. If one deletes the first column, there are two types of rows: (1, 1, 0) and (0, 0, 0). One may then define the functions a and b:

$$a(e_3, e_0) = e_0 \oplus e_3$$

and

$$b(e_2, e_1) = \bar{e}_1 \vee \bar{e}_2.$$

The functions y_0 and y_1 are defined as follows:

$$y_0(x_3, x_0) = x_0 \oplus x_3,$$

$$y_1(x_2, x_1, y_0) = (1 \oplus x_1 \oplus x_2 \oplus x_2 x_1) \oplus y_0(1 \oplus x_1 \oplus x_2).$$

One can verify that f actually admits the simple disjunctive decomposition

$$f(x_3, x_2, x_1, x_0) = y_1 [x_2, x_1, y_0(x_3, x_0)].$$

Conclude this subsection by some remark concerning the case of binary discrete functions, that is mappings from $S_{n-1} \times \ldots \times S_0$ to B_2.

Given a binary discrete function f, a simple disjunctive decomposition of f is characterized by an equation of the type (11.7), but where y_0 is a binary function, namely a mapping from $S_{q-1} \times \ldots \times S_0$ to B_2, and y_1 is a binary function, namely a mapping from $S_{n-1} \times \ldots \times S_q \times B_2$ to B_2.

The concepts of bound set and free set are identical. Note however that if x_i is not a binary variable, then the singleton $\{x_i\}$ is not necessarily a bound set.

For every partition $(\boldsymbol{x}_1, \boldsymbol{x}_0)$ of the set of variables one may again define a partition matrix in which the rows correspond to the points of $S_{n-1} \times \ldots \times S_q$, and the columns to the points of $S_{q-1} \times \ldots \times S_0$. Theorems 11.5 and 11.6 may be stated, without any change, in the case of binary discrete functions.

One could also associate a partition matrix with the Newton expansion of f at point $\mathbf{0}$. Theorem 11.6 still holds true; the functions y_0 and y_1 must be defined as follows:

$$y_0(\mathbf{x}_0) = \sum_{\substack{\mathbf{e}_0 \in S_{q-1} \times \ldots \times S_0 \\ \mathbf{e}_0 \neq \mathbf{0}}} a(\mathbf{e}_0) \binom{\mathbf{x}_0}{\mathbf{e}_0},$$

and

$$y_1(\mathbf{x}_1, y_0) = f(\mathbf{x}_1, \mathbf{0}) \oplus y_0 \left[\sum_{\mathbf{e}_1 \in S_{n-1} \times \ldots \times S_q} b(\mathbf{e}_1) \binom{\mathbf{x}_1}{\mathbf{e}_1} \right].$$

11.2.2. Application of the differential calculus

In the proof of theorem 11.6 one has already been able to note that there is a relation between the existence of a bound set for a switching function f and the possibility of "factoring" some differences of f. This point will be more deeply investigated in this subsection.

We first state some theorems for simple decompositions (not necessarily disjunctive). Then we propose an algorithm for simple disjunctive decompositions.

Theorem 11.7 (Thayse [1972c]. *Let $(\mathbf{x}_2, \mathbf{x}_1, \mathbf{x}_0)$ be a partition of the set of variables. A switching function f has a simple decomposition of the form*

$$f(\mathbf{x}) = y_1[\mathbf{x}_2, \mathbf{x}_1, y_0(\mathbf{x}_2, \mathbf{x}_0)]$$

iff for every x_i in $\mathbf{x}_0$ there exists a switching function g_i, depending on the variables in $\mathbf{x}_0$ and $\mathbf{x}_2$ only, such that

$$\frac{\Delta f}{\Delta x_i} = \frac{\delta f}{\delta \mathbf{x}_0} g_i(\mathbf{x}_2, \mathbf{x}_0). \tag{11.9}$$

Proof. The condition is necessary. Suppose indeed that

$$f(\mathbf{x}) = y_1[\mathbf{x}_2, \mathbf{x}_1, y_0(\mathbf{x}_2, \mathbf{x}_0)];$$

then the following two relations evidently hold:

$$\frac{\Delta f}{\Delta x_i} = \frac{\Delta y_1}{\Delta y_0} \frac{\Delta y_0}{\Delta x_i}, \qquad \forall x_i \in \mathbf{x}_0$$

and

$$\frac{\delta f}{\delta \mathbf{x}_0} = \frac{\Delta y_1}{\Delta y_0} \frac{\delta y_0}{\delta \mathbf{x}_0}.$$

Since $(\delta y_0/\delta \boldsymbol{x}_0) \geqslant (\Delta y_0/\Delta x_i)$, for every x_i in $\boldsymbol{x}_0$, one has also

$$\frac{\Delta y_1}{\Delta y_0}\frac{\Delta y_0}{\Delta x_i} = \frac{\Delta y_1}{\Delta y_0}\frac{\Delta y_0}{\Delta x_i}\frac{\delta y_0}{\delta \boldsymbol{x}_0} = \frac{\delta f}{\delta \boldsymbol{x}_0}\frac{\Delta y_0}{\Delta x_i},$$

and thus

$$\frac{\Delta f}{\Delta x_i} = \frac{\delta f}{\delta \boldsymbol{x}_0} g_i(\boldsymbol{x}_2, \boldsymbol{x}_0) \tag{11.10}$$

where

$$g_i(\boldsymbol{x}_2, \boldsymbol{x}_0) = \frac{\Delta y_0}{\Delta x_i}.$$

The condition is sufficient. Suppose that condition (11.9) holds. From the fact that the variation of f with respect to $\boldsymbol{x}_0$ is a function that does not depend on $\boldsymbol{x}_0$, one deduces that

$$\frac{\Delta f}{\Delta \boldsymbol{x}_0^{e_0}} = \frac{\delta f}{\delta \boldsymbol{x}_0} g_{e_0}(\boldsymbol{x}_2, \boldsymbol{x}_0)$$

for every non-zero $\boldsymbol{e}_0$.

Then, from the partial Maclaurin expansion of f with respect to $\boldsymbol{x}_0$ one deduces that

$$f(\boldsymbol{x}) = f(\boldsymbol{x}_2, \boldsymbol{x}_1, \boldsymbol{0}) \oplus \frac{\delta f}{\delta \boldsymbol{x}_0} y_0(\boldsymbol{x}_2, \boldsymbol{x}_0)$$

where

$$y_0(\boldsymbol{x}_2, \boldsymbol{x}_0) = \sum_{\boldsymbol{e}_0 \in \boldsymbol{O}} g_{e_0}(\boldsymbol{x}_2, \boldsymbol{0})\, \boldsymbol{x}_0^{e_0}.$$ ■

Condition (11.9) of theorem 11.7 leads to several other decomposition conditions which were derived by different authors.

Theorem 11.8 (Akers [1959]). *A switching function f has a simple decomposition of the form*

$$f(\boldsymbol{x}) = y_1[\boldsymbol{x}_2, \boldsymbol{x}_1, y_0(\boldsymbol{x}_2, \boldsymbol{x}_0)]$$

iff

$$\frac{\Delta f}{\Delta x_i} = \frac{\delta f}{\delta \boldsymbol{x}_0}\frac{\Delta y_0}{\Delta x_i}, \quad \forall x_i \in \boldsymbol{x}_0. \tag{11.11}$$

Proof. The proof is already implied in the proof of the preceding theorem. ■

This last condition is however of little practical use since it is generally assumed that the function y_0 is unknown; therefore, Akers transformed the condition of theorem 11.8 into the following.

Theorem 11.9 (Akers [1959]). *A switching function f has a simple decomposition of the form*

$$f(\boldsymbol{x}) = y_1[\boldsymbol{x}_2, \boldsymbol{x}_1, y_0(\boldsymbol{x}_2, \boldsymbol{x}_0)]$$

iff

$$\frac{\delta}{\delta \boldsymbol{x}_1}\left(\frac{\delta f}{\delta \boldsymbol{x}_0}\right)\frac{\Delta f}{\Delta x_i} = \frac{\delta f}{\delta \boldsymbol{x}_0}\,\frac{\delta}{\delta \boldsymbol{x}_1}\left(\frac{\Delta f}{\Delta x_i}\right)$$

for every x_i in $\boldsymbol{x}_0$.

Proof. We only prove the necessity of that condition. The second part of the proof may be found in the original paper of Akers.

By making the operator $\delta/\delta\boldsymbol{x}_1$ act on both members of (11.11) one obtains:

$$\frac{\delta}{\delta \boldsymbol{x}_1}\left(\frac{\Delta f}{\Delta x_i}\right) = \frac{\delta}{\delta \boldsymbol{x}_1}\left(\frac{\delta f}{\delta \boldsymbol{x}_0}\right)\frac{\Delta y_0}{\Delta x_i};$$

then, by multiplying both members of the last expression by $\delta f/\delta\boldsymbol{x}_0$ and by using again (11.11), one obtains the expected relation. ■

Theorem 11.10 (Lapscher [1972]). *A switching function f has a simple decomposition of the form*

$$f(\boldsymbol{x}) = y_1[\boldsymbol{x}_2, \boldsymbol{x}_1, y_0(\boldsymbol{x}_2, \boldsymbol{x}_0)]$$

iff there exists a switching function A depending on the variables in $\boldsymbol{x}_2$ and $\boldsymbol{x}_1$ only, and a switching function B depending on the variables in $\boldsymbol{x}_2$ and $\boldsymbol{x}_0$ only, such that

$$f(\boldsymbol{x}_2, \boldsymbol{x}_1, \boldsymbol{x}_0) \oplus f(\boldsymbol{x}_2, \boldsymbol{x}_1, \boldsymbol{0}) = A(\boldsymbol{x}_2, \boldsymbol{x}_1)\, B(\boldsymbol{x}_2, \boldsymbol{x}_0).$$

Proof. The condition is obviously sufficient. It is necessary: the partial Taylor expansion of y_1 with respect to y_0 at point $y_0(\boldsymbol{x}_2, \boldsymbol{0})$ yields:

$$y_1(\boldsymbol{x}_2, \boldsymbol{x}_1, y_0) = y_1[\boldsymbol{x}_2, \boldsymbol{x}_1, y_0(\boldsymbol{x}_2, \boldsymbol{0})] \oplus [y_0 \oplus y_0(\boldsymbol{x}_2, \boldsymbol{0})]\,\frac{\Delta y_1}{\Delta y_0};$$

it suffices to choose:

$$A(\boldsymbol{x}_2, \boldsymbol{x}_1) = \frac{\Delta y_1}{\Delta y_0}$$

and

$$B(\boldsymbol{x}_2, \boldsymbol{x}_0) = y_0(\boldsymbol{x}_2, \boldsymbol{x}_0) \oplus y_0(\boldsymbol{x}_2, \boldsymbol{0}).$$ ■

Note that a similar theorem was also proved by Pichat [1968].

By taking the difference with respect to $x_k \in \boldsymbol{x}_1$ of both members of (11.9) one successively obtains:

$$\frac{\Delta f}{\Delta x_k x_i} = \frac{\Delta}{\Delta x_k}\left(\frac{\delta f}{\delta \boldsymbol{x}_0}\right) g_i$$

$$\frac{\Delta f}{\Delta x_j}\,\frac{\Delta f}{\Delta x_i x_k} = \frac{\delta f}{\delta \boldsymbol{x}_0}\,\frac{\Delta}{\Delta x_k}\left(\frac{\delta f}{\delta \boldsymbol{x}_0}\right) g_i g_j, \qquad (x_i, x_j \in \boldsymbol{x}_0, x_k \in \boldsymbol{x}_1)$$

and thus

$$\frac{\Delta f}{\Delta x_j}\,\frac{\Delta f}{\Delta x_i x_k} = \frac{\Delta f}{\Delta x_i}\,\frac{\Delta f}{\Delta x_j x_k}.$$

This last relation constitutes the necessary conditions for disjunctive decompositions by Shen, McKellar and Weiner [1971]. The Akers and the Shen theorems, initially proven only for the disjunctive case, remain valid thus even for the non-disjunctive one.

Algorithms for obtaining disjunctive decompositions of switching functions and which are based on the above theorems have been derived by Pichat [1968], Shen *et al.* [1971], Thayse [1972c] and Lapscher [1972]. We now propose an algorithm grounded on theorem 11.7 and on the computation formulae for obtaining the variations (see section 7.2).

The use of theorem 11.7 for the detection of simple decompositions requires that the set of variations of a given switching function be easily available. The computational formulae of theorem 7.12 may be used in this respect. We also know that the knowledge of the prime implicants and of the prime implicates of a switching function allows an immediate computation of the variations in view of the formula:

$$\frac{\delta f}{\delta \boldsymbol{x}_0} = \left(\frac{\overline{pf}}{p\boldsymbol{x}_0}\right)\frac{qf}{q\boldsymbol{x}_0}. \tag{11.12}$$

The formal expression of (11.12) will now be slightly modified in order to allow for building of iterative computation scheme for the set of variations of a switching function. Let us define $\hat{p}_{\boldsymbol{x}_0}(f)$ and $\hat{q}_{\boldsymbol{x}_0}(f)$ as follows: $\hat{p}_{\boldsymbol{x}_0}(f)$ is the disjunction of all the prime implicants of f degenerate in $\boldsymbol{x}_0$ and which contain *all* the variables of $\boldsymbol{x}_1(\boldsymbol{x}_1, \boldsymbol{x}_0$ is a partition of $\boldsymbol{x})$;

$\hat{q}_{\boldsymbol{x}_0}(f)$ is the conjunction of all the prime implicates of f degenerate in $\boldsymbol{x}_0$ and which contain *all* the variables of $\boldsymbol{x}_1$.

The following equality then directly derives from (11.12):

$$\frac{\delta f}{\delta \boldsymbol{x}_0} = \bigwedge_{x_i \in \boldsymbol{x}_1} \frac{\delta f}{\delta \boldsymbol{x}_0 x_i}\,[\overline{\hat{p}_{\boldsymbol{x}_0}(f)}\,\hat{q}_{\boldsymbol{x}_0}(f)]. \tag{11.13}$$

This expression allows us to compute immediately the variations $\delta f/\delta \boldsymbol{x}_0$ when the variations $\delta f/\delta \boldsymbol{x}_0 x_i$ and the prime implicates and implicants of f are known. Since for a non-degenerate switching function $\delta f/\delta \boldsymbol{x} = 1$, all the variations may trivially be computed when starting with the variations $\delta f/\delta \boldsymbol{x}_0$ with the highest cardinality of the set $\boldsymbol{x}_0$. Let us note that the computation scheme based on (11.12) requires to take into account each of the prime implicants and prime implicates once and only once.

Algorithm 11.1. Disjunctive decomposition detection.

(a) Compute the set of variations of the switching function f to be tested by applying relation (11.12) if the sets of prime implicants and prime implicates of the function are known, by using the formulae of theorem 7.12 otherwise. Since one is only concerned with non-trivial decompositions, that is decompositions whose bound set $\boldsymbol{x}_0$ contains at least two variables, only the variations with respect to at most $n-2$ variables are to be computed.

(b) Verify if the conditions of theorem 11.7 are satisfied for the candidate bound sets $\boldsymbol{x}_0$. This verification can be performed, for example, by using the following computation scheme derived from theorem 11.7. The variations are naturally obtained by the intermediate of (11.12) as a product of implicates. One has:

$$\frac{\Delta f}{\Delta x_i} = \frac{\delta f}{\delta \boldsymbol{x}_0}\, y_i.$$

The prime implicants of $\delta f/\delta \boldsymbol{x}_0$ and of g_i are obtained from their conjunctive forms respectively. Each of the prime implicants of y_i is the product of two cubes $A_{ij}(\boldsymbol{x}_1)$ and $B_{ij}(\boldsymbol{x}_0)$, A_{ij} being the product of variables $x_j \in \boldsymbol{x}_1$ and $B_{ij}(\boldsymbol{x}_0)$ being the product of variables $x_j \in \boldsymbol{x}_0$. The conditions of theorem 11.7 become then:

$$A_{ij}(\boldsymbol{x}_1) \geqslant \delta f/\delta \boldsymbol{x}_0, \quad \forall\, i, j$$

or equivalently

$$\frac{\delta f}{\delta \boldsymbol{x}_0}\left[\bigvee_{i,j} \bar{A}_{ij}(\boldsymbol{x}_1)\right] = 0$$

which can trivially be verified.

Example 11.3. Consider the switching function of example 3.7. Obtain first this function as a disjunction of all its prime implicants and as a conjunction of all its prime implicates, i.e.

$$\begin{aligned} f &= \bar{x}_4\bar{x}_0 \vee \bar{x}_4\bar{x}_2\bar{x}_1 \vee \bar{x}_4x_3x_2x_1 \vee \bar{x}_4\bar{x}_3\bar{x}_1 \vee x_5\bar{x}_0 \vee x_5\bar{x}_2\bar{x}_1 \vee x_5x_3x_2x_1 \vee \\ &\quad x_5\bar{x}_3\bar{x}_1 \vee \bar{x}_5x_4\bar{x}_2x_1x_0 \vee \bar{x}_5x_4x_3x_2\bar{x}_1x_0 \vee \bar{x}_5x_4\bar{x}_3x_1x_0 \\ &= (x_4 \vee \bar{x}_3 \vee \bar{x}_2 \vee x_1 \vee \bar{x}_0)(\bar{x}_5 \vee \bar{x}_3 \vee \bar{x}_2 \vee x_1 \vee \bar{x}_0)(x_5 \vee \bar{x}_4 \vee \bar{x}_3 \vee \bar{x}_2 \vee \bar{x}_1) \\ &\quad (x_4 \vee x_2 \vee \bar{x}_1 \vee \bar{x}_0)(\bar{x}_5 \vee x_2 \vee \bar{x}_1 \vee \bar{x}_0)(x_4 \vee x_3 \vee \bar{x}_1 \vee \bar{x}_0) \\ &\quad (\bar{x}_5 \vee x_3 \vee \bar{x}_1 \vee \bar{x}_0)(x_5 \vee \bar{x}_4 \vee x_2 \vee x_1)(x_5 \vee \bar{x}_4 \vee x_3 \vee x_1)(x_5 \vee \bar{x}_4 \vee x_0). \end{aligned}$$

The variations are gathered in the table of Figure 7.2.

The following sets of variables satisfy to the conditions of theorem 11.7:

$$(x_3, x_2, x_1, x_0), (x_3, x_2, x_1), (x_3, x_2), (x_5, x_4).$$

The function f may, for example, be designed as follows:

$$f = F[y(x_3, x_2, x_1, x_0), x_5, x_4]$$

$$F = y \oplus (\bar{x}_4 \vee x_5)$$

$$y = x_0(x_1 \oplus x_3 x_2)$$

$\{i \dots j\}$	$\Delta f/\Delta x_i \dots x_j$	$\{i \dots j\}$	$\Delta f/\Delta x_i \dots x_j$	$\{i \dots j\}$	$\Delta f/\Delta x_i \dots x_j$	$\{i \dots j\}$	$\Delta f/\Delta x_i \dots x_j$
0123	1	012	1	01	1	0	$x_1 \oplus x_2 x_3$
0124	1	013	1	02	$x_1 \vee x_3$	1	x_0
0125	1	014	1	03	$x_1 \vee x_2$	2	$x_0 x_3$
0134	1	015	1	04	$\bar{x}_5 \vee (x_1 \oplus x_2 x_3)$	3	$x_0 x_2$
0135	1	023	1	05	$x_4 \vee (x_1 \oplus x_2 x_3)$	4	$\bar{x}_5$
0145	1	024	$x_1 \vee x_3 \vee \bar{x}_5$	12	x_0	5	x_4
0234	1	025	$x_1 \vee x_3 \vee x_4$	13	x_0		
0235	1	034	$x_1 \vee x_2 \vee \bar{x}_5$	14	$x_0 \vee \bar{x}_5$		
0245	1	035	$x_1 \vee x_2 \vee x_4$	15	$x_0 \vee x_4$		
0345	1	045	1	23	x_0		
1234	$x_0 \vee \bar{x}_5$	123	x_0	24	$\bar{x}_5 \vee x_0 x_3$		
1235	$x_0 \vee x_4$	124	$x_0 \vee \bar{x}_5$	25	$x_4 \vee x_0 x_3$		
1245	1	125	$x_0 \vee x_4$	34	$\bar{x}_5 \vee x_0 x_2$		
1345	1	134	$x_0 \vee \bar{x}_5$	35	$x_4 \vee x_0 x_2$		
2345	1	135	$x_0 \vee x_4$	45	1		
		145	1				
		234	$x_0 \vee \bar{x}_5$				
		235	$x_0 \vee x_4$				
		245	1				
		345	1				

Figure 11.5. The set of variations of f

11.2.3. Lattice of the bound sets

In this section we prove that the set of bound sets for a binary discrete function f is a closure system on the Boolean lattice $\mathscr{P}(x)$ of all the subsets of $\boldsymbol{x}$. According to theorem 1.29 one concludes that the set of bound sets for f is itself a lattice. This property is then exploited in order to develop a non-exhaustive method for finding all the bound sets: by non-exhaustive we mean that it is not necessary to check all the subsets $\boldsymbol{x}_0$ of $\boldsymbol{x}$. Furthermore the lattice is closely related to a disjunctive tree-like composition of f.

First state two theorems that can be proven by the same techniques as theorems 11.7 and 11.10 and hardly deserve to be classified as new theorems.

Theorem 11.11. A binary discrete function f undergoes a simple disjunctive decomposition of the type

$$f(\boldsymbol{x}) = y_1 [\boldsymbol{x}_1, y_0(\boldsymbol{x}_0)]$$

iff there exists a binary discrete function A depending on the variables in $\boldsymbol{x}_1$ only, and a binary discrete function B depending on the variables in $\boldsymbol{x}_0$ only, such that

$$f(\boldsymbol{x}_1, \boldsymbol{x}_0) \oplus f(\boldsymbol{x}_1, 0) = A(\boldsymbol{x}_1)\, B(\boldsymbol{x}_0).$$

Theorem 11.12. A binary discrete function f undergoes a simple disjunctive decomposition of the type

$$f(\boldsymbol{x}) = y_1 [\boldsymbol{x}_1, y_0(\boldsymbol{x}_0)]$$

iff there exists a binary discrete function A depending on the variables in $\boldsymbol{x}_1$ and p binary discrete functions B_i depending on the variables in $\boldsymbol{x}_0$ only, such that

$$\frac{\Delta f}{\Delta x_i} = A(\boldsymbol{x}_1)\, B_i(\boldsymbol{x}_0), \qquad \forall x_i \in \boldsymbol{x}_0.$$

In the sequel, we make use of the concept of prime implicate of a binary discrete function. This concept is quite obvious for a switching function. However, for a binary function of non-binary variables it may mean either prime anticube or prime antiblock or prime convex antiblock; the various results obtained in this subsection remain valid for any choice between the three possible meanings.

We first state the following lemma:

Lemma 11.1. If the binary discrete function f admits a disjunctive decomposition of the form

$$f(\boldsymbol{x}_1, \boldsymbol{x}_0) = g(\boldsymbol{x}_1)\, h(\boldsymbol{x}_0),$$

then every prime implicate of f is either a prime implicate of g or a prime implicate of h. If furthermore neither g nor h is a constant function (0 or 1) then the set of all the prime implicates of f is the union of the set of all the prime implicates of g and of the set of all the prime implicates of h.

Proof. Write down the conjunction of all the prime implicates of g and of all the prime implicates of h. The only case in which there may be inclusion between prime implicates of g and h is when either g or h is a constant function. In that case it is obvious that every prime implicate of f is either a prime implicate of g or a prime implicate of h.

In the case where g and h actually depend on $\boldsymbol{x}_1$ and $\boldsymbol{x}_0$, respectively, it suffices to note that no consensus may exist between prime implicates of g and prime implicates of h since they depend on different variables. ■

Note that in the case where f is not identically equal to 0 ($f \neq 0$), the functions g and h are uniquely defined: g is either the conjunction of the prime implicates of f

that depend on $\boldsymbol{x}_1$ only, if any, or is the constant 1; h is either the conjunction of the prime implicates of f that depend on $\boldsymbol{x}_0$ only, if any, or is the constant 1.

The following theorem is due to Ashenhurst. The proof is based on theorem 11.12 and lemma 11.1.

Theorem 11.13. Let f be a binary discrete function that actually depends on all its variables and admits $\boldsymbol{x}_0$ *and* $\boldsymbol{x}_0'$ *as bound sets:*

(1) $\boldsymbol{x}_0 \cap \boldsymbol{x}_0'$ *is a bound set;*
(2) *iff* $\boldsymbol{x}_0 \cap \boldsymbol{x}_0'$ *is not empty, then* $\boldsymbol{x}_0 \cup \boldsymbol{x}_0'$ *is also a bound set;*
(3) *if furthermore neither* $\boldsymbol{x}_0 \cap \overline{\boldsymbol{x}}_0'$ *nor* $\boldsymbol{x}_0 \cap \overline{\boldsymbol{x}}_0'$ *are empty, where the upper bar denotes the set complement with respect to* $\boldsymbol{x}$*, then f admits a decomposition of the type:*

$$f(\boldsymbol{x}) = y_3\{\overline{\boldsymbol{x}}_0 \cap \overline{\boldsymbol{x}}_0', \quad [y_2(\boldsymbol{x}_0 \cap \overline{\boldsymbol{x}}_0') \top y_1(\overline{\boldsymbol{x}}_0 \cap \boldsymbol{x}_0') \top y_0(\boldsymbol{x}_0 \cap \boldsymbol{x}_0')]\}$$

in which $\top$ *stands for the sum modulo-2 or for the conjunction.*

Proof. If $\boldsymbol{x}_0 \cap \boldsymbol{x}_0'$ is empty, it is a bound set. If $\boldsymbol{x}_0 \cap \overline{\boldsymbol{x}}_0'$ is empty, that means that $\boldsymbol{x}_0$ is included in $\boldsymbol{x}_0'$ and thus both $\boldsymbol{x}_0 \cap \boldsymbol{x}_0' = \boldsymbol{x}_0$ and $\boldsymbol{x}_0 \cup \boldsymbol{x}_0' = \boldsymbol{x}_0'$ are bound sets. Similarly, if $\overline{\boldsymbol{x}}_0 \cap \boldsymbol{x}_0'$ is empty, $\boldsymbol{x}_0 \cap \boldsymbol{x}_0' = \boldsymbol{x}_0'$ and $\boldsymbol{x}_0 \cup \boldsymbol{x}_0' = \boldsymbol{x}_0$ are bound sets.

We may thus directly consider the case where

$$\boldsymbol{x}_0 \cap \boldsymbol{x}_0' \neq \phi, \quad \boldsymbol{x}_0 \cap \overline{\boldsymbol{x}}_0' \neq 0 \quad \text{and} \quad \overline{\boldsymbol{x}}_0 \cap \boldsymbol{x}_0' \neq \phi.$$

Use the notation $\boldsymbol{x}_1$ for $\overline{\boldsymbol{x}}_0$ and $\boldsymbol{x}_0'$ for $\overline{\boldsymbol{x}}_0'$.

Consider a variable x_k that lies in $\boldsymbol{x}_0 \cap \boldsymbol{x}_0'$. According to theorem 11.12 we may write:

$$\frac{\Delta f}{\Delta x_k} = A(\boldsymbol{x}_1)\, B_k(\boldsymbol{x}_0) = A'(\boldsymbol{x}_1')\, B_k'(\boldsymbol{x}_0') \not\equiv 0; \tag{11.14}$$

every prime implicate of $\Delta f/\Delta x_k$ that is neither a prime implicate of A nor a prime implicate of A' must be a prime implicate of B_k and B_k' (see lemma 11.11); it depends thus on variables of $\boldsymbol{x}_0 \cap \boldsymbol{x}_0'$ only. Denote by B_k'' the conjunction of these implicates. Therefore

$$\frac{\Delta f}{\Delta x_k} = A(\boldsymbol{x}_1)\, A'(\boldsymbol{x}_1')\, B_k''(\boldsymbol{x}_0 \cap \boldsymbol{x}_0'), \quad \forall x_k \in \boldsymbol{x}_0 \cap \boldsymbol{x}_0'.$$

We deduce also from (11.14) that

$$A(\boldsymbol{x}_1) = a(\boldsymbol{x}_1 \cap \boldsymbol{x}_1')\, b(\boldsymbol{x}_1 \cap \boldsymbol{x}_0')$$

and

$$A'(\boldsymbol{x}_1') = a(\boldsymbol{x}_1 \cap \boldsymbol{x}_1')\, c(\boldsymbol{x}_0 \cap \boldsymbol{x}_1'),$$

where $a(\boldsymbol{x}_1, \boldsymbol{x}_1')$ is either 1 or the conjunction of the prime implicates of $\Delta f/\Delta x_k$ that are common to A and A'.

We may thus write:

$$\frac{\Delta f}{\Delta x_i} = a(\boldsymbol{x}_1 \cap \boldsymbol{x}_1')\, b(\boldsymbol{x}_1 \cap \boldsymbol{x}_0')\, B_i(\boldsymbol{x}_0) \not\equiv 0, \qquad \forall x_i \in \boldsymbol{x}_0, \tag{11.15}$$

$$\frac{\Delta f}{\Delta x_j} = a(\boldsymbol{x}_1 \cap \boldsymbol{x}_1')\, c(\boldsymbol{x}_0 \cap \boldsymbol{x}_1')\, B_j'(\boldsymbol{x}_0') \not\equiv 0, \qquad \forall x_j \in \boldsymbol{x}_0', \tag{11.16}$$

$$\frac{\Delta f}{\Delta x_k} = a(\boldsymbol{x}_1 \cap \boldsymbol{x}_1')\, b(\boldsymbol{x}_1 \cap \boldsymbol{x}_0')\, c(\boldsymbol{x}_0 \cap \boldsymbol{x}_1')\, B_k''(\boldsymbol{x}_0 \cap \boldsymbol{x}_0') \not\equiv 0, \qquad \forall x_k \in \boldsymbol{x}_0 \cap \boldsymbol{x}_0'. \tag{11.17}$$

Note that at this point we have already proven that $\boldsymbol{x}_0 \cup \boldsymbol{x}_0'$ is a bound set (see (11.15) and (11.16)), and that $\boldsymbol{x}_0 \cap \boldsymbol{x}_0'$ is a bound set (see (11.17)). We now consider two cases.

(a) Consider three variables

$$x_p \in \boldsymbol{x}_0 \cap \boldsymbol{x}_1', \quad x_q \in \boldsymbol{x}_1 \cap \boldsymbol{x}_0' \quad \text{and} \quad x_r \in \boldsymbol{x}_0 \cap \boldsymbol{x}_0'$$

and suppose that either

$$\frac{\Delta f}{\Delta x_p x_q} \equiv 0 \quad \text{or} \quad \frac{\Delta f}{\Delta x_p x_r} \equiv 0 \quad \text{or} \quad \frac{\Delta f}{\Delta x_q x_r} \equiv 0.$$

We prove that

$$\frac{\Delta f}{\Delta x_t x_u} \equiv 0, \quad \frac{\Delta f}{\Delta x_t x_v} \equiv 0 \quad \text{and} \quad \frac{\Delta f}{\Delta x_u x_v} \equiv 0, \tag{11.18}$$

for every choice of

$$x_t \in \boldsymbol{x}_0 \cap \boldsymbol{x}_1', \quad x_u \in \boldsymbol{x}_1 \cap \boldsymbol{x}_0' \quad \text{and} \quad x_v \in \boldsymbol{x}_0 \cap \boldsymbol{x}_0'.$$

Suppose that either $\Delta f/\Delta x_p x_q \equiv 0$ or $\Delta f/\Delta x_p x_r \equiv 0$. In view of (11.16) and (11.17) this implies that

$$\frac{\Delta c}{\Delta x_p} \equiv 0. \tag{11.19}$$

We may write successively the following implications:

$$\text{(11.16) and (11.19)} \Rightarrow \frac{\Delta f}{\Delta x_p x_u} \equiv 0 \Rightarrow \frac{\Delta b}{\Delta x_u} \equiv 0; \tag{11.20}$$

$$\text{(11.15) and (11.20)} \Rightarrow \frac{\Delta f}{\Delta x_t x_u} \equiv 0 \Rightarrow \frac{\Delta c}{\Delta x_t} \equiv 0. \tag{11.21}$$

From (11.20) and (11.21) one deduces (11.18).

The case where either $\Delta f/\Delta x_p x_q \equiv 0$ or $\Delta f/\Delta x_q x_r \equiv 0$ may obviously be handled in the same way.

From the partial Newton expansion of f with respect to $\boldsymbol{x}_0 \cup \boldsymbol{x}_0'$ and from relations (11.15), (11.16), (11.17) and (11.18) one then deduces that

$$f(\boldsymbol{x}) = f(\boldsymbol{x}_1 \cap \boldsymbol{x}_1', 0) \oplus a(\boldsymbol{x}_1 \cap \boldsymbol{x}_1')\,[y_2(\boldsymbol{x}_0 \cap \boldsymbol{x}_1') \oplus y_1(\boldsymbol{x}_1 \cap \boldsymbol{x}_0') \oplus y_0(\boldsymbol{x}_0 \cap \boldsymbol{x}_0')].$$

(b) Suppose that for every choice of

$$x_p \in \boldsymbol{x}_0 \cap \boldsymbol{x}_1', \quad x_q \in \boldsymbol{x}_1 \cap \boldsymbol{x}_0' \quad \text{and} \quad x_r \in \boldsymbol{x}_0 \cap \boldsymbol{x}_0'$$

one has

$$\frac{\Delta f}{\Delta x_p x_q} \not\equiv 0, \quad \frac{\Delta f}{\Delta x_p x_r} \not\equiv 0 \quad \text{and} \quad \frac{\Delta f}{\Delta x_q x_r} \not\equiv 0.$$

From (11.15) and (11.16) one deduces that

$$\frac{\Delta f}{\Delta x_p x_q} = a(\boldsymbol{x}_1 \cap \boldsymbol{x}_1')\,\frac{\Delta b}{\Delta x_q}\,B_p(\boldsymbol{x}_0) = a(\boldsymbol{x}_1 \cap \boldsymbol{x}_1')\,\frac{\Delta c}{\Delta x_p}\,B_q'(\boldsymbol{x}_0') \not\equiv 0;$$

therefore

$$B_p(\boldsymbol{x}_0) = \frac{\Delta c}{\Delta x_p}\,\beta_p(\boldsymbol{x}_0 \cap \boldsymbol{x}_0'),$$

and

$$B_q'(\boldsymbol{x}_0') = \frac{\Delta b}{\Delta x_q}\,\beta_q'(\boldsymbol{x}_0 \cap \boldsymbol{x}_0'),$$

where $\beta_p = \beta_q'$ is either 1 or the conjunction of the prime implicates of $\Delta f/\Delta x_p x_q$ that are common to B_p and B_q'. Note furthermore that for every other choice of x_t in $\boldsymbol{x}_0 \cap \boldsymbol{x}_1'$ and x_u in $\boldsymbol{x}_1 \cap \boldsymbol{x}_0'$ one obtains: $\beta_t = \beta_q'$ and $\beta_p = \beta_u'$. Hence, by putting $d = \beta_p = \beta_q'$, one deduces that

$$\frac{\Delta f}{\Delta x_p} = a(\boldsymbol{x}_1 \cap \boldsymbol{x}_1')\,b(\boldsymbol{x}_1 \cap \boldsymbol{x}_0')\,\frac{\Delta c}{\Delta x_p}\,d(\boldsymbol{x}_0 \cap \boldsymbol{x}_0'), \quad \forall x_p \in \boldsymbol{x}_0 \cap \boldsymbol{x}_1', \tag{11.22}$$

and

$$\frac{\Delta f}{\Delta x_q} = a(\boldsymbol{x}_1 \cap \boldsymbol{x}_1')\,\frac{\Delta b}{\Delta x_q}\,c(\boldsymbol{x}_0 \cap \boldsymbol{x}_1')\,d(\boldsymbol{x}_0 \cap \boldsymbol{x}_0'), \quad \forall x_q \in \boldsymbol{x}_1 \cap \boldsymbol{x}_0'. \tag{11.23}$$

From (11.22) and (11.17) one deduces that

$$\begin{aligned}\frac{\Delta f}{\Delta x_p x_r} &= a(\boldsymbol{x}_1 \cap \boldsymbol{x}_1')\,b(\boldsymbol{x}_1 \cap \boldsymbol{x}_0')\,\frac{\Delta c}{\Delta x_p}\,\frac{\Delta d}{\Delta x_r}\\ &= a(\boldsymbol{x}_1 \cap \boldsymbol{x}_1')\,b(\boldsymbol{x}_1 \cap \boldsymbol{x}_0')\,\frac{\Delta c}{\Delta x_p}\,B_k''(\boldsymbol{x}_0 \cap \boldsymbol{x}_0') \not\equiv 0,\end{aligned}$$

and thus

$$B_k'' = \frac{\Delta d}{\Delta x_r}.$$

Therefore

$$\frac{\Delta f}{\Delta x_r} = a(\boldsymbol{x}_1 \cap \boldsymbol{x}_1')\, b(\boldsymbol{x}_1 \cap \boldsymbol{x}_0')\, c(\boldsymbol{x}_0 \cap \boldsymbol{x}_1')\, \frac{\Delta d}{\Delta x_r}. \tag{11.24}$$

From the partial Newton expansion of f with respect to $\boldsymbol{x}_0 \cup \boldsymbol{x}_0'$ and from relations (11.22), (11.23) and (11.24) one then deduces that

$$f(\boldsymbol{x}) = g(\boldsymbol{x}_1 \cap \boldsymbol{x}_1') \oplus a(\boldsymbol{x}_1 \cap \boldsymbol{x}_1')\, y_2(\boldsymbol{x}_1 \cap \boldsymbol{x}_0')\, y_1(\boldsymbol{x}_0 \cap \boldsymbol{x}_1')\, y_0(\boldsymbol{x}_0 \cap \boldsymbol{x}_0')$$

where $g(\boldsymbol{x}_1 \cap \boldsymbol{x}_1') = f(\boldsymbol{x}_1 \cap \boldsymbol{x}_1', \boldsymbol{0}) \oplus a(\boldsymbol{x}_1 \cap \boldsymbol{x}_1')\, b(\boldsymbol{0})\, c(\boldsymbol{0})\, d(\boldsymbol{0})$ and, for instance,

$$y_2(\boldsymbol{x}_1 \cap \boldsymbol{x}_0') = \sum_{\boldsymbol{e}_{10}}^{\oplus} \left(\frac{\Delta^{\boldsymbol{e}_{10}} b}{\Delta \boldsymbol{x}_{10}}\right)_{\boldsymbol{0}} \binom{\boldsymbol{x}_{10}}{\boldsymbol{e}_{10}},$$

where $\boldsymbol{x}_{10}$ stands for $\boldsymbol{x}_1 \cap \boldsymbol{x}_0'$. ■

Remark. The last theorem may be stated even for a function f that is degenerate in some of its variables. A condition like $\boldsymbol{x}_0 \cap \boldsymbol{x}_0' \neq \phi$ is then replaced by: $\boldsymbol{x}_0 \cap \boldsymbol{x}_0' \neq \phi$ and f is not degenerate in all the variables of $\boldsymbol{x}_0 \cap \boldsymbol{x}_0'$.

We may now state the following theorem.

Theorem 11.14. For every binary function f, the set of bound sets for f is a closure system on the Boolean lattice $\mathscr{P}(\boldsymbol{x})$ of all the subsets of $\boldsymbol{x}$.

Proof. This is a direct consequence of the remark following theorem 1.28, of theorem 11.13 and of the fact that $\boldsymbol{x}$ is a bound set for every binary discrete function f. ■

With every binary discrete function f is thus also associated a closure operator J that associates with $\boldsymbol{x}_0 \in \mathscr{P}(\boldsymbol{x})$ the minimum element of

$$\{\boldsymbol{x}_0' \in \mathscr{P}(\boldsymbol{x}) \mid \boldsymbol{x}_0' \supseteq \boldsymbol{x}_0, \boldsymbol{x}_0' \text{ is a bound set for } f\},$$

(see theorem 1.27 (a)).

In other words, $J(\boldsymbol{x}_0)$ is the smallest bound set for f that contains $\boldsymbol{x}_0$.

From theorem 1.29 we deduce then the following theorem.

Theorem 11.15. For every binary discrete function f, the set of bound sets for f is a lattice in which the conjunction is the set intersection and the disjunction is defined as follows:

$$\boldsymbol{x}_0 \circledV \boldsymbol{x}_0' = J(\boldsymbol{x}_0 \cup \boldsymbol{x}_0')$$

for every pair $(\boldsymbol{x}_0, \boldsymbol{x}_0')$ of bound sets of f. If furthermore $\boldsymbol{x}_0 \cap \boldsymbol{x}_0'$ is non-empty and if *f is not degenerate in all the variables of $\boldsymbol{x}_0 \cap \boldsymbol{x}'_0$, then*

$$\boldsymbol{x}_0 \circledV \boldsymbol{x}'_0 = \boldsymbol{x}_0 \cup \boldsymbol{x}'_0.$$

We now give two methods, based upon theorems 11.11 and 11.12, respectively, that allow to compute $J(\boldsymbol{x}_0)$ for a given $\boldsymbol{x}_0$ in $\mathscr{P}(\boldsymbol{x})$.

Both methods are based on the computation of the prime implicates (anticubes, antiblocks or convex antiblocks) of some binary discrete functions. It will always be supposed that in the expression of a prime implicate like

$$x_{i_1}^{C_1} \vee \ldots \vee x_{i_q}^{C_q} \tag{11.25}$$

every C_j is a proper non-trivial subset of S_{i_j}, that is:

$$\phi \subset C_j \subset S_{i_j}, \quad \forall j = 1, \ldots, q.$$

In other words, the implicate (11.25) actually depends on all the variables in $(x_{i_1}, \ldots, x_{i_q})$.

Lemma 11.2. (1) *If x_i is in $\boldsymbol{x}_0$ and if $(x_{i_1}^{C_1} \ldots x_{i_q}^{C_q})$ is a prime implicate of $\Delta f/\Delta x_i$ containing some variable(s) of $\boldsymbol{x}_0$, then $J(\boldsymbol{x}_0)$ contains all variables in $(x_{i_1}, \ldots, x_{i_q})$.*

(2) *If x_i and x_j are in $\boldsymbol{x}_0$, and if $(x_{i_1}^{C_1} \ldots x_{i_q}^{C_q})$ is a prime implicate of $\Delta f/\Delta x_i$ that is not a prime implicate of $\Delta f/\Delta x_j$, then $J(\boldsymbol{x}_0)$ contains all variables in $(x_{i_1}, \ldots, x_{i_1})$.*

Proof. It is a direct consequence of theorem 11.12 and lemma 11.1.

The two statements of the last lemma constitute what we call Rule 1 and Rule 2, respectively. Let us illustrate these two rules by an example; consider the four-variable binary discrete function f defined as follows:

$$f(y_4, y_3, x_2, x_1) = y_4^{(1,2)}\,\bar{x}_1 \vee y_4^{(1,2)}\,y_3^{(0,1)}\,\bar{x}_2 \vee y_4^{(1,2)}\,y_3^{(2)}\,x_2 \vee y_4^{(0)}\,y_3^{(0,1)}\,x_2 x_1 \vee y_4^{(0)}\,y_3^{(2)}\,\bar{x}_2 x_1, \tag{11.26}$$

where x_1 and x_2 are binary variables, y_3 and y_4 are ternary variables, $\bar{x}_i$ holds for the negation of x_i, and the conjunction symbol has been deleted.

In order to illustrate Rule 1, compute $J[(x_2, x_1)]$;

$$\frac{\Delta f}{\Delta x_1} = (y_3^{(2)} \vee x_2)\,(y_3^{(0,1)} \vee \bar{x}_2); \tag{11.27}$$

we observe that y_3 appears with x_2 in the prime implicate $(y_3^{(2)} \vee x_2)$ of $\Delta f/\Delta x_1$. Therefore, according to Rule 1, every bound set containing x_1 and x_2 must also contain y_3, that is

$$J[(x_2, x_1)] \supseteq (y_3, x_2, x_1).$$

Now compute $\Delta f/\Delta x_2$ and $\Delta f/\Delta y_3$:

$$\frac{\Delta f}{\Delta x_2} = x_1, \quad \frac{\Delta f}{\Delta y_3} = y_3^{(1,2)}\,x_1. \tag{11.28}$$

The three differences $\Delta F/\Delta x_1$, $\Delta F/\Delta x_2$ and $\Delta F/\Delta y_3$ thus have the general form $A(y_4)\,B_i(y_3, x_2, x_1)$, where $A(y_4) \equiv 1$. According to theorem 11.12 the set (y_3, x_2, x_1) is a bound set and $J[(x_2, x_1)] = [(y_3, x_2, x_1)]$.

In order to illustrate Rule 2, compute $J[(y_4, x_1)]$;

$$\frac{\Delta f}{\Delta y_4} = y_4^{(0,2)}; \tag{11.29}$$

comparing $\Delta f/\Delta x_1$ and $\Delta f/\Delta y_4$, one observes that $(y_3^{(2)} \vee x_2)$ is a prime implicate of $\Delta f/\Delta x_1$ that is not a prime implicate of $\Delta f/\Delta y_4$. Therefore, according to Rule 2, every bound set containing x_1 and y_4 must also contain x_2 and y_3, that is

$$J[(y_4, x_1)] \supseteq (y_4, y_3, x_2, x_1),$$

and since this last set is obviously a bound set, $J[(y_4, x_1)] = (y_4, y_3, x_2, x_1)$.

It is obvious from the latter example that given a binary discrete function f and a set $\boldsymbol{x}_0$ of variables one can find $J(\boldsymbol{x}_0)$ by applying repeatedly Rules 1 and 2. This is the basis of the following algorithm.

Algorithm 11.2

Step 1. Obtain $\Delta f/\Delta x_i$ as the conjunction of all its prime implicates, for each x_i in $\boldsymbol{x}_0$.

Step 2. Enlarge $\boldsymbol{x}_0$ by applying Rule 1, and obtain $\Delta f/\Delta x_i$ as the conjunction of all its prime implicates for the new variables x_i added to $\boldsymbol{x}_0$. Step 2 is performed until no new variables are found.

Step 3. Enlarge $\boldsymbol{x}_0$ by applying Rule 2, obtain $\Delta f/\Delta x_i$ as the conjunction of all its prime implicates for the new variables x_i in $\boldsymbol{x}_0$, and go back to Step 2.

The computation is completed when no new variables can be added by applying Rules 1 and 2.

The following lemma suggests another algorithm.

Lemma 11.3. If $(x_{i_1}^{C_1} \vee \dots \vee x_{i_q}^{C_q})$ is a prime implicate of the function $[f(\boldsymbol{x}_1, \boldsymbol{x}_0) \oplus f(\boldsymbol{x}_1, \boldsymbol{0})]$, and if that prime implicate contains some variables of $\boldsymbol{x}_0$, then $J(\boldsymbol{x}_0)$ contains all variables in $(x_{i_1}, \dots, x_{i_q})$.

Proof. Suppose that

$$\boldsymbol{x}_0 = (x_{q-1}, \dots, x_0) \quad \text{and} \quad J(\boldsymbol{x}_0) = (x_{t-1}, \dots, x_q);$$

according to theorem 11.11

$$f(\boldsymbol{x}) \oplus f(x_{n-1}, \dots, x_t, 0, \dots, 0) = A(x_{n-1}, \dots, x_t)\,B(x_{t-1}, \dots, x_0).$$

Therefore

$$f(\boldsymbol{x}_1, \boldsymbol{x}_0) \oplus f(\boldsymbol{x}_1, \boldsymbol{0}) = A(x_{n-1}, \dots, x_t)\,B'(x_{t-1}, \dots, x_0) \tag{11.30}$$

where

$$B'(x_{t-1}, \dots, x_0) = B(x_{t-1}, \dots, x_0) \oplus B(x_{t-1}, \dots, x_q, 0, \dots, 0).$$

The proposition is a direct consequence of relation (11.30) and lemma 11.1. ■

Let us illustrate that last statement by the same function f as above; suppose that one wishes to compute $J[(x_2, x_1)]$:

$$f(y_4, y_3, x_2, x_1) \oplus f(y_4, y_3, 0, 0) = x_1(y_3^{(2)} \vee x_2)(y_3^{(0,1)} \vee \bar{x}_2);$$

since y_3 appears with x_2 in the prime implicate $(y_3^{(2)} \vee x_2)$, we conclude according to lemma 11.3 that any bound set containing x_1 and x_2 also contains y_3, and thus

$$J[(x_2, x_1)] \supseteq (y_3, x_2, x_1).$$

Then compute

$$f(y_4, y_3, x_2, x_1) \oplus f(y_4, 0, 0, 0) = x_1(y_3^{(2)} \vee x_2)(y_3^{(0,1)} \vee \bar{x}_2).$$

According to theorem 11.11, one deduces that (y_3, x_2, x_1) is a bound set, and thus $J[(x_2, x_1)] = (y_3, x_2, x_1)$.

The next algorithm yields $J(\boldsymbol{x}_0)$ for a given subset $\boldsymbol{x}_0$ and for a given binary discrete function f.

Algorithm 11.3

Step 1. Obtain $[f(\boldsymbol{x}_1, \boldsymbol{x}_0) \oplus f(\boldsymbol{x}_1, \boldsymbol{0})]$ as conjunction of prime implicates (not necessarily all).

Step 2. Enlarge $\boldsymbol{x}_0$ by applying lemma 11.3, and go back to Step 1.

The computation is completed when no new variables have to be added by application of lemma 11.3.

Given a binary discrete function f, we are able to compute $J(\boldsymbol{x}_0)$ for every $\boldsymbol{x}_0$ in $\mathscr{P}(\boldsymbol{x})$. Furthermore we know that the singletons $\{x_i\}, i = 0, \ldots, n-1$, form a $\cup$-generating set of $\mathscr{P}(\boldsymbol{x})$. We are thus in a position to find all the bound sets for f: it suffices to use the solution of the problem 1.3. One obtains so the following algorithm that gives the list of bound sets of f.

Algorithm 11.4.

Step 0. Delete from $\boldsymbol{x}$ the variables in which f is degenerate.

Step 1. Compute $J[(x_i)]$ for all variables x_i in $\boldsymbol{x}$. One obtains the list A_1 of bound sets.

Step i. Compute

$$\begin{aligned} \boldsymbol{x}_0 \circledcirc \boldsymbol{x}_0' &= \boldsymbol{x}_0 \cup \boldsymbol{x}_0' \quad \text{if} \quad \boldsymbol{x}_0 \cap \boldsymbol{x}_0' \neq \phi \\ &= J(\boldsymbol{x}_0 \cup \boldsymbol{x}_0') \quad \text{if} \quad \boldsymbol{x}_0 \cap \boldsymbol{x}_0' = \phi \end{aligned}$$

for all unordered pairs $(\boldsymbol{x}_0, \boldsymbol{x}_0')$ of members of A_{i-1}. Delete from the list thus obtained the bound sets that already are in one of the lists $A_1, \ldots, A_{i-1}$. One obtains the list A_i.

The algorithm stops after step i if A_i is empty or is a singleton, that is after at most n steps. The set of bound sets for f is the union of the lists $A_1, A_2, \ldots$, if one does not take into account the variables in which f is degenerate.

Note that the computation of $J[(x_i)]$ and $J[(x_0 \cup x_0')]$ may be performed by employing either Algorithm 11.2 or Algorithm 11.3.

Remarks. (1) Advantage can be taken of the properties of a closure operator. Consider for instance the function f defined by (11.26) and suppose that one must compute $J[(y_4, x_2)]$. From (11.28), (11.29) and Rule 2 one deduces that

$$J[(y_4, x_2)] \supseteq (y_4, x_2, x_1).$$

If one already knows by a previous computation that

$$J[(y_4, x_1)] = (y_4, y_3, x_2, x_1),$$

one may directly conclude that $J[(y_4, x_2)] = (y_4, y_3, x_2, x_1)$.

(2) When x_i is a binary-valued variable, it is obvious that $J[(x_i)] = (x_i)$; hence, for a switching function the list A_1 is known *a priori.*

Example 11.4. The following switching function has been studied by Lapscher [1972];

$$f(x_5, x_4, x_3, x_2, x_1, x_0) = x_2x_1x_0 \vee x_3x_1x_0 \vee x_4x_1x_0 \vee x_5x_1x_0 \vee x_5x_2 \vee x_5x_3 \vee x_5x_4.$$

Compute its first differences as conjunctions of all their prime implicates:

$$\frac{\Delta f}{\Delta x_0} = (\bar{x}_5 \vee \bar{x}_2)(\bar{x}_5 \vee \bar{x}_3)(\bar{x}_5 \vee \bar{x}_4)x_1(x_5 \vee x_4 \vee x_3 \vee x_2);$$

$$\frac{\Delta f}{\Delta x_1} = (\bar{x}_5 \vee \bar{x}_2)(\bar{x}_5 \vee \bar{x}_3)(\bar{x}_5 \vee \bar{x}_4)x_0(x_5 \vee x_4 \vee x_3 \vee x_2);$$

$$\frac{\Delta f}{\Delta x_2} = (\bar{x}_5 \vee \bar{x}_1 \vee \bar{x}_0)(x_5 \vee x_0)(x_5 \vee x_1)\bar{x}_4\bar{x}_3;$$

$$\frac{\Delta f}{\Delta x_3} = (\bar{x}_5 \vee \bar{x}_1 \vee \bar{x}_0)(x_5 \vee x_0)(x_5 \vee x_1)\bar{x}_4\bar{x}_2;$$

$$\frac{\Delta f}{\Delta x_4} = (\bar{x}_5 \vee \bar{x}_1 \vee \bar{x}_0)(x_5 \vee x_0)(x_5 \vee x_1)\bar{x}_2\bar{x}_3;$$

$$\frac{\Delta f}{\Delta x_5} = (\bar{x}_2 \vee \bar{x}_1 \vee \bar{x}_0)(\bar{x}_3 \vee \bar{x}_1 \vee \bar{x}_0)(\bar{x}_4 \vee \bar{x}_1 \vee \bar{x}_0)(x_4 \vee x_3 \vee x_2 \vee x_0)(x_4 \vee x_3 \vee x_2 \vee x_1)$$

Step 1. $A_1 = \{(x_0), (x_2), (x_3), (x_4), (x_5)\}$.

Step 2. One has to perform the fifteen disjunctions

$$(x_0) \circledV (x_1) = J[(x_1, x_0)], \ldots, (x_4) \circledV (x_5) = J[(x_5, x_4)].$$

Let us summarize the results:

$J[(x_1, x_0)] = (x_1, x_0)$;

Rule 1 $\Rightarrow$ $J[(x_2, x_0)] = J[(x_3, x_0)] = J[(x_4, x_0)] = J[(x_5, x_0)] = J[(x_2, x_1)] =$
$J[(x_3, x_1)] = J[(x_4, x_1)] = J[(x_5, x_1)] = (x_5, x_4, x_3, x_2, x_1, x_0)$;

$J[(x_3, x_2)] = (x_3, x_2)$;

$J[(x_4, x_2)] = (x_4, x_2)$;

Rule 1 $\Rightarrow J[(x_5, x_2)] = (x_5, x_4, x_3, x_2, x_1, x_0)$;

$J[(x_4, x_3)] = [(x_4, x_3)]$;

Rule 1 $\Rightarrow J[(x_5, x_3)] = J[(x_5, x_4)] = (x_5, x_4, x_3, x_2, x_1, x_0)$.

$A_2 = \{(x_1, x_0), (x_5, x_4, x_3, x_2, x_1, x_0), (x_3, x_2), (x_4, x_2), (x_4, x_3)\}$.

Step 3. It is not necessary to perform disjunctions with the bound set $(x_5, x_4, x_3, x_2, x_1, x_0)$ since it is the greatest element of the lattice.

$(x_1, x_0) \circledV (x_3, x_2) = J[(x_3, x_2, x_1, x_0)]$;

since we already know that $J[(x_2, x_0)] = (x_5, x_4, x_3, x_2, x_1, x_0)$, we may directly conclude that

$(x_1, x_0) \circledV (x_3, x_2) = (x_5, x_4, x_3, x_2, x_1, x_0)$;

$(x_1, x_0) \circledV (x_4, x_2) = J[(x_4, x_2, x_1, x_0)] = (x_5, x_4, x_3, x_2, x_1, x_0)$;

$(x_1, x_0) \circledV (x_4, x_3) = J[(x_4, x_3, x_1, x_0)] = (x_5, x_4, x_3, x_2, x_1, x_0)$;

$(x_3, x_2) \circledV (x_4, x_2) = (x_3, x_2) \circledV (x_4, x_3) = (x_4, x_2) \circledV (x_4, x_3) = (x_4, x_3, x_2)$.

$A_3 = \{(x_4, x_3, x_2)\}$.

The list of bound sets for f is thus:

$\{\phi, (x_0), (x_1), (x_2), (x_3), (x_4), (x_5), (x_1, x_0), (x_5, x_4, x_3, x_2, x_1, x_0),$
$(x_3, x_2), (x_4, x_2), (x_4, x_3), (x_4, x_3, x_2)\}$.

The corresponding lattice is given in Figure 11.6.

Definition 11.3. Consider the lattice of the bound sets for some binary discrete function f. The *maximal bound sets* for f are the elements of the lattice that are covered by $\boldsymbol{x}$.

For instance, the maximal bound sets for the function f of the previous example are (x_1, x_0), (x_4, x_3, x_2) and (x_5).

The set of maximal bound sets enjoys some important properties that are gathered in the next theorems in which $\bar{\boldsymbol{x}}_i$ stands for the complement of $\boldsymbol{x}_i$ with respect to $\boldsymbol{x}$.

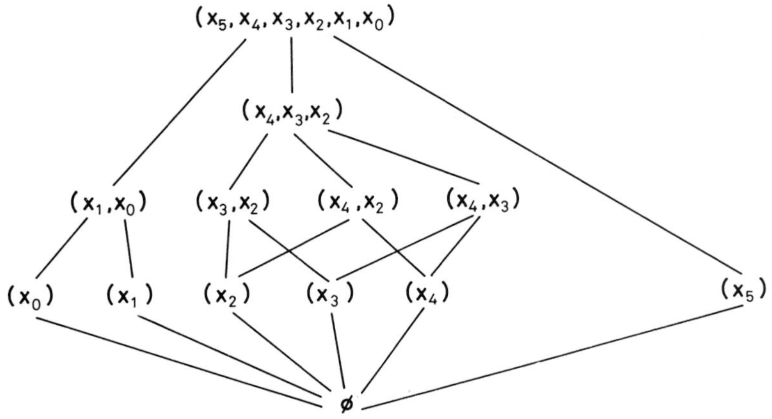

Figure 11.6. Lattice of the bound sets for f

Theorem 11.16. Let f be a binary discrete function that actually depends on all its variables and $\{x_0, \ldots, x_{M-1}\}$ the set of its maximal bound sets. One of the two following properties is verified:

(1) $x_i \cap x_j = \phi$, *for every i and j in $\{0, \ldots, M-1\}$, $i \neq j$;*
(2) $x_i \cap x_j \neq \phi$, $x_i \cup x_j = x$ *and thus* $\bar{x}_i \cap \bar{x}_j = \phi$, *for every i and j in $\{0, \ldots, M-1\}$, $i \neq j$.*

Proof. Suppose that for some indices i and j in $0, \ldots, M-1$, with $i \neq j$, one has $x_i \cap x_j \neq 0$. Hence, by theorem 11.13 (2) one deduces that $x_i \cup x_j$ is also a bound set; by maximality of x_i and x_j one obtains:

$$x_i \cup x_j = x,$$

and thus

$$\bar{x}_i \cap \bar{x}_j = \phi.$$

Consider now a third indice k (if any) in $\{0, \ldots, M-1\}$. One may write successively:

$$x_k = x_k \cap x = x_k \cap (x_i \cup x_j) = (x_k \cap x_i) \cup (x_k \cap x_j). \tag{11.31}$$

This last equality allows us to establish that

$$x_k \cap x_i \neq \phi \quad \text{and} \quad x_k \cap x_j \neq \phi. \tag{11.32}$$

Suppose indeed that $x_k \cap x_i = \phi$; then, by (11.31), one has

$$x_k = x_k \cap x_j \quad \text{and thus} \quad x_k \subseteq x_j.$$

By maximality of x_k this would imply that $x_k = x_j$.

From (11.32), from theorem 11.13 (2) and from the maximality of $\boldsymbol{x}_i$, $\boldsymbol{x}_j$ and $\boldsymbol{x}_k$ one deduces that

$$\boldsymbol{x}_k \cup \boldsymbol{x}_i = \boldsymbol{x}, \quad \boldsymbol{x}_k \cup \boldsymbol{x}_j = \boldsymbol{x},$$

and thus

$$\bar{\boldsymbol{x}}_k \cap \bar{\boldsymbol{x}}_i = \phi, \quad \bar{\boldsymbol{x}}_k \cap \bar{\boldsymbol{x}}_j = \boldsymbol{x}.$$

At this point we have obtained a set $\{\boldsymbol{x}_i, \boldsymbol{x}_j, \boldsymbol{x}_k\}$ of three mutually non-disjoint maximal bound sets. It is obvious that a similar reasoning allows us to enlarge this set in a step by step way. ■

This theorem yields a classification of the binary discrete functions in *type 1* and *type 2* functions according to the fact that the property (1) or (2) is verified.

The type 2 functions belong to a very particular class as proven by the next theorem.

Theorem 11.17. Let f be a type 2 binary discrete function that actually depends on all its variables, and $\{\boldsymbol{x}_0, \ldots, \boldsymbol{x}_{M-1}\}$ *the set of its maximal bound sets. Then f admits a disjunctive decomposition of the type*

$$f(\boldsymbol{x}) = y_{M-1}(\bar{\boldsymbol{x}}_{M-1}) \top \ldots \top y_0(\bar{\boldsymbol{x}}_0)$$

where $\top$ *stands either for the sum modulo-2, the conjunction or the disjunction.*

The proof of this property is divided in several lemmas.

Lemma 11.4. (1) *Every subset of variables of the type*

$$\bar{\boldsymbol{x}}_{i_0} \cup \ldots \cup \bar{\boldsymbol{x}}_{i_{m-1}}, \quad \textit{with} \quad i_j \in \{0, \ldots, M-1\}, \quad \forall j \in \{0, \ldots, m-1\},$$

is a bound set for f;

(2) $(\bar{\boldsymbol{x}}_0, \ldots, \bar{\boldsymbol{x}}_{M-1})$ *is a partition of* $\boldsymbol{x}$.

Proof. (1) Consider two maximal bound sets $\boldsymbol{x}_i$ and $\boldsymbol{x}_j$.

We already know by theorem 11.16 that

$$\boldsymbol{x}_i \cap \boldsymbol{x}_j \neq \phi \quad \text{and} \quad \boldsymbol{x}_i \cup \boldsymbol{x}_j = \boldsymbol{x}$$

and thus

$$\boldsymbol{x}_i \cap \bar{\boldsymbol{x}}_j = \bar{\boldsymbol{x}}_j \neq \phi \quad \text{and} \quad \bar{\boldsymbol{x}}_i \cap \boldsymbol{x}_j = \bar{\boldsymbol{x}}_i \neq \phi.$$

Therefore, by theorem 11.13 (3) one concludes that

$$f(\boldsymbol{x}) = y_3\,[y_2(\bar{\boldsymbol{x}}_j) \top y_1(\bar{\boldsymbol{x}}_i) \top y_0(\boldsymbol{x}_i \cap \boldsymbol{x}_j)];$$

therefore

$$\bar{\boldsymbol{x}}_i, \bar{\boldsymbol{x}}_j \text{ and } \bar{\boldsymbol{x}}_i \cup \bar{\boldsymbol{x}}_j$$

are three bound sets.

Consider now a third maximal bound set $\boldsymbol{x}_k$ (if any); one proves similarly that

$$\bar{\boldsymbol{x}}_k, \bar{\boldsymbol{x}}_i \cup \bar{\boldsymbol{x}}_k \quad \text{and} \quad \bar{\boldsymbol{x}}_j \cup \bar{\boldsymbol{x}}_k$$

are bound sets, and thus also

$$\bar{\boldsymbol{x}}_i \cup \bar{\boldsymbol{x}}_j \cup \bar{\boldsymbol{x}}_k = (\bar{\boldsymbol{x}}_i \cup \bar{\boldsymbol{x}}_k) \circledV (\bar{\boldsymbol{x}}_j \cup \bar{\boldsymbol{x}}_k).$$

A similar reasoning allows to prove the property in a step by step way.

(2) We already know that $\bar{\boldsymbol{x}}_i \cap \bar{\boldsymbol{x}}_j = \phi$ for every i and j in $\{0, \ldots, M-1\}$, $i \neq j$. It remains thus only to prove that

$$\bar{\boldsymbol{x}}_0 \cup \ldots \cup \bar{\boldsymbol{x}}_{M-1} = \boldsymbol{x}.$$

We know by part (1) of the lemma that $\bar{\boldsymbol{x}}_0 \cup \ldots \cup \bar{\boldsymbol{x}}_{M-1}$ is a bound set. If it is not the set $\boldsymbol{x}$, it must be included in some maximal bound set, say $\boldsymbol{x}_i$. But then

$$\bar{\boldsymbol{x}}_0 \cup \ldots \cup \bar{\boldsymbol{x}}_i \cup \ldots \cup \bar{\boldsymbol{x}}_{M-1} \subseteq \boldsymbol{x}_i;$$

therefore

$$\bar{\boldsymbol{x}}_i \subseteq \boldsymbol{x}_i$$

that is

$$\boldsymbol{x}_i = \boldsymbol{x}.$$

This contradicts the fact that $\boldsymbol{x}_i$ is a maximal bound set. ■

Note that this last lemma gives us an indication about the lattice of the bound sets for a type 2 binary discrete function: it contains a sublattice isomorphic to the Boolean lattice B_2^M.

Lemma 11.5. There exists a set of M binary discrete functions $\{A_0, \ldots, A_{M-1}\}$, *where* A_i *depends on the variables in* $\bar{\boldsymbol{x}}_i$ *only, for every* $i = 0, \ldots, M-1$, *such that*

$$\frac{\Delta f}{\Delta x_k} = A_{M-1}(\bar{\boldsymbol{x}}_{M-1}) \ldots A_{l+1}(\bar{\boldsymbol{x}}_{l+1})\, b_{lk}(\bar{\boldsymbol{x}}_l)\, A_{l-1}(\bar{\boldsymbol{x}}_{l-1}) \ldots A_0(\bar{\boldsymbol{x}}_0)$$

for every x_k *in* $\bar{\boldsymbol{x}}_l$.

Proof. Taking into account the fact that

$$\bar{\boldsymbol{x}}_0, \bar{\boldsymbol{x}}_1 \cup \bar{\boldsymbol{x}}_0, \ldots, \bar{\boldsymbol{x}}_{M-2} \cup \ldots \cup \bar{\boldsymbol{x}}_0$$

are bound sets, we may write

$$\begin{aligned}\frac{\Delta f}{\Delta x_i} &= a_1(\bar{\boldsymbol{x}}_{M-1}, \ldots, \bar{\boldsymbol{x}}_1)\, b_{0i}(\bar{\boldsymbol{x}}_0)\\ &= a_2(\bar{\boldsymbol{x}}_{M-1}, \ldots, \bar{\boldsymbol{x}}_2)\, b_{1i}(\bar{\boldsymbol{x}}_1, \bar{\boldsymbol{x}}_0)\\ &\ \ \vdots\\ &= a_{M-1}(\bar{\boldsymbol{x}}_{M-1})\, b_{M-2i}(\bar{\boldsymbol{x}}_{M-2}, \ldots, \bar{\boldsymbol{x}}_0) \not\equiv 0\end{aligned}$$

for every x_i in $\bar{x}_0$. By an iterative application of lemma 11.1 one obtains

$$\frac{\Delta f}{\Delta x_i} = A'_{M-1}(\bar{x}_{M-1}) \ldots A'_1(\bar{x}_1)\, b_{0i}(\bar{x}_0)$$

for every x_i in $\bar{x}_0$. Consider now a variable x_j of $\bar{x}_1$. A similar reasoning yields:

$$\frac{\Delta f}{\Delta x_j} = A''_{M-1}(\bar{x}_{M-1}) \ldots A''_2(\bar{x}_2)\, b_{1j}(\bar{x}_1)\, A''_0(\bar{x}_0) \not\equiv 0.$$

Taking into account the fact that $\bar{x}_1 \cup \bar{x}_0$ is also a bound set, one concludes that

$$A''_{M-1} = A'_{M-1}, \ldots, A''_2 = A'_2.$$

It suffices then to put

$$A_{M-1} = A'_{M-1}, \ldots, A_2 = A'_2, A_1 = A'_1, A_0 = A''_0.$$

Consider finally a third variable x_k that lies in $\bar{x}_l$:

$$\frac{\Delta f}{\Delta x_k} = A'''_{M-1}(\bar{x}_{M-1}) \ldots A_{l+1}(\bar{x}_{l+1})\, b_{lk}(\bar{x}_l)\, A_{l-1}(\bar{x}_{l-1}) \ldots A_0(\bar{x}_0) \not\equiv 0;$$

from the fact that both $\bar{x}_l \cup \bar{x}_0$ and $\bar{x}_l \cup \bar{x}_1$ are bound sets, one deduces that

$$A'''_p = A_p, \quad \forall p = 0, \ldots, l-1, l+1, \ldots, M-1.$$ ∎

Lemma 11.6. If there are two variables x_i and x_j, belonging to different blocks of $(\bar{x}_{M-1}, \ldots, \bar{x}_0)$, and such that $\Delta f/\Delta x_i x_j \equiv 0$, then $\Delta f/\Delta x_u x_v \equiv 0$ for every pair of variables x_u and x_v belonging to different blocks of $(\bar{x}_{M-1}, \ldots, \bar{x}_0)$.

Proof. Suppose that $x_i \in \bar{x}_0$ and $x_j \in \bar{x}_1$. Therefore

$$\frac{\Delta A_1}{\Delta x_j} \equiv 0 \quad \text{and} \quad \frac{\Delta A_0}{\Delta x_i} \equiv 0.$$

Suppose now that $x_u \in \bar{x}_l$; one has either $l \neq 0$ or $l \neq 1$. In the first case one may write successively:

$$\frac{\Delta f}{\Delta x_u x_i} \equiv 0 \quad \text{since} \quad \frac{\Delta A_0}{\Delta x_i} \equiv 0;$$

hence

$$\frac{\Delta A_l}{\Delta x_u} \equiv 0 \quad \text{and thus} \quad \frac{\Delta f}{\Delta x_u x_v} \equiv 0.$$

The case where $l \neq 1$ may be handled similarly. ∎

We have proven that either $\Delta f/\Delta x_i x_j \equiv 0$ for every pair of variables appearing in different blocks of $(\bar{x}_{M-1}, \ldots, \bar{x}_0)$ or $\Delta f/\Delta x_i x_j \not\equiv 0$ for every pair of variables. In that last case one has the following property.

Lemma 11.7. If $\Delta f/x_i x_j \neq 0$ for every pair of variables appearing in different blocks of $(\bar{x}_{M-1}, \ldots, \bar{x}_0)$, then

$$\frac{\Delta f}{\Delta x_k} = A_{M-1}(\bar{x}_{M-1}) \ldots A_{l+1}(\bar{x}_{l+1}) \frac{\Delta A_l}{\Delta x_k} A_{l-1}(\bar{x}_l) \ldots A_0(\bar{x}_0),$$

for every x_k in $\bar{x}_l$.

Proof. Consider for instance $x_i \in \bar{x}_0$ and $x_j \in \bar{x}_1$:

$$\frac{\Delta f}{\Delta x_i x_j} = A_{M-1}(\bar{x}_{M-1}) \ldots A_2(\bar{x}_2) \frac{\Delta A_1}{\Delta x_j} b_{0i}(\bar{x}_0)$$

$$= A_{M-1}(\bar{x}_{M-1}) \ldots A_2(\bar{x}_2)\, b_{1j}(\bar{x}_1) \frac{\Delta A_0}{\Delta x_i} \neq 0$$

and thus

$$b_{1j} = \frac{\Delta A_1}{\Delta x_j}, \quad b_{0i} = \frac{\Delta A_0}{\Delta x_i}. \qquad \blacksquare$$

We are now in place to prove the theorem 11.17. Introduce for that purpose a new notation:

$$\boldsymbol{\xi}_i = \bar{x}_i, \quad \forall i = \{0, \ldots, M-1\},$$

while $\boldsymbol{\epsilon}_i$ will stand for a particular value of $\boldsymbol{\xi}_i$.

If we are in the situation of lemma 11.6, we obtain the following Newton expansion for f:

$$f(\boldsymbol{x}) = f(0) \oplus \sum_{i=0}^{M-1} \left[\sum_{\epsilon_i \neq 0} \left(\frac{\Delta^{\epsilon_i} f}{\Delta \boldsymbol{\xi}_i}\right)_0 \prod_j \binom{\xi_{ij}}{\epsilon_{ij}} \right], \quad \xi_{ij} \in \boldsymbol{\xi}_i,\ \epsilon_{ij} \in \boldsymbol{\epsilon}_i$$

$$= \sum_{i=0}^{M-1} y_i(\bar{x}_i).$$

In the situation of lemma 11.7 one has:

$$f(\boldsymbol{x}) = f(0) \oplus \sum_e \left(\frac{\Delta^e f}{\Delta \boldsymbol{x}}\right)_0 \prod_j \binom{x_j}{e_j}$$

$$= f(0) \oplus \prod_{i=0}^{M-1} A_i(0) \oplus \prod_{i=0}^{M-1} \left[\sum_{\epsilon_i} \left(\frac{\Delta^{\epsilon_i} A_i}{\Delta \boldsymbol{\xi}_i}\right)_0 \prod_j \binom{\xi_{ij}}{\epsilon_{ij}} \right]$$

$$= e \oplus \prod_{i=0}^{M-1} z_i(\bar{x}_i).$$

If $e = 0$

$$f(\boldsymbol{x}) = \prod_{i=0}^{m-1} z_i(\bar{\boldsymbol{x}}_i);$$

if $e = 1$

$$f(\boldsymbol{x}) = \bigvee_{i=0}^{m-1} y_i(\bar{\boldsymbol{x}}_i)$$

with $y_i = \bar{z}_i$, $\forall i = 0, \ldots, M-1$.

This completes the proof of theorem 11.17.

In the case where f is a switching function, every singleton $\{x_i\}$ is a bound set that is contained in at least one maximal bound set. Therefore the union of the maximal bound sets of a switching function is $\boldsymbol{x}$, and for a type 1 switching function the set of maximal bound sets is a partition of $\boldsymbol{x}$. From corollary 11.1 we deduce then the following theorem.

Theorem 11.18. Let f be a type 1 switching function that actually depends on all its variables, and $\{\boldsymbol{x}_0, \ldots, \boldsymbol{x}_{M-1}\}$ the set of its maximal bound sets. Then f admits a disjunctive decomposition of the type

$$f(\boldsymbol{x}) = y_M[y_{M-1}(\boldsymbol{x}_{M-1}), \ldots, y_0(\boldsymbol{x}_0)].$$

If f is a type 1 binary function of non-binary variables it can arise that the union of its maximal bound sets does not contain all the variables. Consider for instance the two-variable function of Figure 11.7. Its bound sets are ϕ, $\{x_1\}$ and $\{x_0, x_1\}$; $\{x_1\}$ is thus the unique maximal bound set.

x_1 \ x_0	0	1	2
0	0	0	1
1	0	0	1
2	1	0	1

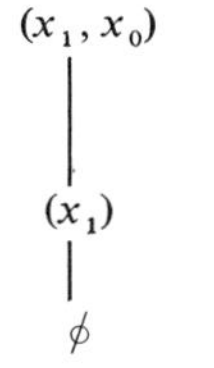

Figure 11.7. Binary function and its lattice of bound sets

We may however state the following theorem that is again a direct consequence of corollary 11.1.

Theorem 11.19. Let f be a type 1 binary discrete function that actually depends on all its variables, and $\{\boldsymbol{x}_0, \ldots, \boldsymbol{x}_{M-1}\}$ the set of its maximal bound sets. Then it admits a disjunctive decomposition of the type

$$f(\boldsymbol{x}) = y_M[\boldsymbol{x}_M, y_{M-1}(\boldsymbol{x}_{M-1}), \ldots, y_0(\boldsymbol{x}_0)]$$

where $\boldsymbol{x}_M = \bar{\boldsymbol{x}}_{M-1} \cap \ldots \cap \bar{\boldsymbol{x}}_0$. ■

The next theorem gives a method for constructing the lattice of the bound sets that is based on theorems 11.17 and 11.19.

Theorem 11.20. Let f be a binary discrete function that actually depends on all its variables, and $\{\boldsymbol{x}_0, \ldots, \boldsymbol{x}_{M-1}\}$ *the set of its maximal bound sets:*

(1) *If f is a type 1 function, then every bound set is a bound set for one of the functions* y_i, $i = 0, \ldots, M-1$, *that appears in the associated disjunctive decomposition of f.*

(2) *If f is a type 2 function, then every bound set is either a bound set for one of the functions* y_i, $i = 0, \ldots, M-1$ *of the associated disjunctive decomposition of f or is of the type*

$$\bar{\boldsymbol{x}}_{i_0} \cup \ldots \cup \bar{\boldsymbol{x}}_{i_{m-1}} \quad \textit{with} \quad i_j \in \{0, \ldots, M-1\}, \quad \forall j = 0, \ldots, m-1.$$

Proof. (1) If f is a type 1 function it may be decomposed under the form

$$f(\boldsymbol{x}) = y_M[\boldsymbol{x}_M, y_{M-1}(\boldsymbol{x}_{M-1}), \ldots, y_0(\boldsymbol{x}_0)].$$

If $\boldsymbol{x}' \neq \boldsymbol{x}$ is a bound set for f, it is included in one of the maximal bound sets, say $\boldsymbol{x}_i$. We may then write:

$$\frac{\Delta f}{\Delta x_k} = A(\bar{\boldsymbol{x}}')\, B_k(\boldsymbol{x}') = \frac{\Delta y_M}{\Delta y_i}\, \frac{\Delta y_i}{\Delta x_k} \not\equiv 0$$

for every x_k in $\boldsymbol{x}'$. Therefore

$$\frac{\Delta y_i}{\Delta x_k} = a(\boldsymbol{x}_i \cap \bar{\boldsymbol{x}}')\, B_k(\boldsymbol{x}')$$

for every x_k in $\boldsymbol{x}'$, and thus $\boldsymbol{x}'$ is a bound set for y_i.

(2) Suppose that f is of type 2 and admits a bound set $\boldsymbol{x}' \neq \phi$. From the fact that $(\bar{\boldsymbol{x}}_0, \ldots, \bar{\boldsymbol{x}}_{M-1})$ is a partition of $\boldsymbol{x}$, one deduces that one may find maximal bound sets $\boldsymbol{x}_{i_0}, \ldots, \boldsymbol{x}_{i_{m-1}}$, such that

$$\boldsymbol{x} \subseteq \bar{\boldsymbol{x}}_{i_0} \cup \ldots \cup \bar{\boldsymbol{x}}_{i_{m-1}} \tag{11.33}$$

with

$$\boldsymbol{x}' \cap \bar{\boldsymbol{x}}_{i_j} \neq \phi, \quad \forall j = 0, \ldots, m-1. \tag{11.34}$$

If $m = 1$, then $\boldsymbol{x}'$ is included in $\bar{\boldsymbol{x}}_{i_0}$ and a reasoning similar to that of part (1) of the proof allows us to show that $\boldsymbol{x}'$ is also a bound set for $y_{i_0}(\bar{\boldsymbol{x}}_{i_0})$.

Suppose that $m \geqslant 2$. The set $\boldsymbol{x}'$ may not be included in any of the $\bar{\boldsymbol{x}}_{i_j}, j = 0, \ldots, m-1$: this is a direct consequence of (11.34) and of the fact that the $\bar{\boldsymbol{x}}_{i_j}$ are disjoint. Therefore

$$\boldsymbol{x}' \cap \boldsymbol{x}_{i_j} \neq \phi, \quad \forall j = 0, \ldots, m-1,$$

and thus $\boldsymbol{x}' \cup \boldsymbol{x}_{i_j}$ is a bound set. Therefore, according to the maximality of $\boldsymbol{x}_{i_j}$ one has either

$$\boldsymbol{x}' \cup \boldsymbol{x}_{i_j} = \boldsymbol{x}_{i_j} \quad \text{or} \quad \boldsymbol{x}' \cup \boldsymbol{x}_{i_j} = \boldsymbol{x};$$

in the first case one obtains

$$\bar{\boldsymbol{x}}' \subseteq \boldsymbol{x}_{i_j} \quad \text{that is} \quad \boldsymbol{x}' \cap \bar{\boldsymbol{x}}_{i_j} = \phi,$$

but this contradicts (11.34). Therefore

$$\boldsymbol{x}' \cup \boldsymbol{x}_{i_j} = \boldsymbol{x} \quad \text{that is} \quad \boldsymbol{x}' \supseteq \bar{\boldsymbol{x}}_{i_j}, \quad \forall j = 0, \ldots, m-1.$$

Hence, from (11.33) one concludes that

$$\boldsymbol{x}' = \bar{\boldsymbol{x}}_{i_0} \cup \ldots \cup \bar{\boldsymbol{x}}_{i_{m-1}}.$$ ■

This last theorem thus suggests a method for generating the lattice of the bound sets of a binary discrete function f based on the computation of the maximal bound sets of a series of binary discrete functions. It runs as follows:

Step 1. Find the maximal bound sets for f.

Step 2. Let $\{\boldsymbol{x}_0, \ldots, \boldsymbol{x}_{M-1}\}$ be the set of bound sets obtained at step 1.

If f is a type 2 function, every subset of the type

$$\bar{\boldsymbol{x}}_{i_0} \ldots \bar{\boldsymbol{x}}_{i_{m-1}}, \quad i_j \in \{0, \ldots, M-1\}, \quad \forall j = 0, \ldots, m-1,$$

is a bound set. One generates in this manner a part of the lattice that is isomorphic to the Boolean lattice B_2^M. The function may be decomposed under the form

$$y_{M-1}(\bar{\boldsymbol{x}}_{M-1}) \top \ldots \top y_0(\bar{\boldsymbol{x}}_0).$$

If f is a type 1 function, it may be decomposed under the form

$$y_M[\boldsymbol{x}_M, y_{M-1}(\boldsymbol{x}_{M-1}), \ldots, y_0(\boldsymbol{x}_0)].$$

Return then to step 1, and successively replace f by $y_0, \ldots, y_{M-1}$. Every function y_i is then also disjunctively decomposed and yields new binary discrete functions, and so on.

It is quite obvious that this procedure describes at the same time a disjunctive tree-like decomposition of f. There is thus an obvious relation between the lattice of the bound sets for f and a kind of "most refined" disjunctive tree-like decomposition of f. If one uses the same notations as in section 11.1.2, this most refined disjunctive tree-like decomposition has the following property: for every bound set $\boldsymbol{x}'$ of f either

$$\boldsymbol{x}' = X_j \text{ for some node } b_j$$

or

$$\boldsymbol{x}' \subset X_j$$

and the output of the building block corresponding to the node b_j realizes a function of the type

$$g(\boldsymbol{x}') \top h(X_j \backslash \boldsymbol{x}').$$

Example 11.5. Consider the function f of example 11.4. Its lattice of bound sets is given in Figure 11.6. Its corresponding disjunctive tree-like decomposition is given in Figure 11.8. It corresponds to the following computation scheme:

$$\xi_0 = x_1 x_0$$

$$\xi_1 = x_2 \vee x_3 \vee x_4$$

$$f(x_5, x_4, x_3, x_2, x_1, x_0) = \xi_0 (\xi_1 \vee x_5) \vee x_5 \xi_1$$

in which ξ_1 corresponds to the sublattice isomorphic to B_2^3.

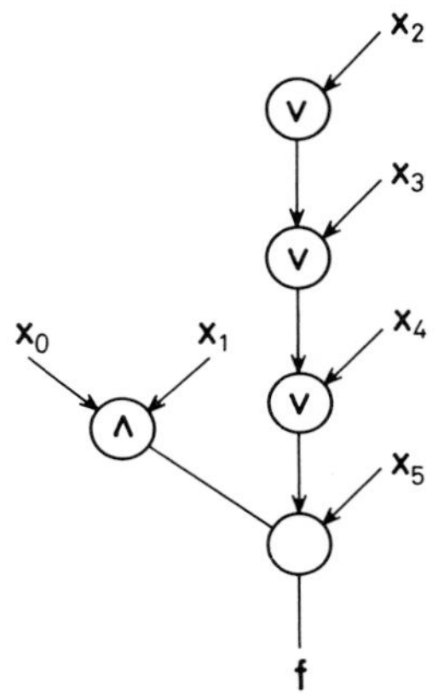

Figure 11.8. Disjunctive tree-like decomposition of f

We conclude this subsection by two remarks indicating possible extensions of the theory developed above.

(1) Consider a binary discrete function f and a simple non-disjunctive decomposition $f(\boldsymbol{x}) = y_1 [\boldsymbol{x}_2, \boldsymbol{x}_1, y_0(\boldsymbol{x}_2, \boldsymbol{x}_0)]$, in which the three subsets of variables $\boldsymbol{x}_0, \boldsymbol{x}_1$ and $\boldsymbol{x}_2$ are disjoint. The subset of variables $\boldsymbol{x}_0$ is called a *bound set with respect to* $\boldsymbol{x}_2$ for f. An algorithm similar to algorithm 11.4 may be developed for finding all the bound sets with respect to $\boldsymbol{x}_2$ for a given binary discrete function f and for a fixed given subset $\boldsymbol{x}_2$ of variables: see Deschamps [1975a].

(2) In the same paper it is shown that an algorithm similar to algorithm 11.4 may also be used for non-binary discrete functions as long as one is concerned with *binary decompositions.* Given a discrete function f, a binary simple decomposition of f is characterized by a relation of the type

$$f(\boldsymbol{x}) = y_1 [\boldsymbol{x}_2, \boldsymbol{x}_1, y_0(\boldsymbol{x}_2, \boldsymbol{x}_0)],$$

where y_0 is a binary discrete function.

11.2.4. Concluding remarks

The material contained in the preceding subsection gives a satisfactory answer to the problem of finding disjunctive tree-like decompositions for a given binary discrete function *f*. It is based on a thorough study of the lattice of the bound sets of *f*. This study is entirely contained in the paper of Ashenhurst, even if we used rather different techniques, issued from the differential calculus, for proving the various theorems.

In what concerns the other types of decompositions, we must certainly quote again the papers of Roth and Karp [1962], Karp [1963] and the book of Curtis [1962] that describe systematic methods for obtaining economical realizations of switching functions; this last book contains a series of theorems that generalize to the case of non-disjunctive decompositions similar theorems due to Ashenhurst.

We guess however that the concept of economical realization is in continuous evolution. At the time of writing these lines, a practical problem could be stated as follows: given a series of large-scale integrated circuits like multiplexers, decoders, and perhaps also read only memories and microprocessors, design a composite digital circuit that realizes some given input—output behaviour. Several years ago, one had to design a circuit with the same external behaviour, but with building blocks that were for instance NAND gates and master-slave flip-flops.

It is quite obvious that the methods that have been proven very efficient in the past for gate oriented circuit realizations are not necessary convenient and efficient if one makes use of l.s.i. circuits.

This is a way for us to justify the rather theoretical and algebraic approach we have chosen all along in this chapter; the material it contains has to be seen as a kind of background that could be useful whatever technological facilities are available.

Chapter 12
Unateness

In numerical analysis one studies monotone functions of a single real variable. Functions which are monotone in all their variables are studied in switching theory. It appears that discrete functions which are monotone in all or in a subset of their variables play an important role in multiple valued logic. These functions not only play a key role in theoretical investigations but have also very simple and useful realizations.

Unate functions are defined in section 12.1; these functions are monotone increasing in a first subset of their variables and monotone decreasing in another subset of their variables. Partially unate functions are functions which are unate with respect to a proper subset of their variables. Much of the material of section 12.1 is probably well known to logicians and switching theorists (see, for example, the papers by McNaughton [1961] and Ying and Susskind [1971]).

Section 12.2 introduces the concept of envelopes associated with a discrete function f. The envelopes are either the smallest unate functions larger than f or the largest unate functions smaller than f; they constitute a straightforward generalization of a concept which was suggested by Kuntzmann [1965]. Envelopes were first used in logic design by Thayse [1975b] and Thayse and Deschamps [1976].

A function f is said to be locally unate if it is unate in a subdomain of f. Hazards in discrete functions and in logic networks may be approached by a common criterion, which was quoted in a paper by Beister [1974] dealing with switching networks: a given transition is hazard-free if and only if the discrete function is locally unate in the transition subcube generated by that transition. Local unateness and hazard-free transitions are studied in sections 12.3 and 12.4 respectively. The particular case of switching functions is studied more thoroughly in section 12.5.

Some applications are gathered in section 12.6. The design of hazard-free networks is an important tool in multiple-valued logic. A procedure for designing hazard-free networks based on the concept of envelope is presented in section 12.6.1. When applied to switching networks, this procedure improves, from a hazard point of view, the well-known two-level realizations obtained by Eichelberger [1965]. The transient analysis of switching networks, already introduced in Chapters 3 and 7 is continued in section 12.6.2. Finally one shows in section 12.6.3 that switching networks realizing unate switching functions present good characteristics from a fault detection point of view; the material presented in section 12.6.3 is due to Betancourt [1971].

12.1. Unate discrete functions

Definition 12.1

(a) A discrete function $f(\boldsymbol{x})$ is *monotone increasing* iff $\boldsymbol{e} = (e_{n-1}, \ldots, e_1, e_0) < \boldsymbol{h} = (h_{n-1}, \ldots, h_1, h_0)$ implies $f(\boldsymbol{e}) \leqslant f(\boldsymbol{h})$ $\forall \boldsymbol{e}, \boldsymbol{h} \in S$; a discrete function is *monotone decreasing* iff $\boldsymbol{e} < \boldsymbol{h}$ implies $f(\boldsymbol{e}) \geqslant f(\boldsymbol{h})$.

(b) A discrete function $f(\boldsymbol{x})$ is said to be *unate* iff there is a (non-trivial) partition $(\boldsymbol{x}_1, \boldsymbol{x}_0)$ of $\boldsymbol{x}$ such that f is monotone increasing in $\boldsymbol{x}_0$ and monotone decreasing in $\boldsymbol{x}_1$.

(c) A discrete function is said to be *partially unate* with respect to, for example, the variable x_{n-1} iff $e_{n-1} < h_{n-1}$ implies either $f(e_{n-1}, x_{n-2}, \ldots, x_0) \leqslant f(h_{n-1}, x_{n-2}, \ldots, x_0)$ or $f(e_{n-1}, x_{n-2}, \ldots, x_0) \geqslant f(h_{n-1}, x_{n-2}, \ldots, x_0)$ $\forall e_{n-1}, h_{n-1} \in S_{n-1}$; a discrete function $f(\boldsymbol{x})$ is said to be partially unate with respect to the variables $\boldsymbol{x}_0 \subseteq \boldsymbol{x}$ iff f is unate with respect to each of the variables in $\boldsymbol{x}_0$.

*Lemma 12.1. A function f(**x**) is monotone increasing iff it has at least one representation as a disjunction of implicants (resp. as a conjunction of implicates) of the form:*

$$f(\boldsymbol{x}) = \bigvee_j \left(l_j \wedge \bigwedge_{i=n-1}^{0} x_i^{[a_{ij}}\right) \tag{12.1}$$

$$\left(\text{resp.} \quad f(\boldsymbol{x}) = \bigwedge_j \left(l_j \vee \bigvee_{i=n-1}^{0} x_i^{[a_{ij}}\right)\right). \tag{12.2}$$

Proof. Since $x_i^{[a_{ij}}$ is monotone increasing and the product and the sum of monotone increasing functions is monotone increasing, the expressions (12.1) and (12.2) represent monotone increasing functions.

Assume now that f is monotone increasing, one has:

$$f(x_i = 0) \leqslant f(x_i = 1) \leqslant f(x_i = 2) \ldots \leqslant f(x_i = m_i - 1)$$

so that the following partial expansion with respect to the variable x_i holds:

$$f = f(x_i = 0) \vee f(x_i = 1)\, x_i^{[1} \vee f(x_i = 2)\, x_i^{[2} \vee \ldots \vee f(x_i = m_i - 1)\, x_i^{[m_i - 1}. \tag{12.3}$$

Now since each subfunction $f(x_i = j)$ is a monotone increasing function, relation (12.1) is obtained from (12.3) by induction on the number of variables.

A similar type of statement holds for proving relation (12.2). ■

*Lemma 12.2. A function f(**x**) is monotone decreasing iff it has at least one representation as a disjunction of implicants (resp. as a conjunction of implicates) of the form:*

$$f(\boldsymbol{x}) = \bigvee_j \left(l_j \wedge \bigwedge_{i=n-1}^{0} x_i^{a_{ij}]}\right) \tag{12.4}$$

$$\left(\text{resp.}\ f(\boldsymbol{x}) = \bigwedge_j \left(l_j \vee \bigvee_{i=n-1}^{0} x_i^{a_{ij}]}\right)\right). \tag{12.5}$$

Theorem 12.1

(a) *The unique representation of every montone increasing (resp. decreasing) discrete function as the disjunction of all its prime implicants is of the form (12.1) (resp. (12.4)): in this representation each prime implicant is essential.*

(b) *The unique representation of every monotone increasing (resp. decreasing) discrete function as the conjunction of all its prime implicates is of the form (12.2) (resp. (12.5)); in this representation each prime implicate is essential.*

Proof. If p is a prime implicant of a montone increasing function, it is necessarily of the form:

$$p = l_j \wedge \bigwedge_{i=n-1}^{0} x_i^{[a_{ij}}.$$

Indeed, assume that

$$p' = l_j \wedge \bigwedge_{i=n-1}^{0} x_i^{[a_{ij}, b_{ij}]}, \qquad b_{ij} \neq m_i - 1$$
$$\geqslant a_{ij}$$

is an implicant of f; since f is monotone increasing p is also an implicant of f and since $p' < p$ the prime implicants are of the form (12.1). If $b_{ij} < a_{ij}$, then l_j (which is a particular case of the form (12.1)) is an implicant of f.

Since all the prime implicants are of the form (12.1) they are necessarily essential prime implicants; indeed a prime implicant of the form (12.1) cannot be obtained from the others by applying, for example, the generalized consensus. A similar type of statement holds for the other points of theorem 12.1. ■

Let us note that the corresponding theorem 12.1 for switching functions was first stated by Quine [1953].

The following theorem 12.2 is an immediate consequence of the above lemmas.

Theorem 12.2. A function $f(\boldsymbol{x})$ is unate iff it has at least one representation as a disjunction of implicants (resp. as a conjunction of implicates) of the form:

$$f = \bigvee_j \left(l_j \wedge \bigwedge_{i=n-1}^{q} x_i^{[a_{ij}} \wedge \bigwedge_{k=q-1}^{0} x_k^{a_{kj}]} \right) \tag{12.6}$$

$$\left(\text{resp.}\ f = \bigwedge_j \left(l_j \vee \bigvee_{i=n-1}^{q} x_i^{[a_{ij}} \vee \bigvee_{k=q-1}^{0} x_k^{[a_{kj}}\right)\right). \tag{12.7}$$

The unique representation of f as a disjunction of all its prime implicants (resp. as a conjunction of all its prime implicates) is of the form (12.6) (resp. (12.7)).

Clearly similar types of expansions hold for partially unate functions; if $f(\boldsymbol{x}, \boldsymbol{y})$ is, for example, partially unate with respect to $\boldsymbol{x}$, the expansions (12.6) and (12.7) hold for these functions but the l_j's are then functions of $\boldsymbol{y}$ instead of being constants.

From the above lemmas and theorems one deduces that the set of prime cubes of a unate function is identical to the set of its prime blocks and to the set of its prime convex blocks. Dually, the sets of its prime anticubes, of its prime antiblocks and of its prime convex antiblocks are also identical. The above assertion evidently does not hold true for the partial unate functions.

The partial unateness of a discrete function may be recognized once its expansion in terms of prime implicants or in terms of prime implicates has been obtained. It seems that no better algorithms exist actually for detecting unateness in discrete functions.

A discrete function $f(\boldsymbol{x})$ is said to be *degenerate* with respect to $\boldsymbol{x}_0 \subseteq \boldsymbol{x} = (\boldsymbol{x}_1, \boldsymbol{x}_0)$ iff:

$$f(\boldsymbol{x}_1, \boldsymbol{e}_0) = f(\boldsymbol{x}_1, \boldsymbol{l}_0) \;\; \forall \boldsymbol{e}_0,\; \boldsymbol{l}_0 \in \mathop{\times}_{i=q-1}^{0} S_i. \tag{12.8}$$

It is convenient to consider the degenerescence as a particular case of the unateness: a *partial degenerate function* is a function which is at the same time monotone increasing and monotone decreasing with respect to the same subset of variables.

A discrete function can easily be tested for partial degenerescence according to the relation (12.8).

12.2. *Envelopes associated with discrete functions*

Definition 12.2. Let ϵ be a vector of n binary elements:

$$\epsilon = (\epsilon_{n-1}, \ldots, \epsilon_1, \epsilon_0), \quad \epsilon_i \in \{0, 1\} \;\; \forall i.$$

(a) The *upper envelope* of $f(\boldsymbol{x})$ with respect to ϵ is the function $\hat{m}_\epsilon(f)$ defined as:

$$\hat{m}_\epsilon(f) = \bigvee_{e} \left[f(e) \wedge \bigwedge_{i=n-1}^{0} x_i^{[\epsilon_i e_i,\, e_i \vee \epsilon_i (m_i - 1)]} \right], \quad 0 \leqslant e_i \leqslant m_i - 1. \tag{12.9}$$

(b) The *lower envelope* of $f(\boldsymbol{x})$ with respect to ϵ is the function $\check{m}_\epsilon(f)$ defined as:

$$\check{m}_\epsilon(f) = \bigwedge_{e} \left[f(e) \vee \bigvee_{i=n-1}^{0} x_i^{[\epsilon_i (e_i + 1),\, (e_i - 1) \vee \epsilon_i (m_i - 1)]} \right], \quad 0 \leqslant e_i \leqslant m_i - 1. \tag{12.10}$$

As usual, it is conventionally assumed in the above expressions that $x_i^{[m_i} = x_i^{-1]} = 0 \;\; \forall i$.

The following theorem states the most important property of the envelopes of $f(\boldsymbol{x})$.

Theorem 12.3

(a) *The function $\hat{m}_\epsilon(f)$ is the smallest unate function larger than or equal to f which is monotone increasing with respect to the variables x_i:{i | $\epsilon_i = 1$} and monotone decreasing with respect to the variables x_j: {j | $\epsilon_j = 0$}.*

(b) *The function $\underset{\vee}{m}_\epsilon(f)$ is the largest unate function smaller than or equal to f which is monotone increasing with respect to the variables x_i:{i | $\epsilon_i = 1$} and monotone decreasing with respect to the variables x_j:{j | $\epsilon_j = 0$}.*

Proof. (a) *Assume first that* $\epsilon = \mathbf{1}$; one has:

$$\hat{m}_{\mathbf{1}}(f) = \bigvee_e \left[f(e) \wedge \bigwedge_{i=n-1}^{0} x_i^{[e_i} \right];$$

$\hat{m}_{\mathbf{1}}(f)$ is thus a monotone increasing function. Moreover, in view of the disjunctive canonical form of f:

$$f = \bigvee_e \left[f(e) \wedge \bigwedge_{i=n-1}^{0} x_i^{[e_i, e_i]} \right];$$

it is the smallest monotone increasing function larger than or equal to f. Assume now that $\epsilon = \mathbf{0}$; one has:

$$\hat{m}_{\mathbf{0}}(f) = \bigvee_e \left[f(e) \wedge \bigwedge_{i=n-1}^{0} x_i^{e_i]} \right]$$

which is the smallest monotone decreasing function larger than or equal to f. The proof of part (a) is achieved in the same way by giving mixed values 0 and 1 to the elements ϵ_i of ϵ.

(b) Similar types of arguments hold for proving part (b); they are grounded on the following relations:

$$\underset{\vee}{m}_{\mathbf{1}}(f) = \bigwedge_e \left[f(e) \vee \bigvee_{i=n-1}^{0} x_i^{[e_i+1} \right]$$

$$\underset{\vee}{m}_{\mathbf{0}}(f) = \bigwedge_e \left[f(e) \vee \bigvee_{i=n-1}^{0} x_i^{e_i-1]} \right]$$

$$f(\boldsymbol{x}) = \bigwedge_e \left[f(e) \vee \bigvee_{i=n-1}^{0} x_i^{[e_i+1,\, e_i-1]} \right].$$

The functions $\underset{\vee}{m}_{\mathbf{1}}(f)$ and $\underset{\vee}{m}_{\mathbf{0}}(f)$ are clearly the largest monotone increasing and monotone decreasing functions smaller than f respectively. ■

The following properties of the envelopes are immediate consequences of the above definition and theorem.

If f and g are two discrete functions:

$$\hat{m}_\epsilon(f \vee g) = \hat{m}_\epsilon(f) \vee \hat{m}_\epsilon(g) \tag{12.11}$$

$$\underset{\vee}{m}_\epsilon(f \wedge g) = \underset{\vee}{m}_\epsilon(f) \wedge \underset{\vee}{m}_\epsilon(g). \tag{12.12}$$

There are 2^n upper envelopes and 2^n lower envelopes of f; these functions are obtained by giving to ϵ its 2^n values.

Definition 12.3

(a) A minimal upper envelope of f (i.e. an upper envelope which does not contain any other upper envelope of f) is also called a *prime upper envelope* of f.

(b) A maximal lower envelope of f (i.e. a lower envelope which is not contained in any other lower envelope of f) is also called a *prime lower envelope* of f.

The prime upper envelopes and prime lower envelopes are concepts which will play a similar role as those of prime implicants and prime implicates in some synthesis problems; this will clearly appear further in this chapter (see section 12.5.1).

We will now briefly describe algorithms for obtaining the upper and the lower envelopes of a discrete function; assume first that the latter is given by means of a lattice expression.

Algorithm 12.1

Obtention of the upper envelopes

Obtain the discrete function $f(\boldsymbol{x})$ as a disjunction of cubes:

$$f = \bigvee_j \left(l_j \wedge \bigwedge_{i=n-1}^{0} x_i^{(C_{ij})} \right).$$

Let a_{ij} and b_{ij} be the smallest and the greatest elements of C_{ij} respectively. (It is recalled that the following ordering holds in S_i: $0 \leqslant 1 \leqslant 2 \leqslant \ldots \leqslant m_i - 1$.) The upper envelope $\hat{m}_\epsilon(f)$ is:

$$\hat{m}_\epsilon(f) = \bigvee_j \left(l_j \wedge \bigwedge_i x_i^{[a_{ij}} \wedge \bigwedge_k x_k^{b_{kj}]} \right)$$
$$\{i \mid \epsilon = 1\}, \qquad \{k \mid \epsilon_k = 0\}.$$

Obtention of the lower envelopes

Obtain the discrete function $f(\boldsymbol{x})$ as a conjunction of anticubes:

$$f = \bigwedge_j \left(l_j \vee \bigvee_{i=n-1}^{0} x_i^{(C_{ij})} \right).$$

Let a_{ij} and b_{ij} be the smallest and the greatest elements of C_{ij} respectively; the lower envelope $\underset{\vee}{m}_\epsilon(f)$ is:

$$\underset{\vee}{m}_\epsilon(f) = \bigwedge_j \left(l_j \vee \bigvee_i x_i^{[b_{ij}+1]} \vee \bigvee_k x_k^{a_{kj}-1]} \right)$$

$$\{i \mid \epsilon_i = 1\}, \quad \{k \mid \epsilon_k = 0\}.$$

Example 12.1. Consider the discrete function:

$$f\colon \{0, 1, 2, 3, 4\}^2 \to \{0, 1, 2, 3, 4\}$$

described by the intermediate of a disjunctive normal form:

$$f(\boldsymbol{x}) = 4x_1^{(2)}\,x_0^{(1,2)} \vee 4x_1^{(1)}\,x_0^{(2,3)} \vee 3x_1^{(0,1)}\,x_0^{(3)} \vee 2x_1^{(2)}\,x_0^{(1,2,3,4)} \vee 1x_1^{(3)}\,x_0^{(2)}.$$

From this normal form one deduces the upper envelopes:

$$\hat{m}_{11}(f) = 4x_1^{[2}\,x_0^{[1} \vee 4x_1^{[1}\,x_0^{[2} \vee 3x_0^{[3}$$

$$\hat{m}_{10}(f) = 4x_1^{[1}\,x_0^{3]} \vee 3x_0^{3]}$$

$$\hat{m}_{01}(f) = 4x_1^{2]}\,x_0^{[1} \vee 4x_1^{1]}\,x_0^{[2} \vee 1x_1^{3]}\,x_0^{[2}$$

$$\hat{m}_{00}(f) = 4x_1^{2]}\,x_0^{2]} \vee 4x_1^{1]}\,x_0^{3]} \vee 2x_1^{2]} \vee 1x_1^{3]}\,x_0^{2]}.$$

Assume now that the discrete function $f(\boldsymbol{x})$ is given by the intermediate of its value vector $[f_e]$; let us denote by $[x_i(\epsilon_i)]$, $\epsilon_i = 0, 1$, the vectors:

$$[x_i(1)] = [r-1, x_i^{[1}, x_i^{[2}, \dots, x_i^{[m_i-1}]^t$$

$$[x_i(0)] = [x_i^{0]}, x_i^{1]}, \dots, x_i^{m_i-2]}, r-1]^t$$

where [$]^t$ means as usual the transpose operation; the negation of these vectors is defined as follows:

$$\overline{[x_i(\epsilon_i)]} = [r-1] - [x_i(\epsilon_i)].$$

Theorem 12.4. (a) *The implicants of the function $\hat{m}_\epsilon(f)$ are the terms of*

$$[f_e] \; \textcircled{\scriptsize $\vee\wedge$} \left\{ \overset{\wedge}{\underset{i=n-1,0}{\otimes}} [x_i(\epsilon_i)] \right\}, \qquad \epsilon = (\epsilon_{n-1}, \dots, \epsilon_1, \epsilon_0). \tag{12.13}$$

(b) *The implicates of the function $\underset{\vee}{m}_\epsilon(f)$ are the terms of*

$$[f_e] \; \textcircled{\scriptsize $\wedge\vee$} \left\{ \overset{\vee}{\underset{i=n-1,0}{\otimes}} \overline{[x_i(\bar{\epsilon}_i)]} \right\}, \qquad \bar{\epsilon}_i = 1 - \epsilon_i. \tag{12.14}$$

Proof. For $n = 1, m = 3$ a routine verification shows that:

(a) $[f(0), f(1), f(2)] \boxed{\vee \wedge} [r-1, x^{[1]}, x^{[2]}]^t = f(0) \vee f(1) x^{[1]} \vee f(2) x^{[2]},$

$$\text{for} \quad \epsilon = 1;$$

$[f(0), f(1), f(2)] \boxed{\vee \wedge} [x^{[0]}, x^{[1]}, r-1]^t = f(0) x^{[0]} \vee f(1) x^{[1]} \vee f(2),$

$$\text{for} \quad \epsilon = 0;$$

(b) $[f(0), f(1), f(2)] \boxed{\wedge \vee} [x^{[1]}, x^{[2]}, 0]^t =$

$[f(0) \vee x^{[1]}] [f(1) \vee x^{[2]}] f(2), \quad \text{for} \quad \epsilon = 1;$

$[f(0), f(1), f(2)] \boxed{\wedge \vee} [0, x^{[0]}, x^{[1]}]^t =$

$f(0) [f(1) \vee x^{[0]}] [f(2) \vee x^{[1]}], \quad \text{for} \quad \epsilon = 0.$

The proof for any n and any m is straightforward and could, for example, easily be obtained by perfect induction. ∎

Clearly, if $f(x)$ is a unate function, increasing in the variables x_i: $\{i \mid \epsilon_i = 1\}$ and decreasing in the variables x_j: $\{j \mid \epsilon_j = 0\}$, the above theorem provides us with an algorithm giving all the implicants and all the implicates of $f(x)$. Theorem 12.4 also points out the simplification that arises in searching the prime implicants and the prime implicates of discrete functions once their unateness has been recognized: instead of dealing with the extended vector (see theorem 3.13) in the matrix products (12.13) and (12.14) one has only to consider the value vector itself.

Consider a discrete function f and its upper and lower envelopes: $\hat{m}_\epsilon(f)$ and $\underline{m}_\epsilon(f)$ respectively. Let $\{\epsilon_\alpha\}$ be the values of the index ϵ corresponding to the prime upper envelopes and let $\{\epsilon_\beta\}$ be the values of the index ϵ corresponding to the prime lower envelopes. The two following functions associated with $f(x)$ will appear of particular importance further on:

$$\bigwedge_{\epsilon \in \{\epsilon_\alpha\}} \hat{m}_{(\epsilon)}(f) = \phi_\alpha(f)$$

is the smallest function larger than or equal to f that can be obtained as a conjunction of unate functions;

$$\bigvee_{\epsilon \in \{\epsilon_\beta\}} \underline{m}_{(\epsilon)}(f) = \phi_\beta(f)$$

is the largest function smaller than or equal to f that can be obtained as a disjunction of unate functions.

Of particular importance is the class of discrete functions such that:

$$f = \phi_\alpha(f) \tag{12.15}$$

or

$$f = \phi_\beta(f). \tag{12.16}$$

These functions not only play a key role in theoretical investigations but have very simple and interesting realizations (see section 12.6.1).

12.3. *Local unateness in discrete functions*

Let us consider two particular values of S_i (it is recalled that the function domain is the Cartesian product $S = \underset{i}{\times} S_i$) namely

$$a_i \text{ and } b_i = a_i + k_i, \quad 0 \leqslant a_i, b_i \leqslant m_i - 1, \quad a_i < b_i .$$

The interval $[a_i, b_i]$ is the set of values $\{a_i, a_i + 1, \ldots, a_i + k_i = b_i\}$.

Definition 12.4. A discrete function $f(\boldsymbol{x})$ is *locally monotone* with respect to x_i and in the interval $[a_i, b_i]$ iff for each k_{i0} and k_{i1} such that:

$$0 \leqslant k_{i0} < k_{i1} \leqslant k_i .$$

One has either:

$$f(a_i + k_{i0}) \leqslant f(a_i + k_{i1}) \quad \textit{(locally monotone increasing function)}$$

or:

$$f(a_i + k_{i0}) \geqslant f(a_i + k_{i1}) \quad \textit{(locally monotone decreasing function)}.$$

Let $(\boldsymbol{x}_1, \boldsymbol{x}_0)$ be a partition on $\boldsymbol{x}$, with $\boldsymbol{x}_0 = (x_{q-1}, \ldots, x_1, x_0)$; the interval $[\boldsymbol{a}_0, \boldsymbol{b}_0]$ is by definition the direct product of q intervals:

$$\underset{i=q-1}{\overset{0}{\times}} [a_i, b_i] .$$

Definition 12.5. A discrete function $f(\boldsymbol{x})$ is *locally unate* with respect to its variables $x_i \in \boldsymbol{x}_0$ and in the interval $[\boldsymbol{a}_0, \boldsymbol{b}_0 + \boldsymbol{k}_0]$ iff it is locally monotone with respect to each of its variables $x_i \in \boldsymbol{x}_0$ in the intervals $[a_i, b_i]$ and when the remaining variables $x_j \in \boldsymbol{x}_0$ $(j \neq i)$ take their value in the corresponding intervals $[a_j, b_j]$ respectively.

Given a discrete function $f(\boldsymbol{x})$, a partition $(\boldsymbol{x}_1, \boldsymbol{x}_0)$ of $\boldsymbol{x}$ and an interval $[\boldsymbol{a}_0, \boldsymbol{b}_0]$, one defines:

$$f_{[\boldsymbol{a}_0, \boldsymbol{b}_0]}(\boldsymbol{x}) = \bigwedge_{i=q-1}^{0} x_i^{[a_i, b_i]} f(\boldsymbol{x}).$$

That function coincides with $f(\boldsymbol{x})$ for all vertices $(\boldsymbol{x}_1, \boldsymbol{e}_0)$ such that $\boldsymbol{e}_0$ is in $[\boldsymbol{a}_0, \boldsymbol{b}_0]$; it takes the value zero in all other vertices.

Theorem 12.5. A function $f(\boldsymbol{x})$ is locally monotone increasing in $\boldsymbol{x}_{00}$ and locally monotone decreasing in $\boldsymbol{x}_{01}$ (with $\boldsymbol{x}_0 = (\boldsymbol{x}_{01}, \boldsymbol{x}_{00})$) in the interval $[\boldsymbol{a}_0, \boldsymbol{b}_0]$ iff the prime implicants (resp. prime implicates) of $f_{[\boldsymbol{a}_0, \boldsymbol{b}_0]}$ are of the type:

$$l_j(\boldsymbol{x}_1) \wedge \bigwedge_{i=q-1}^{m} x_i^{[a_i, b_{ij}]} \wedge \bigwedge_{k=m-1}^{0} x_k^{[b_{kj}, b_k]}, \quad 0 < m < q$$

$$\left(\text{resp. } l_j'(\boldsymbol{x}_1) \vee \bigvee_{i=q-1}^{m} x_i^{[a_i, b_{ij}]} \vee \bigvee_{k=m-1}^{0} x_k^{[b_{kj}, b_k]}\right).$$

It is also a function locally unate in $\boldsymbol{x}_0$.

Proof. The proof directly follows from theorem 12.2 applied to the function $f_{[a_0, b_0]}$. ■

The following remark may be useful for practical computations. Consider, for example, f given as a disjunction of prime convex blocks:

$$l_j(\boldsymbol{x}_1) \wedge \bigwedge_{i=q-1}^{0} x_i^{[k_i, l_i]}. \tag{12.17}$$

Then, the prime convex blocks of $f_{[a_0, b_0]}$ are of the type:

$$l_j(\boldsymbol{x}_1) \wedge \bigwedge_{i=q-1}^{0} x_i^{[a_i \vee k_i, b_i \wedge l_i]} \tag{12.18}$$

iff $a_i \vee k_i \leqslant b_i \wedge l_i \; \forall i$, and are 0 otherwise.

Indeed, let

$$l'(\boldsymbol{x}_1) \wedge \bigwedge_{i=q-1}^{0} x_i^{[k_i', l_i']}$$

be a prime convex block of $f_{[a_0, b_0]}(\boldsymbol{x})$; it must be included in some prime convex block of $f(\boldsymbol{x})$, say, for example (12.17), with $l(\boldsymbol{x}_1) \geqslant l'(\boldsymbol{x}_1)$ and $[k_i, l_i] \supseteq [k_i', l_i'] \; \forall i$.

Furthermore, thanks to the definition of $f_{[a_0, b_0]}(\boldsymbol{x})$, one has:

$$[k_i', l_i'] \subseteq [a_i, b_i] \; \forall i.$$

Therefore

$$[k_i', l_i'] \subseteq [k_i, l_i] \cap [a_i, b_i] \; \forall i.$$

It is obvious that the function (12.18) is included in $f_{[a_0, b_0]}(\boldsymbol{x})$: it coincides with a prime convex block of f for $\boldsymbol{x}_0$ in $[\boldsymbol{a}_0, \boldsymbol{b}_0]$ and takes the value zero otherwise. By maximality of a prime convex block one has thus:

$$l(\boldsymbol{x}_1) = l'(\boldsymbol{x}_1), \quad [k_i', l_i'] \text{ is maximal in } [k_i, l_i] \cap [a_i, b_i].$$

The function (12.18) is thus a prime convex block of $f_{[a_0, b_0]}(\boldsymbol{x})$.

As a consequence, if f is given as a disjunction of all its prime convex blocks, the prime convex blocks of $f_{[a_0, b_0]}$ are obtained by deleting in the list of convex blocks of the type (12.18) all the blocks smaller than other blocks.

If these prime convex blocks are also prime implicants of $f_{[a_0, b_0]}$, the function $f(\boldsymbol{x})$ is locally unate with respect to $\boldsymbol{x}_0$ and in the interval $[\boldsymbol{a}_0, \boldsymbol{b}_0]$.

A discrete function $f(\boldsymbol{x})$ is *locally degenerate* with respect to its variables $x_i \in \boldsymbol{x}_0$ and in the interval $[\boldsymbol{a}_0, \boldsymbol{b}_0 = \boldsymbol{a}_0 + \boldsymbol{k}_0]$ iff:

$$f(\boldsymbol{x}_1, \boldsymbol{e}_0) = f(\boldsymbol{x}_1, \boldsymbol{l}_0) \quad \forall \boldsymbol{e}_0, \boldsymbol{l}_0 \in [\boldsymbol{a}_0, \boldsymbol{b}_0].$$

12.4. *Hazard-free transitions of discrete functions*

Consider two vertices $\boldsymbol{c}$ and $\boldsymbol{d}$ of $\boldsymbol{x}$:

$$\boldsymbol{c} = (c_{n-1}, \ldots, c_{q+1}, c_q, c_{q-1}, \ldots, c_1, c_0)$$
$$\boldsymbol{d} = (c_{n-1}, \ldots, c_{q+1}, c_q, d_{q-1}, \ldots, d_1, d_0)$$

with $c_i \neq d_i, i = q-1, \ldots, 1, 0$. These two vertices involve a partition $(\boldsymbol{x}_1, \boldsymbol{x}_0)$ on $\boldsymbol{x}$; define $\boldsymbol{c}_1, \boldsymbol{c}_0, \boldsymbol{d}_1, \boldsymbol{d}_0$ as follows:

$$\boldsymbol{c}_0 = (c_{q-1}, \ldots, c_1, c_0), \boldsymbol{c}_1 = (c_{n-1}, \ldots, c_{q+1}, c_q) = \boldsymbol{d}_1$$
$$\boldsymbol{d}_0 = (d_{q-1}, \ldots, d_1, d_0)$$

and assume, without loss of generality, that $c_i < d_i \; \forall i: 0 \leqslant i \leqslant m-1$ and that $c_j > d_j \; \forall j: m \leqslant j \leqslant q-1$; this again involves a partition $\boldsymbol{x}_{01}, \boldsymbol{x}_{00}$ on $\boldsymbol{x}_0$ and on $\boldsymbol{c}_0, \boldsymbol{d}_0$:

$$\boldsymbol{c}_{01} = (c_{q-1}, \ldots, c_{m+1}, c_m), \boldsymbol{c}_{00} = (c_{m-1}, \ldots, c_1, c_0)$$
$$\boldsymbol{d}_{01} = (d_{q-1}, \ldots, d_{m+1}, d_m), \boldsymbol{d}_{00} = (d_{m-1}, \ldots, d_1, d_0).$$

Definition 12.6. (a) The function $f(\boldsymbol{x})$ is *hazard-free* for a transition between the vertices $\boldsymbol{c}$ and $\boldsymbol{d}$ iff the discrete function $f(\boldsymbol{c}_1, \boldsymbol{x}_0)$ is either:

a locally monotone increasing function with respect to $\boldsymbol{x}_{00}$ and in the interval $[\boldsymbol{c}_{00}, \boldsymbol{d}_{00}]$ and a locally monotone decreasing function with respect to $\boldsymbol{x}_{01}$ and in the interval $[\boldsymbol{d}_{01}, \boldsymbol{c}_{01}]$

or:

a locally monotone decreasing function with respect to $\boldsymbol{x}_{00}$ and in the interval $[\boldsymbol{c}_{00}, \boldsymbol{d}_{00}]$ and a locally monotone increasing function with respect to $\boldsymbol{x}_{01}$ and in the interval $[\boldsymbol{d}_{01}, \boldsymbol{c}_{01}]$.

It must be pointed out that the above definition implies that the hazards are defined between two vertices $\boldsymbol{c}$ and $\boldsymbol{d}$ and not from an initial vertex ($\boldsymbol{c}$ or $\boldsymbol{d}$) to a final vertex ($\boldsymbol{d}$ or $\boldsymbol{c}$).

Definition 12.6 (b). If a hazard on $f(\boldsymbol{x})$ occurs between the vertices $\boldsymbol{c}$ and $\boldsymbol{d}$, it will be called a *static hazard* iff $f(\boldsymbol{c}) = f(\boldsymbol{d})$; otherwise it will be called a *dynamic hazard.*

Theorem 12.6. Given a discrete function $f(\boldsymbol{x})$, the transition between the vertices $\boldsymbol{c}$ and $\boldsymbol{d}$ is hazard-free, iff $f_{[\boldsymbol{d}_{01}\boldsymbol{c}_{00}, \boldsymbol{c}_{01}\boldsymbol{d}_{00}]}$ has prime implicants of the type

$$l_j(\boldsymbol{x}_1) \wedge \bigwedge_{i=q-1}^{m} x_i^{[c_i, d_{ij}]} \wedge \bigwedge_{k=m-1}^{0} x_k^{[d_{kj}, c_k]}$$

or of the type

$$l_j(x_1) \wedge \bigwedge_{i=q-1}^{m} x_i^{[c_{ij}, d_i]} \wedge \bigwedge_{k=m-1}^{0} x_k^{[d_k, c_{kj}]}$$

but not of both types.

Proof. It is a direct consequence of theorem 12.5 and of the definition of hazard-free transition. ■

Example 12.2. Consider the discrete function described by the table of Figure 12.1.

$x_1 \backslash x_0$	0	1	2	3
0	0	1	0	0
1	1	2	1	1
2	2	2	0	2
3	2	2	0	2

Figure 12.1. Value table

The disjunction of the prime convex blocks of this function is:

$$f = 2x_1^{[2,3]}\, x_0^{[0,1]} \vee 2x_1^{[1,3]}\, x_0^{(1)} \vee 2x_1^{[2,3]}\, x_0^{(3)} \vee 1x_1^{[1,3]}\, x_0^{[0,1]} \vee 1x_1^{(1)} \vee$$
$$1x_0^{(1)} \vee 1x_1^{[1,3]}\, x_0^{(3)}. \qquad (12.19)$$

(a) Consider the interval $[\boldsymbol{a}, \boldsymbol{b}]$ with $\boldsymbol{a} = (a_1, a_0) = (0, 0)$ and $\boldsymbol{b} = (b_1, b_0) = (3, 1)$. From (12.19) one deduces

$$f_{[\boldsymbol{a},\boldsymbol{b}]} = 2x_1^{[2,3]}\, x_0^{[0,1]} \vee 2x_1^{[1,3]}\, x_0^{(1)} \vee 1x_1^{[1,3]}\, x_0^{[0,1]} \vee 1x_0^{(1)}.$$

The function f is thus a partially monotone increasing function in the interval $[(0, 0), (3, 1)]$.

Consider the transitions between $\boldsymbol{c} = (3, 0)$ and $\boldsymbol{d} = (0, 1)$; in view of theorem 12.6 these transitions contain a dynamic hazard. On the contrary, the transitions between $\boldsymbol{c} = (0, 0)$ and $\boldsymbol{d} = (3, 1)$ are hazard-free.

(b) Consider the interval $[\boldsymbol{a}, \boldsymbol{b}]$ with $\boldsymbol{a} = (0, 1)$ and $\boldsymbol{b} = (2, 2)$; one has:

$$f_{[\boldsymbol{a},\boldsymbol{b}]} = 2x_1^{[1,2]}\, x_0^{(1)} \vee 1x_1^{(1)}\, x_0^{[1,2]} \vee 1x_1^{[0,2]}\, x_0^{(1)};$$

the function $f(\boldsymbol{x})$ is not unate in the interval $[(0, 1), (2, 2)]$.

12.5. Switching functions

Unate switching functions were studied by McNaughton [1961] and Harrison [1965]; most of the theorems and definitions quoted by these authors are a particular case of corresponding statements of section 12.1. The concepts of upper and lower envelopes for switching functions were suggested in the book by Kuntzmann [1965] while they were more thoroughly defined and studied by Thayse [1975b]. The following theorem provides us with a simplified formulation for the upper and lower envelopes.

Theorem 12.7

$$\text{(a)}\quad \hat{m}_\epsilon(f) = \bigvee_e \left[f(\bar{\epsilon} \oplus e) \wedge \bigwedge_{i=n-1}^{0} (x_i \oplus \bar{\epsilon}_i)^{e_i} \right], \quad 0 \leqslant e_i \leqslant 1. \tag{12.20}$$

$$\text{(b)}\quad \underset{\smile}{m}_\epsilon(f) = \bigwedge_e \left[f(\epsilon \oplus e) \vee \bigvee_{i=n-1}^{0} \overline{(x_i \oplus \epsilon_i)^{e_i}} \right], \quad 0 \leqslant e_i \leqslant 1. \tag{12.21}$$

Proof. For $n = 1$ a routine verification shows that:

$$\text{(a)}\quad \bigvee_{e=0,1} [f(\bar{\epsilon} \oplus e) \wedge (x \oplus \bar{\epsilon})^e] = f(\bar{\epsilon}) \vee f(\epsilon)\,(x \oplus \bar{\epsilon})$$

$\epsilon = 0$: $f(1) \vee \bar{x}\, f(0)$ is the smallest function larger than or equal to f and monotone decreasing in x.

$\epsilon = 1$: $f(0) \vee xf(1)$ is the smallest function larger than or equal to f and monotone increasing in x.

$$\text{(b)}\quad \bigwedge_{e=0,1} [f(\epsilon \oplus e) \vee \overline{(x \oplus \epsilon)^e}] = f(\epsilon)\,[f(\bar{\epsilon}) \vee (x \oplus \bar{\epsilon})]$$

$\epsilon = 0$: $f(0)\,[f(1) \vee \bar{x}]$ is the largest function smaller than or equal to f and monotone decreasing in x.

$\epsilon = 1$: $f(1)\,[f(0) \vee x]$ is the largest function smaller than or equal to f and monotone increasing in x.

The proof is then achieved by perfect induction on n. ■

Theorem 12.8. (a) *Any switching function f is the conjunction of its prime upper envelopes.*

(b) *Any switching function is the disjunction of its prime lower envelopes.*

Proof. For $n = 1$ a routine verification shows that:

$$[f(0) \vee xf(1)]\;[f(1) \vee \bar{x}f(0)] = f(0)f(1) \vee \bar{x}f(0) \vee xf(1) = f$$

$$f(1)\;[f(0) \vee x] \vee f(0)\;[f(1) \vee \bar{x}] = f(0)f(1) \vee \bar{x}f(0) \vee xf(1) = f.$$

The proof could again be achieved by perfect induction on n. ■

Further in this chapter one will be interested in two canonical representations of a switching function f grounded on the concept of envelope:

(a) the canonical representation of $f(\boldsymbol{x})$ as a disjunction of all its prime lower envelopes, each of these envelopes being expressed as the conjunction of their prime implicates;
(b) the canonical representation of $f(\boldsymbol{x})$ as a conjunction of all its prime upper envelopes, each of these envelopes being expressed as the disjunction of their prime implicants.

Theorem 12.9. The upper envelope $\hat{m}_\epsilon(f)$ is obtained from the Reed–Muller expansion of f at $\bar{\epsilon}$, that is (see notation of section 6.1.1.2):

$$\mathrm{RM}_{\bar{\epsilon}}(f) = \sum_{e} \left(\frac{\Delta f}{\Delta \boldsymbol{x}^{e}}\right)_{\boldsymbol{x}=\bar{\epsilon}} \left[\prod_{i=n-1}^{0} (x_i \oplus \bar{\epsilon}_i)^{e_i}\right]$$

by replacing the summation symbols $\sum_{e}$ by $\bigvee_{e}$, i.e.

$$\hat{m}_\epsilon(f) = \bigvee_{e} \left(\frac{\Delta f}{\Delta \boldsymbol{x}^{e}}\right)_{\boldsymbol{x}=\bar{\epsilon}} \left[\prod_{i=n-1}^{0} (x_i \oplus \bar{\epsilon}_i)^{e_i}\right]$$

with $\bar{\epsilon} = (\bar{\epsilon}_{n-1}, \ldots, \bar{\epsilon}_1, \bar{\epsilon}_0)$.

Proof. The method of proof is based on a repeated use of the equality:

$$a \vee (a \oplus b)\, x = a \vee bx.$$

Indeed, for $n = 1$, one has:

$$\mathrm{RM}_{\bar{\epsilon}}(f) = f(x = \bar{\epsilon}) \oplus [f(x = \bar{\epsilon}) \oplus f(x = \epsilon)]\,(x \oplus \bar{\epsilon})$$

$$f(x = \bar{\epsilon}) \vee [f(x = \bar{\epsilon}) \oplus f(x = \epsilon)]\,(x \oplus \bar{\epsilon}) = f(x = \bar{\epsilon}) \vee f(x = \epsilon)\,(x \oplus \bar{\epsilon}) = \hat{m}_\epsilon(f).$$

The proof is achieved by induction on n. ■

Example 12.3. Consider the function

$$f = x_0 x_2 \vee x_1 \bar{x}_2.$$

The Reed–Muller expansions and the upper envelopes of this function are gathered in the table of Figure 12.2; the prime upper envelopes have been underlined.

The above theorem 12.9 thus provides us with a computational means for obtaining the upper envelopes of a switching function when the latter is given in its Reed–Muller form. If $f(\boldsymbol{x})$ is given as a lattice expression or by means of its truth vector, the method for obtaining its envelopes derives immediately from the material presented in section 12.2.

It must finally be pointed out that the concept of hazard, defined for discrete

$\epsilon_2\epsilon_1\epsilon_0$	Reed–Muller expansion at $(\epsilon_2\epsilon_1\epsilon_0)$	$\hat{m}_{(\bar{\epsilon}_2\bar{\epsilon}_1\bar{\epsilon}_0)}(f)$
0 0 0	$x_0x_2 \oplus x_1 \oplus x_1x_2$	$\underline{x_1 \vee x_0x_2}$
0 0 1	$x_2 \oplus x_2\bar{x}_0 \oplus x_1 \oplus x_1x_2$	$x_2 \vee x_1$
0 1 1	$x_2\bar{x}_0 \oplus 1 \oplus \bar{x}_1 \oplus \bar{x}_1x_2$	1
0 1 0	$x_2 \oplus x_2x_0 \oplus 1 \oplus \bar{x}_1 \oplus \bar{x}_1x_2$	1
1 1 0	$\bar{x}_2 \oplus x_0 \oplus x_0\bar{x}_2 \oplus \bar{x}_1\bar{x}_2$	$\bar{x}_2 \vee x_0$
1 1 1	$1 \oplus \bar{x}_0 \oplus \bar{x}_2\bar{x}_0 \oplus \bar{x}_1\bar{x}_2$	1
1 0 1	$1 \oplus \bar{x}_0 \oplus \bar{x}_2\bar{x}_0 \oplus \bar{x}_2 \oplus \bar{x}_2x_1$	1
1 0 0	$x_0 \oplus \bar{x}_2x_0 \oplus \bar{x}_2x_1$	$\underline{x_0 \vee x_1\bar{x}_2}$

Figure 12.2

functions under section 12.4, reduces, when applied to switching functions, to the concept of function hazard already defined in section 3.3.3.1. It was Beister [1974] who first pointed out, in the restricted scope of switching functions, the relation between the concepts of hazard and of unateness. The approach used by Beister to derive hazard detection methods relies heavily on the work of McCluskey [1962] and McGhee [1969]. Clearly the concepts of static and of dynamic hazard are related to those of local degenerescence and unateness respectively.

Yau and Tang [1971a] presented the following algorithm for identifying partial degenerescence in switching functions. When applied to the appropriate function it can be used to detect local degenerescence and thus also (function) static hazards.

Algorithm 12.2. Let $f(\boldsymbol{x})$ be a switching function under testing for partial degenerescence and let m be the number of minterms of $f(\boldsymbol{x})$.

(a) If m is odd, there is no partial degenerescence in $f(\boldsymbol{x})$; if m is even perform step (b).

(b) Form a table T with m rows and n columns, whose columns correspond to the variables and whose rows correspond to the minterms; a 1 in the ith column of a given row corresponds to the presence of x_i in the minterm while a 0 corresponds to the presence of $\bar{x}_i$ in the minterm. Let c_i be the number of 1's in the ith column (corresponding to the variable x_i of T). If there exists a c_i such that $c_i = m/2$ go to step (c); otherwise $f(\boldsymbol{x})$ is free of partial degenerescence.

(c) When a $c_i = m/2$, let D_{i0} be the set of $m/2$ decimal numbers representing the $m/2$ minterms, each of whose corresponding rows in T has a 0 in the ith column, and let D_{i1} be the set of $m/2$ decimal numbers representing the other $m/2$ minterms. Let $D_{i1} - 2^{n-i-1}$ be the set of integers formed by subtracting 2^{n-i-1} from every element of D_{i1}. For every $c_i = m/2$, find D_{i0} and $D_{i1} - 2^{n-i-1}$. If $D_{i0} = D_{i1} - 2^{n-i-1}$, then $f(\boldsymbol{x})$ is degenerate in x_i; otherwise $f(\boldsymbol{x})$ depends on x_i.

It can easily be shown that the above algorithm 12.1 is correct since

$$f(x_i = 0) = f(x_i = 1)$$

(condition of degenerescence in x_i) can be satisfied by x_i only if $D_{i0} = D_{i1} - 2^{n-i-1}$ and because $D_{i0} = D_{i1} - 2^{n-i-1}$ requires that m is even and $c_i = m/2$. The example below is due to Yau and Tang [1971b].

Example 12.4

$$f = x_5\bar{x}_4\bar{x}_3\bar{x}_2\bar{x}_1\bar{x}_0 \vee x_5 x_4\bar{x}_3\bar{x}_2\bar{x}_1\bar{x}_0 \vee x_5\bar{x}_4\bar{x}_3\bar{x}_2 x_1\bar{x}_0 \vee x_5 x_4\bar{x}_3\bar{x}_2 x_1\bar{x}_0 \vee$$
$$x_5\bar{x}_4 x_3\bar{x}_2\bar{x}_1 x_0 \vee x_5 x_4 x_3\bar{x}_2\bar{x}_1 x_0 \vee x_5\bar{x}_4 x_3\bar{x}_2 x_1 x_0 \vee x_5 x_4 x_3\bar{x}_2 x_1 x_0.$$

Since $m = 8$, we form the table T shown in the left of Figure 12.3. Each c_i is given at the bottom of the ith column. We find that $c_0 = c_1 = c_3 = c_4 = 4$. According to step (c) of algorithm 12.1, find D_{i0} and $D_{i1} - 2^{n-i-1}$, $i = 0, 1, 3, 4$, which are given at the right part of Figure 12.3. The decimal representation of each minterm has been written to the right of the table T at the corresponding row of the minterm in order to facilitate manual manipulation at the step (c). It is seen that $D_{i0} = D_{i1} - 2^{6-i-1}$ is satisfied when $i = 1$ and 4, and hence f is degenerate in x_1 and x_4.

It has already been pointed out in section 7.3.1 that the difference and differential calculus could be used for detecting static hazards in switching functions; the following proposition has been stated (see theorem 7.18).

A transition between the input states $\boldsymbol{x} = \boldsymbol{a}$ and $\boldsymbol{x} = \boldsymbol{b}$ and involving a change in the variables $\boldsymbol{x}_0 \subseteq \boldsymbol{x}$ gives rise to a (function) static hazard for the function $f(\boldsymbol{x})$ iff

$$\left(\frac{Sf}{S\boldsymbol{x}_0} \oplus \frac{\delta f}{\delta \boldsymbol{x}_0}\right)_{\boldsymbol{x}=\boldsymbol{a}} = 1. \tag{12.22}$$

A similar type of formula holds for detecting (function) dynamic hazards. An interesting theorem on hazard detection arises from the fact that a dynamic hazard may occur for a given transition iff one of its subtransitions contains a (function) static hazard. The following theorem then immediately results from this observation and from relation (12.22).

Theorem 12.10. A transition between the input states $\boldsymbol{x} = \boldsymbol{a}$ and $\boldsymbol{x} = \boldsymbol{b}$ and involving a change in the variables $\boldsymbol{x}_0 = (x_{q-1}, \ldots, x_1, x_0) \subseteq \boldsymbol{x}$ gives rise to:

(a) *a (function) dynamic hazard for the function $f(\boldsymbol{x})$ iff:*

$$\left\{\frac{Sf}{S\boldsymbol{x}_0}\left[\bigvee_{\boldsymbol{e}_0}\left(\frac{Sf}{S\boldsymbol{x}_0^{\boldsymbol{e}_0}} \oplus \frac{\delta f}{\delta \boldsymbol{x}_0^{\boldsymbol{e}_0}}\right)\right]\right\}_{\boldsymbol{x}=\boldsymbol{a}} = 1, \quad 0 \leqslant e_i \leqslant 1,$$

$$\boldsymbol{0} < \boldsymbol{e}_0 = (e_{q-1}, \ldots, e_1, e_0) < \boldsymbol{1}; \tag{12.23}$$

T						Minterm	x_0		x_1		x_3		x_4	
x_0	x_1	x_2	x_3	x_4	x_5		D_{00};	$D_{01}-32$	D_{10};	$D_{11}-16$	D_{30};	$D_{31}-4$	D_{40};	$D_{41}-2$
0	0	0	0	0	1	1	1		1		1		1	
0	0	0	0	1	1	3	3		3		3		17	2
0	1	0	0	0	1	17	17			1	17		17	
0	1	0	0	1	1	19	19			3	19			17
1	0	0	1	0	1	37		5	37			33	37	
1	0	0	1	1	1	39		7	39			35		37
1	1	0	1	0	1	53		21		37		49	53	
1	1	1	1	1	1	55		23		39		51		53
4	4	0	4	4	8				Degenerescence in x_1				Degenerescence in x_4	

Figure 12.3. An example for illustrating the algorithm for identifying partial degenerescences

(b) *a (function static or dynamic) hazard for the function f(x) iff:*

$$\bigvee_{e_0} \left(\frac{Sf}{Sx_0^{e_0}} \oplus \frac{\delta f}{\delta x_0^{e_0}} \right)_{x=a} = 1, \quad 0 \leqslant e_i \leqslant 1, \quad 0 < e_0 \leqslant 1. \tag{12.24}$$

Example 12.5. Consider the switching function

$$f = \bar{x}_0 x_2 \vee \bar{x}_1 x_2 x_3$$

and the transition between the input states $\{x_3, x_2, x_1, x_0\} = \{0, 1, 0, 0\}$ and $\{x_3, x_2, x_1, x_0\} = \{1, 0, 1, 0\}$. The function to be tested in order to detect dynamic hazards is:

$$\frac{Sf}{Sx_3x_2x_1} \left[\left(\frac{\delta f}{\delta x_3 x_2} \oplus \frac{Sf}{Sx_3x_2} \right) \vee \left(\frac{\delta f}{\delta x_3 x_1} \oplus \frac{Sf}{Sx_3x_1} \right) \vee \left(\frac{\delta f}{\delta x_2 x_1} \oplus \frac{Sf}{Sx_2x_1} \right) \right] =$$

$$(\bar{x}_0 \vee \bar{x}_1 x_2 x_3 \vee x_1 \bar{x}_2 \bar{x}_3) \, [x_0 x_3 (\bar{x}_1 \oplus x_2) \vee x_0 (\bar{x}_2 x_3 \vee x_1 x_2) \vee$$

$$x_0 \bar{x}_1 (x_2 \oplus x_3)] \equiv 0.$$

Since the above function is identically zero, any transition involving a change in the three variables x_3, x_2, x_1 is free of dynamic hazard.

Let us finally note that unateness detection for switching functions was also considered in a paper by Liss [1973].

We shall now briefly consider the problem of representation of arbitrary switching functions by means of monotone increasing functions. The idea underlying the present remark appears in Von Neumann [1956] where it is called the *double line trick*; the main result is stated in the following proposition.

Any switching function $f(\mathbf{x})$ of n variables may be replaced by a couple of switching functions $\{f_0(\mathbf{x}_a, \mathbf{x}_b), f_1(\mathbf{x}_a, \mathbf{x}_b)\}$ of monotone increasing functions of 2n variables: $\mathbf{x}_a = (x_{n-1a}, \ldots, x_{1a}, x_{0a}), \mathbf{x}_b = (x_{n-1b}, \ldots, x_{1b}, x_{0b})$.

We shall give a constructive proof of this statement; we first define the new variables and functions. To each $x_i \in \mathbf{x}$ we associate the couple of variables (x_{ia}, x_{ib}) such that:

$$(x_{ia}, x_{ib}) = (1, 0) \quad \text{iff} \quad x_i = 0$$

$$(x_{ia}, x_{ib}) = (0, 1) \quad \text{iff} \quad x_i = 1.$$

In a similar way, the functions f_0 and f_1 are defined by:

$$(f_0, f_1) = (\bar{e}, e) \quad \text{iff} \quad f = e.$$

We note that the functions f_0 and f_1 are not completely specified functions: the above definitions just specify f_0 and f_1 at the points $(\mathbf{x}_0, \mathbf{x}_1) = (\bar{\mathbf{e}}, \mathbf{e})$. Further:

$$\{f_0(\bar{\mathbf{e}}, \mathbf{e}), f_1(\bar{\mathbf{e}}, \mathbf{e})\} = \{\bar{f}(\mathbf{e}), f(\mathbf{e})\}.$$

The canonical disjunctive expansion of the functions $f_0(\boldsymbol{x}_a, \boldsymbol{x}_b)$ and $f_1(\boldsymbol{x}_a, \boldsymbol{x}_b)$ is then written down as:

$$f_i(\boldsymbol{x}_a, \boldsymbol{x}_b) = \bigvee_e \left[(f_e)^{(i)} \wedge \bigwedge_i x_{ai}^{(\bar{e}_i)} \wedge x_{bi}^{(e_i)}\right] \vee$$

$$\bigvee_{l \neq h} \left[\phi\,(l) \wedge \bigwedge_i x_{ai}^{(l_i)} \wedge x_{bi}^{(h_i)}\right], \quad i = 0, 1.$$

The point is now that it is always possible to make use of the don't care terms $\phi(\boldsymbol{l})$ in order to leave a monotone increasing expression for $f_i(\boldsymbol{x}_a, \boldsymbol{x}_b)$. If for a given $\boldsymbol{e}$, $[f(\boldsymbol{e})]^{(i)} = 1$, the minterm $\bigwedge_i x_{ai}^{(\bar{e}_i)} \wedge x_{bi}^{(e_i)}$ is present in the above expression. Note that this minterm has exactly n uncomplemented variables. In order to form the conjunction $\bigwedge_i x_{ai}^{\bar{e}_i}\, x_{bi}^{e_i}$ of these variables one should add to this minterm the $2^n - 1$ minterms $\bigwedge_i x_{ai}^{(l_i)} \wedge x_{bi}^{(h_i)}$ such that $(\boldsymbol{l}, \boldsymbol{h}) > (\bar{\boldsymbol{e}}, \boldsymbol{e})$ which actually appear in the unspecified part of the above expression. The proof is thus completed.

It is worthwhile noting that the above proposition does not lead to unique expressions of f_0 and f_1 as monotone increasing functions since a part of their expression is possibly left unspecified: it is thus possible to make use of these terms in order to achieve an additional goal such as, for example, to find the simplest disjunctive normal form.

Binary functions

Hazard detection in binary functions may be performed by using theorems very similar to theorems 7.18 and 12.10 for switching functions. Since binary functions will be used in this chapter for detecting transient phenomena in switching networks, theorems on hazard detection in binary functions will be stated in the corresponding section devoted to these applications.

12.6. Applications

12.6.1. Hazard-free synthesis of logic and of switching networks

The material presented in this section will be a further development of applications already considered under sections 3.3.3 and 7.3.1. One will first introduce briefly the concept of *logic hazard* in the frame of logic networks; it is a straightforward generalization of the corresponding concept for switching networks (see definition 3.18). One will then use the concept of envelope of a discrete function in order to synthesize networks having a good behaviour from a hazard point of view.

Consider a given network which realizes the discrete function $f(\boldsymbol{x})$: an input change from an initial input $\boldsymbol{x} = \boldsymbol{c}$ to a final input $\boldsymbol{x} = \boldsymbol{d}$ occurs when one or more input variables change simultaneously. A first type of hazard arises from the fact that there will be an inherent time delay associated with the operations of input change so that the input variables practically never change simultaneously. Moreover we assume that, when a given input variable x_i changes from a value c_i to a value d_i, the physical realization of the network is such that any value between c_i and d_i may be reached by the variable x_i. The following definition takes these two facts into account.

Definition 12.7. A transition between the vertices $\boldsymbol{c}$ and $\boldsymbol{d}$ is *function-hazard-free* for a network realizing the discrete function $f(\boldsymbol{x})$ if and only if $f(\boldsymbol{x})$ is hazard-free for the same transition (see definition 12.6).

A *function hazard* is evidently only meaningful for multiple input changes or for single input changes between non-adjacent values of the changing input variable.

The function hazards take into account the delays inherent in the input wires of a network and the fact that any input variable cannot change from one value to another without reaching any intermediate value. Now other types of hazards may occur because the internal wires and gates of a network obey the same laws as the inputs, that is that they may contain delays and that they cannot change directly from one value to another one. The hazards which are due to this phenomenon are called *logic hazards.* Since logic hazards are closely related to internal propagation times on the signal paths, it is obvious that these hazards cannot be detected only by means of some tests on the output expressed as a discrete function $f(\boldsymbol{x})$ of the input variables. The presence of delays in a network requests to treat internal discrete signals as independent variables during an input transition, even if this independence does not exist when the system remains static. It follows that the effect of delays in a network may be simulated by means of auxiliary discrete variables. How to introduce these variables and to obtain a function $g(\boldsymbol{x}, \boldsymbol{y})$ simulating the behaviour of a network realizing $f(\boldsymbol{x})$ has been extensively treated in section 7.3.2.2 for switching functions. It is however clear that all what was said in this section for binary signals also holds for discrete signals since the type of signal was never used in order to build the function $g(\boldsymbol{x}, \boldsymbol{y})$.

In view of the above it is clear that hazard detection methods can be obtained by building algorithms able to detect the local unateness or the local degenerescence of discrete functions. These algorithms were developed in preceding sections of this chapter (see, for example, theorem 12.6).

Let us now consider the problem of hazard-free design of switching and of logic networks; for sake of simplicity, the theorems and examples will first be developed for switching networks. Their generalization to logic networks then is straightforward.

The design problem that will be considered may be summarized as follows. Consider first the problem of designing a switching network free of logic static hazard; we know (Eichelberger [1964] and theorem 3.29) that:

(a) A two-level AND-OR network has no logic static hazards if its AND-gates are in one-to-one correspondence with the prime implicants of the function being realized.
(b) A two-level OR-AND network has no logic static hazards if its OR-gates are in one-to-one correspondence with the prime implicates of the function being realized.

Unger [1969] has moreover shown that the above networks are free of logic dynamic hazards involving changes in single input variables; the situation is however greatly complicated when multiple input changes are permitted. This is illustrated by means of the following example.

Example 12.6. Consider the function $f = x_0x_2 \vee x_1\bar{x}_2$ realized by

(a) An AND-OR network described by means of Figure 12.4(a) or equivalently by means of the expression (considered as the structural description of a network):

$$x_0x_2 \vee x_1\bar{x}_2 \vee x_0x_1.$$

(b) An OR-AND network described by means of Figure 12.4(b) or equivalently by means of the expression:

$$(x_0 \vee x_1)(x_0 \vee \bar{x}_2)(x_1 \vee x_2).$$

Both realizations are free of logic static hazards; they contain however a lot of transitions experiencing a logic dynamic hazard (see Figure 12.5):

(a) Dynamic hazard containing transitions for the AND-OR network of Figure 12.4(a):

$$7 \leftrightarrow 5,\ 2 \leftrightarrow 4,\ 3 \leftrightarrow 5,\ 2 \leftrightarrow 6.$$

(b) Dynamic hazard containing transitions for the OR-AND network of Figure 12.4(b):

$$7 \leftrightarrow 5,\ 2 \leftrightarrow 4,\ 1 \leftrightarrow 7,\ 4 \leftrightarrow 8.$$

It is clear, from the above example, that the logic dynamic hazards are produced by function static hazards in the prime implicants or in the prime implicates of the function.

Some of the above hazards may be avoided by grounding logical design on other canonical forms of the function to be realized; these canonical forms are:

(a) the disjunction of the prime lower envelopes of $f(\boldsymbol{x})$, each of these lower envelopes being expressed as the conjunction of their prime implicates;
(b) the conjunction of the prime upper envelopes, each of these upper envelopes being expressed as the disjunction of their prime implicants.

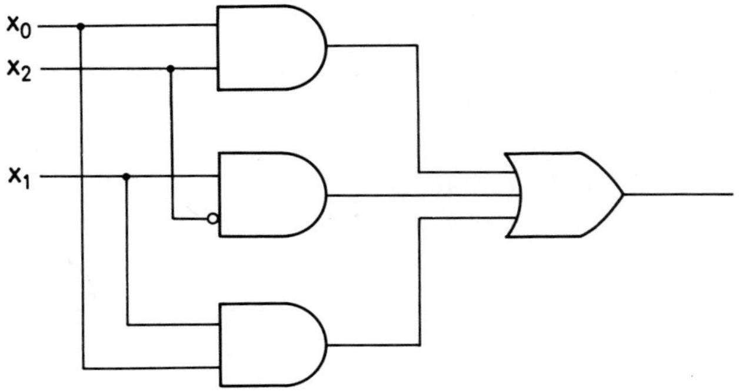

(a)

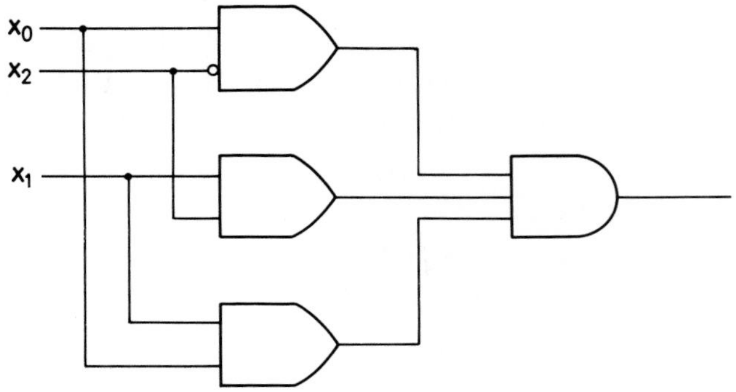

(b)

Figure 12.4. Two-level realizations

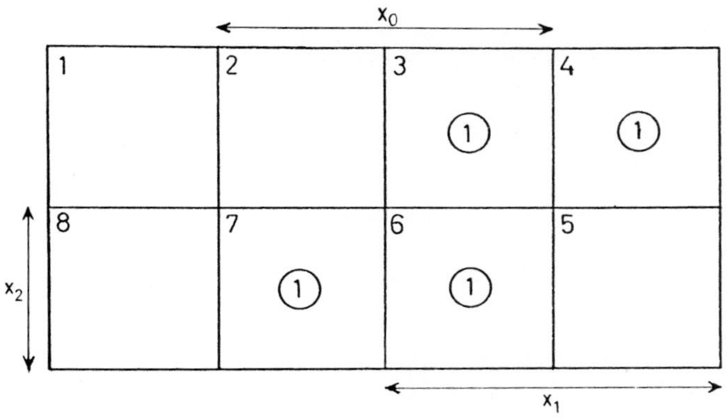

Figure 12.5. Truth table

The following theorem was stated by Unger [1969].

Theorem 12.11. Given any algebraic expression $\mathscr{E}$, if we transform it into a normal form (disjunctive or conjunctive) $\mathscr{N}$, through the use of the associative, distributive and De Morgan laws, then networks corresponding to $\mathscr{E}$ and $\mathscr{N}$ respectively have precisely the same static logic hazards.

The following theorem will now be used for building three-level networks containing less logic dynamic hazards than the corresponding two-level networks.

Theorem 12.12

(a) *Consider a three-level OR-AND network realizing $f(\mathbf{x})$ and built-up as follows:*

the AND-gates are in one-to-one correspondence with the prime lower envelopes of $f(\mathbf{x})$;
the first-level OR-gates, the outputs of which being the inputs of a given AND-gate, are in one-to-one correspondence with the prime implicates of the prime lower envelope realized by that AND-gate.

Then the network thus obtained is:

free of logic static hazards,
contain a less (or equal) number of logic-dynamic hazard than the AND-OR network the AND gates of which are in one-to-one correspondence with the prime implicants of f.

(b) *Dual statement.*

Proof. (a) In view of theorem 12.11, the network is free of logic static hazards. Moreover it contains a less number of logic dynamic hazards than the network realized as the disjunction of the prime implicants of f. Indeed, these last hazards are produced by the fact that some of the prime implicants contain a function static hazard of the form 0–1–0 for a given transition. Since the prime lower envelopes are the *largest* unate functions smaller than f they have necessarily a smaller number of function static hazards than the prime implicants of f. The fact that each lower envelope is realized as a conjunction of prime implicates implies that the function static hazards of these functions are of the form 1–0–1 which cannot produce logic dynamic hazards at the network output. ■

Example 12.6 (*continued*). (a) Assume that f be given as a conjunction of implicates, i.e.

$$f = (x_0 \vee \bar{x}_2)(x_1 \vee x_2); \tag{12.25}$$

then, according to algorithm 12.1, $\mathfrak{m}_\epsilon(f)$ is the expression obtained by deleting in the implicates the letters $x_i^{(\bar{\epsilon}_i)}$. Evidently if an implicate is of the form $\bigvee_i x_i^{(\bar{\epsilon}_i)}$, then $\mathfrak{m}_\epsilon(f) = 0$.

From (12.25) one deduces:

$$m_{001}(f) = x_1(x_0 \vee \bar{x}_2)$$

$$m_{000}(f) = x_0(x_1 \vee x_2).$$

Since $m_\epsilon(f) \leqslant m_{000}(f)$ or $m_{001}(f)$ $\forall \epsilon$, one has:

$$f = x_1(x_0 \vee \bar{x}_2) \vee x_0(x_1 \vee x_2). \tag{12.26}$$

Expression (12.26) is the structure formula corresponding to the network of Figure 12.6(a).

(b) Assume that f be given as a disjunction of implicants; then $\hat{m}_\epsilon(f)$ is the expression obtained by deleting in the implicants the letters $x_i^{(\bar{\epsilon}_i)}$. Evidently if an implicant is of the form $\bigwedge_i x_i^{(\bar{\epsilon}_i)}$, then $\hat{m}_\epsilon(f) = 1$.

From

$$f = x_0 x_2 \vee x_1 \bar{x}_2$$

one deduces:

$$\hat{m}_{000}(f) = x_0 x_2 \vee x_1$$

$$\hat{m}_{001}(f) = x_0 \vee x_1 \bar{x}_2.$$

Since $\hat{m}_\epsilon(f) \geqslant \hat{m}_{000}(f)$ or $\hat{m}_{001}(f)$ $\forall \epsilon$, one has:

$$f = (x_0 x_2 \vee x_1)(x_0 \vee x_1 \bar{x}_2). \tag{12.27}$$

Expression (12.27) is the structure formula corresponding to the network of Figure 12.6(b).

Both realizations 12.6 (a) and (b) are free of logic static hazards, and contain dynamic hazards for the transitions

$$2 \leftrightarrow 4 \quad \text{and} \quad 7 \leftrightarrow 5.$$

It is important to note that the above realizations grounded on the use of prime envelopes do not provide us necessarily with a three-level logical design having a minimal number of logic dynamic hazards. For example, if a function contains disjoint subcubes of 1's, each of the functions defined by 1's on a subcube and 0's otherwise may be realized by a network which computes the upper envelopes of this function. The disjunction of the realizations corresponding to the different disjoint subcubes respectively may then be better than the one which would be obtained by computing the prime envelopes of the function f itself. The importance of the above proposed realizations however is due to the fact that they are canonical and hence easily comparable and realizable; they were first proposed by Thayse (Thayse [1975b], Thayse and Deschamps [1976]). The problem of eliminating logic dynamic hazards in networks free of logic static hazards was also studied by Bredeson and Hulina [1970, 1972], and Bredeson [1973].

The extension of the above procedure to (multiple-valued) logic networks is straightforward within some minor restrictions. First of all, theorem 12.11 by Unger

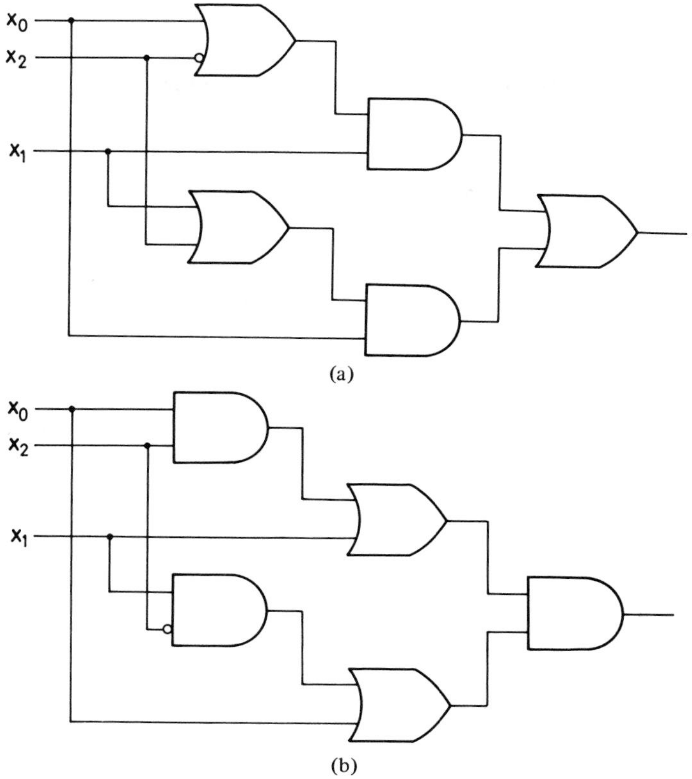

Figure 12.6. Three-level networks

applies to discrete functions as well as to switching functions. Theorem 12.12 only holds for discrete functions of the type $f = \phi_\alpha(f)$ or $f = \phi_\beta(f)$ (see relations (12.15) and (12.16)); for other types of discrete functions it is always possible to realize it, for example, as a disjunction of prime lower envelopes plus some prime implicants which are necessary to cover completely the functions. These realizations improve, from a hazard point of view, the classical two-level realizations.

Example 12.7. (Multipositional switch design.)

The multipositional switch to be designed is described by means of its value table (see Figure 12.7).

The representation of this function as a conjunction of its prime antiblocks is:

$$x_1^{(1,2)}\, x_0^{(1,2,3)}\, (x_1^{(1)} \vee x_0^{(1,2)})\, (x_1^{(2)} \vee x_0^{(2,3)}). \tag{12.28}$$

The representation of this function as a conjunction of its prime upper envelopes is:

$$(x_1^{1]}\, x_0^{3]} \vee x_1^{2]}\, x_0^{2]})\, (x_1^{2]}\, x_0^{[1)})\, (x_1^{[1}\, x_0^{[2} \vee x_1^{[2}\, x_0^{[1)}\, (x_1^{[1}\, x_0^{3]}). \tag{12.29}$$

$x_1 \backslash x_0$	0	1	2	3	4
0					
1	1		3 ①	①	
2		2 ①	①	4	
3					
4					

Figure 12.7. Value table

To the representations (12.28) and (12.29) correspond the realizations of Figures 12.8 and 12.9 respectively. Both realizations are free of logic static hazards; it could easily be verified that the realization of Figure 12.8 experiences logic dynamic hazards for the transitions

$$1 \leftrightarrow 2, 3 \leftrightarrow 4$$

while the realization of Figure 12.9 is free of these hazards.

12.6.2. Transient analysis of switching networks

12.6.2.1. Hazard detection

Function hazard detection has been developed in section 12.5; one will briefly present formulae able to detect logic hazards. First of all one has shown (see theorem 7.21) that a transition involving a change in the variables $\boldsymbol{x}_0 \subseteq \boldsymbol{x}$ gives rise to a logic static hazard for the network represented by $g[\boldsymbol{x}, \boldsymbol{y}(\boldsymbol{x})]$ and realizing the function $f(\boldsymbol{x})$ iff:

$$\left(\frac{\delta f}{\delta \boldsymbol{x}_0} \oplus \frac{\delta g}{\delta \boldsymbol{x}_0}\right)_{\boldsymbol{x}=\boldsymbol{a}} = 1 \tag{12.30}$$

where $\boldsymbol{x} = \boldsymbol{a}$ is the initial or the final input state.

How to obtain the function $g[\boldsymbol{x}, \boldsymbol{y}(\boldsymbol{x})]$, associated with a given network realizing $f(\boldsymbol{x})$, was explained in section 7.3.1: one has only to cut some connections in order to obtain a network without fan-out reconverging structure. The set of variables $\boldsymbol{y}$ represents then the set of functions realized by these connections.

Let us now turn to the detection of dynamic hazards. The function $g[\boldsymbol{x}, \boldsymbol{y}(\boldsymbol{x})]$, associated with a given network and used in relation (12.30) for detecting logic static

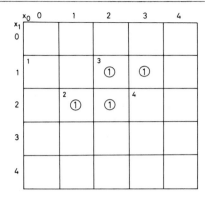

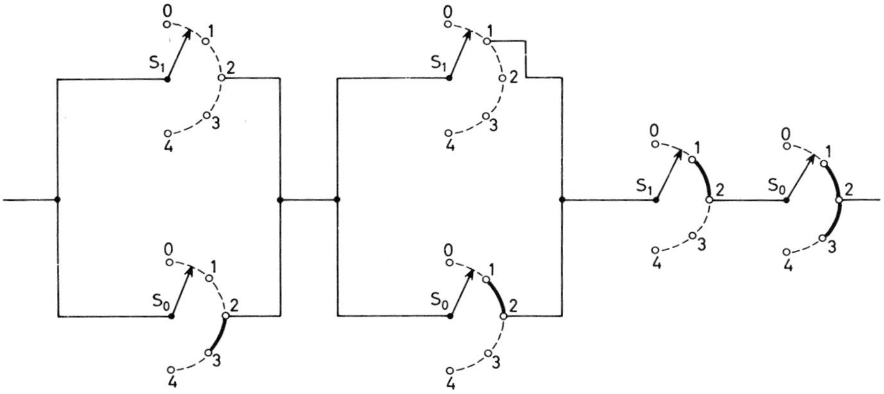

Figure 12.8. Two-level realization of a multipositional switch

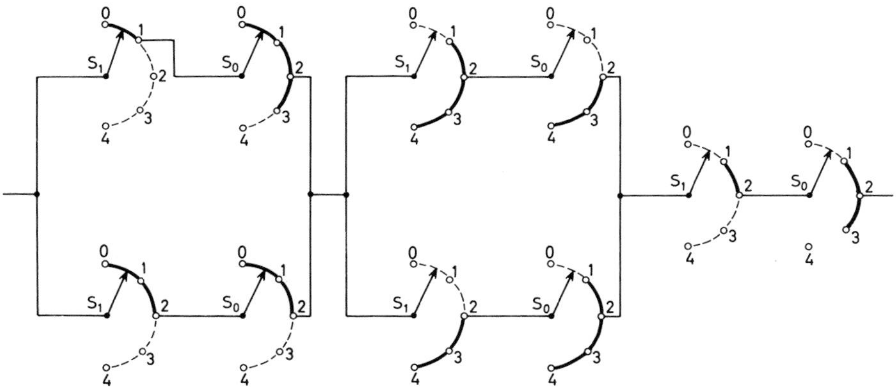

Figure 12.9. Three-level realization of a multipositional switch

hazards, contains functions $y_i(\boldsymbol{x})$ which depend on an arbitrary subset of $\boldsymbol{x}$. The function $h[\boldsymbol{x}, \boldsymbol{y}(\boldsymbol{x})]$ to be used in a similar type of formula for detecting the logic dynamic hazards of a network must be constructed in the same way as the function g but the functions $y_i \in \boldsymbol{y}$ may depend only on at most one variable $x_i \in \boldsymbol{x}$. To each switching network may be associated at least one function $f[\boldsymbol{x}, \boldsymbol{y}(\boldsymbol{x})]$ satisfying the above condition (see, for example McCluskey [1962] and Beister [1974]). Let us compare the network models $f(\boldsymbol{x}, \boldsymbol{y})$ and $h(\boldsymbol{x}, \boldsymbol{y})$ considered above by means of an example.

Example 12.8. Consider the network of Figure 12.10 realizing the switching function:

$$f = x_1(x_2 \vee x_3) \vee x_0\bar{x}_2\bar{x}_3.$$

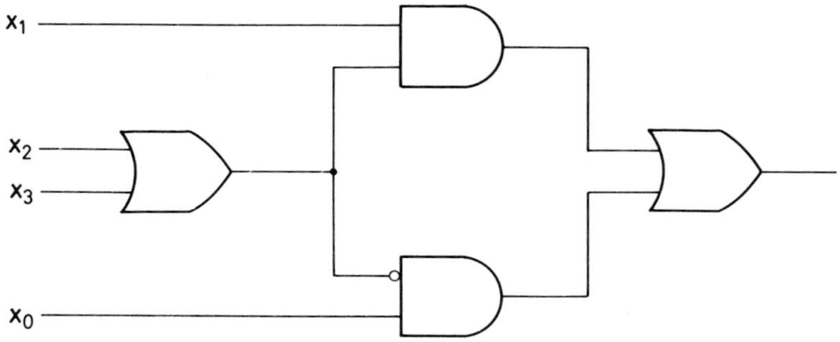

Figure 12.10. Switching network

One obtains, for example:

$$g = x_1(x_2 \vee x_3) \vee x_0 y$$
$$y = \bar{x}_2 \bar{x}_3$$
$$h = x_1(x_2 \vee x_3) \vee x_0 y_0 y_1$$
$$y_0 = \bar{x}_2$$
$$y_1 = \bar{x}_3.$$

The following theorem, the form of which is similar to that of theorem 12.10, then holds for detecting the function and logic hazards.

Theorem 12.13. A transition between the input states $\boldsymbol{x} = \boldsymbol{a}$ *and* $\boldsymbol{x} = \boldsymbol{b}$ *and involving a change in the variables* $\boldsymbol{x}_0 = (x_{q-1}, \ldots, x_1, x_0) \subseteq \boldsymbol{x}$ *gives rise to:*

(a) *A function or logic dynamic hazard for the network represented by* $h(\boldsymbol{x}, \boldsymbol{y})$ *and realizing the function* $f(\boldsymbol{x})$ *iff:*

$$\left\{\frac{Sf}{S\boldsymbol{x}_0}\left[\bigvee_{e_0 e_1}\left(\frac{Sh}{S\boldsymbol{x}_0^{e_0}\,\boldsymbol{y}_0^{e_1}} \oplus \frac{\delta h}{\delta \boldsymbol{x}_0^{e_0}\,\boldsymbol{y}_0^{e_1}}\right)\right]\right\}_{\boldsymbol{x}=\boldsymbol{a}} = 1, \tag{12.31}$$

$$0 \leqslant e_i \in (e_0 e_1) \leqslant 1, \quad \boldsymbol{0} < (\boldsymbol{e}_0 \boldsymbol{e}_1) < \boldsymbol{1},$$

$$\boldsymbol{y}_0 : \{y_i(x_j) \mid x_j \in \boldsymbol{x}_0\}.$$

(b) *A function or logic hazard for the network represented by* $h(\boldsymbol{x}, \boldsymbol{y})$ *and realizing the function* $f(\boldsymbol{x})$ *iff:*

$$\bigvee_{e_0 e_1}\left(\frac{Sh}{S\boldsymbol{x}_0^{e_0}\,\boldsymbol{y}_1^{e_1}} \oplus \frac{\delta h}{\delta \boldsymbol{x}_0^{e_0}\,\boldsymbol{y}_1^{e_1}}\right)_{\boldsymbol{x}=\boldsymbol{a}} = 1. \tag{12.32}$$

The logic hazards are isolated by modulo-2 addition of the expressions present in theorems 12.10 and 12.13 respectively.

Example 12.5 (continued). Consider the function of example 12.5 and the transition between the input states $\{x_3, x_2, x_1, x_0\} = \{0, 1, 0, 0\}$ and $\{x_3, x_2, x_1, x_0\} = \{1, 0, 1, 0\}$. This transition is free of function dynamic hazard; let us now detect the eventual logic dynamic hazards for the same transition. The function h to be considered is:

$$h = \bar{x}_0 x_4 \vee \bar{x}_1 x_2 x_3$$

with $x_4 = x_2$.

In view of theorem 12.13, the function to be tested is:

$$\frac{Sf}{Sx_3x_2x_1}\left[\left(\frac{\delta h}{\delta x_4x_3} \oplus \frac{Sh}{Sx_4x_3}\right) \vee \left(\frac{\delta h}{\delta x_4x_2} \oplus \frac{Sh}{Sx_4x_2}\right) \vee \left(\frac{\delta h}{\delta x_4x_1} \oplus \frac{Sh}{Sx_4x_1}\right) \vee \right.$$
$$\left(\frac{\delta h}{\delta x_3x_2} \oplus \frac{Sh}{Sx_3x_2}\right) \vee \left(\frac{\delta h}{\delta x_3x_1} \oplus \frac{Sh}{Sx_3x_1}\right) \vee \left(\frac{\delta h}{\delta x_2x_1} \oplus \frac{Sh}{Sx_2x_1}\right) \vee$$
$$\left(\frac{\delta h}{\delta x_4x_3x_2} \oplus \frac{Sh}{Sx_4x_3x_2}\right) \vee \left(\frac{\delta h}{\delta x_4x_3x_1} \oplus \frac{Sh}{Sx_4x_3x_1}\right) \vee$$
$$\left.\left(\frac{\delta h}{\delta x_4x_2x_1} \oplus \frac{Sh}{Sx_4x_2x_1}\right) \vee \left(\frac{\delta h}{\delta x_3x_2x_1} \oplus \frac{Sh}{Sx_3x_2x_1}\right)\right]_{x_4 = x_2} =$$
$$\bar{x}_0\,[(x_2 \oplus x_3) \vee x_1x_3 \vee \bar{x}_1\bar{x}_3].$$

The transition considered contains thus a logic dynamic hazard. Moreover there are other transitions involving a change of the three input variables x_1, x_2 and x_3 which contain a logic dynamic hazard: e.g. the transition: x_3, x_2, x_1, x_0: $\{0110\} \rightarrow \{1000\}$.

Remark. An alternate method can be used in order to detect hazards. Given a switching function $f(\boldsymbol{x}_1, \boldsymbol{x}_{01}, \boldsymbol{x}_{00})$, the transition between $(\boldsymbol{a}_1, 1, 0)$ and $(\boldsymbol{a}_1, 0, 1)$ is free of function hazards iff $f(\boldsymbol{a}_1, \boldsymbol{x}_{01}, \boldsymbol{x}_{00})$ is either increasing in $\boldsymbol{x}_{00}$ and decreasing in $\boldsymbol{x}_{01}$, or decreasing in $\boldsymbol{x}_{00}$ and increasing in $\boldsymbol{x}_{01}$. If f is given as the disjunction of its prime implicants, the unateness of its subfunctions can easily be tested by using the results of theorem 12.6.

A similar method can be used for detecting logic hazards; it suffices to consider the associated function of functions.

Apply for instance this method to the study of the logic dynamic hazards of the function of example 12.5.

Example 12.5 (continued). We have to consider the function

$$h = \bar{x}_0 x_4 \vee \bar{x}_1 x_2 x_3$$

where $x_4 = x_2$. Suppose that x_0 remains fixed and that x_1, x_2 and x_3 undertake a transition. Consider first the case where the fixed value of x_0 is 0:

$$h(x_0 = 0) = x_4 \vee \bar{x}_1 x_2 x_3;$$

it is increasing in x_2, x_3 and x_4, and decreasing in x_1; there is no hazard during a transition for which $x_0 = 0$ iff

$$\bar{x}_1 x_2 x_3 x_4 \vee x_1 \bar{x}_2 \bar{x}_3 \bar{x}_4 = \bar{x}_1 x_2 x_3 \vee x_1 \bar{x}_2 \bar{x}_3 = 1.$$

Similarly consider the case where $x_0 = 1$:

$$h(x_0 = 1) = \bar{x}_1 x_2 x_3;$$

there is no hazard during a transition for which $x_0 = 1$ iff

$$\bar{x}_1 x_2 x_3 \vee x_1 \bar{x}_2 \bar{x}_3 = 1.$$

The condition is the same for $x_0 = 0$ and for $x_0 = 1$. By complementing the first member of the last expression, one obtains the condition under which hazards occur:

$$\bar{x}_1(\bar{x}_2 \vee \bar{x}_3) \vee x_1(x_2 \vee x_3) = 1.$$

Finally, the dynamic hazards can be isolated by performing the product of the last expression with

$$\frac{Sf}{Sx_1 x_2 x_3} = \bar{x}_0 \vee \bar{x}_1 x_2 x_3 \vee x_1 \bar{x}_2 \bar{x}_3;$$

this yields the following condition:

$$\bar{x}_0 \bar{x}_1(\bar{x}_2 \vee \bar{x}_3) \vee \bar{x}_0 x_1(x_2 \vee x_3) = 1.$$

12.6.2.2. Detection of malfunctions

12.6.2.2.1. Definitions and network model

Hazards are defined as a possible departure from the ideal behaviour of a network due to a given distribution of some delays. Thus if a hazard exists in a network, it may result in a wrong output of this network if the distribution of the delays is such that the hazard is materialized, but a network containing hazards may also have a correct behaviour for another delay distribution. In other words a hazard is said to exist if there is at least one delay distribution in a network which materializes this hazard as an error at the network output. A hazard is thus a concept which is independent of any assumption on the delays.

Malfunctions will now be defined as a departure from the ideal behaviour of a network when the values of some delays are known or when an ordering in the delay values is given. It is thus obvious that malfunctions must be defined in the context of a given delay assumption: a network may have a malfunction under one delay assumption, but not under another.

Definition 12.7. A function hazard-free transition from an initial input state $\boldsymbol{c}$ to a final input state $\boldsymbol{d}$ presents a *malfunction* for a network realizing the Boolean function $f(\boldsymbol{x})$ and for a given delay assumption iff the output does not change monotonically during the transition.

Definition 12.8. If a malfunction occurs for a transition from $\boldsymbol{c}$ to $\boldsymbol{d}$ and for the network realizing $f(\boldsymbol{x})$, it will be called a *static malfunction* iff $f(\boldsymbol{c}) = f(\boldsymbol{d})$; otherwise it will be called a *dynamic malfunction.* It must be pointed out that the above definitions imply that the malfunctions are defined from an initial input state $\boldsymbol{c}$ to a final input state $\boldsymbol{d}$ and not between two input states $\boldsymbol{c}$ and $\boldsymbol{d}$ as the hazards were defined.

The following delay assumption will be considered further on in this section: the time duration for a signal to propagate from a network input to a network output is proportional to the number of logical gates encountered by the signal along its propagation path.

Given a network, a mathematical model which takes into account the delay assumption defined above, will now be built.

Consider for example a two-level AND-OR network and assume that there exists k different paths in this network starting from the input x_i and ending at the network output. This network realizing a switching function $f(\boldsymbol{x})$ can be represented as follows:

$$f(\boldsymbol{x}) = A \vee x_i \left(\bigvee_{j=0}^{p-1} B_j \right) \vee \bar{x}_i \left(\bigvee_{j=p}^{k-1} B_j \right), \quad p < k,$$

where A and B_j are switching functions independent of x_i. The terms $x_i B_j$ and $\bar{x}_i B_j$ represent the binary signals along the k paths between the input x_i and the output of $f(\boldsymbol{x})$. Assume now that these k paths can be partitioned in l sets of paths ($l \leqslant k$), such that the paths in each set have the same delay value and that the paths in different sets have different delay values. The function of the network can now be written as follows:

$$f(\boldsymbol{x}) = A \vee \bigvee_{j=0}^{l-1} (x_i B_{1j} \vee \bar{x}_i B_{0j}),$$

where each B_{1j} and B_{0j} is the disjunction of some of the B_j's.

Assume further that the ordering in the l delay values corresponds to the ordering of the index j in the above equation, and that the network is assumed to work in the fundamental mode: the network model becomes:

$$F = A \vee \bigvee_{j=0}^{l-1} \left[y_i^{[j \oplus 1, l \oplus j]} B_{1j} \vee \left(\overline{y_i^{[j \oplus 1, l \oplus j]}} \right) B_{0j} \right]$$

$$= A \vee \bigvee_{j=0}^{l-1} \left[y_i^{[j \oplus 1, l \oplus j]} B_{1j} \vee y_i^{[l \oplus j \oplus 1, j]} B_{0j} \right]$$

with y_i a $2l_i$-ary discrete variable taking its values in the set $\{0, 2l_i - 1\}$.

Summarizing the above results, one sees that if an input variable x_i is connected to the network output through the intermediate of l_i sets of paths, each set containing the paths with an identical delay value, the binary variable x_i must be replaced by a $2l_i$-ary variable y_i taking its values in the set $\{0, 2l_i-1\}$. To the values 0 and 1 of the binary variable are associated the values 0 and l_i of the $2l_i$-ary variable respectively. These will be called the stable values of y_i. To a change from 0 to 1 of the binary variable x_i is associated a change between 0 and l_i of the $2l_i$-ary variable y_i in the interval $[0, l_i]$; similarly to a change from 1 to 0 of x_i is associated a change between 0 and l_i of y_i in the interval $[l_i, 0]$.

From the network scheme one has obtained a discrete function in the discrete variable y_i and in the binary variables $x_j (j \neq i)$; this function takes into account the differences in the delay values for the paths between x_i and the output of the network.

What was done for the variable x_i and for a two-level AND-OR network will now be performed for all variables of $\boldsymbol{x}$ and for any type of network.

The following algorithm will provide us with the discrete function $F(\boldsymbol{y})$ which is the mathematical model of a switching network for the given delay assumption.

Algorithm 12.3. (a) To each gate of the network scheme, associate a variable z_j and obtain the expression of these variables in terms of their input variables which are either the network input variables or other auxiliary variables z_k. Indicate explicitly in the expressions the gates from which the signals (or variables) are issued.

(b) Substitute iteratively in the expressions obtained after step (a) the z_j's by their expression in terms of their input variables so that the network output is finally given as a function of its input variables and of the gates encountered by each signal from every network input to the network output.

(c) For each variable $x_i \in \boldsymbol{x}$, the number l_i of paths between the input x_i and the network output, having different delay values gives the number of states, that is $2l_i$, of the discrete variable y_i. The discrete function $F(\boldsymbol{y})$ is then built as was explained before.

This algorithm can best be illustrated by an example.

Example 12.9. Consider the switching network of Figure 12.11.

(a) (The gates encountered by each variable are indicated in an exponentiation form.)

$$f = z_9 = (z_4 \vee z_8)^{(9)}$$
$$z_4 = (x_1 z_5)^{(4)}$$
$$z_8 = (z_7 z_6)^{(8)}$$
$$z_5 = (x_0 \vee z_1)^{(5)}$$
$$z_7 = (\bar{x}_0 \bar{z}_1)^{(7)}$$

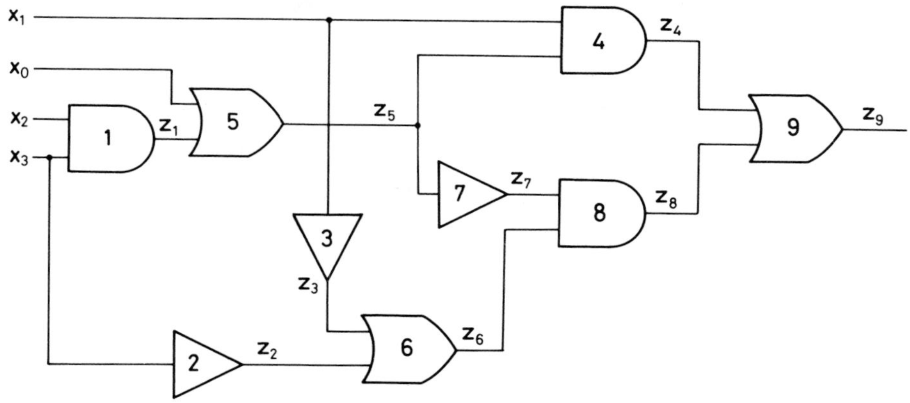

Figure 12.11. Switching network

$$z_6 = (z_3 \vee z_2)^{(6)}$$
$$z_3 = (\bar{x}_1)^{(3)}$$
$$z_2 = (\bar{x}_3)^{(2)}$$
$$z_1 = (x_2 x_3)^{(1)}.$$

(b) $f = x_1^{(49)} (x_0^{(495)} \vee x_2^{(4951)} x_3^{(4951)}) \vee$
$(\bar{x}_0)^{(5789)} [(\bar{x}_2)^{(57891)} \vee (\bar{x}_3)^{(57891)}] [(\bar{x}_1)^{(3689)} \vee (\bar{x}_3)^{(2689)}].$

In view of the above expression, the following table can then be built (see Figure 12.12).

(c) $F = y_1^{[1,2]} (y_0^{[1,2]} \vee y_2^{[1,2]} y_3^{[1,2]}) \vee y_0^{1]} (y_2^{1]} \vee y_3^{1]}) (y_1^{1]} \vee y_3^{[3,0]}).$

The function F obtained is thus a binary function of four 4-ary variables; the stable states of this function are the vertices:

$$\{y_3, y_2, y_1, y_0\} = \{e_3, e_2, e_1, e_0\}, \quad e_i = 0, 2.$$

Variable	Number of gates encountered along the paths from x_i	Number of paths having different delay values	Number of states of the discrete variable y_i
x_0	3, 4	2	4
x_1	2, 4	2	4
x_2	4, 5	2	4
x_3	4, 5	2	4

Figure 12.12. Table associated with the network of Figure 12.11

Remarks

1. The expression obtained after steps (b) or (c) is such that to each path in the network corresponds a letter x_i. This is however only true if the expression has not been rearranged by using, for example, the distributivity or the absorption laws.

2. In the above delay assumption it has been considered, for each variable x_i, l_i sets of paths having different delay values. It has been assumed that the delay values for paths in different sets are different and moreover that an ordering exists between these delay values. Finally it has been assumed that the paths in each set l_i have strictly the same delay value.

12.6.2.2.2. Theorems and computational methods

Consider the switching function $f(\boldsymbol{x})$ and let $F(\boldsymbol{y})$ be the binary function associated with a switching network realizing $f(\boldsymbol{x})$; assume further on that each of the discrete variables $y_i \in \boldsymbol{y}$ are $2l_i$-ary valued variables. Let $(\boldsymbol{x}_1, \boldsymbol{x}_0)$ be a partition on $\boldsymbol{x}$ and $(\boldsymbol{y}_1, \boldsymbol{y}_0)$ be the corresponding partition on $\boldsymbol{y}$; to the transition:

$$(\boldsymbol{x}_1, \boldsymbol{x}_0): (\boldsymbol{e}_1, \boldsymbol{e}_0) \rightarrow (\boldsymbol{e}_1, \bar{\boldsymbol{e}}_0), \quad (e_i = 0, 1)$$

of $\boldsymbol{x}$ corresponds the set of the possible values of $\boldsymbol{y}$:

$$(\boldsymbol{y}_1, \boldsymbol{y}_0): [(\boldsymbol{l}_1\, \boldsymbol{e}_1, \boldsymbol{l}_0\, \boldsymbol{e}_0), (\boldsymbol{l}_1\, \boldsymbol{e}_1, \boldsymbol{l}_0\, \bar{\boldsymbol{e}}_0)]$$

with

$$(\boldsymbol{l}_1; \boldsymbol{l}_0) = (l_{n-1}, \ldots, l_{q+1}, l_q; l_{q-1}, \ldots, l_1, l_0).$$

It is recalled that

$$[l_i\, e_i, l_i\, \bar{e}_i] = [l_i, 0] = \{l_i, l_i \oplus 1, \ldots, l_i \oplus l_i = 0\}$$

for $e_i = 1$;

$$[l_i\, e_i, l_i\, \bar{e}_i] = [0, l_i] = \{0, 1, \ldots, l_i\}$$

for $e_i = 0$.

Since the stable states of the discrete variables $\boldsymbol{y}$ are:

$$\boldsymbol{y} = \{\epsilon_{n-1}, \ldots, \epsilon_1, \epsilon_0\}; \quad \epsilon_i \in \{0, l_i\}$$

knowing the value of $F(\boldsymbol{y})$ at these particular vertices is generally sufficient to deal with the problem considered here. In this respect, the switching function $[F(\boldsymbol{y})]_2$ will be defined as follows:

The switching function $[F(\boldsymbol{y})]_2$ is obtained from the discrete (binary) function $F(\boldsymbol{y})$ by substituting each discrete variable y_i by a binary variable x_i as follows:

$$y_i^{(0)} \rightarrow \bar{x}_i$$
$$y_i^{(l_i)} \rightarrow x_i$$
$$y_i^{(j_i)} \rightarrow 0, \quad j_i \neq 0, l_i.$$

Theorem 12.4. A transition from the input state $\boldsymbol{a}$ *to the input state* $\boldsymbol{b}$ *and involving a change in the variables* $\boldsymbol{x}_0 \subseteq \boldsymbol{x}$ *gives rise to a static malfunction for the network represented by* $F(\boldsymbol{y})$ *and realizing the function* $f(\boldsymbol{x})$ *iff:*

$$\left[\frac{\delta f}{\delta \boldsymbol{x}_0} \oplus \left(\frac{\delta^{\boldsymbol{l}_0} F}{\delta \boldsymbol{y}_0}\right)_2\right]_{\boldsymbol{x}=\boldsymbol{a}} = 1, \quad \boldsymbol{l}_0 = (l_{q-1}, \ldots, l_1, l_0). \tag{12.33}$$

Proof. Similar proof to that of theorem 7.21.

Theorem 12.15. A transition from the input state $\boldsymbol{a}$ *to the input state* $\boldsymbol{b}$ *and involving a change in the variables* $\boldsymbol{x}_0 \subseteq \boldsymbol{x}$ *gives rise to a dynamic malfunction for the network represented by* $F(\boldsymbol{y})$ *and realizing the function* $f(\boldsymbol{x})$ *iff:*

$$\left[\!\!\left[\frac{Sf}{S\boldsymbol{x}_0}\left\{\left[\bigvee_{\boldsymbol{\epsilon}_0}\left(\frac{S^{\boldsymbol{\epsilon}_0}F(\boldsymbol{y})}{S\boldsymbol{y}_0} \oplus \frac{\delta^{\boldsymbol{\epsilon}_0}F(\boldsymbol{y})}{\delta\boldsymbol{y}_0}\right)_2\right] \oplus \left[\bigvee_{\boldsymbol{e}_0}\left(\frac{Sf(\boldsymbol{x})}{S\boldsymbol{x}_0^{\boldsymbol{e}_0}} \oplus \frac{\delta f(\boldsymbol{x})}{\boldsymbol{x}_0^{\boldsymbol{e}_0}}\right)\right]\right\}\right]\!\!\right]_{\boldsymbol{x}=\boldsymbol{a}} = 1$$

$$0 \leqslant e_i \leqslant 1, \quad 0 \leqslant \epsilon_i \leqslant l_i$$

$$\boldsymbol{0} < \boldsymbol{e}_0 = (e_{q-1}, \ldots, e_1, e_0) < \boldsymbol{1}$$

$$\boldsymbol{0} < \boldsymbol{\epsilon}_0 = (\epsilon_{q-1}, \ldots, \epsilon_1, \epsilon_0) < \boldsymbol{l}_0.$$

Proof. The proof follows from theorem 12.14 and from the fact that a dynamic malfunction may occur for a given transition iff one of its subtransitions contains a static malfunction. ∎

Corollary. A transition from the input state $\boldsymbol{a}$ *to the input state* $\boldsymbol{b}$ *and involving a change in the variables* $\boldsymbol{x}_0 \subseteq \boldsymbol{x}$ *gives rise to a malfunction for the network represented by* $F(\boldsymbol{y})$ *and realizing the function* $f(\boldsymbol{x})$ *iff:*

$$\left[\bigvee_{\boldsymbol{\epsilon}_0}\left(\frac{S^{\boldsymbol{\epsilon}_0}F}{S\boldsymbol{y}_0} \oplus \frac{\delta^{\boldsymbol{\epsilon}_0}F}{\delta\boldsymbol{y}_0}\right)_2\right]_{\boldsymbol{x}=\boldsymbol{a}} = 1, \quad \boldsymbol{0} < \boldsymbol{\epsilon}_0 \leqslant \boldsymbol{l}_0.$$

The conditions to be verified in the above theorems imply the computation of several differential operators. This computation can, for example, be performed by using the following relations which are obtained from general formulae derived in Chapter 7.

$$\frac{\Delta^{\boldsymbol{l}_0}F}{\Delta\boldsymbol{x}_0} = \sum_{\boldsymbol{e}_0}\left[\binom{l_0}{e_0}\binom{l_1}{e_1}\cdots\binom{l_{q-1}}{e_{q-1}}\right] F(\boldsymbol{x}_1, \boldsymbol{x}_0 \oplus \boldsymbol{e}_0), \quad \boldsymbol{0} \leqslant \boldsymbol{e}_0 \leqslant \boldsymbol{l}_0$$

$$\frac{\delta^{\boldsymbol{l}_0}F}{\delta\boldsymbol{x}_0} = \bigvee_{\boldsymbol{e}_0}\frac{\Delta^{\boldsymbol{e}_0}F}{\Delta\boldsymbol{x}_0}, \quad 0 \leqslant e_i \leqslant l_i, \quad \boldsymbol{0} < \boldsymbol{e}_0$$

$$\frac{S^{\boldsymbol{l}_0}F}{S\boldsymbol{x}_0} = \sum_{\boldsymbol{e}_0}\left[\binom{l_0}{e_0}\binom{l_1}{e_1}\cdots\binom{l_{q-1}}{e_{q-1}}\right]\frac{\Delta^{\boldsymbol{e}_0}F}{\Delta\boldsymbol{x}_0}, \quad 0 \leqslant e_i \leqslant l_i, \quad \boldsymbol{0} < \boldsymbol{e}_0.$$

A remark similar to that of section 12.6.2.1 can now be made. Given a discrete function $F(y_1, y_{01}, y_{00})$ representing a network that realizes the switching function $f(x_1, x_{01}, x_{00})$, the transition from $\boldsymbol{x} = (\boldsymbol{a}_1, \boldsymbol{1}, \boldsymbol{0})$ to $\boldsymbol{x} = (\boldsymbol{a}_1, \boldsymbol{0}, \boldsymbol{1})$ is free of function hazards and of malfunctions iff the discrete function

$$F_{[(a_1, l_{01}, 0), (a_1, 0, l_{00})]}$$

is either increasing in $\boldsymbol{y}_{00}$ and decreasing in $\boldsymbol{y}_{01}$, or decreasing in $\boldsymbol{y}_{00}$ and increasing in $\boldsymbol{y}_{01}$, in the set of values $[(\boldsymbol{a}_1, \boldsymbol{l}_{01}, \boldsymbol{0}), (\boldsymbol{a}_1, \boldsymbol{0}, \boldsymbol{l}_{00})]$. If F is obtained as the disjunction of its prime blocks, the unateness of its subfunctions can be tested by using theorems 12.5 and 12.6. This method will be illustrated in section 12.6.2.2.3. An example of hazard and of malfunction detection will be extensively treated in this section.

12.6.2.3. Example of transient analysis of a logical network

Let us consider the switching function

$$f = x_0 x_4 \vee x_1 \bar{x}_4 \vee x_2 \bar{x}_4 \vee x_3 x_4$$

which is realized by means of the logical network described in Figure 12.13. One will

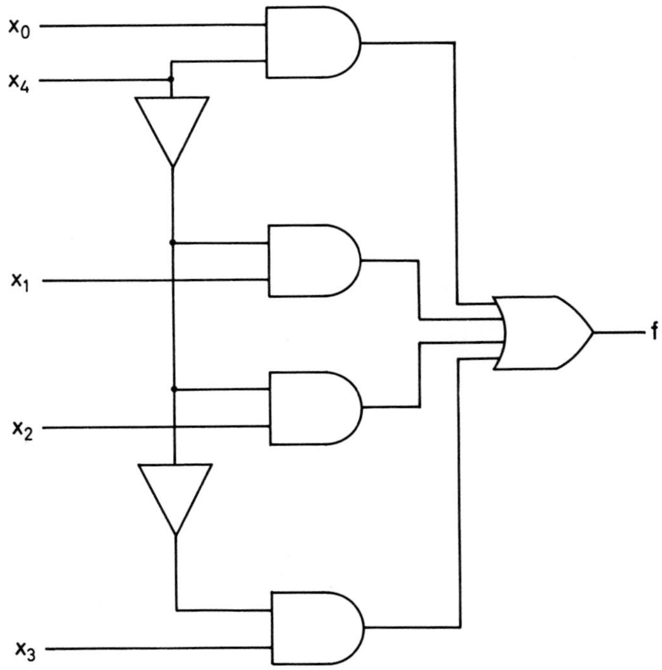

Fig. 12.13 Switching network

successively be interested in the following changes of variables:

(a) single change of the variable x_4;
(b) multiple change of the variables x_0, x_4;
(c) multiple change of the variables x_0, x_1, x_4.

Functional analysis

First, we compute the various differences of f with respect to x_0, x_1 and x_4.

$$\frac{\Delta f}{\Delta x_0} = \bar{x}_3 x_4;$$

$$\frac{\Delta f}{\Delta x_1} = \bar{x}_2 \bar{x}_4;$$

$$\frac{\Delta f}{\Delta x_1 x_0} = 0;$$

$$\frac{\Delta f}{\Delta x_4} = (x_0 \vee x_3) \oplus (x_1 \vee x_2);$$

$$\frac{\Delta f}{\Delta x_4 x_0} = \bar{x}_3;$$

$$\frac{\Delta f}{\Delta x_4 x_1} = \bar{x}_2;$$

$$\frac{\Delta f}{\Delta x_4 x_1 x_0} = 0.$$

1. Detection of the function static hazards

Since function static hazards only occur for a change of at least two input variables, one has to consider the changes (b) and (c).

$$\text{(b)} \quad \frac{Sf}{Sx_4 x_0} = \frac{\Delta f}{\Delta x_0} \oplus \frac{\Delta f}{\Delta x_4} \oplus \frac{\Delta f}{\Delta x_4 x_0} = \bar{x}_3 \bar{x}_4 \oplus (x_0 \vee x_3) \oplus (x_1 \vee x_2);$$

$$\frac{\delta f}{\delta x_4 x_0} = \frac{\Delta f}{\Delta x_0} \vee \frac{\Delta f}{\Delta x_4} \vee \frac{\Delta f}{\Delta x_4 x_0} = \bar{x}_3 \vee \bar{x}_1 \bar{x}_2;$$

according to theorem 7.18, a function static hazard occurs for

$$\frac{Sf}{Sx_4 x_0} \oplus \frac{\delta f}{\delta x_4 x_0} = 1,$$

that is:

$$\bar{x}_3(x_0 \oplus \bar{x}_4 \oplus \bar{x}_1\bar{x}_2) = 1.$$

Transitions containing a function static hazard

Changing variables	Fixed variables
x_4, x_0: $(0, 0) \leftrightarrow (1, 1)$	$\bar{x}_3(x_1 \vee x_2) = 1$
$(0, 1) \leftrightarrow (1, 0)$	$\bar{x}_1\bar{x}_2\bar{x}_3 = 1$

(c)
$$\frac{Sf}{Sx_4x_1x_0} = \frac{\Delta f}{\Delta x_0} \oplus \frac{\Delta f}{\Delta x_1} \oplus \frac{\Delta f}{\Delta x_4} \oplus \frac{\Delta f}{\Delta x_4x_0} \oplus \frac{\Delta f}{\Delta x_4x_1} \oplus \frac{\Delta f}{\Delta x_1x_0} \oplus \frac{\Delta f}{\Delta x_4x_1x_0}$$
$$= \bar{x}_3\bar{x}_4 \oplus \bar{x}_2x_4 \oplus (x_0 \vee x_3) \oplus (x_1 \vee x_2);$$
$$\frac{\delta f}{\delta x_4x_1x_0} = \frac{\Delta f}{\Delta x_0} \vee \frac{\Delta f}{\Delta x_1} \vee \frac{\Delta f}{\Delta x_4} \vee \frac{\Delta f}{\Delta x_4x_0} \vee \frac{\Delta f}{\Delta x_4x_1} \vee \frac{\Delta f}{\Delta x_1x_0} \vee \frac{\Delta f}{\Delta x_4x_1x_0}$$
$$= \bar{x}_2 \vee \bar{x}_3;$$

a function static hazard occurs for

$$\frac{Sf}{Sx_4x_1x_0} \oplus \frac{\delta f}{\delta x_4x_1x_0} = 1,$$

that is

$$\bar{x}_2\bar{x}_4 \oplus \bar{x}_3x_4 \oplus \bar{x}_2\bar{x}_3 \oplus (x_0 \vee x_3) \oplus (x_1 \vee x_2) = 1.$$

Transitions containing a function static hazard

Changing variables	Fixed variables
x_4, x_1, x_0: $(0, 0, 0) \leftrightarrow (1, 1, 1)$	$x_2\bar{x}_3 = 1$
$(0, 0, 1) \leftrightarrow (1, 1, 0)$	$\bar{x}_2\bar{x}_3 = 1$
$(0, 1, 0) \leftrightarrow (1, 0, 1)$	$\bar{x}_2 \vee \bar{x}_3 = 1$
$(1, 0, 0) \leftrightarrow (0, 1, 1)$	$\bar{x}_2x_3 = 1$

2. Detection of the function dynamic hazards

Since function dynamic hazards only occur for a change of at least three input variables, one has to consider the change (c).

$$\frac{Sf}{Sx_1x_0} = \frac{\Delta f}{\Delta x_0} \oplus \frac{\Delta f}{\Delta x_1} \oplus \frac{\Delta f}{\Delta x_1x_0} = \bar{x}_3x_4 \oplus \bar{x}_2\bar{x}_4;$$

$$\frac{\delta f}{\delta x_1 x_0} = \frac{\Delta f}{\Delta x_0} \vee \frac{\Delta f}{\Delta x_1} \vee \frac{\Delta f}{\Delta x_1 x_0} = \bar{x}_3 x_4 \oplus \bar{x}_2 \bar{x}_4;$$

$$\frac{Sf}{Sx_1 x_0} \oplus \frac{\delta f}{\delta x_1 x_0} = 0;$$

$$\frac{Sf}{Sx_4 x_0} = \frac{\Delta f}{\Delta x_0} \oplus \frac{\Delta f}{\Delta x_4} \oplus \frac{\Delta f}{\Delta x_4 x_0} = \bar{x}_3 \bar{x}_4 \oplus (x_0 \vee x_3) \oplus (x_1 \vee x_2);$$

$$\frac{\delta f}{\delta x_4 x_0} = \frac{\Delta f}{\Delta x_0} \vee \frac{\Delta f}{\Delta x_4} \vee \frac{\Delta f}{\Delta x_4 x_0} = \bar{x}_3 \vee \bar{x}_1 \bar{x}_2;$$

$$\frac{Sf}{Sx_4 x_0} \oplus \frac{\delta f}{\delta x_4 x_0} = \bar{x}_3 (x_0 \oplus \bar{x}_4 \oplus \bar{x}_1 \bar{x}_2);$$

$$\frac{Sf}{Sx_4 x_1} = \frac{\Delta f}{\Delta x_1} \oplus \frac{\Delta f}{\Delta x_4} \oplus \frac{\Delta f}{\Delta x_4 x_1} = \bar{x}_2 x_4 \oplus (x_0 \vee x_3) \oplus (x_1 \vee x_2);$$

$$\frac{\delta f}{\delta x_4 x_1} = \frac{\Delta f}{\Delta x_1} \vee \frac{\Delta f}{\Delta x_4} \vee \frac{\Delta f}{\Delta x_4 x_1} = \bar{x}_2 \vee \bar{x}_0 \bar{x}_4;$$

$$\frac{Sf}{Sx_4 x_1} \oplus \frac{\delta f}{\delta x_4 x_1} = \bar{x}_2 (x_1 \oplus x_4 \oplus \bar{x}_0 \bar{x}_3);$$

$$\frac{Sf}{Sx_4 x_1 x_0} = \bar{x}_3 \bar{x}_4 \oplus \bar{x}_2 x_4 \oplus (x_0 \vee x_3) \oplus (x_1 \vee x_2);$$

according to theorem 12.13, a function dynamic hazard occurs for

$$\frac{Sf}{Sx_4 x_1 x_0} \left[\left(\frac{Sf}{Sx_1 x_0} \oplus \frac{\delta f}{\delta x_1 x_0} \right) \vee \left(\frac{Sf}{Sx_4 x_0} \oplus \frac{\delta f}{\delta x_4 x_0} \right) \vee \left(\frac{Sf}{Sx_4 x_1} \oplus \frac{\delta f}{\delta x_4 x_1} \right) \right] = 1,$$

that is:

$$\bar{x}_2 \bar{x}_3 (\bar{x}_0 \oplus x_1) = 1.$$

Transitions containing a function dynamic hazard

Changing variables		Fixed variables
x_4, x_1, x_0:	$(0, 0, 0) \leftrightarrow (1, 1, 1)$	$\bar{x}_2 \bar{x}_3 = 1$
	$(1, 0, 0) \leftrightarrow (0, 1, 1)$	$\bar{x}_2 \bar{x}_3 = 1$

Structural analysis

Let us consider the network realizing f (Figure 12.13). The discrete function associated with this network is:

$$F = x_0 y_4^{[1,3]} \vee (x_1 \vee x_2) y_4^{[5,1]} \vee x_3 y_4^{[3}.$$

The variables x_0, x_1, x_2, x_3 are binary variables while y_4 takes its values in {0, 1, 2, 3, 4, 5}. The stable states of y_4 are thus: $y_4 = 0, y_4 = 3$, which correspond to the values 0 and 1 of the binary variable x_4 of f respectively. The discrete function which will be derived from F must thus only be evaluated at the vertices $y_4 = 0, y_4 = 3$. Only the coefficients of $y_4^{(0)}$ and of $y_4^{(3)}$ will thus be written in the expressions of this section.

We compute first the various differences of F with respect to x_0, x_1 and y_4.

$$\frac{\Delta F}{\Delta x_0} = \bar{x}_3 y_4^{(3)};$$

$$\frac{\Delta F}{\Delta x_1} = \bar{x}_2 y_4^{(0)};$$

$$\frac{\Delta F}{\Delta x_1 x_0} = 0;$$

$$\frac{\Delta F}{\Delta y_4} = x_0 \bar{x}_1 x_2 y_4^{(0)} \vee x_0 \bar{x}_3 y_4^{(3)};$$

$$\frac{\Delta^2 F}{\Delta y_4} = [x_0 \oplus (x_1 \vee x_2)]\, y_4^{(0)} \vee \bar{x}_3 [x_0 \oplus (x_1 \vee x_2)]\, y_4^{(3)};$$

$$\frac{\Delta^3 F}{\Delta y_4} = (x_0 \bar{x}_1 \bar{x}_2 \vee \bar{x}_0 x_3)\, y_4^{(0)} \vee (x_0 \bar{x}_3 \vee \bar{x}_1 \bar{x}_2 x_3)\, y_4^{(3)};$$

$$\frac{\Delta F}{\Delta x_0 y_4} = \bar{x}_1 \bar{x}_2 y_4^{(0)} \vee \bar{x}_3 y_4^{(3)};$$

$$\frac{\Delta^{12} F}{\Delta x_0 y_4} = y_4^{(0)} \vee \bar{x}_3 y_4^{(3)};$$

$$\frac{\Delta^{13} F}{\Delta x_0 y_4} = (x_3 \oplus \bar{x}_1 \bar{x}_2)\, y_4^{(0)} \vee \bar{x}_3 y_4^{(3)};$$

$$\frac{\Delta F}{\Delta x_1 y_4} = x_0 \bar{x}_2 y_4^{(0)};$$

$$\frac{\Delta^{12} F}{\Delta x_1 y_4} = \bar{x}_2 y_4^{(0)} \vee \bar{x}_2 \bar{x}_3 y_4^{(3)};$$

$$\frac{\Delta^{13}F}{\Delta x_1 y_4} = x_0\bar{x}_2 y_4^{(0)} \vee \bar{x}_2 x_3 y_4^{(3)};$$

$$\frac{\Delta F}{\Delta x_1 x_0 y_4} = \bar{x}_1 y_4^{(0)};$$

$$\frac{\Delta^{112}F}{\Delta x_1 x_0 y_4} = 0;$$

$$\frac{\Delta^{113}F}{\Delta x_1 x_0 y_4} = \bar{x}_2 y_4^{(0)}.$$

1. Detection of the static malfunctions

Let us consider successively the transitions (a), (b) and (c).

(a) $$\frac{\delta^3 F}{\delta y_4} = \frac{\Delta F}{\Delta y_4} \vee \frac{\Delta^2 F}{\Delta y_4} \vee \frac{\Delta^3 F}{\Delta y_4}$$

$$= [x_0\bar{x}_1\bar{x}_2 \vee \bar{x}_0 (x_1 \vee x_2 \vee x_3)]\, y_4^{(0)} \vee [\bar{x}_1\bar{x}_2 x_3 \vee \bar{x}_3(x_0 \vee x_1 \vee x_2)]\, y_4^{(3)}.$$

A static malfunction occurs for

$$\frac{\Delta f}{\Delta x_4} \oplus \left(\frac{\delta^3 F}{\delta y_4}\right)_2 = 1,$$

that is:

$$\bar{x}_0 x_3 (x_1 \vee x_2)\bar{x}_4 \vee x_0\bar{x}_3 (x_1 \vee x_2) x_4 = 1.$$

Transitions containing a static malfunction	
Changing variables	Fixed variables
x_4: $0 \to 1$	$\bar{x}_0 x_3(x_1 \vee x_2) = 1$
$1 \to 0$	$x_0\bar{x}_3(x_1 \vee x_2) = 1$

(b) $$\frac{\delta^{13}F}{\delta x_0 y_4} = \frac{\delta^3 F}{\delta y_4} \vee \frac{\Delta F}{\Delta x_0} \vee \frac{\Delta F}{\Delta x_0 y_4} \vee \frac{\Delta^{12}F}{\Delta x_0 y_4} \vee \frac{\Delta^{13}F}{\Delta x_0 y_4}$$

$$= y_4^{(0)} \vee (\bar{x}_3 \vee \bar{x}_1\bar{x}_2)\, y_4^{(3)}.$$

A static malfunction occurs for

$$\frac{\delta f}{\delta x_0 x_4} \oplus \left(\frac{\delta^{13}F}{\delta x_0 y_4}\right)_2 = 1,$$

that is:

$$\bar{x}_4 x_3(x_1 \vee x_2) = 1.$$

Transitions containing a static malfunction	
Changing variables	Fixed variables
x_4: $0 \to 1$, x_0: $0 \leftrightarrow 1$	$x_3(x_1 \vee x_2) = 1$

(c) $$\frac{\delta^{113}F}{\delta x_1 x_0 y_4} = \frac{\delta^{13}F}{\delta x_0 y_4} \vee \frac{\Delta F}{\Delta x_1} \vee \frac{\Delta F}{\Delta x_1 y_4} \vee \frac{\Delta^{12}F}{\Delta x_1 y_4} \vee \frac{\Delta^{13}F}{\Delta x_1 y_4} \vee \frac{\Delta F}{\Delta x_1 x_0} \vee$$

$$\frac{\Delta F}{\Delta x_1 x_0 y_4} \vee \frac{\Delta^{112}F}{\Delta x_1 x_0 y_4} \vee \frac{\Delta^{113}F}{\Delta x_1 x_0 y_4}$$

$$= y_4^{(0)} \vee (\bar{x}_2 \vee \bar{x}_3)\, y_4^{(3)}.$$

A static malfunction occurs for

$$\frac{\delta f}{\delta x_1 x_0 x_4} \oplus \left(\frac{\delta^{113}F}{\delta x_1 x_0 y_4}\right)_2 = 1,$$

that is:

$$x_2 x_3 \bar{x}_4 = 1.$$

Transitions containing a static malfunction	
Changing variables	Fixed variables
x_4: $0 \to 1$, x_0: $0 \leftrightarrow 1$, x_1: $0 \leftrightarrow 1$	$x_2 x_3 = 1$

2. *Detection of the dynamic malfunctions*
Consider successively transitions (a), (b) and (c).

(a) *Change of* x_4

$$\frac{\delta^2 F}{\delta y_4} = \frac{\Delta F}{\Delta y_4} \vee \frac{\Delta^2 F}{\Delta y_4} = [x_0 \oplus (x_1 \vee x_2)]\, y_4^{(0)} \vee \bar{x}_3\, [x_0 \vee x_1 \vee x_2]\, y_4^{(3)};$$

$$\frac{S^2 F}{S y_4} = \frac{\Delta^2 F}{\Delta y_4} = [x_0 \oplus (x_1 \vee x_2)]\, y_4^{(0)} \vee \bar{x}_3\, [x_0 \oplus (x_1 \vee x_2)]\, y_4^{(3)}.$$

According to theorem 12.15 the condition under which a dynamic malfunction can occur is given by

$$\frac{\Delta f}{\Delta x_4}\left(\frac{S^2F}{Sy_4}\oplus\frac{\delta^2F}{\delta y_4}\right)_2 = 1,$$

i.e.

$$[(x_0 \vee x_3)\oplus(x_1 \vee x_2)]\ [x_0\bar{x}_3(x_1 \vee x_2)x_4] = 1.$$

Since this equation is never satisfied, there does not exist any dynamic malfunction for a change of the variable x_4.

(b) *Change of* x_0 *and* x_4
The condition under which a dynamic malfunction can occur is given by

$$\frac{Sf}{Sx_0x_4}\left[\left(\frac{S^2F}{Sy_4}\oplus\frac{\delta^2F}{\delta y_4}\right)_2 \vee \left(\frac{S^3F}{Sy_4}\oplus\frac{\delta^3F}{\delta y_4}\right)_2 \vee \left(\frac{S^{11}F}{Sx_0y_4}\oplus\frac{\delta^{11}F}{\delta x_0y_4}\right)_2 \vee \left(\frac{S^{12}F}{Sx_0y_4}\oplus\frac{\delta^{12}F}{\delta x_0y_4}\right)_2\right] = 1.$$

$$\left(\frac{S^2F}{Sy_4}\right)_2 = \left(\frac{\Delta^2F}{\Delta y_4}\right)_2;$$

$$\left(\frac{\delta^2F}{\delta y_4}\right)_2 = \left(\frac{\Delta F}{\Delta y_4}\right)_2 \vee \left(\frac{\Delta^2F}{\Delta y_4}\right)_2;$$

$$\left(\frac{S^2F}{Sy_4}\oplus\frac{\delta^2F}{\delta y_4}\right)_2 = x_0\bar{x}_3(x_1 \vee x_2)x_4;$$

$$\left(\frac{S^3F}{Sy_4}\right)_2 = \frac{\Delta f}{\Delta x_4};$$

$$\left(\frac{\delta^3F}{\delta y_4}\right)_2 = \left(\frac{\Delta F}{\Delta y_4}\right)_2 \vee \left(\frac{\Delta^2F}{\Delta y_4}\right)_2 \vee \left(\frac{\Delta^3F}{\Delta y_4}\right)_2;$$

$$\left(\frac{S^3F}{Sy_4}\oplus\frac{\delta^3F}{\delta y_4}\right)_2 = \bar{x}_0x_3(x_1 \vee x_2)\bar{x}_4 \vee x_0\bar{x}_3(x_1 \vee x_2)x_4;$$

$$\left(\frac{SF}{Sx_0y_4}\right)_2 = \left(\frac{\Delta F}{\Delta x_0}\right)_2 \oplus \left(\frac{\Delta F}{\Delta y_4}\right)_2 \oplus \left(\frac{\Delta F}{\Delta x_0y_4}\right)_2;$$

$$\left(\frac{\delta F}{\delta x_0 y_4}\right) = \left(\frac{\Delta F}{\Delta x_0}\right)_2 \vee \left(\frac{\Delta F}{\Delta y_4}\right)_2 \vee \left(\frac{\Delta F}{\Delta x_0 y_4}\right)_2;$$

$$\left(\frac{SF}{Sx_0 y_4} \oplus \frac{\delta F}{\delta x_0 y_4}\right)_2 = x_0 \bar{x}_1 \bar{x}_2 \bar{x}_4 \vee \bar{x}_0 \bar{x}_3 x_4;$$

$$\left(\frac{S^{12}F}{Sx_0 y_4}\right)_2 = \left(\frac{\Delta F}{\Delta x_0}\right)_2 \oplus \left(\frac{\Delta^2 F}{\Delta y_4}\right)_2 \oplus \left(\frac{\Delta^{12} F}{\Delta x_0 y_4}\right)_2;$$

$$\left(\frac{\delta^{12}F}{\delta x_0 y_4}\right)_2 = \left(\frac{\Delta F}{\Delta x_0}\right)_2 \vee \left(\frac{\Delta F}{\Delta y_4}\right)_2 \vee \left(\frac{\Delta F}{\Delta x_0 y_4}\right)_2 \vee \left(\frac{\Delta^{12} F}{\Delta x_0 y_4}\right)_2 \vee \left(\frac{\Delta^2 F}{\Delta y_4}\right)_2;$$

$$\left(\frac{S^{12}F}{Sx_0 y_4} \oplus \frac{\delta^{12} F}{\delta x_0 y_4}\right)_2 = [x_0 \oplus (x_1 \vee x_2)]\, \bar{x}_4 \oplus \bar{x}_3 [\bar{x}_0 \oplus (x_1 \vee x_2)]\, x_4;$$

$$\frac{Sf}{Sx_0 x_4} = \frac{\Delta f}{\Delta x_0} \oplus \frac{\Delta f}{\Delta x_4} \oplus \frac{\Delta f}{\Delta x_0 x_4} = \bar{x}_3 \bar{x}_4 \oplus (x_0 \vee x_3) \oplus (x_1 \vee x_2).$$

A dynamic malfunction occurs for

$$x_0 \bar{x}_1 \bar{x}_2 x_3 \bar{x}_4 \vee \bar{x}_0 (x_1 \vee x_2) \bar{x}_3 x_4 = 1.$$

Transitions containing a dynamic malfunction

Changing variables	Fixed variables
$x_4\colon 0 \to 1, x_0\colon 1 \to 0$	$\bar{x}_1 \bar{x}_2 x_3 = 1$
$x_4\colon 1 \to 0, x_0\colon 0 \to 1$	$(x_1 \vee x_2)\, \bar{x}_3 = 1$

(c) *Change of x_0, x_1 and x_4*

In this last case, we use the method based upon the observation of the unateness of some subfunctions of F.

The disjunction of the prime blocks of F is given by

$$x_0 y_4^{[1,3]} \vee x_1 y_4^{[5,1]} \vee x_2 y_4^{[5,1]} \vee x_3 y_4^{[3} \vee x_0 x_1 y_4^{[5,3]} \vee x_0 x_2 y_4^{[5,3]} \vee$$
$$x_0 x_3 y_4^{[1} \vee x_1 x_3 y_4^{[3,1]} \vee x_2 x_3 y_4^{[3,1]} \vee x_0 x_1 x_3 \vee x_0 x_2 x_3.$$

1. $x_2 = x_3 = 0$

$$F_{[y_4=0,\, y_4=3]}(x_2 = x_3 = 0) = x_0 y_4^{[1,3]} \vee x_1 y_4^{1]} \vee x_0 x_1 y_4^{3]};$$

that function is not unate in y_4.

$$F_{[y_4=3,\, y_4=0]}\ (x_2 = x_3 = 0) = x_0 y_4^{[3,3]} \vee x_1 y_4^{[5,0]};$$

that function is not unate in y_4.

2. $x_2 = 1, x_3 = 0$

$$F_{[y_4=0,\, y_4=3]}\ (x_2 = 1, x_3 = 0) = x_0 y_4^{3]} \vee\ y_4^{1]};$$

that function is increasing in x_0 and decreasing in y_4. The corresponding transition is free of function hazards and of malfunctions iff $x_0 = 1$.

$$F_{[y_4=3,\, y_4=0]}\ (x_2 = 1, x_3 = 0) = x_0 y_4^{[3,3]} \vee y_4^{[5,0]};$$

that function is not unate in y_4.

3. $x_2 = 0, x_3 = 1$

$$F_{[y_4=0,\, y_4=3]}\ (x_2 = 0, x_3 = 1) = x_0 y_4^{[1,3]} \vee x_1 y_4^{1]} \vee y_4^{[3,3]} \vee x_0 x_1 y_4^{3]};$$

it is not unate in y_4.

$$F_{[y_4=3,\, y_4=0]}\ (x_2 = 0, x_3 = 1) = y_4^{[3} \vee x_1 y_4^{[3,0]};$$

the corresponding transition is free of function hazards and of malfunctions iff $x_1 = 1$.

4. $x_2 = x_3 = 1$

$$F_{[y_4=0,\, y_4=3]}\ (x_2 = x_3 = 1) = y_4^{1]} \vee y_4^{[3,3]} \vee x_0 y_4^{3]};$$

it is not unate in y_4.

$$F_{[y_4=3,\, y_4=0]}\ (x_2 = x_3 = 1) = y_4^{[3,0]};$$

the corresponding transition is free of function hazards and of malfunctions.

By taking into account the preceding results, one obtains the following conclusion: a function hazard or a malfunction can occur iff

$$\bar{x}_2 \bar{x}_3 \vee x_2 \bar{x}_3 (\bar{x}_4 \bar{x}_0 \vee x_4) \vee \bar{x}_2 x_3 (\bar{x}_4 \vee x_4 \bar{x}_1) \vee x_2 x_3 \bar{x}_4 = 1.$$

The dynamic malfunctions can be isolated by summing (modulo-2) the first member of the last expression with the first member of the expressions giving the static hazards, the dynamic hazards and the static malfunctions, respectively. One obtains then the following condition:

$$x_2 \bar{x}_4 (x_0 \oplus x_3) \oplus \bar{x}_0 x_2 \bar{x}_3 x_4 = 1.$$

Transitions containing a dynamic malfunction

Changing variables	Fixed variables
$x_4\colon 0 \to 1, x_0\colon 0 \to 1, x_1\colon 0 \leftrightarrow 1$	$x_2 x_3 = 1$
$x_4\colon 0 \to 1, x_0\colon 1 \to 0, x_1\colon 0 \leftrightarrow 1$	$x_2 \bar{x}_3 = 1$
$x_4\colon 1 \to 0, x_0\colon 0 \to 1, x_1\colon 0 \leftrightarrow 1$	$x_2 \bar{x}_3 = 1$
$x_4\colon 1 \to 0, x_0\colon 1 \to 0, x_1\colon 0 \leftrightarrow 1$	—

12.6.3. Fault detection in unate switching networks

The results presented in this section are due to Betancourt [1971]. *Unate switching networks* are networks realizing unate switching functions. Test (sets) for irredundant unate switching networks will be derived; these tests detect all stuck-at-0 and stuck-at-1 faults in all realizations with no internal inverters of a given unate function. They can be obtained easily from the product of the prime implicates form or from the sum of the prime implicants form.

Definition 12.9. (a) A *zero-bias function* is the function realized by a switching network when a connection is stuck-at-0.

(b) A *one-bias function* is the function realized by a switching network when a connection is stuck-at-1.

Theorem 12.16. In a non-redundant monotone increasing network that realizes $f(\mathbf{x})$, the zero-bias functions are monotone increasing and are smaller than f.

Proof. Assume a connection j is stuck-at-0. Remove that part of the network that feeds the stuck connection. Call g the function realized by the pruned-out part. Expressing f in normal form as a sum of products and factoring g, we get:

$$f = gf_1 \vee f_2$$

where g, f_1 and f_2 are obviously monotone increasing functions (it is recalled that only AND and OR gates are present in the network). Then:

$$f_{(j \text{ stuck-at-0})} = g_{(j \text{ stuck-at-0})} f_1 \vee f_2 = f_2 \leqslant f.$$

Since the network is non-redundant, the fault is detectable and $f_2 < f$. ■

Theorem 12.17. In a non-redundant monotone decreasing network that realizes $f(\mathbf{x})$, the one-bias functions are monotone decreasing and are greater than f.

Proof. Similar proof to that of theorem 12.16.

Theorem 12.18. Let $f(\mathbf{x})$ be a monotone increasing function, p^i a vertex of the n-cube, and:

$$S_0 = \{p^i \mid f(p^i) = 1 \quad \text{and} \quad p^i > p^j \quad \text{implies} \quad f(p^j) = 0\}.$$

Then S_0 is a test for the class of all single stuck-at-0 faults in any non-redundant monotone increasing network that realizes $f(\mathbf{x})$.

Proof. Suppose $p^j \notin S_0$ detects a stuck-at-0 fault and g_0 is the zero-bias function corresponding to that fault. By theorem 12.16, $g_0 < f$ and consequently $f(p^j) = 1$ and $g_0(p^j) = 0$. Since $f(p^j) = 1$ and $p^j \notin S_0$, there exists a $p^k \in S_0, p^k < p^j$ such that $f(p^k) = 1$. Now g_0 is monotone increasing; thus $g_0(p^j) = 0$ implies $g_0(p^k) = 0$.

Hence $p^k \in S_0$ is also a test vector for that fault. ■

Theorem 12.19. Let $f(\mathbf{x})$ be a monotone increasing function, p^i a vertex of the n-cube and:

$$S_1 = \{p^i \mid f(p_i) = 0 \quad \text{and} \quad p^j > p^i \quad \text{implies} \quad f(p^j) = 1\}.$$

Then S_1 is a test for the class of all single stuck-at-1 faults in any non-redundant monotone increasing network that realizes $f(\mathbf{x})$.

Proof. Similar proof to that of theorem 12.18. ∎

In a monotone increasing function, all the prime implicants are essential, and to determine uniquely a monotone increasing function, it is only necessary to know the smallest vertex in each prime implicant. This follows from the fact that if $p^j > p^k$ and $f(p^k) = 1$, then $f(p^j) = 1$.

These smallest vertices correspond to the elements of S_0 and therefore we have that to each prime implicant corresponds one and only one element of S_0.

Similarly, in every prime implicate the largest vertex corresponds to an element of S_1.

The sets S_0 and S_1 can be found directly from the Karnaugh map or the sum of prime implicants and product of prime implicates expressions of $f(\mathbf{x})$.

To obtain S_0 by this last method, substitute any present variable in each prime implicant by a 1 and substitute a 0 for every variable not present. To obtain S_1, in each prime implicate substitute any present variable by a 0 and any variable not present by a 1.

Example 12.10

$$f = x_0x_2 \vee x_0x_3 \vee x_1x_2 \vee x_2x_3$$
$$= (x_0 \vee x_2)(x_2 \vee x_3)(x_0 \vee x_1 \vee x_3)$$
$$S_0 = \{(x_3x_2x_1x_0) = (0\ 1\ 0\ 1), (1\ 0\ 0\ 1), (0\ 1\ 1\ 0), (1\ 1\ 0\ 0)\}$$
$$S_1 = \{(x_3x_2x_1x_0) = (1\ 0\ 1\ 0), (0\ 0\ 1\ 1), (0\ 1\ 0\ 0)\}.$$

It has been shown above that S_0 and S_1 are sufficient to detect all single stuck-faults, but there are networks that can be tested completely using subsets of S_0 and S_1, while other realizations need all the tests given by S_0 and S_1.

Theory developed so far for monotone increasing functions applies also to monotone decreasing functions with the following modifications:

$$S_0 = \{p^i \mid f(p^i) = 1 \quad \text{and} \quad p^j > p^i \quad \text{implies} \quad f(p^j) = 0\},$$
$$S_1 = \{p^i \mid f(p^i) = 0 \quad \text{and} \quad p^j < p^i \quad \text{implies} \quad f(p^j) = 1\}.$$

From the sets S_0 and S_1 for monotone increasing and monotone decreasing functions, one deduces correspondent sets for unate functions. Consider, for example, a unate function $f(\mathbf{x}_1, \mathbf{x}_0)$, monotone increasing in $\mathbf{x}_1$ and monotone decreasing in $\mathbf{x}_0$; to find the sets S_0 and S_1 the following procedure is used.

Let f be given as a disjunction of prime implicants; in each prime implicant every $x_i \in \mathbf{x}_1$ present is substituted by 1 and the missing $x_i \in \mathbf{x}_1$ by 0, and every $x_j \in \mathbf{x}_0$

present by 0 and the missing $x_j \in \boldsymbol{x}_0$ by 1. The binary vectors so obtained are the elements of S_0.

Let f be given as a conjunction of prime implicates; in each prime implicate every $x_i \in \boldsymbol{x}_1$ present is substituted by a 0 and the missing $x_i \in \boldsymbol{x}_1$ by 1 and every $x_j \in \boldsymbol{x}_0$ present is substituted by a 1 and the missing y_i by 0, giving the elements of S_1.

The sets S_0 and S_1 are sufficient to detect any single stuck-at-0 or stuck-at-1 fault in any realization of f using AND and OR gates.

Example 12.11

$$f = \bar{x}_0 x_3 \vee \bar{x}_0 x_2 \vee \bar{x}_1 x_2 = (\bar{x}_0 \vee \bar{x}_1)(x_2 \vee x_3)(\bar{x}_0 \vee x_2)$$

$$\boldsymbol{x}_1 = (x_3, x_2), \quad \boldsymbol{x}_0 = (x_1, x_0)$$

$$S_0 = \{(1\ 0\ 1\ 0), (0\ 1\ 1\ 0), (0\ 1\ 0\ 1)\}$$

$$S_1 = \{(1\ 1\ 1\ 1), (0\ 0\ 0\ 0), (1\ 0\ 0\ 1)\}.$$

Chapter 13
Symmetry

This last chapter is devoted to the study of a very important functional property: the symmetry. On the one hand, many discrete functions encountered in the representation and synthesis of digital systems present indeed some symmetry. On the other hand, one may take advantage of the symmetries that a function presents in order to obtain more concise representations and more economical realizations.

We suppose that these two reasons alone justify the writing of a chapter on symmetry.

The main definitions and concepts are introduced in section 13.1; the definition of partial symmetry is introduced and related to the notion of ρ-symmetric function. The second section (13.2) emphasizes the algebraic structures of lattice and module that may be conferred to the set of ρ-symmetric discrete functions. The main result of section 13.3 is that every n-variable discrete function may be imbedded in a totally symmetric discrete function depending on at most 2^n variables. Section 13.4 gives some indications concerning the detection of partial symmetries: it also introduces the concept of generalized ρ-symmetric function that is a function that becomes ρ-symmetric after some change of variables. Section 13.5 describes some cellular circuits for realizing totally symmetric functions while the last section (13.6) is concerned with switching functions.

13.1. Introduction of the main concepts

13.1.1. Definitions

We have defined an n-variable discrete function as a mapping from $S = S_{n-1} \times \ldots \times S_0$ to L, where

$$S_i = \{0, \ldots, m_i - 1\}, \quad \forall i = 0, \ldots, n-1$$

and

$$L = \{0, \ldots, r-1\}.$$

There are thus inclusion relations between the factors of S:

$$S_k \subseteq S_l \quad \text{iff} \quad m_k \leqslant m_l.$$

In that last case one may find n-tuples like

$$e = (e_{n-1}, \ldots, e_l, \ldots, e_k, \ldots, e_0) \text{ and } e' = (e_{n-1}, \ldots, e_k, \ldots, e_l, \ldots, e_0)$$

that both lie in S; it suffices that e_l belongs to S_k. A discrete function f has the *partial symmetry* $x_k \sim x_l$ iff for every pair of n-tuples like e and e' one has

$$f(e) = f(e').$$

In other words, the function f has the partial symmetry $x_k \sim x_l$ iff

$$f(x_{n-1}, \ldots, x_l, \ldots, x_k, \ldots, x_0) = f(x_{n-1}, \ldots, x_k, \ldots, x_l, \ldots, x_0), \ \forall x_k$$

and $x_l \in S_k \cap S_l$.

Let us now consider a partition ρ of the set $\{x_0, \ldots, x_{n-1}\}$ into s blocks, and suppose for instance that

$$\rho = (\boldsymbol{x}_{s-1}, \ldots, \boldsymbol{x}_0),$$

with

$$\boldsymbol{x}_i = (x_{i\,n_i-1}, \ldots, x_{i\,0}), \quad \forall i = 0, \ldots, s-1.$$

In the sequel one will suppose that the variables $x_0, \ldots, x_{n-1}$ have been ranged in such a way that $f(\boldsymbol{x})$ can be written under the form $f(\boldsymbol{x}_{s-1}, \ldots, \boldsymbol{x}_0)$.

Given a block $\boldsymbol{x}_i$ of the partition defined above, and a permutation Π_i acting on $\{0, \ldots, n_i-1\}$, i.e. $\Pi_i \in S_{n_i}$, one uses the following notation:

$$\Pi_i(\boldsymbol{x}_i) = (x_{i\,\Pi_i(n_i-1)}, \ldots, x_{i\,\Pi_i(0)}),$$

that is the same block as $\boldsymbol{x}_i$ where the variables are ranged in a different order.

It can arise that two n-tuples like

$$(\boldsymbol{e}_{s-1}, \ldots, \boldsymbol{e}_0) \quad \text{and} \quad (\boldsymbol{e}'_{s-1}, \ldots, \boldsymbol{e}'_0),$$

where $\boldsymbol{e}'_{s-1} = \Pi_{s-1}(\boldsymbol{e}_{s-1}), \ldots, \boldsymbol{e}'_0 = \Pi_0(\boldsymbol{e}_0)$ for some well-chosen permutations $\Pi_{s-1}, \ldots, \Pi_0$, lie both in S. A discrete function is *ρ-symmetric* iff for every pair of n-tuples like $(\boldsymbol{e}_{s-1}, \ldots, \boldsymbol{e}_0)$ and $(\boldsymbol{e}'_{s-1}, \ldots, \boldsymbol{e}'_0)$ one has

$$f(\boldsymbol{e}_{s-1}, \ldots, \boldsymbol{e}_0) = f(\boldsymbol{e}'_{s-1}, \ldots, \boldsymbol{e}'_0).$$

That means that if two points of S can be deduced from each other by a permutation of their components acting inside the blocks of ρ, then the function takes the same value at these two points.

A ρ-symmetric function f for which ρ is the trivial partition in one block is a *totally symmetric function.* Thus given two points of S that can be deduced from each other by a permutation of their components, the function f takes the same value at these two points.

Another definition of the partial symmetry had been proposed by Davio and Deschamps [1972]: the discrete function f has the partial symmetry $x_k \sim x_l$ iff its value at point $(x_{n-1}, \ldots, x_0)$ can be computed from the knowledge of the values taken by each x_i ($i \neq k$ and $i \neq l$) and by the real sum $x_k + x_l$, without necessarily knowing the individual values of x_k and x_l. Notice however that this definition is less general than that introduced above. The two definitions only coincide in the case of discrete functions of binary variables.

13.1.2. Partial symmetry and ρ-symmetry

We now establish the relation between the two main concepts introduced above: partial symmetry and ρ-symmetry. Let us first introduce the following notations:

S_{ij} is the set in which x_{ij} takes its values, for every $j = 0, \ldots, n_i - 1$;

$S^{(i)} = S_{i\,n_i-1} \times \ldots \times S_{i\,0}$;

therefore, for a suitable ordering of the variables one has:

$$S = S_{n-1} \times \ldots \times S_0 = S^{(s-1)} \times \ldots \times S^{(0)}.$$

Lemma 13.1. Consider two points $\boldsymbol{e}_i$ *and* $\boldsymbol{e}_i'$ *in* $S^{(i)}$ *for which there exists a permutation* Π_i *such that* $\boldsymbol{e}_i' = \Pi_i(\boldsymbol{e}_i)$. *Then one can find a series of transpositions* $\tau_1, \tau_2, \ldots, \tau_p$ *such that*

$$\tau_1(\boldsymbol{e}_i) \in S^{(i)}, \tau_2[\tau_1(\boldsymbol{e}_i)] \in S^{(i)}, \ldots, \tau_p\{\ldots[\tau_1(\boldsymbol{e}_i)]\ldots\} = \boldsymbol{e}_i'.$$

Proof. Let us describe a construction method. Suppose that α is the greatest integer appearing as component in $\boldsymbol{e}_i$. If there is an index k such that

$$e_{ik} = \alpha \text{ and } e_{ik}' \neq \alpha,$$

there must exist another index, say j, such that

$$e_{ij} \neq \alpha \text{ and } e_{ij}' = \alpha.$$

This is a direct consequence of the fact that $\boldsymbol{e}_i$ and $\boldsymbol{e}_i'$ are deduced from each other by a permutation of their components. We have thus

$$e_{ik} = e_{ij}' \in S_{ij}$$

since $\boldsymbol{e}_i' \in S^{(i)}$.

On the other hand, by maximality of e_{ik} we may write

$$e_{ij} < e_{ik} \in S_{ik}$$

and thus

$$e_{ij} \in S_{ik}.$$

From the fact that e_{ik} lies in S_{ij} and e_{ij} in S_{ik}, we deduce that the transposition τ_{kj} of e_{ik} and e_{ij} yields a new point of $S^{(i)}$. Use the notation $\boldsymbol{e}_i''$ for $\tau_{kj}(\boldsymbol{e}_i)$. We have the two following properties:

(a) $e_{ij}'' = e_{ij}' = \alpha$.

(b) $e_{il} = e_{il}' = \alpha \Rightarrow l \neq k$ and $l \neq j \Rightarrow e_{il}'' = e_{il}' = \alpha$.

Therefore

$$\#\{l \mid e_{il}'' = e_{il}' = \alpha\} = 1 + \#\{l \mid e_{il} = e_{il}' = \alpha\}.$$

We can use the same construction with the point $\boldsymbol{e}_i''$ as starting point. After a finite number of transpositions, one obtains a point $\boldsymbol{e}_i'''$ of $S^{(i)}$ such that:

$$e_{il}''' = \alpha \quad \text{iff} \quad e_{il}' = \alpha.$$

The construction is continued in the same way by considering in $\boldsymbol{e}_i'''$ and $\boldsymbol{e}_i'$ the components that are not equal to α. Let β be the greatest integer different from α and appearing as component in $\boldsymbol{e}_i$. At the end of this second part of the construction one gets a point $\boldsymbol{e}_i^{iv}$ with the following property

$$e_{il}^{iv} = \alpha \quad \text{iff} \quad e_{il}' = \alpha,$$

$$e_{il}^{iv} = \beta \quad \text{iff} \quad e_{il}' = \beta.$$

Finally one obtains the point $\boldsymbol{e}_i'$ by a series of transpositions and without having ever left the domain $S^{(i)}$. ∎

We may now state and prove the following theorem.

Theorem 13.1. The discrete function f is ρ-symmetric iff it has the partial symmetry $x_{ik} \sim x_{ij}$ *for every pair of variables* x_{ik} *and* x_{ij} *appearing in the same block of ρ.*

Proof. The condition is obviously necessary; its sufficiency is a direct consequence of the preceding lemma. ∎

With every discrete function f may be associated a binary relation $R(f)$ on the set $\{x_0, \ldots, x_{n-1}\}$:

(a) $(x_i, x_i) \in R(f)$, $\forall i = 0, \ldots, n-1$;
(b) if $i \neq j$, then $(x_i, x_j) \in R(f)$ iff f has the partial symmetry $x_i \sim x_j$.

The relation $R(f)$ is a compatibility relation, but generally not an equivalence relation. The theorem 13.1 may be reformulated as follows:

Theorem 13.2. The discrete function f is ρ-symmetric iff every block of ρ is a compatibility class of R(f).

Corollary. The discrete function f is ρ-symmetric iff every block of ρ is included in a maximal compatibility class of R(f). ∎

13.1.3. *Logic functions; carrier functions*

In this subsection we first consider the particular case where

$$S_0 = \ldots = S_{n-1} = E = \{0, \ldots, m-1\};$$

the functions from E^n to L will be referred to as logic functions though E and L are not necessarily identical. In the case of logic functions, the definitions introduced above become somewhat simpler:

(a) the n-variable logic function f has the partial symmetry $x_k \sim x_l$ iff

$$f(x_{n-1}, \ldots, x_l, \ldots, x_k, \ldots, x_0) = f(x_{n-1}, \ldots, x_k, \ldots, x_l, \ldots, x_0);$$

(b) the n-variable logic function f is ρ-symmetric iff

$$f(\boldsymbol{x}_{s-1}, \ldots, \boldsymbol{x}_0) = f[\Pi_{s-1}(\boldsymbol{x}_{s-1}), \ldots, \Pi_0(\boldsymbol{x}_0)]$$

for every s-tuple of permutations $(\Pi_{s-1}, \ldots, \Pi_0)$, i.e. it is invariant under the set of permutations of $\{x_0, \ldots, x_{n-1}\}$ acting inside the blocks of ρ.

If f is a logic function, the binary relation $R(f)$ is an equivalence relation over $\{x_0, \ldots, x_{n-1}\}$; this is a direct consequence of the following theorem.

Theorem 13.3. If the logic function f has the two partial symmetries $x_j \sim x_k$ and $x_k \sim x_l$, then it has also the partial symmetry $x_j \sim x_l$.

Proof. From the partial symmetry $x_j \sim x_k$ one deduces that

$$f(\ldots, x_l, \ldots, x_k, \ldots, x_j, \ldots) = f(\ldots, x_l, \ldots, x_j, \ldots, x_k, \ldots,); \qquad (13.1)$$

from the partial symmetry $x_l \sim x_k$ one deduces that

$$f(\ldots, x_l, \ldots, x_j, \ldots, x_k, \ldots) = f(\ldots, x_j, \ldots, x_l, \ldots, x_k, \ldots); \qquad (13.2)$$

finally, using again the partial symmetry $x_j \sim x_k$ yields:

$$f(\ldots, x_j, \ldots, x_l, \ldots, x_k, \ldots) = f(\ldots, x_j, \ldots, x_k, \ldots, x_l, \ldots). \qquad (13.3)$$

By combining (13.1), (13.2) and (13.3) one obtains

$$f(\ldots, x_l, \ldots, x_k, \ldots, x_j, \ldots) = f(\ldots, x_j, \ldots, x_k, \ldots, x_l, \ldots)$$

that is

$$x_j \sim x_l.$$ ■

This last theorem shows that $R(f)$ is a transitive relation; since furthermore it is both reflexive and symmetric, it is an equivalence relation. Let ρ be the partition of $\{x_0, \ldots, x_{n-1}\}$ associated with $R(f)$; the logic function f is then ρ-symmetric, and ρ is the greatest partition such that f has that property.

Let us now introduce the notion of *carrier* of a ρ-symmetric logic function f; that is the function that gives the information just necessary to define f once it is known to be ρ-symmetric. For that we need some new definitions.

Definition 13.1. The subset $\mathcal{E}_{n_i}$ of E^{n_i} is defined as follows:

$$\mathcal{E}_{n_i} = \{(e_{n_i-1}, \ldots, e_0) \in E^{n_i} \mid e_{n_i-1} \leqslant \ldots \leqslant e_0\}.$$

The number r_i of points in $\mathcal{E}_{n_i}$ is given by the number of combinations with repetitions of m elements taken n_i by n_i, that is

$$r_i = \frac{(n_i+m-1)!}{n_i!(m-1)!} = \binom{n_i+m-1}{n_i}.$$

Definition 13.2. The function θ_{n_i} from E^{n_i} to $\mathcal{E}_{n_i}$ associates with the n_i-tuple $\boldsymbol{e}_i = (e_{n_i-1}, \ldots, e_0)$ of E^{n_i} the unique n_i-tuple of $\mathcal{E}_{n_i}$ deduced from $\boldsymbol{e}_i$ by ordering its components.

Definition 13.3. Given a ρ-symmetric logic function f, the *carrier* of f is a function f_c from

$$\mathcal{E} = \mathcal{E}_{n_{s-1}} \times \ldots \times \mathcal{E}_{n_0} \text{ to } L$$

that is defined as follows:

$$f_c(\boldsymbol{e}'_{s-1}, \ldots, \boldsymbol{e}'_0) = f(\boldsymbol{e}'_{s-1}, \ldots, \boldsymbol{e}'_0), \quad \forall \boldsymbol{e}'_{s-1} \in \mathcal{E}_{n_{s-1}}, \ldots, \quad \forall \boldsymbol{e}'_0 \in \mathcal{E}_{n_0}.$$

Furthermore, it is obvious that

$$f(\boldsymbol{e}_{s-1}, \ldots, \boldsymbol{e}_0) = f_c[\theta_{n_{s-1}}(\boldsymbol{e}_{s-1}), \ldots, \theta_{n_0}(\boldsymbol{e}_0)], \quad \forall \boldsymbol{e}_{s-1} \in E^{n_{s-1}}, \ldots, \boldsymbol{e}_0 \in E^{n_0}.$$

Therefore, to every ρ-symmetric logic function f corresponds exactly one function f_c from $\mathcal{E}$ to L that contains all the information necessary to define f.

In other words, one could define an equivalence relation $\overset{i}{\equiv}$ on E^{n_i}:

$$\boldsymbol{e}_i \overset{i}{\equiv} \boldsymbol{e}'_i \quad \text{iff} \quad \boldsymbol{e}'_i = \Pi_i(\boldsymbol{e}_i) \text{ for some permutation } \Pi_i,$$

and an equivalence relation $\equiv$ on E^n:

$$\boldsymbol{e} = (\boldsymbol{e}_{s-1}, \ldots, \boldsymbol{e}_0) \equiv (\boldsymbol{e}'_{s-1}, \ldots, \boldsymbol{e}'_0) = \boldsymbol{e}'$$

iff

$$\boldsymbol{e}_{s-1} \overset{s-1}{\equiv} \boldsymbol{e}'_{s-1} \quad \text{and} \quad \ldots \quad \text{and} \quad \boldsymbol{e}_0 \overset{0}{\equiv} \boldsymbol{e}'_0.$$

If f is ρ-symmetric, then

$$\boldsymbol{e} \equiv \boldsymbol{e}' \Rightarrow f(\boldsymbol{e}) = f(\boldsymbol{e}').$$

Every class of $E^{n_i}/\overset{i}{\equiv}$ can be represented by the unique element of $\mathcal{E}_{n_i}$ it contains, and f_c can be considered as the function of

$$(E^n/\equiv) = (E^{n_{s-1}}/\overset{s-1}{\equiv}) \times \ldots \times (E^{n_0}/\overset{0}{\equiv}) \text{ to } L$$

that is naturally associated with f.

Let us now turn back to the general case of discrete functions and denote by

$$E = \{0_i, \ldots, m-1\}$$

the set union

$$S_0 \cup \ldots \cup S_{n-1},$$

i.e.

$$m = \max(m_0, \ldots, m_{n-1}).$$

It is obvious that every discrete function f from $S = S_{n-1} \times \ldots \times S_0$ to L can be imbedded in a logic function f' from E^n to L:

$$f'(e) = f(e), \quad \forall e \in S,$$

the value of $f(\boldsymbol{e})$ is arbitrarily chosen if $\boldsymbol{e} \notin S$ (i.e. $\boldsymbol{e} \in E^n \setminus S$).

The next theorem proves that with a ρ-symmetric discrete function f can be associated a ρ-symmetric logic function f'.

Theorem 13.4. If f is a ρ-symmetric discrete function, then there exists a ρ-symmetric logic function f' from E^n to L such that

$$f'(e) = f(e), \quad \forall e \in S.$$

Proof. As it has been seen above, it suffices to define the carrier f'_c of f'. Consider a point $\boldsymbol{e}$ of $\mathscr{E}$. If the equivalence class of $E^n/\equiv$ that contains $\boldsymbol{e}$ also contains an element $\boldsymbol{e}'$ of S, then

$$f'_c(e) = f(e'),$$

and since f is ρ-symmetric there is no ambiguity: suppose indeed that $\boldsymbol{e}''$ is another point of S in the same equivalence class; by definition of the equivalence $\equiv$ the points $\boldsymbol{e}'$ and $\boldsymbol{e}''$ are deduced from each other by a permutation of their components inside the blocks of ρ, and thus $f(\boldsymbol{e}') = f(\boldsymbol{e}'')$.

If the equivalence class containing $\boldsymbol{e}$ does not contain any point of S, then the value taken by f'_c at this point is arbitrarily chosen. ■

The proof of the last theorem suggests the definition of a carrier function even for a discrete function. Denote indeed by $\mathscr{E}'$ the subset of $\mathscr{E}$ consisting of all the points of $\mathscr{E}$ equivalent to at least one point of S:

$$\mathscr{E}' = \{\boldsymbol{e} \in \mathscr{E} \mid \exists\, \boldsymbol{e}' \in S \quad \text{such that} \quad \boldsymbol{e} \equiv \boldsymbol{e}'\}.$$

More precisely,

$$\mathscr{E}' = \mathscr{E}'_{n_{s-1}} \times \ldots \times \mathscr{E}'_{n_0}$$

where

$$\mathscr{E}'_{n_i} = \{\boldsymbol{e}_i \in \mathscr{E}_{n_i} \mid \exists\, \boldsymbol{e}'_i \in S^{(i)} \quad \text{such that} \quad \boldsymbol{e}_i \overset{i}{\equiv} \boldsymbol{e}'_i\},$$

for every $i = 0, \ldots, s-1$.

The carrier f_c of f is then a function from $\mathcal{E}'$ to L defined as follows:

$$f_c(e_{s-1}, \ldots, e_0) = f(e'_{s-1}, \ldots, e'_0)$$

where $\boldsymbol{e}' = (e'_{s-1}, \ldots, e'_0)$ is an element of S equivalent to $\boldsymbol{e} = (e_{s-1}, \ldots, e_0)$. By definition of $\mathcal{E}'$ there exists at least one point $\boldsymbol{e}'$; furthermore, as shown in the proof of theorem 13.4, the definition of f_c is unambiguous.

Let us illustrate by an example these various definitions.

x_2	x_1	x_0	f
0	0	0	0
0	0	1	1
0	1	0	1
0	1	1	2
1	0	0	1
1	0	1	2
1	1	0	2
1	1	1	3
2	0	0	4
2	0	1	5
2	1	0	5
2	1	1	6

Figure 13.1. The totally symmetric function f

Example 13.1. The function f of Figure 13.1 is totally symmetric ($n = 3$, $m_0 = m_1 = 2, m_2 = 3, r = 7$); note indeed that

$$f(0, 0, 1) = f(0, 1, 0) = f(1, 0, 0) = 1;$$

$$f(0, 1, 1) = f(1, 0, 1) = f(1, 1, 0) = 2;$$

$$f(2, 0, 1) = f(2, 1, 0) = 5.$$

The functions f', f'_c and f_c are given in Figures 13.2, 13.3 and 13.4 in which α, β and γ may be arbitrarily chosen.

13.2. Algebraic structures

As it has been seen above, with every ρ-symmetric discrete function f is associated a carrier function f_c from $\mathcal{E}' = \mathcal{E}'_{n_{s-1}} \times \ldots \times \mathcal{E}'_{n_0}$ to L that entirely defines f. It is obvious that conversely every function from $\mathcal{E}'$ to L defines a ρ-symmetric discrete function. There thus exists a bijection between the set of ρ-symmetric discrete functions and the set of functions from $\mathcal{E}'$ to L.

x_2	x_1	x_0	f'
0	0	0	0
0	0	1	1
0	0	2	4
0	1	0	1
0	1	1	2
0	1	2	5
0	2	0	4
0	2	1	5
0	2	2	α
1	0	0	1
1	0	1	2
1	0	2	5
1	1	0	2
1	1	1	3
1	1	2	6
1	2	0	5
1	2	1	6
1	2	2	β
2	0	0	4
2	0	1	5
2	0	2	α
2	1	0	5
2	1	1	6
2	1	2	β
2	2	0	α
2	2	1	β
2	2	2	γ

Figure 13.2. The totally symmetric logic function f'

$\mathcal{E}$	f_c'
(0, 0, 0)	0
(0, 0, 1)	1
(0, 0, 2)	4
(0, 1, 1)	2
(0, 1, 2)	5
(0, 2, 2)	α
(1, 1, 1)	3
(1, 1, 2)	6
(1, 2, 2)	β
(2, 2, 2)	γ

Figure 13.3. The carrier of f'

$\mathcal{E}'$	f_c
(0, 0, 0)	0
(0, 0, 1)	1
(0, 0, 2)	4
(0, 1, 1)	2
(0, 1, 2)	5
(1, 1, 1)	3
(1, 1, 2)	6

Figure 13.4. The carrier of f

Let us denote by r_i' the number of points in $\mathcal{E}_{n_i}'$ and by $r' = r_0' \times \ldots \times r_{s-1}'$ the number of points $\mathcal{E}'$.

One can confer to L the structure of distributive lattice; therefore, the set of ρ-symmetric discrete functions is also a distributive lattice isomorphic to $L^{r'}$.

One can also confer to L the structure of ring, namely the ring of integers modulo-r; therefore, the set of ρ-symmetric discrete functions is an L-module isomorphic to $L^{r'}$.

Let us describe these two algebraic structures in more detail.

13.2.1. The lattice structure

The points of every set $\mathcal{E}'_{n_i}$ may be enumerated in lexicographical order, $i = 0, \ldots, s-1$; this has been seen in section 1.5.1. In that way, every set $\mathcal{E}'_{n_i}$ is totally ordered and the points of $\mathcal{E}'$ may thus also be enumerated in lexicographical order: this is a kind of recursive definition of the lexicographical order.

Every function from $\mathcal{E}'$ to L may thus be represented by an r'-component row vector given the value taken by the function at each of the points of $\mathcal{E}'$ enumerated in the lexicographical order. Therefore, every ρ-symmetric discrete function may also be represented by a row vector with r' components in L:

With the ρ-symmetric discrete function f is associated the row vector $[f_c(\boldsymbol{e})]$, $\boldsymbol{e} \in \mathcal{E}'$; it is called the *characteristic vector* of *f*.

Theorem 13.5. The set of ρ-symmetric discrete functions is a sublattice of the lattice of all the discrete functions.

Proof. It suffices to note that the set of ρ-symmetric discrete functions is closed under the two lattice operations of disjunction and conjunction. ■

Note that to the disjunction (conjunction) of two ρ-symmetric discrete functions corresponds the component-wise disjunction (conjunction) of their characteristic vectors.

Definitions 13.4. For every $\boldsymbol{e}_i \in \mathcal{E}'_{n_i}$ let us define a function $\sigma_{\boldsymbol{e}_i}$ from $S^{(i)}$ to L:

$$\sigma_{\boldsymbol{e}_i}(\boldsymbol{x}_i) = r-1 \quad \text{iff} \quad \boldsymbol{x}_i \overset{i}{\equiv} \boldsymbol{e}_i,$$
$$= 0 \text{ otherwise.}$$

For every $\boldsymbol{e} = (\boldsymbol{e}_{s-1}, \ldots, \boldsymbol{e}_0) \in \mathcal{E}'$ define the *elementary ρ-symmetric discrete function* $\sigma_{\boldsymbol{e}}$ from S to L as follows:

$$\sigma_{\boldsymbol{e}}(\boldsymbol{x}) = r-1 \quad \text{iff} \quad \boldsymbol{x} \equiv \boldsymbol{e},$$
$$= 0 \text{ otherwise.}$$

The following theorem gives two obvious properties of these functions.

Theorem 13.6. For every $\boldsymbol{e} = (\boldsymbol{e}_{s-1}, \ldots, \boldsymbol{e}_0)$ *in* $\mathcal{E}'$ *and* $\boldsymbol{x} = (\boldsymbol{x}_{s-1}, \ldots, \boldsymbol{x}_0)$ *in S one has*

(a) $\sigma_{\boldsymbol{e}}(\boldsymbol{x}) = \sigma_{\boldsymbol{e}_{s-1}}(\boldsymbol{x}_{s-1}) \wedge \ldots \wedge \sigma_{\boldsymbol{e}_0}(\boldsymbol{x}_0)$;

(b) $\sigma_{\boldsymbol{e}_i}(\boldsymbol{x}_i) = \bigvee (x_{i\,n_i-1}^{(e'_{i\,n_i-1})} \wedge \ldots \wedge x_{i\,0}^{(e'_{i\,0})})$,

the disjunction being extended to all elements $\boldsymbol{e}'_i = (e'_{i\,n_i-1}, \ldots, e'_{i\,0})$ *of* $S^{(i)}$ *such that* $\boldsymbol{e}'_i \overset{i}{\equiv} \boldsymbol{e}_i$.

Proof. The point (a) is a direct consequence of the fact that

$$\boldsymbol{x} \equiv \boldsymbol{e} \quad \text{iff} \quad \boldsymbol{x}_{s-1} \overset{s-1}{\equiv} \boldsymbol{e}_{s-1} \quad \text{and} \quad \ldots \quad \text{and} \quad \boldsymbol{x}_0 \overset{0}{\equiv} \boldsymbol{e}_0,$$

while the point (b) is a simple translation of the definition. ■

We can now give a canonical representation for the ρ-symmetric discrete functions.

Theorem 13.7. Every ρ-symmetric discrete function f admits the following canonical representation:

$$f = \bigvee_{e \in \mathcal{E}'} [f_c(e) \wedge \sigma_e] \tag{13.4}$$

where f_c is the carrier of f.

Proof. Compute the value taken by the second member of (13.4) at point $\boldsymbol{x}$ of S and let $\boldsymbol{e}'$ be the unique member of $\mathcal{E}'$ equivalent to $\boldsymbol{x}$; then

$$\sigma_{e'}(\boldsymbol{x}) = r-1$$

and

$$\sigma_e(\boldsymbol{x}) = 0, \qquad \forall \boldsymbol{e} \neq \boldsymbol{e}'.$$

The second member of (13.4) thus takes the value $f_c(\boldsymbol{e}')$ at point $\boldsymbol{x}$; by definition of the carrier f_c of a ρ-symmetric discrete function f, and taking into account the equivalence of $\boldsymbol{x} \in S$ and $\boldsymbol{e}' \in \mathcal{E}'$, one obtains

$$f(\boldsymbol{x}) = f_c(\boldsymbol{e}') = \bigvee_{e \in \mathcal{E}'} [f_c(e) \wedge \sigma_e(\boldsymbol{x})]. \qquad \blacksquare$$

Let us now consider the particular case of totally symmetric discrete functions. We shall relate the n-variable elementary totally symmetric functions to the $(n-1)$-variable elementary totally symmetric functions. For that purpose one uses the following notations quite similar to those already introduced above:

$$\mathcal{E}_n = \{(e_{n-1}, \ldots, e_0) \in E^n \mid e_{n-1} \leqslant \ldots \leqslant e_0\},$$
$$\mathcal{E}'_n = \{\boldsymbol{e} \in \mathcal{E}_n \mid \exists\, \boldsymbol{e}' \in S_{n-1} \times \ldots \times S_0 \quad \text{such that} \quad \boldsymbol{e} \equiv \boldsymbol{e}'\},$$

where $\boldsymbol{e} \equiv \boldsymbol{e}'$ means that $\boldsymbol{e}$ and $\boldsymbol{e}'$ may be deduced from each other by a permutation of their components. One similarly defines $\mathcal{E}_{n-1}$ and $\mathcal{E}'_{n-1}$ as follows:

$$\mathcal{E}_{n-1} = \{(\epsilon_{n-2}, \ldots, \epsilon_0) \in E^{n-2} \mid \epsilon_{n-2} \leqslant \ldots \leqslant \epsilon_0\},$$
$$\mathcal{E}'_{n-1} = \{\epsilon \in \mathcal{E}_{n-1} \mid \exists\, \epsilon' \in S_{n-2} \times \ldots \times S_0 \quad \text{such that} \quad \epsilon \equiv \epsilon'\}.$$

In order to distinguish between the n-variable and the $(n-1)$-variable elementary totally symmetric functions, one uses notations like σ_e^n and σ_ϵ^{n-1}.

Theorem 13.8. The n-variable elementary totally symmetric functions are related to the (n−1)-variable elementary totally symmetric functions by the following relations:

$$\sigma^n_{(e_{n-1}, \ldots, e_0)} = \bigvee (x_{n-1}^{(e_i)} \wedge \sigma^{n-1}_{(e_{n-1}, \ldots, e_{i+1}, e_{i-1}, \ldots, e_0)}) \tag{13.5}$$

the disjunction being extended to all e_i such that

$$e_i \in S_{n-1}$$

and

$$(e_{n-1}, \ldots, e_{i+1}, e_{i-1}, \ldots, e_0) \in \mathcal{E}'_{n-1}.$$

Proof. First note that if $(e_{n-1}, \ldots, e_0)$ is in $\mathcal{E}_n$ then $(e_{n-1}, \ldots, e_{i+1}, e_{i-1}, \ldots, e_0)$ is in $\mathcal{E}_{n-1}$. The relation (13.5) is then a simple translation of the following fact:

The n-tuple $(x_{n-1}, \ldots, x_0)$ of $S_{n-1} \times \ldots \times S_0$ is a permutation of the n-tuple $(e_{n-1}, \ldots, e_0)$ of $\mathcal{E}'_n$ iff x_{n-1} is equal to some e_i and if the $(n-1)$-tuple $(x_{n-2}, \ldots, x_0)$ of $S_{n-2} \times \ldots \times S_0$ is a permutation of the $(n-1)$-tuple $(e_{n-1}, \ldots, e_{i+1}, e_{i-1}, \ldots, e_0)$ of $\mathcal{E}'_{n-1}$. ■

Let us now illustrate this last theorem by an example.

Example 13.2. We consider the case where

$$n = 3, m_2 = 4, m_1 = 3, m_0 = 2.$$

The sets $\mathcal{E}'_3$, $\mathcal{E}'_2$ and $\mathcal{E}'_1$ are described in Figure 13.5.

$\mathcal{E}'_3$:

0	0	0
0	0	1
0	0	2
0	0	3
0	1	1
0	1	2
0	1	3
0	2	2
0	2	3
1	1	1
1	1	2
1	1	3
1	2	2
1	2	3

$\mathcal{E}'_2$:

0	0
0	1
0	2
1	1
1	2

$\mathcal{E}'_1$:

0
1

Figure 13.5. The sets $\mathcal{E}'_3$, $\mathcal{E}'_2$ and $\mathcal{E}'_1$

Let us now write the recurrence relations of theorem 13.8 in this particular case:

$$\sigma^3_{000} = x_2^{(0)} \wedge \sigma^2_{00},$$

$$\sigma^3_{001} = (x_2^{(0)} \wedge \sigma^2_{01}) \vee (x_2^{(1)} \wedge \sigma^2_{00}),$$

$$\sigma^3_{002} = (x_2^{(0)} \wedge \sigma^2_{02}) \vee (x_2^{(2)} \wedge \sigma^2_{00}),$$

$$\sigma^3_{003} = x_2^{(3)} \wedge \sigma^2_{00},$$

$$\sigma^3_{011} = (x_2^{(0)} \wedge \sigma^2_{11}) \vee (x_2^{(1)} \wedge \sigma^2_{01}),$$
$$\sigma^3_{012} = (x_2^{(0)} \wedge \sigma^2_{12}) \vee (x_2^{(1)} \wedge \sigma^2_{02}) \vee (x_2^{(2)} \wedge \sigma^2_{01}),$$
$$\sigma^3_{013} = x_2^{(3)} \wedge \sigma^2_{01},$$
$$\sigma^3_{022} = x_2^{(2)} \wedge \sigma^2_{02},$$
$$\sigma^3_{023} = x_2^{(3)} \wedge \sigma^2_{02},$$
$$\sigma^3_{111} = x_2^{(1)} \wedge \sigma^2_{11},$$
$$\sigma^3_{112} = (x_2^{(1)} \wedge \sigma^2_{12}) \vee (x_2^{(2)} \wedge \sigma^2_{11}),$$
$$\sigma^3_{113} = x_2^{(3)} \wedge \sigma^2_{11},$$
$$\sigma^3_{122} = x_2^{(2)} \wedge \sigma^2_{12},$$
$$\sigma^3_{123} = x_2^{(3)} \wedge \sigma^2_{12},$$

$$\sigma^2_{00} = x_1^{(0)} \wedge \sigma^1_{0},$$
$$\sigma^2_{01} = (x_1^{(0)} \wedge \sigma^1_{1}) \vee (x_1^{(1)} \wedge \sigma^1_{0}),$$
$$\sigma_{02} = x_1^{(2)} \wedge \sigma^1_{0},$$
$$\sigma_{11} = x_1^{(1)} \wedge \sigma^1_{1},$$
$$\sigma_{12} = x_1^{(2)} \wedge \sigma^1_{1}.$$

The first group of relations yields the circuit of Figure 13.6.

13.2.2. The module structure

As noted above, every ρ-symmetric discrete function f is characterized by its characteristic vector $[f_c(\boldsymbol{e})]$, $\boldsymbol{e} \in \mathcal{E}'$, with r' components in L. By considering L as the ring of integers modulo-r one thus confers to the set of ρ-symmetric discrete functions the structure of L-module isomorphic to $L^{r'}$. It will be denoted $[L^{r'}]$.

Definition 13.5. For every $\boldsymbol{e}_i \in \mathcal{E}'_{n_i}$ let us define a function $\tilde{\sigma}_{\boldsymbol{e}_i}$ from $S^{(i)}$ to L:

$$\tilde{\sigma}_{\boldsymbol{e}_i}(\boldsymbol{x}_i) = 1 \quad \text{iff} \quad \boldsymbol{x}_i \overset{i}{\equiv} \boldsymbol{e}_i,$$
$$= 0 \text{ otherwise.}$$

For every $\boldsymbol{e} = (\boldsymbol{e}_{s-1}, \ldots, \boldsymbol{e}_0) \in \mathcal{E}'$ one defines the *Lagrange ρ-symmetric function* $\tilde{\sigma}_{\boldsymbol{e}}$ from S to L as follows:

$$\tilde{\sigma}_{\boldsymbol{e}}(\boldsymbol{x}) = 1 \quad \text{iff} \quad \boldsymbol{x} \equiv \boldsymbol{e},$$
$$= 0 \text{ otherwise.}$$

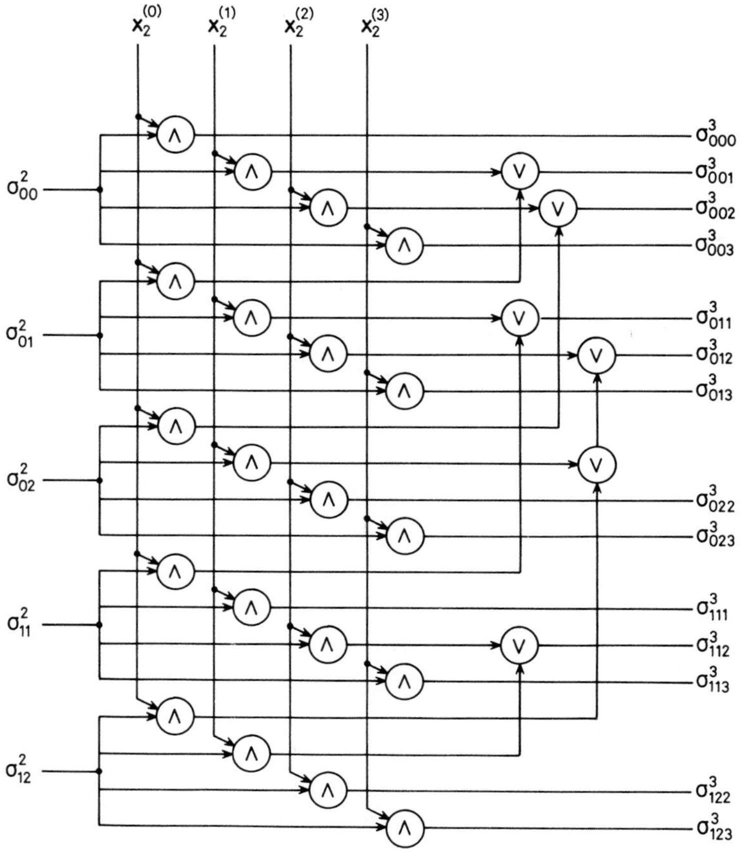

Figure 13.6. Realization of elementary symmetric functions

The following theorem gives two obvious properties of these functions; its proof is quite similar to that of theorem 13.6.

Theorem 13.9. For every $\boldsymbol{e} = (e_{s-1}, \ldots, e_0)$ *in* $\mathcal{E}'$ *and* $\boldsymbol{x} = (\boldsymbol{x}_{s-1}, \ldots, \boldsymbol{x}_0)$ *in* S *one has*

(a) $\tilde{\sigma}_{\boldsymbol{e}}(\boldsymbol{x}) = \tilde{\sigma}_{e_{s-1}}(\boldsymbol{x}_{s-1}) \ldots \tilde{\sigma}_{e_0}(\boldsymbol{x}_0)$;

(b) $\tilde{\sigma}_{e_i}(\boldsymbol{x}_i) = \sum \tilde{x}_{i\,n_i-1}^{(e'_{i\,n_i-1})} \ldots \tilde{x}_{i\,0}^{(e'_{i\,0})}$,

the sum being extended to all elements $\boldsymbol{e}'_i = (e'_{i\,n_i-1}, \ldots, e'_{i\,0})$ *of* $S^{(i)}$ *such that* $\boldsymbol{e}'_i \equiv \boldsymbol{e}_i$. ∎

The proof of the next theorem is similar to that of theorem 13.7.

Theorem 13.10. (Lagrange expansion for ρ-symmetric discrete functions.) Every ρ-symmetric discrete function f admits the following canonical representation:

$$f = \sum_{e \in \mathcal{E}'} f_c(e)\, \tilde{\sigma}_e,$$

where f_c is the carrier of f. ■

The theorem 13.8 also admits a counterpart; the relation 13.5 then becomes

$$\tilde{\sigma}^n_{(e_{n-1}, \ldots, e_0)} = \sum \tilde{x}^{(e_i)}_{n-1}\ \tilde{\sigma}^{n-1}_{(e_{n-1}, \ldots, e_{i+1}, e_{i-1}, \ldots, e_0)}.$$

In the sequel of this section we describe a method yielding bases for the module $[L^{r'}]$ of the ρ-symmetric functions that are deduced in a very natural way from bases of the module $[L^M]$, with $M = m_0 \times \ldots \times m_{n-1}$, of the discrete functions. In fact the basis of the Lagrange ρ-symmetric functions is already an example of the method.

Let us recall that E denotes the set union $S_{m_0} \cup \ldots \cup S_{m_{n-1}}$ that is

$$E = \{0, \ldots, m-1\}$$

with

$$m = \max(m_0, \ldots, m_{n-1}).$$

We now consider a basis

$$b_m = \{g_0, \ldots, g_{m-1}\}$$

of the module $[L^m]$ of the functions from E to L.

Every function g_j may also be restricted to a function from S_{m_i} to L, for every $j = 0, \ldots, m-1, i = 0, \ldots, n-1$. One does not use a new notation for the restriction of g_j to S_{m_i}.

In some cases it may arise that the set

$$b_{m_i} = \{g_0, \ldots, g_{m_i-1}\}$$

is a basis of the module $[L^{m_i}]$ of the functions from S_{m_i} to L or, more precisely, of the discrete functions that degenerate in all variables except x_i.

Let us quote two important cases:

Case 1. If $m_0 = \ldots = m_{n-1} = m$ that is in the case of logic functions.
Case 2. If the functions g_j have the following property:

$$e < j \Rightarrow g_j(e) = 0.$$

Indeed, every function f from S_{m_i} to L may be imbedded in a function f' from E to l defined as follows:

$f'(e) = f(e)$ for every $e \in \{0, \ldots, m_i - 1\}$,

$f'(e)$ is arbitrarily chosen for every $e \in \{m_i, \ldots, m-1\}$.

The function f' may then be represented in the basis b:

$$f' = \sum_{j=0}^{m-1} l_j g_j.$$

At every point e that lies in $\{0, \ldots, m_i - 1\}$ one has

$$g_j(e) = 0, \quad \forall j \geqslant m_i$$

and thus

$$f(e) = f'(e) = \sum_{j=0}^{m_i-1} l_j g_j(e).$$

The function f may thus be written under the form

$$f = \sum_{j=0}^{m_i-1} l_j g_j$$

where g_j stands in fact for the restriction of g_j to S_{m_i}.

Let us suppose that we are either in case 1 or in case 2. The set

$$b = \{g_e \mid e \in S\}$$

defined by the following Kronecker product

$$[g_e] = [g_{e_{n-1}}] \otimes \ldots \otimes [g_{e_0}]$$

where

$$[g_{e_i}] = [g_0 \ldots g_{m_i-1}]$$

is thus a basis of the module $[L^M]$.

The dual basis

$$b' = \{g'_e \mid e' \in S\}$$

is defined by the following Kronecker product

$$[g'_e] = [g'_{e_{n-1}}] \otimes \ldots \otimes [g'_{e_0}]$$

where

$$[g'_{e_i}] = [g'_0 \ldots g'_{m_i-1}]$$

and

$$b'_{m_i} = \{g'_0, \ldots, g'_{m_i-1}\}$$

is the dual basis of b_{m_i}.

Let A_i be the $(m_i \times m_i)$ matrix that relates the basis b_{m_i} to the Lagrange basis $\{\tilde{x}_i^{(0)}, \ldots, \tilde{x}_i^{(m_i-1)}\}$:

$$[g_{e_i}]^t = A_i [\tilde{x}_i^{(e_i)}]^t;$$

the coefficient of indices (e_i, e_i') in A_i is thus equal to $g_{e_i}(e_i')$, $\forall e_i$ and e_i' in S_{m_i}.

The inverse matrix A_i' relates the dual basis b_{m_i}' to the Lagrange basis; its coefficient of indices (e_i, e_i') is thus equal to $g_{e_i}'(e_i')$, $\forall e_i$ and e_i' in S_{m_i}.

It is important to note that if A_i is triangular, that is $g_{e_i}(e_i') = 0$ if $e_i' < e_i$, so is also A_i' that is $g_{e_i}'(e_i') = 0$ if $e_i' < e_i$.

The basis b is thus related to the Lagrange basis $\{\tilde{x}^{(e)} = \tilde{x}_{n-1}^{(e_{n-1})} \ldots \tilde{x}_0^{(e_0)} \mid e \in S\}$ by an $(M \times M)$ matrix A:

$$[g_e]^t = A\, [\tilde{x}^{(e)}]^t$$

where

$$A = A_{n-1} \oplus \ldots \oplus A_0.$$

The matrix A admits an inverse A' that relates the dual basis b' to the Lagrange basis:

$$[g_e']^t = A'\, [\tilde{x}^{(e)}]^t$$

where

$$A' = A_{n-1}' \otimes \ldots \otimes A_0'.$$

At this point it is important to note that if we are in case 2 above the various matrices A_i, A_i', A and A' are all triangular matrices.

In order to simplify the presentation of the theory, we first consider the case of totally symmetric functions.

Definition 13.6. For every ϵ in $\mathcal{E}_n'$ define the discrete functions γ_ϵ and γ_ϵ' as follows:

$$\gamma_\epsilon = \sum_{\substack{e \in S \\ e \equiv \epsilon}} g_e;$$

$$\gamma_\epsilon' = \sum_{\substack{e \in S \\ e \equiv \epsilon}} g_e'.$$

These functions will yield condensed canonical representations for symmetric discrete functions.

Theorem 13.11. The functions γ_ϵ and γ_ϵ' are totally symmetric discrete functions, for every ϵ in $\mathcal{E}_n'$.

Proof. One must prove that the following implication holds true:

if e' and e'' are two points of S such that $e' \equiv e''$,

then

$$\gamma_\epsilon(e') = \gamma_\epsilon(e'') \text{ and } \gamma'_\epsilon(e') = \gamma'_\epsilon(e'').$$

According to lemma 13.1 it suffices to prove the property in the case where e' and e'' may be deduced from each other by a simple transposition. Suppose for instance that

$$e' = (e'_{n-1}, \ldots, e'_2, e'_1, e'_0)$$

and

$$e'' = (e'_{n-1}, \ldots, e'_2, e'_0, e'_1).$$

We now prove that to every non-zero term appearing in

$$\sum_{\substack{e \in S \\ e \equiv \epsilon}} g_e(e') \tag{13.6}$$

corresponds an equal term in

$$\sum_{\substack{e \in S \\ e \equiv \epsilon}} g_e(e''). \tag{13.7}$$

Let us consider a term of (13.7):

$$g_{e_{n-1}}(e'_{n-1}) \ldots g_{e_2}(e'_2)\, g_{e_1}(e'_0)\, g_{e_0}(e'_1). \tag{13.8}$$

If $e_1 \in S_0$ and $e_0 \in S_1$, then the two points

$$(e_{n-1}, \ldots, e_2, e_1, e_0) \quad \text{and} \quad (e_{n-1}, \ldots, e_2, e_0, e_1)$$

both lie in S and are equivalent. Therefore the term

$$g_{e_{n-1}}(e'_{n-1}) \ldots g_{e_2}(e'_2)\, g_{e_0}(e'_1)\, g_{e_1}(e'_0) \tag{13.9}$$

appears in (13.6).

Suppose that $e_1 \notin S_0$. This is impossible in the case of logic functions. We are thus in the case 2 defined above, but then we may write successively

$$e_1 \notin S_0 \Rightarrow e_1 \geqslant m_0 \Rightarrow e_1 > e'_0 \Rightarrow g_{e_1}(e'_0) = 0;$$

the term of (13.7) under consideration is thus equal to zero. A similar reasoning yields the same conclusion if $e_0 \notin S_1$.

We have thus proven that every non-zero term of (13.6) is equal to a term of (13.7). Furthermore, the rule by which one has associated (13.9) to (13.8), i.e. a transposition of the two last factors, obviously defines a one-to-one mapping from the set of non-zero terms of (13.7) to the set of non-zero terms of (13.6).

A similar reasoning allows to construct a one-to-one mapping from the set of non-zero terms of (13.6) to the set of non-zero terms of (13.7). There is thus a bijection between the two sets of non-zero terms and thus

$$\gamma_\epsilon(e') = \gamma_\epsilon(e'').$$

A similar proof yields the second equality. ∎

Theorem 13.12. Every totally symmetric discrete function f admits the following canonical expansion:

$$f = \sum_{\epsilon \in \mathcal{E}_n'} l_\epsilon \gamma_\epsilon,$$

where

$$l_\epsilon = \sum_{e \in \mathcal{E}_n'} f_c(e)\, \gamma_e(\epsilon), \qquad \forall e \in \mathcal{E}_n'.$$

Proof. The function f admits the following representation in the basis b:

$$f = \sum_{e \in S} l_e g_e$$

where

$$l_e = \sum_{e' \in S} f(e')\, g_{e'}'(e).$$

Furthermore, since f is totally symmetric we may write:

$$l_e = \sum_{\epsilon \in \mathcal{E}_n'} f_c(\epsilon) \left[\sum_{\substack{e' \in S \\ e' \equiv \epsilon}} g_{e'}'(e) \right]$$

$$= \sum_{\epsilon \in \mathcal{E}_n'} f_c(\epsilon)\, \gamma_\epsilon'(e);$$

this proves in particular that

$$e' \equiv e'' \Rightarrow l_{e'} \equiv l_{e''}$$

since γ_ϵ' is totally symmetric (theorem 13.11).

The last implication allows us to write

$$f = \sum_{\epsilon \in \mathcal{E}_n'} l_\epsilon \left(\sum_{\substack{e \in S \\ e \equiv \epsilon}} g_e \right)$$

$$= \sum_{\epsilon \in \mathcal{E}_n'} l_\epsilon \gamma_\epsilon. \qquad \blacksquare$$

The set of functions $\{\gamma_\epsilon \mid \epsilon \in \mathcal{E}_n'\}$ is thus a basis of the module of the totally symmetric discrete functions. We now study the matrix transformations relating the bases of this kind. Let us introduce for that purpose three new notations:

$\Theta = [\theta_{\epsilon e}]$, with $\epsilon \in \mathcal{E}'_n$ and $e \in S$, is a matrix of type $(r' \times M)$ defined by

$$\theta_{\epsilon e} = 1 \quad \text{iff} \quad e \equiv \epsilon,$$
$$= 0 \text{ otherwise;}$$

ψ is a mapping from $\mathcal{E}'_n$ to S that associates with the element ϵ of $\mathcal{E}'_n$ one arbitrarily chosen element $\psi(\epsilon)$ of S that is equivalent to ϵ, that is, $\psi(\epsilon) \equiv \epsilon$;

$\Psi = [\psi_{e\,\epsilon}]$ is a matrix of type $(M \times r')$ defined by

$$\psi_{e\,\epsilon} = 1 \quad \text{iff} \quad e = \psi(\epsilon),$$
$$= 0 \text{ otherwise.}$$

With these new notations we may write:

$$[\gamma_\epsilon]^t = \Theta\,[g_e]^t;$$
$$[\gamma'_\epsilon]^t = \Theta\,[g'_e]^t;$$
$$[\tilde{\sigma}_\epsilon]^t = \Theta\,[\tilde{x}^{(e)}]^t;$$
$$[f_c(\epsilon)] = [f(e)]\,\Psi.$$

First prove the following lemma.

Lemma 13.2. If A is the matrix that relates the basis b of $[L^M]$ to the Lagrange basis, then

$$\Theta A = \Theta A \Psi \Theta.$$

Proof. The coefficient of indices (e, e') in A is equal to $g_e(e')$. The coefficient of indices (ϵ, e) in ΘA is thus equal to

$$\sum_{e' \in S} \theta_{\epsilon e'}\, g_{e'}(e)$$

i.e.

$$\sum_{\substack{e' \in S \\ e' \equiv \epsilon}} g_{e'}(e) = \gamma_\epsilon(e).$$

The coefficient of indices (ϵ, ϵ') in $(\Theta A)\Psi$ is equal to

$$\sum_{e \in S} \gamma_\epsilon(e)\, \psi_{e\,\epsilon'} = \gamma_\epsilon(\epsilon').$$

Finally, the coefficient of indices (ϵ, e) in $(\Theta A\,\Psi)\Theta$ is equal to

$$\sum_{\epsilon' \in \mathcal{E}'_n} \gamma_\epsilon(\epsilon')\theta_{\epsilon' e} = \gamma_\epsilon(\epsilon'')$$

where ϵ'' is the only element of $\mathcal{E}'_n$ equivalent to e; it is thus also equal to $\gamma_\epsilon(e)$, i.e. to the corresponding coefficient in ΘA. ■

Note that the preceding lemma also holds for the matrix A' since it relates the dual basis b' to the Lagrange basis.

We may now state the following theorem:

Theorem 13.13. If the basis $\{g_e \mid e \in S\}$ *of* $[L^M]$ *and the Lagrange basis are related by the relations*

$$[g_e]^t = A\,[\tilde{x}^{(e)}]^t \quad \textit{and} \quad [\tilde{x}^{(e)}]^t = A'\,[g_e]^t,$$

then the bases $\{\gamma_\epsilon \mid \epsilon \in \mathcal{E}'_n\}$ *and* $\{\tilde{\sigma}_\epsilon \mid \epsilon \in \mathcal{E}'_n\}$ *of* $[L^{r'}]$ *are related by the following relations:*

$$[\gamma_\epsilon]^t = (\Theta A \Psi)\,[\tilde{\sigma}_\epsilon]^t$$

and

$$[\tilde{\sigma}_\epsilon]^t = (\Theta A' \Psi)\,[\gamma_\epsilon]^t.$$

Proof. It suffices to write the following series of equalities

$$[\gamma_\epsilon]^t = \Theta\,[g_e]^t = \Theta A\,[\tilde{x}^{(e)}]^t = \Theta A\,\Psi\Theta\,[\tilde{x}^{(e)}]^t$$
$$= (\Theta A\,\Psi)\,[\tilde{\sigma}_\epsilon]^t.$$

A similar series of equalities yields the second relation. ■

Corollary. If the bases $\{g_e \mid e \in S\}$ *and* $\{G_e \mid e \in S\}$ *of* $[L^M]$ *are related by the relations*

$$[g_e]^t = B\,[G_e]^t \quad \textit{and} \quad [G_e]^t = B'\,[g_e]^t$$

then the corresponding bases $\{\gamma_\epsilon \mid \epsilon \in \mathcal{E}'_n\}$ *and* $\{\Gamma_\epsilon \mid \epsilon \in \mathcal{E}'_n\}$ *of* $[L^{r'}]$ *are related by the following relations:*

$$[\gamma_\epsilon]^t = (\Theta B\,\Psi)\,[\Gamma_\epsilon]^t \quad \textit{and} \quad [\Gamma_\epsilon]^t = (\Theta B'\,\Psi)\,[\gamma_\epsilon]^t.$$

Proof. The bases $\{g_e\}$ and $\{\tilde{x}^{(e)}\}$ are related by the matrices C and C'.

$$[g_e]^t = C\,[\tilde{x}^{(e)}]^t \quad \text{and} \quad [\tilde{x}^{(e)}]^t = C'\,[g_e]^t;$$

the bases $\{G_e\}$ and $\{\tilde{x}^{(e)}\}$ are related by the matrices D and D':

$$[G_e]^t = D\,[\tilde{x}^{(e)}]^t \quad \text{and} \quad [\tilde{x}^{(e)}]^t = D'\,[G_e]^t.$$

Therefore

$$B = CD' \quad \text{and} \quad B' = DC'.$$

From theorem 13.13 one deduces that

$$[\gamma_\epsilon]^t = (\Theta C \Psi)\,[\tilde{\sigma}_\epsilon]^t$$

and

$$[\tilde{\sigma}_\epsilon]^t = (\Theta D' \Psi)\, [\Gamma_\epsilon]^t;$$

hence

$$[\gamma_\epsilon]^t = (\Theta C \Psi \Theta) D' \Psi\, [\Gamma_\epsilon]^t,$$

and by lemma 13.2

$$[\gamma_\epsilon]^t = (\Theta C D' \Psi)\, [\Gamma_\epsilon]^t$$
$$= (\Theta B \Psi)\, [\Gamma_\epsilon]^t.$$

The second relation can be proven similarly. ■

It is important to note that the bases of Lagrange, Newton, Nyquist and Kodandapani that have been studied above in Chapter 4 are characterized by triangular transformation matrices; they are thus suitable for applying the theory presented in this section.

We now give an example.

Example 13.3. Let us consider the two functions s and c defined in Figure 13.7. They are the functions that realize the elementary cell of a ternary adder: s is the sum and c the carry. We are thus in the case where

$$n = 3, m_2 = m_1 = 3, m_0 = 2, r = 3.$$

x_2	x_1	x_0	s	c
0	0	0	0	0
0	0	1	1	0
0	1	0	1	0
0	1	1	2	0
0	2	0	2	0
0	2	1	0	1
1	0	0	1	0
1	0	1	2	0
1	1	0	2	0
1	1	1	0	1
1	2	0	0	1
1	2	1	1	1
2	0	0	2	0
2	0	1	0	1
2	1	0	0	1
2	1	1	1	1
2	2	0	1	1
2	2	1	2	1

Figure 13.7. The functions s and c

These functions are obviously totally symmetric. The carrier functions are described in Figure 13.8.

Choose the Newton basis

$$b_3 = \left\{\binom{x}{0}, \binom{x}{1}, \binom{x}{2}\right\}$$

for the module of the functions from {0, 1, 2} to {0, 1, 2}, and the Newton basis

$$b_2 = \left\{\binom{x}{0}, \binom{x}{1}\right\}$$

$\mathcal{E}'_3$	s_C	c_C
0 0 0	0	0
0 0 1	1	0
0 0 2	2	0
0 1 1	2	0
0 1 2	0	1
0 2 2	1	1
1 1 1	0	1
1 1 2	1	1
1 2 2	2	1

Figure 13.8. The functions s_C and c_C

for the module of the functions from {0, 1} to {0, 1, 2}.

We now compute the various matrices defined above:

$$A_2 = A_1 = \begin{bmatrix} 1 & 1 & 1 \\ 0 & 1 & 2 \\ 0 & 0 & 1 \end{bmatrix}, \qquad A_0 = \begin{bmatrix} 1 & 1 \\ 0 & 1 \end{bmatrix},$$

$$A'_2 = A'_1 = \begin{bmatrix} 1 & 2 & 1 \\ 0 & 1 & 1 \\ 0 & 0 & 1 \end{bmatrix}, \qquad A'_0 = \begin{bmatrix} 1 & 2 \\ 0 & 1 \end{bmatrix},$$

$$A = A_2 \otimes A_1 \otimes A_0 = \begin{bmatrix}
1&1&1&1&1&1&1&1&1&1&1&1&1&1&1&1&1&1\\
&1&&1&&1&&1&&1&&1&&1&&1&&1\\
&&1&1&2&2&&&1&1&2&2&&&1&1&2&2\\
&&&1&&2&&&&1&&2&&&&1&&2\\
&&&&1&1&&&&&1&1&&&&&1&1\\
&&&&&1&&&&&&1&&&&&&1\\
&&&&&&1&1&1&1&1&1&2&2&2&2&2&2\\
&&&&&&&1&&1&&1&&2&&2&&2\\
&&&&&&&&1&1&2&2&&&2&2&1&1\\
&&&&&&&&&1&&2&&&&2&&1\\
&&&&&&&&&&1&1&&&&&2&2\\
&&&&&&&&&&&1&&&&&&2\\
&&&&&&&&&&&&1&1&1&1&1&1\\
&&&&&&&&&&&&&1&&1&&1\\
&&&&&&&&&&&&&&1&1&2&2\\
&&&&&&&&&&&&&&&1&&2\\
&&&&&&&&&&&&&&&&1&1\\
&&&&&&&&&&&&&&&&&1
\end{bmatrix}$$

$$A' = A'_2 \otimes A'_1 \otimes A'_0 \quad \begin{bmatrix}
1&2&2&1&1&2&2&1&1&2&2&1&1&2&2&1&1&2\\
&1&&2&&1&&2&&1&&2&&1&&2&&1\\
&&1&2&1&2&&&2&1&2&1&&&1&2&1&2\\
&&&1&&1&&&&2&&2&&&&1&&1\\
&&&&1&2&&&&&2&1&&&&&1&2\\
&&&&&1&&&&&&2&&&&&&1\\
&&&&&&1&2&2&1&1&2&1&2&2&1&1&2\\
&&&&&&&1&&2&&1&&1&&2&&1\\
&&&&&&&&1&2&1&2&&&1&2&1&2\\
&&&&&&&&&1&&1&&&&1&&1\\
&&&&&&&&&&1&2&&&&&1&2\\
&&&&&&&&&&&1&&&&&&1\\
&&&&&&&&&&&&1&2&2&1&1&2\\
&&&&&&&&&&&&&1&&2&&1\\
&&&&&&&&&&&&&&1&2&1&2\\
&&&&&&&&&&&&&&&1&&1\\
&&&&&&&&&&&&&&&&1&2\\
&&&&&&&&&&&&&&&&&1
\end{bmatrix}$$

$\Theta =$

	000	001	010	011	020	021	100	101	110	111	120	121	200	201	210	211	220	221
000	1																	
001		1	1				1											
002					1								1					
011				1				1	1									
012						1					1			1	1			
022																	1	
111										1								
112												1				1		
122																		1

$\Psi^t =$

	000	001	010	011	020	021	100	101	110	111	120	121	200	201	210	211	220	221
000	1																	
001		1																
002					1													
011				1														
012						1												
022																	1	
111										1								
112												1						
122																		1

$$\Theta A \Psi = \begin{bmatrix} 1&1&1&1&1&1&1&1&1\\ 0&1&2&2&0&1&0&1&2\\ 0&0&1&0&1&2&0&1&2\\ 0&0&0&1&2&1&0&2&2\\ 0&0&0&0&1&1&0&2&0\\ 0&0&0&0&0&1&0&0&1\\ 0&0&0&0&0&0&1&2&1\\ 0&0&0&0&0&0&0&1&1\\ 0&0&0&0&0&0&0&0&1 \end{bmatrix} \qquad \Theta A'\Psi = \begin{bmatrix} 1&2&1&1&2&1&2&1&2\\ 0&1&1&1&0&2&0&2&2\\ 0&0&1&0&2&2&0&1&1\\ 0&0&0&1&1&1&0&2&1\\ 0&0&0&0&1&2&0&1&0\\ 0&0&0&0&0&1&0&0&2\\ 0&0&0&0&0&0&1&1&1\\ 0&0&0&0&0&0&0&1&2\\ 0&0&0&0&0&0&0&0&1 \end{bmatrix}$$

The functions $\gamma_{e_2 e_1 e_0}$, with e_2 and $e_1 \in \{0, 1, 2\}$ and $e_0 \in \{0, 1\}$ are defined by the following relation:

$$[\gamma_{e_2 e_1 e_0}]^t = \Theta \left[\binom{x_2}{e_2} \binom{x_1}{e_1} \binom{x_0}{e_0} \right]^t;$$

they are related to the Lagrange functions by the matrix $\Theta A\,\Psi$:

$$[\gamma_{e_2 e_1 e_0}]^t = (\Theta A\,\Psi)\,[\tilde{\sigma}_{e_2 e_1 e_3}]^t.$$

The functions s and c may be represented as follows:

$$s = \{[s_c(\epsilon)]\,(\Theta A'\Psi)\}\;[\gamma_{e_2 e_1 e_0}]^t, \qquad (13.10)$$

and

$$c = \{[c_c(\epsilon)]\,(\Theta A'\Psi)\}\;[\gamma_{e_2 e_1 e_0}]^t,$$

with $\epsilon \in \mathcal{E}'_3$;

$$[s_c(\epsilon)] = [0\ 1\ 2\ 2\ 0\ 1\ 0\ 1\ 2],$$

$$[c_c(\epsilon)] = [0\ 0\ 0\ 0\ 1\ 1\ 1\ 1\ 1],$$

$$[s_c(\epsilon)]\,(\Theta A'\,\Psi) = [0\ 1\ 0\ 0\ 0\ 0\ 0\ 0\ 0],$$

$$[c_c(\epsilon)]\,(\Theta A'\,\Psi) = [0\ 0\ 0\ 0\ 1\ 0\ 1\ 0\ 0],$$

and one deduces so the following expressions for s and c:

$$s = \gamma_{001} = \binom{x_2}{0}\binom{x_1}{0}\binom{x_0}{1} \oplus \binom{x_2}{0}\binom{x_1}{1}\binom{x_0}{0} \oplus \binom{x_2}{1}\binom{x_1}{0}\binom{x_0}{0}$$

(this is quite obvious since $\binom{x}{0} = 1$ and $\binom{x}{1} = x$);

$$c = \gamma_{012} \oplus \gamma_{111} = \binom{x_2}{0}\binom{x_1}{2}\binom{x_0}{1} \oplus \binom{x_2}{1}\binom{x_1}{2}\binom{x_0}{0} \oplus \binom{x_2}{2}\binom{x_1}{0}\binom{x_0}{1} \oplus$$

$$\binom{x_2}{2}\binom{x_1}{1}\binom{x_0}{0} \oplus \binom{x_2}{1}\binom{x_1}{1}\binom{x_0}{1}.$$

This example shows the advantage of taking into account the symmetries of a function when computing expansions like the Newton expansion. In fact, the Newton expansion of a function like s, is given by the following expression

$$s = \{[s(e_2, e_1, e_0)]\,A'\}\left[\binom{x_2}{e_2}\binom{x_1}{e_1}\binom{x_0}{e_0}\right]^t,$$

in which A' is a (18×18) matrix.

The same result is achieved by using the relation (13.10) in which $(\Theta A\,\Psi)$ is a (9×9) matrix.

Nevertheless, this procedure may only be applied in the case where one uses the same Newton basis for each variable.

We now turn back to the case of ρ-symmetric discrete functions. We shall not describe in detail the module of the ρ-symmetric discrete functions; indeed the generalization of the theory developed above for totally symmetric functions is almost trivial, thanks to the properties of the Kronecker product, but would require the introduction of rather heavy notations. Let us give some indications:

From theorems 13.9 and 13.10 one deduces that the set of Lagrange ρ-symmetric functions

$$\{\tilde{\sigma}_e \mid e \in \mathcal{E}'\}$$

is a basis of the module of the ρ-symmetric discrete functions, and that

$$[\tilde{\sigma}_e] = [\tilde{\sigma}_{e_{s-1}}] \otimes \ldots \otimes [\tilde{\sigma}_{e_0}].$$

Furthermore, the functions $\tilde{\sigma}_{e_i}$ can be considered as Lagrange totally symmetric functions depending on the n_i variables $x_{i\,0}, \ldots, x_{i\,n_i-1}$.

Let us now suppose that for every $i = 0, \ldots, s-1$ we have obtained a new basis

$$\{\delta_{e_i}^{(i)} \mid e_i \in \mathcal{E}'_{n_i}\}$$

for the module of the n_i-variable totally symmetric discrete functions. That new basis is related to the Lagrange basis by the matrices $A^{(i)}$ and $(A^{(i)})'$:

$$[\delta_{e_i}^{(i)}]^t = A^{(i)}\,[\tilde{\sigma}_{e_i}]^t \quad \text{and} \quad [\tilde{\sigma}_{e_i}]^t = (A^{(i)})'\,[\delta_{e_i}^{(i)}]^t.$$

One may thus construct a new basis of the module of the ρ-symmetric discrete functions; it is defined by a Kronecker product:

$$[\delta_e] = [\delta_{e_{s-1}}] \otimes \ldots \otimes [\delta_{e_0}].$$

The new basis is related to the Lagrange basis by the matrices $A = A^{(s-1)} \otimes \ldots \otimes A^{(0)}$ and $A' = (A^{(s-1)})' \otimes \ldots \otimes (A^{(0)})'$:

$$[\delta_e]^t = A\,[\tilde{\sigma}_e]^t \quad \text{and} \quad [\tilde{\sigma}_e]^t = A'\,[\delta_e]^t.$$

Let us recall that every matrix $A^{(i)}$ is of the type:

$$A^{(i)} = \Theta\,(A_{i\,n_i-1} \otimes \ldots \otimes A_{i\,0})\,\Psi.$$

13.3. Imbedding in a totally symmetric function

It is well known that any n-variable switching function can be represented as a totally symmetric function of at most 2^n-1 variables; see for instance Yau and Tang [1971a]. This property is now generalized to discrete functions.

Let us again consider a partition $\rho = (\boldsymbol{x}_{s-1}, \ldots, \boldsymbol{x}_0)$ of $\{x_0, \ldots, x_{n-1}\}$, with $\boldsymbol{x}_i = (x_{i\,n_i-1}, \ldots, x_{i\,0})$, $\forall i = 0, \ldots, n-1$. Every integer y that lies between 0 and $N-1$, where

$$N = (n_0 + 1) \times \ldots \times (n_{s-1} + 1),$$

admits a unique representation under the form

$$y = y_0 w_0 + \ldots + y_{s-1}\, w_{s-1},$$

with

$$w_0 = 1, w_1 = n_0 + 1, \ldots, w_{s-1} = (n_0 + 1) \times \ldots \times (n_{s-2} + 1),$$

and

$$0 \leqslant y_i \leqslant n_i, \quad \forall i = 0, \ldots, s-1;$$

this is the representation of y in basis $(n_0 + 1, \ldots, n_{s-1} + 1)$: see section 1.5.1.

We now introduce two new notations. Given a variable x_{ij} that takes its values in S_{ij}, then $\boldsymbol{x}_{ij}$ is a row vector with w_i identical components while $\boldsymbol{S}_{ij}$ is the Cartesian product of w_i identical sets:

$$\boldsymbol{x}_{ij} = (x_{ij}, \ldots, x_{ij}) \text{ and } \boldsymbol{S}_{ij} = S_{ij} \times \ldots \times S_{ij}.$$

Note in particular that $\boldsymbol{x}_{0j} = x_{0j}$ and $\boldsymbol{S}_{0j} = S_{0j}$, for every $j = 0, \ldots, n_0 - 1$. Our aim is to associate with every ρ-symmetric discrete function f a function

$$g: \boldsymbol{S} = \boldsymbol{S}^{(s-1)} \times \ldots \times \boldsymbol{S}^{(0)} \to L,$$

where

$$\boldsymbol{S}^{(i)} = \boldsymbol{S}_{i\, n_i - 1} \times \ldots \times \boldsymbol{S}_{i\, 0},$$

that has the two following properties:

(a) g is totally symmetric;
(b) $g(\boldsymbol{x}_{s-1\; n_{s-1}-1}, \ldots, \boldsymbol{x}_{s-1\; 0}, \ldots, \boldsymbol{x}_{0\; n_0-1}, \ldots, \boldsymbol{x}_{0\; 0})$
$= f(x_{s-1\; n_{s-1}-1}, \ldots, x_{s-1\; 0}, \ldots, x_{0\; n_0-1}, \ldots, x_{0\; 0})$.

Note that g depends upon $n_0 w_0 + \ldots + n_{s-1} w_{s-1} = N - 1$ variables.

The following lemma shows that the two preceding properties are compatible.

Lemma 13.3. If $\boldsymbol{A} = (\boldsymbol{a}_{s-1\; n_{s-1}-1}, \ldots, \boldsymbol{a}_{s-1\; 0}, \ldots, \boldsymbol{a}_{0\; n_0-1}, \ldots, \boldsymbol{a}_{0\; 0})$ *and* $\boldsymbol{B} = (\boldsymbol{b}_{s-1\; n_{s-1}-1}, \ldots, \boldsymbol{b}_{s-1\; 0}, \ldots, \boldsymbol{b}_{0\; n_0-1}, \ldots, \boldsymbol{b}_{0\; 0})$ *are two points of* $\boldsymbol{S}$ *that can be deduced from each other by a permutation of their components, then the corresponding points* $\boldsymbol{a} = (a_{s-1\; n_{s-1}-1}, \ldots, a_{s-1\; 0}, \ldots, a_{0\; n_0-1}, \ldots, a_{0\; 0})$ *and* $\boldsymbol{b} = (b_{s-1\; n_{s-1}-1}, \ldots, b_{s-1\; 0}, \ldots, b_{0\; n_0-1}, \ldots, b_{0\; 0})$ *of* S *can be deduced from each other by a permutation of their components that acts inside the blocks of* ρ.

Proof. Let us denote by $\alpha_i(e)$ and $\beta_i(e)$ the number of occurrences of $e \in (S_{i\, n_i-1} \cup \ldots \cup S_{i\, 0})$ among $\boldsymbol{a}_i = (a_{i\, n_i-1}, \ldots, a_{i\, 0})$ and $\boldsymbol{b}_i = (b_{i\, n_i-1}, \ldots, b_{i\, 0})$, respectively.

The number of occurrences of e among $\boldsymbol{A}$ is thus

$$\alpha_{s-1}(e)\, w_{s-1} + \ldots + \alpha_0(e)\, w_0,$$

and the number of occurrences of e among $\boldsymbol{B}$ is

$$\beta_{s-1}(e)\, w_{s-1} + \ldots + \beta_0(e)\, w_0;$$

since furthermore $\boldsymbol{A}$ and $\boldsymbol{B}$ can be deduced from each other by a permutation of their components, they both contain the same number of occurrences of e, that is

$$\alpha_{s-1}(e)\, w_{s-1} + \ldots + \alpha_0(e)\, w_0 = \beta_{s-1}(e)\, w_{s-1} + \ldots + \beta_0(e)\, w_0,$$

with

$$0 \leqslant \alpha_i(e) \leqslant n_i \quad \text{and} \quad 0 \leqslant \beta_i(e) \leqslant n_i, \qquad \text{for every } i = 0, \ldots, s-1.$$

By definition of the numeration system in basis $(n_0 + 1, \ldots, n_{s-1} + 1)$ one concludes that

$$\alpha_i(e) = \beta_i(e), \qquad \text{for every } i = 0, \ldots, s-1.$$

Since this holds for every e in $S_{i\,n_i-1} \cup \ldots \cup S_{i\,0}$, one may conclude that a_i and b_i only differ by a permutation of their components, for every $i = 0, \ldots, s-1$. ■

The set $\boldsymbol{S}$ can be divided in equivalence classes: two points of $\boldsymbol{S}$ are equivalent iff they differ by a permutation of their components. The function g is defined as follows:

(a) If $\boldsymbol{A} \in \boldsymbol{S}$ and $\boldsymbol{a} \in S$ are defined as in lemma 13.3, then g takes the value $f(\boldsymbol{a})$ at all the points of the equivalence class containing $\boldsymbol{A}$. As proven by lemma 13.3 there is no ambiguity in that definition.

(b) If an equivalence class of $\boldsymbol{S}$ does not contain any point like $\boldsymbol{A}$, the function g takes a same arbitrarily chosen value at all the points of the class.

The main result of this section is summarized by the following theorem.

Theorem 13.14. If f is a ρ-symmetric discrete function, with $\rho = (\boldsymbol{x}_{s-1}, \ldots, \boldsymbol{x}_0)$ and $\boldsymbol{x}_i = (x_{i\,n_i-1}, \ldots, x_{i\,0})$ for every $i = 0, \ldots, s-1$, then it can be represented by a totally symmetric discrete function of $N-1$ variables where $N = (n_0 + 1) \times \ldots \times (n_{s-1} + 1)$. ■

Remark. If f has no partial symmetry, that is if ρ is the trivial partition in n blocks, then $n_i = 1$ for every $i = 0, \ldots, n-1$, and $N = 2^n$. Any n-variable discrete function can thus be imbedded in a totally symmetric discrete function of at most $2^n - 1$ variables.

Example 13.4. Let us consider the case where $n = 2, m_1 = 2, m_0 = 3, r = 6$. The Figures 13.9 and 13.10 describe a function $f(x_1, x_0)$ and the totally symmetric function $g(y_2, y_1, y_0)$ associated with f. The value taken by α may be arbitrarily chosen. One can easily verify that

$$f(x_1, x_0) = g(x_1, x_1, x_0).$$

Note that one could also define a totally symmetric function $h(z_2, z_1, z_0)$ such that

$$f(x_1, x_0) = h(x_1, x_0, x_0);$$

x_1	x_0	f
0	0	0
0	1	1
0	2	2
1	0	3
1	1	4
1	2	5

Figure 13.9. The function f

y_2	y_1	y_0	g
0	0	0	0
0	0	1	1
0	0	2	2
0	1	0	1
0	1	1	3
0	1	2	α
1	0	0	1
1	0	1	3
1	0	2	α
1	1	0	3
1	1	1	4
1	1	2	5

Figure 13.10. The totally symmetric function g

the truth table of h would have 18 rows instead of 12 for g. Hence one observes the advantage of according the smallest weights to the variables having the greatest numbers of possible states.

13.4. Detection of the symmetries

As it has been seen in section 13.1, the problem of finding the symmetries of a discrete function f is reduced to that of finding the classes induced by the relation $R(f)$. The knowledge of the maximal compatibility classes of $R(f)$ then allows to find all the partitions such that f is ρ-symmetric: see theorem 13.2 and its corollary.

The first point of any symmetry detection method is thus to define $R(f)$; for that purpose one must be able to check whether a pair (x_k, x_l) is in $R(f)$ that is whether the function f has the partial symmetry $x_k \sim x_l$.

The second point of the method then consists in finding the maximal compatibility classes of $R(f)$. It remains to look for the maximal partitions of the set of variables that are composed of blocks each of which is included in at least one maximal compatibility class of $R(f)$.

One obtains in that way all the maximal partitions ρ such that f is ρ-symmetric.

The main point of the method is thus the finding of all the compatible pairs (x_k, x_l). This problem has been studied by several authors in the case of switching functions. Let us quote some of them: Davio, Thayse and Bioul [1972] have proposed a method based on the computation of the Fourier transform. Mukhopadhyay [1963] has described a method using decomposition charts. Another method due to Das and Sheng [1971] is based on the computation of subfunctions. Yau and Tang [1971b] have described a method for identifying the redundant variables and the partial symmetries of a switching function.

Some other authors have developed algorithms that allow us to decide whether a switching function is totally symmetric or not. Let us again quote some of them: Caldwell [1958], McCluskey [1956a], Marcus [1962], Sheng [1965], Kostopoulos [1975].

Very little has been written on symmetry detection in the case of discrete functions. It is likely however that many efficient methods for switching functions will be generalized in the future to the case of logic and discrete functions. We do not intend to perform here that work of generalization and rather consider that this is still an open problem that certainly deserves the attention of the scientists in the field of discrete mathematics and multiple valued logic.

Let us however state a theorem that, along with its corollary, suggests a method for checking whether a given discrete function f has the partial symmetry $x_k \sim x_l$. It uses the differential operators $\Delta/\Delta x$ (difference) and S/Sx (sensitivity) introduced in Chapters 4 and 7 respectively.

Theorem 13.15. The discrete function f has the partial symmetry $x_k \sim x_l$ iff

$$\left(\frac{S^k f}{Sx_k} - \frac{S^k f}{Sx_l}\right)_{x_k=x_l=e} = 0$$

for every k and e in $S_k \cap S_l$.

Proof. The condition is necessary by symmetry. It is sufficient: consider two points e_k and e_l that both lie in $S_k \cap S_l$; suppose furthermore that $e_l \geqslant e_k$. Thus

$$0 \leqslant h = e_l - e_k \leqslant e_l \in S_k \cap S_l;$$

therefore

$$h \in S_k \cap S_l.$$

We may successively write:

$$\begin{aligned}
f(\ldots, e_l, \ldots, e_k, \ldots) &= f(\ldots, e_k \oplus h, \ldots, e_k, \ldots) \\
&= f(\ldots, e_k, \ldots, e_k, \ldots) \oplus \left(\frac{S^h f}{Sx_l}\right)_{x_k=x_l=e_k} \\
&= f(\ldots, e_k, \ldots, e_k, \ldots) \oplus \left(\frac{S^h f}{Sx_k}\right)_{x_k=x_l=e_k} \\
&= f(\ldots, e_k, \ldots, e_k \oplus h, \ldots) \\
&= f(\ldots, e_k, \ldots, e_l, \ldots).
\end{aligned}$$

■

Corollary. The logic function f has the partial symmetry $x_k \sim x_l$ iff

$$\left(\frac{\Delta^h f}{\Delta x_k} - \frac{\Delta^h f}{\Delta x_l}\right)_{x_k = x_l = e} = 0$$

for every h and e in $S_k \cap S_l$.

Proof. The condition is necessary by symmetry. It is sufficient by theorem 13.15 since

$$\left(\frac{S^h f}{S x_k}\right)_{x_k = e} = \sum_{h'=1}^{h} \left(\frac{\Delta^{h'} f}{\Delta x_k}\right)_{x_k = e} \binom{h}{h'}$$

$$= \sum_{h'=1}^{h} \left(\frac{\Delta^{h'} f}{\Delta x_l}\right)_{x_l = e} \binom{h}{h'}$$

$$= \left(\frac{S^h f}{S x_l}\right)_{x_l = e},$$

for every h and e in $S_k \cap S_l$. ■

We also state a very classical theorem on totally symmetric logic functions. Its proof is similar to that of the corresponding theorem for switching functions (see for instance Harrison [1965]).

Theorem 13.16. A logic function f is totally symmetric iff

(a) $f(x_{n-1}, \ldots, x_2, x_1, x_0) = f(x_{n-1}, \ldots, x_2, x_0, x_1)$,
(b) $f(x_{n-1}, x_{n-2}, x_{n-3}, \ldots, x_1, x_0) = f(x_{n-1}, x_0, x_{n-2}, \ldots, x_2, x_1)$. ■

An important remark is due now. All along in this chapter we have never considered the possibility that a function be symmetric after some change of variables have been performed. In the case of switching functions this remark yields the concept of symmetry centre and the definition of partial symmetries like $x_k \sim x_l$.

We conclude this section by giving a generalized definition of the partial symmetry in the case of logic functions. This new definition covers a.o. the notion of *mixed symmetric logic function* (S. Lee and E. Lee [1972]).

Let us consider a group G of permutation acting on the set $\{0, \ldots, m-1\}$; it is thus a subgroup of the group S_m of all the permutations of $\{0, \ldots, m-1\}$. We shall use the prefixed notation $x\pi$ for the image of $x \in \{0, \ldots, m-1\}$ by $\pi \in G$.

Definition 13.7. Given two permutations π_k and π_l of G, a logic function f has the partial symmetry

$$x_k \pi_k \sim x_l \pi_l$$

iff

$$f(x_{n-1}, \ldots, x_l \pi_l, \ldots, x_k \pi_k, \ldots, x_0) = f(x_{n-1}, \ldots, x_k \pi_l, \ldots, x_l \pi_k, \ldots, x_0).$$

Lemma 13.4. If a logic function f has the partial symmetry $x_k \pi_k \sim x_l \pi_l$, then for every π in G it has also the symmetry $x_k(\pi\pi_k) \sim x_l(\pi\pi_l)$.

Proof. Putting $y_k = x_k\pi$ and $y_l = x_l\pi$ we may write:

$$\begin{aligned} f(\ldots, x_l(\pi\pi_l), \ldots, x_k(\pi\pi_k), \ldots) &= f(\ldots, y_l\pi_l, \ldots, y_k\pi_k, \ldots) \\ &= f(\ldots, y_k\pi_l, \ldots, y_l\pi_k, \ldots) \\ &= f(\ldots, x_k(\pi\pi_l), \ldots, x_l(\pi\pi_k), \ldots). \end{aligned}$$ ■

Note in particular that if f has the symmetry $x_k \pi_k \sim x_l \pi_l$, it has also the symmetries

$$x_k \sim x_l(\pi_k^{-1}\ \pi_l) \quad \text{and} \quad x_k(\pi_l^{-1}\pi_k) \sim x_l.$$

Lemma 13.5. If a logic function f has the two partial symmetries $x_j \sim x_k \pi_k$ and $x_k \sim x_l \pi_l$, then it has also the partial symmetry $x_j \sim x_l(\pi_k \pi_l)$.

Proof. Since f has the partial symmetry $x_k \sim x_l \pi_l$, we may write

$$f[\ldots, (x_l\pi_k)\,\pi_l, \ldots, x_k, \ldots, x_j, \ldots] = f(\ldots, x_k\pi_l, \ldots, x_l\pi_k, \ldots, x_j, \ldots); \tag{13.11}$$

from the partial symmetry $x_j \sim x_k \pi_k$ one deduces:

$$f(\ldots, x_k\pi_l, \ldots, x_l\pi_k, \ldots, x_j, \ldots) = f(\ldots, x_k\pi_l, \ldots, x_j\pi_k, \ldots, x_l, \ldots); \tag{13.12}$$

by using again the partial symmetry $x_k \sim x_l \pi_l$ one obtains:

$$f(\ldots, x_k\pi_l, \ldots, x_j\pi_k, \ldots, x_l, \ldots) = f[\ldots, (x_j\pi_k)\,\pi_l, \ldots, x_k, \ldots, x_l, \ldots]; \tag{13.13}$$

combining (13.11), (13.12) and (13.13) yields

$$f[\ldots, x_l(\pi_k\pi_l), \ldots, x_k, \ldots, x_j, \ldots] = f[\ldots, x_j(\pi_k\pi_l), \ldots, x_k, \ldots, x_l, \ldots]$$

that is

$$x_j \sim x_l(\pi_k\pi_l).$$ ■

We now give the definition of a new binary relation on the set of variables.

Definition 13.8. Given a logic function f and a group G of permutations, one defines the binary relation $R(f, G)$ on the set $\{x_0, \ldots, x_{n-1}\}$ as follows:

(a) $(x_j, x_j) \in R(f, G), \quad \forall j = 0, \ldots, n-1;$
(b) if $k \neq l$ then $(x_k, x_l) \in R(f, G)$ iff there exists a permutation π in G such that f has the partial symmetry $x_k \sim x_l \pi$.

Theorem 13.17. For any logic function f and for any group G the binary relation R(f, G) is an equivalence relation.

Proof. (a) The relation is reflexive by definition.

(b) It is symmetric: if f has the partial symmetry $x_k \sim x_l\pi$, it has also the partial symmetry $x_l \sim x_k\pi^{-1}$.

(c) It is transitive: suppose that f has the two partial symmetries $x_j \sim x_k\pi$ and $x_k \sim x_l\pi'$; by lemma 13.5 it has also the partial symmetry $x_j \sim x_l(\pi\pi')$. ∎

Definition 13.9. With the equivalence $R(f, G)$ is associated a partition ρ of the set $\{x_0, \ldots, x_{n-1}\}$. The function f is then a *generalized ρ-symmetric function* (with respect to G).

Let us now suppose as above that

$$\rho = (\boldsymbol{x}_{s-1}, \ldots, \boldsymbol{x}_0)$$

with

$$\boldsymbol{x}_i = (x_{i\,n_i-1}, \ldots, x_{i\,0}), \qquad \forall i = 0, \ldots, s-1.$$

We now state the main theorem concerning the generalized ρ-symmetric functions.

Theorem 13.18. If f is a generalized ρ-symmetric logic function, then there exists an n-tuple $(\pi_{n-1}, \ldots, \pi_0)$ of permutations belonging to G such that the function $f(x_{n-1}\,\pi_{n-1}, \ldots, x_0\,\pi_0)$ is ρ-symmetric.

Proof. Let us consider the block $\boldsymbol{x}_i$ of ρ. By definition of the partition ρ one has:

$$(x_{i\,0}, x_{ij}) \in R(f, G), \qquad \forall j = 1, \ldots, n_i-1;$$

thus for every j in $1, \ldots, n_i-1$ there exists π_{ij} in G such that

$$x_{i\,0} \sim x_{ij}\,\pi_{ij}.$$

The function

$$f(\boldsymbol{x}_{s-1}, \ldots, x_{i\,n_i-1}\,\pi_{i\,n_i-1}, \ldots, x_{i\,1}\,\pi_{i\,1}, x_{i\,0}, \ldots, \boldsymbol{x}_0)$$

has the partial symmetry

$$x_{i\,0} \sim x_{ij}$$

for every $j = 1, \ldots, n_i-1$, and thus, according to lemma 13.5 it has the partial symmetry

$$x_{ik} \sim x_{il}$$

for every k and l in $\{0, \ldots, n_i-1\}$.

Performing that construction for all blocks completes the proof. ∎

Note that in the construction described above one has in fact associated the unit element of G with every variable $x_{i\,0}$, $\forall i = 0, \ldots, s-1$. One may obviously associate any other element of G with $x_{i\,0}$. The number of suitable n-tuples of permutations is thus at least equal to $(\#G)^s$.

We now give some examples of permutation groups.

The m permutations $\{\alpha_0, \alpha_1, \ldots, \alpha_{m-1}\}$ defined by

$$x\alpha_i = x \oplus i \text{ modulo-}m, \qquad \forall x \in \{0, \ldots, m-1\},$$

form a group of permutations. If f is a generalized ρ-symmetric logic function with respect to that group of permutations, then there exists an n-tuple $(e_{n-1}, \ldots, e_0)$ of elements of $\{0, \ldots, m-1\}$ such that the function

$$f(x_{n-1} \oplus e_{n-1}, \ldots, x_0 \oplus e_0)$$

is ρ-symmetric. The point $(e_{n-1}, \ldots, e_0)$ is called the *symmetry centre* of the function. The number of different symmetry centres is at least equal to m^s.

The generalized totally symmetric logic functions with respect to that group are called *mixed symmetric logic functions* (S. Lee and E. Lee [1972]).

Another example is given by the two-element group of permutations $\{\beta_0, \beta_1\}$ where

$$x\beta_0 = x \text{ and } x\beta_1 = \bar{x} = (m-1)-x, \qquad \forall x \in \{0, \ldots, m-1\}.$$

If f is a generalized ρ-symmetric logic function with respect to that group, then there exists an n-tuple $(j_{n-1}, \ldots, j_0)$ of elements of $\{0, 1\}$ such that the function

$$f(x_{n-1}\,\beta_{j_{n-1}}, \ldots, x_0\,\beta_{j_0})$$

is ρ-symmetric. One then say that f is ρ-symmetric with the *polarity* $(j_{n-1}, \ldots, j_0)$. The number of different polarities is at least equal to 2^s.

Note that the two groups coincide in the case where $m = 2$.

A third example is obtained by combining the two concepts of symmetry centre and polarity. Let us first note that

$$\beta_1\alpha_i = \alpha_{m-i}\beta_1, \qquad \forall i = 1, \ldots, m-1; \tag{13.14}$$

furthermore, in the case where $m \geqslant 3$, we prove the following lemma.

Lemma 13.6. If $\alpha_i\beta_j = \alpha_{i'}\beta_{j'}$, with i and i' in $\{0, \ldots, m-1\}$, j and j' in $\{0, 1\}$, then $i = i'$ and $j = j'$.

Proof. If

$$\alpha_i\beta_j = \alpha_{i'}\beta_{j'}$$

then

$$(\alpha_{i'})^{-1}\alpha_i = \beta_{j'}(\beta_j)^{-1};$$

furthermore, there exists i'' in $\{0, \ldots, m-1\}$ and j'' in $\{0, 1\}$ such that

$$(\alpha_{i'})^{-1}\alpha_i = \alpha_{i''},$$
$$\beta_{j'}(\beta_j)^{-1} = \beta_{j''},$$

and

$$\alpha_{i''} = \beta_{j''}.$$

If $j'' = 0$ it is obvious that i'' must also be equal to 0; but then

$$\alpha_i = \alpha_{i'} \text{ and } \beta_j = \beta_{j'}, \quad \text{i.e. } i = i' \text{ and } j = j'.$$

If $j'' = 1$, then

$$\alpha_{i''} = \beta_1;$$

hence

$$i'' = 0\,\alpha_{i''} = 0\beta_1 = m-1,$$

and thus

$$0 = 1\,\alpha_{m-1} = 1\beta_1 = m-2,$$

but this is impossible in the case where $m \geqslant 3$. ■

From (13.14) and from the preceding lemma, we conclude that in the case where $m \geqslant 3$ the set

$$\{\alpha_i\beta_j \mid i \in \{0, \ldots, m-1\} \text{ and } j \in \{0, 1\}\}$$

is a permutation group acting on $\{0, \ldots, m-1\}$. If f is a generalized ρ-symmetric logic function with respect to that group, then there exists a symmetry centre $(e_{n-1}, \ldots, e_0)$ and a polarity $(j_{n-1}, \ldots, j_0)$ such that the function

$$f[(x_{n-1} \oplus e_{n-1})\,\beta_{j_{n-1}}, \ldots, (x_0 \oplus e_0)\,\beta_{j_0}].$$

is ρ-symmetric.

Conclude this section by noting that the problem of symmetry detection becomes very difficult to solve in the frame of that general, but rather natural definition. However, a positive result is already provided by theorem 13.17; it proves that the main point of any detection method is to find a number of pairs of $R(f, G)$ that along with the knowledge that $R(f, G)$ is an equivalence relation allow to find the associated partition ρ.

13.5. Cellular synthesis

In this section, one shows how to associate a finite automaton with any totally symmetric discrete function. One obtains then an iterative circuit that realizes the given totally symmetric discrete function: see for instance Hennie [1968]. That method of synthesis can be used even for partially symmetric discrete functions as proven by the theorem 13.14.

Recall first some notations already introduced in section 13.1:

$S = S_{n-1} \times \ldots \times S_0,$

$E = S_0 \cup \ldots \cup S_{n-1} = \{0, 1, \ldots, m-1\},$

$\mathcal{E}_n = \{(e_{n-1}, \ldots, e_0) \in E^n \mid e_{n-1} \leqslant \ldots \leqslant e_0\},$

$\mathcal{E}'_n = \{e \in \mathcal{E}_n \mid \exists\, e' \in S \text{ such that } e \equiv e'\}$

where $e \equiv e'$ iff there exists a permutation π acting on $\{0, \ldots, n-1\}$ such that $e' = \pi(e)$.

θ_n is a function from E^n to $\mathcal{E}_n$ that associates with the n-tuple e of E^n the unique n-tuple of $\mathcal{E}_n$ deduced from e by ordering its components.

Let us now consider a totally symmetric discrete function f. One associates with f a finite automaton $A(f)$ defined as follows:

The set of internal states of f is $\mathcal{E}'_n$;
The input alphabet is E;
The output alphabet is L;
The transition function δ maps $\mathcal{E}'_n \times E$ into $\mathcal{E}'_n$ according to the following rules:

(a) $\delta\,[(0, e_{n-2}, \ldots, e_0), e] = \theta_n(e, e_{n-2}, \ldots, e_0)$ if $\theta_n(e, e_{n-2}, \ldots, e_0) \in \mathcal{E}'_n$;
(b) $\delta\,[(e_{n-1}, \ldots, e_0), e]$ is unspecified in all other cases, i.e. if $e_{n-1} \neq 0$ or if $\theta_n(e, e_{n-2}, \ldots, e_0) \notin \mathcal{E}'_n$;
the output function λ from $\mathcal{E}'_n$ to L is the carrier of f, i.e.

$$\lambda(e) = f_c(e), \quad \forall e \in \mathcal{E}'_n.$$

The Figure 13.11 describes the automaton $A(f)$ in the case where $n = 3, m_2 = 3, m_1 = m_0 = 2$.

e	$\delta\,(e, 0)$	$\delta(e, 1)$	$\delta\,(e, 2)$	$\lambda(e)$
(0, 0, 0)	(0, 0, 0)	(0, 0, 1)	(0, 0, 2)	$f(0, 0, 0)$
(0, 0, 1)	(0, 0, 1)	(0, 1, 1)	(0, 1, 2)	$f(0, 0, 1)$
(0, 0, 2)	(0, 0, 2)	(0, 1, 2)	—	$f(2, 0, 0)$
(0, 1, 1)	(0, 1, 1)	(1, 1, 1)	(1, 1, 2)	$f(0, 1, 1)$
(0, 1, 2)	(0, 1, 2)	(1, 1, 2)	—	$f(2, 0, 1)$
(1, 1, 1)	—	—	—	$f(1, 1, 1)$
(1, 1, 2)	—	—	—	$f(2, 1, 1)$

Figure 13.11. Finite automaton associated with f

To this automaton corresponds the iterative circuit of Figure 13.12 in which every cell T realizes the mapping δ from $\mathcal{E}'_n \times E$ to $\mathcal{E}'_n$ defined in Figure 13.11.

In order to realize the circuit of Figure 13.12 one must choose a coding for the internal states of $A(f)$. The most simple way to code the members of $\mathcal{E}'_n$ is in using

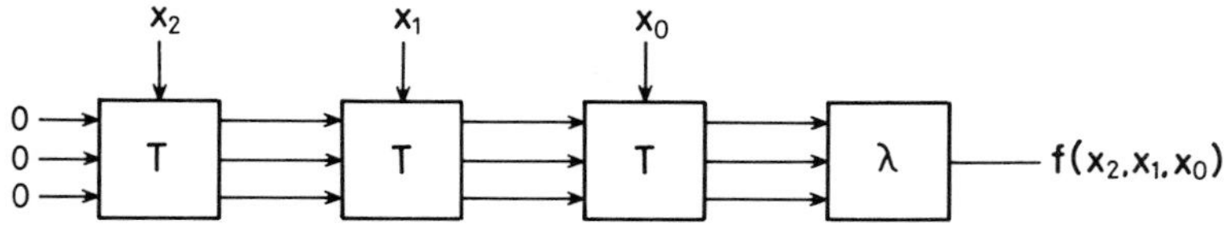

Figure 13.12. Iterative realization of a totally symmetric discrete function

n state variables $y_0, \ldots, y_{n-1}$ defined by

$$y_0(e) = e_0, \ldots, y_{n-1}(e) = e_{n-1}, \qquad \forall e \in \mathcal{E}'_n.$$

The n functions $\overset{+}{y_i}$, $i = 0, \ldots, n-1$, realized by the cell T may then be chosen as follows:

$$\overset{+}{y_0} = y_0 \vee x \tag{13.15}$$

and

$$\overset{+}{y_j} = y_j \vee (x \wedge y_{j-1}), \qquad \forall j = 1, \ldots, n-1, \tag{13.16}$$

where the disjunction and the conjunction are performed in E. Let us indeed consider an n-tuple $e = (0, e_{n-2}, \ldots, e_j, e_{j-1}, \ldots, e_0) \in \mathcal{E}'_n$ and an input state $e \in E$ such that $\theta_n(e, e_{n-2}, \ldots, e_0) \in \mathcal{E}'_n$. They are three cases:

(a) $e \leqslant e_j$. The variable y_j must remain unchanged in $\delta(e, e)$; that corresponds to the values given by the equations (13.15) and (13.16) above:

$$\overset{+}{y_0} = e_0 \vee e = e_0 \quad \text{if} \quad e \leqslant e_0;$$
$$\overset{+}{y_j} = e_j \vee (e \wedge e_{j-1}) = e_j \quad \text{if} \quad e \wedge e_{j-1} \leqslant e \leqslant e_j.$$

(b) $e_j < e \leqslant e_{j-1}$. The variable y_j must take the value e in $\delta(e, e)$; that again corresponds to the values deduced from equations (13.15) and (13.16):

$$\overset{+}{y_0} = e_0 \vee e = e \quad \text{if} \quad e_0 < e,$$
$$\overset{+}{y_j} = e_j \vee (e \wedge e_{j-1}) = e_j \vee e = e \quad \text{if} \quad e_j < e \leqslant e_{j-1}.$$

(c) $e_j \leqslant e_{j-1} < e$. The variable y_j must take the value e_{j-1}, and one indeed observes that

$$\overset{+}{y_j} = e_j \vee (e \wedge e_{j-1}) = e_j \vee e_{j-1} = e_{j-1} \quad \text{if} \quad e_j \leqslant e_{j-1} < e.$$

The cell T can thus be divided in n subcells like that of Figure 13.13. Note that the subcell realizing $\overset{+}{y_0}$ is obtained by putting $y_{-1} = 1$ in the subcell of Figure 13.13.

One finally obtains the cellular array of Figure 13.14(a) that can be transformed into the triangular array of Figure 13.14(b).

Given a totally symmetric discrete function f, instead of realizing f by means of a canonical circuit like those of Figure 13.14, one could also search for an automaton that covers $A(f)$ and has a minimum number of internal states. Let us illustrate that fact by an example.

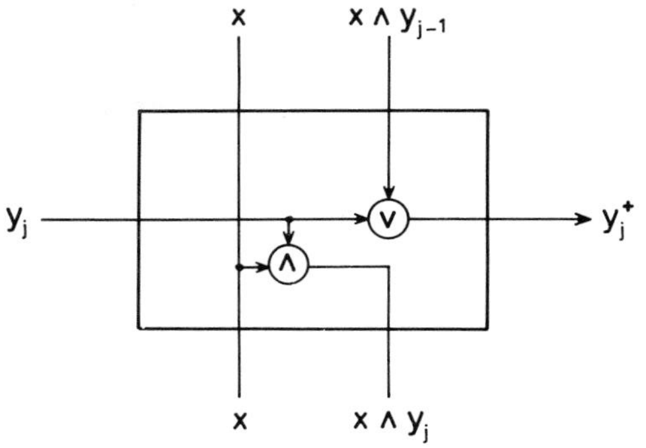

Figure 13.13. Subcell of T

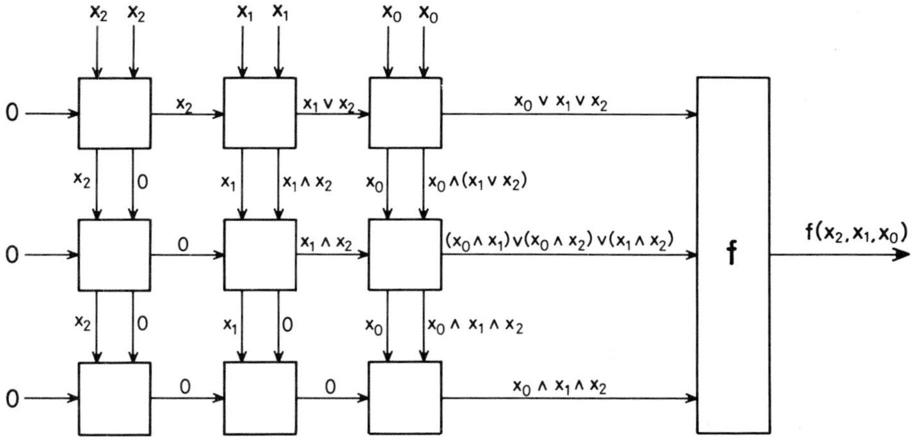

Figure 13.14 (a). Cellular array

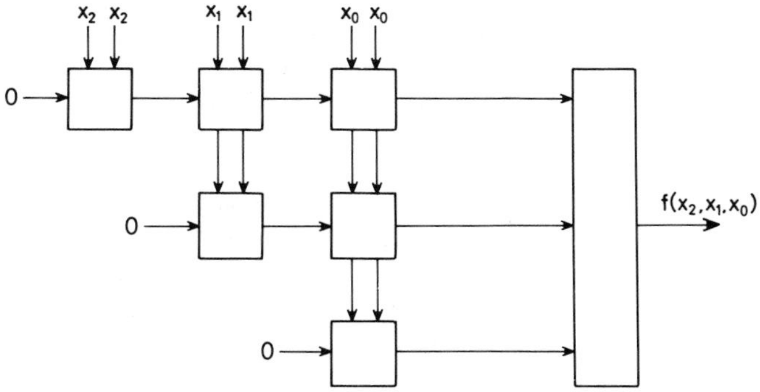

Figure 13.14 (b). Triangular array

Example 13.5. Consider the automaton of Figure 13.15 that corresponds to a totally symmetric discrete function f for which $n = 3, m_2 = 2, m_1 = 3, m_0 = 4, r = 2$.

Let us now look for the maximal classes of compatible states; there are six maximal classes:

e	$\delta(e, 0)$	$\delta(e, 1)$	$\delta(e, 2)$	$\delta(e, 3)$	$f(e)$
(0, 0, 0)	(0, 0, 0)	(0, 0, 1)	(0, 0, 2)	(0, 0, 3)	0
(0, 0, 1)	(0, 0, 1)	(0, 1, 1)	(0, 1, 2)	(0, 1, 3)	1
(0, 0, 2)	(0, 0, 2)	(0, 1, 2)	(0, 2, 2)	(0, 2, 3)	1
(0, 0, 3)	(0, 0, 3)	(0, 1, 3)	(0, 2, 3)	–	0
(0, 1, 1)	(0, 1, 1)	(1, 1, 1)	(1, 1, 2)	(1, 1, 3)	0
(0, 1, 2)	(0, 1, 2)	(1, 1, 2)	(1, 2, 2)	(1, 2, 3)	0
(0, 1, 3)	(0, 1, 3)	(1, 1, 3)	(1, 2, 3)	–	1
(0, 2, 2)	(0, 2, 2)	(1, 2, 2)	–	–	1
(0, 2, 3)	(0, 2, 3)	(1, 2, 3)	–	–	1
(1, 1, 1)	–	–	–	–	1
(1, 1, 2)	–	–	–	–	1
(1, 1, 3)	–	–	–	–	0
(1, 2, 2)	–	–	–	–	1
(1, 2, 3)	–	–	–	–	1

Figure 13.15. Finite automaton of example 13.5

$A = \{(0, 0, 0), (0, 1, 1), (1, 1, 3)\};$
$B = \{(0, 0, 1), (1, 1, 1), (1, 1, 2), (1, 2, 2), (1, 2, 3)\};$
$C = \{(0, 0, 2), (0, 1, 3), (1, 1, 1), (1, 1, 2), (1, 2, 2), (1, 2, 3)\};$
$D = \{(0, 0, 3), (0, 1, 1), (1, 1, 3)\};$
$E = \{(0, 0, 3), (0, 1, 2), (1, 1, 3)\};$
$F = \{(0, 2, 2), (0, 2, 3), (1, 1, 1), (1, 1, 2), (1, 2, 2), (1, 2, 3)\}.$

The classes A, B, C, E and F are essential, while the class D is included in the union of A and E. The five classes A, B, C, E and F thus form a cover of the set of states. Furthermore, one can easily verify that they form a closed cover and yield thus at least one quotient automaton that covers the automaton of Figure 13.15. One of them is described in Figure 13.16.

The states of the quotient automaton could be coded by means of three binary variables. Consider for instance the coding described in Figure 13.17; it has been chosen in such a way that z_0 is at the same time the output variable. One obtains in that way the iterative circuit of Figure 13.18 the elementary cell of which must realize the three partial functions f_2, f_1 and f_0 described in Figure 13.19. It then remains to synthesize the elementary cell that is to obtain an optimal realization of a partial generalized discrete function.

	0	1	2	3	
A	A	B	C	E	0
B	B	A	E	C	1
C	C	E	F	F	1
E	E	C	F	F	0
F	F	F	–	–	1

Figure 13.16. Quotient automaton

	z_2	z_1	z_0
A	0	0	0
B	0	0	1
C	0	1	1
E	1	0	0
F	1	0	1

Figure 13.17. Coding of the internal states

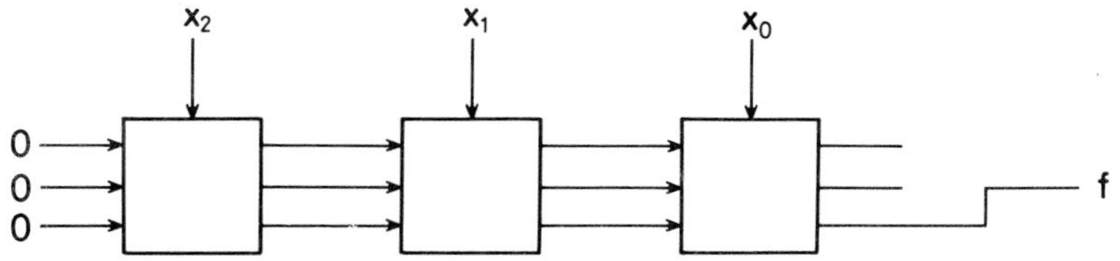

Figure 13.18. Iterative circuit

Note that one has not entirely taken into account the fact that the automaton of Figure 13.15 only receives words of length three. Suppose for instance that it comes into the state (0, 2, 2); that means that it has already received a word of length at least equal to two. If the next input letter is 0, it will have received an input word of length three and it must not necessarily remain in the state (0, 2, 2); it may undergo a transition towards any state to which corresponds an output 1, for instance towards the state (0, 0, 1).

It is possible to take this fact into account by introducing new states, for instance one could write

$$\delta[(0, 2, 2), 0] = (0', 2, 2),$$

$$\delta[(0', 2, 2), e] \text{ is undefined for every } e = 0, 1, 2, 3,$$

$$\lambda[(0', 2, 2)] = 1.$$

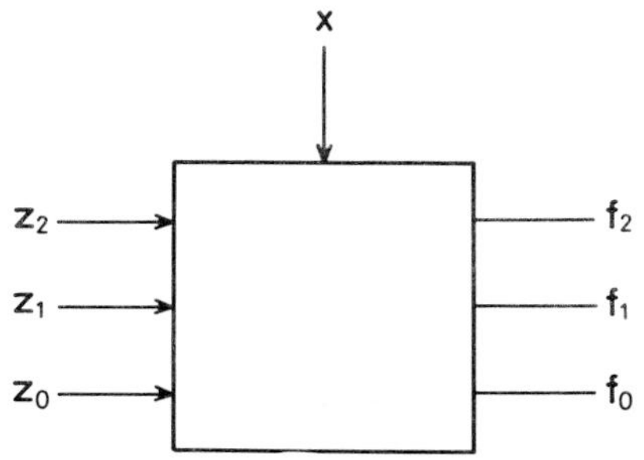

(a)

$f_2f_1f_0$		x 0	1	2	3
$z_2z_1z_0$	000	000	001	011	100
	001	001	000	100	011
	010	–	–	–	–
	011	011	100	101	101
	100	100	011	101	101
	101	101	101	–	–
	110	–	–	–	–
	111	–	–	–	–

(b)

Figure 13.19. Elementary cell

It is then obvious that the state $(0', 2, 2)$ is covered by any other state like $(0, 0, 1)$ to which corresponds an output 1.

This last remark suggests replacing the automaton of Figure 13.15 by that of Figure 13.20; note however that this process would become very tedious when n is increasing.

Another remark is that one may replace the Moore automata of Figures 13.15 and 13.20 by proper Mealy automata. Then one may delete the five states $(1, 1, 1)$ to $(1, 2, 3)$ in the automaton of Figure 13.15 and the fourteen states $(0', 0', 0')$ to $(1, 2, 3)$ in that of Figure 13.20. One then obtains an iterative circuit like that of Figure 13.21.

We now return to the automaton $A(f)$ as it was primarily defined and consider the particular case where f is an n-variable logic function. In that case, the transition function from $\mathcal{E}_n \times E$ to $\mathcal{E}_n$ may be defined as follows:

(a) $\delta[(0, e_{n-2}, \ldots, e_0), e] = \theta_n(e, e_{n-2}, \ldots, e_0)$;

(b) $e_{n-1} \neq 0 \Rightarrow \delta[(e_{n-1}, \ldots, e_0), e]$ is unspecified.

e	$\delta(e, 0)$	$\delta(e, 1)$	$\delta(e, 2)$	$\delta(e, 3)$	$f(e)$
(0, 0, 0)	(0, 0, 0′)	(0, 0, 1)	(0, 0, 2)	(0, 0, 3)	–
(0, 0, 0′)	(0, 0′, 0′)	(0, 0′, 1)	(0, 0′, 2)	(0, 0′, 3)	–
(0, 0, 1)	(0, 0′, 1)	(0, 1, 1)	(0, 1, 2)	(0, 1, 3)	–
(0, 0, 2)	(0, 0′, 2)	(0, 1, 2)	(0, 2, 2)	(0, 2, 3)	–
(0, 0, 3)	(0, 0′, 3)	(0, 1, 3)	(0, 2, 3)	(0, 3, 3)	–
(0, 0′, 0′)	(0′, 0′, 0′)	(0′, 0′, 1)	(0′, 0′, 2)	(0′, 0′, 3)	–
(0, 0′, 1)	(0′, 0′, 1)	(0′, 1, 1)	(0′, 1, 2)	(0′, 1, 3)	–
(0, 0′, 2)	(0′, 0′, 2)	(0′, 1, 2)	(0′, 2, 2)	(0′, 2, 3)	–
(0, 0′, 3)	(0′, 0′, 3)	(0′, 1, 3)	(0′, 2, 3)	–	–
(0, 1, 1)	(0′, 1, 1)	(1, 1, 1)	(1, 1, 2)	(1, 1, 3)	–
(0, 1, 2)	(0′, 1, 2)	(1, 1, 2)	(1, 2, 2)	(1, 2, 3)	–
(0, 1, 3)	(0′, 1, 3)	(1, 1, 3)	(1, 2, 3)	–	–
(0, 2, 2)	(0′, 2, 2)	(1, 2, 2)	–	–	–
(0, 2, 3)	(0′, 2, 3)	(1, 2, 3)	–	–	–
(0′, 0′, 0′)	–	–	–	–	0
(0′, 0′, 1)	–	–	–	–	1
(0′, 0′, 2)	–	–	–	–	1
(0′, 0′, 3)	–	–	–	–	0
(0′, 1, 1)	–	–	–	–	0
(0′, 1, 2)	–	–	–	–	0
(0′, 1, 3)	–	–	–	–	1
(0′, 2, 2)	–	–	–	–	1
(0′, 2, 3)	–	–	–	–	1
(1, 1, 1)	–	–	–	–	1
(1, 1, 2)	–	–	–	–	1
(1, 1, 3)	–	–	–	–	0
(1, 2, 2)	–	–	–	–	1
(1, 2, 3)	–	–	–	–	1

Figure 13.20. Second automaton associated with example 13.5

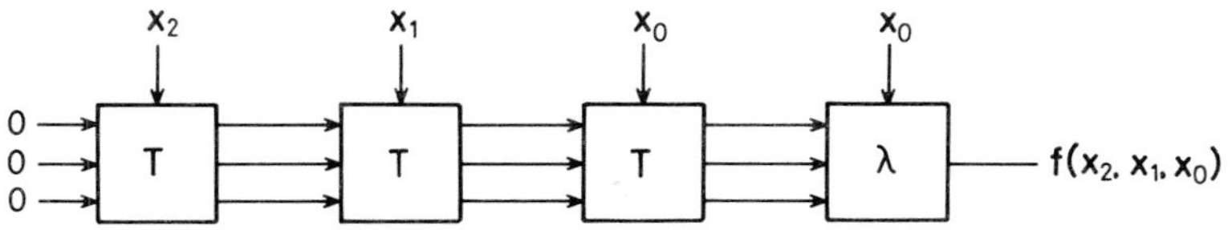

Figure 13.21. Iterative realization of a Mealy automaton

We now prove that when f is a logic function, the set of maximal compatibility classes of $A(f)$ is an irredundant cover of the set of the internal states of $A(f)$. It then suffices to find the maximal compatibility classes of $A(f)$ in order to obtain a quotient automaton with a minimum number of states and it is no longer necessary to solve a CC-table. Let us introduce for that purpose two new notations:

$\preccurlyeq$ is the lexicographic order on $\mathcal{E}_n$,

z is a mapping from $\mathcal{E}_n$ to $\{0, 1, \ldots, n-1\}$ that associates with $\boldsymbol{e} \in \mathcal{E}_n$ the number $z(\boldsymbol{e})$ of 0's in $\boldsymbol{e}$.

Furthermore, one will use the classical notation E^+ for designating the set of words over the alphabet E, i.e. the set of finite sequences of members of E. One can then extend δ to a mapping from $\mathcal{E}_n \times E^+$ to $\mathcal{E}_n$: this has already been seen in section 8.2.3, with a slightly different notation for the transition function.

We first state three lemmas.

Lemma 13.7. Two elements $\boldsymbol{e}$ *and* $\boldsymbol{e}'$ *of* $\mathcal{E}_n$, *such that* $\boldsymbol{e} \prec \boldsymbol{e}'$, *are compatible states of* $A(f)$ *iff*

$$\lambda(\boldsymbol{e}) = \lambda(\boldsymbol{e}')$$

and

$$\lambda[\delta(\boldsymbol{e}, w)] = \lambda[\delta(\boldsymbol{e}', w)], \qquad \forall w \in E^+$$

such that

$$\lg(w) \leqslant z(\boldsymbol{e}').$$

Proof. The states $\boldsymbol{e}$ and $\boldsymbol{e}'$ are compatible iff

$$\lambda(\boldsymbol{e}) = \lambda(\boldsymbol{e}')$$

and if

$$\lambda[\delta(\boldsymbol{e}, w)] = \lambda[\delta(\boldsymbol{e}', w)] \tag{13.17}$$

for every word w such that $\delta(\boldsymbol{e}, w)$ and $\delta(\boldsymbol{e}', w)$ are both defined. Furthermore, it is obvious that the effect of a word w containing some 0's is identical to the effect of the reduced word in which all the 0's have been deleted. It thus suffices that the relation (13.17) holds for every word w that contains no zero and such that $\delta(\boldsymbol{e}, w)$ and $\delta(\boldsymbol{e}', w)$ are both defined.

If the word w does not contain any 0, it is obvious that $\delta(\boldsymbol{e}, w)$ is defined iff $\lg(w) \leqslant z(\boldsymbol{e})$. The proof is then completed by noting that

$$\boldsymbol{e} \prec \boldsymbol{e}' \Rightarrow z(\boldsymbol{e}) \geqslant z(\boldsymbol{e}'). \qquad \blacksquare$$

In the sequel one denotes by $\boldsymbol{e} \sim \boldsymbol{e}'$ the fact that $\boldsymbol{e}$ and $\boldsymbol{e}'$ are two compatible states of $A(f)$.

Lemma 13.8. Let e, e' *and* e'' *be three members of* $\mathcal{E}_n$ *such that*

$$e \prec e' \prec e''.$$

Then

(a) *the fact that* $e \sim e'$ *and* $e \sim e''$ *implies that* $e' \sim e''$;
(b) *the fact that* $e \sim e'$ *and* $e' \sim e''$ *implies that* $e \sim e''$.

Proof. (a) If e and e' are compatible states of $A(f)$ then

$$\lambda(e) = \lambda(e') \text{ and } \lambda[\delta(e, w)] = \lambda[\delta(e', w)],$$

for every word w in E^+ such that $\lg(w) \leqslant z(e')$; similarly, if e and e'' are compatible then

$$\lambda(e) = \lambda(e'') \text{ and } \lambda[\delta(e, w)] = \lambda[\delta(e'', w)]$$

for every word w in E^+ such that $\lg(w) \leqslant z(e'')$.
Therefore, since $z(e'') \leqslant z(e')$, one has

$$\lambda(e') = \lambda(e'') \text{ and } \lambda[\delta(e', w)] = \lambda[\delta(e'', w)]$$

for every word w in E^+ such that $\lg(w) \leqslant z(e'')$.
Thus, by lemma 13.7 one concludes that e' and e'' are compatible states of $A(f)$.
(b) Similar proof. ∎

Given some e in $\mathcal{E}_n$, let us denote by H_e the following set:

$$H_e = \{e' \in \mathcal{E}_n \mid e' \succcurlyeq e \text{ and } e' \sim e\}.$$

Lemma 13.9. For every e *in* $\mathcal{E}_n$, *the set* H_e *is a compatibility class.*
Proof. This is a direct consequence of lemma 13.8(a) and of the fact that $\mathcal{E}_n$ is completely ordered by $\preccurlyeq$.
We are now able to prove the following theorem.

Theorem 13.19. The set of maximal compatibility classes of A(f) is an irredundant cover of the set of internal states of A(f).
Proof. Consider a maximal compatibility class C of $A(f)$ and let e be the smallest element of C under $\preccurlyeq$. Every member of C being greater than e under $\preccurlyeq$ and being compatible with e, one has

$$C \subseteq H_e;$$

since furthermore H_e is a compatibility class (lemma 13.9) and since C is maximal one deduces that

$$C = H_e.$$

The class C is thus entirely defined by the smallest element e that it contains.
Let us now suppose that another maximal class, say $H_{e'}$, contains also e. Then

$$e' \prec e \text{ and } e' \sim e.$$

By lemma 13.8(b) one concludes that $\boldsymbol{e}'$ is compatible with all the members of H_e. Since furthermore $\boldsymbol{e}'$ is smaller than all the elements of H_e one has:

$$H_{e'} \supset H_e,$$

but this contradicts the fact that H_e is maximal.

Thus, if H_e is a maximal compatibility class, it is the only maximal class that contains $\boldsymbol{e}$. ∎

The proof of the last theorem suggests a method for finding the maximal compatibility classes of $A(f)$; the general step of the method runs as follows:

Look for the smallest $\boldsymbol{e}$ under $\preccurlyeq$ that lies in none of the classes that have already been found, and compute

$$H_e = \{e' \in \mathcal{E}_n \mid e' \succcurlyeq e, e' \sim e\}.$$

Example 13.6. Let us consider the automaton $A(f)$ of Figure 13.22, where f is a ternary function of three ternary variables. The members of $\mathcal{E}_3$ are numbered from 0 to 9.

	0	1	2	f
(0, 0, 0) → 0	0	1	2	0
(0, 0, 1) → 1	1	3	4	0
(0, 0, 2) → 2	2	4	5	1
(0, 1, 1) → 3	3	6	7	0
(0, 1, 2) → 4	4	7	8	0
(0, 2, 2) → 5	5	8	9	0
(1, 1, 1) → 6	–	–	–	2
(1, 1, 2) → 7	–	–	–	0
(1, 2, 2) → 8	–	–	–	0
(2, 2, 2) → 9	–	–	–	1

Figure 13.22. Automaton of example 13.6

There are five maximal compatibility classes:

$$H_0 = (0, 5, 7, 8),$$
$$H_1 = (1, 4, 7, 8),$$
$$H_2 = (2, 9),$$
$$H_3 = (3, 7, 8),$$
$$H_6 = (6).$$

One of the quotient automata is described in Figure 13.23. One thus only needs two ternary variables in order to code the internal states of that automaton.

	0	1	2	f
H_0	H_0	H_1	H_2	0
H_1	H_1	H_3	H_1	0
H_2	H_2	H_1	H_0	1
H_3	H_3	H_6	H_0	0
H_6	—	—	—	2

Figure 13.23. Quotient automaton

We conclude this section by an important remark concerning the case where f is a ρ-symmetric discrete function. One thus supposes that

$$\rho = (\boldsymbol{x}_{s-1}, \ldots, \boldsymbol{x}_0)$$

with

$$\boldsymbol{x}_i = (x_{i\,n_i-1}, \ldots, x_{i\,0}), \qquad \forall i = 0, \ldots, s-1.$$

As it has been seen in section 13.3, one can associate with f a totally symmetric discrete function g that depends on $N = (n_0 + 1) \times \ldots \times (n_{s-1} + 1)$ variables. The method described above then yields an iterative synthesis of g by means of cells performing some transformation T: see Figure 13.24.

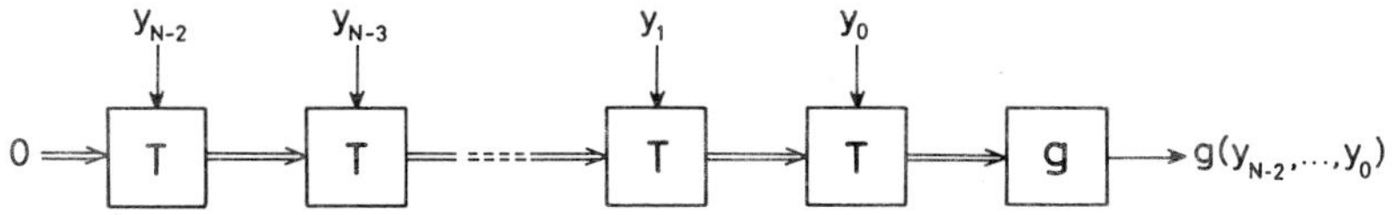

Figure 13.24. Iterative synthesis of g

If we assign the $w_i = (n_0 + 1) \times \ldots \times (n_{i-1} + 1)$ occurrences of the variable x_{ij} to w_i consecutive cells of the obtained synthesis, we may obviously replace these w_i cells by a single cell that performs the transformation T^{w_i}, for every $i = 0, \ldots, s-1$ and $j = 0, \ldots, n_i-1$: see Figure 13.25. This yields the cascade network of Figure 13.26 that realizes the ρ-symmetric discrete function f; it contains $N-1$ cells and s types of cells.

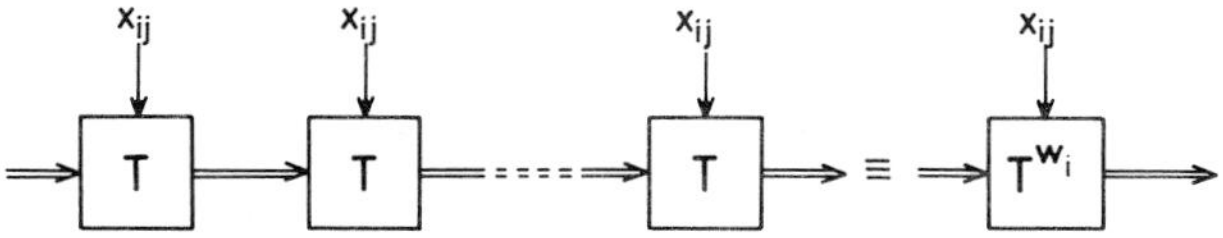

Figure 13.25. Definition of the transformation T^{w_i}

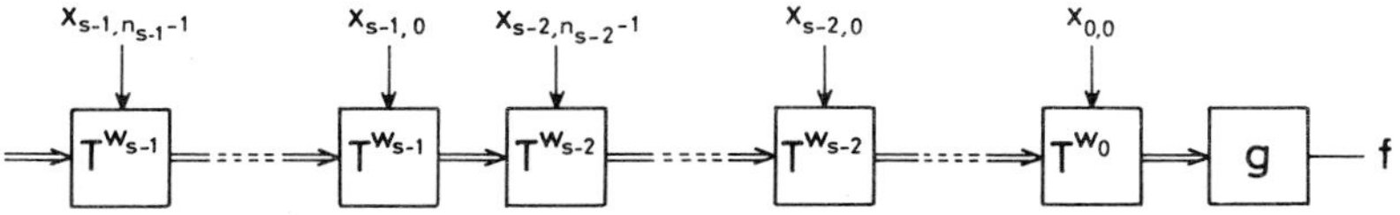

Figure 13.26. Cellular synthesis of f

13.6. Switching functions

This last section is devoted to some particular properties that hold in the case of switching functions, that is the functions from B_2^n to B_2, with $B_2 = \{0, 1\}$.

13.6.1. The carrier function

Let us consider a ρ-symmetric function f, with $\rho = (\boldsymbol{x}_{s-1}, \ldots, \boldsymbol{x}_0)$ and $\boldsymbol{x}_i = (x_{i\,n_i-1}, \ldots, x_{i\,0})$, $\forall i = 0, \ldots, s$. The carrier f_c of f is a function from

$$\mathcal{E} = \mathcal{E}_{n_{s-1}} \times \ldots \times \mathcal{E}_{n_0} \text{ to } B_2$$

where

$$\mathcal{E}_{n_i} = \{(e_{n_i-1}, \ldots, e_0) \in B_2^{n_i} \mid e_{n_i-1} \leqslant \ldots \leqslant e_0\},$$

for every $i = 0, \ldots, s-1$: see definition 13.1.

The main point is to note that every element $\boldsymbol{e}_i$ of $\mathcal{E}_{n_i}$ is entirely defined by its weight $w_i(\boldsymbol{e}_i)$ that is the number of 1's it contains; let us indeed consider a typical point of $\mathcal{E}_{n_i}$:

$$(\underbrace{0, \ldots, 0}_{n_i - w_i},\ \underbrace{1, \ldots, 1}_{w_i});$$

there is clearly no other point in $\mathcal{E}_{n_i}$ with the same weight. Furthermore, for every integer w_i that lies between 0 and n_i there exists a point in $\mathcal{E}_{n_i}$ the weight of which is w_i. Therefore, we may establish a bijection between $\mathcal{E}_{n_i}$ and

$$L_i = \{0, \ldots, n_i\}$$

for every $i = 0, \ldots, s-1$.

The carrier f_c may thus be considered as a function from

$$L = L_{s-1} \times \ldots \times L_0 \text{ to } B_2;$$

it is defined as follows:

$$f_c[w_{s-1}(\boldsymbol{x}_{s-1}), \ldots, w_0(\boldsymbol{x}_0)] = f(\boldsymbol{x}_{s-1}, \ldots, \boldsymbol{x}_0).$$

The function f_c is thus an n-variable discrete function. We now establish the relation that exists between the convex blocks of f_c and the implicants of f.

For every $i = 0, \ldots, s-1$, let us denote by $P_i(v, t)$ the disjunction of all the product terms containing v uncomplemented variables and t complemented variables taken in $\{x_{i\,0}, \ldots, x_{i\,n_i-1}\}$, i.e. the disjunction of all the product terms of the type

$$x_{i\,j_1} \wedge \ldots \wedge x_{i\,j_v} \wedge \bar{x}_{i\,j_{v+1}} \wedge \ldots \wedge \bar{x}_{i\,j_{v+t}}, \tag{13.18}$$

with

$$\{j_1, \ldots, j_{v+t}\} \subseteq \{0, \ldots, n_i - 1\}.$$

We now consider two vectors,

$$\boldsymbol{\nu} = (\nu_{s-1}, \ldots, \nu_0) \text{ and } \boldsymbol{t} = (t_{s-1}, \ldots, t_0)$$

where the ν_i's and the t_i's are integers that satisfy the following inequalities

$$0 \leqslant \nu_i \leqslant n_i, 0 \leqslant t_i \leqslant n_i - \nu_i,$$

for every $i = 0, \ldots, s-1$. Then we denote by $P(\boldsymbol{\nu}, \boldsymbol{t})$ the disjunction of all the product terms containing ν_i uncomplemented variables and t_i complemented variables among the variables taken in $\{x_{i0}, \ldots, x_{i\,n_i-1}\}$, for every $i = 0, \ldots, s-1$. In other words, $P(\boldsymbol{\nu}, \boldsymbol{t})$ is deduced from the conjunction

$$P_{s-1}(\nu_{s-1}, t_{s-1}) \wedge \ldots \wedge P_0(\nu_0, t_0)$$

by using the distributive law.

Lemma 13.10. The disjunction $P_i(\nu, t)$ takes the value 1 at point $\boldsymbol{x}_i$ iff

$$\nu \leqslant w_i(\boldsymbol{x}_i) \leqslant n_i - t.$$

Proof. Let us consider the term (13.18) of $P_i(\nu, t)$; it takes the value 1 at point $\boldsymbol{x}_i$ iff

$$x_{i\,j_1} = \ldots = x_{i\,j_\nu} = 1$$

and

$$x_{i\,j_{\nu+1}} = \ldots = x_{i\,j_{\nu+t}} = 0;$$

if the remaining variables are all equal to 0, the number of 1's in $\boldsymbol{x}_i$ is equal to ν; if the remaining variables are all equal to 1, the number of 1's in $\boldsymbol{x}_i$ is equal to $n_i - t$. Thus

$$\nu \leqslant w_i(\boldsymbol{x}_i) \leqslant n_i - t.$$

This proves the necessity of the condition. The sufficiency comes from the fact that $P_i(\nu, t)$ contains all the product terms of the type (13.18). ■

As a straightforward consequence we may state the two following lemmas.

Lemma 13.11. The disjunction $P(\boldsymbol{\nu}, \boldsymbol{t})$ takes the value 1 at point $\boldsymbol{x} = (\boldsymbol{x}_{s-1}, \ldots, \boldsymbol{x}_0)$ iff

$$\nu_i \leqslant w_i(\boldsymbol{x}_i) \leqslant n_i - t_i$$

for every $i = 0, \ldots, s-1$. ■

Lemma 13.12. The disjunction $P(\boldsymbol{\nu}, \boldsymbol{t})$ defines a ρ-symmetric switching function the carrier of which is represented by the following convex block:

$$w_{s-1}^{[\nu_{s-1},\, n_{s-1}-t_{s-1}]} \wedge \ldots \wedge w_0^{[\nu_0,\, n_0-t_0]}.$$ ■

The next lemma may be seen as a direct consequence of the definitions of ρ-symmetry and of $P(\boldsymbol{\nu}, \boldsymbol{t})$.

Lemma 13.13. If the product term m is a prime implicant of the ρ-symmetric function f and if m is one of the product terms of $P(\boldsymbol{v}, \boldsymbol{t})$, then every product term of $P(\boldsymbol{v}, \boldsymbol{t})$ is a prime implicant of f. ■

The disjunction of the prime implicants of a ρ-symmetric switching function may thus be written in a concise way; instead of finding all the prime implicants, it suffices then to find all the pairs $(\boldsymbol{v}, \boldsymbol{t})$ such that $P(\boldsymbol{v}, \boldsymbol{t})$ is a disjunction of prime implicants. The following theorem plays the key role in the finding of the pairs $(\boldsymbol{v}, \boldsymbol{t})$; it is a direct consequence of lemmas 13.12 and 13.13.

Theorem 13.20. $P(\boldsymbol{v}, \boldsymbol{t})$ is a disjunction of prime implicants of the ρ-symmetric switching function f iff the convex block

$$w_{s-1}^{[v_{s-1},\, n_{s-1}-t_{s-1}]} \wedge \ldots \wedge w_0^{[v_0,\, n_0-t_0]}$$

is a prime convex block of f_c. ■

We are now in place to describe an algorithm that allows to find the prime implicants of a ρ-symmetric switching function f.

Algorithm 13.1

Step 1. Compute the carrier f_c of f.
Step 2. Find the prime convex blocks of f_c.
Step 3. With each prime convex block

$$w_{s-1}^{[v_{s-1},\, u_{s-1}]} \wedge \ldots \wedge w_0^{[v_0,\, u_0]}$$

associate the disjunction $P(\boldsymbol{v}, \boldsymbol{t})$ where

$$\boldsymbol{v} = (v_{s-1}, \ldots, v_0),$$

and

$$\boldsymbol{t} = (n_{s-1}-u_{s-1}, \ldots, n_0-u_0).$$

Example 13.7. The six-variable switching function

$$f = \{x_0 \wedge [x_1 \oplus (x_2 \wedge x_3)]\} \oplus (x_4 \vee x_5)$$

is ρ-symmetric, with

$$\rho = [(x_5, x_4), (x_3, x_2), (x_1), (x_0)].$$

Let us compute its prime implicants by algorithm 13.1.

Step 1

$$f_c = [w_0^{(1)} \wedge (w_1^{(1)} \oplus w_2^{(2)})] \oplus w_3^{(1,\,2)}$$

with

$$w_0 \text{ and } w_1 \in \{0, 1\},\ w_2 \text{ and } w_3 \in \{0, 1, 2\}.$$

Step 2

f_c has five prime convex blocks:

$$w_3^{[0,0]} \wedge w_2^{[0,1]} \wedge w_1^{[1,1]} \wedge w_0^{[1,1]},$$

$$w_3^{[0,0]} \wedge w_2^{[2,2]} \wedge w_1^{[0,0]} \wedge w_0^{[1,1]},$$

$$w_3^{[1,2]} \wedge w_0^{[0,0]},$$

$$w_3^{[1,2]} \wedge w_2^{[0,1]} \wedge w_1^{[0,0]},$$

$$w_3^{[1,2]} \wedge w_2^{[2,2]} \wedge w_1^{[1,1]}.$$

Step 3

To the five prime convex blocks of f correspond the five following disjunctions of prime implicants of f:

$$P[(0,0,1,1),(2,1,0,0)] = (\bar{x}_5\bar{x}_4)(\bar{x}_3 \vee \bar{x}_2)(x_1)(x_0)$$
$$= \bar{x}_5\bar{x}_4\bar{x}_3x_1x_0 \vee \bar{x}_5\bar{x}_4\bar{x}_2x_1x_0;$$

$$P[(0,2,0,1),(2,0,1,0)] = (\bar{x}_5\bar{x}_4)(x_3x_2)(\bar{x}_1)(x_0)$$
$$= \bar{x}_5\bar{x}_4x_3x_2\bar{x}_1x_0;$$

$$P[(1,0,0,0),(0,0,0,1)] = (x_5 \vee x_4)(1)(1)(\bar{x}_0)$$
$$= x_5\bar{x}_0 \vee x_4\bar{x}_0;$$

$$P[(1,0,0,0),(0,1,1,0)] = (x_5 \vee x_4)(\bar{x}_3 \vee \bar{x}_2)(\bar{x}_1)(1)$$
$$= x_5\bar{x}_3\bar{x}_1 \vee x_5\bar{x}_2\bar{x}_1 \vee x_4\bar{x}_3\bar{x}_1 \vee x_4\bar{x}_2\bar{x}_1;$$

$$P[(1,2,1,0),(0,0,0,0)] = (x_5 \vee x_4)(x_3x_2)(x_1)(1)$$
$$= x_5x_3x_2x_1 \vee x_4x_3x_2x_1.$$

The main characteristic of the algorithm presented above is that it avoids to compute some prime implicants of a ρ-symmetric switching function that can directly be deduced from other prime implicants already found and from the ρ-symmetry. Furthermore the list of prime implicants is presented in a concise form. The method is particularly efficient for functions having a large partition associated with them.

Let us now consider a representation of the carrier f_c of the ρ-symmetric function f as a disjunction of cubes:

$$f_c = \bigvee_{k \in K} (w_{s-1}^{C_{s-1\,k}} \wedge \ldots \wedge w_0^{C_{0k}})$$

where K is some index set and $C_{ik} \subseteq L_i$, $\forall k \in K$ and $i \in \{0, \ldots, s-1\}$.

Each cube $w_i^{C_{ik}}$ is the carrier of a totally symmetric function S_{ik} depending on $\boldsymbol{x}_i$:

$$S_{ik}(\boldsymbol{x}_i) = 1 \quad \text{iff} \quad w_i(\boldsymbol{x}_i) \in C_{ik};$$

it is obvious that f then admits the following expression

$$f = \bigvee_{k \in K} (S_{s-1\,k} \wedge \ldots \wedge S_{0\,k})$$

to which corresponds the logical diagram of Figure 13.27. Each function S_{ik} may be realized in two levels; one obtains a four-level realization of f. Each function S_{ik} may also be realized by means of a universal module for the synthesis of symmetric functions.

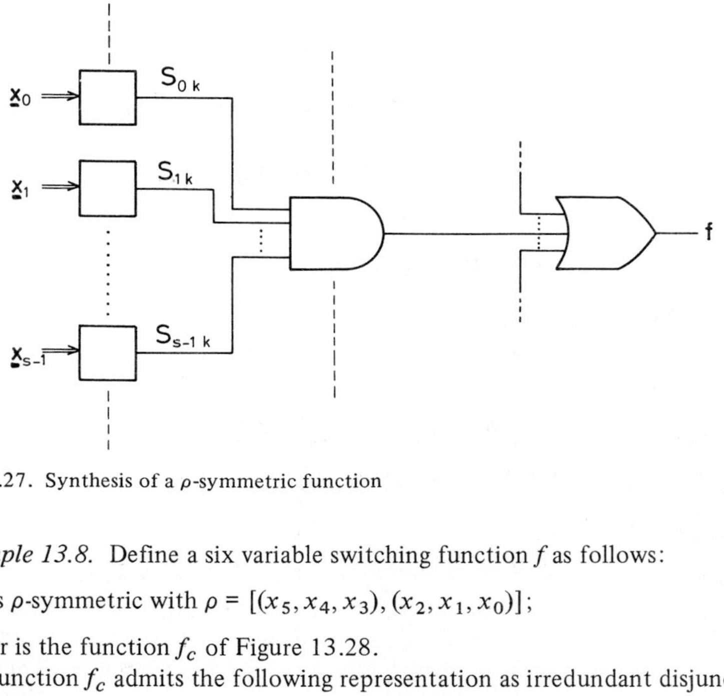

Figure 13.27. Synthesis of a ρ-symmetric function

Example 13.8. Define a six variable switching function f as follows:

f is ρ-symmetric with $\rho = [(x_5, x_4, x_3), (x_2, x_1, x_0)]$;

its carrier is the function f_c of Figure 13.28.

The function f_c admits the following representation as irredundant disjunction of prime cubes:

$$f_c = (w_1^{(0,2)} \wedge w_0^{(2)}) \vee (w_1^{(0,3)} \wedge w_0^{(3)}) \vee (w_1^{(2)} \wedge w_0^{(1,2)}) \vee (w_1^{(1)} \wedge w_0^{(0)});$$

therefore

$$f = (S_{10} \wedge S_{00}) \vee (S_{11} \wedge S_{01}) \vee (S_{12} \wedge S_{02}) \vee (S_{13} \wedge S_{03})$$

where

$$S_{10}(x_5, x_4, x_3) = \bar{x}_5 \bar{x}_4 \bar{x}_3 \vee x_5 x_4 \bar{x}_3 \vee x_5 \bar{x}_4 x_3 \vee \bar{x}_5 x_4 x_3,$$

$$S_{11}(x_5, x_4, x_3) = \bar{x}_5 \bar{x}_4 \bar{x}_3 \vee x_5 x_4 x_3,$$

$$S_{12}(x_5, x_4, x_3) = x_5 x_4 \bar{x}_3 \vee x_5 \bar{x}_4 x_3 \vee \bar{x}_5 x_4 x_3,$$

w_1	w_0	f_c
0	0	0
0	1	0
0	2	1
0	3	1
1	0	1
1	1	0
1	2	0
1	3	0
2	0	0
2	1	1
2	2	1
2	3	0
3	0	0
3	1	0
3	2	0
3	3	1

Figure 13.28. The carrier of f_c

$$S_{13}(x_5, x_4, x_3) = \bar{x}_5 \bar{x}_4 x_3 \vee \bar{x}_5 x_4 \bar{x}_3 \vee x_5 \bar{x}_4 \bar{x}_3,$$

$$S_{00}(x_2, x_1, x_0) = x_2 x_1 \bar{x}_0 \vee x_2 \bar{x}_1 x_0 \vee \bar{x}_2 x_1 x_0,$$

$$S_{01}(x_2, x_1, x_0) = x_2 x_1 x_0,$$

$$S_{02}(x_2, x_1, x_0) = x_2 \bar{x}_1 \vee \bar{x}_2 x_1 \vee x_2 \bar{x}_0 \vee \bar{x}_2 x_0 \vee x_1 \bar{x}_0 \vee \bar{x}_1 x_0,$$

$$S_{03}(x_2, x_1, x_0) = \bar{x}_2 \bar{x}_1 \bar{x}_0.$$

13.6.2. Algebraic structures

We may obviously confer to the set of functions from

$$L_{s-1} \times \ldots \times L_0 \text{ to } B_2$$

either the structure of Boolean algebra or the structure of linear algebra.

The set of ρ-symmetric switching functions is thus a Boolean algebra isomorphic to B_2^M, where $M = (n_0 + 1) \times \ldots \times (n_{s-1} + 1)$. The atoms of this Boolean algebra are the M elementary ρ-symmetric switching functions σ_l defined as follows:

$$\sigma_l = \sigma_{l_{s-1}} \wedge \ldots \wedge \sigma_{l_0}$$

where

$$\sigma_{l_i}(\boldsymbol{x}_i) = 1 \quad \text{iff} \quad w_i(\boldsymbol{x}_i) = l_i,$$
$$= 0 \text{ otherwise},$$

for every $\boldsymbol{l} = (l_{s-1}, \ldots, l_0) \in L_{s-1} \times \ldots \times L_0$.

The set of ρ-symmetric switching functions is a vector space on the field GF(2) of scalars. It is obvious furthermore that the product of two ρ-symmetric switching functions is still a ρ-symmetric switching function, and that the bilinear law holds. The set of ρ-symmetric switching functions is thus a linear algebra.

Let us now describe some bases of that linear algebra. As it has been seen in section 13.2.2, it suffices to consider the case of totally symmetric functions; bases for the set of ρ-symmetric functions are then obtained by Kronecker products.

The simplest basis is obviously the set of Lagrange totally symmetric functions that coincide in this case with the elementary totally symmetric switching functions $\sigma_l, l = 0, \ldots, n$.

Every totally symmetric switching function f admits the following expansion in that basis:

$$f = [f_c(l)] \; [\sigma_l]^t.$$

Let us now denote by $\gamma_{l,1}^n$ the complete homogeneous ring polynomial of degree l in the variables $x_0, \ldots, x_{n-1}$:

$$\gamma_{l,1}^n(\boldsymbol{x}) = \bigoplus x_{n-1}^{e_{n-1}} \ldots x_0^{e_0}$$

the sum being extended to all $\boldsymbol{e} = (e_{n-1}, \ldots, e_0) \in B_2^n$ the weight $w(\boldsymbol{e})$ of which is equal to l, and with the following definition of the exponentiation

$$x^0 = 1, \; x^1 = x.$$

Similarly, we denote by $\gamma_{l,0}^n$ the complete homogeneous ring polynomial of degree $n-l$ in the complemented variables $\bar{x}_0, \ldots, \bar{x}_{n-1}$:

$$\gamma_{l,0}^n(\boldsymbol{x}) = \bigoplus (\bar{x}_{n-1})^{e_{n-1}} \ldots (\bar{x}_0)^{e_0}$$

the sum being extended to all $\boldsymbol{e}$ in B_2^n such that $w(\boldsymbol{e}) = n - l$.

For instance

$$\gamma_{2,1}^3(x_2, x_1, x_0) = x_2 x_1 \oplus x_2 x_0 \oplus x_1 x_0$$

and

$$\gamma_{3,0}^4(x_3, x_2, x_1, x_0) = \bar{x}_3 \oplus \bar{x}_2 \oplus \bar{x}_1 \oplus \bar{x}_0.$$

Theorem 13.21. (a) *The set of functions* $\{\gamma_{l,1}^n \mid l = 0, \ldots, n\}$ *is a basis of the linear algebra of the totally symmetric switching functions.*

(b) *Similar statement for the set of function* $\{\gamma_{l,0}^n \mid l = 0, \ldots, n\}$.

Proof (a) Express the functions $\gamma_{l,1}^n$ in the Lagrange basis:

$$\gamma_{l,1}^n = \sum_{j=0}^{n} a_{lj}\, \sigma_j^n.$$

Hence, at any point $\boldsymbol{x}$ such that $w(\boldsymbol{x}) = k$, one has:

$$\gamma_{l,1}^n\,(\boldsymbol{x}) = a_{lk};$$

the coefficient a_{lk} is thus equal to 1 iff the number of terms equal to unity in the expansion of $\gamma_{l,1}^n$ is odd in the points of weight k. Clearly

$$a_{lk} \equiv \binom{k}{l}, \text{ modulo-2.}$$

The transformation matrix $A_1^n = [a_{lk}]$ is thus the Pascal triangle, computed modulo-2; since it is its own inverse on GF(2), one concludes that the functions $\gamma_{l,1}^n$ also form a basis.

(b) Similar proof. The transformation matrix is

$$A_0^n = [a_{(n-l)\,(n-k)}].$$ ■

It is important to note that in the case where $n = 2^m - 1$, the matrix A_1^n is obtained by Kronecker product of m identical matrices

$$\begin{bmatrix} 1 & 1 \\ 0 & 1 \end{bmatrix};$$

see for instance Calingaert [1961] or Davio [1971]. This suggests an easy construction of A_1^n whenever $n < 2^m - 1$:

(a) compute $A_1^{2^m-1}$ by Kronecker product;

(b) delete in $A_1^{2^m-1}$ the $(2^m - 1 - n)$ last rows and columns.

Let us now introduce two new families of functions. Denote by $\delta_{l,1}^n$ the complete homogeneous Boolean polynomial of degree l in the n variables $x_0, \ldots, x_{n-1}$:

$$\delta_{l,1}^n\,(\boldsymbol{x}) = \vee\; x_{n-1}^{e_{n-1}} \ldots x_0^{e_0}$$

the disjunction being extended to all $\boldsymbol{e}$ in B_2^n such that $w(\boldsymbol{e}) = l$.

Similarly, denote by $\delta_{l,0}^n$ the complete homogeneous Boolean polynomial of degree $n - l$ in the n complemented variables $\bar{x}_0, \ldots, \bar{x}_{n-1}$:

$$\delta_{l,0}^n\,(\boldsymbol{x}) = \vee\, (\bar{x}_{n-1})^{e_{n-1}} \ldots (\bar{x}_0)^{e_0}$$

the disjunction being extended to all $\boldsymbol{e}$ in B_2^n such that $w(\boldsymbol{e}) = n - l$.

For instance

$$\delta_{2,1}^3(x_2, x_1, x_0) = x_2 x_1 \vee x_2 x_0 \vee x_1 x_0$$

and

$$\delta^4_{3,0}(x_3, x_2, x_1, x_0) = \bar{x}_3 \vee \bar{x}_2 \vee \bar{x}_1 \vee \bar{x}_0.$$

Theorem 13.22. (a) *The set of functions* $\{\delta^n_{l,1} \mid l = 0, \ldots, n\}$ *is a basis of the linear algebra of the totally symmetric switching functions.*

(b) *Similar statement for the set of functions* $\{\delta^n_{l,0} \mid l = 0, \ldots, n\}$.

Proof. (a) Let us express the functions $\delta^n_{l,1}$ in the Lagrange basis:

$$\delta^n_{l,1} = \sum_{j=0}^{n} b_{lj}\, \sigma^n_j .$$

Hence, at any point $\boldsymbol{x}$ such that $w(\boldsymbol{x}) = k$, one has:

$$\delta^n_{l,1}(\boldsymbol{x}) = b_{lk};$$

it is obvious from the definition of $\delta^n_{l,1}$ that

$$b_{lk} = \delta^n_{l,1}(\boldsymbol{x}) = 1 \quad \text{iff} \quad k \geqslant l,$$
$$= 0 \text{ otherwise.}$$

It then suffices to note that the matrix $B^n_1 = [b_{lk}]$ has an inverse $(B^n_1)^{-1} = [b'_{lk}]$ defined as follows:

$$b'_{lk} = 1 \quad \text{iff} \quad k = l \quad \text{or} \quad k = l + 1,$$
$$= 0 \text{ otherwise.}$$

(b) Similar proof. The transformation matrices are

$$B^n_0 = (B^n_1)^t, (B^n_0)^{-1} = [(B^n_1)^{-1}]^t.$$ ∎

One could also look for methods allowing to compute the minimum cost Taylor expansion(s) of a given totally or partially symmetric switching function. For that purpose it is possible to take advantage of the symmetries of the function in order to avoid superfluous computations: see Davio [1973].

13.6.3. Cellular realization

In the case where f is a totally symmetric switching function, one associates with f a finite automaton $A(f)$ defined as follows (see section 13.5):

the set of internal states is $\{0, \ldots, n\}$;

the input alphabet is $\{0, 1\}$;

the output alphabet is $\{0, 1\}$;

the transition function δ is defined as follows:

$$\delta(l, e) = l + e, \quad \forall l = \{0, \ldots, n-1\},$$

$\delta(n, e)$ is unspecified;

the output function is the carrier of f.

l	$\delta(l, 0)$	$\delta(l, 1)$	$\lambda(l)$
0	0	1	$f(0, 0, 0, 0, 0, 0,)$
1	1	2	$f(0, 0, 0, 0, 0, 1)$
2	2	3	$f(0, 0, 0, 0, 1, 1)$
3	3	4	$f(0, 0, 0, 1, 1, 1)$
4	4	5	$f(0, 1, 1, 1, 1, 1)$
5	–	–	$f(1, 1, 1, 1, 1, 1)$

Figure 13.29. Automaton $A(f)$

For instance, in the case where $n = 5$ one obtains the automaton of Figure 13.29.

As it has been seen in section 13.5, this automaton describes the elementary cell of an iterative cascade of n cells that realizes f. In order to effectively realize the iterative circuit, one must first encode the $(n + 1)$ internal states of $A(f)$.

These internal states can be encoded by means of $(n + 1)$ binary state variables $y_0, \ldots, y_n$; the assignment corresponding to the state l is defined by:

$$y_l = 1, y_j = 0, \quad \forall j \neq l. \tag{13.19}$$

This assignment yields a simultaneous realization of the $(n + 1)$ functions σ_l^n: indeed, at the output of the last cell, one clearly has

$$y = 1 \quad \text{iff} \quad w(x) = l$$

if one applies the input word $x_{n-1} \ldots x_0$.

Clearly too, the cell $k-1$ computes the functions σ_l^k as functions of the σ_l^{k-1} and x_{k-1} according to the relations

$$\sigma_l^k = \bar{x}_{k-1}\, \sigma_l^{k-1} \vee x_{k-1}\, \sigma_{l-1}^{k-1}.$$

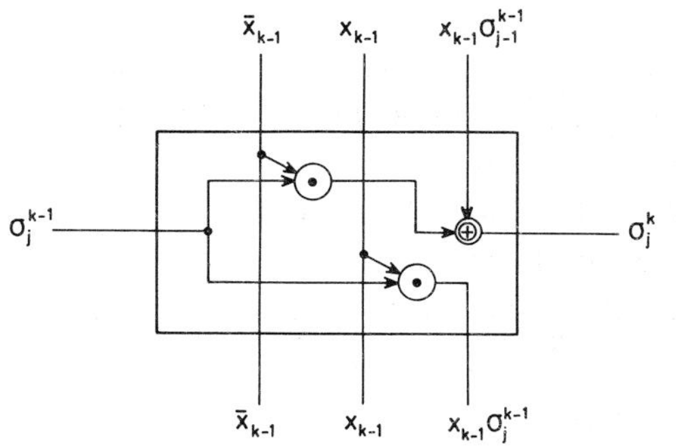

Figure 13.30. Subcell of the elementary symmetric function array

The cell corresponding to the variable x_{k-1} may thus be made up of $(n+1)$ sub-cells of the type shown in Figure 13.30. Since at the input of that cell one has

$$y_k = y_{k+1} = \ldots = y_n = 0,$$

a truncation of the cascade is possible, yielding the *triangular elementary symmetric function array* of Figure 13.31.

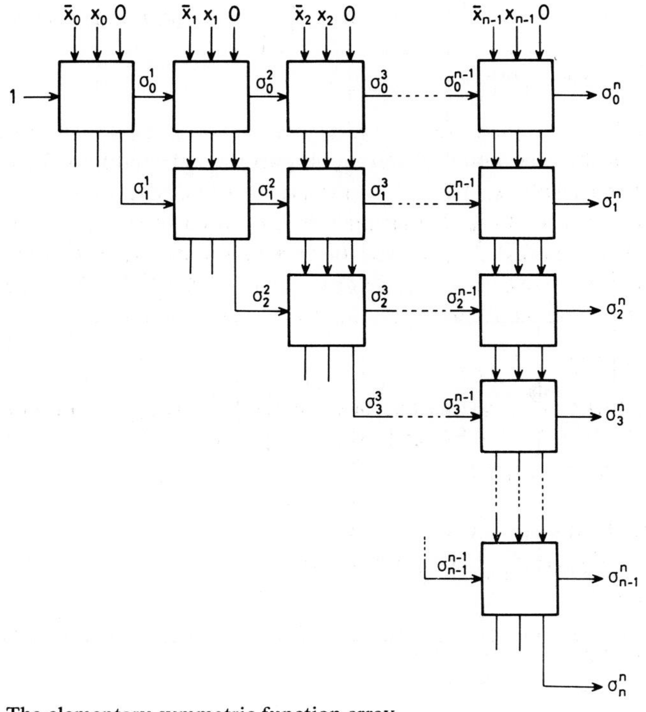

Figure 13.31. The elementary symmetric function array

The following encodings of the variables $y_0, \ldots y_n$ are some possible meaningful alternatives to the assignment (13.19) of the internal state l.

(a) $y_j \equiv \binom{l}{j}$, modulo-2, $\forall j = 0, \ldots, n,$ (13.20)

(b) $y_j \equiv \binom{n-l}{n-j}$, modulo-2, $\forall j = 0, \ldots, n,$ (13.21)

(c) $y_j = 1$ iff $j \leqslant l,$ (13.22)

$\quad = 0$ iff $j > l;$

(d) $y_j = 1$ iff $j \geq l$, (13.23)

$= 0$ iff $j < l$.

These assignments yield simultaneous realizations of the functions $\gamma^n_{l,1}$, $\gamma^n_{l,0}$, $\delta^n_{l,1}$ and $\delta^n_{l,0}$ respectively. In particular, under assignment (13.20), the functions $\gamma^n_{l,1}$ are computed according to the relations

$$\gamma^k_{l,1} = \gamma^{k-1}_{l,1} \oplus x_{k-1}\, \gamma^{k-1}_{l-1,1}\,,$$

and under assignment (13.22), the functions $\delta^n_{l,1}$ are computed according to the relations

$$\delta^k_{l,1} = \delta^{k-1}_{l,1} \vee x_{k-1}\, \delta^{k-1}_{l-1,1}.$$

The two last formulas yield iterative triangular arrays quite similar to that of Figure 13.31; the corresponding subcells are however somewhat simpler: they are displayed in Figure 13.32.

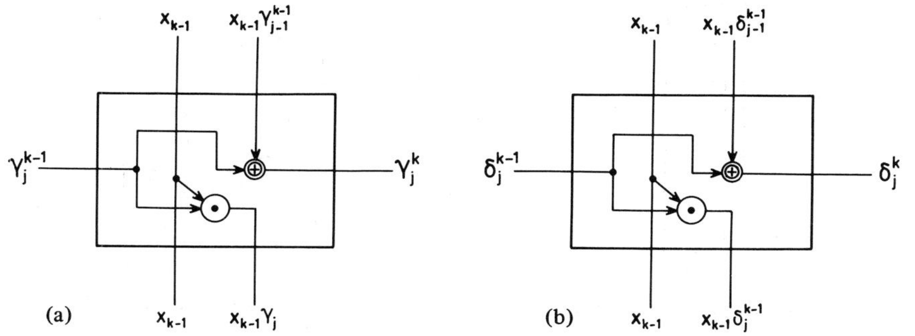

Figure 13.32. Subcells of the γ and δ arrays

Note also that the functions $\delta^k_{l,1}$ are related by the series of inequalities

$$1 = \delta^k_{0,1} \geq \delta^k_{1,1} \geq \ldots \geq \delta^k_{k,1};$$

therefore they may also be computed according to the following relations:

$$\delta^k_{l,1} = \bar{x}_{k-1}\, \delta^{k-1}_{l,1} \vee x_{k-1}\, \delta^{k-1}_{l-1,1}, \qquad \forall k \neq 0.$$

A quite different type of state assignment will now be discussed. Since the automaton $A(f)$ has $(n+1)$ states, it is possible to achieve its state assignment by means of $m = \lceil \log_2 (n+1) \rceil$ state variables $\Gamma_0, \ldots, \Gamma_{m-1}$, where $\lceil a \rceil$ stands for the smallest integer greater than or equal to a. Choosing to associate with the state l the binary representation of the integer l, and denoting by Γ^k_j the value taken by Γ_j at the input of the cell corresponding to x_k, we may write the following algebraic relation:

$$\left(\sum_{j=0}^{m-1} \Gamma^{k-1}_j\, 2^j\right) + x_{k-1} = \sum_{j=0}^{m-1} \Gamma^k_j\, 2^j.$$

Hence the typical cell of the cascade is a particularly simple adder since the augend x_{k-1} has only one significant figure; it actually reduces to a carry propagation circuit. Finally, each cell of the cascade may be implemented as an iterative circuit (Figure 13.33(a)), the subcell of which is represented in Figure 13.33(b).

The complete cascade thus realizes the m functions $\Gamma_j^n, j = 0, \ldots, m-1$, defined as follows:

$\Gamma_j^n(\boldsymbol{x}) = 1$ iff the digit of order j in the binary representation of $w(\boldsymbol{x})$ is equal to 1;
$= 0$ otherwise.

The next theorem relates these functions to the functions σ_l^n and $\gamma_{l,1}^n$.

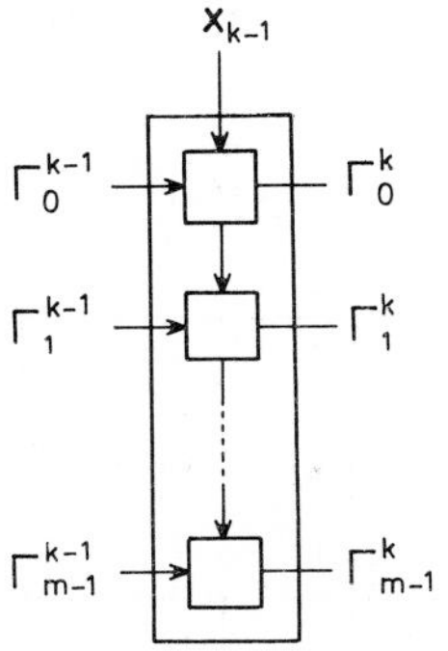

Figure 13.33 (a). Elementary cell of the Γ-array

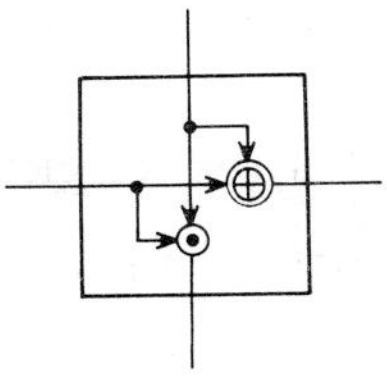

Figure 13.33 (b). Subcell of the Γ-array

Theorem 13.23. If l admits the following representation in basis two

$$l = l_0 + 2l_1 + \ldots + 2^{m-1} l_{m-1}$$

then

$$\text{(a)}\quad \sigma_l^n = \prod_{j=0}^{m-1} (\Gamma_j^n)^{(l_j)},$$

$$\text{(b)}\quad \gamma_{l,1}^n = \prod_{j=0}^{m-1} (\Gamma_j^n)^{l_j}.$$

Proof. Recall first that

$$x^{(1)} = x^1 = x, x^{(0)} = \bar{x} \text{ and } x^0 = 1.$$

Consider now a point $\boldsymbol{x}$ and suppose that

$$w(\boldsymbol{x}) = w_0 + 2w_1 + \ldots + 2^{m-1} w_{m-1}.$$

Therefore

$$\Gamma_j^n(x) = w_j, \qquad \forall j = 0, \ldots, m-1.$$

(a) We may write the following series of implications:

$$\begin{aligned}\sigma_l^n(x) = 1 &\Leftrightarrow w(x) = l\\ &\Leftrightarrow w_j = l_j, \qquad \forall j = 0, \ldots, m-1,\\ &\Leftrightarrow (w_j)^{(l_j)} = 1, \qquad \forall j = 0, \ldots, m-1,\\ &\Leftrightarrow \prod_{j=0}^{m-1} (w_j)^{(l_j)} = 1,\\ &\Leftrightarrow \prod_{j=0}^{m-1} [\Gamma_j^n(x)]^{(l_j)} = 1.\end{aligned}$$

(b) We already know that

$$\gamma_{l,1}^n(x) = 1 \quad \text{iff} \quad \binom{w(x)}{l} \equiv 1, \text{modulo-2}.$$

The proof is then completed by using a property of the binomial coefficients:

$$\binom{w(x)}{l} \equiv \binom{w_0}{l_0}\binom{w_1}{l_1}\cdots\binom{w_{m-1}}{l_{m-1}}, \text{modulo-2};$$

furthermore

$$\begin{aligned}\binom{w_j}{l_j} &= 1 \quad \text{if} \quad l_j = 0,\\ &= w_j \quad \text{if} \quad l_j = 1.\end{aligned}$$

Therefore

$$\binom{w_j}{l_j} = w_j^{l_j} = [(\Gamma_j^n(x)]^{l_j},$$

and thus

$$\gamma_{l,1}^n(x) = 1 \quad \text{iff} \quad \prod_{j=0}^{m-1} [\Gamma_j^n(x)]^{l_j} = 1. \qquad \blacksquare$$

We now turn back to the problem of finding the maximal compatibility classes of $A(f)$ in the particular case where f is a switching function.

Note that the lexicographic order $\preccurlyeq$ on $\mathcal{E}_n$ is replaced by the usual order $\leqslant$ on $\{0, \ldots, n\}$. Furthermore, the extended mapping δ from $\{0, \ldots, n\} \times (B_2)^+$ to

$\{0, \ldots n\}$ is defined as follows:

$$\delta(l, x) = l + w(x) \quad \text{if} \quad w(x) \leqslant n - l,$$
$$\delta(l, x) \quad \text{is undefined if} \quad w(x) > n - l, \qquad \forall x \in (B_2)^+.$$

The statement of lemma 13.7 becomes then: *two elements* l *and* l' *of* $\{0, \ldots, n\}$, *such that* $l < l'$ *are compatible states of* $A(f)$ *iff*

$$\lambda(l + k) = \lambda(l' + k), \qquad \forall k = 0, \ldots, n - l'.$$

This last remark allows to prove the following lemma.

Lemma 13.14. If l *and* l' *are two compatible states of* $A(f)$ *such that* $l < l'$, *then there are at most* l' *maximal compatibility classes.*

Proof. If $l \sim l'$, then

$$(l + 1) \sim (l' + 1), \ldots, [l + (l' - l - 1)] \sim [l' + (l' - l - 1)], \; l' \sim [l' + (l' - l)],$$
$$(l' + 1) \sim [l' + (l' - l + 1)], \ldots, [l' + (l' - l - 1)] \sim \{l' + [2(l' - l) - 1]\},$$

etc. . . .

One thus obtained the following compatibility classes (see lemma 13.8):

$$K_0 = \{l, l + (l' - l), l + 2\,(l' - l), \ldots\},$$
$$K_1 = \{l + 1, l + 1 + (l' - l), l + 1 + 2(l' - l), \ldots\},$$
$$\vdots$$
$$K_{l' - l - 1} = \{l' - 1, l' - 1 + (l' - l), l' - 1 + 2(l' - l), \ldots\};$$

these $(l' - l)$ classes, together with the singletons $\{0\}, \ldots, \{l - 1\}$ cover the set of states. Therefore, the number of maximal compatibility classes is at most equal to $l + (l' - l) = l$: this is a direct consequence of theorem 13.19. ■

We may now prove the following theorem. Let us recall that H_l denotes the set of elements l' such that:

$$l \leqslant l' \quad \text{and} \quad l \sim l'.$$

Theorem 13.24. If $A(f)$ *has* q *maximal compatibility classes, then these classes are* $H_0, \ldots, H_{q-1}$.

Proof. We already know that the sets $H_0, \ldots, H_{q-1}$ are all compatibility classes (lemma 13.9); if one of them, say $H_{l'}$ is not maximal, it is included in another class H_l, with $l < l'$. We have thus

$$l < l' \quad \text{and} \quad l \sim l'.$$

Therefore, by lemma 13.14, we obtain: $q \leqslant l'$, and that contradicts the fact that l' lies between 0 and $q - 1$. ■

The foregoing theorem has direct consequence on the state graph structure of the reduced automaton $A_r(f)$ associated with $A(f)$. Assume for instance that the characteristic vector $[f_c]$ of f is pseudo-periodic, with an aperiodic part $h_0, \ldots h_{k-1}$

and a periodic part $[h_k, \ldots, h_{k+p-1}]$, that is

$$[f_c(0)\ldots f_c(k-1)] = [h_0 \ldots h_{k-1}]$$

and

$$\{f_c(k+rp)\ldots f_c[k+(r+1)p-1]\} = [h_k, \ldots, h_{k+p-1}]$$

for every $r = 0, 1, \ldots$

The maximal compatibility classes are then

$$H_0, \ldots, H_{k-1}, H_k, \ldots, K_{k+p-1},$$

and the corresponding state diagram is given in Figure 13.34.

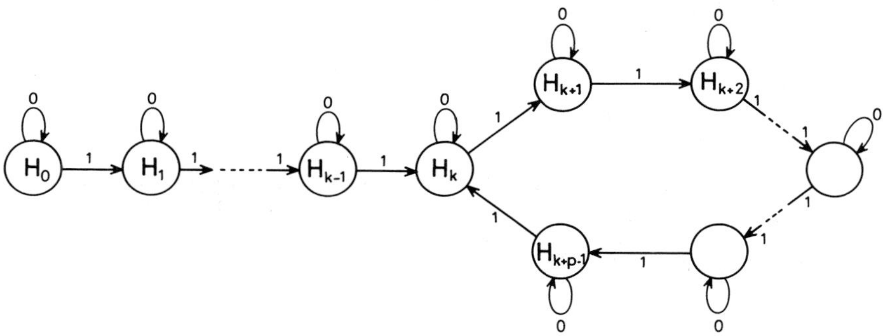

Figure 13.34. State diagram of $A_r(f)$

We conclude this chapter by an important remark concerning the ρ-symmetric switching functions. Consider a switching function f that is ρ-symmetric, with

$$\rho = (\boldsymbol{x}_{s-1}, \ldots, \boldsymbol{x}_0);$$

one may realize f by a cascade of the type described in Figure 13.26. The question arises then whether the cells realizing the transformations $T^{w_0}, \ldots, T^{w_{s-1}}$ are all different. We shall prove that in the case where ρ is the maximum partition, then all the cells are different.

We need for that purpose the following lemma.

Lemma 13.15. Let T denote a pseudo-periodic transformation of the set $\{0, \ldots, k-1, k, \ldots, k+p-1\}$, with aperiodic part $(0, \ldots, k-1)$ and periodic part $(k, \ldots, k+p-1)$. Then

$$T^a = T^b \ (a < b) \quad \textit{iff} \quad a \geqslant b \quad \textit{and} \quad a \equiv b, \textit{modulo-}p.$$

Proof. The condition is obviously sufficient. Let us assume that $T^a = T^b$. If $a < k$, then $(0)T^a = a$ while

$$(0)T^b = b \quad \text{if} \quad b \leqslant k-1,$$

and

$$(0)T^b \geqslant k \quad \text{if} \quad b \geqslant k;$$

in both cases $(0)T^a \neq (0)T^b$. Hence $a \geqslant k$. It then suffices to note that

$$(k)T^a = k + (a)_p \quad \text{and} \quad (k)T^b = k + (b)_p$$

where $(l)_p$ stands for the unique element of $\{0, \ldots, p-1\}$ equivalent to l, modulo-p. The equality of T^a and T^b thus implies

$$(a)_p = (b)_p \quad \text{that is} \quad a \equiv b, \text{ modulo-}p. \qquad \blacksquare$$

With the ρ-symmetric function f is associated the totally symmetric function g:

$$f(\ldots, \boldsymbol{x}_j, \ldots) = g(\ldots, \boldsymbol{x}_{j0}, \ldots, \boldsymbol{x}_{j\,n_j-1}, \ldots)$$

where

$$\boldsymbol{x}_{jr} = \underbrace{(x_{jr}, \ldots, x_{jr})}_{w_j \text{ times}}.$$

Let us suppose that the characteristic vector $[g_c]$ is pseudo-periodic with aperiodic part $(0, \ldots, k-1)$ and periodic part $(k, \ldots, k+p-1)$. Recall also that

$$f(\boldsymbol{x}_{s-1}, \ldots, \boldsymbol{x}_0) = g_c(X)$$

where

$$X = \sum_{h=0}^{s-1} \left(\sum_{i=0}^{n_h-1} w_h \, x_{hi} \right).$$

We may then state the following theorem.

Theorem 13.25. If the two transformations T^{w_j} and T^{w_l} are identical then f has the partial symmetries

$$x_{jr} \sim x_{ls}$$

for every r in $\{0, \ldots, n_j-1\}$ and s in $\{0, \ldots, n-1\}$.

Proof. Suppose that $j < l$ and thus $w_j < w_l$. We deduce from lemma 13.15 that

$$w_j \geqslant k \quad \text{and} \quad w_j \equiv w_l, \text{ modulo-}p.$$

Let us compute f at points

$$\boldsymbol{x} = (\boldsymbol{x}_{s-1}, \ldots, x_{l\,s+1}, 1, x_{l\,s-1}, \ldots, x_{j\,r+1}, 0, x_{j\,r-1}, \ldots, \boldsymbol{x}_0)$$

and

$$\boldsymbol{x}' = (\boldsymbol{x}_{s-1}, \ldots, x_{l\,s+1}, 0, x_{l\,s-1}, \ldots, x_{j\,r+1}, 1, x_{j\,r-1}, \ldots, \boldsymbol{x}_0);$$

for that purpose compute

$$X = w_l + Y \quad \text{and} \quad X' = w_j + Y$$

where

$$Y = \sum_{\substack{i=0 \\ i \neq s}}^{n_l - 1} w_l x_{li} + \sum_{\substack{i=0 \\ i \neq r}}^{n_j - 1} w_j x_{ij} + \sum_{\substack{h=0 \\ h \neq j \\ h \neq l}}^{s-1} \left(\sum_{i=0}^{n_h - 1} w_h x_{hi} \right).$$

One has

$$X \geqslant w_l > w_j \geqslant k, \; X' \geqslant w_j \geqslant k$$

and

$$X - X' = w_l - w_j \equiv 0, \text{modulo-}p.$$

Therefore, according to the pseudo-periodic character of $[g_c]$, we deduce that

$$g_c(X) = g_c(X')$$

and thus

$$f(\mathbf{x}) = f(\mathbf{x}'). \qquad \blacksquare$$

Clearly, the use of the additional symmetries $x_{jr} \sim x_{ls}$ detected in theorem 13.25 would have led directly to a synthesis having one cell type less than the foregoing one.

Bibliography

Abramowitz, M and Stegun, I. 1964 "Handbook of mathematical functions" (National Bureau of Standards, Washington, DC, USA).

Akers, S. 1959 On a theory of Boolean functions, *SIAM J.*, 7, 487–498.

Akers, S. 1972 Universal test sets for logic networks, *Proc. 13th international symposium on switching and automata theory,* 177–184.

Allen, C. and Givone, D. 1968 A minimization technique for multiple-valued logic systems, *IEEE Trans. Comput.*, **C-17**, 182–184.

Amar, V. and Condulmari, N. 1967 Diagnosis of large combinational networks, *IEEE Trans. Electron. Comput,* **EC-16**, 675–680.

Armstrong, D. 1966 On finding a nearly minimal set of fault detection tests for combinational logic nets, *IEEE Trans. Electron. Comput.,* **EC-15**, 66–73.

Ashenhurst, R. 1957 The decomposition of switching functions, *Paper presented at the international symposium on switching theory; reprinted as appendix in:* Curtis, A. "A new approach to the design of switching circuits" (Van Nostrand, Princeton, 1962).

Ashkinazy, A. 1970 Fault detection experiments for asynchronous sequential machines, *Proc. 11th international symposium on switching and automata theory,* 88–96.

Balas, E. 1965 An additive algorithm for solving linear programs with zero-one variables. *Oper. Res.,* **13**, 518–546.

Balinski, M. 1965 Integer programming: methods, uses, computation, *Manag. Sci.,* **12**, 253–313.

Bartee, T. and Schneider, D. 1963 Computation with finite fields, *Inf. and Control,* **6**, 79–98.

Batni, R., Russell, J. and Kime, C. 1974 An efficient method for finding an irredundant set cover, *J. Assoc. Comput. Mach.,* **21**, 351–355.

Beister, J. 1974 A unified approach to combinational hazards, *IEEE Trans. Comput.* **C-23**, 566–575.

Bellman, R. 1960 'Introduction to matrix analysis" (McGraw-Hill, New York).

Benjauthrit, B. 1974 Design and diagnosis of Galois logic networks, *Ph.D. dissertation,* USC, Los Angeles, USA.

Benjauthrit, B. and Reed, I. 1976 Galois switching functions and their applications, *IEEE Trans. Comput.,* **C-25**, 78–86.

Berge, C. 1968 "Principes de combinatoire" (Dunod, Paris).

Berlekamp, E. 1968 "Algebraic coding theory" (McGraw-Hill, New York).

Bernstein, B. 1928 Modular representations of finite algebras, *Proc. 7th international congress of mathematicians,* **I**, 207–216.

Betancourt, R. 1971 Derivation of minimum test sets for unate logical circuits, *IEEE Trans. Comput.*, **C-20**, 1264–1269.

Bioul, G. and Davio, M. 1972 Taylor expansions of Boolean functions and of their derivatives, *Philips Res. Rep.*, **27**, 1–6.

Bioul, G., Davio, M. and Deschamps J.-P. 1973 Minimization of ring-sum expansions of Boolean functions, *Philips Res. Rep.*, **28**, 17–36.

Birkhoff, G. 1967 "Lattice theory" (American Mathematical Society, Providence, USA).

Birkhoff, G. and Bartee, T. 1970 "Modern applied algebra" (McGraw-Hill, New York).

Bordat, J. P. 1975 Treillis de Post. Applications aux fonctions et aux équations de la logique à p valeurs, *Thèse,* Université des sciences et techniques du Languedoc, Montpellier, France.

Bowman, R. and McVey, E. 1970 A method for the fast approximate solution of large prime implicant charts. *IEEE Trans. Comput.*, **C-19**, 169–173.

Bredeson, J. 1973 Synthesis of multiple input change hazard-free combinational switching circuits without feed-back, *IEEE Group Repository System,* R73–118.

Bredeson, J. and Hulina, P. 1970 Elimination of static and of dynamic hazards in combinational switching networks, *Proc. 11th international symposium on switching and automata theory,* 28–30.

Bredeson, J. and Hulina, P. 1972 Elimination of static and dynamic hazards for multiple changes in combinational switching circuit, *Inf. and Control,* **20**, 114–124.

Breuer, M. 1972 "Design automation of digital systems" (Prentice-Hall, Englewood Cliffs, USA).

Breuer, M. 1974 The effects of races, delays and delay faults on test generation, *IEEE Trans. Comput.*, **C-23**, 1078–1092.

Brown, A. and Young, H. 1969 Toward an algebraic theory of the analysis and testing of digital networks, *AAS and ORS Annual Meeting,* AAS paper 69–236, Denver, USA.

Brown, A. and Young, H. 1970 Algebraic logic network analysis: toward an algebraic theory of the analysis and testing of digital networks, *Report TROO-1974,* IBM Systems Development Division, Poughkeepsie, USA.

Brusentzov, N. 1965 A ternary arithmetic machine (in Russian), *Moscow University Vestnik,* **2**, 39–48.

Brzozowski, J. 1962 Properties of regular expressions and state diagrams, *Internal report No 15,* Department of Electrical Engineering, Digital Systems Laboratory, Princeton University, USA.

Bubenik, V. 1972 Weighting method for the determination of the irredundant set of prime implicants, *IEEE Trans. Comput.*, **C-21**, 1449–1451.

Burks, A. and Wright, J. 1953 Theory of logical nets, *Proc. IRE 41,* **10**, 1357–1365.

Cadden, W. 1959 Equivalent sequential circuits, *IRE Trans. Circuit Theory,* **CT-6**, 30–34.

Caldwell, S. 1958 "Switching circuits and logical design" (John Wiley, New York).

Calingaert, P. 1961 Switching functions: canonical forms based on commutative and associative binary operations, *Trans. AIEE,* **80**, 808–814.

Canaday, R. 1964 Two dimensional iterative logic, *Report ESL-R-210,* MIT Electronic Syst., Massachussetts, USA.

Chang, H., Manning, E. and Metze, G. 1970 "Fault diagnosis of digital systems" (Wiley-Interscience, New York).

Chaudhury, A., Basu, A. and Desarkar, S. 1969 On the determination of the maximal compatibility classes, *IEEE Trans. Comput.,* **C-18**, 665.

Clegg, F. 1972 Use of SPOOF's for faulty logic network analysis, *Digest International symposium on fault-tolerant computing,* 143–147.

Cobham, A., Fridshal, R. and North, J. 1961 An application of linear programming to the minimization of Boolean functions, *AIEE International symposium on switching theory and logical design,* 3–10.

Cohn, M. 1960 Switching functions: canonical forms over integer fields, *Ph.D. dissertation,* Harvard University, Cambridge, USA.

Cohn, M. 1962 Inconsistent canonical forms of switching functions, *IEEE Trans. Electron. Comput.,* **EC-11**, 284–285.

Crawley, P. and Dilworth, R. 1973 "Algebraic theory of lattices" (Prentice-Hall, Englewood Cliffs, USA).

Csanky, L. 1973 On the existence of terms in the generalized Reed–Muller canonical form of the Boolean functions, *IEEE Group Repository,* R-73-201.

Curtis, A. 1962 "A new approach to the design of switching circuits" (Van Nostrand, Princeton, USA).

Das, S. 1971 An approach for simplifying switching functions by utilizing the cover table representation, *IEEE Trans. Comput.,* **C-20**, 355–359.

Das, S., Banerji, D. and Chattopadhyay, A. 1973 On control memory minimization in microprogrammed digital computers, *IEEE Trans. Comput.,* **C-22**, 845–848.

Das, S. and Sheng, C. 1969 On finding maximum compatibles, *Proc. IEEE,* **57**, 694–695.

Das, S. and Sheng, C. 1971 On detecting total or partial symmetry of switching functions, *IEEE Trans. Comput.,* **C-20**, 352–355.

Davio, M. 1968 Méthodes de synthèse des circuits logiques combinatoires utilisant une opération linéaire, *Thèse,* Université catholique de Louvain, Belgium.

Davio, M. 1969 Algebraic research of the maximal compatibility classes for incompletely specified sequential machines, *MBLE Internal Report,* R118.

Davio, M. 1971 Ring-sum expressions of Boolean functions, *Proc. symposium on computers and automata,* **21**, 411–418.

Davio, M. 1973 Taylor expansions of symmetric Boolean functions, *Philips Res. Rep.,* **28**, 466–474.

Davio, M. and Bioul, G. 1970 Representation of lattice functions, *Philips Res. Rep.,* **25**, 370–388.

Davio, M. and Bioul, G. 1974 Taylor expansions computation from cube arrays, *Philips Res. Rep.,* **29**, 401–412.

Davio, M. and De Lit, Ch. 1970 State minimal covers of deterministic Mealy automata, *MBLE Report,* N69.

Davio, M. and Deschamps, J.-P. 1972 Symmetric discrete functions, *Philips Res. Rep.,* **27**, 405–445.

Davio, M. and Piret, Ph. 1969 Les dérivées Booléennes et leur application au diagnostic, *Revue MBLE,* **12**, 63–76.

Davio, M. and Quisquater, J. J. 1972 Affine cascades, *Philips Res. Rep.,* **27**, 109–125.

Davio, M. and Quisquater, J. J. 1973a Rectangular universal iterative array, *Electron. Lett.,* **9**, 485–486.

Davio, M. and Quisquater, J. J. 1973b Iterative universal logical modules, *Philips Res. Rep.,* **28**, 265–293.

Davio, M. and Quisquater, J. J. 1975 Complexity of discrete functions, *MBLE Internal Report,* R292.

Davio, M. and Thayse, A. 1969 Analysis of logical circuits using discrete delays, *MBLE Internal Report,* N48.

Davio, M. and Thayse, A. 1973 Representation of fuzzy functions, *Philips Res. Rep.,* **28**, 93–106.

Davio, M., Thayse, A. and Bioul, G. 1972 Symbolic computation of Fourier transforms of Boolean functions, *Philips Res. Rep.,* **27**, 386–403.

Decroly, J. C., Fosséprez, C. and Thayse, A. 1969 A procedure for analysing digital circuits with fixed transition delays, *MBLE Internal Report,* R107.

de la Vallée-Poussin, Ch. 1959 "Cours d'analyse infinitésimale", tome I (Gauthier-Villars, Paris).

Delsarte, Ph. and Quisquater, J. J. 1973 Permutation cascades with normalized cells, *Inf. and Control,* **23**, 344–356.

Deschamps, J. 1974 Application de la notion de fermeture à l'étude des decompositions des fonctions booléennes. *Thèse,* Université des sciences du Languedoc, Montpellier, France.

Deschamps, J.-P. 1973 Partially symmetric switching functions, *Philips Res. Rep.,* **28**, 245–264.

Deschamps, J.-P. 1974 On a theory of discrete functions, Part III: decomposition of discrete functions, *Philips Res. Rep.,* **29**, 193–213.

Deschamps, J.-P. 1975a Binary simple decompositions of discrete functions, *Digit. Proc.* **1**, 123–140.

Deschamps, J.-P. 1975b The module structure of discrete functions, *MBLE Internal Report,* R310.

Deschamps, J.-P. and Thayse, A. 1973a On a theory of discrete functions, Part I: The lattice structure of discrete functions, *Philips Res. Rep.,* **28**, 397–423.

Deschamps, J.-P. and Thayse, A. 1973b Applications of discrete functions, Part I: Transient analysis of combinational networks, *Philips Res. Rep.,* **28**, 497–529.

Deschamps, J.-P. and Thayse, A. 1975 Representation of discrete functions, *International symposium on multiple-valued logic,* 99–111.

Dickson, L. 1957 "Introduction to the theory of numbers" (Dover, New York).

Dietmeyer, D. 1971 "Logic design of digital systems" (Allyn and Bacon, Boston, USA).

Druzeta, A., Vranesic, Z. and Sedra, A. 1975 Application of multi-threshold elements in the realization of many-valued logic networks, *IEEE Trans. on Comput.,* **C-23,** 1194–1198.

Eichelberger, E. 1964 Hazard detection in combinational and sequential switching circuits, *Proc. 5th international symposium on switching and automata theory,* 111–120.

Eichelberger, E. 1965 Hazard detection in combinational and sequential circuit, *IBM J. Res. Develop.,* **9,** 90–99.

Ellison, J. and Kolman, B. 1970 Galois logic design, *Internal Report,* Univac Division of Sperry Rand Corp.

Elspas, B. 1971 The theory of multirail cascades, *in* "Recent developments in switching theory", Ed. A Mukhopadhyay (Academic Press, New York).

Elspas, B. and Stone, H. 1967 Decomposition of group functions and the synthesis of multirail-cascades, *IEEE Conf. Rec. 8th Ann. Symp. on Switching and Automata Theory,* 184–196.

Euler, L. 1772 Lettre à une princesse allemande.

Even, S., Kohavi, I. and Paz, A. 1967 On minimal modulo-2 sums of products for switching functions, *IEEE Trans. Electron. Comput.,* **EC-16,** 671–674.

Fadini, A. 1961 Operatori che estendono alle algebre di Boole la nozione di derivata, *Giorn. Mat. Battaglini,* **89,** 42–64.

Fisher, L. 1974 Unateness properties of AND-EXCLUSIVE-OR logic circuits, *IEEE Trans. Comput.,* **C-23,** 166–172.

Fosséprez, C. and Noé, M. 1966 An algorithm for the optimal covering problem; application to the minimization of Boolean functions, *MBLE Internal Report,* R53.

Gazalé, H. 1959 "Les structures de commutation a m valeurs et les calculatrices numériques" (Gauthier-Villars, Paris).

Gimpel, J. F. 1967 The minimization of TANT networks, *IEEE Trans. Electron. Comput.,* **EC-16,** 18–38.

Ginzburg, A. 1968 "Algebraic theory of automata" (Academic Press, New York).

Goethals, J. M. 1965 Un algorithme pour la programmation linéaire (totalement) en nombres entiers, *MBLE Internal Report,* N16.

Golomb, S. 1959 On the classification of Boolean functions, *IRE Trans. Inf. Theory,* **IT-5,** 176–186.

Golomb, S., Welsch, L., Goldstein, R. and Hales, A. 1967 "Shift register sequences" (Holden-Day, San Francisco, USA).

Grasselli, A. and Gimpel, J. 1966 The synthesis of three-level logic networks, *Internal Report* 49, Princeton University, Department of Electrical Engineering, Digital Systems Laboratory.

Grasselli, A. and Luccio, F. 1965 A method for minimizing the number of internal states in incompletely specified sequential networks, *IEEE Trans. Electron. Comput.,* **EC-14,** 350–358.

Green, D. and Dimond, K. 1970 Polynomial representation of nonlinear feedback shift-register, *Proc. IEEE,* **117,** 56–60.

Green, D. and Kelsch, R. 1973 Non-linear ternary feedback shift-registers, *Comput. J.,* **16,** 360–367.

Green, D. and Taylor, I. 1974 Modular representations of multiple-valued logic systems, *Proc. IEE,* **121**, 409–417.

Hammer, P. and Rudeanu, S. 1968 "Boolean methods in operations research" (Springer, Berlin).

Harao, M., Noguchi, S. and Oizumi, J. 1971 Realization of multi-valued logical functions with multi-stage logical networks, *Electron. Commun. Japan,* **54-C**, 121–130.

Harrison, M. 1965 "Introduction to switching and automata theory" (McGraw-Hill, New York).

Hartman, F. 1967 Boolean differential calculus, *IBM Internal Report,* TR22.526.

Hatmanis, J. and Stearns, R. 1966 "Algebraic structure of sequential machines" (Prentice-Hall, Englewood Cliffs, USA).

Hennie, F. 1964 Fault detecting experiments for sequential circuits, *Proc. 5th international symposium on switching theory and logical design,* 95–110.

Hennie, F. 1968 "Finite state models for logical machines" (Wiley-Interscience, New York).

Hill, F. and Peterson, R. 1974 "Introduction to switching theory and logical design" (John Wiley, New York).

Hsiao, M., Sellers, F. and Chia, D. 1970 Fundamentals of Boolean difference for test pattern generation, *Proc. 4th annual Princeton conference on information sciences and systems,* 50–54.

Huffman, D. 1954 The synthesis of sequential switching circuits, *J. Franklin Inst.,* **257**, 161–190 and 275–303.

Huffman, D. 1957 The design and use of hazard-free switching networks, *J. of the ACM,* **4**, 47–62.

Iablonski, S. 1958 Functional constructions in the *k*-valued logic, *Trudy Mat. Inst. Steklov,* **T.51**, 5–142.

Jordan, C. 1947 "Calculus of finite differences" (Chelsea Publishing Company, Chelsea).

Kandel, A. 1973 On minimization of fuzzy functions, *IEEE Trans. Comput.,* **C-22**, 826–832.

Kandel, A. 1974 Application of fuzzy logic to the detection of static hazards in combinational switching systems, *Int. J. Comput. Inf. Sci.,* **3**, 129–140.

Karnaugh, M. 1953 The map method for synthesis of combinational logic circuits, *Trans. AIEE, Part I, Communication and Electronics,* **72**, 593–599.

Karp, R. 1963 Functional decomposition and switching circuit design, *SIAM J.,* **11**, 291–335.

Kautz, W. 1965a Concerning the minimization of modified ring sum expansions, *Stanford Research Institute Internal Memorandum,* May 13, USA.

Kautz, W. 1965b "Linear sequential switching circuits" (selected papers) (Holden-Day, San Francisco, USA).

Kautz, W. 1968 Fault testing and diagnosis in combinational digital circuits, *IEEE Trans. Comput.,* **C-17**, 352–366.

Kautz, W., Levitt, K. and Waksman, A. 1968 Cellular interconnection arrays, *IEEE Trans. Comput.*, **C-17**, 443–451.

Keister, W., Ritchie, A. and Washburn, S. 1951 "The design of switching circuits" (Van Nostrand, New York).

Klir, G. 1972 "Introduction to the methodology of switching circuits" (Van Nostrand, New York).

Kodandapani, K. 1974 A note on easily testable realizations for logic functions, *IEEE Trans. Comput.*, **C-32**, 332.

Kodandapani, K. 1976 Generalization of Reed–Muller canonical forms to multivalued logic. Private communication.

Kodandapani, K. and Setlur, R. 1975 Reed–Muller canonical forms in multivalued logic, *IEEE Trans. Comput.*, **C-24**, 628–636.

Kohavi, I. 1969 Fault diagnosis of logical circuits, *Proc. 10th international symposium on switching theory and logical design,* 166–173.

Kohavi, Z. 1970 "Switching and finite automata theory" (McGraw-Hill, New York).

Kohler, W. and Steiglitz, K. 1974 Characterization and theoretical comparison of branch and bound algorithms for permutation problems, *J. of the ACM,* **21**, 140–156.

Kolp, O. 1972 The synthesis of multivalued cellular cascades and the decomposition of group functions, *IEEE Trans. Comput.*, **C-21**, 489–492.

Kostopoulos, G. 1975 "Digital engineering" (Wiley, New York).

Ku, C. and Masson, G. 1975 The Boolean difference and multiple fault analysis, *IEEE Trans. Comput.*, **C-24**, 62–71.

Kuntzmann, J. 1965 "Algèbre de Boole" (Dunod, Paris).

Kuntzmann, J. and Naslin, P. 1967 "Algèbre de Boole et machines logiques" (Dunod, Paris).

Lapscher, F. 1972 Sur la recherche des décompositions disjointes d'une fonction booléenne, *Rev. Fr. Automat. Inf. Rech. Opér.*, **6**, 92–112.

Lazarev, V. and Piil, E. 1961 Synthesis method for finite automata, *Automat. i Telemeh.*, **22**, 1194–1201.

Lazarev, V. and Piil, E. 1962 A method for synthesizing finite automata with voltage-pulse feedback elements, *Automat. i Telemeh.*, **23**, 1037–1043.

Lazarev, V. and Piil, E. 1963 The simplification of pulse-potential forms, *Automat. i Telemeh.*, **24**, 271–276.

Lechner, R. 1963 Transformations among switching function canonical forms, *IEEE Trans. Electron. Comput.*, **EC-12**, 129–130.

Lechner, R. 1971 Harmonic analysis of switching functions, *in* "Recent developments in switching theory", Ed. A. Mukhopadhyay (Academic Press, New York).

Lee, C. 1954 Switching functions on an *n*-dimensional cube, *Trans. AIEE, Part I,* **73**, 287–291.

Lee, S. and Lee, E. 1970 Fuzzy nemons and automata, *Proc. 4th Princeton conference on information sciences and systems.*

Lee, S. and Lee, E. 1972 On multivalued symmetric functions, *IEEE Trans. Comput.*, **C-21**, 312–316.

Lewin, D. 1968 "Logical design of switching circuits" (Nelson, London).

Lin, S. 1970 Heuristic techniques for solving large combinatorial problems on a computer, *in* "Theoretical approaches to non-numerical problem solving", 410–418 (Springer, Heidelberg).

Liss, D. 1963 A test for unate truth functions, *IEEE Trans. Electron. Comput.*, **EC-12**, 405.

Lukasiewicz, J. 1920 O logice trojwartosciowcj, *Ruch Filozoficzny*, **5**, 169–171; *translated in* "Polish logic, 1920–1939", Ed. McCall, S. 16–18 (Oxford, 1967).

Lupanov, O. 1958 Ob odnom metode sinteza skhem, *Isvestiya VUZ (Radiofizika)*, 120–140.

Lupanov, O. 1965 Ob odnom podkhode k sintezu upravlyayuschikh sistem – printsipe lokalnogo kodirovaniya, *Problemy Kibernetiki*, **14**, 31–110.

Lyngholm, C. and Yoourgrau, W. 1960 A double iteration property of Boolean functions, *Notre Dame J. Formal Logic*, **1**, 111–114.

Mal'cev, A. 1967 On a strengthening of Slupecki's and Iablonskii's theorems, *Algebra i Logika*, **6**, 61–75.

Maley, G. 1970 "Manual of logic circuits" (Prentice-Hall, Englewood Cliffs, USA).

Malgrange, Y. 1962 Recherche des sous-matrices premières d'une matrice à coefficients binaires. Application à certains problèmes de graphes. Recherche des formes normales minimales d'une fonction booléenne. *Deuxième congrès de l'AFCALTI* (Gauthier-Villars, Paris).

Mange, D. 1973 Modèles asynchrones des bascules bistables, Systèmes logiques, *Cahiers de la C.S.L.* Numéro 5, 256–286.

Marcus, M. 1962 "Switching circuits for engineers" (Prentice-Hall, Englewood Cliffs, USA).

Marcus, M. 1964 Derivation of maximal compatibles using Boolean algebra, *IBM J. Res. Develop.*, **8**, 537–538.

Marincovic, S. and Tosic, Z. 1974 Algorithms for minimal polarized form determination, *IEEE Trans. Comput.*, **C-23**, 1313–1315.

Marinos, P. 1969 Fuzzy logic and its application to switching systems, *IEEE Trans. Comput.*, **C-18**, 343–348.

Marquand, A. 1881 On logical diagrams for n terms, *Philosophical Magazine*, **12**, 266–270.

McCluskey, E. 1956a Detection of group invariance or total symmetry of a Boolean Function, *Bell System Tech. J.*, **35**, 1445–1453.

McCluskey, E. 1956b Minimization of Boolean functions, *Bell System Tech. J.*, **35**, 1417–1444.

McCluskey, E. 1962 Transients in combinatorial logic circuits, *in* "Redundancy techniques for computing systems", Ed. Wilcox and Mann, 9–46 (Spartan Book Company, Washington, DC, USA).

McCluskey, E. 1963 Fundamental mode and pulse mode sequential circuits, *Proc. IFIP congress 1962*, 725–730.

McCluskey, E. 1965 "Introduction to the theory of switching circuits" (McGraw-Hill, New York).

McCoy, N. 1948 "Rings and ideals" (Mathematical Association of America, Menasha, USA).

McGhee, R. 1969 Some aids to the detection of hazards in combinational switching circuits, *IEEE Trans. Comput.*, **C-18**, 229–246.

McLane, S. and Birkhoff, G. 1967 "Algebra" (McMillan, New York).

McNaughton, R. 1961 Unate truth functions, *IRE Trans. Electron. Comput.*, **EC-10**, 1–6.

Mealy, G. 1955 A method for synthesizing sequential circuits, *Bell System Tech. J.*, **34**, 1045–1080.

Meisel, W. 1967 A note on internal state minimization in incompletely specified sequential networks, *IEEE Trans. Electron. Comput.*, **EC-16**, 508–509.

Menger, K. 1969 A transform for logic networks, *IEEE Trans. Comput.*, **C-18**, 241–250.

Miller, R. 1965 "Switching theory, Volume I: Combinational circuits" (Wiley, New York).

Minnick, R., Short, R., Goldberg, J., Stone, H., Green, M., Yoeli, M. and Kautz, W. 1966 Cellular arrays for logic and storage, *Project 5087*, Stanford Research Institute.

Moisil, G. 1972 "Essais sur les logiques non chrysippiennes" (Editions de l'Académie de la République Socialiste de Roumanie).

Montangero, C. 1974 An approach to the optimal specification of read-only memories, *IEEE Trans. Comput.*, **C-23**, 375–389.

Moore, E. 1956 "Gedanken-experiments on sequential machines in automata studies", Ed. Shannon, C. and McCarthy, J. (Princeton University Press).

Mott, T. 1960 Determination of the irredundant normal forms of a truth function by iterated consensus of prime implicants, *Trans. Electron. Comput.*, **EC-9**, 245–262.

Muehldorf, E. 1958 Ternary switching algebra, *Arch. Elek. Übertr.*, **12**.

Muehldorf, E. 1959 Multivalued switching algebras and their applications in digital systems, *Proc. national electronic conference*, **15**, 467–480.

Mukhopadhyay, A. 1963 Detection of total or partial symmetry of a switching function with the use of decomposition charts, *IEEE Trans. Electron. Comput.*, **EC-12**, 553–557.

Mukhopadhyay, A. and Schmitz, G. 1970 Minimization of exclusive-or and logical equivalence switching circuits, *IEEE Trans. Comput.*, **C-19**, 132–140.

Mukhopadhyay, A. 1971 Lupanov decoding networks, *in* "Recent developments in switching theory", Ed. Mukhopadhyay, A. (Academic Press, New York).

Muller, D. 1954 Application of Boolean algebra to switching circuit design and to error detection, *Trans. IRE*, **PGEC-3**, 6–12.

Muller, D. 1956 Complexity in electronic switching circuits, *Trans. Electron. Comput.*, **EC-5**, 15–19.

Muller, D. 1959 Treatment of transition signals in electronic switching circuits by algebraic methods, *Trans. Electron. Comput.*, **EC-8**, 401.

Muzio, J. and Miller, D. 1973 Decomposition of ternary switching functions, *International symposium on multiple-valued logic*, 156–165.

Ninomiya, I. 1961 A study of the structures of Boolean functions and its applications to the synthesis of switching circuits, *Eng. Magoya Uni.*, **13**, 149–363.

Noé, M. 1968 Computer experiments with the optimal covering algorithm, *MBLE Internal Report,* R80.

Nyquist, H. 1928 Certain topics in telegraph transmission theory, *Trans. AIEE,* **47**, 617–644.

Paull, M. and Unger, H. 1959 Minimizing the number of states in incompletely specified sequential circuits, *Trans. Electron. Comput.*, **EC-8**, 356–367.

Perrin, J., Denouette, M. and Daclin, E. 1967a "Systèmes logiques; tome 1: Systèmes combinatoires et introduction aux systèmes séquentiels" (Dunod, Paris).

Perrin, J., Denouette, M. and Daclin, E. 1967b "Systèmes logiques; tome 2: Systèmes séquentiels" (Dunod, Paris).

Peterson, W. 1961 "Error-correcting codes" (MIT Press, Cambridge, USA).

Peterson, W. and Weldon, E. 1972 "Error-correcting codes" (MIT Press, Cambridge, USA).

Pichat, E. 1968 Décompositions simples de fonctions Booléennes, *Rev. Fr. Automat. Inf. Rech. Opér.*, **2**, 61–70.

Piret, Ph. 1969 Dérivatives of discrete functions, *MBLE Internal Report,* N51.

Poage, J. 1963 Derivation of optimum tests to detect faults in combinational networks, *Proc. symposium on computers and automata,* **13**, 483–528.

Post, E. 1921 Introduction to a general theory of elementary propositions, *Amer. J. Math.*, **43**, 163–185.

Post, E. 1941 Two valued iterative systems of mathematical logics, *Ann. of Math.*

Pradhan, D. 1974 A multivalued switching algebra based on finite fields, *International symposium on multiple-valued logic,* 95–112.

Pradhan, D. 1976 On the structure and minimization of Galois switching functions, Private communication.

Pradhan, D. and Patel, A. 1975 Reed–Muller like canonic forms for multivalued functions, *IEEE Trans. Comput.*, **C-24**, 206–210.

Preparata, F. and Muller, D. 1969 On the delay required to realize Boolean functions, *Report R421,* University of Illinois.

Preparata, F. and Muller, D. 1970 Generation of near-optimal universal Boolean functions, *J. Comput. System Sci.*, **4**, 93–102.

Preparata, F. and Yeh, R. 1971 On a theory of continuously valued logic, *International symposium on multiple-valued logic,* 124–132.

Preparata, F. and Yeh, R. 1972 Continuously valued logic, *J. Comput. System Sci.*, **6**, 397–418.

Preparata, F. and Yeh, R. 1973 "Introduction to discrete structures" (Addison-Wesley, Reading, USA).

Prior, A. 1974 Extension of Boolean differentiation to define a test for a specific logic fault in a combinational logic network, *Electron. Lett.*, **10**, No 17, 353–354.

Prior, A. and Bennets, R. 1974 Application of the Boolean difference technique to sequential logic, *Electron. Lett.*, **10**, No 23, 486–488.

Quine, W. 1952 The problem of simplifying truth functions, *Amer. Math. Monthly,* **59**, 521–531.

Quine, W. 1953 Two theorems about truth functions, *Bol. Soc. Mat. Mexicana,* **10**, 64–70.

Quine, W. 1955 A way to simplify truth functions, *Amer. Math. Monthly,* **62**, 627–631.

Quisquater, J. J. 1973 Universal array based on the crossbar switch, *MBLE Internal Report,* R228.

Rao, V. and Nordstrom, W. 1971 Heuristic minimisation of AND-EXCLUSIVE-OR realization of switching functions, *Report No 36,* University of Iowa.

Rasiowa, H. 1974 "An algebraic approach to non-classical logics" (North-Holland, Amsterdam).

Reddy, S. 1972 Easily testable realizations for logic functions, *IEEE Trans. Comput.,* **C-21**, 1183–1188.

Reed, I. 1954 A class of multiple-error-correcting codes and the decoding scheme, *Trans. IRE,* **PGIT4**, 38–49.

Reese, R. and McCluskey, E. 1973 A gate equivalent model for combinational network analysis, *International symposium on fault-tolerant computing,* 79–84.

Reischer, C. and Simovici, D. 1971 Associative algebraic structures in the set of Boolean functions and some applications in automata theory, *IEEE Trans. Comput.,* **C-20**, 298–303.

Rescher, N. 1969 "Many-valued logic" (McGraw-Hill, New York).

Riordan, J. 1968 "Combinatorial identities" (Wiley, New York).

Rosenberg, I. 1965 La structure des fonctions de plusieurs variables sur un ensemble fini, *C. R. Acad. Sci. Paris Sér. A–B,* **260**, 3817–3819.

Rosenberg, I. 1970 Über die funktionale Vollständigheit in den mehrwertigen Logiken (Struktur der Funktionen von mehreren Veränderlichen auf endlichen Mengen), *Rozprary Ceskoslovenské Akad. Ved. Rada Mat. Prirod. Ved.,* **80**, 3–93.

Rosenberg, I. 1973 The number of maximal closed classes in the set of functions over a finite domain, *J. Combinatorial Theory,* **14**, 1–7.

Rosenberg, I. 1974 Minimization of pseudo-Boolean functions by binary development, *Discrete Math.* **7**, 151–165.

Roth, J. 1960 Minimization over Boolean trees, *IBM J. Res. Develop.,* **4**, 543–548.

Roth, J. and Karp, R. 1962 Minimization over Boolean graphs, *IBM J. Res. Develop.,* **6**, 227–238.

Roth, R. 1969 Computer solutions to minimum-cover problems, *Oper. Res.,* **17**, 455–465.

Rousseau, G. 1967 Completeness in finite algebras with a single operation, *Proc. Amer. Math. Soc.,* **18**, 1009–1013.

Rudeanu, S. 1974 "Boolean functions and equations" (North-Holland, Amsterdam).

Rutherford, D. 1965 "Introduction to lattice theory" (Oliver and Boyd, Edinburgh).

Salomaa, A. 1962 and 1963. Some completeness criteria for sets of functions over a finite domain I-II, *Ann. Univ. Turkunensis, Ser. AI,* **53**, (1962) 1–9 and **63**, (1963).

Saluja, K. and Reddy, S. 1975 Fault detecting test sets for Reed–Muller canonic networks, *IEEE Trans. Comput.*, **C-24**, 995–998.

Saucier, G. 1972 Structure facilement testable. Réseau NI à parité, *Colloque international: Conception et maintenance des automatismes logiques.*

Savage, J. 1972 Computational work and time on finite machines, *J. ACM*, **19**, 660–674.

Schofield, P. 1969 Independent conditions for completeness of finite algebras with a single generator, *J. London Math. Soc.*, **44**, 413–423.

Sellers, F., Hsiao, M. and Bearnson, L. 1968 Analysing errors with the Boolean difference, *IEEE Trans. Comput.*, **C-17**, 676–683.

Servit, M. 1975 A heuristic method for solving weighted set covering problems, *Digit. Process.*, **1**, 177–182.

Shannon, C. 1948 A mathematical theory of communication, *Bell System Tech. J.*, **27**, 279–423 and 623–656.

Shannon, C. 1938 A symbolic analysis of relay and switching circuits, *Trans. of the AIEE*, **57**, 713–723.

Shannon, C. 1949 The synthesis of two-terminal switching circuits, *Bell System Tech. J.*, **28**, 59–98.

Shen, V. and McKellar, A. 1970 An algorithm for the disjunctive decomposition of switching functions, *IEEE Trans. Comput.*, **C-19**, 239–248.

Shen, V., McKellar, A. and Wiener, P. 1971 A fast algorithm for the disjunctive decomposition of switching functions, *IEEE Trans. Comput.*, **C-20**, 304–309.

Sheng, C. 1965 Detection of totally symmetric Boolean functions, *IEEE Trans. Electron. Comput.*, **EC-14**, 924–926.

Shinar, I. and Yoeli, M. 1969 Group functions and multi-valued cellular cascades, *Information and Control*, **15**, 369–376.

Sinha Roy, P. and Sheng, C. 1972 A decomposition method of determining maximum compatibles, *IEEE Trans. Comput.*, **C-21**, 309–312.

Slupecki, J. 1939 A criterion of fullness of many-valued systems of propositional logic, *Studia logica*, **30**, 153–157 (1972).

Smith, J. and Roth, C. 1969 Differential mode analysis and synthesis of sequential switching networks, *Report 63*, Elec. Res. Cen., Univ. Texas, Austin.

Smith, J. and Roth, C. 1971 Analysis and synthesis of asynchronous sequential networks using edge-sensitive flip-flops, *IEEE Trans. Comput.*, **C-20**, 847–855.

Spira, P. 1971a On time-hardware complexity trade-offs for Boolean functions, *Proc. 4th Hawaii international conference on system sciences*, 525–527.

Spira, P. 1971b On the time necessary to compute switching functions, *IEEE Trans. Comput.*, **C-20**, 104–105.

Spira, P. 1973 Computation times of arithmetic and Boolean functions in (d, r) circuits, *IEEE Trans. Comput.*, **C-22**, 552–555.

Stern, T. and Friedland, B. 1961 The linear modular sequential circuit generalized, *IEEE Trans. Circuits and Systems*, **CT-8**, 79–80.

Stone, M. 1935 Subsumption of Boolean algebras under the theory of rings, *Proc. Nat. Acad. Sci., USA*, **21**, 103–105.

Stone, M. 1936 The theory of representations for Boolean algebras, *Trans. Amer. Math. Soc.*, **40**, 37–111.

Stone, H. 1971 Universal logic modules, *in* "Recent developments in switching theory", Ed. Mukhopadhyay, A. (Academic Press, New York).

Su, S. and Cheung, P. 1972 Computer minimization of multivalued switching functions, *IEEE Trans. Comput.*, **C-21**, 995–1003.

Su, S. and Dietmeyer, D. 1969 Computer reduction of two-level multiple-output switching circuits, *IEEE Trans. Comput.*, **C-18**, 58–63.

Su, S. and Sarris, A. 1972 The relationship between multivalued switching algebra and Boolean algebra under different definitions of complement, *IEEE Trans. Comput.*, **C-21**, 479–486.

Svoboda, A. 1956 Graphico-mechanical aids for the analysis and synthesis of contact networks (in Czech.), *IPM*, No 4, 9–21.

Svoboda, A. 1960 Analysis of Boolean functions by logical punch-cards, *IPM*, No 7, 13–20.

Talantsev, A. 1959 On the analysis and synthesis of certain electrical circuits by means of special logical operators, *Automat. i Telemeh.*, **20**, 898–907.

Thayse, A. 1969 Minimization of signal width in sequential circuits with fixed transition delays, *MBLE Internal Report*, N50.

Thayse, A. 1970 Transient analysis of logical networks applied to hazard detection, *Philips Res. Rep.*, **25**, 261–336.

Thayse, A. 1971 Boolean differential calculus, *Philips Res. Rep.*, **26**, 229–246.

Thayse, A. 1972a A variational diagnosis method for stuck-faults in combinatorial networks, *Philips Res. Rep.*, **27**, 82–98.

Thayse, A. 1972b Testing of asynchronous sequential switching circuits, *Philips Res. Rep.*, **27**, 99–106.

Thayse, A. 1972c A fast algorithm for the proper decomposition of Boolean functions, *Philips Res. Rep.*, **27**, 140–150.

Thayse, A. 1972d Multiple-fault detection in large logical networks, *Philips Res. Rep.*, **27**, 583–602.

Thayse, A. 1973a Disjunctive and conjunctive operators for Boolean functions, *Philips Res. Rep.*, **28**, 1–16.

Thayse, A. 1973b On some iteration properties of Boolean functions, *Philips Res. Rep.*, **28**, 107–119.

Thayse, A. 1974a New method for obtaining the optimal Taylor expansions of a Boolean function, *Electron. Lett.*, **10**, No 25/26, 543–544.

Thayse, A. 1974b Differential calculus for functions from $(\mathrm{GF}(p))^n$ into $\mathrm{GF}(p)$, *Philips Res. Rep.*, **29**, 560–586.

Thayse, A. 1974c Applications of discrete functions, Part II: Transient analysis of asynchronous switching networks, *Philips Res. Rep.*, **29**, 155–192.

Thayse, A. 1974d On a theory of discrete functions, Part IV: Discrete functions of functions, *Philips Res. Rep.*, **29**, 305–329.

Thayse, A. 1974e Applications of discrete functions, Part III: The use of functions of functions in switching circuits, *Philips Res. Rep.*, **29**, 429–452.

Thayse, A. 1975a La détection des aléas dans les circuits logiques au moyen du calcul différential booléen, *Digit. Process.*, **1**, 141–169.

Thayse, A. 1975b Cellular hazard-free design of combinatorial networks, *MBLE Internal Report,* R293.

Thayse, A. 1976 Difference operators and extended truth vectors for discrete functions. *Discrete Math.*, **14**, 171–202.

Thayse, A. and Davio, M. 1973 Boolean differential calculus and its application to switching theory, *IEEE Trans. Computers,* **C-22**, 409–420.

Thayse, A. and Deschamps, J.-P. 1973a Derivatives of discrete functions and their applications to switching theory, *MBLE Internal Report,* R221.

Thayse, A. and Deschamps, J.-P. 1973b On a theory of discrete functions, Part II: The ring and field structures of discrete functions, *Philips Res. Rep.*, **28**, 424–465.

Thayse, A. and Deschamps, J.-P. 1976 Logic properties of unate and of symmetric discrete functions, *International symposium on multiple-valued logic,* 79–87.

Thelliez, S. 1973 "Introduction à l'étude des structures ternaires de commutation" (Gordon and Breach, Paris).

Tison, P. 1964 Recherche des termes premiers d'une fonction booléenne, *Automatisme,* **9**, 15–17.

Tison, P. 1965 Théorie des consensus, *Dissertation doctorale,* Grenoble.

Tison, P. 1967 Generalization of consensus theory and application to the minimization of Boolean functions, *IEEE Trans. Electron. Comput.*, **EC-5**, 126–132.

Tison, P. 1971 An algebra for logic systems; switching circuits application, *IEEE Trans. Computers,* **C-20**, 339–351.

Tosic, Z. 1972 Analytical representations of m-valued logical functions over the ring of integers modulo *m, Publications de la faculté d'électrotechnique de l'université de Belgrade,* No 410–425.

Tucker, J. 1974 "A transition calculus for Boolean functions" (Virginia Polytechnic Microfilms Xerox Univ. Microfilms, Ann Arbor, USA).

Unger, S. 1959 Hazards and delays in asynchronous sequential switching circuits, *Trans. Circuit Theory,* **CT-6**, 12–25.

Unger, S. 1969 "Asynchronous sequential switching circuits" (Wiley-Interscience, New York).

Ungern, E. 1972 Minimization of exclusive-or switching circuits, *IEEE Repository,* R72–79.

Veitch, E. 1952 A chart method for simplifying truth functions, *Proceedings ACM,* 127–133.

Venn, J. 1876 Boole's logical system, *Mind,* **1**, 479–491.

Venn, J. 1894 "Symbolic logic" (London).

Vinogradov, I. 1961 "An introduction to the theory of numbers" (Pergamon Press, New York).

Von Neumann, J. 1956 Probabilistic logics and the synthesis of reliable organisms from unreliable components *in* "Automata Studies", Ed. Shannon, C. (Princeton University Press).

Vranesic, Z. and Smith, K. 1974 Engineering aspects of multi-valued logic systems, *Computer,* **7**, 34–41.

Wee, W. and Fu, K. 1967 A formulation of fuzzy automata and its application as a model of learning systems, *Proceedings 5th Allerton conference on circuit and system theory,* 47–56.

Winograd, S. 1967 On the time required to perform computer operations, *Ph.D. Thesis,* Dept. Mach., University of New York.

Yau, S. and Tang, Y. 1970 Universal logic modules and their applications, *IEEE Trans. Comput.,* **C-19**, 141–149.

Yau, S. and Tang, Y. 1971a Transformation of an arbitrary switching function to a totally symmetric function, *IEEE Trans. Comput.,* **C-20**, 1606–1609.

Yau, S. and Tang, Y. 1971b On identification of redundancy and symmetry of switching functions, *IEEE Trans. Comput.,* **C-20**, 1609–1613.

Yeh, R. 1973 Toward an algebraic theory of fuzzy relational systems, *Report,* University of Texas, Austin, USA.

Ying, C. and Susskind, A. 1971 Building blocks and synthesis techniques for the realization of *M*-ary combinational switching functions, *International symposium on multiple-valued logic,* 183–205.

Yoeli, M. 1970 The synthesis of multivalued cellular cascades, *IEEE Trans. Comput.,* **C-19**, 1089–1090.

Yoeli, M. and Rinon, S. 1964 Application of ternary algebra to the study of static hazards, *J. of the ACM,* **11**, 84–97.

Yoeli, M. and Rosenfield, G. 1965 Logical design of ternary switching circuits, *IEEE Trans. Electron. Comput.,* **EC-14**, 19–29.

Zadeh, L. 1965 Fuzzy sets, *Information and Control,* **8**, 338–353.

Zahnd, J. 1969 Homomorphisms et recouvrements de machines de Mealy, *Systèmes Logiques,* No 1, 16–18.

Zahnd, J. and Mange, D. 1975 Réduction des tables d'états incomplètement définies, *Systèmes logiques,* No 6.

Author Index

Subject Index